The
Corrupting
Sea

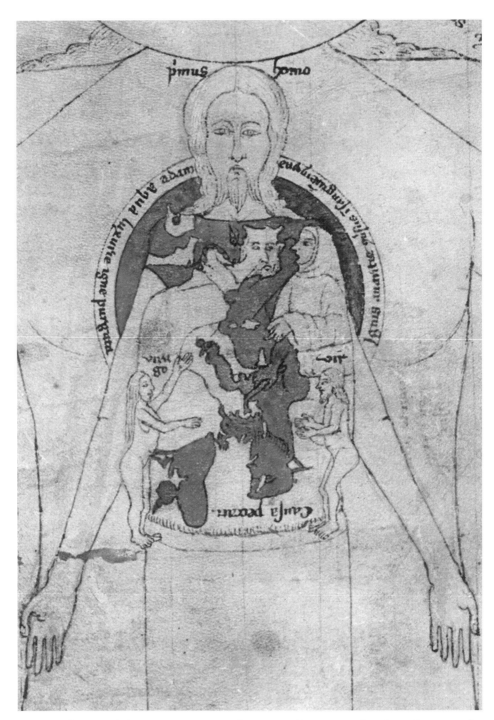

A medieval vision of the corrupting sea. Anthropomorphic cartography, drawn in reverse, by the tormented Italian priest, Opicino de Canistris (1296–c.1350), showing a male Europe (Adam) leaning towards a female Africa (Eve). The scene of their fall will be the Strait of Gibraltar, entrance to the Mediterranean, which has a devil's head at its Levantine end, and is labelled *causa peccati*, the cause of sin. Biblioteca Apostolica Vaticana MS Pal. Lat. 1993 f. 2v, reproduced by permission. See Salomon (1936) 155–60.

The Corrupting Sea

A STUDY OF MEDITERRANEAN HISTORY

Plato thinks that those who want a well-governed city ought to shun the sea as a teacher of vice (*ponerodidaskalos*).

Strabo, *Geography*, 7.3.8

Whereat he said firmly: 'When your Excellency writes a book, you will not say: "Here there is a beautiful church and a great castle." The gentry can see that for themselves. But you shall say: "In this village there are no hens." Then they will know from the beginning what sort of country it is.'

Gertrude Bell (1907) *The Desert and the Sown*, 93

PEREGRINE HORDEN

AND

NICHOLAS PURCELL

BLACKWELL
Publishers

First published 2000
Reprinted 2001

Blackwell Publishers Ltd
108 Cowley Road
Oxford OX4 1JF
UK

Blackwell Publishers Inc.
350 Main Street
Malden, Massachusetts 02148
USA

British Library Cataloguing in Publication Data

A CIP catalogue record for this book is available from the British Library.

Library of Congress Cataloging-in-Publication Data

Library of Congress data is available for this book.

ISBN 0–631–13666–5 (hbk); 0–631–21890–4 (pbk)

Typeset in 10.5 on 12pt Galliard
by Graphicraft Limited, Hong Kong
Printed in Great Britain by MPG Books Ltd, Bodmin, Cornwall

This book is printed on acid-free paper

Contents

MAPS

ACKNOWLEDGEMENTS

A predictable consequence of the size of this work is that we owe a great deal to very many colleagues and friends for help with ideas and bibliography. If we do not mention them all by name, that is partly to avoid embarrassing them by making explicit what we have done with their advice, which often goes far beyond what is normally implied in the customary exculpation, 'remaining errors are our own'. The more prosaic reason for omitting their names is that there are so many of them that it would be difficult to list all and invidious to select. May we simply offer here our warmest thanks? The final text has been read by no one except our exemplary and unflagging computer and word-processing assistant, Humaira Erfan Ahmed, our meticulous copy-editor, Henry Maas, and ourselves; and we (the authors) have been jointly responsible for the wording of all the chapters, even where the material was initially gathered and shaped by one rather than the other, so we really do share the blame for their eccentricities and imperfections. A much earlier version of the whole text has, however, benefited at every point from the constructive scrutiny of Peter Garnsey, and drafts of Parts Four and Five have also been read with the most helpful care by Emily Kearns and John Davis. We are extremely grateful to them, as also to Richard Smith, for his bibliographical omniscience and unwavering enthusiasm for the project. For our knowledge of Braudel's unpublished monograph we are indebted to Oswyn Murray. Alan Johnston very generously drew our attention to the remarkable customs record of 475 B.C. described in Chapter V. In the last stages of preparing the typescript, Sarah Cobden rendered invaluable assistance by cross-checking references and bibliography, and Robert Hoyland kindly examined our transliteration of Arabic. David Cox has been a splendid cartographer, Jane Baun a scrupulous reader of proof. All Souls and St John's Colleges, Oxford, gave the project most generous financial support at various stages. Publication was also greatly facilitated by a grant from the late Miss Isobel Thornley's bequest to the University of London. The forbearance of our publishers must also be noted; we have much appreciated the toleration and helpfulness of Philip Carpenter, Tessa Harvey, Louise Spencely, Jason Pearce and Brian Johnson.

The final acknowledgement should perhaps be that due to the late Arnaldo Momigliano. When we described our undertaking to him he simply laughed.

NOTE ON REFERENCES

There are four kinds of reference in this book.

(1) The largest category identifies apposite *scholarly literature*. In Chapters such works are cited by author and date, and in Bibliographical Essays by author, date and short title. Full details, as appropriate, will be found in the Consolidated Bibliography.

(2) The second type of citation refers mainly to the *primary evidence*.
   - An entry under the editor's name will be found in the Consolidated Bibliography for any work of which a particular edition is cited.
   - Where the passage may readily be consulted in any edition or translation, we have given only the name of the author and the title of the work. The latter is translated into English except in cases where this would make the original work hard to identify.
   - Collections of primary evidence – most notably the multi-volume corpora in which ancient inscriptions are published – are cited in both Chapter and Bibliographical Essay in abbreviated form.

(3) All abbreviations, including the periodical and series titles cited in the Consolidated Bibliography, have separate entries in the list of Abbreviations.

(4) Cross-references from one part of the text to another are given by Chapter (or Bibliographical Essay) and Section number – e.g. VII.3 or BE VII.3.

We are responsible for all translations except those from Aramaic and Arabic.

ABBREVIATIONS

AA	*Antiquités Africaines*
AAAG	*Annals of the Association of American Geographers*
AmAnth	*American Anthropologist*
ABSA	*Annual of the British School at Athens*
AC	*Archeologia Classica*
AE	*L'Année Épigraphique*
AEA	*Archivio Español de Arqueología*
AG	*Annales de Géographie*
AHB	*Ancient History Bulletin*
AHR	*American Historical Review*
AION	*Istituto Orientale di Napoli: Annali del Dipartimento di Studi del Mondo Classico e del Mediterraneo antico. Archeologia e storia antica*
AJA	*American Journal of Archaeology*
AJAH	*American Journal of Ancient History*
AJP	*American Journal of Philology*
AM	*Archeologia Medioevale*
AnnA	*Annuario della Scuola Archeologica Italiana di Atene*
ANRW	*Aufstieg und Niedergang der Römischen Welt*
AntC	*Antiquité Classique*
ANYAS	*Annals of the New York Academy of Sciences*
AQ	*Anthropological Quarterly*
ARA	*Annual Review of Anthropology*
AS	*Anatolian Studies*
ASNP	*Annali della Scuola Normale di Pisa*
ASPN	*Archivio Storico della Provincia di Napoli*
BAGF	*Bulletin de l'Association de Géographes Français*
BAR	*British Archaeological Reports, International Series*
BASOR	*Bulletin of the American Schools of Oriental Research*
BCH	*Bulletin de Correspondance Hellénique*
BF	*Byzantinische Forschungen*
BMGS	*Byzantine and Modern Greek Studies*
BSA	*Bulletin on Sumerian Agriculture*
CAH	*Cambridge Ancient History*

CAJ	*Cambridge Archaeological Journal*
CIG	*Corpus Inscriptionum Graecarum*
CIL	*Corpus Inscriptionum Latinarum*
CQ	*Classical Quarterly*
CR	*Classical Review*
CRAI	*Comptes-rendus de l'Académie des Inscriptions et Belles-Lettres*
CSSH	*Comparative Studies in Society and History*
CT	*Cahiers de Tunisie*
CW	*Classical World*
Dd'A	*Dialoghi d'Archeologia*
DHA	*Dialogues d'Histoire Ancienne*
Diels-Krantz	*Die Fragmente der Vorsokratiker*, ed. H. Diels and W. Krantz
DOP	*Dumbarton Oaks Papers*
EA	*Epigraphica Anatolica*
EcHR	*Economic History Review*
EI	*Encyclopaedia of Islam*, 2nd edn
EJ	*Encyclopaedia Judaica*
EHR	*English Historical Review*
FGH	*Fragmente der Griechischen Historiker*
GJ	*Geographical Journal*
GR	*Greece and Rome*
HSCP	*Harvard Studies in Classical Philology*
HTR	*Harvard Theological Review*
IESS	*International Encyclopedia of the Social Sciences*
IG	*Inscriptiones Graecae*
IGRR	*Inscriptiones Graecae ad Res Romanas Pertinentes*
IGSK	*Inschriften griechischer Städte aus Kleinasien*
IJB	*Israel Journal of Botany*
IJMES	*International Journal of Middle East Studies*
IJNA	*International Journal of Nautical Archaeology*
ILS	*Inscriptiones Latinae Selectae*
JAS	*Journal of Archaeological Science*
JAT/RTA	*Journal of Ancient Topography/Rivista di Topografia Antica*
JDAIAA	*Jahrbuch des Deutschen Archäologischen Instituts: Archäologischer Anzeiger*
JEA	*Journal of European Archaeology*
JEEH	*Journal of European Economic History*
JEH	*Journal of Economic History*
JESHO	*Journal of the Economic and Social History of the Orient*
JFA	*Journal of Field Archaeology*
JFH	*Journal of Family History*
JHS	*Journal of Hellenic Studies*
JIH	*Journal of Interdisciplinary History*
JMA	*Journal of Mediterranean Archaeology*
JMGS	*Journal of Modern Greek Studies*
JNES	*Journal of Near Eastern Studies*
JPS	*Journal of Peasant Studies*
JRA	*Journal of Roman Archaeology*
JRS	*Journal of Roman Studies*

JTS	*Journal of Theological Studies*
LCM	*Liverpool Classical Monthly*
LIWBM	*Leichtweiss-Institut für Wasserbau der technischen Universität Braunschweig: Mitteilungen*
LS	*Libyan Studies*
MAAR	*Memoirs of the American Academy in Rome*
MAH	*Mélanges d'Archéologie et d'Histoire*
MCV	*Mélanges de la Casa de Velázquez*
MDAIA	*Mitteilungen des Deutschen Archäologischen Instituts: Athenische Abteilung*
MEFRA	*Mélanges de l'École Française de Rome (Antiquité)*
MEFRM	*Mélanges de l'École Française de Rome (Moyen Âge)*
MES	*Middle Eastern Studies*
MHR	*Mediterranean Historical Review*
NRS	*Nuova Rivista Storica*
ODB	*Oxford Dictionary of Byzantium*
OJA	*Oxford Journal of Archaeology*
PAPS	*Proceedings of the American Philosophical Society*
Pauly-Wissowa	*Real-encyclopädie der classischen Altertumswissenschaft*
PBSR	*Papers of the British School at Rome*
PCPS	*Proceedings of the Cambridge Philological Society*
PdelP	*Parola del Passato*
PG	*Patrologia Graeca*
PL	*Patrologia Latina*
PP	*Past and Present*
PPS	*Proceedings of the Prehistoric Society*
P Turin	*Turin Papyri*
PVatGr	*Vatican Papyri (Greek)*
QJEG	*Quarterly Journal of Engineering Geology*
QS	*Quaderni di Storia*
RAC	*Reallexikon für Antike und Christentum*
REA	*Revue des Études Anciennes*
REG	*Revue des Études Grecques*
RHES	*Revue d'Histoire Économique et Sociale*
RIL	*Rendiconti dell'Istituto Lombardo*
RL	*Rendiconti dell'Accademia dei Lincei*
RPP	*Review of Palaeobotany and Palynology*
RSI	*Rivista Storica Italiana*
RSL	*Rivista di Studi Liguri*
SEG	*Supplementum Epigraphicum Graecum*
SIG	*Sylloge Inscriptionum Graecarum*
SS	*Settimane di Studio del Centro Italiano di Studi sull'Alto Medioevo, Spoleto*
TAPA	*Transactions of the American Philosophical Association*
Topoi	*Topoi Orient-Occident*
TT	*Tools and Tillage*
WA	*World Archaeology*
ZG	*Zeitschrift für Geomorphologie*
ZPE	*Zeitschrift für Papyrologie und Epigraphik*

The intolerable melancholy, the dinginess, the corruption of that tainted inland sea overcame him. He felt the breath of centuries of wickedness and disillusion . . .

Cyril Connolly (1981) *The Rock Pool*, 91

The world is a visitation and an abode of transition. Be you then travellers in it and take warning from what remains of the traces of the early ones.

Yaqut ibn Abd 'Allah al-Hamawi (d. 1229)
Geographical Onomastics, ed. Jwaideh (1959), 2

INTRODUCTION

When the redoubtable Sir James Frazer was preparing, in his blind old age, the *Aftermath* (1936) to that *summum opus* of Victorian anthropology, *The Golden Bough* (1911–35), his amanuensis read him an account of some rituals of the Borneo Dyaks. The head of a new-born Dyak, Frazer learned, is held by its father in such a position that the mother's blood drips on it. 'I never realised', Frazer said, 'that blood could be shed at child-birth' (Downie 1970, 19).

As our project has expanded, at times seeming to threaten rivalling Frazer's in inclusiveness, we have frequently been conscious of the likelihood that we shall display a comparable ignorance of fundamentals. But such fears inevitably attend an enterprise of comparison that takes both the broad and the long view, and that in traversing several usually distinct disciplines must, on many issues, make what it can of the reports of others.

Not that we have ever thought to produce a measured, synoptic, account either of the whole Mediterranean past or of the scholarly reports that it has generated. The best way to introduce what we do intend – and to explain our title – may be to recount the project's genesis.

This work originated in a simple observation – that, in his celebrated *The Mediterranean and the Mediterranean World in the Age of Philip II* (1972a), Fernand Braudel had proclaimed the enduring unity and distinctiveness of his subject; but he had mostly confined his supporting evidence to what he thought of as the facts of geography and to sixteenth-century documents. (Only very recently have we become aware of the existence of Braudel's substantial study of the *prehistoric* and *ancient* Mediterranean, left unpublished at his death; cf. II.3.) Our simple observation concerning *The Mediterranean* induced a simple question. Could such a work have been written taking as its eponymous ruler an imperial potentate from Antiquity or the Middle Ages? If the Mediterranean had indeed, as Braudel suggested, constituted a distinct unity in earlier centuries than the sixteenth, it ought to be possible to demonstrate the fact. It ought also to be possible to discover how that unity subsisted, and what kinds of continuity were involved in the process.

The answer to our simple question was (we imagined) simply sought. We embarked on a seminar, at each meeting of which one or other of us discussed a theme such as those reflected in our chapter headings here. Given that our brief was to assess the unity of the Mediterranean in periods earlier than Braudel's, and given that ours was a collaboration between a medievalist and an ancient historian, it was natural for us to conceive our period as Antiquity and the Middle Ages. We searched for evidence from any part of that long stretch, and from anywhere within the region. We were looking for material that would, at the very least, display the Mediterranean as an area which could yield novel and fruitful comparisons across extremes of time and space – an area within which established distinctions such as those between Antiquity and the Middle Ages or East and West were ripe for reconsideration. Yet we also, of course, intended to establish how far, and in what respects, this area had indeed possessed unity and distinctiveness in ages earlier than that of Philip II. Our original scope, chronologically speaking – and the title of our seminar – was 'Before Braudel'. The result of those meetings was certainly no imitation of Braudel's method (of which Chapter II.2 supplies a reminder). But it did take the first part of *The Mediterranean*, on the 'constants' of human geography, as a frequent point of reference. Our theme was the relationship of 'man and environment'; and the subtitle of the publication that we hoped would eventuate from the seminar should, we thought, probably include both that phrase and 'Antiquity and the Middle Ages'.

The papers written for that original seminar have slowly been transformed into chapters. And the chapters have so grown in size and number that it has been expedient to publish our findings in two separate instalments. Not surprisingly, moreover, the scope of the project has significantly evolved. Under the sign of the microecology, we have tried (starting in Part Two) to elaborate a conception of how Mediterranean unity has actually worked – of what has, for so much of its past, made the region a discriminable whole. This conception differs markedly from the first part of Braudel's work; and it can neither depend on a simple dichotomy such as that implied by 'man and environment', nor rest content with the standard definitions of human geography. In keeping with this different approach, we have instead been prompted to start from a distinction of subject matter between, on one hand, history *in* the region, contingently Mediterranean or best conceived under some other heading, and, on the other hand, history *of* it – history either of the whole Mediterranean or of an aspect of it to which the whole is an indispensable framework. Part of what happens in the Mediterranean is, *in this very particular sense*, not Mediterranean history. But to an understanding of the rest, knowledge of microecologies and their interrelations is, we argue, essential. That 'in/of' distinction affects our presentation of evidence. All kinds of history – political, social, economic, religious – come to be included in our microecological investigations ('history of'). There is, however, no chapter on Mediterranean political, social, economic, or religious history *per se* – such as might reasonably be expected of a broad survey – because we see all that as belonging to 'history in'. This omission should not be taken as implying a judgement about the relative importance of such topics. While certainly linked in a multiplicity of important ways to its microecological setting, 'history in' is not deterministically to be thought of as a mere by-product of that setting. We are far from wanting to claim that microecologies explain everything.

Putting it that way applies the distinction between 'history of' and 'history in' synchronically. We propose that it be applied *diachronically* too. As work has proceeded we have found it essential to move well beyond the bounds of Antiquity and the Middle Ages: back into later prehistory, most notably in

Chapter V and throughout Part Three; forward into the early modern period, especially in Chapter IV; and even to the later twentieth century in Part Five, which considers the contribution of social anthropology. To a minor extent, this expansion of scope reflects shortages of appropriate and accessible evidence from classical Antiquity or the Middle Ages – shortages that have forced us to look elsewhere, usually to later periods. The main reason for expansion, however, has been our growing belief that the kinds of unity and continuity described in the following chapters extend well beyond our initial termini. One way to capture our rationale for the still vaster period that we have thus embraced would be to liken our discussions to those of archaeologists, who often seek to illuminate their results by drawing comparisons with historical and ethnographic works. The comparisons are effective because the comparanda all derive from 'traditional' or 'pre-modern' cultures. In what follows, we often move in a similar way between prehistory, history and ethnography; and we devote the last two chapters of this volume to exploring just how far ethnography helps us understand the durability and unity of Mediterranean microecologies. It was tempting, therefore, to indicate our revised chronological scope by somehow including 'traditional' (or 'pre-modern') in the subtitle of this book as a substitute for 'Antiquity and the Middle Ages'. To do so would, however, have been to leave the choice of comparative material unexplained: why should the comparisons chiefly be intra-Mediterranean rather than involve evidence from other parts of the world? It would also, more importantly, have been to rest far too much weight on a category which has proved notoriously hard to define, and which, although we inevitably use it now and then as an established and convenient shorthand, we would be loath to turn into a conceptual cornerstone.

Instead, we prefer to think that the range of evidence on which we draw, its particular dispersal in time and space, relates not only to the continuity of Mediterranean history but also to its twentieth-century attenuation. The writing of Mediterranean *historiography* may, so we argue in Chapter II, be seen as having reached a pause with Braudel's work (in that respect we are 'after Braudel', not before him). Historiography *of* the Mediterranean – the type of which Braudel was the greatest exponent – has mostly vanished from the scene. During the twentieth century, the Mediterranean region itself has also to a considerable extent been disintegrated, and the network of its microecologies radically reconfigured, by the involvement of its coastal nations in the credit economies, political alliances, technologies and communications networks of the North and West or the Far East. That is perhaps one, but only one, ingredient in the complex process often called modernization. For us, though, it means something slightly different: the gradual transmutation of our subject matter into something requiring a very different book from this one, and thus a suitable – if very approximate – end-point for our enquiry. We naturally hope that our approach may continue to be useful to the study of Mediterranean lands into the third millennium. But the Mediterranean region as a distinct whole is *not*, we think, the indispensable framework within which to conceptualize the *very recent* history and likely future of its peoples. That is why our subtitle is simply and provocatively *A Study of Mediterranean History*. We allude, of course, to Toynbee's now little-read and largely-discredited *A Study of History* (12 vols. 1934–61) – a work even larger in scope than Frazer's, and perhaps a more dangerous precedent. But the following chapters, we hope, betray nothing at all in common with Toynbee's vision of the past in terms of the growth and decline of civilizations. We rather wish to imply that what we study is Mediterranean history as a whole, the history *of* the region. In every usual sense, of course, history 'keeps on happening': reports of its death are exaggerated. Yet in our very special sense (cf. Fukuyama 1993), Mediterranean history, as exemplified in the sorts of evidence we use below – prehistoric, ancient, medieval, early modern – can be deemed to have reached a close. What we catch in the ethnographies to which Part Five draws attention – ethnographies that were in several cases already historical documents by the time of their publication – can perhaps be regarded as a vestige of it. There seemed no need, then, to include dates in our subtitle. About the prehistory that came before the earliest evidence cited, there is too little that can usefully be said; while the very 'modern' periods and topics not fully represented here belong not in a history *of* the Mediterranean but in some other analysis.

For all these changes of theme and scope, the work that we now present follows the pattern of our original seminar in one major respect: what we have written remains in many ways essay-like. On none of the topics selected for discussion can we claim to have come anywhere near to completeness, although we have certainly not avoided detail. Even some of the more recherché matters touched on – fishing, peak-sanctuaries, earthquakes, cognitive geography – let alone areas of debate such as deforestation, shame, or pastoralism, have generated copious scholarly discussion. Those more expert in such areas are asked to forgive the superficiality that arises from brevity of treatment as we try to engage all these subjects with a larger whole. On the other hand, many of the topics that we find important fall into the gaps between disciplines and have attracted very little attention. We have therefore mostly eschewed the even-handed 'literature survey' in favour of hypotheses and arguments of our own. Rather than attempt uniformly full documentation at every stage – often an impossibility – we have incorporated only essential references into the text, and have kept lists and appraisals of our sources to the Bibliographical Essays. But even these Bibliographical Essays – which should be read in conjunction with their respective chapters – are intended to complement our discussions rather than to note everything pertinent. We make no apology for omission or *Tendenz*. On the other hand, we have felt it important where possible to provide support for our frequently heterodox arguments by generous citation of discussions that seemed to echo our way of thinking. Our bibliography is long but not, we believe, redundant.

Now that the work has grown to two volumes, the caveat about completeness of treatment must extend to the scope of this, the first of them. Several central topics have been reserved for Volume 2: climate, disease, demography and, underlying all these, the relations between the Mediterranean and other major areas of the globe. One way to capture the difference of emphasis between the two volumes would be to say that Volume 1 moves from inside the Mediterranean to outside, beginning with the smallest constituents and their interaction and touching only occasionally on more far-flung links; while Volume 2 will proceed in the reverse direction, from outside in, looking predominantly at those larger systems within which the Mediterranean has been situated and at their effects on its microecologies. A second instalment will also allow us an opportunity to respond to criticisms of the first, in the interests of the debate that we should like to promote.

In this volume, then, we offer only a part of the whole, and only provisional conclusions. Here in Volume 1, by way of preamble to our own foray, we first discuss the nature of Mediterranean history as others have perceived it. Part One begins to outline our unevadable inheritance of Mediterranean historiography. The emerging themes are developed in Part Two, where we have set out the rudiments of our own overall interpretation. The distinctiveness of Mediterranean history results (we propose) from the paradoxical coexistence of a milieu of relatively easy seaborne communications with a quite unusually fragmented topography of microregions in the sea's coastlands and islands. It was a commonplace among Greek and Roman writers that the effects of this easy interaction by sea were profoundly damaging to good social order: hence this volume's title. In Part Three some of the implications of the microregional landscape and its ready connectivity are explored, especially the conditions in which the resources of the environment and human labour combine to produce and distribute the means of survival. Against interpretations that emphasize radical change and violent discontinuity in the Mediterranean past, our approach sustains the hope that valuable comparisons can be drawn, and certain continuities inferred, across extremes of time. In Parts Four and Five, finally, we move from the environmental to the social, though the complex interaction of the two remains a prominent theme. Both the religious aspect of the environment and the controversial conclusions of ethnography are used as touchstones for more general issues.

Our wish to subordinate particular topics to the investigation of large overarching questions has entailed returning to certain important topics and areas in several different places. Pages on exchange or pastoralism, to give only two examples, will be found dispersed in various chapters. This, to repeat, seemed preferable to a division of subject matter textbook-style. Such a division would have lent an illusory appearance of comprehensiveness to an essentially serendipitous enterprise and would also, more significantly, have suggested a very different conceptualization of our subject from the one actually espoused. Recourse to the index, in which major subjects are carefully distinguished, is consequently indispensable. As for times and places, we hope that we have been catholic in including most parts of the Mediterranean and most epochs of our chosen span in at least some discussion. But it is obvious that there will often be many possible illustrations of our contentions from different regions and periods, and that we have been able to include only a few. We can say with Epiphanius, 'the discoveries which our insignificant intelligence . . . has been able to make come from the times and opportunities available; we in no way promise information about everything in the world' (*Panarion* [*Medicine Chest*], preface II, trans. Amidon 1990, 21). Evidence is chosen to exemplify a theme rather than to complete a dossier. We have attempted to avoid, if possible, already familiar instances, in order to remind the reader that Mediterranean history as we understand it should above all concern itself with the numerous small localities rather than the few famous ones. The dazzle of classical Athens, imperial Rome, metropolitan Constantinople, cosmopolitan Venice is responsible to a large extent for the relative obscurity in which our ecological subject matter has for so long been wrapped. By choosing rather to discuss Cefalù, Melos or Cagliari, the Biqa and the Albufera, we hope that, if nothing else, some compensation can be made.

PART ONE

'FROGS ROUND A POND': IDEAS OF THE MEDITERRANEAN

We inhabit a small portion of the earth . . . living round the sea like ants and frogs round a pond.

Socrates, in Plato, *Phaedo*, 109B

Most of all it is the sea that delineates precisely the layout of the land, creating gulfs, sea-basins, traversable narrows and, in the same way, isthmuses, peninsulas and capes; in this the rivers and mountains also play their part.

Strabo, *Geography*, 2.5.17

When God created the Mediterranean he addressed it, saying, 'I have created thee and shall send thee my servants. When these will ask for some favour of me, they will say "Glory to God!" and "God is Holy!" and "God is Great!" and "There is no God but God!" How wilt thou then treat these?' 'Well, Lord', replied the Mediterranean – 'I shall drown them.' 'Away with thee – I curse thee – I shall impoverish thy appearance and render thee less fishy!'

Al-Muqaddasi, *The Best Arrangement for the Understanding of the Lands*, 37, trans. Miquel (1963) 43

The continuum is magnificent. The peoples around the Mediterranean and over to the Gulf of Persia are really one animate being.

Jakob Burckhardt (1959) *Judgements on History and Historians*, 23

Today in 1972, six years after the second French edition, I think I can say that two major truths have remained unchallenged. The first is the unity and coherence of the Mediterranean region. I retain the firm conviction that the Turkish Mediterranean lived and breathed with the same rhythms as the Christian, that the whole sea shared a common destiny . . . And the second is the greatness of the Mediterranean, which lasted well after the age of Columbus and Vasco da Gama.

Fernand Braudel (1972a) Preface to English translation, *The Mediterranean and the Mediterranean World in the Age of Philip II*, 14

CHAPTER I

A GEOGRAPHICAL EXPRESSION

The subject of this work is the human history of the Mediterranean Sea and its coastlands over some three millennia. Its immediate contention is that this history can profitably be treated as material for a unified and distinct discipline. Its purpose is to discover, first, how far the region so treated has displayed over this long period any unity and distinctiveness of its own, and second, what kinds of continuity could have been involved: these two questions form the backbone of our work.

In the Introduction we have drawn a distinction that embraces both senses of the word history – the past and the historian's record of it. There is history *in* the Mediterranean, and there is (or can be) history *of* the Mediterranean. The first need not comprise a large area, time-span, or topic, and is related only contingently or indirectly to its geographical setting. By contrast, history *of* the region presupposes an understanding of the whole environment. And the environment in question is the product of a complex interaction of human and physical factors, not simply a material backdrop or a set of immutable constraints. It is this history *of* the Mediterranean that concerns us.

The ambitious chronological scale on which we therefore operate is hard to delimit exactly. The Introduction, again, indicates in general terms how we have come to conceive our period. But the extent of the enquiry must vary from topic to topic and respond to various characteristics of the appropriate evidence. Instead of relating our coverage to established chronological categories, however, we prefer to see our chosen time-span whole. This time-span cannot, at least for our purposes, adequately be described in terms of different ages – prehistoric, classical, early medieval, and so on – with clear divisions between them. Thus, if we consider material remains, the basis of archaeology, our main period is the Iron Age – that is, from the weakening of the predominance of bronze technologies to the arrival of widespread alternatives to metal in our own century (cf. Chapter IX). If, by contrast, we think in terms of the history of political culture, our range extends from the polity formation of the second millennium B.C. to the origins of nation-states in the later Middle Ages and their subsequent superimposition on the political geography of the Mediterranean. If, more specifically, we look to the history of colonies (VII.6), then attention could range from the Hyksos and the neo-Assyrians to nineteenth-century British and French Mediterranean involvement. If, again, we take the Homeric poems and the records of

the Mycenaean and Phoenician worlds as precursors, then the phenomenon of
the text, in the broadest sense, defines the beginning of the enterprise; and, in
the same terms, our investigation may be said to end with the enormous increase
in the production of bureaucratic documents in the eighteenth to nineteenth
centuries, and the contemporary ideological creation of a 'Romantic Mediterranean' (cf. II.1). The more recent of these termini mark, in their different ways,
a transition to something different in Mediterranean history – a new phase that
seems to us so unlike its predecessors that the broad distinction between it and
them is not one whose usefulness we propose to question: a phase for which
history *of* the region becomes inappropriate and quite different explanatory
frameworks need to be devised.

   The chronology, inclusive and flexible as it is, may need less justification than
the area that we have chosen. What makes the region of the Mediterranean Sea
a promising subject for so broadly based an enquiry?

1. What is the Mediterranean?

Obviously no single brief answer can be given to that question; in a sense, the
whole of this book is a response to it. But we can, at this preliminary stage,
introduce two essential topics to which we shall have to return frequently,
though not in the form in which we set them out here. The first of them is the
long history of how the Mediterranean Sea has been envisaged, beginning with
the earliest traceable origins of the notion that its waters constitute a single
entity. The second, which we would not separate too sharply from the first but
instead interpret as its modern sequel, is the 'scientific' definition of the Mediterranean's physical geography: the established answer to the question of what
makes it a region as well as a sea.

   These related topics allow us also to introduce the two principal ways in which
Mediterranean unity has been characterized: by reference either to ease of communications, which we may conveniently label the *interactionist* approach, or
to common physical features, the *ecologizing* approach. An interactionist theory
is likely to emphasize the sea; an ecologizing one is likely to offer generalized
description of Mediterranean hinterlands. The two approaches are, of course, by
no means mutually exclusive, and indeed Parts Two and Three below will set
out our own particular way of combining them, under the signs of the *microecology*
and *connectivity.*

First, then, perceptions of the sea. We should not take its unity as an uncontroversial geographical datum. Before the development of satellites, the Mediterranean as a whole was invisible: its component waters were each more naturally
experienced as independent. Thus, although the Mediterranean has been a geographical expression for many centuries, the expression originates at a learned,
somewhat abstract, level. By the beginning of the first millennium B.C., in the
Semitic languages of the Levant, the term 'Great Sea' is quite widely diffused,
and it is probably from this tradition that it reached the Greeks. Not surprisingly, it is in the fragments of the pioneer of geography, the philosopher Hecataeus
of Miletus, that the phrase is first attested in Greek, around 500 B.C. – in a
milieu closely linked to the cultures of the eastern Mediterranean. A Greek

comic poet called Ephippus mocks the obscurity and pretension of such abstract thinking in a scene of a fourth-century Athenian play; here the coast-dwellers of the Mediterranean help the monster Geryon to make use of the whole sea as a great cauldron for boiling a fish the size of the island of Crete (Athenaeus, *The Philosophers at the Dinner Table*, 8.346–7). In the ancient geographical tradition the sea shapes the land, not the other way about – a fundamental notion made explicit in the passage from the Augustan geographer Strabo that serves as an epigraph above.

This logical priority of the sea was not, however, solely the creation of abstract thought. It resulted principally from the centrality of the sea to communications. Despite the obvious dangers, sea transport so far surpassed land communications in ease as to make of the Mediterranean a milieu of interlocking routes onto which the coastlands and harbours faced. In a continuum of experience through which the thought of the Levantine and Greek worlds mingled, the practice of navigation brought into existence another representation of the unity of these waters – an alternative geography, less imaginative and more pragmatic than that of the philosophers. A specialized terminology of land- (or sea-) forms was elaborated, a Mediterranean topographical expertise that has displayed striking continuity over the centuries. The circumstances of navigation are, for instance, closely registered in the early development of that influential expression of geo-graphical coherence, the coastwise voyage or *periplous*: the space of the sea is conceived as a linear route defined by a sequence of harbours or natural features. The Mediterranean came indeed to be regarded as like a great river. And so it appears on a late Roman map, the Peutinger Table, where the sea is grossly elongated. Gulf, river and sea are imaged as varying extensions of the same medium, not conceptually divided as they are in modern geomorphology.

Most importantly, the requirements of navigation generated the sophisticated direction-finding art based on segmenting the discernible horizon according to the names of prevailing winds. In the creation in archaic and classical Greece of such a systematic practice – a wind-rose – we can again begin to see some-thing of the cognitive response to the business of navigation, the building up of a framework of reference akin to that found in other seafaring societies. The abstraction found in Hecataeus and his successor Herodotus, who had a clear idea of the place occupied by the Great Sea in the whole pattern of the cosmos, was only one end of a spectrum of approaches to the problem of understanding so large a body of water and how to sail across it.

It was natural, however, to elaborate at the same time much more relativistic concepts of the Mediterranean. The sea was local to many ancient cultures, and the two most vocal of these called it their own. From the time of Plato and Aristotle, the Greeks referred to the Mediterranean as the 'Sea over by Us'; the Romans more simply came to regard it as *Mare Nostrum*, 'Our Sea'. 'We' of course has many different meanings. The divisions of the Mediterranean re-flected in the relativism of the fourth-century B.C. Greek phrase, like some of their modern successors discussed in Section 2 below, serve to make statements about the comparative importance of different parts of the world. Certainly it is possible to trace a whole complex of ideas from Homer to the Hellenistic age that conceptualize the Western Mediterranean as a kind of Near and Far West; and indeed this all-too-familiar enshrining of geographical relativism in official designations is an onomastic trait that originates in Antiquity.

Roman self-centredness was rather more aggressive. The claim of the Romans to 'their' sea was part of a political and cultural process by which they progressively defined the place of Rome at the heart of an Inhabited World – an *Oecumene* or *Orbis Terrarum* with the Mediterranean at its centre. This ever larger claim in the end weakened the relativism of earlier attitudes, and it was during the Roman Empire that the term 'Mediterranean Sea' itself emerged – first explicitly used, in surviving texts, as late as the sixth century of our era in the encyclopaedic writings of Isidore of Seville (*Etymologies*, 12.16.1).

This clear notion of the Mediterranean, part of the 'scientific' world-view of the time, is the one that persists in the learned traditions of the medieval European *Mappae Mundi* and of the Arab geographical writings, from one of which we have taken an epigraph. The Arab tradition portrayed the sea as poor, alien and uninviting, but by and large as a unity – a single sea, full of islands, whose integrity was maintained by its geographers despite obvious pressures to divide it conceptually between Islam and the rest of the world. 'Nos auteurs considèrent la Méditerranée comme une ensemble, et comme un sous-ensemble les îles de cette mer, qu'elles soient d'est ou d'ouest' (Miquel 1967–88, 2.377).

The alternative geographical system – the sum of the concepts of practical navigation – is quite distinct after Antiquity from the geographers' grander vision; it forms the background of the coast-wise orientations of the Arab geographers or the wind-rose-based portolans of the central Middle Ages. As one excellent account has put it, these remarkable charts constitute 'a living vehicle of Mediterranean self-knowledge' (T. Campbell 1987, 373). It was not until the fifteenth and sixteenth centuries, when the methods and ideas of the Atlantic world and its 'voyages of discovery' were turned in on the Mediterranean, that the two geographies – the abstract and the pragmatic – were welded together again. Even then, the older type of thought, deriving from navigation, survived in some of the less accessible parts of the Mediterranean basin. The distribution of traditional practice – whether in ship-design, rigging, or terminology – reflected distinctive social groupings around islands, gulfs or straits, and continued to do so until a 'levelling' was effected by comprehensive changes such as the advent of fossil fuels. Introducing the second edition of his text of Thucydides, Thomas Arnold of Rugby appositely wrote: 'it will be strange if the establishment of steam-vessels on the Mediterranean does not within the next ten years do more for the geography of Thucydides than has ever been done yet, for it will enable those who are at once scholars and geographers to visit the places of which he speaks personally' (1840, iii–iv).

The Mediterranean has been a geographical expression in yet a further, more modern, sense. It brings us to the second of the two established ways of answering the question 'what is the Mediterranean?', and substitutes a mainly ecologizing approach for the interactionism implicit in much ancient thought.

There is, so the argument goes, a set of common features in the physical geography of Mediterranean lands. Since the development of systematic human geography in the nineteenth century (its origins associated with the names of Carl Ritter and Friedrich Ratzel and its Mediterranean application with that of Alfred Philippson), these common features have made it tempting to discuss the lands as an ensemble (cf. VIII.1). The Mediterranean climate, of hot dry summers and mild rainy winters, is the most famous such feature; but the climatic effect of the sea, the recurring structural and petrological patterns of the coastlands, or the distinctive natural vegetation that reflects soil as well as climate, can all be advanced to complement it. Thus the natural distribution of the olive or certain isohyets have often been used to delineate the boundaries of the Mediterranean (Map 1). Physical peculiarities of this kind have been taken as diagnostic of something harder to summarize: an habitual, though certainly not inevitable, relationship of man to environment, in the extraction of either subsistence or surplus from the land; a set of seasonal variations, affecting movement across and around the sea. From this angle – of a history 'close to the soil' – it becomes possible to envisage what Fernand Braudel was thinking of when he wrote that, in the heyday of Ottoman power, the Turkish Mediterranean 'lived and breathed with the same rhythms as the Christian' (1972a, 14).

This will not be our approach, though. Rather than treat physical characteristics one by one at greater length, or tease out common rhythms of history, we shall emphasize pronounced local irregularity: the minutely subdivided topography, for instance, which fractions the sweep of a mountain range or river basin, and the effects of interannual variation in temperature and rainfall, which make next to useless the average annual figures for any small topographical unit (Table 1). A definition of the Mediterranean in terms of the unpredictable, the variable and, above all, the local will indeed be explored throughout this book. It is in that context, we propose, that Plato's simile of the pond, with its connotations of habitat or ecological niche, offers such an appropriate image (VIII.5).

The descriptions and conclusions of modern physical geographers, on which any such analysis must to some extent depend, can no more be taken as uncontroversial data than are the concepts of ancient navigators. Both ancient and modern perceptions should, in the first instance, be seen as belonging equally to the history of ideas; before we test their applicability, that is, we should interrogate their sources. The chief among these sources are the province of the next chapter. Here, though, we must address the perhaps disturbing fact that, outside the long and various traditions of geographical thought which we have begun to introduce, the Mediterranean has not obviously suggested itself as a

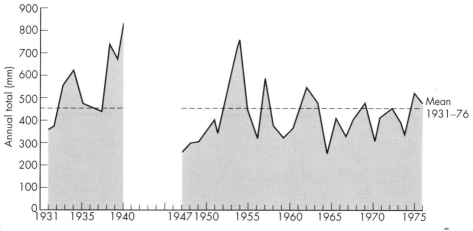

Table 1   Interannual variability of rainfall

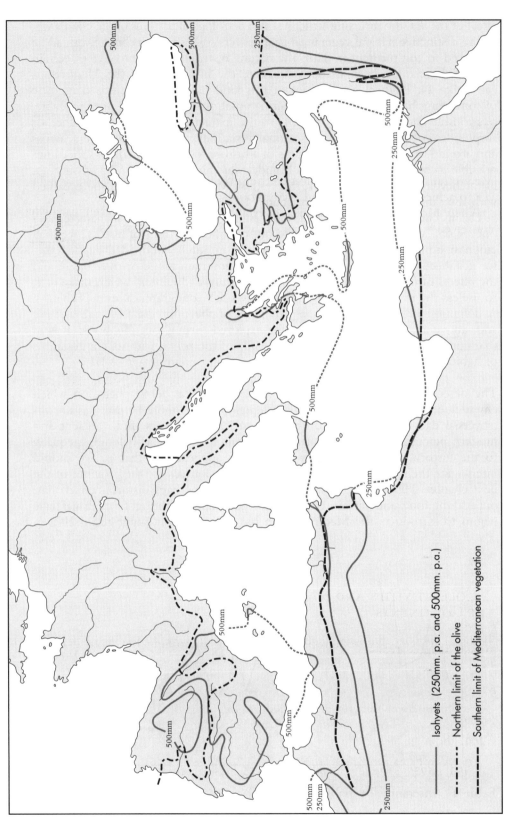

Map 1 Physical definitions of the Mediterranean region

Isohyets (250mm. p.a. and 500mm. p.a.)

Northern limit of the olive

Southern limit of Mediterranean vegetation

single area of investigation. Only archaeologists of the Bronze Age and historians or archaeologists of Greece and Rome customarily treat the area as a whole;
and their respective disciplines have suffered by being insulated both from each
other and from the study of later periods. The sea, its islands, and the countries
that surround it, communicate across it, and share its climate, still seem to many
historians to be far less worth studying as a collectivity than is Europe or the
Middle East, Christendom or Islam. These, not the Mediterranean, form the major
units of enquiry and determine the characteristic orientation of more specialized
research – with damaging consequences for intra-Mediterranean comparisons. For
all the frequency with which it is referred to (or simply invoked on title pages),
Mediterranean history is a division of the subject of history as a whole that has
yet to achieve full articulacy and recognition.

When Mediterranean history is undertaken, moreover, it is often narrowly
conceived – as history in rather than of the region, piecemeal or abstracted from
its locale; as a southerly emphasis within the usual limits of European history;
or as fundamentally *inter*disciplinary in character, an admirable yet still slightly
awkward straddling of some seemingly obtrusive boundary. There remains only
one significant exception to that generalization, now far from recent, Fernand
Braudel's classic account of the Mediterranean region in the age of Philip II, the
first edition of which appeared in 1949. *The Mediterranean and the Mediterranean World* is irradiated throughout by its author's conviction of the essential
unity of his subject, whatever the divisive claims of other historians of the sixteenth century, and nothing that Braudel subsequently wrote about the region
(e.g. 1977a; or his unpublished monograph) surpassed that early *chef d'oeuvre* in
subtlety and conviction.

Braudel's method is not, however, to be followed uncritically (Chapter II).
Nor does his rare achievement single-handedly justify the adoption by other
historians of a Mediterranean perspective. The unity that we have outlined – a
unity ultimately deriving from very ancient geographical ideas – remains precarious. Any further exploration of perceptions of the Mediterranean past must
next address the two historical traditions that implicitly deny the value – even
the possibility – of a genuinely pan-Mediterranean approach. We confront those
traditions with two simple questions. Why 'European' history? Why that of 'the
Middle East'?

2. COLLECTIVITIES AND SUBDIVISIONS I: THE CHALLENGE OF THE CONTINENTS

'Anyone who speaks of Europe is wrong – it is nothing but a geographical
expression.' Bismarck's assertion (an adaptation of Metternich's description of
Italy) scribbled on the back of a telegram in 1876 is that designations such as
'Europe' are empty and arbitrary. Historians have frequently quoted Bismarck's
dictum. Moreover they have, increasingly, endorsed it. After all, since the Germanic migrations which brought about the collapse of the Roman Empire in the
West, the map of Europe has always been complex in the extreme. Only twice
has a substantial part of it been politically unified – by Charlemagne in the eighth
century and Charles V in the sixteenth – and even then the unity derived from
the person of the ruler rather than from any single governmental structure.

The Bismarckian dismissal of Europe does not seem likely to embody much respect for the Mediterranean unity that we have begun to outline, for that too must seem a mere geographical expression. Yet Bismarck's scorn can at least be redirected – against a persistent opinion that is even more damaging to the notion of a unitary Mediterranean. Bismarck was criticizing those who, in accordance with a notion of the continents that predates Herodotus, have been inclined to believe in a transcendent European identity, such as would make nonsense of the idea of Mediterranean history. Students of the European past have preserved the integrity of their subject, in the face of the almost unremitting complexity of the political map, by emphasizing the overarching cultural unity of Europe, exemplified historically in the idea of Christendom.

From the end of classical Antiquity, on this single continent, there have after all been peoples mostly of the same religion and sharing a culture and a notion of law more or less indebted to that of Rome; their languages have, with a few obvious exceptions, belonged to a single family; they have been fundamentally quite similar for most of their history in economy, technology, and social and political structures; and all this because they have been perpetually in close contact with one another, if not always peaceably. They have thus (it is argued) formed an area within which comparisons are particularly illuminating and about which generalizations are both possible and desirable. The local variations which might threaten to defeat such generalizing can even be transformed into a virtue. According to a tradition in European thought that may have roots deep in the Middle Ages, that was developed by the Romantics, and that perhaps finds a modern exemplar in scholarly discussion of 'the European miracle', the very diversity of Europe is a sign of its collective superiority, its extraordinary inventive genius.

None the less, Bismarck is not readily gainsaid. There are serious weaknesses in all attempts at defining European integrity. The chief of them is to take the cultural delimitation as relatively uncontroversial: the continent's peculiarities are often held to be quite readily detectable through a simple survey of the historical landscape. The extent to which the idea of Europe has a history of its own – often convoluted, nearly always politically charged, highly various in the supporting 'facts' adduced – is, for the most part, conveniently ignored. Yet this history – the changing product of imperial and papal ideologues, of predators, crusaders, conquerors from Charlemagne to Napoleon, of federalist visionaries from (say) Voltaire to Delors – shows just how flimsy are all claims to objective definition. Another weakness, arising from the first, is that the European entity as most often construed fails to embrace the whole continent. Europe has never been an unambiguously bounded geographical expression, and its modern historiographies reflect the fact. Between the age of the Vikings and that of Gustavus Adolphus the Scandinavian world was perhaps of relatively little consequence for other European states. Synoptic histories of Europe can almost be forgiven for dealing with it only briefly and circumspectly. A further and more reprehensible narrowing of focus is represented by the long-established, but now more than ever obsolete, tendency to treat eastern European history as a world apart, essentially peripheral. This is more than a matter of being hesitant about whether or not Russia should be seen as part of Europe. It often involves virtually ignoring Slavic history altogether. For nineteenth-century writers on history as opposed in method and philosophy as Hegel and Ranke, for twentieth-century ones as different as Arnold Toynbee and Marc Bloch, European history has meant the history of Roman and Germanic cultures.

> . . . the Romano-Germanic world was itself by no means homogeneous. Differences arising from their different backgrounds had deeply marked the various societies of which it was composed. Yet, however pronounced these differences may have been, how can we fail to recognize, over and above them, the predominant quality of a common civilization – that of the West? If in the following pages [of *Feudal Society*] where the phrase 'Western and Central Europe' might have been expected, we say simply 'Europe', this is not merely to avoid the repetition of cumbersome adjectives. (Bloch 1962, xx)

Yet if historians of Europe may neglect the Balkans they do not neglect Greece, if only because in the established schema of 'European history' it holds an inalienable place as the fountainhead of European culture. If they sometimes emphasize too much the isolation from the rest of Europe of the Iberian peninsula (whether under Christian or under Islamic rule) they could hardly be accused of ignoring Italy. Together with southern France, the three great peninsulas (as Braudel calls them) are seen as an inseparable part of a greater whole extending northwards far beyond anything that might be called Mediterranean. It is not, however, entirely obvious why the Mediterranean south should be regarded as more a part of Europe than the Baltic north or the Slavic east. Intensity of north–south political and economic contacts might be part of a justification. One has only to think of Franco-German involvement in Italy from Carolingian times onward. But have east–west contacts been so much less? In any case, it is clear that historians of Europe would not lightly delegate the writing of 'southern' history to some neighbouring discipline such as 'Mediterranean studies' whose practitioners might also – impartially – embrace North Africa and the rest of the Middle East.

Here, within these areas on the other side of the Mediterranean seemingly so remote from Europe, is the material for a geographical expression of a rather different order, and another collectivity whose links with its neighbours have often been vigorously stressed at the expense of its participation in the Mediterranean world: tracts of precarious habitation in a mosaic of more or less fertile zones between sea and Saharan or Syrian desert stretching from Morocco to Turkey. This geographical expression is the domain of scholarly traditions with which the historiography of Europe has, largely for linguistic reasons, had little genuine contact. They are, though, traditions to which the Mediterranean region sets no agreed limits. Their representatives may focus on Mediterranean coastlands to the general exclusion of the remainder of Africa, largely because the Sahara is so often – though misleadingly – put forward as a resilient cultural and economic frontier. But they may, on the other hand, have as much to do with central Asia and the Arabian peninsula as with the Levant. And this is of course mainly due to the overriding significance of the expansion of Islam for every level of their enquiry, an expansion that has imparted a greater homogeneity – of a kind – to the politically fragmented Middle East than Christianity has ever managed to give to Christian Europe.

Adequate historical definition of this large area extending south and east from the Mediterranean remains hard nevertheless. Identifying it with the area politically unified under Umayyad and Abbasid caliphs or Ottoman sultans requires that no account be taken of the remainder of Islamic history, both later medieval and twentieth-century, when rather different maps apply. Recourse to the modern geography of Islam yields an area extending to equatorial Africa and Indonesia that, even on the scale adopted in the present work, seems far too large to be considered as a single whole. Nor is 'the Middle East' – the general term most commonly used by historians, geographers and anthropologists – particularly satisfactory. Coined in 1902 by the American naval historian Alfred Thayer Mahan, it derived from the strategic thinking of nineteenth-century Europe, alongside the 'Far' and 'Near Easts', and was usually taken to mean Persia and its surrounding territories. Its gradual extension westwards, and the consequent redundancy of the term 'Near East' by the end of the Second World War, have not made its proper application any clearer. And it is also undoubtedly redolent of 'orientalism', as classically if intemperately denounced by Edward Said (1978) – that European tendency (part of Europe's slow self-definition) to image a wide range of 'exotic' cultures as an undifferentiated single 'other'. Some have therefore sought a neutral alternative (SWANA – south-west Asia and North Africa – for example). Yet it is far from clear what such a substitution would really achieve even if it gained widespread acceptance, or what the scope of any new term should be. There is, perhaps, a 'core area consisting of northern Arabia, Syria and northern Iraq' (Wagstaff 1985, 5) – the Middle Eastern equivalent of the north-western core of Europe – to which Iran and Egypt are natural adjuncts. But the decision on whether Afghanistan and formerly Soviet Asia at one extreme and the Maghreb at the other ought also to be included apparently remains a matter for individual scholarly preference. Meanwhile, the cultural and environmental criteria for inclusion that have been proposed – criteria such as 'semiaridity', 'all-pervasive religiosity', or 'competitive individualism' (Keddi 1973; Patai 1952; Lindholm 1996; Eickelman 1998) – are either too vague or too hard to localize for definition to seem any less arbitrary.

On closer inspection, the characterizations of Europe and the Middle East that have usually been offered come to seem disconcertingly imprecise. Few arguments in favour of the categories seem powerful enough to forbid their dissolution, or at least their temporary abandonment; and this is not least because advocates are seldom clear about quite how the general features proposed contribute to unity 'on the ground', in any given locality. None the less the categories continue to be used. And when they do come up for scrutiny, it is, as we have seen, generally only one aspect that is scrutinized: the eastward extension.

Bismarck, we may feel, did indeed have a point. It will be our task to discover whether, at both the general and the local level, there are more convincing arguments to be advanced in defence of Mediterranean unity than his opponents were able to marshal on behalf of Europe or their congeners on behalf of the Middle East.

3. COLLECTIVITIES AND SUBDIVISIONS II: THE MEDITERRANEAN DISINTEGRATED

'The distinction of North and South is real and intelligible . . . But the difference of East and West is arbitrary and shifts round the globe.' Thus Edward Gibbon, annotating the second (1782) edition of *The Decline and Fall of the Roman*

Empire (1896, xxxvi). Discussion focuses, as we have seen, on longitudinal divisions; the one boundary most commonly accepted is that separating North and South. And this boundary seems to fall somewhere across the Mediterranean. Whatever doubts may arise about the integrity of Europe or the Middle East, it remains inescapable that between the sea's northern and southern shores there has long been a major cultural dissonance. Even when the challenge of the continents has been faced, this additional challenge presents itself.

Its earliest manifestation derives from a strand in ancient geographical thought to which we have not so far referred: the 'cosmological' tradition of reflecting on the earth as a whole and on its place in the universe (as distinct from what should properly be called the 'chorographic' tradition that confines description to particular areas of the globe's surface). The ancient cosmological conception of the latitudinal *klima* (or step) gives us the word climate and lies behind the modern theory of the climatic zone. In Antiquity none of the recognized *klimata* into which the surface of the world was divided could be mapped easily onto the notion of 'Our Sea' (Nicolet 1988, ch. 3). And the same could be said of their medieval successors. In that great thirteenth-century Muslim polymath Ibn Khaldun's division of the world into zones, for instance, the Mediterranean is not identified with the 'Middle Zone': rather, the sea straddles three of them (Rosenthal 1967, 1.128–53).

The geographical divisions imposed by cosmology did not, however, initially undermine the ancient conception, described at the beginning of this chapter, of the Mediterranean as a unified topographical phenomenon. Nor did subsequent refinements of the distinctions between zones pose difficulties for the 'scientific' tradition – the current of nineteenth- and twentieth-century thought according to which the Mediterranean could be defined by the common physical characteristics of its coastlands. And yet the notion that the region is latitudinally divided, rather than a unity in itself, seems ultimately to have triumphed among geographers. A tradition whose origins can be discerned in the writings of nineteenth-century human geographers such as Ratzel seems to have petered out in the later twentieth century – during the lifetime of Braudel.

To put it summarily, and in ancient terms, cosmology has finally prevailed over chorography. The distinction of North and South remains what it was for Gibbon: 'real and intelligible'. For neither human nor physical geography, as practised around the turn of the millennium, has much time for the Mediterranean area as a distinctive whole. Until fairly recently, surveys of the region appeared with some regularity. Nowadays, in contrast, the textbooks, the more ambitious synopses of 'the natural regions of the globe', and the newer explorations of cognitive geography have little to say about it. Their typical briefs are either Europe or the Middle East: an old division of labour continues to be observed.

Much the same could be said of the conception of the sea evinced by a number of other disciplines. The social anthropology of its borderlands is intense and lively (cf. Part Five). Ethnographic studies of communities around the Mediterranean proliferate (ethnography 'in', to echo our earlier distinction). Yet comparison both within and across the accepted boundaries of the region – ethnography 'of' – remains rare and controversial. Many anthropologists hold that the region does not really delimit a coherent field of study – that it is, if anything, 'in the first place, a concept of heuristic convenience not a "culture area" in the sense given this phrase by American cultural anthropology' (Pitt-Rivers 1977, viii). Some indeed, most notably Herzfeld (especially 1987b), have argued that it is not even that (cf. Chapter XII). Rather, according to this view, the Mediterranean is a category foisted upon a variety of distinct cultures by the more advanced industrial (and colonial) powers of Europe. Far from being a convenient geographical designation, the term 'Mediterranean' is, in Herzfeld's view, a none too subtle political weapon: a means of distinguishing 'us' – northern European, advanced, diverse – from 'them' – southern, backward, uniform. (Herzfeld might have adduced the geographer Theobald Fischer's *Mittelmeerbilder* (*Mediterranean Images*) in which the justification for the work is explicitly sought in its potential for enhancing German power: Mediterranean countries are seen as undeveloped, easily able to come to the future aid of their great near neighbour to the north (1913, iv).) Alongside 'orientalism', in other words, can be set the comparable ideology of 'Mediterraneanism'. But North and South within the region actually have little in common beyond their essentially subordinate status. In this account, the challenge for anthropology is to resist the allure of the sea and to devise a politically responsible rationale for the ethnography of Europe (Goddard et al. 1994).

Most political scientists would not, it seems, challenge that judgement. When they concern themselves with 'the Mediterranean', they usually take the term to mean something much narrower in focus or more restricted in character than the region as a whole. Still less do they consider it a unity – largely because of the variety of its political regimes. The Mediterranean remains NATO's southern flank, though its place in global strategy is now unclear. It is certainly not a single 'theatre of strategic military action'. In the new era of international relations that has succeeded the Cold War, attention is rather concentrated on the potential 'flashpoints' of the eastern Mediterranean and the Balkans, rather than the sea as a whole. The Mediterranean coastlands have of course also been the world's main arena for international terrorism. But overall the region apparently continues to be reducible to numerous 'tension zones' to which no 'common parameter of political and strategic analysis can be applied' (Cremasco 1984, 207).

Something similar might, finally, be said by economists. The Mediterranean can again be characterized in terms of major routes. But these, unlike the 'routes' of pre-modern economic history (cf. Chapter V), are genuinely isolated channels of movement – as with the great gas pipeline connecting Algeria with the Po valley. It is no longer a question of the complex chains of interaction of (mainly) shore-hugging voyagers. Here, then, the Mediterranean is no more than a collection of conduits, a few straight lines on the map. Alternatively, it may be firmly divided into two regions, as by development economists. The relatively newly industrialized – and 'democratized' – nations of southern Europe are taken to constitute a sensible unit of study. North Africa and the eastern Mediterranean constitute other such units. There is, however, little thought given to the possible rewards of transmarine comparison, let alone of treating the Mediterranean as a single unit; and this despite the legacy of colonial ties between North and South, and despite the 'global Mediterranean policy' developed by the European Community in the 1970s, a policy that has led to a network of trade agreements and the like between EC members and other littoral states.

Small encouragement, then, for Mediterranean historiography from the social sciences – those disciplines that have recently done much to alter traditional modes of historiographical perception. From whatever theoretical vantage point we view the region it apparently remains ineluctably divided. Indeed, within the whole field of current academic thinking and social policy the only context in which the Mediterranean has been treated as a single entity appears to be that of environmental concern. The Mediterranean Action Plan, implemented in 1975 and theoretically involving (among others) all Mediterranean states, had as its goals a wide-ranging protection of the sea against pollution and the promotion of 'environmentally sound development' on its littoral. It is worth noting, however, that the environmental problems in question and their anthropogene sources are exceedingly diverse. The unity that Mediterranean environmentalists have claimed for their subject matter derives far less from peculiarities of the discipline than from some very old clichés of Mediterranean description, such as blue waters and clear skies (on which see Chapter II).

Need all this deter? We have conceded in the Introduction and at the beginning of the present chapter that history *of* the Mediterranean is not the appropriate way of conceptualizing the region in the 'modern' or 'post-modern' periods – however modernity is to be defined. To that extent the reluctance of the disciplines just passed in review to take the region as their frame of reference should neither surprise nor concern us. History, whether 'modern' or 'pre-modern' is – or ought to be – a seamless garment, heuristically divisible in numerous different ways. At one extreme the traditional territories of research could be vastly expanded – through attention to the Atlantic seaborne empires of the western European powers in the later Middle Ages; to the medieval trans-Saharan trade and the penetration of Islam into sub-Saharan Africa; to Rome's contacts with India and China; to Dark Age trade between the Caliphate and Baltic countries via Russia; to the connections between settled Europe and the Asian steppe from the age of the Huns to that of the Mongols. (Something of this order will be attempted with respect to the furthest reaches of the Mediterranean in Volume 2.) At the other extreme we could take advantage of inherent weaknesses in existing conceptions of Europe and the Middle East and wholly redraw the boundaries of investigation to produce units that might at the very least prove refreshing. The Baltic could be taken as a unitary region, with the sea perhaps sustaining a unity in diversity comparable to that of the Mediterranean (cf. Malowist 1972). More to our purpose, southern Europe – Spain, Mediterranean France, Italy and the Balkan peninsula – could also be explicitly 'detached' from the rest of the continent.

The boundary between North and South, the boundary that Gibbon thought real and intelligible, would in this account fall across Europe, not across the Mediterranean. There would thus be no further need to consider southern Europe's littoral as a natural or cultural frontier. Southern Europe might indeed be seen as an enlargement of Auden's Spain (as in the poem 'Spain 1937'), 'nipped off from hot Africa, soldered so crudely to inventive Europe'. (Compare the popular Torinese saying that Garibaldi did not unite Italy, he divided Africa.) The Sahara rather than the sea would then constitute a second latitudinal frontier. Moreover, if we no longer respected the always doubtful integrity of Europe and redrew the line between North and South in this way, we might approach the 'Middle East' with comparable irreverence (XII.7). The boundary between East and West – which was for Gibbon arbitrary and shifting – might be taken as separating the Mediterranean part of the Arab world from the rest: there would be as much justification for that division as for, say, one which separated Egypt from North Africa or Iran from Soviet Asia.

To take advantage of the vulnerability of existing geographies is not, of course, to establish the validity of our own: we have merely opened up a possibility. Clearly, a good deal of theoretical revision remains to be done.

4. Collectivities and Subdivisions III: Intimations of Unity

An account of 1483 illuminates the supposed North–South boundary, and points towards a more satisfying conception of the Mediterranean. Friar Felix Faber, journeying to the Holy Land from Ulm, comes with his noble companions to the south side of the Alps. He describes the moment of arrival in vivid terms:

> while dinner was being prepared I went across with my lords into the court of the house and looking out said, 'Look, if anyone stood on the summit of that mountain, he would be able to see the Great Sea.' When my lords heard this they said, 'Let us go up and behold the sea which perhaps is destined to be our tomb.' And at once my three masters, two of their retinue and I climbed the mountain, which was a good deal higher than it had looked. Casting our eyes out across the region which lay to southward, we looked from the mountains into the Italian plain, and beyond the plain saw the Mediterranean Sea; at the sight of which my lords, being young and sensitive, were appalled and stood still, contemplating the sea and their future dangers. And in fact I too was struck by some qualms at that sight, for all that I had tasted its bitterness thoroughly [on his previous voyage]. For the view from the mountain did have a sufficiently wild appearance. What was near could be seen clearly and the evening sun displayed all the forward part – but all the rest, whose bounds no one could detect, seemed to be towering clouds, thick, gloomy and darkling in atmosphere and colour . . . (*Voyage to the Holy Land* [*Evagatorium Terrae Sanctae* . . .], 7.75)

The sight of the water constitutes the moment when northern Europe and the mountains are left behind and a new region is approached. The decisive point on Felix Faber's journey towards Venice, and thence across the Mediterranean, is this vision of the new world that he and his companions have entered. It is a world characterized by its communications (terrifying as the prospect of them may be), by its climate, and above all by the spectacle of the sea itself – the same sea that washes the shores of his destination, the Holy Land. This sea does indeed form a barrier between Friar Felix's native world and the world of his pilgrimage. But the barrier is here seen to be a zone of transition defined by its potential communications, and not an abrupt discontinuity.

Felix Faber's perception can be pressed into service as we confront a major difficulty inevitably attendant upon history of the Mediterranean: the region's political past. The most sharply defined boundaries, and the ones that have customarily been taken to fracture any concept of the wholeness of the Mediterranean basin, are in every sense political.

There are several long-standing reasons for this emphasis on politics. The first of them is a perhaps undue respect for the usual lines on the political map. Such respect derives from the ideology of the nation-state and its concern with 'natural frontiers' and ethnic inclusiveness, both of which, if achieved, would lend its boundaries a far greater significance than that arising from mere political or military force. The second reason underlies the first. It is that the earliest texts on which Mediterranean narrative history depends – Herodotus, Thucydides, and their precursors – are explicitly concerned with the settling of political demarcation disputes through warfare. The delineation of sharp political boundaries is the subject of historical, and hence of general, learned discussion in Mediterranean lands from the archaic Greek period on (cf. Momigliano 1991, ch. 2). The third reason arises from the long history of profound religious division between Christendom and Islam, which has promoted the division between North and South in the realm of scholarship that we have already considered. Polities like Muslim Spain or the Crusader states in the Levant, or the brief Norman foothold in North Africa (Abulafia 1985a), seem anomalous. They represent a crossing of the sharp politico-religious frontier.

In this context the most disturbing feature of the Mediterranean past must be the infrequency with which even a significant part of the sea and its hinterlands have constituted anything remotely like a political entity. The empires whose sphere of control or influence has embraced some Mediterranean shores have nearly all had centres of gravity well beyond the region. That is certainly true of the earliest hegemonies of the Middle East (as we must continue to call it) from the third millennium B.C., most of which (Hittite and Egyptian apart) were centred on, or attracted towards, the Fertile Crescent of Mesopotamia. It would also apply to the Persian Empire in more than one period of its turbulent history; to the empire of Alexander the Great and to the Hellenistic kingdom of the Seleucid dynasty, which succeeded to the Mesopotamian and Syrian part of Alexander's empire after his death; to the Abbasid caliphate, the Islamic empire centred on Baghdad in the eighth and ninth centuries; and to the empire of the Ottoman Turks from the fourteenth century onwards. The single conspicuous example of the pan-Mediterranean empire is that of Rome.

From the end of the third century B.C. until the fall of her western empire nearly seven centuries later, Rome dominated the Mediterranean region and gradually extended her power well beyond its boundaries – notably to Britain, Gaul and the Danube basin. Yet not even the celebrated *pax Romana* could hope to eradicate the immense diversity of provincial loyalties and cultures. There is indeed a strong sense in which the Roman Empire was not Roman (and, we might add, in which the succeeding Byzantine Empire was not Greek) or at least was only patchily, thinly so. Rome's was an empire in which the precarious unity of Greek and Roman language and culture and an economy of exaction and coinage were totally dependent on communications; and for all the fame of the Roman road, the most basic and the most vital lines of communication lay across the sea.

At this point we may revert to Bismarck's antithesis of the geographical expression and the political reality. In the case of Europe, the geographical expression served to denote an ideal, a formula of unity in diversity that has long been potent in political ideology. The political reality, on the other hand, must clearly be envisaged in more subtle terms than those required for the demarcation of modern states, which have at their disposal cartographic, legal and military facilities of a precision and power unimaginable to earlier epochs. An adequate political map of, say, later medieval Europe – that included all minor authorities and jurisdictions – would present an extremely complex image. And at no point would its character have been determined simply by the physical environment. There may be cultural, ethnic or linguistic frontiers; but there are no natural ones. There are only those frontiers that have arisen out of the interaction between political centres and their peripheries. Frontiers are created slowly, not given; they are very often better conceived as fluid zones of transition between jurisdictions than as clear-cut lines on landscape or map. And even where they remain geographically fixed for a considerable time, the entities that they separate may be in constant evolution. In this sense frontiers are nearly always far less permanent than they may seem. The political map is therefore, above all, a map of the horizon of communications.

If that can be true of Europe, how much more should it apply to a region such as the Mediterranean. The paradox of the Mediterranean is that the all-too-apparent fragmentation can potentially unite the sea and its coastlands in a way far exceeding anything predicable of a continent. The Mediterranean is, in Trump's apt phrase (1980, 3), 'a peninsula in reverse', but one whose possible cohesion and sense of identity exceed anything normally associated with real peninsulas. The minutely subdivided topography bound by a vastly ramified complex of seaways constitutes a geographical expression. And, huge as it is, this geographical expression can be at least *conceived* as a political entity in the same way as can any of the smaller units whose political domain is defined by their horizon of communications. So the Mediterranean is something that the imperialist would willingly bid for or lay claim to, however hard that claim may be to realize. The Roman Empire of course provides the conspicuously successful example; but Saladin's dream of retaking the Syrian coast and then crossing the sea to carry the Holy War to the 'islands of the Franks' implies comparable aspirations (Cameron Lyons and Jackson 1982, 372–3). So too does the visionary programme urged on the count-kings of Barcelona by Arnald of Vilanova around 1300: conquest of Jerusalem, extirpation of Islam, unification with Byzantium – and the foundation of a universal Christian empire with its capital in Sicily (Fernández-Armesto 1991, 67).

There is therefore some truth to the assertion that the Mediterranean was for many centuries a unity by virtue of being successively a Roman, a Muslim, a Christian and a Turkish lake (cf. Trevor-Roper 1972; A. R. Lewis 1951), even if the actual degree of control exercised by the dominant powers was nearly always uneven or limited (II.2; V.2, 4). But the idea is of more general significance. The Greek historians of the fifth century B.C. had already conceived of the past as a sequence of 'sea-powers' or thalassocracies, with the secret of imperial success residing in control of the connecting medium. The prime example was Athens in the fifth century, binding together many dozens of scattered settlements across the Aegean Archipelago and on the inaccessible coasts of that sea, by virtue of being, as a contemporary put it, 'the Power that rules the Sea' ([Xenophon] *Constitution of the Athenians*). What was ruled was, as we have stressed, a network of communications. But it was also the network along which staples were moved to counteract in part the accidents of glut and dearth that the combination of climate and topography made inevitable (cf. Chapters V, VI, IX). This was, in another prominent ancient tradition, the corrupting sea of our title.

Such control of the movement of resources has always been an essential aspect of Mediterranean power at every period. Prehistorians have interpreted seaborne redistribution as the crucial element in the formation of early states and civilizations, and even in the development of agriculture. These tempting theories help remind us that the history of naval supremacy in the Mediterranean – a complex interaction of fleets, pirates, mercenary captains and privateers – is not a simple matter of political confrontation. Nothing short of control of the integrating medium across whole tracts of the sea is at stake, and the prize is one that transcends local interests. Seen in this light, then, Rome's success may appear spectacular only in its completeness and duration. Carthaginians, Ptolemies, Caliphs, Byzantine Greeks, Aragonese, Venetians, and various colonial powers of north-western Europe have all attempted to dominate the mechanics of interaction between the multitude of particular places in the coastlands and islands of this sea. The geography of their respective empires of course differed; in means and intentions they were perhaps quite similar.

The states of the modern Mediterranean, all now independent of empire, are as divided from each other as they have ever been. Yet even the twentieth century, during the course of which the Mediterranean has ceased to possess (in our special sense) a history of its own, has seen various examples of pan-Mediterraneanism, when these separate polities bid for at least an ideological prominence in the wider unity of the whole sea. And this wider unity is conceived in terms that derive from the ancient traditions outlined above. Northern powers have advanced the claims of the heirs of classical civilization; those to the south and east have found indigenous precedents for their location of themselves in a Mediterranean-wide frame. Paradoxically, by virtue of their common aspiration, the separatist states have conduced to the perpetuation of an ancient ideal of thalassocracy – and thus to the maintenance of at least a *residual* sense of Mediterranean unity. It is not, therefore, the obvious limitations of the history of nation-states – the arbitrariness of their frontiers with regard to social, economic or geographical phenomena – that enable us to claim the coastlands of the Mediterranean as a political unit at least as intelligible as 'Europe' or the 'Middle East'. Rather than being a problem whose relevance we should contest, the political and ethnic untidiness of the Mediterranean could turn out to be inspiring. Dense fragmentation complemented by a striving towards control of communications may be an apt summary of the Mediterranean past.

CHAPTER II

A HISTORIAN'S MEDITERRANEAN

It might seem that there is a simple answer to the sceptics who would, in effect, dismember the Mediterranean – simpler than the one advanced at the end of the previous chapter. Has the Mediterranean not been a fruitful concept since those testimonies from the first millennium B.C. already cited? And has it not, until quite recent times, been a noteworthy object of research in its own right?

Simple answers are rarely satisfactory. We must approach the literary and scholarly tradition about the Mediterranean, and in particular its historiography, in a less trusting spirit. Reviewing some of the principal exponents of this historiography, we shall be enquiring into what they have taken to be the particular characteristics of the region. And we shall suggest that some of the seemingly obvious ingredients of a Mediterranean history are better regarded for the moment as facts about various strands of research and popular thought. Because the Mediterranean has been the focus of such prolonged attention from so many different angles, almost every important notion about the region carries its own peculiar burden of cultural history – a burden that renders perilous its further unreflective use.

Take the obvious characteristics of the Mediterranean landscape and environment that constituted the second aspect of the Mediterranean as geographical expression in the opening part of Chapter I. These characteristics have been signalled in the descriptive tradition from its very beginnings. In the Homeric epics the agriculture of olive and vine which shapes so much of even the very modern conception of the Mediterranean is already prominent; and also there in the earliest European literature are the effects of unpredictable rainfall – flash-floods, sudden roaring torrents and boulder-clogged streams whose loads alter the contours of the landscape (cf. VIII.2–3). Another lastingly seductive image is that of the Mediterranean as a region sealed by physical frontiers: to the north, chains of fold-mountains, their passes blocked in winter with ice and snow; deserts to the south and east. Here the tradition may be said to begin with the first literary recollection of Hannibal (Cato, *Origins*, fragment 85). At this level of description the continuity from Antiquity to the age of Braudel is impressive.

Such continuity must, however, be seen first of all precisely as an aspect of the literary tradition. Any investigation of environmental and climatic fluctuation, or of mobility across the proposed boundaries of the region, must reckon with the possibility that the terms with which it instinctively operates – not to mention its conclusions – may have been prescribed in advance, perhaps over two millennia in advance. The yardstick against which it will be measuring fluctuation or mobility may owe more to the literature of the Mediterranean than to its landscape.

1. THE IMAGINARY SEA

The 'classical world'

The all-embracing hegemony of Rome, and its imposition of the values and ideology of a Graeco-Roman elite, has given rise to perhaps the most resonant of Mediterranean images – that of the region as the homeland of classical culture. We have already seen how, through its geographical beliefs, Hellenic and Roman society in various ways appropriated the Mediterranean. For the Greeks and Romans themselves, the Mediterranean was indeed in a strong sense home territory. And it remained so whatever more localized allegiances they might also have owned to. The famous exultant shout of Xenophon's soldiers as they caught sight of open water after a long march back through the mountains of eastern Anatolia – 'thalatta, thalatta', 'the sea, the sea' (Xenophon, *Anabasis of Cyrus*, 4.7.24) – was actually a recognition of the Black Sea; but it can stand as a symbol of the attachment of many ancient peoples to a determinate Mediterranean world.

This home territory was unified by Rome. Writing of the end of the third century B.C., when Rome had survived the threat of Hannibal's invasion, the Greek historian Polybius describes the beginnings of that process of unification – the creation, in effect, of a Mediterranean world (*History*, 1.3.3–4):

> Previously the doings of the world [*oikoumene*] had been, as one might say, dispersed . . . but as a result of these events [Rome's conquests] it is as if history has come to acquire an organic unity [*somatoeides*] and the doings of Italy and Libya [i.e. Africa] are woven together with those of Asia and Greece, and the outcome of them all tends toward one end.

At the centre of this *oikoumene*, of course, lay Italy:

> A land which is at once the foster-child and parent of all other lands, chosen by divine providence to make heaven itself more renowned, to unite scattered empires, to tame savage customs, to draw the discordant and barbarous tongues of numerous peoples together into the conversation of a single language, to give mankind civilization, in short to become the single fatherland of all the races of the earth.

Thus the elder Pliny (*Natural History*, 3.5.39), writing in the first century A.D. when the Roman Empire was approaching the height of its power. In accordance with a theory of the determinants of political success that goes back to the Ionian philosophers and Herodotus, Roman supremacy was often held to derive from environmental advantage (VIII.1).

To some extent since the Renaissance, and certainly since the early nineteenth century, scholarly attempts to grasp the history of the ancient world have very often involved a willingness to deal with evidence from every province of the Roman Empire, to shift attention from Italy to Africa, from Spain to Cyrenaica, their environments as well as their human deposits – to a degree that few students of later periods would contemplate. That there was a homogeneous Mediterranean culture under the Romans is an assumption which (as we noted in I.4) ancient historians have only comparatively recently begun to challenge – faced as they nearly always have been with a material culture which hardly seems to have varied from one end of the Mediterranean to the other.

The Romantic Mediterranean

Partly thanks to the educational dominance exercised by 'the classics' from the Renaissance until the middle of the twentieth century, the scholarly propensity to envisage the Mediterranean region as a distinctive unity has had a 'lay' counterpart. In describing this lay vision we must be careful not to fabricate a single tradition out of an enormous diversity of germane writings. Some of them specifically concern Greece or Rome, others southern Europe (held to be distinct from the 'oriental' world of North Africa and the Levant), and a few explicitly describe the Mediterranean as a whole. None the less, despite their differences of scope they radiate the common conviction that the Mediterranean region is a world set apart from that of northern Europe, whence most of their authors originated.

These literary traditions about the Mediterranean further suggest that the inhabitants of this world exhibit a certain distinctively Mediterranean character; that this character derives substantially from the nature of the Mediterranean environment, the climate especially; and also that it has not changed very much since Antiquity. This claim is typically accompanied by more or less explicit allusion to a wide repertoire of images and commonplaces about life in the Mediterranean – always positive, sometimes near-idolatrous – which may be labelled the Romantic tradition about the region.

The origins of this northern sense of the particular quality of the South might perhaps be traced to the sundering of Catholic Europe by the Protestant reformers (Jenkyns 1980, 41). But it is not until the eighteenth century that such views first reveal themselves clearly. The eighteenth century was, of course, the century of the Enlightenment, and of the development of a line of thought about the determining powers of the environment of which Montesquieu's *The Spirit of the Laws* is a major representative. An eloquent later instance of it is the passage in *The Stones of Venice* (2.6.7) where Ruskin surveys the Mediterranean and the northern worlds as if from a great height, contrasting first their climate and fauna, then their flora, and finally their architecture (1851–3, 2.155–8).

The vocabulary with which Ruskin sets forth his Mediterranean geography ('for the most part a great peacefulness of light, Syria and Greece, Italy and Spain, laid like pieces of a golden pavement into the sea-blue . . .') belongs in a tradition that also flourished in the eighteenth century, the era of the Grand Tour. The famous opening of Goethe's 'Mignon' ('Do you know the land where the lemon trees blossom . . . a soft wind blows from the blue sky . . .') is the blameless forerunner not only of several of the best-known Mediterranean images in Byron and Lawrence Durrell, but also of innumerable tourist- or reader-enticing clichés. Such imagery can also beget academic theory. For the first noteworthy historian of climate, Ellsworth Huntington, the starting point for an investigation into the causes of the burial of ancient Olympia beneath river sediments could even be the fact that Attica was not beautiful enough: it disappointed the Romantic traveller (cf. Chapter VIII). That failure could only be explained in terms of environmental catastrophe (Huntington 1910).

The eighteenth century has other traditions of 'Mediterraneanism' to offer. Traceable back to Winckelmann's magisterial writings on Greek art (e.g. 1755), and to the beginnings of impassioned Hellenism, is the notion that the Greeks, and by extension their Mediterranean neighbours, are a peculiarly natural people – lovers of the open air, happy, hospitable, unreflective, their society simple and harmonious. It is this cluster of qualities that has been held to mark out the 'Mediterranean type'. Acknowledgement of some version of the idea can be discerned in a line of European intellects: Goethe again, Schiller, Schlegel, Marx, Nietzsche, and (as an epigraph to this Part of the book hints) Burckhardt. Its influence is also detectable in those nineteenth-century geographers, such as Friedrich Ratzel, who first systematically – albeit for political ends – treated the Mediterranean as a distinct region of the globe (Peet 1985). And it becomes a commonplace in the less formal writings of contemporary travellers, who found Mediterranean people to be refreshingly classless, unreflective, passionate, open, free of corruption and addiction, light-hearted and pious – all the still familiar stereotypes.

Another major theme of Romantic Mediterraneanism is continuity. At the climax of their Grand Tour, travellers from the North came upon a world hardly industrialized in comparison with their own, and therefore perhaps inevitably more redolent of an earlier age. They had travelled in deliberate search of the distant past: they sought out the topography of the New Testament, the pseudo-classical landscapes that they had already admired in the paintings of Poussin and Claude, the rustics of whom they had read in classical texts. Yet again, early signs of the tendency may be sought in the writings of Goethe, who never visited Greece but did find on his celebrated Italian journey that the South preserved much of its ancient character.

'It is astonishing what a good guide old Herodotus still is in that land', observes a character in a Disraeli novel (*Lothair*, ch. 48), 'that land' being Egypt. 'On the Mediterranean shores . . . the same occupations have been carried on for centuries with little interruption. The same fields are being ploughed, the same vineyards tilled, the same olive-gardens planted, as those in which Theocritus played as a child'. So John Addington Symonds wrote, discussing the permanence of 'rustic manners' in the Mediterranean world (1877, 330). The similarities between rustic manners today and those of Antiquity, beginning with the way in which they struck Braudel, will be one of our concerns in Chapters XI–XII. For the moment it is enough to suggest how a conception of the Mediterranean world as a distinctive unity has often been derived from observing aspects of it that, thanks to supposedly unmitigated economic stagnation, seem not to have changed since classical times.

The scholarly Mediterranean

The special place of the Mediterranean in the educational sophistication of northern Europe could have been nourished just on libraries of the classics, without widespread travelling in the region. The whole Mediterranean would then have served as an extended Arcadia, a place born entirely of the classicizing imagination. In practice, however, the aristocratic Grand Tour and the first-hand experience that it gave were central to the promotion of both the classical ideal and the romance of the area. By the early nineteenth century, moreover, such experience had ceased to be the prerogative of the aristocracy. And the political and economic advantages of contacts with the Mediterranean world could increasingly be perceived alongside the old cultural and aesthetic ones.

Out of the nobleman's Romantic journey to the Mediterranean, therefore, came at least three kinds of progeny: an ever-widening wish to travel; an increasing practical interventionism in the affairs, economic and political, of the region; and, intertwined with both, the systematic study of the material remains of the classical world. Characteristic figures, in this context, of the late nineteenth century are thus the foreign resident or consul taking an active interest in archaeology as well as politics, and the pioneering scholarly explorer. The latter is a type seen at its most developed in the age of D. G. Hogarth and Sir William Ramsay (Chapter X), it finds a most distinguished representative in Mikhail Rostovtzeff (cf. Section 2), and it has achieved an influence reaching into our own time; indeed Louis Robert (1904–85), master of the study of Greek epigraphy, may in some senses be regarded as its last exemplar. The heyday of the Romantic Mediterranean coincides moreover with the period when the Mediterranean was starting to become a prominent subject for the geographer. The search for precise scientific definitions of a region that has already been perceived as a cultural entity thus also belongs in this context. The tracing of isohyets and croplines (Map 1) seems scientific enough; but it may be deployed in the service of ideas that have been generated in a wholly different way.

The once-vaunted detachment of the scholarly method has proved particularly fragile in the field of economic history – the field in which, significantly, many of the most influential syntheses of Mediterranean history have been created. From the early Greek *periploi* onward, the literary response to Mediterranean economic life has been overwhelmingly concerned with seaborne redistribution – what one might, recalling Eliot, call the tradition of Phlebas the Phoenician. Mediterranean historiography has been permeated and directed by the potent image of the sea in the western European cultural tradition, and the seafarer is naturally central to that image. The seafarer represents economic activity. But the seafarer does not – usually – make anything; it is striking how much of the economic historiography of the Mediterranean has concerned itself not with production but with exchange. Redistribution, in its commonest image as trade, has been made the key to understanding not just the economy of the Mediterranean but everything else in the region as well:

> Traders were the apostles of civilization in the Mediterranean Basin. Every commercial center in greater or less degree disseminated elements of civilization or higher culture. Familiarity with life in Athens and Piraeus reveals these two cities as teeming centers of thought and progress. The same was true of Massilia. The Rhone valley people brought raw materials to market there, but they took back with them various elements of Hellenic culture. The great universities, poets, philosophers and artists of the ancient world were found in commercial cities like Athens, Corinth, Rhodes, Miletos, Tarsus, Alexandria and Massilia, for here the currents of thought flowed full and fast. (Semple 1932, 686)

2. Four Men in a Boat

The most influential figures in the twentieth-century historiography of the Mediterranean, and the cardinal reference points for any further discussion of the region as a whole, all accept the centrality of redistribution to the understanding of its history. Their interest is primarily in the 'interactionist' approach. They could, in the sense that we have used the expression, be said to have enlarged the concept of the 'Romantic Mediterranean', giving new life to much of its central imagery.

Rostovtzeff

The first of the four figures with whom the historiography of the ancient and medieval Mediterranean inevitably engages is that of Mikhail Rostovtzeff. His two major works, *The Social and Economic History of the Roman Empire* (1957, but first published 1926) and *The Social and Economic History of the Hellenistic World* (1941), have exercised an extraordinary influence on the economic history of the ancient world. Rostovtzeff was a Russian liberal who had taught in the University of St Petersburg until 1918, and who had gone into exile in the West when the Bolsheviks seized power. Before he left Russia his work had involved, among many other topics, the history of nomadism in south Russia, as well as agrarian history. The pre-revolutionary Russian economy had largely escaped urbanization. What attracted Rostovtzeff in the classical Mediterranean world was what has attracted so many others from the North: the enduring vitality of Mediterranean cities. And what a Russian liberal found so compelling in those cities during an exile first, briefly, at Oxford and then from 1925 at Yale was the cultural and economic achievements of their bourgeoisie. The originality of the two *Histories* lies in their account, both chronological and analytical, of the economic activities of this urban middle class, and of its achievement in unifying the respective empires of Alexander the Great and of Rome.

It may none the less seem strange to regard Rostovtzeff as a Mediterranean historian. His economic history is certainly, in our terms, history 'in' rather than 'of' the region. Braudel tellingly said of him in his last published interview: 'Rostovtseff n'avait pas la formation suffisante. Il fait une histoire économique événementielle' (1986, 17). Mediterranean trade was, for him, strongly affected by major political changes, whether the creation of the Greek colonies (1941, 92) or the increasing dominance of Italy (1941, 778; cf. 1241); it did not possess a vigour of its own. Nor did he relate it very much to its geographic setting. Also, it extended far beyond the Mediterranean: his analysis of the workings of the Hellenistic economy embraced much of Asia. In his discussion of Rome, meanwhile, the Mediterranean world is only specifically evoked in a pessimistic passage dealing with the allegedly inevitable decline of the ancient economy (1957, 470). Seaborne trade is certainly primary and unites the Mediterranean on a focus such as Rhodes or Delos (1941, 1239, 1265–8); in his account of great Mediterranean ports Rostovtzeff is not so far from the position of Semple quoted above. Yet interaction as he interprets it is very much a cultural process largely independent of the accidents of the physical environment. Paradoxically, the Mediterranean as a unitary concept is brought out more clearly in the powerful – and strongly anti-Romantic – attack on Rostovtzeff delivered by Moses Finley (1985a, 33, 191–6). For Finley, the constraints of a prominent Mediterranean ecology act as one check on the classical historian's tendency to exaggerate the volume and importance of ancient trade. The ecologizing tendency is set against the interactionist. One traditional image is counterposed to another – the primitive and unchanging countryman; the restless Phlebas (IX.1).

In the late 1890s Rostovtzeff had been an indefatigable traveller, inspecting antiquities in almost every part of the Mediterranean. And if he did not confine his gaze to the region, and is not quite (on our definition) a Mediterranean historian, in one sense a Romantic Mediterraneanism was fundamental to his vision of the past. The archaeological emphasis in his writings reflects a perception of Antiquity as a field of ruins – a perception closely akin to that of a Grand Tourist. In 1937 Rostovtzeff wrote in a letter of his first visit to India: 'what struck me above all . . . is the life of that what [*sic*] I have studied all my life as a destroyed ruined past. The life of the pagan religion and cult . . .' (Wes 1990, 80).

Rostovtzeff's vision of the structure of ancient society is now obsolete. His bourgeoisie was a chimaera. But his careful combination of literary, epigraphic and archaeological data – with the archaeology presented in the illustrative panels that he insisted on as integral parts of his text (1957, xvii) – in fact represents the only way forward in this field. It is, however (as we shall see in Chapter V and Part Three below), better deployed to illustrate the perennial features of an interaction that is not a matter of great trade routes plied by bourgeois merchants, but something much more closely bound up in the environment and topography of the Mediterranean.

The grandly interactionist conception of Rostovtzeff – of the Mediterranean as a network of 'channels of trade' – was shared by the still more influential figure of Henri Pirenne.

Pirenne

Pirenne was another Northerner, born in 1862 in Belgium. Whereas Rostovtzeff did his greatest work in exile, Pirenne first conceived what is now destined always to be referred to as 'the Pirenne thesis' in a German concentration camp during World War I. Since Gibbon's *Decline and Fall,* if not since the Renaissance, it had been habitual to assume that the end of the Roman Empire in the West must have been cataclysmic, that the Dark Ages began in effect in 476 when the last ruling emperor (actually a usurper) was deposed by the barbarian invaders. However thoroughly Romanized some of the Mediterranean barbarians became, the unity of the region achieved under the Roman Empire was supposed to have given way to a sharp division between East and West – a division that was as much social and economic as political. And out of that arose the lasting configuration of medieval Europe. Meditated under a German occupation, the Pirenne thesis unexpectedly asserts that the 'occupation' of the Western empire by the Germanic barbarians in the fifth century A.D. had far less to do with 'the making of the Middle Ages' than had the Arab conquests of North Africa and the Middle East during the seventh and eighth centuries. It was the rise of Islam to naval dominance in the Mediterranean that, indirectly, shaped the northern economy of Charlemagne's empire, and hence the whole of subsequent medieval society. The title of the book which summarizes Pirenne's thought (a rather more slender work than any of the others assessed in this section), and left only in draft on his death in 1935, is thus *Mohammed and Charlemagne* (1939).

It argues that, in preserving as much as they could of classical culture, the Western barbarians also preserved the classical trading connections between their part of the Mediterranean and the surviving Byzantine empire in the East. The world pictured by Rostovtzeff is thus interpreted as being the world of the early Middle Ages also. For Rostovtzeff, decline was already evident in the third century. For Pirenne, in contrast, the unity of the Mediterranean world survived into the seventh century. It was then destroyed by the sea-captains of Islam, to whom Rome and Byzantium had to yield mastery of the Mediterranean, thereby allowing themselves to be economically cut off from one another.

The rise of the Carolingians, Pirenne went on to propose, was facilitated by the fact that their economic base, the source of their wealth, lay in north-western Europe and consisted in land rather than in gold coinage from the East. Unlike their Merovingian predecessors therefore, whose centre of power lay further south, they were unaffected by Mediterranean economic disruption. Their success finally led the Pope to seek an alliance with the Carolingians; that diplomatic initiative bore fruit on Christmas Day 800 when the Pope crowned Charlemagne emperor. 'It is therefore strictly correct to say', Pirenne wrote in a now famous passage,

> that without Mohammed Charlemagne would have been inconceivable. In the seventh century the ancient Roman Empire had actually become an Empire of the East; the Empire of Charles [Charlemagne] was an Empire of the West . . . The Carolingian Empire . . . was the scaffolding of the Middle Ages. (1939, 234)

Like that of Rostovtzeff, Pirenne's insight is both invigorating and mistaken. He explains too much in terms of towns and long-distance trade, too little in terms of production and aggregate demand. For the caesura in Mediterranean economic history asserted by those who overestimated the destructive inclinations of the Germanic barbarians, he substitutes another – a later, but equally emphatic, break. He envisages Mediterranean history in terms of a sequence of thalassocracies – reasonably enough – but he confuses aspiration and achievement (I.4; V.4).

Mohammed and Charlemagne may, however, still be immensely valued for its assertion of continuity in Mediterranean history from the ancient into the early medieval world, and hence for its partial emancipation of the subject from established chronological categories. As Peter Brown has written, in a passage reminiscent of our epigraph from Braudel:

> whatever the weaknesses of Pirenne's thesis from the point of view of the commercial and maritime history of the Mediterranean, his intuition of the basic homogeneity of Mediterranean civilization deep into the early Middle Ages still holds good. The history of the Christian Church is a history of *Romania à la Pirenne*. It is the history of a religion which identified itself almost from its origins with a Mediterranean-wide style of urban civilization; that penetrated the sprawling countryside of Western Europe along trade routes that linked it to the boom towns of Asia Minor. It fed its imagination on Palestine and Syria; its intellectual power-

house in the Latin world was North Africa, and in this Africa, Carthage, 'Rome in
Africa', remained, like Rome, a great Mediterranean town, moving to rhythms
strangely similar to those of Alexandria, Antioch and Constantinople . . . Any
divergence along the East–West spectrum of the Mediterranean was always dwarfed
by the immensity of the gulf which separated the Mediterranean itself from the
alien societies which flanked it. (1982a, 168–9)

To an extent still largely unrecognized, that judgement concerning the 'horizontal unity' of the Mediterranean might also be applied to the commercial and
cultural history of the Mediterranean in the central Middle Ages – from the late
tenth to the thirteenth century.

Goitein

The work of Shlomo Dov Goitein has shown how the discovery of new evidence
can transform our image of a period of which at least part was seemingly barren.
And it alerts us to the possibility that our ideas about other centuries might be
as mistaken as they were about Goitein's period before he began his work. More
than any other student of the central Middle Ages in the Mediterranean, Goitein
has brought to life again the thoughts and activities of one sector of a prosperous, wide-ranging mercantile 'middle' class which might almost have stepped
from the pages of Rostovtzeff.

The archive that made possible Goitein's feat of imaginative recreation is
that of the Geniza of old Cairo. A Geniza is a storeroom commonly attached to
synagogues in the Middle East, as well as to Christian and Muslim sanctuaries.
Writings that might include the name of God, or that use the Hebrew alphabet,
are deposited in it to preserve them from desecration. The Geniza in one of the
synagogues at Cairo was found to contain documents of all kinds, sacred and
secular, from copies of the Bible to bills of sale and personal correspondence,
dating from the eleventh century until virtually the 1890s, when the storeroom
was emptied and the old synagogue demolished. The archive is unique for two
reasons; first because the storeroom was exceptionally large and can hardly have
been intended for any other purpose than as a repository of documents, so that
it never needed the periodic spring-cleaning common in more humble establishments; secondly because, like the papyri accumulated in the rubbish dumps of
Roman Egypt, its contents have been preserved rather than destroyed by the
environment. Nowhere else have circumstances been so propitious for the survival of a large number of medieval ephemera.

The man whose multi-volume survey, *A Mediterranean Society* (1967–88),
has made the contents of the Cairo Geniza generally accessible was born in
1900 in Bavaria, in a small village that at the time still had a stagecoach service
for travel into the nearby mountains. His academic career took him to Frankfurt
and Berlin during and after World War I, then in 1923 to the new state of
Palestine, and finally, in 1957, to the American academic world, within which he
remained until his death in 1985.

Goitein's fields of interest before he became involved with the publication
of the Geniza archive had been mainly ethnographic and philological. He had
produced a first-hand account of the strictly isolated Yemenite immigrants to
Palestine, 'those most Jewish and most Arab of all Jews' (1967–88, 2.viii). And

while still in Jerusalem he had directed the critical edition of a major medieval Arab writer, al-Baladhuri. Although it too required an exacting combination of ethnographic and philological expertise, Goitein's work on the Geniza contrasted with his previous scholarly undertakings. Here was an opportunity to use texts that opened up a world of vast dimensions and incessant movement. Goitein began his investigation with the study of documents concerning the medieval trade of the Indian Ocean. He then realized that understanding of these presupposed a knowledge of the Mediterranean origins of the merchants who largely sustained the Indian trade, and he enlarged his brief to 'a survey of the documentary Geniza *in toto*' (1967–88, 1.viii). Goitein's Mediterranean world brings together what seem to have been his three abiding concerns: his Jewish heritage, the history and culture of the Islamic Middle East, and the values of liberal humanism. An autobiographical essay of 1975 evinced a marked optimism about the future of mankind; and that optimism may, at least to some extent, have been fuelled by the traces that Goitein discovered in the Geniza of what he calls a medieval free-trade community (1.61) and democracy (2.vii). The Jews living among Arabs who people *A Mediterranean Society* enjoyed a mobility that was often Mediterranean-wide, and that did not by any means exclude contact with European traders, even during periods of open hostility between Christendom and Islam. Goitein declined to venture any judgement about the absolute value of free enterprise (2.viii–ix). Yet it is hard not to sense in his work a humane appreciation of the power of commerce to dissolve, if only for a time, the deepest political or religious divisions.

A Mediterranean Society offers a detailed, deeply pragmatic account, concerned to pass on the intimate revelations of the enormous Geniza archive rather than to expound a broader conception of Mediterranean history. Goitein described himself as a sociographer (5.xvi), perhaps implying a more descriptive approach than might be required of a historical sociologist. And when he came in the last volume of his work to offer a summing up of the community on which he had been working for over thirty years, he proved disconcertingly reliant on some of the stereotypes of the Romantic tradition: the clarity of the Mediterranean sky, the innate sociability of the 'natural' Mediterranean type (5.xx, 7). It is significant that Goitein considered Rostovtzeff a towering figure, took no clear stand in the debate over the Pirenne thesis (to which he could surely have contributed much), and did not properly absorb Braudel's work on the Mediterranean until the English translation was available in paperback (from 1975) and two volumes of his own project had already been published (vol. 5, epilogue).

Beyond the sphere of medieval Islamic and Judaic studies, Goitein's presentation of the Mediterranean has not perhaps commanded the attention that its novelty and suggestiveness merit. And this may be because it lacks a geographical setting other than the one incidentally provided by its documents. The restrictions on freedom of movement to which it gives prominence tend to be navigational. Comparable charges could thus be levelled at three of the 'four men in a boat' whom we have so far considered. They are all too narrowly interactionist. That is, among possible forms of interaction they give undue prominence to long-distance trade. And they neglect ecology, the indispensable context of interaction. The last of our four men and, in the late twentieth century, the most widely acclaimed, could not be accused of giving too little weight to Mediterranean ecology.

Braudel

'When I think of the individual', Fernand Braudel famously wrote in the concluding paragraph of the second edition of *The Mediterranean and the Mediterranean World in the Age of Philip II*,

> I am always inclined to see him imprisoned within a destiny in which he himself has little hand, fixed in a landscape in which the infinite perspectives of the long term stretch into the distance both behind him and before. In historical analysis as I see it, rightly or wrongly, the long run always wins in the end. Annihilating innumerable events – all those which cannot be accommodated in the main ongoing current and which are therefore ruthlessly swept to one side – it indubitably limits both the freedom of the individual and even the role of chance. I am by temperament a 'structuralist', little tempted by the event, or even by the short-term conjoncture which is after all merely a grouping of events in the same area. But the historian's 'structuralism' . . . does not tend towards the mathematical abstraction of relations expressed as functions, but instead towards the very sources of life in its most concrete, everyday, indestructible and anonymously human expression. (1972a, 1244)

That is a revealing summary of the philosophy behind a work whose presentation merely as a thesis was said to mark 'an epoch in world historiography' (Labrousse 1973, 11) – a strong leaning towards environmental determinism, the tautological air of 'the long run always wins in the end', the contempt for mere events, and yet, withal, a humane concern with life in its everyday expression. 'I have loved the Mediterranean with passion' is the work's unambiguously Romantic opening, over twelve hundred pages earlier than the above quotation. And it has often been remarked that the heroes of Braudel's magisterial account are abstract terms or inanimate things personified: the sea itself, first and foremost; the climate and the surrounding landscape; Space, Time, Man – and 'the long term', *la longue durée*. It is this last concept above all others that informs the entire book, making it into a piece of human geography of vast historical compass.

The Mediterranean is in three parts. The first, that of the *longue durée*, is a history of man in relationship to his environment, 'a history in which all change is slow, a history of constant repetition, ever-recurring cycles' (1972a, 20). Reflecting on the reception of his book since its first edition appeared in 1949, Braudel remained confident in the validity of this first 'geohistorical' part, and continued to express his confidence in somewhat Romantic terms.

> None of my critics has reproached me for including in this historical work the very extended geographical section which opens it, my homage to those timeless realities whose images recur throughout the whole book, from the first page to the last. The Mediterranean as a unit, with its creative space, the amazing freedom of its sea-routes . . . with its many regions, so different yet so alike, its cities born of movement, its complementary populations, its congenital enmities, is the unceasing work of human hands; but those hands have had to build with unpromising material, a natural environment far from fertile and often cruel, one that has imposed its own long lasting limitations and obstacles. All civilization can be defined as a struggle, a creative battle against the odds; the civilizations of the Mediterranean basin have wrestled with many often visible obstacles, using sometimes inadequate human resources, they have fought endlessly and blindly against

the continental masses which hold the inland sea in its grip . . . I have therefore
sought out, within the framework of a geographical study, those local, permanent,
unchanging and much repeated features which are the 'constants' of Mediterranean history; the reader will not find here all the unspectacular structures and
recurrent patterns of life in the past, but the most important of them and those
which most affect everyday existence. These provide the reference grid as it were.
(1972a, 1239)

They are, to revert to the earlier metaphor, the prisons, the everyday constraints on human initiative in the Mediterranean. To the general emphasis on
the unifying effect of shipping lanes characteristic of Rostovtzeff, Pirenne and
Goitein, Braudel made a notable addition: the physical environment as both
defining the contours of the region and as delimiting freedom of movement
within it.

Braudel was not, however, content with a simple assertion of the landscape's
ruling influence. The first part of *The Mediterranean* is intended to furnish 'the
reference grid' for the second part, and this in turn should be the reference grid
for the last. If the *longue durée* is time moving at its slowest and least perceptible
pulse, the second part presents a medium term of cycles lasting for anything up
to around fifty years – *conjonctures* as Braudel calls them, borrowing a (somewhat outmoded) term from economics to distinguish them from the structures,
or 'geohistory', of the *longue durée*. *Conjonctures* involve wars and economic
systems; secular trends, in short, in every aspect of social history.

And at the end of the book, least original in substance yet most controversial
in its positioning, the rapid lapse of time; the history of particular persons and
events, *l'histoire événementielle*, the stuff of traditional political and diplomatic
narrative, the realm of individual consciousness in all its blindness. Such history
is seductive. It tempts the historian into supposing that he can explain the actions
of historical characters by referring only to their motives or to the immediate
context, ignoring the underlying structures and *conjonctures*. It is

> a dangerous world, but one whose spells and enchantments we shall have exorcised
> by making sure first to chart those underlying currents, often noiseless, whose
> direction can only be discerned by watching them over long periods of time.
> Resounding events are often only momentary outbursts, surface manifestations of
> these larger movements and explicable only in terms of them. (1972a, 21)

Thus does the long term win out in the end.

This bracing vision of Mediterranean history has been frequently appraised.
There is no need for us to undertake yet another comprehensive review. Our
discussion of the work's qualities will be related to two questions. First: how did
the work come about? And second (the question addressed in the next section):
why for all its fame and influence does it seem to have marked an end rather
than a beginning in Mediterranean studies?

Rather like Pirenne's most seminal writing, *The Mediterranean* was the fruit
of incarceration: its espousal of the *longue durée* may well, as is frequently conjectured, have been a way of averting the pessimism engendered by 'events'
within a German prisoner-of-war camp. Equally, its preoccupations perhaps
reflect Braudel's upbringing. Although his parents lived in Paris, he was born in
a small village in Lorraine and spent his first seven years there, living with his
paternal grandmother:

A very old bell used to strike the hour . . . the village pond drove an old mill wheel; a stony path, as old as the world, plunged down like a torrent in front of the house; the house itself had been rebuilt in 1806, the year of Jena, and hemp used to be retted in the stream at the bottom of the meadows . . . (Braudel 1981–4, 1.559; cf. P. Braudel 1992)

A lovingly detailed picture of life close to the soil, unchanging or slowly moving: one component in Braudel's Mediterranean. The other, which will by now be familiar, is the romance of the sea and of seafaring, the 'amazing freedom' of Mediterranean shipping lanes – something to which a Northerner may be more susceptible than a native.

To remark that there is a poetic element in Braudel's scholarly vision, or that he has a novelist's eye for significant detail, is not merely to comment on his style or on the way in which he organizes his material. It is a recognition that there are, perhaps, two inner voices to which Braudel has attended in writing history (compare Carrard 1992). One voice is insistent on the primacy of historical imagination and passionate involvement; it explicitly admits that the division of history into three layers or time-scales is merely a heuristic device, an arbitrary way of dealing with a complex and indivisible subject (1972a, 21); it concedes that the separation of material into the book's three parts can never be exact; it does not press its determinism too far ('by stating the narrowness of the limits of action, is one denying the role of the individual in history? I think not': 1972a, 1243). The other voice represents the historiographical tradition in which *The Mediterranean* stands – the tradition associated with the French historical journal *Annales.* Its aspirations are scientific: there is far less scope for poetry or passion.

Two aspects of *Annaliste* history are essential to an understanding of *The Mediterranean*. One is the concern to integrate geography and history as closely as possible. There is of course (as we hinted in Section 1 above) a long tradition of geographical determinism in historical writing that stretches from Herodotus to Montesquieu and beyond. (In 1915 Ellsworth Huntington could still claim, with Herodotus, that the 'higher' forms of civilization were necessarily to be found only in the temperate zone.) And in France, more so than elsewhere, a strong link between geography and history has been forged by the structure of the higher educational curriculum – so that regional histories which begin with a chapter on the flora and fauna, functioning as a backdrop to the historical discussion that follows, have long been common.

This explains why two outstanding influences on Braudel's thought were Paul Vidal de la Blache and Lucien Febvre. To name them is not of course to deny Braudel's equal indebtedness to Pirenne (among historians) for his demonstration of the need to study both Christian and Muslim Mediterraneans (Daix 1995, 91–3), or to older masters such as Michelet. Nor is it to underestimate the depth of Braudel's response to the nineteenth-century geographical tradition in Mediterranean scholarship, exemplified for him in the work of Alfred Philippson (Braudel 1972a, 1273). But the writings of Vidal and Febvre seem to have been decisive in shaping Braudel's historical philosophy. Vidal was the geographer (or, rather, historian turned geographer) who most forcefully and persuasively suggested that the Mediterranean region was a unity with an enduring personality of its own. The section on the Mediterranean in Vidal's *Principles of Human Geography* (1926) prefigures Part 1 of Braudel's work in most of its ahistorical essentials (cf. Braudel 1972a, 1273). Febvre was the historian whose *A Geographical Introduction to History* (1925) had elaborated a 'possibilism' that sought to purge geographical history of its previous deterministic excesses, partly by stressing how often human action had been instrumental in modifying the landscape, partly by suggesting that the environment merely set outer limits to the range of possible forms of exploitation (cf. Chapter VIII).

Febvre was one of the founding fathers of the *Annales* school. And his work, ranging in subject from landscape to religion, is exemplary of a second strand in *Annaliste* thinking that gave shape and substance to *The Mediterranean*: the desire for *histoire totale*, total history. In practice that ambition resolved itself into an emphasis on integrating history and the sciences – sociology, anthropology, demography, biology and so on. Its ultimate effect on the *Annaliste* historiographical approach was a somewhat dogmatic substitution of analysis for narrative; statistics for impressions; comparativism and methodological self-consciousness for naive positivism; and above all, as befits a broadly sociological approach, a concentration on the anonymous masses instead of conspicuous individuals, and on continuities and regularities instead of rapid changes. In its search for the hidden depths of the historical process, the long-term determinants of action (economic, social, psychological), *Annales* history has certain obvious affinities with Marxist history. But it is a history without class struggles and without inevitable revolutions – Marxism denatured, static history: 'histoire immobile' as Emmanuel Le Roy Ladurie notoriously labelled one of its manifestations (1978).

This sketch of the genesis of *The Mediterranean* may show how it can be regarded as a simultaneous recapitulation of the major themes that we have previously identified in the history of Mediterranean studies. To the interactionist vision it adds an ecologizing perspective. To the tradition of Romantic evocation it lends the analytical weight of a social science. And these come together in the ultimately Romantic project of an all-inclusive *chef d'oeuvre*, in which an entire world is subordinate to its creator-historian.

3. THE END OF THE MEDITERRANEAN

Rehearsing all these themes, Braudel's book can also be seen as bringing to summation and close an entire epoch in Mediterranean scholarship. Approximately since the time of the publication of *The Mediterranean* in its second edition (1966), as our discussion in Chapter I may already have suggested, what amounts to a Kuhnian paradigm shift has occurred. First, the Mediterranean region as a whole has apparently ceased, at least for the time being, to attract the attention of historians and geographers; major *synoptic* works are rare. Nor, with the partial exception of social anthropology, is the region widely recognized as a major division of their respective fields by practitioners of other social sciences (I.3; Part Five). This state of affairs can be interpreted in two connected ways. First, it can be related to a fundamental change in the overall nature of the Mediterranean region and, as we argue (Introduction), in the appropriate way of writing its history (less 'history of' than 'history in'). Second, it can be seen in more narrowly literary terms as the withering of a scholarly tradition that goes back to the founding fathers of regional geography in the first half of the nineteenth century, Carl Ritter and Friedrich Ratzel. The Romantic current in Mediterranean writing, out of which (we have proposed) the geographical one emerged, may also be taken as having reached its apogee in Braudel's work. Although it is not without adherents – or victims – today, this Romanticism too has withered to a cluster of lame topoi. The likely cause of this paradigm shift was the appearance of *The Mediterranean*.

Several reasons can be hazarded for such paradoxical influence. The most obvious are the magnitude of Braudel's achievement and the twenty-five years that it required of him. Neither encourages anything like an attempt at emulation. It may have been recalled that the two Chaunus' study of just one outreach of the Mediterranean, the Atlantic trade of Seville (1955–9), with its three volumes of text and five more of statistics, contained descriptions only of *conjonctures*, not of the *longue durée*; and it was criticized by the master for in any case failing to deal with the entire ocean.

The second possible reason is that Braudel seems once and for all to have done the job of asserting Mediterranean unity and characterizing it in human geographical terms. A work ostensibly devoted to the reign of Philip II also embodies a substantial amount of 'timeless' environmental description, lastingly useful to historians and geographers alike. Considered in isolation, the geographical opening part of *The Mediterranean* is in many respects the least controversial. It is its 'gravitational pull' on the other two parts of the book that provokes significant disagreement. The broad picture has therefore apparently been filled in: it may appear to need only minor, piecemeal revision.

So, at least, Braudel himself perhaps felt. During the late 1960s or early 1970s (to judge by internal evidence) he brought to near-completion a substantial monograph entitled 'La Méditerranée: la longue marche d'une civilisation'. It was actually a narration of several civilizations of the *prehistoric* and *ancient* Mediterranean, beginning, remarkably, with the Lower Palaeolithic age and working its way, culture by culture, through to Greece and Rome. More emphasis is placed on technological change than on war and conquest; and, as we should expect, the text begins with, and seldom moves far away from, consideration of the physical environment. But, by comparison with Part 1 of the earlier *Mediterranean*, this is unsurprising stuff. The work's chief claim to originality lies rather in its refusal to equate ancient history with that of the Greeks and Romans, and in the sheer amount of space allowed to prehistory. In his last published interview, Braudel stated indeed that the transition from prehistory to Antiquity, particularly in Gaul, interested him far more than that from Antiquity to the Middle Ages (Braudel et al. 1986, 7), an interest also demonstrated in print in the first volume of *The Identity of France* (1988–90). In the unpublished monograph, however, beyond showing how long the *longue durée* can be, Braudel had little to add to his earlier environmental history of the region – one reason, perhaps, why the work remained unpublished during his lifetime.

It is not only to its author that *The Mediterranean* has seemed the last word. When an eminent economic historian of Antiquity wishes to sum up the Mediterranean environment whom else should he cite but Socrates – and Braudel (Finley 1985a, 30–1)? Whom else, again, when archaeologists seek justification for concerted survey projects in the region and intellectual frameworks within which to locate their discussion of evolving settlement patterns (Cherry 1983; Bintliff 1991; Barker et al. 1995)? The few historical studies of parts of the

Mediterranean world that could, as Braudel realized (1972a, 1240), be said to test or extend his ideas about the historical geography of the region do not do so by taking *The Mediterranean* as an exemplar. Baehrel on Provence (1961), Le Roy Ladurie on Languedoc (1966), Delumeau on Rome (1957–9), Vilar on Catalonia (1962), Bresc on Sicily (1986b) – to name only a few of those over whom Braudel's shadow looms – are regional studies cast in a much more restricted mould, and each rather different in method and organization. Only Braudel himself, in his unpublished prehistory of the Mediterranean and then in *Civilization and Capitalism* (1981–4), effectively continued discussing the area as a whole – and he did that, in the first instance, by repeating himself and, in the second, by incorporating his discussion of the area into a global economic analysis.

Concomitant with this neglect of Braudel's subject matter, a more general lack of interest in all-embracing geographical history became evident. For example, Georges Duby and Jacques Le Goff among medievalists pursued 'ruralization', the shift of emphasis from town to countryside in economic, social and cultural history, and thereby pioneered new forms of history 'close to the soil'. But they, like many others, also preferred to study the *mentalités* or thought-worlds of relatively small groups over confined periods – a more intimate, less ambitious, form of history than anything to be found in *The Mediterranean*. Le Roy Ladurie's immensely popular study of a village of medieval heretics, *Montaillou* (1975), can stand here as a symbol of a trend that it helped originate. Among theorists of history meanwhile, Michel Foucault (1972) took the lead in directing interest to abrupt *dis*continuities in the history of systems of thought or structures of power. In succeeding periods of philosophical fashion, so far as it is possible to generalize about them, historiography was dominated by post-modern or 'new historicist' attention to the minutiae of texts (Veeser 1989). In an intellectual climate ruled by poetics, the duller rhythms of the geographical *longue durée* command relatively little attention.

The shift of emphasis away from Braudel's subject matter has been inextricable from an avoidance of his method. And so the third possible reason why *The Mediterranean* marks an end rather than a beginning is that subject and method have become confused with one another. The method has attracted considerable criticism; the subject has perhaps suffered from association with it.

For our purposes, the most significant criticism has been focused on the degree to which Braudel endorses environmental determinism. His contempt for 'mere' events and 'mere' individuals like Philip II, whose personal history is relegated to *The Mediterranean*'s closing pages, has been frequently attacked on conceptual grounds – not only for its determinism but also for its confusion of 'dryasdust' facts, the (sometimes) dispensable stuff of traditional history, with the 'events' that any form of history has to find space for. Moreover as one critic (cited by Hexter 1979, 137–8) has pointed out, Braudel's taxonomic linking of the *longue durée* with geography and of events with politics and diplomacy is arbitrary and easily contradicted: a political structure such as monarchy could have a *durée* of millennia; a geographical event like an earthquake could last only a few minutes and produce no long-term effects. There have also been empirical attempts to refute Braudel's theory about the minimal role of the individual in history and the primacy of economics over politics. Taking issue with Braudel on a subject very close to that of *The Mediterranean*, Jonathan Israel (1982) for example set out to show how economic considerations were determined by political decisions during the war between the Spanish and the Dutch in the earlier seventeenth century. Finally, the charge has been brought that, because Braudel's human geography (unlike Febvre's) admits causation in only one direction, there is little scope for considering the effects of man on the environment. The first geohistorical section of the work is thus, for all its usefulness, too nearly static.

A further major criticism concerns the way in which Braudel deploys his evidence. Those who would accept his vision of historical man as imprisoned by the structures of the environmental *longue durée* may still reasonably doubt whether he has entirely succeeded in translating that vision into historiography. Because he has chosen *histoire totale* which must be set out schematically topic by topic, Braudel has denied himself the opportunity to address particular problems (*histoire problème*) of the sort that could thematically bind together the book's many short sections. *The Mediterranean* can after all quite easily be approached as a series of discrete essays – and with the essays taken in no particular order. Braudel does not quite succeed in creating the cumulative effect he hoped for. Reading the last section of the book on the events in which Philip II was embroiled, we are only occasionally reminded by the author of the vast environmental limitations on human action described over a thousand pages previously. This also means, importantly, that the ecologizing and the interactionist perspectives cannot satisfactorily be integrated; for although interaction is evidenced in all three parts of the book, the ecological material is largely confined to Part 1. *The Mediterranean* is thus best seen as a historical panorama, a massive picture full of engaging detail. Its author's achievement is less to have advanced specific hypotheses – about the economic history of the sixteenth century, about Philip II's foreign policy – than to have enriched our imaginary tableau of the period. When Braudel was taxed in an interview with a failure consistently to link his exposition to the solution of particular problems, he replied that the problem throughout had been to demonstrate the different *durées* of his three levels of history. He thus implicitly admitted that his problem was methodological rather than substantive, and that the solution to it was virtually predetermined in the book's very layout.

Recognition that *The Mediterranean* is more panoramic than problem-solving encourages a further, related criticism. It may seem hard to complain that a work in two volumes of over twelve hundred pages has left vital topics out and misplaced its emphasis. But the complaint is a powerful one, and must be registered. If the structures that delimit the sphere of human initiative are to be fully described (as *histoire problème* suggests) must they not include psychological as well as geographical ones (as *histoire totale* surely requires)? In an article written during the long period when *The Mediterranean* was being revised for its second edition, Braudel was clear, if only as an afterthought, that they should: 'mental frameworks too can form prisons of the *longue durée*' (1980, 31). Yet mental frameworks – *mentalités* – are precisely what *The Mediterranean* to a quite remarkable extent neglects. It is material life – especially towns, ships, and long-distance trade – that mainly captures Braudel's imagination as it did those of Rostovtzeff, Pirenne and Goitein. Perceptions, attitudes, beliefs and symbols; the Reformation, the Counter-Reformation, the Baroque; the clash of Islam and Christianity: all these are reduced to a relatively few pages.

The Mediterranean is, then, widely held to be a major yet flawed achievement. And the most famous piece of modern historical writing has, for the most part, borne fruit outside the field of Mediterranean studies.

4. Mediterranean History

We have now several times drawn a distinction between history *in* the Mediterranean – contingently so, not Mediterranean-wide, perhaps better seen as part of the larger history of either Christendom or Islam – and history *of* the Mediterranean – for the understanding of which a firm sense of place and a search for Mediterranean-wide comparisons are both vital. We have suggested that, during the twentieth century, the Mediterranean has in many ways ceased to be an intelligible unity. As far as the 'contemporary historian' is concerned, history *in* it seems more *à propos* than history *of* it. Indeed, a certain tradition in the historical scholarship of the Mediterranean may plausibly be seen as having come to an end, or at least as having reached a low point, in the period following the publication of Braudel's book. We have raised the further possibility that *The Mediterranean* may, for reasons that are not hard to envisage, also have brought about the decline of other traditions of writing about the region, notably among geographers. None of this of course means what the title of the preceding section mischievously suggests: the end of 'Mediterranean studies'. For their burgeoning is undeniable. It does mean that, as we have already put it, in its own particular field *The Mediterranean* has been more an end than a beginning. Work that has been done since its appearance is, in the main, fragmented. Some of it takes the unity and geographical framework of its subject matter for granted (perhaps on the assumption that Braudel has done what needed to be done); some of it implicitly denies that such unity has ever existed; some of it ignores such large topics altogether.

Our exploration of the principal ways in which the Mediterranean has been conceived, which began with the early first millennium B.C., can now therefore suitably close with a consideration of a publication of 1966. But that is not the end of the matter. The history of ideas about the Mediterranean is hardly a subject that, once tackled, can be entirely set aside like a preliminary 'literature survey'. Its complexities are not a mist through which we can feel our way to emerge on the far side in a clear – let alone a Mediterranean – light that will enable us simply to perceive the region's history for ourselves. The ideas that we have reviewed are an inescapable and essential part of our inheritance. Inescapable, because there can be no unconditioned vision of a historical topic of this size and kind, no entirely independent return to the evidence. Essential, because many of the ideas discussed are far more than historiographical. They must be reckoned a part of the primary object of our enquiry: they have not only reflected but also influenced the beliefs and behaviour of Mediterranean people in the past. In this sense, we might assert, the *Odyssey* has been the creator of the Mediterranean. There is, then, no detached vantage point from which the ideas earlier reviewed can be simplistically interpreted as just temporarily arising between us and our subject in some cognitive no man's land. We cannot get away from them; we can only attempt to remain highly self-questioning in our responses – always aware of their tenacious hold on our thinking, sidestepping their more blatantly misleading imagery or generalizations. That we cannot hope to achieve complete independence of approach certainly does not entail our conceptual passivity.

To specify at this early stage the forms that our efforts to outwit tradition will take would be to offer something in the nature of a detailed programme or methodology. And that we prefer to avoid: there have already been too many in the history of Mediterranean studies. We stated at the outset that our choice of period would have to respond to the changing characteristics of the appropriate evidence. Flexibility must also be the watchword in our approach to subject matter.

First, the lesson to be learned from the discussion elicited by Braudel's work is that *histoire problème* must be preferred to *histoire totale*. *Histoire totale* on a Braudellian scale, but explicitly embracing more than twenty centuries rather than Braudel's two or three, would be unfeasible, unrewarding, and unpublishable. There can, as we have already stressed in the Introduction, be no question of completeness or evenness of coverage, geographical or chronological. We need to be able to address specific questions, and therefore to gather evidence select-ively – from a limited range of periods and places. Nor must we shackle our-selves in advance with some grand vision of the significance of our work for the entire 'historical process' in the Mediterranean. If, in what follows, attention is concentrated on 'constants' of Mediterranean history, Braudellian or otherwise, this is not because we too hold that the *longue durée* wins out in the end, or indeed that it necessarily wins out at all. What is lasting in human affairs is not inevitably decisive.

In an essay on Braudel, W. H. McNeill has criticized 'an approach to history that systematically denigrates conscious behaviour' as being 'as deficient in its way as were the dry-as-dust narratives of conscious policy-making against which Braudel and his mentors rebelled so successfully half a century ago' (1986, 224). This criticism is not entirely appropriate to a work that paid considerable atten-tion to Spanish wars of aggression in the Maghreb and elsewhere had even more to say about conscious responses to environmental stimuli. But the overall point is well made; and it might be applied to our endeavour in this book, for we deal much of the time with unintended patterns of behaviour. We can only anticipate criticism similar to McNeill's by emphasizing that we never seek formally to exclude other forms of history from involvement with the topics or approaches discussed here. Rather what we outline are intended to be the general ecological principles with which the more usual kinds of Mediterranean history – eco-nomic, social or political – should mesh.

The second lesson to be learned from the fate of Braudel's work is that *histoire problème* should avoid determinism, environmental or otherwise (cf. Chapter VIII). Whatever chains of cause and effect it tries to disclose will not all lead in one direction. There must certainly be scope for investigating the effects of man on the environment as well as of the environment on man. And there must, further, be genuine *histoire*, a discipline with its own identity that cannot, we contend, be reduced to the procedures of the biological sciences.

Thirdly, therefore, no limits must be set in advance to the kinds of evidence and topic that will be admissible. History of the Mediterranean – as we have defined it – will be in large measure a history 'close to the soil' – and the sea: a historical equivalent of human geography. But such history cannot be 'mindless', for all its attention to subconscious patterns of behaviour. *Mentalités* must clearly find their place.

That stipulation applies most forcefully to the study of interaction in the Mediterranean – a subject which, fourthly, we must attempt properly to integrate with the ecologizing approach. Interactionist and ecologizing approaches have been detached from one another in many of the currents of thought that we have reviewed. As we have already indicated, Braudel's way of at last bringing them together is not wholly adequate.

Fifthly, it is in keeping with this requisite flexibility of approach that we shall expect conclusions that are neither absolute nor all-embracing. Our task is the investigation of unity in space and continuity over time: these are the prerequisites of a distinctively Mediterranean history. But we shall not presuppose either unity or continuity: both remain to be demonstrated (or denied) topic by topic. And if we find them we shall not suppose them to be measurable in other than loose and relative terms. To borrow an evocative term from mathematics, the Mediterranean is a 'fuzzy set'. A certain vagueness should be of the essence in the way that it is conceived. Unity is obviously unlikely to be hard and fast, exhibiting clear external boundaries and internal homogeneity. It can only be assessed by reference to recurrent features that are more frequently found within the region than outside it. And, most importantly, it should be allowed that, if the Mediterranean past turns out to exhibit any unity at all, then the region may have been far more unified in some respects than in others. Continuity will similarly involve such patterns, and may be of several different kinds. These should ideally be specified, generously documented, and measured against change. Continuity in history will not really resemble immobility. In other words, like unity it will not be an 'all or nothing' matter. Far too much debate on these twin issues has been clouded by the implicit assumption that it will.

Finally, we must state our preference for a broadly ecological model in interpreting the kind of Mediterranean history that concerns us: history of, not just in, the region. But we must take this earliest opportunity of making clear the model's heuristic limitations and the extent of our reliance on it.

5. HISTORICAL ECOLOGY

Ecology is the scientific study of the relationship between living organisms and their animate and inanimate environment. There is as little place in it for, on one hand, simple environmental determinism (now, fortunately, both theoretically and empirically discredited) as for vague popular concern with pollution on the other. An ecologist is customarily involved in the detailed – and usually quantified – study of niches, systems, food chains, transfers of energy, the size and distribution of animal or human populations, and so on. For us to draw on the terminology of such a discipline will therefore be first and foremost a way of indicating that it is here a question of the many-faceted interaction between humanity and environment, rather than of environmental primacy, of human autonomy, or of the limited responsiveness to surroundings implied by 'possibilism'. To that extent an 'ecosystemic' approach clearly has much to commend it. Can ecology however offer anything more specific to Mediterranean history? Can the models and techniques devised by ecologists be rendered 'operational' for historians? We take up our position in the continuing debate on such questions by asserting that a genuine human ecology, both scientific and historical, and also embracing the whole Mediterranean, is at once obviously desirable and utopian. Ecology is not a *deus ex machina* capable of solving the historian's problems with a dose of scientific rigour. It shows us the topics with which we should be concerned, and more especially the likely kinds of connection between them; it is not yet clear that it can do more.

We conclude this chapter by indicating why that should be by looking at one classic example of the ecological analysis of a human society. Roy Rappaport's *Pigs for the Ancestors: Ritual in the Ecology of a New Guinea People* (1984, first published 1968) may still represent ecological anthropology at its most sophisticated. It makes plain just how much the discipline can offer and it has been widely influential. Yet *Pigs for the Ancestors* has also been much criticized on empirical, methodological and conceptual grounds, from both within the discipline and outside it; indeed, Rappaport felt constrained to add one hundred and seventy pages of self-defence to the second edition of his book. Reading the apologia, therefore, as well as the original *Pigs for the Ancestors*, the historian soon realizes how narrow are the absolute limits of what can be achieved – and also how far a historical ecology must fall short of reaching them.

Pigs for the Ancestors concerns the Tsembaga, a clan group of (at the time of Rappaport's writing) about two hundred people occupying an area of some three square miles in the highlands of New Guinea. As Rappaport presents the Tsembaga – we are not here concerned with what has happened to them since 1968 – they are mainly horticulturalists, creating their gardens in cut and burnt areas of secondary forest. But pig husbandry is also nutritionally important to them; and pigs are the focus of their cycle of ritual activity. This cycle culminates in the *kaiko*, a year-long festival during which the vast majority of the group's pigs are slaughtered and eaten. Rappaport attempts to explain the cycle in ecological terms. The details do not matter here; but the conclusion does:

> The Tsembaga ritual cycle has been regarded as a complex homeostatic mechanism, operating to maintain the values of a number of variables within 'goal ranges' (ranges of values that permit the perpetuation of a system, as constituted, through indefinite periods of time). It has been argued that the regulatory function of ritual among the Tsembaga ... helps to maintain an undegraded environment, limits fighting to frequencies that do not endanger the existence of the regional population, adjusts man–land ratios, facilitates trade, distributes local surpluses of pig in the form of pork throughout the regional population, and assures people of high-quality protein when they most need it. (1984, 224)

Many ecologists would now prefer explanations of group behaviour in terms of individual decision-making rather than of Rappaport's so-called 'neofunctional' emphasis on optimal population size. But such questions apart, what must first always strike the lay reader is the amount of detailed and laborious scientific field work upon which the analysis rests. As only one small part of that work, Rappaport recorded the activities involved in transforming an area of 11,000 square feet of secondary forest into garden. He conducted complex time-and-motion studies, and estimated crop yields through the daily weighing of harvests from more than twenty-five gardens for a period of over a year. Having calculated the food value of produce and the metabolic rates for the performance of everyday tasks, he estimated that the input energy of each sex is approximately equal (some 28,000 kilocalories per hectare). He also calculated energy inputs for clearing undergrowth, weeding, planting taro and yams, and so on. Combining all the different inputs he concluded that the calorific yield to input ratio was about 16.5:1 in taro–yam gardens and around 15.9:1 in sugar–sweet potato gardens. Even so, and on this apparently limited empirical front, Rappaport has been taken to task by his critics: for the inadequacy of his data about energy flow, the number of variables he failed to consider, the small scale of his original field work, and the incompleteness of his use of systems theory.

The second notable feature of Rappaport's study is his confidence that 'there should be no conceptual difficulty in treating culture much as one would the behaviour of other animals' (1984, 5). Though Rappaport does not attempt to explain either the origin or the ethnic significance of Tsembaga religious behaviour, the charge of reductionism seems justified. Despite the importance attached to religious ritual, which is, so far as we know, a specifically human phenomenon, animal ecology supplies the frame of reference within which religion and other components of culture are viewed in his study. The Tsembaga have been regarded as a population in the animal ecologist's sense: a unit composed of an aggregate of organisms having in common certain distinctive means whereby they maintain a set of shared trophic relations with other living and non-living components of the biotic community in which they coexist (224).

The problems that would beset imitation of such an approach by Mediterranean historiography seem insuperable. Like the criticism levelled at Rappaport, it is a matter partly of evidence, partly of interpretation.

Gathering evidence in the field is obviously difficult enough for an anthropologist able to spend months, even years, making close observations and accurate measurements, working with small groups whose economy is relatively uncomplicated and geared almost entirely to self-sufficiency. How much greater are the difficulties involved in finding any data at all from the remote past. Not only that: the data must adequately represent large and fluid communities – communities that display complicated and far-flung ties with a still wider world. The Mediterranean region does not, we shall suggest, offer the 'local populations', the clearly bounded environments on which ecologists conceptually speaking thrive (Chapters III–V). Yet without such closed systems, estimates of trophic exchanges or of 'carrying capacity' (signifying either the available resources or the level of population that these will sustain) are clearly impossible.

Vigorous comparativism may of course be a partial solution to the problem of evidence. The strategy has for example informed a very substantial monograph arrestingly entitled _The Ecology of the Ancient Greek World_ (Sallares 1991). Mustering copious models and statistics from the journals of modern ecology can certainly suggest the possible forms that answers to ecological questions about Antiquity may take (Sallares 1991, 8). Yet historical evidence is still needed to decide which of the suggested forms can appropriately be projected back onto the past; and that evidence is rarely sufficient to the task. The requisite demographic particulars are lacking for any period before the early modern one (cf. Volume 2). And the palaeobotany and palaeozoology that would, for an ecologist, be their essential complements are simply not available on a sufficient scale to permit a properly scientific ecological history of the Mediterranean spanning millennia. As we shall hope to show, the character of Mediterranean ecosystems can certainly be indicated – but it cannot be described with anything like the degree of specificity that an ecologist would consider respectable.

The so-called New Archaeology developed in the 1960s, along with the intellectual fashions that have succeeded it, might seem to have progressed towards an alternative solution to this problem set by dearth of evidence. Anxious to acquit itself of the charge of obsession with mere objects, archaeology has performed its own version of the *Annaliste* feat of embracing models derived from the social and natural sciences, thereby hoping to establish itself as 'the past tense of anthropology' (Hodges and Whitehouse 1983, 15). But where it has successfully elaborated autonomous techniques for attempting to reconstruct the environment – and even the psychology – of prehistoric communities through a scientific treatment of the limited data at its disposal, it still has only occasional contributions, on quite specific topics, to make to the larger project of Mediterranean ecological history. It has not yet been able to provide results across a broad enough spectrum from which useful generalizations could be inferred and analogies drawn.

The limitations of archaeology in this context have of course sometimes been transcended. Renfrew and Wagstaff's pioneering study (1982) of Melos makes the bold attempt to apply the 'new' methodology to the archaeological history of an Aegean island from the earliest times to the present (cf. III.4, V.2, IX.5). No facts about Melos can be irrelevant to the project: the Melian Dialogue of Thucydides becomes an artefact like a statue or a potsherd. The difficulty with this fascinating tour de force of *archéologie totale* is that, once again, what is barely possible for a tiny area cannot straightforwardly be carried out on any larger scale. And Melos, though an island, is far from isolated. The sheer complexity of the relationships between thousands of very different environmental niches make this approach as imperfect as that of human ecology *à la* Rappaport. We shall, in what follows, use all the Mediterranean archaeology that we can – but only as one kind of evidence among many, not as the discipline that has provided an overarching model.

Finding the right evidence is none the less hardly the greatest problem that faces Mediterranean ecology. The strictly ecological approach to history is, for us, disabled by the undesirability of treating human beings solely as organisms forming part of a biological system, even one of very wide and uncertain boundaries. When considering such relatively restricted topics as modes of subsistence or demographic regimes, the ecologist has already to omit, gloss over, or reduce to evolutionary terms precisely what the historian is most interested in: apparently autonomous cultural 'variables'. In the long-standing debate over whether or not history can be assimilated to the natural sciences we wish, for all our ecological leanings, to uphold its distinctiveness.

> Human ecosystems differ from model biological ecosystems in kind as well as in degree. For one thing, information, technology, and social organization play inordinately greater roles. More critically, human individuals and groups have unique capacities for purposive behaviour involving (a) the matching of resources with objectives, (b) the transforming of natural phenomena in order to meet these objectives, and (c) the capacity to think about these processes objectively without actually implementing them. The pivotal role of human cognition is illustrated . . . both by value systems and goal orientation that are not characteristic of simple ecosystems and by the significance of group attitudes and decision-making bodies

in the complex societies of the historical record . . . it is important to appreciate at this time that goals, values, and perceived needs are critical in understanding human actions and that culture, perception, and behaviour condition the way in which individuals and societies interact with their environments. (Butzer 1982, 32)

That – from, let it be stressed, an ecological archaeologist – is to put it mildly. And none of the available theories of 'ethno-ecology' (native understanding of the environment), 'cognitive factors', structures of decision-making, food systems or similar abstractions, seems adequate to the task of fully assimilating cultural to scientific explanation – certainly in the ecological sphere (contrast Sallares 1991, 212, on the 'naturalness' of slavery and the evolutionary reason for its historical rarity). Just as there is (or has been) a new archaeology, so also there is a 'new ecology' which involves dynamic evolution, the ecology of nature's ineluctable contingency. Such an ecology concerns itself with instabilities, disequilibria and chaotic fluctuations (Zimmerer 1994). It is thus opposed to the older systems ecology, with its concepts of competitive exclusion and niche specialization (for an instance, Hardesty 1975). In this older ecology homeostatic ideas of systems adaptation became teleological, changes could not be explained, and there was no historical dimension. The 'new ecology', on the other hand, sees no possibilty of estimating generalized carrying capacity, because of local and temporal variability (cf. VII.4).

> Historical time with its emphasis on the irregular periodicity of environmental variations and ecological functioning has replaced the cyclical time of systems ecology. Disturbances such as fire, wind, drought, pest outbreaks, disease epidemics, volcanic eruptions and landslides take place relentlessly across a wide range of biotic and biophysical landscapes. (Zimmerer 1994, 110)

But to ennumerate chaos-inducing factors is not to incorporate them into a coherent model. It is merely to confirm that the historical ecology of the Mediterranean cannot, in the end, however 'new' it becomes, stand as a scientific pursuit. The dynamics and flux of social allegiances and ordered behaviour in the Mediterranean region will defy scientific modelling. Historical ecology, as opposed to other kinds, will therefore investigate these processes in a different spirit. The study of them may clearly be enhanced by frequent invocation of the natural ecologist's terms, procedures and self-reinventions. But without sustained attention to what is distinctively historical about the place of humanity within the environment, and particularly to the complexity of human interaction across large distances, the study of the Mediterranean past will ultimately not have advanced very far beyond Plato's simile of the frogs round a pond.

PART TWO

'SHORT DISTANCES AND DEFINITE PLACES': MEDITERRANEAN MICROECOLOGIES

It is not the resemblances, but the differences, which resemble each other.
Claude Lévi-Strauss (1963) *Totemism*, 77

Geography, like grace, works through people.
Chris Wickham (1988b) *The Mountain and the City*, 6

Examine this region of short distances and definite places . . .
W. H. Auden, 'In praise of limestone'

CHAPTER III

FOUR DEFINITE PLACES

'Physically, the country may be divided into four belts', the Arab geographer al-Muqadassi wrote of Syria and the Lebanon.

> The first belt is that on the border of the Mediterranean sea. It is the plain country, the sandy tracts following one another and alternating with the cultivated land . . . The second belt is the mountain country, well-wooded and possessing many springs, with frequent villages and cultivated fields . . . The third belt is that of the valleys of the Ghaur, wherein are found many villages and streams, also palm trees, well-cultivated fields and indigo plantations . . . The fourth belt is that bordering on the desert. The mountains here are high and bleak and the climate resembles that of the waste. But it has many villages, with springs of water and forest trees. (adapted from Miquel 1963, 85)

Coastal plains of intermittent fertility backed by wooded mountains and desert plateaux, mixed cultivation, sporadic settlement – all qualities of Mediterranean landscape as familiar to the traveller as to the geographer. The problem is that even such fastidious generalizations as al-Muqadassi's no more than hint at an infinitely complex local reality. Worse, they give an impression of uniformity, of fundamental resemblance between one region and another, that is disastrously misleading. We can never hope to come to an understanding of what can usefully be said of the Mediterranean-wide human or physical landscape until we are fully sensitive to the enormous variety and diversity of environments within the basin of the sea, not just to the constants that apparently underlie the chaos. For reasons which we began to examine in Part One, the distinctive texture of Mediterranean lands is not to be sought in the listing of typical ingredients of the visible landscape, a strategy in which observation is all too easily overpowered by tradition. It is rather to be found in the phenomenon of 'subdividedness' – or, to paraphrase our epigraph from Lévi-Strauss, in the continuum of discontinuities. How is that continuum to be described and explained?

At the end of the previous chapter we explored the senses in which an ecological approach might be of service to the historian. To the difficulties there seen to arise, we must add further problems that emerge from the examination of particular localities. This enables us to progress towards an exemplification of what the 'historical' in our 'historical ecology' might mean, as we outline the nature of Mediterranean interaction and the character of the microecological regions of which that interaction should be predicated. A properly *historical*

ecology will certainly not be content with either the enumeration or the classification of local features. At the least it will also have to look at the dynamics
of their interplay with human and animal populations. But that will only turn it
into a *human* ecology – of a kind that may, we have suggested, pay a heavy price
for its inclusion of humanity in terms of the biological reductionism and the narrowness of focus that are alike required of it. *History* has to be brought into the
ecological picture in two ways: first, most importantly, in the avoidance of reductionism through the invocation of as full a political, social or economic context
– spanning as lengthy a period – as the locality seems to require; secondly, in the
pursuit of that context, through the 'unbounding' of the systems on which it is
to be brought to bear, so that the 'definiteness of places' is always qualified by
their 'interdependence'. The image of the fuzzy set, mentioned in II.4 as appropriate to the Mediterranean as a whole, can now, as we hope to show in this
Part, be extended to the microecologies of which the region is comprised. They
will be seen to have their foci and their margins; but these are always changing,
can seldom be easily related to aspects of geography, and are at all times responsive to the pressures of a much larger setting.

Our emphasis in this chapter is thus very different from that of the 'geographical background' that introduces so many historical works. It enables us to
step a little aside from what we have broadly identified as the Romantic tradition of Mediterranean description, with its seductive but misleading imagery. It
avoids an unprofitable scientism. It begins to close the gap – to which we shall
briefly return at the end of the chapter – between the specialized interests of
the ecologist and more traditional political, social and economic concerns in the
study of the past. And it leads naturally into the subsequent discussion of the
degree to which the ecological approach can be extended, first to larger settlements (Chapter IV), then to the region as a whole (Chapter V).

In what follows, then, we approach Mediterranean history by way of its
microfoundations – its shortest distances. We look at four localities in the Mediterranean world – to show how complex is the interplay of ecological factors
that gives each its apparent identity or definition; and to suggest that the principal elements in a microecology's character derive as much from its changing
configuration within the web of interactions around it, across aggregates of
'short distances', as from any long-lasting physical peculiarities.

1. THE BIQA

As melancholy political events of our own time have emphasized, one of the
principal ingredients of the topography of the Levant is the great valley between
the Lebanon and Anti-Lebanon mountains in which the Orontes rises, inland
from the south Phoenician coast (Map 2). It is known as the Biqa (or Bekaa), an
immemorial name applied also to other abrupt valleys and derived from a Semitic
root signifying a split. Aptly; because this great valley, some 100 kilometres long
and about 25 kilometres wide, is a great down-faulted trough, part of a tectonic
system stretching from the Taurus mountains of Anatolia to the lakes of East
Africa by way of the even more pronounced rift valleys of the Jordan, the Red
Sea, and of Kenya and Tanzania. On either side the valley is bounded by the
steep cliffs of the mountains, which rise from the valley floor at 2,000–3,000

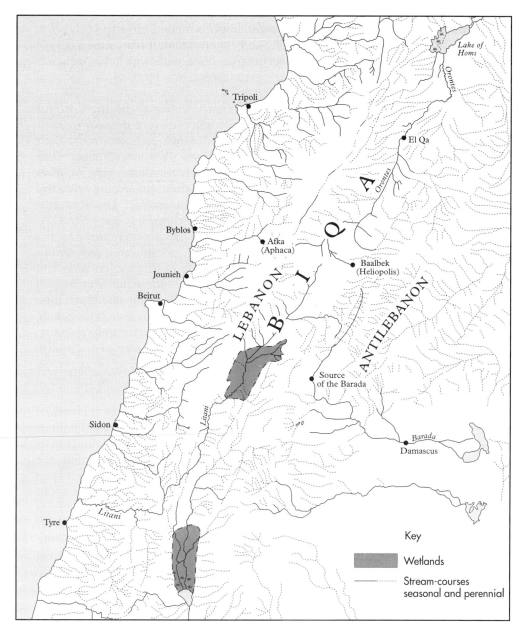

Map 2 The Biqa and its setting

The map is simplified from the magnificent geomorphological cartography of de Vaumas (1954). The effects of the steeply declining rainfall from west to east and from south to north are apparent. In addition there is very marked variability from year to year. In 1878 Beirut received 1,234 mm; in 1933 only 438 (de Vaumas 1954, 224).

feet above sea level to summit levels of more than 12,000 feet in the high Lebanon. For many reasons, this apparently simply bounded geographical region has a bewildering diversity of topography and environment; it represents a degree of fragmentation that makes it an excellent example with which to open our sequence. And, as a further advantage, it has been the object of detailed and provocative academic study (Marfoe 1979).

The complex ecology of this valley is dominated above all by the different influences of the adjacent mountains, which produce varying degrees of rain-shadow and of shelter from prevailing winds, and which each create, by their particular aspect, extremely local climatic conditions. Altitude, exposure and precipitation combine to form a spectrum of microenvironments, ranging from the supposedly classic 'Mediterranean' conditions of the south to the semi-arid plains of the north. Hydrology further complicates the picture. The abundant rainfall of the Lebanon mountains feeds numerous springs, but the bedrock is the limestone which gives rise in so many parts of the Mediterranean to the scenery known as *karst* (VIII.2). The distribution of groundwater and springs in this type of landscape is highly erratic, and there are both waterless areas and oases or marshy bottoms. The streams draining from the mountains have formed terraces and fans of usually fertile alluvium, although in the semi-arid north their valleys are more like wadis. Any list of environments must, however, also include the valleys parallel to the Biqa in the high mountains, the summit plateaux, and the rocky cliffs and slopes of the fault scarps on both sides of the valley. Altogether, climate and geology have produced a dense pattern of extremely local environments. And these offer humanity the widest selection of ecological niches.

A survey of that kind inevitably gives an over-flattering picture of the natural endowments of the region. Modern geographers using average rainfall figures, like their ancient or medieval predecessors (such as Al-Muqaddasi) looking at perennial springs and well-tilled fields, have had no hesitation in labelling the Biqa as fertile. But fertility is not an absolute of scientific measurement; it is an impressionistic, culturally laden, term (VII.1). Moreover, generalizations about regional fertility ignore particular conditions – in this case, not only conditions in the areas where rainfall is consistently well below average, but also those created within the areas of above-average precipitation by immense annual and seasonal variability in the weather. Winter floods and summer droughts are the perennial hazards of a Mediterranean landscape; a village too dry for habitation one year can be almost washed away the next. And the Biqa has extra problems: unusually poor rains in the spring, with consequently low discharge of water sources; strong prevailing winds that erode the soil in areas unsheltered by the mountains; a high carbonate horizon; malarial swamps in the south. The swamps are the remains of a lake artificially drained between 1320 and 1339, a lake whose capricious rise and fall had led to the localization in the vicinity of tales of the Flood and of Noah and his sons (Dussaud 1927, 402).

This valley is not then an area that can readily be irrigated. Even the advent of modern technology – dams, bore-holes, pumps, all the means of soil improve-ment – has apparently affected no more than a quarter of the total land under cultivation. Systems of the type usually labelled 'dry farming' have always been the norm – in so far as the valley can be said to display a norm. For the cata-logue of economic strategies is naturally as diverse as that of the conditions that necessitate them. Overall only one third of the valley is cultivated; and within each of the many zones into which a geographer or an ecologist divides it, the land under cultivation varies from less than a fifth to barely more than a half of the surface area. The means of livelihood can take the form of highland terrace agriculture, lowland cereal dry farming, or (more rarely) swamp drainage or spring irrigation. Land is productive and profitable only sporadically; and it is these isolated patches that are generally devoted to crops like cereals and legumes.

Irrigation remains so expensive and inefficient that only lucrative cash crops make it worthwhile. The place with which it has been longest associated is Baalbek, the ancient Heliopolis, where prosperity has always depended on a zone of intensive irrigated cultivation. It is from centres like this that irrigation can be extended, and to which it can retract, depending on the circumstances governing the choice of agricultural strategies and the degree of intensification (or abatement) that are appropriate from one period to another (VI.1; VII.4). In the Biqa are prominent centres of horticulture or arboriculture, such as El Qa' at the source of the Orontes – its ancient name, Paradeisos, being an eloquent expression of its fertility. And such environments lend themselves to the highly visible production of specialized cash crops, among them the narcotics for which the region has been notorious in very recent times. But pockets of abundance should not be allowed to determine our estimate of the whole area's potential. The pockets are too isolated; their economic effects do not radiate far enough. Baalbek, it is worth noting, has functioned as a symbolic focus for the area both through the religious importance of its temples, and also because it has been a centre of environmental improvement (two functions that we shall see associated in Part Four below). It does not follow that Baalbek has been decisive in shaping the overall social and economic patterns of the valley's history. Despite having a major 'central place', the Biqa does not behave as the territory, the ecological hinterland, of a city – dispersed or fragmented though we shall find that sort of hinterland to be (IV.8). 'Une civilisation agricole a bien pu s'y développer, celle ci n'est jamais arrivée à donner naissance à une petite région politique comme il existe tant dans le proche-Orient. Fait typique: aucune ville important n'y existe' (Dussaud 1927, 315).

Contrary to what glowing accounts of a Mediterranean region's fertility may thus lead us to expect, agriculture is very often hazardous and yields are low. The twentieth-century alternatives to agriculture have been the usual ones: animal husbandry, migration to the largest settlements, emigration. Until comparatively recently the first alternative has been the predominant recourse. So, to the already long list of types of livelihood, we have to add transhumance and nomadism. These are in effect a low-risk form of capital investment – far less susceptible to annual variation than is dry farming; mobile enough to escape disastrous changes in the local ecology; mobile enough, also, to facilitate tax evasion. That is why the largest concentrations of sheep and goats have been found in what are, in agricultural terms, the poorest, the most risk-laden environments: an intensively cultivated area can still also sustain a small herd.

The Biqa has to be summed up not as one microecology but rather as a collection of microecologies. The best account of these is a modern archaeological field survey (Marfoe 1978). But that too, however nuanced its description, however alive its author to local variation, is necessarily misleading as evidence for the distant past. This is probably not because the character of the environment has changed so dramatically in historical times. We return to the subject in Chapter VIII below; but it is a fair provisional assumption that neither climate nor any aspect of the geography has altered so markedly that the *range* and *number* of the microecologies would have been very different in Antiquity or the Middle Ages from what is observable today. What has changed, however, and changed repeatedly – so that it could not be accounted for by reference to any single environmental catastrophe or secular evolution – is the subtle interrelation of different means of survival.

These have not, of course, always been internally determined; the direction and nature of the demands made upon the region from outside have also changed frequently. The Biqa is 'le plus beau couloir de circulation entre le Nord et le Sud du Levant' (Dussaud 1927, 315); and the umbilical route across Mount Lebanon to the port of Beirut has been of lasting importance (IX.7). But when, for example, Beirut and Baalbek were part of a single Roman city territory, farmed – at least initially – by veteran soldiers (Millar 1990), the environment had different demands made on it from any that have arisen since (VII.6). Indeed, this example illustrates the important truth that the ways in which microregions interact and cluster in the Mediterranean are as important as their distinctive internal features. Rural communities have frequently maintained a broad continuum of economic activities, shifting from dispersed nomadism on the northern steppes and the piedmont to highly concentrated transhumance around the zones of intense cultivation, altering the balance between pastoral and arable as and where necessary (cf. Section 6). The descendants of those who, a century ago, were among the few cash-crop farmers in the entire region may now be predominantly nomadic – or the reverse. In the central Biqa tribes of bedouin who were once exemplary camel nomads have used their wealth to purchase land – even though their average income must, in the past, have been a good deal higher than that of many farmers.

All this is a clear reflection of an unstable, treacherous ecology. The fittest who survive are those keeping their economic options open and reviewing their portfolios frequently. And that is most probably how it has always been in historical times: immense variation in space, from one microecology to another; equally immense chronological variation, as individual microenvironments alter subtly (or not so subtly) or the human communities associated with each adjust their division of effort. Here, as in Greece, 'each year the farmer may be aiming for a different production target, from a different area of land, with a different labour force and with the cushion of a greater or lesser amount of produce in store' (Halstead 1987, 85). A case like that of the Biqa certainly helps us to understand how it has come about that Mediterranean agricultural geography has been dominated since Antiquity by certain economic labels (*saltus*, high pasture; *silva*, woodland pasture; *arbustum*, productive orchard terrain; *helos*, marsh pasture or water-meadow, and so on). Yet the Biqa shows emphatically that, for all this labelling, what matters is not the static formula but the entire spectrum of available strategies; and not fixed points on the spectrum but movement along it. Flexibility is all.

One case study is obviously not enough to establish our general view of the Mediterranean environment; and the Biqa might after all be dismissed as a marginal area (though cf. VI.3), at the point of transition between the coastland of the Mediterranean sea and the semi-arid regions to the East. But the essential incoherence of its human geography, which seems to have been characteristic of the area in all periods, encourages us to look at other parts of the Mediterranean, asking whether a comparable degree of ecological fragmentation is discernible elsewhere.

2. SOUTH ETRURIA

The major part of the modern Italian province of Lazio, the region of Rome, covering South Etruria and ancient Latium, offers another tempting local case study in Mediterranean ecology (Maps 3 and 4). Indeed, as a constituent of west-central Italy (the other part being Campania, to the south) it features in many regionally based analyses. Part of the appeal of the area to the historian is undoubtedly that it has received a good deal of scholarly attention; and this again includes a particularly thorough and revealing archaeological survey, designed to elucidate the transition from a classical landscape of dispersed dwellings to a medieval one of nucleated, defensive, hilltop settlement – essentially the process known as *incastellamento* (Potter 1979).

The topography of Latium has been described as a recapitulation in miniature of the characteristics of the entire peninsula (Toubert 1973, 137). The region certainly displays a remarkable complexity and diversity of geology, soil and relief. Broadly it comprises two large volcanic complexes that separate the marsh and shingle of the coast from the limestone ranges of the Apennines and their outliers. The more southerly volcanic group, the Alban Hills, forms a conspicuous focal point for much of the region (V.1). The rainfall is abundant, particularly on the higher ground; and the volcanic tuffs are dissected by hundreds of gullies carrying perennial streams, many of which drain into the Tiber, a major river flowing in a wide flood plain between the two clusters of volcanic craters. The summers are dry and very hot, the winters quite cold. The rain, between 700 and 1200 mm *per annum* over the greater part of the region, falls mostly in autumn and early spring. Some of the alluvial and volcanic soils are agriculturally productive, and the area has been intensively farmed since the Bronze Age with a wide range of strategies suggested by the diversity of terrain: vines, olives or fruit trees where the soils are best, cereals everywhere, animals in the waterlogged meadows or the beech, oak and chestnut woods of the steep slopes, transhumance in summer to the high Apennine pastures – all these existing side by side often within the minutest regions.

This local variety, reduplicated across the whole zone, makes it attractive to consider the region as a unit. The environment is not, however, so obliging. The heavy qualifications made above about the fertility of the Biqa are appropriate here too. The volcanic soils are far from uniformly fertile. Many are very thin and unretentive of water; others – and this is also true of the alluvial soils – tend to be too sticky and waterlogged for the light ploughs which have been customary. These difficulties are compounded by hydrology. The rainfall is abundant but varies considerably from year to year in quantity and distribution. It is naturally highest on the mountains where it is least used, and in any case falls most often at the end of the agricultural year in torrents that can be enormously destructive. So the soils which might, with irrigation, be fertile, and the water itself, are both available. But irrigation is extremely difficult. On the ridges the

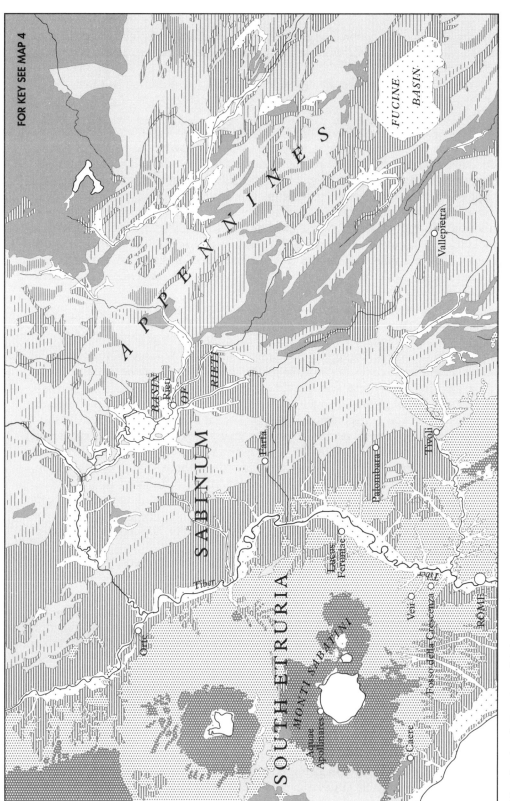

Map 3 South Etruria and Sabinum: physical structure

soils are too thin and dry; the slopes are too steep; and the valley bottoms are too wet. In addition, the force of the run-off causes soil erosion and maintains the steep sides of the gullies, which separate one locality from another to a surprising extent (cf. VIII.2).

The topographical microecologies thus created may not be as varied as those of the Biqa, but they are each none the less distinct. As in the Biqa, moreover, pastoral can often be more attractive than arable farming. Pigs feed in the woods on the steep slopes; cattle and sheep can be grazed on the wetlands in the winter and the high pastures in the summer. Full advantage is thus taken of the range of environments made available by differences in altitude: the mountain pastures, inaccessible in winter, come into their own when the lowlands are at their driest and most prone to fever.

In Antiquity, certain parts of these terrains were indeed proverbial for their agricultural intransigence. The Romans, invoking the environmental determinism common in ancient cultures, attributed the hardihood of their early generals and soldiers to the difficulties of tracts like the Ager Pupinius, in the plain east of Rome. And at their most extreme, these local disadvantages of arable cultivation even led, between the seventeenth and nineteenth centuries, to the virtual desertion of the relatively flat and dry area to the south and east of Rome, the Campagna (a social, political and geographical development of the highest interest, to which we shall return in Volume 2).

Archaeological work has helped to clarify another aspect of the instability of the landscape: in historical times the rivers have changed their nature and their course along the valleys with surprising frequency. Most of them now flow in steep-sided channels that are deeply cut into a broad, level flood plain. Flooding, always a potential danger with Mediterranean rivers swollen unpredictably by winter rain, is therefore rare in the area today. When in spate the rivers tend to dig a yet deeper channel into their underlying deposit. But conditions have not always been like this. Evidence from excavations has shown both the marked topographical changes resulting from rivers' shifting their channels, and also the alterations in the pattern of erosion and deposition that have affected every stream valley and river flood plain in this deeply dissected area. The potency of erosive damage and of the constant deposition of mud through endlessly repeated flooding is most impressive.

Such environmental mutability is also to be expected – and is increasingly being demonstrated – in other parts of the Mediterranean. It is a forceful reminder that the valley floors and alluvial coastal plains which are today so often the centres of Mediterranean population were virtually unusable until the early modern period – indeed in most cases until the twentieth century – a theme to be considered in much greater detail in Chapter VIII. The geographer Strabo had already noticed in the time of Augustus that Rome was the only city on the Tiber (*Geography*, 5.3.7). And Rome's floods were notorious until the 1890s.

In the case of South Etruria, then, what appeared to be a relatively coherent and comprehensible region, with which the historian or archaeologist could usefully operate, proves disconcertingly subject to environmental mutability. This mutability is, moreover, superimposed on the type of microregional difference that we have already found breaking up the conceptual unity of the Biqa. West-central Italy, too, has developed highly flexible and opportunistic responses to the possibilities of the landscape. Polyculture – mixed farming – is the first

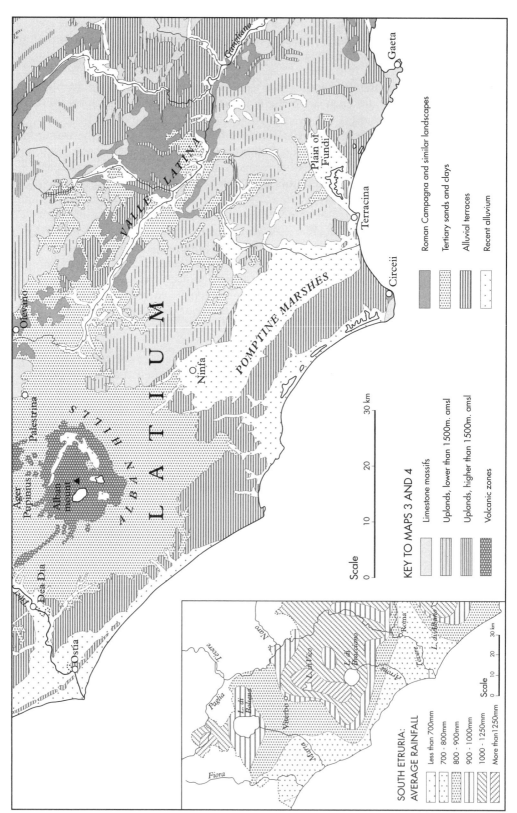

Map 4 Latium: physical structure

KEY TO MAPS 3 AND 4

Limestone massifs

Uplands, lower than 1500m. amsl

Uplands, higher than 1500m. amsl

Volcanic zones

Roman Campagna and similar landscapes

Tertiary sands and clays

Alluvial terraces

Recent alluvium

Scale

0   10   20   30 km

SOUTH ETRURIA:
AVERAGE RAINFALL

Less than 700mm

700 - 800mm

800 - 900mm

900 - 1000mm

1000 - 1250mm

More than 1250mm

Scale

0   10   20   30 km

LATIUM

VALLE LATINA

ALBAN HILLS

POMPTINE MARSHES

Plain of Fundi

Gaeta

Terracina

Circeii

Ninfa

Olevano

Palestrina

Ager
Pupinius

Alban
Mount

Dea Dia

Ostia

Fiora

Poglia

L. di Balsena

Tevere

Marta

Ravenni

L. di Vico

L. di Bracano

Nera

Roma

Tevere

Aniene

L. di Albano

Muju

ingredient of this response, a predictable reflection of the variety of terrain. The second ingredient is, as we have seen, pastoralism, which because of that variety and its topographical distribution, is closely interwoven with the differing forms of cultivation.

Below the walls of the hill-settlement of Pienza, in the more northerly sector of Etruria, remains of a Neolithic settlement have suggested a precocious origin for pastoralism in the region, and even for the developed form of long-distance environmental exploitation, transhumance (G. W. W. Barker 1975, 146). Grains of emmer, wheat and barley were recovered from a series of occupation sites. The proportions of livestock bones found were: 62 per cent sheep and goats, 16 per cent cattle, 12 per cent pig, 8.5 per cent dog, and 1.5 per cent deer. The minimum number of animals that could have created these remains, and their probable age at death, bears a strong resemblance to the normal requirements of more recent periods: mixed farming; a few cattle for traction; a few sheep grazing round about the settlement and killed when fat; cereal cultivation; sheep and goats for milk and wool – with the emphasis on sheep. Not only that; the sites must, in the Neolithic as now, have been situated well above the winter snowline, and they could not therefore have been permanently inhabited. Intermediate between upland and lowland pastures, they lie pretty much on what would, in the very different conditions of the later Middle Ages, again become an established transhumance route.

The conclusion that the long-term history of pastoralism in Pienza can simply be 'read off' from the topography and a few archaeological finds is none the less to be resisted. There has been a persistent scholarly tendency to lay too much emphasis on a pastoral, pre-agricultural phase in the later prehistory of the Mediterranean – a tendency that perhaps bears the continuing stamp of very ancient notions of human progress (see Section 6 below). Pressure of population is sometimes invoked as the determining factor here, as if the environmental location of animal husbandry were identical to that of cultivation. Growing populations could supposedly not afford the luxury of animals and therefore turned to agriculture. In this complex environment, though, the range of niches for humans and their plants and animals is too broad for that argument to be readily persuasive. As we saw in the previous chapter, the reality of the past defies strictly ecological modelling. When presented with data like those from Pienza, therefore, we should not invoke some familar general image – either of a heroic world of pastoral carnivores or of an 'ur-transhumance' anticipating the Neapolitan Dogana by millennia.

In its simplest form transhumance involves the seasonal movement of animals from lowland to adjacent upland and back; but in many places the distances travelled are far greater, and the routes taken by the herders and their animals sometimes become major thoroughfares that may remain in use for centuries. The similarity of pastoralism in Italy within living memory to the practices that can perhaps be glimpsed in prehistory, and that are relatively well known in ancient times, can naturally suggest that this long-distance form of transhumance has been a constant of Italian life. But our description of the Biqa should prompt extreme caution. The management of relations over even the distance between low water-meadow and snowline pasture is a complex social and political matter, and over long distances it is still more so. In landscapes such as those of South Etruria, *pastoralism* is an obvious ingredient in the range of local possibilities. *Transhumance*, in so complex an ecology, is a very different matter, requiring particular social and economic – and political – conditions (VI.7). Understanding how the microecologies work enables us to distinguish the two, and to be chary of rash assertions of the continuity or straightforwardness of agrarian response. No strategy can simply be predicated of the landscape.

Each microecology has its physical characteristics, which may be discernible in a number of different periods by means of archaeological or documentary evidence. But their significance can change radically between one period and the next through alterations in the networks that bind the microecology to its neighbours. A pasture in South Etruria may exist for millennia. Its contribution to its locality will, however, vary enormously as the animals on it change from being those of a local proprietor to those of a large-scale investor from the city of Rome whose flocks are scattered across southern Italy; or to those of a Roman veteran soldier with interests in a nearby city; or to those of the dependants of a papal estate. The grass and the goats comprise only a small part of the overall picture.

Pastoralism conceived on the grand scale and managed across the length and breadth of a plurality of microregions is a potentially unifying force in a region as fragmented as South Etruria. Yet it could not have helped to shape the patterns of allegiance and contact across that region in the absence of a strong central authority. In the archaic period, there is a clear difference in settlement geography between the areas to the north and the south of the Tiber, despite the similarities of the landscape. As in the Biqa, settlement history turns out to be a poor reflector of microtopography. Ultimately, it was the rise of Rome, rather than any predominantly economic feature such as pastoralism, that came to weld this area into something approaching a unity. That unity functions on the ideological as much as on the ecological level. In the late nineteenth century the simplistic comparison of past glories with present decay did much to conceal the inherent variety and instability of the landscape: it was politically expedient to believe that human activities bore the sole burden of explanation for post-classical dereliction. Again, the political and cultural facilities of Rome have themselves been responsible for the scholarly work that makes the region feel so much more intelligible than many others. Above all, the fame and success of the inhabitants of Rome the city, whether as conquerors of the world in the late Republic or as spiritual guides in the Middle Ages, have had enormous consequences for expectations about the city's neighbourhood.

It is to those expectations, and to some extent to their economic consequences – the leisure architecture of the elite for instance, its buying in of large quantities of raw materials from far afield (IX.4), and the enhanced attraction of the city for mobile populations (IX.5) – that west-central Italy owes much of its apparent coherence. The management of water in the area shows a further response to Rome's gravitational pull. Although precipitation is so much greater in aggregate, here as in the Biqa, water control represents the way in which humanity can most readily modify the environment so as to intensify production. The hydraulic works of the Etruscan and, still more, the Roman period – for drainage, storage, transportation and irrigation – are eloquent testimony to the power of the centre to subsume a variety of local efforts into a wide-ranging system (VII.2).

In South Etruria we can, therefore, glimpse the interplay of external and local factors both on the functioning of microecologies and on the way in which they are perceived. The territory of Tivoli, say, on the border between the limestone mountains and the Roman plain, or that of the Etruscan city of Veii, can only be fully understood in terms of their relationships with influences from altogether outside their own ecologies, as well as on the basis of the local variables that we learned to emphasize in considering the Biqa (IV.8). Of these outside influences, the dominant one has been the privileged access to the sea and its continuum of communications. Both the Etruscan centres and the little settlements of Latium usually each had a *scala*, a beach or landfall-point, perhaps a marshy inlet behind a spit of shingle, where contact with the world of Mediterranean redistribution might be maintained. In the long run, these were overshadowed by the especially privileged route provided by the Tiber and reflected in the status of Rome, the Tiber port (IX.7). But if Rome's network of influences permeates the areas around it, transforming and shaping them in various ways from age to age, that is not to say that these areas can simply be considered as an isolated, readily definable city territory. Nor, in the absence of evidence for interdependence, should we be quick to postulate a primitive autarky (IV.7). To emphasize that point still further, and to show that the pull of Rome is only an extreme version of a more common Mediterranean phenomenon, we turn to two other case studies. In these, isolation – of a kind – is much more apparent. One involves a virtual island, the other a real one.

3. The Green Mountain, Cyrenaica

In *Wanderings in North Africa* (1856) James Hamilton contrasted 'the monumental industry of fallen civilization with the slothful hut of victorious barbarism'. Prior to the discovery of petroleum, bedouin Cyrenaica was a land of tents: these are the slothful huts. As in South Etruria, the fallen civilization is that of classical Antiquity. Ancient remains are a prominent feature of parts of the Cyrenaican landscape (Map 5). Systematic archaeological research has revealed the complexity of production and the density of settlement from the seventh century B.C. onwards: several important cities, many large villages, scattered farmsteads – amounting to a response to the potential of the Green Mountain's environment which was certainly markedly different from anything that succeeded it after the sixth century A.D.

This particular sort of prosperity was, however, fragile. An indigenous plant, local to the region, was for example developed in Antiquity as a highly specialized cash-crop – *silphion*. From the sixth century B.C. this umbelliferous plant was a renowned and valuable commodity. Scarce, distinctive and costly, it had numerous culinary and medical uses. Its identity remains, however, an enigma to modern botanists. The human impact on the landscape of Cyrenaica has combined with the heavy demand for *silphion* to render the plant extinct, though it is not clear precisely when the damage was done. The story is instructive. *Silphion* is in some ways a typical Mediterranean commodity. Accidental speciality of a single set of environments, it offers a highly attractive opportunity to producers with wide horizons who can adapt to the advantages of particular localities. The agriculturalists of Greek Cyrenaica also specialized in cumin: another culinary/medical commodity which, although not botanically so singular as *silphion*, derived its value only from its potential for redistribution. More

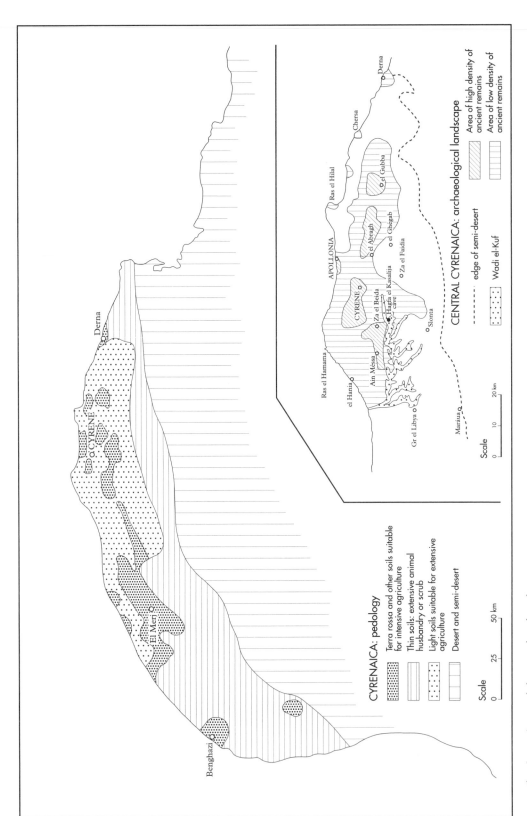

Map 5 Cyrenaica: pedology and archaeology

conventionally, ancient Cyrenaica also produced a notable surplus of cereals, whose value depended in part on the precocity of the harvest by comparison with those of the Aegean.

Choices about primary production in this area, then, turn out to have been the result of a combination of very specific local circumstances on one hand, and the changing network of relationships which the area enjoyed with the wider Mediterranean world on the other. Environmental opportunism, moreover, entails a spectrum of responses to environmental variability through space and time. Against this background, major transitions between widespread agriculture and much greater emphases on animal husbandry no longer appear so catastrophic.

Cyrenaica is a striking region, and one which appears to be isolated. Certainly it is separated from its African neighbours by desert: 700 kilometres of it before the Nile delta is reached to the east, the coastal strip being only slightly more hospitable than the interior; and almost as great a distance to the relatively fertile territory of Tripolitania to the west. Otherwise the hinterland is some half a million square kilometres of Sahara. The homogeneity of the desert margin can make Cyrenaica appear a unitary frontier zone. But the appearance misleads. In terms of climate and vegetation, it is as if a fragment of some Mediterranean archipelago had been uneasily wedged against the African continent – Mediterranean not just in its characteristic rainfall and temperature, but in being a tangled and minutely subdivided complex of interdependent environments: plateaux at different altitudes, intermontane basins, deep wadis. Ultimately it owes this intense microfragmentation to its location, which, in the terminology of plate tectonics, is a subduction zone (Bousquet and Péchoux 1983). The sea itself of course provides a ready network of communications: along the coast to east and west, by way of chains of watering-places and small harbours on a proverbially dangerous shore (V.3), and across the relatively narrow seas (almost a strait) to Greece and the Aegean – the island of Crete being less than 300 kilometres away. Indeed, in the Roman period, Cyrenaica formed part of a province with Crete and was governed from Gortys, just inland from the ports of that island's southern shore. Cyrenaica itself, for all that, is in another sense insular in that its coastal zone is unexpectedly inhospitable: the more productive environments are those further south and further inland, where the rainfall is higher.

For Cyrenaica (Map 6), with all its complexity, is essentially a mountain rising from the steppe-like terrain of the deserts to the plateau of the Jebel Akhdar (sometimes known as *al-ghaba*, the forest, since its vegetation includes patches of evergreen forest and maquis). The plateau is about 400 kilometres long, 150 kilometres from north to south; and it consists of a series of terraces sometimes reaching a height of more than 800 metres above sea level. There is a narrow strip of coastal plain, barely a kilometre wide, from which the first intermediate terrace (to the west) is accessible to animal transport only through a very small number of precipitous ravines. This terrace is a succession of wooded ridges and broad wadis. The main terrace, the tableland, is where the classical ruins, and the deserted farms of early twentieth-century Italian colonists, are to be seen; it rises to a narrow third terrace overlooking the area of former settlement. The plateau then slopes southwards gradually down to the steppe through a belt of juniper trees, a zone of rich vegetation to which the *silphion* may at first have been native.

There are no permanently flowing rivers in this karstic landscape. The only watercourses are seasonal wadis, some of them (notably in the complex of the

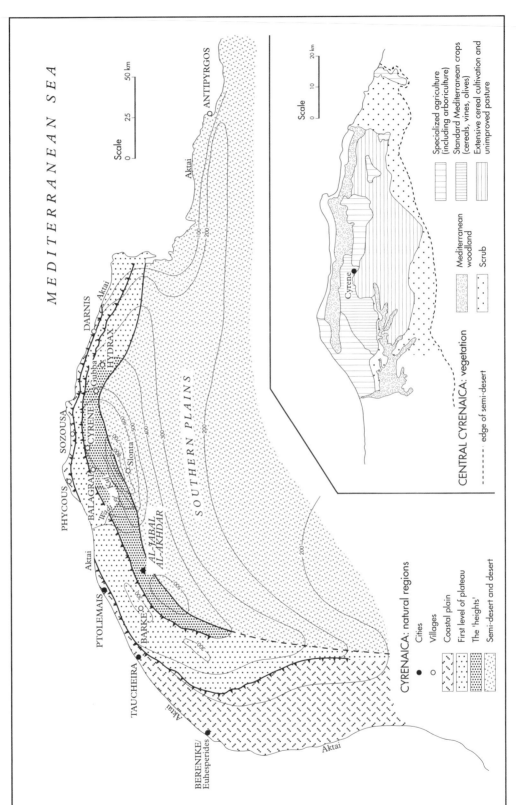

Map 6 Cyrenaica: natural regions and vegetation

Wadi el-Kuf) very deeply incised and favouring north–south over east–west communications. In the margins of the desert steppe, dew is a vital additional source of moisture. On the terraces of the Jebel Akhdar itself, the relatively high rainfall (up to 600 mm per annum) feeds numerous springs. Yet Map 7 shows how limited is the area which benefits from that rainfall. It is also markedly seasonal, in an extreme version of the Mediterranean pattern; and interannual variation is very high (local wisdom predicts one drought year in four). Especially in the less elevated areas where annual average precipitation is lower, the fragmented topography entails that surplus and near-drought can be found only short distances apart. As usual in Mediterranean lands, the pattern of the winds is both distinctive and crucial to each year's production. Winds from the south, laden with Saharan sand (*qibh*, the ancient *notos*: Roques 1987, 70–2) have enriched the mineral content of many local soils (cf. Map 5) – another reason for microenvironmental variability. Yet the sandstorms of spring and autumn can be disastrous if the spring rains have ceased early.

In modern times, bedouin tribes have competed for those north–south 'strips' of the region that will each command the full range of resources to be found, in east–west zones, between high plateau and semi-desert. Most families have mixed agriculture and pastoralism (cattle, goats, sheep, camels). Wheat is grown for family consumption. Barley and straw are fed to cattle: the majority of landowners have in recent times not sold their harvest on the market. But the relation between arable and pastoral is more complex than that, because the ecologies of favoured species are very different, and suitable land for each species is likely to be scattered. Cattle need barley, straw and plentiful supplies of water: the nomadism characteristic of other parts of Africa such as the Sudan is impossible in Cyrenaica. Goats are less particular in their demands, but the juniper forest serves them best. Sheep of course need good pasture, and they must spend the winter on the steppe and the summer on the plateau. Camels want shrub to eat but can easily travel for over a week without taking water.

So how, given this diversity, are animal husbandry and cultivation combined? First, agriculture has been emphatically a subsidiary activity for the Cyrenaican bedouin; its most important tasks can be quite comfortably fitted into even a semi-nomadic pastoralist's schedule. The move southward from plateau to steppe does not take place until December, after ploughing. The sheep may have been moved on ahead with a portion of the workforce; but the majority of people remain in the family tents until the crop has been sown. Secondly, the cereal fields on both steppe and plateau are concentrated near major water supplies, so that even if cattle and goat herders did not have to harvest their fields during summer they would naturally arrive at the same parts of the region in order to water their cattle. Finally, agricultural land can be used as pasture when appropriate. Cattle, goats, sheep and camels will all happily graze field stubble, especially to the north where the alternative flora are (for them) unappetizing. Access to so wide a range of environments has the advantages of resilience to the conditions of a bad year and the possibility of mixed herding. The seasonal movement of the animals, moreover, dovetails unusually neatly with the raising of an arable crop. For the herd's presence in the zone where winter moisture enhances crop yield coincides with the dry summer. The herd thus fertilizes the fields with manure while these are unplanted.

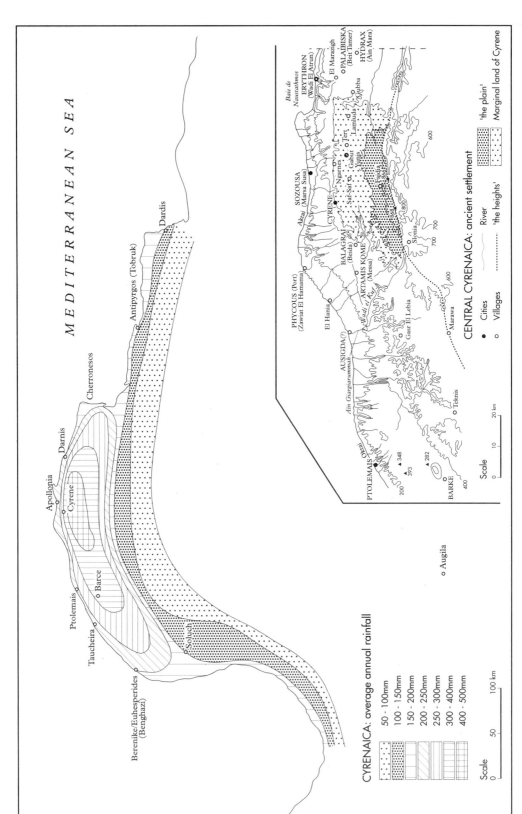

Map 7 Cyrenaica: rainfall and settlement

MEDITERRANEAN SEA

Berenike/Euhesperides (Benghazi)
Taucheira
Ptolemais
Barce
Soluch
Cyrene
Apollonia
Darnis
Cherronesos
Antipyrgos (Tobruk)
Dardis
Augila

CYRENAICA: average annual rainfall

50 - 100mm
100 - 150mm
150 - 200mm
200 - 250mm
250 - 300mm
300 - 400mm
400 - 500mm

Scale
0   50   100 km

CENTRAL CYRENAICA: ancient settlement

● Cities   ~~~ River
○ Villages   ······· 'the heights'

'the plain'
Marginal land of Cyrene

Scale
0   10   20 km

PHYCOUS (Port) (Zawiat El Hamama)
El Hania
AUSIGDA(?)
Ain Giargiarummah
PTOLEMAIS   Okrai
200   ▲393   ▲348
▲282
BARKE
400
Teknis
Marawa
600
650
700
700
Slonta
800
Gasr El Lebia
ARTAMIS KOME (Messa)
Wadi el Kuf
BALAGRAI (Beida)
Safsaf   Gabut
Ngarnes
CYRENE
Akrai   SOZOUSA (Marsa Susa)
Baie de Naustathmos
ERYTHRON (Wadi El Atrun)
El Marazigh
Taulud
Lamluda
Tert
Ayubba
600
PALAIBISKA (Beit Tamer)
HYDRAX (Ain Mara)

The later twentieth-century life of the bedouin may hint at the likely means of survival in the past: the combination of strategies, the necessary adaptation of patterns of settlement and migration to a jumbled mosaic of ecologies – these fundamental complexities have apparently not altered greatly since Antiquity, despite the varying portion of land under the plough. In particular, it must be emphasized that agriculture and pastoralism are (here as elsewhere) closely inter-locked. The apparently independent pastoralists are part of the society of the cultivators. This is not to say that the two automatically co-operate. In the earlier fourth century A.D. for instance, Roman Cyrenaica was periodically overrun by nomads or semi-nomads from southern Numidia and Tripolitania. But such antagonism is not incompatible with various forms of interdependence, some of them quite subtle. On one occasion the raiders are reported to have deployed 5,000 camels to carry away their booty. Turning from horses to camels may have enhanced the seriousness of their incursions. But the change should also be interpreted as a reflection of the increasing marginality of the land, beyond the range of sheep and goats, to which the nomads had to resort as the frontiers of agriculture were advanced by Roman power (Liebeschuetz 1990, 229). The propagation of new forms of production often involves conflict between the innovators and other groups. The groups may in addition be differentiated along ethnic lines – as in Cyrenaica, at the time of the consolidation of the Greek presence, and again in late Antiquity. The interdependence between the two ecological strategies remains none the less salient.

Not only the main features of the environment, but the Roman response to it also, have continued to make their mark on tribesmen of the peninsula. Modern cemeteries still register the geography of classical agriculture. For 'burial' has usually been on the surface, with the body covered by a stone cairn; and ruined farm sites are the best source of loose, easily worked stones with which the cairn can be constructed. Old collapsed cisterns, similarly, can be exploited for their rich soil and made into pear and olive gardens (VI.10); while some of the classical structures (renovated after the oil boom of the 1960s) have again proved capable of proper use. Even if unused, cisterns have remained a valuable guide to navigation in what is otherwise likely to be a featureless landscape. The ancient Greek and Roman roads are still habitually used for seasonal movements of people and animals. Barbarism and civilization are less remote than the anti-quarian, and Romantic, contrast of tent and ruined temple suggests.

Indeed, that comparison (with which we began this section) both reflects a procedural error and announces an important theme. If, despite earlier caveats, we take Cyrenaica as a single area – of the order of 2,000 square kilometres of productive land and a much larger extent of marginal terrain – it is easy to say of it that, for instance, it was prosperous under the Battiad kings of the archaic and classical periods in Greece, or during the late Republic and early Empire, and that subsequently it went into decline. Yet the 'prosperity' which that verdict attributes to 'Cyrenaica' in Antiquity is an impressionistic generalization that bears only very inadequately on the region as a whole – the region as it is familar in large-scale maps.

Consider first the outline of the story. The society that emerged during the first two centuries of Greek 'colonialism', with the creation of a new settlement pattern and the introduction of new productive aims and methods, commanded by the end of the fourth century B.C. a surplus equivalent to the yield of several

thousand square kilometres of wheat fields (Map 8). The key to this rapid success appears to have been the early harvest time, a month earlier than that of
most of Greece and well before that of the Black Sea, which became another
recourse for Greek cities in times of cereal shortage (Brun 1993, 525–6). Over
the following centuries, the economy of the productive microregions of Cyrenaica
continued to yield surpluses for redistribution, though individually they waxed
and waned in prosperity. An aside in a legal text of the Roman imperial period
(*Digest*, 19.2.61) thus attests the commercial export of wheat and oil. The images
of prosperity still feature in the writings of Bishop Synesius of Cyrene in the
early fifth century A.D., but the density of Cyrenaica's ties with the rest of the
world was greatly lessened (Roques 1987, 409–31). Synesius could offer as a
plausible excuse for non-payment of tribute the lack of ships sailing from Cyrene
to Rome. And the bishop reports finding, little more than a day's journey from
the Mediterranean, country folk who had never glimpsed the sea and could not
believe that it was able to support life: they fled at the sight of fried fish, thinking them serpents (*Letters*, ed. Hercher 1871, nos. 147–8). Towards the end of
the millennium, however, the geographer Ibn Hawqal found Barca and its fertile plain prospering from substantial commerce with other areas, but especially
Egypt (trans. Kramers and Wiet 1964, 1.62–3). And his testimony is corrobor-
ated not only by other Arabic sources, but by archaeology, which reveals a
further and previously unsuspected commerce with Sicily from perhaps the late
tenth century onward (Kennet 1994). Nor were the significant outside links only
the seaborne or coast-wise ones; due attention must be paid to the Saharan *koine*
and to the distribution of goods – slaves, dates, cloth and the like – across the
waste, along the routes to the oasis of Augila or beyond (Stucchi 1989; cf. Brett
1969). Quite rapid fluctuations in economic fortune, depending on connections
of varying kinds in a number of different directions, are thus a normal feature of
what appeared at first sight to be a region quite separated from the rest of the
Mediterranean world and about which generalizations of unambiguous scope
could safely be ventured. At the ends of the transects of ecological opportunities
are the multiple routes that lead into the desert and the ports which open onto
the world of the sea. Both sorts of 'gateway' (IX.7) can be realized more or less
vigorously, and the fortunes of the ports of Cyrene, at Apollonia, or the inland
basin of Barca, at Ptolemais, have fluctuated with those of the clusters of microregions inland.

The causes of change in such an economy should not be conceived in too
straightforward a manner. In part, perhaps, because of Ibn Khaldun's memorable imagery in the *Muqaddimah* (trans. Rosenthal 1967, 1.305, 2.289), the
transition from prosperity to decline has often been presented in catastrophic terms
and attributed simply to the progress of the pastoralist. Advance of transhumants
in the wake of the first Arab conquests has been held responsible for the

---

Map 8 Cyrene deploys its cereal surpluses, 330–26 B.C.
'Those to whom the city gave wheat, when the wheat-shortage occurred in Greece' is the
heading of an inscription probably originally from the sanctuary of Cyrene's patron deity
Apollo. The wide horizons of the city's generosity are remarkable, and probably reflect the
normal distribution patterns of the Cyrenaean cereal surplus. Even if this gift had no strings
attached, those who determined the destinations of the fruits of Cyrenaean production, and
who could dispose of such influential favours on this scale, stood to gain enormously in
diplomatic and political prestige (*SEG*, 9.2).

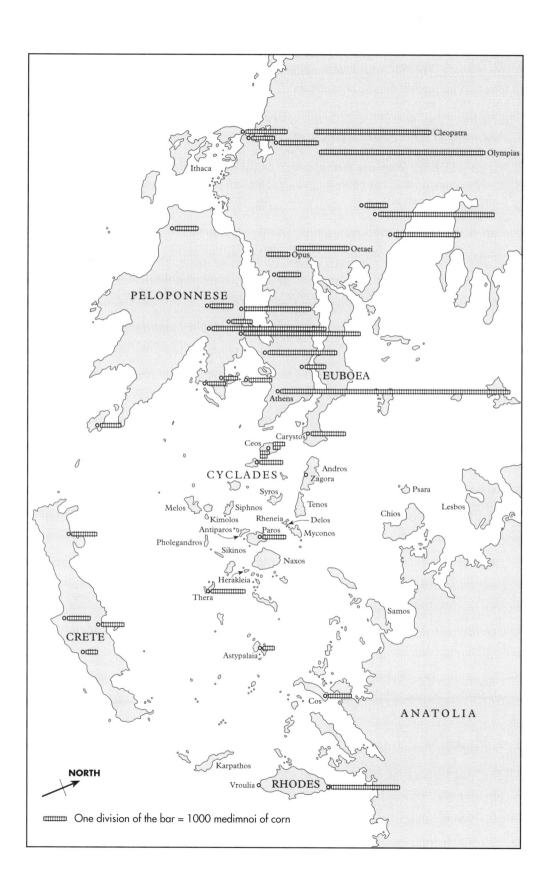

Ithaca

PELOPONNESE

Cleopatra

Olympias

Oetaei

Opus

EUBOEA

Athens

Carystos

Ceos

CYCLADES

Andros

Zagora

Syros

Tenos

Psara

Lesbos

Melos

Siphnos

Kimolos

Rheneia

Delos

Chios

Antiparos

Paros

Myconos

Pholegandros

Sikinos

Herakleia

Naxos

Thera

Samos

CRETE

Astypalaia

Cos

ANATOLIA

NORTH

Karpathos

Vroulia

RHODES

One division of the bar = 1000 medimnoi of corn

collapse of the North African export of olive oil (Frend 1955). The invasion of the nomadic Hilali has been supposed to have brought to a sharp end a period of renewed prosperity in the mid-eleventh century. Relations between immigrants and natives can now, however, as we have already suggested, be envisaged in less dramatic terms. It is not simply a matter of shifting the emphasis away from the violence of invasion and on to broad ecological matters, such as the desiccation potentially caused by increased grazing. For doing that still fails to capture the way in which the nomads variously grasped the opportunities provided by their newly occupied lands. In order to gain 'protection money' they might enhance the prospects for agriculture in a particular area, not destroy it. Some groups might be employed as guardians of crops against other immigrant tribes. Where the markets for animal products were in decline – markets sustained by agricultural-ists – it was hardly in the transhumant's interest to enlarge his herd. Pastoralists, in other words, do not inevitably force land out of production. They are more a symptom than a cause of economic change. The vicissitudes of agriculture in Cyrenaica have owed as much to the strength of central government as to the activities of camels and goats (Cahen 1973).

The vocabulary of prosperity or desolation as applied to whole geographical regions should be seen as part of the rhetoric of political authority and central management. (It was for instance favoured by the Italian colonists of the Fascist period.) Its proper application is only to specific centres of production (from which, as in the Biqa, expansion is possible) and to the extremes of a spectrum of economic possibilities. To understand how movement along that spectrum is possible, the focus of analysis must be sharpened, and the interrelationship of small-scale phenomena more clearly held in view. It is the frequency of change from year to year, in both production and distribution, that makes Mediterran-ean history distinctive. That history must therefore be founded on the study of the local, the small-scale – the specific ('definite') wadi, cove or cluster of springs and wells. But in the pursuit of that study it must never be forgotten that such tiny units are not crisply bounded cellular entities with their own destinies. They are not definite in the sense that they have fixed boundaries. Rather, their defini-tion is always changing as their relations with wider wholes mutate. In the case of South Etruria, Rome provided the most obvious example of a unifying force at work within a region. Like the Biqa, Cyrenaica has had its Romes: not just one centre, that is, but several; shifting ecological foci that have by no means necessarily been cities, that may by now have left few visible traces of their significance, and that have not inevitably been constrained by geographical boundaries of sea or desert.

What is moreover true of isolated pockets of landscape, and of quasi-insular regions on the larger scale, such as Cyrenaica, is even more true of genuine islands, set in the all-influencing sea.

4. MELOS

The small island of Melos, in the Aegean, lies in a cluster with three other yet smaller ones on the south-western edge of the Cyclades. It is about 20 kilometres long and has a surface area of some 150 square kilometres. Unlike most of the other Cyclades, it sits on one of the two bands of still active vulcanicity that stretch from the Greek mainland almost to the Turkish coastline. Volcanic rock therefore covers around four-fifths of the island. At some early stage after the end of the last glaciation, this rock would have been overlain by fairly deep soil. But the hill slopes have since been eroded almost everywhere. Sediment has gradually accumulated both on low-lying inland areas and at various coastal sites. At best, all that has remained on high ground is a very thin soil cover or a layer of loose rock. Most often, though, the volcanic rock is completely exposed. Meanwhile in the valleys the sediment is now dissected by streams.

This pattern of erosion and deposition obviously has much in common with the geomorphology of the valleys in southern Etruria. The chronology is, however, wholly different. Erosion seems to have begun, not in late Roman imperial times, as we would expect from the Italian evidence, but at the end of the Bronze Age. And this process was more or less continuous from then on. It ceased around A.D. 500 – just when it was beginning in some other places. Until the early Middle Ages, the lowest-lying areas must have been largely uninhabitable. But a change in fluvial regime from alluviation to incision opened the valleys and plains to steady cultivation. Why this change occurred is obscure. It might conceivably be visualized as having begun when Bronze Age farmers deforested the uplands and cultivated rather too intensively the soil that they exposed, and thus loosened – although we shall later, in Chapter VIII, see that explanations of this kind have to be treated with enormous caution. Periods of heavy rainfall and severe flood did not help matters. Numerous hillside terraces, artificially 'damming' the movement of soil down to the valleys, remain as witnesses to the struggle of early populations to arrest that progress towards apparent disaster. Only after A.D. 500 could the ecology have stabilized; and even in stability it was not altogether easy to manage.

Nowadays 40 per cent of the island's surface is bare rock, and almost 80 per cent of the total is unused. The fertile soil is largely on the eastern half of the island but it is very unevenly distributed there. Widely scattered fields and terraces are the typical modern farm holding – some indication of the scarcity of usable land, and of the difficulty that has perennially faced farmers since erosion on the hills began. In 1975 eighty-nine farmers were asked how long it took them to walk to their most distant plot. The answers ranged between five minutes and six hours; the average was two hours. Yet distance is not the farmer's only problem. Even where there is good soil the underlying volcanic rocks are porous. Nor is the supply of water ideal in any case (maximum winter rainfall averages 450 mm and there is an interannual variation of almost 50 per cent; cf. Table 1). The winter soil is therefore dry by Mediterranean standards.

Prospects for animal husbandry, just as much as for agriculture, are diminished by all this. The only animals that can be kept in large numbers are goats; transhumance is rare. This is in part because the distance that farmers have to travel to the fields compels them to keep only a few animals so that they can be easily tended close to the farmstead at the beginning and end of the working day. It is also because of the scarcity of pasture and the risks involved in any major shift away from mixed farming (wheat and barley, vine and olives, legumes and gourds, sheep and goats). At first sight, therefore, we have here a simple isolated cluster of niches, exploited with tenacity and ingenuity since time immemorial. Melos might be typical of the precarious nature of Mediterranean life; it might serve as an example of the most ordinary and obscure backwater, where traditional rhythms and often-repeated patterns are easily discernible.

The difficulty is that the history of Mediterranean islands, marginal environments though in some senses they may contain, confounds expectations of insignificance that an analysis of the environment on its own might raise. The admirable research project on 'the archaeology of exploitation' on Melos (Renfrew and Wagstaff 1982) placed considerable emphasis on the 'intra-systemic relations' of the island, in particular those involved in the prehistoric deployment over a wide area of a scarce local resource, volcanic obsidian. The assumption underlying the project was, none the less, that Melos represented a fundamentally self-sufficient unit, isolated enough from the complexities of mainland systems for the archaeologist to discern the processes of human organization with relative ease. That assumption is revealed in the deployment by Renfrew and Wagstaff of the Melian dialogue of Thucydides (*History*, 5.84–116), which might have been thought tangential to the realities of life on Melos. They implicitly accept the idea that the Melians were naturally autonomous and that Athenian aggression constituted a subversion of that autonomy. Yet the Melians' statement of this case (*History*, 5.112), which serves as an epigraph to the 1982 volume, was intended by its author, Thucydides, not to be self-evident but to form part of a debate in which the Athenians' position – that there is a certain necessity to the accretion of influence by the power that rules the sea – is designed ultimately to achieve a terrifying plausibility.

The findings of the research project itself suggest that the vulnerability of Melos in the late fifth century B.C. has been more typical of its long-term history than has any quiet autarky. In particular the relatively high populations – high in terms of any likely 'carrying capacity' of the environment – speak of a rather different state of affairs, in which Melos is an outpost of the demographic and economic dynamics of a wider world. From the classical period, when they believed themselves offshoots of the mainland peoples, to the early modern era when the population size fluctuated with extreme rapidity (that of mid-eighteenth-century Melos falling from c.5,000 to c.1,000 in just a few years), the fortunes of the islanders responded to the wider maritime continuum. Melian assertions of political self-determination do not represent the norm. It is rather the conflicting pulls of the various other regions whose meeting-point is the Aegean that have given shape to the island's history. Far from being unusually quiet and remote, an area such as Melos, or one of its component microecologies, is actually more subject to the shifts and shocks of change than many mainland areas. More clearly, even, than the districts of west-central Italy, with their easy interconnections and their privileged access to far-flung networks through the success of their political centre of gravity, Melos owes its distinctive character not to the accidents of its own geology or climate so much as to its relationships, changing over time, with the fluid patterns of communication in the midst of which it is situated.

Islands are places of strikingly enhanced exposure to interaction, and are central to history of the Mediterranean (V.2, VI.11, IX.2–3). But what is required of the Mediterranean historian is the ability to recognize, in places that are not literal islands, the insular quality of being 'in the swim' of communications. It is this recognition that we have now sought to promote in four examples: an inland district that proves less coherent and definite than its physical geography initially suggested; a seemingly natural region that derives its varying ecological responses from places far beyond it; an isolated territory which also reacts to the networks that it belongs to, overcoming still greater barriers of distance and aridity; and a real island, physically cut off and in that sense totally distinct, yet not in the least isolated.

5. 'LA TRAME DU MONDE'

'When I want to understand Italian history,' Arnaldo Momigliano wrote, 'I catch a train and go to Ravenna. There, between the tomb of Theodoric and that of Dante, in the reassuring neighbourhood of the best manuscript of Aristophanes and in the less reassuring one of the best portrait of the Empress Theodora, I can begin to feel what Italian history has really been' (1969a, 181).

Regions like our four 'definite places' are the Ravennas of Mediterranean history. For Momigliano, among the definitive features of Italy's past that Ravenna encapsulates are the presence of a foreign invader, the memory of pagan and imperial Antiquity, and the enduring force of the Catholic tradition. A selective environmental survey does not reveal cultural traits of that order. But our definite places have indeed introduced a number of equally arresting themes, and our examination of these in more detail should begin to reveal what kinds of continuity, similarity, or generality must preoccupy Mediterranean historians. And not just those interested in geographical or environmental history. Properly understood and interpreted, we suggest, these matters which seem so far removed from the associations of Theodoric and Dante may in fact prove to be contiguous to the historian's 'traditional' spheres of interest – church, society, cultural life, politics – and indeed sometimes essential to their proper understanding.

We shall develop that idea at the end of this chapter and in Parts Three and Four. Momigliano's remark, we may at this stage add parenthetically, is itself of considerable historiographical interest. Whether a vivid *façon de parler* or species of genuine Romanticism, his assertion that the particular collocations of historically eloquent monuments have an especial significance for the historian of Italy puts him in a position – odd for a Piedmontese – rather like that of an outsider looking in at the Mediterranean. It aligns him (emphasizing as he does the *process* of travel and the choice of vehicle) with the mobile, touristic tradition in which the particularity of places is so important. As Momigliano was no doubt well aware, his remark also associates him with a notable statement by a much earlier cosmopolite, St Jerome. In the preface to his first translation of 1 Chronicles, he advised that intellectual understanding would come only through physical travel – travel to Athens for Greek history, to the Ionian Islands for the wanderings of Aeneas, to the Holy Land for the Scriptures (*PL*, 29, col. 401A). As we suggested in Chapter II, many aspects of modern Mediterranean historiography have been grounded in the experience of the scholar-explorer-pilgrim.

Our own particular 'tour' of four localities was intended to promote a number of related ideas. The most important by far is that the 'Ravennas' of Mediterranean history are *normal*. History of this region, as we propose it, concerns localities which have experienced the equivalent in social and economic relations of the exquisite particularities of culture and politics that are to be savoured at

Ravenna. Italian history, like Anatolian history or the past of the Maghreb, has indeed 'really been' microlocal. The most perceptive synthesis of Mediterranean geography expresses the fact memorably. The Mediterranean world is 'a mosaic',

> in which the mean size of each homogeneous unity is of the order of ten kilo-
> metres. Nowhere else is the weave of the world's surface [*la trame du monde*] so
> fine – not even on the islands of Japan, where, if the elements of topographical
> unity are comparable, their content is infinitely less various. (Birot 1964, 3)

Geographical surveys always have to wrestle with complexity. Fragmentation is common enough in landscapes everywhere. But it is the *degree* to which it is subdivided, as Birot pointed out, that distinguishes the Mediterranean world. Indeed, this point may be taken a stage further: the zones and localities that jostle in the Mediterranean can be differentiated in the intensity of their frag-mentation (Medeiros 1988). The nature of the diversity itself is diverse. In any given locale, relatively more uniform tracts of plateau or plain may mesh with the almost absurd variability of the broken topography in which every slope or terrace of a valley-side, each hollow, dune and pool of a coastal lowland, may have its own identity.

Ultimately, there are geophysical reasons for the geological variety of the Mediterranean basin and for the violence of its relief. In the layout of the continents, this sea and its immemorial forebear the inland sea Tethys have had a place which is hard to parallel for importance and longevity. Movements of the plates across the surface of the globe have, over geological time, resulted in many subduction zones, which have been replaced with chains of fold moun-tains. But there are some grounds for the claim that nowhere else in the world's palaeogeography has there been so complex or enduring an example of the pro-cess as in the Mediterranean basin and its precursors (VIII.2). The climates that are known around the globe as 'Mediterranean' are also remarkable for their variability year by year and season by season. Hence the extremely local char-acter of the effects – on soils, hydrology, relief – that result from the interplay of tectonic movements such as faulting, earthquake or orogeny, with the 'physico-climatic forces of denudation'. Although there are other combinations of young fold-mountains with climates of this type, it can be argued that the effect of the physical variety of landscape on the already capricious weather is uniquely pro-nounced across the Mediterranean (Houston 1964). And that must, to an extent, be the result of the strangely fragmented map of the sea itself – as microregional, in many areas, as the adjoining land. Something of a *reductio ad absurdum* of microtopography is consequently to be found among the Mediterranean archipelagos (VI.11).

There is little reason for the earth scientist to go beyond discussing fractured landscapes in convenient macroregional clusters such as the Iberian or Italian peninsulas, or thematically according to one or more of the principal physical variables – mountain terrains, karstic topography, littoral climates, and the like. In investigating *la trame du monde*, however, the historian needs to press fur-ther than the physical geographer. The second lesson that our four examples have helped us comprehend is that the historian must examine the texture of the landscape in terms of the attempt to satisfy human needs from the resources of the environment. Study of *la trame* will, like the life of the overwhelming majority of Mediterranean people in the past, be 'close to the soil'. It will involve minute attention to the varying constraints upon production. Areas where agriculture is at all possible are often limited in their extent and highly fragmented in their disposition.

The constraints are many – pedological, topographical, climatic, botanical – and they are not easy to overcome. Human responses, over history, have been extraordinarily subtle and various, although less comprehensively efficacious than a Romantic optimism might predict. Producers – and agriculture *sensu stricto* is only one element in the portfolio of Mediterranean production – have responded to the fragmented environment with their own 'microstrategies'. It is the kaleidoscopic landscape of production which ultimately constitutes the weave of the world, and although it is shaped by the environmental constraints, it is more pointilliste even than the physical world itself in the specificity and precision of its subdivisions – by field, spring, lane, pasture, garden-ground, pond or copse. One of the most striking botanical microregions of Italy is a hollow of a mere 156 by 188 metres, in which in the nineteenth century a flora of 420 species, many quite alien to the Tyrrhenian coast, was recorded. This is no accident of nature, however, but the cavernous ruins of the Colosseum in Rome – a man-made environment, albeit accidentally so. Where landscape modification has been deliberate, the effects are equally striking. It will be sufficient to cite the example of the control of water, which we saw illustrated in three of our four 'definite places'. In the Mediterranean climate, the single most vital resource for the producer, as well as the most capricious, is water. And water has been managed in a bewildering variety of ways which in themselves offer criteria for a minute subdivision of the landscape in all the periods in which we are interested (VII.2).

The most important way of responding to the constraints of the Mediterranean environment is not to attempt to overcome them, but to adjust to their full intricacy, suiting the means of production to the subtlest complexities of the ecology. By making use of each niche, however small, in minutely subdivided polycultural systems, the environment can be used to its greatest productive capacity. But the subdivision is only part of the story. The third point which we might make after our survey of four representative Mediterranean areas is the paradox that the kaleidoscopic mosaic of the Mediterranean is distinguished by the 'structures' which overcome the fragmentation, and above all by maritime communications. But that is a theme to which we shall return (especially Chapters V, IX).

We are not, therefore, simply offering a revision of Mediterranean regional geography in which the units of study are smaller than has been usual. With the Mediterranean microecologies of this Part's subtitle – the elements of our *trame du monde* – it matters that they are kaleidoscopic; it does not matter what their actual size might be. The fragmentation is more important than the scale. So we shall not attempt to propound a typical size for our microregions, like the 10 kilometres of Birot's rather vague prescription quoted above. We shall, without hesitation, use the term impartially of adjacent fields and of the territories of neighbouring political communities, of individual islands, and of minuscule pockets of intensive cultivation. The underlying concept, rapid variation in the reaction of the producer to the surrounding world in all its complexity (variation which can take place over time as well as over distance), is fluid and inconstant. So it is unreasonable to expect that scale will not be an additional variable, alongside all the others.

Our definition of the microecology, therefore, is a locality (a 'definite place') with a distinctive identity derived from the set of available productive opportunities and the particular interplay of human responses to them found in a given period. It is not the solid geology or the characteristics of the climatic zone, the relief or the drainage, that of themselves define microecologies. It is rather the interaction of opportunities: for animal husbandry, foraging, hunting, intensive agriculture, forest management, horticulture, fishing, or whatever – and, as the final but by no means the least ingredient, for engagement in larger networks of redistribution.

There are two major advantages to this ecological conception of the tessellation of spaces into which the Mediterranean world divides. One is its flexibility over time: it makes change easier to understand. The other is its spatial indeterminacy: it avoids presenting geographical boundaries as permanent or uncrossable. This applies as much to boundaries attributed to the region as a whole as to those presumed to lie within it. It should no longer be a matter of envisaging the Mediterranean in terms of, for instance, Map 1, through the distribution of the olive or a certain climatic regime (definitions that exclude too much territory to be useful or convincing). The Mediterranean of the microecologist is at once more softly edged and less crudely identified.

6. Mountains and Pastures

To test the practicability of this microregional approach, which puts people before physical geography, we may turn to the high mountain zones, 'disadvantaged absolutely in most respects' (Lewthwaite 1981, 60). Mountains have the reputation of being bleak, windy and cold, subject to high precipitation and intense weathering and erosion, dissected and impenetrable, a barrier to communication. Among other forms of marginality, topographic fragmentation in these places is often thought to be so extreme as to prohibit the day-to-day contacts which make production worthwhile (V.1).

Human opportunism and ingenuity have, however, very frequently succeeded in integrating these environments into the productive system. Such integration, while perhaps yielding only a small contribution to the nutritional aggregate, has often had important historical consequences, and helps to show with some clarity the characteristics of environmental opportunism in the system as a whole. Nowhere, in fact, is it easier to see that even the niches with the greatest physical individuality – an isolated upland pasture, a well-watered hollow sheltered by precipitous cliffs – must be understood by the historian not simply in terms of their geomorphological or climatic identity, but as places in which the ecological responses of human populations intersect in a distinctive way. The 'personality of the place' lies not in the bald facts: 'here is a chestnut wood, there a spring, and there a track leading to the summer meadows.' It derives from the presence in this microecology of people engaged in using the spring in agriculture, leading sheep or goats to and from the upland, or exploiting the forest as forage for their pigs.

It derives also from interdependence. Mountain societies can no longer be characterized, as they were by Braudel (1972a, 33), primarily in stark Malthusian terms: of cultural and economic poverty and isolation, with the pressure of expanding population on scarce, overwhelmingly agrarian, resources being relieved in the last resort only by permanent emigration. Mountain microecologies, like almost all microecologies, are parts of greater ecological networks (as Braudel conceded, but with regard only to transalpine trade routes and to a few other, somewhat picturesque, examples: 1972a, 45–6, 206). This interdependence is, moreover, especially pronounced where the fragmentation is most intense. Mountains can seem hostile and marginal areas; yet they are actually closely integrated into the patterns of production and communication that abut them. That explains why mountain zones unexpectedly – and even paradoxically – become regions with wide internal coherence and close contact and interchange across what appear, to the outsider, to be formidable physical obstacles.

The complexity and unpredictability of, for example, Alpine ecologies has been most forcefully brought out by those anthropologists who can combine ethnography with demographic history. Some villages, such as Törbel in the canton of Valais, seem to have been virtually self-sufficient, economically stable (at a very modest level) and autonomous, from the time that the historical record begins (in the thirteenth century) until the aftermath of World War II (Netting 1981). The isolation emerges from the statistics: 'only three men appear to have settled in Törbel, married and had children there since 1700' (1981, 9). Yet other Alpine communities conform far less to the Braudellian stereotype. On the basis of both local ethnography in Alagna (in the Piedmontese Alps) and a wide command of the secondary sources for the whole area, Viazzo (1989) has emphasized that Alpine environmental diversity – even within a single slope – is too great for any broad generalizations about mountain economies to have much purchase on reality. He has suggested that the impoverishment habitually attributed to Alpine villages may be a property more of the land than of the people and their economy. And he has shown that Törbel is far from typical in its isolation. Not only the long history of transalpine commerce, but also that of seasonal – as distinct from permanent – emigration, shows that Alpine communities have developed very extensive ties with their surrounding plains. Since the middle of the nineteenth century, if not earlier, the major part of Alagna's grain supply was for example purchased from outside the area. A large portion of its cattle herd also had to be stabled in the lowlands throughout the winter (the procedure known as inverse transhumance). Over a still longer period perhaps stretching right back to the Bronze Age, moreover, the mining of precious metals in the Alps has at least periodically been both a stimulus to immigration and a source of market-orientated production (IX.2).

Alongside this perhaps unexpected Alpine panorama could be set vignettes of other mountain societies: that for instance created by Fowden (1988) in his study of the practical role played by Mounts Parnes, Pentelicus and Hymettus in the economy of late antique Athens; or that conjured up by Wickham (1988b) of the complex ties engendered by gifts to churches, by political affiliations, and through landownership, between two Apennine valleys and the cities of Lucca and Arezzo during the earlier Middle Ages. Wickham indeed offers a most telling observation – that the marginality of mountain environments can make them more, not less, sensitive to larger commercial pressures, to such an extent that they are 'capable of altering their very geography to fit them' (359). We should not, however, expect that, in the absence of such pressures, mountains display any inherent tendency towards economic isolation.

Mountain societies may be as closely related with others nearby as they are with the plains. The homogeneity of communications in mountainous regions, the dense net of capillaries that (as it were) ties the individual mountains together, makes of some of these areas a curious analogue of the sea. Points where the mountains debouch into the coastlands can parallel the significance of great gathering ports. The upland economy of the Taurus mountain chains in the southern Anatolian peninsula has often displayed this sort of coherence. An arresting example of a gateway between that area and the world of the coastlands and sea in the third century B.C. has come to light in documents concerning the foundation of a city, Arsinoe, by the Ptolemaic rulers of Egypt. This city would not only provide them with another toehold on the coast of Anatolia. It would also institutionalize the relationship between the new port and the societies of the mountain hinterland, particularly the community of Nagidos and its dependants (Opelt and Kirsten 1989).

The difficulties of communications in the mountains concern armies most of all, and to a lesser extent people involved in the bulk redistribution of materials. Those difficulties have, however, often been exaggerated in the literary record to magnify the endurance of those transcending them. From the thirteenth century at least, large quantities of grain and salt were for instance passing on mule-back from the Romagna to Florence across the Apennines. And by the second half of the fourteenth century there was a large-scale transit trade in Spanish wool from the Tyrrhenian to the Adriatic in the same apparently unpromising area (Larner 1990). The less well documented everyday redistribution of people, animals, materials and foodstuffs, though on an individually small scale, can be still larger in aggregate. It is this above all that binds mountain zones together, just as it does islands and sea coasts.

When we use the label 'mountain' in a Mediterranean context, therefore, we are identifying a visually or geomorphologically distinctive landform. But we must be chary of making assumptions about the ecological or demographic structures to be associated with it: these cannot be taken for granted. Generalizing about mountain economies should therefore be undertaken in terms, not of the intransigent actualities of geomorphology, but of a pattern of productive strategies. Most upland areas will, as we have seen, exhibit a high degree of micro-environmental complexity. As Lucien Febvre long ago asserted, there is no sort of mountain unity, no single human-geographical mountain type (1925, 200).

Pastures

One of the numerous ways in which upland ecologies may have been emphatically patterned is through animal husbandry. Wickham for instance, to remain with medieval Italian evidence, is able to show that horses and cows were being wintered 150 kilometres down the coast from one of his valleys perhaps from the eighth century, with quite extensive transhumance of sheep becoming apparent in the twelfth century (1988b, 24–5). Viazzo (1989, 122–6) can sketch a long-term history of animal husbandry in the Alps that begins at the close of the Neolithic period, as the remains of domesticated animals come to outnumber those of wild ones in the archaeological record, and as the movement of flocks and herds across modest distances presumably took on a seasonal pattern.

Yet in a chronology resembling that of the medieval Apennines, long-distance transhumance does not seem to be attested until the turn of the first millennium A.D. (An inscribed altar discovered in the sand of a lake at Graubünden and dedicated to a group of divinities called simply *Pastores* (*AE* 1966, 272–5, with Frei-Stolba 1988) may suggest a much earlier development of pastoralism – around A.D. 200 – but hardly indicates the scale on which it was being practised.) And the particular combination of pastoralism and intensive agriculture known simply as *Alpwirtschaft*, characteristic of the high valleys in modern times, becomes apparent only in the later Middle Ages.

Transhumant pastoralism is perhaps more often associated with mountains than with any other kind of landscape. The association is based on the juxtaposition of markedly different productive opportunities – fertile valley floors and steep forests or high pastures – and not on the other more specific attributes of mountains. Yet, as we have seen, the coexistence within a single microecology of widely different forms of environmental exploitation is typical of many types of landscape: wetlands, stony plains, oases or sandy heaths all offer comparably long spectra of productive choice (cf. VI.7). And pastoralism in particular, if by that we mean the response to ecological locations where the biomass can be made available to human needs only by way of animal diet, is a strategy common to many microenvironments. It cannot be deterministically linked with a restricted number of physically very distinctive environmental niches, such as mountain pastures.

The context of mountain environments provides, none the less, a suitable opportunity at which to summarize observations about pastoralism that were included at various stages in the treatment of four exemplary places. It is also an opportunity to stress again the diversity, extreme mutability, and pervasive interdependence of Mediterranean microecologies.

Modern historiography and archaeology have made it overwhelmingly clear that the image of the pastoralist as a primitive and alien figure must be decisively rejected. A very ancient set of preconceptions will otherwise continue to exercise a damaging influence on our thinking. Although they were originally elaborated with reference to fully nomadic peoples, these preconceptions have proved easily extensible to pastoralists of all kinds. Indeed, they can sustain prejudices against those 'on the move' quite generally, disguising a good deal of what we shall (in IX.5–6) find to have been a perennial instability of Mediterranean populations.

A powerful set of stereotypes dates from the time of the early Greek ethnographer-historians (to look no further than the classical tradition). First, the agriculturalist and the pastoralist each represent pure and unmixed ethnic types, with whole peoples neatly classifiable as either one or the other. Secondly, these unmixed types are polar opposites, with the agriculturalist as superior in virtue of being civilized and the pastoralist as barbarian, although perhaps possessed of a certain noble purity (cf. Jeremiah 35) or even more than that (as with Abel). Thirdly, hardly surprisingly, pastoralism is more ancient than agriculture and in some sense primeval. Even Ibn Khaldun, much the most subtle and penetrating of pre-Enlightenment social analysts, took nomadic society as the starting point for his history, as the 'fertile soil' from which sprang every subsequent form of society. For him, nomads were virtuous. They had the power to generate and, when necessary, regenerate agricultural society. But there was no possibility of their being integrated into it. They still emerge from the *Muqaddimah* (1.2) as distinct in society and economy – and as primitive. This enduring typology was revised in the eighteenth century. The hunter-gatherer displaced the pastoralist as the practitioner of the earliest form of economy. Yet pastoralism had still not 'caught up' with agriculture: it remained a humble forerunner. The image of the pastoralist as lawless and uncouth is perpetuated in the complaints of Mediterranean farmers about the depredation wrought by flocks and herds.

Against these nicely discrete and hierarchical images, whose tenacious history has been traced by B. D. Shaw (1982–3), can now be set, in the form of eight points, a modern vision of the comparable sophistication and essential interconnectedness of pastoralism and agriculture in the Mediterranean. That is, pastoralism and agriculture must, *first* of all, be envisaged as far more likely to have functioned in symbiosis than in isolation. The purely pastoral societies of ancient Greek thought are extremely rare. Moreover they are not to be found within the Mediterranean region: one has to look to the inhabitants of Viking Greenland, or the modern Inuit or Masai, to find groups whose diet and other everyday needs have been derived overwhelmingly from their animals. *Second*, pastoralism is if anything a more complex form of economy than agriculture, not an underdeveloped substitute for it in areas too poor for cultivation. Since it can rarely exist in isolation, it must involve quite sophisticated connections with its surrounding worlds of production and exchange. Some of those connections may involve the pastoralist in violence and predation; yet it should be remembered that accusations on that score may be less a reflection of actual provocation than of the agriculturalist's view of the pastoralist's place in the social hierarchy (Koster and Koster 1976, 283). *Third*, following on from that, there is nothing in any sense of the word primitive about pastoralism. It is subsequent to agriculture on any evolutionary time-scale: the agriculturalist was the first to domesticate animals.

To these refutations of the classical stereotype of the backward alien can be added other points that may bring out more clearly the characteristic forms of Mediterranean pastoralism. *Fourth* then, the close integration of pastoralism and agriculture should be envisaged across a very wide range of functions. Pastoralists must either rely on agriculturalists for a substantial portion of their necessities or engage in some agriculture themselves (a possibility even for fully nomadic peoples). Agriculturalists look to livestock – pigs, oxen and cattle as well as ovicaprids – for manure, traction and threshing as much as for wool, cheese or meat. *Fifth*, as the four definite places have between them already implied, this symbiosis should be recognized as extremely responsive to changing economic opportunities. The sense of cultural difference and the bitterness that cultivator and herder have so often aroused in one another, and that underpin the classical stereotype, should not be allowed to conceal the ease with which even the extreme specialists on either 'side' have partaken of the 'opposing' form of livelihood: 'the herder whose flocks damage crops is a neighbour and rival, a temporary apostate from the settled misery; the irate farmer is a renegade who last year saw no harm in allowing his herds on to other men's fields' (J. Davis 1977, 21).

To sum up this degree of interdependence we might consider the emblematic significance of porridge. It has long been a feature of Mediterranean pastoralists to process cereal products into a hard, durable form which will keep, and which can be rendered edible by soaking or boiling. This preparation, known under many names of which the Greek *trachana* may be the most familiar, makes available the staples of the arable world to the transhumant shepherd when he has to leave the world of agriculture behind (Bryer 1985). Something similar may lie behind the origins of pasta. There is always a symbiosis between animal husbandry and other forms of environmental management.

Sixth: suppose we divide the continuum of Mediterranean pastoral practices roughly into four parts. These correspond to (a) small-scale husbandry where the few animals in question remain on the farm all year round, (b) 'vertical' transhumance, by which herds of only moderate size move seasonally to nearby upland pastures, (c) the far grander 'horizontal' transhumance associated with the Spanish Mesta or the Neapolitan Dogana, involving at the extreme the seasonal movement of millions of sheep over several hundred miles, and finally (d) the less predictable movements of fully nomadic groups, mostly on the Mediterranean's eastern fringes. Of these four, at least since the beginning of historical times the distinctively Mediterranean form of pastoralism has been the second: vertical transhumance between upland and adjacent plain.

That conclusion differs slightly from the one implied in much modern discussion. Most attention has usually been given to (c) – not so much its more spectacular manifestations in the Mesta and Dogana as the generality of large-scale transhumance. This type has seemed to reflect the potential of the Mediterranean environment more closely than do other forms of pastoralism, and thus to offer (according to taste) either an attractive picture of a 'natural' and long-lasting economic practice, or the opportunity for an attack on environmental determinism. Interest has also been focused on its 'high-profile' Roman precursors in the Italy of the late Republic and early Empire. One landowner, an ex-slave called Caecilius Isidorus, is reported to have had 257,000 sheep and goats (Brunt 1975). There is relatively abundant evidence for the maintenance of drove roads and the extension of a lucrative ovicaprine pastoralism deep into the recesses of the Apennines.

It has become customary to distinguish a 'Mediterranean' transhumance of more or less this kind from the vertical 'Alpine' variety, in which animals move to high ground during the summer to free the low-lying fields for the production of the winter fodder that will be consumed in the stable. We prefer to emphasize the variety of Alpine as well as of more obviously intra-Mediterranean pastoral strategies, not drawing too sharp a distinction between them. We prefer also, of course, to direct attention to the 'short distances', the highly local forms of livelihood which both unite microecologies and bind them to their neighbours. In contrast, then, to a body of modern scholarship that tends to be pre-occupied with the largest pastoral networks and to glance occasionally 'down' the scale, we would place the centre of interest at the humbler end of the continuum. It remains debatable just how far highly localized animal husbandry was part of the Mediterranean small farmer's basic means of support in Antiquity (BE VI.7). But the practice has a clear enough history from the early Middle Ages onward, although it would require a vastly extensive survey of the documentary and archaeological record to yield any worthwhile generalizations about regional and chronological patterns (cf. Chapter VI). Problems of evidence notwithstanding, it is this history, especially the circumstances in which it has included some form of transhumance, rather than the history of the Mesta and Dogana, that should provide the starting point for analysis.

Seventh, no form of husbandry can simplistically be related to the pressures of the environment. Each has to be conceived within a far richer context, as 'over-determined' as a Freudian neurotic symptom. No pastoral strategy, we have said, can be simply predicated of the landscape. Therefore no such strategy can be seen as 'natural'. The mountain summer pasture, for example, which is at the heart of transhumance is itself by no means always part of the 'given' environment. It may have to be created by deforestation. Nor can transhumance be interpreted as a straightforward function of any other environmental feature. Predictions about where transhumance will have been most suited to the environment, for example in the comparison of Sardinia and Corsica (Lewthwaite 1981), are nearly always confounded by the historical or archaeological evidence. (Although Sardinia seems much the less well fitted for pastoralism, large-scale sheep grazing and movement have been considerably more prevalent there than in Corsica.) Climatic determinism is a particularly vulnerable type of analysis in this context. The rationale of the transfer of animals to the uplands during the hot, dry, Mediterranean summer may certainly lie in the need to escape the aridity of the plains. But as Wickham (1983–5, 442) has pointed out, 'almost all transhumant systems englobe small groups of non-transhumant stock-raisers, with stock capable of staying in the same place all year.'

Simple determinism must be replaced by a far more complex explanatory setting. The generalization that 'mediterranean pastoralists are constrained as much by government as by grass' (J. Davis 1977, 21) should be extended to political conditions in the broadest sense. These have already emerged as crucially important in the ecological histories of South Etruria and Cyrenaica (Laronde 1996b). The fortunes of pastoralists have been to some degree connected with levels of security and governmental ability to regulate – and, above all, tax – in most other parts of the region as well. The proximity of markets is another part of the scene that deserves just as much emphasis as any environmental feature: pastoralists flourish where they can exchange, not just where they can find grazing. Finally, at the humbler end of the continuum the pattern of human settlement may have a powerful effect. Nucleated settlement associated with extensive farming can make it very hard for individual farmers to look after more than a few animals locally, partly because they cannot devote enough time to them and partly because bare fallowing drastically reduces the availability of fodder. Farmers may thus resort to communal herding, sharing the labour or jointly employing specialists, in order to remove their animals to summer pasture. Conversely, dispersed settlement with intensive farming of immediately adjacent land enables farmers to maintain their animals nearby.

The relative significance of these factors will of course vary with the wealth and location of the pastoralist. And it would be fair to suggest that, on the whole, the rise to prominence of large-scale pastoral systems in particular periods, such as the central Middle Ages in both the Alps and the Tuscan Apennines, reflects a more thorough 'overdetermination' than do the smaller-scale operations of a group of poor farmers. Yet the features of the latter's husbandry are far from easy to explain: we dare not assume that the political and economic conditions sustaining the flocks of an aristocrat are inherently more complex than the combination of tenurial obligation, field system, settlement pattern, market geography, and soil chemistry that might impinge on the decision-taking of the lowly. Our *eighth* and last point is therefore that, if we wish to gauge the sophistication of even quite tiny systems of animal husbandry, we should allow the largest systems their say. The archival detail upon which a study of the Neapolitan *Dogana delle pecore* may for instance depend (Marino 1988), the variety of political and economic topics upon which it must dwell, the way in which the pastoral regime of the early modern kingdom of Naples may be found to provide a possible solution to the question of southern backwardness that has so vexed historians of modern Italy – all this can be taken to signal not just the ramifications of the Dogana but the centrality of pastoralism in some form to Mediterranean history quite generally, and the sophistication of its workings across the *entire* spectrum of pastoral practices. In that sense, the spectrum is not as broad as might have been imagined, the two extremes not so far removed:

> from its foundations in the mid fifteenth century, the system of transhumance in southern Italy was a large-scale cash-cropping enterprise dependent upon private wealth (capitalist graziers, capitalist merchants, capitalist agriculturalists) and public patronage (royal management, royal demesne, and royal justice). In controlling the movement of sheep from summer to winter pasture, the state placed itself in the center of a timeless tradition that amalgamated the realities of capitalist agriculture with the rationale of Arcadian pastoralism. (Marino 1988, 7)

7. THEODORIC AND DANTE

The conception of Mediterranean history initially derived from a selection of 'definite places' and elaborated under the sign of *la trame du monde* has now been applied to mountain economies and to the broader phenomenon of pastoralism. It was described at the outset as an approach to the Mediterranean past by way of its microfoundations. It was not intended to encompass directly the likes of Theodoric and Dante, between whose tombs Momigliano could begin to feel what Italian history had really been. An approach that is broadly ecological, but that does not aspire to produce an all-embracing model on the basis of inadequate data, is not going to explain the collapse of the Roman Empire, or the policies of Philip II of Spain, solely in ecological terms. Nor, as was stressed in Chapter II, will it pay lip-service to what would bulk large in any other form of history merely by leaving a vacant space in the model for 'mental factors' – when what this phrase usually means is the entirety of human culture.

None the less, the wider political context has had to be invoked on a number of occasions: the imperial powers of Athens and Rome; major, if transient, cities such as ancient Cyrene; the political structures that underpinned the (to much more than the accepted degree) exemplary Neapolitan Dogana. We begin to see the possible extent of the connections between the narrative historian's concern with the rise and fall of complex societies and, at the microecological level, a change in the balance of productive strategies, between arable cultivation or arboriculture and pastoralism. Let us return for a moment to the Lebanese valley described at the beginning of the chapter. Here the social and political history of the area is complicated: space would have to be found, in a narrative of successive Hellenistic, Roman and Islamic hegemonies, for a pattern of local politics as complex and unstable as that so cruelly evident at the end of the twentieth century. The various partitions of Syria – between Egyptians and

Hittites in the Bronze Age; between Seleucids and Ptolemies in Hellenistic times; between Fatimids and Hamdanids in the earlier Middle Ages; between Seljuks, Western Crusaders, and Ayyubids – may all be seen as the outcome of political competition, across the centuries, for broadly unchanging human resources: for the allegiance of small, highly elastic local familial and political groups who managed the diverse microecologies, pastoral or agricultural, upon which any larger power ultimately depended.

> The Biqa was thus a political no-man's-land, characterized by a diffuse assortment of political leaders and allegiances, ethnic identities, economic relations, and socio-cultural syncretisms . . . In effect, each rival nullified any degree of administrative or economic integration achieved by the other – and, considering the intrinsic socio-economic disequilibrium of the lowlands, this was seldom difficult. Thus the penetration of bedouin tribes . . . into the settled zone is explained not so much by aggression on their part as by the absence of local authority and the decline of rural settlements. (Marfoe 1979, 18)

Such an interpretation (that echoes in its closing lines the analysis of the Hilali invasions offered in Section 3 above) can only tentatively link the political instability of the Biqa lowlands with the intense local variability of the micro-ecologies there. It is not a basis for generalization across other less fragmented parts of Syria – still less across other parts of the Mediterranean world. But it does, once again, point to the ways in which political and ecological change can be bound up with each other; and it emphasizes the contribution that a study of microenvironments might make to the broader understanding of Mediterranean history. Appreciation of *la trame du monde* offers the possibility of a systematic approach to the task of relating the mutable patterns of productive choices and the formation of networks of power, cooperation, allegiance and dependence. In the chapters that follow we plan to test the concept further. And we start in the world in which Theodoric and Dante must be primarily located – although with some words of Dante that immediately project the topic in an unfamiliar but, to us, congenial light.

Chapter IV

Ecology and the Larger Settlement

sempre la confusione delle persone
principio fu del mal delle cittade
come del corpo il cibo che s'appone ...

Se tu riguardi Luni e Orbisaglia
come sono ite, e come se ne vanno
di retro ad esse Chiusi e Sinigaglia

udir come le schiatte si disfanno
non ti parrà nova cosa né forte
poscia che le cittadi termine hanno.

[it is always the mingling of people that has been the beginning of evil for cities, as, for the body, it is the food that is set before it ... If you look at Luni or Urbisaglia, and at the way that they have gone, and at the way that Chiusi and Senigallia are following behind them on the same path, then hearing how families disintegrate will appear neither new nor remarkable, inasmuch as cities themselves come to an end.]

Dante, *Paradiso*, 16.67–9, 73–8

... fragilités des cités, peuplées d'une masse mobile, vagabonde, mal fixée.

Henri Bresc (1986b) *Monde méditerranéen*, 66

'Routes et Villes, Villes et Routes.' Such was Lucien Febvre's comment on first reading the chapter in Braudel's *Mediterranean* discussing the region as a human unit (Braudel 1972a, 277 n.1). As we began to see in Chapter II, much of the most significant – and romantic – Mediterranean scholarship has been devoted to the region's economic history, and in particular to its towns and their communications. With them, it has seemed to leading representatives of the Romantic tradition, lies the essence of the Mediterranean past and the source of Mediterranean unity. Both *routes* and *villes* have, moreover, been conceived above all in terms of high commerce. Towns and communications are, then, topics on which our overall interpretation of Mediterranean history must clearly be brought to bear. Do towns, in all their seeming solidity, resist consideration in the fluid microecological terms that have been espoused by preceding chapters and will be developed in later ones (VI–IX), or can they fruitfully be embraced by them? How are communications between microecologies best understood (V)?

Our reference in the previous chapter to the worlds of Theodoric and Dante was intended, at the least, to suggest ramifications of our own microscopic approach for the more usual stuff of political and social narrative. In turning to urban and economic history we cannot be so tentative. We shall adopt a stance diametrically opposed to that of (among others) our 'four men in a boat' (II.2). Rather than merely seek points of contact between microregions and the larger world of towns and trade routes, we shall argue that all these subjects can profitably be accommodated within a single analytical framework – much as Dante accommodates cities, families and bodies in the lines quoted above. We place no special emphasis on *routes* conceived as grand commercial links that can be mapped with clear sweeping lines – ribbons laid over sea or landscape (Braudel 1972a, 277; Chapter V). Nor do we give particular, separate, attention to *villes* conceived either as the nodal points of such lines or as the fixed centres of simply determinable hinterlands.

For our immediate purpose, indeed, neither route nor town is a particularly helpful category. Both can be 'dissolved' into less readily mappable kinds of microecological functioning and interaction. Like the special case of ports to which we come later (IX.7), towns can be seen as 'epiphenomenal' to larger ecological processes. Similarly, in the next chapter we shall suggest that the Mediterranean region derives unity and cohesion less from its network of routes in the Braudellian sense than from the more general *connectivity* of its microregions. Here, we begin the process of dissolving Febvre's categories by considering towns. We argue that towns require an ecological history, but not one of a special kind. There is no particular quality of urban space that automatically colours belief and action within it. For our present project, a town is an address, an arena, an architectonic agglomeration: distinctive – sometimes – for the volume and density of its buildings, or the bustle and variety of its population, but not, we propose, for the way in which its microregions work.

1. AN URBAN TRADITION

Carthage, Athens, Rome, Alexandria, Antioch, Constantinople, Marseille, Córdoba, Barcelona, Pisa, Florence, Venice . . . the list could be extended a long way, and its items could be so ordered as to stand for a quite effective summary of many aspects of the Mediterranean past. After all, the Mediterranean has probably been the most durably and densely urbanized region in world history. No other comparable area can boast so many towns and cities of such antiquity. The major cities have, moreover, been the sites (or addresses) in which the fortunes of its populations have principally been determined. Power, civilization and prosperity seem always to have radiated from them. This is the world evoked at the close of the previous chapter. It is also the historiographical world inhabited by the 'four men' of Chapter II.

First there was Rostovtzeff's bourgeoisie and its role in an ancient economy that spanned the Mediterranean and Asia. Then there were Pirenne's early medieval merchants, who virtually made and unmade clusters of cities as their long-distance trading connections flourished or foundered. It was in the nature of things, thirdly, that Goitein's Geniza documents should represent 'an intrinsically urban population' (1967–88, 4.1). Its horizons could almost be defined in terms of a list of cities whose names recur frequently in the texts – from Samarkand to Narbonne. Braudel's purview, finally, was of course hardly so narrow. Yet towns and cities remained at the very centre of his vision, colouring his perception of what lay beyond. In the first volume of *Civilization and Capitalism* (1981–4) towns were portrayed as 'electric transformers', 'watersheds of human history' (479). Yet the conviction that they had been the driving force in not only the industrial, but also the preindustrial, world economy derived from work done on the Mediterranean decades previously:

> The prevailing human order in the Mediterranean has been one dictated primarily by towns and communications, subordinating everything else to their needs. Agriculture, even on a very modest scale, is dictated by and directed towards the town . . . It is because of the towns that man's life has taken on a faster rhythm than it would under natural conditions. (1972a, 278)

The historiographical tradition of the Mediterranean town is weighty, then. And its weight is provided not just by the four men who dominate modern thinking about the Mediterranean but also by other 'stars' in the firmament of social and economic thought whose interests were far from bearing directly upon the region: Smith, Marx and Weber to name only three. This tradition elevates towns into a highly distinctive and supremely significant historical category, precisely because they have become increasingly set apart from the countryside. It implies forcefully that our introduction to the Mediterranean past through a description of rural microecologies – four 'definite places' – was literally eccentric.

The eccentricity was calculated and now needs defending. As we indicated in the previous chapter, we do not wish to create the impression that the Mediterranean past is somehow divisible into two, with microecologies in one category and the rest of 'the historical process' – so much of it created in towns – in the other. A microecological approach, we suggested, reaches out into the more usual domains of research. Urban history should certainly be reckoned one of these domains. And yet we shall not be particularly concerned to establish interdisciplinary connections with it. Indeed, in the full discussion of Mediterranean settlement patterns reserved for Volume 2, towns will not be allocated a particular subsection to themselves; nor, after this chapter in the present volume, will the words 'town' or 'urban' be used with reference to anything more than their architectonic distinctiveness or their legal status. This strategy, paradoxically, is not designed to show that town life is here somehow of only marginal interest. On the contrary: urban history is far from being mere 'superstructure' on a microecological base. The point is precisely that it is indivisible from the broader canvas. In that case, should a town, or a part of a town, not have been included among our examples in Chapter III?

A partial response to the question might be to assert that there is at least scope for a history of the region which starts from its countryside and, as it were, looks inwards to the town – as against one which, in Braudellian fashion, implicitly surveys the area from the vantage point of a city wall. Towns have perhaps dominated the historiography of the Mediterranean – as they are supposed to have dominated its landscape – for too long. The 'ruralization' of European history referred to in our earlier discussion of the *Annales* school (II.3) could, for all the field surveys and village studies now available (BE III, BE VI.2), be prosecuted still more vigorously in a Mediterranean setting.

Further response to the question thus requires something stronger than a mere shift of emphasis. First of all it must involve recalling the number of areas and periods that cast doubt on the degree of urban orientation typical of the Mediterranean past. There were, for instance, few towns in the extensive regions of classical Greece that were classified as *ethne* (peoples). Again, since Antiquity, much of Mediterranean Africa or Spain has been only barely urbanized for quite long stretches of time. The same could be said of central Anatolia. Counter-examples such as these could still, however, be dismissed as peripheral – to an urban 'core'; they evade the question of whether the prominence traditionally allowed to the urban history of the Mediterranean can be accepted, even in modified form. An alternative, but still 'ruralizing', approach might take its cue from the estimated proportion of Mediterranean populations that did not reside in towns. That would necessitate more than just a shift of emphasis, or an attentiveness to non-urbanized areas and periods. But speculating about this extra-urban proportion of course raises another large question: one of definition. Our estimate of the characteristic urban population of the preindustrial Mediterranean – 3, 5, 10 per cent: a figure of that order – will naturally depend on the kinds of settlement that we are prepared to count as towns and the number of them that we thus identify. But what is a town?

2. Definitions

Urban geographers and historians have typically sought a definition in terms of concentration of population and diversity of non-agricultural pursuits. To qualify as a town, that is, a settlement must have reached a certain size and density; it must include a substantial number of people not primarily engaged in producing their own food; and the occupations of the latter must be sufficiently various – aristocratic leisure, government, administration, religion, trade, manufacture, service, and so forth. The great difficulty is of course that these four criteria – population size and density, size and diversity of non-agricultural sector – each refer to a continuum. There is no readily agreed size or proportion that will distinguish a town from, say, a large village, a royal manor, a self-sufficient temple-complex, a 'mega-monastery' (e.g. San Vincenzo al Volturno: Hodges 1997). Indeed it is a commonplace of urban history that many settlements usually identified as towns have been smaller than large villages of the same period, and that the greatest diversity of occupation may be regularly exhibited in a rural market or coastal emporium. No exquisitely extended catalogue of possible urban functions – and some of them contain as many as a hundred – can dispel the unease created by such awkward cases. Any definition of a town is bound to contain arbitrary elements.

These difficulties have, however, usually not been allowed to call into question the validity of urban studies (historical, sociological, geographical, or whatever) as a distinctive branch of scholarship. Reassurance has been sought in the simple – and, so far as it goes, quite compelling – argument that it is possible to distinguish most towns from most other forms of settlement without being able to decide all hard cases. In other words, the extremes of the continuum can clearly be differentiated from one another even if its middle range is ambiguous. But this argument, though persuasive, is generally confounded by lack of evidence.

Since reliable statistics about population density and occupational structure in the preindustrial past are usually lacking, studies of urban systems have tended to invoke a crude demographic criterion: only settlements of more than 10,000 people – or a figure of that order – qualify for discussion. This strategy has the clear advantage of eliminating a good many potentially difficult cases. But numerous smaller settlements, many of which might well in other circumstances have been categorized as towns, are also excluded. And that exclusion is particularly unwelcome so far as the Mediterranean is concerned. So many of the settlements on which its reputation as a highly urbanized region must largely depend have sheltered no more than one or two thousand people – 'small towns' on certain definitions but towns none the less. Moreover, some densely packed villages, for instance the 'agro-towns' of southern Italy, remain within the terms of reference despite their inhabitants' narrow range of occupations, and despite the uncertainty about their status expressed in that ungainly label.

Political, legal, social or architectural criteria have also frequently been advocated by students of urbanism. One possible advantage of this strategy is that it in effect shifts responsibility for definition onto the past: it substitutes indigenous for modern analytic categories. A town is what each age takes it to be. Each town becomes, as the title of a stimulating monograph has it, an 'argument in stone', a statement of civilized values, a declaration of the local nature of urbanism (Carver 1993). It 'constructs', some might be tempted to say, a particular kind of space (H. Lefebvre 1991). But this approach is ultimately no less troublesome. First, it leaves out settlements that would normally qualify as towns in social or economic terms but which did not frame their arguments in the expected way, lacking the requisite status or the appropriate buildings (such as, in pagan Antiquity, temples and baths); or conversely, it uncomfortably includes very minor settlements which resembled the larger towns only in that – to take a medieval example – they were the seats of bishops. Secondly, when essentially historical criteria are invoked, there is a danger that historians may carry over one particular age's or culture's 'construction' into other periods for which it may well be unsuitable. If that particular anachronism is avoided, then we are still left with urban history as a kind of fashion parade, in which one urban 'style' succeeds another for no deeper reason than changing taste. Long-range comparisons of the type that we attempt in this book become very hard. The circuit of walls, the public amenities, the charter in the archive: these tell us about inflections in the history of values more than about the history of settlement – which is more to our purpose here. The early medieval village huddling beneath the still imposing defences of an otherwise derelict ancient city, and still 'hiding' behind its name, furnishes the clearest reminder that neither location nor nomenclature confer uncontroversial urbanity on a site. Classical criteria have bedevilled the evaluation of early medieval settlements (B. Ward-Perkins 1997). Such criteria create the impression that specific architectural styles and forms are diagnostic of true urbanism. Yet architecture is not that reliable a guide. With respect to early medieval Rome, for example, it emerges that the apparent caesuras in architectural activity which seemed quite nicely to reflect phases of extreme political turbulence were in fact almost as full of building projects as was the 'Carolingian Renaissance'. Ecclesiastical patronage of church construction proves to have been no respecter of Dark Ages (Coates-Stephens 1997; cf. Krautheimer 1980, ch. 4;). Quite generally, moreover – not just with regard to the early Middle

Ages – adopting a historicist definition can tend to promote exaggerated interest in simple continuity or discontinuity from one period to another: more subtle alterations in the character of settlements are overlooked in favour of a simplistic answer to the question of whether or not one particular feature survived (e.g. a regular street plan: but cf. B. Ward-Perkins 1995). And the corollary is that insufficient attention may be given to new settlements of urban character that lacked the appropriate rank and appearance.

Definition in historical (indigenous) terms is thus no more satisfactory than reliance on an arbitrary demographic threshold. A fault more evident in the historical approach but actually common to both definitions – and one that deserves emphasis in the present context – is the insufficient attention paid to variety and change. *Geographical* variety first of all: subtly differing kinds of settlement have coexisted within a very short distance of one another. But this is partly because of *chronological* variety: settlements in the Mediterranean, many of them extremely small, have slipped in and out of whatever category may be established to contain them – and it would be rash to assume that, in doing so, they have necessarily undergone some important transformation – across a qualitative frontier from, say, urban to non-urban. We should imagine them as being in flux from year to year, even from day to day – just like other microregions made by mobile Mediterranean people (IX.5–6). They may evolve at a very great pace, exhibiting frequent changes of population density and disposition, social institution or economic function – all perhaps beneath a relatively immutable architectural carapace. They are indeed, we suggest, the ultimate microenvironments, taking anthropogene effects on the landscape to their extreme conclusion, while remaining as fickle in their forms as any of the ecologies already encountered.

Relatively short-term variations in the number and hierarchy of urban settlements within any given region can be quite striking in scale. The processes of *synoicism* and *dioicism* (by which villages respectively aggregate into a city or emerge from its fragmentation) are well known to ancient historians. A celebrated example is provided by Mantinea in the centre of the Peloponnese (Hodkinson and Hodkinson 1981). During the sixth century B.C. a city developed there out of a conglomeration of small agricultural settlements that supported a previously dispersed elite. Yet in 386 B.C. – Xenophon (*Hellenica*, 5.2.6–7) gives a vivid account – an alien political force, finding this arrangement unsatisfactory, arbitrarily abolished that city and at a single stroke returned the region to a village settlement pattern. Mantinea the town is a precarious conceptual tool.

So much for the ancient world. It may less often be appreciated that urban settlements have been comparably fluid in later periods of Mediterranean history (though cf. Bintliff 1998). Terranova, in Sicily's Val di Noto, is for instance listed as having over 4,000 hearths in the tax return of 1276–7; 'by the late fourteenth century, Saracen attacks and the plague had reduced it to little more than a hamlet' (S. R. Epstein 1991, 24). During roughly the same period Prato lost over 75 per cent of its population (Herlihy and Klapisch-Zuber 1985, 62). It would be unwise to assume that the various visitations of the Black Death render these demographic losses utterly exceptional. Anatolia supplies several telling examples. In the twelfth century the small settlements of the Menderes valley were regularly evacuated as Greeks, Turks or Western Crusaders began their campaigning season: the population simply removed to the surrounding hills (Whittow n.d.). Of course, not all demographic fluctuations were so rapid. A place such as

Erzurum required about a century to empty and fill up again during the early modern period (Faroqhi 1984, 73). In rather less time, between about 1560 and 1610, the seaport of Izmir (ancient Smyrna) changed from a sluggish harbour peopled only by a few Turks into one of the most significant of Levantine emporia. The transformation was brought about by enterprising local officials, who took advantage of slackening Ottoman control to break Istanbul's commercial monopoly (Goffman 1990). A final example: the gateway city, Šaltiš, which processed and exported the fabulous metal resources of south-west Spain, bloomed and withered within a few generations (Bazzana and Trauth 1997; IX.2).

Simple enumeration of the central places of past landscapes can thus be very hard. Because of their *fragilité*, locations of great social or economic significance may for one thing be invisible to the source tradition, whether juridical, archaeological or descriptive. The demographic graph of secular fall and increase moreover tells nothing like the whole story. Some communities for instance create an architectural façade for their shared activities which can look like that of a town even though it reflects no lasting social life or economic function: except on a few special occasions the population lives elsewhere. In the eleventh century for example, according to its bishop, John Mauropous, the Anatolian city of Euchaita was transformed from a wasteland into a populous market centre by the great feast of St Theodore (Haldon 1990, 117; X.10). It would have reverted to waste once the fair was over: 'le cittadi termine hanno.'

A more complex instance of labile 'urbanism' – from the Roman imperial period – is provided by Oenoanda in the mountains of Lycia. Although not particularly grand, its remains are well preserved; and it is clear that, as a nucleated settlement, it did not have a large permanent population. Its inscriptions are unique, however; they show how the self-expression of a local elite could flourish even in the absence of the economic and social institutions of a city. The discovery of the longest known ancient genealogy, of a complete philosophical text, and of a great dossier of regulations for a festival – all of them inscribed on stone – make the workings of this apparently insignificant centre visible to us with an unusual clarity. Here are some of the festival regulations.

> The following will process through the theatre and will sacrifice together for the days of the festival . . . The Organizer of the Festival, one bull; the priest of Zeus, one bull; the three festival supervisors, one bull; the secretary of the council and the five magistrates, two bulls; the two market-supervisors of the city, one bull; the two officials in charge of the gymnasium, one bull, the four treasurers, one bull; the two rural police officers, one bull; . . . of the villages, Thersenos with Armadu, Arissos, Merlakanda, Big Mountain, [ ]lai, Kirbu, Euporoi, Oroata, [ ]rake, Valo and Yskapha, with their associated farmsteads, two bulls; Orpenna Sielia with associated farmsteads, one bull; Ogarsan [ ]ake with Lakistaunda and Kakasboi Killu . . . (trans. [slightly adapted] Mitchell 1990, 185–6; cf. Wörrle 1988)

A city that had seemed little more than a symbolic focus, the setting of elite display, is now revealed in the full complexity of its relations with the countryside where its population resided for most of the time – a hinterland of some thirty distinct settlements, no doubt in at least as many separate microecologies, with names redolent of a non-Greek past. And all this in a mountain environment that can hardly be regarded as one of the most productive in the Mediterranean (cf. III.6).

Such shifting and paradoxical forms of settlement might of course be more effectively categorized by reverting to the criterion of occupational diversity, than by considering only size and status. Yet even if, in any given case, the details of occupational structure could be known, the percentages that they comprised would often create an entirely misleading impression of stability – stability of occupation, in a world in which the maxim of survival is 'diversify' (Chapter VI); stability of people, second, who are actually very likely to be 'on the move' (Chapter IX). Worse, to look at occupational structure would still be to under- write an attempt to separate towns from other kinds of settlement by establish- ing a different, yet no less arbitrary, threshold. The criterion of diversity does not therefore respond to what, in looking at its economic aspect in Chapter III and its demographic aspect just now, we have already identified as the 'fluidity' of Mediterranean forms of habitation. The mobility that we shall see to have been common among Mediterranean populations undermines all attempts at clearly distinguishing settlement types.

3. THE URBAN VARIABLE

Given such problems of definition, it is worth asking the obvious yet rather neglected question of why it is important sharply to differentiate towns and cities from the remainder of the continuum. There seem to be only two plaus- ible and intellectually respectable answers to that. One of them depends on a simple matter of heuristic convenience. For the historian at least, many settle- ments are extremely poorly documented, and for practitioners of any relevant discipline the total number may be too large to be manageable; it is therefore sensible, if arbitrary, to restrict study to the 'upper reaches' of the hierarchy: the larger, denser, more diverse instances. In that case, a synoptic account of Mediterranean habitation (such as we propose for Volume 2) can ignore the restriction and attempt to embrace the entire range of settlement types.

Mere heuristic convenience is, however, not likely to be the sole or even the principal reason for attempting to exclude many sites from discussion. The major objective – common to urban historians and social scientists of all kinds – is surely to register the conviction that, despite its obscurity, there really is some distinctive urban variable, some feature of town life that makes it qualitatively, and not just quantitatively, different from that of other settlements. If this vari- able is known, the value of urban studies as a separate discipline will be self- evident. If the variable has yet to be identified, then (so it might be argued) a narrow focus will be necessary to isolate and display it.

We must, however, ask whether there is indeed such an urban variable. What is achieved by predicating of a given instance of social or economic behaviour that it happened in a town? 'A town is a town wherever it is', Braudel famously wrote (1973, 373). And a great deal of urban sociology and history has rested on the assumption that the town does constitute a kind of space, a generic social entity. After all, population densities are likely to be higher in towns than elsewhere; more urban dwellers depend on the market for food than would the inhabitants of other settlements; economic activity, because confined within a smaller area, is likely to be more intense; levels of social interaction generally are likely to be much higher and (perhaps) less bound by tradition; urban demo- graphy – and even psychology – are likely to be distinctive, the former dominated by immigration, the latter by the supposed effects of social atomism, the 'lonely crowd'.

Yet once the analysis is pressed beyond the enumeration of such basic, and far from inevitable, features, it is hard to avoid the conclusion that the urban variable has still not been defined with any rigour. Grant that the town's properties include concentration and intensification (cf. H. Lefebvre 1991, 101). If the question be raised of *what* is concentrated, and by *whom*, then the town immediately becomes too large a unit of analysis: the discussion must turn to particular social groups (burghers, entrepreneurs, aristocratic financiers, artisans, unskilled labourers, visiting smallholders, and so forth) and to particular forms of action (bureaucracy, conspicuous consumption, investment, manufacture, migration . . .). The supposed generic social entity disappears and something much more particular and various takes its place.

In another sense, however, the town is too *small* a category. Description of the forms of interaction observable within it must inevitably draw on the terminology and conclusions of a wider social history: it will not be claimed by even the most radical urbanist that towns provide the setting for unique, uncontaminated, forms of life. No longer seen by medievalists as 'islands in a feudal sea', towns should perhaps not be conceived in insular terms at all (any more, we argue, than real islands should: V.2, VI.11, IX.2–3). Artisan manufacture, for instance, has hardly been a purely urban activity. It certainly was not so in Antiquity (V.4); nor, it seems, for much of the Middle Ages. In any case, in order to characterize its urban peculiarities, if it has any, extra-urban comparisons would have to be drawn; there could be no other way to bring the peculiarities into focus. And to establish its sources of material and manpower and the extent of its markets, the historian would have to range well beyond the urban scene. In short, nothing is achieved by considering urban-based activity in isolation from the wider economic world. If the town is too big a unit of analysis it is also, for different reasons, not nearly large enough.

Empirical support for that paradoxical contention can be found in the direction taken by the historiography of the origins of capitalism, industrialization or modernity (all variously defined) in late medieval to early modern Europe. This historiography reflects a debate that is tangential to the study of the ancient or medieval Mediterranean, but that has, none the less, gained considerable influence over the way in which the region's towns have been conceived. Three traditions of research can be loosely discriminated – and, in Hegelian spirit, we can identify them as thesis, antithesis, and synthesis. Each of the three can conveniently be associated with a different 'star' name. Adherents of the *thesis*, who may count Pirenne among their number, take as starting point the apparently close correlation in Europe between levels of urbanization and economic precocity (*vide* northern Italy and the Low Countries). They emphasize the 'heterogeneity' of urban social and economic life, its detachment from that of the surrounding countryside (supposedly the crucial division of labour), and its consequent potential for self-transformation. According to this tradition the rural economy has nothing progressive to contribute. It can only respond passively to the electric shocks aimed at it by nascent capitalists in the towns.

> The modern capitalist economy, with its motivation of investment, bourgeois and proletarian classes, the penetration of production by machines and of exchange by

price-fixing markets, developed from and in the autonomous economic systems of
the towns. The rebirth and extension of Classical property rights and money, and
the exchange relationships which they encouraged . . . could only develop in urban
enclaves where the needs and will of merchants prevailed. This renaissance was,
therefore, necessarily an urban phenomenon: the capitalist economy of the modern
world could only be born, expand and ramify in the towns of western Europe.
(Langton and Hoppe 1983, 13)

What is significant about those ideas, there presented in the inevitably bare
summary of a survey article (and by no means representative of its authors' own
opinions), is how few of them can still be accepted. There is no need here to
rehearse the terms and vicissitudes of what has come to be called 'the Brenner
debate' about the agrarian origins of capitalism (Aston and Philpin 1985; cf.
VII.4). The mere mention of its subject matter is sufficient to indicate a radical
alteration of emphasis in the search for the beginnings of modernity – from the
towns to the countryside.

That is the *antithesis* in the Hegelian triad. Although its representatives have
gained the advantage only comparatively recently, in this second tradition Marx
(that is, the Marx of *Kapital*, vol. 1) might replace Pirenne as symbolic lumin-
ary because so much of the discussion concerns the consequences of the end
of feudalism (Holton 1986, 41–8). Yet it is of no particular significance in the
present context whether the terms of any agreed conclusions bear interpretation
in Marxist terms; whether the genesis of rural capitalism be ascribed to certain
English landlords or, in an alternative proposal mainly associated with the term
'proto-industrialization', to small farmers in pastoral areas: for us, the salient
feature of this line of enquiry is that it effectively dispels the notion of towns as
the only begetters of the modern European economy. Their creative heterogeneity can no longer be upheld.

Even so, neither Brenner nor his critics have really arrived at a durable solution
to the problem of origins. The third of the three traditions referred to therefore
offers something like a *synthesis* of the opposing schools of Pirenne and Marx
(cf. Holton 1986). The presiding deity is now, perhaps unexpectedly, Weber. In
his long, posthumously published, essay on the city (1958) he was not, in the
end, seduced by the idea of the town as a distinct empirical entity or analytical
construct. Instead, he offered a comparative account of the social structures to
be found *within* cities, locating these where necessary in the far more ample
historical setting of the development of capitalism. In Weber's own projected
outline for Part 2 of *Economy and Society*, the substance of the essay was to bear
the significantly longer title 'Non-legitimate domination. (The typology of cities)',
and it was to be only one section of a much larger portion of the text devoted
to 'domination' (1968, 1.lx). Weber's interest lay in the particular form of
power, not in the city as a *Ding an sich* (cf. Finley 1981, 16).

Towns, as we have said, taking our cue from Weber and applying this lesson
of historiography to the matter of urbanism as a whole, are arenas, addresses.
And addresses, in themselves, make nothing happen. Rather than stress either
urban or rural dynamism, therefore, locating the first stirrings of transformation
in one or other sector, the adherents of the synthesis tend to dispense with the
urban–rural dichotomy altogether. What matter are social institutions or processes (or, we add, ecologies) – on which town walls do not necessarily impinge.

Concerning a conference on 'towns and economic growth' held in the mid-

1970s, the implications of which have still to be fully assimilated, it was concluded, optimistically, that the papers revealed 'a new sense of how urban history might proceed'.

> And it was one which involved a quite radical redefinition of the town as an object
> of study; a redefinition which sought to undo the conceptual separation of town
> and country and re-unite the town with its larger social environment . . . The
> debates of the previous decade . . . and the accompanying concern to tease out an
> 'urban factor' in economic and social history seemed to have lost their momentum
> – at least in their familiar terms. The tendency, rather, was to move away from any
> attempt to treat towns as variables in themselves – whether dependent, independ-
> ent or merely intervening – and also from the attempt to regard the town as a
> generic social reality, and to see cities and towns instead as fields of action integral
> to some larger world and within which the interactions and contradictions of that
> larger world are displayed with special clarity . . . The town, then, is an *explanandum*,
> not an *explanans*. Within the analysis of a chosen social system the relationships
> concentrated spatially within towns present themselves for explanation. But . . . they
> should present themselves specifically in relation to our understanding of the sys-
> tem in which they occur and not as exemplars of an autonomous urban reality.
> (Abrams 1978, 2–3, 30)

Fields of action integral to a larger world: it is instructive to note the extent
to which that way of conceiving towns has come to be applied even to the most
dominant or dynamic of great cities. A London or a Madrid must be viewed in
the same systemic terms as should the average 'small town'. 'London, a mighty
beating heart, causing everything to move at its own rhythm, capable of creating chaos or calm by turns' (Braudel 1981–4, 1.528). And yet, as it turns out,
the stimulus given to the demography and economy of seventeenth- to early
eighteenth-century England by the most rapidly growing major city in Europe
cannot be analysed in terms of any discrete metropolitan variable. Its only convincing interpretation derives, on one hand, from the general context of state
and society in England under the Tudors and Stuarts and, on the other, from an
awareness of particular changes within the city, for instance among its merchant
classes (Campbell et al. 1993; Wrigley 1978a; 1987, 190; Morley 1996, 28). As
for the succeeding period: Daniel Defoe's observation in his *Tour through England and Wales* (1724–6) that all the gentlemen of the Vale of Aylesbury were
graziers, but not all the graziers were gentlemen, shows something of the economic changes wrought by Georgian Londoners' demand for boots and shoes
(Reed 1996, 66). Their manufacture would have been carried out on a small
domestic scale, 'as likely to be found in the country as in the town', and their
marketing, before being transported to the capital, would have occurred in a
shifting variety of settings, from markets in the small 'feeder cities' of London's
immediate hinterland to inns and private shops (1996, 68–9).

A comparable degree of influence, but of a less beneficial kind, has been
ascribed to a leading city of the Mediterranean world during a slightly earlier
period:

> In the sixteenth century Madrid undermined the economic position and central-
> place functions of the manufacturing towns of the Spanish interior. In the seven-
> teenth, Madrid encouraged the development of a rural society based on local
> power, low-order central places, and markets and land usage that left few incent-
> ives for the peasant to increase productivity . . . The capital city extracted resources

from all over the interior, both by subsidizing its own urban market and by administratively redirecting regional commodity flows . . . In brief, the rise of Madrid between 1560 and 1630 contributed to the decline of the Castilian economy. (Ringrose 1983, 14–15)

That seems overwhelmingly to make the 'urbanist's' case. Madrid's impact must, however, also be estimated with reference to a considerable number of other factors contributing to the area's stagnation: imperial policy, weight of taxation, the virtual disappearance of the Castilian textile industry, and suchlike. And to embark on such a catalogue is, once again, to broaden the analysis well beyond Madrid towards an investigation of the entire regional economy, and to conceive the city as the point at which the frictions and failures of the whole system are best revealed (contrast Morley 1996, 30). Moreover, the appropriate complement to this approach must surely be an examination, perhaps through Weberian lenses, of particular intra-urban 'modes of domination' – the complex of political, administrative and social institutions for which the name 'Madrid' is such inadequate shorthand.

We cannot generalize in *economic* terms from Madrid to other Mediterranean capitals: by the later eighteenth century, for instance, the hinterland of Naples presents a far less dispiriting picture (Marin 1996, 160–1). But, at the *conceptual* level, Madrid is exemplary. For it can be said that, if a damagingly dominant early modern city such as Madrid has to be treated in the way just outlined – at once set in the widest possible context and conceptually dismantled into its socio-economic components – then it is unlikely that *any* preindustrial Mediterranean town is rightly understood as an independent variable. To take two obvious examples from earlier periods, the cities of Rome and Constantinople undoubtedly constituted extremely important elements in the economies of their respective empires: their populations' food requirements necessitated far-reaching governmental schemes for extraction and transport which have seemed to some to form the armature of the Mediterranean economy (BE V.4). And these will have been an important stimulus to production and settlement in particular areas such as Italy or North Africa or north-western Anatolia. But it cannot be said that either of the two great cities, or indeed the ensemble of towns in their successive empires, was responsible for empire-wide economic development (Hopkins 1978a). Like Madrid or London, they can be analysed only as parts of a system – a system in which, it increasingly seems, the distinction between town and countryside is not an important one to make:

> The phenomenon of urbanism cannot be separted from its historical context; it is not an independent cross-cultural variable . . . The growth of the city of Rome and the changes which it brought about in the economy of the peninsula must be seen in the context of changing structures of power in Italian society . . . (Morley 1996, 185)

Our microecological model answers, then, to the direction that some urban economic historiography has hesitantly taken. It encourages us to conceive towns less as separate and clearly definable entities and more as loci of contact or overlap between different ecologies. Towns are settings in which ecological processes may be intense, and in which the anthropogene effect is at its most pronounced. But they are not – or not simply by definition – more than that. And they should not be presented as conceptually detachable from the remainder of the spectrum of settlement types. Towns, it would not be entirely fanciful to suggest, are rather like mountains (III.6). The distinction between mountains and hills and downs must be essentially arbitrary, and the range of ecologies to be associated with them is very much less narrow and predictable than might have been expected.

Agreement on that cannot, of course, resolve all the conceptual difficulties attendant upon the project to 'ecologize' towns. The larger framework within which they should be set needs more exact delineation. There are, moreover, other bodies of urban theory that must briefly be confronted and, so far as this project is concerned, either modified or explicitly rejected.

4. TYPES AND THEORIES

Since this chapter is 'against *villes*', the gist of our argument at this point might described as 'against typologies'. The most enticing typology would be that which differentiated Mediterranean towns from those in northern Europe or the non-Mediterranean Middle East. But if we are not here concerned with towns as such, we shall not *a fortiori* hope to be able to identify the essence of Mediterranean urbanism. We plan, rather, to indicate some characteristic features of Mediterranean *settlement*. It is worth remarking that not even Braudel ventured to pronounce on '*the* Mediterranean town'. He reasonably contented himself with sketching the common demographic and political fortunes of Mediterranean towns in the age of Philip II (1972a, 326). Even at the most element-ary topographical or architectonic level, there are no specifically Mediterranean urban forms. Only under the Romans, after all, did larger settlements around the sea even begin to approximate to uniformity of architecture and status, let alone to socio-economic function. And they shared that uniformity with provinces remote from the Mediterranean, such as Britain. Moreover, the classical pattern of regular street plans and open spaces surrounded by public buildings was not extraordinarily durable: in some places, it may, on one influential appraisal, already have begun to be eroded in the later Roman period before the Arab conquests (Kennedy 1985a, 12; though cf. B. Ward-Perkins 1996, 150–1). Thereafter, for the historian of urban form, all is divergence. Even where medieval European towns lay on classical sites, they departed from the ancient norm in an immense variety of ways, none of them peculiar to the Mediterranean or indeed especially noticeable in the region. Few would want to draw close parallels between pre-historic Boğazköy, one of the first 'cities' of the region, where public access to premises took place over the roofs of the neighbouring buildings, and classical Athens. But the topographical and functional differences between major settle-ments in *post-classical* times are scarcely less far-reaching.

It is therefore no surprise that the often-vaunted 'Islamic city' – supposedly common in, but of course not peculiar to, southern Mediterranean lands – seems to have proved a chimaera (Eickelman 1998, 96–110). The debate on it is in any case repetitive, ambiguous in its terms, and limited in scope to architec-ture and forms of association – bazaars, street plans, artisan quarters, guilds, and so forth. The first Islamic cities retained, as neighbourhoods, the identities of the villages from which their inhabitants came; what first united them was little more than their address. Even in a developed form, the Islamic city as a type has little to contribute to an ecological approach. A study entitled *Muslim Cities in the Later Middle Ages* is to be read, its author tells us 'less in terms of "urban" history, a case examination of the functioning of cities, and more as a partial contribution to the study of a wider history of Islamic societies . . .' (Lapidus 1984, xvi). The same should be said of works invoking typologies of European cities. Weber's patrician and plebeian cities (1958); Braudel's bureaucratic, clerical, commercial, and industrial towns (1972a, 323) or his later, still essentially Weberian, political distinction between open (ancient), closed (medieval), and subject (early modern) towns (1981–4, 1.507–20) – these and equivalent taxonomies have the merit of directing attention away from the idea of the town as a unitary thing in itself (an idea to which Braudel none the less committed himself when he wrote that 'a town is a town'); they nudge our attention towards the processes at work within specific social settings. They help to bring out something of the distinctive sociological features of different periods in the history of settlement: for instance, the absence of clear *political* and *cultural* separation between city and countryside during much of Antiquity (Wallace-Hadrill 1991; Purcell 1995c). But their ecological correlates remain to be demonstrated. Deployment of their component terms achieves very little on its own.

A similar criticism might be levelled at two other theoretical approaches to urbanization that ought to be considered here. Both are of increasing interest to historians as well as to geographers and economists. Both have implications for the future study of settlement distribution. And yet neither can be pressed into service on this occasion. We do not presume to contribute to the general debate about their progress and prospects; we simply need to indicate why their usefulness is, for present purposes, limited. They do not meet the criteria of applicability to the microecological model already set out: they are not fluid enough; they yield notions of the historical landscape that are too easy to represent graphically.

The first of these bodies of thought is *central place theory*. This has the distinct merit in the present context of relating smaller 'places' to their hinterlands and larger ones to subordinate (or 'tributary') settlements. That is, it sees each settlement as part of a system. The system is interpreted as hierarchical, and the degree of centrality achieved by a place is defined in terms of the goods and services that it offers and its role as a mediator between tributaries and larger system. Thus any given place (or node) will be included in a number of overlaid – nested – larger regions. The model is indeed theoretically susceptible of global extension.

Now there are clear reasons why settlements might become loosely arranged in such a hierarchy. Larger settlements will meet a wider range of needs than smaller ones and therefore be more widely spaced: their services will be required both by the local population and by those who have travelled from parts of the surrounding region. Most villages need a baker but only more substantial places can support a tailor (Wrigley 1991, 10). Yet, if the model be considered at a less abstract level, then its usefulness to the historian of the preindustrial past is not immediately striking.

There obtrudes, first of all, the basic difficulty of finding sufficient evidence about the functions of particular settlements to specify their position in the presumed hierarchy. We have already seen how plastic any functional definition of a Mediterranean site must be. Secondly, consequent upon that, there is the difficulty of defining the regions within which centrality is to be measured. Such definition should be the goal of enquiry, not its starting point. Thirdly, even were the right evidence about functions and regions apparently available it would, we contend, be the wrong way to envisage the Mediterranean landscape. Our arguments to be presented in following chapters (especially V and IX) about the wide horizons and mobility of Mediterranean 'settlers', together with our earlier adumbration of the essential mutability and rapidly shifting contours of microregions and the links between them (Chapter III and Section 2 above), imply that central place theory offers an image of settlement patterns that is too narrowly, and too statically, conceived. Despite attempts to embody it in arithmetic rather than geometry, the theory usually resolves itself into a diagram of nodes surrounded by polygons (representing hinterlands) and connected by simple lines (representing communications). Space is assumed to be uniform and simply divisible. This is 'Routes et Villes' by other means: quite different from the image of the Mediterranean that we wish to convey.

A fourth source of concern is the origins of the model in the study of modern, integrated, industrial economies. This is the domain to which it seems most suited, either as analytical tool or as means of predicting where new services should be located. Yet even here its proponents are often hard-pressed to account for empirical departures from the 'norms' that the model specifies. And historians of the comparatively recent past and of industrialized areas have also found it at best incomplete, and at worst wrong, as an explanation for the geography of habitation and function.

Finally, the model in any event ought to be evaluated in the light of the second, associated, body of ideas which students of urbanism have found attractive yet which we must also sidestep. This again deals with the spatial distribution and systemic interrelation of settlements, but (usually) in terms of population rather than goods and services (or at least with crude aggregates, the number rather than the variety of services offered). An obvious feature of settlements in a particular territory is that those of largest population size are fewest in number and that, conversely, for any given population size the smaller it is the more numerous are the settlements that correspond to it. The simplest form of the relationship that can thus be detected between towns and cities when ranked in order of size is that the second largest city will be half as big as the largest, the tenth largest one tenth as big, and so forth. More generally, if the sizes of settlements in a modern urban system are plotted logarithmically against their rank they are often found to adhere more or less closely to a straight line. They are then said to obey the *rank-size rule*, evincing 'lognormal distribution'.

Like central place theory, this analytical technique has the merit of treating individual settlements as part of a larger whole, and of emphasizing the continuum of settlement types. Applied to urban systems of the last few centuries it has yielded some highly significant results. These systems are shown to have been surprisingly regular. Beneath the apex formed by the great cities there lay 'a pyramid, rather than a mound of variable and indeterminate shape' (Wrigley 1991, 110). Regional differences in the shape and slope of the logarithmic graph have also been demonstrated – differences between, for example, North and South in western Europe during the early modern period (de Vries 1984, ch. 6).

Grave difficulties none the less attend the analysis of rank-size distribution in earlier centuries. Quite apart from problems of counting posed by mobility (IX.5), the population of ancient and medieval settlements is impossible to estimate with enough exactitude. Equally damaging, the boundaries of the regions in question are once again impossible to specify. Modern national ones are unlikely to be appropriate (though historians have often failed to acknowledge the fact); geographical ones will not necessarily be any better; and if the specification be left to intuitive judgement as to what is to count as a single system, then the results will have no independent force because the curve of the graph is bound to reflect the size and shape of region that the analyst has chosen. The model becomes feebly self-validating.

It might further be questioned whether size of population is the best indicator of a city's importance within its system. Populations may concentrate in particular settings for any combination of a variety of reasons – and, around the Mediterranean at least, sometimes very ephemerally. The selection of a different criterion of rank, such as the scale on which some economic or cultural function is fulfilled, can produce a graph of far different curve or gradient from that obtained by the usual demographic measure. Worse, the whole theory is coloured by a teleology which sets up as the goal of all economic development a lognormal distribution with a particular slope (in demographic terms, when the tenth largest city is one tenth the size of the very largest: a slope of −1). All other curves are implicitly held to be departures from, or anticipations of, this norm – which is, significantly, that of modern, integrated, industrial society. Thus a premodern slope may be adjudged 'immature' if its slope is less than −1. Cities represented on it are 'too small' or 'too large'. And yet, although the goal has been stipulated, the variety of paths towards it remain to be disentangled. And the reasons for recurrent forms of 'deviation' – such as that of *primacy*, where the metropolis is larger than the rank-size rule predicts – remain to be clearly established.

Given these problems of evidence, definition and explanation, our particular reservations about the heuristic usefulness of invoking the rule in the study of Mediterranean settlement may seem relatively trivial. From our point of view, an initial problem is that too much attention is in practice given to the upper reaches of the settlement hierarchy, and that an arbitrary demographic threshold is usually required to make the calculations manageable. The pronounced downward turn occasionally taken by an otherwise lognormal graph when it reaches a certain low rank has been held by some analysts to be an indication of the transition from urban to rural settlement. But it is salutary (and, for us, comforting) to find that no full and acceptable explanation of the phenomenon seems to have been provided. The relatively smooth continuum that we should prefer to envisage between megalopolis and hamlet remains, from this point of view, theoretically intact.

The image of a settlement system associated with that continuum is, nevertheless, for us an inappropriate one. It is again static, incapable of responding to a Mantinea as in a very short time it jumps from the top of the rank order to the bottom. It brings us back – disadvantageously – to nodes and their linear connections: drawing pins of different sizes, as it were, stretching ribbons between them. That is not ecology as we have defined it. Towns are not singularities, routes are not ribbons; a proper conception of both will resist the kind of systemic and mathematical approach that is as fundamental to rank-size analysis as it is to central place theory.

Rank-size theory does have one advantage for us. The analyses that have been produced of modern settlement systems strengthen our suspicions about the usefulness of *cultural* and *political* typologies as indicators of ecological difference:

> Since the existence of an urban hierarchy obeying the rank-size rule appears to be so widespread, it follows that it is compatible with a wide range of different political, social, economic and other characteristics, and this has important implications for some long-running debates about the city and its functions . . . (Wrigley 1991, 111)

A certain form of *economic* typology must now also be placed under suspicion. One of the long-running debates to which Wrigley refers has focused on a simple and apparently clear-cut distinction between cities that promote economic development and those that do not.

In one influential formulation this is a distinction between 'generative' and 'parasitic' cities (Hoselitz 1954–5). But the dichotomy takes several forms. It underpins Sjoberg's (1960) characterization of the preindustrial city (generally parasitic) and thereby gains a chronological dimension. More specifically, and of greater significance for our project, it resolves into an implied contrast within an earlier age: between the 'consumption city' of Antiquity and its more productive medieval successors.

5. CONSUMPTION

'By a consumption city', Werner Sombart famously wrote in *Der moderne Kapitalismus* (1916–27, 1.142–3), 'I mean one which pays for its maintenance . . . not with its own products, because it does not need to. It derives its maintenance rather on the basis of a legal claim, such as taxes or rents, without having to deliver return values' (trans. Finley 1981, 13).

In an obvious sense all cities are centres of consumption: civilization (in the strict sense) is possible only where the urban few can live on the surplus produced by the rural many. But Sombart was making a stronger point. On his definition the consumption city is a centre of consumption above all else. It does not reciprocate its economic 'debt' to the countryside in production or services. Naturally, these are available within it; but they are brought into being and principally maintained by the spending power of those in receipt of taxes and rents. Great city-based consumers dominate economically as well as politically. The countryman can buy produce and services from the city with the profits of selling his surplus grain in its market. But the effect of such transactions will still, at best, be no more than to return to him some of the wealth that he has already given up in rent or tax: a rebate, not a reciprocation. This model of urban society, refined and given prominence by Weber as an 'ideal type' most applicable to Antiquity, was revived by Finley and has often seemed so persuasive that 'consumption city' and 'ancient city' have been treated as virtually synonymous.

It is, of course, widely acknowledged that there have also been medieval or early modern cities that could be taken as satisfying Sombart's definition; Madrid provides a good example. The implied distinction between the ancient world and subsequent periods is therefore not a hard and fast one. It is also – less often – acknowledged that neither Sombart's nor Weber's writings about cities merit the selective and simplifying accounts of them that have formed the basis of much subsequent discussion. For example, both men rested as much analytical weight on the *origins* of urban societies as on their mature configurations, which could be very different. Weber's ideal types, more particularly, were attempts to isolate, in pure form, select features of a complex social reality. They are heuristic devices: we should not expect them to have been empirically exemplified in full. In that sense, Weber did not intend us to think that consumption cities actually existed. (It has none the less been held (cf. Finley 1981, 20–1) that Mantinea in the Peloponnese was, unusually, a genuine instance because of the ease with which its inhabitants could be dispersed into villages. By contrast, we take Mantinea to instantiate a more widespread phenomenon: the blurring of categories through the mutability of settlement.) Nor did Weber neglect the similarities between ancient and medieval cities in his attempt to isolate their differences (Capogrossi Colognesi 1995, 36).

Yet, if any generalization can be hazarded about the city in Antiquity as a juridical, architectural and sociological category, it is after all that it was primarily the home of a governing class living off rents, taxes and agricultural yields. Manufacturing and commercial sectors were subsidiary, and relatively small. Sombart's model seemingly conforms to the contours of ancient cities so nicely. We are urged to contrast the medieval city in its most memorable form: 'the excavators of Tarsus have found no Cloth Hall . . . ancient cities lacked the Guildhalls and Bourses which, next to the cathedrals, are to this day the architectural glories of the great medieval cities . . .' (Finley 1985a, 137, pardonably overlooking the fact that Tarsus has not been excavated). The medieval city, it is there implied, was a 'production city'. For Finley, as for Weber and others before him, the immediate value of the consumption city was that it contrasted so well with medieval urban dynamism.

The major part of our response to the model, as to the distinction between ancient and medieval that it entails, will be set out in V.4. There, we consider the 'primitivist' or 'minimalist' conception of the ancient economy as a whole (a conception of which the consumption model has been a close ally) and we attempt to show why ancient and medieval economies can more profitably be compared rather than compartmentalized. The argument of Chapter V, however, makes no great distinction between urban and non-urban forms of economic production, organization or exchange, and presupposes the relinquishing of towns as a separate category. Here, then, we have to confront the model more explicitly.

It is worth observing, first, that this characterization of the ancient city is quite ancient itself. Indeed, with age, it has become a rather blunt instrument. It was first elaborated, with slightly differing emphases, during the decades round 1900, not only by Weber and Sombart but also by Karl Bücher (Morley 1996, 14–21). Its scope has varied. Sombart, reacting to Pirenne's optimistic assessment of the trading capacities of earlier medieval cities, invoked it to contrast the Dark and the later Middle Ages. Bücher used it for a broader distinction between ancient and medieval. In this he was followed by Weber, and much later (in the 1970s) by Finley, who was himself partly reacting to a *bourgeois* vision of cities, this time Rostovtzeff's, when he gave the model new life, with reference especially to the Greek *polis* (Lomas 1995, 1).

Such divergences notwithstanding, what these scholars all had in common, and what now above all 'dates' the model, is the explanatory task that they set it. The point of their respective typologies of cities was to account for capitalism. The underlying argument seems to have been of this order: capitalism originated in the (later) Middle Ages, not in Antiquity (or the early Middle Ages). Its cradle was the producer city. Capitalism is economic growth, and the opposite of growth is stagnation. The ancient economy was non-capitalist; therefore it must have been stagnant. The source of this inertia was the cities. Ancient cities must have been the opposite of producers, i.e. consumers. So we arrive at a pleasing symmetry: consumption cities were the cause of economic failure in Antiquity, just as medieval producer cities were later the cause of capitalism.

The primary objection is an obvious one. As we have seen above, when medieval historians now try to explain the genesis of capitalism – which is not that often – they no longer do so by exclusive reference to cities. Nor (as we shall see in the next chapter) is it any longer thought profitable to evaluate the ancient economy in terms of its presumed failure to be exactly like the later Middle Ages – that is, according to what it was *not*. Between capitalism and stagnation, there are other possible kinds of productive development, and at least some of these can be discerned in Antiquity. The example of that arch-consumer, imperial Rome, shows that a city of this kind can interact with regional economies in ways that are far more thoroughgoing than Sombart, Weber or Finley would have allowed. 'Its [Rome's] effects on the economy of its hinterland were far-reaching, and can indeed be described as progressive . . . The city of Rome . . . became a driving force in the development of the Italian economy' (Morley 1996, 185). No stagnation there; and even if the conclusion needs qualifying (Section 3), it is hard to imagine that the older Finleyan view could ever be reinstated.

Cities will be 'brakes' or 'accelerators' of the economy (Wrigley 1990) according to individual circumstances, not simply according to the historical period in which they belong – this is what accounts for the contrast between London and Madrid. But one general way to assess whether the consumption could ever have had the deleterious effects ascribed to it is to ask what difference its sudden disappearance would have made. Put another way: if nothing like a consumption city had ever existed in Antiquity, would it have been useful to invent it? Without the city nearby, the taxpayers would still have had to pay in cash or kind for the single greatest charge on the state, its army. They would also still have had to support the aristocracy in its rural residences: ancient *rentiers* 'consumed' everywhere, not just in cities. On the other hand those same taxpayers would probably have lacked the convenience of a large and regular market and a point of contact with long-distance trade. Their roads would have been neither so numerous nor so well maintained. And they would have had to cope with the presence among them of those who might have otherwise migrated to the city, thus potentially depressing *per capita* income. Even the pure consumption city would have had some advantages for those compelled to feed it.

If the consumer city model is robbed of its explanatory force, however, there is not much else that can be said in favour of its retention. For our purposes, it rests too heavily, and by no means appositely, on a few major examples – for instance ancient Rome as against medieval Genoa – to make its point (Finley 1985a, 125). It fails, that is, to evoke the full range of settlement types. And although Sombart predicated his original analysis on the activities of a specific class of people, his model encourages reification of what should have remained abstract. It turns 'the consumption city' into an entity seemingly capable of independent action. It tries to reduce what in the ancient world, let alone the medieval one, were multifarious civic *economies* to a single balance sheet (cf. Osborne 1991a, 119).

The model is also usually taken to exclude non-economic benefits from its calculus. Yet if we must think of relations between city and countryside in terms of debt or reciprocation, then the religious, legal, military, administrative, sexual and medical services to be found within the city ought to be included in the reckoning. The emphasis would thereby be shifted away from what cities supposedly failed to do, and on to what their inhabitants actually did.

We prefer to conceive of settlements (rather than cities) as the sites of shifting, overlapping ecologies. So we question whether it is possible, or indeed desirable, to calculate and compare the net productivity of particular sites or categories of site. The rank-size regularity displayed by supposed consumption cities in modern times has already suggested that Sombart's model may embody a distinction without a significant difference. Further, the economic functions that inhabitants of ancient cities did in fact provide for their surrounding countryside may be found less wanting when weighed in a balance not prejudicially tipped by Bourses and Cloth Halls, a very culturally specific expression of economic dominance (V.4). Processing of raw materials, artisan manufacture, regular markets in which money could be earned to pay taxes as well as goods purchased, casual employment in building or carrying, servicing the survival strategies of storage and redistribution which we explore further in Chapter VI – these sectors of ancient civic economies were not as meagre as devotees of the consumption city have liked to suppose. Nor, as archaeology increasingly shows, did they minister so overwhelmingly to the demands of a civic aristocracy and its rural tenantry. Goods from some cities and from 'small towns' or *vici* are being found quite literally far afield, too much so to have been the effects of a 'rebate' (cf. Whittaker 1990; Barker and Lloyd 1991).

For all its faults, the consumer city as a type may well capture more of how flows of goods within cities were engendered and directed than do any of its more recent rivals, such as the 'processor city' or the 'service city'. Whether it any longer prompts scholars to ask important questions is another matter. We may remark in concluding this section that even the consumer city's most subtle and astute defender since Finley ends his defence on a truly Weberian note, with an admission that the framework that the model provides is not quite the right one: 'the study of cities is only an imperfect way of studying the operations of power in society' (Whittaker 1995, 22).

6. Settlement Ecology

To venture such criticism of the consumption city as a model is not to assert that ancient and medieval towns were in all crucial respects similar. It is rather to suggest that differences between settlements cannot helpfully be conceptualized in this grand manner and that close comparisons across the supposed ancient/ medieval divide really are possible. The essence of urbanism in any particular period – let alone in those larger historiographical constructs, 'Antiquity' and 'the Middle Ages' – is not indeed something that we shall be concerned to discover. We want instead to see what results may be obtained when the town is dissolved as a category and the full range of Mediterranean settlement is approached from an ecological standpoint and viewed in its entirety. So far the present chapter has of necessity been mainly devoted to 'clearing the ground' for that project. It has therefore had less to do with specific examples than with general theories, and it has rejected many more of these than it has endorsed. That emphasis seems appropriate. If we are intent on abandoning 'the town' as a distinct settlement type, we should not reasonably be expected to produce an urban theory of our own. Some more positive indication of the direction in which we shall later proceed should, however, now be added – in a way which may for convenience refer to cities as legal entities, or to towns as useful short-hand for architectonic agglomerations, but otherwise avoids discriminating too sharply among concentrations of people.

To proceed outwards from the centre of what has been at issue, it would be helpful first of all if the processes of microecological interaction and overlap *within* major settlements could be displayed. These processes are hard to bring into focus, partly because of lack of specific evidence. Something of them can perhaps be seized, if only in passing, in examples of the phenomenon of *dioicism* referred to earlier, when a 'town' such as Mantinea begins to reveal the component 'villages' into which it is to be split; but even records like those from Oenoanda (Section 2 above) give no more than an inkling of the complexity of the process of dispersal. To refer to the geography of markets and occupations or the delineation of residential quarters, of networks of reciprocity among kin and neighbours is to point towards the sort of information required but does not really tell us enough about the communities (defined in ecological terms) that made up the larger conglomeration.

Archaeology can sometimes be suggestive. The internal connectivity (on which see Chapter V) of Pompeii, as well as its permeability to 'outsiders', has for example been given imaginative archaeological definition by Laurence (1995). The 'syntax' of the city is defined in terms of its doorways and its graffiti:

> The highest occurrence of doorways and street messages [graffiti and dipinti] were to be found along the through routes from the city gates into the centre of the city. This implies that the social relationship between the inhabitant and the visitor was strong in Pompeii. In other words interaction with the city's hinterland or even other cities is stressed in the spatial structure of Pompeii. (1995, 72)

Much of what is lacking even from such ingenious archaeology can be made good only in imagination. Consider a deed of sale of a share in a house, drawn up in 1009/10, that survives among the earliest deposits in the Cairo Geniza (cf. Chapter II). The house lay in a neighbourhood known as the Wool Hall (which would have pleased Finley), and it was flanked by properties named after a wax maker, a raisin seller, a belt maker and a glass manufacturer. It had three small inner courts which are likely to have been used for further commercial or artisan undertakings. The man who bought the shares was a money changer (Goitein 1967–88, 4.16). Could it ever be reconstructed, the scale and complexity of the ecological history of that cluster of dwellings – the local contacts and wider sources of supply and demand of its changing population – would surely be daunting. And yet that is one of the kinds of history to which we should, however unsuccessfully, aspire.

Another kind would give proper emphasis to the 'agricultural' sector within Mediterranean settlements of every type and size, not just those that have been classified as villages or agro-towns. *Rus in urbe* – the countryside within the city – was, possibly to a greater degree than in adjacent regions, prominent within major settlements right across the ancient and medieval Mediterranean, even during times of relatively high population density. *Rus* in two senses: first, open land devoted to primary production; and second, the living space of those who worked in the countryside. There were large open spaces – uncultivated, agricultural land, or orchards – in even the largest and apparently most crowded of Mediterranean cities: Pompeii, Rome, Barcelona, Milan, Cairo, to name only some.

> The land which lies about the Church is not only fitted for the growing of plants, and for the sowing of seed, but you may see in it trees growing to a great height and laden with fruit and with the vines which climb up in them, and crops growing under the trees; for all the land around this Church is full of strength and rich in wheat.

No minor church or settlement described there but the sanctuary of the Holy Apostles in the heart of Constantinople; and not Constantinople ravaged by the Black Death but the City of the early 1200s, at hardly less than the height of its medieval prosperity (Downey 1957, 863, 897–8).

Rus in urbe implied the presence of cultivators as well as the availability of space. Yet the number of agriculturalists was often larger than the intra-mural space would support and their land, to which they commuted, often lay at some distance from the city. In such cases, a city address became the equivalent of a farmstead at the focus of a collection of scattered holdings. According to the Tuscan census of 1427 for instance (Herlihy and Klapisch-Zuber 1985, 128), among those who declared an occupation, small-scale agricultural proprietors were the third most common in Pisa (6 per 1,000 households), the second most common in Pistoia (10.9 per 1,000), and the commonest of all in Prato, Volterra and Cortona (12.2, 34.7 and 13.8 per 1,000 respectively). The distribution of their holdings is not recorded. But it is reasonable to presume that a substantial portion of them were extra-mural. And this has been a feature of Mediterranean settlements into comparatively recent times – from which, inevitably, the only relatively precise statistics derive. In the Cairo of 1877, for example, 57 per cent of the economically active resident citizens reportedly cultivated fields outside the city (Abu-Lughod 1969, 164).

Insecurity naturally played some part in concentrating sizeable proportions of the agricultural population within the defensive networks of cities; but in the Mediterranean world as elsewhere, it was also common for cities to be flanked by extensive suburbs, often stretching so far as to provide a very gradual topographical transition from city centre to more open countryside. And attention to this kind of settlement should form yet another strand in the ecological history that might, we suggest, replace that of too great a concentration on towns.

In Athens of the fifth and fourth centuries B.C. for instance, as one moved outwards from the political centre of the *agora* into the fertile surrounding plain, the density of settlement declined relatively evenly. The coastal strip that ran in both directions away from Hellenistic and Roman Alexandria was comparably inhabited. In the case of Rome itself this 'suburban' belt extended over a very wide area indeed, and joined Rome to its satellite settlements ten and fifteen miles away. Here is how it seemed to Dionysius of Halicarnassus, a learned Greek antiquarian of the age of Augustus:

> the districts around the city, numerous and extensive as they are, are all built up, despite the fact that an enemy could easily occupy them because they are exposed and unwalled. Suppose that you want a general notion of the size of Rome. Confusion is unavoidable – you will not even have any idea of how far the city extends or when it leaves off being a city. It is the fact that town is so interwoven with country which gives the observer some idea of the endless urban sprawl. (*Roman Antiquities*, 4.13)

It would, moreover, be a mistake to assume that a sprawl of this kind constituted a simple ecology focused within the enceinte. Antioch of the fourth century A.D., with a population estimated at as many as 300,000 people, had spread across an area some 300 times greater than that enclosed by its circuit of walls. The resulting settlements were more like large independent villages than suburbs; and, as the contemporary orator Libanius explained, if perhaps with some exaggeration, their inhabitants had little need for the city, thanks to exchange among themselves (*Oration* 11.230; cf. Kaplan 1992, 94–5). In other words, although the city could hardly be said to have been redundant (Garnsey and Whittaker 1998, 333), the ecology was decentralized.

What flows of goods would help make up such an ecology? A prime instance of the limitations of conventional urban history is the extent to which, in answering that question, it has concentrated on foodstuffs, and especially on supplies of grain. But settlements depend on many other things too, and a properly ecological approach should make at least some attempt to bring them into the account (VI.4, VIII.5). It has for instance been claimed (Bairoch 1990, 145) that each city-dweller in preindustrial Europe consumed between 1 and 1.6 tons of firewood per annum. A settlement of 10,000 inhabitants would thus require the daily arrival of between 30 and 50 cartloads, each cart carrying one ton of wood. (A more specific estimate: around 1300, Londoners were consuming more than 386 tonnes of fuel per day, of which a quarter went on brewing and baking: Galloway et al. 1996; Murphy 1998, 122; VI.4.) By contrast, assuming a daily intake of one kilogram of grain per head per day – a quite generous allowance by historical standards – then a settlement of 10,000 would expect the daily arrival of only ten one-ton cartloads of grain (van der Woude et al. (eds) 1990, 8). In a Mediterranean environment, average needs would of course have been less, perhaps substantially so; and materials other than firewood – for example dung and straw – would be burnt for winter warmth. But neither the statistics of demand nor the geography of supply are likely to be available for very much of the preindustrial Mediterranean. A thirteenth-century eulogist of Milan asserted that the city consumed more than 150,000 cartloads of firewood annually (Lopez and Raymond 1955, 68). Such figures are hardly to be relied on. The importance of fuel to an ecology should be appreciated none the less, the more so because it helps to show the connections between the wilder, uncultivated parts of a locality and its principal settlements (VI.6). In default of more precise sources, anecdotal evidence must be pressed into service. The sixteenth-century traveller Reinhold Lubenau has for instance left a vivid description of villagers gathering firewood from nearby mountains for transport by boat to Istanbul, where the sultan extracted substantial profits from its sale. Indeed, so expensive was it there that, in many thousands of households, no fire was lit. All cooking would be taken to one of the city's 2,276 bake-houses and shops; for these had cauldrons or pans embedded in brick and therefore needed only a minimal fire (Koder 1988, 146).

7. AUTARKY

The workings of ecologies at the very centre of settlement; *rus in urbe*; extra-mural sprawl; the variety of goods whose movement helps make up an ecology – these are four topics considered so far, the study of which may contribute to the dissolution of 'the town' into a less arbitrarily bounded, and rapidly mutable, area of enquiry. The principal task will, however, be to identify the characteristic scale of the ecology of Mediterranean settlement. Exact or unchanging frontiers are not of course to be expected; evidence is too sparse for that – and ecologies too fluid. Towns are no more 'definite' than the places surveyed in Chapter III. Indeed, the thrust of the argument will be that it is a mistake to expect larger settlements to have been dependent for supplies on a distinct area such as a subject territory or a 'natural' hinterland. If the term hinterland is to be retained, then the presumption should be that what is in question is fragmented, not a compact domain that can be mathematically modelled and limned on a map, a 'zone d'approvisionnement' (Grantham 1997). The *dispersed*, changeable, hinterland has, we suggest, been the Mediterranean norm.

Now if we were restricting discussion to certain extreme cases that assertion would hardly be controversial. As for extremes of *size*, first of all, it is freely acknowledged that an Alexandria or a Constantinople has to draw its essential supplies from far afield and from a number of different directions. Take once more the outstanding example of Rome. With around one million inhabitants in the time of Augustus, Rome was – and, until the nineteenth century, remained – the largest city in Mediterranean history. Under the early Empire its inhabitants' food came, in varying proportions, from Gaul, Spain, North Africa, Sicily, Sardinia, Egypt, Cyprus and the Chersonese, as well as Italy (Garnsey and Saller 1987, 95; Morley 1996).

Secondly, for all our cavils at the consumption city, it is beyond dispute that the productive wealth and purchasing power of what can be called the extreme of *society* – the aristocracy or the religious or mercantile elite – added a special dimension to the hinterland of its civic residences. This dimension was perhaps of greatest significance under the Romans, when the wealthiest citizens consumed in the countryside as well as the city, and might own estates scattered right across the empire and thus all round the Mediterranean. Yet in the thirteenth century too,

> nobles who were at home in Rome . . . had major holdings and palazzi in smaller towns, and they had great country estates and fiefs throughout central Italy in places like Palombara, Palestrina, Terracina, and Ninfa . . . *So, in a way, a realistic map of Rome would not be bounded by the walls, but rather it would stretch out into the surrounding provinces in a series of superimposed networks following personal connection and the interests of real property.* (Brentano 1974, 17, italics added)

The special hinterland created by a city's merchants might enlarge its ecologies in other, more startling ways. That of the circulation of coinage is one. Describing his city's fiscal resources, the Renaissance Florentine Gregorio Dati asserts that between 1375 and 1405 the civic government disbursed 11.5 million florins on its major wars alone – an average of 380,000 per war. In response to the incredulous, Dati reports that, although such a vast sum could not be found within the city at any one time, the continuous circulation of its gold allowed the government to spend the same coinage over and over again. It was the exports of Florentine merchants that brought the gold back. 'The florins which are spent in one year', Gregorio explains in nicely ecological fashion, 'return in large part the next or following year, as does the water which the sea scatters through clouds upon the earth by rain, and which by rivers returns to the sea' (Herlihy 1978, 142–3).

Thirdly, it is acknowledged that the extent of the hinterland brought into play by governments and merchants will be at its highest during extremes of *scarcity*. Faced with the prospect of famine the efforts of the grain officers of Mediterranean cities knew no bounds, whether of ethics or of geography. Braudel nicely pictures the desperate piracy of some early modern cities (1972a, 331). But their anxieties were hardly novel. Let us add, as a medieval example, the Florentine import of grain from Apulia in 1329, a year when many parts of Italy were stricken by famine, yet when the starving Apulians would even so have been able to feed themselves had not their surplus been stored away ready for shipment north (Abulafia 1981, 381–2, 387; cf. VI.8).

Our source for grain prices and policies in that year is a contemporary Florentine corn-chandler. In his memoir he remarks that Florence could usually feed itself from the produce of its own *contado* for five months a year (Pinto 1978, 317). Even in the context of the high population levels prevalent in Europe on the eve of the Black Death, that information is striking: it aligns early Renaissance Florence with imperial Rome, placing it among the settlements that could not expect to support themselves from a nearby hinterland. Does it also take us from the realm of extremes into that of the usual? Florence was certainly not alone among Italian cities in its periodic reliance on imported grain (Section 8 below). Lucca was better able to support itself from its hinterland than was Florence. Yet even in good years it still had to import. The demographic disaster of the Black Death made little difference: between 1369 and 1376 and again between 1380 and 1385, there was some shortage or difficulty of supply in every year (Meek 1978, 97). Were such statistics indeed close to the norm? Addressing that question brings us up against what we shall provocatively label 'the myth of autarky' (cf. VII.5).

Writing in the time of Augustus, the great architectural theorist Vitruvius includes in his *On Architecture* (bk 2, preface) a report of a conversation between Alexander the Great and Deinocrates of Rhodes, who had designed the Egyptian city which still bears Alexander's name. He suggests to Alexander the founding of a magnificent city on Mount Athos in Greece. Alexander immediately asks whether there are fields round about which could provide the city with its food supply. Deinocrates replies that the new foundation would have to be supplied from a distance, using sea transport. Alexander therefore rejects his proposal out of hand. Just as a child needs milk, he says, so a city without fields and abundant produce from them cannot grow, or maintain a large population.

As a postscript to the account, Vitruvius reminds his readers that not only is Alexandria a great emporium; it has the abundant cornfields of Egypt irrigated by the Nile on which to depend for its victuals.

Both the apocryphal story and its author's postscript embody a conception of the ideal city whose history in Europe can be traced from Plato's and Aristotle's discussion of the *polis* to von Thünen's theoretical model of the isolated state, the city around which various agricultural products are grown in concentric circles (1966, first published 1826–63). In periods such as Antiquity and the early expansion of Islam, the temptation is often to demonstrate power or earn prestige through the foundation of cities. But this lust for civic splendour has (it is argued) always to be tempered by a respect for elementary economics. That is, the inhabitants of a city must be able to obtain sufficient staple commodities from their immediate surroundings through tribute, forced levies, taxation, rents or the open market. Supplies should come from nearby to minimize transport costs; for without cheap food the citizens will not have the wherewithal to engage in artisan production, commerce, politics and government, or civilized cultural pursuits. On this view, the city and its hinterland, defined either polit-ically or geographically, should therefore form a single unit. That unit must be autarkic – self-sufficient – or nearly so if the city is to endure in both safety and independence. Of course it is unlikely that a city will be autarkic in everything that it requires: luxuries, minerals or metals for instance. But self-sufficiency in essentials (usually equated with cereals: VI.8) has been the ideal – and, it is often held, an ideal normally attained. Only two categories of town could supposedly flourish without being autarkic, and these two categories substantially overlap: first the megalopolis, too large for autarky; second the major seaport, too well-placed for it (although even a seaport will need sufficient agricultural resources close by in its early stages). The megalopolis had the purchasing power to render the expense of transport costs negligible. The seaport could avoid the higher cost of transport overland.

Leaving aside for the moment the whole question of such relative costs (cf. IX.4), one comment that might immediately be hazarded is that autarky is like rank-size regularity: it depends on prior specification of the region, the hinter-land, in question. If the region is defined in terms of political control then it has to be borne in mind that the control may well have been sought with autarky in mind. (Of course the growth of a settlement or its political circumstances might frustrate such a drive to self-sufficiency: witness the partial incapacity of four-teenth-century Florence.) If the region is defined in geographical terms then its frontiers are as likely to be suggested by the area within which autarky seems possible as by any 'natural' phenomena. The argument for a given settlement's autarky can thus turn out to be circular.

Even supposing that the usual political and geographical definitions remain acceptable, however, two points deserve emphasis. One of them, hinted at already, is that the question of whether or not a settlement is self-sufficient may not be a particularly worthwhile one. Indisputably, provisions will always be brought to the settlement from as nearby as possible. That may make the hinterland *temporarily* compact. But turning as occasion warrants to supplies from further afield does not necessarily betoken a significant change in the character of a settlement's ecology. The notion of autarky entails an unrealistic distinction be-tween concentrated and scattered resources. It also entails a separation of what are taken to be basic necessities from other requirements; this certainly matches the emphasis placed on foodstuffs in historical conceptions of the ideal city, but is none the less arbitrary in ecological terms (Chapter VI). And yet historians tend to present autarky as something absolute, a state of ecological grace – from which there can only be an irrevocable and deleterious departure.

The other point to be emphasized is the extent to which, considering Mediterranean history as a whole, the prevalence of autarky has been deduced from its persistence as an ideal: practice has been inferred from rhetoric (V.4). Evidence for the ecology of the great mass of such settlements has not seemed plentiful enough to call into question the validity of the inference. Yet when, say, the inhabitants of Jerez de la Frontera near Seville stated in answer to an enquiry in 1582 that 'the town has only its harvests of wine, corn, oil and meat' – just sufficient to maintain its trade and its workers (Braudel 1981–4, 1.487) – they should not necessarily be taken exactly at their word. In attempting to minimize their fiscal obligations, they perhaps appealed as much to an ancient image as to a contemporary reality.

Some further examples, starting (like this one) at the very end of our period and moving increasingly further back in time, may suggest an alternative approach to the questions of self-sufficiency and the shape of hinterlands.

8. DISPERSED HINTERLANDS

The network of settlements in central Turkey of the sixteenth and seventeenth centuries reveals something of the scale of local exchange, and thus the fragility of the autarkic ideal (Faroqhi 1984). A fundamental determinant of this network's configuration was the unremitting growth of Istanbul. That growth began early: Mehmet II assured food supply by bringing in slaves to replace defaulting cultivators on his own estates. Perhaps several times the size of its largest Mediterranean contemporaries, the Ottoman capital's population was soon absorbing provisions, raw materials and manufactured goods on a scale that affected the structure of trade and production throughout large tracts of Anatolia (and well beyond). In that respect it resembled imperial Rome. Another general feature of the first importance was that the one supposed prerequisite of a dispersed hinterland, ease of access to water-borne transport, was often lacking. Caravans of horses and camels had to make good the deficiency. A third feature was instanced above in asserting the fragility of Mediterranean settlements: an extremely mobile population. Settlements might grow and contract dramatically within a quite short period.

This last feature, coupled with the unbalancing effect on regional production of Istanbul's vast size, ought to have outweighed the problems of overland communication and promoted substantial interregional trade, one settlement making good the shortfall of another. It was not an economic environment in which self-sufficiency would have been easy. That is why markets seem to have proliferated during the early modern period. That, again, is why the Ottoman government had to legislate to *enforce* self-sufficiency on every small administrative unit or *kaza* (Faroqhi 1984, 56, 191). Commerce in grain from one *kaza* to another required special permission from the centre, which normally granted it only in favour of the capital or to help chronically deficient areas such as the

Aegean islands. A settlement that was suffering unduly from this restriction could try to capture more of the grain that would otherwise be sold in surrounding markets; it could impose illegal exactions on its taxpayers; it could extend its *kaza*; or – what amounted to the same thing in terms of supply – it could presumably defy the government and trade with its neighbours.

The possibility that an Ottoman settlement could enlarge its administrative hinterland provides a telling reminder of the arbitrary element in definitions of autarky. Hinterlands are not easily read off the landscape, even when situation and environment seem apt to satisfy a latter-day Alexander the Great. Sixteenth-century Algiers was a classic Mediterranean new city. It had a prime location for the coastwise trade of the Maghreb; and, thanks to the great trough of the Mitijda plain, behind and beside it, there was a fine agricultural hinterland within apparently easy reach. But it was unable to make effective use of any of this until the political action of the *condottiere* Kheir-ed-din Barbarossa brought together a major and varied population from all over the Mediterranean. Its neighbourhood then rapidly became famous – but for intensive rather than extensive agriculture: gardens and orchards that were serving the needs of the new population (G. Fisher 1957, 60–5).

The region of Córdoba in the later Middle Ages (to shift northward and back in time by way of further illustration) was, like much of Andalusia, an exporter of grain. Yet the sources of those exports, as of the supply of Córdoba itself, were somewhat patchy. The region of the city is not to be thought of as a single more or less homogeneous von-Thünen-like hinterland, nor even as an amalgamation of three geographically distinct regions (Edwards 1982, 2–6). A survey of larger holdings in grain rent undertaken for the Crown in September 1502 reveals a more complex distribution of areas of surplus and near-starvation in the vicinity of Córdoba's subordinate settlements. Many of these will have been hard-pressed to meet their own needs locally. The capital was certainly under such pressure in the early sixteenth century. Emergency measures to prevent export of grain from the region and to ensure the capital's supply were being taken before the end of 1502. By 1506 the city council was petitioning the Crown for help and negotiating in Seville the purchase of grain imported from Sicily. What had gone wrong? The harvests of the early 1500s were not, it seems, particularly bad. There were, instead, three minor ingredients in the crisis: locally rising population, an extension of grazing land, the Crown's attempt to set limits to the price of grain. And there was one major ingredient: the reluctance of great landlords to bring their grain to market when prices were being thus artificially depressed. The worst general famine of the period, embracing supplies of meat as well as grain, was caused above all by speculative zeal (Edwards 1982, 113; 1987, 23). The concept of a stable – and mappable – administrative or geographical hinterland seems inappropriate to these essentially political vicissitudes.

A clutch of related examples that demonstrate the complexity of the problem of food supply can be found in the later medieval Italian communes. We have already mentioned Florence and Lucca. The history of governmental supervision of grain production and trade – to subsidize imports as well as to profit from exports – can be traced in a number of cities such as Cremona and Parma back into the early thirteenth century (Peyer 1950, ch. 2). Cities can also be found pairing off with one another and making treaties of mutual assistance in ensuring adequate grain supply (for instance Modena and Ferrara or Bologna and Imola).

In the early fifteenth century, to narrow the focus, the commune of Pescia in the Valdinievole (some forty miles north-west of Florence) was one of those that had probably attained normal self-sufficiency in wheat and was able to export considerable quantities of wine and oil. Yet this achievement depended not only on the efforts of its *contadini* but on the commune's successes in boundary disputes with its neighbours which had been in train since *c.*1200 if not earlier (J. C. Brown 1982, 68–71, 9–10). And it was a precarious achievement. By 1546, a year of good harvest, the supply of wheat had become inadequate, and autarky was made possible only by resort to other grains and alternatives such as chestnuts: exactly the sort of shift along the spectrum of possibilities that has always been essential to the survival of the individual Mediterranean producer (Chapters III, VI). By the early 1600s the area could support only half of the city's population. Pescia's hinterland, like that of Florence and the rest of Tuscany, now in a sense extended to Poland. The commune, caught in the toils of the Florentine state and the regional specialization and commercialization that it by no means evenly or benevolently promoted, had transferred most of its 'eggs' to a basket lined with silk. That in 1549 an ordinary shoemaker purchased 70 pounds of silkworm eggs brought from Palermo 'vividly attests to the density of economic networks that linked Pescia to the international economy by the mid-sixteenth century' (76).

That expansion of horizons should not inevitably be envisaged as signalling a radical *ecological* change, still less a fall – as it were from a state of nature (autarky) into one of culture (international commerce). Specialized silk production is not less natural than that of wheat (IX.3). And in making the transition from one to the other Pescia may have suffered less from Florentine domination than did a good many other communes. Nor should the collective history of these Italian cities be thought of as moving only in one direction, away from self-sufficiency in food. Indeed the imperialism of Renaissance Florence might better be seen as representing, in its regional consequences, an extreme of one particular swing of a slowly moving pendulum.

A previous swing towards dispersal of hinterland had been exemplified in the most obvious setting for such dispersal, the seaport. In such places as Amalfi, Genoa or Pisa, settlement has been presumed to flourish because the ports lay at advantageous 'nodes' on long-distance shipping lanes (contrast V.3, IX.7). Yet the original ecology of such stars in the history of medieval commerce does not suggest that long-distance luxury trade was the dominant element in their early growth. Nor, on the other hand, does it suggest that seaborne supply was a merely secondary extension of an already firm agricultural base. Rather, trade (in both luxuries and staples) and the development of a rural hinterland seem to have exercised powerful influences on each other. The hinterland turns out to be a complex notion. For, as in most other Mediterranean ecologies, production and redistribution were inseparable (IX.1).

Consider Amalfi of the eighth, ninth and tenth centuries (Kreutz 1988; 1991, ch. 5). Here is a site that must, initially, have had little to commend it to settlers or traders. Its beach front, a precarious strip between cliff and water, is less than 400 metres long. There is no natural harbour or protective hook of land, and local wind conditions are far from encouraging. On shore, the distribution of settlement and hinterland would have displayed few of the predicted attributes. First, Amalfi was barely distinct from the village of Atrani, immediately the other side of a bend in the cliff, which perhaps had a harbour of its own. Thus, to a degree, the settlement was itself dispersed. Secondly, although there were no obvious sources of food, plentiful timber was near at hand, and hemp and flax were to be had in the vicinity of Naples: ships could be cheaply built and rigged. Immediate staple requirements would have come, we can only speculate, mainly from the often quite distant farms that Amalfitans were buying, but also from the other ports, possibly not very distant, into which Amalfitan ships were initially putting.

Early Amalfi – Amalfi of the eighth century – can be envisaged only as a very minor stopping point in the coastwise trade of the Tyrrhenian Sea, one of many such for *caboteurs* (V.3). Its attractions were its convenient spacing from other such points and its proximity to the Islamic world, from which it would soon derive considerable profit (V.6). There was no specialized mercantile community, self-conscious and proud of its status. Occupational 'structure' would, predictably, have been hard to describe. The *calonna* system of financing maritime expeditions – by which profits were shared among the entire crew – ensured that taking to the sea was a useful way for almost any man to accumulate sufficient wealth to buy some land. Objectives were limited; so too was growth. And yet where settlement ends and hinterland begins is now hard to determine. For the destination of imports – whether staples for consumption, luxuries for exchange or coinage for purchase – was both Amalfi–Atrani and those inland holdings.

That the development of such a dispersed hinterland could indeed have a considerable effect on the commercial character of a city is reinforced by the contrasting early histories of Genoa and Pisa. It might seem that Genoa, first, could never have developed an extensive food-producing hinterland, confined as it is between sea and mountains. Yet mountains can facilitate more communication than they hinder (V.1). And in the archaic period Genoa already lay within the *économie du littoral* of the substantial Etruscan trade with Gaul (Milanese 1987, Bonamici 1995). In Roman times the city (Genua) was to become 'a port of respectable size' (Garnsey 1976, 17), with lines of communication to Emilia and the upper Po valley by way of the Passo di Giovi. Strabo (*Geography*, 4.6.2) describes Genua as the emporium of Liguria, where wood, wool, hides and honey from the surrounding hills were exchanged for incoming oil and wine (cf. BE IX.4 for shipwreck evidence). The convergence on Genoa of consignments of grain brought by both land and sea is perhaps also to be included in the reckoning. Certainly in the sixth century Procopius would think of Genoa as well placed for voyages to Gaul and Spain (*History of the Wars*, 6.12.29).

The next centuries are obscure. Under Ostrogothic rule, the city was home to a Jewish community, some of whose members presumably traded; and it may be significant that one of the Greek words that passed into the local vulgar Latin as a legacy of the succeeding period of Byzantine rule was *stolus* – fleet. Muslim raiders from North Africa sacked the city in 934–5, and an Arabic text (unfortunately written much later but possibly reliable) implies that there was silk and linen worth looting there (S. R. Epstein 1996, 13–14). The pertinent part of the story resumes in the eleventh century. On the eve of the First Crusade, with the supposed 'commercial revolution' well under way, Genoa's commercial activity was still somewhat restricted to the western Mediterranean – the redistribution across the western Mediterranean of salt from Provence and Sardinia and of grain (its movement now clearly evidenced) from southern Tuscany and Sicily, all of this not so different from the local *cabotage* that had perhaps been the norm during the preceding early medieval centuries. Suddenly, the advance of the crusaders opened up trading opportunities in the Levant, particularly trade in oriental spices and dyestuffs. A rapid expansion of markets will not, however, in itself explain why Genoa was able to make so much of these, and other commercial openings in the Mediterranean, during the twelfth and thirteenth centuries. More important in Genoa's development was that landowners of the early eleventh century were already investing surplus derived from rents, feudal dues or piracy against the Saracens, not in land – for there was probably little extra land to be had – but in trade. In a manner reminiscent of Amalfi, the leaders of Genoese expansion were members of a rural aristocracy rather than a mercantile class of 'new men'. Free from imperial interference (which blighted the prosperity of so many medieval Italian towns) and living on good terms with their archbishop (another potential source of frustration), these feudal-mercantile families were able to concentrate political and economic authority in their own hands. Trade could therefore be directed to their personal profit. And one of the easiest sources of profit was on their doorstep: 'Rather than postulating outside, "oriental" inspiration for the commercial growth of Genoa, we can look to the basic needs of the population and to the ability of the moneyed class to satisfy these needs to its advantage' (Abulafia 1977, 50; cf. S. R. Epstein 1996, 25–6). The development of an expanded hinterland stimulated commerce, not the other way around.

The contrast between Genoa and Pisa lends credibility to that contention. In the eleventh or twelfth century Pisa was third in importance as an Italian commercial centre after Venice and Genoa. She had, however, notably in the Tuscan Maremma, a vastly more productive immediate territory than either of the others. Certainly Lucca and Florence independently encroached on it: by the end of the thirteenth century self-sufficiency from this territory had clearly become impossible and Pisa was importing grain from Sicily. But until then its commercial activity seems to have been not nearly so vigorous as that of the Genoese. One reason for this comparative inertia may well have been that the ecological imperative to establish a dispersed hinterland was not so urgent in the eleventh and twelfth centuries – the period when a flourishing long-distance trade was otherwise within the limits of possibility.

These instances have been drawn mostly from later medieval to early modern times. The phenomenon was not, however, new to them. An elegant study (Figueira 1981) has provided a useful example from a very early period. The island of Aegina in the Saronic Gulf has only limited agricultural potential (slightly more than Melos, considered in Chapter III). By conventional calculations its own resources can support at minimal nutritional levels only some 5,000 people. Incidental evidence from around 500 B.C. makes it certain that the population was then at least seven times as large, and by no means existing precariously. The conclusion that Aegina was heavily dependent on a complex, reliable and large-scale trade in staples seems inescapable.

Nor do we need to search beyond the traditional matter of ancient Greek history to find comparably telling evidence. Scholars have debated the question of whether or not Athens at the height of its imperial power regularly imported grain (Garnsey 1988a, ch. 6; Whitby 1998) as if the norm, from which only a great city might conceivably need to depart, were self-sufficiency. Moreover, the city-states which constituted the Athenian empire in the second half of the fifth century B.C. were among those polities for which the Aristotelian ideal of self-sufficiency was originally prescribed. In them, if anywhere, that ideal might have been most commonly cherished and exemplified. Yet the diversity of their resources implied in the varying amounts of tribute payable to Athens – wine, vinegar, fish, salt and precious metals, as well as agricultural produce – makes that exemplification unlikely: 'The modern preoccupation with economic self-sufficiency . . . needs rethinking . . . As the evidence of harbour taxes shows, inter-state trade was routine and few *poleis* were truly self-sufficient. We should not confuse the Aristotelian ideal of autarky with economic reality' (Nixon and Price 1990, 166).

The regular movement of grain is not specifically attested in the sources of the fifth century B.C. But we perhaps draw close to it in the evidence – itself by no means abundant – for the assistance clearly offered by one *polis* to another or one daughter settlement to its home territory in times of scarcity (Garnsey 1988a, 70–3). The tendency of the examples just assembled has after all been to diminish whatever gap might have been envisaged between the extreme and the norm. Food crisis, as has emerged from a number of different studies, and as the example of Córdoba showed, is to be interpreted as a failure of organization as much as of a freak of nature: famines are made by people as much as by harvests (VII.4). Lesser food crises can arise from small alterations to the very mechanisms that had been set up to avert them. Such crises may well necessitate imports of food. And, thanks to that climatic variability which cannot be overestimated as a factor in Mediterranean history, food crises have by all accounts been frequent in the Mediterranean. Therefore we should not place too much trust in the concept of a normal year. There were perhaps not that many of them. And even during such years, the above examples invite us to conclude, 'normality' cannot easily be equated with self-sufficiency. The argument for a substantial trade in commodities that has been elaborated by ancient historians should be extended to the whole of the preindustrial Mediterranean past: the proximity of surplus-producing areas to those in need of staples ought to have generated interregional trade throughout our period. Redistribution is an imperative of survival (Chapters VI, IX).

If in addition to blurring the distinction between the normal and the critical in the history of food supply, we bring together the differing concerns of the inhabitants of, say, a city or commune then a still more dispersed hinterland has to be imaged. Earlier on we treated mercantile elites as extreme examples; but we then argued that it is a mistake to concentrate on grain supply at the expense of that of other commodities. The argument should now be extended to embrace the interests of those whose contacts were most far-flung: the example of the medieval Italian emporia has shown the extent to which the develop-ment of distant trading connections in high-value goods was inextricable from the search for additional sources of food (IX.4). To the overall picture that would consequently emerge one final touch can again be anticipated from a later discussion (IX.5): the mobility of Mediterranean populations. That people may have arrived in a given settlement after travelling some considerable distance should be reckoned no less a feature of its ecology than the concentration or dispersal of its food sources. Braudel wrote in his last major work that nothing is more eloquent in this respect than a map of immigrants' origins (1988–90, 1.185; cf. Reyerson 1979). Yet settlements lose people to far-flung locations as well; those locations too should be included on the map, which would represent a short period only, such could be the rapidity of Mediterranean settlements' demographic 'turnover' (Map 23).

Removing the analytical space that is so easily created between crisis and normality, or between elite and the remainder of a settlement's population, or between stable and migrant groups, we have also implicitly been reducing the distance between a Constantinople and a Pescia. The first rank of settlements, we have been urging, were not aberrant exceptions to a prevailing rule of autarky created by extraordinary environmental demands or social and political circumstances. They were simply the most developed examples of a tendency which could be widely exemplified from any region and any period in Mediterranean history. Autarky in all basic requirements cannot be predicated of the majority of settlements. Nor should autarky in food supply. If a norm must be envisaged, let it be that of the tentacular settlement.

Estimation of the number and scale of dispersed hinterlands does not, however, take us far enough in our ecologizing. Just as the site of a town should be reconceived as a number of overlapping ecologies, so should its hinterland be thought of as a complex set of smaller entities, an accumulation of short distances and definite places. If the dynamics of the extended hinterlands that supported an Athens or a Genoa could be considered in detail, rather than by overview, what at first appeared a grand system, operating as if by some careful plan, would be revealed as a huge accumulation of very local phenomena. The often tiny communities within the Athenian empire did not have to function in a wholly novel way when they became part of 'the power that rules the sea'. The larger entity was simply a direction, or impetus, given to the previously less formed, less patterned, ecological interaction of several hundred settlements, several thousand microregions. The routes that supplied medieval Genoa comprised dozens of possible way-stations. Each of these functioned in its own fashion as a local environmental system, the product of which was given an altered function, a new set of relations, by its inclusion on the sea route that led to the northern Tyrrhenian. Tiny islands with sheltered lee-shores or small coves in the mountainous peninsulas of the southern Peloponnese became parts of a Mediterranean-wide network – like loose beads piled at random yet suddenly acquiring order and meaning when the string that threads them is tightened (Balard 1974 and Map 12). That process is intermittent. Harbours such as Porto Caglio near the tip of Cape Matapan, or islands such as Prote near Pylos, show from the inscriptions of Roman traders that they were part of a network in ancient times as they were to be once more in the age of the Genoese (*IG*, 5/ 1.309–11). Those two sources of evidence serve in effect to pull the threaded beads into order for the historian to see. At other times the thread may not be discernible, or there may be no thread, or the threads may run in quite different directions.

When, however, they are visible in their ordered complexity, these sets of relations interweave and bind together the smallest human places of production and consumption – the least stable and the most widely dispersed – into the same web as the most complex, perennial and densely packed. To emphasize: imperial Athens, Rome, Constantinople or Venice are not freaks, departures from a norm

of straightforward self-sufficiency. Far smaller settlements, even ones as intermittent as Oenoanda, could also form the symbolic and economic foci of substantial yet dispersed territories. It is therefore the common processes by which
microecologies interact, rather than the presumed distinctions between one kind
of settlement and another, or one period and another, that should hold the
Mediterranean historian's attention. We emphasize, with Holton (1986, 117),
that 'this does not mean the complete dissolution of any sense of "urban" and
"rural". These terms retain a limited importance both as demographic markers
of the spatial distribution of populations, and as cultural symbols.' None the
less, we prefer the example implied by Dante's analogy (in this chapter's first
epigraph) between cities and families, the macro- and microcosm of human
settlement. The supply of eighteenth-century Melos ought to be envisaged as an
Athenian imperial carrying trade in miniature, the economy of Etruscan Veii as
an illustration of the types of contact with other places that, on an incomparably
larger scale, formed the horizons of Renaissance Venice. As with the various
kinds of pastoralism (cf. III.6), the grander systems are – perhaps unexpectedly
– indicative of the nature of the rest. So far as settlement is concerned, the
details will of course vary with area and period. The unifying feature is not the
accident of a nucleated pattern, whether or not this qualifies as urban; it is
the intricate and often far-flung engagement with a wider, kaleidoscopic, world.

CHAPTER V

CONNECTIVITY

The intricate local patterns within the dispersed hinterlands of Mediterranean settlements provide a suitable point of transition in our enquiry into 'routes et villes . . .', Febvre's lapidary response to Braudel. From *villes*, we turn to *routes*. In the preceding chapter we argued that the study of towns should, for the purposes of ecological history, be replaced with a much more open conception of the ways in which larger settlements are nourished. Towns have been seen as a defining feature of Mediterranean history. But, as such, they have usually been understood in conjunction with sharply defined lines of communication and redistribution, on which they have been seen to depend. These Mediterranean routes have therefore also attained a constitutive role in notions of the Mediterranean past. Our emphasis on the processes which sustain more or less transient agglomerations in the Mediterranean entails that we should also attempt to set routes in a much broader interpretative context.

We certainly do not mean to imply that defined highways or sea-lanes have never existed; on the contrary, their functioning more or less throughout our long period is well documented. Rather, just as we proposed in Chapter IV that the town is not a readily discriminable category of settlement and has no distinct ecological history of its own, we now want to suggest that the kind of route which Febvre and Braudel envisaged is best seen as a special instance of a far larger phenomenon: the *connectivity* of microregions. By this term, we understand the various ways in which microregions cohere, both internally and also one with another – in aggregates that may range in size from small clusters to something approaching the entire Mediterranean.

We have argued that microregions always need to be understood with reference to some wider setting (Chapter III); and we have extended our microregional approach to the study of larger ('urban') settlements (Chapter IV). Here, then, we complete the exposition of our basic model of the Mediterranean past, by attempting to show how microregions can coalesce on a grand scale. This coalescence – which begins across the 'short distances' corresponding to the 'definite places' in the title of this Part of the book – encourages that history *of*, rather than merely *in*, the Mediterranean which we defined right at the outset. In the present chapter our aim is chiefly to *describe*. The *explanation* of connectivity, and its consequences for the timbre of Mediterranean cohesiveness, will emerge in the course of Chapters VI–IX.

1. LINES OF SOUND AND LINES OF SIGHT

Our account of those definite places was intended to demonstrate that the characteristics of microregions are best captured, not by any enumeration of topographical or climatic features, but through an understanding of the highly complicated and always changing interaction of human productive opportunities. This interaction could give highly varying significance to even the simplest local feature – so much so that environmental determinism had no place in the analysis. In the study of connectivity, similarly, establishing which aspects of the physical environment might have been the most important in the choice of paths of communication is perhaps the least important aspect. Relief, vegetation, sea current or coastline will of course frequently have delimited the particular channels available to people, ships and goods. Yet meticulously plotting the occasions on which that has happened (were it possible with our period) would not actually promote greater understanding of how Mediterranean ecologies interact. Of far greater significance than the (as it were) 'vertical' relation of traveller to immediate physical setting is the 'horizontal' one that binds ecologies together. And this complex connectivity within and between microenvironments is more closely analogous to the inhabitants' shifting, potentially all-round perceptions of their environment than to specific routes marked on a contoured map.

Some idea of the multiplicity of reference points in the perceptual world of the microregion will therefore be an essential guide to the nature of Mediterranean communications. So we begin with an unusual, but by no means extreme, example of the way microregions cohere – in apparent disregard of physical geography:

> If any business do put them upon a visit to their neighbour, they come not close to his door, but stand off at a great distance, and call aloud to him; if he make them answer, they discourse the business they came about, standing off at the same distance; except they be earnestly invited to come in. And this way of discoursing at a distance they practise more in the fields and mountains; their voices being so strong, that 'tis ordinary to talk at a mile's distance; sometimes at four or five, where the valleys interpos'd between two hills, give advantage to the voice. Sometimes they can discourse at that distance, that the carriage of the sound through the winding of the valleys, shall require half a quarter of an hour's time; and yet they make distinct, and proper answers, both audible and intelligible, without the help of a *stentorophonical* trumpet. (Georgirenes 1678, 64–5)

Human interaction across great distances, quite unassisted by technology, may seem even more astonishing to us than it did to Joseph Georgirenes, archbishop of Samos. We find it hard to conceive of space without maps and aerial photographs; the nature of communications before they could be enhanced artificially is equally hard to intuit. Who would have stressed unprompted the acoustic element in the development of the networks of interaction that, during the early modern period, bound together the settlements of the mountainous Aegean island now called Ikaria?

In the conceptualizing of locality and space, sight can play a still greater part than sound. Substantial areas may be defined by places visible from afar:

places often – and not coincidentally – of great religious significance, as we shall see in Chapter X. The highest volcanic summit of the Alban hills, Monte Cavo, provides a useful example (III.2). This most conspicuous peak was the site of the Temple of Jupiter Latiaris, the federal sanctuary of the archaic League of the cities of Latium. Quite generally, Mediterranean microregions are patterned by ties of mutual visibility. The watch tower or look-out has been a prime constituent of the region's landscapes, and has given its name to many prominent features, as is reflected for example in the modern Greek toponym Vigla, from *vigilia*. Chains of beacons or signal stations could convey simple messages very rapidly, and were often used by the Greeks and Romans as part of their network of communications. The distance from Troy to Mycenae is powerfully evoked in this manner at the beginning of Aeschylus's *Agamemnon* of 458 B.C. There can be little doubt that an essentially visual ordering of geography was one of the earliest ways by which the individual might understand the relationship between his own sphere of movements and far broader horizons (Tracy 1986).

Fields of perception and their foci are characteristic ingredients in the definition of Mediterranean microregions because these microregions can never be sufficiently understood solely in their local context. The chains of perceptibility created by looking from one vantage point to the next serve both to express the relationship of individual localities to one another and, as with Friar Felix's vision of the Mediterranean quoted at the end of Chapter I, to make sense of the wider world. Faced with the difficulty of comprehending the layout of whole mountain-ranges, ancient geographers even carried the notion to its extreme, and offered exceedingly optimistic assessments of mutual visibility – for example, Strabo's assertion that from the heights of the Balkan ranges west of Macedonia it was possible to see both the Aegean and the Adriatic (*Geography*, 7, fragment 6).

In Chapter I we explored some of the earliest documented ways in which the Mediterranean came to be understood as an entity. We emphasized the coastwise voyage and the listing of features that punctuate the shore. For the coasting mariner, the list was made possible by the visibility of seamarks. The Isola di Camerota off the Tyrrhenian coast of Elea, for example, can be shown to have acted as a visual reference point for the definition of this ancient city's seaboard (De Magistris 1995, 60–76). Like lines of intercommunicating watch towers, the mariner's lines of sight express the greater unity of what lies beyond the bounds of perceptibility. Along the mountainous coast of the ancient Maghreb, the cities that lay in a sequence of safe anchorages took their names from the headlands which identified them for the seafarer: Rusazu, Rusippisir, Rusuccuru, Rusguniae, Rusaddir (Mackie 1983; Map 23). Well into the Roman period, they retained the toponym – related to the later Arabic *ra's* or head – that they had been given centuries before by westbound Phoenician mariners. In this case the names that had reflected the early sailors' perceptual continuum were used for the Roman cities that made this coast part of the empire. The seafarers' perception was institutionalized in the administration of the area, and contributed to another kind of unity, that of a province of the *imperium Romanum*.

Under the Roman thalassocracy, the coastal villas of the rich often took over the locations of seamarks, and their confident display came to symbolize

the quality of life in an age that had tamed the sea's perils. It was a particular
pleasure to own pairs of villas that looked along the coast from promontory to
cape or from island to mainland, lending the proprietor a sense of control over
the maritime landscape. Moreover, the owners who adapted the landscape in this
way were also deliberately appropriating the architecture with which Hellenistic
cities had embellished their harbours. Port monuments such as lighthouses
and moles or the famous colossus of Rhodes all belong in this context – as only
the most developed expressions of the idea that the identity of a powerful Mediterranean figure depends on how his territory is perceived from its maritime
approaches.

    Mutual visibility is at the heart of the navigational conception of the Mediter-
ranean, and is therefore also a major characteristic of the way in which microregions interact across the water, along the multiple lines of communication that
follow those of sight. There are only relatively restricted zones where, in the
clearest weather, sailors will find themselves out of sight of land. And these
unintelligible 'deeps' of the sea are the areas that have held the greatest terror for
the Mediterranean seafarer, from Odysseus onward. Yet a map of them shows how
confined they are. Thanks to the mountainous nature of so many coastlines,
much of the Mediterranean basin is linked quite easily by lines of sight (Map 9)

    The sequences of fixed points that pattern lines of visual communication
between microregions are most obvious, and are easiest to use, in the maritime
sphere. The shores, with their usually clear unilinearity and their easily intuited
sequence of prominent features, readily assist the conceptualization of space. On
land, by contrast, there are so many complications that lines are less easy to
determine. Indeed, in its unhelpful jumble, the interior bears a certain resemblance to those deeps of the sea. The abundance of features and directions promotes perceptual confusion. Away from the coasts, fewer topographical features
are dominant enough to provide an equivalent armature for the patterns of
human interaction. Only a very small number of mountain passes, some isolated
peaks, and certain great river valleys approximate the effect of seashores. By
means that are analogous to the provision of artificial seamarks, however, the
gaps in the perceptual network of terrestrial communication can be improved:
landmarks can be emphasized architecturally, and lines can be elaborated too.

    The Roman road, the most developed form of overland interconnection in
Mediterranean history, was surveyed as a set of links along lines of sight. The
course of the road was a highly artificial choice. In its most frequent ancient
conception, indeed, it can be defined simply as the shortest distance between
two prominent seamarks or navigable rivers (Purcell 1990b). In this it was quite
unlike the great channels of trans-Saharan or Asiatic communication, formalized
in the latter case as the Royal Road of the Persians. Operating on an intercontinental scale, these routes were locally very variable in their exact course; they did
not have so close a relationship to the regions which they traversed and to which
they did not really belong. Clearly the geometric simplicity of the concept,
and the power displayed in ignoring physical obstacles, were both part of the

Map 9 Visibility of the land from the sea
   This revealing cartography (after Chapman 1990) may be contrasted with Braudel's
eloquent, if somewhat misleading, analogy (1972a, 103): 'great stretches of the sea were as
empty as the Sahara.'

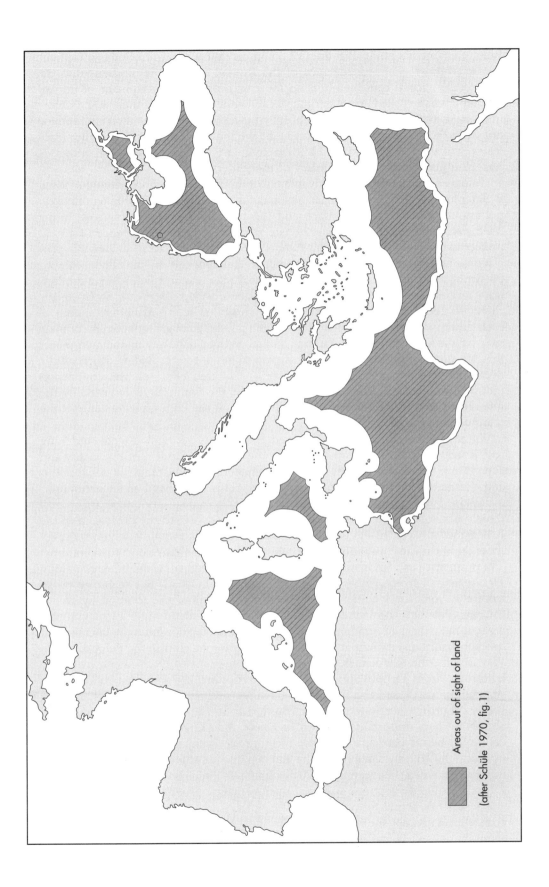

Areas out of sight of land

(after Schüle 1970, fig.1)

Roman engineer's point. But lines of communication always embody an element
of the arbitrary. The nonchalance of the Roman engineer reminds us that the
supposedly natural route is often no more of a physical determinant of human
behaviour than is the natural geographical frontier (cf. I.2). If there was a determinism at work in the Romans' choice of direction for major roads, it derived
not from the incomprehensible jumble of the local topography, but rather from
features of the reliable and well-known geometry of coasts and watercourses. It
was, in other words, a determinism of the understanding.

Claims about the economic advantages of the Roman road are often dismissed
by reference to the non-utilitarian rationale of its creation, as well as to the likely
poor state of repair of its surface and the paucity of evidence for road-borne
commerce in classical times. The debate is misplaced: the importance of a road
project in the Mediterranean landscape is the effect that it achieves through proclaiming and encouraging interaction between microregions – an effect achieved
by symbolism and the establishment of social relations as much as by any physical movement of goods and people. Compare a likely coastal case: in two ports
there are goods to be exchanged, people whose interests and understanding of
each other promote friendly association, and a short passage between. A compact
may be made to encourage exchange, and physical facilities in the two places
may be improved. For a time the two localities interact. Bad weather or the
decay of the harbour mole will have only a limited effect on the connection
that has been set up. With a road it is similar; the compact represented by the
investment in *this* link between *these* two places is the important aspect, not the
'hardware' that goes with it.

Where such a compact has acquired the solidity of high esteem and long
use, it may continue to function against the apparent dictates of rationality and
expediency. Classical Athens, famously, enjoyed the advantage of a capacious
and defensible 'natural' harbour, at Piraeus. This functioned as its gateway to
a dispersed hinterland in the network of Mediterranean communications and
rapidly developed into a major hub within that network, to the great gain of the
Athenian state. Yet smaller, less well endowed landings and anchorages, more remote from the city, none the less continued to play a vital role in the economy.
The strangest case is Oropos, on the opposite, northern, coast of Attica (Map
10), separated from Athens by twenty miles of hilly road. For seaborne traffic
from the north, it would seem preferable to continue the journey by sea to
Piraeus. Although the rounding of Cape Sounion entails a longer journey, somewhat at risk from bad weather, this route can hardly have failed to be cheaper and
quicker than transhipment at Oropos. Yet, we are told, during the Peloponnesian
War, when Athens' enemies occupied the strongpoint of Decelea and made the
land-route from Oropos unusable, the interruption of the movements of tran-
shipped goods caused the Athenians grave inconvenience (Thucydides, *History*,
7.28.1). Further, we now discover (Blackman 1997, 14–16) that Oropos had
already been an important centre of exchange and of metalworking in the eighth
century, when it participated in the forming of complex economic connections
between the communities of nearby Euboea and far-flung parts of the Mediterranean. As a link between early Attica and this precursor of the Piraeus hub,
Oropos acquired functions and relationships which proved highly durable.

The path of actual movement between places, like the simple perceptions of
contact and juxtaposition that underlie it, is therefore a selection of just one

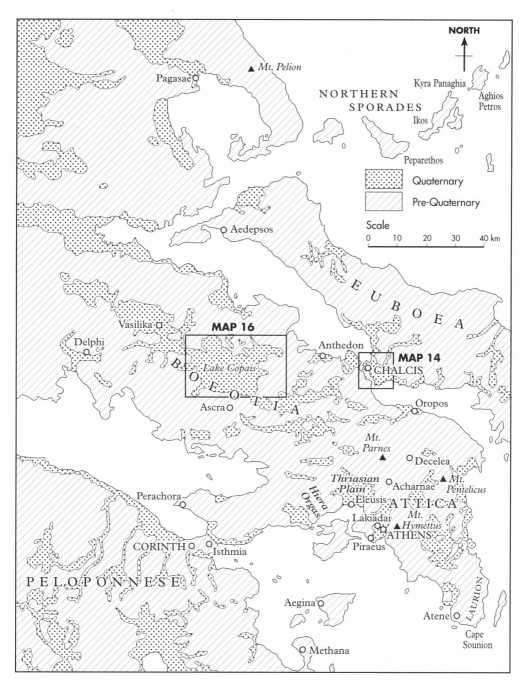

Map 10 Central Greece

strand in that potentially omni-directional connectivity between ecologies best exemplified in ties of visibility. It is a selection made for any one of a variety of possible reasons. The significance of a strand will ebb or endure as the ecologies, in all their contingency, mutate. That is why, at the extreme, routes may be invisible to the untutored eye: they are defined by local knowledge and current practice, not by physical peculiarities.

That is also why modern studies of the communicability of Mediterranean regions – even of so physically individual a landscape as the Peloponnese – have shown some striking differences between the communications networks of classical and of modern times. The configuration of passes, plains, fords, ports and minor paths has remained substantially unchanged; but the relationship between them and the major lines of transportation has varied considerably over time. In the Peloponnese, an *impression* of great continuity between ancient and modern networks is created by the recorded efforts of nineteenth-century travellers to retrace the steps of the ancients. If the classical routes had altogether disappeared (the travellers surmised) the landscape could show where they must have run. And yet this impression of continuity is deceptive. For what matters in assessing the communications of the area is not the fate of particular routes but the relative significance of each part in the workings of the whole. Now in theory this can be measured. When dealing with a fully specifiable network, connectivity may be defined (far more narrowly than we do) as one of several possible mathematical functions of the proportion of nodes to links and of the likely journey times. A comparison, in these terms, of the connectivity of the Peloponnese displayed, on one hand, in the Peutinger Table, probably dating in its original form to Augustan times, and, on the other, in George Gennadius's map of the Balkans of 1822, shows how much has changed. In particular, the increasing value placed on speed of travel has, contrary to all received wisdom about Mediterranean transport, lent a new importance to routes through the northern mountains, and caused a relative decline in the part played by coastwise traffic (Sanders and Whitbread 1990; III.6, with Section 3 below; Map 32).

If the scope for comparison is extended back into pre-Roman times, a yet more striking contrast emerges. It seems that the ancient Spartans may have controlled and exploited their territory (of over 8,000 square kilometres) by a dense system of wagon tracks, quite different in character from Roman networks, let alone from more recent ones. Nineteenth-century travellers had occasionally noticed parallel grooves traversing the landscape and acting rather like railway lines for wagon wheels. But it has required a modern topographical investigation (Christien 1989) to reveal the full extent and the antiquity of the system. It seems to have been created especially for the safe transport of goods across the Taygetus Mountains, enabling the Spartans to enjoy the wealth of the Plain of Messenia. At its most developed, it integrated the whole of the southern Peloponnese, contradicting the poor connectivity that might be ascribed to Sparta simply on the basis of the Peutinger Table (Sanders and Whitbread 1990, 348). Such findings should encourage a more sympathetic reading of Thucydides's 'mythistorical' claim that the Greeks once travelled more by land than by sea (*History*, 1.13.5).

Thus, even routes that cross difficult terrain, and that might be expected to prove ineffective as lines of communication, often turn out to admit of surprisingly fluent and varied interchanges between regions. A further illustration to set alongside the survey of Peloponnesian wheel ruts comes from Larner's (1990) study, already cited in III.6, of the Apennines inland from Rimini during the Renaissance. It nicely reinforces the conclusions derived from Sparta; it shows once more that Mediterranean mountains are not necessarily barriers; and it adds another chronological period to our set of examples.

The Apennine routes were described as 'difficult and harsh' by more than one eminent Renaissance observer; and the difficulties involved in the movement of goods and people could certainly be enormous. Yet there is sufficient evidence to show that, as channels of redistribution, these routes were of great significance for the regional interaction of the period. 'We went through the mountains of the Apennine, which last for around twelve miles, but it is an easy mountain (*è montagna facile*).' So wrote Francesco Guicciardini on crossing the Cisa Pass in 1511 – and not during the summer of that year, but in cruel February (Larner 1990, 148–9). Armies moved around as Guicciardini could, albeit with far greater effort. In 1495, the invader Charles VIII of France had taken a force of some 10,000, with fourteen heavy artillery and twenty-three smaller pieces, across the very same pass. Trade routes, too, could be found when necessary, for instance the one negotiated between Florence and Rimini in 1402, when most of the usual Florentine channels had been cut by her war with Milan. The secret of such relative ease of passage lay in the knowledge of a dense and evolving network:

> a network of tracks leading from one valley to another, from the hill pastures to the valley bottoms, and over the high watersheds . . . Again, wherever there was a castle, village, church, or monastery, there was a track leading somewhere else, and wherever a commune or local lord extracted tolls, smugglers would seek out obscure paths across the highest passes in order to avoid paying them. (Larner 1990, 152–3)

Even mountainous regions, as we have earlier argued, are not as impenetrable as classical and medieval opinion, reinforced by a Romantic sensibility to desolation, would have them. This is a fact which Islamic geography, perhaps because it was less oriented towards the sea, always recognized (Miquel 1980, 3.59–69). By and large, the Mediterranean world before railways did not depend on the wheel (W. H. McNeill 1987; Bulliett 1975). Pack-animals have been the preferred solution, and their versatility is responsible for the complexity of the geography of communications in areas of high relief. We may add that it is important to distinguish zones of high relief from zones of high altitude. In the Mediterranean lands high mountains are commonly plateaux and massifs of ancient limestone, surrounded by tumbled lower foothills of softer, more recent rocks. It is the foothills that create difficulties of communication. Except when they are under snow, summits can offer very easy routes (Butzer 1994, 23). The inhabitants of mountainous regions travel through them with striking ease, making use of surprisingly short and level routes among the summit plateaux and ramified watershed ridges which in many Mediterranean mountains form a relatively coherent surface across hundreds of miles. The high Pindus and the central Apennines provide good examples of that coherence, as do some of the cultural unities formerly to be found across the Yugoslav mountains (Milojević 1939). There have also been notable cases of unity within and between regions linked only by high-altitude communications – in the Lebanon, for instance, which long coherently resisted the Hellenistic kingdoms and Rome, or the cultural realm of the Algerian Kabyle. We should, in addition, mention the mountain-based state of the rebellious Italian allies of Rome at the beginning of the first century B.C., with its aspiring capital at Corfinium high in an intermontane basin; or the ease with which the Lombard presence in Italy was maintained along the dorsal ridge and its outliers, from the Cisalpine settlements in the north, through the Duchy of Spoleto, to the Duchy of Benevento in the central south.

It is with the points of transition between mountain and lowland that the picture becomes more complicated. Transhumant herding, linking high and low pastures, which we encountered in our 'definite places', and to which we shall return in the next chapter (Section 7), helps integrate upland zones. But on most Mediterranean mountains only a relatively restricted summit level is rendered quite useless during the season of snow, and relations between the middle mountain-zone and the coast, or between the middle zone and the high pastures are more common than movement all the way from high pasture to coast or vice versa. This is partly because both the summer pasture and the coastal wetlands are particularly good for the animals; and country folk will have had to be content with access to only one of what were, in any case, often widely separated areas. There is nothing unusual about such cases. Just as most microregions have some environments whose potential is to be realized only through animal husbandry, so too most have some access to mountains – a fact which has been adduced to explain the slow development of the luxury snow-trade in the Mediterranean (de Planhol 1995).

The main hindrance to the movements of people and goods by land has usu-ally been social rather than physical (VII.4–5). Some tracts are, however, rela-tively free from this problem because aridity makes them so sparsely populated. This effect reinforces the paradoxical ease of communications of Mediterranean mountains. Dry levels and bare plains, some at high altitudes, such as the Spanish Meseta, may be isolated by their height and rugged fringes, but still offer vast areas of easily traversed countryside. Communications across the great deserts themselves, to the east and south of the Mediterranean lands, have also often been easier than might be supposed (a theme to which we hope to return in Volume 2; cf. III.3 for Cyrenaica and the Sahara).

Mediterranean places are doubly identified. First, they have their own dis-tinguishing features that are perceptible to their inhabitants (although perhaps not to the stranger, who can register only the 'natural' physical environment). Yet, secondly, these local characteristics derive at least some of their significance from being part of more extensive networks. Such networks often abut on the unexpectedly connective tracts which form the skeleton of the Mediterranean peninsulas and islands, ridges, plateaux, plains. But much more important is the role played by the sea itself, and particularly by coastwise navigation. If we are seeking to illustrate connectivity in the Mediterranean area at its most com-prehensive, its most variable in direction, then we must clearly look to the sea, and particularly to its islands and peninsulas. Their dense and convoluted inter-action provides a more appropriate image of Mediterranean routes in general than could any network of lines and vertices, suggestive of perennial, physically determined channels of contact.

2. EXTENDED ARCHIPELAGOS: THE CONNECTIVITY OF THE MARITIME

The lines of visibility that bind places across the Mediterranean Sea create, as we have now begun to show, a distinctive maritime milieu – a milieu that dominates pockets of the land world with which it comes in contact. The Greeks called those pockets that lie opposite islands *peraiai* (Dilke 1985, 74–5); and the terminology, defining a piece of the mainland in terms of its relationship to an offshore island rather than vice versa, strikingly reflects the conceptual primacy of the maritime world. The sea, as we saw in Chapter I, unites the Mediterranean conceptually as well as topographically. It is no barrier to communications, but the medium of all human intercourse from one region to another. Moreover, to the sea in the literal sense we must add the very important cases in which water-borne contacts extend the sea into the land. Navigable rivers – Ebro, Rhône and Tiber, Po, Adige and Narenta, Axios, Strymon and Hermus, Maeander, Pyramus, Orontes and Nile – and dozens of smaller but often partly navigable streams, with the coastal wetlands where land and sea mingle, together constitute another zone of communications (VI.5). The advantage of maritime transportation, economical of energy, relatively quick, wide open and unobstructed, is not outweighed by its risks, terrible though these often are. As the ancient interpreter of dreams Artemidorus of Daldis (a land-locked town of Anatolia) says, sea-travel is a far better dream to have than land-travel because of its greater facility (*On the Interpretation of Dreams*, 2.23). Maritime communications have been regarded as a necessary (though not a sufficient) condition for growth in the Mediterranean economy (Finley 1985a, 129). The sea is also the foundation of our case for the distinctiveness of Mediterranean history: deeply implicated in the unpredictability of the conditions of life, it is also of course the principal agent of connectivity.

In the patterns of relationship between microregions, the coastal enclaves that are part of the world of the sea but interact with the 'depths' of the hinterland have always played a special, if highly volatile, part (IX.7). They function as what geographers have labelled gateway settlements, through which goods and people are 'funnelled' in both directions (Hodges 1988, 42–52). The ensemble of Mediterranean lands is not just a gigantic peninsula in reverse (cf. I.4); it has an inside-out geography in which the world of the sea is 'normal' (the interior), and the land is the fringe, its marginality increasing with its distance from the water. Distance is, in effect, inverted: places linked by sea are always 'close', while neighbours on land may, in terms of interaction, be quite 'distant'. The influential theories of Wallerstein (1974–89) about the nature of large-scale social and economic systems will therefore apply to the Mediterranean, if at all, in a curious way: the core territories may be composed of far-flung coastlands whose functional proximity is the product of seaborne connectivity. Peripheral regions will be found in the interstices of this network as well as in geographically remote areas (G. Woolf 1990). Hence the differences in cost between land and sea transport characteristic not only of the ancient world but of any period in Mediterranean history before the advent of railways (IX.4).

The study of maritime connectivity is one subject in which the Mediterranean historian has most to learn from prehistory. The degree of intercommunication displayed by the islands of the Mediterranean in the second millennium B.C. is well known (A. B. Knapp 1990). Already in the Mycenaean period, the unpromising offshore islet of Vivara on the north shore of the bay of Naples acted as the depot for seafarers in their interactions with the rich Italian mainland, just as Pithekoussai, a few kilometres away, was to do from the eighth century (Frederiksen 1984, 65–7; IX.7). In the fourteenth century B.C., Ustica, a small volcanic island north of Palermo, was regularly in the swim of Mediterranean-wide exchange and had been equipped with a fortified enceinte and rectilinear ground plan (Ross Holloway and Lukesch 1991). Still earlier, in the Gulf of Mirabello at the eastern end of Crete, a Minoan city flourished on an islet, modern Pseira, that had virtually no productive potential. The community served as a gateway to a fertile area on the mainland, that would once again focus on Pseira when it prospered in the early Byzantine period and supported an island monastery (Harrison 1990).

At the dawn of the historical period, when the textual evidence is at its scantiest, archaeology produces further instances of the precocious existence of Mediterranean-wide interdependence. On the other side of Crete from Pseira is the port of Kommos, where notable connections with the Phoenician milieu as it grew to embrace the whole Mediterranean basin have been revealed. Examination of the ancient graffiti shows that Greeks from different places, including both Euboea and central Greece, were to be found there in the eighth century B.C. (Csapo 1991, J. W. Shaw 1989). In the Euboean ambit during the same period, the site of Zagora, in an unwelcoming corner of Andros, is revealed as sharing in the continuum of redistribution – more, to owe to it its very existence (Cambitoglou 1988).

A further example from the Phoenician world, and from just outside the Mediterranean region, is provided by the city of Gades, now Cadiz. It was founded from distant Tyre, most likely in the mid-eighth century B.C., on a small group of islands commanding access from the coastal routes to the wide estuary of the Guadalquivir. It flourished as the entrepôt through which the increasingly complex local cultures of the mainland, with their rich resources of silver, were tied in to the redistributive networks of the Mediterranean (Aubet 1993; Chamorro 1987; IX.2).

With Pithekoussai, the successor of our first instance, Vivara, and with Gades, we have of course arrived in the mainstream of what is usually called Greek colonization, one of the most complex manifestations ever of the interactive potential that has been central to Mediterranean maritime history. As a result of the intricacy and all-pervasiveness of seaborne interaction and the development from it of the more formal practice of establishing daughter-settlements, by the fifth century B.C. the whole sea had become virtually a single hinterland – the extended archipelago of the title of this section. The Greeks and Romans themselves recognized the world of the Greek maritime settlements as a cultural and social continuum. Cicero provides a memorable simile with which to register, retrospectively, the seaborne character of the spread of Greek culture: 'the shores of Greece are like hems stitched on to the lands of barbarian peoples' (*On the Republic*, 2.9).

Cicero wrote in the knowledge that the maritime world that he was describing had, thanks to Pompey's thalassocracy, become Roman.

For some time now [since Pompey's defeat of the pirates] we have seen that immeasurable sea, by whose disturbance not only the maritime routes [*cursus maritimi*] but even the cities and the military lines of communication were afflicted, by the courage of Gnaeus Pompeius and the Roman People kept safe and controlled from the Ocean to the furthest recess of the Black Sea, just as if it were a single harbour. (*On the Consuls' Provinces*, 12.31)

Little more than a century later, as reflected in St Paul's 'odyssey' in Acts, the foundations had been laid for the extended archipelago to be christianized. The islands and peninsulas that had been the sites of Hellenistic ports or Roman villas, proclaiming the power of the rulers of the sea, came in time to be the sites of holy communities such as Lérins or Athos. The Mediterranean network became a Christian one – informed by pilgrimage and crusade and by the wanderings of saints and their relics; sacralizing, and further demonstrating the coherence of, seaborne communications (Chapter X). The rulers of the sea began to define themselves by their religious allegiance: but their political behaviour continued to follow a 'logic' that had been observed for centuries. The maritime empire of classical Athens had once known a strategy called *epiteichismos*. This involved the fortification of beachheads supplied from the sea with which the adjacent land-powers could be harried. Islamic enterprise now fought to establish pockets of control on Christian shores, at Garde-Freinet in Provence, for instance, during the years 891–973, or in the marshes at the mouth of the river Garigliano in Italy. Christian leaders, whose aspiration to control the maritime milieu found its most ambitious expression in the Knights of St John, came to establish similar bases on the shores of the Maghreb, some of which – e.g. Melilla and Ceuta – have proved tenacious.

For the story does not end with the early modern period. In the waters where the term *epiteichismos* was coined, the insurgents of the Philhellene Fabvier made use of the Methana peninsula of the north-east Peloponnese as a base for occasional raids into Turkish territory in just the same way; they christened it the Cadiz of Greece, referring explicitly to similar events at the other end of the Mediterranean in the Spanish revolution of 1823 (Forbes 1982, 57). Up until the Second World War, Mediterranean *Realpolitik* remained as much a matter of the manipulation of extended hinterlands as it had been in the first millennium B.C. And although Tangier, Port-Mahon and Malta have now settled back into a more local frame of political reference, the divisions of Cyprus, the contested status of the Rock of Gibraltar, and the importance during the final years of the Cold War of military enclaves such as the American naval base at Cretan Soudha can still remind us of the more distant past. Since the advent of new maritime technologies in the nineteenth century, and above all since the advent of air travel and intercontinental ballistics, such reflections of Mediterranean unity can no longer be seen as the product of the totality of water-borne interactions between microregions. But they offer a potent reminder of how significant that totality has been (I.4).

In connectivity of this type, what is the place of sea routes as conventionally conceived? We have suggested that they can be treated as just a special instance of a broader phenomenon. Yet, while few doubt that land routes have been extremely various and resist mapping, Mediterranean sea routes have often been taken to be quite clearly defined. How then does our interpretation relate to the more usual image of the Mediterranean as ribbed with shipping lanes?

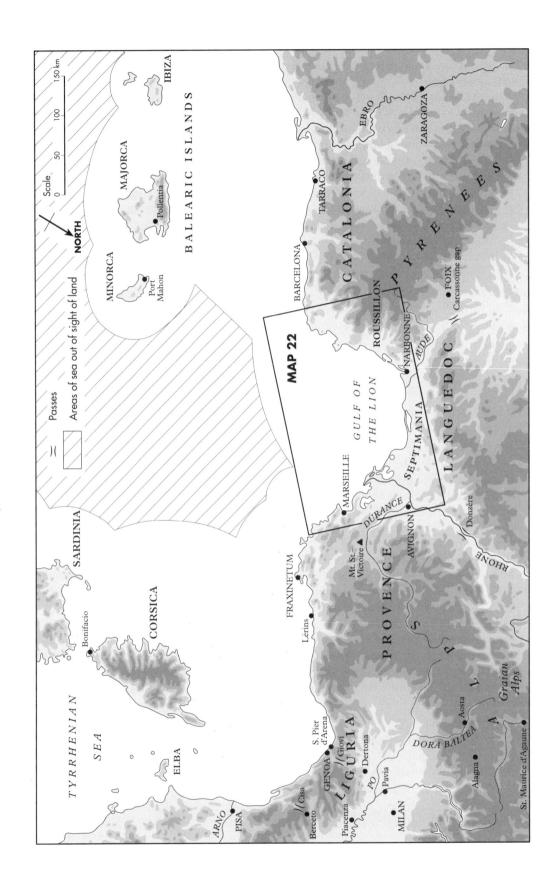

TYRRHENIAN

SEA

SARDINIA

CORSICA

Bonifacio

ELBA

BALEARIC ISLANDS

IBIZA

MAJORCA

Pollentia

MINORCA

Port
Mahon

NORTH

Scale
0   50   100   150 km

Passes

Areas of sea out of sight of land

EBRO

ZARAGOZA

CATALONIA

TARRACO

BARCELONA

PYRENEES

ROUSSILLON

FOIX
Carcassonne gap

NARBONNE

AUDE

MAP 22

GULF OF
THE LION

SEPTIMANIA

LANGUEDOC

MARSEILLE

DURANCE

AVIGNON

Donzère

RHONE

FRAXINETUM

Mt. St.-
Victoire ▲

PROVENCE

Lérins

A   L   P   S

Graian
Alps

Aosta

DORA BALTEA

Alagna

St. Maurice d'Agaune

S. Pier
d'Arena

GENOA

Giovi

Dertona

PO   Pavia

MILAN

LIGURIA

Cisa

Berceto

Piacenza

ARNO

PISA

3. SHIPPING LANES

Our answer can begin by returning to Cicero. His assessment of Pompey's achievement refers explicitly to *cursus maritimi*, sea routes. And this might well appear to be an ancient testimony to the wisdom of Febvre's remark about 'routes et villes'. The context is highly instructive, however. In Part One above we included the preconceptions of political and military power among those that have been most influential in forming historical attitudes to the Mediterranean, and that need to be treated with caution by the student of the *longue durée*. Here, in Cicero, is an example of their effect. For the requirements of naval might are vastly more specialized than the infrastructure within which everyday microregional interaction occurs. The ensemble of dockyards, arsenals, victualling stores, deep-water anchorages, and battle-zones will come to be linked by well-defined routes that are suitable for major warships. It is to routes of that kind that Cicero refers. And it is to routes of that kind that the attention of maritime historians has principally been drawn.

Onto the blurred and complex picture of communications that we derived from lines of sight can, then, be superimposed a far sharper image. It owes little to the versatility of ocular contacts and much to the capabilities of larger ships and to the imperatives of weather and current. The best presentation of this sharper image has been given by John H. Pryor (1988). His discussion is intended to apply to the period running from late Antiquity until the fourteenth century at least, and in many respects on into the early modern period. Let us look at some of its details. We shall suggest that Pryor mistakes the special case of large vessels, above all war ships, for the generality of navigation and thus exaggerates the constraints on the latter.

Pryor depicts merchant and war ships, sailing and oared vessels in the medieval Mediterranean as substantially determined in their habitual courses by a combination of technology, climate, and current: 'to a large degree man had to make his crossings of the sea in harmony with the forces of nature rather than in spite of them or against them' (1988, xiv). Summer and winter alike, nearly all the prevailing winds right across the Mediterranean sea blow from somewhere between north-west and north-east. The exception is the scirocco; but that is

---

Map 11   A *façade maritime*: from the Arno to the Ebro

From the coast of Liguria to the delta of the Ebro is a single *façade maritime*. High mountains or tumbled coastal chains lie close behind the shore over almost all of this area, and are interrupted only by small coastal plains. Over these four hundred kilometres of Mediterranean coastline, there are just four important corridors leading into continental space: the passes behind Genoa which give access to the upper Cisalpine plain; the Rhône valley, leading into the heart of France and to the upper Rhine; the Carcassonne gap, an easy route to the Garonne basin and the Atlantic coast of France; and the Ebro valley, which communicates with all the northern and central parts of Iberia. The focus of this *façade* is the embayment into which the Rhône debouches. Here the coastal plains are much wider, and are fringed with a noteworthy series of lagoons from the delta of the Camargue to the marshes at the mouth of the Ter in Catalonia. This area is portrayed in more detail on Map 22. The Golfe du Lion itself is a shallow continental shelf on which focus sea routes from the northern Tyrrhenian, from Tunisia via the west coast of Sardinia, and from the Strait of Gibraltar by the Spanish seaboard or the Balearic archipelago. The height of the mountains renders most of these waters visible from land.

too violent to be of much navigational help (20). Meanwhile, apart from currents flowing between Sicily and Libya, the general direction of the movements set up by the inflow of Atlantic water through the Straits of Gibraltar is anticlockwise. Winds and currents are therefore two potent and often opposing forces in the Mediterranean. In addition to these, the medieval mariner also had to take account of the dangers of many of the sea's southern lee-shores: numerous reefs and sandbanks (such as the Syrtes), a frequent lack of natural deep-water anchorage, coasts often too low-lying to afford clear landmarks (cf. Pryor 1988, 21, with Udovitch 1978, 543–4). Navigation was further complicated by the limitations of the ships themselves. 'They could maintain a real course at 90° to the wind only with great difficulty, even when that wind was by no means a gale force' (Pryor 1988, 35). This applied not only to earlier medieval vessels with lateen sails, shallow keels and rounded hulls, but also, to a considerable extent, to the cogs, carracks and galleys of later centuries. They all lacked windward capability (33–6, 51). Technological development made relatively little difference (Section 4 below).

So it becomes clear why long-distance voyages, above all voyages from east to west and south to north, could be made more safely and speedily along the chain of islands and coastlands in the northern waters of the Mediterranean (Pryor 1988, 14, fig. 2). Mariners would take advantage of the currents and of the daily cycle of coastal breezes to make their way against the prevailing winds that could otherwise render northern and western voyages impossible. In very general terms, if we could plot the results of navigators' decisions, we would arrive at a relatively uncluttered chart of maritime trunk routes or highways, zones within which medieval captains very commonly set course. For east–west voyages, the trunk routes ran from Alexandria to Tyre or Beirut. They then diverged – north to the area of Antioch and along the Lycian coast, or west to the south coast of Cyprus. The routes merged again at Rhodes and ran thence via Karpathos across to the south coast of Crete. From Crete they bent north into the Ionian Sea past Cephalonia, then across the Straits of Otranto, and around the Italian coast to the eastern end of Sicily. From Sicily, shipping could either turn north into the Tyrrhenian Sea and follow the Italian, French and Spanish coasts around to Gibraltar; or it could proceed south-west through the Sicilian channel, north-west again to the coast of Sardinia, and thence either north to the Provençal coast or due west across the open sea to the Balearics. From the Balearics, the routes made either west towards Gibraltar or southwards to the African coast (Pryor 1988, 7).

For voyages from west to east and north to south, the currents would have made a southern route faster. The prevailing winds were also generally more favourable and they allowed a greater choice of route. None the less, Mediterranean shipping still preferred to follow those northern lanes – even during the later Middle Ages, when more manoeuvrable cogs and carracks, a little better able to point into the wind, became, in Christian waters at least, increasingly common. Scattered along the northern lanes were the major ports and naval bases – Malaga, Bonifacio, Malta, Naxos, Rhodes, Attalya and others. These continued to exercise a 'gravitational pull' on shipping, and hence to define the shipping lanes, even when advances in design and in navigation had made a wider choice of route conceivable (1988, 54). Also on these lanes lay, not surprisingly, the chief battle zones of the various wars between Christian and Muslim forces from the eighth to the sixteenth centuries (7–8, 54).

In Pryor's pages we thus find in essence a scholarly amplification of Cicero's vision of the Mediterranean sea as marked out by *cursus maritimi*, adherence to which was made attractive by a combination of wind, current and technology. It is a substantive picture that would have been familiar not only to the orator but to Herodotus five centuries earlier. So far as it goes, therefore, there is nothing in this analysis from which we could reasonably dissent. In both Antiquity and the Middle Ages, Mediterranean shipping undoubtedly had its *preferred, long-distance*, commercial and naval routes which it followed – *other things being equal*. As soon as attention focuses on the words in italics, however, it becomes clear that some qualification must be entered, some complexity added to the simple chart of delimitable shipping lanes. This can be done here very largely on the basis of the evidence that Pryor himself offers. For of course, as he writes, geographical and technological factors were not the only ones that entered into the calculations of Mediterranean captains: 'economic and other considerations constantly induced ships to voyage away from the main trunk route sea lanes' (38). By giving still greater emphasis to the caveat, we can perhaps show how the supposedly clear definition of those trunk routes can be blurred. The apparent distance between Pryor's conception of maritime communications and our own might then diminish.

Two initial points of qualification concern the degree of contrast between north and south. First: the relative significance of the southern lanes should not be underestimated. Muslim navigators, cartographers, and geographers certainly knew about them. And those in a position to do so used them when they could – that is, when political circumstances permitted. The routes that followed the southern lee-shores were hardly unfamiliar. In the writings of the early Muslim geographers they are rather, as we should expect, the more fully recorded ones (Lewicki 1978, 447–8). Like the northern routes, they too had their insular ports and anchorages (Pryor 1988, 24). Moreover, if we look to the massive documentation of the Geniza archive for details of actual nautical practice, we can see there that direct routes between Egypt and the Maghreb were easily frequented by ships travelling in both directions, not just eastwards with the current (Section 7 below; cf. II.2). Indeed, the Arabic-speaking Jewish merchants whose enterprises loom so large in the Geniza were largely confined to the realm of Islam: they seem to have tested the northern routes hardly at all (Udovitch 1978, 562; Goitein 1967–88, 1.211–12).

Secondly: if the southern lanes should not be underestimated, nor should the northern ones be overpraised; they were by no means uniformly conducive to easy passage. The Palestinian coast, for example, proved extremely rough and challenging (Goitein 1967–88, 1.320). The eastern part of the south Anatolian coast was rocky and reef-strewn (Pryor 1988, 90, 98). The Italian side of the Adriatic was also unwelcoming: few landmarks, natural anchorages or sheltering offshore islands; and some dangerous shallows (93). North Africa had no monopoly of navigationally demanding coastline.

The discrepancies between northern and southern routes in the Middle Ages were not, then, quite so great as might have been suggested by the outline presented above. The south certainly had its fair share of accessible and popular shipping lanes. But giving due weight to them is not the only way in which the map of nautical communications must be more densely filled in. For one thing, some indication has to be added of the routes that crossed the open sea. These were especially attractive for vessels moving from north to south and, in the eastern Mediterranean, from east to west because they would have the prevailing wind behind them (Pryor 1988, 37, 95; Lewicki 1978, 452–67). Our suspicion is that underwater archaeology will increasingly reveal that the dangers of the open sea routes were far less of a deterrent to pre-modern mariners than has customarily been assumed (BE IX.4).

It is, however, even more important to stress quite how much choice faced the captain of a Mediterranean ship even when he had already made the decision broadly to follow one of the lanes that we have described. There were, in other words, routes within routes – a multitude of them. This was particularly so in the western part of the sea; the eleventh-century Muslim geographer al-Bakri (ed. de Slane 1965) for instance knew of some twenty ways of crossing from North Africa to his native Spain (Lewicki 1978, 458). We can simply point to the enormous diversity of courses that could be set through the Cyclades to show that the east was not so different (Pryor 1988, 91, 97).

In addition to these routes within routes, there were other routes quite different in type from the main shipping channels. Not so much in those 'deeps' out of sight of land, but rather across every stretch of Mediterranean coastline, the sailors whose practice defined these marine byways risked the dangers of shallows, headwinds or contrary currents for political or economic gain. Routes of this kind were too various in direction ever to be fully recorded. The myriad possible combinations of port, shelter, detour and accident comprised by even short journeys could hardly be mapped or set in writing – although some remote indication of them is perhaps to be found in the large number of minor anchorages and landmarks recorded, for example, by al-Bakri as defining the itinerary between al-Mahdiyya (in Tunisia) and Alexandria (cf. Udovitch 1978, 545). What was required in making such a journey was the maritime equivalent of that local knowledge of the Romagnol Apennines to which we referred earlier (Section 1). Such knowledge informed the navigation of innumerable small vessels.

These vessels could be engaged in any combination of a range of possible ventures: *cabotage* (or tramping), petty piracy, the transport of travellers and pilgrims. Although individually they operated on a small scale, they were probably responsible in aggregate for many more of the movements of goods and people around the sea than was *le grand trafic maritime* (Heers 1958). Braudel aptly called them 'proletarians of the sea' (1972a, 296). He emphasized how perennial their activity has been, and how dense: 'the importance of the shore was such that the coastal route was scarcely different from a river' (105). Indeed, as we have suggested, real rivers made a crucial contribution to Mediterranean connectivity. The 'fluvialization' of land transport which has been discerned in both the early Roman Empire and the later Middle Ages can be seen as an extension of the domain of *cabotage* deep into the heart of the continent (Lopez 1956, 22). Islands too have a vital part to play in the network of coastal

Map 12   Records of connectivity in Genoese ships' logs, 1351–70
'La mer est l'aventure; l'escale, la sécurité et l'occasion de fructueux profits' (Balard 1974, 258). Simone Lecavella was captain of a warship acting as rearguard to the fleet of Paganino Doria. His voyage in 1351–2 took 135 days and covered 5,480 nautical miles. Pellegro Maraboto sailed on a diplomatic mission in the winter of 1369–70, with merchants on board; he covered 3,700 nautical miles in 81 days, and about a third of his nights were spent at sea.

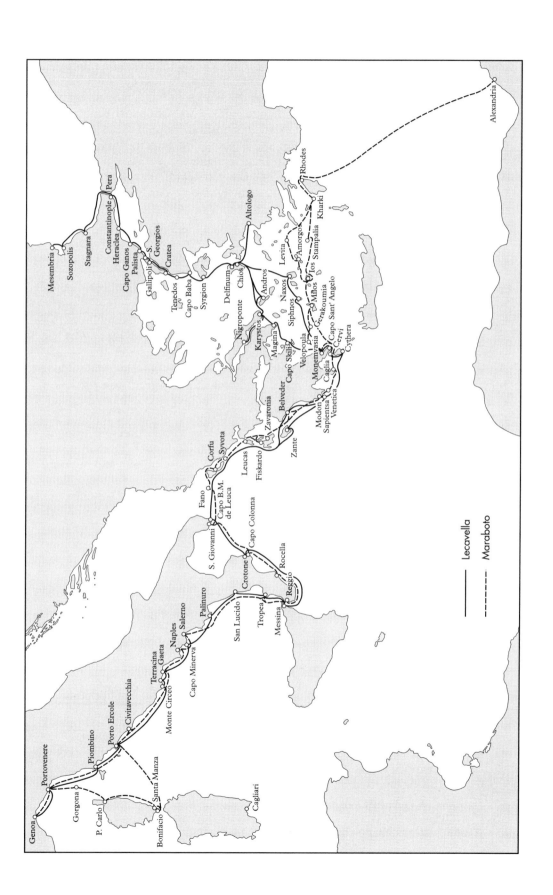

Genoa
Portovenere
Gorgona
P. Carlo
Piombino
Porto Ercole
Santa Manza
Bonifacio
Cagliari
Civitavecchia
Monte Circeo
Terracina
Gaeta
Naples
Capo Minerva
Salerno
Palinuro
San Lucido
Tropea
Messina
Reggio
Rocella
Crotone
Capo Colonna
S. Giovanni
Fano
Capo B.M. de Leuca
Corfu
Syvota
Leucas
Fiskardo
Zante
Zavaronia
Belveder
Modon
Sapientsa
Venetica
Capo Skilli
Velopoula
Monemvasia
Caglia
Cervi
Cythera
Capo Sant' Angelo
Gerakoumia
Mflos
Ios
Siphnos
Naxos
Amorgos
Levita
Stampalia
Kharki
Rhodes
Altologo
Andros
Chios
Delfinum
Karystos
Magina
Nigroponte
Syrgion
Capo Baba
Tenedos
Cratea
S. Georgios
Gallipoli
Palista
Capo Ganos
Heraclea
Constantinople
Pera
Stagnara
Sozopolis
Mesembria
Alexandria

Lecavella
Maraboto

contacts: 'les îles ont longtemps servi de carrefours et de tremplins de cabotage' (Kolodny 1974, 129). Commerce of this kind has an accidental, casual flavour about it; destinations, cargoes, the speed of the voyage, what was available and what was wanted in each locality all change, season to season. In the preceding chapter we used the image of a beaded string rather than Braudel's river: the beads are the dozens of anchorages and harbours on each journey, different each time because of the accidents of wind, current and the mariners' preferences. Map 12 illustrates something of this from the records of voyages made from Genoa in the fourteenth century. But the activity can be hard for the historian to see, especially in generally ill-documented times or places. The informal harbour – for which the Venetian label *scala*, literally a flight of steps, has become widespread in the Mediterranean – is of greater overall significance than the great naturally endowed port, a Piraeus or a Marseille.

The vessels frequenting informal harbours would mostly have been lateen-rigged: so at least was the two-master, only 15 metres long, that sank with its diverse cargo of glass and amphorae off the Turkish coast at Serçe Liman in the early eleventh century, and that is perhaps the best surviving example of this kind of ship (van Doorninck 1991; IX.4). It may be that the advantages of the lateen sail are easy to overstate. Once claimed as an innovation of the Middle Ages but actually attested in Antiquity (L. Casson 1971), its potential was seldom fully realized because of the dynamics of medieval ship design. None the less it can still reasonably be said that a small lateen sail is readily deactivated in sudden bad weather (Kreutz 1976, 98). Hugging the shore or island hopping for safety and for ease of navigation, vessels of *cabotage* could therefore respond quite rapidly to changing winds and currents. It is their 'Brownian motion' on the Mediterranean's perimeter that does most to fill the conceptual gap between potentially all-round communications (with which we began) and the restricted shipping lanes connecting major harbours that form Pryor's starting point.

A similar conclusion can be reached by turning, finally, from geography to the temporal dimension of maritime activity. The sailing season, the period from roughly early April to late October, is the chronological equivalent of shipping lanes: the clear limits within which maritime activity was commonly reckoned both safe and profitable. The annual winter standstill, when mariners often found the sea too stormy and visibility too poor, was, indeed, more honoured in the observance than in the breach. Changes in design and navigation during the later Middle Ages potentially extended safe sailing into earlier spring and later autumn (IX.4). Yet, whatever its timing, the contrast between open and close seasons remained quite pronounced. And it is no surprise to find its most vivid presentation in the pages of Braudel (1972a, 248–53, 260–4). On this score the broad continuity between Antiquity and the later medieval to early modern period is striking.

None the less, as with the summary of shipping lanes, some quite strong qualification must be introduced (Pryor 1988, 89). If the winter standstill was universally observed, why should various authorities have sought to enforce it through legislation? Why should al-Bakri have referred to a number of obscure points on the North African coast as suitable winter harbours (cf. Udovitch 1978, 548)? Large, strong ships could of course always put out during the winter months if travel was essential. Small tramping vessels could continue to avoid major winter hazards by keeping close to the shore (Braudel 1972a, 249).

Raiders – Dark Age Muslim pirates, for example (Kreutz 1976, 97) – could attack unexpectedly by risking a winter voyage. A bar chart of all nautical ventures (were records of them available) would then, in all probability, show both seasonal peaks, when masters *preferred* to put to sea, and a lower level of more or less constant activity throughout the year, the reflection of avarice, cunning or necessity. Certainly the registers of a tax levied on incoming ships to the capital of Majorca in the early fourteenth century show that the seasons had relatively little effect: 'almost any month could rate as a busy one' (Abulafia 1991, 46; cf. Abulafia 1994, 132–3). We shall see later in the chapter (Section 4) how that appears to have been equally true two millennia earlier. Potentially all-round connectivity was matched by potentially year-round enterprise.

4. Economies Compared

> Pray that yours will be a long voyage; and that there will be many summer mornings when you arrive – very gladly, and with the most grateful thanks – arrive at havens not known to you before. Drop anchor at Phoenician trading-ports and acquire beautiful wares, mother-of-pearl, coral, amber and ebony, and pleasurable perfumes of every kind, the most you can, amass the perfumes of pleasure. You will go to many of the cities of the Egyptians, and learn, learn from those who know.
> (Kavafy, *Ithaki*, 13–23)

So far in this chapter we have been discussing exchange in the context of communications in general. Focusing on the specifically economic concerns of Mediterranean communities does not, though, require any change of emphasis. The pattern of the redistribution of commodities can be seen as analogous with a dense mesh – too dense to imagine in terms of ribbons on a map. Sections of Chapter III, on 'four definite places' and on mountain environments and pastoralism, have already shown how rapidly the boundaries of Mediterranean microregions can shift. They have also suggested the variety of ways in which the economy of a microregion may be bound up with that of others. To the emergent picture we have added the typically dispersed hinterlands of larger settlements (Chapter IV) and the kinds of communication exemplified by acoustic and visual geography (Sections 1–2 above). All these can be aligned under the heading of the aggregates of 'short distances' that correspond to the definite places.

Also in Chapter III, we saw how a microecological approach could be brought into relation with the established narrative of Mediterranean *political* history. We should next begin to look at the concomitant narrative of *economic* history. 'Four definite places' pointed several times to the problems inherent in wide-ranging judgements about regional prosperity. So it is appropriate here to return to that theme, and to examine in a more general way how connectivity relates to the conventional narrative outline of Mediterranean exchange. Can the apparent gap between the two be narrowed?

On one hand there is the Brownian motion of *caboteurs*. On the other, there is a narrative outline that begins with the development under the Romans of a Mediterranean-wide exchange principally generated by the interests and purchasing power of aristocracy, state and army. The story moves on to the decline and fragmentation of that exchange in late Antiquity as a consequence of first Germanic and then Muslim invasion. There follows the recovery and boom of the high Middle Ages associated with the names of a handful of Italian cities and often considered a commercial revolution. Then, perhaps, the narrative allows an excursus – to the Muslim world and to the commercial primacy of Fatimid Egypt, epitomized in the activities of the Jewish communities in Cairo or the Karimi merchants. We return, however, to Europe for the height of medieval Western prosperity and domination represented by Italian colonies in Byzantium and the Caliphate. And the final chapter expounds the later medieval decline heralded by the Black Death. Told in these summary terms, the story is one of waxing and waning empires, of clear growth and decline in the volume and complexity of trade. It mainly involves the shipping of goods over long distances; and it dwells most on trade in luxuries – furs and delicate fabrics, precious metals and spices, exotic slaves. This is the commerce of Mediterranean poetry, of the Romantic images of 'Phlebas the Phoenician' type, juxtaposing the Odyssean struggles and tragic risks of seafaring with the precious fruits of the journey. The passage of Kavafy at the head of this section is a characteristic example. This is the elite trade by comparison with which – and the comparison is effectively a transfer to historical analysis of the Romantic schema – the *caboteur* is a 'proletarian'.

Such a 'high commerce', often prestigious, usually of great economic value, can indeed be discerned in many periods of Mediterranean history. Its glamour has encouraged scholars to study it in isolation. Here we wish to stress five ways in which harm can result from that.

First, the glamour of high commerce may detach particular instances of it from their real social context and idolize them: 'Nous connaissons déjà ce type de commerce, ou plutôt, ce type de représentation économique, qui voit les échanges surtout dans un sens et imagine le négoce international comme une sorte de pompe aspirante au bénéfice d'un monde musulmane qui ne rendrait rien' (Miquel 1967–88, 2.462).

Our aim, by contrast, has been to replace the almost mystical attachment of French geographical historians to the concept of routes with a notion of shifting webs of casual, local, small-scale contacts radiating from slightly different centres in different ages but constant in their economic and social effect – with something nearer, in fact, to Braudel's own formulation: 'the whole Mediterranean consists of movement in space' (1972a, 277). We hope thereby to undercut the dualism of existing approaches to Mediterranean trade, which are founded on a clear distinction between the world of 'high commerce', *la grande navigation*, and small coastwise movements. Insistence on this dualism (we believe) makes the sophistication of the one end of the spectrum harder to explain, and distracts attention from the humbler movements at the other end, although these are a fundamental ingredient in the social and economic history of the Mediterranean. (The same dualism also renders the economy of demand more obscure. In this work, we shall mostly be stressing supply, but the attention which the social and economic history of demand is beginning to receive is naturally welcome; cf. Foxhall 1998a.)

A second problem arising from a concentration on high commerce is that, among the ordinary redistributive processes which are overlooked, there is a whole set of highly effective but illegal, informal, arbitrary movements. These have, at some periods, exceeded regular commerce in importance, and include the activities of the pirate, the brigand or the plunderer. In reality, the seizure of passing goods or travellers by simple force is a perennial form of the redistribution which we have been describing; it is easier and perhaps more natural than trade, and has the merit for the historian of being attested throughout the ages (Section 5 below; IX.6).

Third, high commerce has usually been closely, if not exclusively, linked with the history of a particular variety of economic sophistication, with topics such as credit, insurance, investment, trade guilds, elaborate port architecture, protectionism, capital growth. Interest in such specialized outgrowths and accompaniments of redistribution has distracted from the study of the latter. Worse, it has created the impression that the two are indissoluble, encouraging a progressivist approach to economic history in which the advent or disappearance of these possible adjuncts of elite exchange calibrates primitiveness or modernity. But sophistication of that sort is not a necessary condition of high commerce. Significant volumes and densities of exchange can exist without such infrastructure. Indeed it is less the absence of that infrastructure (in periods of supposed decline) than its presence at other times which needs remark – as has been excellently well demonstrated for ships of large tonnage. These served a very specialized economic purpose in the grain trade of ancient Rome (when ships reached 600 tonnes' burden quite frequently), but were not to be met again until the inception of that striking phenomenon, the alum trade of fifteenth-century Genoa. Their absence in other places and at other times, for example the earlier Middle Ages, cannot, however, be taken as a symptom of economic primitivism or recession. '"Un navire trop grand pour un marché donné coûte vraiment trop cher" . . . c'est à partir du moment où il faut acheminer régulièrement des produits pondéreux ou volumineux sur un long parcours que les gros tonnages deviennent intéressants' (Pomey and Tchernia 1977, 251).

From the elements of economic sophistication, it is worth identifying the history of nautical technology as giving rise to a fourth way in which the privileging of high commerce has led to distortions. It is true that ships were relatively expensive. The ancient historian Ammianus Marcellinus (*History*, 14.8.4) regarded as a wonder the fact that Cyprus could build ships entirely from its own resources; construction usually depended on existing shipping to assemble the raw materials for new vessels and their equipment. But these are the ships of high commerce, at the top end of the scale. The norm is the little boat of the *caboteur*. And with respect to this norm (as to other aspects of technological history: Chapter VII), we can stress again that technological improvements appear local and ephemeral: they have been less profoundly revolutionary than enthusiastic historians in search of turning-points have claimed; or, where they have had a brilliant future in front of them, it has been many years before their potential has been realized. In medieval Italy of the eleventh to thirteenth centuries, 'improvements in naval architecture were made with respect to increase in size and to modifications to long-established designs rather than to any radically new features' (Pryor 1988, 31; contrast P. Jones 1997, 183). We have already considered the case of the lateen sail (Section 3). As for the compass, 'navigation out of sight of land without a compass had never been very difficult in the Mediterranean. Even after the compass was well known and widely available, shipping continued to navigate the Mediterranean without it because it was not really essential there' (Pryor 1988, 53). The size of ships, and in particular their capacity to carry supplies (above all, water), was much more important than their navigational equipment in determining the extent to which direct passages across the deeper sea were attempted in addition to *cabotage* by way of coasts and islands.

And this brings us to the fifth and most serious issue, which is nothing less than that of how Mediterranean history should be periodized. We have seen some of the distortions that arise from rigidly separating the ancient 'consumer' city from its 'productive' medieval successor (IV.5). In analogous fashion, the presence or absence of high commerce has been one of the touchstones by which epochs have been classified. The classification has usually had a more or less Whiggish, teleoscopic intent: to investigate primarily those parts of economic history which may be regarded as precursors and perhaps ancestors of economic institutions and practices that have been central to the European economy and its worldwide ramifications since the sixteenth century. The consequence has inevitably been to devalue practices which cannot be usefully seen as embryonic modernity – practices which are quite different in kind and may be more interestingly comparable with forms of economic behaviour in, say, Asia or the pre-Columbian Americas. An openness to such comparisons enables us to see what is distinctive and interesting about Mediterranean history – what is there, rather than what is missing. For the teleoscopic perspective encourages the itemizing of absences and shortfalls: a historiographical strategy which is helpfully, if pejoratively, labelled minimalism.

In the case of the Mediterranean, minimalism originated primarily in the age of the 'Battle of the Books', in the Enlightened vindication of Modernity against the all-too-potent and essentially reactionary glorification of Greek and Roman Antiquity (VIII.1). In the twentieth century, it has taken the form of a series of claims about the economic primitiveness of the distant Mediterranean past which find some justification in contemporary inflated and anachronistic visions of a mercantile Golden Age in Antiquity. On this minimalist view the vast majority of the people of the ancient Mediterranean were engaged in essentially self-supporting agriculture which created little surplus and small aggregate demand. Transport costs were cripplingly high, technology stagnant. Such interregional trade as there was concerned mainly luxuries for the tiny aristocratic elite, though there was from time to time a command economy supplying staples to a few favoured centres. Traders were despised, and the institutional and physical infrastructure of trade was inadequate. On this foundation, established by A. H. M. Jones (1964), Finley (1985a, published first in 1973) built the vision of an 'ancient economy' which could be identified and distinguished from (especially) its medieval successors. Informed by social anthropology, and especially by the work of Karl Polanyi, Finley pursued the laudable project of exploring the distinctive features of ancient Mediterranean cultures. His work embodied a galvanizing imperative not to make retrojections into Antiquity of the characteristics of later forms of economic organization. Ultimately, however, the project was sabotaged by the use of the 'minimalizing' comparative technique. Its thrust remained essentially negative: a generation was taught – in a very emphatic way – what was *not* important in the pre-medieval Mediterranean (cf. Foxhall 1990b, 22–3).

Adding the notion of 'the ancient economy' to an already progressivist account of social and economic history makes sensible periodization very difficult. First, it lumps together the actually extremely diverse economic systems of the first millennium B.C. and the first half of the first millennium A.D., inhibiting their proper interpretation. In the process, it reifies the divisions between

'Antiquity' and later prehistory on the one hand, and the early Middle Ages on the other. In the interests of long-term comparative Mediterranean history, we believe, on the contrary, that it is essential to overcome the prejudices and traditional hostilities which have hindered prehistoric archaeologists, classical historians and medievalists in learning from one another. The concept of 'the ancient economy' makes this type of comparison much more fraught. And the problem is an unavoidable, structural consequence of the strategy involved in *classifying economies chronologically*. The search for common denominators using the comparative approach across wide spans of space and time seems to us more promising than asserting schizophrenic splits of historical experience created around 'turning-point' events on the teleoscopic scale. The notion of an ancient economy is inextricably compromised by that species of historiography (cf. VIII.1 for its equivalent in the history of catastrophe). Apart from mere chronology, in the economic behaviour of the Etruscans, Carians, Romans, Spartans, Carthaginians, Mycenaeans, Tartessians or Vandals, there was nothing which deserves the title 'ancient'. But there was much that merits the label Mediterranean.

A further flaw in minimalism is that many aspects of it owe less to economic actuality than to normative wishful thinking on the part of the ancient persuaders. The elites of Antiquity whose opinions are best represented in the surviving literature went to great lengths to marginalize those who engaged in commerce (as they did those who received pay for their work). Changes in prevailing sentiments of this type are not to be confused with changes in the character of an economy. It would be rash, for instance, to make much (with Lopez 1959, 84–5) of the apparent contrast between the ancient-style prejudice against commerce of Byzantine Greeks and the hardy and modern-sounding opportunism of Venice.

Not that the ancient authors presented a united front on this topic: there are many evocations of practices which closely resemble those of high commerce as we see them in later periods. The hymns of praise to profit which we know from the Hellenistic period – including the extreme 'let me be called a bad man, so long as I make a profit' – are perhaps wilfully paradoxical inversions of the literary and philosophical orthodoxies (Diodorus Siculus, *Historical Library*, 37.30). But there are other arresting passages too. In the *Odyssey* the hero is appalled to be thought a trader. By contrast his divine patron, the wise Athena, disguises herself as a roving warrior-captain with a cargo of iron. The goddess may suitably stand at the head of a tradition of heroic merchants that is integral to the weave of Mediterranean historiography. In overtly Odyssean fashion, the historian Herodotus criss-crosses his Mediterranean with the tracks of wanderers: among the *condottieri* and 'culture heroes', he gives a special place to Kolaios of Samos and Sostratos of Aegina, the most redoubtable traders known before his time, fabulously successful in their dealings in southern Spain and in Etruria. Later, the captains of the acme of Athenian connectivity appear in the oratorical writings of the fourth century, their achievements prefigured by the faint praise of that reluctant thalassocrat, the 'Old Oligarch':

> and if we are to recall smaller advantages too, it is through the rule of the sea that the Athenians have been quick to research the varieties of good living, mixing with different people in different places: whatever is pleasurable in Sicily or in Italy, in Cyprus or in Egypt, in Lydia or Pontus or the Peloponnese, or anywhere else, it is all gathered into one place – through the rule of the sea. ([Xenophon] *Constitution of the Athenians*, 2.7)

In the Roman imperial period, connectivity became one of the wonders of pan-Mediterranean power, for all its banausic associations. The encyclopaedist Pliny grudgingly explains the arcana of meteorology; he thinks these are unjustly despised by the vast crowd of so many thousands who make voyages, using the open sea and 'the welcoming reception of all the coastlines' (*hospitalis adpulsus litorum omnium*) (*Natural History*, 2.118). The inscriptions of both the Hellenistic and Roman periods reflect this recognition of the paradoxical glory of seaborne communications, and attest the commercial achievements of some of those who used the ever more lavish port facilities and larger vessels of the time:

> If you don't mind, guest, stop and read. I have often run across the Great Sea in sail-winged ships; I have visited very many lands, but this is the final boundary-marker which the Fates once sang for me as I was born. Here have I laid down my worries and all my labours: here I have no anxieties about the stars or clouds or the rough sea, and I do not fear that expenses might outweigh my profit. Kindly Credit, I thank you, most holy Goddess: three times you restored me when I was exhausted by the foundering of my luck. You are worthy to be chosen personally by every mortal. Life and health to you, guest, and may you always get the better of your expenses, since you have not despised this stone and thought it a worthy memorial. (*CIL*, 9.60, Brundisium)

It is natural to juxtapose this text, from the end of the first century, with the archives of the Cairo Geniza or the literary relics of the great traders of the late medieval Mediterranean. The dazzling fame of a Kolaios or a Sostratos seems readily comparable with the reputations of the great Italian merchant patricians such as Benedetto Zaccaria (cf. Braudel 1986, 11–12). Nor, in making the comparison, would we be setting up a handful of ancient examples against a plethora of medieval ones. Such men were, after all, not commonplace in Christendom, nor do they have easily discoverable counterparts in the medieval Islamic world. And there may have been many more of them in ancient times than has customarily been supposed.

The archive of wax tablets, roughly contemporary with the inscription just quoted, that was discovered in the middle of the twentieth century at Murecine near Pompeii shows the complexity and value of the trading interests of the port of Puteoli (Wolf and Crook 1989). Such interests, too, begin to seem comparable with those of the Merchant of Prato. Their social and cultural framework was, however, quite different: the principle of Roman business-life appears to have derived from the duties that were owed at law by the freed slave to his former owner. For these enabled a reliable form of agency to exist in the absence of other kinds of commercial association – while carefully preserving the invisibility of the notables at the top end of the tiers of freedmen and freedmen's freedmen. As Finley protested (1985a, 137–8), the excavators of ancient cities have indeed found no Cloth Halls, or other quasi-medieval symbols of the political standing of entrepreneurs (IV.5). But that cultural difference is not germane to the comparative study of levels of economic connectivity.

Minimalist accounts of the Mediterranean economy before the Middle Ages have been accustomed to draw attention to the alleged absence then of high commerce, and to suggest that only high commerce would do to establish a comparison between the later Middle Ages and what went before. At the same time, such accounts have been inclined to belittle ancient trade – for all the world like the Old Oligarch – as the frivolous support of a leisured elite. Yet as Braudel showed long ago, in discussing the economic importance of the spice trade (1972a, 442), the very high values of the cargoes of high commerce represent very considerable movements of capital; their social history is of far greater overall importance than the practical significance of the activities that they represent might suggest (Sherratt and Sherratt 1991). We must not be misled into thinking that, because its bulk was small and its recipients few, 'luxury' trade was economically insignificant. Nor, in a study of levels of connectivity, should we be particularly concerned that much ancient trade (and not only ancient trade) was 'directed' trade, or the result of a command economy, aimed at the supply of the state or the army. The 'market' is among those features of modernity whose presence or absence in the past is principally of interest from the progressivist point of view. (Which has not deterred proponents of one response to minimalism from attempting to reinstate the market, alongside other aspects of formalist economics, even in the Bronze Age.)

It is certainly a 'state document' that provides the most unexpected and arresting new evidence for many years about eastern Mediterranean commerce in the mid-first millennium B.C. For sheer completeness, this document will find few (if any) parallels before the early modern period (cf. Lopez and Raymond 1955, 135). Painstaking editorial work on an Aramaic palimpsest from Elephantine in Upper Egypt has revealed the official record of the customs dues exacted by the Persian government of Egypt at a port of the Delta in the year 475 (Porten and Yardeni 1993, 82–195, and Excursus 3, xx–xxi). The repetitive nature of this long text enables reconstruction of the complete roster of arrivals and departures during that year, with the nature of both inbound and outbound cargoes, and the origins of the ships. Forty-two vessels paid duty between February and December 475 – across, it should be noted, a very long sailing season (Section 3). Thirty-six of them were Ionian Greek, and six Phoenician. The level of duty was high, including nearly a tonne of silver. The imports were varied, embracing wine, oil, wood, wool, various metals and empty jars, which were perhaps used for the export cargoes, in every case solely composed of mineral soda (*natron*), the raw material of much textile processing. We shall return to various aspects of this particularly interesting text in later chapters. For now, it is simply worth stressing how a single document corrects the prevailing picture of primitivism in archaic Greek commerce. Here is a port wholly devoted, it appears, to the export of a single valuable raw material (which shows that we are not dealing with one of the major gateway-ports of Egypt but with somewhere less grand). The sophistication of the commercial relationships that are revealed accords with what letters on lead tablets from the Black Sea and the western Mediterranean have begun to show us about the nature of Greek trade with non-Greeks in the sixth century. But it is striking also that the ships engaged in this specialized and high-value trade away from Egypt not only had diverse origins, but were also relatively small – to judge from plausible reconstruction of the total size of the cargoes, no larger than a few dozen tonnes' burden. Moreover, the inbound cargoes were the extremely varied ones that we should expect of commerce which retained, despite the sums of money involved, close links with *cabotage*.

Thus far luxuries for the most part; but yet another way in which the minimalist orthodoxy has come to be questioned concerns the volume of interregional trade in staples, especially as revealed by the ubiquitous archaeological evidence. This evidence suggests that under the Romans (if not before) empire-wide trade – over land as well as sea – seems to have been much more voluminous and pervasive than Finley or Jones would have conceded. 'Ecology, history and society all find a new role through a shift in focus from the exclusively regional to the more broadly Mediterranean' (Papadopoulos 1997, 207). During the later Empire for instance, the type of pottery known as African Red Slip ware (ARS) achieved a remarkable degree of market penetration:

> there were some places, like northern Italy, that ARS did not reach until late, but inside the areas it did reach, such as those covered by the central Italian field surveys in Etruria [cf. III.2] and Molise, the latter by no means easily accessible or prosperous, it can be found even on the smallest sites, thus indicating that it was available even to peasants: a mass-produced, long-distance commodity, only semi-luxury, cheap enough for everyone to buy, just the sort of product in fact that Jones and Finley tended to ignore. (Wickham 1988a, 190)

We return to the whole subject of redistribution in much more detail in Chapter IX, where we shall encounter many other instances of the increasing *rapprochement* between the economies of the Greeks and Romans and other parties in the ancient and prehistoric Mediterranean on the one hand, and their medieval successors (Byzantine, barbarian or Islamic) on the other. The Finleyan orthodoxy is thus being eroded by the simple accumulation of contrary evidence – the natural fate of overbold, negative asseverations. A single find such as the Elephantine Palimpsest can have a devastating effect. The more telling argument against minimalism has, however, been theoretical. It is based on the closer comparison of Mediterranean connectivity across the millennia, and it is to be sought in the Brownian motion of the world of what we can call 'low commerce'.

Even when its high counterpart was at its highest, the volume of *cabotage* probably exceeded that of the great commercial ventures (Heers 1958). And the relatively 'small' traders involved in it were quite capable of dealing in a tremendous variety and quantity of goods, as is amply demonstrated by the documents from the Cairo Geniza (Goitein 1967–88, 1.153–5; cf. Hopkins 1978a, 51–2). Our estimate of the characteristic levels (as against the peaks) of economic activity in the Mediterranean may therefore have to be reduced a little; but we shall be drawing a fairer picture of the medieval norm than is implied by a study of, say, Benedetto Zaccaria. And doing that will, in this respect, again bring Antiquity and the Middle Ages quite close to one another. In either, the movements of goods associated with connectivity across 'short distances' take up a far larger portion of the overall picture than the usual narrative would suggest. After all, the more glamorous high commerce itself involved numerous small commercial outlets, as even the poetic image of Kavafy suggested. 'Short distances' stand for what is not directly comprehended in the standard glamorous story of commercial networks: frequent overnight stops; an extremely dense and mutable pattern of movement; and the redistribution of a great variety of goods, not just luxuries. In sum, the profound, widespread, and lasting interdependence of Mediterranean microregions. We shall be pressing this argument further at several points in Part Three. At this stage, it is enough to suggest how reference to short distances brings into focus the more or less constant 'background noise' to the history of Mediterranean exchange across both Antiquity and the Middle

Ages: the invisible currents – to use Braudellian metaphor – beneath the swell of great commercial empires.

In emphasizing this repetitive background we are by no means implying that the usual story embodies an illusion, that there were not some changes of the utmost importance in the volume and objects of trade, or in the institutions and cultures associated with it: the Genoese or Venetian empires are hardly to be written out of significant existence. Rather, the point is simply that the obvious fluctuations in Mediterranean high commerce can usefully be approached – and indeed explained – as it were from the bottom up: by looking, in Braudellian manner, at their recurrent, less glamorous, features instead of working from the top downwards. 'High' and 'low' commerce are inextricable, and the former is best seen as depending on the latter (IX.4), arising out of it, declining into it, in overlapping phases (to anticipate VI.1 and VII.4) of what might be labelled intensification and abatement.

Some characteristics of the 'low' background are described in later chapters and need only brief rehearsal here. *First*, even to think in terms of exchange over any significant distance – *cabotage* and the like – is not necessarily to be 'touching bottom' in analytical terms. At that fundamental level, we should envisage the kinds of diversification and year-by-year adjustment that we have already seen being achieved by the producers met in Chapter III (cf. VI). These responses to environmental risk often simulate the results of redistribution, even when they do not reflect its conscious practice (Chapter IX). Just as important a response to risk is the habit of storing surpluses: an interannual exchange, in effect, operating within a single enterprise. And all this is, of course, in addition to the highly localized but genuine exchanges embodied in customary reciprocity between neighbours, or between smallholder and lord or patron. Engagement in the wider world of redistribution has no more glamour than the other vital means of diminishing risk. It need not be popular or 'smart'. On the contrary, it is often stigmatized as uncertain, dangerous, demeaning or immoral, too closely involved with the corruption induced by the sea. Contact with wider horizons is not necessarily embraced with enthusiasm. The necessity of redistribution does not erode the charm of autarky. Rather the reverse – it makes that charm comprehensible (IV.7). Here is a further example of that dazzle of ancient arguments to which we have already alluded. The enthusiasm for self-sufficiency of the ancient literary tradition – and its medieval inheritors – is a sure sign that this was a goal hard of attainment, a goal which needed high levels of persuasion before it was even attempted.

Secondly, the importance of land transport to Mediterranean redistribution should not be underestimated (IX.4). Even goods mainly transported by sea usually had to be moved overland to or from harbours. And where necessary, bulky goods could be taken across extremely arduous terrain, for example the Romagnol Apennines (Section 1). Land transport was always relatively expensive: only very modern technologies would alter that. But it must not be assumed that its high cost was inevitably prohibitive. Above all, as we saw with the example of the road from Oropos to Athens (Section 1 again), local circumstances could induce patterns of microregional interaction quite different from what is apparently dictated by simple physical realities. It was to accommodate just such imponderables that, in Chapter III, we replaced a geographically determined microregional picture with our own conception of the ecology.

Thirdly, even in periods when overall demand was at its slackest, and the movement of luxuries least in evidence, the requirements of the relatively poor could remain very large in total and generate an interregional trade in cloth, foodstuffs and perhaps other commodities too. We shall find signs of this in the next section and much more detail in Chapter IX.

Finally, such demand was quickened by minute spatial and temporal variation in the environment. The four local examples in Chapter III show how Mediterranean rainfall varies immensely from one year to another and from one place to another (cf. Table 1). To the notion of a microecology must be added that of a microclimate (to be developed in Volume 2). Hopkins (1978a, 1983b) and Garnsey (1988a, ch. 2), for example, have used modern agricultural statistics to emphasize what Braudel had already made clear in his study of sixteenth-century famine (1972a, 328–32): years of glut and severe shortage follow each other in a Mediterranean microregion, not only with alarming unpredictability, but in a sequence that may be quite different from that of adjacent regions. Consider the recent order of magnitude of average interannual variations in wheat yields in Mediterranean lands. Egypt has the lowest variation (12 per cent) and was therefore probably not only the most substantial but also the most reliable producer of wheat in ancient and medieval times, her yield dependent on the varying height of the Nile flood rather than on microclimatic conditions. Other countries fare rather worse: Lebanon (42 per cent), Tunisia (67 per cent), Italy (21 per cent) and so on. Moreover, these national averages conceal enormous and still more local variations, such as those of the Biqa valley (III.1). If wheat yields varied thus, from both year to year and place to place, crops of other grains would have been comparably unpredictable. Wine and oil production would have fluctuated still more. All this could create sudden local demand that a microenvironment could not satisfy but local traders perhaps might. A Roman legal authority writing at the period when the Roman Empire made possible maximum interdependence could still rule that

> This suit is left to the discretion of the Judge, because we are aware how greatly prices vary between one community and another, and between regions: above all in the case of wine, oil, and cereals. Even granted, moreover, that currency does have a uniform value everywhere, in some places it can be raised easily and at low interest, while in others only with more difficulty and at a high rate of interest. (*Digest*, 13.4.3 *preamble*, Gaius, *Commentary on the Provincial Edict*, bk 9)

A reminder that money is also part of the capricious environment, another Mediterranean resource of very uneven distribution. In many periods, even recent ones, Mediterranean lands have, moreover, not even enjoyed the monetary sophistication that Gaius takes for granted.

To emphasize the lowest common denominators of redistribution is not, to repeat, intended as a denial of the obvious cultural differences between Minoan palace officials, Hesiodic landowners and early Byzantine senators, or between the commercial networks of Hellenistic Rhodes and tenth-century Cairo. But it does offer a genuine opportunity, first, for identifying the degree of continuity that can defensibly be predicated of Mediterranean redistribution and therefore, secondly, for making a contribution to the debate on a very vexed question of Mediterranean history, the transition between Antiquity and the Middle Ages.

5. THE EARLY MEDIEVAL DEPRESSION

To what extent can the Mediterranean Sea be said to have displayed continuous connectivity throughout the ancient and medieval periods, and at what level? The answer to that is best sought from the very early Middle Ages.

To judge by the evidence of shipwrecks, the late Roman Republic and early Empire may well have witnessed more trans-Mediterranean commercial shipping than did the next millennium. By the late Empire, the fourth to sixth centuries, long-distance exchange was thus (by the same measure) very much reduced, especially in the western Mediterranean. According to the archaeology of settlement meanwhile, demand was, as we should expect, shrinking; and much of the demand that remained was determined, however indirectly, by the exactions of the government. Traditional civic life entered a decline, contraction, reconfiguration – earlier in the west than in the east. Overall population levels fell noticeably, although parts of the Byzantine Empire enjoyed a temporary boom until bubonic plague arrived in the mid-sixth century and Persian and Arab invaders in the seventh. Exchange networks became highly circumscribed. In short, the Mediterranean maritime economy was entering a severe depression from which it would not begin to emerge until, at the earliest, the very end of the ninth century. Even then, recovery would be visible only in the newer ports of Italy; and, to judge by the size of harbours such as Amalfi's (Kreutz 1988; IV.8), transmarine shipping and commerce were still extremely small in scale.

Such, more or less, is the least controversial picture that can be painted of Mediterranean exchange during the obscure transition from late Antiquity to the early Middle Ages. It is worth noting, parenthetically, how far its validity depends on acceptance of the revisions to the Finley–Jones orthodoxy mentioned earlier: unless, that is, a substantial volume of interregional redistribution is conceded to the *ancient* Mediterranean, there can have been no preceding apogee from which the early Middle Ages could markedly decline. In another sense, however, this agreed picture of late Antiquity and the early Middle Ages is closer to the old orthodoxy than to its revisions. The 'minimalist' view of ancient trade has not been entirely abandoned; it has just been transferred to a slightly later period. According to this newer minimalism, it is the seventh century rather than the second in which aggregate demand was small, merchants were lowly, and only luxuries could profitably be moved over long distances.

For all that, the early medieval depression is of course inextricably associated with neither Jones nor Finley but rather with Henri Pirenne, whose 'thesis' about its causes was outlined in Chapter II. This depression makes an excellent test case for our own theses – about the essential connectivity of Mediterranean microregions, and about the quite high degree of transmarine interaction generally to be expected in the pre-modern Mediterranean. Our main concern with the Pirenne period is not to produce a revised theory of the origins of decline – warfare, Vandal or Muslim piracy, over-taxation, general insecurity, demographic collapse, the weakening (in the east) or disappearance (in the west) of the late Roman state. Some doubts about many of these supposedly disastrous features of the period will emerge parenthetically in what follows (and in IX.4). For reasons already given, we are particularly resistant to the 'top-down' approach which sees the whole spectrum of economic life in late Antiquity as epiphenomenal to state transfers of goods; we might rather envisage the Pirenne period in terms of a complex tangle of 'abatements' (VII.4; Gunderson 1976). But the principal task here, more simply, is to see how much interregional as well as local exchange continues to be evident, for whatever reason. That is, we are more concerned with the results than with the explanation of economic changes in the early Middle Ages. The Pirenne period should enable us to hear, and assess the volume of, the constant 'background noise' of economic life more accurately than is possible during periods, both earlier and later, dominated by strident commercial networks. We shall certainly *not* expect to find unbroken continuity: the broad similarities between ancient and medieval economies that we have just been emphasizing certainly do not entail that. But, if we are right about the common factors behind the redistribution of commodities, from the microecological level upwards, and about the nature of connectivity, then we ought to find, widespread, a certain amount of movement on more than a tightly regional scale. It does not have to be strictly commercial: seizure in war, piracy, state intervention, aristocratic gift-exchange or ecclesiastical poor relief can be just as effective in promoting the satisfaction of demand. Persistent signs of activity should however be detectable – and at something greater than those exceedingly low levels that have so often been postulated for so many parts of the post-Roman Mediterranean. 'We . . . have progressed a long way down the road to destroying the myth of the Dark Ages as a depopulated, self-sufficient, wilderness covered era' (Moreland 1994, 107).

To begin to support that confident verdict, we should leave aside the 'declining years' of the ancient economy (roughly from the collapse of the western Empire – earlier in some accounts – to the Muslim conquests). We need instead to develop some general points concerning the period that has chiefly engaged Pirenne and his critics, roughly the later seventh to earlier ninth centuries. This, as Pirenne famously argued, was the period during which the advances of Muslim pirates brought about the gradual disappearance of the trade in papyrus, spices, wine and textiles that the western Roman Empire and its barbarian successor states had previously elicited from the east. Pirenne and his numerous commentators differ over the vitality of Mediterranean economies in the preceding period, the sixth or early seventh centuries; most archaeologists and historians now see those centuries as ones of severe economic recession in the West and (at best) incipient decline in the eastern Mediterranean. They agree with Pirenne, though, on this, that the 'long eighth century' (cf. Wickham and Hansen forthcoming) witnessed the nadir of exchange networks in the region. That was the period, they argue, when east–west trade in the Mediterranean thinned to the merest trickle – when connectivity was at its lowest. Our response to such arguments can begin by focusing on the piracy and naval warfare of the period, so crucial to Pirenne's account but somewhat neglected since.

(1) We should be aware at the outset how far conclusions of the type that we are challenging stand in a venerable tradition. 'The Muslims gained control over the whole Mediterranean . . . The Christian nations could do nothing against the Muslim fleets, anywhere in the Mediterranean. All the time, the Muslims rode its waves for conquest.' Ibn Khaldun's hyperbole (trans. Rosenthal 1967, 2.41) is not simply the forerunner of Pirenne's account of the belated collapse

of the ancient economy. It also reinforces that tendency, on which we commented earlier (I.4), to view Mediterranean maritime history simply as a sequence of achieved thalassocracies. The ninth century can thus become 'the Islamic imperium', an age of 'undisputed [Muslim] mastery over the whole Mediterranean' (cited from Kreutz 1976, 87). Yet even granting the usefulness of 'thalassocracy' as a descriptive term, a more nuanced account of its application to the Pirenne period is clearly desirable.

That, then, is the first general point to make about the early medieval depression: whatever the effects on commerce of maritime hostilities between Christendom and Islam in the early Middle Ages, they were far from constant in magnitude or distribution. Long periods of *de facto* truce or stalemate alternated with outbursts of hostility. Areas of supposed dominance showed themselves surprisingly variable in their allegiance. In the western Mediterranean basin, for example, Muslim pirates had been operating since the conquest of North Africa in 698, but their activities had declined by the middle of the eighth century as they encountered first Byzantine and then Frankish resistance; there followed almost half a century of maritime quiet. This phase ended in 798 with a raid by Spanish Moors on the Balearic islands, which had been conquered by Muslim forces from Tunisia as long previously as 707 but were, by this stage, under nominal Byzantine rule. The attack prompted the islanders to transfer their loyalty to Charlemagne.

The fact that the Frankish king was seen as able to ensure their defence may be surprising. Time and again in Mediterranean history, supposed landlubbers take to the sea with a success that astonishes historians because they forget the sheer normality of engagement with maritime connectivity. The Frankish response in the western Mediterranean generally has, therefore, often been underrated: 'the Franks had no fleet', as Pirenne influentially wrote (1939, 166). Yet they proved to be vigorous, and at times aggressive, sailors for several decades. In 828, for instance, some Frankish ships moved around Corsica searching for pirates. Finding none, they sailed to Sardinia, where they took on local pilots who could guide them to North Africa. They landed between Utica and Carthage, and only after several victorious battles were they forced to withdraw by a combined force of Arab coastguards and bedouin. Later in the ninth century Frankish naval power undoubtedly waned. By 849 the Balearics had become a protectorate of the Umayyad caliphate in Córdoba. Yet the islands were not considered fully part of the *dar al-Islam* in 902, when a wealthy individual still thought it necessary to obtain permission from the emir of Córdoba to organize his own *jihad* against their inhabitants (J. Haywood 1991, 113–16).

(2) The next point to be made about the Pirenne period is the obvious one that, even when naval superiority could temporarily be established, it was likely to be a highly localized phenomenon, without implications for the overall fortune of one side or the other. The forces of Christendom were clearly under no single direction. But nor were those of Islam, although it is always tempting for Western scholars to generalize about them as if they were. As Ibn Khaldun acknowledged, under the Fatimids and Umayyads, 'the fleets of Ifrîqiyah [North Africa] and Spain constantly attacked each other's countries' (trans. Rosenthal 1967, 2.40). That was happening by the beginning of the ninth century – witness the occupation of Alexandria by Spanish Moors in 814. For much of the

tenth century North Africa, previously united with Egypt under the Aghlabids, was politically divided, and Fatimid and Aghlabid forces waged naval war on each other. In such circumstances, Muslim maritime dominance was hardly likely to be as complete as it has sometimes been depicted.

(3) Even when allowance is made for that fragmentation, to conceive the commercial history of the period in political terms at all is still probably mistaken. Intermittent hostility between Byzantine or western forces and those of some part of Islam was by no means a great hindrance to maritime redistribution. Trade did not narrowly follow the flag in this period any more than it would in later centuries (objects found in the living quarters of the Serçe Liman wreck for instance raise the possibility that the vessel had a mixed Muslim–Christian crew: Section 3 above with van Doorninck 1991). In the earlier Middle Ages there were, to look no further, Jewish merchants to act as commercial intermediaries between Christendom and Islam. But no Christian authority forbade trade with non-Christians; and in neither the Koran nor the sayings of the Prophet is there any prohibition on trade with infidels. Cyprus, a condominium of Baghdad and Constantinople neutralized for purposes of exchange between 688 and 965 (Kyrris 1984), was by no means the only zone of sustained interaction. Venice and Amalfi, the outstanding examples, were quite regularly in contact with Africa, Egypt and Syria. As Wickham writes (1981, 150) Amalfi 'seems to have established its position . . . by more or less consistently siding with the Arabs in their raids on the Italian coast in the ninth and tenth centuries, and thus obtaining special concessions and opportunities in the Arab world'. A Muslim source written around 840 records a decree ascribed to the Caliph 'Umar (634–44) by which foreign merchants from outside the Caliphate were to pay the same duties – 10 per cent – as were imposed by their own governments on Muslim merchants (Gibb 1958, 230). The supposed date of the measure may well be too early; its contents are, however, entirely plausible. They are confirmed by a number of anecdotal references in Arabic sources to trade between the Caliphate and Byzantium in the seventh and eighth centuries.

(4) The next general point relates particularly to those pirates – mainly Arab, but also Slav and Greek – who are sometimes seen as a major cause of declining redistribution. By their repeated depredations they supposedly reduced regular trade to a mere trickle. In Pirenne's eyes, piracy destroyed Mediterranean economic vitality; in the eyes of his critics, it markedly confirmed a decline already widely in evidence. And even if piracy did not do that, it might alternatively be argued, its prevalence in the period is the clearest index we have of that widespread insecurity which was entirely inimical to commerce.

  Now it can hardly be denied that Muslim corsairs posed a substantial threat to commercial voyaging and added to the problems of maintaining ports. Witness the reference to pirates in the Rhodian Sea Law of the eighth or ninth century (ed. Ashburner 1909, cxliii–cxliv). None the less, contemporary reports of, for example, Byzantine and Muslim ships plundering each other's coastal settlements, or of Byzantine ships lying in wait for Muslim merchantmen off the Levantine coast, should not be interpreted with undue pessimism (*pace* Ashtor 1976, 104; McCormick 1995, 357–8). *Pace* – in different ways – both Pirenne and his critics, such reports suggest the dogged maintenance of trading links and institutions – on a scale worth plundering – rather than catastrophic decline (Abulafia 1987, 415).

The point is worth dilating on (see also IX.6). First, the capability of the typical pirate vessel should not be exaggerated. It was no more or less the prisoner of technological limitations and the victim of current and weather than were its potential victims. As in later centuries, so in the Pirenne period, these victims could minimize their risks by arming themselves and travelling in convoys. Pirates might pick off one or two ships but were highly unlikely to capture the whole lot. 'The scourge of piracy, while fearsome indeed for an unfortunate victim, did not result in any paralysis of maritime commerce' (Udovitch 1978, 541, with Goitein 1973, 322–3). There is no overwhelming reason to suppose that the circumstances making that judgement true of the eleventh century, as illuminated for us by the Geniza records, would not have obtained three hundred years previously.

To reduce our estimate of the pirates' threat on the grounds of their limited nautical capability is, however, to see the problem only in the traditional terms of a permanent opposition between commerce and predation. Pirates are, in that sense, somewhat analogous to pastoralists (III.6). They are easily *imaged* as 'the other', the dangerous inversion of the values of the settled world – or, in this case, of the world of trade. Yet, like pastoralists, pirates *actually* flourish only in profound symbiosis with that world: too much so to be seen simply as its opposite. Evidence for piracy, it should hardly need stressing, is also evidence for persistent exchange; and reports of the repeated devastation of coastal settlements, the pirates' other chief target, are signs of resilience, not collapse. Raiders clearly have no interest in permanently eradicating sources of livelihood. They may make particular areas of the sea or coast too risky and force changes in the pattern of redistribution, pushing networks inland or changing the rhythm of commercial voyages. The Elder Pliny, for example, alleges that it was fear of pirates that first encouraged winter sailing, although the same effect in his own decadent times was achieved by greed (for him, interestingly, adverse weather had nothing to do with it: *Natural History*, 22.125). Some ports decline in consequence of a pirate threat; others, less prosperous, less obvious targets, slowly take their place – and the volume of *cabotage* relative to grander enterprises will doubtless increase (Ahrweiler 1978, 276). But generalized catastrophic decline does not necessarily follow (III.3).

Raiders need traders upon whom to prey, then. But those raiders are also, in a stronger sense, part of the world of trade; they are not just parasites. Like the transfer of goods between aristocratic estates or like government requisitions, piracy is simply another form of redistribution in an economic environment where markets are often scarce (IX.6). Aristotle rightly listed piracy and brigandage as a mode of production alongside the more usual forms, such as hunting, fishing and agriculture (*Politics*, 1256a). Strabo even observed how piracy and *agriculture* were interdependent (*Geography*, 11.2.12–13). Again like pastoralism, piracy is not an exclusive calling: one season's predator is next season's entrepreneur. Piracy can be a means of capital accumulation, a prelude to more legitimate ventures (Lewis 1978, 2). It can supplement income during difficult times. Perhaps that is why, for instance, Crete of the ninth century A.D. could be at one and the same time a notorious pirate base and a centre of 'international' exchange. Finally, like pastoralism, piracy seldom exists in pure form: few are willing or able to live entirely from the profits of raiding. Pirates need to sell or exchange some of their booty in order to acquire whatever they cannot plunder. Markets are as useful to them as muscle.

In preference to such ecological considerations, the more straightforward concept of a 'pirate coast' has been invoked to explain the *longue durée* of Mediterranean marauding. Certainly, some localities have been seen as especially suitable for pirates: a chronicler of the 1320s will speak with horror of 'the coast of Amalfi – and this coast is inhabited by the worst people and the greatest pirates there are in the world, especially a village called Positano' (Ramon Muntaner, *Chronicle*, ed. Lanz 1843, 149). Now for the lawless, a complex coastal topography may be an advantage. But, beyond their complexity, the coasts of Cilicia and Dalmatia and 'Barbary' – the coast of the Maghreb – do not in fact have much in common. These supposedly classic pirate zones are actually typical clusters of intensely fragmented microecologies, cut off from their hinterlands by difficult relief, but with easy access to the milieu of connectivity through anchorages and coves as numerous as the microregions which they serve. The continuity of Mediterranean redistribution provides, we submit, a better explanation for the structures of piracy and their longevity than does the geographical determinism implicit in the notion of the 'pirate coast'. Piracy is the continuation of *cabotage* by other means.

So it will not do to invoke piracy, in the Pirenne period or in any other covered by this book, as confirmation that basic redistribution has broken down. If that redistribution had already declined in the Mediterranean as grossly as Pirenne's critics assert, piracy would not have flourished. When public order fails, pirates may certainly make the bulk grain trade or the regular supply of spice difficult to maintain; they act as redistributors of high-value goods too (Brulé 1978, 159). But it was not on Cyprus sugarcane or Venetian glass that the Barbary pirate supported family and community. If the 'Dark Ages' in the Mediterranean are characterized by piracy, then it is a fair presumption that they are not so dark that the background glow of coastwise communication is extinguished. The activities of raiders cannot be invoked to explain more than local reductions in trade and redistribution. They are not an independent variable, separable from the rest of economic life. The anonymous Continuator of the *Chronicle* of Theophanes (5.63–4, ed. Bekker 1838, 304–5) provides, from the late ninth century, a nice vignette showing how all the intermittent warfare and piracy of the period was compatible with – and even dependent on – the maintenance of trading links. A Byzantine fleet had just defeated an Arab force off the Lipari islands, campaigning, as historians would like to think, to make the seas safe for trade. Its next move was to seize a passing merchant ship laden with olive oil and presumably, therefore, on its way from Muslim North Africa (Frend 1955, 62). But as Kreutz comments (1976, 87 n.33), 'we are not told [in the source] whose ship it was, and one suspects no one much cared.'

(5) The combined effect of warfare and piracy (perhaps coupled with diminished demand) may well have been an increased regionalization and mutability of the pattern of redistribution – beyond even the levels of local complexity that we have proposed as the Mediterranean norm. The need to avoid zones of warfare, a consequent relative increase in coastal tramping, and the unpredictability of commercial opportunities – these will all have made the task of traders

in the 'Pirenne period' more hazardous than it would have been in the heyday of the Roman Empire, when the Mediterranean was largely free of pirates. How the differences between the two periods are best summed up remains unclear, however. Was there for example a loss of unity and cohesion in the Mediterranean economy?

It is always tempting to equate ancient trade with the transfer of goods right across the Mediterranean, particularly from east to west. Trade of that kind can then be used as a yardstick against which to measure, and find wanting, the apparently more fragmented Mediterranean of the early medieval depression. There was, though – and this is the next general point – nothing startlingly new about such a lack of integration. In Antiquity, some degree of integration was often promoted by the requirements of states; and even when the framework for integration was provided by the all-embracing Roman Empire and its Mediterranean-wide elite, it seldom extended the redistributive network in its most complex form to the majority of coastlines and hinterlands. A study of the distribution of cheap signed oil lamps under the Roman Empire (Duncan-Jones 1990, ch. 3; cf. Foraboschi 1994) suggests that much ancient trade was limited to distinct zones within the Mediterranean – somewhat as it would be in the ninth century when that oil-laden vessel encountered a Byzantine task force. So far as overall patterns of redistribution are concerned, therefore, it may be unwise to draw too sharp a contrast between Antiquity and the Pirenne period. Very various degrees of regional and interregional integration have been found in the Mediterranean throughout prehistoric and ancient times, as well as in the later Middle Ages, or the early modern age for that matter.

(6) The picture that is emerging of the Pirenne period is a complex one. How far is it consistent with an interpretation that sets greater store by shipping lanes than we have been doing? Undeniably, much of the history of the early medieval depression can be written in terms of which power enjoyed mastery of the lanes. From the late seventh century to the early ninth, Christian forces generally lost their capacity to police the more important passages in the northern part of the Mediterranean. Sometimes the Muslims controlled the lanes instead, in virtue of their conquest of strategic islands or beachheads; sometimes the lanes were under no single authority and use of them was commensurately uncertain. Eventually, the Christians regained control – in part because the northern channels and islands were too far away from Muslim mainland bases, and galleys attacking them were thus, in terms of food and water supplies, at the very limit of their range (Pryor 1988, 8–9, 109; cf. Ehrenkreutz 1972, 98). But interpretation in this vein leaves out numerous other ingredients in Muslim fortunes; it is hardly sufficient to account for a growth and decline that spanned at least two centuries; and it relies too heavily on the conviction that lasting thalassocracy was genuinely possible – something which we have already questioned. That is, it takes too little notice of connectivity – which means, in this context, the numerous strategies that small *caboteurs* might devise for evading pirates, and for finding new courses through dangerous waters, largely by hugging the shore and making full use of its refuges. If, as we have previously urged, shipping lanes were not quite the indispensable channels of communication, then the 'loss' of them to piracy or Muslim conquest during the early medieval depression may not have been so devastating to maritime redistribution.

That possibility remains to be demonstrated, of course. We can, meanwhile, summarize the stage that the argument has reached so far. To conceive the Pirenne period in terms of centuries of outright dominance by Christendom or Islam, with damage to trade in proportion, is misleading on several counts. It ignores the intermittent nature of maritime hostilities; the political fragmentation of both 'sides' and the still greater mutability of the political map of any one area of the sea; the extent to which economic ties cut across, and indeed could be largely unaffected by, even the most local of political boundaries; the interdependence of piracy and 'settled' exchange; and the degree to which the Mediterranean economy had, since Antiquity, always to some extent functioned in distinct zones. Above all, it ignores the resilience and adaptability of maritime communication in the Mediterranean (which Pirenne and his critics have perhaps both underestimated), and hence underrates the capacity of traders to endure the most adverse political circumstances.

6. CONNECTIVITY MAINTAINED?

The preceding section has necessarily been somewhat abstract. It explores what Hopkins has called 'the logic of the situation' (1983a, 107 n.15). Low-level connectivity proves hard enough to document in any period because it is of its essence to leave few traces in the official record. There is, further, an abiding difficulty arising from the way in which the whole Pirenne period has been divided by scholarly tradition. Students of the economic history of late Antiquity may pursue their theme into the period of the early Islamic conquests – but then they often stop, in the seventh century, occasionally in the early eighth. A gap remains between their interests and those of historians concerned with the next major phase in Mediterranean economic history, the 'commercial revolution' of the tenth century onward associated with the growth of north Italian cities such as Venice.

This gap in the historiography is understandable. It is prompted by the nature and general paucity of the evidence for the seventh to eighth centuries. Written sources yield, as we shall see, a few hints – but, until we come to the period suddenly illuminated by the Cairo Geniza, no more than that. The evidence of coinage is too sparse and ambiguous to be of more than occasional use, not least because so many of the contacts with which we are concerned will have involved non-monetary exchange. Other archaeological evidence of this period, meanwhile, speaks a little more volubly, but its drift is still hard to catch. Too few shipwrecks have been recovered for any secure conclusions to be based on them. On land, the main problem is the sparseness of modern field surveys and excavations. The criterion of modernity is essential here because only quite recently have archaeologists shown the will and capacity to distinguish and interpret late Antique or early medieval strata, particularly of wooden buildings. This is an archaeological realm in which finds are extremely hard to date. Pottery, that unsurpassed aid to precision in other periods (IX.4), seems either to have become stylistically quite crude, and thus chronologically indeterminate, or gradually to have given way to perishable container materials such as leather and wood – annoyingly for the archaeologist. Such changes may well of course be a sign that something radical was happening to the economy: it is disquieting, to say the least, that in some parts of the post-Roman world whole populations almost become archaeologically invisible. But it would be rash to infer that the substitution of wooden for stone buildings and of barrels for amphorae is inevitably a symptom of collapse in the volume of redistribution.

What can be said, then? Relying of necessity for the most part on written texts, we shall sketch an answer to that question first by looking as far as possible at the Mediterranean as a whole, and then by narrowing the focus and proceeding region by region.

Some of the most eloquent evidence of connectivity maintained across the Mediterranean comes from hagiography. In around 670 for instance – well after the beginning of the circum-Mediterranean advance of Islam – the Burgundian bishop, Arculf, did not find it especially difficult to gain passage from Christian to Muslim territory and back again. At Alexandria, moreover, he reportedly found 'the commerce of the whole world': some hyperbolic indication, perhaps, of the enduringly 'international' flavour of redistribution in the eastern Mediterranean (Adamnan, *On the Holy Places*, 30.16, ed. Meehan 1958, 102–3; Bede, *Ecclesiastical History*, 5.15).

More revealing is the only pilgrimage narrative to survive from the eighth century, the *Hodoeporicon* or *Itinerary* of St Willibald, a record of a journey undertaken during the early 720s, first to Rome and then to Jerusalem (trans. Talbot 1954, 153–77). From Gaeta, the saint and his companions took ship to Naples and stayed there for two weeks. Then they found in the harbour a vessel from Egypt, which carried them to Reggio di Calabria. After two days they crossed to Catania in Sicily; three weeks later they sailed down the coast to Syracuse; thence they crossed the Ionian Sea to Monemvasia; they moved on to Chios; and finally (passing Samos) they reached Ephesus. They made several more short journeys by ship along the Levantine coast, crossed to Cyprus ('which lies [in condominium] between the Greeks and the Saracens') and, after three weeks in Paphos, returned to the mainland, entering Muslim territory with no apparent difficulty. They were, admittedly, twice arrested as spies; but on each occasion they gained their release – the first time at the prompting of a local elder, the second (after a merchant had failed to redeem them) through the joint intercession of the captain of the ship on which they had sailed from Cyprus and a powerfully connected Spaniard (whether Muslim or convert is unclear). What is noteworthy in the account, a nun's transcription of Willibald's much later oral testimony, is first the circumstantial detail, which has no obvious theological or metaphorical purpose and so may be taken as broadly trustworthy; second, the number of short coastal 'hops' that the saint and his companions were able to make; third, the presence of an Egyptian ship, surely Muslim, in an Italian port; and lastly the permeability of the Christian–Muslim frontier in both Cyprus and Syria.

Of the other, similar, narratives that could be set beside Willibald's we mention just one. From around 829, when he exchanged his birthplace in southern Anatolia for Ephesus, until 842 when he died, Gregory the Decapolite travelled extensively by ship around the Byzantine eastern Mediterranean – Proconnesus, Constantinople, Thessalonica, Christopolis, Corinth, Reggio di Calabria, Rome, Syracuse, Otranto. Inevitably, as his hagiographer tells us, there were hazards. Because of Muslim pirates waiting offshore, the sailors at first refused to leave Ephesus. Later, on the voyage to Thessalonica, the saint encountered Slav pirates who pursued any merchant ship that passed the mouth of their river. And only the saint's guarantee of divine protection could persuade his crew to undertake the voyage from Corinth across to Calabria, on the open expanses of the Ionian Sea (Map 9). The risks seem obvious – but how great were they? We should remember that it was perhaps in the hagiographer's interest to magnify them, and hence display to the full the virtues and the miraculous achievement of his subject. Whatever the actual threat from pirates, the saint's journeys were, it seems, successfully completed. The sailors, though reluctant, are represented as, at least, available; indeed, the whole narrative depends for its plausibility on the existence of a maritime 'infrastructure' (Dvornik 1926, 53–8; Malamut 1993, 247–8).

Gregory, it should be noted, travelled during the century in which the Muslims were supposedly masters of the sea. The most striking testimony to the enduring possibility of Mediterranean-wide exchange in the Pirenne period does indeed involve traders from Islam (Gil 1974); but it hardly suggests commercial stagnation. It is the much-discussed report of the Jewish al-Radhaniyya, or Radhanites:

> These merchants speak Arabic, Persian, Roman [presumably meaning Greek], Frankish, Spanish, and Slavonic. They travel from the East to the West and from the West to the East by land as well as by sea. They bring from the West eunuchs, slave girls, boys, brocade, beaver skins, marten furs and other varieties of fur, and swords. They embark in the land of the Franks [northern Italy?] on the western Sea, and they sail toward al-Farama. There they load their merchandise on the backs of camels and proceed by land to al-Qulzum [on the Nile delta] . . . They embark on the Eastern sea and proceed from al-Qulzum to al-Jar and to Jidda [the port of Mecca]; then they go to Sind, Hind, and China . . . On their return from China . . . some of them sail for Constantinople in order to sell their merchandise to the Romans. Others proceed to the residence of the king of the Franks to dispose of their articles . . . These different journeys may likewise be made by land . . . (Lopez and Raymond 1955, 31–2)

The account of these commercial supermen by Ibn Khurdadhbih cannot be entirely trustworthy. For one thing, his knowledge of the European West, like that of so many of his fellow geographers, is disturbingly vague – partly a reflection of the fact that Muslim merchants did not usually venture beyond the *dar al-Islam* and expected 'pagan' traders to come to them. But if, as has been argued (Ashtor 1977a), Ibn Khurdadhbih's account belongs to the first edition of his work, dating from 846, then it may be just as significant that he thought such commerce possible in the early ninth century than that it actually happened on the scale described. Were the Radhanites unique? Or were they, on one suggested (Persian) etymology of their name, not from Radhan in Mesopotamia, but simply 'those who know the trade routes' – know them best (1977a, 268)? And is Ibn Khurdadhbih therefore presenting a selective account of a more widespread phenomenon, albeit an account heightened from life? One indication that there may be contemporary realism in his account lies in the sheer eccentricity of the choice of routes that he ascribes to the Radhanites. They do not seem to have passed through Alexandria or Fustat, for example. Al-Farama, which they used instead, was hardly a major entrepôt, although a ninth-century caliph did construct a fort there (Ashtor 1970, 183–4; 1977a, 252). The Radhanites begin, indeed, to look a little like those *caboteurs* whom we sketched above, and on whose services they would presumably have depended. As with the *Life* of Gregory, the narrative would only have been credible if its intended readership took for granted the existence of an appropriate infrastructure. Moreover the Radhanites are shown as operating in an environment which is at least consistent with the picture of the eastern Mediterranean urged by several historians and archaeologists – a picture in which many of the great names among Middle Eastern ports had declined centuries before these 'super-traders' appeared and more obscure coastal centres came into their own (Ashtor 1970, 170–72; Kennedy 1985b).

Another much-scrutinized text that implies comparably wide-ranging networks of exchange between East and West comes from the dark centre of the Pirenne period, the early eighth century. It is a text to which Pirenne himself devoted considerable attention, seeing in it the last documented gasp of trans-Mediterranean commerce (1939, 89–91, 168, with translation). Founded in the reign of the Merovingian Chlothar III (657–73), the Abbey of Corbey enjoyed the privilege of collecting a substantial annual rent from the royal customs house at the port of Fos, near Marseille (Maps 11, 22). (The settlement's name derived from the *Fossa* which Gaius Marius had built eight centuries before to improve the navigability of the Rhône delta's easternmost arm.) The rent took the form of desirable imports. Presumably those goods not collected by customs-men as tolls in kind were purchased with the proceeds of monetary taxes in the local market. Everything was to be stored in the royal *cellarium* (warehouse?) for collection by the abbey's agents (Pertz 1872, no. 86).

The merchandise in question is impressive in quantity, in variety, and in likely provenance ('a veritable delicatessen': Loseby 1998, 219): 10,000 pounds of oil, 30 hogsheads of the fish-based condiment *garum*, 30 pounds of pepper, 150 pounds of cumin, 100 pounds each of figs, almonds and olives, and so on. The list ends with 10 skins of Córdoba leather and 50 quires of papyrus. In all, it has been estimated (Doehaerd 1978, 191), these are very substantial quantities of luxury goods (beside the oil, leather and papyrus), and many of these goods would have originated in the Levant.

We know the details of this levy, not from the original grant of Chlothar III, but only from its later confirmation, by Chilperic II, in April 716. Nor does the original survive of an only slightly less spectacular grant, also confirmed by Chilperic, of a rent from the royal customs dues at Marseille to be converted into oil and paid to the Abbey of Saint-Denis (Pertz 1872, no. 82). How realistic, then, were these displays of royal munificence? At the least, they expressed a belief that the Provençal ports remained attractive to merchants from far afield; they reveal, that is, an *expectation* of continuing Mediterranean-wide connectivity, from which the rents described would presumably form only a proportion of the aggregate yield. Moreover the fact that such privileges were confirmed by the Merovingian king is a sign of his, or his magnates', strength, not of the government's slackening grip on reality: the original grants were theoretically perpetual, but kings could in practice often resume what they had once given away. An example: the rent originally granted in the 630s and regranted in 691 to Saint-Denis on the Marseille customs was for some reason renounced by the abbey only a few years later in exchange for an estate in Berry (Ganz and Goffart 1990, 914). A sign of commercial malaise in Marseille? Not necessarily, it would seem; for in 716 the original grant was reconfirmed. On this particular matter at least, there was no mindless rehearsal of empty dispositions. Such confirmations were sought, not volunteered; and they would surely not have been sought had the beneficiaries not thought their privileges worth reasserting (*contra* Loseby forthcoming a). The quantities in question were doubtless highly optimistic; it does not follow that the entire grant represents a fantasy. Some earlier indication of the weight that kings attached to the rent on imports at Fos is given by the *Formulary* of Marculf, a collection of model letters drawn up for the guidance of the royal writing office around 700: it includes (1.11) a very similar list of oriental luxuries to that granted to Corbey (Zeumer 1886, 49).

Some scholars think that the Corbey grant can thus be taken seriously as a reflection of the state of one particular facet of the Merovingian economy (Wood 1994, 215–16). Others, from Pirenne onward, think it an anachronism, a mere 'propaganda ploy', showing only 'what the commercial possibilities of the Provençal ports had once been' (Loseby forthcoming a; 1992, 175). The basis for this pessimistic conclusion is first that, after the Corbey grant, we hear no more of such matters in eighth-century texts; second, that the archaeological context which would enhance its credibility is, as we shall see, so limited; third, that the Merovingian king Chilperic II was too weak to exact customs in southern France; and finally, that the imports envisaged were no longer available: papyrus had already ceased to be used by the Merovingian writing office some years before the grant was made and, as Pirenne had it, 'it is . . . impossible that African olive oil can still have been imported at this time' (1939, 168). Certainly the evidence supporting the grant is meagre. But one import, papyrus, cannot be used as an index of an entire trading connection; and as for olive oil, Pirenne's argument is *a priori*: it rests on his previous assertion – which we have already called into question – that the Arabs had rapidly become masters of the Mediterranean and brought maritime movement in the western Mediterranean to a standstill. The amphorae in which the oil might previously have arrived disappear from the archaeological record just too early to provide plausible context; but that does not of course preclude a change to perishable containers (such as were perhaps used by that early ninth-century ship mentioned above). Moreover, Chilperic seems to have been the last Merovingian king to confirm grants of the sort in question, so that it is no surprise that the Corbey list does not re-emerge in the documents. But even if this really was a final propagandist gesture, the question still has to be answered of what political advantage accrued to the king or his powerful advisers from making quite worthless dispensations.

For a more rounded view of the fortunes of Fos and Marseille, we ought to be able to turn to archaeology (Loseby 1992). Doing so offers a useful case study in the limits of archaeological evidence and explanation in this period. Modern excavations, principally in the area of the Bourse at the north-eastern end of Marseille's harbour, have revealed a city growing larger during the sixth century, a time when many comparable settlements were contracting. Even more striking, an extramural suburb in the region of the Bourse was still expanding around 600, and the assemblage of small finds suggests that this was an active industrial quarter. None the less Marseille's primary function was that of a gateway community, an emporium. There is nothing to be learned from the spade about its exports – presumably slaves, wood and so forth. Its visible imports are dominated by goods carried in African Red Slip ware; eastern amphorae diminish in number as we approach the seventh century and then disappear altogether, a phenomenon that might loosely be correlated with the apparent ending of papyrus imports to Francia. Meanwhile, however, the link with Africa endured in the seventh century, and traces of imported goods from *c*.700 are still being found by the excavators, forming at least some archaeological background to the original Corbey grant (Hesnard 1995, 77; Bonifay et al. 1998, 358, 419).

Also part of the context for that grant are the enigmatic quasi-imperial and the royal gold coinages minted at Marseille and other centres in the Rhône valley from around 575 until the 670s, seemingly for important local trans-actions, though perhaps not commercial ones (Loseby 1998, 223–7). Marseille continued to function as a major mint, after the collapse of the gold coinage and its replacement by a silver one, until well into the eighth century (Hendy 1988, 68–9). All this seems to bear out the references that we find, in the earlier writings of Gregory of Tours, to Marseille's prominent position as a conduit of commerce and communication between the Mediterranean and north-western Europe in the sixth century, and suggests the city's continuing – even growing – political significance.

Archaeology can, however, only take us a certain way along the road we wish to travel. One clear example of its limitations is given by the amphorae. These, apparently so eloquent of the scale of the city's imports, do not match the evid-ence of Gregory, or of the royal grants already mentioned, that oil was arriv-ing in significant quantities. The large majority of the fifth-century amphorae were coated on the inside, suggesting that they did *not* contain oil. The interior coatings of amphorae from the sixth to seventh centuries simply do not sur-vive, so that we cannot tell for what goods they might have been used. Perhaps the texts are completely misleading, or the oil was being brought to Marseille from sources other than Africa – or, more plausibly though discomfitingly for archaeologists, the stuff was being carried in containers of which nothing could survive. It is worth remembering also that modern excavations have covered (so far) only one corner of the harbour, confined to vessels of shallow draft: the bigger ships were docking elsewhere. The harbour's facilities also remain undug, which may be why no trace has so far emerged of the royal customs depot and storage facilities. We have to bear these problems in mind when interpreting the archaeological muteness of Marseille in the period from the end of the seventh to the tenth centuries: 'It is impossible to be certain how far this lacuna reflects urban collapse and the real absence of the population, and how far it is an index of their archaeological invisibility, as they cease to build in durable materials, and the supply of datable artefacts dries up' (Loseby 1992, 170). One of the last *archaeological* signs of the economic resilience, if not of Marseille then at least of a harbour quite nearby, is provided by the so-called Saint-Gervais B wreck which sank off the now submerged port of Fos during the second half of the seventh century, with a cargo that included fine oriental pottery, common table ware, pitch, and above all, impressively, grain (Jézégou 1982, 1998; cf. BE IX.4).

For the succeeding century or so we have to go back to the texts (mostly assembled in Ganshof 1938). Marseille appears several times in Frankish and papal sources of the eighth century as the port linking northern Europe with Italy. This implies its continued connectivity – without, of course, telling us anything about the scale of its commerce. If Muslim raiders attacked the ports of Provence and even conquered territory there during the first half of the eighth century, then we might surmise that the region was not as economically stag-nant and impoverished as the Pirenne school would have it. Marseille is referred to as a port in a charter of 781, about the time that the Saxon merchant Botto is reported by the Petau Annals (*sub anno* 790) to have been active there as a *negotiator* or merchant.

But we should not concentrate too narrowly on one city. Even in the geographically privileged outlet of the Rhône corridor to the Mediterranean, Marseille had always had rivals, such as Arles. For example when, shortly before 800, in the reign of Charlemagne, the court poet and scholar Theodulf of Orleans wanted to satirize the corrupt Arlesian judges of his day, he included among the bribes offered to them: oriental gems, Muslim gold coins, luxury cloths sent by 'the grim-faced Arab', and skins from Córdoba (Lopez and Raymond 1955, 36; cf. Doehaerd 1978, 196–7). Archaeology is moreover beginning tentatively to render Theodulf's verse indictment less implausible than it once sounded. Dassargues (Lunel), between Nîmes and Maguelonne, 'livre encore entre le milieu du VIIe et la fin du VIIIe s. plus de 15 per cent de céramique importée, principalement des amphores' (Citter et al. 1996, 126). More remarkably still, at Bouquet/San Peyre (Gard), an elevated rural site 40 kilometres north of Nîmes, a burnt-out, probably aristocratic, house has yielded African amphorae and lamps, cruder amphorae of Byzantine type, and a seal bearing characters in Kufic script. All are datable, thanks to the fire, to the end of the seventh or the early eighth centuries – testimony to 'un certain dynamisme des échanges et des activités portuaires de la Provence à l'aube du VIIIe s.' (1996, 32). There is nothing here to match the social and geographical penetration of African Red Slip ware in its heyday. But the finding of Mediterranean pottery from this date some way inland is striking none the less.

Detailed consideration of southern French evidence has led us from the sources most redolent of Mediterranean-wide exchange (such as the Corbey privilege) into a more narrowly regional approach. Having looked at evidence of exchange in and around Marseille, we can move on around the sea in a roughly clockwise direction. The next area we come to is thus the central Mediterranean. We have already touched on aspects of Italian trade, not least that of Amalfi with Muslims (Section 5). Our suggestion now is that the development of Italian emporia in the ninth to tenth centuries, often taken to mark the beginnings of the recovery of the European economy after the Dark Ages and indeed to herald a Commercial Revolution (Lopez 1976), is more intelligible when seen against the background of the fragmentary eighth-century evidence: as the end of the Pirenne period rather than the dawn of something new.

Two particular areas within the Italian peninsula are of interest, the north-east and the south-west. In 715, coincidentally the year of the last Corbey grant, the merchants of Comacchio at the mouth of the Po made a 'commercial treaty' with the Lombard kings which allowed – for a price in tolls – trade in pepper, oil, salt, marinated fish, and presumably other, unnamed, products along the Po plain (Hartmann 1904, 123–4; Balzaretti 1996, 219–25). The salt and fish were doubtless local; but the pepper and oil do suggest more far-flung contacts. Moreover in the Lombard kingdom itself, the mid-eighth-century Edict of Aistulf also envisages that all kinds of person might be doing business with Roman (that is, Byzantine) citizens; it mentions customs houses; and it stipulates that those involved in trade by land or sea should carry written authorization from the king or one of his judges (Lopez and Raymond 1955, 37–8). Some of this trade, too, will surely have been 'international' and transmarine.

As for Venice, in the mid-sixth century the inhabitants of Venetia and Istria more broadly had figured in the letter collection of the greatest servant of the Gothic regime in Italy, Cassiodorus, as exporters of wine, oil, grain, fish and salt (*Variae*, 12.24). Thereafter we lose sight of them for some time. They resurface, however, in the middle of the eighth century. In 747, for instance, their merchants were in Rome buying up slaves for sale to 'pagans', that is, Muslims (*Book of the Popes* [*Liber Pontificalis*], 93.22, trans. R. Davis 1992). Excavations on the Venetian island of San Lorenzo hint at what already in that period may have been a substantial emporium with extensive links to the Muslim and Byzantine worlds (Hodges 1994, 123). But the first clear sign of the prosperity resulting from exchanges of wheat, salt or slaves for oriental products *apparently* come in 829 (the document's authenticity is not unassailable). In that year a *dux* (doge) famously seems to have left property in his will to the value of 1,200 pounds in gold – wealth partly derived from investment in overseas trade (Lopez and Raymond 1955, 39–41). Eighth-century connections between the Adriatic, northern Italy and, via the Alps, northern Europe in general, were perhaps sufficient to yield substantial rewards for some of those involved and to generate the expansion of strategically placed settlements. As might be expected, archaeological confirmation of this is slow to follow, although sites such as Ferrara both hint at what may wait to be found and also warn of the difficulties of interpretation likely to be involved (B. Ward-Perkins 1988, 25).

The second area to look at is of course the south-west of Italy, whose coastal centres seem to form a central commercial axis in the Mediterranean, the Muslims of North Africa being their most valued trading partners in the ninth and tenth centuries. What we find is in effect a sequence of flourishing emporia forming a perhaps unbroken link with classical Antiquity. First in the sequence is Naples, which retains to this day a substantial part of its Graeco-Roman street plan, and which was in the Pirenne period the seat of a *de facto* autonomous Byzantine duke as well as of a bishop. Excavations in one of the city's Roman baths show that coins and imported foodstuffs continued to arrive in the city well into the seventh century. Olive oil and wine came in amphorae from North Africa, and also, in increasing proportions, from further east: Gaza, Antioch, the northern Aegean and the Black Sea, although these were all apparently declining in quantity towards the middle of the century. It is as if we can see Naples turning its commercial face more to its Byzantine parent state as its overseas contacts in the central Mediterranean became relatively enfeebled. By the later seventh century, these contacts, if they were maintained, become archaeologically invisible (Kreutz 1991, 2). But finds from around the Tyrrhenian – fragments of amphorae (still!) or of glazed ceramics – trace, across the long eighth century, supra-regional exchange networks involving Naples as well as a number of smaller ports, and reaching perhaps to the San Peyre site mentioned above. This is exactly the sort of low-level, but yet much more than local, exchange that we should now expect (Citter et al. 1996, 122–5; Arthur and Patterson 1994, 416–20). One final text to mention from the end of the Pirenne period: in 836 the city concluded a treaty (the *Pactum Sicardi*) with its threatening Lombard neighbour Sicard of Benevento (Lopez and Raymond 1955, 33–5). In this treaty, the Neapolitans agreed not to buy Lombards for resale overseas, clearly as slaves. Where would these have been sold? Possibly to Muslim North Africa or Sicily (like the slaves that the Venetians bought in Rome), for Naples had already sought the help of Arab mercenaries from Sicily in its struggle against Benevento; conceivably to Byzantium, because we have one reference to Greek slavers operating off the Campanian coast in the late eighth century (Kreutz 1991, 20–1).

So much for Naples. As we move out of the eighth century, the light of the always fragmentary evidence now flickers further to the south. Amalfi appears in the *Pactum Sicardi* simply in a heading that is unexplained but at least suggests wide-ranging activities: 'concerning the Amalfitans, how they travel around' (Kreutz 1991, 21). We commented earlier (Chapter IV) on the relatively abundant ninth- to tenth-century evidence for Amalfi's involvement in trade with Islam and Byzantium, and also on the obscurity of the reasons for the rise to commercial prominence of a port so unpromisingly situated. And this could happen, it is worth emphasis, despite the operations of pirates who are pictured, for example, in the Frankish 'Royal' Annal for 820 as seizing merchant ships en route from Sardinia to the Italian mainland (Kreutz 1991, 25).

Why this efflorescence of Italian emporia trading in slaves, timber, grain and metals (Doehaerd 1978, 192–3)? A standard answer is that the axis joining Italy to North Africa was the sole major channel of Mediterranean exchange left free and commercially viable. The transalpine connection was possible only when the Lombards allowed the routes to be opened; to the west Muslim pirates, to the east a Byzantine blockade, alike rendered maritime trade relatively unattractive. In short, the central Mediterranean connection was the only one available (Barnish 1989, 394). Putting it that way would, as we have argued, overestimate the possibilities of thalassocracy – or for that matter of control of overland traffic. It would surely be better to think in terms of the novel demand created by the various Muslim conquerors' consolidation of their hold on the southern Mediterranean shores and their extension of political control to major islands. The initiative in satisfying that demand seems to have lain with the Christian merchants. It was, after all, they who travelled to Muslim ports, not Muslim merchants who ventured into the *dar al-harb* (Udovitch 1978, 562). But why particular ports were the ones to take fullest advantage of these novel opportunities remains hard to understand. Why Amalfi rather than Naples (Kreutz 1991, 87)? The answer we must give in the current state of our knowledge is simply: access at the time to connective networks that were of their essence changing in ways that must to us, at this remove, remain mysterious. Mediterranean ports, we shall later argue (Chapter IX) are 'epiphenomenal' to the world of maritime connectivity. Their situations reflect the logic of the sea and are not wholly, or even mainly, explicable in terms of the more readily intuited physical features of their hinterlands.

The ports we know about a little are best conceived as visible intensifications of the wider network (IX.7), not as functions of some large abstraction such as the western Mediterranean. The networks will always be poorly evidenced. But we can see some traces at least of the commercial 'hinterland', the connective region from which the prosperity of a centre like Venice emerges by moving on round the Mediterranean and by looking more closely at the Adriatic in the Pirenne period.

The Adriatic reminds us how the obvious forms of political dominance can be irrelevant to the evolution of local networks of communication. From the later sixth century onward, the Byzantine Empire lost much of its hold on the countries either side of the sea: Avars raided, Slavs took over most of the Balkans, Lombards the greater part of Italy; Ravenna and the papal states asserted their independence in central Italy, as did Venice in the north and the duchy of Naples in the south; in the ninth century, the Arabs began attacking Sicily and southern Italy in earnest. And yet, through it all, the Greeks maintained their access to the maritime connectivity of the coastlines with their multitudinous peninsulas and islands. As the Emperor Constantine Porphyrogenitus wrote, of Dalmatia, 'only the townships on the coast held out . . . and continued to be in the hands of the Romans [that is, Byzantines], because they obtained their livelihood from the sea' (*On Administering the Empire*, 30.58–60, ed. Moravcsik and Jenkins 1967, 142). Such places were fortified, and used as bases not only for exchange along the coast but also for attacks on the Slavs. So apparently successful were these attacks that only one Slav naval action is known in the period. 'Under the control of Dalmatia is a close-set and very numerous archipelago, reaching as far as Beneventum [southern Italy], so that ships never fear rough seas in those parts' (29.285–7; 1967, 138–9). The archaeological vestiges of that local control are meagre yet instructive: amphorae, glass and ceramic objects and iron utensils, all probably of Byzantine origin are strewn along the Dalmatian coast (Ferluga 1987, 42–3, 47). That is maritime connectivity at work, in despite of the most unfavourable political circumstances.

Discussion of the Adriatic moves the regional focus from Italy towards the heart of the Byzantine Empire, in the Balkans, Asia Minor and, until they were lost to the Arabs, Syria, Egypt and North Africa. We have noticed some aspects of the overseas exchange that Byzantium maintained throughout the Pirenne period, especially with Islamic lands. No proper treatment is attempted here, partly because the main general points have already been made, partly because a coherent account is hardly possible in the present state of our knowledge (Wickham forthcoming). Once again the archaeology is limited and ambiguous. Also the texts are few: partly because of the dearth of hagiography, we learn more about Byzantine trade with Islam from Arabic than from Greek sources. So not even occasional vignettes, of the sort that can be offered of the early history of Venice, are readily available here. Discussions of the Byzantine economy in the Pirenne period have therefore been focused elsewhere – particularly on the timing of the transition from the classical city to the Dark Age village or fort as the major form of settlement.

On the theme of maritime connectivity there is little that can be added. The Byzantine navy remained strong until the second half of the eighth century – although it was never perhaps capable of the sort of blockade with which, despite a lack of clear evidence for any such project, it has been credited (Lilie 1976, 273 n.262). We may infer that there were a fair number of substantial commercial captains or ship owners in the early ninth century because the Emperor Nicephorus forced them to accept a loan (in gold) from the state at a high rate of interest (16.66 per cent) – either because he was trying to reinvigorate the economy or, more likely, because he was in desperate need of new sources of revenue (Frances 1966; Hendy 1985, 627). A certain amount is known, also, about the taxation of commerce more generally in the period. But direct evidence of the scale or intensity of maritime connectivity in the Pirenne period is rare. To envisage what *may* have been going on, we have to look further back.

The circulation of fine ceramics and amphorae in the Aegean shows the complexity of the patterns that result even in the seventh century, and also their penetration inland, even if the movement of only a handful of different goods is plotted on a map (Abadie-Reynal 1989). Morsels of specific evidence – textual, archaeological, epigraphic – suggest that both interregional and local exchange networks survived the political and social upheavals of the age far better than has been suspected. Merchants from Rhodes, Chios, the Black Sea and the Aegean are for instance well attested in mid-seventh-century Constantinople (Lopez 1959, 71) – but then Constantinople is always something of a special case. More representative, perhaps, is the customs law from Cagliari which presents a vivid vignette of the local redistribution of a Sardinian settlement at the dawn of the seventh century (Durliat 1982).

A shipwreck discovered at Yassi Ada, off the south-east coast of Turkey, provides still more telling evidence of the character of everyday provincial movement (Hodges and Whitehouse 1983, 64–5; Bass and van Doorninck 1982, 316; BE IX.4). The boat drew some 30 or 40 tonnes. It was shipping 900 amphorae of wine southwards along the west coast of Asia Minor when it struck a reef and sank, in around the year 625. The kitchen wares from its galley are just as significant as the cargo of wine. There were various tablewares (some of them glass) and storage amphorae; also stone mortars and copper cauldrons. In the galley's cupboard were sixteen gold and fifty copper coins.

The local background to such a find is obscure. But there are signs in other parts of the Byzantine world that merchants were continuing to serve a sizeable market for standard inexpensive goods. Excavations of the rural settlement of Castellu, in the district of Corte that lies at the heart of Corsica, have uncovered sixth- to seventh-century amphora fragments that show how regional trading networks could reach inland to sites far from the sea and accessible only by mountain tracks, just as they had in classical Antiquity (Pergola and Vismara 1989; compare the San Peyre site above). On a grander level, Abydos, the main Byzantine customs station on the Hellespont, seems to have remained in operation from the fifth century to the tenth, when it was praised by the Muslim geographer Idrisi above all other Byzantine cities for its broad streets, beautiful houses and magnificent bazaars. Abydos was one of those relatively few Byzantine settlements that retained its classical street grid from late Antiquity into the Middle Ages (Angold 1985, 14, though cf. B. Ward-Perkins 1995).

A regional network from the other end of the dark period that engendered the Pirenne thesis is hinted at by the remains of a ninth-century Arab house close to Knossos on Crete (Warren and Miles 1972). The Arabs' occupation of the island in 828 may have led them to establish – or to take over – a local trading network in the southern Aegean. Nine coins of an Arab emir of Crete were found on the house's floor. Three similar ones are known from the Athenian *agora*, eight from Corinth, one at Gortyn, two at Vizari in the remains of a Byzantine basilica, one at Arkhanai and ten at Herakleion – besides several others on Crete itself. It is at least consistent with what we know of the economic organization of Arab Crete, and also with the ceramic evidence from the island slowly being brought into focus, that the distribution of these finds should be the result of small-scale commercial activity.

Crete turns our attention from Byzantium to Islam and thus helps to complete this rapid clockwise Mediterranean tour. So far we have been concentrating on maritime connectivity, because it is by sea if anywhere that the enduring connectivity of the Mediterranean region as a whole is most likely to be evident, even in periods of sparse evidence and reduced interaction such as the one associated with Pirenne. But, around the sea's shores, overland networks should also have been important in maintaining the interdependence of microregions during the seventh and eighth centuries, and of these overland networks the Islamic ones are, for all the Radhanites' knowledge of seaways, the most visible:

> Grain was shipped from Northern Mesopotamia to Southern Iraq, olive oil from Syria, Palestine and Tunisia to Egypt. Dates from Iraq were exported to many provinces of the Moslem world. Khuzistan, Makran and Yemen produced sugar, Syria was famous for its fruit-culture, the products of which were highly appreciated in Iraq and in Egypt. Barca supplied Egypt with cattle for slaughter. The textile industries of Khurasan, Bukhara and Samarkand exported their cotton goods to all the provinces of the Near East. The cotton cloth of Herat, Meraw and Nishapur was sold everywhere. The Caspian provinces produced silk and woollen stuffs renowned in all parts of the Abbasid empire. Khuzistan and Fars, the two provinces of South-western Persia bordering on the Persian Gulf, exported precious silk and cotton fabrics, Armenia its famous carpets. Egypt had from time immemorial a highly developed linen industry, and when it was united, under the sceptre of the caliphs, with Iraq and Persia, these latter countries became a big market for its products. The North African provinces, lastly, exported coarse woollen fabrics, destined for the lower classes of Oriental society. (Ashtor 1976, 78)

That description is now decades old; but archaeology has tended to confirm rather than to invalidate it. Conquered areas such as North Africa and Syria were reorientated into complex sets of exchanges that are evident, often, in the fine or semi-fine ceramics that continue to survive (Wickham forthcoming). These exchanges might involve new axes – the Sudan in North Africa's case, western Iraq for Syria – as much as the eastern Mediterranean; and they throve on it. The vigorous settlements of the early Islamic period (of the Umayyad and early Abbasid caliphates) were thus mostly inland. Pella, Damascus, Aleppo, Antioch, Jerash, Amman, Qinnasrin – these are the success stories, either newly flourishing or developments based on earlier, Byzantine, prosperity. The contrast has been drawn with Tyre, Sidon, Beirut and Laodicea (Lattakia), which seem to have declined well before the coming of Arab invaders and to have remained dormant thereafter (Kennedy 1985).

And yet we must not be too hasty in judging the extent to which the extension of Islam shifted the emphasis in southern Mediterranean connectivity from seaborne to overland communications. The Caliph 'Umar II proclaimed: 'dry land and sea belong alike to God; He hath subdued them to His servants to seek of His bounty for themselves in both of them' (Gibb 1955, 6). We have already seen evidence of maritime traffic between Muslim North Africa and both Italy and Byzantium. That evidence can now be reinforced by the results of excavations at Ostrakine (El-Felusiyat), which show that the 'Sinai corridor' continued as the vehicle for staple goods from Tunisia and the Byzantine eastern Mediterranean well after the Arab conquest of Egypt (Arthur and Oren 1998). Such connections seem to have been as important to the exchanges of the early Islamic world as those between the islands that the Arabs conquered, or on which they gained a foothold, especially from the eighth century. The regional network that we find centred on Crete is a small part of that world, the medieval counterpart of those prehistoric archipelagos referred to in Section 2 (Lewicki 1978, 454–7, 466).

7. CONCLUSION

'A journey from Spain to Egypt or from Marseille to the Levant was a humdrum experience' (Goitein 1967–88, 1.42). The documents recovered from the Cairo Geniza (cf. II.2) preserve for us the conceptual map of the Mediterranean common amongst later generations of Mediterranean merchants and seafarers than those of the Pirenne period. 'The West' was a long way away, the documents imply. But 'the West' was not only Christian Europe or al-Andalus: it included the Maghreb as well. Little distinction was made between Islamic and infidel parts of this distant region. On the other hand, this distant West was far from inaccessible. The chief lesson of the commercial information that the Geniza contains is that the Mediterranean was looked on as a single region – despite pirates, politicians, or technological constraints. In this chapter we have been exploring the varied forms of communication, from the acoustic to the commercial, which help make that unity, that humdrum ease of movement, possible, even in periods – such as that associated with Pirenne – when it has seemed least to be expected.

We could hardly deny that it can be helpful for specific purposes to use the terminology of the routeway in describing channels of connectivity – as we found Cicero doing, for instance. The annual movement of grain from Alexandria to imperial Rome can usefully be conceived in such a way. Even in this instance, however, the vagaries of the journey meant that the economic impact of this specialized form of redistribution was felt in hundreds of harbours 'along the route' in quite different ways each season. And it is our contention that the normal rhythms of Mediterranean exchange, the 'background noise' of coastwise movement which we have found in supposed Dark Ages, are vastly more fluid in their patterns; and that, whether they take the form of *cabotage*, slave-raiding, piracy or pilgrimage, they act to bind the microecologies together even when the phenomena that answer to the description of routes have – actually or apparently – ceased.

We must not, however, leave the impression that the continuum of communication was unvariegated and all-embracing. The *existence* of such a continuum has, we believe, been a constant from at least the second millennium B.C. onwards; which is why the medieval and the prehistoric have alike provided the material for detailed examples in the preceding pages. But the point of our definition of the microecology (Chapter III) and our discussion of extended hinterlands (Chapter IV), and (here) of the patterns of interaction too various and detailed to be called routes, has been to emphasize that the clusters and series of points of contact are constantly changing, and that the degree of connectivity is locally very changeable too. These – to allude once more to an earlier epigraph – are the differences which resemble each other.

PART THREE

REVOLUTION AND CATASTROPHE

I'd pop over to California, too . . . only I promised some editor to make a detailed study of the problem of Mediterranean trade. You may say the subject is dull, a specialist's subject, but that's what we need, we need specialization – we've had enough of philosophizing.

Turgenev, *On the Eve*, trans. Gardiner (1950) 221

CHAPTER VI

IMPERATIVES OF SURVIVAL: DIVERSIFY, STORE, REDISTRIBUTE

Quails and prickly-pear are their principal resource;
There is no water anywhere in all the Inner Mani.
It bears only beans and thin wheat:
This the women sow, the women reap:
The women gather the sheaves to the threshing-floor
The women winnow it with their bare hands
The women thresh it with bare feet
Their hands and their feet are cracked with drought
Like tortoises', coarsely thickened.

> Niphakis, Poem in praise of Tsanetbey Grigorakis,
> late eighteenth century, version collected by Leake
> (1830) *Travels in the Morea*, 1.332–9

1. THE HISTORY OF MEDITERRANEAN FOOD SYSTEMS

We have identified extreme topographical fragmentation as one of the two key environmental ingredients – along with the connectivity provided by the sea itself – in a distinctively Mediterranean history. The claim needs to be tested further. The primary production of food can legitimately claim to be a basic human activity (although we shall again be resisting the claims of 'calorific determinism' (II.5)). Dramatic variation – over the shortest distances and within the briefest times – in the practices of primary production is characteristic of the Mediterranean landscape. If, as we suspect, the core of Mediterranean history is the control and harmonization of chaotic variability, then that should be manifest in the history of food production. The distinctiveness that we stressed in Chapter III should make it worthwhile to compare the different periods of Mediterranean history, in the hope of understanding similarities in the conditions of production within a network of fragmented and ever-changing environments. That comparison, through a selection of some patterns in the agrarian past of the Mediterranean lands, is the subject of the present chapter. We offer an outline statement of what we take to be the parameters for a history of Mediterranean agriculture – some well-known, others more controversial.

Success in our project of tracing intrinsically Mediterranean factors in the history of primary production will entail assigning revolutionary changes in techniques or organization a reduced role. If the types of continuity for which we are arguing find general acceptance, then some at least of the turning-points and revolutions familiar from orthodox analyses may prove to have been more apparent than real. To some extent the historiography of discontinuities has been powered by a sense of intractable differences between periods: the transitions from one to another in such cases have needed to be sufficiently dramatic to account for them. In this chapter we purpose to nuance the investigation of qualitative differences through time in Mediterranean social history, and in the next two (VII–VIII) will look again at some of the alleged turning-points between periods in the light of what we have found. Until the last quarter of the twentieth century, there has been an unresolved problem in this area. On one hand, agronomical theorists have not found it too difficult to identify characteristic Mediterranean agricultural behaviour: although this project has sometimes been tinged with Romantic Mediterraneanism, discussed in Part One, many of the similarities in the cultivation of olives, wheat or vines between ancient Greece and late Antique Syria, Islamic Spain or early modern Italy do seem to be more than superficial. On the other hand, there has of course been a tendency of great theoretical force on the part of economic and political historians to divide up this same range of cultures precisely on the grounds that the means of obtaining and distributing the primary products on which life depends have been radically different in each. By contrast with the associative, almost picturesque, approach of the first school of thought, such analyses have often ultimately been based on comparison with places environmentally very different from the Mediterranean.

In general, a tendency to simplify the essential diversity of Mediterranean landscapes has also led to over-schematic interpretations of the agrosystem. Accounts have tended to privilege a rather limited number of strategies, and therefore to attribute too great a significance to possible transformations of those activities – transformations through technical improvements, as it might be. The complexity of the Mediterranean environment suggests that what is needed from scholarship is a more organic and ecological account of how the effects of human activity intertwine with the processes of geomorphology and the life-cycles of other living things. Investigation of the agricultural production of a rather limited range of 'staples' seems to us to be much less interesting and fruitful than holistic approaches to the problem of human survival, such as those which use concepts of the sort familiar to the social anthropologist (e.g. 'food system': LaBianca 1990, 1–20). But towards the end of the chapter, and still more in Chapter 7, we shall move into those parts of the agrosystem where the effects of the pursuit of power and wealth are as marked as any environmental constraints.

2. THE NEW ECOLOGICAL ECONOMIC HISTORY

Diversity is now widely perceived as central to the study of historical Mediterranean food systems. Three principal currents in scholarship have brought this about.

The first is landscape archaeology (BE III). This is essentially a result of the combination of new techniques (ranging from air photography to the computer processing of large quantities of data) with the escalating costs of traditional excavation and with new opportunities – or emergencies – in the development of large tracts of the rural landscape. The sophistication of the means by which material is recovered from wide segments of landscape, and of the techniques by which it is interpreted, is now very considerable. Not the least of the beneficial outcomes has been a tendency (developing for other reasons also) towards chronological period-inclusiveness. Earlier neglect of certain periods at the expense of others – often of early medieval at the expense of classical – has been corrected, and huge strides have been made in the identification, provenancing and dating of diagnostic artefacts (which have often been of primary importance for the economic and social historian in themselves). Most important perhaps, the practice of survey archaeology has entailed a *complete* understanding of the whole gamut of changes in the landscape through time, and has therefore generated a salutary holistic approach to the history of the environment. This development in archaeology has brought about a quantitative revolution in the amount that we know about Mediterranean rural landscapes in the past. It is not too much to say that the present book could not have been written before this revolution; and we should register the effect of its absence from almost all works of Mediterranean economic and social history written before about 1980.

The second and third currents are in some ways side-effects of the first. In the pursuit of a holistic comprehension of the landscape, archaeologists have revived interest in two other avenues to the understanding of past environments. One of these is the systematic study of the literature and documents produced by travellers in the Mediterranean from the later Middle Ages onwards. The other, which has in some ways made the greatest contribution of all, is ethnography – contemporary, historical, archaeological (the last sometimes called ethno-archaeology). The debate on one phase of Mediterranean productive history, the agriculture of ancient Greece, has for example been totally transformed by methods derived from social anthropology: through the interest of archaeologists in anthropological theory, and through the comparison of ancient productive systems with the data of modern ethnographic research.

There are some difficulties which should be registered in relation to each of these new approaches. Archaeological survey is skewed towards certain sorts of recognizable material, and the sites which it identifies are not always easy to reconstruct in imagination as a functioning social landscape. More seriously, accidents of survival prevent effective survey in many of the most fertile areas of the Mediterranean, where continuous human use has obliterated the record; equally, the changing geomorphology (which we shall examine in more detail in Chapter VIII) has buried important landscapes wholesale or allowed their removal by erosion. The accounts of travellers are often tralatician, tendentious and misleading; they suffer from the characteristic purblindness of the literary observer to the processes of production. Ethnography meanwhile privileges a certain sort of country person, who will usually live in a more or less unfavourable location, relatively, and untypically, as we shall argue, little integrated into networks of redistribution – because by and large those are the places where country life has changed least (cf. Chapter XI). This has also skewed the picture. For ethnographic analysis of the centres that are much more normal in Mediterranean history – that is, the central places of lowlands with easy access to the sea, rather than the remoter mountain villages – the only raw material available is derived from the vanished past, and must be interpreted by the historian. Ethnographic accounts of small producers underplay relations with the state or with powerful members of the community, and exaggerate autonomy and independence and the values of the household. Their remarks too may be tendentious or untrue, and are in any case hard to build into narratives with a chronological dimension. But when all these caveats have been entered, it remains the case that no other single influx of knowledge has ever had the transforming power of comparative ethnography in the field of Mediterranean history. And that is simply because it illuminates and expounds the basic logic of survival in the Mediterranean. Which is that, in the face of the highly unpredictable delivery – microregion by microregion – of the rain on which all production depends, unpredictable both in overall quantity year by year and in terms of its distribution over the winter months, the producer is faced with an ineluctable triple imperative: diversify; store; redistribute.

The material which is presented in this chapter will amply illustrate the theme of diversification. Nor is it hard to find evidence for the central role that storage has played, which suggests a notable degree of over-insurance against risk. To give only one introductory example, Ramon Muntaner recorded in his *Chronicle* (ed. Lanz 1843, 223) that in the 1320s, after their disgusting atrocities at Rodosto, the Catalan Grand Company settled in eastern Thrace and proudly subsisted there for five years on the stored provisions that they had seized – without ploughing, digging the vineyards or pruning the vines. The implications of storage for relations of dependence and decision-making in Mediterranean landscapes receive fuller attention in Chapter VII.

Historically, the most important strategy for coping with risks of all kinds to the provision of food and the maintenance of production, and especially for coping with the unpredictability of the weather, has probably been redistribution. Redistribution from one part of a microenvironment to another – the 'low-level' connectivity of the previous chapter – is one of the normal and obvious ways of responding to risk. Larger-scale networks of distribution offer proportionally more thoroughgoing remedies. In nutritional terms, swapping my peas for your barley is a relatively egalitarian manoeuvre. But if I can sell my peas to the city, with the cash I may perhaps be able to invest in more barley than would have been available to me from local exchange. The strategy of entering a market may thus be seen as an ingredient in the repertoire of responses to risk. We suggest that the degree of participation of a microregion in the networks of exchange and supplementary supply – its *redistributive engagement* – constitutes another helpful scale of variation on which to assess the agrarian history of that place. Agrarian history is closely entwined with connectivity, and should not be considered in isolation. That theme will be specifically addressed in Chapter IX.

3. UNDERSTANDING THE MARGINAL

> Dans de nombreuses régions et pendant de nombreux siècles l'agriculture a été . . . *l'art de ne pas cultiver la terre.*
>
> Sigaut (1975) 215, his italics

The newer approaches to Mediterranean production just described have strongly emphasized risk: principally the risk that is inherent in the meteorology of the

Mediterranean, with its marked intra- and inter-annual variability of precipitation (although there are many other uncertainties of life in such a complex landscape to which we shall return in more detail in Chapter VIII). The patterns of risk avoidance in production, through the myriad complexes of crop choice, inter-cultivation, processing, redeployment of residues, and interaction of agriculture with animal husbandry, are one of the most interesting factors differentiating microregions. This is in turn precisely because Mediterranean environments have very different and very local conditions of aspect, moisture-retention in the soil, natural vegetation, or accessibility.

Describing diversification in British agriculture since the fourteenth century, Joan Thirsk writes of

> a sequence of movements from mainstream farming to alternatives, and then back again. Major disjunctures have recurred, obliging farmers to divert their attention from the primary pursuit of grain and meat, to investigate other activities. On each occasion, when diversification has been necessary, farmers' ingenuity has been taxed, but it has successfully produced solutions which enabled them to survive until the old order returned. (1997, 2–3)

The essential difference between Mediterranean and north-west European production is sharply visible here: in the Mediterranean those disjunctions are typical accidents of everyday experience, and, rather than 'a sequence of movements', we find a coexistence between 'normal' and 'alternative' agriculture. The coexistence itself takes such various forms as to make such a classification as Thirsk implies almost unworkable.

Another way of expressing the omnipresence of risk is to regard all Mediterranean environments as 'marginal'. This marginality comes in three forms. First, the structural marginality of those places whose average climatic conditions, above all their aggregate precipitation, are only just sufficient for the usual range of productive activities: the semi-arid and arid fringes, or the areas of continental winter cold at the edge of the Mediterranean climatic zone. It is relatively easy to understand the marginality of those places where the zone of Mediterranean-type production – classically defined by the practicability of oleiculture (see Map 1) – shades off into areas differentiated by summer rainfall or greater aridity, or by lower winter temperatures. In fact, the complexity of Mediterranean topography makes the application of even this simple standard more difficult than might be expected. Witness the climate of the north Aegean island of Samothrace with its year-round gales, summer rain and cold winters; or the extreme aridity of the hinterland of Valencia in south-east Spain; or the tough conditions of production in the Mani of southern Greece, as they appear in the epigraph to this chapter.

Within each microregion, moreover, even away from the limits of the 'Mediterranean' climatic region, the accidents of relief and lithology, hydrology and soil, produce, under the influence of changing weather patterns, a second kind of marginal transition, in which the scale is purely local, or even microlocal. Examples include small-scale rock-formations such as the surface travertine beds of the Plain of Antalya, or the fossil dunes of the coast of Palestine and the microtopography of the hard limestone *karst* regions. On the coasts, salinity, dune formation, or exposure to the wind also multiply the zones of seasonal risk. All these have frequently produced areas of increasing difficulty into which human productive effort is extended with diminishing returns. The accidents of the unpredictable Mediterranean year do not all derive from shortage of rain: the formation of marshes through heavy precipitation and poor drainage or exposure to unexpected cold may be equally hazardous. Sometimes, perversely, there is too much rain – as in Tunisia in 1761 when it rained from August to May and all the crops rotted (Valensi 1985, 142).

Risks which may intensify through time constitute the third type of marginality, reinforcing the difficulties of an uneven environment. Some such risks are sudden: the unexpected local transformation. In the unstable landscape of the Mediterranean, at each locality the temporally marginal is only moments away – beyond the landslide, or the earthquake – or hours away – after the flash-flood or the wildfire. Beyond the sudden event, routine but unforeseeable, normal but tragically disruptive, the relentlessly haphazard meteorology and the ecological threats of disease or insect-infestations recalibrate the scale of difficulty of production from month to month and field to field. The other type of temporal marginality is more gradual and foreseeable but no less ineluctable: the process by which productive terrains become less and less easy to use as the seasonal shifts of the year's weather move towards the drier or the colder. This fourth and last form of marginality is replicated in almost every microregion, during every season: few localities are so sheltered as to be wholly immune to winter frost; few have water so perennial and so abundant as to render them immune to complete productive incapacity in the summer.

These forms of marginality interact with each other, and require the utmost adaptive flexibility on the part of producers. The balance between complex agricultural activities and simpler forms of foodstuff collection is one reflection of the shifting conditions of time and locality. Thus, as every summer's drought approaches, the interdependence of the world of the farmer and the world of the gatherer is restated – as we see from the following traveller's description of the Mani in the early nineteenth century:

> To botanize in search of esculent wild herbs in the spring and early summer, is a common occupation of the women of Greece, those herbs forming an important part of the food of the poor during the fasts of that season. In the summer they have no such resource, and in the long fast which precedes the feast of the Panaghia, on the 15th of August s.v., the patient has little but the gourd tribe to depend on. The summer productions of the garden, however, which depend on irrigation, such as gourds, cucumbers, badinjans, water-melons, etc., are too dear for the poor, or rather are not to be had, as gardening, the produce of which is so liable to be plundered, can never flourish in a country where property is so insecure as in Turkey. The chief food of the lower classes, therefore, in the summer fast, is salted star-fish, olives, goat's cheese and bread of maize, seasoned with garlic or onion and washed down perhaps with some sour wine. No wonder that the great summer's fast sometimes proves fatal, especially to women. (Leake 1830, 1.258–9)

The crops have changed from one period to another, but the desperation has arisen in every period of Mediterranean history before our own times.

In this chapter we consider how the omnipresence of the marginal has enforced diversity, flexibility and opportunism in managing the environment, re-examining the relationships between extraction of food from the uncultivated environment and the formal procedures of agriculture *sensu stricto*. In Chapter VII we shall be able to move on to the consideration of what all this implies for the qualification of production as 'subsistence' or 'cash-crop'. Throughout, the level of 'redistributive engagement', the locality's degree of involvement with other places, will be seen to be of high importance. Our aim is to show how analysis of this sort can offer a way of cutting some of the Gordian knots of debate on the Mediterranean economy. Understanding environmental responses can suggest alternatives to the polarity between primitive and modernist in the discussion of the ancient economy, and help to find common ground between Antiquity and the Middle Ages or between the Islamic and Christian worlds. It also promotes a deeper understanding of the productive regimes from which the changes of the early modern period emerged.

Maintaining the maximum variety of resources is an obvious response to the variety of risk, and it is most economical to allow fissiparous Nature, that has been so prodigal in its environmental diversity, to provide a solution. In a highly differentiated ecology, the repertoire of 'extras' for the gatherer has been extremely large. The natural setting itself is rich in potential contributions to the pursuit of survival, as Leake's description suggested – the foraging for herbs and edible vegetation, and the salting of starfish from the rocky seashore. The place of such simple gathering in the nutritional history of the Mediterranean must be acknowledged: an early twentieth-century list for example includes 621 plants for casual gathering (Garnsey 1988a, 53). Each tiny region has to augment its food supplies in difficult times with what chance offers – tortoises in places where starfish were clearly not available, according to the rural informants of one ethnographer (we must, however, recall the predilection of Greek countryfolk for the colourful exaggeration of plights of this kind: Halstead 1990a, 153). And when a Greek comic poet of the fifth century B.C. pictured a townsman retiring to rural comfort – to an enterprise including a yoke of oxen for ploughing, wine presses, goats and sheep – he imagined the man's satisfaction at being able to eat as relish (with the staples of his diet) not old fish from the urban market, but the tasty finches and thrushes that inhabited the countryside (Aristophanes, *Islands*, frag. 387).

Paradoxically, then, the environments in which the more complex manipulations of human agriculture would be most difficult offer a different kind of resource which is crucial when preferred strategies fail. Gathering from such areas is augmented by specialized extension of planned production, through olive-trees planted in the crevices of hillsides where nothing else will grow, or vines, carobs and figs (to all of which we shall return). But the starfish and tortoises offer an even more important lesson: the usefulness of animals, small or large, in carrying the nutrition available in winter over into the summer drought. There are many animal species which perform this function more effectively by far than those two strange instances, and it is in this strategy that we have the key to that great symbiosis between animal husbandry and agriculture which is at the heart of Mediterranean agrosystems (thus, for instance Butzer 1996, 142; cf. also III.6). Not the least of the benefits of environmental intricacy in the periphery of the Mediterranean is the range and quality of the niches that it offers for humans' domesticated animals.

The peripheral environment of marsh, mountain, forest or sea was long undervalued by historians influenced by the cultural prejudice that privileges, as being more civilized, tilling the soil over other productive activities (Fumagalli 1992, 99–101). An agrarian history which stresses the interdependence of agricultural activities with other strategies for maintaining nutritional input from the environment is to be preferred. Archaeological discussion of the nature of early agriculture, in revealing, for instance, the great importance of the prehistoric occupation of Mediterranean wetlands, has promoted such an approach (Delano Smith 1979, 290–1).

In point of fact, the areas that we often dismiss as least hospitable, or perceive as residual fragments of a landscape that was once hostile to humanity, are among the most diverse and complex portfolios of complementary productive opportunities. They offer, in most dramatic fashion, the opportunity of harnessing natural variety to buttress against natural risk. Woodlands and wetlands are prime examples, and the next two sections are devoted to them.

4. THE INTEGRATED MEDITERRANEAN FOREST

To this day, forests survive in the remoter Mediterranean mountains – in the Taurus or the Pontic range, or in some parts of Pindus or Rhodope – which suggest to us the 'natural vegetation' of the region. They survive either as forest in the strict sense, or in the altered states known as *maquis* or *phrygana* (or other such local names), the bushy, thorny and impenetrable scrub which forms so immediate an impression on the visitor to the Mediterranean (Margaris 1981). It is tempting to regard these wood- and shrublands as a hostile natural environment, to be set against the tamed product of human cultivation. In fact, of course, the forest is not a static isolated piece of original nature being vandalized by careless mankind, but a tremendous resource which can be used to a whole range of intensities according to human needs, and which is in a constant state of change according to the different demands made upon it.

It follows from this openness to human activity that little, if any, Mediterranean woodland is actually in its natural state (and that was probably already true in Antiquity: Delano Smith 1996). There is virtually no 'primeval' wilderness. Every part of the environment has been used, abandoned, reoccupied to various degrees and at varying rhythms. This makes microregions what they are: 'a region's landscape reflects the essentially episodic nature of both human activity and geomorphological process' (1996, 176). The genuine wilderness has, moreover, always been a good deal less amenable than sentiment suggests:

> Much of the wildwood may have consisted of small, stout, hard and intractable trees, casting a dark dry shade beneath which nothing would grow, and yielding nothing but wood and small amounts of pasture. What has replaced it is by no means the useless 'scrub' that geographers often suppose. It is a complex, beautiful and resilient mosaic of vegetation . . . Meat, wool, cheese, honey, edible plants, drugs, dyes, etc. are products not of wildwood but of the historic vegetation of Greece. (Rackham 1983, 347)

It is wrong to regard change to the natural vegetation as being automatically 'damaging'. In the first place, causing rapid and irreversible simplification of an ecological system needs to be distinguished from making major changes through introducing new symbioses. Even in seemingly wild forest, the less useful trees are gradually thinned to the advantage of the more desirable species, such as those whose fruit (acorn or chestnut) is useful. In late Antiquity we hear of a 'large village' on Mount Lebanon where the principal productive activity was the gathering of walnuts, presumably from managed wild trees. The people engaged in this activity (whose local centre was the prosperous city of Emesa (Hims)) are interestingly described as 'having no master', unlike the country people of most parts of Syria, who were more tightly bound into structures of dependence. Forest-margin exploitation was opportunistic and relatively uncontrolled, a strategy that called for collaboration but which did not invite domination (Theodoret, *History of the Syrian Monks* [*Historia Religiosa*], 17.2–3).

In this case the nuts were being gathered for trade as a quality foodstuff. But the nuts and fruits of the woodland are also of great importance for animals. It is crucial not to take this as a sign that the wood is part of the outer darkness, any more than are the mountains which are also so frequently linked with pastoralism (III.6). Animal husbandry is almost everywhere integral to the diversity of Mediterranean production, and it is husbandry more than anything which binds the forest to other productive zones. Nothing could be less helpful than to urge, in the context of the forest, an 'appreciation . . . of the change from a predominantly tillage economy to one in which pastoralism has played a major part, and of the decline of the classical culture' (Thirgood 1981, 8). A revealing juxtaposition, that – and an unhelpful one, reflecting the equation of agriculture with civilization and the deep-seated cultural hostility to the shepherd in any manifestation that we have already had occasion to criticize. A corrective comes from a careful study of the pollen of the woodland of the *dehesa*, the coastal margin of the wetlands of the Guadalquivir plain in southern Spain. Here an ecology which is characteristic only of Iberia and the Maghreb turns out to have been adapted for extensive animal husbandry since well before the Bronze Age. The peaks of sophistication of this usage coincide with the moments when the economy of Spain has been most 'urbanized' and its societies most complex (Stevenson and Harrison 1992). We return in Chapter VIII to the effects that misunderstanding of the uncultivated landscape have had on the long-term history of Mediterranean environments.

Throughout Mediterranean history up to the nineteenth century, woodlands and scrublands have constituted a major source of energy. The combustion of vegetation has been essential to the survival of Mediterranean people in the often very cool winters, not least the poorer inhabitants of cities (IV.6). In the absence of cheap wood for fuel, there are many other possible recourses which have been important in the Mediterranean past. On a microregional scale, the litter of local woodland or maquis can be drawn upon. Brushwood, leaves and twigs are sources of fuel the collection of which need do no harm to the ecology; they form part of a complex array of recycling activities which also make use of the residues of a number of other productive techniques. The bath-houses of twentieth-century Syria are for instance fuelled with *tezek*, a mixture of camel-dung and straw from cereal crops (Robert 1980, 276). The bake-houses of the Middle East often used dried olive-pulp, straw and small twigs. Locally and periodically these small-scale demands can in aggregate be greater than the capacity of the immediate environment (Bresc 1986b, 87–98). But that is precisely why the portfolio of fuel resources, like that of food resources, is everywhere diversified. On Cyprus highly specialized use of particular maquis species is recorded: the smoke of *Pistacia lentiscus* is valued for curing meat, and its fruit is used to flavour sausage; *Arbutus andrachne* provides an important fuel resource because it coppices so freely, regrowing rapidly after fire damage or cutting; and the ladanum gum which is produced by *Cistus villosus* is collected by shaving off and processsing the beards of goats that have been browsing in these low bushes (Hayes 1995).

Trees also provide an extremely valuable raw material for human artefacts, underestimated with respect to the more distant past because of their poor survival rate. What does remain in a few favoured contexts justifies the use of the term 'civiltà del legno' for Antiquity as much as for the Middle Ages (Fumagalli 1992, 4–5; for wooden barrels, cf. the discussions of the 'container revolution' in Chapters V and IX). The omnipresence of wood in myriad small-scale objects and devices was, like the ordinary requirements of human communities for fuel, maintained by symbiotic coexistence with forested areas, and benefited substantially from the natural variety of species.

All such uses can be intensified and planned – by selective clearance, by attentive regimes of felling and cutting, and by replanting where necessary: systematic forestry, in fact. This can, in principle, enormously extend the capacity of the woodland environment to fulfil the demands made on it – as by metallurgy, which depends on the combustion of charcoal for its high temperatures. One ton of refined iron may have consumed 65 cubic metres of wood. We should however recall that metallurgy has often been more intermittent, shifting and opportunistic than we readily imagine from modern analogy (cf. IX.2). Therefore even these demands may be met from the concerted woodland resources of quite large numbers of microenvironments; and silvicultural management, and particularly the practice of coppicing, is capable of notable yields. One hectare of good coppice will yield 84 cubic metres in 16 years (Bechmann 1990, 151–4). The fuel needs of even a sustainable metallurgical establishment might therefore be reckoned at some 12 hectares of coppicewood per ton of annual product. In a fragmented topography, and in a society not consuming large quantities of refined metal, local needs could no doubt often be supplied in this way. Similar silviculture has no doubt regularly been able to supply most ordinary demands for wood as a constructional material (the special cases of timber for ship building and major architectural projects are discussed in Chapter VIII).

Cities and other large settlements form another test case, because of the intensity of their demands (IV.6). A traveller in Naples in 1777–80 (Swinburne 1790, 81) reported finding himself in the Posilippo Tunnel, one of the main entrances to the city, in danger of being 'hurt by the faggots which asses are continually bringing from the woods' – maintaining supplies for a substantial city from local resources in relatively recent times. We know that in the Roman Empire there was sufficient woodland in Italy for specific tracts to be assigned by the emperors to the provision of fuel for the enormous bath-complexes of the city of Rome (*Augustan History: Alexander Severus*, 24, 5; cf. Hemphill 1987). Such woods, probably in former times public property of the Roman People, could be deployed wholesale, whether (as seems more likely in this case) for planned extraction or for asset-stripping. The effect of fragmentation in local topography and the distribution of forest between jurisdictions – whether of cities, villages or estates – will elsewhere generally have acted to protect forest from wholesale exploitation.

In most periods it has been relatively unusual for forests to have been indiscriminately and destructively exploited for long enough to abolish them.

According to one calculation, a population of fifty million in the Mediterranean basin would require 75,000 tonnes of wood every day; the aggregate of 27 million tonnes per annum would represent about half the likely primary productivity of Mediterranean woodlands (Le Houerou 1981). The aggregate is impressive: that such quantities were forthcoming is eloquent testimony to the importance of the complex extractive relationship with the woodlands in which so many Mediterranean producers have regularly participated, and on which all inhabitants of the region have depended. There have undoubtedly been instances of over-exploitation and deforestation, sometimes on a quite large scale. No mystical equilibrium between human demands and natural resources in the Mediterranean has ever existed, however subtle and flexible extractive strategies may seem; and the sudden demands of a commercial opportunity such as the sugar-cane industry of medieval Cyprus or a state-led intervention such as a Roman silver mine have sometimes had irreversible effects. We shall set out our assessment of the place of such developments in the wider context of Mediterranean environmental history in Chapter VIII. But it can be asserted here that, before the nineteenth century, the urgency of societies' needs for woodland products led to the active integration of forest or scrubland into the managed environment more often than it caused irreversible loss of so flexible and varied a resource.

Extraction of forest products is not, of course, entirely fragmented by the topography of the microregions. Access to the forest depends on the nature of the systems of redistribution which can tie together processes of exploitation across thousands of microregions. Rivers, especially where they are suitable for the flotation of timber, privilege adjacent forests (Petts 1990). The forests of the uncleared lowland plains were a convenient resource for the fleets and architects of the Mediterranean: in Albania the Venetians, for instance, took ship-timber from the marshy coastal plain of Durazzo (Ducellier 1981). The belief that Mediterranean lowland forest was 'certainly never so productive as that of the mountains' (Thirgood 1981, 13) is simply false, an instance of that underestimation of the wet lowlands in Mediterranean history of which we shall see more in the next section. There is a productive zone where the forest meets the Mediterranean seaboard – or, to put it another way, where the accessibility which makes the seabord a region of high potential for communication shades off into the less accessible and more mountainous interior. Here, in this zone, two sets of environmental responses abut, in an interaction which is locally dependent on specific microregional characteristics. No doubt in the prehistoric period the zone of exploitation was narrow; by the Middle Ages, however, it had in many places expanded to near the environmental limits of the most important cultivated species (Toubert 1973, 181).

Let us return, finally, to the relationship between Mediterranean forests and traditional 'tillage'. Many of the woodland products that we have met are integral to other forms of production: making equipment for instance (there is a particularly interesting symbiosis with viticulture: Bechmann 1990, 88–92), and the provision of fuel for food-processing, or preservatives, flavourings and additives. In those ways, the managed wood complements the open field. But there has always been the possibility of using the forest as a buffer zone into which tillage can be extended when necessary, through the clearing of forest and woodland on a short- or long-term, cyclical or permanent basis (for instance, by various intricate procedures of burning: Bechmann 1990, 55–68). The new, rich, unworked soils are highly productive, and the forest-edge habitats are particularly rich in possibility (Bechmann 1990, 4). If every microregion has usually had its woodlands and scrublands, in every microregion the last three millennia have seen numerous ebbs and flows of the area under formal cultivation, and dramatic fluctuations of the blurred boundary at the edge of the managed landscape. In some ways, Mediterranean agriculture in its shifting opportunism has retained aspects of the slash-and-burn or swidden systems which are found elsewhere in the world, and which are sometimes predicated of earlier and supposedly more primitive phases in the history of this region.

The various means of increasing the yield of the forest are themselves naturally often cyclical or intermittent. Even attempts at wholesale reclamation may be practised in any one environment at sufficient intervals to allow recovery. A certain beneficial regularity of flux and reflux of forest margins over time is recognizable (Bechmann 1990, 76–8). Much more common is an ebbing and flowing, *within* the woodland, of the less destructive patterns of exploitation, according to the demands of production and the calculation of the best technological means, all within the context of the microregion. The uncultivated environment, like the cultivated, is subject to the periodical intensifications and relaxations of human intervention which form one of the basic rhythms of Mediterranean agrarian history (VII.4).

The full range of procedures can be seen in the forest margins of medieval Latium, which were exploited with every degree of intensity, including management which closely resembled gardening (Toubert 1973, 266): 'une présence aussi diverse et affirmée témoigne de l'ingéniosité attentive avec laquelle le paysan latial a su tirer parti de l'extrême discontinuité des sols et des microclimats' (1973, 197). It is noteworthy that this use of the marginal is a sign of sophistication rather than primitiveness. Where the productive system has not had the advantages of redistribution to reinforce its pursuit of variety, the wilder woodlands have indeed been less attractive. An example is the forests in Pontic Anatolia that were avoided by Neolithic settlers (Roberts 1982).

The productive potential of woodland has been neglected by scholars for too long: 'The study of the human exploitation of Post-glacial Mediterranean woodland is . . . compromised by the lack of inter-disciplinary communication and an unwillingness to consider models of land-use not advocated by Hesiod or Columella' (Lewthwaite 1982, 217). Ancient economies, like medieval ones, were never among those in which activities other than 'tillage' played only a minor part. Flexibility of production has been essential for survival in the Mediterranean.

5. THE UNDERESTIMATED MEDITERRANEAN WETLAND

Among the widespread environments of local marginality in the Mediterranean, wetlands have been, if possible, more underestimated by scholars than even forests have. Modern reclamation of them was first aimed at fighting malaria and was subsequently motivated by the profitability of intensive horticulture or arboriculture, or by the settlement expansion associated with tourism. It has so greatly reduced their frequency and extent that few people would regard wetlands as a canonical feature of the Mediterranean landscape. But a glance at the coast of Albania, which did not undergo any modernization until after the fall of its communist regime, reveals the previous state of affairs. The great wetlands at the mouths of the major rivers, such as the Rhône, Po, Strymon, Nestos, Hebrus, Maeander, Pyramus, Nile or Bagradas, are especially distinctive and significant. The delta of the Ebro provides a classic case. Thousands of hectares of alluvial soil, so heavy that it reportedly needs three horses to pull effectively a single-bladed plough, are surrounded by great belts of tall reeds and, in the outer fringes, by fishy salt-lagoons. The air is so humid that wooden buildings are impracticable and reed or brick must be used; this part of eastern Spain has not suffered from shortage of water. Huge numbers of insects feed a vast population of frogs and toads which in turn feed great flocks of migratory birds. Apart from the care of a few scrawny cattle, fishing and fowling almost entirely supported the scattered human population until the advent of modern drainage. The twentieth century saw the introduction of intensive horticulture (*huerta*) of the sort long characteristic of other places on the east coast where environmental management posed less extreme problems (cf. Chapter VII).

Highly distinctive and relatively extensive landscapes of this kind are important; but in some ways the smaller and more local wetlands have made a greater contribution to Mediterranean history. As with woodlands and scrublands, they form a part of the repertoire of environments available in a great many different microregions. Wherever a seasonal watercourse backs up behind beach deposits, wherever the accidents of topography render a valley floor less quick to drain, or wherever fault-lines have created intermontane basins, zones of inland drainage (as with the *ghouta* of the Orontes valley, Map 15), there is a potential wetland, ranging in degree of saturation from perennial pool or lake to marsh which dries out in summer. The flood-plains of any perennial river can provide an extended chain of environments constantly shifting according to the river geomorphology, length of winter inundation, and the permeability of the soil, and creating what ecologists call 'hydraulic disturbance patches' (Petts 1990). Mutability is characteristic: each season, at a different rate according to the weather, the layout of reed-bed and lagoon, salt-flat and sand-bank changes, and with it changes vegetation and wildlife. Thus the coastal *sebkha* of the Maghreb – flooded during the winter, but dried out completely by evaporation in the heat of the summer. The wetness of any wetland, its salinity, the frequency and effect of flood, the details of the topography of levée and watercourse or pool and pasture – all are liable to change according to vicissitudes in the catchment areas of the streams that feed them. The resulting diversity has actually offered multiple opportunities for gradual management of conditions in the margin, and it is this flexibility that makes the wetlands so important, particularly as part of a chain of resources involving neighbouring regions of different types. So it is those who make use of such chains of resources who particularly need wetlands (which for the ancient dream-interpreter Artemidorus (*On the Interpretation of Dreams*, 2.28) are positive only in the dreams of shepherds). In west central Italy, the wetlands afford winter grazing for sheep excluded by snow from the uplands, to which they move during the malarial summer. In Palestine, it is the moisture that forms the special resource in the dry heat of summer: the eighth-century St Willibald was impressed to see sheep immersed in the wetland at the source of the Jordan to keep them cool through the heat of the day (cf. Hodkinson 1988, 47). These environments are all ultimately the product of the alluvium created by the erosion and weathering of the hills and mountains, and they are therefore highly prone to dramatic changes during winter floods, with consequences for human activity which will require our attention in Chapter VIII below.

Wetlands resemble forests, then, in their normality: few microenvironments lack a spectrum of conditions ranging from the well-drained to the – at least seasonally – very moist. They are also like the woodlands in their internal variety, and even more kaleidoscopic in that that variety is more prone to intra-annual fluctuations. It is not surprising, therefore, that people have made use of them in a huge variety of ways. Just as the destruction of forest for fields was only the most extreme of a great series of interactive involvements with woodland, so reclamation is only the most transformative of a whole range of symbiotic techniques for using the wetland environment. The wholesale reclamation of marshes and lagoons to provide crops for the swollen cities of today disguises the potential of such environments for much less draconian forms of productive intervention. The fowler, fisherman, huntsman and reed-cutter, like the woodland shepherd, charcoal-burner or beekeeper, should not be relegated to the fringes of a world whose centre is misleadingly defined by a single sort of agriculture.

The coastal wetland offers four general levels of opportunity. The first is as an environment for gathering – of the characteristic plant and animal species. One of the wild plants gathered for food in Antiquity was an unusual type of water-chestnut local to the marshes of the lower Strymon valley in Thrace (Theophrastus, *Enquiry into Plants*, 5.14.5). It achieved a certain fame in the ancient world as a particularly estimable bonus to the local diet, comparable to the abundant and nutritious marsh-vegetation of the Egyptian Delta, above all the lotus. Like the tropical wetland crops that have been introduced in more recent times, plants of perennially waterlogged habitats were available during the summer dearth. But that type of habitat has not been given the place it deserves in Mediterranean historiography – despite the possibility (Sherratt 1980) that it had at the dawn of human agriculture been the cradle of cereal-gardening (*contra*, Limbrey 1990, preferring self-mulching basaltic vertisols, the highly fertile tracts of black clay soils locally found in parts of the Fertile Crescent). More obviously, and more importantly, the wetland is a major location for the acquisition of extra nutritional resources from hunting and fowling (as is the forest) and, above all, from fishing, to which we shall turn in more detail in the following sections.

The second type of opportunity concerns the marginal aspect of humid environments. Like the forest edge, the wetland edge offers locations for the occasional and local extension of productive activities – moving towards the open water as the fringes dry through the spring, or opportunistically improving sections of marsh with drains or dykes to make wet pasture more manageable. The annual movements of the edges of lakes in intermontane basins (such as that of the Fucine Lake in the Central Apennines, or Lake Copais in Boeotia: Map 16) have particularly lent themselves to this sort of use. On the Pomptine Marshes south of Rome a part of the whole vast tract was more or less suitable for cereal cultivation – of the most shifting, desultory and extensive kind. About a quarter of the possible cereal lands would be cropped at any one time, while the rest were used for rough pasture: great herds of oxen were allowed to roam, fulfilling no immediate function except manuring. The cycle of wheat growing was a long one. A band of seasonal migrants from the nearby mountains would break the soil in spring; it was left bare all summer; after the autumn rains, having been ploughed a second time, it was finally sowed for harvest the following year. More intensive, but equally shifting and transitory, use was made of wetter areas near settlements:

> the people of Terracina have the civil right to reclaim any plot of terrain that is inundated and that seems suitable to them, and every year in the summertime they drain a twentieth part with small ditches which they surround with dikes. They sow maize and vegetables and collect fruits in great quantity – in general these little reclamations do not last, since when the winter comes, the rivers carry so much water that they overflow the low dikes and destroy the work of the farmer, who in the good season starts again and thinks it worth his efforts and investment in view of the money that the provisionally reclaimed land yields him. (Attema 1993, 50, quoting a description of 1759; cf. 34–5 for cereals)

The third type of exploitation makes use of the perennial characteristics of permanent wetlands, as places in which water is reliably available for pastoral or arable production. In the pursuit of protective diversity, it is very useful to have access to environments of guaranteed special characteristics, and there are many instances of interlocking productive systems which make use of adjacent but quite different physical milieux. The case of south and east Spain illustrates the repertoire of environments well. The basic division is between the dry upland *sierras* where *secano* dry farming is practised and the well-drained but well-watered plains, the *campiñas* of Andalusia. The tracts where rivers make irrigation possible are known as *vegas*; on them is found intensive agriculture and in places the horticulture of the *huertas*. Wettest of all are the coastal wetlands, *marismas*, where today rice-paddying is practised – a modern way of exploiting an environmental extreme beyond the point where even the extension of *huerta* can reach. The possibility of agriculture actually within the wetland environment is not to be neglected. That is revealed by the systematic use of wet lowlands in pre-Columbian Central America, which have received the sort of study that the Mediterranean so sadly needs. In Central America, ditching and mounding to control the soil-moisture, and to provide a 'nutrient sump', made wetland one of the most important productive landscapes (Sluyter 1994). Roman centuriation of wet lowlands, as in Cisalpine Gaul, and the control of valley-bottom moisture in fragmented wetland environments through underground drains, as in west central Italy, may be seen as partial Mediterranean equivalents (VII.2). Medieval evidence shows that such high estimation of Italian wet bottomland continued: 'the Lucchese charters are documents for people who considered marshes alongside vines, olive groves, arable fields, and vegetable gardens to be viable resources' (Squatriti 1995, 39). In this case willows, yielding withies for vine-ties, were of special importance.

This reminder of the way in which the interdependence of productive strategies promotes the interaction of microregions leads naturally to the fourth advantage of the wetland: because of its position between land and sea it is often especially well endowed as a place of communication, a node in networks of redistribution. Its outlets to the sea may be used as harbours, its channels provide natural routes of communication behind the dunes along the seaboard, and navigable rivers may debouch into it. The setting of medieval Tinnis in the Egyptian Delta, of Ravenna from the Roman period on, and still more so of Venice among the lagoons and river-channels of a deltaic wetland, poised between reclaimable *terraferma* and the world of the sea are the acme of this effect (Cosgrove 1990). An observer in the early sixth century of our era saw the Venetian complex of waterways as the channel by which the agricultural abundance of Istria might be made available to Ravenna and to the cities of the Po plain – to the benefit of the inhabitants of the lagoons (Cassiodorus, *Variae*, 12.22–4).

Each facet of the wetland's usefulness can be managed in a more or less intense and complex fashion, and all were notably important in the economy of the Roman coastal villa (Purcell 1995c). Here aviaries, fish-ponds and game-reserves were a stylized and controlled extension of the gathering practices of a normal wetland environment (Parain 1936, 56–9). Irrigated meadows and specialized cultivations, such as the wet vineyard on the Tyrrhenian coast which produced the famous Caecuban wine, used drainage and local reclamation to develop the pastoral and arable use of wetlands to a high point of artifice. But the proprietor did not live off his fieldfares or lampreys: they were sold through the luxury foodstuffs market to which the villa also had access. The art of the villa consisted in managing and improving that access too, through harbour-works or road construction: Mediterranean ports, such as Ostia or Minturnae, often located beside the marshes at or near river-mouths, came to be the centres of networks of villa estates. The intensification of production is naturally closely associated with what has been called the 'delocalization of diet' (LaBianca 1990, 16). That can be characteristic of environments which at first sight seem unacceptably marginal. Increasingly intense exploitation of the environmental diversity of the wetland is structurally linked with the opportunity offered, through the topography, of easy involvement with networks of redistribution that reach beyond the immediate locality. Exploitation of marsh or wet-pasture resources may only be worth carrying beyond a certain point if a market is available. It often is, however, because the wetland provides an entrée to the sea.

6. 'THESE PLACES FEED MANY PICKLING-FISH AND EXULT IN THEIR ABUNDANCE OF FISHES' (Cassiodorus, *Variae*, 12.22.15, on Istria)

The labours of the months which form such a familiar ingredient of the art of the medieval calendar offer a vivid evocation of the life of primary producers. In Italian examples, both hunting and fishing scenes are prominent. In French ones they do not feature. Italy has on these grounds been called 'primitive' (Mane 1983, 247): rather, it is Mediterranean.

The starfish of the Mani remind us that the sea itself is among the productive 'marginal' environments of the Mediterranean. Many a microregion has turned to the sea for sustenance: but Mediterranean fishing has suffered from a poor press. Braudel, for whom the meagre resources of the sea were the inadequate counterpart of the scant resources of the land (1972a, 144), spoke of its waters in powerful, but meaningless, evolutionist terms as 'geologically too old . . . biologically exhausted'. He contrasted the Mediterranean unfavourably with the North Atlantic (138): when supplies did not equal the demand of a city such as Genoa (138–9), or when changing shoaling-habits deprived Dalmatian communities (158), there were no long-distance fishing-fleets to relieve the crisis. But that these dearths mattered to the inhabitants is significant too. They suggest that a sufficiency was more usual.

Seen overall, the Mediterranean is indeed an 'oligotrophic ecosystem' (Cruzado 1985, 144–5), ungenerous in the food it offers to marine species, especially by comparison with the nearby Atlantic. It has been called a 'negative estuary', in which salinity levels are high because of the excess of evaporation over precipitation (Estrada et al. 1985, 149–51). Yet Braudel's notion that the sea parallels the land is right in a very important way that he did not intend. Oceanographically, the Mediterranean displays a very marked variety of conditions. The weather and the highly fragmented topography of coast and sea floor produce complex surface currents, a varied vertical distribution of temperature in the water, and above all a differential distribution, vertically as well as horizontally, of the saline water entering from the Atlantic and the nutrient-rich fresh water supplied by the rivers.

The plankton populations exhibit a pronounced spatial heterogeneity (Estrada et al. 1985, 165–8). The fish that form a human resource are unevenly distributed too, according to their preferences for, as it might be, the layers of water of differing temperature grading down to the warm but inhospitable still waters of the deeps, or for the zones of contact with waters of different temperature or salinity, such as the great Atlantic influx that washes along the African coast as far as Cape Bon. The apparently uniform, if turbulent, sea is thus as fragmented into ever-shifting microregions as the land. The place of fishing in the annual cycle of production also varies dramatically according to species' life-cycles (T. Lefebvre [1929]), reinforcing the fragmentation. The topography of fisheries in Mediterranean history has reflected the need to respond flexibly to this microregional ecology as much as has the exploitation of any terrestrial environment. The Hellenistic and Roman fish-pickling plants of the approaches to the Strait of Gibraltar were for example dependent on the oceanography of the Alboran Sea.

Even after the advent of steam and diesel engines made catching deep-sea fish safer than ever before, they remain unimportant for Mediterranean diet. The total catch of west Mediterranean waters, notwithstanding today's demands and methods, has been estimated at 200,000 tonnes p.a. (Bas et al. 1985). Fish that are relatively common in modern fish-markets, such as the *rhombus* (turbot), were great rarities in the ancient world and became the stuff of fable and the delight of the gastronome. But the extravagant luxury of eating such rarities should not mislead us.

The problem, as a geographer puts it, is that 'the contrast [with the Atlantic] is rather one of the relative difficulty of fishing than one of relative scarcity of fish' (Houston 1964, 40–3). The fish-species of easier waters are naturally the most important. Nearly a fifth of the sea is continental shelf, such as La Planasse in the Golfe du Lion; and there are many places where their life-cycle brings important species of fish into frequent contact with the shore. Thus shoaling fish in season have locally been of considerable economic potential. Indented coasts (Iasus in western Asia Minor is a good example: Strabo, *Geography*, 14.2.21) and islands such as the Cyclades are particularly favoured in that respect. In the late nineteenth century the impressive fisheries of the rocky north-eastern Adriatic yielded some 9,000 tonnes p.a., of which half was consumed locally (Faber 1883; cf. Ferluga 1987, 45). In the third quarter of the twentieth century, a productive fishery was deliberately established on the Fournoi islands of the eastern Aegean, in a local intensification of exploitation (Kolodny 1974, 301–8).

The most important element in the ecology of Mediterranean fisheries, however, is undoubtedly the wetter parts of the ubiquitous wetlands. Where rivers – above all the Rhône, Po and Nile – discharge into the sea, the high levels of plankton support sizeable populations of fish. The same locations usually offer sheltered lagoonal waters, and the teeming mullet, carp and eel whose migrations make use of these habitats constitute a more substantial and more accessible resource than the shoals of the open sea or the species of the coastal rocks. In the marsh which separates the island of Leukas from the mainland of north-west Greece, for instance, the abundant mullet, sole, eel and shrimps were controlled in the early nineteenth century by wicker partitions in water less than one metre deep (Goodisson 1822, 56). On one estimate the lagoons are twice as productive as the open sea in their natural state, while capable when managed of *twenty* times that productivity (at 100 to 130 kg/ha p.a). The Adriatic lagoons in fact produce 150 kg/ha p.a., which is high for any waters outside the tropics.

Marshy lagoons once represented perhaps 6,500 sq. km of Mediterranean coastland. It is not therefore surprising that lagoon fisheries have formed a considerable part of the revenues and alimentation of cities. The Albufera at Valencia (Map 13), for instance, where the open water (3,000 ha in winter contracting to 2,000 in summer) is separated from the sea by the densely wooded strip of the Dehesa de El Saler, supports three fishing communities on eels and four species of mullet. (Yields p.a. in the years 1900–10 were about 130 tonnes and 43 respectively.) The lagoons of Bizerta in Tunisia can yield up to 3,000 kg of fish in a day, but the yearly totals remain very variable.

Such exploitation is not new. Later medieval Catania developed the fisheries of the Lentini lagoon (Bresc 1986b, 101). Two freshwater lakes provided important fisheries for tenth-century Thessalonica (John Cameniates, *De expugnatione Thessalonicae*, ed. Böhlig 1975, 5.10–15). In Antiquity, Artemis at Ephesus derived a very considerable part of her temple revenues from the fish of the lagoons at the mouth of the Cayster (Strabo, *Geography*, 14.1.25). The oyster contract of the Lucrine Lake in Campania had pride of place among the public revenues of Rome; while Strabo tells us of a lake near Calydon, 'large and well-endowed with the raw materials of pickling (*euopsos*), which is controlled by the Roman colonists of Patrae' (10.2.21). The elder Pliny (*Natural History*, 9.29) gives us a vivid illustration of one of these publicly managed fisheries, the *stagnum Latera*, in the territory of Nîmes; he alleges that tame dolphins, for all the world like sheep-dogs, helped to catch the shoaling mullet.

We are not primarily concerned to assess the aggregate contribution made by fisheries to the feeding of such communities. Rather we aim to show how they illustrate the potential of the marginal in times of crisis. The dramatic interannual fluctuations to which fisheries are vulnerable do not make fishing useless, but accommodate it to the normal rhythms of production (Powell 1996, 14). This fragmentation of the resource is typical of Mediterranean opportunities, and has been reflected in the organization of human responses: the seventy-two fishing republics that were the precursor of Venice, or the 270 *volis* with which the Ottoman Sea of Marmara was organized. In order, moreover, to take advantage of this resource through redistribution, a willingness to move and to adapt is important, and this too is a characteristic of Mediterranean history (Parain 1936, 65–9). Diversity and redistribution alike entail mobility (IX.5–6) and fishermen have been among the most prominent of Mediterranean sailors. Marino Sanudo

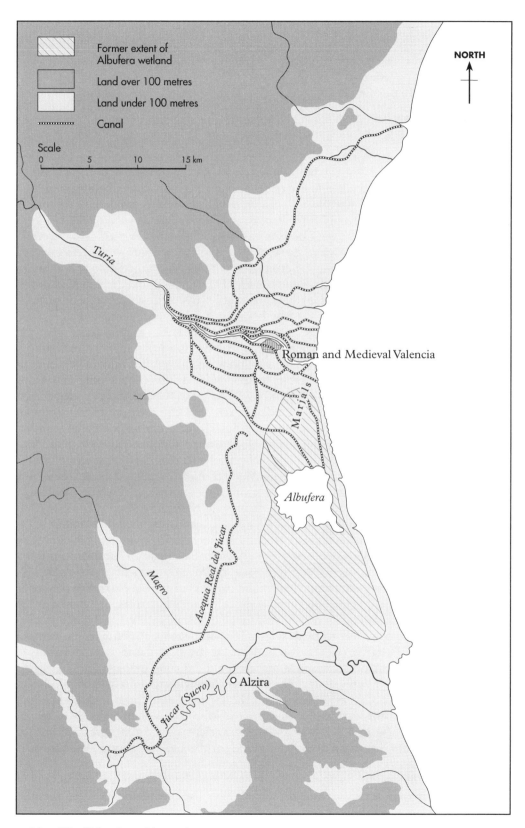

Former extent of
Albufera wetland

Land over 100 metres

Land under 100 metres

Canal

Scale
0   5   10   15 km

NORTH

Turia

Roman and Medieval Valencia

Marjals

Albufera

Mogro

Acequia Real del Jucar

Jucar (Sucro)

o Alzira

Map 13   Valencia and its setting

recorded the very numerous fishermen of the islands in the lagoons of the mouth of the Maeander; they used to pay a substantial revenue to the Byzantine emperor from their fisheries. A few survived in his time, and were known as 'valenti marinari' (Marino Sanudo, *Istoria del Regno di Romania*, fol. 16r, ed. Hopf 1873, 145).

The Corcyraean Bull and the question of glut

The first statue on the right as a visitor entered the sacred precinct of Apollo at Delphi was that of a great bull dedicated in about 480 B.C. by the people of Corcyra (modern Corfu). The city, as the inscription on the base declared, dedicated the statue to Apollo out of a tithe of the takings from the sale of a miraculous draught of tunny-fish (Pausanias, *Description of Greece*, 10.9.3–4; Habicht 1985, 75–6). The episode is informative. Fish-shoals on this scale were an unexpected and erratic gain, an eagerly exploited treasure-trove. As community wealth, the tunnies may be compared with the Athenians' contemporary windfall of a newly discovered vein of silver. The catch, its sale and the record were all systematic, the result of organized collective action. Most important, however, the fish were – already at the beginning of the fifth century B.C. – an asset capable of being turned into disposable wealth. They clearly fetched prices out of proportion to their nutritional value: there was a lively market for them.

The fertility and movements of the fish population and the human response to them are all highly unpredictable: in the years 1600–1605 tunny exports from Palermo ranged between 675 and 1353 tonnes (Gotteri 1969). Such unpredictability mirrors that of other kinds of extractive effort, at the mercy of the weather (Estrada et al. 1985). As Braudel perceived, years of dearth and glut are both common. But historians should not undervalue fisheries just because there are few places where a population can afford to rely on fishing alone. For similar reasons, fishing even outside the Mediterranean rarely serves as an independent subsistence activity; and there are no other strategies on which the wise Mediterranean primary producer relies exclusively either.

Environmental opportunism can draw on sea resources in bad periods, but it is more usual to conceive them as an optional extra – a means of gaining nutritional credit through deploying the occasional windfall in local or longer-distance redistribution systems. As Strabo said of Velia on the southern Tyrrhenian coast of Italy: 'they are compelled by the badness of the land to work the sea for the most part, and set up pickling-works and other enterprises of that kind' (*Geography*, 6.1.1). Recourse to the sea does not entail eating what you catch; it has been more common to process it, sell it, and eat what you get in return, supplying what Plutarch calls in the context of the fish, game and wild birds available at the resort of Aedepsos 'a market for the quality dinner-table' (*Topics for Discussion at the Dinner-Party* [*Quaestiones Conviviales*], 4.667c). As at Velia, the response to the sea has usually taken the form of quite high investment in traps for shoaling fish such as the tunny – the *madragues* of the west Mediterranean or the *dalyan* of the east and their ancient precursors (Bresc 1986b, 264–73). The good fortune of Corcyra stands at the head of a long tradition of investment and organization in tunny-fishing.

The economics of disposing of such windfalls have been invoked to explain the emergence of complex societies and interaction in the prehistoric Mediterranean

(Bintliff 1977b, 117–9; 1977a, 71). These theories have been attacked on the grounds that fish is a nutritionally inefficient resource (one kilogram of fish supplies only about two-thirds the calories of a kilogram of wheat) and that it has not overall played a major role in diet (Gallant 1985). Thus even today in Italy, the consumption of fish averaged across the whole peninsula and all social classes is only 10.4 kg. p.c. p.a. (Beckinsale and Beckinsale 1975, 18). But averages which iron out the difference between Campobasso and Palermo will not help understanding of the local perspectives that are central to Mediterranean history; and we shall be arguing that the history of Mediterranean diet cannot afford to operate with an exclusive attention to a narrow range of 'staples'.

The episode of the Corcyraean bull illustrates the importance of the local perspective, but it also makes the decisive point about fish, that you sell it for far more than it is worth to you in nutritional terms. Those who deny the dietary importance of fish in the Mediterranean remark, quite correctly, that it is economically close to a cash crop (Gallant 1985). Fish can be sold or consumed, when times are bad, at its 'nutritional price'; but it has usually been, like the Corcyraean tunny, an asset which has maintained its producers through its exchange value when fitted into the network of Mediterranean redistribution. The insight is far-reaching in its relevance for Mediterranean production. Cash crops are 'subsistence' strategies too. In Antiquity culturally complex practices were associated with the production and distribution of the important cash crops, and particularly oil and wine. It is instructive that in some contexts (such as the Sea of Marmara and its approaches, or southern Spain), similar practices were associated with the organizing of fishing and its capital-intensive infrastructure and with the creation of a sophisticated retail network for fish products (Purcell 1995b).

Diversity, opportunism, and specialization: the centrality of salt

It is not hard to find parallels in terrestrial environments for the unstable resource of the sea fisheries, but the fisheries of inland waters can in fact be somewhat more predictable. Between 20 August 1353 and 3 May 1354 the single fishery of Marta on Lake Bolsena produced 1,035 eels for salting and sale, and it despatched 1,120 to the papal court at Avignon on 3 March 1363, with another 885 in December that year (Lamonelli 1990). The eels were picked up at Corneto by a galley from Porto Venere, but because it was the winter season the journey took from 23 December to 4 April: a vignette of the management of a local resource for a distant luxury market (V.3). Where the Orontes issues from the Amuk wetland, catches of eels have reached 500,000 or 600,000 at the migration season, and, salted, they have been exported as far as Cyprus or even Malta; upstream, the marshes of the Ghab produce abundant freshwater *Silurus*, which are sent to the urban markets of Aleppo and Damascus (Weulersse 1940a, 60–1; Map 15). During the early sixth century, to return to Italian evidence, the nets of fishermen were found to be seriously obstructing navigation on five Italian rivers, the Mincius, Ollius, Anser, Arno and Tiber (Cassiodorus, *Variae*, 5.17; cf. 20).

On land, using the aleatory resource of the sea is more closely paralleled by the pursuit of game in mountain, forest and marsh than by inland fishing. Fowling is a special case of this, and in particular the seasonal snaring of migratory birds in the places, mainly on the coast, where they make their first landfall after crossing the Mediterranean in vast flocks. On Cape Matapan, the name Porto Caglio confirms what the poet of our epigraph says about the importance of migratory quail in the economy of the Mani; the bunting of late medieval Cyprus were exported pickled in vinegar in thousands of barrels a year to Rome and Venice (di Lusignano 1573, 88r; BE Section 6); and the southern cliffs of Malta are to this day hung with nets for the migratory north-bound bird population. On Capri scores of thousands of quail used to be trapped every summer. The number varied very extremely from one year to another: on this tiny island 12,000 quail were taken in bad years, 60,000 in good; and there was a record year of 150,000 with 45,000 in a single day (Swinburne 1790, 2.7). As with the fish so with the birds: the resource is an unreliable bonus. It is of most use if it can be made to do more than fulfil its basic nutritional potential – through storage against crisis, or through redistribution.

The principal way of rendering the bonus of extra fish, fowl or game less perishable and therefore more valuable was pickling in salt. Literary sources and archaeology – in the form of the study of containers, and, more strikingly, of the physical remains of the pickling plants themselves – leave us in no doubt as to the extent to which the perhaps unpromising output of Mediterranean and Black Sea fisheries was converted into a commodity of major economic importance. That happened above all in the Black Sea from the sixth century B.C. and, in the Roman period, along the shores of the eastern approaches to the Strait of Gibraltar. The process not only preserves the perishable fish: it uses the parts that would be unpalatable when the fish was fresh, and it makes transportation more efficient by eliminating the weight of water and concentrating the protein. The pickle also forms a very helpful supplement to a diet high in cereals (Curtis 1991, 7–9, 22–3). These considerations should be set against the relatively high energy cost of obtaining and processing the product.

The centrality of salt reinforces the importance of the coastal wetland environment. Because of the low tidal range, the very shallow fringes of the more maritime marshes turn in the summer heat into natural salt-pans, providing salt just where it is most needed. The famous *taricheuai* or pickling installations of the Black Sea were sited beside the very shallow lagoons and estuaries, where the great rivers of the Russian steppes debouch. A similar combination of salt and fish supported the public revenue of Istros at the mouth of the Danube and promoted the flourishing of medieval Comacchio between Venice and Ravenna. Salt, the means of turning animal biomass of all kinds into a commodity for redistribution, was itself a commodity of the highest importance in Mediterranean history (IX.2).

The source both of useful produce and of the means of greatly extending its usefulness, the coastal wetland functions as a gateway to the world outside: we have seen how the marsh of the Garigliano mouth and the woods of Garde-Freinet acted as beach-heads for the seaborne Saracens in the early Middle Ages (V.2). Whether in the Veneto or the Delta, the watercourses of the coastal wetland have offered a privileged access point between the sea and the land and have often constituted nodes in the networks of movement and redistribution (Laven 1989). The diverse roles of such places moreover encourage the development of appropriately complex societies. A remarkable example can be derived from the Étang de Berre near the Rhône delta in the later Middle Ages. The productive life of the region was founded firmly on the ecology of the wetland, but this was entwined with the activities of small traders and pirates – like those other denizens of the wetlands, the hunter, fowler or fishermen, figures who have been on the fringes of every historical society (Grava 1980).

The example of the Corcyraean tunny enforces two important points: that the aleatory nature of Mediterranean production does involve glut as well as dearth; and that it cannot be understood in detachment from the context of connectivity, which is invoked equally in conditions of overproduction and shortfall. A theoretically very helpful analysis of responses to fish-glut in traditional communities of the Atlantic remarks that

> glut poses in a particularly acute form a problem . . . How can they maintain the integrity of local ways despite a lack of economic and political isolation? . . . the most important parameters [of different responses to glut] are the status and ideological orientation of mediators between local society and the outside world, the prevalence of egalitarian ways in everyday affairs, and the manner in which uncertainty is conceived of and dealt with. (Wylie 1993, 386)

Engagement in the wider world of redistribution possesses no more glamour than the other necessary routes to diminishing risk. It need not be popular or 'smart': it is often stigmatized as uncertain, dangerous, demeaning or immoral – as too closely involved with the corruption induced by the sea. It is not a matter of embracing far-flung contact with open arms. The necessity of redistribution does not erode the charm of autarky (V.4). But we hope that our survey has helped to indicate why the exploitation of what has seemed to be the marginal cannot be isolated from other parts of the economy.

7. THE MOVEABLE MICROREGION: MEDITERRANEAN ANIMAL HUSBANDRY

Several times in the previous pages we have noticed that the gathering of animals in the wild has played a part in human survival. The ecology of some animal species, we observed, produces occasional gluts. These can offer useful resources in times of scarcity if the means of preserving perishable meat can be found: drying, in the sun or over brushwood fires; pickling in its various forms; above all, salting. A wild animal killed and eaten in the summer dearth represents biomass from the more abundant winter vegetation stored without human input of labour or skill. As a way of converting plant material into human nutrition, it may be inefficient; but that inefficiency is partly outweighed by the convenience and opportunity offered to small communities vulnerable to risk, especially through the large quantities involved with shoaling fish or migrating fieldfares. The calculation is not the abstract one of overall nutritional yield (II.5): risk and shortage skew the values out of all recognition.

We have also observed above that, in the range of human uses of wetland or woodland, accessibility and ease of movement played a formative role. Improving these is an obvious simple step towards organizing the contingent resources of the wild. Simple techniques include the use of fish-hooks, weapons, nets or poisons. But the spectrum of increasing complexity and cost leads through sophisticated and costly fish-traps or hunting-preserves to the controlled reproduction of the life of the wet or wooded margin in fish-pond, aviary and game-park that became a feature of ancient elite investment: what the Romans called

pastio villatica, 'country-house husbandry'. Alongside these practices, and related
to them, is ordinary *pastio*, the management of completely domesticated animal
species. We had occasion to set out some of the larger historical questions about
this subject in III.6. But it is essential to return to it at this point, since it needs
to be fitted into the ethnoarchaeological framework of the present discussion.

Domesticating animals, naturally, offers exactly the same basic nutritional insurance as eating wild animals in summer. But whereas the quest for the bunting
or the mullet mostly involves going to the places to which that creature's life-
cycle happens to have brought it, the incomparable advantage of domestication
is that you take your animals with you, and you decide on the environment in
which their life-cycle will take place. Again, we have already seen something of
how this may be done in marsh and forest, systematically rather than through
the accidents of wild habitat and hunting. Given the imbrication of untillable land
with cultivable soils characteristic of the majority of Mediterranean landscapes,
animals everywhere have a contribution to make to increasing production and
fending off risk. This fact has not prevented a widespread and serious misunderstanding of the subject. It is true, as we have said, that processing plants for
human food by way of animal husbandry is highly inefficient: growing wheat,
feeding it to animals and eating the animals is absurd. If all your land is cultivable for human food plants, then you will only keep animals if you have so much
land that they do not compete with you for nutrition. If they do compete in that
way, when human populations increase, animal husbandry should be a luxury
which has to be forgone. But this is where the characteristics of the Mediterranean landscape come into play. It is, first, always sensible to keep a few animals
as stored food against unexpected shortages of vegetable products. More importantly, the omnipresence of landscapes which support ovicaprids (such as the
ubiquitous scrublands or the lush wetland fringes) or pigs (the oak or chestnut
woods) means that animals do not *need* to compete with humans for land. Which
is not to deny that in many cases this theoretical balance has been destroyed
by the attraction of more resource-intensive husbandry; but it does refute the
notion that animals and crops are mutually exclusive except in conditions of very
low population density.

The other hindrance to understanding is the persistent belief that animal husbandry somehow belongs in a particular part of the Mediterranean environment
which is not the shifting, readjustable, adaptive marginal world of our previous
discussion but a static and unchanging zone, physically determined. We have
already seen (III.6) how mistaken it is to regard pastoralism as the characteristic
activity of the inhospitable mountain, determined by the poverty of natural resources. Rather, mountain pastoralism, and above all long-distance transhumance,
is a novel opportunistic exercise extending the reach of the producers of the
more comfortable landscapes – a kind of displaced intensification. In many cases,
moreover, it appears that the mountain pastures, so far from being the environment which determined the practice *ab origine* are in fact a consequence, and
a relatively recent one at that, of large-scale transhumance (Cherry 1988, 15).
Such initiatives may respond to hard times. In ancient Crete, where communities underwent intense competition for scarce resources, increasing the scale
of transhumance was an important but intermittent way of increasing the number of microregions accessible for exploitation. So the intensification of the
effort involved in husbandry was a strategy which could be, and was, introduced

in response to crisis – to be allowed to lapse when better times came (Chaniotis 1995). Such initiatives may also be more ambitious in scope. Where dairying is the desired recourse for the management of ovicaprids, the use of wetland pasture has nothing of the marginal about it. The exploitation of oak, beech or chestnut woods for swine does not necessarily represent the desperate gleaning of scraps of nutrition from unpromising second-rate environments, since that exploitation may well convert a rich natural resource into a high-status and high-value product for redistribution. Pastoralists, just like fishermen, can produce 'cash crops'. There is, then, a stability and a normality about Mediterranean animal husbandry. But it is not that of a Manichaean world order; it is the endlessly recreated ingenuity of the truly diverse primary producer.

In fact, the advantages of husbandry in fulfilling the trio of Mediterranean imperatives – diversify, store, redistribute – are much subtler and more complex than this schematic beginning suggests. Managed animals are an incomparably flexible resource. Apart from their flesh (and other post-mortem benefits such as leather, bone and horn), species domesticated in the Mediterranean during our period have offered milk, clothing, manure, and energy for traction, transportation and water-lifting. Here is one strand in the complexity: 'modest flocks of ovicaprids clean and fertilize the cultivated fields near the settlement and – in the process – convert unusable plant-materials into meat and milk serving as dietary supplements or fall-backs in times of crop-failure' (Cherry 1988, 21).

Animals can be switched from one strategy to another very rapidly, according to circumstance, and made to intersect with varying patterns of cultivation in many different ways: they are so readily moveable according to the vagaries of season, the resources of the microregion and its neighbours, and the opportunities for redistribution (including markets). Which is not to say that the mobility has to involve great distances: it is the possibility of redeployment, rather than the regularity of massive displacement, that is usual (cf. Cherry 1988, 16). Animals can be treated simply as storage-batteries for summer slaughter, or intensively managed for breeding and sale as a cash crop, depending on the economic climate; and when they need to be realized as capital, they can be moved with their own energy, sent for sale on the hoof. As with fish, then, the nutritional input of an animal after exchange may be much greater than could have been provided by consuming it directly.

The adaptive nature of animal husbandry thus invites reaching beyond the microregion towards a more comprehensive spectrum of environments. It also offers the possibility of supplying something closely resembling the bonuses of the margin to distant consumers. The imperative to be adjustable and adaptable applies just as much to pastoralism (as, indeed, to the 'marginal exploitations' of fishing and gathering) as to any other form of production. It is this that makes it so unhelpful to separate schematically pastoralism from agriculture. When interdependence is high and intensification desirable, animals not only make it possible to exploit zones of forest, steep slope, or marshland which would otherwise yield much less nutriment, but through the addition of labour into the processing and marketing of animal products, they can readily take their place in the world of storage and redistributive gain. Hence the importance of the recognition that pastoralism as a system does not indicate underdevelopment, but rather the opposite: it is 'a specialization of economic activity predicated on a certain amount of exchange' (Wickham 1983–5, 449). When we hear that the priestess of Athena Polias in classical Athens had for ritual reasons to eat only cheese that had come over the sea (Strabo, *Geography*, 9.1.11), we get a small insight into the economy of the islands of the Aegean and into the way that, even in their restricted environments, high-quality animal products could be one of the forms that it was useful for microecological intensification to take. On islands such as Ceos in the classical period, as (for example) on Minorca in the early modern, the advantages of islandness (to which we return in Section 11) have made possible pastoral specialization of a considerable degree of sophistication.

There is no better index of the engagement of husbandry with the world of redistribution than the perennial importance in Mediterranean history of salt. The primary use of salt was to render animal products storable: products from the wild, as we have already seen; from living beasts, as with salted cheeses; and variously processed meats (such as sausages). Salted victuals facilitated their own production and redistribution – as food for shepherds, away from cultivated lands, or for seafarers (Dubois et al. 1987). It is not hard to document the scale and political and cultural significance of salt production. The salt-pans of medieval Provence for instance yielded some 10,000 tonnes per annum; in the eighteenth century, production at Aigues-Mortes alone reached 17,000–19,000 tonnes (Delano Smith 1979, 389, cf. 399–400). In the nineteenth century Santa Maura (Leukas) on the west coast of Greece produced some 5,000–6,000 tonnes p.a. (H. Holland 1815, 62). The figures reflect the ineluctable necessity, if risk was to be reduced, of preserving and exchanging animal products.

In our view, then, animal husbandry lies at the heart of the Mediterranean agrosystem. Indeed the intricate complex of productions which we have so briefly outlined was, it has been persuasively argued, a decisive ingredient in the early development of agriculture itself (Sherratt 1983). Pastoralism has coexisted with other strategies from the first (III.6). Moreover, its refinements have been given important roles in the processes of social stratification and elite-formation in later prehistory. There remains, however, a residual reluctance to accept that this is the way that the ancient Mediterranean 'worked'. Based in part on misapprehension of the 'competition' between humans and animals, this reluctance is also clearly linked with the primitivist/minimalist conception of ancient Mediterranean production which was orthodox before the changes of perspective with reference to which we opened this chapter (V.4). It draws on the stereotyped opposition of pastoral and arable, and on the misconception that the environmental opportunism of animal husbandry is most typically expressed in long-distance movements of animals, both views that we discussed in Chapter III.

The occasional periods during which transhumance has taken place on a macroregional scale, and the tensions between pastoral and arable which have given rise to the dualist vision, are in fact features of the ways in which the omnipresent animal husbandry intrinsic to the system has been manipulated to the gain of particular individuals or powerful institutions. But those periods cannot be understood unless they are seen as superfetations of the underlying range of normal animal husbandry – and indeed of other productive systems too, since through manuring, plough-traction, and as beasts of burden, animals are involved in every large question of agrarian history. The processes by which major extrapolations from the basic repertoire take place – whether 'intensification', 'extensification' or some other term is appropriate for them – will receive further attention in the next chapter (VII.4).

8. Cereals and the Dry Margin

Our resistance to a 'Manichaean' separation between the worlds of pastoral and arable is partly based on rejecting the notion of a geographically determined 'bad' zone where animals belong. We should now turn to the other side of the supposed dichotomy, and show that the cultivated world of the Mediterranean environment has been just as subject to caricature. It is now the turn of dry farming to be seriously re-evaluated (cf. Garnsey 1988a, 93–4). Summer drought and unreliable precipitation used to be thought to dictate a standard response, everywhere oriented solely towards the conservation of soil-moisture by a relatively restricted range of techniques, of which the most characteristic and unavoidable was biennial fallow. Once again, it is the ethnographic revolution that has enabled us to see these practices as only part of an enormously more varied and flexible response on the part of producers. The productive behaviour which we found in places that have sometimes been regarded as fringes will actually prove to be characteristic of the whole: 'the medieval economy was primarily founded on the exploitation of uncultivated territory, on husbandry, hunting, and fishing, which noticeably reduced the contribution of cereals to the economy and the diet [l'economia altomedievale era basata in primo luogo sullo sfruttamento dei spazi incolti, sulle attività di allevamento, della caccia, della pesca, che sensibilmente limitavano il ruolo economico e alimentare della cerealicoltura]' (Montanari 1985b, 50).

Ordinary production turns out to be surprisingly similar to the management of the special locations of wetland, forest or mountain pasture. A wide-ranging account of the original domestication of cereals has argued for 'an often protracted phase of small-scale surface- and groundwater based horticulture which ultimately differentiated into hydraulic and rainfed systems of both extensive and intensive kinds' (Sherratt 1980). And we shall increasingly see that the setting of Mediterranean production often more closely resembles the garden than anything which we should normally associate with the word 'farming'. That term, like 'arable', is one which does more harm than good in the study of Mediterranean landscapes.

Most scholars would agree that, over much of our period, a strikingly central role in Mediterranean nutritional systems has been played by cereal crops, and by wheat and barley in particular, satisfying perhaps up to some 65–70 per cent of nutritional needs (Gallant 1991, 63–4). This centrality has encouraged belief in a relatively uniform system of dry farming (III.1). But of course a significant overall dietary contribution does not entail a standardized system of production. One reason is that the foodstuffs that form the core of a nutritional system may themselves be more diverse than appears at first sight, for instance because they require rather different labour regimes. Cereals are, by comparison with other Mediterranean food plants, relatively low in their demand for labour (1991, 75–6), but they are still susceptible to a great many quite different production relations. Moreover, Mediterranean climate and topographical diversity entail that it would be madness to attempt to fulfil so important a dietary need with a single way of growing a single type of crop. Subsistence monocultures bring disaster in most Mediterranean environments. The agrarian history of Sardinia for example shows a chiaroscuro of deadly famine and notable surpluses of wheat produced for export (Rowland 1990). The two are linked: specialization is potentially lethal; it is far better not to put too many eggs in the same basket. In Sardinia, as in other places of which we shall see more (VII.6), the pressure to specialize has been imposed from outside the decision-making ambit of the primary producers themselves, to their grave danger. The pre-eminence of cereals – their organized role as a preferred staple – is to be explained by a 'logic' that extends well beyond the productive environment itself. The scholarly tendency to represent cereals as a dominant ingredient in diet, in the face of abundant evidence, from many places and periods, for considerable dietary diversity is encouraged by the very high cultural profile that cereals have attained. Their centrality to the ideologies of the city in Antiquity gave them a peculiar place in the ancient sources, as has been revealed by work on the size of the conventional rations used for distributions in Greek and Roman communities (Forbes and Foxhall 1982). The culture of bread eating was an equally complex social phenomenon in the medieval West. We hope to make clear how this is in turn the result of the centrality of these foodstuffs to the economic and political management of production. The regularity of the provision of cereal products throughout our period has been assured not by uniformity in the productive process but by the management of collection, storage and redistribution. In independent production, the first rule has been the one that we have already seen so widely applied: diversify.

Variety and flexibility are indeed the thing. In a world fissioned into microregions, that is not too hard to achieve. In different corners, you grow different plants. It is even possible to grow them in the same corner: one of the principal ways of spreading the risk is mixed cropping – by sowing mixed seed, or by the more systematic planting side by side of different species (intercropping), or by using the same land subsequently for a second or third crop during the season. Each has its own benefits and drawbacks (Gallant 1991, 38–41). Microregional diversity has encouraged a much greater variety of cereals than we might expect (Garnsey 1988a, 49–53). This applies both to local varieties, and to the different species of cereal themselves. The survival of emmer in Roman Italy (Spurr 1986, 10–13), despite the advantages offered by other cereals, is a case in point; around Roman Herculaneum a mixture of emmer and barley was sometimes sown (Pagano 1994).

'Agriculturalists should keep in store these kinds of wheat and emmer because it is unusual indeed to find a property which is situated so that we can make do with a single type of seed: some waterlogged or arid part is sure to get in the way.' Thus Columella (*On Agriculture*, 2.6.4), a man who knew his microregions. Some species, both cereals and other crops, were particularly adapted to being sown in an emergency if the winter rains had been poor: among them, according to Theophrastus (*Enquiry into Plants*, 8.1.4), millet (*kenchros*), Italian millet (*elumos*) and sesame (Gallant 1991, 114–6). The gradual spread of hard wheat, *Triticum durum*, also illustrates well the variety of practice and the subtle reasons for cereal choices. The ambiguity of the terminology for cereal crops and the lack of archaeological information long combined with the instinctive wish to believe in qualitative separations between Antiquity and the Middle Ages to produce confident assertions that hard wheat was not known or not important in the ancient Mediterranean. Yet its rise to prominence in Ptolemaic Egypt can be documented in the papyri (D. J. Crawford 1979); there now seems little doubt that it was the principal wheat of Roman Italy (Spurr 1986, 15–17); and careful analysis of the emergence of new types of cereal crop has confirmed such accounts, while helpfully explaining the slowness of the process by which hard wheat reached its post-classical importance in terms of the evolution of the species itself (Sallares 1991, 333–51).

Diversification also, naturally, entails growing many food plants other than cereals. Ethnographic research on Crete has shown country people drawing only 49 per cent of their protein and 39 per cent of their calories from cereals (Allbaugh 1953). Legumes have been the most important complement. Their cultivation is abundantly attested from all parts of the Mediterranean through-out our period but has been generally underestimated. The presumed logic of subsistence dry farming made it difficult for scholars to see how agriculturalists could afford to replace autumn sowing of wheat with legumes (Spurr 1986, 103–5), which have the disadvantage of relative invisibility to archaeology and archaeobotany. In fact, it seems that a group of cereals and legumes (emmer, barley, einkorn; pea, lentil, chickpea, bitter vetch) and, interestingly, flax, were originally domesticated at more or less the same time in the Fertile Crescent (Zohary 1989). The Romans moreover believed that legumes had been the principal complement to emmer in their earliest ancestors' diet. Legumes feature prominently in Biblical and Talmudic texts (Dar 1995). In second-millennium B.C. Israel, cereals and legumes are attested as having been grown side by side with a view to local redistribution of the surplus – although the same evidence reflects the perils of specialization, in that the beans grown on alluvial bottom-lands here were found to have been very prone to attack by bruchids (Chernoff 1993). Legumes also appear to be of equal agricultural importance to cereals in Byzantine sources (Teall 1971, 52). They serve as a very helpful buffer crop between cereals, store well, and can be used as fodder. It has been suggested that they should be given a place alongside the grape and the olive as standard ingredients in Mediterranean agriculture (Sarpaki 1992). Even in the reasonably predictable conditions of Egypt, records from around 116–115 B.C. show only 55 per cent of the inner core of irrigable land around the village of Kerkeosiris under wheat; 11 per cent was devoted to lentils, the same again to beans, and 10 per cent to vetch (D. J. Crawford 1971, 130–1; 1979, 142). The cultivation (and rapid evolution) of varieties of the bean *Phaseolus* has been seen as a central contribution to the agricultural prosperity of Muslim Spain (Bolens 1990c, 70).

There are, it should be recalled, also other staples in play. A salutary reminder comes from the study of the chestnut economy which spread so widely in medieval Italy. A country boy apprenticed as a draper in thirteenth-century Genoa could be expected to return home in October to help gather the nuts that were the source of the flour on which the family depended (S. A. Epstein 1988, 126). Here is a flour that was a nutritional staple without even being derived from a cereal or indeed from cultivation in the strict sense, but which is comparable to cereals in nutritional value. Indeed the chestnut has provided an alternative economy in various parts of the Mediterranean basin since Antiquity (it is wrong to think that it is incompatible with limestone-derived soils). Even acorns have been used in a similar way. Much more important, it is only relatively recently, and thanks in part to the ethnological approach once again, that the crucial nutritional role played in the Mediterranean diet by oil and wine themselves has begun to be recognized (Amouretti 1986).

Two examples may serve to illustrate the diversity. The first is from Byzantine Thessalonica. There is an interesting aside in the record of the miracles of St Demetrius, where it is said that, when grain gives out, it is not customary to call it famine while there is still a supply of other goods available in the market. In a large seventh-century city, then, sufficient quantities of other foodstuffs were usually available to avert starvation. Variety at the nodes of the networks of exchange and consumption is a natural result of the connectivity for which we have argued. But it is striking to find evidence that, even in a period when networks of redistribution were hardly at their most developed, the quantities implied by that miracle narrative could be relied on to such an extent (V.6).

The second example is the diversity of diet of the primary producers in the *Euboicus*, a set piece by the early second-century A.D. orator Dio Chrysostom. This paints an elaborate, clever and amusing picture of rustic simplicity contrasted with urban decadence. There is a good deal of imagined detail, which can obviously not be taken to be an ethnographic description of any specific time or place. Dio is playing up the poverty and marginality of his country folk, but his presentation, though stylized, needs to be plausible. The country folk here enjoy a very varied diet. The householder claims to have in store some two *medimnoi* (108 litres, *c*.80 kg) of wheat, twice that amount of barley, and 216 litres of millet; but only a tiny quantity of beans 'because they didn't grow this year' (45). If this had all been wheat, it would have represented approximately the yearly subsistence minimum for two people, and the public distribution allowance for one, which is perhaps how Dio arrived at it. He has increased verisimilitude by making the majority of the store the lesser-status crops. Of these, the millet is less rich in protein than wheat (Spurr 1986, 99), the barley comparable in nutritional value. The family's other resources include a garden with fruit trees and vegetables, which they are specifically said to have added to their repertoire; two vines but no olives; and the produce of hunting and browsing cattle in woods and meadows, which are represented as being in a natural rather than a managed state. The exchanges between one household and another in a family network are also discussed. Redistribution and diversification blend:

> We don't [the woman of the house speaks] want for anything: but they [the daughter who married a man of some substance in the local village] take a bit of game when we have it or fruit or vegetables – they don't have a garden. And last year we had some of their wheat, threshed seed, and gave them it back as soon as harvest was in. (*Euboicus*, 69; cf. Garnsey 1988a, 56–7)

Storage

So much for diversification. Cereals have a special role to play in the second canonical response to risk: storage. The practices of storage are as diverse as those of cultivation. The techniques chosen and their implications will depend on the nature of the plant, the method of harvesting, and the degree of subsequent processing. The amount of grain required for seed is another important variable, since it is the keeping of live cereals that poses the greatest problems (Sigaut 1988, 4). Whether milled, as flour, parboiled, as bulgur, turned into pasta, porridge, trachana (Hill and Bryer 1995) or some sorts of bread, cake or biscuit, cereals offer very greatly enhanced storage and transportation potential.

The variety, which reflects regional characteristics very strongly, is enormous. Two Mediterranean storage practices may be emphasized here, although we shall return to the question in our discussion of harvesting techniques in the next chapter (Section 1). First, small-scale producers, storing for their own needs, have at their disposal a method which has not been well known: the hermetically sealed underground store (Sigaut 1988, 10–12). This is highly effective against insect damage, and therefore encourages relatively high estimates of disposable surpluses. But equally characteristic, second, is the showy store-place of the powerful figure who has acquired the right to dispose of the cereals produced by many microregions. Building such places has formed a continuing theme – from Mycenaean palaces, through Roman villas on their high platforms composed of storerooms, the granaries of tax-grain in Hellenistic cities or Roman ports, to medieval monasteries and their barns (for storing whole sheaves, a strategy with various advantages if there are sufficient draught animals to move the extra weight). An eloquent early example comes from a ninth-century B.C. tomb in Athens: among the grave goods was a detailed pottery model of a great beehive-shaped granary building, a very suitable memento of status in the community to accompany the dead woman (Coldstream 1995).

Storage architecture is a sure diagnostic of the principal distinctive function of cereals: they lend themselves to being collected, counted, stored and exchanged, and therefore they become the normal instrument for the extraction of surplus from hapless producers. Storage buildings often reflect a monocultural regime imposed from 'above' for the benefit of consumers far away. The granaries of the major settlements of Hellenistic Sicily provide a good example (Deussen 1994, cf. Livy, *History*, 24.21.11–12, for the royal granaries on Ortygia). The view that cereals were prominent in the origins of agriculture because of their orientation towards storage and redistribution (Runnels and van Andel 1988) therefore seems to us acceptable but anodyne: the 'orientation' is no structural facet of a neutral ecology pursuing its natural course, but the awakening of a type of exploitative system that would endure for millennia. How many famines and food-crises have taken the form not of absolute scarcity, but of the hoarding of foodstuffs by cynical entrepreneurs or officials awaiting really high prices (VII.4–5)?

Redistribution

An ancient Greek proverb illustrates a transition towards the state in which substantial quantities of produce are stored and exchanged: 'Attic-style storage: market and buy in' ([Aristotle] *Oeconomica*, 1.1344 b 31–3: *Attike phylake: polountas oneisthai*). In other words, in the ancient Athenian system – relatively unusually still at that point – the market replaces the usual function of storage for small establishments. Which brings us on to the question of redistribution.

There was always a market for food, either in the cities or in places where shortages had occurred, and one of the most convenient ways in which redistribution to them could be ensured was by growing, storing and shipping cereals. This naturally varied in scale and efficacy from one period to another, but (as we have argued in Chapters IV and V) we see no reason to think that it has ever been insignificant during the long period under consideration. The difficulties attending production in bad years or unsuitable localities have been magnified, inducing

pessimism about average yields, rather than being taken as further evidence of
the normality of risk and of the necessity of providing for it. The evidential basis
for calculations of comparative yield is extremely unsure; it can easily happen
that yields are both high in terms of quantity of seed sown and low in terms of
area (Valensi 1985, 125–7). And it needs to be reiterated that, although there
are no doubt many roughly egalitarian exchanges, redistribution does not take
place by some ecological magic. It is usually mediated through the control exercised by the powerful – landlords, entrepreneurs, or officials – who seek out the
areas of shortfall in order to dispose advantageously of what they have accumulated. There is a nexus here between, on one hand, the control of what is readily
stored and redistributed (and counted, calibrated and measured in the process)
and, on the other, the exercise of ultimately exploitative control, whether the
mechanism be share-cropping, slave labour, rent, tribute, religious offerings, tax
or market-controlled sale. It seems to us odd that more attention has not been
given in the study of Mediterranean production to a given product's degree of
suitability to the extractive process, and indeed to the mechanisms of (in a broad
sense) political power.

Underestimating the role of politically motivated movements of staples has
indeed produced malign distortion in Mediterranean historiography. It is not
in the end the needs of the *autoconsommateur* that have promoted cereal cultivation to such a high level of prestige and importance. The proof of this is
paradoxically to be found in the way in which the convenience of the network of
redistribution outweighs the optimum suitability of crops to local ecologies in
the history of Mediterranean cereals: emmer, well fitted to the wetter conditions
of Italian hills, and barley, much better adapted to the semi-arid areas, have both,
in such environments, lost ground repeatedly to wheats. The main advantage of
wheats, whatever is said about taste and cultural fashion, and even nutritional
return, must be the ease with which they may be managed as a general commodity, facilitating the development of Mediterranean-wide redistribution (though
cf. Lombardo 1995). The climatically less vulnerable productions of the extra-
Mediterranean zones of south Russia or Egypt do much to maintain the stability
of the resulting market in cereals (see further Volume 2).

Figures from the Ottoman Empire of 1863 (Table 2) show both the diversity of
land use and the multiplicity of grains. While some of the crop was undoubtedly
consumed by those who grew it, no grain was reserved for *autoconsommation*.
Statistics relating to the district of Amasya on the Black Sea coast (Issawi 1980,
259–60), show that, in 1841, 315 of the 542 tonnes of wheat produced, and
116 of the 205 tonnes of barley, were available for export. Nor do these figures
reflect only recent centuries: the Ottoman Empire had long exhibited economic
conditions very like those of Antiquity, with glut and acute shortage coexisting in neighbouring microregions, and wide differentials of price that reflected
the relative difficulty of moving foodstuffs overland. Prices in the seaports were
noticeably more stable (1980, 211). Still more revealingly, in food-crises such
as that of 1845, exports of cereals, though forbidden, were still attempted by
the entrepreneurs who had hoarded supplies (213–14). We might as well be in
Thessalonica towards the end of the seventh century, when the miraculous intervention of St Demetrius relieved the besieged city from a wholly avoidable food
crisis. There was plenty of grain in the granaries, but the responsible authorities
sold it all off, to their great private profit, to merchants on board the foreign

Table 2 Crops in three Ottoman provinces

Crop-type	Salonica	Acre	Cavalla
Barley	29%	9%	
Millet	5%	7%	
Wheat	38%	40%	
Sesame	10%	13%	
Legumes	1.7%	5%	
Maize	10%		
Cotton		6%	3%
Tobacco		2%	8%
'Grains'			55%
Rye	6%		
Olives		14%	
Oilseed, beans, olives, vines			8%
Fodder and pasture			25%
Watermelons, vines, figs		4%	

Source: Issawi (1980) 199–200.

ships that happened to be in the harbour just before the siege started (Lemerle 1979a, 244).

The slowness with which preferred cereal crop-types have changed is surely in part attributable to their role in networks of exchange. Since cereals lend themselves to storage and shipping, they have also responded more to the exigencies of participation in a Mediterranean redistribution system than to the day-to-day needs of the cultivator. Plurality of cereals is well suited to reducing risk, but is likewise also frequently dictated by the convenience of redistribution. In the Mesara in Crete during the nineteenth century for instance, barley was grown for domestic use, and wheat for the Heraklion market (Watrous 1993). But that is not an inevitable pattern. In many contexts barley too will be exported; and if not, it may serve as a link in other forms of engagement with the market, such as the production of fodder for animals. Every crop is for both 'subsistence' and 'cash', and the balance at any one time depends totally on the season in each locality and on the network that joins it with its neighbours. Sicily sent barley to Rome in the last two centuries B.C., but producers faced irksome pressure over this period to increase wheat production instead (Mazzarino 1961; cf. Gallo 1983). The resentment caused by that pressure fuelled public disorder by the beginning of the first century B.C. (Gallo 1989). A later example: over the period 1300–1450, substantial production of barley for sale gave way to production principally for animal feed (Bresc 1986b, 128–9). *Triticum durum* from Apulia, the preferred import cereal in medieval Florence, was some 5 per cent more costly than its competitors and, in times of shortage, cheaper varieties from the Romagna or Sardinia had the edge over it (Abulafia 1981, 385). All the rival producers were orientated towards export.

Something of the normal level of complexity can be seen in the slow and piecemeal reception of arrivals from the New World during the early modern period. Their appallingly confusing nomenclature reflects the chaotic process of their introduction. After its transfer to Egypt from other Turkish provinces in the eighteenth century, maize (*Zea mays*) was known as Turkish, Syrian or Peloponnesian *sorghum* – to which it is unrelated (Darby et al. 1977, 460). By contrast, in Italy the name 'saracen grain' is applied to a millet-like plant (*Polygonum fagopyrum*) with a short season well suited to upland areas; but it is indigenous, and may well have been cultivated in Antiquity (Spurr 1986, 60–1). The story of the erratic and unpredictable reception of maize in Italy is instructive, and closely reflects the economic circumstances of the time (Cazzola 1991). An earlier introduction to the north Italian countryside, *Holcus sorghum*, had found a niche in the agrosystem as a fodder crop which was eaten in times of famine. In Ferrara in 1451–1459 it formed 27 per cent of the crop, with wheat at 53, barley 8 and oats 2 per cent. This famine-fodder role could readily be usurped by maize. Despite the low esteem in which such crops were held (deriving also from their greedy feeding habit), they succeeded and spread because of a logic which swayed both independent small producers and rural bosses: when wheat prices rise, sell as much of the wheat as you possibly can (or force your increasingly dependent labour force to do so), and survive by eating your sorghum or maize. The problem was that Italian producers cooked the maize in the way that they had previously cooked sorghum: as a *polenta*, which (unlike its treatment in its American parent-culture) destroys the vitamins that prevent pellagra. Hence a cycle of increasing impoverishment and malnutrition.

Sorghum, which is an excellent crop for hot dry climates (Harlan 1989), was known in Coptic Egypt and spread rather slowly in the Maghreb under Islam. Climate, rather than social differences, has prevented its use in north-western Mediterranean lands, where the closely related millet was a much more suitable lower-quality grain, and long remained of great importance. The advent of rice has been even slower. Known in classical times, and widely cultivated in Mesopotamia, it became widespread in the Mediterranean only in the early modern period. Nothing suggests that the dynamics of acceptance of new cereal crops in historical times have been significantly different from the faltering pattern by which diploid and then tetraploid varieties of ordinary wheat spread during the first (prehistoric) centuries after their domestication.

Because of their convenience for storage, transportation and therefore city-maintenance, cereals have – as long as there have been cities – formed the most attractive of all the monocultural cash crops to the typical wealthy managers who have been the architects of intensification in the Mediterranean. The history of cerealiculture in this region is not a history of subsistence production. That point is made with equal force by the notorious case of the grain-estates that fed ancient Rome (Rickman 1980) or the sad story (which the evidence allows us to read in much more detail) of how the economy of Sicily in the late Middle Ages was transformed by the opportunity of purveying grain to the cities of the Tyrrhenian and Catalonia (Bresc 1986b, 523–44, cf. 919–22). Islands, being particularly accessible, were favoured locations for this enforced, colonial, specialization, which is found in Roman Sardinia as well as in Sicily (Villedieu 1984). From at least the development of the infrastructure that transported very substantial quantities of *Triticum aestivum* to Athens in the fourth century B.C. the redistribution of cereals has been a major feature of Mediterranean life, and it serves to introduce a number of the other characteristics of redistribution which we shall study in Chapter IX. In medieval Lazio, the cerealiculture of the poor was founded on a plurality of the lower-status, more resilient crops; it was the domains of the larger landowners – such as monasteries – which could afford the risk of specializing in hard wheat for the civic market (Toubert 1973, 250–5). As the story of the introduction of maize showed, however, independence in these matters was precarious. During the early Middle Ages in general, the people of the countryside subsisted between garden and forest: it was their misfortune to be forced to join the 'civilization of bread' as the control exercised by city-based elites over the countryside and the diminishing wild increased (Montanari 1985a). Apulia could provide shipments of 45,000 tons of grain for Florence in 1311; in the lean year of 1329 Apulians starved while the merchants stock-piled what grain there was in their cities waiting to sell it at an inflated price (Abulafia 1981, 382).

9. Adjustable Agriculture: The Case of the Tree-Crop

> The Arab general, after the death of the patrician Gregory [at Sbeïtla, 647], had the curiosity to enquire about the source of all the booty. He looked at the coin and asked where it came from. A local began to hunt round about, clearly looking for something. He found an olive and brought it to Abd Allah. 'It is with this that we acquire our wealth', he said. 'How so?' 'The Greeks have no olives themselves, and therefore their custom is to come over here and buy oil, which we sell them. That is the source of our wealth.' (Ibn Abd al-Hakam, *The Conquest of North Africa and Spain*, adapted from A. Gateau 1947, 46–8)

The olive, *Olea europaea, var. sativa*, domesticated at least since the third millennium B.C., is among the most conspicuous symbols of Mediterranean landscape and life. It offers numerous advantages in the economy of risk. The habitat of the tree is limited by temperature rather than precipitation, so that it requires cool but frost-free winters. It is tolerant of drought; but it is also a natural performer of exactly that acrobatic adjustability to which the canny human producer aspires, automatically responding to any benefit of extra moisture that may be available by cropping more generously without further help. The tree comes slowly to fruiting but is very long-lived. This has greatly slowed the effect of human selection on improving the species (Sallares 1991, 307), and also makes optimism about security an essential ingredient in the decision to grow it. Olives can be left without much attention (Virgil, *Georgics*, 2.420: 'contra non ulla est oleis cultura'). They return investment in labour and cultivation; yet should that not be available, they will survive perfectly well until an opportunity for increasing human effort arrives. They are easily combined with other crops in polycultural systems.

Oil is a highly versatile product whose contribution to diet in the Mediterranean has been very substantial indeed. It stores well ('oil good for treasuring [*euthesauron elaien*]', Leonidas of Tarentum, *Palatine Anthology*, 6.300.3) and forms a medium in which other things – such as cheese or vegetables – may be preserved. It has served a number of highly significant purposes other than food – anointing the body and filling lamps for illumination being the two most important. On the less positive side, its yield is very variable: roughly equivalent to cropping in alternate years, except under very favourable conditions, such as irrigation. This variability makes it highly suited to opportunistic redistribution (Sallares 1991, 308), with the qualification that, compared with dry goods, oil is a relatively difficult substance to transport. Oleiculture, alongside other productions of the margin, is a classic strategy of occasional, opportunistic activity for local consumption, as part of the microregional producer's portfolio.

The unique cultural significance of olive oil makes it easy to overlook the parallels for this type of enterprise. They include the fig and the carob. No major Mediterranean food-plant has been so unfairly neglected as the fig: weight-by-weight it is about five times as rich calorifically as cereals or olives (Foxhall, forthcoming [69]). It offers a vital resource – sugar – at vastly less expense in social and environmental terms than does sugar-cane; and, like organized apiculture, it represents a way of making use of the margins, for it characteristically grows in unpromisingly arid corners of the cultivated ground. The carob, *Ceratonia siliqua*, tolerates very xeric conditions and (as, in abundance, in Israel today) is often a plant of agricultural abatement. On a 'desert mountain (onely beholding to the locust [i.e. carob] tree)' George Sandys, who had clearly never encountered terraces before, saw St John's cave:

> A place that would make solitarinesse delightfull and stand in comparison with the turbulent pompe of cities. This overlooketh a profound valley, on the far side hemd with aspiring mountains, whereof some are cut (or naturally so) in degrees like allies, which would be else unaccessably fruitlesse, whose levels yet beare the stumps of decayed vines, shadowed not rarely with olives and locusts. (1615, 182–3, cf. Liphschitz 1987)

The carob, however, was cultivated in Antiquity. (Theophrastus, *Enquiry into Plants*, 4.2.4, cf. 1.11.2 and 14.4, tells us of the alternative name 'Egyptian fig', although giving as its distribution Syria and western Asia Minor.) It was a prominent orchard crop in the period represented by the Mishnah despite the limited prestige of its fruit, which served as poverty-fare or animal fodder. Equally, the fig, characteristic although it is of derelict sites, is often an orchard crop, grown in association with the labour-intensive vine (cf. Toubert 1973, 260). Crops of the margins may be a response to shortage of labour or to other tendencies associated with abatement. But they may also be attempts to push cultivation to its limits in a phase of intensification. And this is certainly true of the olive too.

On Mediterranean islands we see these trees in their adaptive role, fitted into a regime of property which is for social and political reasons ultra-fragmented (Kolodny 1972 and 1974). They take their place among the resources that are minutely enumerated – like the trees of the orchard of Laertes on Ithaca in the *Odyssey* (1.190; 11.187; 24.205, 336) – whereas ploughland and pasture are described much more summarily. Two estates owned on the island of Leros in the eleventh century by the monastery of Patmos also reveal how significant even small numbers of trees could be (Malamut 1988). Temeneia in the south had 156 cultivated olives, 326 oaks, 12 carobs, 3 pear-trees, 4 fig-trees, 9 quinces (with two others in vineyards), 10 pomegranate-trees and 4 almonds. Parthenion at the other end of the island had 150 cultivated olives, 5 oaks, 1 fig, 3 pear-trees, 24 carobs and some vines and pomegranates. Just as every tiny patch of really productive soil can count, so every tree is a significant resource.

This worthy but limited role is, however, by no means the end of the story for the olive. For all its usefulness on the microecological scale, the olive has been among the most conspicuously successful species for investment agriculture in the Mediterranean (cf. Bresc 1986b, 170–1, on Sicily). In fourth-century Attica, in the deme of Atene, the cultivation of olives on large estates deploying considerable labour in terracing can be traced in the archaeological landscape (Lohmann 1992). Olive cultivation spread relatively slowly before the beginning of the Archaic Greek period. It is not, for instance, mentioned in Hesiod's *Works and Days*, though it would be to take our scanty evidence far too literally to deduce from this silence an arboricultural revolution in the decades which followed (Sallares 1991, 31–4). The olive appears to have been significant in late Bronze Age Phoenicia and in Minoan Crete, but it triumphed in Egypt (which was previously largely dependent on castor-oil) only towards the Roman period (Sandy 1989, 35–54). That is not surprising given the slow life-cycle of the plant, and the amount of stability needed if producers are to grow it. Such slow and uneven spread may be important for understanding its eventual successes.

For Aristotle, olive-cultivation provided a prime example of shrewd investment in a monopoly: the philosopher Thales was said to have been moved to demonstrate that his ingenuity could have worldly fruits and successfully predicted (astronomically!) a glut in olive-production. He bought up all the presses of his native Miletus and of the island of Chios and duly made a fortune (*Politics*, 1.10.8–10, 1259a). The tale may not be plausible for Thales's actual lifetime (sixth century B.C.); the interesting feature, rather, is Aristotle's conception of the economic nature of oil production. The presses were available, and could be cornered by outside investment, even (in the case of Chios) from outside the *polis*, so they were not private adjuncts of the producers. But they were at the mercy of the famously aleatory cropping-habits of the olive (more or less every other year, but not with absolute certainty). What was superimposed was authority from outside, informed by a lucky guess and by a sense of the market. The essential precondition for that, the real revolution in the olive's history, was the possibility of intervention in a supra-local way, and the ability to ensure the movement of the product. The one was the product of political authority, the other of the widespread use of the amphora.

Something of the olive's role in Mediterranean economies may be seen in three further ancient examples. They all, as it happens, come from Attica, where cult and myth articulated a belief in the antiquity of oleiculture, and where its cultivation was a part of the ideological framework of being Athenian (reflected in the prizes of substantial quantities of olive oil given at the Panathenaic festival). The Athenian lawgiver Solon (early sixth century) was held to have forbidden the export of all Attic produce except for oil. It has reasonably been suggested that the principal aim of such a measure was preventing 'good-time dearth' caused by producers, especially of cereals, who preferred to sell away from home at a profit (Garnsey 1988a, 111–12). Olive oil is excepted, then, from Solon's law not because it is obviously the most valuable export, or to encourage producers to make it so, but because Athens, as one of the places where the olive had been established, could usually supply at least its own needs, and in glut years there would be a surplus whose export it would have been absurd to prohibit. The second example: an honorary decree of the early second century B.C. records the moderation of a merchant who was on his way to the Black Sea, from an uncertain origin, with 56,000 litres of oil which he was going to use for the purchase of grain for Athens. Stopping at Piraeus on the outward leg, he found an

unexpected shortage of oil, which he helped to remedy by selling at the ordinary
rather than the dearth price. This need have been only a poor off-year in the
Attic olive-cycle; and his action was hardly altruistic, since he would probably
have got a similar price for the oil in Pontus and saved himself a long journey
(Gauthier 1982). Finally, the Emperor Hadrian, in A.D. 124/5 decreed that a
third of Attic oil production should be made available in the first instance for
sale to the city-government of Athens: a measure which also seems to reflect
the need to prevent shortages resulting from the wish to sell elsewhere at higher
prices than would be possible in Athens (Garnsey 1988a, 75–6). Hadrian's
measure, it is worth noting, envisages that a substantial number of infringements
will take the form of shiploads of less than about 1,000 litres, a clear reflection
of the normal role of *cabotage* in maintaining connectivity between adjacent
microregions (V.3).

From Diodorus Siculus (*Historical Library*, 13.81.4–5), we happen to have a
vivid picture of the prosperity derived from heavy (but not exclusive) investment
in oleiculture on the part of the Greek elite of Acragas (Agrigento) on the south
coast of Sicily during the fifth century B.C. The trade was orientated towards
the single market of Carthage. It seems very likely that a number of the other
expansions of oleiculture which are conspicuous in the ancient archaeological
or literary evidence were also responses to the formation of particular markets
of this kind, instances, essentially, of 'directed trade' (IX.4). The most extreme
ancient case was the supply of imperial Rome. There, the strange hill of broken
transport amphorae behind the Tiber wharves, Monte Testaccio, appears to
represent a staggering total import, over a couple of centuries, of 6,000,000,000
litres of oil, at first from Italy, but then mainly from southern Spain and North
Africa. The gradual decay of the oleiculture of the Belus massif in north Syria,
which had been directed at the needs of Antioch and other substantial cities of
the Levant, and the environmental disaster which is said to have accompanied it,
show the effects on production of the disappearance of the customized market.
It was hard to achieve a sufficient diversification of markets to prevent vulnerability to this problem. Tripolitania, the Tunisian Sahel or the Guadalquivir
valley in the Roman imperial period, or Cilicia in the early Byzantine, also show
spectacularly how demands for oil in mass-markets linked by reliable distribution
networks could be reflected in the transformation of a landscape to the profit
of large-scale specialized estate owners (Mattingly 1996). Oleiculture was sometimes therefore essentially a colonial exploitation, realizing the quick profits to
be had in the first generation from new planting of even marginal lands because
of their fertility (Mattingly 1994). In these cases, moreover, planting substantial areas for the first time and setting up the infrastructure of processing which
has left so many remains to this day was much more demanding of capital and
labour than the usual microregional cultivation.

We may, then, observe several important points in the ancient history of olive
oil. First, it resembles cereals to a surprising extent: it has been more of a nutritional stand-by, and cereals less of a subsistence norm, than is often imagined.
Second, in stable conditions, it represents a useful way of extending both the range
of productions and the cultivated area, without – the 'colonial' case excepted –
committing very much labour. Third, as Aristotle saw, its irregularities make it
lucrative; the accidents of its slow distribution and the vagaries of its cropping-
cycle constitute a gift to an aleatory redistribution system. Fourth, the prerequi-

site for the use of any of these opportunities has been maritime transportation and the use of the amphora; so the development of those from the end of the second millennium B.C. (Heltzer 1993) enabled changes to take place which had not been possible before (cf. Sallares 1991, 31–4). Fifth, all these aspects have invited overseeing by the elite – which was structurally associated with the large-scale management of the ancient environment.

The olive appears to have a double life. On the great estates of the Guadalquivir valley, it produced the thousands of litres of oil poured, for despatch to distant Rome, into the Dressel 20 amphorae, which were still, after a millennium, using more or less the volume-module of their distant Phoenician precursors. On the little island holdings of Byzantine Patmos, by contrast, individual trees provided a few carefully counted basket-loads of fruit. We should, however, hesitate to invoke a twofold interpretation: this is a single phenomenon. Mediterranean production characteristically specializes in crops of precisely this kind, which can be used at any level of connectivity as well as at differing levels of labour supply and environmental variety. We should not, therefore, consider the olive an ingredient of an unsophisticated agriculture which it was inadvisable to expand into a major cash crop (*pace* Sallares 1991, 309: 'that the Athenians relied so heavily on such a crop is evidence for a very low level of development of the agrarian economy'). Equally, it is incautious to view the complexities of the more highly developed examples of directed trade in oil as a harbinger of a commercial economy. For although the olive lent itself to tremendous speculative investment, it was only locally and periodically, in the event of colossal focused demand, that it produced more than modest returns. In the medieval economy, the olive was of relatively little importance in many regions. Its cultivation had spread pretty uniformly across the Mediterranean, and the major markets which had produced the phenomenal olive booms of Antiquity were no more – with the result that medieval historians can find it hard to understand, or even to accept, the scale of the ancient redistribution of this product. There are major differences between periods at the level of large-scale directed commerce. Which is salutary: long-range comparison is essential precisely because there were economic processes which operated in the pre-medieval Mediterranean with a much greater intensity than they did in the Middle Ages. The direction of change is far from predictable.

The vine, *Vitis vinifera*, was originally a plant of the forest margin. It is therefore found in as many habitats as is woodland, and constitutes an outstanding example of the domestication of the products of the wildwood (Olmo 1995, 37–8). It will thrive in very moist conditions (wooded wetlands are among its natural habitats), and indeed one of the most famous Roman fine wines, Caecuban, was grown in the marshes behind the coastal strip in the Plain of Fundi. More famously, it lends itself to cultivation on stony, gravelly ground (Courtot 1989, 83: 'la vigne, colonisatrice par excellence des terres peu fertiles, des sols minces, sablonneux ou caillouteux'; cf. Bolens 1990b, 3). The variety of its habitats makes it a quintessentially microregional species, and it has produced an enormous multiplicity of individual types, often the result of local independent domestication (Yanuchevitch et al. 1985, 117–19). If land is short, the vine is quite happy in a variety of polycultural regimes. It combines very happily with the olive, since the cycles of the year's tasks for the two plants fit snugly together, accommodating the growing of cereal crops at the same time (Amouretti 1992), especially given the olive's tendency to biennial cropping. Its leaves and trimmings can be used as fodder or kindling. Its fruit is sweet and nutritious, and fermented, as wine, still more so. Wine will keep over the months before the next vintage, and wine or vinegar can help to preserve other perishable products, fruits or meats (Amouretti 1990). Made to a higher specification, and stored in airtight containers, wine will keep for very much longer: it lends itself to storage against bad times. We shall return to the circumstances under which this has been possible.

So, once more, one would expect a little viticulture everywhere.

> There is probably no region where wine was consumed which cannot itself practice viticulture. This product travels over long and short distances equally, with a mobility and an identity shared with few others . . . the example of the vine shows how definitively it has been human intervention rather than climatic or geological conditions that have determined agrarian structures. (Zug Tucci 1978, 311)

Viticulture certainly seems ubiquitous. Thus a contract made by sons for the maintenance of their father in an Apennine village above Modena in the late Middle Ages: 380 litres of flour, 305 litres of wine, 2 kg salt, 4 kg cheese, 25 kg salt pork, 2 kg olive oil, and one of walnut oil each year (Pini 1989, 45–6). Or again: 'This is Kleiton's little shack; this is his tiny plough-strip; this is the scanty patch of vines close by here; this is the bit of brushwood: this is where Kleiton spent eighty years' (Leonidas of Tarentum, *Palatine Anthology*, 6.226).

The prominence of wine in all periods of the history of the Mediteranean is, then, like that of oil, somewhat unexpected. The vine has become emblematic of Mediterranean agriculture; the wine trade is the most celebrated of Mediterranean commercial activities. Here again is a product which was stored and exchanged on a particularly massive scale during Antiquity, in a way which can surprise even by comparison with the wine trade of the Christian Middle Ages, let alone with that implied by the (admittedly intermittent and imperfect) prohibitions and restrictions on wine consumption in the Islamic Mediterranean. Consider a potentate such as Tellias of Acragas in the fifth century B.C., whose town-house was built over cellarage for some 600,000 litres of wine (Diodorus Siculus, *Historical Library*, 13.83.3; Vandermersch 1994, 94). Or the proprietor of the Roman villa at Donzère (where the Rhône emerges into the lowlands of Provence) whose storerooms held 250,000 litres. Unlike the olive, the vine was indeed grown everywhere. So why such storage capacity?

Oil and wine, like the cereals, and above all wheat, have been so intricately wound into the social fabric of Mediterranean cultures that it can be hard to isolate their characteristic place in the logic of primary production. And, as with cereals, cultural explanations have been advanced for their prominence (Unwin 1991, 9; Pini 1989). There is little doubt that the increasing prominence of *Triticum aestivum* and *Triticum durum* among cereal types reflected the adoption of their products as part of a complex of status symbols by city elites and their imitators in the ancient world. Something similar might be said in very general terms about the choice of cereals over pulses. But it would not ultimately be satisfactory to look just at taste; we saw that the expression of taste was inseparable from a set of production relations which amounted to a more nearly inescapable pressure to increase grain production.

Cultural explanations in the history of wine have included the simple predilection for an attractive psychotropic comestible, Dionysiac symbolism, and
the Christian significance of the vine and of wine (including, most implausibly,
the actual demand for eucharistic wine itself: Herlihy 1974, 15; *contra*, Barceló
1988, 205–6). On such a view, the prominence of oil and wine in Mediterranean history would be explained like this. The aristocratic society of the Homeric
poems is already defined by the ritual consumption of wine and uses oil in the
anointing which accompanies the ablutions preparatory to the ritual. The values of
that society became for various reasons dominant throughout the Mediterranean
basin; they were extended through the institutions of the city to relatively large
numbers of citizens who wished to participate in the oil- and wine-consuming
life; the scale of production necessary to cater for this taste established these
goods firmly in the agrosystem, and it was helped to survive by the cultural legacy
which the ancient city and its elites passed on to Byzantium, Islam and the Christian West. There is no doubt that that account is in some senses true. But it has
something of a 'just-so' quality. Expounding the ways in which a thing has been
important does not explain the importance. There are, moreover, objections to
the view that wine's status derives principally from some intrinsic merit, such as
its psychotropic properties. Many other Mediterranean fruits can be fermented
but few have been, to any significant extent. It is at least somewhat remarkable,
given the importance to the diet of cereals, that wine has been so exclusive in
the Mediterranean for so much of its history. The contrast with beer-drinking in
Mesopotamia and in northern Europe is very apparent (though beer may have
been more difficult to make at the time that fermentation was first discovered:
Singleton 1995, 72). As with the other economic strategies that we have examined, the particularities of production relations offer a more promising route.

'Aparecen de vez en cuando como fantasmas veloces y silenciosos, algunas
referencias a "agricultores"' (Barceló 1988, 203 n.2). Extraordinarily, in view of
its labour-intensiveness, histories of viticulture (like many technical histories,
as we shall see in Chapter VII) often reduce to Barceló's 'mute and fleeting
apparitions' the people who devoted their energies to it. 'Le vigneron n'est pas
un agriculteur comme les autres' (Amouretti 1988, 14). The vine, likewise, is
not like the carob or the olive – it needs constant attention. Year-round creative
responses are required as well as strategic decisions. Turning grapes into their
main storable and redistributable form, wine, is not like threshing barley, drying
beans or salting cheese; it requires additional expert knowledge and more hard
work. Worse, there is the risk that, in a world without chemistry, it can, despite
labour and expertise, very easily go completely wrong, and that the vintage will
be ruined (cf. Amouretti 1990 on boiling the must to reduce this risk). Finally,
wine production shares with that of oil the problem that liquids are relatively
difficult to store and transport. As far as the avoidance of risk is concerned, viticulture sounds like an enterprise to be avoided.

What it offers, however, to outweigh these dangers, is the opportunity for the
conversion of labour and skill and environmental advantage into low-bulk high-
value commodities. When times are right – when the weather is clement and
the supply of labour adequate – it is expedient to put more effort into improving
the quality of the crop. This is the logic of intensification. While conditions are
favourable, it is also expedient to grow more difficult, more recherché crops.
The suggestion has been made that we should carefully distinguish the domestic

economy of subsistence polyculture from market-orientated production in response to external demand (Unwin 1991, 11). Quite the reverse! The agrarian
history of the Mediterranean will be intelligible only if we recognize that there is
a single spectrum of resource management in which pressures from outside bear
upon a portfolio of risk-avoiding gambits. You always have olives and vines and
a multiplicity of cereals, because that is wise in a precarious environment. You
increase your production according to the external pressure that is brought to
bear and the distinctive variables governing each crop; and viticulture is preferred
when labour is relatively abundant, oleiculture when it is not. Where there is an
opportunity to turn fish-gluts into fine pickles, or to make gourmet Lucanian
sausage out of animal products, it is worth adding the extra labour – converting
what might have been rather inadequate basic resources into commodities worth
much more than their weight in 'staples'. Viticulture and wine-making turn labour-
glut into storage and redistribution credit.

If Mediterranean producers were indeed more like the independent peasants that some scholars have made them, wine-making might indeed have been
rarer (VII.5). But they were part of a network of connectivity, and the opportunities of redistribution transformed the calculus of prudence within the
microregion – especially when impelled by the interests of the powerful. 'Moins
que la "culture" . . . c'est . . . l'intégration par le pouvoir politique de l'expansion
agricole avec une libération des dynamismes individuels bourgeois et/ou aristo-
cratiques' (Bolens 1989, 72). We might contend that the imposition of intensification involves control and manipulation, perhaps, rather than 'libération', but
it was certainly not merely a matter of 'culture'. The products of opportunistic
intensification characteristically wax and wane. In the Mediterranean, fashion-
able crues have been highly labile. By late Antiquity, for instance, the famous
Italian wines of the Roman Empire had vanished, and the Gothic court savoured
a new oenological canon: Acinaticium from Verona for the royal table, and
Palmatian from Bruttium, as good as the wine of Gaza (Cassiodorus, *Variae*,
12.4; cf. 12.12).

As so often, islands are especially revealing here (cf. VI.11). In many periods,
some of the principal centres of wine-production have been located on Mediterranean islands – Thasos, Chios, Cos or Rhodes, Crete under Roman and Venetian
rule, Lusignan Cyprus. Island wine-production realizes the advantages of good
niches in a continuum of redistribution; but it also turns to protective advantage
the high densities of population that those qualities of island life often promoted
(IX.5). The availability of the 'human resource', redeployable labour, and its
typical mobility across the shifting ecology of a microregional Mediterranean,
emerge again as crucial variables. This need to convert temporary, local labour-
surplus into the wherewithal of survival through stock-piling and exchange has
been responsible for the tenacity, from the second millennium B.C., of the
culture of oil and wine. There may thus be a structural connection between the
limited engagement in the world of the sea of many of the Islamic cultures of
the Mediterranean and their lack of participation in the civilization of wine
(Sherratt 1995b, 22; though cf. V.6). The effect is no crude environmental
determinism: the production and transportation of wine are given their importance by the special contribution offered by viticulture, the commoditization of
surplus labour.

The nature of both the production and the redistribution of wine in the Mediterranean is illuminated by the study of containers. For Antiquity, as we shall see, the archaeological study of amphorae has been the richest source of information on this subject (IX.4). Indeed, it is worth recalling how the relative decline in importance of this container after Antiquity has shifted the evidential base for medieval trade (V.5). This decline reflects a crucial difference between Antiquity and the Middle Ages in the West: the demise of the practice of ageing wine (Singleton 1995, 69–70). When sealed with pitch, the transport amphora which the Phoenician Levant bequeathed to the Mediterranean was air-tight. Wine could therefore be aged and stored for many years. The barrel which became the normal means of transport for liquids in the western Middle Ages (Zug Tucci 1978) made this impossible: whence a taste for young wine, and the disappearance of the phenomena of mass storage and redistribution until the invention of the corked glass bottle.

The contrast should not be made too sharp. The Elephantine Palimpsest (V.4) shows the importance of trade in the wine of the current season and the previous one in the eastern Mediterranean of 475 B.C. Barrels were certainly employed in Antiquity too. And the barrel has its own contribution to make to the economics of redistribution, since the process of vinification continues in it, the volume of the contents changes, and the container itself – at customs-posts, through reuse or resale – is an element in the calculation of profit and loss, an ingredient in the gambling margin of the astute merchant (Zug Tucci 1978). Meanwhile, Byzantine and other amphorae continued the ancient tradition, which survived through the Middle Ages in Cyprus, to the amazement of western observers commenting on the sixty to eighty years' age of the local wines (di Lusignano 1573, 85). The point is that the modalities of redistribution add another vast set of options to be reckoned in the calculus of production.

An important consequence of the study of the containers has been the realization that they offered an easy means of standardizing the packaging of commodities. Amphora-held products were more easily calibrable, and this naturally transformed the ways in which they were exchanged. In turn, production for amphora-filling was also more readily measurable, equivalences were easier to establish. The great medieval fairs which became so famous for the exchange of textiles began as wine-marts: 'le vin semble d'ailleurs avoir acquis . . . le rôle et la signification d'une valeur d'échange courante' (Doehaerd 1947, 277). In the Middle Ages, wine became a commodity of choice for rents and dues in kind, and a preferred medium of exchange, which it served to calibrate, for instance through providing standard measures for the capacity of ships (Zug Tucci 1978, 314–7). This function is the key to understanding the role of wine in Antiquity too – for instance in Hellenistic Magna Graecia (Vandermersch 1994, 24). Given that the Greek cities were autonomous, it is instructive to observe a tendency towards uniformity in commodity packaging which began in the archaic period and survived through the Hellenistic age into the Roman Empire. Production was in the hands of people who regarded themselves as citizens of their city-states; but the uniformity and comparability of their product imply much wider structures. Now it is implausible to suggest that it was mainly commercial ambition which brought about this effect: the wit displayed by Thales in Aristotle's tale (rehearsed above in the discussion of the olive) was unusual, or the story would have little point. Rather, we should seek the origins of the commoditization reflected by the amphorae not in the pursuit of commercial profit but in the regularization of surplus extraction.

Wine was thus *the* quintessential object of redistribution between microregions: a privileged expression of interdependence. The keeping quality of ancient wine meant that this role was fulfilled most emphatically in Antiquity, but it appears to be common enough in the Middle Ages too. Wine, in other words, came to have a structurally distinctive role in the commoditization of surplus (Pini 1989, 62–3). It became a convenient medium for calibrating every kind of obligation in the relations of production, storage and redistribution. And the convenience of the tax-man (or the rent-collector), if we may put it like that, ultimately helped to establish these products as the indispensable cultural identifiers which they undoubtedly became, and so in the process confirmed them as commodities as well as means of paying what the producer owed to the powerful. This double potential came to outweigh even the avoidance of risk, and has been responsible for the extraordinary overproduction of wine which has characterized so many periods of Mediterranean history – overproduction in large units and small, by independent producers and hired hands, slaves and coerced smallholders (Vandermersch 1994, 104–6). The life of small-scale viticulturalists, as we evoked it at the beginning of this discussion, may not have been so idyllic after all.

The role of wine in the extraction of rent, tax or tribute is easily illustrated. In A.D. 598, a levy of 20 *urnae* of wine a year for the Count of Misenum was disputed by the people of the island of Procida, who were presumably producing for the still buoyant market of Naples (Gregory the Great, *Collected Correspondence*, ed. Norberg 1982, 9.53). The wine-rents of medieval landlords enabled them to supply major markets (Unwin 1991, 168). From ancient Cherronesos on the coast between Cyrenaica and Egypt, a late second-century A.D. papyrus (*PVatGr*, 11) records the annual tax-payments in jars of wine (ranging between 34 and 404 litres) of twenty-two little properties (Catani 1985). But a millennium and a half before, the economy of the Minoan palaces had made wine an important part of its system of tax or tribute (Palmer 1995, 283–4). A judgement about the dues owed to the city of Genoa by a people of the Ligurian Apennines in the late second century B.C. included the payment of one sixth of the wine that they produced (*CIL*, 5.7749, l. 27).

The history of cerealiculture may offer a further parallel. We suggested that the nexus storage–rent–tribute–commodity was important to understanding the production of cereals; that seems to be even more true of the olive and the vine. The peaks of redistribution of wine and oil are thus analogous to those moments of maximum dependence on the networks of cereal production that we cited in the last section; and of course, they sometimes coincide with them, as when Rome or Constantinople attracted huge quantities of oil and wine as well as of cereals. Whatever the period, then, the production of wine for the market had something of the institutional about it as well as something of the commercial. Both Antiquity and the Middle Ages offer examples of zones of specialized production whose vineyards and amphora-kilns or harbours were directed at sale in particular markets, often those of great cities. Island wines in the fifth- and fourth-century B.C. Aegean were destined for the Athenian market; the product of many of the fine vineyards of Republican and early imperial Italy was primarily aimed at Rome; on the shores of the Sea of Marmara, specialized vineyards

made wine for Constantinople (Günsenin 1993). Some of this directed production was low-bulk and high-quality; in other places the quite different policy of
producing larger quantities of cheaper wine was selected. Producers remained,
however, highly vulnerable, both because of the special requirements of viticulture and vinification which we have noted, and because, like oil producers, they
tended to be 'directed' – dependent, that is, on particular markets (IX.4).

One of the more singular episodes in the history of Mediterranean wine is its
provision by imperial Venice for the workers in the Arsenal (R. C. Davis 1997).
In the seventeenth century, up to 600,000 litres of wine were supplied each year
for a workforce of only some 1,200. The wine was procured from the territories
of Venice's interests overseas, and its consumption by the workers who more
than any others perpetuated that empire had a forceful symbolic value. This is a
remarkable instance of a connection between the collection and movement of
wine and the maintenance of large-scale structures of power which is a significant theme in Mediterranean history.

Even more than oleiculture, viticulture has been associated with the settlement of new areas and the taking in hand of new productive landscapes. If the
capacity of the vine to cope with difficult environments is partly responsible for
the association, it is hard not to see the opportunities for the deployment of new
sorts of control over labour as an ingredient too. Once cash-crop viticulture had
been established for the convenience of local elite consumers, the vine became a
crop of choice wherever pressure could be brought to bear effectively on production. That is why it has been associated particularly with 'colonial' landscapes
or areas of resettlement (VII.6). The aggressive development of the natural
resources of the Aegean island of Thasos and its mainland *peraia* by Greeks in
the seventh and sixth centuries culminated in one of the first highly organized
production and distribution systems for which we have good evidence. In the
western Mediterranean of this period, too, there is a striking connection between the establishment of new settlements and investment in cash crops, with
the increasing prominence of viticulture and the transfer of genetic material to
establish new vineyards (Vandermersch 1996).

Viticulture and the new settlements of the Greeks and Romans are indeed
very closely linked. In Italy, archaeology is beginning to reveal the extraordinarily
labour-intensive conversion of land for vineyards through trenching, or through
the digging of planting pits in rocky ground (Quilici 1988: Pannàconi, near
Vibo Valentia). Another striking example from the Tyrrhenian coast of Italy is a
vineyard in the Plain of Fundi (very close to where the famous Caecuban wine
was made). Here huge labour forces were deployed in constructing field-drains
out of unused transport amphorae (Quilici Gigli 1987). These examples date from
the period of the massive subdivision of the agricultural landscape through the
allotment schemes known as 'centuriation'. It is hardly unexpected to find that
in other regions too (Provence is a case in point) there is a relationship between
the creation of a settled, subdivided landscape in the later Roman Republic and
the establishment of local viticulture.

One place where Roman authority disposed of the local resources was Crete:
Augustus assigned territory around ancient Knossos as an endowment for the
Italian city of Capua. The Cretan wine-amphorae which have been found in
Campania reveal that the link was expressed through the wine-trade (Marangou
1994). The medieval wine-trade of Venetian Crete or Lusignan Cyprus is

prefigured here; as is the immediate introduction of exchange-oriented viticulture into Majorca after its Christian subjugation in 1229 (Barceló 1988, 204). Yet beyond doubt, the outstanding example from Antiquity of such 'colonial' viticulture is the extraordinarily well-preserved landscape of the Greek *apoikia* of Chersonesos in the Crimea. Here the annual production of wine for the Mediterranean market, during the third century B.C., from a complex viticultural landscape involving minute subdivision into intensive, garden-like lots and the capital-intensive construction of wind-breaks, has been estimated as 20,000,000 litres (Randsborg 1994, 186–7).

Mediterranean viticulture has been 'colonial' in a second important sense. It has provided a commodity the sale or exchange of which has constituted a brutal cultural leverage on the inhabitants of areas outside the political sphere of the vineyard controllers and the zone in which the wine is produced. The best-understood instance of this is the acculturation of Gaul which prefigured the Roman conquest. Wine produced in the high-investment vineyards of Roman Italy in the second century B.C., perhaps originally for the supply of the Roman army, became a high-value status symbol and the source of vigorous inter-necine conflict between Gallic communities. At the peak of this development, an amphora of wine of 25 litres is said to have been exchanged against one slave. In such cases, the conquered region eventually acquires the practice of viticulture itself. The history of Mediterranean viticulture can indeed be represented cartographically as a sweeping movement taking in new areas by progressive stages (Vandermersch 1994). Creating new areas of production and abandoning old ones are features of a productive strategy which is both opportunistic and essentially oriented towards redistribution.

10. THE MEDITERRANEAN GARDEN

> Here the garden rather than the field was the focus of sedentary life.
> Vidal de la Blache (1911) 205; (1926) 129

The wetlands of the coasts of south-east Spain have, as we remarked in Section 5, been converted to *huerta*: 'garden'. The unit of surface measurement of the irrigated landscape is the *hanegada*. The *hanegada* is 0.0831 hectares (Courtot 1989). At Punat, on the Dalmatian island of Krk, tiny olive or vine cultivations are surrounded by stony wilderness. Such pockets of workable soil in the limestone landscapes (hollows made by the solution of the rock) are known as *bogaz* or karstic garden (*Milieux calcaires* 1991, 21). Both are extreme cases of microregional fragmentation, and of the seizing of every opportunity for diversification. It is such localities that the most rococo schemata of polyculture are to be found – and the most dazzling displays of productivity. Of an oasis in Tunisia during the Roman period, we have this famous fabulous picture:

> There is a city of Africa in the middle of the sand on the way to the Syrtes and Leptis Magna, called Tacape [modern Gabés] advantaged in its soil beyond all wonder. A spring provides abundant water for a space of some three miles in each direction; it is generous, but still assigned to the inhabitants by fixed allotments of time each day. Beneath a great palm-tree here there grows an olive, beneath that a fig, under that a pomegranate, then a vine; below the vine wheat is sown, with

legumes in between and here and there leaf-vegetables, all in the same season, all reared beneath the shadow of another cultivated plant. Four cubits of that soil in a square – measured with fingers closed – are sold for four *denarii*. The most amazing thing is having two vintages each year from double-cropping vines. (Pliny, *Natural History*, 18.188–9; cf. Bousquet and Reddé 1994; Pavis d'Escurac 1980)

Unfortunately, excessive cultivation and poor care were ruining this natural abundance.

The agriculture of what has been called the 'microfundium' is in some ways the natural result of that topographical, environmental, fragmentation which is so significant in the Mediterranean landscape. But it also accords with the logic of risk-avoidance. The consequences are important. First, the effect of the diversificatory imperative is that the Mediterranean 'garden' is a location, a type of use of labour and resources and not a particular selection of 'horticul-tural' crops (although those will no doubt be grown there). The garden is, for instance, often associated with irrigation (Bolens 1989, 73). It participates in all aspects of the agrosystem and interacts with the economy of less intensive production around it. Second, the necessity of storage and redistribution means that the Mediterranean garden is no *hortus conclusus*: it must participate in the processes of the market, more or less complex as they may be, according to the period.

The familiar physical fragmentation of the productive landscape is reinforced by the characteristically minute subdivision of property units. At Santa María del Monte near León, before inept consolidation of the lots by modern planners, 459 ha of garden land was held as 148 holdings – but divided into 3,681 parcels, with an average size of only 0.123 ha (Behar 1986; XI.3). This is not a survival of incompetent and outmoded ways, or the malign product of part-ible inheritance, but a sensible and responsible way of managing intensification in a risky environment. Even in temperate regions something similar applies. McLoskey shows how the usefulness of fragmentation underlies the apparently inefficient open-field system of the English Middle Ages. Quite apart from the climatic, hydrological and pedological microtopography, 'one place could be hit by flooding, insects, birds, rust, rabbits, moles, hail, hunting-parties, thieves and wandering armies, to name a few more of the reasons an English peasant might want insurance, while another close by would go free' (1976, 125). How much more diversity there has been in the Mediterranean. There, with intensive agri-culture, reduced productivity per unit of labour can be an acceptable choice if productivity per unit of land is increased (Bentley 1990, 53).

The usefulness of Mediterranean orchard/garden agriculture as part of the portfolio even of mainly nomadic pastoralists can be seen in the apparently most unpromising conditions of the volcanic mountains of the desert tract of southern Sinai. Here it was introduced by the community of the monastery of St Catherine, constructed by the Emperor Justinian (Perevolotsky 1981). Until recently the Jebaliyah bedouin, using flood and well irrigation (VII.2), grew a huge variety of fruit trees in small plots (440 were recorded, ranging in size from 0.6 ha to about 6 ha), and maintained vegetable gardens in about half of them; formerly cereals were also grown around the fringes. The complementar-ity of these two very different types of production is important. There have been many places and times in Mediterranean history at which the garden has been the principal form of agriculture, and other effort has been devoted to the economy of the forest, the mountain or the marsh. That seems for instance to have been the case during much of the early Middle Ages (Andreolli 1990). In Aetolia until very recently, out of sixty-four villages only fourteen were self-sufficient in wheat, and twenty-one in oil; but they were virtually all self-supporting in meat, wine and vegetables (Bommeljé and Doorn 1987). A eulogy of Rhegion (Reggio di Calabria) in late Antiquity can concede that its territory is not much good for grain: its economy does well on intensive high-value arboriculture (Cassiodorus, *Variae*, 12.14). Five hundred years later this was still true, although the commodities had changed. The Reggio *Brebion* is a unique census for tax purposes of 6,425 mulberry trees for silk production scattered in ecclesiastical and other properties in the immediate environs of the city (Muthesius 1997, 113–15).

We have already seen that, arguably, it was in garden locations that cereals were domesticated. Far from being associated firmly with extensive dry farming, they have since often been cultivated in garden conditions. In the Valencian *huerta*, for instance, cereals were prominent among the impressive variety of crops of the irrigated plain (Glick 1970, 27–30). In the Arno valley of Roman Italy the finest *siligo* (soft bread wheat, *Triticum aestivum/compactum*) was grown in conditions not unlike those of the irrigated belt (*regadio*) of Valencia; and the legendary productivity in wheat of parts of ancient Campania are to be linked with long-lasting soil moisture as much as with the mineral-rich soil. The example of Campania is a telling one. Accounts of the early modern agriculture of the area describe it as 'un jardin méditerranéen', where polycropping was taken to its limits: wheat and legumes were grown among vines trained on trees, without any fallow (Delille 1985, 377–8; Swinburne 1790, 1.148).

> And all this way from *Capua* to *Naples*, is a most fruitful plain of corne, and vines growing high upon Elme trees, according to the tillage of *Lombardy*, one and the same yeelding corne, and wine, and wood to burne, but the other wines of this Country, growing upon hills and mountains, and all the other fruites, cannot be worthily praised. (Moryson 1617, 106–7)

Here is a favoured set of ecological niches where the opportunities for intensification have allowed the development over a wide region of a highly intricate agricultural complex. Such 'coltura promiscua', which is 'fondée sur un minimum de création technique et sur un maximum d'adaptation empirique aux conditions naturelles' (Toubert 1973, 258–9), requires both certain natural preconditions – above all a reliable water-supply – and certain socio-economic ones – for instance Italian *mezzadria* share-cropping. The connection between irrigated garden cultivation and the social relations of production will receive detailed attention in the next chapter. Even in the 'jardin méditerranéen' of early modern Campania, however, we note that the resources of pastoralism were managed in close tandem with those of intensive agriculture, and extended through the reclamation of wetland in the coastal plain of the Volturno (Lepre 1978).

One particularly instructive analysis of this form of agrarian landscape concerns medieval Palermo (Bresc 1972). Here the eloquently named Conca d'Oro has several lessons for us. First, although the plain is wide and was indeed the territory that largely maintained the city, the present ubiquity of intensive market-gardening is no guide to the past: only the most favoured sections of this favoured environment were previously reserved for cultivation in this way (1972, 126–7). Irrigation and drainage were indeed both important (57–67). The lots were small, and the cultivators low in status, but the people from whom they leased their holdings – thus providing us with the evidence for their activities – were of the highest means and standing (104–11). For them, moreover, their stake in this uniquely prestigious environment was nothing less than part of their identity as members of the community.

The labour regime of the garden has meant that it is often closely associated with denser clusters of population. Quite extensive belts of horticultural properties surrounded ancient cities such as Rome or Alexandria, or Islamic ones such as Córdoba or Granada (Dickie 1992). It can be shown that even a city of the size of Constantinople could have been self-supporting in fresh vegetables (Koder 1995; 1993). The *huerta* today is the biggest vegetable-growing area of the Mediterranean and produces a quarter of Spain's rice and onions. Such prosperity should not be retrojected on too large a scale. But the ability of horticulture to produce specialized foods which were important for city markets has played a significant part in risk-reduction.

Mediterranean production relies on diversification between wild and cultivated, animal- and plant-resources, intensive and extensive production; on quality of care in production, multiple varieties of animal or plant, processing and packaging for storage and redistribution. Even staples may be specialized; even weeds may be cultivated. A parasitic weed of the thorny maquis, one of the dodders (*Cuscuta spp.*), was first collected and then cultivated widely in the Fertile Crescent in the second half of the first millennium B.C. Its principal use appears to have been as an ingredient in beer (Stol 1994, 175–9). Despite the oddity of its biology and use, it was sufficiently highly regarded to be one of the six commodities whose prices were ceremoniously noted in the Astronomical Diaries maintained by the scribes of Babylon (*kasû*: Slotsky 1997, 31–4), along with barley and dates (from which the beer was made), cardamom, sesame and wool. Although Babylon is hardly Mediterranean, the plant grew in Syria too, and was reported from the Long Walls of Athens (Pliny, *Natural History*, 13.129). More importantly, the economic importance of an (at least originally) wild species, which was used in *materia medica* and as a flavouring, makes a point that is significant in a Mediterranean context. The silk-mulberries of Reggio, the *silphion* and cumin of Cyrene (III.3), the storax of Gabala and the mastic of Chios are, like the narcotics of the modern Biqa, not obscure accidents of Mediterranean production, but illustrate the acme of the intensification and specialization which are to be seen in the Mediterranean garden, and which represent one of the most important protections against omnipresent risk.

We should recall that the exploitation of the margins which forms so important an ingredient in the autarkic systems available for study today has been made possible, despite the risks, by state-guaranteed prices for commodities (Kolodny 1974, 386). Pre-welfare societies relied far more on growing a little of everything in prime locations and selling it in markets of some form.

In this way the economy of sedentary groups, far from being autarchic [*sic*], always had an outlet, either to other local economies which provided supplementary products, or to the town, which provided money, luxury items and manufactured goods . . . None of these specialized crops mattered in terms of the general macroeconomy of the country. Had there been a shortage of figs from the Jabal Matmata or melons from Sfax the country would have remained unaffected. On the local level, however, that of a microeconomy, such products were the safeguards without which people at the mercy of a capricious climate and poor equipment would have been unable to secure their subsistence. (Valensi 1985, 110–16)

Such a microeconomy may, however, have more implications even for the macroeconomy than this account allows, when the strategy of diversification and intensification is used to ward off risk across vast tracts. It seems to have been characteristic of the fragmented production of Roman Egypt, for instance, that the small producers were constantly trading off their surpluses even while they aimed at autarky (Bowman 1986, 91). It has been suggested that diversity of production (as opposed to specialization or commercialization) may sometimes be promoted in order to encourage speculation by making available a large number of different products at several different levels of quality. We must also remember that it was always possible for self-sufficiency to be 'not the result of successful peasant smallholder aspirations, but . . . a deliberate strategy pursued by urban landholders' (S. R. Epstein 1991, 39).

'The economy has a normal surplus' (Halstead 1989), the product of regular overproduction to avoid risk in an unpredictable environment, and it creates the possibility of using surplus – through 'social storage', exchange, or trade – to provide a more diverse insurance cover for the future. The Mediterranean garden, therefore, is the more typical image of primary production than the wheat field or the grazed hillside. Diversity, of labour technique or intensity, as well as of the quality and quantity of what is tended on the small scale, are structural features of Mediterranean history.

11. THE CASE OF THE SMALLER MEDITERRANEAN ISLAND

In Sections 9 and 10 we have had occasion to name eight islands – and two places called 'almost island' (Cherro-/Chersonesos). In many respects, the smaller Mediterranean islands exemplify admirably the concept of the marginal that we were exploring earlier in this chapter. They tend to instantiate especially well the variety of landscape – aspect, geology, relief, soil, altitude, hydrology – that creates a microregional topography. Most contain some very productive niches, which have sometimes been highly renowned. Theophrastus for example records the spot on the islet of Chalkia off the west coast of Rhodes where barley cropped twice in the length of time that barley all around took to do so once (*Historia Plantarum*, 8.2.9–10). The case illustrates how tiny these niches often are, constrained as they are especially by the limitations of island aquifers (Kolodny 1974, 75–92). Extending production involves opportunism and ingenuity.

It has been common in different periods of Mediterranean history to make use of island resources in the same way as those of mountain or wetland – as adjuncts to the more accessible landscape, places into which expansion can take place when times seem suitable. 'Clazomenae', says Strabo of the city in the Gulf of Smyrna, 'has in front of it eight cultivated islets' (*Geography*, 14.1.36). The inhabitants of neighbouring microregions exploit island resources in classic fashion as extra opportunities in the margin: as pasture for instance, on the outlying Lipari islands in the fifth century B.C. (Thucydides, *History*, 3.88). As early as the *Odyssey* (12.134–5), occupation of the pastoral resources of an island – in this case occupation of the mythical island of Thrinakie by the Daughters of the Sun-god, looking after their divine father's cattle – is eloquently called 'overseas settlement', *apoikesis*.

The next step beyond the seasonal and occasional exploitation of island resources is instantiated by the mid-twentieth-century history of Kyra Panagia, the most remote of the Northern Sporades in the north Aegean. A hermitage-dependency of Mount Athos, the island had been uninhabited (occasional monks apart) when it was let in 1969 to three families (10 individuals) from nearby Halonnesos. They took on the 2,000 goats and 600 olive trees, and produced 1,500 kids for sale to neighbouring islands, as well as 3,000 kg of oil. Forty beehives each yielded 60–80 kg of honey annually. The six men of the population took 500 kg of milk each day for cheese; the sheep were pastured using a microtranshumance system, moving uphill from the shore some 300 metres in July. Except for trips to sell their produce and buy staples, the tenants lived in great isolation (Efstratiou 1985, Appendix VI, 168–9). As it happens, a tiny island in a bay of the larger Kyra Panagia is the site of one of the most important Neolithic settlements of the Aegean, a striking testimony to precocious human appreciation of the resources of a whole chain of islands important as a route across the northern Aegean.

Such tiny niches of high potential for intensification have been long recognized as special features of the Mediterranean landscape. In an archaic Greek poem a plain on Euboea (Map 14), which became notorious as the object of hot contention between rival communities and their aristocratic leaders, is labelled with a technical term 'vine-ground', *oinopedon* (Theognis, *Elegies*, 891–4). Two and a half millennia later, at the beginning of the nineteenth century, the *oinopedon* of central Zante (Zakynthos), which had once been a wetland (Goodisson 1822, 176), exported seven million pounds of dried grapes to Britain (H. Holland 1815, 21). In the Peloponnese of the early nineteenth century, another such microregion, a small alluvial basin in the barren and grindingly poor mountains of the Mani, where the opportunity had been taken to develop an intensive vineyard plot, could be poetically called a 'wine-spring', *krasivrysi* (Leake 1830, 1.266). From the beginning of the historical period onward, we hear of the association of some of the islands with specialized production of certain high-value commodities destined for a wide market. What is it that makes island productions especially important, so that from them are derived all the most famous wines of ancient Greece – Pramnian (from the island of Ikaria), Thasian, Chian and Coan, and some famous in more recent times, such as the Byronic Samian? How was it that islets such as Peparethos and Ikos in the Northern Sporades can be shown archaeologically to have had an abundant viticulture serving, as the distribution of their distinctive amphorae shows, a substantial market in the Black Sea (Doulgéri-Intzessiloglou and Garlan 1990)?

The answer can only be connectivity. Islands are uniquely accessible to the prime medium of communication and redistribution. It is not that island niches are usually really much more productive in themselves than similar environments on the mainland. It is rather that they have the simple advantage of being located on islands. And despite a malign tendency to see islands as isolated and remote, characterized principally by their lack of contamination and interaction, they

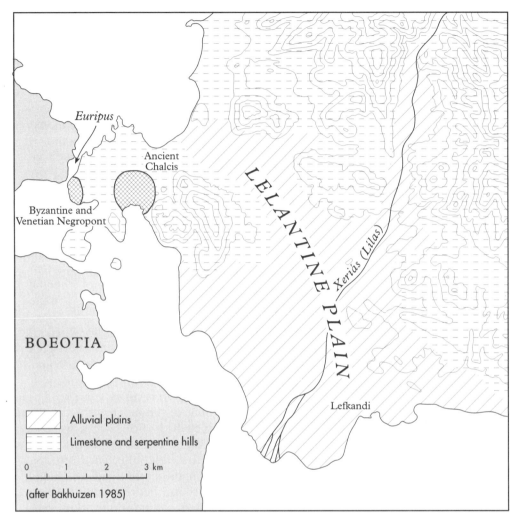

Map 14 *L'ochio e lo zardin de Nigroponte*

In the sixth century B.C., the aristocratic Theognis lamented the 'shaving' of the vine-plain of Lelanton and the destruction of the interests of the birth elite who controlled intensive cash-crop production in central Euboea. The map makes clear the complexity of the surrounding topography and the variability of the settlement pattern. Map 10 displays the wider geographical context. In 1439 Venice granted an appeal about precisely the same sliver of land. The crisis was caused by the disappearance of a salaried officer called streamwarden (*potamarchos*), in whose absence the powerful were taking more than their share of the irrigation water: 'and so many plots have remained unirrigated, and if things continue like this, the place Lilanto, which is the life of this island, will turn into a desolation – a place which provides more utility to the Signoria than any other, through being the eye and garden of Euboea' ('per esser l ochio [*sic*] e lo zardin de Nigroponte'. Deliberazioni miste no. 1041 [indexed as 1049], 2 May 1439: Sathas 1882, 455, ll. 6–23). A paradigmatic Mediterranean microregion.

in fact lie at the heart of the medium of interdependence: they have *all-round connectivity* (V.2).

This helps to explain the special importance of the opportunistic exploitation of resources such as the fish and fowl which we noticed earlier in this chapter, and the curious prominence, far beyond their intrinsic worth, of many other island products: resin, wax and honey, minerals such as Lemnian earth, Cean ruddle, Melian obsidian, Thasian metal-ores, Parian or Proconnesian marble, the iron of Elba or the copper of Cyprus. Some of these commodities were among the islands' earliest enticements to settlers. And in the case of high-bulk substances, exploitation in the heart of the medium of redistribution offers real advantages: the marble of Thasos and Proconnesos was worked from ships or barges at sea-level.

In the heart of the medium of redistribution, moreover, so much value is added to all forms of production as to make improvements on the provision of nature well worth attempting. Hence arrangements such as the dovecotes of Tenos, enhancing the yield of island fowling. Animal husbandry can be practised at a level of intensity comparable to that of the most specialized horticulture. On Delos the tiny terraces were also used for animal pens; and from the late Middle Ages Minorca evolved a highly developed cattle-rearing economy (Bisson 1975). But many islands have sold the dairy or meat products of more extensive pastoralism, especially where they have had the good fortune to be quite well placed for a major market. Thus, during the early modern period, the islands of Cres and Losinj in the northern Adriatic paid their taxes to Venice out of the cash received from the sale of the produce of as many as 150,000 sheep (Imamović 1987, 171–9).

Wine has pride of place among the 'island monocultures', as they have been called. But the list, continuing down virtually to our own times, is long, and reflects all the specializations of the Mediterranean. Fresh vegetables, such as garlic and onions, are the speciality of some of the Cyclades. When population rises to a sufficient density, even tiny and rocky islands such as Delos and its neighbour Rheneia can be adapted to intensive market-gardening, producing barley, grapes, figs, pomegranates and vegetables on narrow terraces facing away from the wind (Brunet 1990a; 1990b). More famous are specialized crops such as the sugar-cane of medieval Cyprus and the mastic of Chios (Perikos 1993), dependent on a sophisticated and quite far-flung market (now largely in the Islamic world). Such exploitation needs to be highly planned. The sacred law of the sanctuary of Zeus Temenites at Arcesine on Amorgos (SIG^3, 963) sets out detailed provision for the productive behaviour of tenants, prescribing compulsory fallow, careful digging around vines and figs, maintaining walls and spreading manure. Another inscription from the small island of Herakleia attempts to regulate the inevitable tension between, on one hand, settlers at the very basic stage of exploitation which we have seen in the case of Kyra Panagia, with their herds of goats, and on the other, those who were attempting something more intensive and more like the prescriptions on Amorgos just described (Robert 1949).

The islands, moreover, produce the wherewithal of trade: clay, salt, timber, and flax. Island potteries have been as prominent in the manufacture of containers for transportation as island shipyards have been in the making of the boats themselves. And finally, dense island populations provide the labour input required to carry out the redistribution – which takes place at times when the Mediterranean agriculturalist is kept from work on the land by the drought. Those are also the times when labour is available for the potteries of islands which specialize in ceramics, such as Iz in the Dalmatian archipelago (Carlton 1988).

Three case studies, of which two actually involve peninsulas, may help to illustrate the nature of these archetypal microregions: the Mani, as we met it in our epigraph from Niphakos; the northern Ionian islands at the beginning of the nineteenth century; and the reoccupation of Mount Athos at the instigation of St Athanasius the Athonite (died *c*.1001).

In the Mani of immediately pre-modern times, we find a place of extremely limited natural resources, colonized because of its remoteness as a stronghold against the mainland of the Peloponnese, and acting as a parasite upon its more productive neighbour. In Niphakos's poem, the epigraph to this chapter, note the stress on women's labour. The men are engaged, by way of an elaborate culture of aggression, conflict and honour (Chapter XII), in transactions which, essentially, deploy their energies beyond the Mani – aggressively or in a mercenary fashion – to bring back the wherewithal for survival. In this case, the distinctive role of the Mani in the network of commodity redistribution, which derives from the danger of its shores to coasting voyagers, is secondary to a more developed and highly specialized exchange of what are basically labour services. The involvement of the mountain populations of south Anatolia, Greece and southern Italy in the exchange economies of the first millennium B.C., often centring on the recruitment of mercenaries, was not so very different. The peninsula is the 'off-shore' refuge from which engagement in a wider world takes place.

Further north and west, a different symbiosis took place. In the early nineteenth century, Holland described how Santa-Maura (Leukas) and its large population (at that time some 18,000 people) survived: 'the island may be said also to traffic in manual labour, as a great number of the peasants pass over every year to the southern parts of Albania to assist in the cultivation of the land: for which service they are chiefly paid in produce' (H. Holland 1815, 62–3). The very fertile alluvial soil of the north shore of the Gulf of Arta (Ambracia) was their main destination: 'The population of this plain is of a very fluctuating kind, and several villages appear in different parts of it which are appropriated to the peasants of Santa-Maura and Cephalonia who come over to assist in the labours of tillage and harvest' (1815, 81).

Further south, the people of Zante had turned over most of their fertile soil to the currant monoculture mentioned above. They still grew a third of their requirements of grain; of the remainder another third came as payment in kind for labouring in the Peloponnese, while the rest was imported to the island and bought with cash gained in payments for such work (1815, 22). We must remember that at this period the Ionian Islands were under quite separate government from any part of the mainland. The running of a high-population commodity-specialized community on a safe and independent island, through the occasional management of the resources of a neighbouring mainland *peraia*, is a pattern which was very common in the first millennium B.C. too.

What we see here is a special instance of a characteristic Mediterranean inversion: the topsy-turvy conditions which develop when the fringes, into which human activity has extended, become the paradoxical centre of population and enterprise because the more obvious niches have been rendered less desirable, usually by political insecurity. Mountains and wetlands, forests and islands have all at times been the location of this paradoxical transposition; but the last have the most to offer, through their engagement with the maritime.

Our third example is also rich in paradox. The eremitic impulse was transformed on Mount Athos into a full-scale re-colonization and intensification of the range of cultivable niches on the Athos peninsula. It made use of the population-gathering force of monastic recruitment to create what was virtually an island sanctuary, from which the produce of intensification could be inserted into the redistributive process and further productive niches progressively colonized (Teall 1971, 54, 56). In the reoccupation of many of the Mediterranean islands, the monastery has played a notable role (Kolodny 1974, 179–88).

It has been the same accessibility to the seaborne that subjects Mediterranean islands to the burdens of what might be regarded as a colonial agriculture (1974, 159–62). Such exploitation divides the productive niches into land-allotments for the benefit of a thalassocratic power; it assigns them to the settlers of a new city (Gaffney and Stančić 1991); it forbids the cultivation of highly productive environments because it is unable to dominate them politically, as when the Venetians (between 1364 and 1463) refused to allow agriculture on the Lasithi and Anopolis plains in the mountains of Crete (J.-P. Richard 1985). In 1815, 5,200 square miles of Sardinia were still owned by Spanish landlords (H. Holland 1815, 6).

This external economic logic has again and again caused the concentration on monocultures to the ultimate detriment of local society, institutions and the environment (Braudel 1972a, 151–8). No wonder that in early modern Corsica the populace of the island begged the authorities of Genoa to spare them economic growth or improvement: it was a palpable sign of subjection and did them no good (Fel 1975). The same process, in less disastrous starkness, can be seen throughout the history of the Cyclades from the Latin conquest to their independence from Turkey (Slot 1982, 18–19, drawing attention to the forced monoculture of grain, but pointing out that some monocultures supported high populations). The inversion which gives islands an unexpected centrality has various demographic consequences, to some of which we shall return (IX.5). One is the characteristic 'pulvérisation' of property into the 'microfundia' that we have met in the two previous sections (Kolodny 1974, 377–88). Islands give an impression of productivity and prosperity – but this has often been at considerable cost to their inhabitants.

The ruthlessness of colonial-type exploitation shows in extreme form that the use of the Mediterranean island, opportunistic and mercurial in its origins, vulnerable and precarious in its continuance, is intrinsically prone to disastrous down-turns and even to extinctions. When abatement occurs and the intensive monocultures are abandoned, the islands revert to being dependent margins. By the Roman period, Ikaria was used mainly for pasture by the Samians (Strabo, *Geography*, 14.1.19) and Ikos had become the domain of a single viticultural-ist from Peparethos (Philostratus, *Heroicus*, 8.9–10 [139]). Or, if the process continues, the islands may be wholly abandoned for a considerable time, giving the impression of catastrophe. Insularity reinforces crisis: islands are characterized by an 'instabilité et vulnérabilité de l'implantation humaine' (Kolodny 1974, 127–37), which enables us to see very clearly the processes which are toned down or confused on the mainland.

The lesson of Mediterranean islands for the historian of production is, therefore, that it is unhelpful to take as the category for discussion either a particular crop-type or even a basic productive regime. Two places growing barley or almonds; two places cultivating fragmented lots with irrigation; two places using unfree labour . . . may be wildly different from each other because of their respective contexts in the wider ecology of connectivity. Excessive concentration on the traditional classification by crop-type or regime will obscure and render unintelligible much of their economic and social history. The true nature of Mediterranean production is its adaptability. We need to assess, in a given place at a given time, what function is being fulfilled by a type of production which we think is familiar. Is there a high degree of redistributive engagement, as often in island environments? Has a set of local conditions made the avoidance of environmental risk the dominant concern? Do political conditions entail that a set of producers are left with their own choices to make, or is there a strong degree of extractive pressure being applied by authorities near or far? Is the activity which looks so similar to ones we have seen elsewhere part, broadly speaking, of a tendency towards intensification or towards abatement?

The effects that are on display so clearly in the islands include, then, the fragmentation of the landscape, the flexibility of human response, the ease with which the processes of intensification and abatement ebb and flow, and above all the central importance of the sea in enabling all of these things to be developed to what is often such an extreme form. Islands usually offer little that cannot be found elsewhere. The attractiveness of using energy and ingenuity in exploiting their scanty resources so painstakingly is wholly dependent on the fact that they are islands, which transforms their potential through the alchemy of engagement in redistribution. Mediterranean islands demonstrate very clearly that intensification is primarily a matter of realizing that potential for entering networks of redistribution which is naturally their salient feature. In these insular cases we can see beautifully demonstrated the principle at the heart of our microregional analysis: that it is not the physical givens alone, but the changing emphases placed upon them according to the quality of interaction, that determine the character of a locality. We have also repeatedly noticed the extent to which the means of survival have been adapted and manipulated in the interests of those who possessed the power to do so: 'in the risky environment of the Mediterranean, the few have repeatedly commandeered the "normal surplus" of the many' (Halstead and Jones 1989, 55).

The economic history of the Mediterranean has thus been formed by the anxieties and precariousness of production, in which neither the problems nor their remedies are easily anticipated, and by the ambiguous forces of exchange – necessary, despised, belonging to the margins, but implicated in the life of most localities. That, however, is a static characterization. It is time to turn to the question of how to model change.

CHAPTER VII
TECHNOLOGY AND AGRARIAN CHANGE

Poseidonius goes on to the farmers and describes with no less eloquence how the soil is cut up and separated by the plough, so that the looser soil may more easily yield to roots: and to sowing and hand-weeding to prevent wild plants from harming the crop. This too he claims needs wise men – as if in our time too it was not the case that agriculturalists are finding very numerous new ways of increasing fertility!

Seneca, *Letters*, 90.21

For the greater part of human history, labor has been more significant than tools, the intelligent efforts of the producer more significant than his simple equipment.

M. Sahlins (1974) *Stone Age Economics*, 81

There would have been a desert if I hadn't captured so many people, and the people I captured would have died of hunger if I hadn't captured so much land.

Manius Curius Dentatus on his conquest of Sabinum (early third century B.C.),
Auctor de viris illustribus [*On Famous Men*], 33.2

1. WORKING THE SOIL

Fertility, productive opportunity, and the soil itself are all of human construction. 'Objet de l'activité agricole, le sol cultivé est en même temps le produit' (Reboul 1989, 31). There is no absolute quality of land anywhere: its value and potential depend on the choices and perceptions of those who make use of it. This is one of the reasons why, in Chapter VI, the schematic separation between prime and marginal environments, which seems so natural at first, proved both unhelpful and relatively easy to dispense with.

In that chapter, we set out the opportunistic character of the pursuit of food in the Mediterranean and described some historical reactions to the all-pervasive marginality of a risk-rich world. The omnipresence of risk is essential background also for the subject of this chapter, which is the history of the process by which productive environments are constructed through the exercise of choices and preferences. This is a study in social history, and it will become apparent that the deployment of *technical* ingenuity is secondary to the *social* relations between human participants. Our belief in treating 'la fertilité comme rapport social' (Reboul 1989, 37–56) will involve us in a quite contentious reconsideration of aspects of Mediterranean production which have, in our view, been mistakenly assigned a determining prominence. The study of inventions and innovations is conceptually subsequent to the relations of control and subservience which have principally shaped decisions about production in the Mediterranean as elsewhere. In the *danse macabre* of *Monsieur le Capital* and *Madame la Terre* (Marx, *Kapital*, 3, ch. 48) it is not the liveries of the musicians that primarily attract our attention.

A stand-by instance of supposed technological determinism in history is the plough. On the traditional view, decisive improvements were made to plough technology in the early Middle Ages. These were so effective that they spread quite rapidly: previously untillable forest-land and the marshier alluvial lowlands were opened up and population boomed. The main ingredients of this alleged revolution are the iron share, the heavier structure of the plough, the introduction of the mouldboard, and a new ability to harness the team of draught animals in file so that they could pull the heavier tool through deeper, stickier soil. Also involved is the abandonment of a biennial fallowing system (which each season took half the land out of production) in favour of more sophisticated crop-rotation techniques, especially the 'three-field system'. The theory gained great prominence. Technological revolution became a fundamental historical datum in this vision of medieval history (L. T. White 1962). Doubts were expressed immediately (Hilton and Sawyer 1963), but the charismatic attractiveness of the theory in itself has meant that it has still frequently been reproduced (e.g. Mokyr 1990, 32).

In this doctrine, the medieval prosperity of northern Europe is juxtaposed on one hand with the economic transformations which produced modernity, and on the other with an irremediably different and wanting condition in Antiquity. The discontinuities of politics and culture between ancient, medieval and modern are thus explained in terms of simple differences of basic production (Lopez 1976, 44–5). The theory is a classic example of a revolution that has been called into existence to negotiate the transition between two periods and cultural systems that are – erroneously – perceived as wholly different and incommensurable.

There are several reasons for a different approach to the history of the plough. To begin at the beginning: the labour of domesticated animals in agriculture through the use of the plough was first harnessed in the late fourth millennium B.C. The change was of the greatest importance, whether or not it should be perceived as a breakthrough. (It has certainly been thought rapid enough to deserve the name revolution: Sherratt 1981.) And it has been persuasively located in the context of the formation of a complex symbiosis between man and domesticated animals (Sherratt 1983, esp. 91–2). Sherratt argued that since the 'secondary products revolution', the interrelationship between pastoralism and plough-agriculture has evolved (as he put it) slowly. That relationship includes the use of animals for burden, textile production and dairying. It also includes the refinement of the adaptation of animal-rearing to the environment through the gradual adoption of transhumance, as well the social forms which reflect all of these. Now, this theory is perfectly suited to explaining the intimate links between animal husbandry and other forms of Mediterranean production which we emphasized in Chapters III.6 and VI.7. But it has a further appeal which sits oddly with its revolutionary terminology. The discovery of such a long interrelationship and process of mutual influence enables us both to reduce significantly the role of revolutionary change in such areas during more recent times, and to explain why revolutionary change has held such an attraction for historians. Seen against so long a history, the innumerable local and periodic modifications of 'plough-use' seem individually less potent as explanations of global transformation. But it is easy to imagine how the irregularities in the staccato rhythm have contributed to theories of technical revolution among specialists in relatively short periods.

Plough technology now appears as a relatively small cog in a much greater machine. 'Events' such as, say, the first mouldboard plough used in Lombardy, or the first water-buffalo bred in Campania, are constituents of a vast series. In a productive system of such complexity, change in one or two parts is slow to affect the whole. The history of plough use is piecemeal and unsystematic. Neither sudden diffusion nor rapid transformation of any aspect of this practice in the Mediterranean world in historical times can now be accepted. Ethno-archaeological fieldwork confirms. A striking technical anomaly has been recorded in the fertile Ropas valley in northern Corfu – in a context, therefore, of a favoured agricultural niche on an island in close contact for centuries with networks of redistibution. Here, very locally, a highly distinctive type of plough was in use until recently (Sordinas 1979). But this was not an instance of tenacious survival of a primitive ard-plough: the design was by local standards sophisticated to an extent that actually rendered it rather unsuitable. We may draw a series of conclusions. Even within an island population, the social domain of an innovation is tightly limited by microregional fragmentation. There is an important mismatch between actual agricultural need, understanding, and response – the 'survival of the mediocre' as it might be called (borrowing the term from Hallpike 1986, ch. 3). As Sherratt predicted, plough technology has a relatively humble place in the spectrum of evolving productive choices. In Mediterranean conditions, an 'improvement' of obvious value elsewhere is not necessarily desired 'here'. The super-networked Mediterranean island (V.2, VI.11, IX.3) and its hyper-exploited microniches can determine the formation of pockets of anomalous – and quite unsuitable – hectic technical 'progress'.

The Ropas valley case also raises the central problem of who benefits from innovations of this sort. Archaeologists have explored parts of the long history of the plough in suggestive ways. The plough is one candidate for the instrument which first enabled the prehistoric elite to accumulate enough wealth decisively to differentiate itself from the rest of society (Pullen 1992). The ecological implications of owning, feeding, and using draught animals have also been invoked to link the scratch-ard to the ways in which elite power in the Mycenaean world may have deliberately encouraged more extensive, rather than more intensive, agricultural production (Halstead 1995: a view to which we shall return). We should recall that the most intensive cultivations of traditional Mediterranean agriculture, such as the *huerta*, are carried out by labour-intensive digging (Bolens 1981, 94–108 and especially 121). The labour regime of Antiquity is often thought to have revolved around the plough, though it also had a conspicuous place for the various operations of deep-digging. Seneca was right to claim, in the passage which stands as the first epigraph to this chapter, that every Mediterranean society in every age finds at every level its own philosophers of production.

The calculus of advantage in improving the plough to exploit new terrain, or deciding whether to use it at all, is complicated for the decision-maker by the usual questions about the productive capacities of the particular portfolio of microenvironments which may be accessible season by season. The microfundial lots of Mediteranean garden belts are dug by hand (VI.10); digging is the principal form of cultivation of olive-groves and vineyards. The different mattocks, spades and hoes, or the tools needed for pruning or harvesting, may be more significant in the repertoire of the primary producer's desired equipment than the plough-share. And even if ploughing is the preferred strategy, in semi-arid conditions the ard-plough remains as effective as the mouldboard. It can be argued that the general efficiency of ard-tillage has remained relatively constant throughout history – even up to the present – varying only in the draft required according to ard-size and soil characteristics (K. W. Russell 1988, 38–40).

Ultimately, the plough is only one among many techniques by which human effort transforms – with varying aims – the physical conditions of production. This limits the extent to which its development can be called decisive in economic history. And that is above all true of the Mediterranean world. At many times, in many environments – differentiated both by their geomorphology and climate on the one hand and their social character on the other – the technical improvements of the various 'plough revolutions' would have contributed little to either intensification or risk avoidance. And risk avoidance may be, as we shall see repeatedly in this chapter, a higher priority than intensifying production. Increasing the yield of a particular product from a given environment (measured in value after redistribution or direct usefulness to the producer) per unit area, per unit labour, or per unit time are common enough goals. But it is highly misleading to regard them as universal.

The terraced landscape

Over generations the plough makes relatively durable changes in the environment. But there are many other forms of landscape modification, some changing entire landscapes and lasting for millennia, or even formally irreversible (cf. Chapter VIII), some lasting for only one season, and microlocal in scale. The most basic form of landscape modification is working the soil. On this subject too, there has been a persistent scholarly interest in finding technologically deterministic differences between cultures. Once again, the thrust has been (as we shall see in Section 3 and Chapter VIII) to blame the ignorance and culpability of ancient societies. The suggestion is that Mediterranean peoples were unable to replace soil fertility before the Middle Ages. A glance at a dream-interpretation of the Roman imperial period alone demonstrates how normal manuring was (Artemidorus, *On the Interpretation of Dreams*, 2.26). Interventions in the structure and distribution of the regolith to make it more suitable for preferred forms of cultivation have in practice been infinitely varied – throughout our period. It is inherently implausible that soil exhaustion, or techniques to counter it such as the application of manure or other structure- or mineral-improving substances, have at any one time been ubiquitous or absent across whole cultures.

Among the simplest techniques are creating a level or gently curved surface, removing stones, and digging. No cut-off point distinguishes this end of the spectrum (where an individual does what he or she can in any time available) from the creation, at the other end, of the terraced hill-slopes that are so familiar a visual element in the recent Mediterranean landscape: using this technique to create, over 10 square kilometres of terrain, 6 square kilometres of new cultivable surface may take twenty to fifty working people eight to twenty years to accomplish (Blanchemanche 1990, 169). Terracing may be spectacular in mountainous areas. It too has a lower register, however: micro-terraces and minor sculptings of fragmented relief, as in the walls and floors of solution-hollows in karstic landscapes (e.g. the terraced dolinas of the lower Murge in Apulia), where it works through an especially sympathetic adaptation to geomorphological process. Particularly intensive and protracted human effort combines with geomorphology to create a type of micro-landscape which is highly distinctive of the Mediterranean world (*Milieux calcaires* 1991, 30; cf. VI.10 and VIII.2).

It is essential to appreciate that we are not usually dealing with once-for-all improvements. The Mediterranean landscape is always unstable, environmental change unceasing. There has never been any question of taking a product finished by the Artificer Divine and deciding what to do with it. If it is now clear that all Mediterranean environments are in some sense anthropogene, we must still recall that the indissoluble bond between human and natural geomorphological process also entails that all human landscapes are constantly being altered by non-human agency. The abandonment of terraces may markedly increase the rate of degradation of the landscape (Parain 1936, 43–4); indeed it is one of the more persuasive arguments for linking the incidence of major periods of valley-bottom alluviation with widespread abatement of productive effort (VIII.3). The relationship between terracing and soil-erosion is, however, complex, and depends on the continuing maintenance of the whole system. Some have suspected that the gain in controlling the movement of the regolith is mainly limited to the period immediately after the creation of the terraces, which subsequently tend to become much less effective.

The problem, made general by the high relief and fragmented topography of so many Mediterranean lands, is 'la tyrannie de la pente'. This is a tyranny whose agents are soil-creep and regolith instability, inseparable from the constant downward movement of groundwater and the much more startling effects of run-off from sudden winter deluges (e.g. Columella, *On Agriculture*, 4.17.7). The close link between water and the soil has two effects. The first is that the disposal of unwanted water before it does any harm and the retention of precious water before it goes to waste are extremely hard to disentangle, so that there is a structural connection between drainage and irrigation (Blanchemanche 1990, 111–32). The second is that historical interpretation needs to consider both the physical moulding of the surface and the tools with which the intended cultivation will be carried out. Also important to the morphology of the Old World plough has been the extent to which arable cultivation on slopes is required, together with the particular characteristics of the slopes themselves (1990, 57). When transverse ploughing of a hillside is possible, that may serve to minimize vulnerability to gullying and soil erosion without the expensive construction of terraces (1990, 43–62; Pliny, *Natural History*, 18.178; Columella, *On Agriculture*, 2.4). Conversely, it has been suggested that in the pre-Columbian New World, where terraces are also prominent and only digging-sticks were available for working light thin soils, the terrace is primarily a means of conserving soil moisture, and its protection against erosion is a bonus (Donkin 1979).

Each of these possibilities has important implications for the type of social organization to be found and its preferred productive strategy. Terraces are well-suited to tree crops, and are often associated with microfundial cultivation (de Reparaz 1990), where they may represent the initiative of landscape-improvement to accommodate small-scale opportunistic diversification. But this initiative might, of course, in turn represent either cautious autarkic risk-buffering, or a venture into an essentially market-orientated commodity. Terraces help to delimit, and make saleable, shares in the productive landscape, marking boundaries in what would otherwise be somewhat contestable parts of the environment (Blanchemanche 1990, 153). But the spaces so delimited are often very small, so that this form of landscape control may be closely associated with the ultra-fragmentation of rights in the productive landscape. We have seen in Chapters III and VI how such fission of property rights helps dilute risk, since the minuscule environments of terraces display local variation in an extreme form. Yet, for a landowner who can dispose of considerable resources of labour, arboriculture is also practicable even on quite steep hillsides, through the alternative strategy of trenching (Foxhall 1996, 53–60); and it has been suggested that the relative lack of references to terraces in ancient evidence reflects their association with small-scale production. The larger producers, whose interests are the most apparent in the ancient evidence, had other ways of dealing with the tyranny of gradient. But in that case, who organized the sometimes very great outlay of capital and labour in the creation of larger terraced landscapes?

Questions of demographic pressure are also germane to the interpretation of terraces. The terraces that we see today in Italy or Greece derive largely from the later nineteenth century. Widespread rural overpopulation was combined with new opportunities for the exchange of Mediterranean tree-products in a conjunction that has only occasionally been found in the more distant past, but which strongly influenced Mediterranean scenery as we now see it (Moody and Grove 1990). The agricultural terraces of Delos between the fifth and first centuries B.C. appear to provide a parallel (Brunet 1990b). As we saw in VI.11, the principal characteristic of the island microregion is not its innate productive capacity but its location in the medium of redistribution. High populations, high levels of capital, and specialization make possible unusual forms of the intensification of productive effort. It is important to note that, in itself, an environmental change involving considerable time and labour and skill is not *necessarily* an instance of intensification: its aim may be to diversify through increasing the available productive area or some other form of risk reduction.

If the evidence from Greece is ambiguous (Foxhall 1996, 45–6), that from Roman Italy appears to be clearer (Quilici Gigli 1995). There it is to be associated with the display of transformative power in the productive landscape which Roman proprietors developed to such an extent. In fragmented environments, it is not usually possible to build a wall with gates and lodges around the parcel of land or even its innermost section, or to mark out ownership through the landscape garden in the manner of Stowe, Badminton or Blenheim. The most eloquent means of displaying control over the productive landscape is to concentrate on the central facilities of storage and distribution. Hence the architecture of the prominently sited Roman villa (Purcell 1995c; V.1). But an alternative is to demonstrate power over nature through the creation of highly visible capital-intensive projects whose purpose is to modify the conditions of production.

Terraced hillsides are prominent among these projects, showing, in the larger cases, that the proprietor is able to transcend the limitations of individual micro-environments, and to override their divisions. The effect is still more marked in the case of irrigation works.

At the simplest level of human intervention, then, we have encountered a group of interconnected questions. They concern the nature, design and use of tools and equipment, the scale with which transformation of the regolith is attempted, and the pressures to adopt various options, arising from demography, the pursuit of collective or individual advantage and the 'necessities' of power. All these themes can be reproduced on a larger scale, and will recur throughout this chapter. Their organic connection with each other is important to remember when we assess the evidence surviving in the landscape for major changes in technique and their impact on social history.

One of the functions of terraces is the simultaneous retention of soil moisture and prevention of waterlogging. Terraces thus attempt to harness the processes of change in the profiles of the hills and valleys, processes which are consequent upon the most potent agency of mutability in the environment, hydrology. Change in the regolith – unstoppable, destructive, omnipresent – does at least for the most part move at a pace which, on human time-scales, can be considered slow. There are infinitely more mercurial hydrological changes. Adjusting meteorological or geological water resources to human interests, principally through irrigation and drainage, is thus a far more complex task (and has a much higher profile in historical discussions). But the group of interconnected questions that have arisen from our glance at ploughing and terracing is also central to the consideration of these more glamorous subjects. Both terracing and irrigation are represented within the microregion as strategies of improvement in miniature, part of that symbiosis between production and the environment which is so characteristic of the Mediterranean world. Both are also closely involved in the extension of human initiative beyond the apparent physical constraints of the locality, whether at the hands of various sorts of collective effort or at the behest of the exploitative powerful. If the technical details of these interventions are made the exclusive focus of the enquiry, irrigation and drainage will be no more intelligible than the history of the plough-share. The nature of the strategy behind the innovation is of the highest importance. Above all, however, it is the ineluctable fact of continuing change everywhere every year which makes a deterministic view of the contribution of technology to Mediterranean history unsatisfactory.

2. The Irrigated Landscape

> There is no doubt that gardens should be attached to a villa, and especially that they should be kept irrigated – watered if possible with the water of a flowing stream, but otherwise from a well with a wheel, valve-pumps, or by drawing with shadufs.
>
> Pliny, *Natural History*, 19.60

Water has some claim to be the most important variable in Mediterranean food production. We saw in Chapter VI to what extent productive strategies have been shaped by the need to cope with the accidents of precipitation. In any micro-environment the soil's retentiveness of moisture, and the distribution and reliability through the seasons of wells, springs and surface watercourses are among the most important topographical markers. The interlocked problems of disposal, storage and redeployment make the control of water a characteristic aspect of microregionally fragmented topography. Its management has therefore been a perennial theme in Mediterranean history, and a fertile field for human ingenuity. It provides an excellent introduction to, and test case of, the social impact of technological innovation. We have a proselytizing zeal on this subject: it seems to us to suffer from a surprising neglect, even with regard to areas such as Egypt, where it might have been expected to form the cornerstone of economic and social history.

The nature of Mediterranean irrigation

One end of the spectrum of possible irrigation practices is inundation agriculture. But only in the wetlands of the Mediterranean has this ever been a genuine possibility, on a limited scale. Somewhat more realistic is what has been called, in the history of Islamic agriculture, the 'invention of summer' – that is, as a growing-season (Section 3). It involves a reliable, perennial, unfailing provision of water in sufficient abundance to extend the winter growing season into or through the months of summer drought. This is, it must be stressed, neither the normal, nor even a very common, aim of irrigation (Farrington 1980, 288). Consumption of water is very variable: figures for nomads in the Negev suggest that a household of six people, two camels, one donkey, two dogs and ten sheep can require as little as 18 cubic metres per year (Scarborough 1991, 102); UNESCO figures allow 25 litres per caput per day, or some 10 cubic metres per person per year. Constant irrigation for the 'invention of summer' is by these standards fantastically prodigal. Applying 20 mm of water each day to 100 ha of irrigated garden would use up the daily supply of 'an average, medium-sized Roman city aqueduct' (Hodge 1992, 247). So the first point about the history of irrigation that needs to be made emphatically is that this type of provision, which is a common image of the technique, is difficult and rare.

    For the most part, Mediterranean hydrological resources are not copious enough to allow irrigation through the summer on a significant scale. Spring-fed summer production is inevitably local, though it may, of course, make a disproportionate contribution to a microregional economy. The abundance and accessibility of waters in oasis agriculture is exceptional. Artificial access to aquifers poses problems. The principal technology is the well-known *qanat*, a system of underground conduits. This taps otherwise inaccessible aquifers, forming a kind of 'artificial spring', which has been seen as a major contribution to the Arab 'invention of summer' (Watson 1983, 103–11). Attention to the nature of particular environments, however, counsels one sort of caution: a *qanat* is best suited to tapping the seasonal aquifers of alluvial fans (because of the relative ease of excavation in the unconsolidated material). It is therefore not immune to variations of flow. The hidden water beneath torrent beds may be reached by catchments of this kind (the *cimbra* of southern Spain) or by wells, but it is not inexhaustible. *Qanawat* are also both technically demanding and costly: one instance in Iran 3 kilometres long, recorded in the mid-twentieth century, delivered enough water for a half-acre to be irrigated once in twenty-four hours; it took seventeen years to complete (English 1968, 174).

Perennial rivers are the most promising providers of abundant water. In Egypt, the management of Nile water through gravity-fed irrigation networks has been practised since the very distant past (the date is still controversial: Luft 1994). The contrast between the arid climate and the abundance of the Nile was extreme by Mediterranean standards and gave the Egyptians pre-eminence among ancient peoples for their skill in irrigation (Diodorus Siculus, *Historical Library*, 1.74.2, referring to inundation, *epirrhysis*). Even in Egypt, maintaining the cultivation of orchards and gardens throughout the year was a practice only gradually extended across the landscape, with the *saqia* proving decisive in the Hellenistic period (Eyre 1994). By the sixteenth century, maintenance of the Egyptian irrigation system occupied 120,000 men full-time (Rabie 1981, 62). Ponds which made ground water accessible were always important. In the Delta, care was needed to prevent salinization (Eyre 1994, 71–2). But the main contribution of the Nile was not to provide water for extra production in months when most Mediterranean regions experienced the dry season: without the Nile, Egypt could not support agriculture at all. Elsewhere in the Mediterranean, only eastern and south-eastern Spain, in the rain shadow of the Iberian peninsula, displays the same combination of (on one hand) annual totals of precipitation too low for agriculture to support significant populations with (on the other) perennial rivers of considerable volume.

There are many perennial rivers, of course, in the parts of the Mediterranean which do receive reasonable quantities of winter rain. The Orontes of Syria (Map 15) is a good example. It drains the powerful springs of the inland trough which we took as one of our 'four definite places' in Chapter III, the Biqa. Then, fed by the aquifers of the Lebanon and Anti-Lebanon and the catchments of the north Syrian mountains, it flows through two further intermontane basins occupied by substantial wetlands, the Ghab and the Amq (cf. VI.5). In the remainder of its course, however, it has the advantage of an unusually steep profile and a fast flow in a stable bed, not subject to very damaging floods (Weulersse 1940a). In the upper sections, barrages of at least Roman date supply irrigation for extensive production of cereals and summer crops, as well as tracts of intensively cultivated Mediterranean garden, of which the most developed example before modern interventions was the area fed by the Lake of Homs (Calvet and Geyer 1992, 27–39). Lower down, the Orontes is distinguished by the frequency of the device known there as the *noria*, a waterwheel driven by the current of the stream from which it lifts water. This device is unusual in that the energy it uses is nearly cost-free, so that in principle it enables the poor to share in irrigation – after the (very considerable) expenditure of the original capital. On the Orontes, even in August, each of these sophisticated machines lifted an average of some 45 litres per second through a height of 15 or 20 metres to irrigate 25 hectares of land (peak figures reached 150 or 200 litres per second, enough for 50–75 hectares: Girard et al. 1990, 368). The *noria* was widely disseminated in the Islamic *koine* (Glick 1970, 177–82), where the necessary technical knowledge and the resources to build both the expensive machine itself and the network of distribution channels were all to be found. But the availability of stable, powerful, perennial rivers was of more significance. Most Mediterranean rivers are not like that: where they are found, they constitute a specialized

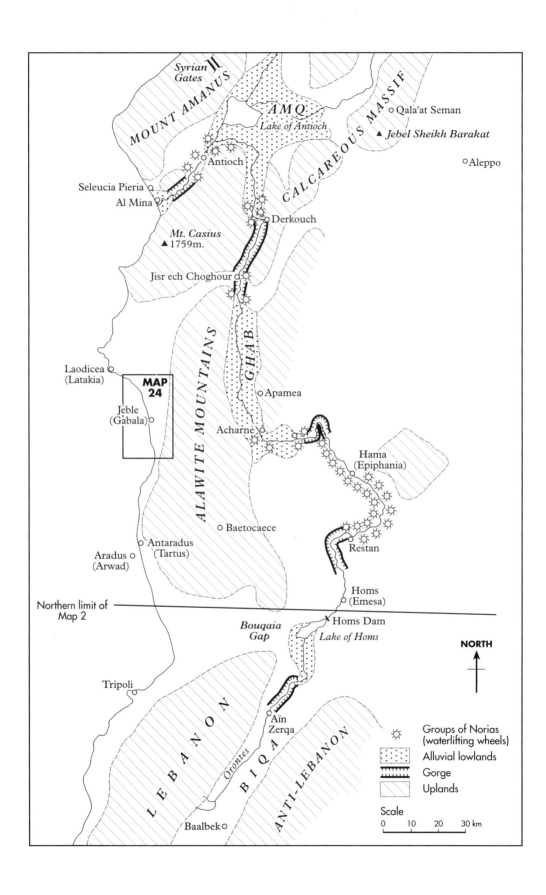

Syrian Gates

MOUNT AMANUS

AMQ
Lake of Antioch

CALCAREOUS MASSIF

○ Qala'at Seman

▲ Jebel Sheikh Barakat

○ Aleppo

Antioch

Seleucia Pieria ○
Al Mina ○

Derkouch ○

Mt. Casius
▲ 1759m.

Jisr ech Choghour ○

Laodicea ○
(Latakia)

MAP 24

Jeble ○
(Gabala)

ALAWITE MOUNTAINS

GHAB

○ Apamea

Acharne ○

Hama
(Epiphania)

○ Baetocaece

Antaradus ○
(Tartus)

Aradus ○
(Arwad)

Restan

Homs ○
(Emesa)

Northern limit of
Map 2

Bouqaia
Gap

Homs Dam
Lake of Homs

NORTH
↑

Tripoli ○

LEBANON

Orontes

BIQA

Aïn
Zerqa ○

ANTI-LEBANON

Baalbek ○

Groups of Norias
(waterlifting wheels)

Alluvial lowlands

Gorge

Uplands

Scale
0   10   20   30 km

resource – in the same way as does a wetland, a harbour, a mineral deposit, a unique plant species – a resource for the microregions which share it to use in their interplay with their neighbours and the larger world.

Gravity-fed water resources from copious springs and rivers are in principle accessible to a wide community. But in practice such springs must be situated at a useful altitude in relation to the workable land, and the river must have a reasonably steep profile. Otherwise the water has to be lifted, and this immediately introduces a major constraint. Of the machines known to traditional technologies, only the *noria* overcame gravity without further input of costly human or animal energy (for some figures on water-lifting capacity cf. Hodge 1992, 246–53). This means that the impact of none of these devices can be considered without full discussion of the labour relations and the economic circumstances of the place and time: like those of the plough and the terrace, their technical specifications are only a limited part of the picture. Until the dissemination of new sources of power in the nineteenth century, no large-scale upward redistribution of water was possible (K. D. White 1984, ch. 6). The exploitation of aquifers inaccessible to gravity-fed systems was thus an important part of the modern transformation of Mediterranean agriculture.

Even in what at first sight appear favourable circumstances, water is much less freely available for copious irrigation than might be supposed. A more usual aim of water management is, therefore, some degree of independence from the vagaries of precipitation that have so all-pervasive an effect on the fortunes of microregions: irrigation for the 'regulation of winter', in other words. In this the elimination of vulnerability to flood or waterlogging, to the problems of water glut, plays a vital part: drainage is, as we have said, inseparable from irrigation (even for southern Spain: Bolens 1981, 16). The replacement of risky uncertainty in the production of staples with assured control has been the purpose of most Mediterranean water technology. This may be sought through an infinite variety of means – from the diversion of natural perennial water resources to the creation of cisterns – and according to all the variables of scale and landscape: relief, altitude, soil type, slope and so on. In semi-arid areas, the control of flash-flooding after winter rainstorms is frequently attempted, to protect the cultivable environment from damage and to deploy the water productively, through wadi-diversion and run-off control with dams (the *boquera* of southern Spain). The collection of mineral-rich sediments from the floodwater may be as significant as

---

Map 15 Irrigation on the Orontes

For the wider context of the Orontes valley, and the location of Heliopolis/Baalbek, compare Map 2. The city of Emesa/Homs is located where the Bouqaia gap gives easy access at low altitude to the Mediterranean coast. The map shows the two major *ghouta* wetlands of the trench-like valley of the lower Orontes: the Ghab (whose most important settlement, Qalaat el Moudiq, is the great ancient city of Apamea) and the Amq (in the territory of Antioch, which is only some five km below the confluence of the Orontes and the Kutchuk Asi). The boundary between the marsh and the open water, and the edge of the marsh itself, are seasonal. Note also the irrigated microregional tracts where the Orontes emerges from the Biqa. Also indicated schematically is the distribution of water-lifting wheels (*norias*). They are all located in the sections where the flow of the river is swifter, and are therefore negatively correlated with the wetland economies of the Ghab and Amq (Weulersse 1940a). The map also provides a wider context for the Plain of Jeble, as presented in Map 24, and locates the limestone massif whose landscape was studied by Tchalenko (1953–8).

the management of the water itself. The perennial rivers, with or without water-lifting devices, are also used for this purpose more often than for the 'invention of summer'.

So only in very favoured conditions has hydraulic control been effective enough to encourage specialization. It has been more natural for it to be drawn on to assist ecological flexibility. A very important tendency has therefore been to use irrigation to extend and diversify those strategies which have been called the 'Mediterranean garden' (Bolens 1989; VI.10). The question arises at once of who benefits from it and how. Like certain forms of terracing, as we have seen, hydraulic works can be very labour- and capital-intensive, and self-consciously showy. At Tuspa, on the east shore of Lake Van, at the end of the eighth century B.C., King Rusa of Urartu provided a complex network of diversions of existing watercourses linked to an artificial lake – which he named after himself. The great inscription which proclaimed his achievement specified that it served vineyards, orchards and vegetable gardens (Garbrecht 1980). No doubt, therefore, about the link here with a form of intensification of production: the investment in higher-status, higher-value crops. But that link is not to be presumed where it is not specified (Farrington 1980, 288).

Irrigated horticulture is only one use of the control of water. The close symbiosis between animal husbandry and other productive strategies makes the improvement of meadows a profitable intervention in a wetland environment, as we saw in the last chapter. A Roman villa-proprietor, something of a specialist in wetter environments (we have suggested), might use irrigation to create pseudo-wetland for rich pasture (Cicero, *To his Brother Quintus*, 3.1.3: 'at the new villa you will easily irrigate 50 *iugera* of *pratum*'). Around eighteenth-century Orange in Provence, a capital-intensive project arranged for the irrigation of peri-urban meadows with water from the river Durance to provide dairy produce for the town (Grosso 1975). G. Ceredi of Piacenza, author of *Tre discorsi sopra il modo d'alzar acque da' luoghi bassi* [*Three Discourses on How to Raise Water from Low-Lying Areas*] of 1567, tells us that in sixteenth-century northern Italy one canal irrigated 250 acres of land for meadow, twice monthly; that Po-side meadows were irrigated from mid-May until mid-August; and that the first crop of hay was cut without irrigation, while the second and third needed water. But his zeal for irrigation was met with the instructive objection that irrigation had resulted in some places in the expansion of profitable meadows at the expense of staple production (Drake 1976, 66–7). In all of these cases hydraulic technology served the interests of a recognizably powerful section of society, concerned with lucrative redistribution rather than prudence. 'Claudite iam rivos pueri; sat prata biberunt' (Virgil, *Eclogues*, 3.111): 'shut off the channels now, lads, the meadows have drunk enough.'

The history of hydraulic technology has offered candidates for Famous Discoveries quite as much as the history of plough technology. Both the *qanat* and the *noria* have been thought to have had a transforming effect on productivity. But both environmental conditions and the aims and objectives of those planning, building and maintaining the system need to be considered before the overall effect of improvements in irrigation can be assessed. The dams of King Rusa had a revolutionary effect on little apart from his own self-esteem. Famous Discoveries history, moreover, always depends on proving a negative case – that the idea was never deployed before the pivotal moment of supposed invention.

In Mediterranean history such cases are especially hard to establish. Indeed, we shall see again and again in this chapter how once-canonical assertions in this kind of technological history have succumbed to the contrary evidence of individual archaeological finds or citations of documentary or literary evidence (such as the Graeco-Roman tendency to dream about manure which we met in the last section). Thus the claim that the ancients were ignorant of the *qanawat* of Iran can be refuted by reference to Polybius (*History*, 10.28; cf. the discussion of the *cuniculi* below). The *noria*, long associated with Islamic technological sophistication, is now attested in north Syria – at Apamea on the Orontes, a few miles north of Hama – in A.D. 469 (Balty 1987, 9–10; cf. Bonneau 1993, 99–102, for the *tympanon* of Hellenistic Egypt).

It is helpful to be able to 'back-date' devices like these because the debate about how much credit we should give to which Great Culture for its technical ingenuity has been too lively. The crude schematizing of cultural history involved should need no further refutation here; but it is apparent that it continues to appeal, for sentimental and often for political reasons. This way of thinking is still implicated in unacceptable assumptions about underdevelopment, backwardness and primitivism with which we shall have occasion to engage again before the end of this chapter. Yet most of the social phenomena which have patterned human interaction with the Mediterranean environment cannot in fact be regarded as ethnically specific.

There has been a most exciting development in the study of irrigation technology in the Mediterranean: a completely fresh start in the analysis of the medieval eastern Spanish material, above all from the archaeological point of view. Distinctive geographically, this area has the advantage of offering an abundant documentary record, to which considerable archaeological material has been added. Its fascinating complexities deserve wider consideration by Mediterranean historians: they are of more general interest than has been apparent to the scholars who know most about them. The remarkable fieldwork which has made historical reconsideration possible found an energetic and outspoken interpreter in Miguel Barceló (for an overview see Kirchner and Navarro 1993). The problem posed for the historian by the fragmented nature of irrigation schemes is one of how to achieve sensible generalizations. Barceló identified a collectivity of transformations across the Iberian landscape, a set of interventions which made it possible for many microregions to become interlocked. It is not unreasonable to adopt Barceló's terms 'hydraulic landscape' or 'hydraulic space' for this kind of effect, which has also been identified as a 'macrosystem' of irrigation (Butzer et al. 1985; Euzennat 1992). Barceló insisted passionately on the necessity of interpreting that landscape from the social and economic perspective; and we shall return in a little to his association of it with a centralized fiscal system dependent on maintaining the autonomy of many relatively small producers and of eliminating competition from 'señores de renta'.

Documentary, toponymic and archaeological evidence closely links the origin of this Iberian water-supply system with Berber resettlement in Spain from the eighth century (Bazzana 1992). But it is of the highest importance to assess whether it was a novelty in the Mediterranean. Some scholars speak cautiously of socio-cultural analogy rather than direct influence from the Maghreb or sources further east in the Islamic world, and Barceló himself inveighs against the pursuit of origins as trivial by comparison with social explanation. Yet it remains a pity that when a historical Mediterranean irrigated landscape outside Egypt at last receives serious study, it is seen in artificial and unnecessary isolation from comparanda in other places and times.

From our point of view, the most conspicuous failing is the reluctance to engage in serious debate about the similarities or differences between the irrigated landscape of pre-Islamic Spain and those of its precursors. To be sure, some archaeologists have attempted the comparison. They have postulated, over the long term, a gradual change in the management of environmental resources accompanying slowly altering agricultural systems (Gilman and Thornes 1985). And they seem to us to have shown entirely convincingly that there were extensive precursors for the irrigated landscapes of Islamic south-east Spain in the Hellenistic and Roman periods (Butzer et al. 1985, 504: Islam 'recreated the Roman agrosystem'). These conclusions have not, however, been widely accepted, perhaps partly because their proponents remain oddly unconcerned with social relations of production and possible changes in them. At the level of local detail, a decisive contribution was made by the discovery in 1970 (but still unknown to Butzer) of a Roman arbitration dating to the first quarter of the first century B.C. about the rights of upstream and downstream communities to the waters of a canal from the river Ebro (J. S. Richardson 1983). Now although it is consoling to have so clear a document from eastern Spain itself, evidence of this kind is of wider importance too. The attribution of such hydraulic control to the local Iron Age cultures, or to the Punic or Roman hegemonies in the Iberian peninsula, has mainly seemed implausible because of a set of major misconceptions about the ancient Mediterranean. It is time that these misconceptions were nailed.

The underrated irrigations of the ancient Mediterranean

'Uncommon in Greece and Italy', says a history of *Greek and Roman Technology* about irrigation 'where the technique of dry-farming prevailed' (K. D. White 1984, 168). 'La gestion de la hydraulique requiert un outillage mental tout à fait étranger aux grecs' (Orrieux 1985). Plato's 'mental tool-kit', on the other hand, includes this prescription for the running of the ideal Hellenic state:

> As for the waters which come from Zeus, and flow down off the high places to collect in the floors of the steep valleys, so that they do not damage the land but do it good, the country wardens (*agronomoi*) should close off the outlets with dams and dikes which will hold back and absorb the rainwater and create streams and springs for the agricultural land which lies below and in every locality, so rendering the driest places rich in good water. Groundwater, on the other hand, either in the form of a river or a fountain, they should adorn with cultivated plants and buildings of the comeliest kind, collecting the separate rivulets in underground catchments so that they form an abundant and unfailing whole. Then, if there should be a sacred grove or precinct there, they can embellish it at all times with the gushing water, letting it flow right into the temples of the Gods. (Plato, *Laws*, 6.8, 761 a–b)

The landscape is broadly that of Attica, containing as it does both karstic springs and steep mountains deeply dissected by torrent valleys which channel flash-floods in the rainy season. Limestone landscapes encourage hydraulic experimentation, and have therefore even been adduced as a hydrogeological explanation for the settlement patterns of archaic and classical Greece (Crouch 1993).

While resisting deterministic explanations, we would certainly endorse the view that, in the ancient Greek agricultural landscape, the systematic management of hydrological resources was normal. The enclosed basins (*polje* is the technical term, derived from Dalmatia) of the limestone uplands are naturally drained by sinkholes or *katavothres*, which invite aetiological speculation as well as improvement or imitation:

> . . . tanto te absorbens vertice amoris
> Aestus in abruptum detulerat barathrum
> Quale ferunt Graii Pheneum prope Cyllenaeum
> Siccare emulsa pingue palude solum
> Quod quondam caecis montis fodisse medullis
> Audit falsiparens Amphitryoniades.
> (Catullus, *Carmina*, 68.109)

[the flowing tide of love had hurled you down from a great height into a precipitous chasm, like the one which the Greeks say at Pheneus, near Mount Cyllene, dried out the rich soil through the draining off of the wetland: report has it that Herakles of the false father had dug it through in the blind entrails of the mountain.]

Despite the natural exits, these basins accumulate run-off and in their natural state, fed by both seasonal torrents and perennial springs, even in summer they form wetlands with extensive areas of open water. We examined some of the productive advantages of even the wilder parts of such environments in VI.5, and saw the importance likewise of systematic responses to the rich alluvial soil, the high moisture, and the annual movement of the shore-line and marshland edge. The mineral-rich soils of seasonal lake-beds are a more familiar feature of the semi-arid belts: we have already met the ebbs and flows of agriculture in the Biqa (III.1). In the Hodna depression in Algeria, there has been huge interannual variation in cultivated area around the 1,000 ha of oasis gardens at the core (Despois 1953, 233–64; Map 20). Here the irregularities of wetland margin cultivation are matched by the very uneven yields of floodwater agriculture in the nearby wadis, reminding us that the fertility of flood-alluvium is not limited to the desert fringes, but can be found in the valleys of the northern peninsulas too (VIII.3–4).

Since at least the Mycenaean period, the human communities of the Greek intermontane basins have shown great ingenuity in managing the environment (Lauffer 1986). Map 16 shows the hydraulic works of the large sequence of *poljes* in central Boeotia, and the way in which flash-flood run-off in the side-valleys was penned back, perennial springs led off in culverts, and marshland and lake dyked to separate wetland resource and water-supply from drained and irrigated valley-floor (Argoud 1987; for the techniques, Gilbertson 1986). They also show the subtlety with which the work was adapted to each local topography. The central wetland, around Lake Copais, provided a resource for a large population over a wide area, and was famous in Antiquity for its agriculture and water management. Something similar appears to have been true of the intermontane basin of the Fucine lake in the central Apennines of Italy (Leveau 1993a; Map 4).

If ancient irrigation has been neglected by archaeologists, the fault lies largely with the vulnerability to decay of the material remains of the hydraulic landscape. Of the hundreds of watermills attested for eleventh-century England in Domesday Book only nine survive today. Over the considerably longer period since Antiquity, the more pronounced instability of Mediterranean conditions

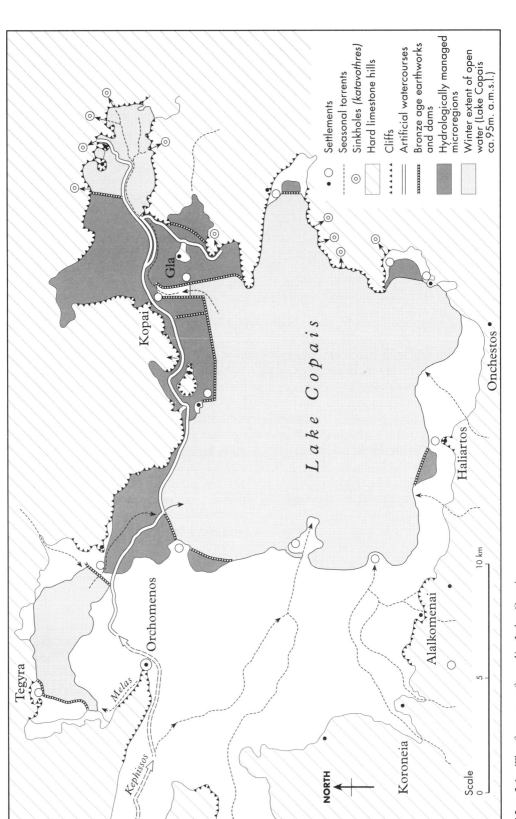

Map 16 The fortunes of a *polje*: Lake Copais

has had an even more marked effect. Only quite recently have archaeologists begun to study the extant remains in detail, and at the points where the mountain valleys debouch into either interior or coastal lowlands, exactly as the *Laws* prescribe, impressive water-management schemes have started to emerge. At Dhamalospilios in western Cyprus, in a remote area where the rural landscape of Antiquity happens to be particularly well preserved, there is report of a local valley-side aqueduct feeding a Roman farm, very similar in configuration to those of Islamic Spain (Fejfer 1995, 23). Literary texts in fact contain some valuable material on the subject: irrigation linked to a landscape of multiple intensification on the estates of the Carthaginian elite, for example (Diodorus Siculus, *Historical Library*, 20.8.4); or the case of the pre-Roman Salassi in the Dora Baltea valley of the Alps in the third and second centuries B.C., whose gold-washing activities so exhausted the river that the farmers downstream could not irrigate their crops and repeatedly had recourse to war (Strabo, *Geography*, 4.6.7). Where they survive, documents also suggest the normality of gravity-fed channels: in the flood-plain of a seasonal river at Herakleia in south Italy (*IG*, 14.645, ll.13–5) or a pocket of small vineyards on the coast of Cyrenaica (Catani 1985). It seems likely that the problem is one of a lack of evidence rather than of accounting for major change after Antiquity.

Central and eastern Greece suffers severely from the unpredictability of winter rain. But west central Italy (another of the definite places of Chapter III), where the rainfall is more abundant and somewhat more reliable, also developed a complex hydraulic landscape early in the first millennium B.C. Over centuries, thousands of galleries, the so-called *cuniculi*, which have long been a puzzle to archaeologists, were dug for both drainage and irrigation in the broken relief of the volcanic hills, using technology essentially identical to that of the *qanat*. The thoroughgoing transformation of the landscape by these methods has plausibly been linked with the Roman state's first systematic settlements of large numbers of its citizens on newly pacified territory, and with the wholesale division of the land into allotments on a regular grid which went with it. If so, it may prove an instructive parallel for the creation of other Mediterranean 'hydraulic spaces'.

We think that the contribution of hydrological management to the landscape of production in the pre-medieval Mediterranean is certain to have more prominence in future discussions. But to foretell this is not simply to correct a bizarre error or propose an antiquarian curiosity. The study of post-classical irrigation systems has posed some remarkably interesting questions about agricultural change, and the ancient Mediterranean has a great deal to contribute to this debate. The great Roman aqueducts, scores of kilometres long, are enormously spectacular examples of Mediterranean water technology. But like the giant *qanawat* of semi-arid districts, they are untypical in the demands that they make in terms of design, construction and maintenance. Hydraulic improvement has much more frequently been closely adapted to the specific circumstances of very small environments.

Why big and expensive water-projects are rare

The Roman aqueduct is one of the most celebrated of historical Mediterranean water technologies (Hodge 1992). It has usually been studied either from the exclusively technical point of view or as a feature of the culture of Roman civic life, to which it was indeed integral. But the contribution of the aqueduct systems of Roman cities to intensive horticulture, whether by fraud or by design, is well attested, and the supply of intensive extra-mural production may be proposed as a more important factor in the genesis and propagation of this technology than is usually admitted. It seems a genuine possibility that this was an significant factor in the creation in the late fourth and early third centuries of Rome's own first long-distance supply lines (Purcell 1996b, 202–3). There is no necessary functional separation of civic provision from irrigation: in the middle of the twentieth century, at Aleppo in north Syria, an ancient conduit, the *Qanaye* of *Hailaan*, bringing in the water of substantial springs, still supplied both the city's needs (for three days a week) and market gardens (four days a week). Sixty-four ha of gardens in three clusters of 21, 14 and 31 properties were watered: the largest unit of horticulture was an estate of just over 5 ha, and the smallest 0.18 ha (Mazloum, n.d.). In the case of Rome's first aqueducts, the technology is the same as that of the *cuniculi* which made possible a 'colonization' of large tracts of the landscape of west central Italy and a substantial concomitant change in productive practices. The local precedent was the harnessing of the crater lakes of the Alban Hills as irrigation reservoirs for the Latin plain. A parallel is also to be found in the drainage for improved pasture of the wetland of the intermontane basin of north Sabinum (Map 3) after its conquest at the beginning of the third century by Manius Curius Dentatus, who also built Rome's second aqueduct. The interesting view that he took of the scope of his activities within both human and physical environments may be seen in the epigraph to this chapter.

Such hydraulic pomp is the descendant of the initiatives of King Rusa of Urartu. It was to be found at the same period in Greece too, where we begin to discern the first really thoroughgoing attempts to change the hydrology of whole regions. Philip II of Macedon drained the marshes near Philippi to make settlement possible – and was reported to have changed the climate of the plain in the process (Theophrastus, *Enquiry into Plants*, 5.14.6; cf. Pliny, *Natural History*, 17.30). King Philip's manipulation of the populations of his realm in 346 B.C. is described in striking terms: practising resettlement like a Persian king, and with the same ruthlessness, he treated people as if they were transhumant animals (Justin, *Epitome of the Philippic Histories of Pompeius Trogus*, 8.5.7–6.2). At his son Alexander's behest, major new drainage-works were undertaken in the Copais basin. The tradition bore further fruit in the famous hydrogeological interventions of the early Roman imperial period: renewed projects in the Copais and, most famously, the huge project to control the hydrology of the wetlands around the lake in the intermontane Fucine basin of the central Apennines, attempted under Claudius and brought to an imperfect conclusion under Hadrian (Leveau 1993a).

In the late nineteenth century, the Copais wetland was finally drained completely. The environmental diversity that had supported local communities for millennia was obliterated in favour of a modern agricultural landscape (Knauss 1990b). In the same period, modern technology also permitted the final obliteration of the Fucine lake. The zeal to reclaim – and its association of itself with the works of the heroes, kings and emperors of the ancient world – was most vividly displayed in the propaganda of the 'battle for the plains' of Mussolini's Italy. The call was made 'to reclaim the land and with the land the men and with the men the race' (Longobardi 1936). It is striking to find similar thinking in

Braudel's analysis of the *longue durée*, as when he writes of the Mediterranean coastlands: 'these great plains represent the essential agricultural history of the Mediterranean, the last, the most difficult and the most magnificent of its successes – that is if one does not look too closely at the cost in human terms of reclaiming them from the marshes' (1972a, 82). Braudel considered the 'battle' for this peripheral landscape typical of the tense relationship between human civilization and the potentially hostile and destructive desert of the Mediterranean environment.

The modern traveller, seeing the vast areas of intensive agriculture on the flat alluvial coasts of Provence, or the Pomptine marshes, or the Gulf of Arta, or the Cilician plain, can assume that such areas must always have been the nuclei of Mediterranean farming, or, more dangerously, that there has indeed been a single millennial war of reclamation whose history has only today been completed. The consequences of that assumption include a blindness to the ecological realities of production in the pre-modern period, with an over-emphasis on the arable and a misunderstanding of the role of the marginal landscapes (Attema 1993, 32–3; cf. 51; VI.3). The sense of struggle which Braudel so clearly understood is ancient enough, and forms a recurrent commonplace of the literature of the Mediterranean right back to Homer (Traina 1988). But its triumphalism is misplaced. This kind of landscape history – in which modern power and know-how succeeds where the puny efforts of the past failed, and tames a monstrous environment of waterlogged, malarial, unreliable soils – is based on a misunderstanding of the sophistication with which traditional responses cope with diversity and mutability – indeed revel in them. Far from being a hostile margin, Lake Copais actually provided an insurance policy against the risks of Mediterranean production, a calibrable response of wonderful flexibility to the exigencies of each season. The ancient technologies applied here were of a wholly different kind from the modern; their users came to enhance the resource, not to annihilate it. In abolishing diversity, moreover, modern root-and-branch schemes have often been found to have highly deleterious effects in the medium term, depleting long-term water resources or causing salinization of coastal areas (N. A. F. Smith 1976, ch. 16). Reclamation triumphalism also entails stressing the dramatic displays of hydraulic power at the expense of the far more important small-scale and ubiquitous modifications. Before the deployment of new sources of energy, the latter were much more effective at producing change in the landscape. Scholars' search for revolutionary improvement or catastrophic decline seriously distorts.

On the one hand, crude interventions on a vast scale, planned and executed by despots or highly centralized political or economic regimes; on the other symbiotic, co-operative, egalitarian, organic growth and communal management of water-systems. It is the first that remind us of the influential thesis of Wittfogel (1957) about the social implications of water management in the riverine civilizations of the ancient Near East. His principal argument was that the construction, maintenance and regulation of expensive hydraulic works requires and maintains authoritarian, monarchic state systems: nothing less than the total transformation of the hydraulic landscape will do to generate the necessary impulse to centralize.

The model has been criticized by Mesopotamianists and Egyptologists, and certainly does not appear to have been generally applicable to Mediterranean landscapes. The irrigation systems of Roman North Africa may be contrasted with the enormous aqueducts that supplied Roman cities. In North Africa the trans-formation of the landscape through the piecemeal management of water resources was achieved locally, and was not dependent on massive state intervention: 'no introduction of special new hydrological techniques was required, no special outsider technologies, and no heavy handed political direction' (B. D. Shaw 1991, 85).

We have seen that it was in fact relatively normal for irrigation technologies not to be particularly complex; much of the detail of even the grandest schemes was, like the creation of a thoroughly terraced landscape, in practice planned, executed and maintained piecemeal by the local population (cf. Brunhes 1902, 427, for the insularity – a good term – of irrigation pockets). Even in pharaonic Egypt, it was private proprietors, able to afford the labour and wanting to improve the productivity of relatively small lots, who contributed more than did central-ized authority to the formation of the artificially irrigated landscape (Eyre 1994, 73–4). Wittfogel's theory was designed to explain relatively uniform and extens-ive productive landscapes: it does not work well in the context of microregional diversity. The techniques of irrigation and drainage must be seen as the answer to the ever-changing challenge of alluviation, run-off and hydrological unpredict-ability which is central to Mediterranean landscape history. The salient point about the history of the management of the Copais basin is that the 'logic' of water control has been, until very recently, essentially local. It can therefore only be appreciated against the background of the ecology of the microregion (cf. B. D. Shaw 1982, 93).

If Alexander the Great and Hadrian intervened to improve or repair a system like that of the Copais (replicating the almost divine status of the heroes to whom myth attributed the original transformations of the landscape), locally, their action was clearly analogous to that of a civic benefactor. The management of ambient hydrology was indeed linked with power – divine or human – but in Antiquity, as we should by now expect, the demonstration of that power tended to be specific to a particular microregion or group of microregions. Even the most ambitious of rulers assumed the character of a local benefactor when improving a region's hydraulic technology. More normally, it was a *local* hero (like Herakles in the wetland basins of the Peloponnesian mountains) who – in myth or record – saw to the needs of the environment (a theme in the geography of religion which we shall explore further in Chapter X). In the post-classical world too, whether it was Caliph Hisham of Damascus regulating the distribution of the Barada river to the oasis of his capital in A.D. 742–3 (Glick 1970, 264–5), or the kings of Valencia ruling in matters concerning the *regadío* of the *huerta*, the local system came first and was merely superintended by the potentates who came after. The emblematic case is not Claudius's ambitions for the Fucine basin, but the appointment of a new king of Sidon by Alexander: Abdalonimus the well-cleaner, whose credentials derived from the management of irrigation horticul-ture (Justin, *Epitome of the Philippic Histories of Pompeius Trogus*, 11.10.8–9).

The conclusion should be clear. As with the choice of strategy (Chapter VI) so with the deployment of technique: many different powers may be found intervening in the life of the microlocality. They vary in scale and in kind. One is the state – in all its various manifestations. But there is no need, whatever the state's pretensions, to assign to it a special place of its own in an ecological Mediterranean history.

Irrigated utopias: smallholder co-operation reconsidered

Land management unites the household: water-management unites the community.
Beardsley (1959) 126

More often than being the megalomaniac dream of kings, Mediterranean water management, in its local complexity, has been linked to co-operative social institutions such as the singular egalitarian legal and institutional arrangements of the Valencian *huerta* (Glick 1970). Water technology is also more often associated with small valuable lots under intensive garden cultivation than with great estates (Pavis d'Escurac 1980). The wet seaward fringes of the *huerta*, the *marjals*, were an environment that offered the prospect of lucrative expansion, but which was actually very difficult to harness (Glick 1970, 44–8; 98–102). While the *huerta* itself protected agriculture against the very frequent droughts of this part of Spain (there were 69 between 1866 and 1926: 1970, 133), it was so fragmented by its topography and the sources of its supply that overall improvement of the irrigation system was very hard to achieve. Mediterranean diversity both protects and limits human interests.

That the opportunity to irrigate promotes a co-operative social response is an axiom of the study of Mediterranean water systems. The response is held to take several different forms. In the piedmont spring-belt of Morocco, microregional variation and the vagaries of the weather are associated with a very adaptable system of the utmost institutional complexity which none the less uses only very simple techniques ('almost technologically embarrassing': Geertz 1972, 33; cf. 25). This system depends on contractual rather than civic obligations, water being managed as an individual right, not a collective necessity. Individual private ownership of water, analogous to but separable from title to land, is the organizing principle. By contrast, collective, corporate ownership of the water-system is characteristic of the inundation irrigation of the wet tropics or the flash-flood management of arid areas (Varisco 1983), even though it should not be ignored by the Mediterranean historian. The maximum fragmentation of production takes place within the irrigated zone; and typically, these water-systems are associated with largely autonomous primary producers, often referred to as 'peasants' (Section 5 below), and not with market-orientated estates belonging to substantial landowners (Glick 1970, 117, for the case of Valencia; English 1968, for a similar effect with *qanawat*).

The co-operative, fragmented system is very suggestive. It underpins the disjunction that has become orthodox between the medieval Islamic agrosystem and its ancient precursors. The older view indeed held responsible for the medieval hydraulic culture the tribal or kinship structures of certain groups – either Islamic society as a whole, or particularly the Berbers who are so clearly linked with the Spanish hydraulic landscape. If we are right in thinking that there was much more local-scale irrigation in Antiquity, does that mean that we should retroject the medieval Islamic social system as we have outlined it? Or extend it to the productive landscapes of the Christian Middle Ages? There are reasons for hesitation in using the Islamic model at all.

First, irrigation has frequently been used to promote the wealth of the large landowner. This should, on the picture that we have been sketching, be linked with the more expensive kinds of technology. Thus in Egypt, Bonneau noted

two phases of technological improvement: an extension of the traditional technology of the *shaduf* in the second century A.D. and a noteworthy increase in the
numbers of powered waterwheels (*saqiya*) in the fifth and sixth. The employment of complex and expensive machines in Roman villas – and their illustration
in elite art, such as the representation of the *noria* at Apamea – may be adduced
here, together with the passage of Pliny with which the present section began.
In this form of agriculture, even quite small properties possessed elaborate pumps,
and might make a display of water-lifting equipment. The necessary expertise is
not always to be found in the communities which rely on the irrigation. The
qanat, for instance, depended on the skill of mobile experts, the *muqanni*, who
roved from place to place undertaking new building or the perpetually necessary
repairs. There is no doubt that wealthy landowners were among their clients.
The fragmented irrigation landscapes also undergo normal change in the patterns of land-ownership and resource control; the size of units owned by the
more powerful, and the degree of control exercised by that group, has ebbed
and flowed at different rhythms in the different *huerta*s of eastern Spain. If the
power of the absentee landlords was at its greatest in the eighteenth century
(Courtot 1989, 88), there is no reason to doubt that it was to be found at some
times and places in the Islamic period too. The development of Roman water
law also reflects the changing needs of a property regime in which the consolidation of portfolios of plots into single holdings became increasingly important
(Capogrossi Colognesi 1981a, 355–7).

Second, it is easy to be too sanguine about the co-operative element in these
social systems. Elsewhere very similar hydraulic landscapes look less egalitarian:
'irrigation . . . connected with stratification systems based in part on differential
control of means of production' (Hunt and Hunt 1976, 398; cf. Hunt and
Hunt 1974). We may note that, in the southern Spain of the recent past, it has
been so obvious that intensification brings difficulties, above all with labour, that
there has been a reluctance to engage in it and a surprising attachment to traditional dry farming – *nostalgia del secano* (Djurfeldt 1993). The principal canal
of the Valencian *huerta*, the *Acequia Real del Jucar*, is indeed administered
by institutions of citizen-style democracy of the sort for which these irrigated
landscapes have become renowned. But there is a property qualification of 30
hanegada (about 2.5 ha), and, since the average lot-size is only 0.8 ha, some
four-fifths of those drawing water from this *acequia* are disenfranchised. These
landscapes appear egalitarian when the eye shifts to them from the *latifundia*.
When the focus is adjusted, however, they reveal in miniature the hierarchies
of control which are characteristic of Mediterranean landscapes. It is an interesting paradox that primary producers in systems of this sort have a degree of
autonomy but simultaneously are locked into social dependence. The process of
mediation between local and global social forms is worth analysing (Mendras
1979). Shared economic interest in a water resource does not necessarily promote co-operation and resolve conflict; outside authority is needed to assure
these (Fernea 1963–4). As Barceló perceives, primary producers who managed to
maintain a certain autonomy were the lucky ones (Barceló and Kirchner 1988).
There has been a marked tendency to idealize the agrarian world of Andalusia
(Lagardère 1993), but this world has much more to offer if we look away from
the fountains, the banana-trees, and the sophistication of soil-classification, and
examine the social relations of production. In Islamic agronomy, as in Roman

and other systems, the main purpose of landowners and their experts, however elaborate the cultural 'packaging' of the skills of the agriculturalist, was self-interest: 'leur souci est . . . de rentabiliser le travail des agriculteurs' (Zakri 1990, 47; cf. 35). We shall revert to this discussion when we come on to the selection of cultivars in the next section.

Even with the relatively good documentation left by medieval Spain, moreover, questions about demography, the crop-types in the irrigated zones, and levels of yield remain open (Kirchner and Navarro 1993, 144–45). There seems to be a mismatch between the Andalusian agronomists and the archaeological evidence, which will not come as a surprise to those who have laboured to reconcile the results of field-survey or excavation with Greek and Roman writings on agriculture – equally intended to divert the literate and leisured. We shall return later in this chapter to the possibility that the milieu for which these traditions were formed was more varied in status and means than any that would really deserve the title 'peasant'. Here too we should conceptually subdivide the hydraulic landscape: there were many different levels of sophistication and investment. The Calendar of Córdoba (of 961) shows, for example, how long-standing local knowledge from before the Muslim conquest was combined with the technical innovations of the Islamic literary tradition (Butzer 1994).

The role of the state helps to explain this uneasy mixture of new and old agrarian behaviour and of aristocratic high culture with a rural population which engaged in more or less co-operative improvement of large tracts of the landscape. For Barceló, 'el eje en torno de cual gira todo el proceso formativo de al-Andalus es la relación entre el Estado y los campesinos' (1988, 245: 'the axis around which the whole process of the formation of al-Andalus turned is the relation between the state and the primary producers'). State fiscal policy excluded competition from *señores de renta*. Other Mediterranean Islamic polities, such as the Ottoman one of the sixteenth century, employed comparable paternalistic policies (Islamoglu-Inan 1988). In certain periods its predecessor, the Byzantine Empire, also did much to maintain smaller property at the expense of great landowners, though the rationale and scope of the measures is a matter for considerable debate (M. Kaplan 1994, 93).

We have already argued that the management of production across the micro-regional matrix by the state is not essentially different in kind from the deployment of other sorts of control. But it may well differ in dimension. The central authority is, first and foremost, making large-scale decisions about the workforce available within the broader landscape: the apparently piecemeal expansion of irrigation to create a collective hydraulic landscape is to be linked with a process of settlement directed from above – in the case of al-Andalus, principally the settlement of Berbers. A further example, from Castellitx on Majorca, shows an integrated design of irrigation system and watermill associated with a woodland clearance of 159 ha (Barceló 1988). The movement of labour in and out of productive spaces by large landowners or other locally powerful bodies is similar except in scale. This may provide us with grounds for making a comparison with the ancient world, and specifically with the phenomenon of allotment which was so closely linked with the notion of citizenship in both Greece and Rome. (Note, in this context, the remarkably communitarian prescriptions for water-law at Plato, *Laws*, 844 a–b). The creation of hydraulic landscape under the auspices of the government at Córdoba can then be set alongside the transformation of the landscape of west central Italy by settlers deployed by the Roman city-state of the fourth and third centuries B.C., through the construction of the *cuniculi*. The hydraulic skills of the Berbers or the Romans are derived from the process of settlement and not from ethnic or social traits of either group.

In these cases the interests of the landlord-state were promoted by relatively complex technology. That was not always the case. The interests of the ancient Egyptian state in irrigation were for example more simply connected with the deployment of labour by time, rather than space, to coincide with the all-important productive opportunity offered by the Nile flood: 'leur constante préoccupation fut de faire respecter une heureuse coïncidence de l'arrivée et du débit local de l'eau avec le moment le plus favorable aux semailles ou à une récupération des produits agricoles adaptée aux circonstances' (Bonneau 1993, 307). (Compare the suddenness of the need for co-operative labour in the *sayl* (seasonal flood) agriculture of the Yemen: Varisco 1983.) For Bonneau, this preoccupation explains the relatively unchanging profile of Egyptian water technology. The concern was overwhelmingly with response tuned to a precise moment, and this was best achieved by the control of the workforce rather than through the use of expensive equipment. The low level of technological complexity in many of the 'co-operative' systems of irrigation management very likely reflects similar priorities. This would help to provide a new kind of explanation for the relatively low rates of technological innovation in ancient hydraulic systems (Bolens 1989, 82). We discern a clear connection between high technology and the intrusive interests of the state (through its colonists or citizen-settlers) or of large landlords. But we also perceive that that connection is only one end of a spectrum of possibilities for improvement of the landscape through hydrological control, the simpler forms of which can be predicated of environments where the state is interested in the control of the timing of work, or where outside pressures on the microregion are less intense. That is why we are reluctant to attribute a pivotal role in transforming Mediterranean production to any particular aspect of irrigation technology.

In the use of more or less complex technical interventions in the productive landscape, the common denominator is the development and planned extrapolation of the basic means of coping with environmental risk. We have observed this taking the form of increasing by artifice the range of environments which are under control, or, in the case of irrigation, of providing an antidote to the principal source of risk in the system, the variability and unreliability of rainfall. It has been held that improvements which resulted in a net gain of understanding and sophistication in the science of production have in Mediterranean history frequently been adopted spontaneously to the overall accruing good of complete societies. We are not satisfied with such a view. The landscape of the microregion is a landscape of power. The display of technology is not the evidence of the ability to do new things; it is designed to gain the maximum kudos – for the great landowner, or for the state which has encouraged the settlement of a new landscape – from what has been spent on attempting to compel greater productivity. The subject here is not the satisfying demonstration of human technical ingenuity. It is the devices of those who control the productive landscape as they pursue either intensification or extensification, demanding now more, now less, per unit area, per unit labour or per unit time. The topic is one which, we feel, needs treatment at some length (Sections 4–6 below).

We have identified a void between two influential approaches in Mediterranean history. One is the view that the development of sophisticated environmental improvements, such as integrated terrace-systems or advanced irrigation projects, can be structurally linked to certain essentially communitarian social forms – the tribe, clan or village. The other looks to the indubitable phenomenon of elite, often 'royal', investment in the kudos to be gained by claiming responsibility for such transformations of the landscape. The incompatibility of these two views turns out to be illusory when the environment is examined from the perspectives which we are advocating in this volume. That is essentially because there is no other way in which we could expect elite power to manifest itself in the Mediterranean landscape except through the intensification or abatement of the adaptations which are – which must be – generated through the day-to-day interactions of local producers and consumers. Thus, optimistically, we might say that, in Mediterranean microregional landscapes, the majority of the population, even when servile, can never be seen as a totally passive recipient of the whimsical plans of the bosses. Pessimistically, we might add that those who think that they can descry self-supporting, self-reproducing, largely self-determining communities of primary producers living in wise harmony with each other and with their natural surroundings, and gradually learning to maintain the equilibrium with less effort through their own ingenious devices, are deceived. It appears that the reality of improvement in productive conditions is almost always the combination of the extractive purposes of the powerful with the co-operative, adaptive behaviour of the labour force: both sides of the apparent interpretative gap are usually found together, if in differing proportions. At the same time, what look like immemorial symbiotic practices are points on the spectrum through which communities pass as they oscillate at greater or lesser speed between inadequate intervention and over-exploitation. The moments that look like balance are only immemorial in that they have been reached again and again only to be lost once more, endlessly recreating forms of behaviour which were first to be seen many centuries before the beginning of history.

Watermills

The water-systems of southern Spain are notable for their watermills, which are as controversial as the other waterworks. The question is: which came first, the mill or the leat (Selma 1991, 73, cf. 97)? And how expensive was the mill, and who paid? And how does control of the mill resemble control of the water system? The close association between the two adds a new dimension to the argument about the respective interests of the small and the large proprietor. Barceló has maintained that mills can be an instance of seigneurial investment and social control (1988, 230–43). Selma, in contrast, has argued the communitarian case: not even control of technology and access to the processing of the staple disturbs the pre-feudal egalitarian peace; necessary and functional mills could be managed 'by the people for the people' without the intrusion of self-interested initiative. The comparative evidence can support either case. On the Orontes in this century, certainly, watermills owned by the larger proprietors were 'un des facteurs de la domination économique que ceux-ci exercent sur les fellahs' (Weulersse 1940a, 59). But a mill excavated in the Alps near Avenches is harder to classify. Precisely dated by dendrochronology to around A.D. 57–8, it was small and relatively cheap and went out of use within 30 years. It milled the traditional *Triticum spelta* at first (although naked wheats increased, perhaps with changing diet, as the period went on). Despite its transience and simplicity, it was probably associated with a substantial suburban villa of the Augustan period, and with the culverts and canals which were transforming the landscape north-east of the town of Aventicum (Castella 1990, 13–29). Watermills in the Byzantine lands seem also to have been at this end of the price-range (M. Kaplan 1992, 53–5).

The watermill used to be advanced as a classic instance of the technological abyss which separated Antiquity from the Middle Ages, a *cause célèbre* in the debate on the impact of technological change. As no mere technique, but a whole new source of energy, the watermill had a considerable stature. It was known in the classical world from at least the first century B.C.: why, then, was its potential realized on any scale only in the early Middle Ages? The debate began in 1935 with an important article by Marc Bloch. Two observations may now be made.

The first concerns evidence: the nature of the record makes the argument from silence extremely hazardous. Ancient watermills, moreover, despite their obvious vulnerabilty to erosion and the absence of documentary material for Antiquity, are becoming less rare than they were. Evidence can even be cited to suggest that such machines could add to the cachet of an ancient community in the same way as did the traditional repertoire of buildings for civic munificence. In A.D. 324–6 Orcistus in Anatolia (in the upper Sangarius valley near Amorium), seeking recognition as a city, adduced both its baths and its 'abundance of watermills on the downflows of the streams that flow past the town' ('ex decursibus praeter-fluentium aquarum aquimolinarum numerum copiosum') (Chastagnol 1981).

The second point is that, as is clearly shown by the Spanish context through which we have come to the subject, questions about the watermill are inseparable from enquiry into the power of landlords, local centralization, the ecology of production, redistribution mechanisms, the availability of capital and of animal and human labour, attitudes to investment, tastes in foodstuffs, settlement patterns, and so on. An account of the technology itself is literally meaningless to the historian unless animated by social history. The complex of watermills at Barbégal near Arles, fed by the aqueducts which supplied that city, is a classic example. Not only do these constitute an impressive early-imperial deployment of the technology; re-evaluation has set them in the context of the systematic reclamation of a wetland microregion and its development for market production, a development linked with the aspirations of new Roman settlers following the foundation of Arles (Leveau 1995; 1996). In the neighbourhood of medieval Lucca, it has been suggested, relative scarcity of watermills reflects the dispersed population (Squatriti 1995, 35). The comparative weakness of landowner power in the Lucchese area might also be adduced.

Braudel considered technological change relatively unimportant as a cause (1981–4, 1.430–5). A case study which aims to correct him has drawn attention to the infrastructure which supported investment in mill technology in medieval Tuscany, and to its apparent contradictions: a self-contained barter economy linked to the business world by a cycle of fairs and markets; rural peasants owning and running expensive hydraulic machinery without the intervention of the urban entrepreneur or the propertied aristocrat; and an advanced technology that does not use the wheel as a means of transporting goods. (Muendel 1985, 62)

This is, in fact, a typical Mediterranean vignette, nicely pointing up the unevenness of technical sophistication and the contrast between the interior of the microregion and the wider world with which it is connected. The elements which are advanced as paradoxes are, however, the normal consequence of the ambiguities of dependence in the Mediterranean landscape, to which we shall return in detail in Sections 4 and 5. As for the historical effects of the mill technology, the example shows that Braudel was right: the contingent fact that there were all these mills in this environment had only a limited effect on its history because of the overriding effects of connectivity or its absence.

Another *cause célèbre* is the windmill, and here some progress has been made (M. J. T. Lewis 1993). The technology was first used, as far as we can see, on the Iranian plateau in the first millennium of our era. The process by which it reached the parts of north-western Europe where it was speedily adopted, integrated into the economy, and improved had not been clear. Now it seems likely that the Aegean is the missing link, and an adaptation through Byzantine learning of an idea familiar to the Seljuk Turks (who arrived in the region at the end of the eleventh century) has been postulated for the most important technological detail, the change from horizontal to vertical arrangements of the vanes. That explains the process of diffusion by invoking the Mediterranean as channel of communications. But we still await the proper integration of the discovery into the economic and social history of the Aegean islands and coastlands. Who learned and practised the new craft? Who made capital available? Was the perceived advantage greater local autonomy through independence of expensive conventional mills, or the greater convenience for storage and redistribution of dealing with milled flour rather than grain (cf. Sigaut 1988, 5, on the significance of central milling, not found in rice or millet areas)? The subject is just beginning. And that is the note on which to end this section: the healthy uncertainties which have replaced grand schemas in the historiography, and which have dethroned technological determinism.

3. On the Diversity of Cultivated Plants

The history of irrigation has introduced to the discussion the material culture of the Islamic West. We have already met, in the context of irrigation, the remarkable revolutionary effect which has been ascribed to Islamic innovations in Mediterranean agriculture. A new agronomics, for some interpreters, permitted self-reliance

> et la commercialisation du surplus; il supposait un savoir botanique et une observation des sols; il était acquis sur une parfaite maîtrise de la gestion de l'eau pour l'irrigation; la nature restée sacrée, aimée comme une femme et respectée en tant que source de bienfaits, l'équilibre . . . sauvait l'environnement de l'abus réifiant déstructeur. (Bolens 1990a, xvi)

Observe the implication that 'commercialisation du surplus' was new. The view is allied to the old idea that overproduction exhausted the unmanured soils of Antiquity (cf. Section 1). Those soils had been tilled by such figures as the hard-working and practical Roman peasant, stolid and unimaginative compared with the Romantic glamour of the agriculturalist imaged in the Islamic treatises (Bolens 1990a, xiii). How can Cato's recipe for cabbage soup to ease urine-retention compete with henna, orange-blossom and pomegranates? The ancient world was primitive economically and backward culturally and (on this caricature) it also devastated the environment. By contrast, one of the principal innovations of the new agriculture was (supposedly) its ecological brilliance (in pedology, for instance: Bolens 1981, 66–78). Now we have already seen something of the problems connected with the idea of 'une parfaite maîtrise de la gestion de l'eau' and the hydrological landscape of al-Andalus. The variety of the sources and the liveliness and originality of the society which they describe clearly attract par-tisanship and encomium. But sentimental attachment to the patina of a culture – of the sort which once gave such a distinctive but misleading colouring to stereotyped perceptions of 'classical Greece', 'imperial Rome' or 'later medieval Europe' – should not be allowed to distort the enquiry into the nature of Medi-terranean economic and social history. Technical ingenuity has figured promin-ently in the delineation of the special characteristics of early Islamic societies, and we shall return to the mechanical inventions attested in medieval Arabic texts (cf. Hill 1980). At this point we wish to consider a type of technical change which lies somewhere between the landscape modifications of our first two sections and mechanical technology: the selection and improvement of food-plant cultivars, which forms a major part of the evidence for an Islamic agricultural revolution.

The introduction into agrosystems of completely new species of plant or animal, or more productive cultivars or more useful strains, is clearly one important variable over time in the history of production. The obvious impact on mod-ern Mediterranean diet of the New World introductions, above all maize and the tomato, makes this a widely known phenomenon. A standard work on the Islamic agronomic revolution has documented the arrival in various parts of the Muslim world of fourteen important species, of which twelve were suited to Mediterranean conditions (Watson 1983). These included crops which are said to have represented major gains in nutritional output per unit area, such as sugar-cane (*Saccharum officinarum*) or spinach (*Spinacia oleracea*); and ones such as the watermelon (*Citrullus lanatus*) which resembled large-scale irrigation in making possible a summer growing season through their resistance to drought (Watson 1983, 123). Some significant introductions among the cereals such as sorghum (*Sorghum bicolor*) or hard wheat (*Triticum durum*) offered both types of advantage.

Consideration of this argument enables us to bring together a number of quite important methodological observations, concerning the nature of innova-tion, the problem of the sources, the role of elite initiative, and the effect of the fragmented Mediterranean environment.

The newer evidence which enables us to retroject the Mediterranean cultiva-tion of some of these plants (for instance, hard wheat) into the centuries before Islam is of relatively minor importance. Equally, we may pass over the fact that the Islamic agronomic literature is heavily tralatician, drawing on – and citing – a variety of Byzantine and Graeco-Roman authorities. (On the other hand, ancient agricultural ignorance, and hence Islamic innovation, can never legitimately be inferred from the silence of the very scanty agronomic literature to survive from Antiquity: recall the case of the watermill.) It is however much more noteworthy that a species-by-species account of agronomic brilliance will leave us where we were with the shape of the plough mouldboard: in possession of interesting details but lacking the framework against which they make sense. Islam was 'a civilization that had a look of newness, fashioned out of elements that for the most part were old' (Watson 1983, 2). Of these elements, the role of the elite in shaping our evidence and in masterminding agrarian change is the one that requires most attention. The crop is of little consequence compared to the production relations which govern its care. We address three aspects of these: the cultural, the economic, and the biological.

First, the question of *high culture*, and the milieu within which the agronomic treatises were composed and perused. The form as well as the content links the agronomists of the Muslim world with those of Antiquity; there are similarities between the 'climates of discovery' in the Islamic world and its classical and Christian equivalents. Is discovery even the right word when it is a question of a learned literary tradition which is essentially recreational, or at best generally informative, rather than in the fullest sense didactic? The specialized gardens sponsored by the Islamic elite (Watson 1983, 117–19) were no doubt an important factor in the evolution and introduction of new cultivars. So were their predecessors in the classical world, such as that of the ex-slave Antonius Castor, who owned a botanic collection in the mid-first century A.D. (Pliny, *Natural History*, 25.9). But in such investigations there was a strong element of the indulgence of leisured curiosity.

In these circumstances, the diffusion of the new ideas was highly erratic, and largely dependent on the whimsical communications of members of the elite (Watson 1983, 88–90). The dissemination of fresh information was so far from being the object of the exercise that the more exotic plants and techniques could remain a guarded secret, as was notoriously the case with sericulture (Lopez 1945; Oikonomides 1986). In Antiquity, when plants were acclimatized in new locations, dissemination reflected the warlord's mastery of exotic Nature and the capacity of his homeland either to supply or to receive a great variety of useful species from elsewhere. This is the background to the botanical investigations of Alexander's generals and, following them, to the introduction to Italy and the West by the victorious Roman generals of the first century B.C. of chestnut, cherry, peach and citron. Fine additions to the Mediterranean repertoire: but we should remember that Alexander had shown just as much interest in attempting to transplant shade-loving ornamental species such as ivy from Europe to Babylon (Plutarch, *Topics for Discussion at the Dinner Party* [*Quaestiones Conviviales*], 3.648 c–d). It is hard for any account of agriculture before the early modern period to compensate for the fact that it derives its material over-whelmingly from the consuming stratum of society, from learned writings composed by the leisured for the leisured.

A minutely subdivided taxonomy of foodstuffs is a sign of the refined taste of elite consumers rather than of flourishing agriculture. Introducing exotics and attempting to improve strains of plants or animals genetically is very often primarily intended to serve luxury consumption. The spectacular improvements and striking professionalism in agriculture found in the privileged environments of the islands or the intensively farmed garden-belts round great cities from classical Greece to the medieval Middle East are hardly evidence of Mediterranean-wide agricultural boom. We should not elevate to the status of 'agricultural revolution' the onset of a lively but fitful interest among city notables in dramatically improving the returns of their estates or in the variety and quality of what they served at dinner.

Agronomic writings were also composed by the greedy for the greedy; and this brings us, secondly, to the *economic* consideration. The surviving Roman agricultural treatises show that sophisticated techniques of grafting were used throughout the Roman period. Here too there is, as we have emphasized for this genre of literature, a streak of frivolous delight in sophistication for its own sake (as with the water-lifting devices of Roman villas). We read in a collection of dinner-time discussions about a pleasure-garden by the river Kephisos outside Athens in the second century A.D., where virtuoso grafting was the main decorative element (Plutarch, *Topics for Discussion at the Dinner Party* [*Quaestiones Conviviales*], 2.640 b). At the same time, it is apparent that grafting and other methods were used for economic purposes too, and selection perhaps became nearly systematic for vines (cf. Purcell 1985) and small fruits. The gradual improvement of varieties – of grapes among other things – in the flourishing intensive agriculture of medieval Languedoc offers a useful corrective. Yet the improvements were subsequent to and dependent on an increase in agricultural effort, and can be seen as only contributory causes of any prosperity which resulted. As in the medieval Islamic world, 'higher and more stable agricultural earnings were achieved . . . by applying more capital and labour to the land unit' (Watson 1983, 128).

Whether innovation concerned new techniques or new species, it was designed to produce great profits for the proprietors rather than to add to the poor man's repertoire of stratagems for avoiding risk. Most of the improvements were concerned with high-return, high-investment crops, and only the more fortunate independent producer could hope to rely on the market for such things in the gamble of survival. We have met (VI.3) the testimony of William Leake on the Peloponnese. The gourds which might in principle contribute so much to the 'invention of summer' were too expensive for the indigent, who could also not afford to protect them against each other's hunger-driven rapacity.

Another feature common to the Roman and the Arabic agronomic traditions is an interest in marvellous and unexpected returns. Here there is, of course, a recreational delight in the exaggerated and the fabulous, but there is an economic dimension too. With anecdotes of astonishing takings in Varro or the elder Pliny we might compare the story in the Arab geographer Ibn Hawqal (213, trans. Kramers and Wiet 1964, 1.207–8) of the doubled revenues won by the innovative techniques of an emir of Mosul. In Ibn Hawqal's story, we hear how al-Hasan ibn Abd-Allah ibn Hamadan took control of Nisibis during the conflicts between Byzantium and the Arabs of the mid-tenth century. He felled the fruit trees and remodelled the watercourses, amassing by confiscation and by purchase vast tracts of the property of those who had fled to the infidel. Very few proprietors were left. In place of arboriculture he introduced cotton and rice and grew cereals and sesame alongside. When the revenues doubled, he could colonize uncultivated land, letting it to the deserving, who became share-croppers owing him half the crop. The populace accepted his rule and that of his son, but was soon reduced to misery by the rapacity of Ibn Ra'i, who took to estimating values in a way that left the cultivator nothing, and who hoarded all the surpluses in his own stores. As an instance of the successful and imaginative introduction of new crops, this tale from upper Mesopotamia could be thought to be a demonstration of the improving zeal of the landlord at its best (Watson 1983, 101). Attention to the anecdote in full shows the all-too-likely context of such introductions: exploitative latifundism. Agrarian change is seen in its true form here: the naked self-interest of the powerful, playing with property and labour in an increasingly cynical way, and incidentally promoting the spread of new crops, and the reoccupation of underused land, in their greed-driven efforts. Historians have tended to echo the landlord's view of these reorganizations. Profits justify the steps taken to gain them; estate owners or rulers who resettle are regarded as 'improvers'. That has certainly been the case with the Byzantine emperors of Nicaea in the years after 1204, who have been credited with agricultural far-sightedness for disposing of estates in the fertile flood-plain of the River Hermus north of Smyrna (Teall 1971). In giving favoured dependants a share in prime productive resources they were in fact playing a game of patronage and demographic manipulation according to the age-old latifundistic logic (Ahrweiler 1958). The running of the great imperial estates of Roman North Africa in the second century A.D. is closely comparable (Kehoe 1988).

The vaunted progressiveness of such innovators seems, then, to be nothing but a specialized and ingenious form of intensification, one step beyond the traditional monoculture. A simple example would be the destructive extraction of a natural plant-resource. The classic Mediterranean case of that is the cultivation for the trade in herbal products of the mysterious Cyrenaican umbellifer *silphion*, so greedily carried out that the plant became extinct (III.3). But new crops can be grown just as destructively. Sugar-cane in the medieval Mediterranean is an obvious instance. An introduction of the Islamic elites, it has been notorious for the social demands made by the intensiveness with which it is grown and the complexity and cost of the refining process (Braudel 1972a, 154–6). It brings the proprietor great returns, but is precarious because of the environmental perils of monocultures in the Mediterranean and the fluctuations of price in the commodity market. Such monocultures can also have a destructive and final impact on fragile environments. In twelfth-century Morocco the refining of sugar so completely exhausted the available fuel supply that its cultivation had to be abandoned (Berthier 1969; cf. Bresc 1986b, 227–52). The disappearance of the valuable sugar business in some parts of the Muslim Mediterranean after Christian reconquest shows not that Islam was especially compatible with serious agricultural improvement, but that such enterprises were dependent on an elite which could and did leave after political or environmental disaster. This is borne out by the fact that the other specialized cultivations of the Islamic lands often markedly waned when there was a change of hegemony such as the *reconquista* in Spain or the loss of Sicily. To explain this, cultural attitudes to novelty have been invoked, combined with demographic determinism: the under-population of Christian Europe was allegedly less conducive to an intensive and innovative agriculture than were Islamic high populations and intensely mobile labour-forces (Watson 1994). But the workers of the land were not the movers behind the sugar industry. They were exploited to set up and run the novel monoculture, and abandoned in destitution when it ceased. The processes of sudden endeavour and equally sudden relaxation of effort, intensification and abatement (Section 4) are prominent in this case. (For both cultural attitudes to innovation and the theory that has innovation promoted by rising population cf. Section 7.)

The third aspect of selection which deserves attention is the *biology* of cultivated plant species. To join the ancient agronomists in concentrating on a few highly visible species is misleading. Innovation of the utmost importance is going on continuously. All cultivars have been steadily improved by simple – and not necessarily conscious – mass selection techniques such as choosing the best individual for seed (thus A. W. Johnson 1972, 154–5, on the interest of traditional primary producers in the collection of seeds and cultivars). This is largely invisible to us precisely because it did not attract the attention of the high literary tradition, but it is of far greater importance than the introduction of cherries or spinach. The 'continuous appropriation of plant genetic resources' is more all-pervasive than any invention, less retarded by what Kloppenburg has called the 'social integument' (Kloppenburg 1988, 8); and, before the early modern period, it could not be described as being imposed from above. The Mediterranean, moreover, has had a special role to play in this essential human activity, which in turn deserves its place in Mediterranean history.

The great profusion of named and distinguishable varieties of fruit and vegetable in the Islamic literature is impressive: Watson (1983, 1) quotes sources for 360 types of date in the market of ninth-century Basra, or a coastal town in North Africa where in the fourteenth century one could find 65 kinds of grape, 36 of pear, 28 of fig and 16 of apricot. The Roman agricultural writers betray a similar tendency, listing multiple varieties of grape, fig and olive, distinguished by place name, or by traditional country words reflecting the shape and size of the fruit. What we find here is not an atmosphere of improvement, or not that alone, but the moment at which a wide-ranging and curious enquirer sets side by side the agricultural practices of scores of localities whose repertoires of crops and of activities were each slightly different (see also Mattingly 1996, 214, for the multiplicity of cultivars, and its relationship to varying environmental conditions). The plethora of 'brands' for an over-stratified luxury market reflects the concerns of the elite. But the diversity itself was far more important, a characteristic of the ecology of cultivation in Mediterranean lands.

Just as the real story of the techniques of crop improvement turns out then to be universal and continuous, but densest where human interaction is densest, so the real history of the introduction of new species has a more ordinary setting than the gardens of Granada. New crops were inserted within a spectrum of pre-existing strategies, and their cultivation took its place alongside other occasional modifications designed to obtain various productive, cultural or security-related goals (for a similar view of agricultural innovation in medieval north-western Europe: Watson 1981). Thus the arrival of a new kind of nut, or a new cultivar, or a new technique for its cultivation – the hazel-nut, say, in the medieval Viterbese or the currant in the Corinthia – is strictly comparable to improvements and adaptations in the pig- or chestnut-economy of the forest-margins, which is where so many nut species were originally domesticated anyway (cf. VI.4 on the walnut villages of late antique Lebanon). Before the early modern period, grains had no special place in these decisions, except in certain areas such as Egypt or south Russia where the relatively greater predictability of the weather rendered monocultures less risky.

Risk, rather than the maximum return per unit land or per unit labour (or any abstract goal such as 'optimum mean yield': Bolens 1981) is, as we saw again and again in the last chapter, the crucial concept. The background to the opportunism of Mediterranean agriculture is in the end the simple fact that monoculture entails starvation in a year when circumstances conspire against that product. Spread the risk by exploiting as many different ecological niches with as many products as possible. This is the maxim that prevents innovation from being revolutionary in Mediterranean history.

4. ABATEMENT AND INTENSIFICATION

The mesmerizing simplicity of focussing on the ratio of food to population has . . . played an obscuring role over centuries.

Sen (1981) *Poverty and Famines*, 8

Our presentation of technical innovation so far has repeatedly sought to correct the bias of evidence and scholarly discussion towards the high-status and the singular. New techniques have either been seen to derive their interest and significance from extraneous considerations such as the social and political setting; or they have been revealed as parts of much larger systems of responses to the need to produce. We have, in short, been looking for common denominators in the study of productive technique. It is now time to turn to a pair of general descriptive terms which have appeared intermittently in the discussion up to this point, and to consider what characteristic forms they might take in the Mediterranean as we have described it. They cover most technical changes because they describe intensity rather than type – the increase and relaxation of productive effort, however defined.

How much better is what kind of more?

The basic constituent of the attempt to get more out of the Mediterranean landscape is increasing the nutritional potential realizable from a unit of physical resource (such as a certain surface area) or a unit of human labour (such as an hour's hard work by an adult woman). 'The fundamental problem of agrarian societies was the efficiency of work' (Delille 1985, 104–5). But if we are to compare the ways in which this has been achieved (or not) in the Mediterranean lands over our long period, some further clarification is in order.

First, observe the cautious phrasing which we have just used. It is easy to talk airily of land- or labour-productivity as if they approximated to precisely quantifiable entities. Imagine, however, comparing an improvement in a water-supply which will require 100 hours' work with the selection of a crop-type which will require the same amount, or planning fifty hours' harvest-work for the women as against fifty hours' minding of animals for the children. The criteria according to which such choices have been made are, naturally, specific to the radically different societies with which we are here dealing. They involve the weighing of non-productive issues such as cultural desirability – nice food, ritually appropriate food – and imponderables such as risk of failure, disease or pest. 'Calculation' will also on many occasions involve decisions about the likely relationship between the cost, in terms of resources and energy, and the various possible outcomes of exchange, gift or sale.

Next, considerable care is appropriate to the question of who makes the decisions about such matters. Within a microregion, patterns of intensification may be adopted almost cyclically, matching household life-cycle (Gallant 1991) or following some strategy of occasional exploitation of marginal land. Complex sequences of occupation can thus be discerned (Roberts 1990). That is the basis of the cultivation of the *eschatiai* ('extremities') of the ancient Greek country-side, and of the continuing process of *adiectio sterilium* or *epibole* (taking in wastelands) in the first millennium of our era (Jones and Woolf 1969, chs. 1–2).

It is vital to appreciate that such patterned, local intensification also entails its reverse, the abandonment of the initiative when it is complete, or when circumstances change. A reflective study of the region of Hesban in Transjordan (LaBianca 1990) has explored in detail how the concepts of intensification and its opposite – in its terminology, 'abatement' – can be used as analytical tools for very long periods of agrarian history. The Levant, where the desolation of the landscape in the later Middle Ages and early modern periods has long been apparent, is a particularly informative starting point for an investigation of this sort (cf. Ashtor 1978, 51). Like 'set-aside', abatement can be environmentally beneficial. It acts as a kind of large-scale fallow, and can make Mediterranean production unexpectedly resemble slash-and-burn or swidden systems: nomads of semi-arid regions, occasionally practising cultivation in different spots, are not so different from many other Mediterranean producers. In some places, even what appear to be well-endowed localities have in more than one epoch displayed a noticeable lability of settlement pattern (Lewthwaite 1988, 179; Day 1975; Chapter IV; further Volume Two).

Some circumstances, such as a strong demand for a certain crop, may result in decisions about the degree of productive intensity arrived at more or less co-operatively, across a landscape comprising many different microregions. Where marginal lands have been opportunistically improved or taken in hand, they are naturally allowed to revert to wilderness when conditions change. Not that wilderness was unproductive (VI.3–4): the transition should not be seen as one between polar opposites. Marginality exists over time as well as in space: it may concern productive environments which have only recently been reawakened, or which are sliding into disuse. This compounds the difficulty which we identified in Chapter VI of rigidly separating the supposedly marginal enterprises of the mountains, woods or wetlands from a fixed domain of 'proper', arable, agriculture. It is hardly surprising that blades for clearance work are such an important part of the repertoire of Mediterranean tools (above, Section 1). In the cycle of intensification and abatement, moreover, it is not always easy to predict which niches will be preferred when.

Locally reducing productive effort per unit area is part of the normal range of exploitations of the microregion. It may take the form of a decision to make less use of those parts of the environment where the most appropriate enterprises are intensive. Valley bottoms can, in the appraisal of a particular season, become too waterlogged to be worth draining, or too vulnerable to flood or prone to disease. The uplands may seem preferable because they are disease-free, because there are particular advantages in strategies suited to their environment, because they offer security from oppressive political and economic structures or from war, or because they lend themselves to oppression and competition. Such motives have been implicated in phenomena as diverse as *incastellamento* and brigandage (cf. Bazzana 1992, 385, on the unstable settlement pattern of medieval southern Spain, with its frequent abandonments). Apparently perverse choices are central to the patterns of occasional intensification and abatement across the Mediterranean landscape and through time. Many monastic foundations in the early Middle Ages represent a similar preference for making available the uncultivated margin (Fumagalli 1992, 15).

That picture of more-or-less co-operative decision-making assumes relatively autonomous producers. Such a happy state of affairs, like conditions of ecological balance and long-lasting stability, is alas unusual. It is of course more likely that the power to make such choices will reside wholly or in part with some authority – a landlord, or local official, or representative of the state. The decision may, indeed, ultimately result from the interests of an authority in a very distant place, when the strategy is intended to satisfy the needs of a political system for supplies in kind (e.g. for the maintenance of an imperial capital). Rulers have used the instruments of constitutional authority to obtain from subjects the advantages, albeit writ large, that any local boss enjoys over the workforce. They have also sometimes used the images and metaphors deriving from control of local production to express the nature of their constitutional power. Recall King Philip's manipulation of the populations of his realm of Macedon: he treated people as if they were transhumant animals. Aristotle's advice to Philip's son Alexander, which he famously ignored, was: treat the Greeks in the style of a leader (*hēgemonikōs*), like friends or household members; treat the barbarians as a master (*despotikōs*) like animals or plants (ed. Rose 1863, fr. 658 = ed. Plezia n.d. fr. 6). The high-profile demands of an aggressively rapacious state are not the only pattern, however. Long chains of dependence may be involved in the implementation of major decisions about reclamation, like those which we examined in Section 2. In medieval Lucca, reclamation of wet waste was organized by the Church through letting to reasonably well-off tenants who sublet (Angeli 1989).

Like all of the previous contexts for intensification in various forms, this one is also fraught with the likelihood of the eventual reversal of the pressure, and of a turn towards abatement (cf. Section 6 below). Many an episode of abatement or intensification in Mediterranean history is directly to be attributed to the strategic decision-making of the powerful: land may be abandoned when labour becomes too scarce, too costly, or too recalcitrant; or after a simple failure of interest or nerve. But there may be more positive reasoning at work here too. Another context in which abatement may be deliberately chosen is extensification, which, it is clear, can be a sensible response when an owner controls a huge tract of land but little labour (Djurfeldt 1993). Abatement is, therefore, as likely as intensification to be associated with centrally managed landscapes, around a Mycenaean palace or a medieval monastery – or with the subdivided terrains of Roman colonization (Chapman et al. 1996, 263).

It is of great service in Mediterranean history to be able to look at both intensification and abatement as strategies which can be applied in good times or in bad, and by producers operating in many different frameworks of decision-making: intensification should not automatically and exclusively be identified with increasing prosperity and success. Take, once again, the case of animal husbandry.

We have noted that it is not necessary for it to be associated with hard times. There are periods – such as phases of Byzantine history – in which there is little doubt about the link between pastoralism and widespread abatement (Whittow, n.d). A proper understanding of intensification and abatement in Mediterranean environments shows that there is no incompatibility between this connection and the view that animal husbandry could be an important and profitable strategy (Wickham 1983–5).

Abatement is, indeed, as normal as intensification. Mediterranean history is full of what late Antique emperors referred to in their legislation as *agri deserti*, abandoned fields. Such fields were usually taken at the time as a melancholy sign of decline. Accounts of ancient travellers (who usually had vested interests of one kind or another), from Tiberius Gracchus to St Ambrose, show them appalled by rural desolation. And conventional laments of this kind have sometimes been accumulated by historians as evidence for economic or social catastrophe. Anecdotal or rhetorical complaints about empty lands are, however, unreliable evidence. What the travellers deplored might have been beneficial: migration to large cities for instance, always regarded as a bad sign, actually *helps* the countryside. The choices that were expressed in cultivating any given zone in any particular way – if at all – were more complex than was likely to be apparent to many a casual elite observer. The supposition that the normal activity of the countryside is a routine of subsistence agricultural production is, as we hope to have shown, mistaken or tendentious. Worries about rural depopulation have been common enough to generate a suspicious multiplication of supposed crises over the centuries: if they are pivotal events, Mediterranean history has been singularly rich in pivots. That there have been times when disaster has affected very wide areas of the Mediterranean landscape is not disputed. But the salient point about the tradition of concern for rural population is that it attests a normal state of affairs. Abatement, the relocation of the labour-force, and the stripping out of elite assets, have kept on happening in the Mediterranean. Even the notorious abandonment of land in the Roman Empire during the period of its decline can be shown to answer very well to this model: 'while certainly some land was going out of use permanently, there was a great deal of marginal land fluctuating in use between good and bad years. This was accompanied by movements of population . . .' (Whittaker 1976, 164). It is inconsistent to describe Roman villa-estates as manifestations of elite land management for profit, and yet also to be surprised that their archaeology frequently reveals abandonment and asset-stripping.

Demography, intensification and abatement

Horizontal movements of population of the kind evoked in that quotation were always important in Mediterranean agrarian history. Underpinning this observation lies the likelihood that, outside some metropolitan concentrations, problematically high population density was rare in the pre-modern Mediterranean. This subject will receive a fuller treatment in Volume 2. Here we shall simply record that we see no important exogenous variables at work promoting really sustained demographic growth over our period. Even in the decades preceding the arrival of the Black Death, demographic decline was always at the very least an imminent possibility.

Population is one of the principal variables in the highly mutable landscape against which intensification and abatement must be viewed: labour resources and the number of mouths to feed are in more than one sense vital elements in the choice of strategy. Demographic determinism, however, has very little place in Mediterranean history as we conceive it. First, the repertoire of ways of minimizing risk is fundamentally adaptive and therefore relatively good at accommodating increased pressure of numbers. There is considerable scope for the intensification of production in most microregions. Second, among the standard risk-reducing options, diversification and storage with redistribution in mind play a significant role. They can both do so, of course, principally because of the connectivity provided by the Mediterranean sea itself. Communications and movement, redressing imbalances and shortfalls, usually burst the Malthusian bubbles. Flexible responses ease the tensions created by population levels far higher than any conceivable carrying capacity of the ambient microregion – as notably, and eloquently, with the high populations which have been common throughout our period on islands. Islanders may own or control estates in larger environments, a particular example of the use of redistribution to allow demographic increase which explains why we shall also deal with latifundism and absentee landholding in a chapter dedicated to productive technique (Section 6 below). But third, and most important, connectivity acts on the otherwise demographically more tightly constrained microregions, making possible substantial horizontal movements of population: people have been mobile as well as their supplies. Demographic pressure, where it has occurred – especially through increases in entitled segments of society such as male citizens – can be remedied in various ways by the movement of population (Garnsey 1988a, 63–8). This is why we shall also consider colonization and allotment in this chapter (Section 6 again). In the Mediterranean, they are analogous to other forms of intensification, and more important than many. In the history of Mediterranean technology, the surveyor's rod is mightier than the watermill.

Two provisional conclusions, therefore. First, in Mediterranean history food crisis has not been caused by demographic growth's outstripping carrying capacity (however that might reasonably be defined). In the Mediterranean environment *any* population exceeds carrying capacity in a bad year. We stressed in Chapter VI that there have been no ecological paradises. The failures are the result of accident, war – and social injustice. 'Starvation is blue-blooded' is how it could seem – *limos eupatridēs*, as an Athenian scratched on the potsherd with which he was trying to banish an aristocratic politician from his city (Willemsen and Brenne 1991, 153). The control of storage, of which we have already noticed instances, gave the store-owners a stranglehold for which they were all too seldom admonished. In late Antiquity, however, Cassiodorus spoke out against hoarding (*Variae*, 9.5); Augustine of Hippo, anticipating the theory of 'entitlement-failure' (Sen 1981), knew well that famines were the fault of people not weather (*Sermons*, 25.4; cf. 311.8); while Ambrose of Milan delivered much the most scathing attack on the habits of landowners known to us from the ancient world. 'To what end do you make the poor wish the land was sterile? I see no advantages accruing from abundance, with you taking charge of redistribution, you fixing the prices, until they had rather that no cereals came up than have you playing the broker with the people's starvation' (*On duties*, 3.37–52 at 41).

The second conclusion is that land-hunger, as opposed to land-greed, is not normally a very helpful category in Mediterranean history. The land itself is only one resource, and 'entitlement' in Sen's sense is what you can get, not what you need (Sen 1993, 30: 'the set of alternative bundles of commodities over which a person can establish . . . command'). Before modern times the environment as a whole, through redistribution and intensification, could accommodate any imaginable demographic increase. Only the population boom of the nineteenth and twentieth centuries significantly changed that state of affairs. In Europe, for instance:

> there were still ecological niches to fill and population levels were to rise without problems for several centuries. Agriculture and economic intensification were not the direct result of increasing population but . . . a socio-political response. (Hodges 1982a, 164)

That was written of the early Middle Ages, but could be applied more widely to our area and period. Similarly, the model for the intensification of production visible from time to time in the record of human exploitation in the southern Argolid 'does not require population pressure, only the pressure of people widely dispersed through many different ecological zones' (van Andel and Runnels 1988).

The adaptability of labour

In a usually underpopulated environment with the strongest incentives to adaptability in the intensity and character of productive effort, it is not surprising to find a great diversity of labour use, to which the labour of women and children has been central (Scheidel 1995; cf. Bennett 1987, Hanawalt 1986). Comparative evidence suggests that women in particular were the labour-force of occasional intensification, just as they were the ordinary workers in the much more 'subsistence-orientated' but still far from classically peasant-like Mani of Niphakis's eighteenth-century vision, the epigraph to this chapter. From the philosopher Poseidonius comes a vivid and horrifying anecdote of women at work as day-labourers in gangs of diggers, probably improving arboricultual yields, in the first century B.C. A woman labourer in Liguria gave birth while at work but, wrapping the child in leaves, went back to her digging so as not to lose the day's pay (Strabo, *Geography*, 3.4.17, cf. Diodorus Siculus, *Historical Library*, 4.20). Diversity of labour use finds a modern expression in the phenomenon of part-time farming, as it has been documented by ethnographers and geographers (Ansell et al. 1984). We have already remarked on the indivisibility of town and country in this context (Chapter IV), and shall return to the artisan agriculturalist in the next section (cf. Delano Smith 1979, 228 on sericulture).

Other kinds of effort than the purely agrarian conduce to security too, above all, as we have stressed, through the redistribution which is made possible by connectivity (cf. Le Roy Ladurie 1966, 60). Among the part-time occupations that may prove attractive to producers, we may cite the processing or packaging of foodstuffs, and transforming the 'secondary products' of food-production, such as leather or wool, into saleable produce. Here too the labour of women and children has played an important part. Indeed, it is one of the structural advantages offered by flexible, adaptive, diverse production that it enables full use to be made of all available labour resources throughout the seasons. A Roman agronomist prescribes that on frosty and wet days when women cannot labour outside, they should be set to wool working (Columella, *On Agriculture*, 12.3.6). These non-agrarian employments, significantly, include undertaking the redistribution itself, as do Hesiod's agriculturalists with their boats for use in the unproductive summer season.

This adaptability of labour has implications for understanding the archaeological record, on which so much of the agrarian history of the period which we are covering must depend. In this record change is prominent. Indeed, one could go so far as to say that agrarian archaeology is the archaeology of change and not of stability. For it is episodes of intensification and abatement, normal as general phenomena although they reflect the most diverse socio-economic and cultural matrices, which create most of the archaeological landscape as we see it today. It is, moreover, impractical to attempt to distinguish archaeologically between production for use and production for exchange (Gamble 1981). The complexity of strategic decisions about the use of labour, wherever they are taken, precludes their being visible in most of the archaeological record.

> Material culture cannot be seen as a simple reflection of past social systems. Nor is it a passive record which methodological advances will allow us to interpret in order to reach the past 'as it really was'. Rather it is and was activated in the creation and protection of social relationships. (Moreland 1992, 116)

We should add that archaeological evidence may be neutral between many different kinds of social relationship, and that it is impermissible to interpret what remains only from a materialistic point of view. There are good reasons for not allowing a 'calorific determinism' to occupy the centre of our study of past societies (Sherratt 1995a, 14–15; cf. B. D. Shaw 1984c, 230; II.5). The archaeological record is always minimalist. The interpretation of material evidence must allow for the more complex 'superstructure' of social activity which accompanied the visible changes: 'In the historical framework of its productive forces, a society is not based on production alone, but on the reproduction of the conditions of production' (Meillassoux 1991, 325).

Conclusion

Much discussion of agrarian technology has taken as its starting point the imperative of raising productivity. Our analysis of intensification and abatement has shown what an inadequate approach that is, and how it neglects the difficulty of classifying agrarian productivity, even when it distinguishes labour productivity from land productivity. Neither a determining environment nor a dictatorial demography can be invoked as the principal factor in the history of productive technique. Within the diverse topography and interlocking ecologies of the Mediterranean, the basic techniques – plough and sickle, water and fire, as Le Roy Ladurie put it (1966, 76–80) – have proved themselves adaptable to many needs. They have done so – and this is a crucial part of our argument – against the background of a sophistication in the system of social and economic interdependence which far outweighs the most showy inventions. It is the technological transformation of that whole system itself, through the mechanization of the redistributive infrastructure and the computerization of its finances, that has brought about the far-reaching changes associated with modernity – not individual innovations.

Within the system of interdependence which binds Mediterranean micro-regions, a vital part remains to be attributed to the relations of power within society, the 'social forces of production' (producers' relations with each other, their tools, and the land), and 'the inherently conflictive relations of property' (the terms are those of Brenner 1976). 'It is the structure of class relations, of class power, which will determine the manner and degree to which particular demographic and commercial changes will affect long-term trends in the distribution of income and economic growth – and not *vice versa*' (1976, 31). Or, as Sahlins put it in the passage from which we have drawn the second epigraph to the chapter, 'for the greater part of human history, labor has been more significant than tools, the intelligent efforts of the producer more significant than his simple equipment' (M. Sahlins 1974, 81). To the producers' intelligent efforts – the social setting of technique – we now therefore turn.

5. Anatomy of the Mediterranean Countryman

> Ignorant men with limited, dull horizons, they all had the same obsession with grey earth, grey days, black bread.
>   (Chekhov, *My Life*, 13, trans. Hingley 1965–80, 8.170)

These primary producers are Russians. In the pages that follow we consider the characteristics of the Mediterranean labourers whose varying efforts in times of abatement or intensification emerged in Section 4. It must be said at the outset that we do not think it helpful to regard them as dull people of monochrome obsessions. But it is useful to begin by quoting this literary stereotype because it is unfortunately common in the historical imagination of Mediterranean scholars.

Take for instance the stereotype of the 'vertues labourieuses du paysan romain rivé à la réussite empirique' which we saw in Section 3 used by Bolens as a foil to her own characterization of the fortunate country people of al-Andalus. Behind this stereotype lies a whole history of the image of the Roman citizen-cultivator, generated during the political turmoil of the late Roman Republic, and far removed from the realities of the Italian countryside at any period. In the early third century B.C. a Roman general was denounced for deploying two thousand of the state's citizen soldiers under his command not against the enemy but in improving his estate through the clearing of woodland (Dionysius of Halicarnassus, *Roman Antiquities*, 17.4.3). Wishful thinking about citizens has done a good deal to obfuscate the study of the ancient economy. Ancient stereotypes also include the shepherd and the fisherman, stigmatized as types of the lone outsider, in contradistinction to the independent citizen cultivator (III.6). The realities of the dependence of all such people and the closeness of their integration into the milieux of consumption and of other kinds of production have been noticed in Chapters III and VI. It has not been uncommon for Mediterranean fishermen to be reduced to near or actual unfreedom in their service of the luxury trade: the lagoon-fishermen of early modern Comacchio, for instance, were liable to summary imprisonment (Parain 1936, 59). It would not take long to compile a register of images of primary producers from the many cultures of our subject matter. The exercise would not greatly help our enquiry.

Acquiescence in cultural stereotypes is often linked with the all-too-common omission from Mediterranean agrarian history or archaeology of the social relations of production, and especially of labour relations. Among the blandest and least analytical of the descriptive terms available is the catch-all heading 'peasant'. A social anthropologist has distinguished two principal references for the term: a 'medieval European cluster' of low-class farmers in a sharply stratified system on one hand, to be distinguished from poor and backward citizen farmers in a nation-state in the early stages of industrialization, cultural modernization and market integration on the other (Dalton 1972, 406). This distinction offers the historian nothing. It encourages us to think that the exercise in long-term, geographically wide comparison which we are undertaking has some protreptic use if it can dissuade others from schematic dichotomies on the grounds of social stratification, market orientation, citizenship or the existence of the nation-state, and teleoscopic concepts like modernization. The category of 'peasant' is the obverse of the coin of which the reification of the city (Chapter IV) is the reverse.

There are three manifestations of peasant-theory which we find particularly unhelpful for Mediterranean history: (1) the notion of subsistence, and the ideas of (2) self-determination and (3) immemorial stability. We shall examine each in turn.

A critique of 'subsistence'

It is commonly assumed that, because nutritionists can define (with some difficulty) a base-line of simple subsistence, a state in which available human labour suffices for human demographic maintenance and no more, some historical societies will be found which can be regularly associated with that state.

Belief in the existence, let alone the normality, of subsistence societies so defined has clearly sometimes been the product of an essentially evolutionist view. To represent the past in suitably backward terms, such a view may draw on images and attitudes which were formed for other cultural settings. To quote Chekhov once again:

> the same thatched roofs with the holes in them, the same ignorance and misery, the same desolation on all sides, the same gloom and sense of oppression. All these horrors had been, still were, and would continue to be, and the passing of another thousand years would make things no better. (*The Student*, trans. Hingley, 1965–80, 7.105)

Such beliefs are also dangerously complacent: they promote a self-exculpatory distancing (J. Woodhouse 1991). Disgust satisfies the viewer's liberalism; and its intensity argues that the state of affairs is unavoidable.

Reflection on the realities points a different way. If a whole society is on the cusp, scarcely surviving, how can it cope with bad times? How can it have survived bad times in the past, to come to our notice today? Societies that are in that position, and there have unfortunately been many, are not societies in whose nature it is to be always on the verge of starvation, but societies undergoing change. Many succumb to disaster in the sequel; some win through. The processes which lead careful overproducers to ruin are occasionally natural, but more often derive from the social relations of production. Everything has to do with access. Just as famines have little to do with food-shortage, one person's subsistence is usually the product of another's greed.

The interaction of humanity with the Mediterranean environment is so variously productive of the means of existence that a stable state of subsistence agricultural production seems to us unlikely to have formed part of the ebb and flow of strategies for the maintenance of life within the region during the period under consideration in this book. For a number of reasons this is not an optimistic statement. In the first place, we have seen that the variety of Mediterranean production is a response to difficulty: 'the strength of the peasantry lay in the multifarious character of their resources, but this was not so much a matter of choice as of necessity, the required counterpoise to the low yields regularly to be anticipated for the sown crops' (J. K. Evans 1980, 162). The necessity and the variety are not in doubt, but they did not always succeed in equipping a rural population with 'strength'. The chronic fickleness of production's fortune could be countered, but there were always losers as well as winners. The inexorable logic of an aleatory environment is that there have to be, regularly, people whose gamble in the choice of strategy does not pay.

The 'peasants' of the usual analyses were the lucky ones: producers for whom the defences that we have analysed worked. Even they could only achieve this through a degree of agility and adaptability which does not fit the usual definitions of a peasantry. Others were compelled to be adaptable and agile too, but were at the mercy of employment by the more fortunate through the numerous forms of unfree and dependent labour attested in Mediterranean history. Often these have required unremitting toil, homelessness, and in extreme cases starvation. While natural mischance, especially meteorological, is often also involved in such downturns of fortune, it is exacerbated by human social systems through innumerable structures of exploitation or conflict. Thus 'subsistence' is not a way of life: it is a state passed through in particular cases of crisis; and it is the widespread result of many systems of political control. To repeat: 'in the risky environment of the Mediterranean, the few have repeatedly commandeered the "normal surplus" of the many' (Halstead and Jones 1989, 55). To see subsistence as a natural stage, justified by its place in the past from which we have evolved, is either unhelpful or downright pernicious.

> They turn the needy out of the way: the poor of the earth hide themselves together. Behold, as wild asses in the desert, go they forth to their work; rising betimes for a prey: the wilderness yieldeth food for them and for their children. They reap every one his corn in the field; and they gather the vintage of the wicked. They cause the naked to lodge without clothing, that they have no covering in the cold. They are wet with the showers of the mountains, and embrace the rock for want of a shelter. (Job 23.4–8)

Some empirical justification for our view may be derived from the fact that it is very hard to point to established subsistence systems in Mediterranean history. Not surprisingly, since to aim at subsistence is suicidal: it makes no provision for the bad year. Even the pursuit of self-sufficiency is an ethical tenet rather than a practice observable in reality (V.4; Foxhall, forthcoming). In Mediterranean

conditions, let us asseverate once more, overproduction is the only safe plan. So
there is no incompatibility between protestations of autarky and producing surpluses for storage, exchange or redistribution: the latter is the way the former
are made plausible. In turn this means that evidence for the pursuit of autarky –
in Antiquity, or in the Byzantine world (M. Kaplan 1994, 94) – does not indicate
economic backwardness, or the absence of investment, opportunism or production for sale. Nor need we question whether producers aimed at a surplus. The
surplus was the unpredictable residue of sensibly ambitious production when
times were not as bad as they could have been.

That subsistence strategies would have been evident at the time of the first
agricultural innovations was once an inevitable tenet of the progressivist school
of thought; but even that is now by no means certain. One attractive suggestion,
based on understanding the necessity of overcompensation to avoid risk, depicts
the specialized products of the first agriculture as high-status disposable goods,
an addition to the portfolio of good things for redistribution and not a desperate stratagem to postpone otherwise inevitable extinction: 'agricultural products can be, and were, forms of wealth: they were first devised for that reason'
(Runnels and van Andel 1988, 102). That perception underlies our insistence
on the centrality of redistribution (cf. Garnsey 1988a, 56–8). Indeed it is not too
much to suggest – as Gallant did for fishing (VI.6) – that, in the Mediterranean,
every crop is a cash-crop. Showing that fish, or wool, or fruit, can function in
some ways like a cash crop helps to dispel the illusion of the subsistence dystopia.
The overcompensation that is unavoidable in all forms of production (since at
least some years are good) creates the problem of glut that we have already met.
The *Liber Pontificalis* [*Book of the Popes*] (90, trans. R. Davis 1989) records for
the years A.D. 708–15 in west central Italy that three famine-years were followed by glut, during which the famine was forgotten. But such alternation of
glut and dearth principally benefits the brokers who can manipulate the processes of storage and redistribution.

The bewildering variety of the landscape and the unpredictability of the seasons
mean that 'l'agriculture traditionelle a été condamnée à être savant' (Toubert
1973, 197) and promote what has been called a 'kaleidoscopic peasant agriculture' (Parain 1936), which is visible in the archaeological and historical record
from at least the Bronze Age. Yet the *savant* humans who form the fragments
in the kaleidoscope must not be taken to be autonomous players working out
their local ecological destinies. Their flawed, quixotic, exogenously manipulated
behaviour in the face of an intuitive and often misplaced calculus of advantage
in production, changing from season to season, imparts to the Mediterranean
microregion as a human phenomenon so much more variety than nature could
have alone (cf. Chapter III). In ecological terms, Mediterranean niches are very
wide (Hardesty 1975, 71).

The traditional language of agrarian history therefore seems to us to underestimate the sophistication and complexity of the response of producers to their
circumstances. It fosters a static and deterministic approach to a reality whose
much more contingent dynamic is often that of exploitation (cf. Dalton 1974),
and whose product is local disaster rather than exhausted but surviving tenacity
(cf. Sen 1981). It is comforting but misleading to think that the rural poor have
been reduced to misery by nature, acting through environment or demography;
or by their own improvidence or stupidity, manifested in the primitivity of their

folkways or their lack of economic rationality – rather than by the ruthless self-interest of the more fortunate.

Self-determination?

So the second aspect of 'peasant thinking' which we consider misleading is the emphasis on certain sorts of self-determination usually associated with the category. The independent producer is an inherently unlikely specimen in the Mediterranean world, where diversification, storage and redistribution are rendered essential by the dangers of an unpredictable environment. Such risk-buffering behaviour has been 'a recurrent stimulus to economic inequality and social change' (Halstead 1990a, 160). In the Mediterranean, domination has taken the form of manipulating the means of avoiding environmental – and other – hazards. Now the independent producer is an adept at discerning the appropriate moment for intervention or for changing strategy – at the philosophy of the opportune time, *kairos* in ancient Greek. But so is the authority who may find it helpful for the smaller-scale producer to be less independent . . . And since, in many conditions, scale is a risk-buffer, the odds may favour the planner who can think big.

The trio of necessary responses generates a series of subsidiary but highly important consequences: the separation between the margin and the cultivated is blurred; the concept of a staple is elided into the varieties of crop quality and the portfolio of related forms of production; and decisions about tillage, irrigation and crop occupy places on spectra of possibilities rather than representing 'on/off' choices. Above all, and encompassing and modifying all these, is the unavoidable and repugnant fact that the individuals providing the labour in the productive process are seldom in a position to make the optimal decisions in their own interest. Each of the strands of Mediterranean production as so far identified has lent itself to creative intervention on the part of organizers, managers, administrators or proprietors, self-interestedly establishing the limits of flexibility in the provision of equipment, expertise, specialization, diversification, intensity of effort, access to markets or whatever. They extract produce, gain in prestige from the very process of directing, or acquire cachet from control of the materials of accumulation or exchange, from which they also draw direct profit.

In his incomparable survey of the archaeological remains of the calcareous massifs of north Syria between Antioch and Aleppo, Georges Tchalenko produced a picture of the agrarian history of the region which gave a prominent role to the larger landowner, whose investments in the area were, he thought, closely associated with the production of olive oil for distant markets as well as for the consumption of cities, above all Antioch (Tchalenko 1953–8; see Map 15). Tchalenko's successors have refined the detail of what we know archaeologically, but have arrived at a counter-intuitive view of the agrarian economy. This area of Syria was densely studded with villages whose domestic architecture is very well preserved. It is elaborate, even city-like in its orientations and aspirations. We can now see that the agrosystem was – no surprise here – less monocultural than Tchalenko had realized, animal husbandry being noticeably significant, but with other normal diverse strategies such as viticulture too. Over the period from the fourth to the sixth centuries A.D. there is a notable stability in the house-lots: little fragmentation or redivision, 'petrification' even. But the buildings become more elaborate, and more rooms are provided, presumably for the accommodation of more people. The conclusion drawn is that with – perhaps because of – increasing population, more land was put down to olive orchards; but, in a primitive economy, the returns from these could not be spent on real improvement of the agrarian base, and they were simply used up on more and more solid domestic architecture. There was no substantive change in the system of production; nor did outsiders take a substantial part of the extra earnings. Neither the cities nor the state, according to this account, had the power to distrain on the product of the successful response to increasing population: the producers, middling peasants in the words of these authors, just got fatter and fatter until the combination of declining markets and continuing Malthusian increase arrested the process.

We find the explicit statement that the weakness of the ancient economy lay in the inefficiency of its power to extract the product of agricultural success simply incredible. It would mean, if true, that the material felicity of the late Antique producers of the limestone hills of north Syria was relatively easy to attain in many another district of the ancient world. On this view, neither the rapacious landowner, nor the city council, nor the imperial government was competent to dent the acccumulative complacency of these satisfied farmers, answerable only to themselves in their Mediterranean garden. The misprision is analogous to that concerning the independent-looking miniature holdings of the *huerta* (above, Section 2). Dependency does not always take crudely obvious forms and, as we saw at the end of the previous section, some varieties in the archaeological record are easy to overlook. Theodoret, we should note, was *surprised* that the people of the walnut village of Mount Lebanon near Emesa had no masters: he represents it as a disadvantage not to have a patron (*History of the Syrian Monks* [*Historia Religiosa*], 17.2–3; cf. VI.4). We find it more plausible that the stone houses of the Belus were owned by Antiochene proprietors of some economic muscle and peopled by dependants of little or no autonomy. What the petrification of the house-lots in this case suggests to us is that the activities of the inhabitants were constrained by an iron control, from outside, of the landscape of property.

Immemorial stability?

The third element in the notion of a normal peasantry which should be applied to Mediterranean history only with caution is the immemorial stability often linked with the alleged self-determination. Most of the Mediterranean has in the course of our period been constantly and continuously affected by episodes of depopulation and repopulation, transfer of inhabitants and redeployment of the labour-force. How long is required for a culture of enrootedness to develop? Of how many localities can one confidently assert, for how many moments, that the last major episode of settlement disruption was more than three generations in the past? On a time-scale of centuries for Mediterranean history, these interruptions begin to appear normal. This is where *histoire événementielle* demands incorporation into the long-term picture. A very schematic generalization may be attempted thus.

The transitions and changes of the period when our study begins are still only imperfectly known. But if the half-millennium before the first Greek inscriptions is no longer as 'dark' as it was once thought, the change has not involved re-instating it as an epoch of continuity and stability. Rather, the processes on which light has fallen have ended the darkness by enabling us to retroject the beginnings of the period of rapid change and dynamic movements of people which we had always associated with the seaborne diasporas of the eighth to fifth centuries, Phoenician and Greek, and with the cultures with which they interacted in Italy, Iberia, Thrace or Gaul. The Hellenistic age saw the violent imposition and re-imposition of the structures of planned settlement on hundreds of local-ities all over the Mediterranean, at the hands of individual cities, the Successor Kingdoms, and Rome. In all these cases the sea was the medium which admitted the intruder, the coastlands the most affected by the constant upheavals. Pros-perity and success were the hectic achievements of opportunistic endeavour; inimical to the development of long-lasting rural institutions, and vulnerable to the next reversal of fortune. Such reversals were brought about by social forms parasitic on sudden success, such as mercenary war or piracy; and by the occa-sional violent involvement, with the coastlands, of peoples from beyond the basin. Often represented as continuing a *Völkerwanderung* of the pre-classical period or foreshadowing one of the early Middle Ages, these episodes appear normal on the longer time-scale, so that there is no reason to disjoin, say, the Cimmerians of the seventh century B.C. from the Seljuk Turks of the eleventh A.D. The gap between the depredations of the Cimbri and the Teutones and those of the Marcomanni is only 250 years. And if the troubles stemming from relations between the Mediterranean Roman Empire and neighbours to east and south are considered, the periods of stability are shorter still. As for the sequel, only the nascent nation-states of the early modern period decisively limited this sort of interruption of rural continuity, thus ending Mediterranean history as we are defining it in this chapter.

But these episodes are only half the picture. It would be quite wrong to imagine that they repeatedly slapped down an ever-renewed aspiration on the part of Mediterranean peoples towards a settled, adaptive, renewable, stable agricul-ture, which would have produced yeomen or middling peasants anywhere that a gap in the political mayhem allowed it to take root. When left in peace for a generation or two, the powerful in the Mediterranean have turned to the mani-pulation of the productive environment and its logic of survival. The result is still more incompatible with the idea of normal peasant production than is the shattering effect of political violence. We have started to see some of the tech-niques involved, and will see more: the encouragement of specialization, the introduction of the cash crop, the exaction of dues in kind, the hoarding of staple foodstuffs, the development of systems of distribution which capitalize on scarcity, and above all the treatment of the microregional landscape and of the resources of available human labour as assets which can be controlled to suit the interests of proprietor or bureaucrat. It has been argued that the failure of settlers in Roman Italy shows that 'il était impossible de devenir paysan: il fallait l'être depuis la naissance' (Łoś 1992, 750). Far from it: the new settlers of ancient Italy succumbed to the same pressures that weighed upon producers born to the life of the countryside. Their misfortunes were not exceptional; rather they were typical of Mediterranean rural conditions. More settled inhabitants and new-comers were alike vulnerable to the burdens of dependency; both could and did fail. Nor, as we argued above, is there any reason to envisage a 'birth peasantry' as normal and the intrusive settler a rarity. Columella (*On Agriculture*, 1.7.3, from Saserna) needs to persuade his reader that there are serious disadvantages to the tenant who lives in a city: he recommends searching out someone who belongs in the area of your estate if you can. Eloquent testimony to common practice and to the rarity of indigenous dependants.

A further result of microregional variation and rapid interregional engagement, therefore, is the reduction, by comparison with other societies, of long-term rural continuities (III, XI.2). This is of course not to deny that there have been *any* examples of rural continuity. Such cases have promoted the social and customary uniformities which can be found in the Mediterranean across space and time (though many of those may be due to spontaneous and fortuitous recreation of similar practices to cope with similar situations: cf. Halstead 1987 and X.1). Sometimes some lucky producers have acquired a security which they can successfully hand on to the next one or two generations. Sometimes the environment and the absence of interruption from outside have together made that normal. But never for long, and never over many regions at the same time. Even without malice or violence it is perfectly usual for the opportunism which is encouraged by the Mediterranean environment to lead to failure, abandonment of the land, emigration, dereliction and impoverishment.

A final clarification is in order here. We have talked in this section and the previous one frequently and sometimes indignantly of 'the powerful'. This general term is certainly not intended to be restricted to 'great landowners', aristocracies, or the very high in status. Many of the people that traditional accounts recognize as 'peasants' are among the powerful of our analysis: those visible to us in the Byzantine evidence, for instance. We read in the *Life* of St Pankratios of Taormina (quoted by Kazhdan 1994, 81) of a 'peasant' (*geponos*) who employed twenty-four hired reapers to harvest his cereal-crop. No agrarian history can be adequate which divides its subject simply into elite and peasantry, with men like this *geponos* as peasants. We might say the same of the 'cheap' watermills which we met in Section 2: anyone who owned a watermill was in a very good position. The Roman archaeological evidence is full of small villas; that does not make their occupants peasants. In praise of late Antique Bruttium it is said that 'the country people dine like towndwellers, and the middling-rich enjoy the abundance of the topmost elite' (Cassiodorus, *Variae* 8.31: 'vivunt illic rustici epulis urbanorum, mediocres autem abundantia praepotentium'). The quadripartite schema, *rustici–urbani–mediocres–praepotentes*, reflects the complexity of economic stratification in more detail than is usual in the literary texts, but it does not seek to include the groups below *rustici*; and it encourages the historian to ponder the state of affairs in less happy Mediterranean countrysides.

Slavery, share-cropping, dependent tenancy, colonization, serfdom, allotment, confiscation: the forms which dependency has taken are very various, and we can naturally not survey them all here. But they embrace a vast range of differentials in power. Some tenancies include in the net of obligations seed, water or traction (Foxhall 1990a, 106); some servile relationships are couched in paternalistic and improving terms:

> Gaius Castricius Calvus, son of Titus, military tribune . . . a man of good will . . . an Agriculturalist; a patron to good ex-slaves, and especially to those who cultivate their fields well and energetically, who keep themselves physically in good condition, which is particularly important for agriculturalists, who feed themselves, and who keep possession of whatever they have . . . true maxims for the person who wants to live well and in freedom; the first thing is duty – you are to wish your

master well, respect your parents, keep good faith; curse not, lest you hear bad things of yourself. The man who does no harm and is faithful will lead a pleasant and untroubled life in uprightness and happiness. These precepts which the Agri-culturalist teaches you to remember he did not learn through the teaching of the learned, but of his own nature and experience. (*CIL*, 5.600)

So says the epitaph of a Roman proprietor from Forlí.

Our plea is for a Mediterranean history that embraces Calvus's ex-slaves and Pancratios's twenty-four labourers too; and our dichotomy is between those who are in a position to make decisions about production, and those whose labour they control. Many of the city-council class who supposedly vanished when the classical *polis* disappeared in late Antiquity were probably no wealthier than St Pankratios's *geponos*. He is on the same side of the divide as the younger Pliny or the emir of Mosul, and we see no merit in calling him a peasant.

6. Colonizations and Allotments: The Unreason of Far-Flung Power

Communemque prius, seu lumina solis et auras / cautus humum longo signavit limite mensor [the careful surveyor has designated with extended boundary the soil that before had been common like the sunlight and the breezes].

Ovid, *Metamorphoses*, 1.135–6

The Golden Age ended with the opening up of the Corrupting Sea. Alongside the callings of mariner and trader, another new employment which symbol-ized the decline in morality and felicity was that of land surveyor. The myth is revealing. The division and maintenance of property are indeed linked with the need to control extraneous landscapes, places at a distance, resources to which control can only be extended by virtue of the connective Mediterranean.

The effect of distance

In the Mediterranean basin, the landscape itself has been deliberately reorgan-ized to match human productive agendas. The reorganization, which began many centuries before the end of the Bronze Age, has been all-pervasive, very varied and frequently random. We saw how an unstable physical framework and a fragile ecology have formed an inherently mobile setting for humanity's search for nutrition. We also saw how the mutability of the physical landscape manifests itself in a chaotic and unpredictable way. The differences across small distances in human experience of the natural world have been compounded by differences of response. Those varying interventions in the landscape have ex-acerbated its lability and vulnerability, making anthropogene process in Medi-terranean geomorphology the vexed subject that it is. The fragmentation and instability of the Mediterranean landscape have been strongly reinforced by human behaviour.

That behaviour has centred on the manipulation of the fragmented landscape to avoid risk and to make a virtue out of the necessity of flexibility and adaptab-ility. The principal variable over time – and we have seen clearly how mutable over time the physical landscape can be – is the intensity with which productive goals are pursued in each microecology. That varying intensity can take the form of extension into the domain of the marginal or in the adjustment of other aspects of production: labour, property, crop-type, technique, physical infrastructure, social structures. The reasons for intensification in any of these ways being highly various too, and not necessarily long-lasting, the process may be discontinuous and may give way to relaxation of pressure on production, the phenomenon for which we have borrowed the term abatement. It is true as a general rule that intensification reinforces the differences between microregions while abatement does something to blur them. In this section we shall have occasion to notice, however, the ways in which the regional specialization associated with monocultures (Bresc 1986b, 250–1), while emphasizing the differences between *regions*, diminishes the smaller-scale variety – to the increased risk of the producer.

The picture overall is therefore one in which creativity and destruction go hand-in-hand. In seeking ways of avoiding risk and guaranteeing the continuation of sources of food, human activity sometimes achieves quite long-lasting gains in productivity; but sometimes it also brings about the rapid degradation of the unstable environment, to which we shall turn in more detail in the next chapter. Only in very recent times has the effect been to increase productive uniformity. If there has been overall movement towards land-saving, taking the Mediterranean as a whole, it was scarcely noticeable between 1500 B.C. and A.D. 1800 (*contra* Persson 1988, whose perspective runs from the origins of agriculture to the present). Over that time, gains in certain regions were always offset by losses elsewhere; a population-mass of comparable size rattled around in an increasingly dog-eared-looking world, deployed by the powerful for new versions of the old games with intensification and abatement. We may even regard the state of affairs today, in which the Mediterranean lands produce a fifth of the planet's vegetables and a third of its fruit but depend on imports for two-thirds of their own grain, as a logical extension of the intensification that we have been discussing (Allaya et al. 1984).

Such a provisional summary account of the nature of the agrarian history of the Mediterranean basin may help answer some very fundamental questions. The factors that have entrenched cereals, oil and wine in Mediterranean cultural history have been briefly sketched (VI.8–9). But why are latifundism and the ideology of allotment both such characteristic features of Mediterranean history? Why was it in a Mediterranean context that there originated the legal sociology of property – Roman law – which has become the dominant model for property rights over much of the planet? Latifundism and allotment are not the opposites that they seem to be. They are in fact interdependent processes, and they are each founded on the same set of pressures and possibilities for the transformation of Mediterranean production. In the first place, an already topographically fragmented landscape encourages a high degree of institutional flexibility in determining the rights of individuals over productive pursuits: who can mine ruddle, gather water-chestnuts, forage pigs, grow olives, draw water, trap buntings *here*? (E. P. Thompson 1976: a helpfully diverse view of heritable rights in the environment). The hydraulic landscape, the system of terraces, the regime of adaptable labour – all invite precise parcelling-up of space. But more important is the broadness of scale that follows from the continuum of redistribution and the mobility of people across it. Redistribution, whether of things or

people, is the ultimate Mediterranean strategy – whence the significance of the
degree of redistributive engagement which we proposed at the beginning of
the chapter.

Structural absenteeism – as we might call it – can be seen as a central feature of Mediterranean agrarian power relations, a macrocosm, one might say, of
the microregional producer and his scattered fields (III.4). The Mediterranean
makes it easy for a geographical separation to exist between the decision-maker
and the labour-provider, as well as between the producer and the consumer.
Another way of looking at the phenomenon of mobility, which we have hitherto
described in rather neutral terms, is to say that labour may be deployable over
great distances. Allotment involves the assigning by remote individuals or collectivities of shares in the productive environment (in the inclusive sense propounded in Chapter VI) to parties who may originate from neither the home of
the assigning power nor the location of the allotment. The distances involved
promote the collection of niches and opportunities into portfolios which often
amount to latifundia. Those distances also assist the dissolution of the portfolios
again. The assignation and the dissolution form one theme; the impulsion to
intensify production or to relax effort is another, playing at the same time and
sometimes, but not always, sharing causes with the patterns of aggregation and
fragmentation.

The effort to increase economic control and the profit that comes from it has
taken extremely varied and often intermittent forms in Mediterranean history.
That is why we are hostile to the progressivist account which measures agrarian
change as a set of steps on a road from primitive underdevelopment to economic modernity, and devotes disproportionate attention to those activities of
the wealthy which seem to differentiate one step from another – for example the
advent and the demise of the Roman villa-estate, or the scattering of fortifications across the medieval landscape in the process which is known as *incastellamento* (see further Volume 2). As far as *incastellamento* is concerned, there are
two quite distinct subjects in question which should not be confused: on the one
hand the creation of fortified strongpoints and the arrangement of the territory
around them on a juridical basis; on the other the much more diverse phenomena of directed settlement nucleation (Wickham 1988c, 415–16, suggesting that
immediately post-Roman nucleations are as interesting from this point of view
as *incastellamento*; cf. Moreland 1993, Dunn 1994). In Chapter IV we argued
that the architectonic identity of towns should not lead us automatically into
supposing that 'the town' is a distinct type of ecology. We are now making an
analogous point about settlement more broadly understood. Despite architectural differences, there is no reason to regard *incastellamento* as essentially unlike
the replacement of small strategically located villages or conurbations in pre-
Roman Italy with the massive villas which dominated the landscape under the
Republic and early Empire. The idea that a whole community had been replaced
by an estate was a commonplace of the literary tradition. The obvious superficial
contrasts between settlement phases obscure the similar structures of production
and its control from a distance beneath. 'L'habitat est l'instrument de la consolidation du pouvoir' (Bresc 1988, 245). The instrument changes; the kind of
power being deployed is much more homogeneous.

Intensification and abatement, as controlled by the interlocking interests
of state and great proprietors, have brought about waves of aggregation and

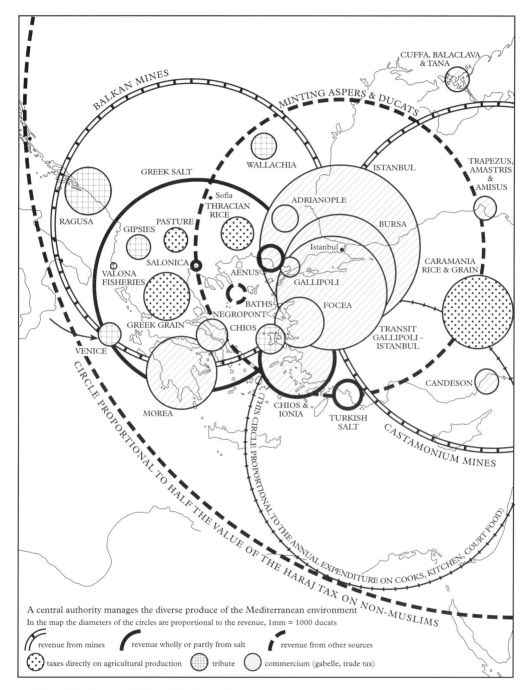

Map 17 The portfolio of the Gran Signor
  A central authority manages the diverse product of the Mediterranean environment: the fiscal system of Mehmet II, Ottoman Sultan, in 1475, after Iacopo del Promontorio (ed. Babinger 1957, 62–9). The relative values to the state of the different economic activities are often quite unexpected.

disaggregation of settlement again and again. Once more, it is possible to generalize from what we have written about towns to the whole range of settlements: 'l'habitat va sempre cristallizandosi e decristallizzandosi in *tutti* i secoli, specialmente nel Mediterraneo, e . . . diversamente in ciascuna microregione. Non dobbiamo temere di ammetterlo' (settlements crystallize out and dissolve again in *every* period, and in different ways in each microregion. We should not be scared of admitting it) (Wickham 1988c, 417). Recall that the vision offered in Chapters III to V, of a fragmented Mediterranean divided into myriad shifting microecologies, was a vision not primarily of the givens of the landscape but rather of human interaction with it. That includes both informal initiatives evidenced in many local alterations of settlement pattern and, at the other end of the spectrum, formal 'colonization' of the sort that is found in the Greek *apoikia* or the Berber settlements of Islamic Spain, as well as state-controlled production, as we find it on Roman public property or in the temple-estates of ancient Anatolia.

The Mediterranean latifundium

Large estates are not, of course, peculiar to the Mediterranean. But, in the Mediterranean world, the accumulation of very substantial interests in the productive landscape does take a sufficiently characteristic form for it to be possible to speak of a Mediterranean latifundism. Despite the name, a latifundium is not a big estate worked as a single unit. In Mediterranean conditions it tends to be a bundle of interests in the productive landscape, comprising several different sorts of enterprise, and as fragmented as a microregional smallholding. Thus the nineteenth-century Barracco estate in Calabria was 'complex and diversified in both production and administration, with a whole mosaic of tenancy forms, a multiple-crop system . . . and a great variety of farming techniques . . . as well as a complex web of markets' (Petrusewicz 1996, 6). More importantly, it had been created by very subtle and delicate intensification out of the existing productive landscape: fusing discrete ecosystems together, 'the *latifondo* proved . . . efficient enough to exploit the pre-existing historical and social infrastructure so as to create a highly profitable enterprise.'

> The *latifondo* did not 'colonize' an 'empty' territory by creating a completely new form of farming enterprise, but embraced and incorporated a densely and stably populated region that had long-standing modes of production and distribution, social hierarchies and models of behaviour. The estate never proposed to effect a radical transformation of the existing equilibria . . . but to harness them for the realization of surplus production. (1996, 72, cf. 74)

This example, for which we have excellent documentation, may help us to understand much earlier instances, such as the scattered villas of the younger Pliny in Italy at the end of the first century A.D. (De Neeve 1990), or the eighth-century Byzantine estate of Philaretus the Merciful in Paphlagonia, with its forty-eight separate properties and 12,000 head of sheep (Auzépy 1993). So how, especially on a very long time-scale and across the whole Mediterranean basin, do we decide what size a portfolio must reach before we want to use the label latifundium?

This is where the effect of distance may help. Mediterranean latifundism is a form of the application of extraneous control, and the fact that the decisions are made elsewhere gives it its characteristic form. Wielding power simultaneously in more than one microregion encourages centralizing of storage, the provision of expensive or unfamiliar techniques, the systematizing of access to external redistribution, and the redeployment of assets between the different parts of the holding. Latifundism of this kind is associated with technical change, compelled mobility of the labour-force, and the shifting pattern of local abatement and intensification. Among many possible instances, note the case of the medieval Levant, where static technology did not impede small-scale producers from obtaining good returns from cereals. Here latifundism took the shape of the *qati'a*, which by contrast used quasi-industrial farming techniques, and all the sophistication of learned Arab agronomy, to make quick profits; associated with the more sophisticated technology, it can be blamed for environmental degradation (Ashtor 1976, 45–60). It is also linked with the connectivity of specialized markets, the 'directed trade' which we shall survey in Chapter IX. Thus, in many ways, the most typical and developed instances of Mediterranean latifundism have been found at those moments when extended political hegemonies allowed the portfolios of proprietors to be scattered not just across a cluster of microregions, but across the whole Mediterranean. Such was the political setting of the estates of Roman imperial senators, or their late Antique successors (which Gregory the Great called *patrimonia sparsa per orbem* (properties scattered across the world): Vera 1986), or of the sugar-plantations and arboricultural estates of later medieval colonialism (VI.11).

This is not to suggest that latifundism and connectivity combine to beneficial effect. Landlords' strategic decisions are self-interested and may – obviously – be irrational or incompetent (cf. S. R. Epstein 1991 for examples from medieval Sicily and Tuscany). Latifundistic logic entails vulnerability to conflict with the state, competition with neighbours, price fluctuations, problems of the control of labour, and exposure to the perils of orientation towards the uncertain world of the Corrupting Sea.

We should not fail to include in our survey the implementing of the will of the powerful through less tranquil means than the management of economic strategy – such as piracy, brigandage, or warfare. The ritualized conflict of citizen soldiers in Archaic and classical Greece was constrained to take place on the tracts of level ground which were at the same time the most coveted prize in the conflict (Osborne 1987, 137–64; Connor 1988). In the fragmented landscape we can observe a 'spécificité méditerranéenne de la guerre [qui] vient tout d'abord de ce que cette guerre s'inscrit dans la structure longue du millénaire médiéval; structure donc d'une longue guerre méditerranéenne qui est aussi souvent maritime' (Toubert 1988, 9). One of the modalities of Mediterranean warfare was to attack 'l'infrastructure arbustive de la vie agricole', though the agricultural landscape in fact has shown considerable resilience in the face of scorched earth tactics. As we should expect, since the diversity of low-risk production also helps insure against war damage. In most of the period under discussion, those who control more than one microregion must address the opportunism of violence, by fortifying estate-centres in particular: 'c'est en effet une forme savante de l'occupation du sol que cet habitat castral' (1988, 9). Defensible strongpoints, used as storage centres for both local use and interregional redistribution (as were the fortifications of the Acciaioli in medieval Messenia), are an element of the microregional landscape too (Lock 1995, 247; cf. 251).

Thus, no consideration of the techniques and equipment in which innovation may take place and investment be made by the Mediterranean producer would be complete without at least a mention of the need to confront violence. In about 200 B.C. the Seleucid King Antiochus III gave permission for the fortification of a strongpoint to protect the estates of his local governor, the High Priest Ptolemy son of Thraseas (Piejko 1991). Ptolemy owned a number of villages near Scythopolis on the west edge of the Jordan valley, and passers-by were damaging the property, and in particular settling on bits of the land and carrying off the population. The world of connectivity can be seen impinging on the productive landscape, in this case a classic example of an agrarian portfolio of interests. Even well away from the sea, we have a vivid sense of the disposability of population, and of the tendency, against the precarious institutions of legal title, for land to be occupied and for the produce – and the producers – to be removed by the mobile.

Eleventh-century Tunisia offers another eloquent example. Over two centuries, huge estate-portfolios (coexisting with both middling and exiguous property) had developed, in which agricultural slaves appear to have played a role comparable with that of the slaves of Roman Italy. Like the abandonment of villas in Roman Italy, indeed, the collapse which began with the terrible famine of A.D. 1004 has been attributed to the occlusion of the supply of imported slaves (Talbi 1981). In fact, the careless disposal of slave labour was only one symptom of out-of-hand great-landownermanship – also interestingly on display in the way in which the elite, like the targets of Ambrose's indignation, responded to crisis by speculating on grain prices rather than by reforming the system of production. The loss of redistributive markets for produce also clearly played a part.

The ecology of colonization

The estates of Ptolemy son of Thraseas lay in an area which had been systematically settled and assigned in lots about twenty years before (Polybius, *History*, 5.70.5). An allotted landscape of independent producers gave way to one of latifundia, as has often happened in Mediterranean history. The process is more than just the inevitable usurpation of control by the powerful. Allotments, we have been arguing, are more like latifundia than one might suppose. They too are a manifestation of absentee power. They too are the expression of a Mediterranean phenomenon: colonization.

In Egypt it was a royal attribute of Pharaoh to be feeder of the people. As late as Saite times the allotment of land was a primary function of kingly power (Menu 1995). Large sections of the landscape can be seen as a latifundium run for the state. In Mesopotamia, the very high ratios of seed to yield recorded are perhaps to be attributed to a distinctive and risky strategy applied on essentially 'public' lands (Halstead 1990b). In Asia Minor, for much of the Hellenistic period, two systems of dependence coexisted: one of them embraced the dependants of kings on royal land and the other the populations that produced the materials needed by the economies of the cities (Corsaro 1983). The distinction might rather be represented as that between the Mediterranean ecology of redistribution and the 'continental' centralized and uniform regime of production. Although the ideology of allotment in Antiquity reflected in part the disposing power of eastern kings over their people, it owed much more to the combination of the principle of the citizen lot and the operation of extraneous power in a world of connectivity: overseas colonization, in other words, as practised especially by the Greek city-states of the seventh to fourth centuries and the Roman state of the fourth to first centuries B.C.

Two aspects of this large subject are of prime importance for our purposes. The first is the way in which the surveying which made allotment possible directly denied the fragmentation inherent in the landscape. It was therefore particularly suited to the drier parts of the coastal plains and alluvial basins and valleys. Linked to hydraulic control, as we saw in Section 2, and to the reclamation of marginal areas such as wetland and wood, it created a unified productive terrain far more effectively than latifundism ever managed. Second, surveying was usually also associated with the ambition of intensifying production, above all through the possibility of supplying external markets. Neither Greek *apoikoi* on the lots which archaeology attests from the seventh century B.C. in Sicily, nor Roman settlers on a landscape divided up by the surveying technique known as centuriation, expected that their new property gave them the opportunity for subsistence production, for reasons which we have seen. As much as that of any latifundium, the production of the subdivided landscape was aimed at redistribution: locally, of course, but also across the sea over which the settlers had come (cf. the 'colonial viticulture' discussed in VI.9). This is why, as we shall see in more detail in Chapter IX, there is the closest link between the new cities on which the allotted landscapes centred and the trade-nodes or *emporia* which also dotted the Mediterranean coasts.

The imperial behaviour of Athens in the fifth century B.C. provides another good example. The islands were of great importance to the Athenian thalassocracy ([Xenophon] *Constitution of the Athenians*, 2.16), and the accessible productive niches of several were surveyed and assigned in schemes which were called 'lot-ownership' (*klerouchiai*: Brunt 1966). In the case of Chalkis on Euboea, the 'land of the Hippobotai' (the previous aristocracy) was divided into 2,000 lots to be let out according to inscribed lists kept at Athens, excepting a sacred precinct of Athena 'in the place called Lelanton' (Aelian, *True History*, 6.1). The detail shows that we are dealing with the plain whose value for viticulture had made it a notorious bone of contention between rival groups of aristocrats (Map 14). Now this famously productive land was assigned to Athenian tenants. The history of Roman settlement has a place for island opportunities too, including the first attested Roman overseas ventures, 500 settlers in 378 B.C. in Sardinia (Diodorus Siculus, *Historical Library*, 15.27.4) and Corsica (Theophrastus, *Enquiry into Plants*, 5.8.2). At a later stage of Roman power, in 123–121 B.C., Metellus Balearicus founded Pollentia on Majorca with the conscious aim of alleviating the corrupting effects of the sea, through replacing the piratical activities of the locals with the agricultural ones of the 3,000 settlers 'from the Romans of Iberia' (Strabo, *Geography*, 3.5.1, commenting on the way in which fertile islands are generally vulnerable to outside intervention – to 'being plotted against').

Like other places which are particularly prone to both intensification and abatement, island territories are easily reoccupied. A tax-register for Naxos, Paros, Syros, Santorini, Melos and Andros for 1670 demonstrates the role of

Frankish landlords in settling new cultivators, including Albanians, on these islands (Slot 1991; compare the deliberate re-colonization of abandoned lots by medieval Albanian settlement in Boeotia: Bintliff 1996, 7). In a classic instance of the canny recognition of the right moment, and treating the population of a whole archipelago as if it were the resource of a single microregion, the Gozzadini family of Siphnos took advantage of a period of high corn prices to settle the inhabitants of Kimolos, Folegandros, and Sikinos in small fortified towns on Antiparos (Slot 1991, 200–1). Famously, imperial powers were just as capable of commanding abatement, as we have seen in the context of Venetian Crete. The agriculture of Sardinia in classical Antiquity had been highly productive, but it was destroyed by the Carthaginians when they conquered the island and forbade the inhabitants on pain of death to grow anything that yielded a profit ([Aristotle] *On Wonderful Reports*, 100: note how misleading is the standard translation (Dowdall 1909), absurdly rendering *prosphora* as food, not profit).

There has been much debate about the causes of the overseas settlement of so many Greeks in the Archaic period. Demographic explanations have been advanced – including land hunger – and climatic difficulties suggested (Cawkwell 1992). But it was not only Greeks who were involved. Phoenician movements, too, have become more and more apparent as a result of archaeological work. As our discussion will have shown, we see no reason to seek special (and, still less, apologetic) explanations here, any more than for Athenian cleruchies, Roman *coloniae*, or Venetian and Genoese settlements in the later Middle Ages. The establishment of cash-crop production in the landscape of the Hellenic overseas settlement is one of the more radical and intrusive dislocations in Mediterranean agrarian history. At this point, we need not engage with the questions of labour relations, crop innovation, market orientation, and productive scale, which we touched on in Chapter III.3 with regard to the history of Cyrenaica, and which were most famously encapsulated for the Hellenic tradition in the fabulous stories of the success of the agriculture of Sybaris. The labour- and planning-intensive allocation of lots in the productive landscape is famously one of that tradition's salient features. It was conspicuous at Metaponto, but is perhaps now even more splendidly demonstrated by the proper publication of the fossilized agrarian landscape of Chersonesos Taurike in the Crimea by Saprykin (1994; cf. VI.9 for the viticulture of this territory).

First-millennium B.C. examples deserve special prominence in our argument because so many of them are essentially maritime in nature, and their link with the Mediterranean itself is not in doubt. We have, however, allowed throughout that the sea has not had a monopoly of connectivity: extraneous power can be seen at work in overland colonizations also. Roman allotment schemes, which used the techniques of land-division pioneered by the Greeks of the western Mediterranean settlements, placed the greatest emphasis on the supplying of an alternative infrastructure of connectivity. Sometimes this involved navigable rivers, more often the celebrated Roman road. Communications technology takes its place in the list of techniques that have been used in the intensification of production. An agrarian system in which the complete transformation of the landscape through geometric land-division happens at all is *per se* not like the Chekhovian images of Section 5.

Finally, we may return to the Berber colonization in al-Andalus which we noticed in Section 2 (Bazzana 1992). There, we observed how another kind of infrastructure, the hydraulic landscape, was to be associated with the settlement of outsiders, at the state's behest, across a landscape which was essentially in need of reclamation. That infrastructure required the dissemination of techniques and skills, and we can now see more clearly how very natural it is for the introduction and spread of such innovations to be subsequent to the processes by which the productive landscape is managed. As with the latifundium, so with colonial landscapes: the rhythms governing changes in technology and practice are the product of social forces, and not autonomous developments in the history of ingenuity.

In the 1320s the Genoese issued an ultimatum to a marauding band of Catalan mercenaries. The intention was straightforward: the Catalans were a major liability to the multiple political and economic interests that made up the Genoese empire in the eastern Mediterranean and Black Sea. But what the Genoese told the Catalans to do was to 'get out of their garden – that is the empire of Constantinople – which was the garden of the commune of Genoa' (Ramon Muntaner, *Chronicle*, ed. Lanz 1843, 227: 'e lo desafiament fo aytal, que ell nos manaua ens deya de part del comu de Genoua, que nos que ixquessem de llur jardi, ço era limperi de Constantinoble, que era jardi del comu de Genoua.' Horticulture and colonialism are alike quintessentially Mediterranean.

7. THE RECEPTION OF INNOVATION AND THE HISTORY OF TECHNOLOGY

Over two long chapters, we have so far attempted in this Part to present a picture of the conditions of production in Mediterranean history. The operations of a distinctive ecology, we have argued, enable the historian to make constructive comparisons across apparently widely divergent Mediterranean societies. Such comparisons are made possible by the fact of omnipresent risk, and by the recurrent ways in which both that risk and its remedies are patterned by the fragmented landscape and the connectivities which help resolve the fragmentation. On our interpretation, therefore, the potential of the productive environment, the media of redistribution, and the control of human labour were not so different in the Mycenaean, Merovingian or Mamluk worlds that comparison between them is unfruitful. In Chapters III and VI, however, we began to see how microregional Mediterranean production has been variously subject to modification or manipulation according to the social and political milieu. In the present chapter, we have been setting out some of the ways in which control over relations of production cause variations in the intensity with which human productive effort is deployed and with which networks of redistribution are brought into play. The outcomes are extraordinarily varied; but the logic underlying them still encourages us to think that these too may sensibly be compared across very wide gulfs of space and time within Mediterranean history. Our attention to common denominators, such as the control of storage or the redeployment of labour, has led us to set the accidents and particularities of the different moments and localities – a certain type of irrigation, or strain of food crop, or method of terracing – in a context which makes individual features seem less decisive. Now, as we have said in discussing some of these productive techniques, this is to contradict an authoritative historiographical tradition.

The tradition maintains that some technological variations – for example in the plough or mill – have been of enormous historical importance. Indeed, many historians have claimed much more: that technological innovation and its revolutionary consequences make it virtually impossible helpfully to compare 'before' and 'after'. Inventions and their effects divide up the past so thoroughly that comparison of say Antiquity and the early Middle Ages in respect of their technologies loses much of its interest.

The combination of new evidence with new methods of interpretation has (we hope) served to show that new forms of plough or mill are more usefully considered as items in a much more extensive repertoire of productive strategies than as departures from or major transformations of that repertoire. The question now deserves a more general statement. Does the Mediterranean historian need to take into account *any* such pivotal, revolutionary transformations or innovations? And if not, why have they had such a pervasive influence on the historiography of the past century?

Reflections on the history of technology

The first point to stress is that the evidence for the history of technical change in the Mediterranean in our period is both deficient and very difficult to use. (The sensible summary of Greene (1994) brings out the contrasts between the Greek, Roman, Islamic and early medieval Western material.) The catastrophes and revolutions of Mediterranean historiography are often primarily phenomena of the literary sources. Apart from a scatter of archaeological and pictorial evidence, much of the technological history of the Mediterranean has been written on the basis of the descriptions of machines in literary texts – the *De architectura* of the Roman writer of the Augustan age, Vitruvius, or Pliny's compendious *Natural History*, and then the Islamic scientific treatises – which themselves subscribed to a particular ideology of technical description. In the ancient world, this literary ideology included a built-in disdain for the products of mere ingenious craft. The actual diffusion of new techniques is almost completely unknown to the literary (and to a large extent the documentary) traditions, because it happened at a social level below the attention of the writers. If we sometimes hear of failures to disseminate useful ideas – such as the exciting metallurgical discovery in Pontus that was lost because the designer never told anyone about it ([Aristotle] *On Wonderful Reports*, 62) – we *never* hear anything about the wholly unglamorous transmissions of craft expertise. Archaeology provides something of a corrective (as we saw with regard to the watermill), especially because its very randomness presents a realistic picture of the messy and piecemeal nature of social change and discourages dramatic simplifications. But its accidental character and the selectivity of the means by which it is preserved make it an unreliable guide to what mattered.

More damaging, however, than the deficiencies of the evidence is a mistaken conclusion from those deficiencies: the conclusion that the processes of the reception and diffusion of ideas were as meagre as are the literary accounts of them. One standard account of the problem of technology in the Roman world puts it thus: 'this contrast between theoretical brilliance and practical incompetence is great and dramatic' (Reece 1969, 32). But the contrast is actually between the rich and stylized details of ancient literature and the scrappy chaos that is all that we can see of the realities of production. The difficulties are not confined to the ancient Mediterranean, though the notion of Greek and Roman technological 'backwardness' is the most prominent consequence of them. The same problem occurs with respect to the Islamic world. Here there is little evidence of the widespread deployment of the ingenious ideas included in the treatises of al-Jazari or the Banu Musa (Hill 1980, 146–52) and, with patently triumphalistic Eurocentrism, technological history is implicated in the presumed divide between a successful West and a failed Orient (Ashtor 1983a). By contrast, the available picture of the medieval Christian world has been highly complicated, and is not dominated by a few major texts; simplistic views of the invention and diffusion of ideas have therefore been advanced much more rarely. A similar caution could usefully be applied to earlier periods.

We have to deal with a very strange kind of historiography. New ideas and their diffusion acquire a life of their own, and start to behave as agents in history. Take an influential instance of this anthropomorphism of ideas: 'it appears that at just this time [the first century B.C.] the ability to harness animals in file was developing simultaneously all over Eurasia' (L. T. White 1962, 15). The language is conventional – as well as being obviously both evolutionist and progressivist – and we know what is intended. But what can such a generalization actually mean with regard to a particular location in space, time and society? How could it happen that the pastoralists of the steppes, Anatolian countrymen, Iberian shepherds, stonecutters in Greek marble quarries, timbermen in South Indian tropical forests were all during those years mysteriously gripped by this transcendent mood of change?

What is the subject matter of this kind of history? We may distinguish three versions. There is History of Inventions. At its crudest, this is a blatantly schematic arranging of certain sorts of often spuriously dramatized event in a chronological order. We may cite the case of Greene (1986, 19): 'the history of the bilge-pump would be sadly incomplete but for the study of material from shipwrecks' (tongue-in-cheek to judge by the same author, 1994). Some accounts of this type display a quite extraordinary introverted mechano-mania. Their titles evince a polemic zeal: *Machines as the Measure of Man* (Adas 1989). It is paradoxical that such thinking, which is particularly inclined to find the technological achievements of the Mediterranean peoples before the Middle Ages wanting, should so clearly derive from the fascination of the Greeks and Romans with the 'first discoverer' and with virtuoso technical curiosities such as Hellenistic automata.

In contrast to History of Inventions, History of Technology is more sophisticated (K. D. White 1984, 14; cf. Landels 1978). It recognizes the need to conceptualize and explain a system within which novelties interact. The difficulty is that it has tended to associate such systems closely with readily identifiable cultural groupings. Hence the entrenched view of a qualitative difference between the technological culture of Antiquity and that of Christian western Europe, on which the deterministic arguments of L. T. White (1962), rather than the sensible views of his critics (such as Hilton and Sawyer 1963) have become to a considerable extent the voice of orthodoxy. The orthodox argument is doubly deterministic. It claims the utmost historical impact for the presence or absence of certain technological capabilities. But it also sees the technological receptivity of a society as being constrained by certain characteristics of the social system (or, more usually, certain facets of the conventional historical description of that system), such as slavery in the case of Antiquity. Religion was another such characteristic: White argued that the alleged animistic piety of the Romans deterred them from 'messing about' with Nature, which would have surprised critics of the emperor Nero. Deterministic accounts of History of Technology involve an unacceptable oversimplification (Mokyr 1990, 14).

There is, of course, no justification for regarding aspects of the organization of labour or of the religious system as analytically prior to a society's degree of receptivity to technological change. The more helpful approach, the third of our trio, is the *histoire des techniques*. This draws on social anthropology and insists 'that techniques are socially produced, and as such are always bedded in some symbolic system' (Lemonnier 1993, 22, cf. 3). It is because techniques are first and foremost social productions that they may not be regarded simply as sets of constraints. It is better to adopt a 'universal conception of human technological activity in which complex social structures, nonverbal activity systems, advanced linguistic communication, the ritual co-ordination of labor, advanced artifact manufacture, the linkage of phenomenally diverse social and non-social actors and the social use of diverse artifacts are all recognized as parts of a single complex that is simultaneously adaptive and expressive' (Pfaffenberger 1992, 513).

Investigating the central question of who is in a position to make what choices shifts the focus of attention back to the realities of power in the landscape. It helps to explain the general lack of variety in the long-term history of techniques (the strange 'convergence' of innovations in areas where there can be no question of influence, as with the harnessing 'revolution' that we have just mentioned or the resemblances between hydraulic systems in the New World and the Iberian peninsula); and it usefully reduces the emphasis customarily placed on efficiency and utilitarian calculation in the process of innovation. It has been argued that stasis should be more characteristic than change in the history of technology, and that the experience of the West in the last two centuries must not be retrojected (Mokyr 1996, 83). But historians of technology have frequently been influenced by the cultural framework of modern science, and by a competitive market economy in which the attainment of optimum returns and the pursuit of efficiency are axiomatic. *Histoire des techniques* has been able, for all this, to show that, in the contemporary world too, there is no reason for regarding techniques as anything other than social productions (MacKenzie and Wajcman 1985). Innovative behaviour should not be seen as an exogenous variable, and it is a great merit of the approach to agrarian change pioneered by Esther Boserup, to which we shall give more attention shortly, that, in her work, neither such behaviour nor the inherent fertility of the soil is considered to be such a factor (cf. Netting 1974b).

Even in the apparently ultra-efficient and socially unencumbered field of the design of military hardware in the late twentieth century, 'engineering traditions and bureaucratic routine relegate the search for material efficiency to the position of a minor factor in . . . design and development' (Lemonnier 1993, 6). It is tempting to use this demonstration in an *a fortiori* argument about the premodern technological history of the Mediterranean. To do so, however, would entail adhesion to another very damaging way of thinking: progressivism. All our period is pre-industrial; it is also pre-aerospace, pre-television, pre-nuclear. It is a sterile exercise to count off aspects of life in the present until, by exclusion, an unredeemed primitive squalor is arrived at. When the past societies of the Mediterranean are compared with each other, there appears little reason to dole out bouquets to some rather than others on the basis of a subjective judgement about innovative capacity. Societies do not have 'technological blocks' or 'a genius for technology'. There is now no place for 'antiquisants qui continuent à être frappés du syndrôme finleyen de "blocage technologique" du monde gréco-romain' (Raepsaet 1994, 326).

Receptivity, rationality and development

In the history of techniques, attention to the circumstances and consequences of choice can ensure that the questions of diffusion and receptivity are posed with considerable sophistication (Meikle 1995a). The first strand in this way of thinking is to recognize that individual choices have relatively little effect; it is *patterns* of choice which, after being maintained for a considerable time, begin to make substantial change possible. The way decision-making associated with bimodal choice relates to innovation across whole societies has been modelled in the light of mathematical catastrophe theory (Renfrew 1978). But attention is now given rather to those conjunctions of political, social and economic circumstances which give a cluster of innovations enough chance to become well enough established for the 'multiplier effect' to make change irreversible. Where communications take place only intermittently, such developments are naturally retarded (P. S. Wells 1980, 77). It has been argued, too, that it is normal for advances in technological systems to be slow, even very slow. Actual stagnation may in fact be very rare, despite appearances. On this view, technological change is immanent in all production. It depends for its realization on complex parallel sequences of small innovations and implementations. These sequences are only effective when they happen to complement one another (Persson 1988). Archaeologists, especially those who deal with periods for which there are no distracting literary traditions, are used to separating the invention from its dissemination. The same is now habitual among those who work on the early modern and modern Mediterranean, and who have taken their cue from ethnographies such as those quoted in Chapter VI, which instructively illustrate how potential users respond to new introductions.

Most strikingly, anthropologists have documented the resistance of some southern European villagers to even economically advantageous change. We may cite as an example the Greek village of Vasilika, in the Boeotian plain beneath Mount Parnassus. When Ernestine Friedl conducted field work there in 1955–6 the inhabitants numbered 216. The village had developed a mixed agricultural economy of cash crops (cotton and tobacco) as well as ones for local consumption. In Vasilika, the desire for new technology could be conditioned by customary attitudes to the city, rather than by so-called rational economic considerations. Women in Vasilika wanted their houses to have electricity, for example, because all houses in Athens had it. They also wanted running water. But those without it continued to draw their water from the well by hauling the buckets up manually. A windlass would obviously have made their task far easier, but, because the windlass had nothing to with technology of the city, it was not seen as desirable (Friedl 1962, 46). A second example: in the Spanish village of Belmonte, to which we shall return in Chapter XI.3, acceptance of technological change in the 1960s was similarly moulded by non-economic considerations. It tended to be sponsored by the *pudientes*, the wealthy and powerful. Those lower down the social hierarchy might then follow their lead. The commanding role custom assigned to *pudientes* was even made clear semantically. The word *chandro* was an insulting one everywhere in Belmonte – sufficient to provoke a fight. But the exact implications of the insult varied. Applied to a labourer *chandro* meant lazy; applied to a *pudiente* it signified backwardness in the adoption of modern farming techniques (Lison-Tolosana 1966, 320).

There is a clear difference between the two communities. Although Vasilika lies only a kilometre from the main road connecting Athens and Thessalonika, contacts with the wider world, commercial and otherwise, were (in the period of Friedl's field work) usually sluggish: significantly, only the festival of the local saint, the *paneyira* (*panegyris*), provided a ritualized moment of engagement with the world of exterior redistribution (X.3). There were no *pudientes* to bear the responsibility for innovation. In a nutshell, Vasilika was very poor, 'the archaism and self-sufficiency of traditional culture being a form of involution characteristic of pauperized communities' (Lewthwaite 1981, 59). But we must stress that communities with a relatively high degree of self-determination are by no means committed to rejecting innovations. Indeed it is at the household level, rather than among the authors of treatises on agronomy, that the significant changes occur – as we have already seen (VII.2) in the case of the hydraulic landscape (J. Langdon 1986, cf. Holt 1996, 118–19). We should recall that, in the Mediterranean environment, even where the goal is recognized as increased productivity of a certain kind, there are many routes towards it which may seem more attractive than raising the level of technology. Very simple existing techniques can be improved by skill or care: 'plus la technique est simple, plus l'observation et la minutie de l'application doivent être de qualité pour une rentabilité accrue' (Bolens 1981, 170). But that *qualité* can be forthcoming. The more complex techniques, as we see at Belmonte, are in contrast part of the domain of the powerful. That example shows clearly how closely the adoption of new technology is tied to the structures of economic and social authority. Technological complexity can be regarded as a form of intensification. Whether independently chosen or more or less forcibly imposed, it can be relaxed as well as increased.

All this makes it hard to assign any technique or invention a position in long-term history on the basis of its contribution to the pursuit of what appears today to be rational economic behaviour.

> Welche Vorteile gewährt die doppelte Buchhaltung dem Kaufmanne! Es ist eine der schönsten Erfindungen des menschlichen Geistes. [What advantages has double-entry bookkeeping afforded the tradesman! It is one of the most beautiful discoveries of the human spirit.] (Goethe, *Wilhelm Meisters Lehrjahre*, bk 1, ch. 10)

The enthusiasm of Goethe's caricature, Werner, helps us assign a context to the theme under discussion. It was in the eighteenth century that the idea of deterministic innovation acquired its definition and autonomous status *vis-à-vis* the less material and more philosophical elements of Enlightenment culture. Double-entry bookkeeping has had a continuing fame as one of the supposedly decisive differentiators between recognizable modernity in economic behaviour, since the mid-thirteenth century, and irremediably alien primitivity before. In many ways, however, as we have argued, the question of differentiation is not of great importance. It is true that, if your figures are likely to be approximate, you round up your demand; on the other hand accurate accounting offers a powerful legal lever which can be deployed with a relentless precision wanting in a rough calculation. Rapacity may be slightly moderated by accounting, but the loser is unwise to rely too much on it. How likely is it that an end to the impressionistic numeracy of the past substantially changed the behaviour of those who aspired to the accumulation of wealth and status? The important question is rather: how does the financial infrastructure serve to express the theory of exaction and legitimate it in relation to the legal and institutional underpinnings on which extractors rely? The thirteenth-century 'revolution' is thus a change in the sophistication of the self-perpetuating and self-justifying paraphernalia of greed; and from the Minoan–Mycenaean tablets, through the Athenian tribute-lists and the Murecine archive (to which we shall return in Chapter IX), there is a very long history of this form of rhetoric.

In those circumstances it is not surprising that technical 'progress', as an element associated with the wider world and, therefore, with the horizons and interests of the larger landowner, often attracts the suspicion and hostility which we saw, in the previous section, directed against the latifundium. In VI.11, we alluded to a petition of the Corsicans to Genoa in which they rejected both agricultural improvement – that is, intensification and an increased emphasis on cash crops – and the involvement in the wider political and social horizons which went with it (Fel 1975). In another response, which we saw in Toubert's analysis of 'coltura promiscua' in the last chapter (VI.10), traditional techniques are designed to be as adaptable and as efficient at intensification as possible, without depending on technical wizardry, precisely because continued access to it may not be guaranteed. The sophisticated risk-avoider will avoid reliance on some complex technical procedure which may be withdrawn or go wrong, or which costs too much, especially in terms of dependence on the favour of those who invested in it.

The rationality of increased productivity, which is so familiar from economic decision-making in modern Western cultures, was formerly universally thought to have had a primacy in the planning of reform in both 'underdeveloped' countries – to recall the terminology of that approach – and in historical societies. We have already come across one instance of the reluctant recognition that what appear to be obviously wasteful practices may serve other sorts of goal than the economic: the ecological usefulness of microfragmentation of rights in the environment (VI.10). In 'underdeveloped' cash-crop production in the tropics, it has been found that

> initial advantages [in resources, status etc.] tend to be self-reinforcing. Wealth-owners are able to put their wealth to use in creating further wealth not primarily for the increased production that this makes possible, but rather for the power, prestige and security granted by titles to income-earning assets. (Ingham 1981, 93)

What has been called the 'allocative efficiency of traditional agriculture' promotes conservatism (A. W. Johnson 1972). In the case of Africa, it is more widely accepted that narrow intensive scientific knowledge about agriculture is simply less efficient than knowledge rooted in the social and ecological setting, both past and present (Arcangeli et al. 1993; Richards 1985). A feature of the study of the ancient economy of the Mediterranean too has been the misplaced investigation of the extent of modern economic rationality. Our earlier discussion of the plough, the terrace, the water-conduit and the mill has brought out some problems that this investigation faces. The cultural background against which decisions are taken about whether or not to adopt a technical change in production-methods is highly complex. It is not always easy to assess where advantage might have lain.

Perceptions of the difference in standards of living between 'First' and 'Third World' countries of the present day underlie and inform many accounts of the difference between the economic and social systems of the distant past and those of the (Western) present. Just as there are considerable difficulties in performing the comparison with contemporary societies, mainly for political and ideological reasons, so this is a transparently unhelpful framework for dealing with the past: 'models . . . of economic backwardness only describe . . . surface phenomena without understanding the hard realities and structural limits of production' (Marino 1988, 11 and n.21). The deficiencies of the evidence make it unwise to retroject preconceptions about the nature of the problems of the world today embodied in terminology such as that of 'underdevelopment'. Plotting the rise and fall of the population of 'ancient Greece' and 'ancient Rome' against numbers of 'discoveries' (on a scale from 0 to 80) each century (J. L. Simon 1981, 196–210) is an extreme example, on which we need not dwell. It does, however, recall the question of the relationship between demography and technology, which does now need a somewhat fuller treatment.

Revolutions and evolutions

Population history has seemed to offer an explanation of several of the most decisive transformations in the Mediterranean historical record. The eclipsing of the classical tradition and the breakdown of the Graeco-Roman social framework at the beginning of the so-called Dark Ages, as well as the secular decline in the number of settlements over most of the Levant since the Middle Ages, have been seen mainly in demographic terms. Demographic growth, on the other hand, has been implicated in the creation of a commonalty of contacts across the Mediterranean during the Bronze Age, and in the rise of various social and economic expressions of that development. Population boom has been postulated on a wildly implausible scale to account for what has been taken as the sudden flowering of archaic Greece and the new presence of Greeks in overseas settlements in the eighth century B.C. (IX.5). But it is on attempts to explain the origins of the medieval world and how allegedly different it was from the classical past that the theories have had most impact. Here also, a close relationship has been traced between population growth and technical innovation.

The organization and control of labour is of vital importance in determining the degree of intensity – in the broad sense of the term – with which the land is exploited. To that extent population totals are an ingredient in the choice of agricultural practice. As Manius Curius Dentatus knew, agricultural strategy and the control of labourers were symmetrically interdependent (see the third epigraph to this chapter). The size of the local workforce strongly affects decisions about production. But it is not an independent variable: as in Sabinum in the third century B.C., it can be an aspect of the strategy over which some people at any rate exercise choice.

On the theory of Malthus about the relationship between population and production, in good times, such as that of an increased surplus, the population would rise; but the rising population would experience greater and greater hardship until the demographic increase was interrupted. One Malthusian interpretation claims that Europe after the Dark Ages was 'an agrarian community depressed economically by its own too rapidly growing population, by the redundancy of labour and deficiency in the utilisation of the soil which result from it.' (Herlihy 1974). For another prominent medieval economic historian, in the same vein modern Egypt, India and China are instances of population growth 'pull[ing] a civilization downward'; in the modern West and in Japan we have been lucky enough to experience an equivalent to the 'resurgence of skill' which brought about the economic revolution of the early Middle Ages (Lopez 1976, 27–55). Whatever the merits of arguing in that way about the twentieth century, in the Mediterranean past it seems however that it has not been the direct impact of malnutrition (or environmental pressure: Brown and Ellis 1995, 47–9) which has usually kept the population low but marriage patterns and general levels of health (Livi-Bacci 1991; cf. Garnsey 1988a). This chapter has touched on numerous factors which would tend to prevent good times from leading to demographic boom.

An influential alternative to Malthus, propounded in 1965 by Esther Boserup in her monograph *The Conditions of Agricultural Growth*, sees rising population as the principal motor of the intensification of productive effort, and with it of technological change. Here again, though, disquiet immediately arises from the historically unimpeachable cases in which demographic growth does not seem to have been accompanied by technical innovation. The rival theories can in fact coexist (R. D. Lee 1986). But though both effects are no doubt sometimes found, it is difficult to regard either as central to the understanding of Mediterranean history. The cultural complexity of the choices involved in the adoption of new techniques, which we have stressed, has a very serious damping effect on any crude demographic pressure. Even more important is the population mobility which we argue to be characteristic of the Mediterranean world. Any imbalance between the population densities of microregions or wider areas can, if conditions are suitable, be more easily modified by the horizontal movement of population than by other demographic – or technological – change.

A presence which has been felt throughout this chapter, though not explicitly addressed until now, is the supposed agricultural revolution of the Middle Ages. In outline, the orthodox view of this revolution has it that there was a dramatic increase in agricultural yields in temperate western and northern Europe in and after the ninth century. This was a consequence of the dissemination of related novel technologies and techniques, specifically the mouldboard plough, new systems of harnessing, and the three-field rotation; and it made possible a very substantial increase in population – 'one of the major developments in the demographic history of humankind' (Verhulst 1990, 21). Although not formulated with the aim of explaining the difference between a primitive Antiquity and an advanced late medieval world, this 'revolution' – like all revolutions – inevitably exaggerated the qualitative dissonance between 'before' and 'after'.

The scholarship that produced it has had an influence on the discipline of Mediterranean history comparable to that of Pirenne in that it has promoted acceptance not only of a pronounced qualitative distinction between Antiquity and the Middle Ages, but of one between North and South as well. How did contemporary Mediterranean societies compare in productivity and demographic vigour with booming north-west Europe? 'D'un tel décollage économique, il n'est pas question dans l'Empire byzantin' (M. Kaplan 1994, 91; cf. Harvey 1995).

It should not require a long summary of this chapter to set out the principal inadequacies of that view for the Mediterranean historian. (Chapter V has already outlined some basic sources of disagreement.) The history of innovation does not work in the way implied; but in a microregional environment, in any case, the productive efficacy of the technologies of traction and tillage, and of the techniques and strategies of production, is dependent on more important variables: labour, power, and connectivity.

The remarkable increase in complexity of interaction between settlements in the Aegean in the fourth millennium B.C. has been interpreted as cause rather than effect of demographic increase (on the basis of evidence from many sites, but principally from the Franchthi cave in the Argolid). Arguing explicitly against Boserup's theory, van Andel and Runnels claim that 'it was economic opportunity that attracted new people rather than the other way around' and that the first agriculture was analogous to the cash crop rather than the subsistence crop (van Andel and Runnels 1988, 243; cf. Runnels and van Andel 1988).

For our present purpose, there are two chief consequences of this movement in the subject. The first is that the role of the transforming technological revolution in explaining change in history has been reduced considerably. The idea or invention is powerless without enabling circumstances, and we would use those circumstances as explanations as readily and with equal logic in explaining the consequences that supposedly flowed from innovation. The improving landowner is at least as interesting a phenomenon as the ideas that he introduces. Having dethroned technological revolutions from the place of honour that they have occupied for so long, scholarship may be able to emancipate itself also from the staccato, melodramatic, progressivist historiographical patterns which have been so closely linked with them.

More positively, technological change has not lost its importance as a subject. Instead, bereft of its suddenness of action and status as a prime mover, it can be reinstated as one of the ingredients in a profoundly complex process. Innovation in technology takes its place in the vigorous debates on the nature and causes of all agrarian change. It has come to be widely accepted that, in general, the introduction of new practices is very gradual at first, then goes through a phase of rapid diffusion, and then slackens off in speed markedly (Grigg 1982). The length of time taken by the gradual phase is quite unpredictable and will depend on many factors. Some of these are quite subconscious and irrational – such as the complicating influences of fashion and accident. Others are hotly debated at the time – such as variations in the extractive strategies of the political elite, or the anticipated effect of different demographics.

It is here that the question of innovation is of particular interest to the Mediterranean historian, or at least to the themes of Mediterranean history that we have chosen to present in this account. Innovation will be seen to operate as one of the key elements in the human articulation of the microregions that were defined in Part Two, and – at the same time – as a vital aspect of the intercommunication that links them together. The sophistication of human responses to the local variability in the geological and meteorological environment is itself very variable, and technology in its strict sense takes its place in a much larger repertoire of expertise and stratagem. For scholars, it will also play an important part in tracing the patterns of intensification of effort and its abandonment and the interplay of pressures which bring them about, themes which we treated in Sections 5 and 6.

The understanding of technological change that we have delineated in these pages leaves little or no place for assigning technology a revolutionary role in Mediterranean history. Indeed, there is little room in such a history for pivotal turning-points of any kind. This negative conclusion should occasion no surprise, because there is an important structural connection between it and the fragmentation of the Mediterranean landscape. Changes, constant and ubiquitous though they are, are local in their effects (and often in their causes too), variable in their intensity over distance and time, evanescent, gradual and partial; they come to have general effects only after their presence has eventually been consolidated over the inexorable disunity of the microregions. Change in other environments may be much more visible because it does have a consolidated character on a large scale. Mediterranean change is much less easy to observe. It follows that one of the very few phenomena of Mediterranean history which may be said to be environmentally determined is the illusion of continuity. For that is fostered primarily by the way in which the moments of change are concealed in the recesses of microtopography, dissolved in the fragmentary diversification of the productive landscape.

CHAPTER VIII

MEDITERRANEAN CATASTROPHES

...a new and more glorious era would open for learning, when men should begin to look for their commentaries on the ancient writers in the remains of cities and temples, nay, in the paths of the rivers and on the face of the valleys and the mountains.

George Eliot, Romola (1863), ch. 6

> emanent subito sicca tellure paludes
> et metat hic iuncos spicas ubi legimus olim
> +coculet+ arguti grylli cava garrula rana . . .
> praecipitent altis fumantes montibus imbres
> et late teneant diffuso gurgite campos
> qui dominis infesta minantes stagna relinquant.
> cum delapsa meos agros pervenerit umbra
> piscetur nostris in finibus advena arator
> advena, civili qui semper crimine crevit.

[Let swamps all at once flow out upon the dry earth, and may they harvest reeds where we once gathered in the ears of corn. Let the frog, with unceasing voice . . . the nest of the shrill grasshopper. May frothing deluges of rain pour down from the mountains, take over the whole expanse of plain with spreading flood, and portend misfortune for the proprietor as they leave behind them lakes! When the flood comes to what were my lands, the outsider ploughman who now has them will go fishing – the outsider, whose gain has always been the consequence of civic injustice.]

Dirae, 72–4, 76–81; cf. Goodyear 1971

1. ON THE HISTORY OF CATASTROPHE

Historia naturalis

In the third quarter of the first century of this era, Gaius Plinius Secundus, a Roman elite functionary of the second rank, composed, in thirty-seven books, an account of everything, mostly arranged under the headings animal, vegetable and mineral, but not neglecting the divine order of the universe and the world, or human societies and institutions. In Pliny's world order the Roman Mediterranean, with Italy as its pivot, was the essential element (*Natural History*, 2.1). He called his synthesis by a highly imaginative name, which has become so familiar a concept that it is hard to discern its original oxymoronic piquancy. His was an Enquiry, a *historia*, of the sort invented by Herodotus half a millennium before. But it was an Enquiry into the workings of Nature. And Enquiries of the Herodotean kind had been concerned for the most part with human affairs, which Greek and Roman thought tended to separate schematically from the order of nature. Pliny's project therefore entailed an intellectually ambitious amalgamation of interpretative traditions.

The task that Pliny undertook is a difficult one in any age. Almost all historiographies are developed for the task of analysing human social, economic, cultural, or political relations and their changes through time. Applying them to change in the physical world – of geology or geomorphology, climate or ecology – immediately raises serious problems of method. But the historiographical metaphor is an obvious one, and it is widely used, at least in popularizing accounts, by natural scientists. Take the following example of geological narrative. Between six and five million years ago, the Mediterranean basin was the site of the epic unfolding of a geological drama. A combination of factors, including the relatively sudden subsidence of the basin of the Alboran Sea, between the Maghreb and the Iberian peninsula, closed the channels to the Atlantic in the vicinity of what is now the Strait of Gibraltar. Within a matter of centuries, evaporation turned the Mediterranean into a vast desert plain far below sea level, covered with great deposits of evaporite from the lakes and pools of the dying sea. As the Gibraltar channel closed, salt waterfalls, decreasing in vigour, bled salt out of the world's oceans, causing the 'Messinian salinity crisis'. Still more amazing must have been the time when the Atlantic poured back in . . . (Maldonado 1985, 26–8, 30). The desiccation of the Mediterranean has been called 'the most spectacular geologic event of . . . global evolution during the Cenozoic' (1985, 35). The past of the Mediterranean thousands of millennia before human history is depicted here in the language of historical writing, and, specifically, in the language of one variety of it, *histoire événementielle*. The device serves both to entertain, and to make comprehensible the vast time-scale of geology.

Such historical presentation of change in the physical world embodies a certain irony. Until the discovery, by nineteenth-century geologists, of the depth of time, the whole of the past, notoriously, was imagined in the West as comprising only a few thousand years (Trautmann 1992). In such a history, great events took on a pivotal role much more easily than they do now that the sheer duration of the immemorially repetitive ordinary has diminished the relative scale of each happening. When time was short, catastrophic events such as floods could be adduced to explain the obvious evidence of – for example – landscape change.

The landscapes of the Mediterranean, in all their bewildering variety and complexity, discontinuous and visibly mutable even in the short term, were among those that most insistently called for a 'natural history', an explanation of radical change which until the nineteenth century had to be accommodated within the frame of a few millennia. Indeed, no examination of the problems of writing Mediterranean history can ever omit consideration of physical change: the subject of the present chapter. The problem of incorporating the physical in a historical narrative remains. None the less, there is no reason to exacerbate this problem by gratuitous retention of ideas which were shaped by ignorance about the depth of time: that is how the use of catastrophe narratives by geologists becomes unhelpful as well as ironic. Disaster history continues to fascinate, and

needs no misleading promotion by casual association with the language of popular science.

Other long-lasting legacies of the interest taken by the Greeks and Romans
in the effects on human affairs of the dispositions of Nature should also make
us wary. Ancient analysis went far beyond the chronicling of natural events: the
interweaving of the natural with human history might reflect deeper meanings
and form part of overarching, possibly purposive, systems. It is worth recalling
that the causes which we would recognize under the heading 'Nature' are only
a part of a much more far-reaching conception of the universe that long out-
lasted the ancient world. In 1186 a Mediterranean-wide hysteria is recorded which
derived from fear of the catastrophes that would follow the conjunction in Libra
of all the planets on 15 or 16 September. The imperial court and the courtesans
of Constantinople dug holes in which to hide from the impending holocaust
(Niketas Choniates, *History*, 220.23–221.43, ed. van Dieten 1975; Kazhdan and
Wharton Epstein 1985, 182). Astrological catastrophe no longer features among
the shattering events which are propounded as punctuations of history. But perhaps it is the punctuation-thinking that should be abandoned as well as belief in
that particular aspect of the working of Nature.

Ancient attitudes to catastrophe were profoundly teleological. Progress, however, was not the normal trend: decline was a more common hypothesis. Indeed,
the sequence of stages by which felicity ebbed away from the Golden Age, first
attested in Hesiod's *Theogony*, was related to the conception of the world of
Mediterranean connectivity as a late and repugnant stage in the slide: the culmina-
tion of worse and worse human behaviour was involvement with the Corrupting Sea (IX.1). Social and economic corruption was mirrored in environmental
degradation and natural disaster. That conception of the past – and its refutation
– have had an important history. Mediterranean historiography must not fail to
make every allowance for the influence this history may continue to exert.

The humour of blaming the past

In 1752 David Hume ruefully concluded his treatise *On the Populousness of
Ancient Nations* (*Essays Moral, Political and Literary*, 11): 'the humour of blaming the present and admiring the past is strongly rooted in human nature and
has an influence even on persons endued with the profoundest judgement and
most extensive learning.' Hume's pamphlet was a passionate and highly rhetorical vindication of modernity, designed to emancipate discussion of the present
from Hesiodic comparison with the exaggerated felicity and prosperity of the
ancient world. It is important to appreciate that the kernel of the historiographical
contribution made by the Enlightenment and its immediate heirs was the decisive differentiation between the present and a relatively distant past (the age was
still quite unaware of the scale of prehistoric time) in the interests of recognizing
progress. Both the reactionary view which Hume was attacking, and the progressivist programme which he advocated instead, survive to present obstacles to
the understanding of Mediterranean history.

The 'humour of blaming the present' has combined in the late twentieth century with a teleological interest in historical catastrophe to encourage search for
the antecedents of the destructive environmental mismanagement of our own age.
Mediterranean regions have seen many episodes of environmental degradation

directly caused by human action, sometimes irreversibly. But although parallels between discontinuous instances of ecological destructiveness are naturally discernible, it may be of only limited interest to draw them. There is certainly no reason to weave them together into a teleological account which leads organically through ancient and medieval abuses to the escalating environmental débâcle of the twentieth century (cf. also Section 6 below). In a village of Roman brick-kilns the air may have been as bad as the modern Athenian *nephos*, but the comparison is not illuminating. Nor is there is any causal or developmental connection between an episode of soil-erosion after timber-felling to fuel sugar-boiling in Lusignan Cyprus and the clear-felling of Amazonian rain-forest.

The opposite humour, the Enlightenment predilection for blaming the past, has had still more malign consequences, through its encouragement of an unreflecting progressivism which has come close to being orthodox. It has sometimes led to a qualitative categorization of great tracts of the past, progressivist to its core, which lies at the heart of many abuses in the study of past landscapes. An instance is the idea that the Mediterranean agrosystem (both at home and when transferred by Iberian colonialism to the New World) was somehow bad, whereas pre-Columbian peoples lived in perfect ecological balance (a view attacked by Butzer 1996). The effects of progressivism continue to be felt in schematic periodizations – such as the notion of 'an Ancient Economy' – which have so hindered fertile comparisons (V.4). Archaeology has been among the principal inheritors of Enlightenment teleology, and specifically, of the subdivision of the past that has been labelled the 'type of block thinking which takes the form of a stadial sequence' (Sherratt 1995a, 6–7). In both archaeology and history, such a conception inevitably pulls the transitions between the blocks into unreasonable prominence. It is time to reconsider those transitions.

The handmaids of teleology are Catastrophe and Revolution. Decline-hypotheses combined with the short time-scale of pre-Darwinian history to render disasters indispensable. Revolution in its modern sense – the upturns, equivalent to catastrophes, by which the opposite goal of progress is attained – was a discovery of the Enlightenment. Yet, as in Hume's treatise, the two competing visions are locked in a rhetorical antinomy which goes back to the antagonism of Nature and Culture characteristic of ancient thought. History that is inclined to play up the drama of human ingenuity by representing – as it might be – the processes of agrarian innovation as rapid and awesome in their power also stresses the might of humanity's avowed or implicit adversary, the force of Nature. The history for which these conceptual tools were made concerns the Steps by which Man Progresses, and the Blows with which Nature makes him Recoil.

We concluded Chapter VII with a brief consideration of the history of technical Revolutions. Moving immediately to the discussion of physical changes in historical time in the Mediterranean environment offers an opportunity to draw a particular set of comparisons between the two themes. The study of environmental change has traditionally been dominated by the invocation of Catastrophe, and we may observe at the outset that rapid transformations of technical capacity and violent alterations in the physical landscape are thus conceptually related as types of explanation. They belong to the same repertoire of historical techniques. Major environmental changes can readily be compared with the effect of technical innovations in production. Indeed, the connection between the two has sometimes been perceived as causal. Thus (to take instances from VII.1 and 2) the creation and abandonment of terraced landscapes have been implicated in major changes in alluviation; new plough technology has encouraged the extension of agriculture onto heavy lowland soils and promoted clearance and reclamation; the 'hydraulic landscapes' made possible by irrigation technology have changed local climate and transformed hydrology. In this synthesis of the different kinds of pivotal transition in history, we see still the long shadow of Enlightenment thinking.

The Romantic historicism of the period from the Enlightenment to the insights of Darwin moulded the early stages of several of the disciplines that have contributed most to understanding the Mediterranean, from oceanography, in the circle of Adolf Dohrn in mid-nineteenth-century Naples (Margalef 1985, 2) to archaeology (in the investigation of the landscape around Rome in the age of Gell and Niebuhr). That period may seem a hardly less remote stage in our understanding of the Mediterranean past, but, as we argued in II.1, it too has had a pronounced and very tenacious effect on the ways in which Mediterranean history has been written; and these include the catastrophe-orientated account of human–natural relations. That is ultimately because of the enthusiasm with which such ideas were received at the time. It was the closely related theory of environmental determinism, in particular, that helped win geography a place in nineteenth-century science because of its usefulness in legitimating, through the concept of 'living space' [*Lebensraum*], the history of capitalist imperialism (just as, it has been persuasively argued, the tenacious biological analogy for human history survived and gained in popularity). In this case the role of geographers such as Ratzel (II.1) in setting the agenda for Mediterranean history acquires extra importance but appears in a somewhat regrettable light (Peet 1985, especially 315–17). Perhaps through the otherwise laudable influence of geography, ancient historians and medievalists have continued to make much of sudden changes in the environment and of rapid transformations in human responses to its productive possibilities brought about by innovations of equipment, know-how and organization.

Humanity and Nature: dissolving the dichotomy

In Chapters VI and VII, we attempted to sketch a backdrop to Mediterranean agrarian history in which the shifting characteristics of the environment produced short-lived conjunctions which were here or now favourable or hostile to productive endeavour. The gradual adaptations of human behaviour which mute, localize and abbreviate the impact of innovations have the same effect on malign changes, whether caused by nature or by people. In the end, it could be said that the central assumption of microregional analysis will be the relative insignificance of the global change which transcends local diversity. A human landscape fragmented in the way that we have described is extraordinarily resilient; it cushions against sudden disaster; it absorbs pressures and defuses stresses; it is malleable and ductile, hard to snap under strain.

We have also argued that productive endeavour likewise ebbs and flows across the diverse mosaic of environmental settings in a way that can seem capricious. This is because the endeavour is a reflection not only of a sometimes imperfect understanding of the shifting circumstances to which it would be prudent to respond, but also of the social pressures on the inhabitants – familial, political, economic, military. Yet those pressures, too, in many respects operate in a fragmented fashion, because of the microregional composition of the Mediterranean landscape. The consequence is that local and periodic episodes of intensification will usually resist incorporation into longer tendencies or processes, such as those identified with 'economic growth'; and, equally, occasional and sporadic phases of abatement should not be soldered together to construct a vision of 'decline' (III.3). In the Mediterranean, an unpredictable environment has been the setting – over and over again – for the improvement of human food-systems and of ecological harmony, and for the deterioration of both as a consequence of accident, aggression and greed. If monolithic periods of Mediterranean history should not be seen to be separated by pivotal revolutions or catastrophes, there is little room for discerning steady, or even intermittent, progress over the millennia either. Things have always got worse as well as better.

We saw how the social constraints characteristic of this environment and other aspects of Mediterranean production combined to inhibit the impact of both new techniques and technological novelties. Our hope was to demote the contribution of major abrupt change to the analysis of such an agrarian history, and to show how Mediterranean historiography could avoid distinguishing cultures, places or periods by means of technical revolutions. Given what we have said about the antecedents and associations of this historiography, we should expect to be able to do something analogous in the field of alleged catastrophic environmental change. It has been remarked that 'abusivement regroupés en un seul événement les phénomènes catastrophiques spatialement dispersés créent une géographie fictive' (Bousquet 1984, 70) – and a history, we might add. Because of the particular ecology of the microregion, as we defined it in Part Two, diversity and change are normal, but sudden convulsions are usually limited in their scale. As the author of the strange curse-poem that forms our epigraph knew well, geomorphological calamity was a frequent enough happening to be the subject of a malediction. Millennial catastrophe makes a poor curse.

To explain change in history, then, and especially in the history of the Mediterranean, we must do without the comforting evolutionism of tracing catastrophes survived and revolutions achieved. Our *historia naturalis* will take a different form. History is best suited to the record of human transactions. Conditions such as fertility and connectivity, which appear to have a strong element of the 'natural', are, as we have seen (III.3 'prosperity'; VII.1 'fertility'), suitable for the historian only because they are actually in a very large measure human constructions. In this chapter, accordingly, we shall stress the effects of human behaviour in shaping the environment, through 'anthropogene process' as it is known to geomorphologists.

We should reiterate at this point an important facet of our notion of the microregion: that it is a unit whose definition at a point in time will derive both from the characteristics of environmental givens (current hydrology, soil-conditions, vegetation cover, the year's weather) and from the prevailing state of human effects on the landscape (intensity of labour-effort, numbers of animals, choices of productive strategy). So a microregion may include the 'obvious' microtopographical identifiers – a plain, or a small valley, one side of an island; but it will also include less visible and less readily intuited elements such as the detached pastures (on nearby mountain-slopes or smaller islands), the claybeds two valleys away, from which all our region's containers are made, the harbour through which redistribution takes place, the homes from which migrant harvest labour comes.

In this chapter, we begin with the aspects of environmental change that are wholly beyond human control, deriving from the geological structure (Section 2) and from the meteorological givens (Section 3). Such accidents of the natural world turn out not to have a free-standing history in their own right. Human responses and symbioses are the subject matter of the historian. Ultimately, of the physical changes which demand attention in the Mediterranean landscape, it is with those with which human actions have been intimately interleaved that the historian can help. There is no history as such of the 'wars' between bands of chimpanzees; nor is there of the volcanic eruption, or the earthquake, let alone the orogeny; of meteorite-falls or eclipses. When we speak of a history of these things we are either using a potentially misleading metaphor, or else actually describing the interaction with these events of human observers, agents, or victims.

Section 4 thus moves on to consider the more complex interactions involved in anthropogene process: the effects on the environment of human actions, which both respond to circumstances and undertake new interventions. In Section 5 we address the particular question of the vegetation history of the Mediterranean lands in our period. The chapter concludes with an assessment of the contribution of human behaviour to environmental change, and returns to the general concept of catastrophe. In the process, we mean to set out something of the current debates on the natural environment of the Mediterranean which are of most interest to historians, and to relate them to the human responses which we attempted to outline in Chapters VI and VII.

2. An Unstable World

> The wall was built against the will of the immortal Gods, and so did not remain intact for very long . . . When the champions of Troy were dead, and many of the Argives, although some survived, and the city of Priam had been sacked in the tenth year and the Argives had departed to their native land in their ships, then Poseidon and Apollo planned the destruction of the wall and turned against it the might of the rivers. All the streams which run down from the Ida massif to the sea, Rhesus and Seven-sources, Caresus and Rhodius, Granicus and Aesepus and noble Scamander, and Simois by which many leather shields and helmets had rolled in the dirt, and many of the half-gods too; the outlets of all these Phoebus Apollo turned together. He sent the flood for nine days against the wall, and Zeus rained without stopping, the quicker to reduce the wall to flotsam on the sea. The Earthshaker wielded the trident he held in his hands and struck into the waves baulk and block from the foundations which the Achaeans had struggled to build; and made them prey to the fierce currents of the Hellespont. Then he heaped up a great beach of sand, completely ruining the wall, and turned the rivers back into their courses, where the water had flowed sweetly before. (Homer, *Iliad*, 12.8–9, 13–33)

None of its inhabitants has been unaware of the unstable nature of the Mediterranean's physical environment. This passage illustrates its presence in the earliest literature of the area, older than literacy itself. The instability is one of the characteristics that distinguish the Mediterranean from its neighbouring regions

– directly, and through being the primary cause of the fragmented topography that, as we have argued in earlier chapters, in turn underlies the distinctive collectivity of microregions. Instability is also, we may note, the cause of the sheer crags and beetling precipices of Mediterranean mountains and coasts – of much, in other words, that has been thought distinctively and Romantically Mediterranean by poets and painters (II.1). Most importantly, it is landscape instability that creates one of the essential features of the microregion: that it is not a fixed entity, but constantly alters the characteristics that are most significant for human perception and occupation. The fragmentation that we have described is not just topographical: it has its chronological dimension too. All microregions change with time. As we indicated in Chapter III, it is not the particular physical characteristics of Mediterranean microregions that make them distinctively Mediterranean, but the extent to which they share a common mutability and diversity: the differences that resemble each other. And the instability of the environment is one of the principal sources of this variability over time. Adapting Heraclitus (Diels-Krantz fragment 12), we might say that you cannot step twice into the same microregion.

Structure and landscape

The instability is the product of several factors, of which the geological structure of the Mediterranean region is the most important. Major faults bound fragmented areas of the earth's crust known today as plates, where mountains of recent creation jostle older mountainous areas being re-elevated by tectonic forces, where some areas of land or seabed gently rise and others tend to fall. The Mediterranean lands are dotted with a huge range of geophysical eccentricities: hot springs, sulphur beds, fumaroli; the ever-burning flame of the vent of natural gas in the mountains of Lycia which became attached to the myth of the monstrous Chimaera; the boiling mud-pools of the Solfatara, 'the Forum of Vulcan', at Pozzuoli in the Phlegraean Fields. Such marvels are eloquent testimony to the structural instability, and have had a considerable religious and social impact (X.2). But, for humanity, the most momentous of tectonic manifestations are the destructive geophysical phenomena of vulcanicity and seismicity.

Catastrophe, in one sense, is readily to be found in Mediterranean history in the scattering of volcanoes and in the wide belts where devastating earthquakes are frequent. The effects of eruption and earthquake are so dramatic that these events are relatively well documented in the literary sources and easily traceable on the ground. The earthquake of 373 B.C., during which the two cities of Helice and Bura slid into the Corinthian gulf, became a commonplace of ancient discussions of Nature (Bousquet et al. 1983, 9–10). But perhaps no event in the physical record of the Mediterranean is as well-known as the eruption of Vesuvius in A.D. 79 which destroyed Pompeii and Herculaneum.

No one would deny these events the label catastrophe. Yet it is striking that no major historical consequences for the economy and society of even the immediately surrounding part of west central Italy can be definitely shown to have followed the eruption of A.D. 79. Although it did not resurrect the vanished cities, recovery seems in fact to have been quite swift (Jashemski 1979b). We should recall that the area was, at the time, a managed landscape of considerable complexity. Producing for redistribution, it was the result of a marked intensification of effort by absentee proprietors over the previous two centuries. Despite their awesome power, the impact of Mediterranean volcanoes has, in historical times, been essentially microregional in scale. Even in the immediate vicinity of eruption, the productive landscape proves quite resilient. Soils derived from airborne volcanic debris are at their most fertile in the early stages of weathering (Ugolini and Zakoski 1979). The largest eruption of our period took place in the late Bronze Age on the Aegean island of Thera/Santorini, probably in 1628 B.C. Despite the (often over-imaginative) connections that scholars have drawn with political changes in the Aegean, even in this case there does not seem to be evidence for widespread environmental transformation. The dendrochronological data on which the date of 1628 is based must, by their nature, be sensitive to changes of this kind, and it is significant that they remain inconclusive (Kuniholm et al. 1996; Renfrew 1996). The contribution of volcanic activity to Mediterranean history lies in the cumulative effect that it has had on the landscape over geological time-scales, greatly adding to the diversity of the environment through the interpolation of totally different rocks among the predominating sedimentaries. We have seen something of landscapes of this sort in considering two of the 'definite places' of Chapter III, Melos and Etruria.

Earthquakes also appear to have had a relatively muted effect. The leading authority on historical seismicity notes a similar environmental resilience:

> modern writers have attempted to use earthquakes to account for gaps in the sequence of civilizations and for movements of peoples, hypotheses for which I can find absolutely no historical justification. Earthquakes in the past twenty-five centuries have had little, if any, serious influence on historical developments in the Middle and Near East. (Ambraseys 1971, 379)

Towns and their individual fortunes are only one manifestation of the microregional history of the Mediterranean as a whole – and not usually a decisive one, as we argued in Chapter IV. Terrible though it is in human terms, the obliteration of Bura or Pompeii would not, on our reasoning, be expected to have had a major effect on the history of the landscapes in which these settlements had functioned. Classical authors were aware that it was as architecture that cities were vulnerable to earthquake. Seneca the Younger contrasted the effects of disease favourably with those of earthquakes: 'a pestilential climate wears cities out; it does not abolish them' (*On the Movement of the Earth* [*De terrae motu*], 8). In a perceptive and revealing passage, Strabo attributed the pattern of dispersed settlement around the Mysian city of Philadelphia to the effect of persistent earthquakes, finding it hard to imagine why a city had been founded in so dangerous a place (*Geography*, 13.4.10). He appreciated how desirable it was to exploit this fertile agricultural niche, and he understood that production and redistribution were less adversely affected by the earthquakes than were the usual forms of city life, which it would have been prudent – and unproblematic – to forgo in such a locality.

In A.D. 141 a severe earthquake caused grave damage in every city of Lycia. To the inhabitants of the region it appeared a *kosmikos seismos*, a 'universal earthquake' (*IGRR*, 3.739.53, ll. 48–9). That at least is how it was described in a vote of thanks for the superabundant generosity of the region's richest proprietors in making some of their colossal wealth available to repair the wrecked architecture of civic prestige. In the historical record, earthquakes have often been

given an epic role, especially when their effects on built environments are politically or symbolically influential. It has been tempting to postulate a parallelism
between patterns in the history of human affairs and those in the movements of
the earth itself (as of the stars). When a Persian fleet for the first time dared to
contravene the 'natural' division of the continents by crossing the Aegean from
Asia to Europe, and set foot on the sacred island of Delos, at the Aegean's mid-
point, the island suffered its only earthquake, portending disaster (Herodotus,
Histories, 6.97–8).

Seismicity is indeed connected with the layout of the continents. It is a consequence of the endless jostling of the crustal plates where Asia and Africa abut
– an active feature of the Mediterranean region as a part of the planet. Twentieth-
century gains in understanding this process have led to changes in earthquake
history. The older idea was that earthquakes and volcanoes in the Mediterranean were somehow the last rumbling of primitive upheaval: the occasional, but
perhaps less and less common, catastrophes of a region that was 'still settling'.
That idea fitted well into a progressivist pattern of thought which will be familiar. The disasters had, in this account, been pivotal historical events, but happily
there were now (or would soon be) fewer of them. As we might expect, analysts have been reluctant to let such dramatic disasters disappear from their
repertoire as a result of new information. Failing individual seismic episodes of
sufficient moment, recourse has been had to the idea of the earthquake cluster.
An instance has been discerned in the sixth century and described as the Early
Byzantine Tectonic Paroxysm (Pirazzoli 1988). Another such paroxysm could
be advanced as explanation of the widespread political crisis of the second half
of the second millennium B.C. But in even the earlier of these two periods,
networks of interaction and interdependence were complex and far-reaching
compared with the structures involved in earthquake-producing tectonic movements. We do not believe that even the accident which produces a fairly tight
clustering of earthquakes is able to overcome the resilience of such networks.
The natural mistake of the Lycians must be shunned by the historian: earthquakes, unlike some climatic changes, and even in clusters, are *never* universal,
never 'world earthquakes'. They are, however, in aggregate something of a
Mediterranean phenomenon.

That German pioneer of Greek geology, the geographer Alfred Philippson
wrote in 1904 that no day passes without an earthquake somewhere in Greece –
in Greece, not to mention the extremely active seismic belts of the rest of the
Mediterranean (1904, 28). The earthquake zones are so extensive, and coincide
with so many regions of great historical importance, that seismicity can be
regarded as a familiar feature of the whole sea. It is another distinctive identifier
of the Mediterranean ambit itself, separating it off from the more stable regions
to north and south. These belts can be differentiated from other types of environment. As a recent study says: 'le séisme . . . acquiert une signification qui, à
l'échelle régionale, lui fait jouer un vrai rôle dans la différentiation de l'éspace
méditerranéenne' (Bousquet et al. 1984, 288). The effect is achieved through
exacerbating the normal local mutability of the environment. In earthquake
zones, topography, pedology and hydrology are all even more labile than normal. Overall, then, seismicity is one of the most important underlying factors
in that impermanence of the landscape which marks off the Mediterranean from
its neighbours. And it is worth reiterating that it is structurally – in the geological

sense – linked with the fact of the sea's existence. But we have argued at some length in the previous two chapters that impermanence and variability are the two factors of Mediterranean living to which its human societies have most elaborately adapted. We would therefore resist even the limited measure of determinism involved in regarding earthquakes as a 'natural constraint' on human action rather than as historical catastrophes (Guidoboni 1989, 22–3).

La tyrannie de la pente

The mutability of the Mediterranean landscape also owes a great deal to the instability of the regolith (the layers of rock-debris and soil which lie above the solid rock), and to rainfall (another aspect recognized in the Homeric passage with which we began this section). Once again, the uneven distribution of Mediterranean precipitation is highly significant: sudden downpours after drought are more potent agents of landscape change than enduring mild drizzle. But the rains are not only seasonal; they are violent and spasmodic. The effects are often violent too. In the mountains, avalanches and the equally destructive mass movements which over a matter of years pull whole slopes into abysses can both be common (J. R. McNeill 1992, 30–1). Reports of villages destroyed in this way are frequent. In 1877 the populous settlement of Agrapha in the high Pindus of northern Greece disappeared into a gorge leaving only a tiny fragment: 'after long-continued rains the whole western half of the village collapsed, and began to slide steadily downwards, finally sinking into the quivering earth' (W. J. Woodhouse 1897, 38). In 1963 another landslip in this region destroyed the ancient Tatarna monastery (Koumolides 1985; X.3).

The terrifying effect of such disasters is naturally reinforced by high relief. In understanding the 'definite places' of the Mediterranean it is not too extreme, therefore, to speak of *la tyrannie de la pente*, the tyranny of gradient (VII.1; Neboit et al. 1984a, 317–30). Gradient apart, the impact of precipitation is shaped by three interrelated factors: the rock-type, the soil structure, and the vegetation-cover, which we shall briefly discuss individually, the first two in this section, and the last in Section 5. At the outset, however, it is clear that with so many variables local experience will be further fragmented. Each season in every microregion brings unique conjunctions of those variables. As we shall see in more detail below, this makes generalizations about environmental change over wide areas – concerning for example deforestation or soil erosion – very difficult.

Hard limestone full of crevices into which water disappears, impermeable volcanic rocks, and unconsolidated clays or gravels each respond differently to flash-flooding. The solid geology (as opposed to the geology of the regolith) of the Mediterranean is extremely varied locally. Once again, the explanation is structural: because of their place in the structures of the crust, Mediterranean lands are subject to continuous uplift associated with the formation of fold-mountain systems such as the Alps or the Taurus. The deformation of the strata in this process results in extreme fragmentation and chaotic variety, which is complicated still further by the inclusion, within the foldings of younger rocks, of re-elevated massifs much older in date. As with the effect of seismicity on the mutability of the surface, then, there is a structural reason why the Mediterranean is a zone of microregions. In all this geological profusion, most of the individual types of rock are not hard to find outside the Mediterranean too. But there is one type of landscape directly controlled by the lithology which has some claim to be thought of as distinctive of the region: the limestone terrains of the Mediterranean. Soluble limestones form very special geomorphologies because of the effect of precipitation in dissolving the rock. Underground streams, sink-holes, copious springs, and cave-systems which in turn collapse to create hollows (sometimes on quite a large scale) are among their characteristic features. The intensity of such processes is affected by mean annual temperature and levels of precipitation. The technical term used by geomorphologists for this type of landscape is *karst* (III.1), and it is applied to the limestone landscapes of the Pennines and of the tropics, as well as those of Provence or Greece. Among the instances of landscape which we used to introduce the microregion in Chapter III, karst was prominent in the cases of the Biqa and the Jebel Akhdar. But the name is derived from an archetypal instance, the limestone plateau called Carso or Karst on the borders of Italy and Croatia. In the Mediterranean, this landscape is sufficiently common for it to be regarded as typical; and it develops a particularly intricate microtopography which has already led us to allude to it several times.

Soils are naturally closely related to the solid geology, and here the imbrication of three principal types is pertinent to the topic of microregional identity. Quite different soils are associated respectively with the alluvial and colluvial valley floors and coastal plains; with the predominant limestones (including both karst and other kinds); and with the areas of igneous rock (which are scattered very widely because of the structural instability of the area, even where there are no signs of volcanic activity in historical times). Relief, gradient and hydrology are of great importance, too; and we have seen in VII.1 how, from the human point of view, the soil cannot be taken as a given, but is capable of being substantially modified to suit productive purposes. Soil is indeed a part of the geology in the development of which living things are continually involved. Human tilling, manuring, terracing and irrigation are only part of a large range of effects in which the character of the vegetation also plays a vital part. Conversely, the survival and reproduction of complex plant-associations such as forest, or the potential for agriculture, is critically affected by the weather, the gradient and the instability of the surface.

After relief, soil structure and precipitation, then, the final factor to mention is human activity, intensifying the instability of an already fragile environment: 'la montagne méditerranéenne est un milieu géographique intrinsèquement instable et fragile, et son remplacement par les formations dégradées du *saltus* et les cultures de l'*ager* ne peuvent que renforcer des processus actifs depuis toujours' (Neboit et al. 1984a, 322). The activity of human beings may be seen as reinforcing the tendencies to change that are latent in the unstable Mediterranean environment, whether it involves carelessly permitting the formation of those upland and hill-slope pastures (highly prone to deterioration) which the Romans knew as *saltus*, or more purposively 'improving' the environment for agricultural production. The interlocking of continuous changes in an inherently unstable environment with the accidental and deliberate effects of human intervention are of the greatest importance in explaining the uncertainties with which human producers have had to cope. But precisely because of the sophistication which those uncertainties have induced on the part of Mediterranean populations, they have not usually caused widespread disaster. Although the irreversible destruction of soil-cover, and the formation of the gullies and barren slopes that are often called 'badlands topography', can be locally devastating, it is important to emphasize just how local the effect may be. There is no reason to assign it a catastrophic role in history (van Andel and Zangger 1990a, 154).

The normality of flood

The other half of the story of mountain degradation is the fate of the eroded soil cover when it reaches the plains. This is inseparable from the way it gets there, which is as the load carried by seasonal inundation. Destructive floods have always been a feature of Mediterranean life: 'this man has perhaps lost his rich soil, while on another's land sand, stones and mud brought by flood have settled' (Agennius Urbicus, *On Disputes about Rural Property*, 42, ed. Thulin 1913). So writes a Roman on the daily difficulties of settling boundary disputes.

To the processes of flooding the nature of the coastline is also crucial. The fluid dynamics of valleys and the behaviour of streams are naturally affected profoundly by even slight changes in sea-level relative to the land (Rapp and Gifford 1982, 27). Since the 'maximum transgression', of the middle of the fifth millennium B.C., sea-levels have overall fallen, by a global process known as eustatic adjustment. Locally, the tectonic instabilities of the Mediterranean have also in many places had significant effects on relative levels (Flemming et al. 1973); coastlines have been drowned or uplifted by as much as several metres within historical times. Sea-level change is clearly potentially capable of producing definite qualitative changes in the environment over long historical periods, and these might, as has sometimes been claimed, be of considerable importance to the historian. At least during the historical period, however, the eustatic readjustment has been found not to be a steady progression, but a series of oscillations around the present level. Like the highly local, and more rapid, tectonically induced changes (as they are found in western Crete or, spectacularly, on the north shore of the Bay of Naples), these alterations are therefore less far-reaching in their impact on human activity, and more easily reversible, than might at first sight appear likely. Rather than being catastrophic events, therefore, they usually more closely resemble the other geomorphological processes, terrestrial or maritime, which constantly modify the coastline and in so doing also change the character of flooding in the lower parts of stream valleys.

Marine erosion and deposition, as seen in complicated deltaic change, affects the lengths and profiles of stream courses. Nor are water processes the only ones involved. On the south coast of Anatolia or the west coast of Italy – and in many other places – the movement of dune belts has had a marked impact on alluviation behind the coastal strip (G. Evans 1973, esp. 93), as well as transforming the topography beyond recognition (compare the anecdote of Moryson, X.2). Dune-accretion and movement is controlled to a large extent by the wind. It is however worth remembering that even the sand involved is not a constant feature of all Mediterranean coastal environments, but often derives from further afield: the supply of wind-blown sand which reaches the south-eastern shores of the Mediterranean from the Sahara is yet another variable over time (Neev et al. 1987).

Rome was the only city on the Tiber, and one of the few great ancient cities on the banks of a perennial river. The Romans' natural preoccupation with the Tiber has given us an unusually detailed picture of its inundations throughout

Roman history from the fifth century B.C. onwards (LeGall 1953, 14–17, 29–33). The picture differs from the more detailed records kept from the late nineteenth century only in the prominence in Antiquity of spring floods, and even occasionally of summer ones (cf. III.2). The epigraph to this chapter is a passage from an anonymous Latin poem developing the theme found in Virgil's *Eclogues* of the expropriation of agricultural land. It takes the form of a curse uttered by the dispossessed, and expresses the hope that the new owner will find his property at the mercy of a readily imagined inundation, leading to the transformation of the landscape.

Incidental episodes of disastrous flooding are not hard to find in later periods. In A.D. 589 the *Liber Pontificalis* [*Book of the Popes*] (65, trans. R. Davis 1989) records terrible autumn flooding all over Italy. Surveys of post-classical landscape history in the eastern Mediterranean draw attention to numerous further notices of this sort (Hendy 1985, 58–68): the high incidence of flooding in sixth-century Anatolia for example gave Justinian the chance to pose as a Master of Waters in the regal tradition that went back to Xerxes and Cyrus (or to the triumphal irrigators whose grandiose schemes we met in Section 2 of the previous chapter). The calcareous massif between Antioch and Aleppo, whose controversial agrarian history we have also discussed (VII.5), was thought to have been denuded of one to two metres of fertile *terra rossa* soil after the abandonment of the prosperous oleiculture which had existed there in late Antiquity (Millar 1993, 251–6). Eleventh-century estate documents provide eloquent testimony for land abandonment in the Maeander flood-plain (Ashtor 1976, 51–8; Hendy 1985, 58–68). And there are occasional instances of really dramatic and long-lasting transformations such as the flooding of the southern basin of the Dead Sea by increased run-off around A.D. 1000 (Neev and Emery 1967).

But the events referred to in such evidence span a millennium, and each instance is actually very different in kind. Some are erosional, some sedimentary, some recurrent, some singular: they are variously the product of meteorology, warfare, and pastoralism – a whole range of human and natural causes. Rather than serving to explain secular changes such as the decline of Byzantium or the early modern dereliction of the Levant, collecting anecdotal material of this kind simply illustrates the perennial instability of the Mediteranean regolith. Given the multiplicity of factors involved, it is scarcely surprising that human strategies of settlement and agriculture have been so frequently disrupted by floods that are locally unexpected. But the disruption, and its remedies, along with so many other social and physical factors, lie within the range of circumstances affecting choices about abatement and intensification. At the height of one of the epochs when flooding has been thought to have been historically important, Cassiodorus speaks positively about concession by the state of flood-damaged and abandoned land for reclamation (*Variae*, 2.21, cf. 32). And the documenting of the events, like the use of earthquakes in historiography, tells us more about the recorders' preoccupations with the relationship of humanity to the natural world than it does about the realities of their economic and social consequences.

In most of the climatic regimes of the Mediterranean, flooding is thus a perennial hazard, ranging from the annual inundation of the Nile, through the periodic flash-floods of the desert margins, to the effects of ill-distributed rainfall in the northern peninsulas. Whatever variations of climate there have been within the historical period, it can be stated confidently that there have always been inundations. Like earthquakes, then, this is a phenomenon which occurs through-out the region but is not usually widespread in its effects. It contributes markedly, however, to the individuality of the localities and moments at which it is present. It enhances the microregional character of the Mediterranean, fragmenting it both historically and geographically, underlining its nearly infinite variety. A striking map, therefore, would be one which depicted the boundaries of all the river-catchments whose waters end up in the Mediterranean. Unfortunately, with alluviation as with earthquakes, there has been a similar tendency to elevate some events into being pivotal catastrophes. We turn next to some of the argu-ments adduced. The historian is bound to consider the possibility that this perennial phenomenon is locally and in some periods more intense, to explain this if it is the case, and to assess its effects on long-term history.

3. ALLUVIAL CATASTROPHE AND ITS CAUSES

The Greek discovery of anthropogene process

In the second century of our era, the traveller and antiquarian Pausanias wrote:

> the fact that the Echinadian islands have not yet been joined to the mainland by the river Achelous is due to the Aetolians, for since they were driven out the whole country has been turned into a wilderness. Hence, Aetolia remained untilled, and the Achelous does not wash down as much mud as it would otherwise do on to the Echinadian islands. In support of this view I can cite the Maeander; flowing through the lands of Phrygia and Caria, which are ploughed every year, it has in a short time reduced the sea between Priene and Miletus to dry land. (*Description of Greece*, 8.24.5)

Pausanias was not the first ancient writer to comment on the wonder of coastal change: we have already seen a passage of the *Iliad* which touches on the same theme. From at least the classical Greek period, the inhabitants of the Mediter-ranean have been conscious of the effect of the continuous denudation of the hills on rapid changes in the line of the coast. Herodotus (*Histories*, 2.10), in the fifth century B.C., was the first to elevate the idea to a general principle. He took three examples from his homeland, the Aegean coast of Asia Minor – the gulf at the mouth of the Scamander by Troy, the Caicus, and the Maeander – and compared them with the Achelous in Aetolia, the longest river of mod-ern Greece, the river of Pausanias's comments above (Map 18). Generalizing from their rapidly prograding mouths, he argued that the Nile valley and delta were another case of a great inlet of the sea which had been filled with the silts deposited by successive floods. His sense of landscape and his reasoning about it from examples earn him the sobriquet of Father of Geomorphology as much as that of Father of History. His near-contemporary Thucydides also addressed the case of the Achelous and the Echinadian islands, in rather more detail than Herodotus (*History*, 2.102). Landscape change was thus a theme of classical historiography in its first generation. But Pausanias is unique in reflecting on what has changed through time during recorded history, and above all in his quite new *explanation* of the phenomenon: it is human activity that has ulti-mately brought about these astonishing transformations. This is the earliest description known to us of 'anthropogene process'.

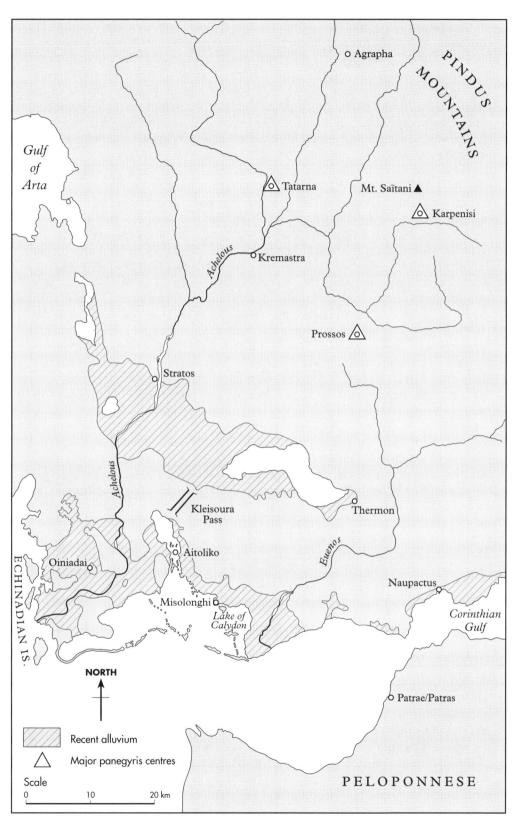

Map 18 The river Achelous and its region

Discussions of geomorphological change in ancient texts help establish the continuity of environmental history, and we shall see that it is important that fifth-century B.C. authors noticed rapid coastal change as a result of alluviation. But ancient presentations of such matters need to be used with the greatest of care by landscape historians – as we shall also see repeatedly in the course of this chapter. It is hardly necessary to point out that these authors lacked any concept of geomorphology, and it is not so easy to assess whether Pausanias's reasoning was as correct as it might seem. Ancient authors' mimetic debts to their predecessors pose serious problems in dating ancient literary evidence. The only *terminus post quem* in Pausanias's obervations is the Roman depopulation of Aetolia in 167 B.C., and his 'short time' for the advance of the Maeander delta is quite impossible to measure. Priene is still attested as a port in the early third century. Nearby Myus was still a port in the fifth century but had been abandoned when its harbour became a swamp infested with biting insects (Pausanias, *Description of Greece*, 7.10–11). Today Miletus, still a port in Pausanias's time, lies inland and the island of Lade, where a sea-battle was fought in 494 B.C., is a land-locked hillock (see Map 19). Similarly, the numerous examples of spectacular alluviation in the Augustan geographer Strabo – such as his suggestion that the delta of the Cilician river Pyramus would soon join Cyprus to the mainland (*Geography*, 1.3.7) – need not refer to his lifetime, since his text is a layer-cake of allusions to authorities as early as the fifth century B.C. The examples chosen are not a random sample either: some of the interest of ancient writers in alluviation derives from the conversion of Island into Mainland – a transformation, after all, of considerable significance for the layout and interaction of the Mediterranean as a network of 'maritime hinterlands'.

Pausanias, at any rate, identifies the principal questions. Upon what basis can we 'read back' from coastal development and valley-floor alluviation to agrarian history? Granted that human activity is important, is it cultivation or its cessation that causes alluviation? We might reason, following Pausanias, that the part of north-west Greece that he describes has been deserted since his time too, for some of the Echinadian islands have still not been joined to the continent. But we can take into account, as he could not, the bathymetric and oceanographic constraints on coastal advance, highly complex as they are (Eisma 1978, 74, 78). The extent of anthropogene process here is of the utmost significance for the historian. If the onset of alluviation, for instance, was principally explicable by global environmental factors, rather than human activity, examples of it would have little to contribute to either *histoire événementielle* or the understanding of the longer term.

From Curtius to Vita-Finzi and his heirs

We have seen that the ancient Greeks first identified the processes of alluviation which result from flooding. Those processes have also played a very important part in our interpretation of the ancient Greeks. They have done so since the discovery, in the German excavations of Ernst Curtius during 1875–81, of how deeply the site of the panhellenic sanctuary of Olympia was buried beneath the alluvium of the river Alpheius, the product of a great number of landscape-transforming floods. The sediments were spectacular enough to catch the imagination, and were widely discussed (cf. Huntington 1910). Although the documentary record

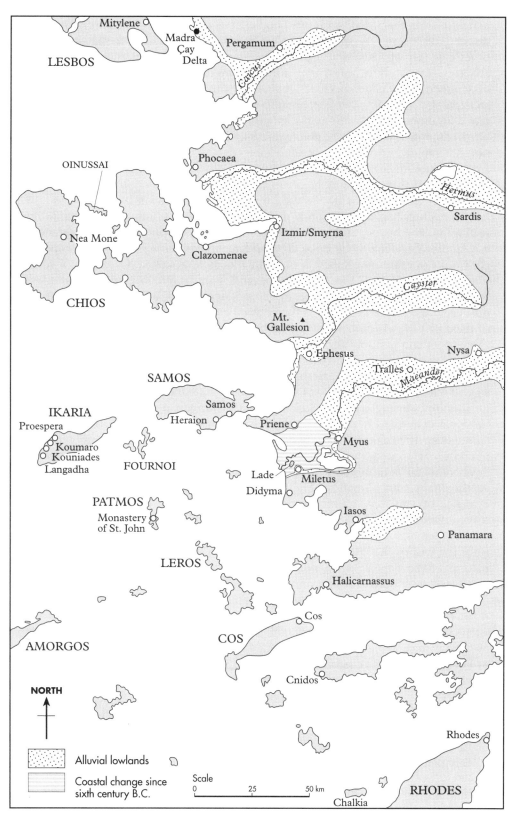

Map 19 The river Maeander and its region

makes it clear that Mediterranean people have always been vulnerable to flood disaster, discoveries as striking as this have invited speculation that at certain times this fact of Mediterranean life acquired greater prominence and became able to transform human history. From the late nineteenth century on, the study of sediments has never been far removed from the practice of Mediterranean archaeology. But after 1969 it became the highly controversial foundation of a set of ambitious claims about the environmental history of the Mediterranean. Neither the revival of interest among archaeologists in the cause of alluvial change nor the rapidly growing body of reliable data has stimulated much response among historians, other than those who work on Archaic and classical Greece. We think that this is regrettable, even though we do not accept the most dramatic claims that have been made for the impact of alluviation on human affairs.

In the English-speaking world, the scholar who has done most to inspire research into the history and nature of recent sedimentation in the Mediterranean is Claudio Vita-Finzi. His book *The Mediterranean Valleys* (1969) juxtaposed the results of examining valley-floor sediments in Tripolitania, Cyrenaica, Jordan, Greece, Italy, Spain, Morocco, Algeria and Tunisia. He concluded that there had been two distinct and coherent phases of deposition, universal and synchronous, each of which was followed by renewed erosion of the valley floor. The first of these phases, which produced what he termed the Older Fill (1969, 92–100), came to an end in about the eighth and seventh millennia B.C.; except for comparison, this phenomenon therefore lies outside our scope. Not so the second phase. The interaction of datable archaeological remains with sediments persuaded Vita-Finzi that there was a second lengthy phase of alluviation. It began, he thought, during or immediately after the Roman period and continued in most places until very recently, although he considered that it had now ended throughout the region (1969, 1–3, 101–2, 116–20).

Vita-Finzi argued that this extended period of alluviation radically altered environmental conditions. His major aim was to explore the effects of such a transformation on humanity. The sedimentary record represented for him clear evidence of a major discontinuity in the physical setting of Mediterranean history: a discontinuity which contradicted the orthodoxy that climatic and general environmental conditions in the Mediterranean have overall not changed greatly since the end of the last glaciation. If his view of the universal and synchronous pattern of the deposition of the Younger Fill was correct, that Fill could have been caused by human action only if it was concerted and universal in its impact to an implausible degree. So he allotted the impact of humanity on the environment the role of 'simply abetting the phase of downcutting that began at the Last Glaciation' (1969, 110). The alternative view, that the alluvial event was essentially anthropogene, he considered a matter of intellectual fashion, 'a swing in the pendulum of culpability' (1969, 106). The only possible explanation remaining was a general change in the climate, which he took as the most likely explanation for the Older Fill too.

Scholars who took up and developed Vita-Finzi's hypothesis used it as the foundation for audacious hypotheses of their own.

> These recent alluvial formations were deposited, in almost their entirety, during and after the Roman period, and up to that time extensive alluvial soils were represented solely by the heavy and generally low fertility Pleistocene formations.

> Those areas of intensive irrigation cropping today occupy land that was of an entirely different character throughout prehistory – Pleistocene colluvium/alluvium, Pliocene marls, open sea, and to a limited extent, lagoon and delta saltmarshes. (Bintliff 1977a, 71)

On this interpretation, the actual process of alluviation disrupted society, depressed agriculture, helped spread disease, and destroyed communications networks. Yet, 'the nature . . . of the younger fill . . . has ultimately in all the areas examined brought improved agricultural production in comparison to the potential of the prehistoric landscape' (Bintliff 1976a, 273); 'while the Older Fill is moderately fertile farming land, and the deltaic fill useful seasonal pasture, the Younger Fill offers unparalleled excellent soil qualities and is the most productive and intensive zone of modern farming. The arrival of this alluvium must therefore be considered as of tremendous consequence to the arable potential of Greece' (Bintliff 1977b, 43).

The suggestion was very radical. Three important propositions were seen to follow from Vita-Finzi's original observation. First, the floods which deposited the Younger Fill brought, over a short period, intense chaos which entailed a terrible crisis for economic and social systems. Second, and still more controversial, the Mediterranean world before this set of events had been geomorphologically quite different. The agricultural potential of the Mediterranean lands at all previous periods would therefore need to be reassessed, and in very many cases would turn out to have been overestimated, through erroneous retrojection of the landscapes created by the deposition of the Younger Fill. Conversely, the third challenging hypothesis stated that the arrival of new soils – or rather of whole new agricultural landscapes – transformed Mediterranean society, and might be thought responsible for major qualitative changes in the social and economic history of primary production over the ensuing centuries (Bintliff 1976a, 273; 1977b, 43).

History since late Antiquity became, on this view, a progress, a triumphant awakening to the ever more productive new environment. The ecology of food-production had been quite different before the Younger Fill. A new lease of life was given to the old qualitative distinction between the Middle Ages and everything that preceded them, and the primitiveness of Antiquity apparently acquired a solid foundation in geomorphological fact. It will be apparent that the intellectual affiliations of this line of reasoning were less radical than the argument itself. Scholars working in the progressivist tradition that we discussed in Section 1 had attempted this gambit before, on much less plausible evidence. The soil has been invoked many times before as the key to the end of Antiquity:

> one single, major and strikingly variable productivity factor suffices to solve the problem. That factor – the exhaustion of Roman soil and the devastation of Roman provinces – sheds enough light for us to behold the dread outlines of its doom. (Simkhovitch (1921) *Towards the Understanding of Jesus and Two Additional Historical Studies: Rome's Fall Reconsidered, and Hay and History*)

Pausanias was right

> And the flash-floods uncover the traces [of human encampments] as though they were writings whose text has been renewed by pens.
>
> Labid ibn Rabi'ah, *Mu'allaqa*, 8, trans. Polk 1974

Vita-Finzi's original preference for a determining climatic change as the explanation of the Younger Fill has not won general support. The climatic history of the Mediterranean is a topic of great complexity and we return to it in Volume 2; but, in brief, we adhere to the widely held view that there has been in historical times no general change in climate of sufficient magnitude to be the cause of a pan-Mediterranean alluvial event. We would also draw attention to one other pan-Mediterranean variable in sedimentary process: sea-level. Fluctuations in the eustatic curve might well provide an explanation of patterns and synchronicities in the alluvial record. Disengaging a general climatic effect from a general sea-level event would, however, constitute a highly intricate research project. And it is not, in fact, principally disagreement with Vita-Finzi's environmental determinism which has motivated critics of *The Mediterranean Valleys.* It is chronology rather than causation that is at issue.

Chronological precision was central to Vita-Finzi's brilliant hypothesis. Subsequent work on the sedimentary record of Greece and Turkey has, however, made it clear that there were periods of intense alluviation at dates which cannot be fitted into the Vita-Finzi scheme. Attempts have been made to save his chronology; but, even for the Aegean world, it seems that the task is impossible. In the western Mediterranean, too, the findings are much more varied than can suit the simple theory of the Younger Fill. To most scholars in this field it has come to seem more likely that the sediments represent a complex sequence of on-and-off episodes of alluviation and its absence, rather than continuous phases, lasting for centuries, and beginning and ending everywhere more or less simultaneously.

The major study carried out in the southern Argolid during the early 1980s is a case in point. A general pattern emerged: a violent alluviation during the first half of the second millennium B.C. was followed by stability until the Hellenistic period; more alluviation then took place, to end with a quiet phase until the early modern age, when another distinct band of alluvium was deposited. This picture could hardly be more at variance with Vita-Finzi's chronology. Yet there was a further important finding: the southern Argolid evidence was notably inconsistent with the findings of other fieldwork nearby, and even varied considerably within the survey area selected (Pope and van Andel 1984, 285). The survey, in other words, beautifully chronicled the classically varied environmental history of the microregional Mediterranean landscape. Or take the case of the fringes of the Pomptine Marshes south of Rome. A detailed Dutch survey of the soils and the archaeological record found that there was indeed support for the argument that the deposition of colluvium had created new agrarian opportunities: but these opportunities opened up during the Roman Republican period, not at the end of Antiquity, and at a time when, as we have seen, the landscape was radically altered through an episode not of chaos but of agrarian colonization (Attema 1993, 131; cf. above, VII.2 and 6).

Another region where sedimentological research has revealed a more intricate and continuous picture than Vita-Finzi's scheme can countenance is that of Homer's Troy, for which the *Iliad*, already quoted on the subject, provides early evidence for the development of a complex lowland environment. The area was claimed as a classic example of the Younger Fill: a marshy marine inlet at the mouths of the Scamander and Simois, where relatively fast alluviation in the post-classical period made available substantial new tracts of fertile soils. The geomorphologists who carried out a more detailed survey, however, speak of a 'continuum of alluviation in the flood plain beginning at least by 9800 B.P.' (Rapp and Gifford 1982, 27–32). They found no trace of any 'relatively short and restricted period of deposition' which might correspond to the Younger Fill. A long arm of the sea which reached well inland past prehistoric Troy has progressively filled up until the coast of the Hellespont shows no indentation. From that point, the continued deposition of material by the Scamander and other streams has been made impossible by the violent currents of the Hellespont. That the *Iliad* can describe this interaction of marine and fluvial processes suggests a noteworthy sensitivity to alluviation in the Archaic Greek period.

There are other examples of the accumulation of sediment over long historical periods. In the hinterland of Carthage, the valley-bottom deposits show constant alluviation from the Punic period right through to late Antiquity. This alluviation is again linked with human agriculture, although also, perhaps, with the effect of increased pluviality (Bourgou and Oueslati 1987). The sediments of the Brádano and Cavone valleys in Lucania were – despite the proverbial desolation of the area in recent times (XI.2) – laid down mainly in periods of agricultural activity rather than abandonment, particularly the fifth to third centuries B.C. (Between the seventh century and the second A.D. the deposit was over 12 metres thick: Brückner 1986.) Later phases are medieval and of the nineteenth to twentieth centuries.

The classic case of Olympia has also been examined afresh. The huts of the first Slavic squatters in the abandoned sanctuary antedate the deposition of the thickest part of the 5-metre-deep Fill (Dufaure 1976). How long before that deposition were they built? An answer comes from one of the headwaters of the Alpheius, the Gortynios, where the great depth of alluvium buries a twelfth-century church as well as the classical ruins on which it stands (Bousquet et al. 1983, 21). The last datable remains at Olympia can be only a *terminus post quem* for the great alluviation, and do not help to date it accurately or measure its duration. The scholars responsible for these findings also offer the telling observation that it is not clear whether the conditions of the great alluviation were wholly different from those preceding them (Bousquet et al. 1983). The careful management of stream and river for the avoidance of floods or the maintenance of water-supply could have had the effect of completely inhibiting whatever factors were already promoting deposition during the classical period just as they would in the Middle Ages.

The archaeological dating of sediments remains highly controversial. As the epigraph to this section suggests, moreover, one sure consequence of alluviation has been a dramatic skewing of the older evidence away from areas where most of the traces of the early productive landscape have been deeply buried by subsequent deposits, especially when these combine with modern patterns of land-use (Ammerman 1985). Even more striking, especially at the key site of Olympia, is the suggestion that changes in human activity may be the principal variable in the local impact of alluvial process.

Further, the singularity of local alluvial conditions, valley by valley, is apparent – as it was already to the Greeks – in the effect of the deposition of sediments on the line of the coast. Deltaic deposition at the mouths of the Maeander and the Caicus in western Anatolia, which (as we have seen) have prograded at many other periods than that proposed by Vita-Finzi for the Younger Fill, does not fit the universal hypothesis at all (Eisma 1978, 67–81). In defence of that hypothesis, a rigid distinction has been drawn between the alluviational regime which produces coastal delta-advance and that which back-fills the lower courses of the valleys. Delta-formation is held to be characteristic of the 'normal Mediterranean' climatic type, prevailing today and throughout Antiquity, whereas the deposition of fill in the valleys is associated with a period of greater run-off from the hills, whether the result of increased total precipitation or of a different distribution during the year (Bintliff 1977b, 38–9; 1981, 13–18). But there is no foundation for such a distinction and the attempt to exclude all delta-formation from the debate is special pleading. The chronological difficulties with the Younger Fill are so great that it is preferable, while accepting delta-advance and valley-alluviation as geomorphologically distinct, to see them both as facets of the whole complex of depositionary phenomena – phenomena whose dynamics are regionally and chronologically very variable.

The intensity of similar processes in the reasonably well-documented early modern and more recent periods confirms this view, as well as further opening up the question of causation. It is very hard to deny an important role to human activity in explaining the very rapid recent growth of some deltas. That of the Ebro, for example, has prograded by as much as 10 metres p.a. in some phases since the sixteenth century. In this case the progradation reflects the effects of agricultural intensification in a semi-arid landscape of the interior (Dupré 1987). Human causes have long been invoked for valley-floor alluviation as well.

The 'arrival of the Younger Fill' was not a single event; it has no place in a 'stadial' narrative of grand phases and catastrophic divides. But accepting that does not eliminate alluvial disaster from Mediterranean history. This is what gives the debate that Vita-Finzi started a continuing importance. The sediments are there, and it is vital to enquire what effect their arrival had on the economy and society of the locality. Even if the fills cannot be synchronized, we should still attempt to assess the impact, in aggregate, of their deposition. The results of human occupation of them might not have been universal and synchronous, but they might still be cumulatively of enormous importance.

The other vital question concerns the causes of deposition. If, in the absence of major physical explanations, the fills are indeed largely the product of human activity, is it possible to deduce the nature of that activity – extending or abandoning hill-slope cultivation, destroying forest, terracing, irrigating or draining – from the fact and configuration of the sediments? If other evidence is wanting, can we 'read back' the nature of the activity from the marked environment, in an application of the new history imagined by George Eliot in the passage which we have used as an epigraph to this chapter? It is time to turn to the other end of the swing of the 'pendulum of culpability', and to consider the geomorphological contribution of the human inhabitants of the Mediterranean landscape.

4. SEDIMENTS AND HISTORY: THE PROBLEMS DISPLAYED

The disruption of flooding

The first aspect of the enquiry concerns the direct effect of floods. Under this heading, we shall need to include waterlogging in ill-drained bottomlands, extension of wetland margins, flash-flooding from torrential winter rain, and large or small perennial rivers bursting their banks. How intense was the historical impact of flooding, and the damage and disruption that it caused? The spectacular thicknesses of fill that attracted the attention of early archaeologists in sites such as Olympia, and that were later to give rise to the theory of Vita-Finzi, represent in historical terms, hundreds or thousands of individual floods (the normality of which we have already asserted in Section 2). Wherever there is a flood there is alluviation. When large volumes of fast-moving water scour a wadi in the semi-arid fringes of the Mediterranean that has been dry for a considerable period, the material distributed may be very coarse and rocky; more usually the flood deposits a fine silt. But even in areas with higher average precipitation, the periods of intense flooding which are identifiable by the deposition of a particular band of fill have been claimed to represent catastrophe for agricultural production – catastrophe of the sort invoked by the curse of the poem quoted at the head of this chapter.

There is no doubt that such deposits can, after particularly intense flooding, be of startling quantities. A single disastrous flood in the Jucar valley near Valencia in eastern Spain (Butzer et al. 1983), to which we shall return, deposited a layer of alluvium a metre thick over the middle course of the valley. Of one locality in the southern Argolid it is possible to state that a 4.8 metre thickness of alluvium could not have been deposited over a period longer than about fifty years (van Andel and Zangger 1990a, 152). On 14 May 1901 the Zakro area in Crete lost its woodland and its soil cover together in a single rainstorm (Rackham 1982, 195).

Events like this are responsible for much of the valley-bottom sediment, and they are the result of essentially local processes. They are obvious examples of the instability that we have seen to be a major factor in creating and maintaining the diversity of Mediterranean microregions. At the same time, they also illustrate how the Mediterranean microregion is a flexible complex of interrelationships between human and natural factors rather than a 'sealed' physical unit at the mercy of natural forces. In the Jucar valley it was possible for agriculture to resume quickly enough for the boundaries of properties and the network of communications to be restored. The settlement pattern, society and economy of the wider region could cope with single events even of this magnitude: the physical microregion in which the damage takes place is characterized also by the nature of its interdependence with other places (Chapters III, V, IX). It is on those patterns of interdependence that its inhabitants draw to redress the physical damage of disastrous floods, just as they draw on a wider environment to redress the natural deficits of agricultural production caused by the usual accidents of meteorology (Chapter VI).

The landscape may be completely transformed in the end, but the pace and intensity of human activity is of a different scale from that of the geomorphology of sedimentation, and in most circumstances seems very capable of adjusting to the vicissitudes of the environment. That adjustment can be seen in practice in some archaeological sites. The archaeological stratigraphy of a Roman villa site beside a stream called Fosso della Crescenza (in the part of South Etruria which we looked at briefly in III.2; see Map 3) is punctuated by layers of flood-alluvium which apparently, for the most part, did not seriously interrupt the occupation of the site until the end of Antiquity. It was only with abatement, and the abandonment of the site, that the alluvium could build up above it unchecked. The flooding was repeated and, no doubt, damaging. Yet, as in the Jucar valley, it could be accommodated; the activity of the settlement continued unbroken. And the more so because even floods large enough to have left conspicuous evidence in the record of the sediments have, as we have argued, always been characteristic of Mediterranean life. The investigators of the Fosso della Crescenza site wish to see the application to the Mediterranean of 'a complex system of stream dynamics in which the alternation between erosion and alluviation is a *normal* part of the functioning of a stream' (Judson 1983, 71, our italics). Both are normal and they alternate in very rapid succession (Neboit-Guilhot 1992–3). Other authorities have similarly remarked that 'not nearly enough information is available on such basic topics as stream flow, let alone sediment yield or sediment content' (Wagstaff 1981, 260), and Pope and van Andel remind us that 'semi-arid stream behaviour is complex and not yet understood well enough to permit predictive models' (1984, 290). The effects of run-off in Mediterranean environments are no more explicable in simple terms than the causes. A study of anthropogene erosion in Morocco demonstrates that most run-off affects only the channels, and does not do as much damage to slopes except in the most extreme circumstances (Laouina et al. 1993). Such a contradiction of the patterns found elsewhere, in similar conditions, is probably to be expected. Processes of this type have been modelled using mathematical catastrophe theory – despite its name, a far cry from the historicizing catastrophes against which we are inclined to argue. The result is a description – not an explanation – which shows how sudden, apparently capricious alteration in the interaction of the human and environmental variables and in their effects in the landscape is to be expected. In that case, the reading of the history of the human agency in a landscape from the evidence of alluvial changes becomes a desperately complex task, and the inconsistencies and conundrums of what has so far been observed in the field should cease to surprise.

Sedimentation and the origins of agriculture

The second aspect of the enquiry is much broader and involves a longer time-scale: does continuing alluviation over long periods produce important changes in the productive environment? Whatever the chronological problems, there is no doubting that the alluvial deposits which Vita-Finzi called the Younger Fill largely postdate the late Bronze Age. So, over 3,000 years – to put it no more precisely – has there been a significant qualitative change in the Mediterranean environment? Materials that once formed soils in the hills and mountains have vanished for ever; they are now present as fill which has changed the topography, drainage and pedology of the lowlands and significantly extended them towards the sea. So much is undisputed. Claims that might be made about the net significance of the change include: the exchange of wetlands for fertile well-watered lowlands where Mediterranean agriculture could boom; a radical alteration in the capacity of Mediterranean coastlands and river-mouths to provide navigable havens; a large-scale obliteration of large sections of the archaeological landscape; and the major effects of soil-erosion and landscape degradation in the interior. We have said enough to make it clear that we do not think that the evidence allows *any* of these changes the combination of geographical scale and suddenness which would require them to be seen as catastrophic. That is certainly the ultimate finding of the Southern Argolid survey, one of the most environmentally sophisticated archaeological projects yet to have been devised: 'human activity has aggravated the erosion of the Greek mountains, but the landscape of Classical times was not much richer in soil than it is now' (Jameson et al. 1994, 194). For all that, the bold claims made about the effects of sedimentation remain important and challenging, even if the changes in question happened in different places at widely different rates and moments.

One of the uses to which alluvial history has been put is in the general description of the Byzantine economy (Hendy 1985, 66–68). Literary and documentary evidence suggests that much of the Byzantine period was characterized by destructive alluviation. The dating of the material – as we have seen – did not endorse a single general episode of deposition (the Younger Fill) followed by stability. The seemingly inevitable conclusion was therefore that Byzantine agricultural history was characterized by the collocation of destructive erosion with an apparent chronic inability to control the plains and wetlands. This amounted to a major agrarian disadvantage for much of the Byzantine empire as compared to its neighbours to east and west and to its classical precursors. A great Mediterranean culture and a long period of history are thus categorized in terms of responses to the changing environment. The argument is strangely familiar. It compares one large tract of Mediterranean history with others, but in a disappointingly judgemental and superficial way: the medieval West, the Arab Levant and, in this case (unusually for this way of thinking), even Greece and Rome, 'succeeded' in some way that Byzantium did not. In VII.7 we met an identical reasoning: Byzantium was again compared unfavourably with the successes of the medieval West, but here the place of alluviation was taken by technological *blocage* (M. Kaplan 1992). This interchangeability of causes is revealing.

Improvement through sedimentation, like damage from flood, has its place in the understanding of the history of individual microregions, or of groups of them. But assessments of such improvement which depend on estimating the average productivity of *very* large numbers of microregions mistake the significance of the microregional ecology of production (III.3). The accidents of runoff and deposition are among the local variables in an unstable environment. Human production in the Mediterranean has to cope with many of these, and we have seen (VII.2) how drainage and irrigation are integrated into overall strategies for working the land under a range of social and political conditions. But since fertility and productivity are such relative concepts, and decision-making is so complex, patterns of intensification and abatement are very unlikely to be simply related to environmental givens. A change in the regime of property, or an episode of colonization or allotment, is likely to have more effect on productivity than the arrival of a thick layer of alluvium on, say, 60 per cent of a district's microregions. Further, we saw in Chapter VI how inadvisable it was to overemphasize arable agriculture on good soil. The repertoire of ways of surviving in the Mediterranean environment is very extensive. It is not clear, for instance, that the loss of wetter environments, often proclaimed as one of the advantages of alluviation, was so very positive. It is also quite unclear what effect the transformation of the bottomlands might have had on the crucial contribution so frequently made to Mediterranean production by animal husbandry. On this score, damage to mountain terrains may have had negative effects. Certainly we would view the reduction of connectivity caused by widespread silting of harbours as deleterious. But we would also insist that these negative consequences of widespread alluviation, like any positive ones, were deprived of significant aggregate effect by the fragmentation of the conditions of production.

Ironically, the gravest consequence of Vita-Finzian alluviation, as we noted in the previous section, has been its effect on the evidence for Mediterranean history. We saw when looking for the hydraulic landscapes of Antiquity in Chapter VII that archaeological survival rates are not good. One of the most important components in estimating the archaeological evidence for ancient landscapes is to allow for the destructive effect of alluviation. It is not too strong a claim that almost all Greek and Roman lowland landscapes are as deeply buried as Olympia, and the record of ordinary production is consequently unavailable. It is thus all the more unacceptable to espouse a unilinear progressive historiography that seeks an evidential base for the primitive character which it would like to predicate of the past; or to draw a sharp division between the useless, unredeemed environment of Antiquity and the endless possibilities of the Mediterranean after the 'second Vita-Finzi alluviation'. This approach also gravely understates the complexity and sophistication of the relationship between humans and their environment.

Not the least of the reasons why that symbiosis is so complex is that human action, as several of our earlier examples have strongly suggested, is a major ingredient in the shaping of the patterns of erosion and deposition. That point now merits further exploration. We have looked at the direct consequences of flood and the overall effects of alluviation. The third aspect of the application of sedimentology to the study of history is the explanation of alluvial phenomena by reference to sudden interventions in the environment by human societies.

Anthropogene process: where history and geomorphology meet

The recognition that human beings have been an effective agent of landscape change was already present in ancient Greek thought. But the role of 'anthropogene' processes has been stressed more and more emphatically in recent years – with the widespread popularization of an ideology of conservation since the late 1960s, as well as with a growing reluctance to see humanity as passive in its relations with nature. We, too, strongly prefer to attribute changes in Mediterranean environmental history within our period to human action, as must be clear by now. But there are dangers in doing so.

Deposits of valley-fill could, on this interpretation, relatively soon be seen as highly authoritative evidence for agrarian history. Indeed, some of the claims made for the effects of anthropogene process rival in grandeur the other global hypotheses which followed Vita-Finzi's discovery. Take for instance the view that a single devastating phase of soil erosion accompanied humanity's first impact on the Greek environment at the transition between the Neolithic and early Bronze Age (Zangger 1992c). Further such episodes have been identified by the Southern Argolid survey: namely two phases of stabilization of the regime of erosion linked respectively with terracing of slopes and damming of gullies, and with the return to natural vegetation of abandoned land; and two phases of destabilization, associated with careless clearing of such vegetation and neglect of the terraces and dams. At the very least, there is a strong temptation to connect sedimentary change with various major episodes in human history (van Andel and Zangger 1990a).

In detail, however, the correlations so far proposed between sediments and economic history have proved as hard to maintain as the claims for catastrophic alluvial events (thus also Butzer 1996, 144). The surveyors of the south Argolid themselves note how weak is the match between major phases of prosperity or decline in conventional history and the alluvial record (Pope and van Andel 1984, 302–3). The same difficulty is apparent elsewhere. We simply cannot share the optimism of the scientist who thinks that a single layer of sediment which contains archaeological material of the classical Greek and late Roman period can be said to correlate well with history (Brückner 1990)! It is worth reiterating the likelihood that sudden change in the whole system is a structural feature of complex environmental process which does not relate in simple ways to alterations in any one variable. Two particular cases will illustrate the delicacy required of the enquiry into anthropogene causation.

The first concerns the neighbourhood of Valencia. Because of the rain-shadow of the Iberian peninsula, south-eastern Spain is one of the driest of Mediterranean coastlands. Its semi-arid landscape is particularly vulnerable to human intervention – and to sudden geomorphological change in general. Here a detailed geoarchaeological study (Butzer et al. 1983) tells a useful cautionary tale. The river Jucar, much the most important perennial water-source (its headwaters lying beyond the semi-arid coastal strip) appears to have been, throughout the Dark Ages, a reasonably well-balanced and predictable watercourse. Its annual floods were a gentle inundation, a wetting of the land and a provision of a little alluvium; no great destruction, no vast layers of mud or gravel. On its lower flood-plain the Moorish predecessor of the city of Alzira flourished, and began to harness the waters of the river for seasonal irrigation in the style of nearby Valencia, as well as to extend agricultural activities into the wooded hills of the watershed. The regime of the river then changed dramatically, and the area has been devastated over the last seven hundred years by a very regular series of extremely destructive floods, so bad that the shape, economy and population of the city have all been profoundly affected.

It might appear that this was a straightforward instance of anthropogene process, a simple case of the evil consequences of human activity (deforestation, to which we return in Section 5) in a precarious environment, as well as an important datum for the history of the region's productive landscape before and after the Arab conquest (VII.2). Yet while the agricultural expansion of the eleventh and twelfth centuries was a factor in the change of regimes, and did indeed involve woodland clearance, the careful study of Karl Butzer and his team has shown that there were other factors that exposed the city to so much flooding: local climatic variations and coincidences, and, most importantly, a geomorphological change which caused a ponding-back of material in the valley above a tributary, thus decreasing the gradient of the river. The correct explanation of the environmental change therefore turns out to be intricate and highly specific. It is unique to the Jucar valley and the microregions which intersect it. It can make us sensitive to what may occur elsewhere, but is not an example of global trends. Human intervention is important, but acts in concert with many other factors. The same conclusion has been reached by sedimentologists elsewhere, and even in the case of a landscape which has had such intense and varied human occupation as the parts of South Etruria near Rome (Brown and Ellis 1995; III.2). The extreme form of anthropogene determinism appears implausible.

Our second example comes from the other end of the Mediterranean. The environmental history of the north-west Peloponnese has been considerably clarified: the ancient landscape has been studied thoroughly and excellent work has been done on the geomorphology. A series of rivers smaller than the Alpheius, which buried Olympia, but still of significant size by Peloponnesian standards, carry the substantial rainfall of this west-facing coast across a complex series of sedimentary deposits down to a highly mutable shore. Here medieval fortifications, one of which protected the settlement and port of Clarentza, famous for its medieval wine trade, rise on isolated masses of limestone, now promontories but once islands. The region is extremely prone to earthquakes. And these sudden events play a major part in changing the balance of the processes at work in a locality, in loosening unconsolidated material and making it vulnerable, in disturbing drainage patterns, or in lowering already low-lying areas so that lagoons may form. The earthquakes do not themselves transform the whole landscape (Section 2), but they act together with the longer-term evolutions of climate and human activity, punctuating the *longue durée* and playing an essential role in bringing about environmental change.

The detailed examination of the sediments and the archaeological topography reveals an extremely complicated history of rivers changing course, or being shortened and steepened by coast erosion; of local flooding; of sequences of alluviation and downcutting. Each small valley has its own story. As for the Younger Fill, Hellenistic sites are usually slightly buried whereas Roman ones are scarcely beneath the surface at all; and in the case of the former it is, as always, very hard to say at what moment after the *floruit* of the site (an approximate date based on the pot chronology at best) the burying took place. Sites of the prehistoric period in this part of the north-west Peloponnese are found on a higher, better-drained band of alluvium above the coastal plain; but it is clear that this may be because the chaotic alluviations and erosions lower down have removed or buried other sites without trace. It may also reflect the choice of a particular agricultural strategy, a turning away from the marshy, heavier soils towards the interior (prehistoric sites along the edges of the Narbonese wetlands provide a partial parallel for both possibilities). In the north-west Peloponnese, we may note in passing, there are Hellenistic and Roman sites even beyond the present shore line, reflecting post-classical erosion of a once more extensive littoral. It cannot be maintained, therefore, that there was no coastal plain below the older alluvium until the great deposition of the Younger Fill in late Roman times and afterwards.

Conclusion: continuities versus events

Historians, as much as environmental archaeologists, are prone to 'over-periodizing' – searching for phases of pivotal importance, usually catastrophic, with which to divide up the past. A merit of Mediterranean history as we propose it is that it so sturdily resists these errors. We must be prepared to see the events which we study on a smooth scale stretching into the distant past. There may be prominent events on the scale, but we should be reluctant to emphasize them too greatly. The erosion of the land, the expansion of human agriculture, the post-glacial rise in sea-level, the instability of the deep structures of Mediterranean geology – these are all very long-term phenomena. They interact cumulatively, and perhaps never in the historical past so quickly as now, although there have been many previous changes in the pace and complexity of interaction. Alluviation is a great constant of Mediterranean life. But this cluster of processes must be seen in perspective: we must pursue 'mutual-caused processes of co-evolution of people and their landscapes', and recognize the 'futility of one-sided deterministic approaches in which certain factors are singled out as the sole explanation of complex, closely interwoven physical, biological and cultural processes' (Naveh 1990, 45 and 49). In particular, we should be alert to interpretations of the environment which present the constraints on human activity in too simple terms. The discussions of Chapter VII on the nature of intensification and the relationship between human productive endeavour and population showed that the connection between the condition and extent of the productive landscape of a particular place and time on the one hand, and population-dynamics on the other, is not as simple as the heirs of Vita-Finzi have sometimes maintained (Brown and Ellis 1995, 47–9). This will become more apparent as we move on to the question of the effect of human activity on natural vegetation.

The interest of the subject lies in contrasting the local fluctuations with the overall trend in erosion, weathering and alluviation (whether anthropogene or not). It lies, in other (Braudellian) words, in the contrast of *événements* with the *longue durée*; this is a historical matter in the first place, and it is not surprising that the parallel between earth science and history has been most subtly drawn by French geographers, their discipline so closely linked to historiography:

> Like all geographical and geological systems [environmental change through history] is a matter of complicated interrelationships: for each constituent part acts, at its own pace, as much as part of the long term (the process might be called mobility in this case) as it does of the short term (when we might speak rather of instability, a matter of sharp divisions, of events) . . . history conveys the same principles of mobility and instability. Is the basic underlying debate of this discipline not the question of the primacy of continuity or dividing-points (which can be seen either as accidental 'events' or as crises which give rhythm to the *longue durée*)? (Bousquet et al. 1983, 3–4)

We firmly believe that anthropogene process has transformed the Mediterranean landscape. But it must be recognized that 'a process' is precisely what it is. It can be discontinuous, although it is normal, persistent and cumulative, operating in numerous different ways at different times in different places. Indeed, there is virtually no Mediterranean landscape that has not been affected, so that the individual messages can be blurred by the universality of the phenomenon. But, regrettably, the 'chemistry' of human reaction to the diversity of an unstable landscape is too complex for the products of anthropogene process to contain an intelligible record of human activity.

The details of the interaction between human agency, the ecology of domesticated animals, and various associations of plants also require very intricate modelling, and are likewise very variable – as we should by now expect – from one locality to another (Thornes 1987). We shall see in the remainder of this chapter how this variability makes the historiography of vegetation-cover in the Mediterranean also an extremely delicate task. The wider objective of Section 5 will be to show how the human ingredient in the complex relationship that we have begun to outline is as flexible and varied as the mutable microregions on which it so multifariously impinges. Choices about production – the theme of Chapter VI – and the deliberate employment of technology to manipulate the conditions of production – the theme of Chapter VII – can be seen both to promote and to respond to the fluidity of the environment. The complex interaction of explanatory themes and the convolution of the relationships involved in the history of each microregion constitutes a far more distinctive Mediterranean-ness than do either the relations of production or the physical parameters considered separately.

5. Ecology in an Unstable Environment: The History of Vegetation

In 1797, the last year of Venetian rule in the Ionian islands, the entire forest cover of the central mountains of the island of Cephalonia was destroyed in a terrifying conflagration which could be seen as far away as Zante. The climatic regime of the island became palpably less equable (Riemann 1879, 4). Strange stories circulated a generation later: the bones of huge serpents had been found on the charred hillside; opportunistically, the country folk had sowed barley on the new land, and reaped a sixtyfold return, followed by another twentyfold on the self-sown relics of that first harvest. By doing so, they created the suspicion that the fire might not have been a natural occurrence (Goodisson 1822, 148–9). Whether naturally occurring (as, most plausibly, here) or abetted by human action, fire has had as important a role in the formation of the unstable and fragmented Mediterranean landscape as have the aspects of weather and geology that we have discussed up to now.

Forest-fire is already a terrifying fact of life in Homer. Such fires can be very widespread. In 809 outbreaks affecting 10 or more ha each, between 1961 and 1970, fires destroyed a quarter of all the forest in three *départements* of Provence (Gödde 1976). In a striking testimony to the fragmentation of holdings – justifiable by reference to this risk as well as to meteorological ones – a fire in the peninsula of Methana in 1985 burned some 50 ha, with the result that 104 families from six villages lost property. The devastation that fire brings to the Mediterranean every summer is all too familiar, with arson implicated in many cases. As a result, plant-scientists and ecologists have come to understand much better the evolving ecology of vegetation in semi-arid Mediterranean landscapes.

Mediterranean scrubland does recover from fire – in about thirty-five years, for instance, in the *tomillares* of eastern Spain (Thornes 1987, 49–50). But the frequency of burnings is sometimes greater than that, and there is no doubt that it has a disastrous effect on soil-retention. We may add that fire is much less bound to microregions than are the effects of weather or hydrology: it ranges across scrublands and woods in a highly capricious way. As on Methana, the more fragmentation of the productive landscape there is, and the more that cultivated land and scrubby grazing-land or managed wood interpenetrate, the more damaging the fire. Only quite specialized cultivations, across open terrain, are relatively immune. Higher-status enterprises – monocultures, allotted land-scapes, estates aiming at redistribution on a substantial scale – may have escaped fire-damage the most often, which could account for the relative lack of anecdotal data on destructive conflagration.

We want, however, to draw attention to a wider context and more positive role for fire in the history of the Mediterranean landscape: the promotion of genetic diversity among plant species. 'Mosaic structure is one of the main characteristics of Mediterranean vegetation and results in a rich niche segregation and a high biotic diversity. Fire is of major importance in determining this mosaic' (Pignatti 1983, 154). Across the globe the genetic diversity of plant species is not uniform. Some areas form centres of inter- and intra-specific diversity, sometimes known after their discoverer as Vavilov centres. These are characterized by 'genetically variable populations that exhibit different responses to pests, diseases and changes in environmental conditions' (Kloppenburg 1988: 46–9; Hawkes 1983, 52–60). The Mediterranean is a Vavilov centre *par excellence*. In a striking phrase, an ecologist has called it an 'evolutionary archipelago', fragmented into islands by the broken topography that derives ultimately from structural instability, characterized by a heterogeneity that applies to time and to human perception as well as to the landscape (Di Castri et al. 1981, 26–7). Points of contact will be immediately apparent between this genetic diversity and the picture that we have sketched of disparate microregions in differing degrees of intercommunication, the archipelagos of the landscape of connectivity which we introduced in Chapter V. The characteristic feature of the gene centre is that it can be identified by the similarities there within homologous series of different species – which recalls our contestation that patterns of human and physical landscape in the Mediterranean are constituted by the 'differences which resemble each other'.

There is little doubt that the ecological history of the human presence in the Mediterranean – humanity's co-evolution with the other species in the vicinity – is one of the principal elements promoting such genetic diversity.

> Throughout the long history of agro-pastoral utilization, the semi-natural and pastoral ecotopes of open forests, shrublands, woodlands and grasslands, together with the agricultural ecotopes of terraces, patch- and hand-cultivated rock poly-cultures have created a mosaic of landscapes. The transfer of fertility, by way of grazing animals, and of seeds, by way of grazing, wild herbivores, and insects, created ideal conditions for introgression and spontaneous hybridizations of wild and cultivated plants and biotypes. (Naveh and Vernet 1991, 23)

Habitual risk-avoidance in an unreliable natural setting – that central feature of Mediterranean production which we have explored in Chapter III and, at much greater length, in Chapter VI – has led to minute differentiation of response to each microecology in each part of each season, and in so doing has reinforced the ecological diversity. The effect is pithily stated by an author of the fifth century B.C.: 'not every piece of land suffers disease at the same time' ([Xenophon] *Constitution of the Athenians*, 2.6). As if by way of illustration, in the 1950s all the almond trees of Cretan Neapolis suddenly died, while almonds elsewhere were untouched (Kolodny 1974, 145). Modern field work does indeed show that the acuteness of insect infestation may vary markedly from field to field (Halstead and Jones 1989, on Karpathos in the southern Aegean).

As with flood and alluviation, changes to the biotope, although locally violent, take their place as ingredients in the elaboration over time of an inordinately complex ecological system (Trabaud 1991; Trabaud and Lepart 1981), a system in which human activity plays an intricate and integral part. Enquiry into it must therefore take the form of an analysis of the nature of particular ecological relationships. Pan-Mediterranean visions of catastrophe must be regarded with the greatest caution: the crisis of a mountainside in Cyprus can only with an unrealistic effort of the imagination be said to affect an entity – such as 'the Mediterranean forest' – which also includes the woods of Catalonia. After many years in which it has been orthodox to postulate very considerable changes in Mediterranean vegetation history over the last three millennia, there is now an increasingly powerful case for very substantial overall stability (Rackham and Moody 1997, 123–39).

As we turn to look at some of the more important specific instances in Mediterranean history of the effect of human activity on vegetation, and, therefore, at forests in particular, the principal difficulty which we face is the oversimplification also made orthodox by some earlier accounts. 'While floristic variety is infinite there is only a limited number of ways in which ecosystems can be treated or maltreated, and a limited number of socio-economic circumstances' (Thirgood 1981, 5). Nothing could be further from the ecological – and therefore the historical – truth.

Propounding the catastrophe

The Mediterranean landscape itself – broken in relief, variable in soil and drainage, made unstable by the accidents of geology – strengthens the effects of the unpredictable meteorology on plant communities, as well, of course, as on human production. While this has obviously promoted the diversity of plant-species, it has also, in the process, ensured that seasonal or annual dearth of rain, freak frosts, unseasonable scorching, an unusual degree of waterlogging, storm, snow and drought modify local margins of survival. Vegetation in the Mediterranean world is therefore very liable to change and degradation, which is easily visible, and is made more intense by human activity: clearing the existing vegetation to use it for fuel or building, or to replace it in part or whole with deliberately selected species. The vulnerability of the most conspicuous vegetation association, forests, has attracted particular attention.

There are many localities which are today barren, but which are described by the writers of the past as having been lushly vegetated. The all-too-obvious vulnerability of existing forest in the Mediterranean – 'une forêt fragile' (Higounet 1966) – has long made it attractive to postulate a formerly extensive forest-cover which human carelessness has turned into wilderness: into the vast tracts of impenetrable thorny aromatic scrub or macchia so typical of the modern Mediterranean. Scrublands strike the visitor from the north as alien and inhospitable, whether they are the evergreen sclerophyllous associations of the somewhat more humid hills that are usually known as *maquis*, or the thorny species of the really arid environments (commonly known as *garrigues*), which dry out to save transpiration in the summer months (Margaris 1981). Apart from producing the *macchia*, the catastrophic degradation of forest is said to have caused a critical shortage of the products of the older vegetation in rapidly degrading forests. It is also thought to have promoted the partial or total denudation of the landscape through assisting the soil erosion which we have already encountered. Since most of the destruction is usually dated within the last three thousand years, it is likely to be of the greatest interest to the Mediterranean historian (as distinct from the prehistorian) with an eye on the long-term.

Very serious charges have been levelled: 'environmental ruin was the price paid for the glory that was [classical] Greece' (Thirgood 1981, 1–2). Rash over-grazing which destroyed woodland, combined with growing demand for timber, has been seen as the origin of a stress which brought along the eventual political and economic eclipse of the Muslim states of the Levant (M. Lombard 1959). A similar timber crisis is supposed to have hastened the relative decline of the Mediterranean and rise of the Atlantic world (Braudel 1972a, 141–4). Mean-while, changes in vegetation-cover have been included in various versions of the theories of alluvial catastrophe which we considered in the previous section.

The most influential classical source for deforestation is a passage from Plato's dialogue *Critias*, written in the fourth century B.C.:

> Many great deluges have taken place during the [last] nine thousand years; [in Attica] and during all this time . . . there has never been any considerable accumula-tion of the soil coming down from the mountains, *as in other places*, but the earth has fallen away all round and sunk out of sight. The consequence is that in comparison with what there then was, there remain only the bones of the wasted body, as they may be called, as in the case of the small islands . . . But in the primitive state of the country, its mountains were high hills covered with soil, and the 'plains . . . of Phelleus' [possibly scrub or macchia] were full of rich earth, and there was abundance of wood in the mountains. (111 a–c, trans. Jowett 1871, slightly adapted; our italics)

This interesting account has been quoted and requoted, with successive modi-fications which have taken it ever further from the sense of the Greek, let alone the context in which the passage occurs (Rackham 1982, 178–9). Plato is con-structing what has been called an 'imaginary prehistoric geography'. This is from one of the places in which he also discourses at length about the ideal city of Atlantis. Both passages are designed to illustrate philosophical arguments, pieces of elegant and highly intelligent invention. Like Thucydides in his account of Greek prehistory, Plato is fashioning the past in accordance with his understand-ing of the present. We should not assume that these writers knew anything about such distant happenings, even if we can independently establish that their accounts are plausible, or even, by coincidence, true. The nine thousand years of deluges in the passage above are a clear sign of the mythographical schematism of Plato's approach; but that sentence is often omitted from modern versions of the passage.

In fact it is not now considered likely that the hard limestone mountains of which he was writing have ever had a soil cover during the millennia since the last glaciation. In a later dialogue Plato is quite happy to say of prehistoric Athens that it was short of timber even in the distant past; and the present passage cannot be pressed as evidence of serious deforestation by the fourth century. (Athens still possessed forest resources at much later dates, even if they were not adequate to its needs: Fowden 1988.) The phrase italicized in the above quotation rather indicates that, elsewhere in Greece, soil erosion was absent and forest throve, and that by contrast some of the Aegean islands were already as bare as they are today.

This cautionary case shows excellently how difficult to use are the scattered classical sources for phenomena such as deforestation. Already rhetorical in flavour, they should not be rendered more so in paraphrase. 'Strabo described Mount Abyla, near Ceuta as clothed with "a mantle of great trees"; today only a few relict Aleppo pines remain' (Thirgood 1981, 41). Strabo (*Geography*, 17.3.6) actually says something less emotive: he refers to 'a mountain called Abile, rich in game, with large trees'. The misrepresentation apart, there is the question of why it should be thought likely that, if the Romans destroyed a forest, it could not ever have grown again – or of why, if a forest is still in existence today, it must be a survivor, against all the odds, of the primeval vegetation. In the same vein, the suggestion is often made that the trees and shrubs of holy places and springs are relicts, preserved by sanctity, of what once surrounded them. On the contrary, in X.2, we shall attempt to suggest that the sacred woods of the Mediterranean are religious articulations of the perceived microenvironment, reflecting the characteristic Mediterranean diversity and plurality of landscape modification. They may be ancient relicts, but there is no reason to think that their simple presence entails that. More extensive collection of the evidence for forest history in the post-classical Mediterranean would very likely help to discourage the sometimes portentous conclusions that have been drawn from the ancient texts.

Why deforest?

To some extent, the case for catastrophic deforestation rests on the assumption that the forest was perceived as a hostile and useless environment. Although the schematic characterizations of literature do sometimes portray woodland in this way, we were able to argue in VI.4 that attitudes to woodland have been much more positive and that it has very often constituted a vital part of the managed environment. Nor is this an eccentric view (see especially Wickham 1990). Failure to appreciate the general importance, in the Mediterranean past, of exploiting the full diversity of environments has promoted a lack of sympathy with woodland. Woodland production has therefore been readily implicated in the explanation of degradation. Woodlands offer food directly, by routes ranging from apiculture to hunting. Its different forms can be used as a primary resource for timber, brushwood, charcoal and so on. It can be managed in many ways, from charcoal-burning to 'modern'-type silviculture. But it can also be used indirectly, again being improved or managed in many different ways, as a reserve of wild food or as a pasture for several different types of domesticated animal, especially pig and goat. These indirect uses increase the potential of the forest without inevitably destroying it: 'un défrichement n'est pas un déboisement' (Chabal 1997, 77).

Some woodlands are so extensive as to constitute whole microregions – some are, indeed, even larger than that. Their importance, however, is first as a resource which impinges on thousands of other microregions, contributing to the distinctive repertoire of production opportunities in each of these; contributing also not just a 'take-it-or-leave-it' bonus, but a set of possibilities of varying intensity of exploitation, capable of modulation according to demand in a quite complex way (VII.4). If the woodland is being managed effectively, it will form a fully integrated part of the productive environment. What looks like a survival of primitive woodland systems is likely to be the product not of ecological but of social marginality (Lewthwaite 1982).

If the forest is seen in this light, the threat posed to it by once-and-for-all clearance for arable cultivation perhaps seems less pervasive. There are, moreover, many environments in which soil, aspect, relief or accessibility reduce the usefulness of reclaimed areas. Reclamation may also be local and temporary. Yet the pressure to disrupt the symbiotic management of the forest more permanently does exist, and it brings us back to the questions of intensification and agricultural change which we faced in the last chapter, and which now enable us to see the problems which Mediterranean woodlands have faced from a more realistic perspective than that provided from the lurid imaginations of catastrophe proponents. The history which depicts human activity as restrained by the remorseless grip of superhuman process is not innocent: it is often interested in reducing the potential contribution of the truly anthropogene causes – the social and political ones.

Over-intensification and its contexts

The *Goats*, a comedy by Eupolis, presents a chorus of these creatures which boasts of the amazing variety of their diet. Twenty-two species of maquis and woodland are listed, confirming the usefulness for husbandry of environments which have no agricultural potential (VI.7). There is no hint of ecological pressure: the full use of the Attic environment is being neutrally, if humorously, portrayed. Yet over-grazing by goats has been most often claimed as the cause of the degradation of forest to scrubland, and of scrubland to barren hillside capable of supporting only a few thorny xerophytes. 'Wherever man, or his animals, can gain access the result is . . . degraded forest, worn-out scrub, retrogressive pasture, eroded land and bare rock' (Thirgood 1981, 7). Now this can be denied even for the drier parts of mainland Greece: 'in Boeotia I can find no evidence to suggest that gariga and steppe [the barrenest landscape] are derived from macchia' (Rackham 1983, 304; cf. Quézel 1981). Soil moisture, a factor which varies extremely from place to place, is the secret; and in very large areas of the Mediterranean the conditions are at least no worse than they are on the hills of Boeotia. We should not doubt that over-grazing is a real possibility, or that it has sometimes brought about environmental damage. The notion that grazing has been widely and severely destructive of the environment has, however, been sustained by the widespread idea that animals somehow 'go' with 'bad' places (VI.7). The normality of symbiotic husbandry seems incredible if goats are associated with deforestation, grazing with soil erosion. In fact, most ecologies have been flexible enough to accommodate even quite developed animal husbandry. And the damage that it may cause is local and temporary, except in infrequent – and mainly relatively modern – examples.

What produces such moments of overload as there have been? Ecological accounts can be given. Thus, on one view, the exploitation of the highly vulnerable mountain margins of the Mediterranean world was restricted to the areas above the reach of malaria but below the timberline, and to the age after the introduction of maize and before the effects of erosion became as palpable as they are today (J. R. McNeill 1992, 352). The evidence of Mediterranean sediments tells a different story about the antiquity of such exploitation, and one that makes it more plausible to assign the exploitation to opportunistic intensi-fication than to a phase of settlement. While such broad ecological factors have undoubtedly been relevant, we consider this type of intensification a more local and occasional phenomenon, and ascribe it to causes other than biological necessity. The message of the physical evidence appears to be that local pressures on fragile environments have been an immemorial feature of Mediterranean life rather than a feature of well-defined phases. They are immemorial, not because of human nutritional prerequisites or demographic behaviour, but thanks to the constant intrusion on productive communities of extraneous pressures towards the redeployment of labour and environmental resources (VII.4). Thus, where forests have been destroyed by the grazing of animals, it has often occurred when pastoral strategies have crossed the crucial upper limit of scale and become the unwieldy and uncontrollable exploitation of the landscape by tens of thou-sands of animals. The harm which such investment pastoralism can inflict on both the economy and the environment is analogous to that of other enterprises at the top end of the scale of intervention, ambition and greed. It should not be laid at the door of the forms of pastoralism that have been far more common in Mediterranean history (III.6).

A similar point can be made with regard to the most acute of the attested woodland crises. It is exemplary of the usefulness of forest landscapes that these crises concern intensified extraction of woodland resources rather than the reclamation of woodland for cultivation. A classic instance is the colonial-style investment in sugar-cane in the eastern Mediterranean during the Middle Ages (VII.3). The degree of specialization here was marked, although it only differed in its novelty and its visibility from many of its precursors among intensification monocultures in the Mediterranean tradition. One of its unusual requirements, however, was a large supply of wood as fuel for refining, which was relatively centralized and highly equipped because of the colonial nature of the enterprise. The demands of this intrusive and exploitative venture certainly did cause local environmental damage.

Opportunities for monocultural specialization in Mediterranean landscapes find a parallel in the accidentally distributed mineral resources which so privilege the microregions in which they are found (a theme to which we return in the next chapter). Both mining (if underground) and the metallurgical process require considerable quantities of wood. One of the standard allusions in a classical author to the destruction of forest refers to the demands of mining copper on Cyprus (Strabo, *Geography*, 14.6.5). It is noteworthy that Strabo quotes the scientific writer Eratosthenes as having said that the plains of Cyprus were 'mad with forest' until systematically tamed by organized felling for metallurgy: the passage, often assumed to be about environmental damage, actually expresses the view that the demands of the mines helped *improve* the landscape. It has been calculated that, during their century of prominence after c. A.D. 50, the enormous Roman silver workings of Rio Tinto in south-west Spain would have required for smelting the felling of two acres of woodland daily (G. D. B. Jones 1980, 161). Charcoal, which is preferred or required for many metallurgical operations, is a greedy user of wood: ten kilograms of wood may yield one of charcoal, which burns to provide the calorific content of only 1.67 kilograms of wood. But its crucial feature, which will be highly relevant to our argument in IX.2, is that it is therefore considerably lighter and easier to transport and store than wood (as well as burning with a gentler heat: Bechmann 1990, 151–4). The needs of metallurgy can be met up to a point by silviculture. Yet they have been more occasional in their impact for much of our period than analogy with recent times might suggest. If mining was – inevitably – very local, smelting could be more flexible (as we shall, once again, see in more detail in IX.2). Metal production was often discontinuous. Altogether, this call on woodland resources does resemble the capricious intensifications of agricultural production. Its effects, sometimes very damaging, never came near to deserving the description 'catastrophic'.

We extend this line of reasoning to other uses of timber. If metallurgy resembled sugar-boiling in the intensity of its local effects on fuel-resources, it also resembled it in being for most places and in most of our period an opportunistic and epiphenomenal exploitation of resources. *A fortiori*, the requirements of making kiln-fired brick, pottery or glass can be regarded similarly. At Sallèles d'Aude, in Languedoc, a Roman complex of pottery kilns represents an unusually developed and specialized intensification of the use of a resource, ceramic-quality clay, which was very widespread in the Mediterranean (Vernet 1997, 180–8). The palaeobotanical evidence suggests that the kilns consumed different species of wood as each was available: first the ash and elm of the coastal plain, then oak from the lower hills, then ilex from further away and higher up. There is, we must concede, little sign here of forest-management – rather the progressive using-up of resources over some two hundred years. But this unusually long-lived and demanding enterprise survived and flourished, engaging, according to changing circumstances, with a range of different landscapes for its provision.

Sallèles, in the rural territory of Roman Narbonne, was not a major nucleated settlement. But the advances in the retrieval and analysis of carbonized botanical remains which have made its impact on the environment so apparent have also shed light on the ways in which centres of denser population, nodes in the networks of connectivity, opportunistically related to an environment which was changing as a result of these very demands. Excavations at the Baños del Almirante site in Valencia, for instance, show that the new Roman city of the Republican period first exploited the copious stands of evergreen oak (*Quercus ilex*) in the territory, but came increasingly to depend on the scrubby woods of Aleppo pine (*Pinus halepensis*) and the other bushes of the *matorral* (Vernet 1997, 173–80). At the same time, with the formation in this region of that hydraulic landscape which we have already briefly studied (VII.2), species from the banks of the watercourses, poplar or *Harundo donax*, the Giant Reed, became more important. The wood of cultivated species, olive, fig and carob, was also increasingly used for fuel.

The specialized demands for woodland products of nucleated centres could thus be met, as their nutritional needs were, through a complex net of fluctuating engagements with neighbouring and more distant microregions – the dispersed hinterlands of our discussion in IV.8. Take the example of fuel for bathhouses: woodlands large enough to produce sufficient fuel from dead wood, even at some distance from the recipient, might be set aside by a benefactor for provision. But it was more common to make do, as the Valencian evidence seems to indicate, with the detritus of non-woodland production. Such is the clear implication of Plutarch's remark (*Topics for Discussion at the Dinner-Party*, 3.658 d–e) that competent civic supervisors permit bathhouse contractors to burn neither olive wood (which damages the baths) nor the arable weed-species darnel (which produces poisonous fumes).

The burden of supplying production could thus be relatively widely spread. Even allowing for a much greater presence of forest resources, whether old or of recent regrowth, in most localities in most parts of our period, the demands for fuel of an unevenly distributed and mobile population undoubtedly generated a fuel trade. Because of the saving in bulk, charcoal was of high importance for this (Bechmann 1990, 151–4). There is some evidence that the adminstrators of ancient cities felt a concern to stock-pile wood in the same spirit that they garnered staple foodstuffs (IV.6): an architectural treatise comments on the functioning of the porticoes behind as stores for wood (Vitruvius, *On Architecture*, 5.9.8). Apart from the simple needs of consumption, wood was a commodity vital for the maintenance of the redistribution which was the *raison d'être* of so many Mediterranean cities: its availability for barrel-making was an essential factor in the geography of the wine trade of the later Middle Ages (Zug Tucci 1978).

Timber for construction – above all of buildings and ships – was the last of the special demands made on the forests by the Mediterranean economy during our period. That these special demands could not, on occasion, be met has sometimes been taken as an indicator of crisis in the forests. The large tall-growing forest trees needed for roof- and ship-timbers were, however, a specialized resource from deep within the forest ecology. The demand for them was quite clearly an unusual instance of a very narrowly focused intensification of production. Timber of this size is, to all intents and purposes, an unrenewable resource; yet it is possible to remove it completely from a forest without affecting the rest of the forest ecology at all. Although shortages of large timber are quite well attested both in Antiquity and throughout the Middle Ages, such crises tell us nothing about the wider history of vegetation.

In the case of the largest timbers, it is obvious that accessibility is a key issue. But that – as should now be clear – is true also of more mundane forest-resources. As with all opportunistic exploitation, the changing webs of communications, which suddenly render a microregion nodal or which return it to relative isolation, have a major part to play. An extreme instance is the building of railways in the forested parts of the Mediterranean peninsulas during the nineteenth century: the projects provided both a huge demand for timber – to be used as sleepers – and the means by which further extractions of timber could much more easily be made. It is at this moment that a real qualitative change in the forest history of the Mediterranean may be seen (Meiggs 1982, 386–97).

The complexity of the networks of connectivity is such that we can safely disregard grand and simple statements about the scarcity of timber, such as the famous case of the alleged deficiency, in this respect, of medieval Islam. An influential account claimed that an inevitable shortage of wood in the Islamic world, deriving partly from natural scarcity, but partly also the result of nomadism and unchecked urban exploitation, led to the eventual decline of the Islamic states in the seventeenth and eighteenth centuries by comparison with the well-wooded Christian world (Lombard 1959). This interpretation fails because it takes an implausibly simple view of forest exploitation, and relies on an insufficiently differentiated picture of the landscape of half the Mediterranean. The sea-captains of different origins who serviced the ports of the Nile delta were already importing substantial and varied cargoes of timber in the early fifth century B.C., according to the Elephantine Palimpsest (Porten and Yardeni 1993).

The historiography of deforestation

Lombard's argument about Islamic timber-supplies evokes the familiar and discredited idea of an Islamic world crippled by the environmental effects of the legacy of nomadism, an idea which we have already examined (III.6). With regard to the eastern Mediterranean, the accusation of causing environmental catastrophe has been levelled at whole cultures with more direct political purpose than is usually the case when the culprits are Greek or Roman. A further example, as presented by Walter Lowdermilk in the late 1930s, is the allegation that Arab rule, and the agriculture practised under it, had caused environmental disaster in Palestine (Selwyn 1995).

The litany of complaints about historiography of this kind will by now be familiar: misuse of anecdotal evidence, unconsidered analogy from modern times to the past, Romanticism, progressivist and evolutionist *parti-pris*, cultural prejudice in favour of agriculture, failure to see the weakness of interregional generalization in the Mediterranean, and above all an assumption of human helplessness in the face of environmental determinism which obscures the central fact that poverty and destitution in Mediterranean environments have more often resulted from human action than from natural process (VII.5, 6).

The near-complete triumph of the catastrophic theory of deforestation in Mediterranean historiography is to be attributed in large measure to the attitudes of the last century. The habit of repeating a few key texts from classical authors is certainly a vestige of that age, when travellers and scholars were keen to shift to historical geography, with the sense of inevitability that it could help create, the blame for the horrors which their own age had actually caused. The tendency was reinforced by the impressively bleak aspect of the hard limestone mountains of the Mediterranean, such as the great Velebit chain in north Dalmatia or the terribly bare hills of Myconos – or of Attica. It was hard to believe that the wildernesses of malarial Latium or the stony slopes of the Greek mountains could have been the setting for the acme of classical culture. A decline since that period had to be postulated, and reasons for the decline sought.

The impact of the twentieth century on the environment must also be added to the reckoning. Travellers have been impressed by the rapid changes visible as the result of logging or the indiscriminate grazing which accompanied the abrupt upswing of the population, and appalled by the devastation brought about in our own age. It is now clearer than ever that, whatever horrors the nineteenth century perpetrated, the damage that we have become able to inflict on the environment is of a wholly different order from the worst efforts of the past (XI.1). The role of Mediterranean history can no longer be to serve as a rogues' gallery of instances of precocious destructiveness (any more than to present accolades to past cultures for ecological or technological sophistication). Rather it is to explore and explain the often sustainable symbioses between humanity and the environment, whether more or less systematically managed. And this is the tendency which may be discerned among the more recent expert opinion on the subject, which is inclined to be strongly critical of the idea of catastrophe through deforestation (Rackham and Moody 1997, 128–31).

Vegetation in Mediterranean history: a balance-sheet

First proposition: even without human action, but still more because of its impact over many millennia, the biology of the Mediterranean has evinced a singularly diverse mosaic. Consequence: generalizations linking Provence and Lebanon, the Aures and the Pindus must concern the 'global' character of the mosaic and not the individual pieces, and this is the reference of terms like 'the Mediterranean forest'.

Second proposition: human interaction with the vegetation – and fauna – of a microregion has often constituted an ecologically balanced relationship, stable and sustainable. Although very varied and sometimes subject to grave crisis, the history of vegetation-cover changes across a qualitative spectrum too wide for it to be clear what a catastrophe – implying as the word does that two of the possible states on that spectrum are much more significant than the others – might really be. Consequence: the instability of vegetation ecology belongs among the many ways in which the history of each small region and locality makes the landscape; it is a constant of Mediterranean life, but a local one. Soil-erosion, forest-fire, over-felling, regeneration, browsing by goats, thinning out of certain types of tree, the introduction of new species and new associations – all these have happened repeatedly, at different rates, in most subregions or microenvironments. Changes occurring *without* human help have had very violent effects on vegetation too.

Third proposition: the symbiosis does produce overall change over time, but it is not necessarily in any sense 'bad'. It is possible to take a positive view of managing the forest, as we did in VI.4.

Fourth proposition: the late nineteenth and twentieth centuries have witnessed a quantitatively different interaction between human communities and the landscape. Previously, the fragmentation of the Mediterranean was so assured as to make very unlikely the simultaneity of major environmental damage across groups of microregions. The remoter forests far from the reach of connectivity still represented a frontier which was not broken until the development of railways, which simultaneously demanded timber and made it more accessible. Huge modern increases in population have further contributed in multiple ways to the degradation of the environment especially where it is most vulnerable. Most of the damage which can be attributed to the goat, for instance, has occurred within this recent period. Consequence: it has been easy to retroject our own difficulties onto the past, either because that exculpates us, or because we cannot abide the idea that anything in history could have got worse rather than better.

6. CONCLUSION: AN ENVIRONMENTAL HISTORY WITHOUT CATASTROPHE

The view that humans have had almost entirely negative impacts on nature – widespread among environmental historians, historical geographers, ecologists and environmentalists – paradoxically perpetuates the old Western stereotypes of humanity as active, dominating, and separate from a nature that is passive and static. A view more in tune with late twentieth-century empirical data and current ecological theory would emphasize that relationships between humans and nature are interactive and embedded within a kaleidoscopic environment in which little or nothing is permanent (Blumler 1995; II.5).

For us, the predisposition to a gradual model for historical change in the Mediterranean derives from the theory of the microregions that we outlined in Part Two. If we are right to stress the crucial and distinctive significance in Mediterranean history of local variability – the 'differences which resemble each other' – then we should expect quick change and slow mutation to coexist, but to be alike limited in their geographical extent. Rapid and radical transformations of whole regions, on the other hand, will be rare or non-existent. A revolution or a catastrophe would need to affect the medium of connectivity, the networks that constitute Mediterranean identity through providing the matrix for micro-regional interaction; and the complexity of such networks entails that the sud-denness of change is likely to be greatly dulled. However terrible and sudden the accidents that may befall each locality, the complexity of the processes of interlocking diffuses the impact of the effect on the ensemble of thousands of 'definite places'.

In this chapter we hope to have given some reasons for accepting a history of the Mediterranean environment over the last four millennia in which there have been endlessly recurrent local crises, but no sudden global changes. The relat-ively frequent repetition of the events studied – their normality – makes us want to associate ourselves with those who are reluctant to use the notion of cata-strophe (Delano Smith 1979, 393–6). We see the relationship between human communities and the environment as a *relatively* stable symbiosis.

Mediterranean historiography should attempt to forgo the luxury of the vision of the past in which differences can readily be explained by pointing to major, sudden discontinuities. We do not, of course, exclude gradual, secular change from history. It is important to recognize that there were indeed more deltaic plains, fewer dense woodlands, more areas of eroded badland, deeper layers of recent valley-fill, more harbourless coasts in the nineteenth century than there had been in the Bronze Age. But those aggregate changes had come about in so piecemeal a way that it is not even possible to attribute them to periods, let alone to moments: and they were mostly susceptible to reversal. If we find the historiography of catastrophe misleading, that is not because we are so foolish as to think environmental catastrophe impossible. Quite the reverse: if anything, we feel that historians should not encourage taking catastrophe's name in vain, especially in an age which is constantly demonstrating its capacity to transform the Mediterranean world on a previously unimaginable scale. It is interesting to see that a plant-scientist periodizes the Mediterranean past with reference to an 'agropastoral phase' lasting from *c.*1000 B.C. until A.D. 1869. It was in that year that the opening of the Suez canal decisively overturned the old bio-geographical order by allowing an exchange of waters between the Mediterra-nean and the Red Sea, and provided a satisfactory historical turning-point to signal the arrival of a qualitatively and quantitatively different epoch of anthro-pogene impact (Pignatti 1983, 152–3). The choice of turning-point would have greatly appealed to Herodotus.

Changes that have shocked the last four or five generations have encouraged historians to retroject the violence of contemporary environmental destruction. To do so, we have argued, obscures the different reality of the environmental changes which can be documented from the pre-modern world. Yet even when those changes obtained – as they sometimes did – on a more than local scale, it does not in fact seem that they succeeded in interrupting the rhythms of interdependence. We prefer to stress the normality of the damaging consequences of environmental instability, and the recurrent failure of human populations to tread the narrow path between environmental destruction and nutritional disaster. The environmental history of the Mediterranean before modern times is certainly not an account of the effortless symbiosis with the rest of Nature of 'ecological angels' (J. R. McNeill 1992, 354), any more than the pre-Columbian peoples of the New World lived in harmony with nature before they were intruded upon by unsound Mediterranean ecologies after 1492 (Butzer 1996). While an analysis of the interaction of humans with their world in Mediterranean history must often be pessimistic, it will, however, benefit from the recognition that the swings of the pendulum were shorter, and the balances easier to achieve, than in the critical instability of the dawn of the millennium.

The major environmental conditions of the Mediterranean world have not in aggregate changed to a historically significant extent over the last four millennia. They have not, in any case, played a determining role in human affairs: as a major survey team has found for the volcanic landscape of the Methana peninsula in the Saronic Gulf: 'it is clear from the location of certain villages and archaeological sites that in the past the chief considerations in deciding where to settle and, at times of lower population, where to farm on Methana have not been directly connected with the physical environment' (James et al. 1997, 31). Or as Lucien Febvre put it: 'do we really have to spend time showing that . . . there is nothing "given ready made" to man by nature and nothing that geography can impose on politics?' (1973a, 215). If tens of thousands of people suffered in every age from undernourishment, that was not because there was less forest or more alluvium across the Mediterranean basin as a whole than there had been five centuries previously, but because of sudden and local environmental crisis or, much more normally, because of those social and political constraints on production that we examined in the previous chapter. Across the Mediterranean, until the population boom of the nineteenth century, there was always in theory enough of the essentials for everybody – as, globally, there still is.

Nor have the malign conditions been the direct physical consequence of environmental disaster provoked by human agency. To the question 'is the history of agricultural change in reality the history of environmental *damage?*' (Chase 1992, 249, his italics) the answer for the Mediterranean must be emphatically negative. Human initiatives, as we have stressed, have been compelled to be varied, opportunistic, adaptive. Both abatement and intensification can cause devastating environmental change. But they both come and go, taking many different forms, with a variety of rhythms. Long-term change is almost never unilinear. Mediterranean environmental history over this period does not exhibit the sad consequences of the unwitting mass behaviour of hosts of primary producers encroaching on fragile zones in an automatic way, with a steady incrementation of the deleterious effects.

The responses which have ensured this relatively high degree of stability across a fragmented landscape have also diminished the impact on human societies of the shocks and crises of the natural world. Among these responses the potential for connectivity and the possibility of mobility play a crucial part. As a human ecologist has put it, 'wide niches are more suitable in environments that fluctuate in time' (Hardesty 1975, 82). It is to the ways in which the redistribution systems facilitate increases in the spatial variety of resources available to the inhabitants – the width of the niches – that we turn in the following chapter.

CHAPTER IX

MOBILITY OF GOODS AND PEOPLE

Nobody sails the seas just to get across them.

Polybius, *History*, 3.4.10

For who does not think that life has improved, because of the exchange of things and the society of happy peace, since the majesty of the Roman Empire united the world?

Pliny, *Natural History*, 14.2

And every shipmaster, and all the company in ships, and sailors, and as many as trade by sea, stood afar off, And cried when they saw the smoke of her burning, saying, What city is like unto this great city! And they cast dust on their heads and cried, weeping and wailing, saying, Alas, alas that great city wherein were made rich all that had ships in the sea by reason of her costliness!

Revelation 18.17–19

The sea is beautiful in the eyes of God especially because it surrounds the islands, of which it is at one and the same time the adornment and the protection; because it brings together the most far-removed continents and gives to sailors unhindered intercourse; through them it furnishes to us the investigation of what was previously unknown (*historia ton agnooumenon*); it provides the fortune of the merchant abroad; it improves easily the needs of life, allowing the well-endowed to export their excess (*exagoge ton peritton*) and to the poor it furnishes the amendment of what they lack.

Basil of Caesarea, *Homilies on the Hexaemeron*, 4.7 (ed. Giet 1968)

1. INESCAPABLE REDISTRIBUTION

The Greeks and Romans thought many things that have darkened the understanding of their interpreters. Among these was their belief that the Golden Age had been marked by the absence of exchange: no ships before 'Argo', no buying and selling, no corrupting seafaring. A consequent gulf separated thinking about trade from thinking about agriculture; and that gulf remains surprisingly deep, wide and treacherous, even in historical scholarship. Yet it is a central part of our argument that the gulf is as unhistorical as the Golden Fleece.

Mediterranean opportunism will by now be familiar – the onus to keep alert to all that you might have in your control so that you can use it to make up for what goods accident denies you. The production of food has always been governed by the logic of this opportunism, and we have seen in Chapters VI and VII three historically influential consequences. First, a surprisingly high value has often been set on gathering the nutriment offered with little or no assistance by a diverse environment. Second, the extreme capriciousness of that environment dictates the basic modalities of storage and redistribution. Finally, human effort and skill in responding to this capriciousness are desiderata with a value which may be compared with that of the environmental opportunities themselves and of the food that may be won from them.

All three of these fundamentals enmesh foodstuffs with the range of non-dietary commodities to be found in the kaleidoscopic Mediterranean. Opportunistic gathering will naturally address the useful but inedible bounty of the environment, as we have already seen clearly in the case of forest products (VI.4). Storage and redistribution, though primarily adapted to the levelling of imbalances in the availability of food, will also *pari passu* embrace any other materials or products whose distribution is irregular enough to give them a place in exchange transactions. The human contribution which adds to the value of a microregion's seasonal yield by increasing its quantity or quality may also be deployed to refine and improve non-edible productions. That human contribution is also exchangeable itself. No Mediterranean history can be complete which does not include the buying and selling of people.

Structurally, then, there are reasons for extending the analysis of exchanges in foodstuffs to other commodities and to the movements of people. All these subjects are essential to explaining the Mediterranean connectivity which we described in Chapter V. It is our view that the generally ecological argument which started in Chapter VI with ethnoarchaeology can usefully be extended to give a cohesive set of general explanations of Mediterranean interdependence and its often very considerable scale. These can in turn strikingly illuminate the history of the individual exchanges which have been prominent in different periods of Mediterranean history. This discussion begins with two of these: metals and textiles (IX.2–3). We then move on to more general observations on the nature of Mediterranean trade (4), which serve to introduce the theme of the reducing of human beings to the status of a commodity. In the last sections of the chapter, we turn to the relationship between the commercial exchange of people and one of the larger themes of this whole study: mobility itself (5–7).

The Mediterranean world at all periods must be understood as a vast conglomerate of tiny sub-regions and larger groups of sub-regions: more fragmented, we have urged, than most of its neighbours. The individual identity of these small areas is human, topographical and environmental: the definition of our 'definite places' is usually far less pronounced than that of islands or plains hemmed by mountains (Chapter III). Now many historical landscapes are best considered piecemeal. But the outcome of such consideration remains essentially a local history unless the relationships of the constituent parts also receive detailed examination. We have maintained that the Mediterranean world is made distinctive not only by its fragmentation but by its connectivity (Chapter V). Is any regularity or pattern discernible in connections across the Mediterranean? Have they tended to generate any distinctive types of intercommunication, transaction or exchange, political, social or economic? Further, what kinds of continuity are there in such patterns? Can we invoke the fact that the very diversity and particularity of the

Mediterranean's myriad constituents has always been intense in order to make historically interesting comparisons between Antiquity and the subsequent centuries? We resume here those questions to which a preliminary and partial answer was attempted in Chapter V.

The physical aspects of the matrix – the patterns of intercommunication facilitated by the environment, the sea itself and its climatic and oceanographic characteristics, its chains of islands, and the landforms of mountain and coastland – will all play some part in establishing the nature of Mediterranean redistribution. There are, moreover, unexpected features which deserve to be more widely appreciated, such as the role of mountain belts as zones of easy communication rather than barriers (III.6, V.1). Yet physical aspects, although they cannot be passed by, are the less important. For one thing, the dictates of physical geography over relations between regions have always been far from absolute (V.1–3). Seemingly natural units have been politically and economically divided (for example Aegean Anatolia in the Seljuk period). The least predictable ties have sometimes been long-lasting, such as those between Egypt and south Anatolia in the Ptolemaic and the Ottoman periods (I.3–4). But, still more significantly, the mere configuration of physical geography has only a trivial, often coincidental effect on social and economic relations. The really complex patterns of ties which underlie the world of the Greek *apoikiai* (overseas settlements) of the eighth to the fifth centuries B.C., or the Byzantine world between the demise of the western Empire and the coming of Islam, or the territories of Genoa or Venice in the high Middle Ages, need a different kind of explanation. It is with this kind that the present chapter is primarily concerned.

Many of the characteristic products of the Mediterranean lands, edible and inedible, are common and widespread. That there are ubiquitous Mediterranean commodities does not, however, entail that there was no redistribution of them (Newbigin 1924, 29). The changing history and geography of connectivity enable the produce of a particular area to become a recognizable commodity even if its source is less elusive than the entrepreneurs who gain from its exportation might claim. The irregular distribution that generates exchange is not, in most cases, the ineluctable consequence of the physical givens. It is highly contingent. It mutates from season to season; but it also responds to the ever-shifting 'social construction' of commodities, which are as much a creation of the social and economic framework as is the fertility of the soil (VII.1). 'Societies construct objects as they construct people' (Kopytoff 1986, 90).

2. ANIMAL, VEGETABLE AND . . .

> Javan, Tubal and Meshech . . . traded the persons of men and vessels of brass in thy market.
>
> Ezekiel 27.13, of Tyre

Heavy commodities in search of a category

Waters and soils are the variables which we have considered in most detail in our discussion of microregions, together with the geology which configures them. Among the distinguishing aspects of a locality – alongside the pockets of deeper alluvium, the maquis slopes, the springs and the reedbeds – is another accident of that geology: mineral resources. The right to dig sand, excavate clay, quarry rock, or mine for rarer materials is another element in that diverse repertoire of entitlements which are found in Mediterranean societies. These minerals are inedible. But they closely resemble the foodstuffs which we have examined hitherto in the place that they occupy in the calculus of risk-avoidance and environmental opportunism. Forest management (as we explored it in VII.4 and VIII.5), likewise proved analogous to food production. We particularly insist that there is no reason to disjoin timber from the category of the present section just because it *grows*. For that matter, although the majority of the bulky commodities under consideration here are inedible, salt might be adduced as another item which helps to bridge the gap between them and the redistribution of foodstuffs (VI.6). Moreover, some inedible commodities are very tightly integrated into the taking of decisions about how to produce and process foodstuffs: the redistribution of millstones is a particularly apposite instance (Williams-Thorpe 1988). Some are implicated in redistribution, such as the timber of which carts and ships are made. Pottery, wood and leather vessels also belong in this list (V.5). Minerals offer the same range of possibilities as do foodstuffs: local, domestic use; storage for occasional redistribution; refining and improvement with redistribution deliberately in mind. These possibilities are further defined by the rarity and quality of the mineral resources, and by the nature and degree of the connectivity enjoyed by their microregions.

In this section, then, we argue that, for the purposes of Mediterranean history, it may be helpful to see all the bulky, heavy, inedible materials that originate in the microregional landscape as a single category. Even when such material is extremely common, like other widespread Mediterranean commodities, it may still find a place in redistribution. Alluvial clays are found everywhere, but ceramics, terracotta revetments, or even brick and tile made from them, may become objects of redistribution and exchange if communications, especially by water, are good. Although some heavy commodities are genuinely rare – like the ores of tin among minerals or the lustrous marble of Paros among building materials – it is helpful to consider them all together (cf. Brun 1997). To do so may seem counter-intuitive. Certain groupings of these materials, and metals especially, have customarily been accorded a very distinctive place in social and economic history. Against that we invoke two related arguments. The first repeats what we said in Section 1 about the culturally specific definition of materials and what is made from them. The reasons for valuing metals in Mediterranean societies have been extremely varied. Only the fact of the value and the effect that that has on the ecology of production, storage and redistribution remain as the basis of the comparison; but, paradoxically, that may offer more to the historian than does the uncritical ascription of a continuous identity to the commodity. The second argument, therefore, is that we would wish to enjoin caution about taxonomy. The range of things that we know to be metals in the strict chemical sense did not necessarily constitute a discrete collectivity in the understanding of earlier cultures, and therefore in their economic and social behaviour. The redistribution of silver, iron and lead cannot automatically be treated together in the same discussion.

For all that, island mineral resources have had a privileged place in the history of Mediterranean exchange. In certain places, isolated sources of precious and otherwise almost unobtainable materials existed. The volcanic obsidian of Melos was one of the earliest Mediterranean commodities and was still sought after in the Middle Ages (III.4). The healing earth of Lemnos, antidote to poison and plague, used to treat the eponymous hero's wound in Sophocles's *Philoctetes*, was on sale under the Sultan's licence in the bazaar of Constantinople in the nineteenth century (X.4). The grey marble of Proconnesus, which gives that island and the sea around it their modern name of Marmara, was floated directly out of the quarries for despatch all over the Roman East. The list could be extended to the alum of the Lipari islands, the fuller's earth of Kimolos, sulphur from Sicily, the ruddle of Ceos, and the marble of Naxos and Paros, as also to the somewhat more celebrated ore deposits – copper on Cyprus or silver on Siphnos. In all these cases the island location is what mattered. When the Hellenistic philosopher Euhemerus imagined the miraculous island of Panchaia, where Zeus had been a human king, he endowed it with extraordinary resources of metals to match (Diodorus Siculus, *Historical Library*, 5.42–6).

This further demonstration of the advantages of islands introduces a characteristic of the Mediterranean world that will form a central theme of this chapter. Contrary to modern geographical theory, commodity production has been centred neither on the places where raw materials were produced nor on the places where finished products were consumed. Rather, it is located within the medium of communication itself. Here too the islands have an important role, because of their communications, which allow them a special place in the network of connectivity and redistribution, and thus enable them to maintain unexpectedly high populations (Sections 5 and 7 below). This is why a great centre of workmanship in bronze was found in what might seem to us to be the most inconvenient of places, the minute Cycladic island of Delos. The island that had itself once, in myth, been a wanderer was a node for the communications of the Aegean and beyond, and its centrality was expressed in, and depended upon, the fame of its cult of Apollo. Another great bronze-working centre of the archaic Aegean was also insular – Aegina in the Saronic Gulf, which had less sanctity but more widely ramified seaborne connections (as we shall see more than once in this chapter). Its famous bronze candelabra were made partly on the island and partly at Taras in southern Italy. Much later, in the third century B.C., we find a bronze-worker from Lucania, in the same region, active on the island of Rhodes ('Botrys Leukanos'; see Morel 1991).

The situation of metal-processing, and other sorts of commodity-manufacture, within the medium of communication naturally gave a major role to islands. But that situation has more general implications. The manufacturers were themselves mobile. Carrying the raw materials, as the wrecks of their vessels have sometimes shown, they sailed the Mediterranean, manufacturing where they found demand. It is essential to stress that Mediterranean redistribution is closely tied to the mobility of the producer: the wandering craftsman is a key figure. That is one of the reasons why the hunt for 'industry' in the ancient world is rather absurd (V.4; IX.4).

Light from prehistory

In modelling regional interdependence, the development of long-distance exchanges, and the contribution made by both to the formation of states, prehistorians have made much of the very limited availability of natural resources such as obsidian, and the growth of systems of distributing them ever more widely. With regard to the Mediterranean, we should want to give priority in such modelling to the redistribution of local surplus to feed equally local shortfall. This is not to say that Aegean civilization was the result of ecological microdiversity (Sherratt and Sherratt 1991, 355, taking exception to this formulation). Rather, important aspects of that civilization's character and especially of its ability to spread must be understood against the need for and possibility of interdependence. We do not see why local movements of foodstuffs should be conceptually separated from the valuable cargoes of princes (V.4; IX.4). The one brought about the web of communications and maritime knowledge which made the other possible. Nor do the relations of production in emmer-patch or vine-ground have less to do with 'civilization' than those of Sidonian textiles.

The specialized commodity that has received most attention from prehistorians is bronze and its constituents. This is, not unnaturally, because it is conspicuous in the archaeological evidence. But the reason for its visibility deserves a moment's attention. A good many ingots in the shape of outstretched ox-hides are known from a wide variety of wrecks and other sites. Physical analysis of the metal (Stos-Gale and Gale 1992) has succeeded in identifying some of the sources of these ingots. Yet the salient point is the simple fact that, across the Mediterranean, and before the end of the second millennium B.C., there is a standard type. It is of the utmost significance that there existed a regime of mutual understanding, to put it no more strongly, which was able to impose, for whatever reason of credibility or convenience, a degree of uniformity on the produce of a group of very widely separated major producing areas – areas which included Cyprus as well as several sources in Anatolia. Moreover, the style of the ingots, and a determinate range of obscure markings, remain the common expression of Mediterranean redistribution until the middle of the first millennium. In the western Mediterranean also, about 1000 B.C., a major quantitative increase in exchanges involving metals has been traced through common types of metal artefact, a development from local small-scale contacts which created a metallurgical *koine* joining Sicily, Sardinia, Italy and the Iberian peninsula (Giardino 1995, 339–41). Continued excavation at the site of Punta d'Alaca on the tiny island of Vivara, on the north side of the Bay of Naples, now reveals dense contacts with the Aegean and major metalworking remains already in the sixteenth century B.C. The nearby island of Pithekoussai was a centre for metallurgy in the networks of movements of Greeks and others in the eighth-century Tyrrhenian – when it appears likely that it was closely linked with the important metalworking site at Oropos, north of Athens – and in the seafaring communities of central Euboea (Blackman 1997, 14–16; V.2).

To give some examples of the archaeological material: in 1967, sixty copper ox-hide ingots, metalworking equipment, and glass were found in the wreck known as Cape Gelidoniya A off the coast of Lycia, dated to about 1200–1150 B.C. (Parker 1992a, no. 208; see BE). That cargo was surpassed by the Ulu Burun wreck in Carian waters, where in 1984 a ship of about 1325 B.C. was found to contain 100 'Canaanite' amphorae with varied high-value contents and 6 tons of copper in 200 ox-hide ingots – 'enough (given tin for alloying) to make the weapons needed to equip a small army' (1992a, 440). A prestige cargo, sometimes thought to have been a special consignment, this wreck raises the two vital questions about metallurgical exchanges in late prehistory. Can they be regarded as commerce? And, whether or not they can, can they be compared meaningfully with the distributive systems of the Greeks and Romans, let alone those of medieval Genoa?

Some scholars magnify prehistoric metallurgy to the extent that an ingot becomes a kind of talisman, and the powers of priest, king and smith blend. Against them, it has been stated that, even in the case of Cyprus, which bears the same name as copper, metallurgy was a 'technological subsystem which must be looked at within the total cultural context' (A. B. Knapp 1990, 150). We would advise caution, for reasons adduced in Chapter VII, about even the less far-reaching arguments which assign metallurgical improvements a decisive role in agricultural productivity (Muhly et al. 1985, on the implications, for agricultural intensification, of the early sophistication of iron-working in Anatolia). Metals are visible: they have not infrequently survived. We feel that it is rash to assign them too singular a role in an epoch from which so much else has been lost. For us their importance is as tracers of networks of connectivity centuries before the Greek overseas settlements. We see little difficulty in inserting them into our model of Mediterranean interaction, and therefore of comparing them with the whole spectrum of later economic history. As late as the early modern period it would not be hard to find cases of redistribution in the Mediterranean which conformed less well to the expectations of mutual understanding among distributors than did the ox-hide ingot.

Metal in the Greek and Roman Mediterranean

The geography of the new cities of the Greeks and Phoenicians in the early first millennium is clearly related to the distribution of sources of metal ores. We know from the excavations at Lefkandi that the island of Euboea was closely connected with Mediterranean redistribution from the very beginning of the millennium. One of its principal cities, Chalkis, shared its name with bronze as Cyprus does with copper, and was probably involved in the movements by which the Greeks settled the Aegean and, particularly, gained access to the silver of the Thracian coast. This process, in which the Phoenicians were also very likely involved, took the form from the seventh century of the settlement from Paros of the island of Thasos, the base from which the opposite coast was subsequently exploited.

The cities of Euboea were (we noted) also involved in the first large-scale settlements in the Tyrrhenian basin – where Pithekoussai formed the base for transactions with the fertile plains of Campania on the nearby mainland, and with the mineral-rich coast of Etruria to the north (Coldstream 1994). Again, the settlement of the mainland opposite followed, and iron from the island of Elba was worked in the ports of the Campanian coast long after Pithekoussai had ceased to be important (Diodorus Siculus, *Historical Library*, 5.13). It has been estimated that the slag-heaps which remain on Elba represent the refining of 10,000–12,000 tons of ore p.a. over 400 years (Gill 1988). Etruscan culture was shaped by the interactions represented by the redistribution of these metal resources, and became famous for its metallurgy, in both gold and bronze (Critias, at Athenaeus, *The Philosophers at the Dinner Table*, 1.28 b–c; cf. Camporeale 1985).

Both Greeks and Phoenicians were involved in the movements of materials in the archaic Tyrrhenian, and both played a vigorous part in seizing the opportunities provided by the metal resources of the Guadalquivir basin in southern Spain (Aristotle, *On Wonderful Reports*, 1.35; Diodorus Siculus, *Historical Library*, 5.35.4). Here too a polity developed out of the new contacts. Known to the Greeks as Tartessos, it was famous for its fabulous wealth of silver (Chamorro 1987). The island city of Gades, a Phoenician settlement, controlled the approaches to the Guadalquivir estuary, and a chain of coastal settlements offered anchorages along the route back into the Mediterranean (V.2). In the Black Sea a similar pattern can be traced. Although scholars have denied that Greek settlement in the land of the Golden Fleece, Colchis, was related to the search for metals, it is highly suggestive that some 400 smelting sites for iron there can be dated to the period immediately preceding the settlement (Tsetskhladze 1995).

In this rapid survey, islands have featured prominently: Vivara, Cyprus, Euboea, Elba, Gades. The significance of the milieu of redistribution has once again been apparent; the far-flung distribution of the sources of metal, and the effects of rarity, are clearly to be seen. Since metallurgy depends on combining the supply networks of diverse raw materials, it is inevitable that the location of metallurgical effort should fluctuate markedly from region to region, like other kinds of productive intensification (Edmondson 1989, 94–6). That metallurgy was an ingredient in overseas settlement by Greeks and Phoenicians poses no problems for our analysis. Far from needing to choose between commercial or agrarian ambitions for such episodes of mobility, we should, by now, be surprised if they were distinguishable. The importance often assumed in the past by the beginning or end of a new vein of ore shows how sudden gluts and dearths affected this form of production too.

Mineral commodities are distinguished also by the ways in which they may be stored. Materials that need to be shipped over long distances but are everywhere in demand lend themselves to stockpiling. For example: in the late sixth century B.C., the people of Delphi sent ambassadors around the Greek world soliciting contributions for the rebuilding of the temple of Apollo after a fire. The Saite pharaoh Amasis contributed 1,000 talents of alum (of the order of at least 26 tonnes). This was regarded as a very substantial gift. In a nice demonstration of the different orders of magnitude of state and individual wealth, the Greeks of the Egyptian port of Naucratis, to which we shall return, added a further one third of a talent (Herodotus, *History*, 2.180.2). Both the garnering of this vital commodity and its value as a medium of exchange are striking confirmations of the widespread manufacture of high-quality fabrics at this date, for alum is an essential ingredient in textile processing (Section 3 below). But they are also valuable glimpses of the management of mineral resources – like the soda exports from that other Egyptian port recorded in the Elephantine Palimpsest (Porten and Yardeni 1993; V.4). The accumulation of scarce commodities to reinforce power is more famously visible in this period in the deposition of iron bullion in Greek temples, and in its successor strategy, the coining of silver. Redistribution of metals was carried out in a vast variety of ways in Antiquity, under state or elite supervision. The particulars of monopoly, coinage, military supply, mine-owning and so on need not concern us here. But it is important to emphasize that the values of gold, silver and bronze as artefacts and as coin fluctuate; and it can be hard to tell what is private exchange and what state accumulation. Similar ambiguity afflicts the exchange of foodstuffs: extraction of tax in kind and distribution as largesse form part of the history of production; control of storage and access to redistribution are part of the structures of rural power (cf. VII.6). There is no reason to regard metals as essentially different.

The last lesson to draw from this brief account of metals in the Greek and Roman world is that we cannot, from the high status of certain metals and their usefulness in the definition of an elite, infer their scarcity. The slag-heaps of Elba have already suggested as much. A single Roman legionary fortress, occupied for a couple of decades, has yielded – nineteen centuries later – 20 tons of iron nails (Pitts 1985). The baths and aqueducts of Rome required thousands of tons of lead, and the roofs of the former, it has recently been shown (DeLaine 1987), were filled with coffering hung on great armatures of cast iron weighing, in each case, scores of tons. Yet we read that in Antiquity 'metal was never the basis for constructing ships, aqueducts, public buildings' (Nef 1987, 695). On the other hand, in the Middle Ages all the forges of Styria, the largest iron-working zone of Europe, produced only 2,000 tons of iron each year. Antiquity and the Middle Ages again converge (V.4).

After the Iron Age?

If we expect timber or lead or terracotta each to have had a single meaning, then we shall be surprised by the vicissitudes of the material over time. Conversely, if we set out to draw comparisons over many centuries, we face the extreme difficulty of having to take into account the changes in meaning, value and use of every material. Some changes are naturally more intense than others. Any material can acquire the social status which encourages hoarding. We have already observed how iron, and even alum, fulfilled that function in archaic Greece. Textiles, as we shall see in the next section, could be used in a similar way. Investment in high-prestige building was another possibility (Tate 1992b, 97, for that of the moderately as well as the outstandingly wealthy). Architecture is a repository of valuable materials which will for the most part be available for later re-use: even roof tiles fall under that description. The huge consumption of lead and iron which we have just noted in ancient Rome was generated by state projects, and, like the consumption of precious marble from all over the empire, also represented the use of wealth in this way. The Middle Ages may compare 'unfavourably' on this score: just as states then made little use of coloured marble, so their demands for iron and lead for culturally-specific prestige projects were different. Equally, there is no point in comparing the earlier Mediterranean valuation of iron with its counterpart after the diffusion of the cannon.

This liability to change of value is to be seen even in the constantly precious metals, silver and gold. In their case, the main variable is the degree to which a particular society uses its stocks of precious metal for an abundant coinage, or for plate and other decorative and cultural functions. Thus it can be argued that the early Byzantine Empire is characterized by the use of gold plate and coin, while it had enough silver only for plate. Contemporary Persia had large amounts of silver coin and plate, but no gold coin or jewellery (Grierson 1992). The mint and market prices for silver differed. Although it can be argued that, for most of Byzantine history, there was no interruption overall to the supply of any important metal (Bryer 1982), the individual mining districts and the networks in which they were engaged varied considerably. The metals of the Balkans found several different outlets at different periods, both to the Adriatic by way of Ragusa, and to the Aegean and Black Seas. Comparison with the other end of the Mediteranean world is helpful: even the outlets of the Rio Tinto deposits and their neighbours display hectic mutability. 'Centre d'une métallurgie de concentration', Muslim Šaltiš, with its 'rôle de recueil, de transformation, et de redistribution de la mer et de la mine', has been revealed by excavations in a thoroughly unpromising island-site amid salt-marshes at the mouth of the Rio Tinto (Bazzana and Trauth 1997). One advantage, apart from connectivity, was access to the wood of coastal pine-forest. The Tartessian gateway at Huelva, through which Iberian silver had passed in the first half of the first millennium B.C., lay nearby but not on the same site. Šaltiš itself proved short-lived, despite being an architecturally complex and economically prosperous agglomeration. Its ephemeral history is that of an authentic Mediterranean town (Chapter IV).

Minerals, therefore, are a very abnormal commodity, if by 'normal' we mean 'given to functioning in a market economy according to the classic laws of economics'. Even in the Middle Ages, they were too valuable to be left to 'real' traders, and have therefore been neglected by scholars interested in the free market – the equivalent of the 'industrial' obsession which we shall meet in the next section when dealing with textiles. Not only do they markedly lend themselves to evaluation in different ways according to different cultural expectations, but they are especially liable to be required for the specialized purposes of individual authorities, such as the state. The accidents of where they are to be found combine with the contingencies for which they are needed to create a more than usually fluid geography of supply and demand.

It is obviously of significance here that northern Europe was relatively self-sufficient in metals, and that sources of metals are quite evenly spread among the lands on which medievalists' attention is focused by the documentary evidence (cf. Goitein 1961, 185–8). The Mediterranean world is quite different. There the accidents of geology have endowed some areas with an abundance of iron or copper or silver, so as to give them, in the language of productive ecology which we have been using, conditions of perpetual glut. Elsewhere, perpetual dearth of the raw materials of weaponry, ornament, coin and construction prevails. Between the ancient and medieval Mediterranean there are real differences of detail in the valuation and distribution of minerals, but they do not derive from a relative underdevelopment on the part of the ancient world. They show us how unstable values are, and how socially determined demand can be. But they also invite us to think the unthinkable – that, far from the usually progressivist picture, of the succeeding ages of metals which we mentioned briefly on the first page of Chapter I, copper might have been historically more important in the Bronze Age Mediterranean, and iron and lead in the Roman world, than either were again before the end of the Middle Ages.

In precious metals we have a commodity which has not been underestimated by ancient historians, but which is strangely absent from the economic histories of the medieval Mediterranean. For the sake of symmetry let us turn next to one which has been prominent in the scholarship of the post-classical Mediterranean, but which has attracted few ancient historians: textiles.

3. The Problem of Mediterranean Textiles

Travelling in peninsular Greece in the mid-second century A.D., Pausanias makes an uncharacteristically detailed allusion to the society of the city of Patrae (modern Patras):

> The women of Patrae are twice as many as the men, and more charming women are nowhere to be seen. Most of them earn their livelihood by the fine flax that grows in Elis [the fertile alluvial plain of the river Alpheius around Olympia, some thirty miles to the south-west of Patrae]; for they weave it into nets for the hair and dresses. (*Description of Greece*, 7.21.7, trans. Frazer 1898)

Patrae had been founded as a Roman *colonia* (one of the highest statuses available to a city at this time) some two hundred years before, and it was recognized that its maritime communications were among its great advantages. It functioned well as a central place for that corner of the Peloponnese and the adjacent coasts and islands (Rizakis 1997). This brief notice introduces the salient features of textile production in the Mediterranean – its specialization, its relationship to redistribution, its place in the regional economy, and its demographic profile. Textiles deserve a prominent place in our discussion of the place of exchange in Mediterranean history.

Inedible crops

Textile production can readily be fitted into the categories which we used for foodstuffs in Chapters VI and VII. To begin, then, as we did before, outside the domain of cultivation: hides, feathers and fur are available from managing the wild, and it is instructive that they could fetch very high prices in certain contexts, rather like the most sought-after fish. And there is, in fact, a maritime textile. Sea-wool, or marine *byssus*, is a very singular case. This shimmering, multicoloured fibre is the product of a scarce shellfish, and its gathering and weaving make a fine example of the full usage of the more recondite resources of the coastal environment. But it was not the shellfish gatherers of the reefs of the Levant who, lacking sheep or flax, dressed in this cloth. The fabric became a famous luxury, almost unobtainable and of nearly unimaginable cost. This instance appears bizarre to us; but it is ecologically no odder than the production of silk, a combination of cultivation skills with opportunistic gathering. Cultivating silk is not less natural than growing wheat, and can form part of the same set of strategic decisions about how to survive.

Along with other animal products such as leather, an underestimated commodity, wool is an important example of a 'secondary product', a bonus available from an animal husbandry of which the principal objective is nutrition. So the production of woollen textiles is potentially ubiquitous (Frayn 1984, ch. 1; Braudel 1972a, 1.89). No economic or technological revolution is needed to increase production for exchange (Riu 1983). This is a form of intensification of effort which can be achieved very rapidly – and which can disappear as quickly. At Safed, the central town of Galilee, immigrant Jews introduced a woollen industry which, by 1535, was yielding 15,000 pieces of cloth each year, although its origins did not go back beyond the beginning of the century, and by 1602 there was no woollen manufacture at all (Braudel 1972a, 1.436–7).

In the Mediterranean world, moreover, animal husbandry was intimately integrated into the economies of most microregions (III.6; VI.7). The competition between human needs and pasture for sheep – starkly expressed in early modern England by the saying 'sheep eat men' – was in principle not so extreme (Schneider 1987, 419). On the other hand, selecting high-quality woollen production – whether independently, or at the behest of a landlord – could entail a preferential treatment for the animals, on improved pasture perhaps, and here strategies might conflict. The same might be said of improving strains of sheep specifically for wool, a choice which (like so many of the species-improvements which we mentioned in VII.3) also belongs in the repertoire of high-value high-risk enterprises. The ancient evidence gives us a relatively clear view of the management, for wealthy Romans, of flocks of sheep thousands strong (Frayn 1984, chs. 6–7). This is the extreme effect of developed commerce in animal products, and brings into play unusual environmental management such as long-distance transhumance. The pattern is that of intrusive direction of the productive landscape from outside, as explored in VII.6.

Other textiles require the cultivation of specialized crops. Flax is the most important (although cotton should also be mentioned in passing: Mazzaoui 1981). It does best in sandy alluvial soils near abundant fresh water supplies, requirements which can be quite frequently met but which are not normal in Mediterranean environments. Flax is, indeed, one of the species which is well suited to the wetland margin, and it is a happy coincidence that it is best produced in the wetlands of the coastal fringe which are the places most open to long-distance water-borne communications. In the fifth century B.C., Herodotus comments on the flax cultivation of Colchis, at the east end of the Black Sea, and Egypt (*History*, 2.105). (The flax of the Egyptian Delta will provide us with a case study at the end of this section.) None the less, an archive of scratched records on pottery fragments from Kafizin in Cyprus shows us the degree of organization (with the consumption of Ptolemaic Egypt in mind) attained by flax production in Cyprus during the third century B.C. (Bruce-Mitford 1980). Here, as with the great flocks of Roman Italy, the direction of specialized production has a colonial flavour.

Patrae, our first example, refounded as a Roman overseas settlement in the Augustan period, furnishes a parallel. The abundance of labour may be a factor in the positive correlation between colonial contexts and certain sorts of textile enterprise. In the case of Patrae we particularly note the importance of the way in which specialized textile production and redistribution has mobilized female labour (VII.5). Women's craft-employment is already prominent in the Pylos tablets of Mycenaean date. In Mamluk Jerusalem, women pedlars were engaged in the sale of cheap cloth items (Lutfi 1985, 290–1). Further parallels may be found in the ancillary weavers of second-century Tarsus, non-citizens but forming a large proportion of the population (Dio Chrysostom, *Oration* 34.21–3; C. P. Jones 1978, 80–1); or in those of the ninth-century household of St Severus of Ravenna (Herlihy 1985, 58, 118).

Labour is also essential to the supply of the peripherals for cloth-processing, as we see from a remark by the elder Pliny (*Natural History*, 19.47) on the appeal of madder and soapwort to the 'filthy mob' as cash crops because of the enormous profit they yield. That profit was presumably earned in the region of Rome. But it is to some extent a coincidence that all the preceding examples are urban.

Notice that we are not trying, with Hume, 'to ascribe the growth of a city to the establishment of a manufacture' (Finley 1985a, 22; IV.5; BE VIII.1). We simply draw attention to the complexity of the ties which linked city and region, and region and region, and to the variety of their possible social and economic results. Ancient literary praise for a city's textiles is not direct evidence for urban processing of wool or flax: it more likely attests the quality of what was produced in the territory (Morel 1978). Textiles are often produced in villages (for a good example, Mount Pelion in Greece, Hourmouziadis 1982, 222) and this enterprise further elides the town–country division (Chapter IV) and blurs 'industry' and 'agriculture' as concepts (cf. Garnsey 1980, 44: 'a continuum existed between agriculture and industrial employment'). Surplus labour can be turned into an item in the repertoire of risk-aversion in a great many different locations: what that conversion always presupposes, however, is the existence of markets.

The nature of textile redistribution

As so often, the regulations for the payment of dues on routine transportation of commodities allow us a vignette of redistribution. Table 3 shows the duties levied from A.D. 202 at a road-station inland in the Maghreb, where a pass in the mountains gives access from the high plains of Numidia, and ultimately from the Algerian coastlands, to an enclosed basin between the more hospitable environments and the desert (Map 20). We are in a location analogous to that of the Biqa, therefore, or the highest zone of the Jebel Akhdar of Cyrenaica (III.3). In the basin lies the salt-lake of the Chott el Hodna, and around it a cluster of environments offering a variety of largely pastoral opportunities (Darmon 1964). The pastoralists of the Hodna are interdependent with the arable cerealiculture of the Cirta plateau, to which they transhume with their flocks. A further advantage for their pastoral enterprise is the availability of the salt of the Chott itself (cf. VI.3; Despois 1953, 290–3). Hence the wide range of animals, textiles and leather-goods in the inscription, which also alludes to the importation of slaves. Through the gateway in the other direction came materials such as alum needed for the processing of the various secondary products of the pastoralism, and all the standard commodities of the Mediterranean redistributive *koine* of the period. The meeting of local and longer-distance redistribution, and the routine place of a wide variety of textiles within it, are very apparent.

At inland Zarai, then, an ordinary bundle of cloth was taxed at the same rate as a hundred-pound lot of untreated hides, a donkey or a hundred-pound load of dates. Even Zarai was no economic island; how much less were the larger communities of the Roman Mediterranean. (We note in passing that Italian raw wool was to be found in transit through the territory of Palmyra in the Syrian desert in the second century A.D.: Matthews 1984; cf. Teixidor 1984).

As an item of consumption, textiles have a very singular sociology (Schneider 1987). They range between luxury and near-necessity, as the Zarai document shows. They are particularly susceptible to 'brand-naming' – to the creation of contingent differences of workmanship and finish and perceived quality according to skill, tradition, and the availability of specialized labour. There is some evidence for such craft specialization in periods from which few textiles have survived, and it is a helpful confirmation of the scale and complexity of their exchange. The diversification of textile quality and character, like the typological virtuosity

Table 3 The Zarai customs tariff

[2 dupondii = 1 sestertius; 2 sestertii = 1 quinarius; 2 quinarii = 1 dinarius]

Poll Tax [sc. on animals]

Slaves, each:	1.5 denarii
Horse, mare:	1.5 denarii
Mule, male or female:	1.5 denarii
Donkey, ox:	1 quinarius
Pig:	1 sestertius
Piglet:	1 dupondius
Sheep, goat:	1 sestertius
Kid, lamb:	1 dupondius
Animals for local re-sale:	duty free

Regulation for non-locally produced clothing

Thick woollen robe for dinner parties:	1.5 denarii
Tunic ?third-quality for dinner parties:	1.5 denarii
Blanket:	1 quinarius
Purple cloak:	1 denarius
Other African cloth, per bundle:	1 quinarius

Regulation for leather goods

Finished leather:	1 quinarius
Rough leather:	1 dupondius
Sheep/goatskin:	1 dupondius
Soft fine leather, 100 pounds:	1 quinarius
Glue, 10 pounds:	1 dupondius
Sponges, 10 pounds:	1 dupondius

Principal regulation of the customs post

Cattle and baggage animals:	are duty free
Other things:	see the specific regulation
Wine, fish-pickle, 1 amphora:	1 sestertius
Dates, 100 pounds:	1 quinarius
Figs, 100 pounds:	1 quinarius
Vatassa, 10 bushels:	[gap]
Walnuts, 10 bushels:	[gap]
Resin, pitch, alum, 100 pounds:	[gap]
Iron?	[gap]

Source: *CIL*, 8.4508; cf. Haywood (1938) 81–3.

of fruit (VII.3), is a sensitive response to a variable redistributive infrastructure and fluctuating demand. Simple calculations of self-sufficiency and 'subsistence' dependence – calculations of how much wool is needed simply to keep the cold out for a given number of people who do not own animals – are only relevant to a small part of the full gamut of textile strategies. Because textiles are so perishable, we must recall throughout the discussion that much of their history is far less apparent to us than are, for instance, the production and distribution of

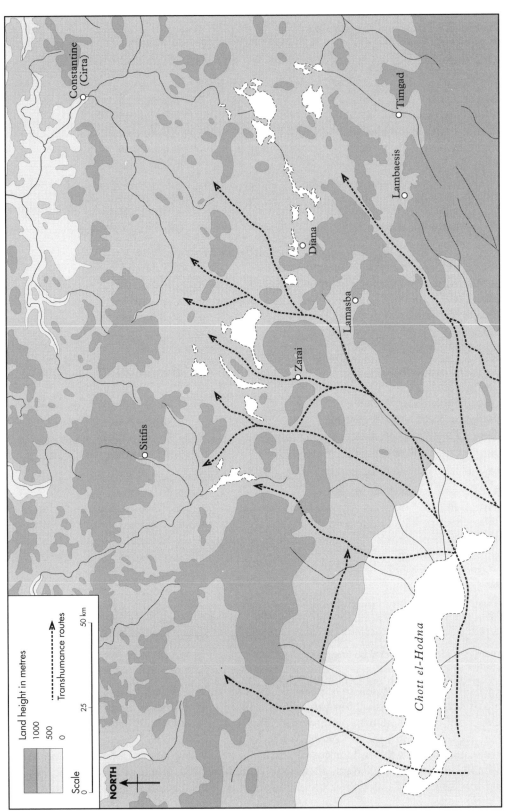

Map 20 The customs table of Zarai in its context

ceramics. The documentary evidence for high-value goods is indeed sometimes hard to interpret: the silk supposedly due to the monastery of S. Giulia at Brescia in the tenth century and recorded in its Polyptych, a vital resource for the economic historian, is revealed actually to have been a red mineral pigment (Toubert 1987).

A Fatimid princess, aunt of the Caliph al-Hakim of Egypt, had in her possession at her death (shortly before 1025) 30,000 pieces of fine Sicilian woollen cloth (Lombard 1978, 54). A Galatian called Claudius, between the years A.D. 102 and 116 sent the Emperor Trajan a selection of fine clothing (including two brooched cloaks and two pairs of embroidered bootees) and received a civil reply which he inscribed on stone in his home town of Pessinus (*IGRR*, 3.228). From two different angles we perceive here what Maurice Lombard has called 'la thésaurisation des tissus' (Lombard 1978, 194–9). The spending of very large sums of money on textiles was a perennial aspect of ancient elite behaviour, and the accumulation of fine textiles has, in much of Mediterranean history, been integral to maintaining a high social standing – a spectacular, easily quantifiable, and pleasing form of real estate. Expensive textiles may be woven and embroidered with the utmost care, tailored and decorated to the highest standards, made beautiful by the craftsmanship of the weave, the design of the whole, the colour of the exotic dye or the rarity of the raw material (as with the marine *byssus*). The high value attached to them as artefacts may be unfamiliar but is not inexplicable. It reflects control of labour and of the productive landscape, and access to many different sources of supply; it stores social credit in a long-lasting and relatively low-bulk form; it stock-piles materials which may sometimes be hard to obtain.

Eleven out of thirty-two sections in the Edict on Prices with which the Emperor Diocletian attempted to rein in inflation in A.D. 301 (BE IX.4) are devoted to textiles, and contain dozens of minutely differentiated items. The prices run from 'loin-cloths of coarse linen for the use of common people or slaves' (200 *denarii*) or shirts of the same for the same (500 *denarii*) to 'second-quality women's dalmatics from Byblus' (in Phoenicia, the third most expensive place of origin) at 7,000 *denarii*, or to a hooded cloak from Canusium in Apulia, patterned, at 4,000 *denarii*. The highest prices which do not involve purple dye are 12,500 *denarii* for a brooched cloak (like the one given to Trajan, but from Raetia) and a doubled Dardanian mantle. But it is felt worth recording that no one is to sell women's hoods with vertical stripes using 1 pound of purple for more than 55,000 *denarii*, or raw silk dyed purple for more than 150,000 *denarii*. For comparison, a litre of wheat was rated at 7.5 *denarii* and a litre of the cheapest legumes at about 4.5; a pint of wine was 8 *denarii*, a pair of chickens 60 – and a shorthand teacher was to receive 75 *denarii* per pupil per month, the approved cost of a pair of soldier's shoes.

Every inhabitant of the Mediterranean needs warm winter clothing; extremely few wear silk. Between the 'cobbling together' by the poorest agriculturalist of a makeshift winter-garment, or the widespread distribution of the cheapest second-hand clothing, and the sale of elaborately woven and embroidered damasks of the finest wool, there is a whole spectrum of demand. The economic history of the textile trade is the history of movements – in both directions, naturally – along that spectrum, as reflected in the capacity to obtain material. In the thirteenth century and in the third (A.D.) it was an easier, cheaper, more natural thing to want an ordinary woollen garment made some dozens of miles from your home than it was in the eighth century B.C. or A.D. But, because textile making is embedded in the normal rhythms of production, there is always some exchange, as there is of foodstuffs, even where it would be inappropriate to speak of markets (Abulafia 1981, 384). Ready-made clothing was sold in great variety at rural fairs in late Antique Italy. Compare Cassiodorus (*Variae*, 8.33) on the Leucothea fair, to which we shall return in Chapter X.3: 'not to mention the garments, arranged in uncountable catgories' ('quid vestes referam innumera varietate discretas?'). In certain periods, levels of production made it possible for there to be a substantial market in second-hand clothes (the commodity dealt in by the *tenuiarii* of Roman Italy for instance), and for expectations of wearing dyed cloth to extend quite far down the social scale: investigation of the technology of dyeing in Graeco-Roman Egypt shows the effects of catering for an ever-widening demand (R. J. Forbes, 1964, 82–98; cf. Reekmans 1994, 126–7). Textile manufacture resembles many other types of production. It aims at overproduction for (indefinite) storage, either for local use or for opportunistic sale. In a harsh and unhealthy Sardinian winter in the second century B.C., the commanders of a Roman army had considerable difficulty in persuading the local communities of this highly pastoral island to provide clothing (Plutarch, *Gaius Gracchus*, 2.2–3). Like many tales of requisitioning or tax in kind, the anecdote is instructive. There was a clear expectation that there would be an available surplus, on a considerable scale. Noting that conditions favoured redistribution, and finding additional domestic use for their textiles, the Sardinians were reluctant to disgorge – at first.

We have argued that sheep and goats are everywhere, so what generates a wool trade? One answer is successful specialization, and this applies particularly to the higher-value end of the spectrum. But for the redistribution of lower-value textiles, the principal explanation must be mobility, causing concentrations of people beyond the local resources of animal husbandry. So this, like the redistribution of some of the foodstuffs which we discussed in Chapter VI, can be regarded as *epiphenomenal to human mobility*.

If we want to test for the importance of mobility, the best places to look, as we have seen several times, are the islands. It turns out that islands are prominent centres of textile production. Leo Africanus observed that Djerba's textiles made it prosperous in the teeth of agricultural poverty (Épaulard et al. 1956, 400). Pantelleria was a centre for textiles in the later Middle Ages (Bresc 1971, 113). Verres, the infamous Roman governor of Sicily, set up a weaving establishment with a three-year contract to provide women's clothing: not on populous Sicily, but across the rough sea on Malta (Cicero, *Against Verres*, 2.4, 103). Malta at much the same period was praised by Diodorus Siculus (*Historical Library*, 5.12) for the quality of the harbours, the wealth of the inhabitants, and the grandeur of their houses, as well as for the excellence of the craftsmen in general, and the linen-workers in particular. The advantages of islands for textile production can only have been the supply of labour and the possibility of easy redistribution.

In the textile business, people as well as goods move constantly from 'rural' to 'urban' settings and back again. The town appears again as the ephemeral abode that we discerned in Chapter IV: how else could Roman Patrae have so disproportionate a female population? The mobility of the roving craftsman is parallel to that of the trader and of the goods in which he deals, and is a vital constituent of Mediterranean life. The cloth-workers of Tarsus are likely to have been a deracinated population, engaged in a productive process related to the agriculture which they had left, under the pressures which so frequently dispossess and compel mobility in Mediterranean history. They operate in a city because the city, like the Mediterranean island, is an agglomeration of population in an accessible place. It is an elegant detail that, in the Mediterranean at least, the vehicles of the redistribution were generally possible only with the aid of the commodity – sailcloth, canvas and ropes.

Pacemakers of industrial progress?

The historiography of textiles has been shaped principally by their contribution to early modern and modern economic history. They have, on this view, 'been pacemakers of industrial progress at least twice in the last thousand years' (Lopez 1976, 130). The medieval cloth trade is always scrutinized for the supposedly pivotal moments of mechanization or the division of labour or the setting up of factories – when these are far from the crucial questions. Textile production and exchange in earlier periods, similarly, are nearly always interrogated in the language of industrialization. Here too, though, technological determinism has found its critics (cf. Chapter VII). The spread of the mechanized fulling-mill turns out to have been marginal to the fortunes of the medieval English cloth trade (Bridbury 1982, ch. 2). As far as the Mediterranean is concerned, the imbalance remains between the study of what medieval textile production made possible and that of what it emerged from.

Interpretation of the evidence for the cloth trade in the ancient Mediterranean has been distorted by both positive and negative comparisons with later periods. Some have looked for factories and a great international market in cloth; others have scrutinized the inscriptions for signs of the sophistication in trade practices which was characteristic of the medieval cloth trade. 'Where are the cloth-halls, the Guildhalls and Bourses?' demanded Moses Finley (1985a, 137; IV.5; V.4). When they are not forthcoming, the case for the irremediable primitiveness of the ancient economy is found proven, and variations of social organization are converted into a major qualitative difference in economic complexity. In fact, the cloth production and exchange of the Middle Ages is increasingly being described in ways which make it sound more and more like Antiquity (V.4). 'To speak of "large scale production" and "capitalist methods" in connection with the famous cloth-making centres of Flanders and North Italy . . . is to give an entirely false impression of the structure of the industry' (Bridbury 1982, 11). From the comparative viewpoint, the alacrity with which medieval historians have hailed the moderate 'booms' of the Italian Middle Ages as steps towards a better future is astonishing. They may be the first of their kind in Europe since the 'Pirenne period' (V.5–6). Yet comparison with the Islamic, Byzantine and ancient worlds suggests that these local paroxysms are at once less singular and more familiar, the hectic and temporary consequence of a vortex of intensification.

Most clothing production remained local. The great expansion of the trade was a gradual process which began only with specialized production of very high-value fabrics (cf. Pounds 1973, 386–94). Local products of a lowly kind could still suddenly find a place on a much wider market in the Braudellian Mediterranean (Braudel 1972a, 1.383). The small-scale, pedlar-borne redistribution of Roman textiles is evoked by a passage of the *Digest* (14.3.5.4–5): 'but it has also seemed reasonable to give the name of business-agent [*institor*] to the people to whom clothes-dealers and linen-merchants give clothing to be carried round and disposed of – the people that we colloquially call travelling vendors [*circitores*].' Such movements, a kind of *cabotage* of the land, are a basic feature of Mediter-ranean economic life.

Of course, the statistics of the medieval cloth trade in its most spectacular manifestations are impressive. Giovanni Villani claimed that, at the beginning of the fourteenth century (thirty years before he was writing), three hundred work-shops supported thirty thousand Florentines from the manufacture of 100,000 pieces of cloth annually (*Chronicle*, 11.94). Such descriptions may be inflated, but the more specific and detailed evidence of the fifteenth and sixteenth cen-turies shows that the order of magnitude does not mislead. It is important to stress, none the less, how low were the levels of labour productivity in this industry. The labour of women and children as well as of surplus manpower was its foundation, and it remained unusual for that labour to be systematically organized. The putting-out system developed only gradually. Moreover, the development of the complex 'rural'–'urban' connection to which we have adverted is – it must be remembered – a local phenomenon. That it happens in one place does not entail that it will also happen in a neighbouring one with identical conditions. When we talk lightly of 'the cloth trade of a medieval city', we should recall that the group of places to which we refer is a very restricted one, and that, even in the heyday of the textile production of Fez or Florence, those places were extremely unusual (V.4). The society and economy of most cities of that epoch must be understood with quite other models, much closer to those appropriate also to the ancient city (as in the case of sixteenth-century Rome: Delumeau 1957–9, 367–83). Favourable conditions for intensification enable; they do not determine.

There is thus no reason to suppose that the ecology of textile production and redistribution in Antiquity was substantially different from that of the later medieval Mediterranean. Two principal approaches may be called upon to help us appreciate the nature of ancient textile production. The first is the document-ary. Papyri from Egypt and inscriptional and archaeological evidence give us a picture of the degree of organization of the wool trade and its place within society. Literary evidence has very often been abused in this area – poetic and generalizing allusions to wool production are rashly taken to entail a textile-industry when, of course, they may only suggest it (see the strict words of Morel 1978). But even the most rigorously sceptical review of the evidence leaves a consistent and vigorous picture of the home- and workshop-production of Italy and Egypt, even if we cannot expect to reach the higher summits of sophistication of the late Middle Ages. We do find the rudiments of the putting-out system (Wipszycka 1965, 98–102) and, not uncommonly, the existence of workshops involving the hiring of groups of labourers, often women (as in the work-tallies – with jocular insults appended – of a dozen such groups scratched into a plaster wall at Pompeii: *CIL*, 4.1507 with 1510).

The fact that urban benefactors spent their money on baths and theatres in Antiquity, and not on guild-buildings or commercial exchanges as they were to do in later medieval Ypres, Padua or Antwerp, tells us nothing whatsoever about the organization of the production and exchange of textiles, positive or negative. It is simply parallel to the aristocratic disdain which makes classical literature ignore smallholder agriculture and urban poverty so thoroughly. The emperor Gallienus is said to have responded to news of a revolt in Egypt 'Quid! sine lino Aegyptio esse non possumus' [however can we manage without Egyptian linen?] (*Augustan History, Gallienus*, 6.4). The narrator's purpose is to criticize the heartless emperor for making light of public disasters by jokingly alluding to the supply of *vilia ministeria*, 'trivial conveniences' (6.7). Egyptian grain is what he should have been alarmed for. But it is interesting that Gallienus's impropriety lay in his anxiety about the trivial and socially inferior provisions of bulk trade, not luxurious baubles for the entertainment of the court. The cheap trade of Egyptian linen and Gallic wool was therefore commonplace enough to find a role in the rhetorical fantasizing of the author of the *Augustan History*. Here, as usual, we have to employ evidence which has not been filtered out by elite prejudice in order to trace the existence of 'a fairly complicated exchange of wool, animals and perhaps workers throughout the Mediterranean area' (Frayn 1984, 171).

When we learn of the striking of a marvellous vein of some mineral, the mercurial success of the pioneer involved, and the dazzling wealth that ensued, to the fascination of potentates, it is natural to suspect that we are reading, as we so often have to, anecdotes which bear upon ancient Mediterranean economic history from the elder Pliny or Strabo. Yet the career of Benedetto Zaccaria and the story of the alum of Phocaea in Turkey (Lopez 1976, 139–44), or the discovery, in 1462, by Giovanni di Castro of the alum of the hills of Tolfa in south Etruria to the interest and benefit of Pope Pius II (Nenci 1982) are narratives of just this sort. Alum is an essential mordant in the dyeing process, and one of those sought-after minerals which so enhance the opportunities of certain favoured microregions, as we saw in the previous section. It is the awkward locations of such materials that renders the production of high-value textiles dependent on redistribution – combined with the aggressive marketing and protection of certain special sources of commodities which are, in reality, not all that rare. This is the phenomenon of a resource that is in fact available in many places, but which acquires the reputation of being very scarce. Before the Genoese developed the alum of Phocaea, it had been an important export of Egypt. Before the alum of Tolfa replaced their 'monopoly', it had in fact already been outflanked by the export of Kütahya alum to Venice in the fourteenth century (Zachariadou 1983, 167–9).

Not only do the adventures of Zaccaria sound like a story in Herodotus, but we have a record of the enormous demand in city after city in the Hellenistic world for the alum of a third source, the volcanic Lipari islands in the Tyrrhenian (Diodorus Siculus, *Historical Library*, 5.10.2; compare Section 2). Alum has therefore been called 'il grande dimenticato dell'economia antica' (Nenci 1982, 183). At least it helps us to compare that economy fruitfully with that of the Mediterranean in other periods.

The cloth production of Antiquity and the textile-cities of the fourteenth-century Mediterranean may none the less seem to be separated by a wide qualitative chasm. This is partly the product of the retrospective, teleological approach which is, we noted, interested principally in the seeds of later industrial organization. It is also partly the result of the inadequate nature of the sources for the earlier Middle Ages. These resemble those for Antiquity in being basically 'anecdotal' (V.5–6). But, as has been observed of the early allusions to the English cloth trade, 'while references of this nature do not prove the existence of an industry geared to an export market they presuppose one able to produce a surplus above purely local needs' (T. H. Lloyd 1977, 1). The early medieval gap could be at least bridged by some consideration of the evidence for textile production in the Islamic world, which is, as a glance at the standard accounts (above all Lombard 1978) reveals, overwhelmingly a Mediterranean phenomenon. There is oddly little sign that scholarship on late medieval textile production in Christian Europe takes into account the degree of complexity and the level of intensity reached several centuries earlier – and reached on the Christian side of the religious frontier too, to judge from the accounts of 'Naples the city of flax' in the tenth-century Arab geographers. And still more revealing cases are available, above all in the Egyptian Delta.

The scale and elaboration of textile production in ancient Egypt was mentioned earlier. Early Byzantine (or late Antique) Egypt was also celebrated for its cloth. The Islamic conquest does not seem to have interrupted this reputation. In the ninth century already there is adequate testimony to flourishing production, and continuity is easier to postulate than re-creation, since styles and techniques persisted, and since in the Islamic tradition in Egypt the skills of cloth-making are often associated with the Coptic populations (Lombard 1978, 163–5; cf. Gervers 1983, 279–315). In this long textile history, description – as exemplified in Lombard's book, based on more or less anecdotal or accidental evidence – is much easier than economic explanation. A continuous tradition of production may indeed, period by period, have many different sets of economic underpinnings. In the Roman cities of northern Italy, the prominence of specialized textile production should be partly explained by the legacy of the Celtic societies of pre-Roman times in the region. In these societies, animal husbandry retained a position that favoured the commercialization of its products. During the Middle Ages the region developed equally specialized textile enterprises. But these now depended on a wholly different set of conditions, among which access to the importation of materials such as cotton was vital. Even before the mid-twelfth century, fustians were made in Lombard cities with imported cotton; and the inland city of Piacenza, a near neighbour in Roman times of the great Gallic sheep-fair of Campi Macri, is found interestingly poised between distant Genoa and Venice for imports of cotton (Racine 1987). By contrast, in the contemporary Islamic Mediterranean, for the most part, the relationship of raw material to processing appears to have been generally closer than it was in northern Italy. That is, the same people were concerned both with the exploitation of the land and with the profitable sale of commodities derived from the product of complex processing of their crops. In such cases, the production of textiles can be seen as a form of agricultural investment, and their storage and 'commoditizing' as a natural development from the deployment and redeployment of more generally consumable agricultural surpluses. Hence the wide distribution of the subdivisions of the cloth 'industry' across the whole range of settlement types.

Tinnis: a case study

Within the whole regions which together produced the various finished products of flax growing, more specialized centres also emerged, above all where redistribution of the cloth – that is by means of commerce proper, and also state management – could take place most easily. One of the more impressive cloth regions was the seaward part of the Delta, and within it the cities of Damietta and Tinnis formed the most conspicuous central places – their names indeed deserving equal prominence in textile history with those of Lucca or Florence. The area is among the most complex of the Mediterranean wetlands, as one of interpenetration of land and sea: a tangle of the greatest ecological distinctiveness, with interlocking islands and fens, waterways and swamps, pasture and irrigated alluvial soil. There are shoals, pools and reefs, sand-spits and fossil dune-belts, and thousands of square kilometres of reedbed (Map 21). Intense summer heat produces an extreme humidity which is of use in the making of linen. The fibres of the flax may be soaked in the waters of the lagoon, which support an ecology of fish and water-birds on which the inhabitants of the region can rely as an important substitute for a purely cereal diet (they cross the marshes in reed boats to trap birds and fish in flaxen nets). The deep soil, of sandy alluvium, always moist, is ideal for flax, hemp and other fibres, and the pastures are good for sheep and goats. The complex topography and its variegated specialities are united by the network of waterways, at whose interstices, where dry sites are to be found on levees or old dunes, rise the cities from which the interlocking activities are co-ordinated.

Chief among these settlements from the sixth to the twelfth centuries was Tinnis, an example which illustrates not only our view of the textile trade but several other of our principal contentions in this volume. Sited on an island in the lagoon, a fossil coastal dune, this was a city of some 30,000 to 50,000 inhabitants wholly dependent on various aspects of the production of textiles, above all linen cloth. The city covered the whole island, and depended for food partly on the animals reared on the pastures of neighbouring islets, but more on the grey mullet of the lagoon. The organization of the textile economy was rudimentary. There is no trace of any 'industrial' development, and the individual artisan remained the basic unit of production. That did not diminish the scale of the production in aggregate. Physically and culturally an island (for centuries after the Islamic conquest it remained predominantly Christian), Tinnis was a 'gateway settlement' of a special kind, at the junction of two economic geographies, beside Egypt rather than of it (cf. Section 7 below). Within the Delta and the network of Nile waterways, it was part of an economy which both produced specialized raw materials and contributed to their processing, and which distributed the end-product to the Egyptian market. But accessible as it was to sea-going ships, Tinnis slotted in also to its produce's overseas distribution network. It depended for some of its food not on local agriculture, but on the surpluses of Crete – geographically distant, but next door on the Mediterranean seaways: a dispersed hinterland of an exemplary kind (IV.8).

The important lessons for our investigation are prominent: one, the local ecology defines the region, its society and its economy; two, large populations are seen to survive independent to a large extent of traditional 'subsistence' farming; three, 'urban' and 'rural' activities form an inseparable whole; four, society and economy depend on exchanges which transcend the boundaries of local regions; five, coastal entrepôts are engaged with a Mediterranean network through long-distance exchanges, not just with their immediate hinterland; six, the specifics mutate, but the generalities remain, in a pattern to which we shall return in Section 7. Ancient Tanis, Buto, Pelusium give way to Tinnis, Damietta and Dabiq – centres which themselves prove transient.

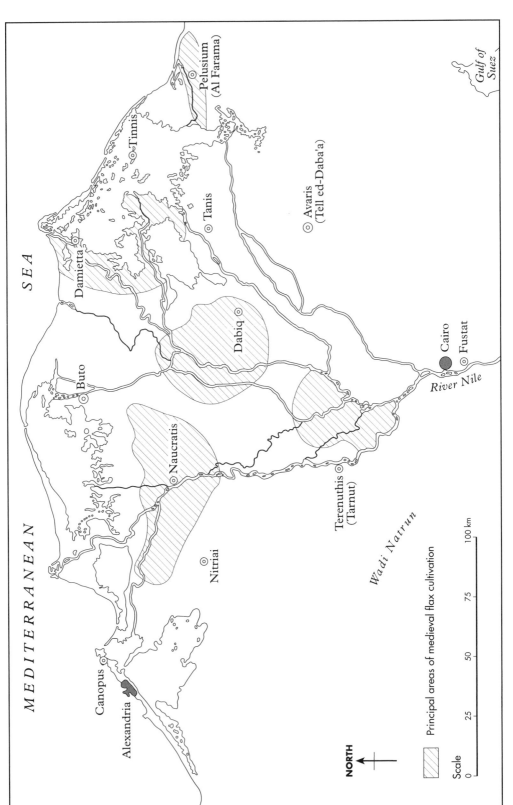

Map 21 Tinnis and the Egyptian Delta

4. Problems with High Commerce: Variety, Specialization and Choice

High and low commerce indissolubly linked

In Chapter VI we showed how Mediterranean production is characterized by glut and dearth, whether of fish or migratory fowl, or of the harvest of the land, whether of the product of agriculture or of simple gathering. The insights that ethnoarchaeological research has offered scholars attempting to understand the history of Mediterranean production can also be used in the study of redistribution. With each year's experience varying so greatly from one pocket-sized microregion to another in the Mediterranean lands, such originally small-scale movements of a few miles between one coastal village and another, or one island and another, need no special explanation. These are the exchanges principally made possible by the sea which Basil of Caesarea, writing in the 360s A.D., describes in our fourth epigraph to this chapter. While the products of the local environment such as minerals or agricultural specialities do have a vital role to play in our exposition, we should also consider the small-scale and unspectacular differences between one small area and another – a better fishing-place, a warmer winter climate, a more reliable well. Variable advantages such as manpower and 'invisible' assets such as defensibility, nodality, religiosity, natural beauty and so on also play their part in connectivity. It would be misleading to give names such as trade or commerce to much of the basic redistribution which is entailed by the fragmented Mediterranean landscape. We may, for instance, be dealing with the part-time activity of a producer who probably spent much of the rest of the year in basically agricultural activities; not unlike the addressees of Hesiod's *Works and Days* (618–94), of the end of the eighth century B.C., whose boat and nautical equipment lie alongside the ordinary resources of the farmer. Founding the Dionysiou monastery on Mount Athos in the fourteenth century, the monks' first steps were to plant vines and to acquire a boat with which to import produce in return for the wine, in a very Hesiodic manner (Oikonomides 1968, 4–5).

The short hops and unpredictable experiences of *cabotage* are, as we argued in Chapter V, the basic modality for all movements of goods and peoples in the Mediterranean before the age of steam. They united diplomats, warriors, pirates, pilgrims and traders in cargoes of all kinds, high- and low-value. They encourage us to take a synoptic view of these movements, one which has more to learn from economic anthropology than from the more restricted subject matter of classic economic history with its preoccupation with prices, markets and economic laws (BE IX.1). The interplay of status and the movements of people are as important to this network of contacts as the sale of commodities. Gift and theft take their place beside barter, loan and purchase. Violent and irregular movements of people or materials must be included in this history as much as the tidier world of (more-or-less) legally regulated commerce.

As we also argued in Chapter V, we must not let the glitter of high commerce devalue these routines of ordinary redistribution. It is high commerce that has done most to promote the misleading dominance in Mediterranean economic history both of the defined trade route and of labelled resources – 'resources', that is, in the sense of the old cartography which marked 'wool', 'horses', 'purple dye', 'furs' over large tracts of land and 'trade routes' designated by arrows pointing away from them. Such specialized productions and movements, like the link between Crete and imperial Venice or the oil trade from Baetica to Antonine Rome, belong to a very distinctive segment of the whole phenomenon of redistribution – directed trade, to which we shall return.

In fact, the glamorous manifestations of high-prestige trade should generally be regarded as outgrowths from or intensifications of the routine patterns of redistribution, just as the most showy and celebrated productive enterprises are of the mundane rhythms of production. If high commerce is the result of specialization, that, as we should by now have made sufficiently clear, does not mean a development out of some autarkic ecological norm. Specialization of all kinds is one of the strategies with which the occupants of a microregion or those who control it from outside may approach the calculus of how to optimize their resources. On this analogy, the local or occasional decline of high commerce (when it is real), so far from inviting us to pronounce redistribution extinct, actually resembles the abatement of elite investment in primary production (above VII.4). That does not signal productive catastrophe in an archaeological landscape, and the abatement of high commerce does not show redistributive disaster: halving the cinnamon trade, like closing the dormouse hutches, need not have so malign an effect. Little and often usually outweighs big and rare. Cassiodorus comments on two malign habits in the relationship between production and redistribution: on the temptation for a community to export more than can be spared, which obviously entails there being the opportunity to do so (*Variae*, 1.34, cf. 2.12); and on deliberate delays by merchants hoping to raise prices (1.35). In both cases the merchant is seen to be playing a very similar game to landowners, and for identical reasons.

Interpreting these conspicuous movements as intensifications of existing universal local and small-scale redistribution systems offers help with several problems. First, with the question of the genesis of high commerce. At the local level, what were the year-to-year experiences of those involved in production, movement and consumption during the periods when the more spectacular, large-scale exchanges about which we are well-informed originated? What is the prehistory, for instance, of the dense network of contacts, the large-scale movement of a very wide range of expensive goods, which we see in full swing in the tenth century in the papyri of the Cairo Geniza? How was it that materials which were actually not hard to find came to be regarded as the speciality of one particular locality? Where a product was thought to be of medicinal value it could fetch prices which made control of important routes between source and principal market extremely valuable (Nutton 1985). The mastic of Chios, that arboricultural island-speciality that we introduced in VI.11, was marketed in the Egyptian linen-capital Tinnis (above, Section 3). In the eleventh century its control was a prize much sought after and won by the Italian traders (Malamut 1988, 388). But botanically, there is actually little that is special about the scrubby plant that is to this day one of the glories of Chiote agriculture. The trade in alum, as we saw in the previous section, also exemplifies artificial rarity.

What, we may ask further, are the gradual, lesser antecedents of the developed practices of moving tens of thousands of tons of grain, olive oil and wine from far-flung producing areas to the privileged consumers of Antiquity such as Rome and Athens? Were these miraculously beneficial leaps in the primitive dark? That has always seemed an unsatisfactory explanation. Such questions about the emergence of high commerce – questions too seldom raised – invite, rather, explanations of the kind we have begun to suggest in our discussion of background redistribution.

Second, and related, is the problem of interpreting how commercial complexity has changed over time. The conventional history of Mediterranean trade shares features with the history of the environment and the history of technology. In particular, it revolves around revolutions and catastrophes – the historiographical *di ex machina* which the theory of intensification and abatement does so much to render redundant. The type-case of the one is the burgeoning of (mainly Italian) trade in the later Middle Ages; of the other, the demise of the redistribution systems of Antiquity. We are in a position to deploy briskly some of the cavils at 'revolution and catastrophe history' which we raised repeatedly in Chapters VII and VIII, with brief allusion to the examples treated there. Is the transformation a genuinely widespread one, or has too much been made of change that was intense but chronologically and geographically circumscribed (the deforestation of Cyprus)? And has that exaggeration come about because the only evidence is evidence from one place and time where something dramatic did happen: has the deadweight of the surrounding silence been properly incorporated in the theory (the eruption of Thera or the Gallic mechanical reaper)? If there is more widespread evidence, does it really fit tightly together, or does the accommodation of numerous instances deprive the transformation of suddenness (the Younger Fill)? Are the evidence and the theory skewed towards impressive, prestigious manifestations (the Archimedean screw and the banana)? Has enough attention been given to what was going on outside the elite: did what had been lost or what arrived harm or benefit primary producers so much in Mediterranean circumstances (the mouldboard plough and the watermill)? In particular, is the change mainly interesting because of a teleoscopic view of historical change (double-entry bookkeeping)?

Hindsight has given high commerce, particularly that of the later Middle Ages, particular significance, because out of it came economic and social movements which proved historically formative in the early modern world. But the elements which were specially significant for the genesis of early modern economic behaviour are not necessarily the most interesting parts even of high commerce for the historian of the earlier Mediterranean. We shall be as resistant to the quest for technological revolutions which enabled the march of progress towards commercial modernity as we were in Chapter VII to the pursuit of their counterparts in the history of agricultural production.

If we are to claim that high commerce is a natural growth from the background of the maritime *koine*, we still need to show in more detail what connections unite redistributing dung on the Lebanese coast (an example to which we revert shortly) or sharing the barley-harvest among a group of islands, with selling purple-dyed linen a thousand miles from where the flax grew and the murex swam. Can we really make the Bronze Age shepherd and the Genoese merchant-prince members of a single hierarchy? How close is the connection between the products of agricultural intensification and the other primary ingredients of Mediterranean redistribution?

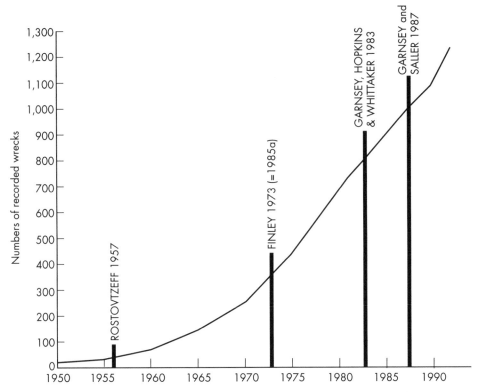

Table 4   The availability to scholarship of Mediterranean shipwreck evidence (after Parker 1992)

Shipwrecks and the normality of the mixed cargo

> naufragium maius restat in litore. erat in summis montium iugis ardua divitis specula: illic iste naufragiorum reliquias computabat, illic vectigal infelix et quantum sibi iratum redderet mare. [A great wreck settles on the shore. On the highest hill-crest a local magnate had a lofty watchtower, and from it he used to calculate the salvage value of wrecks, his inauspicious toll and the rate of return of the angry sea.] (Seneca the Elder, *Controversies*, 8.6)

Just as archaeology and social anthropology have combined to transform the study of the productive environment, in ways which are now reaching the scholarship of the medieval Mediterranean, so those disciplines are capable of reshaping the study of redistribution, even that of the trading cities of the late Middle Ages and early modern period. Underwater archaeology, in particular, has made an enormous contribution. It is interesting to note, for instance, the relationship between the huge expansion of data on shipwreck finds and the history of publication on the ancient economy (Table 4). The deeper waters of the Mediterranean are now also becoming accessible to this kind of investigation.

The variegated small cargoes of the wrecks reflect admirably the haphazard conditions of trade in all the periods represented, which range from the middle of the second millennium B.C. to the Middle Ages. They have served to redirect the attention of historians towards *cabotage* and small-scale redistribution, and they overwhelmingly attest the importance of highly heterogeneous cargoes. Take the following four examples (a résumé of more important instances will be found in the Bibliographical Essay). The Cyrenia wreck from Cyprus, of the end of the fourth century B.C., contained 343 Rhodian amphorae and fifty-odd from Samos, twenty-nine corn-grinders of volcanic rock, and 10,000 almonds, spilled from their sacks. A small African ship of about 100 B.C., wrecked near Antibes in Provence (La Baie de la Cavalière) while probably making for Marseille, had picked up wine from Apulia and Campania, and a large quantity of salt pork, probably from Genoa; most of the wine had been sold, since the ship had needed to take on basalt from the Provençal coast as ballast. The ship of 'captain Georgos' with its 900 wine-amphorae was wrecked near Halicarnassus in about A.D. 525; and we have already drawn attention (V.3) to the nearby eleventh-century wreck at Serçe Liman that had been carrying wine from Constantinople and cullet for glass-making, and is placed firmly in an 'international' milieu by the presence in it of Arab weights and Byzantine coins, side-by-side. On the evidence of what survives – durable goods, especially amphorae – half the wrecks of which we currently know carried mixed cargoes (Parker 1992a, 20–1).

This type of traffic can be attested elsewhere too. A passage in the *Digest* (19.2.61.1) could be a description of one of the ships whose wrecks we have described: it envisages the contract-shipping of 3,000 measures of oil and 8,000 bushels of wheat from Cyrenaica to Aquileia, and a delay of nine months before the ship ever left its home port. But evidence is available from much earlier times too:

> List of the freight which is in the ship of the first prophet of Amun under the authority of the scribe of the treasury Hori, the scribe Pra'emhab and the guard Amenkha'u: sesame-oil, *msh* jars; 7 . . . wine, great *kb* jars; 3: olives *kb* jar; 1: seed-corn of emmer, sacks; 60 . . . gourds, sacks, 27¼: papyrus-rolls; 50: salt, sacks; 40: rushes, bundles; 550: sedge, bundles; 110: head of gutted waterfowl; 100 . . . gutted fish; 5000. (Janssen 1961, 82–3: *P Turin* 2008, 2016 Part VIII)

This is the bill of lading of a Nile river-boat from around 1137 B.C. The text affords a rare glimpse of the internal economy of ancient Egypt, of the complex redistribution of ordinary goods in middling quantities from one part of the valley to another. It is not known to what extent the exchanges implied can be called trade, nor how independent the ship-people were; little can be said about producer or recipient or about the determination of value. A sacred setting seems more plausible than a 'commercial' one. Yet the social forms of the exchange are less important than the simple fact of the redistribution. As the editor of this papyrus says, we are led to the conclusion that the 'transport of goods for the daily subsistence of the inhabitants formed part of the economic structure of Egypt under the New Kingdom . . . a proof of the non-existence at the period of the so-called "closed economy" with complete self-sufficiency' (Janssen 1961, 98). Indeed, here is another instance of the complex and important inter-dependence of agricultural producers within regions which are unified by adequate communications (in this case the Nile).

Specialized high commerce may promote other movements of goods: thus, the *routes maritimes* of the Adriatic were a natural generator of local exchange in the Middle Ages (Thiriet 1981, 75ff). Conversely, *cabotage* locally redeploying microregional productions may provide opportunities for the small-scale movement also of high-value goods. Most importantly, the need for ballast and the wish to fill up the boat around a principal commodity allow the bulk movement of very low-price goods, which we should otherwise scarcely imagine to have repaid being carried hundreds of kilometres. Marble of unusual colour or earths believed to have special properties, like many metals, may be valuable enough to transport even from very remote and inaccessible sources. At the other end of the scale, both coarse and fine pottery was moved in bulk as an epiphenomenon to the trade in the agricultural goods; its clay was another product of the land, another intensification of the use of nature's gifts. This is just as true of the glazed Arab plates built into the *campanili* of Romanesque Italy – a case in which the themes of ceramic cargo and building material meet – as it is of the Attic black-figure vases found in the cemeteries of Etruria.

There is a close relationship between pottery and commercial redistribution in classical Antiquity. We saw already in Chapter V how the sheer quantity of extraneous ceramic fragments in the archaeological environment is one of the principal tokens of connectivity. The island of Aegina, which has served as an example of a highly connective location for metallurgy (Section 2 above), provides an unusual instance of a classical literary reflection on basic ceramic redistribution. Aeginetan horizons were proverbial by the late fifth century, when Herodotus (*History*, 4.152) narrated the tale of the island's miraculously successful merchant-captain Sostratos. They found a place even in the myth-history of inland Arcadia, which was said to have been linked to the sea and the outside world by the enterprise of Aeginetans: they communed with the acorn-eating mountaineers by means of trains of pack-animals from the port that they had established at Cyllene. The *mythos* of the origin of the island community was clear to the fourth-century historian Ephorus (*FGH*, 70 F 176; Strabo, *Geography*, 8.6.16): the first islanders had lived a strange life, excavating the good soil from some depth and scattering it on the stony surface, wasting nothing by living in the holes from which they had dug it (a story which nicely illustrates the fact that soils are made not given). So poor was the land that the Aeginetans were compelled to turn to the life of 'trader-like sea-working' as Strabo calls it – which is why, he says, cheap pottery is referred to as Aeginetan goods. The link between pottery and trade needed no explanation. To move from myth to history: the fifth-century politician and philosopher Critias, no friend to those who needed to earn their livelihood, regarded Athens as inventor and centre *par excellence* of the pottery trade (Athenaeus, *The Philosophers at the Dinner Table*, 1.28 b–c) – not surprisingly, given the wide horizons of the shippers who from the Archaic period onward used Attic ports. The commercial significance of manufacturing cheap pottery is even expressed in an unusual short poem: 'may the cups and all the bowls turn out well and fetch the gain of sale, many in the *agora*, many in the streets, and bring a great profit, and for us too who sing for the potters' ([Herodotus] *Epigrams of Homer*, 14.3–6). Wandering potters who imitated the styles of their homeland have done much to complicate the typology of the ceramics which are our most abundant testimony to the Archaic Greek period. The Corinthian Demaratus, who brought his pottery skills to Etruscan Tarquinii, is the type: the most successful of the *demiourgoi*, the mobile craftsmen of Section 2, whose heirs became Kings of Rome (Dionysius of Halicarnassus, *Roman Antiquities*, 3.46; Zevi 1995).

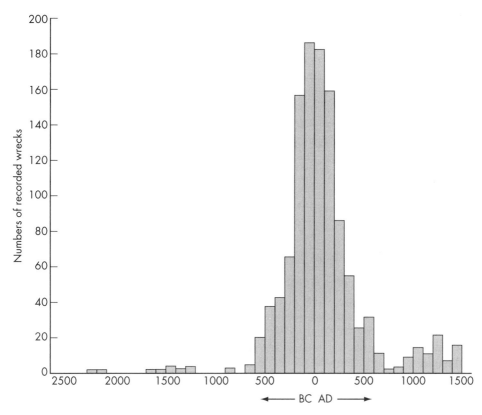

Table 5 Mediterranean shipwrecks by period (after Parker 1992)

Casual observation has yielded a twentieth-century example of the pottery-trade from the Levant (Mallowan 1939). Hereditary shippers collect amphorae from Sidon, where they are made, in boats capable of carrying from 200 to 1,500 each, and exchange them, without money, but at a fixed traditional rate, against sheep-dung from the Alaouite Mountains. On their return journey they sell the dung for fertilizer to the horticulturalists and arboriculturalists of the coastal settlements. Here we see empty amphorae used in a characteristically low-value exchange, intimately bound up with other productive strategies (which, it should be noted, connect, at a considerable physical distance, animal husbandry with the cultivation of the 'Mediterranean garden'). Comparison with other similar movements of pottery in the modern Mediterranean has greatly illuminated the extraordinary dispersal of mass-produced pottery, whether containers or tableware, characteristic of all periods revealed by Mediterranean archaeology. The typology and distribution of pottery gives us a special sort of information about the contacts between Mediterranean regions. It has been greatly assisted by the practice of surface survey; and it has been further refined by the huge expansion of shipwreck archaeology.

One arresting feature of the shipwreck evidence is the relatively poor showing made by the commercial boom which, on the conventional view, began in the thirteenth century. We know of many more imperial Roman wrecks than late medieval or early modern ones (Table 5). And we should not hesitate to consider the possibility that this pattern reflects a real quantitative difference. Our argument throughout has been designed to re-open the possibility that on some notional scale of quantities or values, second-century trade was significantly greater than trade at any other time before the nineteenth century. Pliny, in our second epigraph, was, after all correct in asserting how unusually favourable the Roman Empire was to interdependence. It is conceivable that the wrecks are a fair reflection of the heyday of connectivity. But we must of course allow some caution. Wrecks are often discovered because they are marked by a scatter of amphorae. Increasing obsolescence of the amphora – the 'container revolution' of the earlier Middle Ages (V.6) – entails greater invisibility of wrecks. Ancient shipping, on the other hand, might be thought the more vulnerable to storm. Our unevenly distributed wreck evidence may be skewed away from important medieval routes and may favour busy connections of the Roman period.

The problem of the history of the amphora

A special place in Mediterranean history is undoubtedly occupied by the transport amphora, a pottery vessel designed for easy accommodation in ships such as those whose wrecks we have just discussed, and whose history, lasting from the Bronze Age to the advent of modern packaging, is the hall-mark of their trade's perennial nature.

Thanks to the intensive work of devoted experts in the intricate field of amphora-typology, we can now begin to see connections which were wholly unknown before. For the classical Greek period, networks of communication are appearing which, as we saw in Chapter VI, have transformed our picture of Greek and Hellenistic viticulture in Italy and Sicily. The extension of the 'amphora habit' into the late Antique Mediterranean is one of the most remarkable trends of recent scholarship: the sequence of types is now little by little filling in gaps, so that (at Marseille, for instance) contacts are apparent between Italy, the eastern Mediterranean and Africa continuously to the moment when the amphorae are found in association with inscriptions in Arabic (V.6; Bonifay and Piéri 1995).

Take a nice example of a study which has been rounded off pending further discoveries: the oil-amphorae of a senator who reached the consulship at Rome in A.D. 40, C. Laecanius Bassus. The oil which reached all over the Po valley and which was so widespread in the middle Danube area came from his Istrian estates; we can place with reasonable certainty both the extremely sumptuous landscape villa of the family, on the island of Brioni Grande, and one of the workshops in which the amphorae were produced under the supervision of some of the forty or so managers whose names also appear on them. The business went back to the Augustan period, was taken over by the Roman emperors in the second half of the first century, and dwindled to serving local needs only by the mid-second century (Bezecky 1995).

When the hundreds of amphora-types that can be studied have been pin-pointed in this way, we shall have acquired a very considerable body of completely new information about the Mediterranean over the first two millennia of our period. Those concerned with the 'post-amphora' Mediterranean will have to ask, as they have not needed to before, what the change away from the amphora meant, and what else changed at the same time. And in doing so, they will expect a clear statement from experts in the earlier period as to what exactly the amphora phenomenon itself in its broadest sense actually is. And this will be harder to achieve than optimism at the discovery of so much new evidence might suggest. For one thing, it is no easy matter to determine what was actually in the amphorae. When lined with pitch, they probably contained wine; but sometimes amphorae characteristic of wine-producing areas turn up un-pitched. The trio of wine, oil and fish-pickle appears to account for a great many amphorae: which is a striking reflection of the productions which we studied in Chapter VI, but seems odd to many commentators. And what of quality, value, price and profit?

To go back to Laecanius: how did his piece of the amphora system begin? What were the means by which he or his family or forebears brought about the required change in the strategies of land and labour on the estates which he owned? What does it mean that the business became part of the productive portfolio of the emperor? What does it mean that, in 150 years, the whole thing had come and gone? Above all, how big was the business? How many original amphorae do the 400 that have been studied represent and how close was their distribution to that of what survives? How many of Laecanius's amphorae lacked the stamps which allow us to trace part of this milieu? How much benefit was there from the growing, processing, sale, distribution and consumption of the oil – for whom, and where? These are the hard questions that have to be put squarely to the evidence. And they are questions that merit consideration in the context of microecologcial fragmentation and mutable connectivity.

What we might call the conservative interpretation of amphorae in the ancient economy yields four methodologically significant points (Whittaker 1989). The first is one which we have ourselves made in a different context. Amphorae are durable and visible; through this accident, we have disproportionately many of them. The second is a general caveat about archaeological material, and concerns the hazards of random preservation, recovery and publication. The third concerns interpretation: do the stamps reflect commercial sale, or consumption by Laecanius's own dependants? The fourth relates to the contingency of the distribution of research (such as the absence of study of deep-sea wrecks, or of wrecks on coasts hostile to sub-aqua tourism). All four points are fair ones; but they should encourage the use of amphora evidence rather than the reverse. Given the inescapable over-prominence of the amphora, we have to make allowances by multiplying the other commodities for which we have so much less evidence, and especially foodstuffs and textiles. And given the indubitable accidents of archaeology, it is the more remarkable not just that we have masses of amphorae but that some patterns, such as that of the jars of the Laecanii, are visible. Such patterning must, on this argument, have been more intense in actuality. Moreover, if the amphorae of the Laecanii do witness the simple provisioning of the far-flung dependants of the family of an undistinguished Roman consul, rather than 'commerce', then we must 'scale up' our estimate of the economic significance of such directed trade. The jar-borne element of the private commissariat of a senatorial family is visible to us across the Mediterranean despite the randomness of survival and the skewing of research. Allow for what was carried *not* in pots, but in perishable containers, and multiply by the likely number of families of comparable wealth . . .

There are two Roman entities which should feature in any brief account of Mediterranean economic history. They are the two examples of the amphora habit which we know as the Dressel 20 olive-oil trade, principally from Baetica to Rome and the Dressel 1 wine trade, which developed out of the export viticulture of Roman Italy from the middle of the second century B.C. (Tchernia 1986; VI.9). They each have a much more than subjective typological coherence, and considerable geographical and chronological definition, although subtypes, imitations and variants are always making the picture look more complex. And, against methodological doubts that we might feel over types where only 400 examples survive, each of these is safe in the fact of totals known to us that are thousands and tens of thousands strong.

The degree of standardization which allows the formation of a typology is itself (as with the ox-hide ingots, above, Section 2) worthy of remark. This standardization resembles the process by which the marketing of mass-produced textiles was achieved in late medieval Italy (above, Section 3). But, as we suggested in Chapter VI.9, the amphora and its standards have a good deal to do with a different incentive to commensurability: the convenience of the exactor, whether official or landlord, rather than that of the dealer in the market-place. As with the Laecanii, so with the Dressel 1 amphorae: there is a hint of officialdom about them, which may originate, in the latter case, in arrangements made for the supply of the Roman army during the second century. Official or not, there is no doubt that, in practice, much of the wine and oil in these amphorae was produced for and sent to centres of consumption specified in advance. Of these the most conspicuous case is undoubtedly the city of Rome in the early imperial period.

The demands of the Roman imperial state succeeded in welding into a single system more of the redistributive networks of the Mediterranean than was ever achieved before or since. Indeed, when dealing with periods of this kind, it may be appropriate to speak not just of a prevalence of directed trade, but of a command economy. The author of the Apocalypse (as in our epigraph to this chapter) was certainly of the view that merchants were synonymous with suppliers of the ruling power. So they would remain even in late Antiquity. Writing in a period when the city of Rome could no longer command its supplies in the earlier style, Cassiodorus recognizes the desirability of natural market pricing arising out of negotiation, but is well aware of the cases in which it still does not happen (*Variae*, 9.14). We must, however, also acknowledge that, even at the acme of Rome's demands, there continued to be many divagations and perturbations of the patterns of directed trade according to mercantile opportunism, and that these secured very numerous and diverse outlets for commodities in the same way that would have been expected of a more market-orientated system. And it should be added that there was a wide multiplicity of centres to which trade might be in the technical sense 'directed' (the enormous consumption of Italian wine in late Republican Gaul was an example which we discussed in VI.9). Quite generally in Mediterranean history, the logic of intensification which underlies the production of goods for redistribution has been linked to a high degree of predictability about the destination, or at least the type of destination.

To argue thus is not, of course, to belittle the historical significance of exchange. The eastern harbour-basin of Apollonia in Cyrenaica is covered with a 30 cm-thick layer of broken amphorae of the years 180–150 B.C. Roughly a quarter are wine amphorae from the viticultural islands of Rhodes, Chios and

Cos, and their mainland neighbour Cnidos. A quarter are fragments of local pottery. And about a tenth reflect the burgeoning production of wine in the Tyrrhenian and Sicily, with the Dressel 1 just beginning (Laronde 1996a, 16). The thickness of the deposit of a single generation's consumption in a single city should be stressed. A likely explanation for it is the introduction of a garrison and the development of the city as a major fortified strongpoint. The very abrupt start and finish in this provision of wine, therefore, seems to reflect a 'directed' trade. Such special imperatives of consumption and redistribution have usually been arising, and dissolving, all over the Mediterranean. Exchanges obey the same fickle logic that we have seen in agriculture.

Intensification, technology and directed trade

In our earlier account of intensification and abatement (VII.4) we saw the wide variety of agencies responsible in the Mediterranean for the particular uses made of the opportunities of each microecology. We find no obstacle to extending that analysis to the opportunity offered by redistribution. The same range of entities is visible.

At one end of the spectrum lies 'the state', and especially the greater states that have controlled a substantial portfolio of Mediterranean environments, with imperial Rome as the *ne plus ultra*. These are the most developed examples of trade 'directed' to the point at which it becomes part of a command economy. We should recall, however, that the 'command effect' is not limited to control of the movement of goods (VII.6). It may begin at the moment of decision-making about production, and extend to the moment of consumption. Requisitioning of many different types, tribute and tax in kind, and illegal exactions by the powerful, are part of the legacy which the Mediterranean world received from its Near Eastern neighbours and adapted to its own conditions. Under the Romans, the cereal surpluses of Cyrenaica (III.3) were channelled into the state supply system. A relative shortage of oil and wine, to be attributed to the increase in cereal production, appears to have ensued. These essential commodities were made available by importers, whose commerce we discern through the Italian coarseware pottery which is abundant in Cyrenaica, and which had travelled epiphenomenally to the trade in oil and wine (Riley 1981). The command import of grain thus benefited the imperial power twice over, and had a more complex effect on the economy than the direct stimulation of what was of greatest importance to the empire, the accumulation of staples. The duties often levied on trade goods, reflected in the customs regulations that we have several times used as evidence, could also have a major impact on economic geography. It would be easy to assume with Cassiodorus, who writes (*Variae*, 4.19) of sailors who fear customs-posts more than storms, that these duties simply acted as a brake on commerce. But their effect may have been more subtle. Levies such as those of Zarai (Section 3 above) were payable in coin, and therefore will have enhanced the commercialization of redistribution on the part of those who could expect to pay them. We may compare Hopkins's (1980) model for the economy of the Roman Empire, according to which the need to produce more so as to earn money to pay taxes generated commerce. Directed trade in the strict sense is only the core of a system of stimuli applied to redistribution by the exactions of central authorities.

At the other end of the spectrum from that of the state, in all periods of Mediterranean history there have been more or less independent brokers, un-trammelled in their opportunistic behaviour by fixed sources of supply and consumption. Most redistribution – and in this aggregate we must remember once again to include piracy and plunder – has in all the periods which we are considering been in the hands of people who belong under neither extreme: warships engaged in piracy, merchants part of whose cargo is subsidized, all those whose cargo is in part directed to a particular market dominated by a cultural or political elite.

A distinction which we hope to be able to by-pass through the application of an essentially ecological methodology is therefore that between private enter-prise and the role of the state, another shibboleth for the recognition of the qualitative superiority of the medieval West. One of the odder consequences of drawing this distinction has been the view that state-managed enterprises are somehow not properly economic, and that they represent a primitive stage in the development which leads to the achievements of the later Middle Ages. State intervention is also held to be a sign of problems: when warships in the eleventh-century Aegean are found intervening in island redistribution, seizing goods and acting as the agents of the exchanges, 'nous apprenons . . . que les îles exportaient avant tout des produits agricoles de base, ce qui confirme tout ce que nous avons dit de l'économie insulaire' (Malamut 1988, 383–469 at 437). The episode is indeed not so different from peacetime trade. But it does not reveal a backward economic state. It is the normal economic life of the sea.

The great variety of forms taken by the very loosely defined intervention of the state in economic life and the difficulty of defining the boundary between state and non-state activity, or between public and private, pose difficulties for 'minimalist' views of the Mediterranean economy (V.4). They also, however, make it hard to accept the attempts associated with the 'New Institutional Eco-nomics' to take advantage of apparent regularities in the state-run economies, particularly of the Fertile Crescent and of Egypt, so as to apply in a formalist spirit the laws of modern economic theory to the ancient world (Andreau et al. 1994). The Gordian knot can readily be cut on the analysis which we propose. We have already seen how response to the conditions of production cannot but create opportunities for management in the broad sense, and these opportun-ities for control, planning and system in the choice of labour, strategy, crop, storage technique and redistribution are naturally embedded in whatever power structures pertain locally at a given moment. It is therefore unsurprising to find every point on the scale of institutional complexity represented in the nexus of production and distribution – from the self-determining family through to the co-ordinated supply systems of thalassocratic empires. At Dia in Bithynia, for example, in the Roman period, a civic benefactor was praised for works at the 'emporium' and for thereby increasing the civic revenues derived from the 'emporium' (*IGRR*, 3.1427, cf. Robert 1980, 74). After the colonization of Patmos in the early twelfth century, the monastery's boats gave shape to an extended maritime hinterland; those of the monastery of Nea Mone on Chios ran the sea route between Chios and Smyrna (Malamut 1988, 452–3). Many consumers, we should also recall, were not independent purchasers (Reekmans 1994, 132): landowners may control consumption as well as production, redis-tribution and storage.

The 'lubricant' required to ease as much as possible the 'friction' of passage by land is as much a matter of social engineering as of communications technology. Establishing the status of the trader, ensuring the safe movement of an envoy, guaranteeing the embassy from harassment are more important to the encouragement of a commonalty of terrestrial regions than technical improvements in bearings, harness or road-surfaces (V.1). A maritime *koine* was 'cheaper' in human terms, and developed much sooner, not just because of energy requirements, but because at sea the incidental hazards of negotiation, protection-money, wilful obstruction and downright violence were so much rarer than in the carrying of goods across region after region, through settlement after settlement, by land. The main result of this is to make it impossible to compare directly the 'real' costs of land and sea transport, since the former always depended on the degree of 'social lubrication' available. It makes little sense to estimate the cost of the movement of grain by land when it might be transferred as tribute, as military requisition, as rent, as part of a single landowner's agricultural strategy, as a crisis-speculation or as 'straight' trade. The expense of the oxen and carts might be constant – the social overheads would be vastly different in each of these cases. One example of scholarly failure to appreciate this fact is the frequently repeated observation about the relative costs of land and sea transport in Antiquity based on figures from Diocletian's Price Edict (cf. Duncan-Jones 1982, 368): for these figures do not concern economic costs but maximum permitted hauliers' rates. It would be an unwise industrial manager who estimated his transportation costs on a quotation of Pickfords. The paradoxical result is that not infrequently land transportation – for the fortunate transporter – is less prohibitively expensive than the most pessimistic modern economic historians have supposed.

The argument of this section supports the coherence, with respect to both place and time, of the various Mediterranean phenomena which it is the business of this book to examine. It was the agents of background redistribution who created the Mediterranean continuum, not the great shipowners of Roman Puteoli or medieval Venice. The patterns of high commerce have been remarkably inconstant. Redistribution remains.

5. The Ultimate Resource

Redistribution takes resources out of one microregion and transfers them to another. The definition of resource that we have used has been largely ecological. Microregions offer soils, minerals, climatic advantages, water, the produce of the wild environment; they offer the yields of crops; they offer the more abstract contributions of safe storage or easy communications. The other variable is human labour, and that, as we have seen, moves in and out of microregions – indeed must do so if redistribution is to take place. Redistribution encourages mobility; crews tend to be heterogeneous in origin (Mollat du Jourdin 1993, 172–4). In the winter of 1369–70, Pellegro Maraboto's diplomatic voyage from Genoa to the Aegean took eight-one days. Twenty-four nights were spent at sea and the remainder in some fifty ports (Map 12). Maraboto lost ten crew in Calabria, at Methone, and on Rhodes, and took on thirteen new recruits. A contemporary, Simone Lecarella, lost seventy-six crew to casualties and desertions

(Balard 1974). Sailing itself can be seen as a seasonal use of excess labour: the annual cycle of work may include redistributive opportunities as well as productive ones.

The conveying of people in itself, an economic activity for which Aristotle created the separate category of 'ferrying' (*porthmeutike*), is an important form of redistribution. Cassiodorus reports an interesting case in which fraudulent ship-owners have earned 280 *solidi* from the sale elsewhere of grain intended as a directed supply for Rome, and 758 from fares of passengers, both sums now being demanded by the king (*Variae*, 5.35). In this instance at least it appears that mobility, in the form of ferrying or passenger transit, was more profitable than trade. Not all economically significant forms of mobility were so relatively benign.

We have seen that it is useful to give an account of the redistribution of materials and foodstuffs which starts with the variable resources of a fragmented microregional landscape. The mobility of people can be analysed in an essentially similar way. Not only is it an obviously inevitable corollary of the moving of other things, but population itself can be seen as a deployable resource within the diversity of the environment. The Mediterranean lands for most of our period have been predominantly underpopulated (VII.4). Mediterranean populations have found it hard to reproduce themselves. And the scarcer the population, the greater the care required in deploying it. This is one of the reasons why abatement is as typical as intensification in the productive landscape. Much of the landscape of the Mediterranean lands has been underused for much of the time because there have simply not been enough people. The Roman census, which aimed at considerable accuracy, was not designed to calibrate population growth but to register the most valuable of a polity's resources: its people. The management of human numbers is a basic political and economic activity. Even states fearful of the foreigner on cultural grounds none the less, almost despite themselves, produce machinery, institutions, which promote assimilation and acculturation. A tolerance of the naturalized foreigner lies, for example, uneasily alongside a paranoid exclusiveness towards the serious alien in Byzantine history (Lopez 1978). Rome's ambiguous openness to new citizens, her development of incorporative structures of citizenship, has been perceived, both in Antiquity and since, as a principal reason for her political success (Sherwin-White 1973). Those states such as classical Athens which could afford exclusive citizenship were those which had the good fortune to be demographically more prosperous; elsewhere, the proud intransigence of Sparta towards new citizens led to demographic catastrophe.

Each season sees a changing distribution of resources, as the accidents of meteorology and the responses of human planning intermesh. People are a key variable in this shifting economic geography. The question at any moment in Mediterranean history must be: where are the people? They may be conspicuous, moving about the landscape – everywhere in the best periods, only more patchily in others. Or they may be inconspicuous, clustered in tight huddles or in remote places, fearing conditions of insecurity and locally suffering from them. They may be more sedentary, based in stable productive settlements, or more mobile, given to joining wandering social entities such as bandit groups, armies, pilgrimages, mercenary-bands, caravans. They can be very hard to see. The ancients, talking about population, talk in visual terms – of crowdedness, *frequentia*, or its opposite, 'sparseness', *infrequentia*. For them, a well-populated area is simply one where plenty of the right sort of people are on show: aggregates are by and large of secondary importance. 'Ubique populus', says Tertullian in *De anima* (30.4) – 'people everywhere'. That was the desired state of affairs. Abundant population is one of the greatest blessings which a city or region can enjoy, and these concepts are a prominent *mentalité* of the Greeks and Romans.

Among the massive handling of all kinds of resource characteristic of the larger states, management of manpower finds an important place. This is a concept that has long been familiar to historians of the ancient Near East. The great empires of the Babylonians, Assyrians and Persians devoted themselves to the organization and redeployment for their own political purposes of all the useful resources at their disposal; and those included not only the usual raw materials of commissariat and arsenal, but also the vital human resource, shifted in tens of thousands through recruitment, conscription and mass-deportation. The familiar constants of Mediterranean history – colonization, slavery and the raising of mercenary armies – continued these ancient 'structures' into more familiar historical epochs (we return to some of them in more detail below). Nor are they limited to the mere pursuit of large aggregates: certain types of person are more valuable to the recreation of the demographic resource. 'In rural communities located in the margins of larger state-societies women formed the most precious and vulnerable part of the patrimony of men' (Blok 1981, 62; Chapter XII). Repugnant as it is to dehumanize the agents of history in this way, the behaviour of Mediterranean communities suggests that such an approach is not alien to the attitudes of the periods under consideration.

'Overpopulation is always a relative, not an absolute, concept' (Slicher van Bath 1963, 12). It has not, even considered relatively, been a common Mediterranean phenomenon (cf. VII.4–5). Plato's celebrated and dramatic 'ancient device', the sending out of colonies (*apoikiai*), was essentially a means of keeping the polity to an optimum size for the working of social institutions (*Laws*, 740 e). If it was occasionally used to counter economic blows such as famine, it remained fundamentally a political solution to the problem of how to share citizens' goods among citizens, rather than an economically motivated response to a real demographic crisis. For one thing, most *apoikiai* were at their inception composed of adult male citizens only. What Greek state in a moment of supposed demographic pinch ever gave up its slaves? The Roman practice of hiving off segments of the citizen population and settling them elsewhere is likewise due to the social tension caused by the problem of having too many poor citizens rather than by that of having overall too many mouths to feed. We should also recall how effective a rhetorical exculpation it is to plead demographic *force majeure* when accused of greed and aggression. There is no reason to invoke population explosion to account for the relatively sudden involvement of the Greeks in making the most of the opportunities of the *koine* of connectivity – they were neither the first nor the last to experience such an inception. Demographic felicity, hard to attain, quick to disappear, is more often the consequence than the cause of such episodes.

So the demography of the cities and regions which were the setting of the social, political and cultural developments of the Archaic Greek period must not be viewed in isolation either from one another or from the world in which they were set. It has been rightly called 'naïve to treat the demography of a society as a result of its economic constitution' (Wrigley 1969, 49). Certainly the effects of the various kinds of local intensification on demography are very often strongly delimited by environmental conditions (e.g. Broshi 1980, on the Negev). But more importantly, demographic bubbles are burst by two processes: the mobility of the population itself, and the redistribution of resources between different localities. As we argued in VII.4, demographic stability was maintained by mobility, and food crisis was more often the social consequence of 'entitlement failure' than the narrowly ecological one of Malthusian growth.

Who was your mother's maternal grandmother?

It is natural to be persuaded by the terrible violence of many episodes of population transfer that they entail demographic catastrophe. They do often entail the extinction of social communities, and are therefore described in final terms by witnesses and commentators. Yet, from a larger perspective, they are often more redistributive than destructive. An Epirote woman who was enslaved by the conquering Romans in 167 B.C. and transported to Italy and who bore five slave-children on a Roman estate, or a Christian farmer seized by corsairs from the Balearics and pressed into a life of drudgery in Algiers, where none the less he could procreate, did not cease to be demographically significant because they were redistributed through violence, because their offspring were not the legitimate product of a legal union in a fixed place of abode. Bartholomew of Yano gives a figure of 400,000 Turkish slave acquisitions between 1437 and 1443. Even allowing for exaggeration, the demographic impact of the episode must have been considerable (Alexandrescu-Drersca 1987, 17). Our conception of the Mediterranean world is one in which it is through just such redeployments of human resources that the spectre of net population decline is averted. We believe neither that most country folk were the grandchildren of country folk in the same region, nor that most inhabitants of nucleated settlements could claim to be third-generation inhabitants.

The term 'depopulation' thus covers both loss to a particular state authority of a certain demographic resource – such as Byzantium's 'huge losses in population by the conquests of the Arabs' (Charanis 1966) – and actual demographic decrease. A major war may well result in both, but the historian needs to distinguish the two carefully. Saracen pirates thus 'depopulated' Athens in the eighth century: closer scrutiny reveals that they in fact were engrossed in the local population (Setton 1944). Much the same happened when Slavic immigrants 'depopulated' the Peloponnese from the sixth century, and during the troubled early medieval period in Sicily, where substantial population continuity can now be maintained against the older view of hiatus (Molinari 1994). Turkish depredations 'depopulated' the Aegean islands (Hasluck 1910–11). But in the sixteenth century, for instance, the inhabitants of Samos were at one point simply relocated on Chios. The 'depopulation theory' has also been comprehensively reconsidered with respect to the Cyclades of this period, and found wanting (cf. Slot 1982).

One source of these interpretative difficulties with depopulation is that historical demography, developed outside the Mediterranean, has usually considered static populations and has not produced models for how populations readjust by lateral movement in conditions of great mobility. And this is because such conditions are not widespread, indeed are perhaps nowhere so well developed as in the Mediterranean coastlands. Another problem is the more general one of specifying to which subset of the Mediterranean population any individual belonged. Who counts as part of the really indigenous population of a microregion, and for how long?

Why islands have large populations

Population belongs in this chapter not only because it is useful to see it as a resource in itself, but because its behaviour is intimately related to the systems of redistribution which we have been examining. Populations 'share' the collective fruits of intensification: in times of trouble, informally by plunder, theft or seizure; in times of greater stability, in the various structures of commerce, tribute, charity, benefaction and the gradual beginnings of a market economy.

The consequence is that population density maps onto communications. The zone of easy movement constituted by the maritime *koine* has the highest concentrations of people, whether these are the product of gentle natural increase or – much more likely – long- or short-term gatherings of the mobile inhabitants of places with easy access to the sea. This is what lies behind the striking phenomenon of the high and dense populations of Mediterranean islands, going far beyond any usual estimate of their 'carrying capacity'.

The island of Naxos in the early fifth century B.C. had a population large enough to field 8,000 hoplites (Herodotus, *History*, 5.30). Populations of 30,000 on each of Minorca and Majorca are suggested for the Hellenistic period (Diodorus Siculus, *Historical Library*, 5.17). We should note also the case of Vroulia, on the southern tip of Rhodes, densely occupied and with copious storage facilities, from 625 to 575 B.C. or thereabouts *only*, and clearly orientated wholly to the sea: a prime instance of settlement instability (I. Morris 1992, 174–99). Ustica, off Sicily, only 8,600 ha in size, supported 3,633 people in the nineteenth century and has been revealed as a major settlement in the Bronze Age too. The island-cities of Aradus off the Phoenician coast, and ancient Tyre with its notorious 'high-rise' developments, are further examples. From Antiquity, the clearest case of all is Aegina (Figueira 1981, esp. 22–64, with 47–52). In 1812–13 Ithaca had 7,000–8,000 inhabitants and by itself could feed about a quarter of them: the trade in currants from the Peloponnese financed the remaining imports (H. Holland 1815, 52).

Another traveller to visit the island in the same period noted how the deep, sheltered harbour at Vathy attracted ships to Ithaca, and created a demand for labour, and especially for mariners, from as far afield as the Kingdom of Naples. While labour was very dear, both arable and pastoral agriculture declined and land prices fell (Gell 1807). The involvement of ancient Aegina in redistribution offers a parallel explanation for its high population. An Athenian treatise of the fifth century opines that the thalassocrat does not need to fear the foundation of new cities to oppose his rule, since if all the islanders gathered in one place they would soon starve ([Xenophon] *Constitution of the Athenians*, 2.2). Yet several islands did concentrate their populations in just this way. Rhodes was the most famous example, and undoubtedly owed its ability to take this step to control of maritime movements. The demographic flux that followed induced the city to attempt to preserve, through social institutions, a core of families of the

presynoicism *poleis* (Rice 1988; IV.2). Comparable social engineering with regard to the aristocracy is recorded from Cyprus under the Venetian dominion
(Arbel 1989).

The pattern is not limited to literal islands: as we have seen, many a coastal
microregion is to all practical purposes an island, its communications maintained
by sea rather than over the mountains. Here too a favoured location may make
possible the use of the redistribution of the *koine* to support a larger population
than would be predicable of the local environment. When we find population-
densities of 3, 4, 10, 12 to the hectare, therefore, we are entitled to ask whether
the Mediterranean landscape generally is so surprisingly supportive, or whether
it is not rather the redistributed abundance of the great overproducing zones
and the places which (that season) have done freakishly well that is maintaining
the population. Island settlements are much more than the refuges for which
they are often taken: the example of Venice is important not as one of abject
flight in circumstances of cultural disaster, but as the nearly incredible success
that could attend settlements favourably placed to enjoy the full benefit of the
maritime *koine*.

Where are the people? On the move. Where then do we count them? This
question is more difficult, and is the cause of considerable wasted effort. (It was
a Mediterranean power which at least in one context came up with the logistic-
ally bizarre solution of counting them at the place where they thought their
family belonged: namely, in the best-attested case, Bethlehem in Judaea.) Since
mobility may take an individual across many important local sub-regions in the
course even of a single year, the aggregate population of a particular regionally
defined unit at any one moment may not be a very helpful statistic – which is
just as well, given that such aggregates are virtually impossible to determine
within our chronological and geographical range. To illustrate: take the notional
population in a defined place at a moment in historical time. As the seasons
change (therefore in a matter of months) many of those assessed in that figure
will be altogether elsewhere – pursuing seasonal agricultural goals ten, a hundred, two hundred miles away; or following the lure or compulsion of political
or military activity two hundred, five hundred or a thousand miles away; on
pilgrimage, sold into slavery, emigrating, engaged in the redistribution of surpluses – all the forms of mobility which we must consider further in their own
right in Section 6 of this chapter. There is no difficulty in imagining momentary
aggregates changing by many per cent through circumstances like these, and no
reason – over a period of years, now, not months – to divide populations into a
large sedentary core and a substantial mobile group. The proportion of those
who are sometimes mobile, in the course of individual lifetimes, may in some
cases be very high.

Hence we will find it theoretically impossible to talk of 'the population of
a city' – such as Rome in Antiquity, for example. At any instant there will be
within its built-up area hundreds who will not be there tomorrow, thousands
who will have left by the end of the year, tens of thousands who will have moved
away in the course of a decade. Some will have travelled only ten miles for casual
manual or agricultural labour; others will have gone to the extremes of the
Mediterranean world. Take Musicus, a slave of the Emperor Tiberius who happened to die at Rome while there on official business, and was therefore buried
there. He held a moderately senior post in the administration of taxes in central

Gaul. His entourage, who dedicated his tombstone (for all that he was a slave), included a business secretary, a major expenses secretary, three personal valets, a doctor, one wardrobe-attendant, two valets de chambre, two footmen, two cashiers, two cooks and a single woman, Secunda, whose role is not specified (*ILS*, 1514). Had Musicus not died, where would these sixteen people have been in six months' time?

Migration of sizeable groups from one region to another has also to be reckoned: for example that from Greece to the overseas settlements of the Archaic Age, or of Romans and Italians to Spain and Africa in the last two centuries B.C., or of the Jews around the Mediterranean in the Hellenistic period (explicitly compared with the Greek *apoikiai* by Philo and Josephus), or the various movements within the Islamic world such as those from Iraq to the Levant from the ninth to the eleventh century (Ashtor 1972, 90–1). In very many of these instances what happens is a grafting of new demographic elements onto the existing population, and a relabelling of the next generation. The fact that a few hundred Corinthians founded Syracuse, which five generations later was a city of tens of thousands of inhabitants, does not signal a natural increase by a factor of twenty each generation. Rather, the populations of Sicily were progressively incorporated in the evolving civic community of Syracuse, and we can account for the growth of that community without assuming that each generation did more than reproduce itself.

As with abatement in the countryside, nucleated populations are not immune to being dispersed. As we have argued with respect to towns (Chapter IV), agglomerations form and dissolve. In medieval Sicily violent changes in urban ranking can be observed for which 'the main cause . . . seems to have been individual mobility' (S. R. Epstein 1992, 70). A study of late medieval Périgueux concluded that 'il est évident . . . que sans l'apport du peuplement étranger la ville n'aurait pu vivre' (Higounet-Nadal 1978, 214). It has been argued that, in similar centres in Spain such as Cuenca, intense mobility was 'based on the dynamic resourcefulness of people who were able to maximize income diversification so as to ensure the maintenance of living standards in the face of on-going rural population growth'. It promoted stability, and proved a highly successful adaptive strategy – on the part of the local population's 'hypermobile subsectors' (Reher 1990, 296–8).

6. ORGANIZED MOBILITY

> This stream [of mountain peasants] submerged lower Languedoc . . . The procession reformed every year, almost every day, and was made up of landless peasants, unemployed artisans, casual agriculture labourers down for the harvest, the grape harvest, or threshing, outcasts of society, beggars and beggar-women, travelling preachers, gyrovagues – vagabonds – street musicians, and shepherds with their flocks. (Braudel 1972a, 47)

Mediterranean mobility vividly pictured. These are the ordinary country people of the Mediterranean environment, the producers who were not fortunate enough, we argued in VII.5, to deserve the label 'peasant' ('another feature we associate with traditional peasantry is geographical immobility': Macfarlane 1984, 342, questioning the dominance of societies of this type in medieval northern Europe too). Those travellers portrayed in medieval Languedoc have little share in the security of the family, its property, its home and its livelihood. Besides geographical mobility, their lot entails wage labour and – as Braudel goes on to hint rather coyly ('in the long run they contributed to the human stock of the lowlands') – exogamy. Braudel further attributed the distinctive characteristics of the peoples of the Dalmatian and Catalan litorals to the marine communications which exposed them to acculturative influences from across the sea (1972a, 57–8). The sea itself intensifies the effect that we have seen in Languedoc, and opens it to other categories of the dispossessed.

In Antiquity too, abandonment of the traditional home had been a genuine option. If there was a cultural predilection for continuity and stability, it often did not outweigh the less welcome conditions of that fixity, especially dependence and exploitation. In the third century A.D., in two cases for which evidence has happened to survive, the villagers of Scaptopara in Thrace (X.3) and Philadelphia in Lydia threatened to desert their ancestral abodes and tombs to avoid local oppression (De Ste Croix 1981, 216). The idea of cutting loose and taking off – *anachoresis* is the usual Greek term – constitutes a characteristic *mentalité* of the time. Indeed, in Egypt, where it was particularly common, it came to refer to religious withdrawal, thus giving us the term 'anchorite'. During late Antiquity, in response to the footloose wanderers, concepts of immobility became part of the repertoire of virtue: both *stabilitas* and the disciplined mobility that is *militia* turned into catchphrases. Soon, within monasticism, a firm distinction was made between settled communities and the reprehensible, mobile, gyrovagues (McDonnell 1980). These attitudes are intelligible only against the background of a very fluid society – just as autarky is valued only in an interdependent world. Neither in sixteenth-century Languedoc nor in late Antiquity was geographical mobility a particularly comfortable option; but it was a perennial reality. Of medieval Spain, 'it is a commonplace that kings of this period governed by itineration. It is less often remembered that their subjects were intensely mobile as well' (Richard Fletcher 1989, 81). Even when it is remembered, the fact has seldom been properly accommodated by historians.

This category of the displaced, driven from the community by violence or need, makes an appropriate beginning for our survey of Mediterranean mobility. The underlying motor of Mediterranean movements was, after all, the temporary or perennial maldistribution of the full range of resources on which life depends. In correcting that unevenness, the anxiety and misery which can be its products coexist with the – by no means inevitable – satisfaction of the want. In the cultural history of the Mediterranean lands these facts have produced many different responses. With regard to ancient Greece, for example, one can point to the evolution of tightly defined notions of citizenship, and the whole extraordinary range of institutions and attitudes concerned with losing and regaining its rights – expulsion, exile, recall and bringing back into the community. One city claimed inalienable autochthony; every other Greek was conscious of being the end-result of movement.

It is not possible to say which type of movement came first, the 'safe, controlled' ones or the 'violent, compelled' ones: both are closely connected and each reinforces the other as part of the range of possibilities available to the inhabitants of the Mediterranean. Braudel (1972a, 454) linked vagrancy and casual mobility with unemployment. But there are many other ingredients, in all the shifting and interlocking fortunes of the different microregions. The common denominator may be no more than the knowledge that movement is an option, and the means, psychological and physical, to undertake it. Voluntary emigration on a large scale, unprompted by economic malaise, has after all been important in some periods, such as the epoch of the consolidation of Rome's power in Italy during the third and second centuries B.C. It may be taken as diagnostic of high levels of general mobility, since 'net migration is almost always only a small fraction of the gross, and hence any pattern of net migration flows may be very far from showing the true levels of actual movement' (Hollingsworth 1969, 105).

Emigration therefore plays an important part in promoting an expectation of mobility in Mediterranean societies. If the movements of the early modern period are anything to go by, these are processes which tend primarily to involve young males: of 27,000 departures from France to Canada between 1608 and 1763 only 1,767 were women (Poussou 1994, 27). That reassures the Mediterranean historian of earlier periods about comparability. It is not difficult to postulate displacements of this order of magnitude for almost any of the centuries that concern us.

The movements which we have been examining – voluntary or not – beat with an irregular, slow pulse. The individual's experience of them comes perhaps once or twice in a lifetime. But this is not the only rhythm of personal mobility. Indeed this large-scale, slow mobility can only be understood against a backdrop of movements at a much quicker tempo, experienced by very many Mediterranean people much more regularly. The most useful heading for these is perhaps 'agricultural mobility'.

In a relatively uniform landscape with little topographical variety and a limited range of soil-types, agricultural exploitation is susceptible of a high degree of centralization. In most Mediterranean landscapes, by contrast, the extreme topographical diversity makes it essential for the population of each microregion to be quite mobile if the full range of environmental opportunities is to be exploited. Various studies have examined the scatter of plots of Mediterranean agriculturalists, and the distances which they may have to travel either seasonally or much more frequently – and often by sea (cf. III.4). The degree of such mobility within a given area is related to the level of the effort made to intensify production. It is also an important ingredient in the evolution of attitudes to 'home' and 'away' which differ markedly from those of perennially immobile agricultural societies in other parts of the world (VII.5). These attitudes underlie that willingness, which we have noted above, to move more thoroughly and more permanently. The fixity attributed to peasant societies is founded on uniform distribution of environmental opportunities and on the low, local, regular mobility which results from it. The reverse is true of the Mediterranean.

Transhumance is a case in point (III.6). No qualitative boundary distinguishes the flexible response to winter and summer pasture resources within a subregion six miles across from the extended versions which exploit the high pastures of whole mountain chains and involve the pastoralist in journeys of dozens of miles. It is simply a question of the width of horizon, of the pastoralist's own view of the size of the environment which he is to use. That view expands and contracts gradually; the movements remain similar in kind. Much the same can be said of nomadism. The nomad, too, is part of a spectrum of strategies for making use of scattered and precarious environmental opportunities. He is not a type to be set in polar opposition to the sedentary agriculturalist but one who operates in symbiosis with a whole range of other practices – including sedentary farming – in an effective and reliable use of the natural landscape as a whole, which allows for the variations between place and place and season and season. The mobility of the most far-wandering nomad is just one extreme of a scale that can be used for measuring the activities of any Mediterranean primary producer.

Further, the movements in the landscape of the primary producer are not simply concerned with the extraction of what the environment offers. They involve also the deployment of what is extracted – at ports, fairs, sanctuaries, villages, markets, cities. The constant 'ebb and flow between country and town' (Braudel 1972a, 338) is part of the overall mobility which characterizes the Mediterranean countryside. Stays in the city may be no longer than a few hours, or they may last half a lifetime: from a brief visit to the cycle of emigration and return. The road to the centre of the microregion and back again is one of the most frequently used channels of Mediterranean mobility.

Not that our mobility demonstrates freedom. This is obviously so in the case of the slave, less so in that of the craftsman, the mercenary, the merchant and the pilgrim. All our mobile types are locked into structures of obligation, whether more or less reciprocal, and are bound with social and cultural ties as much as any completely stationary peasant cultivator – even when they are travelling hundreds of miles from the place where they were born. Indeed their travelling reinforces, extends, diversifies the networks of reciprocity and the structures of self-definition, and furthers the cultural, intellectual and social homogeneities which have been so prominent a part of the history of the Mediterranean. The dense 'interactivity' (I.1) which is linked in Antiquity with the great athletic or cultural festivals is an outgrowth of this aspect of Mediterranean life. It had a noteworthy religious dimension, as did the journeyings of people to spas and resorts in the Roman period. Along with the still more important religious manifestation of Christian and Islamic pilgrimage, we shall examine this in more detail in the next chapter (Section 4).

The wandering artisan is a product of a *koine* which draws its energy in part from the irregular distribution of material resources. Both craftsmen, as with the potters discussed in Section 4, and raw materials, as we saw in the case of metalworking (above, Section 2), moved freely in this *koine*. Among the characteristic Mediterranean figures are therefore the *demiourgos*, the artisan or professional whose craft marked out a special status that was often stateless, and the *metoikos*, the 'person who has changed abode', as the principal entrepreneurs of Greek *poleis*, above all Athens (Whitehead 1977). If less formally institutionalized in later ages, travelling craftsmen – people such as Flavius Zeuxis of Phrygian Hierapolis, who rounded Malea 72 times on his way to Italy (*IGRR*, 4.841) – remain important to the culture of the fair and the market from the Roman period into the Islamic and Christian Middle Ages (see further below, Section 7). Like the movements of seafarers and the emigrant, these are patterns which are essentially male (Jacoby 1994a, 550).

The destructive arts, too, are practised by the wandering specialist. The individual *condottiere* is another familiar Mediterranean figure, whether Dorieus the Spartan in the Ionian Sea in the sixth century B.C. (Herodotus, *History*, 5.41– 8), or Dragut the corsair in the same waters in the sixteenth (Braudel 1972a, 907–11), perhaps leading a band of settlers or robbers. Crusader, pirate, colonist, or heroic trader-adventurer; Carthaginian, Milesian, Norman, or Turk – such individuals took advantage of the freedom of the *koine* to explore its various openings and opportunities. Sometimes independent, they were also often engaged in the more or less assiduous service of Mediterranean states, which organized mobility in the interests of their own military manpower. Greek soldiers from Ionia who were rewarded for their individual valour expressed in inscriptions their pride and wide horizons. A striking example from near Priene speaks of the gift of a city as the mercenary's reward for his services to an early sixth-century B.C. pharaoh (Şahin 1987). At the same date the poet Alcaeus's brother was fighting in the Fertile Crescent (fr. Z27, ed. Lobel and Page 1955). The Saite pharaohs employed Carians from Anatolia; Italian mercenaries served a wide range of Hellenistic states; Carthage drew soldiers from Liguria and the Celtic lands north of the western Mediterranean, and experienced acute disruption in the late third century from the volatility of the ethnic mix that it had created (Polybius, *History*, 1.79). Densely populated islands offered this lucrative use for their manpower alongside the others that we have met (Herodotus, *History*, 7.165 (Corsica); Pausanias, *Description of Greece*, 10.17.5 (Sardinia)). Rome's armies contained more non-Romans than Romans at most periods; armies in the medieval period likewise were usually of bewildering ethnic variety. Sometimes summoned, employed, discharged and sent home, mercenaries also frequently became settlers, engaging in new demographic relationships by killing the men of a settlement and taking over the women (Diodorus Siculus, *Historical Library*, 14.9.9; Polybius, *History*, 1.7.2–8). They might also function as bandits, robbers, or traders, their activities shading into the other manifestations of mobility. Mercenary service and piracy have, in particular, been instructively interdependent (Gabbert 1986). So it is to piracy that we now turn.

Pirates and brigands

Mediterranean history should include the forcible, arbitrary and irregular movements of materials and people alongside those that have the sanction of commerce, gift exchange or tribute. So we have chosen to use the term 'redistribution' to cover both types. Mercenaries have appeared to be as integral to an ecological history as other mobile groups. The same may be said of pirates and brigands. A normal manifestation of Mediterranean production and redistribution, piracy can be seen as the continuation of *cabotage* by other means (V.5), although pirates can deal in high-value goods also (Brulé 1978, 159). It has been a systemic epiphenomenon of connectivity, suppressed by powerful states only for brief intervals in Mediterranean history. Like other skilled manpower, pirates have been employed (as privateers) in the defence of polities, or even as their *raison d'être*. In the first century B.C., piracy, and especially that from Cilicia, was so far from being the accidental result of local criminal opportunism that it was represented as an organized threat to Roman supremacy. The elite of archaic Samos developed its own value-system of plunder and ransom (Bravo 1980), and, in the same period, the oracle of Apollo at Didyma advised that it was right for pirates to do as their fathers did (A. H. Jackson 1995). Their activities, like those of the mercenary, were a calling of some potential stature.

Like *caboteurs* and traders, pirates are always parasitic on the communities with which they interact (V.5), and in this they resemble land-based brigands, whose economic dependence on ordinary communities was noticed in the sixth-century *Digest* (1.18.13 *preamble*, Ulpian). The brigand gang of the third-century A.D. folk hero, Bulla Felix, operating in southern Italy, 'learned of everybody that was setting out from Rome and putting in to Brundisium, who they were, how large a party, what goods they had with them, and in what quantity' (Cassius Dio, *Roman History*, 77.10.2). But this dependence, like specializing in any form of redistribution, was only one item in the ecological portfolio of alternatives. Attempts have been made at certain periods to encourage or to compel pirates to turn away from the sea towards a greater emphasis on primary production. Evidence on Crete for the recolonization of pirate landscapes may even suggest an oscillation between production and redistribution, analogous to other characteristic cyclical shifts in patterns of exploitation (Rackham and Moody 1997, 197–9).

The aspect of pirate behaviour that particularly concerns us here is the way in which it has served to wed the movement of materials and the mobility of people. Pausanias relates an anecdote which illuminates a number of the themes of this chapter. In the late third century B.C., Illyrians arrived in several ships at Mothone in Messenia and offered to buy local wine against their own cargo, but (untypically) at the local price. The inhabitants were enticed by the possibility of profit as the exchange continued into a second day. In the end, when the crowd was large, and came to include many women, the Illyrians seized them and sailed off 'leaving Mothone desolate' (Pausanias, *Description of Greece*, 4.35.6–7). Illyria is a good distance from Methone: in their engagement with the milieu of redistribution Mediterranean pirates reflect the tremendous connectivity of the sea by having startlingly wide horizons. In the fourth and third centuries B.C. pirates from the Tyrrhenian were a nuisance in the Adriatic and Aegean (Tarn 1913, 85–6). In the early seventeenth century, Pelaguza (now Palagruṣá) in the mid-Adriatic formed a base for pirates from distant Algiers (Moryson 1617, 270). Excavations suggest that during the first millennium B.C. this had been an important stopping-place for shipping from the equally remote Aegean, and that it should be identified with the sacred Island of Diomedes. Islands were naturally as important to piracy as to other forms of seaborne traffic. This is most clearly the case with the form of redistribution most characteristic of the Mediterranean pirate, the trade in human beings.

Understanding Mediterranean slavery

The forms of slavery which are characteristic of the Mediterranean are shaped by its connectivity. Demographic resources are valuable and uneven. Redistribution between microregions is easy and normal. Slavery is therefore indeed a 'structural feature of Mediterranean society' (Braudel 1972a, 754–5).

As in all slave studies, distaste, pity and guilt pattern the discussion (Bresc 1989; Meillassoux 1991). Yet, in our antipathy, we should not overlook the fact that enslavement was often the best available mechanism of escape, the most effective way of realizing potential mobility, for desperate people in hard times. Cassiodorus observed parents selling their children, in order to better them, at the fair of Leucothea in south Italy, to which we return in the next chapter (*Variae*, 8.33). Slavery occasionally provided a route for voluntary emigration from the medieval Maghreb. Alongside the numerically underrated practice of voluntary slavery, there were the slower but equally effective ways of gathering the human resource, such as the Turkish *devshirme*, the capturing and rearing as Turks of Christian children, common from the fourteenth century (Vryonis 1956). Slave-breeding was important in the Roman world, although it is impossible to estimate its demography (Scheidel 1997). But, in most ages, the most substantial contribution to the slave population was made by slave-raiding and exchange. And to that, as to other forms of redistribution, the sea was central.

Magister Nicetas, ambassador to the Arabs of Crete from the Byzantine emperor Leo VI (886–912), met a single aged monk in the ruins of Paros. This monk had been told of the miraculous encounter of a Euboean hunter, visiting Paros when it was totally deserted, with the aged Theoctiste. She had been seized from Lesbos by Cretan pirates but escaped into the wilderness of Paros, where she had lived ever since as an anchorite (*Vita S. Theoctistae*, 12–15, Acta Sanctorum, Nov., 4.228–9). Nearly two millennia before, the mother of Odysseus's swineherd Eumaeus was imagined as having been seized by Phoenican traders from the neighbouring island of Syros (Homer, *Odyssey*, 15.415–29). 'The most precious and vulnerable part of the patrimony of men', in the words quoted in the last section (Blok 1981, 62), have indeed suffered more than most from the pressures of redistribution. At the price of a fine, women in Ceos in the early third century B.C. were forbidden to wander around the island, so as to prevent their being seized by pirates (Mendoni 1989). Another inscription records the theft of women by pirates from Amorgos and Naxos (*SIG*[3], 520–1). There is no useful way of calibrating the demographic effect of the Roman slave-trade: we know that it involved, all told, millions of human beings (W. V. Harris 1980; Hopkins 1978b); but we have no idea of the reproductivity of slave *familiae* or of the demographic consequences of slave–free liaisons in various social contexts. But, given the medieval parallels, it is not unreasonable to expect that slaves played a notable part in maintaining the relatively stability of population levels in Roman Italy.

It has been argued that 'the medieval traffic in slaves was overwhelmingly a traffic in women' and that

> this sea-borne migration of unfree female labour anticipated the larger sea-borne migration across the Atlantic Ocean which began in the sixteenth century. In fact Mediterranean slaves, men and women alike, were employed on the plantations of Crete and other islands – a dress-rehearsal, so to speak, for their introduction on to the plantations of the New World. (Stuard 1995, 3, 27–28)

In the fourteenth-century Aegean and Peloponnese, women slaves were much more valuable than men (Lock 1995, 256, recording ratios of 17:8 hyperpers for 1317; 43:30 in the 1330s, and 96:64, 1380s). For Greek writers such as Ducas (9.1: Magoulias 1975, 73), the preference of Turks for Greek or Italian women was overwhelming. Already in the 1320s Ramon Muntaner (*Chronicle*, ed. Lanz 1843, 202) had described in less overstated terms how in the Hellespontine region the Turks took the local women to wife. The demographic consequences of Islamic elite polygamy were potentially very significant, especially in a society where there was a substantial influx of newcomers through the importation of the unfree (cf. Phillips 1985, 73–4). In the Maghreb of the fourteenth century we find thousands of slave-artisans of Christian origin at Tlemcen (Dufourcq 1975, 133); naturalization and procreation were inevitable.

At the same period, on the other side of the religious divide, at Perpignan most 'enfants trouvés' were offspring of Muslim slave women (1975, 142–3).

The ancient slave trade produced a major redistribution of population. 'The wealth that Rome has received from tributary Asia threefold shall Asia receive again from Rome . . . and for each of those who toil in the land of the Italians, twenty Italians shall labour in Asia as needy slaves.' So ran a subversive poem from the Roman East (*Sibylline Oracles*, 3.350ff). In the Middle Ages the slave-population of Provence and Catalonia came from all over the eastern Mediterranean, by no means exclusively from Muslim states (Dufourcq 1975, 142–3). The great redeployment of Black Sea slaves by Italian traders serving the needs of Muslim Egypt resulted in the end in the seizure of political power there by the Mamluks (Verlinden 1977, 949–63). The ubiquitous Balkan slaves shipped through the Adriatic ports in the late Middle Ages gave our language, among others, the use of the word Slav(e) for *servus* (1977, 797).

These demographically crucial movements were not usually the product of abrupt actions on the part of the powerful, by comparison with (say) the 'trawling' of the entire populations of Aegean islands by the Persians in the early fifth century B.C. (Herodotus, *History*, 3.149, cf. 6.31). The huge numbers of slaves – up to 150,000 from Epirus alone after 167 B.C. – imported to Italy during Rome's conquest of the Mediterranean in the second century B.C. (Hopkins 1978b) are rivalled by the consequences of medieval wars: the 40,000 enslaved at the Christian capture of Majorca (Bresc 1989) or the great gluts on the Mediterranean-wide market after the battle of Kosovo in 1389 and after the fall of Tripoli in 1510 (Braudel 1972a, 665, cf. 754–5). But these were untypical: the more normal scale was a continuous trickle involving a few captives at a time – ten, twelve, or twenty to a boat. As we see it clearly in the medieval documentary evidence (Verlinden 1977), it was a profitable sideline for those who exploited the *koine* in other ways: an additional cargo, like the others noted in Section 4. Such gradual relocation was maintained in a number of ways, all analogous to, and closely connected with, other forms of redistribution. A striking example is provided by the meeting of Roman and Gaul in the second and first centuries B.C. The peoples of non-Mediterranean Gaul became a specialized market for the wine trade of the Dressel 1 amphorae (Section 4 again), adopting wine consumption as a status symbol in aristocratic competition. They paid, we are told, in slaves, at the rate of one slave per 25-litre jar. The slaves thus acquired by Romans helped provide the manpower for the agricultural intensification of which this viticulture was a part; while, at the Gallic end, the quest for the slaves and the sharpened aristocratic competition engendered those internecine hostilities and debilities which eventually made the Roman conquest relatively easy (Diodorus Siculus, *Historical Library*, 5.26.3, with Tchernia 1983). Parallels may be found in Tartar exchanges of slaves for textiles in northern Black Sea ports (*PG*, 158.1061).

It is in the context of the normal networks of redistribution that we should observe how islands – a characteristic home, as we have seen, of the pirate – have also played a prominent part in the history of Mediterranean slavery (Bresc 1986b, 112, cf. 114). Thucydides observed that the number of slaves in the territory of the *polis* of Chios at the end of the fifth century B.C. was greater than that of any other city-state, except for the (very special) case of Sparta (*History*, 8.40.2). Slaves were also present in large numbers in the countryside round the island-*polis* of Corcyra (3.73). In both instances it is reasonable to see the precocious development of chattel slavery as the provision of a source of labour for the intensification of agricultural production: we have noted how well suited island locations are to that, because of the ease of redistribution. But they are advantaged likewise because the same patterns of connectivity that disperse their produce bring them the people whose labour alone can make it possible to increase production. Chios developed further in this direction; the details that are given of its slave practices during the fourth century by Theopompus and Nymphodorus, and of the eventual revolt against the freeborn by the slave Drimacus (*FGH*, 572 F 4: Athenaeus, *The Philosophers at the Dinner Table*, 265 d–f), include the interesting view that the Chiotes had been the first Greeks to buy barbarian slaves. (For exchanges of Chiote produce, especially wine, already by this period, see Sarikakis 1986). The slave-market of Delos, like its archaic importance as a centre of metallurgy (above, Section 2) was also the consequence of its maritime centrality (Bruneau 1988). Writers of the Hellenistic period give a further pertinent vignette of a characteristic Mediterranean island, Majorca. A population of 30,000 is alleged, while production is specifically said not to have included cash crops such as oil and wine. Mercenary pay, above all from Carthage, was vital: and the Majorcans used it to remedy a striking gender imbalance in the population, buying women captured by pirates from merchants at four to five times the going rate for men ([Aristotle] *On Wonderful Reports*, 88; Diodorus *Historical Library*, 5.17.2–3). Enclaves of the coastlands which formed 'islands not surrounded by sea' played a similar role to that of real islands in this context. The *Itinerarium Bernardi Monachi* describes the large-scale export of Christian slaves through the toe-holds established by the Arabs on the Italian coasts, for example one consignment of 9,000 Beneventans sent to Alexandria (Avril and Gaborit 1967; Tucciarone 1991).

The history of slavery is another area, for all that, in which attempts have been made to divide the phenomenon qualitatively into ancient and medieval, according to the extent to which the commoditization of slaves had developed, as distinct from the casual raiding for unfree labour (so Bensch 1994). Those attempts are related to the sometimes acrimonious debate, already hinted at, concerning the extent to which Mediterranean slavery in the later Middle Ages should be seen as precursor to the Atlantic slave trade (Stuard 1995, 27–8). Yet, as with other examples of the varying degrees of commoditization which we have examined in this chapter, the different modalities of buying and selling people can be fitted into a single overall ecological picture of Mediterranean history; they do not make useful markers for its periodization.

7. PLACES OF REDISTRIBUTION

Harbourlessness and the epiphenomenal port

'Italy . . . easily reached by all peoples, its shores abounding in harbours, its winds favourable and light' (Pliny, *Natural History*, 37.201) was bound to have a privileged place in Mediterranean history. 'The fact that [Italy] is in general harbourless combines with the wonderful capacity and quality of the harbours which do exist to promote the extraordinary scale of trade.' The second, more complex, variation on the theme is that of the geographer Strabo (*Geography*, 6.4.1). Which ancient witness is right? Did Italy abound in harbours or did it have only a few, but excellent ones? And which state of affairs is better, from which point of view? The examination of redistribution which has been undertaken in Sections 1–6 of this chapter may help us to resolve the apparent contradiction and answer those questions.

At the beginning of Chapter VII, we insisted on seeing 'la fertilité comme rapport social'. Connectivity – as we propounded it in Chapter V – is as much a 'rapport social' as fertility. Both are 'constructed' from the accidents of the physical environment by human endeavour; and the varying patterns of that endeavour are more important to the understanding and, above all to the historical interpretation, of relations such as fertility and connectivity, than the physical givens. The topography of easy communications, therefore, no more determines the history of redistribution than petrology and pedology determine that of primary production. There is a parallel, indeed, between the two relations. Both fertility and connectivity may be regarded as interlinked strategies for the avoidance of risk and insurance against uncertainty of livelihood. Strabo, then, in his counter-intuitive but perceptive association of the rarity of harbours with the volume of exchanges, may have an idea of how the social and institutional concentration which is characteristic of nodal centres promotes the growth of the exchange-functions which he calls *emporie* (cf. Casevitz 1993). The critical mass of people involved, and the complexity of their institutional relations, may be as important as the topographical givens.

In this final section, we revert to the geography of microregions and their interaction with which we started the sequence of four chapters that make up Part Three. In all of them we have stressed the paramount importance of human society against the various claims of environmental determinism. In assessing the '*place* of redistribution', in conclusion, we hope to draw on the arguments of this chapter so far. The first, to repeat, is that redistribution is an extension of the strategies of production and storage; and the second, which follows from it, is that the history of Mediterranean redistribution is therefore inseparable from that of the people who produce, store, process, transport and consume. For all these activities are carried on by people who are often profoundly mobile. It follows that, as Strabo saw, access to the sea is not a simple matter, not a matter of asking 'is there a harbour here or not?'

In this geography of connectivity, through which people and their goods move, the nodal points may be regarded as ports. These ports do not, therefore, exclusively lie at the abutment of land and sea. The gateways to the Alpine passes, Verona and Turin, are in this sense as much ports as Venice and Ravenna. The harbours of Smyrna or Miletus may be compared with the portals of the Anatolian plateau, Tarsus below the Cilician Gates, or Apamea Celaenae at the headsprings of the Maeander, which 'remained, for long ages, the most considerable city of the interior, outdistancing even the ports of the coasts with the sole exception of Ephesus' (Syme 1995, 17, cf. 335–9).

That notion of a port is of course reminiscent of Polanyi's idea of the 'port-of-trade', adopted to good effect by archaeologists under the name 'gateway settlement'. The concept has been applied, for the most part, to settlements which control the point of contact between two rather strongly contrasted economic and social systems, and we have seen that there is a place for it in our analysis of redistribution (above, Section 3). An excellent instance is to be found at the mouth of the river Narenta in Croatia, where a river giving access to the Balkan interior penetrates the high limestone mountains fencing the Mediterranean coast. Here there was an important settlement of traders both in the late Roman Republic (Sherwin-White 1973, 225–6) and under the rule of medieval Ragusa (Stuard 1995, 16). Two further points can also be made.

First, it is not necessary for the separation between the systems either side of the gateway to be social and economic: it can be ecological. Heterogeneity in value-systems promotes interregional exchange, even without a gateway (Sherratt and Sherratt 1991, 377 n.11). And ecological variety conduces to that sort of heterogeneity. The ecological definition will allow us to see the same 'gateway' effect at work at the interface of zones differentiated by the microregional pattern of production, storage and redistribution. It will also cover caravan cities such as Aleppo or Palmyra, ports on the edge of the desert-sea, and the gateway cities between two seas of the Tripolitanian littoral in both Antiquity and the Middle Ages, as well as the larger-scale potential differences between the Mediterranean and non-Mediterranean worlds represented in Antiquity by the trade of the Black Sea or Egypt. (In the nineteenth century, once again, the foundation of the Greek merchant marine was the opening up of the Black Sea and the Hellespont: Harlaftis 1995.) Each microregion has its own 'ports'. Kioni, the westernmost anchorage on Cyprus, a classic stopover for *caboteurs*, also serves as a perfect example of a microregional outlet (J. R. Leonard 1995). Attending to the requirements of redistribution is an aspect of the large-scale manipulation of the environment. Improving ports is yet another form of intensification. On the Levantine coast, as early as the second millennium B.C., local communities engaged in relatively sophisticated landscape engineering – not only to help drain the coastal plains, but also to improve access to the havens at the mouths of streams where they were impeded by the aeolianite karkar ridges that are a feature of the area (Raban 1990). The small ports sometimes linked to Mycenaean settlements are a close parallel (Zangger 1998).

Second, and as a result of the first point, we can detach the idea of a gateway from that of a settlement. Like towns, on the 'ecologized' account given in Chapter IV, they are simply nodes of density in the matrix of connectivity. Ports of all kinds obey a regional logic; they cannot be understood as solitary and fixed points. The offshore island of Dia, insignificant in terms of its productivity, has the best four harbours of all Crete. Its advantages, unexpectedly, may explain the importance of the site of Knossos/Candia on the mainland of Crete directly opposite (Rackham and Moody 1997, 200). Near Genoa, the 'misfit port' of San Pier d'Arena displayed ship-building, village and resort functions, but never developed into a centre of population of the kind usually thought appropriate for a port (Heers 1989). Even Ostia, the gateway of imperial Rome at the mouth of the Tiber, has something of the misfit about its economic and social character.

Such detachability ultimately derives from the fact that nodes within and between microregions are very changeable. It is this intrinsic mutability of microregional 'interfaces' that explains how, on many Mediterranean *façades maritimes*, the principal ports, residential foci, storehouses, and subsidiary centres have seemed to wander among the microregions. Carthage, Tunis, La Goletta and Utica near the Bagradas, Ambracia, Nicopolis, Preveza, Vonitsa around the Gulfs of Ambracia and its mouth, Aquileia, Grado, Torcello, Venice or Narbonne

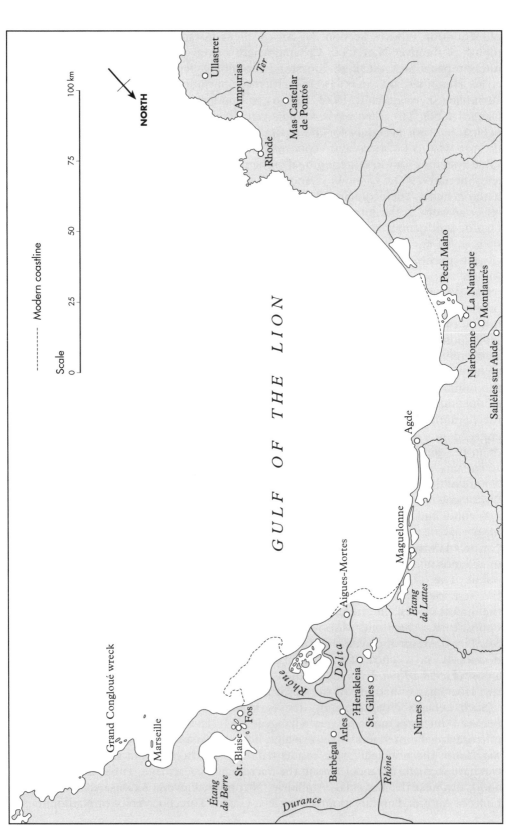

Map 22　The lagoon coast of the Golfe du Lion

and its subordinate ports, in their respective zones of estuaries and lagoons, are all further instances (Map 22). The mouths of great rivers provide access to inland communication networks, but even so, they tend not to determine the siting of gateway settlements. The settlements on the rivers flowing into the Black Sea; Al Mina and Seleucia Pieria near but not on the mouth of the Orontes; Marseille, Saint-Blaise, and Fos, or Aigues-Mortes, Rhodanousia, Saint-Gilles and Arles on the way to the Rhône – these are all examples of such mutability. We could also cite the cases of Tinnis and Šaltiš introduced in Sections 2 and 3 above. In the early modern period, goods for Rome were transferred from large ships to small at Civitavecchia, well away from the Tiber mouth. From here trade proceeded straight through to the river harbour of Ripa Grande (Delumeau 1957–9, 1.105). Civitavecchia had originally been developed as a harbour by the Emperor Trajan, presumably with just this function in mind.

Alluviation makes the topography of such localities mutable and their neighbourhood unsafe (cf. VIII.3–4). Avoidance of the institutions of authority may also be a factor assisting the detachment: in the later Middle Ages, Sicilian grain merchants used *scale* to dodge cities (Bresc 1986b; V.3). But it is the tendency of the adjacent microregions to mutate that here too results in the instability of settlement history. A nearby city may maintain a sanctuary at the river mouth (cf. Chapter X.2), as did ancient Paestum at the mouth of the Sele, or Minturnae at the mouth of the Liris, in a classic demonstration of the detachment of urban architectonic forms from ecological topography.

The emporion *and the colony*

Given these factors, it is natural also to find a mismatch between the geography of redistribution and the geography of commercial exchange, which we have already met in the case of Oropos and Athens (V.1). The island-city of Arwad off the coast of Syria was, in the mid-twentieth century, exclusively the home, not the market, of the sailors based there, although their carrying trade spanned the eastern Mediterranean. Some of the Aegean islands, such as Psara and Oenoussae, are, likewise, 'îles de navigateurs' whose own harbour facilities and productive capacity are exiguous (Kolodny 1974, 365–76). Conversely, there are places which are advantaged in the geography of exchange, being well placed to serve *caboteurs*, but whose inhabitants do not participate in it. Much of Crete in the Archaic Greek period, like Corsica for a good deal of its history, presented 'façades aveugles à la mer' (Kolodny 1968, 229); ports such as Kommos were enclaves managed from the world of the sea (J. W. Shaw 1989). In the fourth century, quite abruptly, Cretan cities began to capitalize on their advantages and to develop new ports, such as Hierapytna (Brulé 1978, 148–9).

Those cases in which the personnel of redistribution are so clearly detached from the processes of production invite us to attempt a generalization. Redistribution depends on connectivity; and connectivity is not a matter of physical geography, but of the patterns of human mobility. There have been many cases in which a mutual interdependence has entailed that redistribution and connectivity are intimately linked; most of the movements of people between the two places are connected in such cases with the exchange of specific products. But such an account is by no means sufficient as a description of Mediterranean trade. In very many cases also, the connectivity is generated by 'mobilities' the primary cause of which is *not* redistribution. In these instances, the patterns of redistribution, the opportunities for the special intensification of production offered by connectivity, will be shaped neither by supply nor by demand but by the accident of channels of human mobility.

Exchange is consequent upon the location of potentially mobile people. Travelling markets accompanying armies are an extreme example, as are the *emporia* that track colonial expeditions (Dalby 1992). It has, however, been common, on the same principles that we have examined in considering wandering centres at the interfaces between microregions, to use as centres of redistribution temporary or mobile markets and fairs. The 'take-off' of fairs in the late fourteenth and fifteenth centuries is not a sign of old-fashioned economic behaviour caused by desperation but the opportunistic seizing of useful chances at a buoyant economic moment (S. R. Epstein 1994, 24). The religious articulation of such occasions will receive further attention in the next chapter (X.3).

We earlier maintained that many of the characteristic episodes of Mediterranean colonial history can be illuminated by applying the simple formula which we perceive in Mediterranean history as a whole: fragmentation by land plus connectivity by sea (VII.6). This perspective enables us – it is worth stressing – to by-pass completely the old debates about the relative importance of agrarian as against commercial aims in those episodes. 'Colonization' – *sensu lato* – results from an ambitious productive opportunism. We further proposed overseas colonization as a characteristic form of the deployability of labour in the Mediterranean, arguing that it represented a continuation of the microregional management of labour in other places. The sea contributes more than just a line of communication with home. It also supports a framework within which labour may be supplied, and the products of the settlers' efforts be redistributed – which is why we return to the theme in the present chapter.

The Mediterranean colony is a direct manifestation of the maritime *koine*: it is always part of a seaborne network, a bridgehead of the easily navigable world in a different social medium, or a gateway settlement where two societies – and their economies – come face-to-face. We introduced these bridgeheads as manifestations of the unity of maritime connectivity in Chapter V.2. They are a type that has all but vanished, with the single-minded territorial claims of the new Mediterranean nation-states and the cultural absolutism which even the more enlightened have shown to enclaves of any kind. The societies and economies of the coastlands change beyond all recognition. What is constant is the nature of the meeting between two different communities, one associated with control of the sea, one which manages the cluster of terrestrial microregions.

The Mediterranean colony is, typically, cosmopolitan. First, the juxtaposition of at least two different communities is axiomatic: the colonist and the indigene. But the seaborne community itself tends to be cosmopolitan too. Although some dominant power provides the nominal foundation or character of the new community, cases in which an exclusive ethnic composition is found are not usual. Rather, the colony relies – necessarily, given the prevailing demographic conditions – on the mobile population of the *koine* at large and it is therefore composed of all-comers, even though political or social privileges within the community may well vary with ethnic background.

The Genoese colonies at Caffa (ancient Theodosia) in the Black Sea from 1275, or at Famagusta in Cyprus are excellent examples of the cosmopolitan nature of such centres (Balard 1987, 1988); the *Bastion de la France* on the coast of the Maghreb, one in a sequence of footholds of the seafaring peoples on this inhospitable coast (see Map 23) was similar. (Contrast the settlement at Chios, VII.6.) In Antiquity, although some of the earlier Hellenic *apoikiai* were composed of various elements, traditions about foundations tended increasingly (and probably misleadingly) to attribute these settlements each to a single mother-city. Mediterranean colonization is better represented in that epoch by the establishments which are usually known as *emporia* (trading places) (Bresson and Rouillard 1993). In these settlements two features are strongly apparent. The first is the close management of the economic opportunity, that control of the movements of goods and people which unites state-run and 'private' economies from prehistoric to early modern times:

> l'*emporion* était un lieu de profit et que l'on soit dans la zone grecque, phénicienne, étrusque ou égyptienne, on voit que dans un souci fiscal en premier lieu les Etats anciens avaient toujours le souci d'exercer le contrôle le plus étroit sur les flux d'hommes et d'objets de commerce ... le contrôle, et non la licence, ait été la règle. (Bresson 1993, 226)

The second feature is the resulting *mélange* of communities and origins, memorably summed up in a *mot* of Michel Gras which deserves to become canonical: 'qui dit *emporion* dit ... confrontation ethnique et culturelle, réussie seulement dans un but économique' (1993, 106).

The most striking example is Naucratis on the westernmost, Canopic, distributary of the Nile, where the Saite pharaohs licensed a community of Greeks from eleven homelands (Bowden 1996; Map 21). This was the gateway between two quite different worlds – indeed in this case not just between colonist and indigene, but between the Mediterranean and a land which is outside it ecologically. Here, the diversity of the settlers' backgrounds was reflected in the institutions of the settlement, which displayed a pattern of tight control that may be regarded as characteristic of *emporia*. It is worth noting that, if we had only the same kind of evidence for Naucratis as we have for most of the hundreds of Greek overseas settlements, we should think it an *apoikia* of the Ionian city of Miletus: Herodotus alone preserves the crucial details of its diverse organization in the sixth century B.C. Those eleven homeland cities were of course engaged in trade, including the redistribution of Egypt's Nile-borne grain to the often-needy communities of the Aegean (Austin 1970). The trade was promoted by their diversity, and by the cultural boundary that was breached at Naucratis. But the movement involved was also, crucially, one of people too: the mercenaries from Caria and Ionia described in the last section, who could enter Egypt solely through this route, and whose service was so important.

That makes a wider point about the colony. The juridical forms of certain institutions, defined against the background of some legal framework, are a quite different phenomenon from the underlying fact of the opportunistic intrusion of outsiders, sometimes people of many different origins. This fact is understood best on a very long time-scale. The medieval institution of the *fondaco* or *funduq* – a distinct and autonomous settlement of foreigners within the port of another culture – can be traced back to the Constantinople of the tenth century and the *mitaton* system with which the Byzantine Greeks attempted to regulate the presence and competition of aliens. It is a striking comment on the

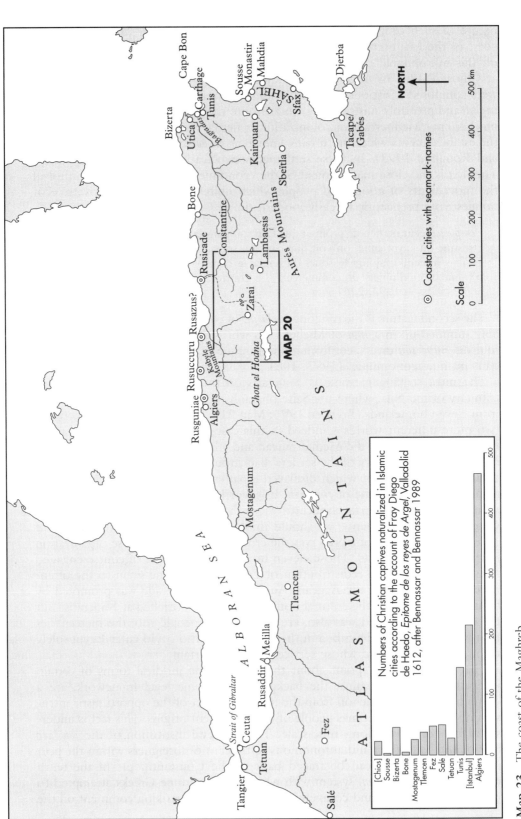

Map 23 The coast of the Maghreb

Tangier

Tetuan

Salé

Ceuta

Rusaddir / Melilla

Strait of Gibraltar

ALBORAN SEA

Fez

Tlemcen

Mostagenum

Algiers

Rusguniae Rusuccuru Rusazus?

Kabyle Mountains

Chott el Hodna

Rusicade

Constantine

Zarai

Lambaesis

Aurés Mountains

MAP 20

Bone

Bizerta

Utica

Bagradas

Carthage

Tunis

Cape Bon

Sousse

Monastir

Mahdia

Kairouan

SAHEL

Sfax

Sbeïtla

Tacape / Gabés

Djerba

A T L A S   M O U N T A I N S

NORTH

Scale

0   100   200   300   400   500 km

◎ Coastal cities with seamark-names

Numbers of Christian captives naturalized in Islamic cities according to the account of Fray Diego de Haedo, *Epitome de los reyes de Argel*, Valladolid 1612, after Bennassar and Bennassar 1989

[Chios]
Sousse
Bizerta
Bone
Mostagenum
Tlemcen
Fez
Salé
Tetuan
Tunis
[Istanbul]
Algiers

0   100   200   300   400   500

unwillingness of medievalists to look further back into the Mediterranean past that one intelligent survey of the origins of the phenomenon is reduced to ascribing them to China (Lopez 1949). The *conventus* of foreigners in the cities of the Hellenistic and Roman worlds and the metics of the early Greek world, communities within states, can scarcely draw their inspiration from so far east. Even the Roman overseas *colonia*, which seems at first sight a more exclusive entity, rather different in its purpose and intention, should be mentioned in this context. To return to the north coast of the Maghreb, the range of coastal *coloniae* established by Augustus and also marked on Map 23 (Mackie 1983) fit well into general Mediterranean patterns. Already in the second century B.C., by founding such settlements as Narbo, in the heart of the crucial zone of exchanges round the Golfe du Lion, and by all but doing so on the site of the ancient redistributive hub of Carthage, Rome inserted itself into this tradition.

The best examples of ethnic variety in what has sometimes been presented as a monochrome, colonial, world, are some of the earliest, however: the Greek *apoikiai* briefly considered above and in Chapter V.2. The first, Pithekoussai, established by the second quarter of the eighth century, was a joint foundation of two cities in Euboea; graffiti prove a Phoenician presence, and the archaeological remains establish the importance of the smelting of (probably) Elban iron. The chosen site lay on the volcanic island of Ischia, point of contact in the *koine* for the agriculturally rich and socially developing Campanian plains. Pithekoussai was foreshadowed by a large Mycenaean settlement on the island of Vivara, still more sea-orientated, since the islet is waterless and almost without soil. Its successors, to which it bequeathed its overseas connections, were daughter settlements in the *peraia* – Cumae, Naples and Dikaiarkheia, which became Roman Puteoli: the gateway between Campania and the sea-world has been a perennial phenomenon, even if it has not always been in the same location (Frederiksen 1984, chs. 2–4). In the last years of the seventh century, sudden famine on the island of Thera led to the foundation of a colony on an island off the coast of Cyrenaica (Cawkwell 1992). This safe site in the mainstream of the *koine* was the forerunner of the city of Cyrene, further inland in the fertile Jebel (III.3) but still a gateway to the outer world, for an agriculture rapidly developed by and for an influx of settlers from all over the Greek world that rapidly submerged the Theran rulers (Applebaum 1979, ch. 2).

Such examples could easily be multiplied: the Greek settlements happen to have displayed a high institutional profile which makes them relatively easy to 'see' even at such a distance (Bresson and Rouillard 1993). But the underlying processes have had a much longer history. And it is important that this is again not exclusively a pattern to be associated with 'colonial' trade: tiny islands off the coast of the Peloponnese appear to have functioned during the late Bronze Age in a way which is strongly reminiscent of Vivara (Lolos 1995). Poros, Hydra and Spetsai, islands in just that location, have more recently provided conspicuous examples of 'îles des navigateurs' (Jameson et al. 1994, 135–9). At the other end of the scale, even great Mediterranean *metropoleis* have resembled these diverse and variegated outgrowths of the realm of mobility and redistribution. 'O farmers, traders (*emporoi*), craftsmen (*tektones*), artisans (*demiourgoi*), metics, foreigners and islanders, come here all the people (*leos*)' (Aristophanes, *Peace*, 296). That was the way to apostrophize the populace of metropolitan Athens in its heyday as hub of a great maritime network.

The extraordinary ethnic variety of the population of the Mediterranean coastlands is, then, a consequence of the structural mobility which we have been describing. The nodes and gateways through which movements pass, and where they are most apparent, display that variety obviously. It is true of the country-side too, especially in microregions such as those of the islands which are especially open to mobility. On the Dalmatian island of Brać, more than half of the population can be traced through their family names to an external origin; and many of the remainder have names which yield no information about origin and so may conceal yet more immigrants (F. W. Carter 1977). Epistolary texts about exchange inscribed on tablets of lead, dating from the sixth and fifth centuries B.C., have been discovered in the lagunar zone of the Catalan–Provençal *façade maritime*. Most are in Greek, but there are also many non-Greek names, and the closest links with Etruscan and Celtiberian participators in redistribution are apparent. Similar documents have emerged from the closely comparable social and economic milieu of the north-western Black Sea at the same period. Two thousand years later in this region, the population of the Genoese city of Caffa was generally 5 per cent Italian and 60 per cent Armenian, with many Greeks; but there were violent fluctuations in these proportions (Balard 1987, especially 225).

The ethnic diversity of the population is the most obvious correlate of mobility, but from it also arise the cultural homogeneities which help make possible the Mediterranean social anthropology that we particularly deploy in the next three chapters. Clearly we cannot unpick the weave of this tangled mass of ethnic origins; nor can we quantify the mobility from period to period and place to place. It is extremely likely that it has been less in remote corners and at certain unfavourable periods. Our contention, though, is that it has never ceased. In VII.5 we argued that the immobility inherent in conventional images of the peasantry has not been common among Mediterranean country-people, and that local continuities over many generations of rural life are not to be expected. But some continuities there are, and the movements which we have just explored offer a key to understanding them. If there have been recurrent features in Mediterranean history, they are not the product of the naked geography of the region. Rather they arise from the underlying rhythms of human response to the physical environment, the rhythms of intensification, redistribution – and mobility.

PART FOUR

THE GEOGRAPHY OF RELIGION

There is a culinary geography of the sea, no doubt, but there is, none the less, a religious geography also.

> Febvre (1925) *A Geographical Introduction to History*, 219

CHAPTER X

'TERRITORIES OF GRACE'

For years I gave no thought to the place we had left or to my tree which had been felled. Then . . . I began to think of the place where the tree had been or would have been. In my mind's eye I saw it as a kind of luminous emptiness, a warp and waver of light, and once again, in a way that I find hard to define, I began to identify with that space just as years before I had identified with the young tree. Except that this time it was not so much a matter of attaching oneself to a living symbol of being rooted in the native ground: it was a matter of preparing to be unrooted, to be spirited away into some transparent, yet indigenous afterlife. The new place was all idea, if you like; it was generated out of my experience of the old place but it was not a topographical location. It was and remains an imagined realm, even if it can be located at an earthly spot, a placeless heaven . . .

Heaney (1988) The Government of the Tongue, 3–4

The most revealing map of Europe [in the early Middle Ages] would be a map, not of political or commercial capitals, but of the constellation of sanctuaries, the points of material contact with the unseen world.

Southern (1953) The Making of the Middle Ages, 133

1. RELIGION AND THE PHYSICAL ENVIRONMENT

Almost every place in the Mediterranean world has at one time or another been pagan, Christian and Muslim (the Italian peninsula is the principal exception). This truth must be important, especially for those who wish to tackle the really large-scale problems of the history of the sea and its coastlands. Geographical language is certainly very commonly employed in discussing the history of religion. But what does it actually mean to say that a *place* has been Christian? What does it presuppose about the social dimension of religion to draw a map entitled, for example, 'The Expansion of Islam' or 'The Spread of the Cult of Serapis'? What does it mean to say that a place underwent a *change* from being pagan to being Christian, or from being Christian to being Muslim?

The previous chapters have all, in different ways, but with cumulative effect, assembled some of the ingredients of a distinctively Mediterranean sense of place. Locality has been identified by the interactions between humanity and the changing set of environmental conditions, by the ecological patterning of productive strategies, by the complex two-way relationship at work in anthropogene change in the landscape, and by the crucial reciprocities and interdependences which are made possible by the sea. Our spatial approach to Mediterranean history has aimed to establish place as a useful instrument of analysis. It is appropriate to try out this approach in the historical investigation of Mediterranean cultures. The geography of religion is an inviting point at which to start. It will not be difficult to show that the religious landscape of the Mediterranean world has always closely reflected a fragmented topography and the geography of the means by which that fragmentation is overcome.

The simplest relationship between space and the holy can be expressed by a map of localities having some particular religious association, a distinctive degree of connection with the divine: churches, for example, holy springs, or the tombs of the Islamic 'saints', or *marabouts* (Map 24 is an example). To the points on the map which indicate the density and distribution of such features can easily be added lines depicting routes, perhaps of a procession or a pilgrimage, a sacred way or a ritual boundary. The density of these nodes and their connections gives us a basic concept of religious geography, and an easy way in which different cultures and periods may be compared. This level of the investigation is principally descriptive. The ensemble of spatial expressions and correlates of religious behaviour is what we designate in this chapter by the term 'landscape'.

In the wider-ranging examination of the structures of religious behaviour which has become increasingly prevalent and sophisticated from the middle of the twentieth century, a more important role has been accorded to space and locality. These are among the concepts which help to transcend restrictive classifications such as Islamic, Christian and 'pagan' in the interests of an understanding based on comparison. It is, however, all too easy for scholarly notions of space to be more abstract than is really helpful, or to be derived from a rather hazy cultural history. Manifestations of religious space have been very various in the different theologies and cultic systems which have been found in the Mediterranean. The very possibility of attaching religious significance to places as such has not

---

Map 24 Sacred topography and the microregional landscape

The coastal plain of north Syria is separated from the interior by the Alawite Mountains, and this section of the plain lies some way from either of the corridors which lead in from the coast, and which give an important nodal role to Lattakia (Laodicea) to the north and the island-port of Arwad (Arados) to the south. For much of Antiquity, the territories of Gabala (Jeble on this map) and Paltos (on the Nahr Sene, a very short but perennial river flowing from the copious headsprings which are marked) therefore depended on Arados and formed part of its *peraia*. The prosperous settlements of the second millennium B.C. were situated at a safe distance from the coast. With the establishment of the cosmopolitan Phoenician town at Tell Sukas in the eighth century, the region began to engage fully in the world of the maritime. A mound in the vicinity of Paltos was a seamark-sanctuary identified by the Greek seafarers as the tomb of the hero Memnon.

The terrain has a history of prosperous arboriculture, being renowned among Greek and Roman authors for the quality of the incense-gum storax which was produced here. The sacred grove of olives and figs overthrown by the miraculous intervention of the holy Thalelaios was located close to Gabala, and its site is quite likely to have coincided with one of the many sacred sites mapped here. The sacred topography of the heretical Muslim Alawite *ziaras* in the Syrian coastal plain makes use of eminences, springs and sacred trees or groves. For the hierarchy of pilgrimage/festival destinations in which they take their place, see Section 5 below. (After Weulersse 1940b, 255, fig. 94; archaeological detail from Riis 1970.)

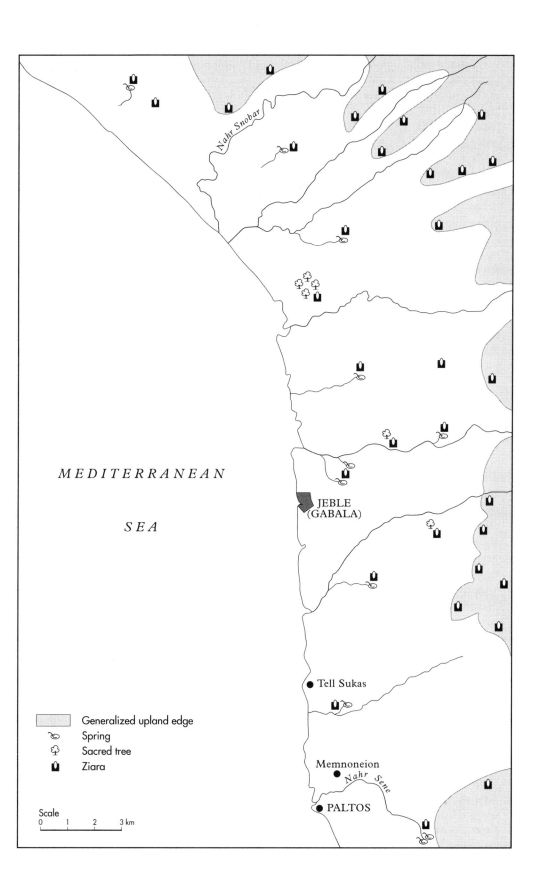

MEDITERRANEAN

SEA

JEBLE
(GABALA)

● Tell Sukas

Memnoneion
● Nahr Sene

● PALTOS

Nahr Snobar

	Generalized upland edge
	Spring
	Sacred tree
	Ziara

Scale
0   1   2   3 km

been doctrinally uncontroversial, and is not automatically to be predicated to the same extent of all the religious systems of Mediterranean history. Indeed the eventual acquiescence in the notion of holy places by Christian thinkers has been regarded as a survival – up to a point – of pre-Christian religious behaviour (Markus 1990, 139–55). Given this divergence, it may be useful to adduce the more tangible set of propositions concerning the nature of the Mediterranean landscape which we hope to have been able to establish by this point in our argument. That should in turn help to provide a more concrete and more comprehensible range of associations for the concept of locality. Other scholars have made pleas for the spatial recontextualizing of cult-places (especially in the ancient world), while remaining mainly interested in the political and cultural, rather than the productive, landscape (Alcock 1993, 173). This seems to us to be a missed opportunity: 'Dieu est lointain, et aussi le triomphe final de la vraie foi. En attendant donc le déroulement immuable des cycles préscrits, il faut à ce peuple de paysans une religion plus tangible et plus proche de sa vie terre à terre' (Weulersse 1940b, 255).

That condescension towards the supposed impoverishment of 'peasants' in religious *mentalités* notwithstanding (cf. VII.5), it is indeed helpful to return to the religiosity of *la vie terre à terre*. A certain type of response to locality in its general sense may be one of the things which the very different religious systems of the Mediterranean have in common. More particularly, it is the rural religious context – the embedding of cult in the microregional landscape and the web of connectivity – that has been observed to mute and blur the doctrinal differences on which historians of religion have been inclined to focus (Mitchell 1993, 2.10 n.3).

Our picture of the conditions of Mediterranean history may have a contribution to make to the history of religion. One possible area is precisely the apparent continuity or repetitive similarity of religious responses to the environment in different periods, under different religious systems – a problem that has often attracted the attention of Mediterranean historians, and to which we shall return shortly. But in turn, the geography of religion should prove an indispensable guide to and illustration of the other patterns discussed in this book. A guide on two different levels. For the religious landscape should respond to the social and economic aspects of Mediterranean geography – the importance of central places, the respect accorded to certain frontiers or boundaries, the allegiances of small districts to wider wholes. It will help us to understand the coalescence of the thousands of Mediterranean localities into some sort of unity. These are patterns that would not necessarily have been apparent to the people who were involved in them. But, on another level, the geography of religion will also reflect the more conscious attitudes of the inhabitants of the Mediterranean lands towards the ecological opportunities that they encounter. Religious systems are often intended to explain; and we stand to gain a great deal in our investigation of Mediterranean history if we listen to the explanations offered (cf. Geertz 1966).

It will become clear that we do not subscribe to any elementary deterministic theory of the relationship between religion and landscape. Here as in earlier chapters, and as in the social anthropology to be presented in Chapters XI and XII, we envisage human perceptions and the actions that arise from them as the major (not the only) ingredient in the creation of microregions. Religious structures do not in any simple way *reflect* social and economic formations – what we might call (with some injustice to its most famous proponent) the Durkheimian view. Nor, however, are they merely, and self-servingly, *imposed* on the human landscape by the manipulative decision-takers and their agents, whose role in the fortunes of the microregion we have already frequently met – the Marxian view. We do not feel obliged to select one of these perspectives in preference to the other, and both leave much to be explained. The ways in which religious patterns *express*, *re-present* or *generate* features of the landscape are too various to be contained by any but a broadly ecological account in which ties of causality run in several directions – and the use of such verbs in what follows cannot be anything other than approximate.

A primary purpose of this chapter is to enquire whether, in the various possible ways in which the geography of religion can be explored, the Mediterranean should be regarded as distinctive; and if so, what the reasons are for any similarities in such potentially diverse forms of behaviour over wide gaps of space and time. In the process we can expect to reveal much about the interaction between culture, history and environment within the Mediterranean world. The discussion will begin with the role of the environment, considering the Mediterranean landscape once again, and reassessing the familiar forms of its small-scale topography in the context of religion (Section 2). Following the order of our earlier analysis in Chapters VI and VII, we shall then turn to the productive landscape and to its social characteristics (Section 3). These too have prominent religious dimensions, which are closely related to cultural views of the landscape and the nature of the human environment. In Section 4 we make the same transition as we did in Chapter IX, out into the world of connectivity and mobility. Beyond that, in the final section of the chapter, we shall turn to the ways in which the geography of religion helps define regions of different sizes and types and the relations between them. Such definition takes place on a variety of scales – through variations in the texture of the human landscape, through connections with boundaries of various kinds, and through the relationship of a religious region to a focal site which may be either inside the region or, in the case of pilgrimage, far beyond its confines. We also look back to an earlier part of our discussion, to the wider concepts of the Mediterranean which we began to examine in Part One. This should make clearer the changing relations between contiguous geographical areas of all sizes and, still more, should illuminate the hierarchies and relationships of regions of different status. Religion has been a means of conveying both relations of dependence such as federalism or empire, and relations of autonomy such as theocracy or sacred neutrality. Even within what appear to be obvious regional units, the geography of cult illustrates important aspects of local ties, above all between town and country, and it will help strengthen our contention in Chapter IV that the connections between a Mediterranean town and the different parts of its hinterland are not qualitatively different from those between one microregion and another.

Finally, and on the larger scale, the sea itself has been the medium of religious differentiation, as it is also the vehicle of religious change. On one hand, it has served to establish rival conceptual claims about the extents and limits of religious influence, as with the Crusader concept of Outremer, or the long struggle between Muslim and Christian for control of the sea in the early modern period. On the other hand, it is the milieu in which the Orientalizing religious forms of the seventh century B.C., Diaspora Judaism and Pauline Christianity were disseminated. In religion, therefore, we see clearly instantiated the important paradox of Part One, that the Mediterranean is both a zone of easy lateral transmission of ideas and practices and a barrier which promotes divisions between cultural systems.

The problem of survivals

The distinctive Mediterranean environment – geology, climate, hydrology, vegetation, even fauna – has underlain most accounts of Mediterranean history which emphasize continuity. It is not surprising, then, that travellers and scholars have long been fascinated by how little at first sight seems to have changed in the practice of religion – above all in the matter of its place in the landscape. Sacred groves and stones are still found in the eastern Mediterranean; whitewashed churches, often on the footings of temples, crown hills and punctuate the visible landscape of modern Greece just as their distant pagan predecessors did. This is one of the aspects of the popular perception of the Mediterranean and its history which seem most to justify the strong claims about continuity which have been made, and the environmental determinism on which it is based.

The similarities have aroused curiosity since at least the time of the pioneering but eccentric historical geographer of Anatolia, Sir William Ramsay, who wrote in 1892 on 'Permanent attachment of religious veneration to localities'. Here is a passage concerning North Africa from a reliable modern textbook:

> there is the example of the hot spring at Hammam Sayada near Beja in Tunisia where miraculous cures are attributed to the intervention of a holy woman, Lella Sayada . . . Work on the spring . . . revealed Roman baths and a dedication by an imperial freedman to the genius or presiding spirit of the place, named Aquae Traianae. It is this spirit who is still invoked under the name of the Moslem holy woman Lella Sayada. (C. Wells 1984, 267)

But is it? This is a nice instance of a common enough phenomenon – the religious significance, at widely different periods, of the sacred spring. The author's opinion would be widely shared. The correspondence between ancient sites and the shrines of Islamic *marabouts* in the Maghreb is in fact very widespread (Siraj 1995, 439–52). Yet on what grounds might one elsewhere make so close an identification of the Roman and the modern objects of cult? To give another example, in the second century A.D. the satirist Lucian describes the importance of fish to the cults of north Syria (*On the Syrian Goddess*, 45). In Urfa, in the same region, are still to be seen great carp-ponds which are now sacred to Abraham (Segal 1970). Does the similarity mean anything?

Ramsay's naive view was that it could only mean survival. But we must be cautious. The Muslim saint Sheikh Ma'shuq 'the loved one', who was venerated near Tyre in the nineteenth century, seemed a plausible survival of the cult of Adonis, the beloved of Venus, for which the region was celebrated in Antiquity. Stranger coincidences are recorded, however, and we must always be aware of the possibilities, over a millennial time-span, of the refreshing of everyday practice from the written tradition: self-conscious revival rather than survival. It is easy to be mistaken in the interpretation of symbols. The carp of Urfa appear so bizarre that continuity is easy to credit: but this may rather be a case of spontaneous regeneration of what is actually a rather common way of expressing sanctity. If a wider perspective is adopted, parallels multiply for even the strangest religious observances. In A.D. 563, for example, the Emperor Justinian's last journey took him to the shrine of St Michael at Germia (Yürme, near Ankara:

P. Brown 1996, 125). Here, it transpires, there was a miraculous healing fishpond not unlike those of Urfa. 'Les poissons sacrés sont la concrétisation vivante de la sainteté du lieu', says an authority on the cult of the *marabout*, who also discusses sacred tortoises, and a huge hairy eel with earrings in a sacred pool (Dermenghem 1954, 145–8). But the freshwater fish is not only a symbol or a sacred object, as we saw in some detail in VI.6. We must be prepared to take productive possibilities as seriously as zoological curiosities. It is easy to misunderstand the material remains of the past when their context is not sufficiently apparent.

A cautionary tale from Tripolitania deserves repetition. The standing stones in clusters of three which dot the inland wastes of Tripolitania, labelled 'trilithons' by early investigators familiar with Stonehenge and attributed by them to an ancient cult, are the frameworks of imperial Roman olive-presses (Mattingly 1988). The attribution of mysterious cultic significance was part of a failure to perceive – in this case – how completely a whole environment had changed. Even when we are confident that we are looking at a sacred stone and not an olive-press we should not be hasty to attribute continuity of meaning to it before we have attempted to locate it at different dates in its interpretative setting.

The interest in survivals taken by earlier scholars is to be linked to that biological, evolutionary, unilinear approach to history which we have already discussed at some length. The quest for earlier 'strata' of culture was characteristic of the end of the nineteenth and beginning of the twentieth century: the metaphor came from geology by way of the new discipline of archaeology (Hodgen 1936). Survivals were throwbacks, glimpses of the systems of the past fossilized by accidents of the environment, marvels or eccentricities which could be held to have had a determining effect on patterns of religious observance. Lucien Febvre rejected such a view in his insistence on a social understanding of the geography of religion, expressed in the quotation which is the epigraph of this Part. Indeed, the special localities at which the apparent survivals occur can only be understood against a broader religious backdrop, which can hardly be said to have been determined by these peculiar cases. Going further, modern social anthropology has no difficulty with an even more thoroughgoing view of the potential primacy of religious behaviour: pilgrimage centres '*may* . . . have played at least as important a role in the growth of cities, marketing systems and roads as "pure" economic and political social factors have' (Turner and Turner 1978, 234, our italics). The hesitation now seems overdone.

While supposed continuities certainly played a part in the creation of a distinctive Mediterranean social anthropology (XI.1), its leading exponents in the second half of the twentieth century ceased to be much interested in such matters. One of them wrote: 'this is not to say that I think anything can be explained by being termed a "survival". On the contrary, the concept of survival is almost a confession of defeat before the challenge to find a contemporary sense in anything' (Pitt-Rivers 1977, vii–viii). It is clearly true that the simple documentation of curious instances of survival may intrigue, but does not on its own help us to explain. The task of the historian is, however, somewhat different from that of the social anthropologist. There are – obviously – some meaningful social and cultural continuities, and some – to put it no more strongly – are longer than others. Tenacity, traditionalism and presumed or invented survival need explanation too, and they are sometimes associated with aspects of the environment such as hot springs.

As anthropologists became more historical in their methods, and more interested in cognitive processes such as the creation of tradition, it became less unfashionable to study survival. Criticism instead was directed against 'caesurism' or the 'temporalization of difference' – the use of turning-points in the narrative of history as a way of representing the boundaries between the familiar and the strange (Pina-Cabral 1992a). Much of our argument in preceding chapters has similarly advocated paying attention more to gradual than to sudden change. In the Mediterranean, the tenacity of the antithesis between 'our way' and 'the wrong way', the new way and the old way, or the local and the alien, seems likely to derive in part from the fragmentation of culture and allegiance whose underpinnings in the productive environment we have traced at considerable length. We have seen how closely structures of power are connected with the logic of production and redistribution: tensions between dominant and dependent groups have often been expressed by means of adherence to newer or older forms of religious behaviour. Thus: 'the veneration of saints provided the cover under which surviving remnants of conquered religions could continue to exist in Islam' (Goldziher 1971, 2.300). It has even been suggested that 'pagan survivals are the products of a struggle for power between the religious creativity of the masses and the Church's need for control' (Pina-Cabral 1992a, 59).

Shifts in the settlement geography of an intricately subdivided landscape such as Lycia loosened the conceptual roots of traditional religion in late Antiquity: in a newly orientated microregional topography it was easier for a new system such as Christianity to form its own space (Fowden 1990a, 369). Dislocations in microregional geography, then, may catalyse religious change. On the other hand, cults have shown themselves, independently of geography, capable of undergoing radical changes in social function and meaning. One example is provided by the Italian sanctuaries which survived from the Samnite countryside of the Hellenistic period to be incorporated in the cities of Roman imperial times: survived, that is, through a complete reorientation of the economic and social net within which they operated (M. H. Crawford 1981, 160). Another case, that of the cult of the goddess Epona, has been traced in early medieval Burgundy (Oaks 1987).

It is too easy to see the manifestations of religious observance in the landscape as a dotting of nature's 'i''s, when it is really a rewriting of the whole text. As we saw in Chapter VIII, for most Mediterranean localities, any moment at which we could really perceive the 'before' and 'after' of the arrival of a human population is so far back beyond recoverable history as to belong in the domain of myth. Millennial processes of interaction have made all Mediterranean landscapes essentially anthropogene. What we have called the religious landscape is the expression or interpretation, in the context of religion, of whole systems of interaction between humanity and the environment. These systems of interaction are often far-reaching in their ambitions for the transformation and management of what nature has provided, which is why we insist that the response articulated through the forms of religion must not be seen as passive. Analysis of the integrative force of religious observance in the microregions of peninsular Greece legitimately adduces the siting of both prehistoric sanctuaries and Byzantine churches (Bintliff 1977a, 102). It does not, however, follow that the landscape may be said to have determined cultic continuity. Prevailing physical conditions no doubt inform the practice of religion in such cases, but they do no more than that. Microregions, as we have argued, are to be predicated of the human uses of the environment, and not of the layout of the physical landscape in isolation.

While it is our view, therefore, that religion expresses the relationship between the Mediterranean landscape and its inhabitants, we do not think that it is the landscape as such which has been responsible for the continuities that may be discernible. The fact that sacred groves occur in widely different cultural contexts in Mediterranean history suggests environmental, productive and topographic resemblances. We may not however argue from these resemblances to religious survival, and still less make ambitious claims about the continuity of ethnic or cultural identity, or of economic practice. As so often in Mediterranean history, the problem is not in finding continuities, but in assessing which ones are significant – and why.

2. A PERILOUS ENVIRONMENT

The starting point of the enquiry should be the same as that of previous chapters: the physical landscape of the Mediterranean lands with its singular congeries of distinctive landforms, the broad constants of its scenery, the extreme particularities of its network of microregions. Because of that topographical and environmental complexity, the *range* of potentially sacred points is remarkably large; but in a heavily subdivided geography, as opposed to a relatively uniform and uninterrupted one, the contexts of each point in social and cultural relationships are also inevitably quite different from one another. There is a whole variety of landscape elements, some of which we shall examine in more detail below, whose nature and identity have been conceived in religious terms, and which have come collectively to compose a religious environment.

With their varied associations in religious practice, springs, pools and watercourses are especially prominent, but they are only part of a repertoire of landforms which in itself, by its staccato pin-pointing, evokes and confirms that particularism and brokenness which is native to Mediterranean landscapes. The religious response to physical space and to the characteristics of the environment takes the form of a perceptible, often highly conspicuous, punctuation or articulation of the natural scene. Thus the Mediterranean religious landscape has long been conceptualized precisely as a collectivity of numerous identifiable individual localities or types of locality. The Athenian ephebes, young citizens undergoing the *rite de passage* to adulthood, swore fidelity to the city by heroes, heroines, rivers and springs, as well as by the cultivated landscape of the Attic countryside (*SIG*, 527.15, cf. Plutarch, *Life of Demosthenes*, 9.4: 'earth, springs, rivers and flowing waters'). For Byzantine Christians, demons dwelt in sea, rivers, wells, cliffs, ponds, marshes, forests, trees and pagan tombs, and must be driven by the exorcist into the uncultivated wilderness (*Euchologion*, ed. Goar 1647, 730–1, 736, 698). The environment was dangerous, and veneration attached to its generalities as well as to its details.

The idea of a repertoire of features in a religious landscape emerges clearly in a philosophical discussion of the first century A.D.:

> Picture a thick grove of ancient overgrown trees, cutting off any sight of the sky
> from below with the shade of their interlocking branches: the rampant woodland,
> the seclusion, and the surprise of finding so thick and complete a shade in open

> countryside all convince you of its sanctity. Or some cave, the foundations of a mountain deeply eroded in the native rock, not hollowed by human labour but, in all its vastness, by purely natural processes – it will forcibly strike you with a sense of religious veneration. We worship the headsprings of the great rivers – the unexpected welling up of a powerful stream out of the unknown is the site for altars – springs of hot water are sacred, and either their murkiness or their vast depth makes some of the lakes holy. (Seneca, *Letters to Lucilius*, no. 41.3)

Seneca argues that the truly good man stands out from the mundane, mediocre, immoral world around him in the same way as do these singularities from the natural order, and that such a man is venerable in an analogous way. In other words, the object of religious attention is the singular in the natural world. On this view, it is the unusual, the distinctive, the individual, about such places – rather than any practical usefulness or contribution to secular activities – which helps to make them holy. The stranger accidents of geomorphology, like other kinds of contradiction, portent, paradox and departure from normality – the category of the 'interstitial' in other words – were readily assimilable to the world of the divine. In any given period of Mediterranean history, the elements of the repertoire can be related to the religious system prevailing at the time.

Holy waters

Prominent springs and pools have been the setting for religious cults from prehistoric times to the present day: 'there is no spring that is not holy [*nullus enim fons non sacer*]' (Servius, *On the Aeneid*, 7.42). When Plato discussed irrigation in the *Laws* (VII.2) the control of water was inseparable from its use for the provision of rural sanctuaries. Water has indeed been indispensable in the ritual activities of most Mediterranean religious systems. No ingredient of the environment is given a higher status by inclusion in them, and if all springs are holy, in an important sense, all holiness is connected with water.

  The apparent 'long durations' of water-cult are particularly noteworthy. At Gerasa in the Decapolis of Jordan, for example, on the desert fringe of the Mediterranean world, a pagan Dionysiac water-into-wine cult associated with natural pools beyond the north gate of the city was quickly succeeded by an annual, equally miraculous, evocation of the Marriage at Cana (Bowersock 1990, 41–53). All over Turkey springs each called *ayasma*, 'the sanctified place', a Greek word used of Christian sacred wells, are still venerated by the Muslim population; at least one, in a still more weird contortion of tradition, is sacred to the philosopher Plato (Hasluck 1929, 363–9, cf. Trombley 1993–4, 1.151). The association of holy waters with pilgrimage is a further case of the importance of religious veneration of springs; the water of the fountain at Lourdes in Aquitaine, or of the spring Zamzam at Mecca, for example. In the latter case, a single spring is the focus for a whole conceptual space of the widest extent. Rivers also share in cults of this type, which, as Seneca said, have often been associated with their headwaters and sources. Springs contributed to and drew from the rich associations of wetland environments: a sacred spring of Apollo Tegyraios formed an important component in the marvellous landscape of the Copais in Boeotia (Plutarch, *Pelopidas*, 16; VII.2 and Map 16). Waters with unusual characteristics have been particularly numinous. The ferruginous foam of Tunisian sacred springs has been venerated because of its red colour (van Binsbergen

1985). Hot springs deserve mention too, a special case to which we shall return shortly.

High Places

Mountain religion is as easy to exemplify from every period of Mediterranean history as water religion. High Places are attested from the Bronze Age in the religious traditions of the Levant, and played a vital role in those of Minoan Crete. Summits in historical periods have been linked with nymphs, heroes and saints; with angels such as St Michael, whose presence is found at prominent mountain-shrines like that of Monte Gargano all over south Italy; with prophets such as Elijah, to whom so many Greek mountain tops are sacred; and even with Satan, the use of whose name attests the hostility felt to the wild Aetolian heights of Mount Saïtani (Woodhouse 1897, 32). Scholars have often claimed to find continuity in such observances, between Zeus and Helios for instance and Elijah (Megas 1958, 142–4). But very different interpretative traditions can easily cluster independently around places of such singular character. At Qadboun, 1,175 metres up on a crest of the Alawite mountains, a ninth-century B.C. high-place sanctuary of Baal is also a powerful Islamic shrine. Here, however, there is as yet no trace of a Christian phase of veneration (Bounni 1997).

One aspect of mountain summits is the strangeness of exposed and weathered rock, fantastically shaped pinnacles, beetling crags or tors. A good example is the domed crags which form the distinctive landscape of the Christian pilgrim shrine at the holy mountain of Montserrat in Catalonia. Montserrat has eastern parallels, too. One case is to be found in the flourishing monastic communities of the Mountain of One Thousand and One Churches (Binbirkilise) in Galatia, an isolated and inaccessible volcanic massif of forbidding appearance which rises above the flat plain of Konya (Ramsay and Bell 1909). Another instance is the rock monasteries of the unusual deformational landscape of the volcanic region of central Cappadocia, which may be most familiar as the setting for much of Pasolini's film *Medea* (Rodley 1985). Mountains apart, there are numerous evocations of the power and majesty of natural rock in religious architecture from megalithism in prehistoric times to the works of New Kingdom Egypt and its imitators (Donohue 1992). The colossal temples of Baalbek, which date from the early Roman imperial period, are among the most striking examples (Hajjar 1985).

The other, related, quality of the more remote and cold mountain-tops is precisely their remoteness, their frightening detachment from the normal conditions of life (though cf. III.6). Mountains have been linked with the time of origins, suitable places for the abode of the divine. Alternatively, they can be associated with death and what follows. Especially sacred in Antiquity was the precipitous black crag down which an Arcadian stream plunges nearly a thousand feet from the summit of Mount Aroania (modern Chelmos). The place was regarded as the headwaters of the Styx – but the water can, despite that river's poisonous reputation, be drunk quite safely. The otherness of the mountain, its security and remoteness, as well as the numinous quality of certain landforms, played a large part in the choice of such places for pagan religion – Mount Olgassys in Pontus (Mitchell 1993, 2.22–3), for example – or for Christian communities such as the famous monastic centres of Athos, Meteora, or Gallesion near Ephesus, and many less well-known, such as the Holy Mountain above Ganos on the north shore of the Sea of Marmara.

Woodland religion

A central role has been played by forest in the natural vegetation of the Mediterranean, and trees have been prominent in the man-made landscape of the region and in its religion throughout history. In ancient Greece, cults connected with undomesticated wilderness were frequently associated with thickly planted groves proverbial for their darkness, silence and mystery. Productive trees, to which we shall return (Section 3), had an entirely different range of overtones. In Christian cemeteries planted with cypress, and in association with many a Muslim holy place, the grove remains an important visual adjunct of the sacred. In the Levant, moreover, single prominent trees have claimed from the most ancient times a marked religious significance, and both they and the sacred groves are hung with scraps of cloth or waste paper as a sign of their sanctity – the *za'rur* or 'tree-altars' of the Muslim tradition (Goldziher 1971, 316–7). Special treatment of individual trees of unusual size or visual impact was a common feature of ancient paganism outside the Semitic world too (cf. Pliny, *Natural History*, 12.3). To maintain a sacred grove of indigenous trees is not just to accept that this wild natural place is holy and good: it is an active, creative strategy which can take its interpretative and social momentum from, for example, the contrast which may be explicitly pointed up between the particular kind of wildness of the grove and the precise character of the carefully tended agriculturally productive fields which surround it in all directions.

In ancient Greece and Rome the different species of tree in the groves of different deities reflected the religious element in the ancients' understanding of the contrast between cultivated domesticated terrain and untamed wilderness (de Cazenove and Scheid 1989). Regular rows of fruit-trees indicated and expressed quite different cults from those that focused on clustering stands of plane or cypress. The waste, to revert to the allusion just made to fauna, was also seen as the world of the hunt and of the animals which were its object. That world too had its religious evocation in Antiquity, for instance in the cult of Artemis. Similar basic cultural distinctions, between the eremitic exterior 'desert' of Christian anchorite and monk and the inhabited world of human lay communities, or between the arid desert and the watered sown, have also found their religious expression in other periods; indeed, the religious expression, we must insist, has often been of great moment in the genesis of distinctions such as these which have confused the interpretations of economic and social historians.

Cults and the underworld

So much for the surface. Beneath it, where springs after all start too, there is even greater potential for close contact between cult and landscape. The conception of the earth's surface as a boundary between two worlds is, perhaps not very surprisingly, to be found equally in ancient, Christian and Islamic thought about the layout of the universe (*RAC*, 'Erde'). The cave is of course an obvious crossing-point from one world to another (it has its obverse in the veneration of outcroppings of natural rock). Examples of sacred caves need no listing, but few are so impressive as the huge swallow-hole in the limestone of Corycus in Cilicia, at the bottom of which, in a deep funnel-shaped cave, the roaring of an underground torrent can be heard uncannily magnified. The place made a deep impression on ancient travellers. Here is the description of Pomponius Mela, a geographer of the age of Nero. It is rich in examples of the language with which the Greeks and Romans of the Empire regularly evoked the wonders of the landscape:

> Above [Corycus] is a cave remarkable beyond easy description. Its enormous open-
> ing pierces the summit of a steep hill a good mile above the shore. Within there is
> a very deep recess, clothed on all its sides with woodland which becomes denser as
> you descend, so that the whole is enclosed by a circle of greenery. The only way
> down is a path of about a mile and a half, rough and narrow and leading through
> agreeable woods and very shady glades; the movement of streams in all directions
> produces a real rustic accompaniment. The inner cave at the bottom is notable in
> a quite different way. A sound of cymbals and a tremendous rattling din afflicts the
> visitor with holy horror; light lasts for a while, but as you descend – if you dare
> – further in, you enter a deep tunnel, continually more lightless as you go down.
> In there is a very large stream which gushes out copiously but briefly, as it quickly
> passes out of sight after only a short course in the cave. The area beyond is too
> terrifying to enter, and so unexplored; but the whole complex is numinous and
> truly holy, a quite suitable place for divine habitation, as it is indeed considered to
> be. (*Geography*, 71–4)

This place was sacred to the serpent Typhon in Antiquity. A Byzantine church closes the access to the inner cave; on the plateau above are the remains of a great Christian pilgrim-sanctuary. The trees at the bottom of the swallow-hole are still hung with the dedications of the local Muslim population. Mela's description remains valuable because of its vivid sense of the contrasts and paradoxes which make the place so shocking, and to which its cultic significance is certainly to be attributed.

The *karst* scenery which is so characteristic of the Mediterranean is especially rich in caves, so that there are many parallels for the Corycian Cave. In the sacred cave of the Qazhayya monastery in Lebanon the mentally ill were tradi-tionally chained up among the stalactites and beaten to assist St Antony in pro-viding a cure (Katchadourian 1984). The cave-sanctuary of the Archangel Michael high on Monte Gargano, both high place and sacred cave (and near a sacred oak-grove), was, from the early seventh century, replicated at other similar points in the south Italian landscape. Perhaps the most famous of them was Mons Aureus, the Olevano grotto/cave (Ado of Vienne, *PL*, 123.368–9, *c.* A.D. 607: Avril and Gaborit 1967). In a cave below the cliff of the Tagliata at Vallepietra in west central Italy, votive offerings from the prehistoric period and Roman Republic show the antiquity of cult; the place has until the twentieth century been the object of Christian pilgrimage every Trinity Sunday (Ashby 1929). Here, however, it has been possible to trace a reawakening of cult-activity from the eleventh century, when the cave became associated with St Dominic of Sora, who 'Christianized the numinous geography of the Central Appennines' (Howe 1997, 71–5, at 71). Appropriating the symbolism of woods, mountain-tops, and caves, Dominic and his followers were very clearly making statements in a lan-guage that was there to be used, rather than, as is sometimes said of their early Christian forebears, directly taking over existing cults.

The various products of tectonic activity share some of the religious characteristics of caves. Hot springs, for example, have been particularly important in
the development of therapeutic cults, and have a prominent role in fostering the
veneration of water-sources in general (cf. [Aristotle] *Problems*, 24.19: 'Why are
hot springs sacred? Is it that they have their origin in two of the holiest of
things, sulphur and lightning?'). At all periods picturesque tales have surrounded
such places. We may cite the hot spring in a gorge near Constantine in Algeria
where the demons of disease lurk in the form of tortoises and can be placated
by the sacrifice of chickens, according to Leo Africanus (Épaulard et al. 1956,
2.368); at nearby Aquae Calidae, in Islamic tradition, the *marabout* who is
venerated there is helped in his task of heating the water by 2,000 phantom
wood-bearing camels who live underground with him. The geographers of the
Hellenistic period, to judge by Strabo (see especially *Geography*, 5.4.5) identified
and named as a type of landform the *Ploutonion* or sacred place where emanations of the underworld could be experienced. At Pythia near Constantinople,
it was a hot-spring cult of Apollo that became another great sanctuary of the
Archangel Michael, whose church was embellished by Justinian.

Spas and watering-places have played a vital, but neglected, role in Mediterranean social history, both when an unusual mineral spring was famous simply
because it was so unusual and so sacred – to be admired, and feared, a source of
cure, or of punishment for perjury – and also when the use of the waters was
surrounded by the more complicated cultural panoply of medicine and luxury-
resort. The hot waters and sulphurous vapours of the north coast of the Bay
of Naples are an excellent example. The site of elaborate and well-known cults
of the underworld from the archaic period, this area, as the notorious resort of
Baiae, became a principal centre of Roman culture. But it also, as is less well-
known, provided an important setting for many of the activities of the medieval
Aragonese court of Naples, and was the principal destination of many a cultured
traveller in the early modern period too. A nineteenth-century account shows
one of the more ordinary mineral springs in action as a central place in a simple
rural region of north-western Greece:

> the springs [of Kremastá] rise in the bed of the river itself, near both banks, and as
> they are considered especially efficacious in cases of rheumatism, large numbers
> from all parts of Aetolia visit them annually. They contain iron and sulphur . . . The
> visitors erect huts for themselves of branches and planks, and take with them
> provisions to last during their stay. (Woodhouse 1897, 24)

The other small-scale side-effects of vulcanicity, such as natural flames of
burning gas (as in the Chimaera of Lycia), fumaroles, sulphurous emanations
and so on, also attract some religious awe throughout. Nor does heat have a
monopoly of sanctity: unusually cold waters are a wonder too, and play their part
in the veneration accorded to caves. The important underlying feature seems to
be pronounced departure from the norm. And in a fragmented topography, that
departure must perhaps be very arresting indeed to attract veneration.

But we should be wary of such interpretations. For what gives pattern to the
religion of locality in Mediterranean history is, in fact, not the recurring irregularities of the physical environment, but the milieux to which the individualities
contribute meaning. The sacred tree is of less significance *en tant que tel* than
because it identifies the area within which it is the special thing, the significant

entity which is associated with the divine. What is of enduring importance is not so much the springs and crags, but the fact that a fragmented environment needs multiple labels, repeated points of contact with the world of the super-natural as with the human world outside. The staccato religious landscape does not reflect the unchanging awe inspired by certain landforms, highly distinctive though they be, but the continuing need to express the character, coherence and interrelationships of the microregions. To illustrate this, we turn to some other environmental inflections of Mediterranean religion.

Dangerous weather

The local weather patterns which we saw, in Chapter VIII, making so unstable the complicated and mountainous topography of the Mediterranean are too often neglected by historians of religion. The pattern of the liturgical year and the visible signs of an unstable environment were tied together in a closer way than is implied in the common understanding of the simple rhythm of the agri-cultural seasons. The June hail at Valencia in south-eastern Spain was called 'St Peter's stones [*les pedres de sant Pere*]'. The water in the conduits on which the whole regional economy depended, changing colour as the different soils of the catchment-areas responded to the seasons, became in a July storm the blood of martyrs, *la sang de les Santes Escudelleres*, that is Justa and Rufina (Glick 1970, 132–3; VII.2). The waters of the stream which flowed from the Aphaca sanctu-ary in the Lebanon to the shore near Byblos flowed every year with the blood of Adonis (Pairman Brown 1969, 65–6). Suffering in the religious domain replicated the throes of the environment. Both ancient cults and their Christian successors have often been associated with winds and tempests, whose effects, conditioned by relief and topography, are localized and predictable to a degree unfamiliar beyond the Mediterranean. In the case of one Anatolian city, the local meteorology, at the hands of its divine associate Zeus Panamaros, actu-ally saved the community from the siege of the renegade Roman Q. Labienus in 39 B.C. by means of a violent summer storm (Roussel 1931). And a record inscribed and dedicated on the acropolis of Lindos on Rhodes relates how Athena saved the city from a Persian siege in 490 B.C. with an unexpected rainstorm (Pritchett 1979, 22–3). Parallels for this type of local story in the lives of saints from Anatolian cities, such as St Thecla, St Nicholas of Myra or St Theodore of Sykeon, are easy to find (Mitchell 1993, 2.133).

The role of weather in divination (for example in the Byzantine *brontologia*) has been important for connected reasons. The weather-cults of the Mediter-ranean have also naturally been concerned with eliciting the meteorological effects on which production and survival depend as well as with the avoidance of meteorological disaster. Redistribution too, even of the most irregular kind, is no exception. Venetian sailors believed that the women of Senj could cause the violent squalls of the area to come to the aid of their pirate men folk by lighting fires in the frightening karstic caverns (Tenenti 1967, 15).

Locusts, sand-dunes and lava: protecting the microregion

> Mercuri sceptripotens, Argifonta, deorum angele
> abige lucustarum nubis de his locis sacrosancta

virga tua, tuum enim simulacrum hoc in loco stat
ponendum ad proventum frugum et ad salutare
remedium locorum et nationum harum.
sis propitius et placatus hominibus cun-
ctis et des proventus frugum omnium rerum.

[Mercury of the powerful staff, slayer of Argus, messenger of the Gods, ward off
the clouds of locusts from these places with thy sacrosanct rod: for thy image
stands in this spot, whose establishment was needful for the increase of the crops
and the healthful cure of the region and these nations. Be kind to all people and
give increase of crops and all things.] (Varilioglu 1988)

We are in the Cilician Gates, the narrow defile in the Taurus where the ancient
Royal Road, even today the only practicable route, crosses from the Anatolian
plateau into the Cilician plain. Route used by innumerable armies, it is also the
access to the rich plains for marauding swarms of insects. The gorge – a singular
landform – is sacred: the aim of the cult proclaimed in this Roman imperial
inscription (in Latin, unusually for the region) is the maintenance of the integrity of the region below from intrusions which might destroy the harvest. This
is an extreme example, in which the boundary-role is very clear. Yet it points
the way towards the interpretation of many aspects of environmental religion.
Enchanted pillars in the sand-dunes among the market gardens of Syrian Tripoli
(probably ancient tombs) were held to protect the city from scorpions and from
the encroachment of the dunes themselves (Moryson 1617, 241) – which we
have seen as a substantial, if relatively uncelebrated, aspect of environmental
danger, for instance to the cities of Lycia and Pamphylia (VIII.2). Theodore
of Sykeon set up crosses on the banks of the river Sangarios to prevent the
further erosion of monastic land (*Life of Theodore*, 141). Theodoret of Cyrrhus
describes how the holy man Aphraates came to the rescue with holy water when
locusts attacked the crops, other plants, wetlands (we should note their inclusion in the list of vulnerable assets), woods and meadows in late Antique Syria
(*History of the Syrian Monks* [*Historia Religiosa*], 8.14). It was *a man with only
a single farm*, but labourers as well as family to support, who appealed to the
saint, we may note, in another revealing glimpse of the gradations of wealth in
the productive landscape.

   The religion of the phenomena which we identify as 'tectonic' is better understood if we conceive of them as points of risk from outside rather than entities
wholly included in and explicable by their context. We think of a hot spring
as something which belongs to the locality, as simply another feature of the
place, although perhaps a distinctive one and therefore helpful in the process of
microregional self-definition. Traditional explanations go further, however. In
his indefatigable attacks on idolatry, the holy man Asclepiades was said, in what
is probably an aetiology of one of the volcanic wildernesses of central Syria, to
have climbed Mount Lebanon; he saw one of the plains beneath green with vines,
as parts of the Biqa might have been, around the great sanctuary of Baalbek
(III.1). He 'blasted it with fire, so that the whole plain turned to ash' (Damascius,
Life of Isidore, frag. 166, ed. Zintzen 1967, 139). In hagiographical tradition,
the third-century martyr Pionius of Smyrna made a district of Lydia in Anatolia
a harbinger of the destruction of the impious. This is the volcanic area known in
Greek, revealingly, as 'Burnt Out' (Katakekaumene): its tectonic features have

attracted both pagan and Christian cult. The serpent Typhon (as at the Corycian Cave, above) was the ancient object of veneration here; in 1895 the inhabitants were found making expiatory pilgrimages along lava-flows to the crater-lip. The Katakekaumene was called 'well-vented and well-shaken' (Strabo, *Geography*, 12.578). It was a place exposed to the danger of earthquake as well as to the alarming manifestations of vulcanicity. As we showed in VIII.2, earthquakes were not perceived just as isolated catastrophes: seismicity itself was a feature of the weakness and instability of the material world. Consequently, the social and religious response to this danger relates not to earthquakes as single disasters, but to seismicity in general. At the same time, since it was a condition which was known to have a geographically varied distribution, seismicity came to serve as another definer of a region's character: vulnerability to earthquake could demarcate the Mediterranean world from the less tectonically active zones which abut it. We shall return to the ways in which this type of landform (and especially volcanoes) expressed the relationship of particular places to the wider layout of the world and indeed the cosmos.

There is serious danger in geographical particularism. When dealing with volcanoes or hot springs, lakes or crags, it is too easy to take each one in isolation, whereas the religious behaviour associated with each is often part of a complex cultural system of explanation and decision. Tectonic activity does not just consecrate this spring or that fumarole; it is an instance of humanity's closeness to the underworld in general. The drainage of obviously transient lakes, pools or swamps has sometimes been attributed to sages, saints or gods – Herakles in the Stymphalian plain in Antiquity, Plato for the Byzantine population of the plain of Konya in the thirteenth century (cf. Lane Fox 1986, 531–2). We met the association of Noah with the principal wetland of the Biqa in the first section of Chapter III. At one level, this is an explanation which is specific to the individual locality, but it is also a statement about the manifestation of supernatural power in the landscape as a whole – a theological as well as a geomorphological observation. We should also note that it, in effect, concerns the potential of the area for modification and improvement by human rather than by superhuman means. Such statements relate very closely to common aspirations for major modification of the landscape, and especially of its hydrology (VII.2). The drainage-mythology of Lake Copais is part of the cultural history of the progressive alterations which have so completely altered the nature of that complex and fascinating cluster of microregions. Something similar can be said of the cult of San Frediano, the wonderful hydraulic saint of early medieval Lucca:

> to define with modern precision Fredianus' rectification of the local hydrology is not necessary. Rather emphasis should fall on the conjuncture between environmental conditions, resilient population and inspired leadership which gave the [river] Serchio a new appearance late in the sixth century. (Squatriti 1995, 21–5 at 25)

In the nineteenth century there is a clear link, before the rise of secularism, between Marian apparitions and Po floods (Fincardi 1995). And St Michael's greatest miracle, that of Chonai, involved the protection of a holy hermit and the archangel's oratory from a sinister attempt by diabolical powers to dam a river and flood the whole area (Meinardus 1980).

Controlling the periphery: the case of water

It must be remembered that, in the better-watered hills of the western Mediterranean, the geographical concept of a river, identified by a name applicable
to one of the innumerable rivulets which form its sources, is a relatively late
arrival, and reflects a developed idea of regional topography. The worship of the
Tiber by the Romans, for example, is an important sign of the organization of
its basin into a homogeneous whole. Where a river has an obvious source or
headwater, that may become the object of worship, as in the springs of the river
Eurymedon in Pisidia (Kaya 1985). Otherwise, a prominent feature on its course,
such as the Tiber Island at Rome, or a waterfall, may be preferable. The ancient
cults associated with the river Timavus near Aquileia derive from its status as
a natural wonder, emerging from renowned caverns in the *karst* (Dyer 1996).
It was, in other words, a river whose upper course and source were less easy to
comprehend than were those of most streams. In turn this made it a conventional
point de repère for the geography of the whole Adriatic basin, whose northern-
most tip it was held to represent (Strabo, *Geography*, 5.1.9).

The water-religion of the Mediterranean made a great impression on the first
students of the subject. Both Robertson Smith and Frazer presented numerous
examples. The sanctuary of Aphrodite at Aphaca in a high valley of the Lebanon
in the territory of ancient Byblos, burial-place of Adonis, where offerings were
hurled into a sacred lake and a strange luminous fire could on occasion be seen
hanging in the air, was remarkable enough without the overworking which Frazer
gave it (1906, 28–50). It was natural to adduce the rarity and indispensability
of water to explain the facts, and scholars of a functionalist turn of mind have
continued to see this as the explanation of the religious significance of springs.
But springs have functions in the landscape which are a good deal more complex than this suggests, and depend on the patterns of use which integrate the
water into the lives of those who depend on it: they provide, as we have already
pointed out, a classic focus for the shifting and mutable topography of the
microregion.

For characteristic proponents of the 'Romantic Mediterranean' (II.1), in the
Mediterranean lands,

> the face of nature is scorched and brown: most of the rivers dry up; and only their
> white stony beds, hot to the foot and dazzling to the eye, remain to tell where they
> flowed. It is at such seasons that a green hollow, a shady rock, a murmuring stream
> are welcomed by the wanderer in the south with a joy and a wonder which the
> untravelled Northerner can hardly imagine. (Frazer 1906, 127)

And this is taken to be the direct explanation of water-cult. The response is
better suited to the poetic traveller than to the historian of the Mediterranean.
As the exorcists of the Byzantine Empire knew well, watery places could equally
be places of danger and the abode of monsters (C. Mango 1992, 219). That the
reactions of those who used these waters were not a simple evocation of their
usefulness (let alone their amenity) was recognized long ago by Robertson
Smith (1889), more sophisticated than Frazer on this subject. Two of his remarks are of particular importance. He observed that water, for all its rarity in
the desert, is less venerated there than in the lands where, since it is more
abundant, it can be used for agriculture. This, he further argued, is because the

sacredness of water goes far beyond simple reaction to its usefulness for the quenching of thirst or the irrigation of crops. Water is very closely associated with ideas of life, and hence comes to have therapeutic connections not directly concerned with its being biologically necessary. For all that, the veneration so conspicuously accorded to springs in North Africa is still often said to be determined by physical conditions, above all relative aridity. But the distinctiveness of the water-cults of the Maghreb lies neither in the hydrology of the region nor in the tenacity of Berber religion.

Recall that water has to come *from* somewhere. Its religion is therefore a religion of provenience. Whether the source of the water is the expected rain, the imagined places whence flow the waters of well or spring, or the discoverable origins of streams and rivers, the very natural concern with maintaining access to water does not depend on a passive admiration of the currently visible pool or rivulet. It entails a far more dynamic concern with the whole environment, an attempt to come to terms with 'the uncontrolled periphery' of the locality (Gose 1993). In other words, the microregion does not make sense unless it is contextualized, and water-veneration helps us see that that process involves the hydrological cycle as much as the network of redistribution.

Visible mountains and the microregion

The individual geographical feature and its religious veneration are thus part of a wider imagining of how whole regions actually 'work' within the known terrain of the world. The visibility of mountains and their summits is not just a curiosity, but a major ingredient in the visualization of space in a broken topography (V.1). This is particularly clear in the case of the high-place sanctuaries which seem to show an impressive continuity from the Bronze Age Aegean through to the Levant in early Christian times and beyond into the Islamic period. A conspicuous example is the holy mountain of Jebel Sheikh Barakhat, which dominates the small plains of the northern part of the calcareous massif of north Syria (Callot and Marcillet-Janbert 1984). Condemned as the abode of demons by Christian authors, it has remained a holy place throughout its subsequent Islamic existence. The location three miles to the north of the cult-centre of St Simon Stylites, which also developed into a significant regional centre, is not coincidental.

The choice of setting for a shrine depends on a wide range of factors and perceptions: where it can be seen from, what can be seen from it, how it complements or contradicts a pattern or atmosphere perceived in the surroundings or understood from their traditional associations. We saw in V.1 how the cult-places of ancient Latium were often oriented towards, or at least provided with a clear view of, the Alban Mount, site of the most important cult-place of the region, the temple of Jupiter Latiaris, one of the formal centres of a loose political federation embracing the whole surrounding area. Sanctuaries of Apollo of Delos in the surrounding islands looked to that sacred island literally as their centre, being located where there was a clear-weather view to it (Rubensohn 1962). The acoustic environment (which we identified at the opening of Chapter V) is one that has been much exploited by religious practice, through the bell, the *semantron* and the muezzin. The role of audibility in the siting of belfry and minaret, both highly expensive adjuncts of sanctuaries, still needs proper study.

But the thoroughness with which conquering Islam denied the use of bells to its Christian subjects is a token of the importance of this often neglected aspect of the religious landscape:

> Bells, primarily a means of communication for religious purposes, soon [in earlier medieval Italy] became the outstanding means of communciation for the municipalities. There is some support for the hypothesis that urban communal life could not have developed without control over the bells. (Haverkamp 1998, 179; V.1)

Out of an estimated 3,248 active pilgrim-shrines in modern Europe, 18 per cent are connected with cities of more than 25,000 inhabitants (Nolan 1990); 30 per cent of those are 'suburban' (peripheral rather than central to the city landscape). Most of the shrines which are related to landscape features – the familiar trees, springs, rocks, summits of our survey so far – are remote from cities, and very few are in their centres. But the two kinds of shrine are united in forming a network which constitutes and makes sense of a whole landscape, rather than stressing its divisions. Ancient and medieval cult-places functioned in the same way.

The mutability masked by apparent survivals

We cannot, of course, be sure of sharing these perceptions of the layout of the holy in the landscape; indeed much of the significance of the choice of sites for ancient temples, Islamic holy tombs and Christian medieval shrines in East and West almost certainly escapes us. And it is not just the basic patterns of regional self-definition that we must attempt to understand but also the ways in which they have been interpreted. Apparent continuity may repose less in resemblance to ancient practice – such as the cave beneath the waterfall in eastern Morocco where the Ait Hamid avert fever by offering *couscous* to the river god (Goldziher 1971, 315) – than in the development of an interpretative tradition. Such a tradition may be to a high degree culturally specific. But it can also be unificatory. In the case of the Maghreb the tradition of that latter kind would run from classical literary texts through African Fathers and Islamic geographers, the colonial explorers of the nineteenth century, the anthropologists and archaeologists who both served them and laid the foundations for contemporary Mediterranean historical scholarship, and the contemporary exegetes of the Tunisian, Algerian or Moroccan past.

The religion of the locality interacts with principles, ideas and traditions which transcend space. The dedication of mountain-tops to Elijah, or the analogy between sacred springs and the River Jordan, cannot be understood without reference to potentially divergent interpretations of the Bible. We should allow for what has been called the 'interpretative charity' which enables even aspects of rather different forms of religious behaviour to be mutually influential and widely comprehended (Pina-Cabral 1992a, 58); and for the fact that the 'hardware' of locality and physical form, including temple, church or tomb, is in practice infused with changing structures of meaning by ritual and observance. Often what we see is a blockish, all too palpable, relic of something that, in the times when it was important, would have been hard to discern through the shimmering screen of constantly altering devotional behaviour (Trombley 1993–4, 1.149–50). Elijah's original holy mountain was Mount Carmel, in Palestine, sacred alike to Jews, Muslims and Christians. In late Antiquity, it was claimed that Pythagoras had lived there in retreat. A landmark of the Crusader state of Acre, its meaning revived in sixteenth-century Catholic spirituality and the antiquarian-geographic tradition simultaneously. No punctuation of the Mediterranean landscape could lend itself so little to simple materialistic explanation (Piccaluga 1990).

Finally, the force of innovation – or revelation – should not be underestimated: the creation of new cults is important in itself, reflecting, in the fresh significance of a locality, the immediacy of some religious vision (as it might be) or the discovery of an image. Mediterranean religious systems are concerned with expressions of change – change since a time of origins, pivotal moments in the major narratives of religious explanation. They are as historical as they are geographical, even where they are inclined to attempt to confront change with a claim to unwavering orthodoxy. In some senses, this 'religion of mutability' might be considered a more lasting, overarching structure than any of the specifics of Mediterranean religion – capable, as it appears to be, of bracketing and embracing the acculturative encounters of the ancient Mediterranean, the 'end of paganism', the fragmentation of early Christianity, and the conversions and counter-conversions of the Middle Ages.

While there are many factors contributing to the distinctive role of mutability in the religious history of the Mediterranean, we maintain that, among them, prominence should be given to the immemorial uncertainties of the microregional environment and its interconnections. An active Mediterranean religious landscape shares in that mutability of the dynamics of microregions which we have constantly stressed as distinguishing them from the static subdivisions of deterministic geography. The punctuated panorama of cult is constantly coming into being and dissolving. With its emphasis on the process of inception, material collected on the Marian cult-places of the Catalan countryside clearly illustrates a part of that (Table 6). It also reminds us of the intersection of such matters with the world of production that we set out in Chapters VI and VII, in which the fragmentation of the landscape in space and time was promoted by local variability, but was crucially reinforced by the varying pressures towards intensification or abatement. It is therefore to the religion of production that we now turn.

3. THE SACRALIZED ECONOMY

The religion of the productive landscape

It would be possible to review the whole survey of Mediterranean production as we set it out in Chapters VI and VII, and examine how religion has expressed the local character of the different elements. Such a survey would be long and inevitably repetitious, and its principal merit would be to stress the multiplicity of productive modalities. Once again, it is the very diversity of manifestations which proves to be the salient characteristic. We shall limit ourselves to a few illustrations.

Rather than the spectrum of intensification and abatement, or the polycultural portfolio of interdependent strategies, it is often thought that what Mediterranean cult has articulated is a sharp division between the desert and the sown, between productive terrain and wilderness. Thus, the older histories of Mediterranean religion were clear that the religion of trees was concerned with an outer

Table 6 Marian apparitions in Catalonia, 1651–3

Of 182 Marian shrines surveyed in Catalonia, 117 had foundation-tales
involving the discovery of a sacred image.

> 95 of these image-tales involved human intermediaries:
>> 67 male herders
>> 10 female herders
>> 4 ploughmen
>> 4 noble hunters
>> 2 female woodcutters
>> 1 male woodcutter
>> 1 carter
>> 1 charcoal-burner
>> 1 hermit
>> 1 slave
>> 1 villager
>> 1 peasant couple
>> 1 noble couple
>
> 62 involved animal intermediaries, including:
>> 34 oxen
>> 15 bulls
>> 1 bull and cow
>> 1 bull and ram
>> 1 sheep
>> 1 lamb
>> 1 goat
>> 3 dogs
>> 2 crows
>
> 88 of these image-tales specified the location of the discovery:
>> 80 in the 'natural' landscape (including 32 caves, 17 trees, 13 springs,
>>   4 hilltops)
>> 8 in the 'human' landscape (including 2 vineyards, 2 wells, 1 garden)

Source: Christian (1981) 16–18.

wilderness, and with delineating a firm line between the domesticated, cultivated
world and the untamed domain of nature. But on closer inspection, instead of a
dichotomy, we find here a representation of the two ends of a finely calibrated
scale. We must be careful to read the ancient texts aright. Consideration of the
uses of the terms reveals that, in the case of sacred groves, 'il ne s'agit pas d'un
autre intégral, mais un autre portant les marques de l'altérité tout en demeurant
complémentaire de la cité et de ses valeurs' (Scheid 1989, 20).

   In other words, sacred groves expressed precisely that complementary integration which we found to be present in relations between people and the
'marginal' landscapes of marsh and woodland. Here, as in our study of animal
husbandry, there can be found no room for environmental Manichaeanism. The

monastic forests of medieval north Italy, equally, were in some senses religious space, protected by curse-sanctions, but that did not make them parts of a schematically conceived outer wilderness (Lagazzi 1988). Moreover, sacred groves do not have to be composed of the trees of the wilder woodland: they may be sacred exemplars of productive arboriculture. A sacred grove of 500 olive and fig trees was destroyed by *daimones* when the late Antique Christian holy man Thalelaios took up residence in Gabala in coastal Syria (Theodoret, *History of the Monks of Syria* [*Historia Religiosa*], 28.1; Map 24).

The idea that the immunity of a sacred grove from cutting represents a straightforward response to general shortage of timber in the locality is an extreme case of simplistic functionalism (Jordan and Perlin 1984). Unfortunately, human social behaviour does not operate instinctively to promote a wholesome ecological balance. There is no state of grace in which – whether unconsciously through religion or semi-consciously through social organization – human productive activity has tended towards a symbiotic equilibrium (compare the accounts of historical ecology in II.5, VI.2, VIII.5). Unreason and environmental damage are more characteristic – and these are just as likely to be expressed cultically as are accidentally beneficial habits. Religion has felt the impress of the full range of interventions in the Mediterranean woodlands, across the whole spectrum of types of natural vegetation. It has concerned itself with both the wilder and the more domesticated environment, and with the uses of woodlands for all their various products, for nutrition and for other purposes. In its inclusiveness and flexibility, it cannot be shown to have articulated a general dichotomy between wild and tame in the productive logic of the Mediterranean, even if those two polar extremes might sometimes be used as *points de repère* within specific cults.

The same blurring of the distinction between food and other products is to be seen outside the forests. The styptic earth of Lemnos, antidote in mythology to the poisoned wound of Philoctetes, and once sacred to Artemis, was also still the subject of a liquefaction miracle (on the feast of the Transfiguration) in the nineteenth century: cakes of it, their authority guaranteed by the Sultan's seal, could be found, as a plague remedy, in apothecaries' shops in Constantinople. Volcanic islands produce commodities which share in the complex sacredness that derives from both the insular and the thaumatological. In the case of marketable goods such as this, we see how the religion of specific places in the Mediterranean goes beyond the landforms themselves, and communicates itself to the whole domain of production within the environment. The rites connected with the reed-harvest in Antiquity at Lake Koloe in Lydia, when the reeds were said to dance around their king, encapsulate the close engagement of this wetland environment with the regional economy (*Opusculum de aquis mirabilibus*, ed. Oehler 1913, 43; Robert 1982).

Among the products of littoral marshes salt has a special role (VI.6). Naturally occurring as salt-springs or the anhydrite deposits which go with them, salt can constitute one of those geological wonders which attracts veneration just because of its oddity: an example is the so called 'salt-Mecca' of the Plain of Konya, in central Turkey, a curious isolated volcanic hill in a desiccated landscape, taking its name from the distant Holy City (Ramsay 1908, 175). Yet salt is of much greater significance because of the essential role that it plays in transforming perishable environmental products into materials suitable for storage and redistribution. Some of the places where it is extracted by evaporation from coastal salt-pans have had a commensurate place in the geography of cult. The salt lagoon at Kition near modern Larnaca in Cyprus is a case in point. The cult of the deities associated with the salt-works goes back to the fourth century B.C., when a Phoenician official in charge of salt-production is attested. It appears still – or again – in the cult of Artemis Paralia of the Roman imperial period. The point has been effectively made that the rhythms of salt-production dove-tail with those of the agricultural year. It is not surprising, then, that this cult resembles the cults of ordinary agrarian production. We have seen on several occasions that all production in the microregion is often conceived of in much the same way, whether it is mineral or vegetable, the fruit of tillage or of gather-ing, consumed in the raw or subjected to complex processing. That uniformity of conception is frequently manifest in religious cult too.

The nutritional significance of salt is often cited as the principal feature of interest in its cultic roles. But its religious significance may be thought to derive rather from its complex role in the ecological geography of production. A similar argument might be applied to the religious applications of the production of the leading ingredients in the Mediterranean diet. The landscapes of pastoralism or intensive horticulture, of great estates or smallholding, of human control or precariously managed wildness, have each their religious expression. Certainly the religious status of wine, like its complex social position, owes a good deal to the conditions of its production, and those in turn, as we saw in Chapter VI, are dependent on the distinctive regime of agricultural choice in a world of flexibly deployable labour and fragmented environmental niches. Such an account of the interaction between this product and the religious matrix seems more convinc-ing than that which has Christian ritual needs determining the distribution of viticulture. Even the possibilities for cultural self-definition offered by wine's symbolic and psychotropic characteristics (Sherratt 1995b, 17–24) are not inde-pendent of the labour-intensiveness of the production of grapes and wine, and the special needs which the latter has as a commodity (Purcell 1994; VI.9). At ancient wine-producing centres such as Jerash, the abundance of wine was celebrated with water-into-wine miracles (Kraeling 1938).

Cereals have their place in Mediterranean religion too, although no one seems yet to have proposed a close explanatory connection between the Christian Eucharist and the cultivation and exchange of *Triticum aestivum*. The ancient cave sanctuary at Hagfa el Kasalija, in the great gorge of the Wadi Kuf near Cyrene, was devoted to the celebration and protection of arable cultivation in general. Its walls were covered with rough representations of ploughs: inscrip-tions alongside show that this was a place of local pilgrimage (*SEG*, 9.736–66). The network of cults which in Antiquity centred on the goddess Demeter and the cultivation of the Thriasian plain at Eleusis – an archetypical example of well-drained, easily cultivated bottomland – was of course closely tied to the consump-tion as a staple of bread (primarily wheaten, but not excluding barley). It would be wrong to think of this observance as the religion of a feature of everyday life whose normality made it sacred. Rather, the myths which express the integration of the cult with the original establishment of settled human existence emphasize the precarious and special nature of cerealiculture; and in many cases, by exten-sion, the cult is found in the context of the introduction of the new crop into areas where it was unfamiliar. Hence, for instance, the significance of Demeter in the world of Greek overseas settlement (Cole 1994, 211–15). It is equally revealing that, for the Romans, the introduction and cult of the essentially Hellenic Demeter as Ceres was strongly linked with dependence on cereals as the commodity whose availability *from outside* is what protects against food-crisis. From the beginning of the fifth century B.C., Ceres's temple stood along-side the earliest river harbour of the city; strikingly, the building also housed the cult of Liber, the Roman god of that other quintessential commodity of Mediterranean redistribution, wine. The religion of cereals, therefore, confirmed the place that they had as the product which became indispensable through being linked with the infrastructure of interdependence. The association in mythology between the cultivation of cereals and the good order of the most civilized human societies reflects the cultural pre-eminence of bread. And that, as we have seen, derives in its turn to a significant extent from the success which controlling the production and exchange of so manipulable a commodity gave to those who influenced the formation of Hellenic and later cultural traditions.

Sacrifice has some claim to be regarded as the central observance of ancient Mediterranean religion. Ancient commentators on the practice wished to make it a relic, in some sense, of a primitive age when pastoral production had been of relatively greater importance than arable, in the same ordering of degrees of civilization which we have just encountered in the case of cereals. That explanation forms part of the complex of ideas which have assigned animal husbandry a misleadingly detached or marginal position in evaluations of the Mediterranean agrosystem (III.6, VI.7). Revolutionary shifts between distinctively arable and pastoral moments in agrarian history have been far rarer than gradual changes in a pattern which usually accommodates both. Contrary to the rationalizations of the ancients, we would rather perceive in the longevity of the importance of animal sacrifice a symbol of the diuturnal complexity and diversity of the normal productive systems of the Mediterranean. This adaptation of ritual to the logic of production provided a set of opportunities for different religious echoes of various aspects of the relationship between animal husbandry and other enterprises. Religion is equally capable of association with less stable economic relations, of the kind that we have described in Chapters VI and VII. It has been argued that the ritual consumption of meat in the ancient Greek regime of animal sacrifice reflected the beginnings of the emancipation of 'bosses' from the trammels of a system in which surplus production for consumption or redistribution was much more limited (Jameson 1988, 107). That may be a helpful insight, but such emancipation was one of very many similar moments in ancient economic history. There is still less justification for describing sacrifice as an 'economically regulated ritual system': the modalities of Mediterranean production are too changeable and too varied for that (Rappaport 1979, 41). Thus, the festival calendars which we are able to reconstruct for ancient Greece reflect the uncertainties of the year. They do not revolve around largely immutable seasons for different operations, but instead allow for precisely that adaptability and diversity in the sequence of tasks (the 'chaîne opératoire') which we have predicated of the risky environment (Amouretti 1991, 125; compare Casevitz 1991). They also allow an important place for the processing of the crop. The neo-Babylonian astronomical diaries, already encountered in the discussion of specialized production (VI.10), celebrate an interesting range of staples, including the principal cereal (barley) and the fundamental textile (wool) as well as extras, such as cardamom and sesame (Slotsky 1997). The context is clearly ritual, but it would be unwise to assume any straightforward relationship between the choice of these substances and their economic or cultural significance.

Religious behaviour and explanation can delineate the degree of marginality in the productive environment – in the sense examined in VI.3 and VII.4, rather than in that which depends on a distinction between the cultivated and the wild. In Chapter VII we set out to show the normality of intensification and abatement as the 'human resource' is redeployed across a wide landscape. In that context, it is worth noting how *not* cultivating has sometimes been an expression of the sanctity of production. Cases in point include: the tracts of land on the borders of ancient Attica, the Hiera Orgas, a rich meadowland whose untilled state did honour to Demeter; the precinct of the hero Protesilaus in the rich (and colonial) territory of the Gallipoli peninsula (Herodotus, *History*, 9.116); the sacred desert island of Apollo at Pordoselene (Strabo, *Geography*, 13.2.5); or, after the Christian Holy Places had become an object of pilgrimage, the plain where the miracle of the Loaves and Fishes had taken place, which was 'for ever' left uncultivated. Ancient veneration of divinities closely linked with the untamed wilderness, such as Artemis or Silvanus, might be practised in large settlements, or on different sorts of productive estate. They offered subtle calibrations of wildness. Christian monasticism, in its various manifestations, in its interest in both wilderness and reclamation, could likewise define zones of productive difficulty and new intensification, sometimes taking over estates which had been allowed to run down, as in late Byzantine Bithynia (Malamut 1993, 110).

Abatement and intensification find religious expression too. It can take the form of deliberate revival of earlier landscapes of cult: another reason for being cautious about too readily assuming that continuities are as long or as simple as they may appear. Religion marks the 'zone' – actually a plethora of dissimilar and uncontiguous localities – where abandoned land or other environmental opportunities may be taken in hand. This is the setting in which it is desirable to deploy the action of a supernatural patron within and against the wildness of the natural world. The superhuman protector is pitted against an unholy geomorphology: *nulla est religio in stagno* ('there is no veneration to be wasted on a pond') as Gregory of Tours insisted (*On the Glory of the Confessors*, 2): but in 'the system of communication with the supernatural' (Flint 1991, 257) such numinous places played an indispensable part. The festival, pagan or Christian, in the remote wilds of the mountains, or the cults which protect seafarers on remote rocky shores, concern in part the *mainmise* of humanity on the natural world and the current extension – sometimes confident, sometimes hesitant – of the enterprises of civilization.

The promotion of fertility and the protection of assets are commonplaces of all religious systems; yet they take a distinctive form within the Mediterranean landscape. Just as it is not simply individual landforms but types of terrain which find their expression in religion, so all the features of the agrosystem also have a religious geography. The diversity of production is again evoked in the rural calendars of the ancient and Christian worlds, through the manifold celebrations of different parts of the productive landscape by processions, rituals and offerings. As we have seen, the oath sworn in ancient Athens at their *rite de passage* by the young men who would as adults defend the state against its foes evoked the physical features of the landscape; that landscape was also in ritual terms defined by its crops, which featured as additional symbolic guarantors of the vow – the list ends 'Zeus, Growth, Income, Leadership, Herakles, the boundaries of the fatherland, wheat, barley, vines, olives and figs' (Siewert 1977). Individually some of these crops received an additional sacred status in Attica, as with the connection between fig-trees and the hero Phytalos (Kearns 1989, 205) or the sacred olive-trees, oil from which was highly prized ([Aristotle] *Constitution of the Athenians*, 60.3).

Two final examples: Around A.D. 300, at Rhodian Lindos, the devoted priest of Athena, Aglochartos, set up a series of inscriptions to record his planting the Acropolis of the city with olives sacred to the goddess. They describe him as the 'field-labourer [*gioponos (sic)*] of Athene' (*IG*, 12/1.779–80). 'Georgos' means farmer, and St George is the Holy Farmer to the present day in Cyprus, where his feast coincides with the onset of the spring rains. Locally he is venerated as George of the Threshing Floor or George of the Carobs. In Lebanon he has close ties with the Muslim heroic figure al Khidr, and his prominent shrine at Jounieh occupies the site of an ancient spring-sanctuary.

The religion of the extractive landscape

As we saw in Chapter VII, the distinctive patterns of Mediterranean social and economic history will include structural variables adapted to the physical environment but not dependent on it – including the regimes of property, the classifications of land, and the systems of control of labour and productive choice. Mediterranean religion sacralizes these too.

Religion and landscape do not, however, interact simply through the sprink-ling of cult-places like a kind of seasoning. Sacralization is not an irradiation or contagion spread by the simple juxtaposition of religious places or people with the world of the secular. The divine and those most involved with its interpreta-tion or worship have an actual role in production and exchange. Ancient gods, Christian churches and monasteries, and Islamic charitable foundations (*waqfs*) all actually managed – directly – production in the environment. Take the re-ligious institutions of Antiquity. Fairs and festivals apart, their economic dimen-sion is too often overlooked. But many prominent temples and cults of Greek and Roman cities – the Vestal Virgins of Rome itself being a case in point – were great landowners. Their revenues were often substantial. Acting as proxy for the gods, temples behaved like private *rentiers*. In so doing, moreover, they legiti-mated the economic behaviour of the urban landowner – and, no doubt, inter-sected with it, since there was a tight overlap between senior officials of the cult and the local elite.

From the eastern Mediterranean, in Antiquity, we may cite another very instruct-ive case of the economy of religion, which remained important for centuries: the great temple estates of Asia and Syria. Here, the religious structures associated with the control of the landscape and its resources became paramount in social and political structures too, so that the personnel of the cult and the institutions of the cult-place were co-extensive with the administration and governance of a whole cluster of microregions. During the Hellenistic period these entities offered some alternative to the traditional city-institutions in the management of production, distribution and consumption; they functioned as centres for the scattered settlements of regions to which urbanization on the Greek model had not spread. Even though rulers interfered in them, the special status of the shrine was often preserved, as in the early third century B.C., when the more familiar forms of the *polis* were imposed on the landscape, through the synoicism of the territory of the great sanctuary at Nysa in the Maeander valley. In this particular case the preservation was achieved through a grant of the status of asylum, making the Plutonium immune from civic burdens and outside interference (Strabo, *Geography*, 14.1.44; cf. the discussion of underworld sanctuaries in the previous section).

The landscape of property was equally evoked in the geography of religion. The subdivided terrains of Roman centuriation schemes were themselves the product of religious deliberation. They were laid out according to the ritual of the augurs, that established a conceptual equivalence between the subdivisions of the sky in which the manifestations of the divine could be observed and the parcelling out of the land on which human activity took place (Torelli 1969). As part of their arcane classificatory science, the augurs likewise developed a complex typology of land-surfaces defined according to their sacral relationship to the Roman state. Like centuriation (VII.6), this bound together the majesty of religion and the assessing of the potential of conquered or conquerable landscapes. Centuriated areas, finally, were also punctuated by points of considerable sanctity, as the treatises of the Roman land-surveyors make clear. Processional rituals such as the *Ambarvalia* in the Roman countryside reinforced property boundaries, and were as much concerned with ownership as with productivity. In the Athenian cleruchies of the fifth century B.C. (VII.6), sanctuaries of Athenian cults could act as symbolic centres of the allotted terrains. Each formed a *temenos* or precinct whose sacred boundaries were marked with boundary-stones, and were drawn with a precision which might serve as an exemplar for the rest of the settlement scheme.

A second-century A.D. author, attacking an opponent as irreligious, provides a picture of the numerous religious features of the agricultural landscape:

> he sets aside none of the crop for the gods of rural production who feed and clothe him; no wine, no firstling from the herd; there is no shrine in his villa, no consecrated place or grove. Sacred places and groves? People who have been there say that they have not seen a single anointed stone or wreath-hung bough! (Apuleius, *Apologia*, 56)

The first point to note here is that the alienation of part of the yield forms one of the basic acts of rural religion. It is a simulacrum and extension of prudent storage, as also of the alienations which are necessary because of other relations of dependence and subordination, and it perhaps makes those more acceptable, or at least more routine. In a quite different example, revealed by the wills of middling-wealthy proprietors on an eighteenth-century Aegean island, we find an equivalent pattern, in which materials for contribution to occasional festivals are prescribed:

> The daughters of the late Ioannes Pylaras, Kale and Maria leave . . . first to Sts Cosmas and Damian at the village of Langada, ten loaves and a goat; to St John at Proespera, four loaves; to St John the Divine at Kouniades, sixteen loaves and a goat; and to St Irene eight loaves and a half a goat; and to St Sideros at Koumaro, four loaves and a half a goat (11 February 1765, Ikaria). (I. Melas 1955, 2.85)

In such wills, vines, individual trees, tiny plots of land, even beehives, are similarly left to the scattered churches of the villages across whose fragmented territories individual portfolios of property were distributed.

Apuleius's list of the absolutely normal adjuncts of an agricultural estate reminds us of how the collectivity of such individual features constituted a visual imagining of the whole productive landscape. The Greeks and Romans, it is clear, identified and artistically portrayed a sacred landscape in which features such as crags, caves, springs, groves and the shrines associated with them are used to depict the ideal rural terrain. It was the frequent sacred punctuations of the landscape which defined the countryside in the aesthetic perceptions of the Hellenistic and Roman worlds. The creation of artificial landscapes, such as the specially built caves in which the rites of Mithras took place (Biamonte 1997), or pools for the worship of nymphs, also belongs in this context: a synecdoche by which salient features picked out in the terminology of religion evoke the whole.

Religious features become the defining element which separates the human landscape from its imagined antithesis, the outer wild. Human devotion to the gods neutralizes the realm of the alien and dangerous, but reinforces features which are especially important: boundaries obviously, but also significant points on the network of communication, such as bridges, road-junctions, columns, and harbours. Another passage of Apuleius is explicit about the way in which the Graeco-Roman visualization of the rural landscape was oriented towards the traveller:

> the general way with a punctilious traveller, when a grove or some holy place appears by the road, is to make a vow, offer an apple, or sit for a little while . . . no more reasonably has an altar bound with flowers, or a cave shaded with branches, or an oak laden with horns, or a beech crowned with fleeces – or even a mound marked off as holy by a fence, or a tree-trunk rudely carved with the axe, or a patch of turf moistened by libations or a stone anointed with oil enjoined an observant rest on the traveller . . . (*Florida*, 1)

The passage also strongly evokes the style of wall-painting popular in Roman houses of the early Empire usually called 'sacro-idyllic'. These conveyed precisely the potential of the landscape to support, through the correct observances enjoined by the world of the divine, the life of those who commissioned and enjoyed such decoration. In these cases it is easy to see that we would be foolish to estimate the sanctity of a boundary-stone without trying to appreciate the web of property-rights, or to assess a crossroads cult without understanding the nature of the road network. In just the same way it was unprofitable to attempt to understand why a single cave or spring has remained holy, without referring to a wider interpretative framework. Of contemporary Morocco Clifford Geertz has pronounced tantalizingly that he can discern 'certain symbolic connections between water sources, sacred places, gardens and Paradise too elusive and complicated to describe in short compass' (1972). The connection that appears to us to be most significant can, however, be put, in simple form, quite briefly: it is the implication of water-rights and the management of the microfundial garden in every facet of the interplay of aspiration and dependence in this zone on the edge of the Mediterranean. Religion and eschatology can alike be expected to have played their part in the cultural formulation of such a state of affairs.

The religion of primary production defines a landscape which in its *pointilliste* topography is highly suited to analysis in microecological terms. We have seen how the religion of the redistributive node – whether the shifting and transient

festival or the rather different forms more usually associated with urban environments – articulates regions of production, consumption and exchange. But the
microregions which we adopted in Part Two were characterized by relative
'fluidity', and by their various interdependences. If religion in some senses mirrors the microregional ecology of the Mediterranean, it should also prove an
intimate corollary of exchange as well as production. The next stage in the
religious response to the ecology is therefore to be found in those central foci of
redistribution and exchange on which the definition of the microregion so much
depends. To that crucial centre of exchange, the religious fair, we now turn in
more detail.

Festivals and fairs

The place of the rural fairground or market-place in the Mediterranean economy was emphasized in Chapter IX. It is not surprising that these temporary
central places, which formed symbolic meeting points for wide areas, should
come to be associated with, and guaranteed by, various religious practices. We
should not imagine that the religious associations were somehow deliberate,
though they may have provided the justification for privileges such as those of
the festival at Aegeae in Cilicia, described by a Jerusalem pilgrim in about A.D.
530 as enjoying a 'tax-break' of forty days each year (Theodosius, *On the Situation of the Holy Land*, ed. P. Geyer 1898, 150). The Byzantine festival, which
used the ancient term *panegyris* to describe an occasion that was usually both
religious and commercial, offers some of the most characteristic examples of this
important phenomenon of Mediterranean history. Some of its elements may also
be observed in Orthodox religion in our own times. But the religious fair is not
unique to the eastern Mediterranean. The fair of St Gilles in Provence in the
twelfth century was based on pilgrim trade, but was also held usefully near the
west distributary of the Rhône delta, so that it could function as an occasional
gateway settlement for the Rhône corridor (compare Map 11). In 1148, 109
moneychangers were present with twenty-five associates and assistants; the fair
was dominated by Italians, but had a notable following from Germany as well
(Wolff 1988).
   A description of the fair of St Demetrius in twelfth-century Thessalonica (from
a work in the style of Lucian called *Timarion*) includes all the salient features.
The author emphasizes how cosmopolitan the crowds were – and the wares as
well, many of which derived from the Islamic Mediterranean. He is struck by
the degree of organization displayed in the regular avenues of tents and stalls.
The cattle and the textiles impress him particularly. Much of the description is,
however, taken up with the very grand religious ceremony in honour of the
martyr, attended by the dignitaries of Church and State. On a more local scale,
and from pre-Christian Italy, we have the younger Pliny's account of rebuilding
the temple of the cereal goddess Ceres on his estates: 'it may be rather old and
small, but on the appointed day it is extremely crowded. On the thirteenth of
September a great gathering of people assembles from the area, much business
is done, many prayers are made, and many answered' (*Letters*, 9.39). Ceres was
performing as patron – patron of Pliny too, of course – just as the founders of
her cult had intended. An observer of the late nineteenth century provides a
comparable case of a festival in the deep countryside, the *panegyris* at the mon-

astery of Tatarna in Aetolia: an extremely remote location, but at the intersection of important routes, and so a focus for the whole region:

> A level tract, called Magúla, stretches along the river and affords an admirable camping ground for the thousands that attend the Fair [which 'seems more largely attended than . . . any other in Northern Greece'] . . . Square open hearths bordered with stones cover the clearings among the shrubs . . . It is pretended that so great is the throng at the time of the Panégyris that the river barely suffices to supply the needs of men and animals. (W. J. Woodhouse 1897, 36)

The paradox that so remote a region attracts more visitors than anywhere in the more prosperous neighbouring areas is one of considerable significance for Mediterranean economic history and demography. Other *panegyreis* in this part of Greece (1897, 21; Map 18) are still more remotely located. Indeed the relative inaccessibility of the festivals can be part of their point: it allows even the farthest-flung regions to participate, albeit occasionally, in the networks of exchange. Even so, the sanctuary at Baetocaece in the Alawite mountains of Syria, which enjoyed two days of tax-exemption each month for its fair, had some difficulty during the Hellenistic and Roman periods in maintaining its independence against the aggressive behaviour of the city of Aradus (Rey-Coquais 1987). Mountains are by no means as remote as they might appear (III.6).

From the years of transition between the pagan and the Christian landscape, in the fifth century A.D., comes Cassiodorus's vivid description of the ancient fair, dedicated to St Cyprian (feast day 16 September), held at the sanctuary of the nymph Leucothea at Consilinum in Italian Lucania (*Variae*, 8.33). For Cassiodorus, Leucothea was Lucania's Jordan, and the beauty of the spring which gave the fair a focus was reinforced by the presence of sacred fish and wonders of Christian cult, as well as by the great *panegyris*. Here was a sacred spring which provided an agreeable and practical meeting-place for the rural population and the merchants who came there to buy their produce. It is clear that the fair was an entertainment as well as an economic necessity, and it achieved such success that the nucleated centre of Consilinum moved down from the fortified heights above to the more accessible fairground by the main road – where, under the name Marcigliana, it remains. An animated fair still took place at Marcigliana in the late nineteenth century – annually on St Bruno's Day (6 October) (Lenormant 1883, 2.138).

Fairs of this kind are usually held at localities which have some topographical singularity. The abundant spring is clearly important: but so is the wider geographical significance of the routes which converge on the area and the movements of people along them. Road-junctions have always been prominent in Mediterranean religion. But there are cases where it is the mobility of people itself that is primarily expressed by the existence of the cult. It is possible to see in this light the way in which the watering-places of the Roman world interacted with the communications network. Hot springs were rare enough to impinge on wide geographical conceptions, and acted as centres and resorts for those whose mobility was widest in scope.

How this might work in detail is admirably illustrated by a petition to the Roman emperor Gordian of A.D. 238 from Scaptopara in Thrace. The village was fortunate in that one of its sons was serving in the Praetorian Guard at Rome; he was given the job of reporting on the state of the village when the appeal was received:

the village . . . is in the best bit of the territory of the city of Pautalia, having a
good share of both mountain country and plain, and in addition baths of hot water
which are extremely well suited not just for luxury but for health and the care of the
body. Nearby a festival is held several times a year and especially around the first of
October, when it has a tax-free status for fifteen days. (*SIG*³, 888, col. 3, 122–38)

Centre of a classic microregional landscape, favoured for communications
as for the landscape variety which permitted a wide range of productive behaviour, and offering the attraction of a natural wonder, this village became – as
we might have predicted – a major centre for redistribution, probably at the
expense of its nominal superior, the city of Pautalia. The religion of the spring
was no doubt related to the religion of the festival. This was, as it turned out, to
be blessed with too many advantages: the community suffered from the over-
popularity of its festival and the excessive interest of the Roman soldiery of the
province, as well as of the governor's staff, who were disinclined to pay for the
services which they enjoyed. The Scaptopareni, we may observe, claimed to be
contemplating horizontal mobility as a solution, abandoning their ancestral tombs
and property; and the praetorian Pyrrhus noted in his report that the number of
landowners had indeed noticeably decreased.

'There is a sanctuary of particular holiness', says Dionysius of Halicarnassus
(*Roman Antiquities*, 3.32), 'whose cult is an observance shared between Sabine
and Latin peoples. Because of the festival [his word is *panegyris*] many merchants, artisans and farmers gathered for financial gain, and the fairs there came
to be the most spectacular of all the similar ones held in various parts of Italy.'
He is describing the Grove of the water goddess Feronia in the Tiber valley
above Rome, which is sited near easy crossing-places of the river whose centrality to neighbouring peoples makes it a neutral point of contact between them
(compare Section 5 below; Map 3). This was a successful enough instance of a
festival for the place also to be chosen, in Dionysius's own time, as the centre of
a landscape of allotted terrain, and to be given the status and architectural
panoply of a city, with the name of the Colony of the Grove of Feronia. It is
time to look briefly at whether religious expressions of economic and social
nodality in larger centres of population are substantially different from those that
we have been studying.

The religion of the epiphenomenal town

The answer is that they are not: as befits the Mediterranean town of our earlier
discussion (Chapter IV), which we have portrayed as an occasional manifestation
of densening in the network of connectivity or a patch of marked turbulence in
the eddies of mobility. We mentioned there (Section 2) how the festival of St
Theodore in the eleventh century transformed Anatolian Euchaita (in Pontus,
near Amaseia) from a desert into a market centre: another demonstration that
the religion of the *panegyris* can actually create a periodic town. In A.D. 795,
the yield in tax of the fair at Ephesus was 100 pounds of gold (Theophanes,
Chronicle, anno mundi 6287). Like St Demetrius's fair at Thessalonica, this
one took place in a city. But that is to some extent an accident. In the eastern
Mediterranean of the sixth and seventh centuries A.D., when the life of the cities
generally underwent rapid transformation, the great rural sanctuaries became
major foci of economic and social activity (Kennedy 1985a, 24). Conversely,

festivals and fairs were essentially labile, and if they happened to be given the appurtenances of civic status, were still apt to move elsewhere, leaving the city without a *raison d'être*. That is what happened to the city of the Grove of Feronia. In IX.7 we considered the close relationship between the opportunistic establishment of centres for redistribution (*emporia*) and the foundation of formal cities (*apoikiai*) in the world of the ancient Greek diaspora. Our example of Naucratis in Egypt showed clearly that cult-places were a major focus of organization and identity in both types of new settlement.

There is, indeed, some reason to argue that – as with the Grove of Feronia – the religious foci which are often so important in the topography of towns are manifestations of patterns of activity which predate the settlement. They are therefore logically prior to the incrustation of architecture, domestic or public, with which they are subsequently encased. This may in some instances explain the way in which urban topography is so frequently shaped and defined by the topography of cult (Carver 1993, ch. 2). It is not, however, only the rituals of the productive and redistributive landscape that can form the religious core of settlement agglomerations. The function of religious central places in the cognitive identification of locality (to which we shall return) can be sufficient; and there are other roles fulfilled by sacred space which *may* be quite independent of other topographical meanings. A very necessary role, for instance, involves the disposal of the dead. There is a 'necrogeography' of the Mediterranean landscape to which nucleated settlements with a certain religiously expressed identity have been central. The absence of burials may define the space of the civic centre itself, as in the ancient Roman world (Harries 1992). Paradoxically, a city so defined, when seen in the wider perspective, is as readily characterized by the burial or cremation places which surround it as by any monument or social pattern of the inner architectural kernel. The meeting-points of the currents of mobility are dangerous because they are epidemiological foci too; they are the places where many Mediterranean people have finally ceased from mobility.

The enquiry into the religious expression of the central processes of production and redistribution may easily be extended into 'urban' space. Mediterranean religion does not reflect any schematic separation of town from country. The contribution of religion has rather been to integrate nucleated settlements with their hinterlands. Religious geography makes little distinction between settlement-types, rather reinforcing the impression of the continuum between city and countryside that was emphasized in Chapter IV. In the medieval Christian Mediterranean, for instance, no strong distinction can readily be drawn between 'urban' and 'rural' confraternities, chantries, or religious festivals (M. Rubin 1992; cf. Caro Baroja 1963). And only with reference to such a continuum can sense be made of the huge variety of intermediate-status settlements which bridge the conventional gap between country and town. The separate identity of these hamlets, villages and subordinate communities of various kinds depended, in an ecology of interacting microregions, on their relation to each other and to more important central places, and is, as one would expect, partly expressed in their religious standing. A suggestive study of a Central American case has shown how the ceremonial centres for a dispersed settlement pattern may be articulated by movements of people and materials, and how the underlying form displays considerable tenacity through subsequent episodes of alternating nucleation and dispersal (Vogt 1968, 170–1).

In cases where we have sufficient evidence for the rural settlements of ancient territories, villages are revealed as cultic microcosms of the more famous *poleis.* The rural demes (*demoi*) (the name, significantly, also applied to parts of the city) or villages of ancient Attica maintained cults celebrating the founder of the community and other aspects of its mythical history – as well as aspects of the distinctive productive regime of the locality. The cult of the hero Beanman (Kyamites) in the Athenian suburban deme of Lakiadai was, for example, the site of a bean market in the zone of intensive horticulture which surrounded the classical city (Kearns 1989, 180). The allotted territories of Hellenic communities overseas were also studded with small sanctuaries (J. C. Carter 1994). The use and decline of such centres parallels the history of intensification and abatement in the management of productive opportunities (Alcock 1994). Elsewhere, documents can help to show similar patterns: the sanctuaries which promoted the identity of villages in the Roman Biqa are an example (Ghadban 1987). But a more abundant type of evidence, common to very many regions, is that of votive deposits from hundreds of rural sanctuaries.

During the Middle Ages, monasteries came to exercise many similar functions in the local human geography. The great monastery of Bobbio in the Lombard Apennines took over the role of the little Roman town of Veleia as the central place in the area; at Farfa in the Sabine hills north of Rome an abbey was inserted into a landscape which had been divided among villages, from one of which, the *pagus Farfensis*, it took its name. Another ambiguous type of settlement is that represented by the submonastic communities called *domuscultae*; these were founded during the seventh and eighth centuries in a vain attempt to correct the decay of villages and arrest the depopulation of the Roman Campagna. From the Islamic world we notice settlements such as Monastir in Tunisia, whose *raison d'être* continued to be that of a fortified religious house or *ribat* after the closure of the eponymous Christian monastery. An uninformed outside observer might often have found it hard to distinguish a medieval monastery from an ancient village. The same goes for the theocratic centres of the 'temple-state' of ancient Asia Minor which we have already met: 'in Morimene at Venasa is the temple of Venasian Zeus which has a settlement of almost three thousand temple servants and also a sacred territory that is very productive, affording the priest a yearly revenue of 15 talents' (Strabo, *Geography*, 12.2.6). Town, or village, or something else?

Among such ambiguous cases, the religious centres which are in some senses suburban or peripheral prove especially informative about the continuum which joins nucleated settlement and productive territory. As in the geography of Christian pilgrimage in Europe today, the accessible religious sites of Mediterranean suburbs formed part of an integrated, hierarchical, system with sanctuaries in much more remote localities (Nolan 1990). Sanctuaries in the ancient world patterned dispersed religious hinterlands: witness the festival of Dea Dia in her grove on the Tiber bank six miles below Rome, to which the populace flocked by boat; the Eleusinian celebrations of Demeter and Persephone in Attica, the procession to which brought into being, in the sixth century B.C., one of the earliest real roads in Greece, the Sacred Way; or the Serapis cult, notorious for its licence, at Canopus beside Alexandria. All these drained the neighbouring metropolis of inhabitants in very much the same way as the feasts of the martyrs would periodically drain the early Christian city. There is no reason to discern a sharp break between Antiquity and the Middle Ages on this score, or a moment when the growing worship of the Christian martyrs in their suburban shrines, located where the martyrs had been interred, effectively turned the city inside out (Jerome, *Letters*, 107.1–2). For all the excitement of the Christian writers of late Antiquity at the novel cult of the martyrs, the urban periphery had long been a 'locus of the holy'. The seeming novelty of suburban martyr-cult derives from a view of the ancient city as a tightly-knit little unit defined by the cults on its acropolis.

Continuity in religious practice across widely different epochs has also been discerned by urban historians of the Mediterranean. Geographical determinism has naturally not been advanced as the direct explanation of these resemblances: the urban landscape is largely man-made. But the apparently resilient religious topography of alleys, open spaces, gates, pools, crossroads and bridges, and similarities between the sacred space of Mediterranean cities in Antiquity, the Middle Ages, and indeed the modern period, have helped reify the Mediterranean town as a concept, and suggested a degree of permanence – and distinctiveness – in urban history which, we argue, is generally overstated.

Certainly some of the coincidences are noteworthy. A catalogue of the minor holy places in Rome in the nineteenth century – Madonnas, 1421; saints, 1381; lamps, 1067 (Lanciani 1893, 34) – is reminiscent of the enumeration of the 255 crossroads cult-places in ancient Rome (322 by the fourth century of our era). Not so surprisingly, perhaps, since Rome has often re-invented itself using earlier models. Such places, moreover, are the product of frequent spontaneous generation, and they are individually ephemeral. This has been brilliantly demonstrated for the Muslim street shrines of modern Istanbul. Accidental veneration has been noted at the tomb of a military officer who died in 1912, and at a grave which transpired to be that of a horse, not a holy man; a shrine full of candles owed its creation to the candle lit by a local grocer on the wall outside his shop as an advertisement for his wares (G. Lewis 1972). Such spontaneous manifestations of cult might, on a more prestigious level, articulate important locations in the topography of urban power. The cult of the miracle-working Madonna of Orsanmichele was for instance established in Florence at the end of the thirteenth century, in that all-important node of Mediterranean power, the grain market, between the headquarters of the civic government and the cathedral (Henderson 1994, 196–7). Conversely, these systems of urban religious topography also decay and mutate. Some of the processes involved are well illustrated in Constantinople. The religious awe and veneration attached there, in a curious and haphazard way, to the relics of the monumental architecture and honorific statuary of three centuries before comes over very vividly in a text of the early eighth century:

> At S. Mamas there once stood a terrifying bridge with about twelve arches and vaults. For a very big river used to pour down at that point, especially, as they said, in the month of February. There too stood a very big bronze dragon, since some said that a dragon lived in that bridge. Accordingly many virgins were sacrificed on it and a great number of sheep and birds and oxen. (*Brief Historical Notes [Parastaseis Syntomoi Chronikai]*, 22, ed. Cameron and Herrin 1984, 84/5)

From Rome of the seventh century A.D. we hear of a procession called the Inchinata, still performed in the early twentieth century (Ashby 1929, ch. 2). Representatives of the different orders of the city (in the tenth century, six shaven men representing the people and six bearded ones who stood for the senate) travelled from one sacred place of the city to another at Ferragosto, bearing images which were periodically anointed with basil, along a route decorated with triumphal arches of greenery and flowers. The old political hub of ancient Rome – the end of the Forum, by the Senate-house, beneath the Capitol – was the starting point for this procession, although, by the time the procession is first recorded, those places had lost any practical significance for the life of the City. This rite changed its style and its details frequently over the twelve hundred years of its existence; it was imitated in neighbouring communities and there was cross-fertilization between its different instances; it was affected by various changes in the social and religious life of the City. But none of this should be seen as unusual. The mutability and flexibility of 'religious space' is one of its salient characteristics.

In many cases the comparable density of religious topography found in cities of very different epochs is to be attributed to cosmopolitanism – that is, to horizontal mobility. The cities' lack of homogeneity will then be one of the underlying reasons for the density and fluidity of their religious landscape. The closest analogues for them will be found not so much in medieval London or Bruges, as in early twentieth-century entrepôts of the Far East, such as Shanghai or Singapore. The diversity of cult reflects the plurality of origins of the short- or very short-term residents of the nodal settlement. Each village in the catchment area, each cluster of microregions, contributes a piece to the urban religious mosaic, as it does to the topography of retail and residence. The city's role as a central place in the definition of networks of connectivity is the one that matters to the Mediterranean historian, and we return to the religious expressions of that function in the final section. First, we should consider the religious dimension of mobility itself.

4. THE RELIGION OF MOBILITY

The mysteries of Euploia

> He gave the Sea that thou mayst sail, lest thou shouldst weary in wayfaring; and not that thou shouldst busy thyself about the deeps therein, and the stones and all such things that thou bringest up out of them. (St John Chrysostom, *Tenth Homily on Philippians*, PG, 62, col. 262)

Chrysostom places the experience of the Christian seafarer in the context of the Corrupting Sea. His attitude to the ambiguous merits of that sea – which is, after all, the medium of blessed pilgrimage – derives from the ancient tradition that gives us our title. One moral peril is the lure of the precious stones that may be won from the deeps. For Chrysostom a more original, and perhaps more insidious, danger is that knowledge of the sea for its own sake may become a paramount attraction – a corrupting oceanography.

The transactions of production and the relationships which go with them are 'anchored' in a landscape whose interstices are frequently the object of cult. In

---

Map 25   The mysteries of Euploia
   Examples of seafaring sanctuaries in remote places are collected on this map, and the destinations of the travellers who left inscriptions on the island of Prote, off the west coast of the Peloponnese.

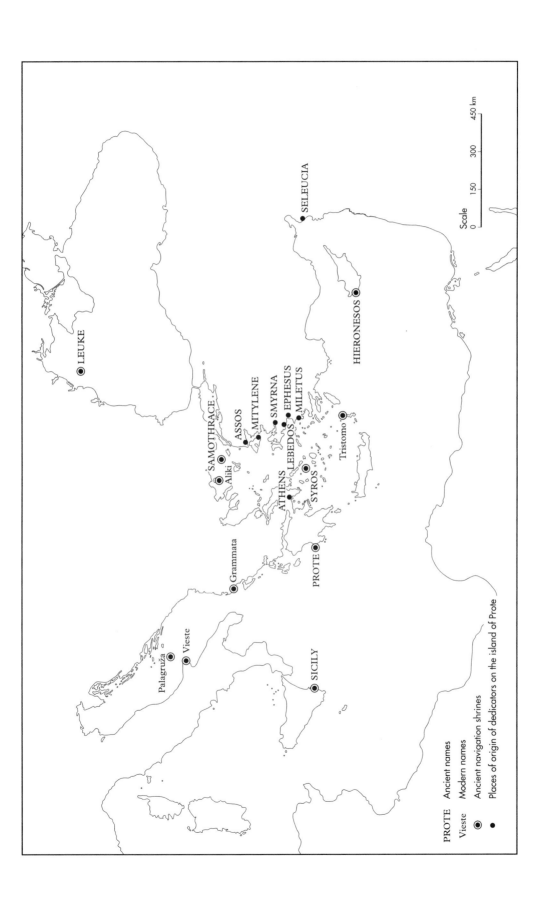

SELEUCIA

LEUKE

HIERONESOS

SAMOTHRACE
Aliki
ASSOS
MITYLENE
SMYRNA
EPHESUS
MILETUS
LEBEDOS
ATHENS
Tristomo
SYROS

Grammata

PROTE

Vieste

Palagruža

SICILY

Scale
0   150   300   450 km

PROTE   Ancient names
Vieste   Modern names
◉   Ancient navigation shrines
●   Places of origin of dedicators on the island of Prote

just the same way, the extension of those processes by means of navigation, which is so essential a component of Mediterranean life, is also paralleled in a cultic topography. Particular features of the sea-voyage are marked as sacred, especially those coastal havens, springs or landmarks that are most significant to the business of navigation. Such cult-places trace a geography of communications that has been obsolete since mechanized transportation (V.2). Yet again we see how the religious response to particular landforms can only be understood in terms of a system that reaches far beyond the locality.

There is, for example, a cove at the remote north end of the island of Syros in the Cyclades, the hub of the archipelago, whose rocky shores, inaccessible from the barren hinterland, are inscribed with invocations to the goddess of fair sailing, Euploia, and her Christian equivalents. The island is of significance only as a node in the maritime route-network; and this cult-place is of any interest only to those in transit. Similar rock-cut inscriptions are found on the desolate islet of Prote off the coast of Messenia. It is now completely deserted, but it was prominent in the logs of medieval travellers; while ancient inscriptions attest contacts with Lebedos, Seleucia, Miletus, Smyrna, Athens, Ephesus, Assos, Mytilene and Sicily (see Map 25). There are other such sanctuaries at Aliki on the south coast of Thasos – at Grammata on the notoriously fearsome Acroceraunian coast of Albania, and on an island off Vieste at the end of the Gargano peninsula. A small island called Holy (Hieronisos), at the extreme west end of Cyprus, whose ancient cult of Apollo appears to have been succeeded on the adjacent mainland by a cult of St George with similar functions, is likely to represent another instance (Connelly 1996). The large Christian basilicas which punctuate the particularly fragmented coastal topography of Lycia – the homeland of that specially maritime saint, Nicholas of Myra – also mark out a landscape of anchorages, sheltered moorings, and coastal towns with access to the interior. The islands have a particularly important role to play in this topography: Gemili, ancient Lebissos, is an example (Tsuji 1995, Foss 1994; Map 26). In this last case, the whole coast from Attaleia to Lindos or Rhodes has acted as a cluster of landfalls for ships making the passage from Cyprus and the Levant or from Alexandria (cf. V.2–3). No one port dominates; it is the plurality of anchorages and havens which is reflected in the fragmented religious topography.

One facet of the sea's presence in Mediterranean religious systems is thus the way in which the island, especially the island in close connection with a coast, is used as a cult-place. Like some sanctuaries on the fringes of mountain, forest or marsh, the sacred island or peninsula partakes of two domains and expresses the difficult zone of transition between them. Wilderness is often less remote and intractable than it appears. Apparently inaccessible, and certainly poor in resources, the islet of Delos was (as we noted earlier) in fact central to Aegean communications, and its centrality was expressed in a cult of Apollo parallel to that at Delphi, which was seen as the navel of the world. The island of Poros was the base of the quasi-federal religious league called the Calaurian amphictyony (Strabo, *Geography*, 8.6.14, with Lolos 1995 for the maritime communications of the area). The sanctuary of Artemis Patmia on Patmos, also at first sight in a marginal location, was of some importance among the scattered islands that constituted the maritime hinterland of Miletus and that offered multiple corridors for navigation in the eastern Aegean (*SEG*, 39.854–5). Its site was to be occupied from the eleventh century by the famous monastery of St John. Other

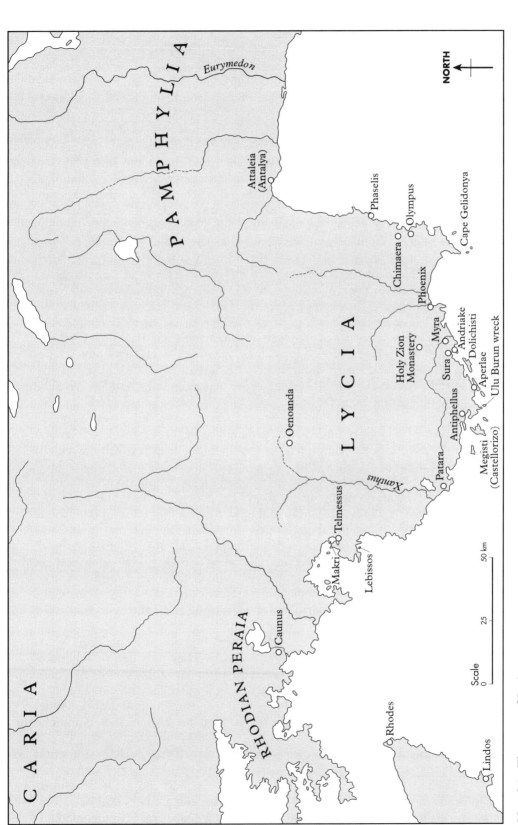

Map 26 The coast of Lycia

monastic enclaves, such as Lérins, provide further parallels, and the argument can be extended to 'îles que n'entoure pas la mer', such as the peninsula of Athos. Maguelonne, the type of that wild margin which is easy of access by water, on the sand-spit between the lagoons of Languedoc and the sea, was claimed by the papacy on the grounds that it was the site of the second church of Christendom after that of Rome.

Some sacred islands are less ambiguously inaccessible. Sanctuaries of the protectors of seafarers might be situated with apparent perversity not in the centres of communication or the indispensable landfalls of the island-hopper, but in places famed for being hard to reach and unimportant to communications. The clearest case is perhaps ancient Samothrace, in the northern Aegean. 'Inportuosissima omnium' to Pliny (*Natural History*, 4.73: 'the island least well-equipped with harbours of all'; cf. Cole 1989), its cult of the Kabeiroi, the great Gods, was widely observed as protection for seafarers, and its sanctuary acted as the centre of a dispersed hinterland. Stranger still was the island of the hero Achilles in the Black Sea, off the mouth of the Danube, which had a similar status, as a federal centre for the communities of the Black Sea, united in worshipping Achilles Pontarches. First mentioned in the epic poem *Aithiopis*, this was the White Island (Leuke) where birds, Achilles' servants, cleaned the temple with their wings, where there was an ancient wooden statue of Helen and Achilles making love, and where sailors approaching the shore would glimpse Achilles running or riding, and might distantly hear his singing. Dedications there were made in both Greek and Latin; Achilles might appear as St Elmo's Fire, like the Dioscuroi, on passing ships (Arrian, *Coasting-voyage around the Black Sea*, 21–3). The island of the hero Diomedes, where there was a sacred grove celebrated for the flocks of migratory birds which gathered there, appears to have played a similar role in Adriatic navigation (it is probably to be identified with the rock of Palagruža: Kirigin and Čače 1998).

Among the offerings at both Samothrace and Delos, whole ships were dedicated. This conspicuous commemoration of connectivity could be seen at other ports too. Aeneas's ship was on show in the river-harbour of late Antique Rome; and the first ship of all, the Argo, which opened up the corrupting sea, was displayed at Corinth (Couchoud and Svoronos 1921). All the main ports of the Mediterranean have celebrated the religion of seaborne communication. In Antiquity, the cults of the maritime powers could be infinitely transferred from their sometimes remote homelands, and sanctuaries of Isis or the Great Gods of Samothrace help map the networks of redistribution in the periods of their popularity. The cults which brought large numbers of travellers across the ancient Mediterranean, especially the healing cults, functioned as places at which acculturation could take place relatively painlessly. They provided an 'interface' between the diverse ethnicities of the ancient world. At sanctuaries of Asklepios such as Epidaurus or Pergamum we can see the cultural effects of mobility being registered in a religious context; Mediterranean-borne communications functioning under the auspices of the divine to promote interchange and community (Chirassi Colombo 1975).

Islamic cultures are sometimes thought to have turned their backs on the world of the Mediterranean, but an Islamic parallel for the patrons of the seafarer can in fact readily be found: the traveller Yaqut referred to the grave of Muhriz near Tunis, dust from which had the property of keeping sailors safe and giving them a speedy return (Goldziher 1971, 2.284). In the medieval Christian Mediterranean, meanwhile, numerous saints protected maritime communications, and some came to have a geographical spread comparable to that of the seafaring cults of Antiquity. Thus, the cult of St Nicholas was of far wider importance than the local context of harbour topography in Lycia which we have already noted. Originating in this pivotal area, Nicholas came to represent the protection of the world of the coasts and of maritime traffic by his own multiple resting-places as well as by the proliferation of his cult-sites. Through the translation of his remains the saint himself, like the images of pre-Christian deities before him, in a very intense expression of the link between religion and redistribution, became a commodity.

The moving of saints' bones is indeed a particular inflection of the sanctity of movement, and the bartering and bargaining that accompanied it is the equivalent in the religious sphere of the secular economic activities which accompanied mobility. Paulinus of Nola speaks of how the movement of relics sanctifies the roads and posting-stations by which they pass (*Poems*, 19.342–52). Dealing in relics, already expressly forbidden in the *Theodosian Code* (9.17.7, A.D. 435–7), became a distinctive epiphenomenon of the medieval Mediterranean economy (Geary 1986). At the same time, especially in the Byzantine world, the narratives of the travels of the saints during their lifetimes became a notable feature of hagiography, in a tradition which could be seen as beginning with St Paul (V.1, 6). The journeying of both saint and relic was fraught with miracle. Tales which echo real webs of communication, such as that of the arrival of St Restituta from Carthage on Ischia, are the medieval equivalents of ancient myths of heroes washed about the sea as infants exposed in chests, or of tales of allegedly historical date, such as that of Arion the singer, thrown into the deepest part of the Ionian Sea between Sicily and Greece, and saved by Poseidon's dolphin which brought him to the sanctuary of Cape Tainaron.

Despite the resistance of elite prejudice, some Christian saints were actually traders too (or some representative Mediterranean entrepreneurs were accorded sainthood). St Omobono of Cremona, who died in 1197, is an unusual example of an artisan/dealer saint, a tailor/cloth-retailer who invested some of his takings in an urban vineyard before *commercia deserens temporalium, mercator efficitur regni caelorum* ['abandoning the exchange of the things of this world, he became the merchant of the Kingdom of the Heavens'] (Vauchez 1987, 118). Just as traders and pilgrims or travellers and saints could be hard to distinguish, so some commodities were more than simply material, but became invested with religious status. The earth of Lemnos, like other medicinal products, falls in this category, but so do some of the other more luxurious and specialized outgrowths of the systems of redistribution, above all silk in the Middle Ages (Liu 1996).

Alongside the religion of safe communications there was a demonology of the forces that hindered them: not only the storms and rocks, the elements whose religion we outlined in the last section, but also the rapacious representatives of authority eager to take their cut of the cargo. The *teloneia* of Greek folklore are demonic forces whose name means 'customs-houses': a transposition to the eschatological and supernatural domain of the concerns of ordinary country people with the impositions and impediments put in their way by collectors of dues, particularly duties on goods moved from place to place. This vivid fear is a curious reaction to a constant of Mediterranean existence (Lawson 1910, 283–7; C. Stewart 1991, 282 n.2). But it reminds us that the religion of mobility has a dark side.

We cannot imagine what travelling and communications felt like in the Mediterranean without at least attempting to empathize with those who held that any journey, *this* journey, had among its genuinely possible destinations the inferno. Eschatological geography patterns the world: north and west are the directions in which to go to Hell. The same geography which includes and makes sense of ports and roadsteads, customs-houses and pirate strongholds, shoals and squalls, includes the accursed and deadly as well as the blessed and the holy. Every journey – as Chrysostom pointed out in the passage which we have quoted – can be a pilgrimage and should therefore not be wasted on the idle and greedy curiosity of the oceanographer. Every place may be a point of communication with the divine.

There is not, in this sense, a 'geography of religion' alongside other geographies. Perhaps anywhere, but certainly in the Mediterranean of our period, geography – that is, any conceptualizing of space – concerns the divine. The dangers of navigation combine with the other hazards of nature to bring together worldly and otherworldly time and space (Gurevitch 1988, 130–44). The sacred and miraculous movements of people and things are not a superficial sprinkling of the holy onto the mundane and normal, but an integral part of the way that the world was experienced. That integration is a firm one, and should not be dismissed as doubtful or ambiguous. It is, moreover, central to Mediterranean religions and not a quaint frill.

Hence it is essential to be prepared, once again (cf. VIII.1), for interpretations of the geomorphology of the Mediterranean that are radically different from those of modern scientific consensus. The pivotal sacred island of Delos, once a wanderer, *per miraculum*, around the seas, but now anchored, was also defined by its special status in relation to earthquakes (a claim sometimes also made for Athens or Attica). Individual earthquakes may have been specifically explained, whether by mythographers or philosophers of nature; but they remained a general aspect of the condition of the physical world and its overall relationship with the divine (VIII.2). Volcanoes, equally, might seem to be a readily understood feature of the environment. On the late Roman map, the Peutinger Table, Stromboli and Lipari appear as scientific-seeming conventional signs – red blobs. Yet it may mislead to call them volcanoes. That is our classification and our rationalization, which derives from a very modern view of the functioning of the physical world. In the pre-modern view, these are places where overworld and underworld are contiguous. Early commentators on the *Odyssey* knew where to locate the detour on that archetypal Mediterranean voyage that took the hero to the Underworld: it was amid the frightening pools of boiling mud and sulphurous exhalations of the Phlegrean fields in Campania.

The volcanic islets in the caldera of the great volcano of Santorini/Thera were thought in the nineteenth century to be the abode of vampires. Souls in purgatory could also be met there – transformed into donkeys endlessly carrying loads of stone (Tozer 1890, 109–10). We would not go far wrong to classify these fiery orifices as 'entrances to the underworld' rather than 'volcanoes'. In his *Dialogues*, Gregory the Great created a Christianized topography locating Sicily both in the heart of the perilous communications of the Mediterranean and in intimate communication with the nether world (Boesch Gajano 1988). In his time, sailing to Sicily was a vividly felt metaphor for death and perdition, since Etna was so palpably a gate of Hell (Gregory, *Dialogues*, 4.36.8–9). Incidentally providing an eloquent testimony to sixth-century communications, Gregory also tells how the father-in-law of his friend Julianus, returning from tax-business in Sicily by ship, put in at the strikingly eruptive Lipari islands. While the crew were busy with the vessel, he visited a hermit who had had a vision, at the moment of Theodoric's death, of the king's being pulled into the crater by his victims Symmachus and Pope John (*Dialogues*, 4.31.2–4).

The sea, then, is another feature of the physical world which needs to be reconsidered, not as an oceanographic assemblage, but as a constituent of a sacred cosmology. Far more widespread, if less terrifying, than volcanoes, it was conceived by the past inhabitants of the Mediterranean world as part of the divine order of the universe.

> Since days of old, when god built Mari, no king residing in Mari had reached the sea. To the Cedar Mountain . . . they had not reached . . . But Yahdun-Lim . . . marched to the shore of the sea in irresistible strength. To the Ocean he offered his great royal sacrifices, and his troops cleansed themselves with water in the Ocean. (Malamat 1998, 45–6)

Thus the first ruler of Mari on the Euphrates in the Old Babylonian period *c.*1800 B.C., at the start of a long tradition of regarding the Mediterranean itself as a divinity.

One of the great general phenomena of the familiar environment, if perhaps the most special of all, the sea derived status from perceptions of a more abstract order too: more than mountains or farmland, marshes or deserts, the sea defined the world. That definition could not be profane: it should centre properly on the sacred focus of the cosmos. Chrysostom's words, quoted at the beginning of this section, foreshadow the *mappae mundi* in which the waterways of the round world converge on Jerusalem. We could scarcely wish for a better testimony to the concept of the Mediterranean as the sum of its maritime communications, to the idea of the sea itself that is created by the experience of travellers crossing it. The pilgrim is well aware of the perils of the deep: the ease of movement is only relative (Deluz 1987). But for the devout Christian, the Mediterranean is the medium of grace, through its assisting the pilgrim to reach his or her goal, a goal which is as otherworldly as the underworld that the traveller can also glimpse in the chthonic wonders of the region. Such beliefs informed the emotional vision of Friar Felix Faber as he looked out from the last outliers of the Alps before taking ship at Venice (I.4).

Unconscious pilgrims

Among the manifestations of sacred mobility which have played a part in Mediterranean history, pilgrimage is pre-eminent. It resembles some of the other ambiguous journeys that we have met in this section, and is intimately connected with the religious cosmologies which shaped ideas about the layout of the world. The salient point about pilgrimage is that it need not always be a journey undertaken exclusively or even principally for religious reasons. 'Hem ziyaret hem tifaret', as the Arabic phrase had it, 'partly pilgrimage, partly trade'. The travellers who invoked divine protection for their essentially non-religious journey shade into the pilgrims whose religious voyage could embrace many material opportunities. The long circuit of the myriad tombs of the saints of Islam converted the journey to Mecca into an extended pursuit of a livelihood which was, for all its pious motivation, indistinguishable from the endless wanderings of the petty overland trader or of the coastal *caboteur* (Goldziher 1971, 2.290). Studies of the rhythms of modern pilgrimage have sometimes reflected on their similarity to those of the involuntary mobility of labour (Werbner 1989, 299–323). The deployment of human resources according to the changing compulsions of production may, conversely, perhaps be linked with the extra-ordinary prominence of sacred mobility in all periods of Mediterranean history.

One of the most significant aspects of religious journeying is the discontinuity of social life which the journey involves: 'in all ritualized movement [there is] at least a moment in which those being moved were liberated from normative demands . . . were between . . . successive lodgements in jural political systems' (Turner 1974, 13). The dislocation can occur in a wide variety of contexts. In pilgrimage, therefore, the journey is not just a means to an end: pilgrimage makes sacred the whole realm of travel and communications and even the notion of geography itself (Turner and Turner 1978, 233). The complex of movements and the habit of mobility are possibly more important than the actual destination. If the older destinations become inaccessible, as after the Islamic conquest of the Holy Land, pilgrimage can be directed elsewhere. Continuity is not therefore especially to be looked for in the places that are the objects of pilgrimage: these are as flexible as the networks of communications themselves. A medieval example, from Palestine, illustrates this well. From the thirteenth century the most frequented pilgrim shrine for Jews in Palestine was at Meiron in Galilee. Recent excavations have clarified its history. While it was a prominent local religious centre in late Antiquity, with a fine synagogue built in a conspicuous position and a much-venerated copious spring, it had then nothing like the status which it would acquire in the Middle Ages. The spring continued to be a very important part of the cult, however, and it has been tempting to see the sanctuary as one instance of geographically determined continuity. But it is rather the discontinuity which is indisputable. Archaeology leaves no doubt about the virtual abandonment of the site in the early Middle Ages. Using the documentary records of healing miracles, a similar picture can be constructed of the violent fluctuations in popularity of the medieval pilgrimage-cult of St Gibrien at Reims (Sigal 1969). The 'rayonnement intermittent' of this cult into its catchment-area is directly comparable to other variations in intensity in the forces which bind complexes of regions together.

Pilgrimage has been viewed as specific to the medieval and post-medieval world, eastern or western. Its inception in Holy Land pilgrimage in fourth-century Christianity, its dissemination among thousands of other cult-places in the centuries that followed, and its enthusiastic adoption as a major aspect of Islam have been taken together as something radically new – which marks a caesura, a sharp break between Antiquity and the Middle Ages. If that is correct, so novel a development in precisely the milieu of interregional communications, a sacralization of mobility itself, must be of importance for our enquiry.

Three points may be made here. First, what is absent from ancient Greece and Rome is not sacred mobility in the broader sense, but a particular terminology and ideological consciousness that is characteristic of medieval Christendom (and, to an extent, of Islam). The pilgrim ideology is a specialized outgrowth from less self-conscious but no less widespread religiously orientated movements. The journey to the local cult-place is easily attested from all periods of Mediterranean history. Second, the apparent absence of a Mecca or a Christian Jerusalem from Antiquity (for all that certain high-profile cults can be shown to have attracted large numbers of devotees from very large catchment-areas) should not lead us to undervalue these lower-key expressions of religion in the context of mobility. In the Middle Ages, too, it is misleading to concentrate exclusively on pilgrimage to the greatest centres. The normal range of pilgrimage included myriad smaller destinations, which declined in popularity or were recreated through the interacting religious initiatives of individuals or groups as geographical horizons changed (McManners 1982, 10–11). Third, in this field Antiquity labours under a special disadvantage in any comparison with more recent periods. That disadvantage is the extreme secularizing tendency among twentieth-century ancient historians, whose preferred use of labels such as 'federal sanctuary' has played down the religious and cultural aspects of ancient social behaviour in favour of the narrowly political or (sometimes) economic. It is high time to reconsider the centrality of cult-places in the Greek and Roman worlds in ways which allow them to be more accurately compared with religious behaviour in post-classical cultures.

Paulinus of Nola wrote of the confluence of pilgrims at the shrine of St Felix in Campania for the patronal feast of 14 January 396: 'look at the confusion of colours, the motley crowds, the ordinary folk on the highways to the shrine: we see with astonishment countless cities here in one city' (*Poems*, 13.24–5). Felix's sanctuary outside the walls of the ancient inland city of Nola was a typical suburban martyr-shrine of the sort described in the previous section. The Christian context was new, and tradition claims that another novelty of this shrine was Paulinus's creative adaptation of the long-standing metallurgical crafts of Campania to the forging of bells, so that this was the first-ever example of an acoustic religious landscape in the Mediterranean (Goldschmidt 1940, 5: cf. V.1). Like the literary tradition in which Paulinus was writing, however, the gathering of the mobile population of southern Italy was not new (Paulinus also presents a mock-heroic but instructive catalogue of the cities from which pilgrims came to Nola, ranging from Rome to Apulia: *Poems*, 14.49–85). Just as at the fair of Consilinum to the south, which we also met in Section 3, so here, the Christian *panegyris* was the successor of numerous very similar gatherings at the cult-places of the older religious system (Map 27; examples from Nola's close neighbour Capua are discussed in the next section). The economic and social interactions of the microregional landscape are indeed a perennial feature of Mediterranean life. Their religious dimension is very likely to display resemblances across doctrinal – as well as supposed chronological – divisions.

Ancient festivals, moreover, also formed a network of a different kind: that of the itineraries of travelling performers and artists, who should be counted among the highly mobile professionals typical of Mediterranean culture (IX.3–4). That dolphin-borne emblem of mobility, the singer Arion, had been on tour around the festival-circuit of Greek south Italy before his eventful homeward journey. In the second century of our era Artemidorus of Daldis claimed to have collected his dream-interpretations in towns and at *panegyreis*, in Greece, Asia, Italy and the larger islands (*On the Interpretation of Dreams, pr.* 2). The numbers journeying to the hundreds, even thousands, of festivals which included cultural or sporting competitions were very large, and the geography of their movement was as religious in character as that of post-classical pilgrimage, since all the festivals did honour to local divinities. At the same time, the hierarchies, rivalries and parities of prestige in these festivals expressed and contributed to political and social competition between communities and regions. In the Archaic Greek

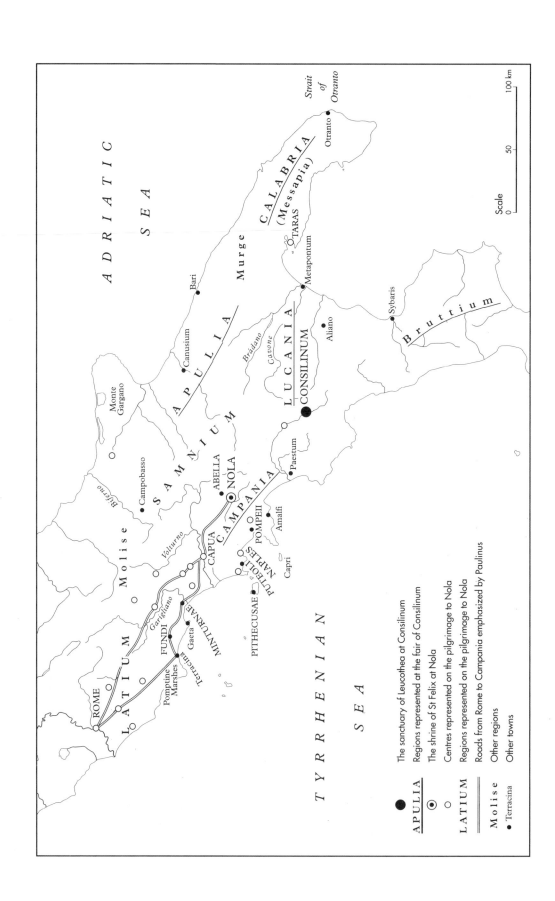

ADRIATIC

SEA

Strait
of
Otranto

CALABRIA
(Messapia)

Otranto

Murge

TARAS

Bari

Metapontum

APULIA

Sybaris

Canusium

Bruttium

Brádano

Cavone

LUCANIA

Aliano

Monte
Gargano

CONSILINUM

SAMNIUM

Campobasso

ABELLA

NOLA

Paestum

Biferno

Molise

CAMPANIA

Volturno

POMPEII

Amalfi

CAPUA

NAPLES

PUTEOLI

Capri

Garigliano

MINTURNAE

PITHECUSAE

FUNDI

Gaeta

LATIUM

ROME

Pomptine
Marshes

Terracina

TYRRHENIAN

SEA

Scale

0   50   100 km

● APULIA   The sanctuary of Leucothea at Consilinum

APULIA   Regions represented at the fair of Consilinum

◉ LATIUM   The shrine of St Felix at Nola

○   Centres represented on the pilgrimage to Nola

LATIUM   Regions represented on the pilgrimage to Nola

═══════   Roads from Rome to Campania emphasized by Paulinus

M o l i s e   Other regions

● Terracina   Other towns

period that was apparent in the tensions from which the Olympic truce and the precarious sacred neutrality of other panhellenic festivals developed. Pilgrimage to these festivals – as we should not hesitate to call it – has been aptly described as 'a symbolic movement not so much from "secular space" to "sacred space" and back again, but rather between "local space" and "panhellenic space"' (Rutherford 1995, 276). The competition for religious prestige continued to play a significant part in the formation of the hegemonies of the more centralized states of the later classical and Hellenistic age. The great monarchies of the age after Alexander played the politics of religious geography with great skill, encouraging certain festivals and guilds of performers at the expense of others.

It is therefore in a context that might at first sight seem surprising that we should look for the most developed equivalents in the ancient world of the great conceptual unification brought about by Christian and Islamic pilgrimage, that wider patterning of the Mediterranean world through sacral movement. The context is the enormously wide pull on Mediterranean communications exerted by that ultimate Hellenistic king, the Roman emperor – a pull centred, through him, on the city of Rome. 'If a person ask you, "Where is your God?", reply to him "In the great city of Rome"' (Talmud, *Ta'anit*, 1.1). The cultic communities, of many different local origins, which developed in the Mediterranean hub came to consider themselves different from their fellows at home, and as much superior as the city of Rome was politically and historically.

In this case it is particularly clear how impossible is the extrication of the 'practical' – political, legal, economic, administrative – reasons for making a journey to the *caput mundi* from their religious setting, since the worship of the Roman emperor, one of the most generally diffused religious practices of Antiquity, was precisely concerned with the overlap between such things and the world of the divine. In the early first century A.D. a traveller from Gades to Rome dedicated four silver goblets to commemorate his journey at the healing sanctuary of the hot springs at Lake Bracciano, just north of Rome (Aquae Apollinares, now Vicarello: Heurgon 1952). The choice of a therapeutic shrine in a place of natural wonder is significant, given the role of healing and protective cults in fostering the religion of acculturative mobility in the Hellenistic period. It celebrated the region of Rome as the centre of the world, the most special of places. The traveller's message to the god was particularly explicit: each of the goblets was embellished with a detailed history of the stages of the long itinerary which had led from Gades to Rome. This is precisely the tradition which moulded the nascent genre of Christian pilgrim literature. Both the Bordeaux pilgrim of A.D. 333 and the Ravenna Cosmographer deploy the road-itinerary as the medium with which to convey the pilgrim's travelling, and change their tone to a more expository and enthusiastic one as soon as they cross the frontiers of the Holy Land. The geography of religion is inseparable from the religion of geography. Both concern 'l'effrontement de l'homme à l'espace' (Dupront 1973).

Map 27 The catchment areas of two late Antique sanctuaries in south Italy
Southern Italy, showing the pilgrimage catchment areas of Consilinum (Cassiodorus, *Variae* 8.33) and Nola (Paulinus, *Poems*, 14.49–85). Paulinus arranges his description of the origins of pilgrims to the shrine of St Felix at Nola according to the two great roads which led from Rome to Campania; but other distant centres are also represented.

5. CONCLUSION: THE RELIGION OF BOUNDARY AND BELONGING

Competing centralities

High in the Graian Alps above Aosta stands the shrine of a saint called Besse. It offers a paradigm case of many of the themes of this chapter. The shrine is situated beneath a conspicuous and unusual outcrop and is surrounded by a detailed ritual topography. It is the centre of a community of five upland settlements, but a focus for the regional aspirations of all the neighbouring mountain-dwellers, and a figure of a rather different kind of prominence in the cities immediately below. There are clear tensions between the different claimants to devotion to the saint, and significant differences in the meaning of the cult for the inhabitants respectively of the adjacent villages, of the high mountains in general, and of the cities of the plains. Locally, Besse is a focus of loyalty for the upland microregions; but he exerts a wider influence as a distinctive and powerful figure who offers the region beyond the environment in which he strictly speaking belongs a sense of distinctive identity *vis-à-vis* the wider Christian world.

Cities such as those in the plains below Besse's shrine have often had prominent patrons. In Antiquity this might be a *poliouchos theos* or city-protecting deity; potent human figures were recruited as patrons too – heroes, sages, philosophers, holy men and women or saints. This sort of patronage is not, however, exclusive. The more complex the relations of a community or locality, and the more fraught with points of anxiety, the more kinds of patronage are called for. The pilgrim literature shows how large the collections might become – the twelve apostles, forty martyrs, and thirty-five saints who protected medieval Verona are catalogued in the *Versus de Verona* in an order according to the city's topography which makes their collocation distinctively Veronese. Such listing might be given a more tangible expression. At Ephesus under the Roman Empire, a benefactor founded a processional ritual to take place once a fortnight, in which the images of the mythical and historical founders of the city together with representations of the different parts of the Roman body politic to which the city was beholden, along with those of other great benefactors, were paraded through the streets and taken to the great temple of Artemis in the suburb (G. M. Rogers 1991).

The patron's supernatural power miraculously protects the community from the hazards of the 'dangerous environment', such as earthquake, flood or disease. It is natural that the protection should also be invoked to avert food-crisis. The patron must exert influence to counteract the perils of the world of connectivity – mercantile fraud, bandits, requisitions, excessive taxes, oppression and war. In the late Roman West the *potentia* of the saint extended the social and cultural influence of cities (P. Brown 1981, 119–27). But cities, as we have argued, are special only in scale; and we have seen how villages and festival-sites or fairgrounds share 'urban' religious forms just as they reproduce 'urban' functions. It was claimed in A.D. 546 that the temple at Daeira in the mountains of Caria near Tralles had formerly controlled 1,500 subsidiary temples and shrines (John of Ephesus, *Ecclesiastical History*, 3.3.36). The supernatural patrons of the nodal place where ecologies impinge upon each other have to see to the continuation of the interaction and to the inclusiveness of its effects across the neighbourhood. In twentieth-century Spain, local shrines played a very significant part in shaping both the attitudes of country people to the regions in which they found themselves and the relationships between one region and another (Christian 1989). The consequence was a proliferation of cult.

Fragmented environments and fragmented religion are linked. Besse is a saint for the mountain, and, no doubt in somewhat different ways in each of them, a saint for the nearby lowland 'agro-towns' too. It is saints of this type who could be enrolled on the distinctive catalogue of a city with a complex and fragmented hinterland such as Verona. The implication is clear: in conceptual terms, as much as in the practical relationships set out in Section 3 above, such centres are compounded of the nesting allegiances to the world around them in which they participate. In their religious organization of space, as in so many other ways, Mediterranean cities can be thought of as 'densenings' of the texture of the fabric of interdependence.

At the more important religious sites, a clustering of small-scale features of the ritual topography may be found – although such features, like the overall religious geography of regions, are regularly found to decay and shift rapidly. And it must not be assumed, from the relatively simple examples of sacred topography which we chose to illustrate Section 2, that this type of religion is not usually much more complex. Some sacred places, for example, are used only on certain very rare occasions; communities may well have divided loyalties. One vivid example from the Mediterranean diaspora, Contella in Mexico, is a settlement of some ten thousand inhabitants, with ten municipal subdivisions, forty religious fraternities, and annual pilgrimages to seventeen different shrines (Turner 1974, ch. 5). Like medieval Verona, this community can be expressed by such an enumeration. The catalogue of religious identifiers may be a more potent description than the delineation of administrative boundaries. As among the bedouin of South Sinai, the aim may be to control not so much 'a clearly bounded territory, but defined points in it and paths leading through it' (Marx 1977, 33).

A document of A.D. 387 from Capua in Italy gives us a beautiful Mediterranean example (Map 31B). It is a calendar of the most important religious festivals of the year (note that Christianity has yet to supersede such observances at this date). They are a mixture of occasions of wider significance within the continuum of Roman religion and of very local celebrations. Thus: 'ritual procession to the river – to Casilinum'; or 'ritual procession to the river – on the pilgrimage to the temple of Diana'; or 'ceremonial setting out on the pilgrimage to Lake Avernus'; or 'the vintage at Lake Acherusia'. Some of these places were an easy walk from Capua; others were more than thirty kilometres away. But the points involved, and the routes to them, defined the unevenly distributed territory of the city and the very different environments which it encompassed: another dispersed hinterland, in the terms of Chapter IV. The identity of Capua was dependent on the religious expression of the constituent parts of its far-flung territory, and that religious expression took the form of participatory rites in which, no doubt, colourful crowds joined: crowds not so different from those which Paulinus evoked at the shrine of Felix at nearby Nola.

The Capua calendar also provides another lesson in how to approach the elements of the physical landscape. It happens that, in this instance, all the punctuations of landscape which define the religious and social domain were connected with water. As the prominence of hydrology in Mediterranean toponyms reveals, there are few more effective ways of characterizing a region: the distribution of

wells, pools or springs is registered both at the level of common practical knowledge and visually too, since stands of plane or oleander conspicuously mark
out the places in the scenery where there is surface water in a largely arid landscape. The religion of water, therefore, works through the contribution made by
hydrology to the topography of resources, and not through the simple veneration
of water as a necessity that is contingently available in certain spots. Microregions,
in other words, exist in the mind as much as on the map.

The religion of economic neutrality

We saw in the previous section that the great pilgrimages to Mecca, Catholic
Rome or Compostela should be conceived as the most developed outgrowth of
religious behaviour which may be discerned at every scale down to the small
localities whose transient observances were described by Apuleius (Section 3).
How is that continuum to be related to the overall geography of microregions?

In north-west Tunisia, the hierarchy of shrines expresses the nesting of the
microregions (van Binsbergen 1985, 208). The focal points of Islamic cult in
the Syrian coastal plain are arranged within a comparable hierarchy of pilgrim-
age/festival destinations, of which one of the most significant is the Khoder al
Bahri at the mouth of the Orontes (Weulersse 1940a, 255). The geographical
relationships which are represented by these practices do not always tally with
the apparently natural cartographic subdivisions. Many quite local pilgrimages in
the Mediterranean have made a point of crossing regional boundaries. The cult-
places of the Apennines, such as Vallepietra (above, Section 2), attract pilgrims
who have to cross a number of quite formidable physical obstacles on their way
to the shrine. Such overcoming of the obstacles of geography by personal mobility makes journeying of this kind the basis for understanding, explaining and
conceptualizing the layout of the world. And the obstacles in question are more
than just interruptions to movement, where physical progress becomes more
arduous; they are zones of transition between ecologies, between regions whose
conditions of production and redistribution are different.

If the spring is generally sacred in regions of dangerous aridity, that (to repeat)
should be seen not as part of a universal separation of the desert and the sown,
since the 'desert' is an exploitable environment too. In arid regions the spring's
contribution to the categorization of the locality is ecological, part of a zoning
according to differences in environmental management. The same can be said of
the forest. Defined through the religious respect paid to trees and to groves, part
of the totality of the known world as articulated by religious systems (whether
the cult of Silvanus or Magna Mater or the practice of eremitic monasticism), the
forest remains an environment in close rapport with the more densely peopled
landscapes of arable agriculture (VI.4). Wetland zones likewise, marginal – but,
as we have seen (VI.3), important in the Mediterranean landscape – have their
own status in systems of religious explanation. Finally, mountains. As zone of
communications, location of boundaries, and vital link in the environmental chain,
the mountain is an important enough part of the Mediterranean cosmos to
receive complex and emphatic treatment in the religion of space. It is here that
the edges of the ancient Greek community are located by the religious orientation of the *ephebeia*, the *rite de passage* by which young men coming of age
begin their military activity on behalf of the *polis* and its crops in the wildest

fringes of the city's territory (Osborne 1987, 146–9; cf. Section 3 above). Between mountain and plain there exist complex relationships the tensions in which (not least demographic) can form the basis for ritualized aggression such as the *ver sacrum* ('sacred spring') of the Italic mountain peoples in the pre-Roman period, a periodic raid. A more peaceable solution is to develop elaborate means of collaboration and tension-alleviation, including some of the pilgrimages and *panegyreis* which we have been discussing. Among these processes, the maintenance of 'sacred neutrality', as it has been called, deserves a little more attention.

Religious observance can defuse hostilities between rival claimants to a contestable set of resources. Given the fluidity of interaction between Mediterranean microecologies and the labile nature of the structures that determine which clusters associate with which other, such disputes are inevitably common. Something of a type-case, determined more than most by the configuration of mountain topography, is that of a much-respected settlement of holy men (*marabouts*) that keeps neutral a vital pass in the Moroccan Atlas through which two groups of transhumant shepherds must travel and in which they would otherwise regularly come to blows (Gellner 1969). A well-known inscription in Oscan, from Abella in southern Italy, sets out the role of a temple of Hercules, also with reference to disputes about the movement of flocks (Prosdocimi 1976); and we know of sanctuaries which marked out boundaries through providing sacred neutrality at the crossing-places between ecological zones from many points in pre-Roman Italy (Zifferaro 1995). In classical Greece, the sensitive border zone between Megara and Athens, the *hiera orgas*, was, as we saw, sacred to Demeter – and its neutrality was expressed by the respect with which its natural vegetation was regarded: it was a valley-bottom irrigable meadow where cultivation was rigorously prohibited.

This essentially privative aspect of sacred neutrality is only part of the picture. In the Mediterranean world, the problems of production, consumption and exchange, dependence, labour and mobility, provide a great many contexts in which a similar effect may be beneficial without there being much danger of open conflict. The bedouin of the late Ottoman period used burial sites for safe storage of agricultural implements because of their sacred neutrality (LaBianca 1990, 83). We have seen that the production of cereals has had its religious aspects; but the collection and storage of cereal harvests at important points in the landscape is also sanctified in some instances. Excavations in north-east Spain have revealed a sanctuary (Mas Castellar de Pontós) which, from the fourth to second centuries B.C., functioned as a collecting point and sacred store, with a series of rock-cut silos, at the boundary between the territories of the Greek coastal cities and the cereal-producing Iberian hinterland (Adroher et al. 1993). Production, gathering and storage may present certain difficulties, but the problems of redistribution are more intense, and there remains, especially, the basic question of whether increasing involvement in connectivity is desirable. Sanctuaries in the ancient Greek world have, accordingly, been seen as 'sacred channels' between cities, offering safer travel and increased opportunities for trade (Sinn 1996). An inscription of 235 B.C. prescribes that soldiers, veterans, suppliants and slaves are not to be retailers (*kapeloi*) in the sanctuary of Hera on the island of Samos, or suppliers of goods to the temple-cult: in so doing, it demonstrates just what the appeal of being such a retailer might have been – even for the low in status among the numerous visitors to this important, and highly accessible, shrine (*SEG*, 27.545; Soverini 1990–2).

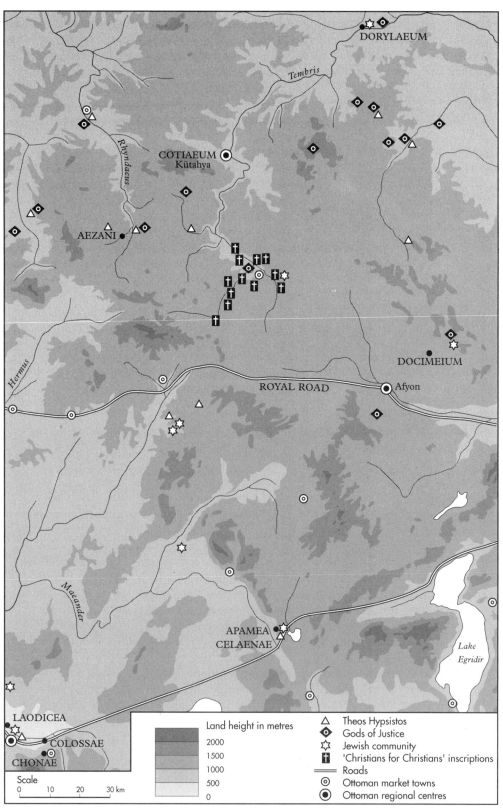

Map 28 Religious cults and microregional topography in west and central Phrygia

The religious manifestations which epigraphy traces in Anatolia of the middle and late Roman Empire are highly regional, but in the Hertzian sense: they express not microlocal differentiation, but the structures which pattern the interaction of microlocalities (Mitchell 1993, 2.16–19; compare Map 28). Here the religion of Mediterranean ecology happens to be fairly well attested. The cult of Zeus Ampelites ('of the grapevine') is an especially informative example because of the orientation of viticulture towards redistribution (VI.9). Still more instructive are Dike, Hosion kai Dikaion, Hosia (literally 'Justice', 'the Just and the Fair', 'the Fair Goddess' – gods who protect the 'dealings of peasant villagers' (Mitchell 1993, 2.18, cf. 25–6), the Phrygian gods of Fairness in Microregional Reciprocity, as we might call them. Note that it is the double accident of the ancient taste for inscriptions and their survival in rural Anatolia which allows us to see here religious behaviour of a kind which is likely to have been quite normal in other fragmented Mediterranean landscapes.

The intersection and 'interface' of zones of cultural, social and economic allegiance on land, and the widespread religious activities associated with them, are relatively familiar. We have argued that the Mediterranean world is also patterned by maritime territories, boundaries and allegiances; and, in places of overlapping or disputed 'territorial' classification, we find religious sites whose singularity works in similar ways. Places of this kind include the promontory sanctuaries of Hera at Perachora near Corinth (Sinn 1990) or Poseidon at Tainaron in the southern tip of the Peloponnese, conspicuously at the very end of the land and much more accessible by sea. Tainaron was an *asylon*, a place of refuge where even the subject-populations of Sparta usually enjoyed immunity, and its geographical distinctiveness was emphasized in cosmological terms by the unexpected location there of an entrance to the Underworld. In the eighteenth century the peripatetic Earl of Sandwich visited another such place, this time an actual island:

> The whole of its inhabitants consists in one single hermit who leads a solitary life in an artificial grotto cut out of the rock, far from the intercourse of mankind, whom he seems desirous to shun. His chief pleasure is in the cultivation of a small garden and vineyard which he maintains with great care and nicety. [Five lines of rustic topos from Ovid's *Metamorphoses* omitted.] Joining to the cavern serving for his habitation is a chapel of the same nature, in which he celebrates mass according to the Roman catholic rite. Opposite to this chapel is another grotto, in which is the tomb of a Turkish saint, who died and was buried here at a time when the Grand Signor's fleet was at anchor before the island. The hermit keeps a lamp always burning at the head of this tomb, upon which account he remains unmolested by the Mahometans who frequently come to Lampedosa to water their ships and gallies. We were assisted by this good old man to the utmost of his power, receiving from him a calf and some other provisions which entirely banished the apprehensions we had of dying for hunger. (Montagu 1799, 988–90)

As parallels for the immunity of this small holy place from the violence of the Mediterranean seaways, we might cite the ancient shrine of the Phoenician goddess Tanit on Malta, inviolate in the wars between Rome and Carthage and untouched by the innumerable pirates of the Hellenistic seas (Cicero, *Against Verres*, 2.4.103) or the monastery on Patmos (Hasluck 1910–11, 167). Yet religion also affirms the separateness of much more complex centres of connectivity, such as the gateway settlements of ancient Naucratis and Islamic Tinnis (IX.7, 3).

These cases inevitably bring us towards the political significance of the religion of space, a modality of religious behaviour which concerns centres of allegiance as much as boundaries. An annual festival attracts worshippers from throughout the neighbourhood. They celebrate their common religious heritage and other shared aspects of the community to which they all belong. The festival comprises sacrifices, games, meals, and more 'political' acts such as the honouring of strangers who have deserved well of the commonalty. The important point is that this commonalty may have no other visible expression. It is created by the sharing, in a topographically significant place, of religious activity. The examples rehearsed in Section 2 above, in which a spectacular landform was confirmed as topographically significant by the observance of a cult-place, concern the problems of regional loyalty and self-definition as much as the inherent awe felt for the character of the locality itself, however remarkable its appearance. The sacred lake of the deities called the Palikoi in Sicily was certainly an unusual feature, but its exceptional status owed something to the ambiguous political position of the Sikeloi, the pre-colonial population, who worshipped there and to whose identity it was central. There may, therefore, be more than one physical focus for allegiance: in pre-Roman Latium the sheltered valley and spring known as the Source of the Ferentine Water served as a hidden centre alongside, but distinct from, the conspicuous cult-place of Jupiter Latiaris on the volcanic cone of Monte Cavo.

Various degrees of formality can be involved in the arrangement, which at its most political becomes a kind of federation; and sanctuaries on which regions focus in this way are often loosely called 'federal' in modern scholarship. These centres express groupings and relationships on a scale far transcending the microregional. They are therefore of the highest interest in the investigation of networks of interaction. In the ancient world some of the greater cosmopolitan shrines functioned as centres precisely because they formed part of the matrix which linked the more significant clusters of productive localities, without being located in any one of those clusters. They became, in various institutional ways, the central places of the catchment-areas from which their worshippers derived. But such focal sanctuaries acquired a role which transcended the networks in which they were physically set: we have already noted Delphic claims to cosmological centrality. Even though land-locked, both Olympia and Delphi acquired a noteworthy pivotal position in respect to the scattered overseas settlements of Greeks, particularly in the West. Other central sanctuaries were from the start located in areas obviously nodal to mainly maritime communications. An example is the Isthmian sanctuary in the territory of Corinth. Cape Tainaron, Samothrace, and the other great Apolline centre, Delos, represent another type; while obviously maritime because of island or promontory location, they developed as centres because of the cult, despite being in barren or dangerous regions. At different epochs they acted as centres of loosely federal allegiances.

Scholars have attempted to trace the ways in which political forms are expressed in religious geography. In one notable case, the topography of cult was thought to have reflected the spatial changes which accompanied the dislocations in hierarchy and allegiance and settlement pattern linked to what is normally called 'the rise of the *polis*' (De Polignac 1984). The sacralization of boundaries through the establishment of sanctuaries between the heartlands of these Greek communities formed an important part of the argument. Subsequently, however, it has been proposed that the remoter sanctuaries were in fact established *earlier* than the cities: at the time of the shrines' construction, they did not lie halfway between *poleis*. The location of cities, then, did not bring about the construction of shrines in between them. Rather, religious imperative led to the construction of shrines in out-of-the-way places: cities subsequently developed on the nodes in the routes joining these sacred places (Malkin 1996). The great sanctuaries of Anatolia and Syria might offer some helpful comparisons.

The general point is that, in the Mediterranean world, the religion of space first, and most basically, relates to the patterns of production and redistribution. Political institutions are also, of course, related to these patterns. But the two relationships need not be straightforwardly connected to each other. One of their common elements is, however, the contribution that both political and religious allegiance make to the understanding of the layout of the world, and it is to that theme, already briefly adumbrated in our discussion of the religion of mobility, that we return.

Territories of grace?

Both Islam and Christianity are geographical religions. They might be said to have expressed the layout of the world religiously in three principal ways: through a sense of the boundaries beyond which the faithful are no longer to be found; through the relationship of the narrative of the origin of the religious system and its locations to the wider world of the faithful; and through the subsequent establishment and maintenance of centres of devotion replicating the original holy places. All three of these geographical expressions can be found in the earlier Mediterranean too.

There is a spatial conception – the 'territory of grace' – within which and across which the religious system can be expected to function in a recognizably orthodox way. The identity of a place or a region within the Christian or Islamic world is established by the character of its distinctive assemblage of cult-places. Thus even the principal core area of Christianity, the Holy Land, is conceived (on a mosaic map of the sixth century A.D., for instance, from Madaba in Jordan, as well as in the pilgrim literature) as a collection of pilgrimage-centres rather than a single focus. Medieval plans of the holy city of Rome likewise define the city by the whole repertoire of its holy places. The peculiar constellation of protectors enjoyed by a medieval city like Verona is another example. Holy places are scattered in multitudes across Christendom, and in order to pin-point the distinctive identity of a locality, the particular density and character of the cluster of holy sites that are associated with it must be described.

The ancient religious continua were notable for the replication of cult-places. Greek *apoikiai* subscribed to cults such as Apollo the Leader or Apollo of the Dolphins. The colonies of Rome contained their versions of the Capitoline Temple of Jupiter, evoking the hill at the heart of the mother city and the ruling god who guaranteed Roman military success. Later the Vatican Hill and the Almo Stream in the environs of imperial Rome became so closely associated with certain cults of eastern Mediterranean origin, and especially that of the Phrygian Mother of the Gods, that they were deliberately recreated in sanctuaries of those deities elsewhere in the empire. Similarly, the cult of the god of Baalbek ceased to be only a local focus for the Biqa (III.1) and spread throughout the Mediterranean. Duplication and imitation posed no conceptual problems. This is a habit of thought which is instructively developed in Indian sacred topography, where the detailed ritual landscape often reflects and recapitulates the wider religious geography of the subcontinent, the Himalayas, the Ganges, and other sacred rivers and mountains. Ancient Mediterranean thought embraced the anatomical imagery of the 'navel' of the earth, the *omphalos* or *umbilicus*: but even a place of that kind was not universally acknowledged and tended to multiply (Mueller 1961).

This was likewise the case to a surprising extent in Islam and Christianity, within which the claims to uniqueness of the authentic focal Holy Places might have been thought dominant. One of the virtues of relics was to render the sanctity of holy places mobile, a process in which they were assisted by associative description and eulogy, such as Cassiodorus's depiction of the Leucothea spring as Lucania's Jordan (above, Section 3). The defining central sacred place becomes in a sense common currency, to be used anywhere. In an extreme instance, an attempt was made in the first century of Islam to suggest that, on one night of the year, the sacred spring of Mecca, Zamzam, abandoned its usual location and emerged instead in the pool of Siloam in Jerusalem. The cult of the Temple Rock was being advanced at the same moment by 'Abd al-Malik, for basically political reasons, as something of an alternative to the Ka'ba in Mecca (Goldziher 1971, 2.44–5). Religion is here being used in formulating definitions of geographical space: definitions which, importantly, come to transcend 'real' space. Something of a parallel is again provided by the sacred geography of the Indian subcontinent. Through being the nodes in the network, the *tirthas* (literally 'fords') which are the goal of the pilgrim define the whole space from the Himalayas to Cape Comorin and articulate its otherwise ungraspable extent.

The categories of religion assist in conceptualizing geographical space beyond what is easily visible, and in making intelligible the vast tracts of land and sea which surround the easily intuited microregion. In the Mediterranean world – an even more culturally and ethnically diverse whole than the Indian subcontinent – such a way of thinking reflects an underlying sense of the unity of the area within which topography can be recreated, and an interestingly open and flexible view of the subordination to that unity of its constituent parts. Precisely because such an interpretation of space is not claimed as simply descriptive or scientifically innocent, it is a convenient vehicle for both hidden and explicit assumptions about the nature of the relationship between the viewer and the world. The geography of religion, then, has often expressed political or social claims, as in the migration of Zamzam to Jerusalem, or the dispersal of the cults of Zeus Olympios or Jupiter Capitolinus. But behaviour of this kind was of much more than political significance. The understanding that, near or far, highly sacred places exist, whether Delphi, Rome, Jerusalem or Mecca, which have a significance for everyone, is one of the cognitive foundations on which mobility rests.

It is sometimes thought that the monotheistic universe which succeeded ancient paganism is wholly different from the kaleidoscopic numinousness of the landscapes which we have evoked in this chapter: 'we tend to look up into the sky and find it empty. We no longer see there a *mundus*, a physical universe as heavy as a swollen cloud (for good or ill) with the presence of invisible beings' (P. Brown 1995, 8–9). The material which we have collected suggests to us that the lower level of the *mundus*, the physical world in which Mediterranean people lived, retained its supernatural populousness for much longer than late Antiquity. We rather agree with the view that sees the Christian discovery of sacred space, which we introduced in Section 1, and its evocation in the religious geography of the Holy Land and other pilgrim destinations, as the transference of a very ancient way of thinking into the newly successful religious system (J. E. Taylor 1993). In the absence of continuity of observance at the Holy Places before the fourth century, the formation of the sacred landscape of Judaea can be envisaged as Constantine's riposte to a pre-existing pagan cultic landscape. And this fast footwork by which the divinized geography of the ancient Mediterranean was perpetuated – in Islam as in Christianity – gives the lie to the view that ancient attitudes to ecology were somehow qualitatively different from those of medieval Christendom because of theological differences between the systems.

Conclusion

It is not more true to say that religion is geographical in the Mediterranean than that geography is religious. We see no reason to reject symmetry in the matter. In the history of Mediterranean religions, there is a cognitive cohesion founded on a certain level of engagement with place and a certain range of ways of conceptualizing it. What, then, of our original problem of continuity and survival in the Mediterranean context? And are any of the religious practices with regard to space and geography that we have described distinctively Mediterranean in any way? Three observations are possible.

First, the dense topographical detail of the fragmented landscape has as distinctive a reflection in religious behaviour as it does in economic and social relations. The religious landscape in the mid-fifteenth century still resembled the picture which, at the beginning of this chapter, we drew of its remoter past from a variety of anecdotal, archaeological or descriptive accounts, a picture comprising 'places of universal significance for agricultural and herding communities: near water, near important trees, on cliffs or peaks' (Christian 1981a, 91). Not every landscape lends itself so readily to the creation of both large and small-scale ritual topography – although the Mediterranean world cannot by any means be called unique in this respect. We have also observed that religion relates to environment through the ways in which it is intimately linked to agriculture. In the passage just quoted, the very general reference to agricultural and herding communities can be analysed into the many distinctive rhythms of Mediterranean agriculture. Each of the various agricultures which were examined in Part Three evinces its own religious geography.

Second, religion expresses regional allegiances, the connections between regions, and the position of regions within hierarchies. In a severely partitioned world such as that of the Mediterranean, with its thousands of microregions, that type of religious observance is predictably of the highest importance. The phenomenon of sacral mobility also of course belongs under this heading. Bernard Lewis has described the Hajj pilgrimage to Mecca as 'the most important agent of voluntary personal mobility before the age of the great European discoveries' (*EI*, 'Hajj'). The indissoluble link between religion and the movements of very numerous individuals over a great variety of distances should be apparent: it is not by any means limited to the greatest international pilgrimages. Understanding something of the relation of religion and space is essential for understanding the way in which cultural unities have developed in Mediterranean history.

Finally, any preconception that geography, geology or topography dictate religious practice must be abandoned. The conspicuous survivals and continuities in Mediterranean cult are not the product of any natural determinism, for all that they relate in complex ways to the physical environment. But by the loss of that explanation we gain a much more useful and important understanding of continuity. It should no longer be possible to accept Hertz's proposal that the survival of cult practice is the result of the stagnation which derives from isolation. Yet that rather patronizing view is shared by Braudel (1972a, 35) in one of the few passages where he refers to the complex of subjects discussed in this chapter. He uses the phrase 'religious geography' in reference to the supposed primitivism of the religion of mountain areas. The recognition of the distinctiveness of mountain regions in the Mediterranean and elsewhere may have been a great strength of his work. But, as we have seen (III.6, V.1), such areas form microregions which are lively and mutable and comparable with those of the lowlands with which they are in perpetual interaction. And that state of affairs is faithfully replicated in religious behaviour, as, paradoxically, Hertz's own study (1913) excellently showed.

Religious forms change too fast for natural determinism; they are essentially unstable and mutable in all contexts; they are continually being recreated after they have disappeared. The observances which distinguish the singularities of the landscape or the dense details of civic topography are highly labile: pilgrimages and shrines in general come and go as easily as the evanescent street venerations of Istanbul, and if the physical reality assists their growth, it is human initiative which plays the decisive role. That there are clear continuities, clear lines of descent even where details change, suggests, however, that the populations of the Mediterranean have passed on elements of their societies from generation to generation with fewer breaks and disturbances than the chaotic political history of three millennia might suggest.

The great theme is that of the Mediterranean's overarching role as mediator and boundary, as zone of transition and agent of comparison and differentiation. Earlier in this section we encountered the hermit of Lampedusa, a precarious neutral on an island, in a sea of religious conflict. The interesting fact is not the contingent accident that a place has been Christian, then Muslim, then once again Christian – many places have changed religious colour over and over again. It is rather that the sea is the medium in which this religious mutability operates. It is because they are coastlands of such a sea that the particular places have had such a history. The vehicle of pilgrimage or of the movement of cult, hero or saint, holy man or relic – the sea is also the medium in which the religious conflicts of armada, crusade or sectarian piracy are played out.

Hertz ended his essay on St Besse like this: 'At the extremities of the high valleys, beliefs and ritual gestures several thousand years old are perpetuated, not in the form of survivals or "superstitions", but in the shape of a real religion ... The main interest of the cult of St Besse is without doubt that it offers us an image ... of the religion of prehistory' (in S. Wilson 1983, 89). Right and wrong: the veneration of Besse is certainly real religion, but it is important not because it shows us an image of an otherwise inaccessible and very distant past (though it does) but because it provides an image of the religion of history: history of, and not just in, the Mediterranean.

PART FIVE

'MUSEUMS OF MAN'? THE USES OF SOCIAL ANTHROPOLOGY

Should more importance be attached to what we know (namely history) than to what we see (ethnography)? In my view, it is a good idea to make full use of all the available data . . .

Germaine Tillion (1983) The Republic of Cousins, 153–4

Here, as elsewhere, it is change which the historian is seeking to grasp. But in the film which he is examining, only the last picture remains quite clear. In order to reconstruct the faded features of the others, it behooves him first to unwind the spool in the opposite direction from that in which the pictures were taken.

Bloch (1954) The Historian's Craft, 46

CHAPTER XI

'MISTS OF TIME':
ANTHROPOLOGY AND
CONTINUITY

1. SURVIVALS REVISITED

'The Mediterranean', Braudel once wrote, 'is a collection of museums of Man . . . One finds there a human milieu, an accumulation of men which the noisiest, most spectacular invasions have shown themselves incapable of biting into deeply.'

That is from the original French edition of *The Mediterranean*, published in 1949 (p. 298). It is omitted from the revised version of 1966 (=1972a). Perhaps Braudel no longer found its metaphors persuasive (though cf. 1972a, 161). His conviction that time is not always 'cette valeur agissante' – that in the Mediterranean time can effectively stand still – is, however, one that he emphatically did carry over from the first to the second edition of his work. Scattered throughout the opening, environmental part of *The Mediterranean* of 1966 are firm indications of Braudel's belief that the past lives on abundantly in the present – with the culture of vendetta in Sardinia for instance; with the egalitarian character of villages of the Moroccan High Atlas; with the ecology of Tuareg nomadism. And right at the end of his second volume Braudel asserts once more, in by now familiar terms, the timeless quality of Mediterranean history. Those 'constants' so dear to him 'are to be found unchanged in Mediterranean life today':

> one may stumble across them in a journey, or in the books of Gabriel Audisio, Jean Giono, Carlo Levi, Lawrence Durrell or André Chamson. All western writers who have at some time in their lives encountered the Mediterranean, have been struck with its historical or rather timeless character. Like Audisio and Durrell, I believe that *antiquity lives on round today's Mediterranean shores* [our italics] . . . I also believe, with Carlo Levi, that the wild countryside which is the true subject of his evocative book *Christ Stopped at Eboli* takes us back into the mists of time. (1972a, 1239)

This idea – that at least some areas of the Mediterranean, or some aspects of Mediterranean life, have, since Antiquity, remained virtually immune to change – is by no means peculiar to Braudel. We noticed some of his Romantic precursors and sympathizers in Chapter II. Another striking representative of this tradition is Germaine Tillion, whose essay in speculative anthropology, *The Republic of Cousins* (1983, but first published, like Braudel's second edition, in 1966), has already provided an epigraph. Here is another excerpt:

> There are foreign customs that 'take' like dye . . . while others do not, but slide off and are wiped out by the launderings of time. So in the Mediterranean basin one reverts to the hypothesis of a very ancient substratum common to the dwellers on its European, Asian, and African shores: in other words, to the Ancient World. (1983, 34–5)

That is why, for Tillion, the history of the many despotic civilizations that have succeeded one another in the region ('what we know' from documentary evidence) is only a part of the whole story. Their despotism was far from complete; it did not 'take'. It was limited by the perduring autonomy of local communities, so that the 'ancient substratum' was never obliterated and is therefore now visible to the social anthropologist or the traveller. For Tillion, as for Braudel, the *longue durée* is out there, waiting to be visited. It is 'what we *see*' (153–4).

Our project, as we explained in the Introduction, began with Braudel. So the concluding part of this volume can appropriately invoke him once more. Not, however, with approbation. It will be clear from preceding chapters that we cannot endorse his (or Tillion's) beliefs about the nature of continuity in the Mediterranean, or about the ways in which social anthropology might contribute to Mediterranean history. Indeed it is important right away to distinguish his approach from our own. We can then go on to enquire what ways remain in which the ethnographic present might instruct us about the historic past.

The writing of history always, trivially, involves finding an appropriate analytical balance between continuity and change. Earlier chapters of this book have deliberately emphasized some of the distinctive continuities of the Mediterranean past, whether in religious practice or rural economy, the response to disaster or the acceptance of technological change. But the continuities, although of several different kinds and degrees, have above all been ones of pattern or configuration; of the overall character of microecologies in their internal workings and their dense interrelation – continuities of structure, we might say, although the term is such a loaded one, and structural history is open to so many varieties of interpretation and opprobrium (C. Lloyd 1993). We have not been searching for instances of immutable human behaviour or environmental stability, still less for some unwavering and deterministic relationship between the two. Similarities over time and space have, most often, been expressed in terms of recurrent variability – in terms, to recall Lévi-Strauss yet again (the epigraph to Part 2), of the differences which resemble each other. In the Mediterranean microregion, we have argued, all is mutability – to a degree that is distinctive, and also that is evident right across the 'pre-modern' centuries. Microregions have certainly not been immune to the 'invasions' and other major historical changes that must figure largely in any short account of the Mediterranean past. Their boundaries, as we have presented them, have been far too shifting and permeable for that. On the contrary, we have emphasized their often far-flung connectivity (Chapters V, VI, IX): that perennial involvement in a much wider world, through the movement of people as well as goods, which is an aspect of their identity, not a threat to it. Thus, at several points, we have tried to show how our microecological approach can be brought into relation with the 'textbook' ingredients of political, social, religious and economic narrative. Sometimes our approach is the obverse of the textbook's; sometimes it furnishes a corrective. In either event, the wider historical context is as potent a factor in the workings of the microecology as is the local physical environment or the human responses to it. So there has been no question of seeing any aspect of the microecology as standing outside time, as inevitably part of the *longue durée*, a preservative of Antiquity against the ravages of exogenous change. The only remotely constant aspect of microecologies is their 'micro-ness', which has been fundamental to our discussion throughout this volume. Beyond that, the one sense in which our conception of Mediterranean history involves timelessness is in its incorporating a number of periods often treated in isolation from one another – the prehistoric and the historic; the ancient, the medieval, the quite recent – within a single conceptual and explanatory framework: history *of* the region, which, we contend, has to be understood in microregional terms.

Throughout, therefore, it has been expedient to turn to the recent past for illumination of remoter periods (cf. especially III, VI.2, X.1, but also VI–X generally). We have suggested that the Mediterranean environment has not changed *so* drastically over two millennia that the livelihood of contemporary Lebanese farmers or bedouin pastoralists bears no helpful resemblance to that of much earlier inhabitants – whatever the continuities, or lack of them, involved. For more information than the historical and archaeological evidence alone could supply, we have looked to the discipline that has long concerned itself above all with the small, 'traditional', settlements – social anthropology. On a wider front, even where ethnographic evidence has not been directly invoked, the discipline has remained a potent background presence, its findings or techniques often having influenced our historical or archaeological sources.

Such involvement of history with anthropology is, of course, hardly novel. Many historians now quite habitually look to ethnographic data for confirmation or amplification of the historical evidence, for novel questions to ask of familiar material, fresh theoretical worlds to conquer, modish methods to try. So too do the ethnoarchaeologists upon whose paradigm-shifting work we drew in Chapter VI. The geographical area to which they look is, at least in the English-speaking scholarly world, not inevitably the same as the area they study. It is equally likely to reflect the location of former colonies; and it may still be justified on the grounds that the anthropology of a Third World country is more provocative to a historian studying, say, medieval rural France than the sociology or ethnography of contemporary northern Europe.

In this respect the Mediterranean has generally been seen as different from more northerly areas of study. There the historian is frequently tempted to compare present and past in much the same locality – and not only to compare, but to note the similarities, and thus to begin to assume direct continuities between the two. This is partly because of the presumed stability of the environment, more perhaps because of the Romantic intellectual traditions that we explored in Chapter II. Up to now we have followed Braudel's example only to the extent of using Mediterranean anthropology selectively, so that some of the recurring features of Mediterranean history can be brought into sharper focus. We have tried not to take apparent similarity of present and past as evidence of survival or continuity, whether in belief or in behaviour; indeed such similarity has often been found to mask profound underlying discontinuity (of which telling examples appeared in Chapter X). So we have – we hope – avoided the rhetoric of museums and mists. And we have certainly not suggested that anthropology (together with travel literature) actually constitutes our best, most vivid, source for the remoter past. It therefore remains to be seen whether in this context anthropology should ever be more than an *ad hoc*, ancillary discipline: whether, by itself, it has its own distinctive contribution to make to the historiography of the Mediterranean world.

Continuity is clearly the theme that should be taken up first. The immediate lure – and potential value – of anthropology is after all that it does seem – somehow, however indirectly – to put us in touch with the *longue durée*. But clearly, if anthropology turns out to be usable independently, and on a broader front than we have up to now envisaged, we should not abandon the discipline there. We should see, in Chapter XII, what it can contribute to discussion of our other two, related, themes of unity and distinctiveness.

2. Balanced Arcadias

The great legal historian F. W. Maitland once wrote that anthropology 'by and by . . . will have the choice between being history and being nothing' (1936, 249). Firmly endorsing his dictum over twenty-five years later, the anthropologist E. E. Evans-Pritchard was in the embarrassing position of having to cite his own *The Sanusi of Cyrenaica* (1949) as still 'one of the few genuinely historical books written by an anthropologist' (1962, 58) – 'genuinely historical' meaning, for him, that it was based on the critical evaluation of written records and oral traditions (our paraphrase). Yet *The Sanusi* has not been an influential monograph. Only towards the close of the twentieth century has Evans-Pritchard's example been widely heeded.

The reasons for that are clear. The kind of modern, professional monograph to which the Mediterranean historian immediately turns does not, inevitably, take its inspiration from the vast evolutionary perspective of a Frazer or a Robertson Smith. In the Anglo-American scholarly world at least, it rather lies in a line of descent from the structural functionalism of Radcliffe-Brown (for whom history was largely an irrelevance) and perpetuates the enduring ideal of studying remote societies small enough to be captured as a whole, and in a brief but intensive period of field work, by a single student. When anthropologists extended the characteristic locations of that field work from Africa and Asia to the countries around the Mediterranean, and eventually thence to 'complex' societies further north, they on the whole preserved the established character of their typical monograph. They tended to confine themselves to single villages or discrete neighbourhoods and to the period of their 'participant observation', which was after all their most valued source of information. The settlements that they chose to study were, moreover, typically marginal, seemingly remote from the centres of power, where 'History' is taken to be generated. They have thus, until quite recently, generally given short shrift to the historical dimension of the institutions and settlements that they describe (J. Davis 1977, 6–8, 19–20).

There are naturally many exceptions to that generalization and they are growing rapidly in number, especially as historiography of certain kinds (like anthropology of certain kinds) seems to have been dissolved into the ampler discipline of cultural studies (J. Goodman 1997, 792–8). Yet the impression that at least some Mediterranean societies have been frozen in time and cut off from the wider world, will, however unintentionally, long be created in the unwary by some of the classics of the Mediterranean ethnography. Reading Pitt-Rivers's *People of the Sierra* (1971, first published 1954), which virtually inaugurated Mediterranean anthropology in English, it requires little more than an imaginative leap to be swallowed in those enticing mists. Du Boulay's *Portrait of a Greek Mountain Village* (1974) only occasionally hints that the Greek mountain village life described was already under pressure from without at the time of publication (e.g. p. 258). Campbell's account of the Sarakatsani (1964), to which we return in Chapter XII, does not usually encourage the reader to bear in mind that the field work from which his monograph derives was conducted in 1954–5 (cf. J. K. Campbell 1992), and thus against the immediate background of the horrors of the Italian invasion and Greek civil war. These ethnographic classics are far from being the only examples (J. Davis 1977, 19–20, 242–4, for others). The much-favoured ethnographic present tense is a seductive rhetorical device. It promotes confusion between the time of observation and timelessness, between a snapshot and a monument.

Travel literature offers comparable inducements to reverie and nostalgia since it frequently describes territories that are at first glance remote and inaccessible. Carlo Levi's *Christ Stopped at Eboli* (first published in 1945), actually more a memoir than a travel book, is a case in point. This undoubtedly splendid piece of writing seems thoroughly to have deserved Braudel's approval by substantiating what he wrote about the survival of 'museums of man'. It is a moving portrait of the stagnant village life of 'Gagliano' (Levi's pseudonym for Aliano) in Basilicata/Lucania, southern Italy – a kind of life unknown to most Italians. Levi, a Torinese Jew, originally a doctor by profession, was for two years banished to this 'deep South' of apparently immemorial backwardness by the Fascist government at the start of the Abyssinian war. 'I am glad,' he none the less confesses at the start of the book, written in Florence several years later and published in 1945,

> to travel in my memory to that other world, hedged in by custom and sorrow, cut off from History and the State . . . where the peasant lives out his motionless civilization on barren ground in remote poverty . . . 'We are not Christians,' they say. 'Christ stopped short of here, at Eboli' . . . Christ did stop at Eboli, where the road and the railway leave the coast of Salerno and turn into the desolate reaches of Lucania . . . Christ never came, just as the Romans never came, content to garrison the highways without penetrating the mountains and forests, nor the Greeks, who flourished beside the Gulf of Taranto. None of the pioneers of Western civilization brought here his sense of the passage of time, his deification of the State or that ceaseless activity which feeds upon itself. No one has come to this land except as an enemy, a conqueror, or a visitor devoid of understanding. The seasons pass today over the toil of the peasants, just as they did three thousand years before Christ. (1982, 11–12)

Braudel is not alone in having succumbed to the charms of this sort of 'survivalism'. Pitt-Rivers's introduction to a volume on *Mediterranean Countrymen*, for example, generalized about islands and mountainous peninsulas that 'isolate and to a certain degree protect [the Mediterranean's] local communities' from the integrative ambitions of their conquerors (1963, 9). The historian of the seventeenth century, Geoffrey Parker, also enlisted Levi in support of a criticism of Braudel's other major work, *Civilization and Capitalism* (1981–4), more specifically of the *Afterthoughts* (1977) to the preliminary version of its first volume (1973). Braudel had supposed in *Afterthoughts* that a sort of 'national accounting' could be applied to past economies in pursuit of a total economic history. Parker uses Braudel's own favoured evidence against him. Levi and his kind have, he says revealed to us a world outside history, a world irrecoverable from historical sources and therefore inaccessible to this national accounting. 'It would be idle to suppose', he wrote of places such as Gagliano, 'that these communities had opted out of modern life only in the 19th century' (1980, 8). More recently, in a work of avowedly *Annaliste* pedigree, Graeme Barker has quoted Levi by way of introduction to the long-term settlement archaeology of a Mediterranean valley (Barker et al. 1995, 15–16).

If such places as Gagliano have really existed, what would it mean for Mediterranean history? It would indeed suggest that certain territories within the region had not been reached and affected by the great 'movements' of history, the stuff of textbooks – that the Mediterranean world is in effect divisible into two: static communities on one side, 'history' on the other. It would not tell us how many such communities there have been. It would be a weaker thesis than those of Braudel and Tillion, which involve whole regions able to resist their invaders, culturally if not politically. But reports such as Levi's could be taken to convey the atmosphere of a secluded society, a society for which history is always 'elsewhere'; and that might be of value to the student of the *longue durée*.

Levi conveys atmosphere, certainly – the atmosphere of stasis which any Mediterranean community may *for a time* generate. But he also does more than that. He gives us, perhaps even without meaning to, materials for a *history* of the area – of the changes that it has witnessed. Look again, more closely, at Gagliano. The stranger here who is treated, as in Homer, 'like a god' is likely to have come from the North. What is first being brought out is the supposedly age-old difference between urbanized north and non-urbanized south, not the peculiar isolation of the village. Gagliano is supposed to be a community cut off from History and the State – yet it is somewhere to which the government has already, before Levi's arrival, several times despatched its political opponents. In one of the village squares stands a sumptuous and monumental public amenity imported from Turin by a Fascist mayor: 'a pig was drinking the stagnant water at the bottom of one receptacle; two children were floating paper boats in another. In the course of the year I never saw it serve any other function' (C. Levi 1982, 50).

The 'great' and the 'little traditions', in Redfield's (1956) classic formulation, rub shoulders. But the important point is that the amenity was there; and that the state which it symbolized had (we learn from Levi) brought economic catastrophe to the peasants around Gagliano by placing a tax on goats. Again, the state with which Gagliano is held to have had no contact for two thousand years could be described by the inhabitants as 'an inescapable evil', reflecting the machinations of those 'fellows in Rome' (C. Levi 1982, 78). It had enforced military service. It had also, in the Fascist period, enhanced the isolation of the area: policies designed to prevent migration had (as in other parts of southern Europe) contributed to an *increase* in the area's agricultural population. During the post-war years, by contrast, 'the young men of promise' had left the village never to return – for America or Naples, as well as for Rome. What presented itself to Levi's eyes was the traces of a vanished order:

> All that people say about the people of the south, things I once believed myself: the savage rigidity of their morals, their Oriental jealousy, the fierce sense of honour leading to crimes of passion and revenge, all these are but myths. Perhaps they existed a long time ago and something of them is left in the way of a stiff conventionality. But emigration has changed the picture. The men have gone and the women have taken over ... Gagliano has twelve hundred inhabitants, and there are two thousand men from Gagliano in America. (1982, 102)

The outside world has therefore impinged rather more than we were initially led to suppose. The stagnation of village life in Gagliano – if such it was – can hardly be taken as an inevitable and long-term feature of the area. Indeed the reverse. On, as it were, the margins of his account, Levi includes precisely what our earlier chapters have shown to be some of the prime ingredients in the normal variability and connectivity of Mediterranean microregions: fluctuating relations between pastoralism and agriculture; the manipulative state with its taxes and its symbols; the mobility of people both voluntary and compulsory (that is, economic migration and military service – not necessarily very distinct). As with almost any Mediterranean settlement, an enquiry into the ramifications of Gagliano's ecologies could not confine itself to local and recent data. The focus would have to be widened chronologically and geographically and deal (at least) with the history of the whole of the south.

It would, then, contrary to what Parker wrote, hardly be 'idle to suppose' that Gagliano had opted out of modern life only in quite recent times – or that it had ever opted out at all. Far from transporting us across static centuries into the mists of time, Gagliano may, even as Levi presents it, just as plausibly recall some of that microregional interdependence which we hope to have established as the Mediterranean norm. Levi describes the 'outside world' as having 'stopped at Eboli', some two millennia before his arrival, with the Greeks 'who flourished beside the Gulf of Taranto'. For its evocative 'poetic licence' his work has been quoted with enthusiasm by an archaeologist (Barker et al. 1995, 16). It is ironic, then, that modern archaeology should refute him. In the sixth to fourth centuries B.C., archaeology shows, Gagliano (i.e. Aliano) was absolutely 'in the swim' of the intense interaction between migrants and indigenes that has passed under the label of 'Greek colonization' (VII.6).

What is the modern equivalent here? Of what contemporary history are these supposedly timeless communities actually part? At this point we are bibliographically challenged. For reasons touched on in I.3, we have very little general historiography of the Mediterranean region in the twentieth century on which to draw. At best we have partial accounts of particular areas. Fortunately, however, the constituents of major change are not hard to name and in this context we need do no more than that: first of all emigration on a massive scale, chiefly to America around the start of the century, also to Australia, and to northern Europe since the last war. Alongside emigration must be placed an unparalleled degree of internal migration, from one portion of the region to another and more particularly, since World War II, from countryside to city. To extensive mobility, an enhanced version of a fundamental constituent of Mediterranean history (IX.5–6), we naturally have to add a number of other factors: widespread, substantial, demographic increase, much of it due to disease eradication and improved health-care; significant environmental degradation, probably more extensive, so we contend (Chapter VIII), in the later twentieth century than in any previous one; expanding literacy; international terrorism; decolonization; the belated and uneven diffusion of industrial, transport and information technology; the revenues from oil which have paid for much of that technology in Islamic countries; on the other side of the Mediterranean the EU policies that have deeply affected the prospects of the smallholder; the growth of tourism as a major industry; the resurgence of Islam in various forms, which has forged new conjunctions of traditional religious behaviour and social transformation; renewed nationalism; the attack mounted by dictatorial regimes of both Left and Right on the cultural and political independence of intranational regions. Finally, to the catalogue of change we should perhaps add that all these seem, in the light of the available statistics, to be occurring with an unprecedented comprehensiveness and at an unprecedented rate. The major change, that is, lies in the dimensions of change itself.

It is easier to list the ingredients than to characterize the whole. We suggested in the Introduction that this congeries of changes is to be associated with a reconfiguring of our subject: the slow disintegration of the Mediterranean unity that we have tried to analyse in the foregoing chapters, the end of history *of* the Mediterranean as other conceptualizations of the area become increasingly appropriate. What remains unclear is when and how the transition from Mediterranean to 'post-Mediterranean' should be conceived as taking place. Sociologists and development economists have rightly become sceptical about the value of the model of evolution enshrined in the 'traditional–modern' dichotomy, according to which all societies are traditional, or modern, or, in some ill-specified way, transitional. But no adequate formulation has been found to replace the model. Talk of the 'late development effect' or of 'post-traditional' cultures populated by 'post-peasants', confuses terminological fertility with conceptual sophistication. Nor can dependency theory, from development economics, with its black-and-white economic morality, be said to have clarified our perceptions in this respect.

In ways we thus cannot adequately generalize about, vignettes such as those provided by Levi, or data in more formal anthropological studies, always need to be interpreted in the light of the many ways that Mediterranean life has profoundly altered in the course of the twentieth century. The necessity must be recognized of constantly juxtaposing ethnography with information from other sources. Context and chronology are essential. No statistic or social fact about a small 'backwoods' community such as Gagliano is automatically a reliable guide to how things have been before the last world war, let alone in the mists of time. And no aspect of its story can be viewed in isolation; it has never been cut off from its neighbours, its overlords, the refuges to which its people have fled – least of all from History.

Alertness to context must therefore involve a refusal to operate with a simplistic dichotomy between individual community and 'the world' beyond. Highly localized variation with time and place will have become a familiar topic and needs only passing reintroduction here. The pre-war inhabitants of Gagliano may sometimes give the *appearance* of being isolated. Yet in post-war Pisticci, not ten miles away to the south-east, the inhabitants can listen at festivals to bands playing Verdi or Puccini and condescend to inform foreigners that 'we Italians are naturally musical' (J. Davis 1973, 8–9). No sense of regional inferiority or radical apartness there. Nor, incidentally, does the more distant historical record suggest that Pisticcesi have kept aloof from cultural fashion. A graffito on a painted pot attests institutionalized aristocratic homosexuality in Pisticci at the end of the sixth century B.C. (Lombardo 1985).

Ethnography has to be grounded in history to be of any exemplary value to Mediterranean studies. Yet at the local level – the level at which the anthropologist engaged in participant observation must operate – such evidence is likely to prove very hard to come by, particularly in the small settlements that anthropologists have so often favoured. Local records may supply tenurial or demographic details, and that is why many of the ethnographic studies of Mediterranean societies that admit historical material frequently do so in chapters on marriage, the household, migration or landholding. But such records are unlikely to give us detail from very much earlier than the end of the nineteenth century, detail of the sort that permits any vividness in the juxtaposition of past and present (J. Davis 1977, 244–5; 1980).

Could historical ethnography on that limited scale none the less be turned to a particular advantage? We might conjecture that a vantage point on the *longue durée* is to be found in the period immediately preceding that of the most striking changes that Mediterranean societies have recently undergone (the ones that announce for us the termination of our subject). A judicious combination of anthropology and nineteenth-century history might take us back to just before the unexampled tumult of 'modernization' began. We would have reached a slightly calmer period. A relatively unimpeded view over the distant past would then be laid out before us – the effect a little like that of viewing the cosmos through a telescope mounted on a satellite rather than on the earth. Without the distortions of the intervening atmosphere, previously known objects suddenly come into sharper focus and new ones are revealed. The obstacles created by recent economic development and profound social transformation would dissolve – and these (we would be assuming) have been the only real obstacles. After all, those nineteenth-century Mediterranean travellers who found themselves in a recognizably 'classical' landscape thought that the region's belated and incomplete industrialization had largely preserved its societies in a seemingly very old routine.

Was it the railway that finally brought this routine to an end, not only consuming unprecedented quantities of timber (cf. VI.4, VIII.5), but so connecting the great and little traditions that the first engulfed the second: acting as an immediate conduit of men, ideas and advanced machinery? Abou-Zaid's (1963) discussion of Kharga Oasis, 150 kilometres west of the Nile valley between latitude 24° and 26° N, has prompted the suggestive phrase from which this section takes its title: he presents what his editor calls a 'balanced, if brutal arcadia' (Pitt-Rivers 1963, 13) – of villages having only limited contact with the valley, each acquiring by barter what it cannot itself produce. The arcadia was disrupted during the early part of this century by the simultaneous advent of the monetized economy and a railway line, which ended the relative isolation and prompted many to emigrate. Before that, perhaps, life was harsh but stable. If so, of course, this Oasis was very unlike most of the microecologies of Chapters III, VI, and IX.

A still more extreme view of the impact of railways can be found in what is now something of a classic within its area, written by an anthropologically minded historian, and belonging here because of its quasi-ethnographic cast. In his *Peasants into Frenchmen* (1977), Eugen Weber set out to describe the integration of the 'traditional' peasant culture and economy of southern France into that of Paris and the 'modern' north during the last quarter of the nineteenth century. For him the railway was, along with schools and roads, the principal agent of change. Reading French folk-lore, Weber recalled, led him 'to discover a new France in the nineteenth-century countryside, a France where many did not speak French or know (let alone use) the metric system, where *pistoles* and *écus* were better known than francs, where roads were few and markets distant, and where a subsistence economy reflected the most common prudence' (1977, xii).

In this France there flourished the customs, superstitions and witchcraft beliefs which we have been accustomed to find in studies of popular belief in the seventeenth century rather than the nineteenth (e.g. K. Thomas 1971). It is a vision of the rural past which Levi would have recognized as akin to his own: the peasantry, fiercely independent, suspicious of all strangers, loathed the distant state and the taxes that it inflicted upon them. Yet in another sense, we are told, their outlook was wholly apolitical and unpatriotic. Even in 1906, 36 per cent of French conscripts interviewed apparently did not know who had won the Franco-Prussian war in 1871; many rural Savoyards in 1894 were convinced that Napoleon III still occupied the throne of France; few peasants had been genuinely interested in the democratic and socialist ideas so vigorously propagated during the 1840s. Their economy, too, reflected none of the major changes usually associated with the nineteenth century:

> There seems to be general agreement that the rural economy changed little with the Revolution, that there was no radical modification of land structure or work techniques or productivity before the middle of the century. The farming methods of the July Monarchy, wrote an agronomist of the period, were comparable to those of the Algerian Arabs. (1977, 117)

About the same time, Weber adds, an officer reconnoitring part of Béarn simply copied out the report of an *Intendant* of 1698, noting that nothing had changed, and that agriculture 'seems to have been in its present state since a very ancient age'. It is as if we are being afforded a view of the *longue durée* that takes us straight back to the world of Le Roy Ladurie's 'peasants of Languedoc' (1966).

Unfortunately, Weber's work is now exemplary in this context precisely because his assertion of the archaism of Mediterranean French rural economy and culture has been proved mistaken. Even in the pre-railway age, the isolated, relatively stagnant Mediterranean society remains as elusive as our discussions above of the ancient, medieval or early modern evidence would have led us to predict. Weber's arresting conclusion that French was a foreign language for almost half the children who would reach adulthood in the last quarter of the nineteenth century has, for example, been shown to be an exaggeration (Berenson 1979). His notion that southern peasants were broadly apolitical in outlook is hardly substantiated by their massive vote for the 'democ-socs' in the elections of 1849. On the other hand, as we shall see in the next section, it is likely that he overestimated the degree of cultural integration and uniformity that the railway line would bring.

More seriously in this context, the strong general implication of his work – that the economy of the southern French countryside was, and long had been, static – is, to say the least, questionable, and questionable not only on the general grounds that previous chapters here entitle us to advance. As one reviewer of the subsequent historiography of rural France has put it:

> The increasing diversification of rural employment was an essential feature of the slow structural transformation of the entire pre-industrial economy. From the end of the middle ages until the early nineteenth century, population increase, the spread of rural industry, limited urbanization, the growing commercialization of agriculture market expansion, and the growth of commercial employment opportunities slowly transformed the rural economy. (Goldsmith 1984, 190)

In many regions, Goldsmith recalls, those who had previously devoted themselves to subsistence agriculture diverted their energies in ways that emerged in Chapters III and VI – to small-scale wine-production, vegetable gardens, industrial crops, the burgeoning rural textile industry. The possibilities of rural employment reached their peak during the first half of the nineteenth century.

> Then further urbanization, the decline of rural industry, and the exodus from the countryside simplified the structure of the rural economy . . . The countryside became once again primarily the residence of peasant farmers. *Historians . . . mistook the apogee of traditional peasant society and agrarian systems, roughly the second half of the nineteenth century, for the eternal order of the fields and read this back into earlier periods.* (1984, 190, our italics)

They forgot, in other words, that the one great 'constant' of the Mediterranean economy has been shifting along a spectrum of possibilities, not standing still. Yet rather than concede, as background to the expansion of rural employment which Goldsmith enumerates, a simple and unchanging 'subsistence' agriculture, we would of course venture much further and stress diversification as the norm in Antiquity and the Middle Ages, quite as much as later. This diversification may have reached one of its periodic extremes at some point between the end of the Middle Ages and the nineteenth century. But it could hardly have been peculiar to that period.

No 'eternal order of the fields', then – not even before railways. It seems that for present purposes anthropology must indeed choose between being history and being nothing. It seems further (the conclusion of Chapters III–X) that this history always reveals flux: that there is no 'balanced arcadia', no ecological state of grace to be viewed, even when we have surmounted the intervening obstacles of modernization. Can Mediterranean anthropology therefore do more than offer occasional confirmation or amplification of what the evidence of the past already suggests? Can it tell us nothing at all about the *longue durée*, the prehistoric, ancient and medieval pasts that have been our focus so far? The prospect seems bleak. But now that we have faced up to what would hinder such a simplistic extrapolation from the present, we can afford to try a more optimistic approach. All that is necessary is to concede the truth of three propositions, none of which could be described as controversial.

The first is that any period or aspect of history is likely to exhibit both continuity and change. The second is that in the late-nineteenth and twentieth centuries the proportion of change to continuity has been greater than ever before. The third is that these modern changes were more profound than any that had preceded them in historical times. The anthropology of this recent period can therefore show us societies undergoing a transformation possibly more far-reaching than any other in their previous history – far from static though that history has clearly been. In some communities the changes will of course have been so overwhelming that the continuities with the pre-industrial world are negligible. But from the remainder – the category from which anthropologists are still the more likely to select their subjects – perhaps there is something to be learned. It will not, of course, be anything like the whole story. But if these concern the processes hidden by that shorthand 'historical change' – resilience or adaptation, the assertion or modification of tradition – then they will have exemplary value on two fronts. First, they will show us the outer ripples (arriving of course at varying times and rates) of what we have conceived, for present purposes, as a historiographical terminus: the end of the Mediterranean. Secondly, more pertinent to the core of our enquiry than to its point of closure, they will show how changes have been experienced, giving us the 'insider', ethnographic view of what earlier chapters have described largely from the outside, from historical evidence: how microecologies maintain their identity despite the mutability and the shifting frontiers which we have attributed to them; how they have cushioned or diffused the impact of revolution and catastrophe (VII.7, VIII.6). If we can gain some idea of all this from historically aware ethnographies, alive to context and therefore confronted with perhaps the greatest changes so far, we might also gain some insight into the effects (or lack of them) of earlier – and lesser – changes.

That is hypothesis, making the logical best of an optimistic case. We must therefore turn next to ethnographic examples in which anthropologists have not shied away from history but have revealed how a present that they observe has grown out of a past that they can document. These examples do not reveal ancient substrata, relics of an unchanging past. More valuably, they hint at characteristic responses to upheaval. We opened up our investigation of Mediterannean ecology with four definite places, in the presentation of which anthropology was subordinate to history. We begin this final part of the present volume with three more local examples, in which the hierarchy is inverted.

3. THE PRESENCE OF THE PAST

We look first at the work of Susan Carol Rogers (1991). This offers a particularly vivid reminder of how fragile and misleading the antitheses between tradition and modernity, nation and locality can be – however we choose to define them. It also, *pace* Weber, emphasizes how little impact the advent of railways and other recent forms of rapid communication can have on local variations in culture and economy. The small community in Mediterranean France that Rogers studied in the mid-1970s and the 1980s was able to revivify an apparently archaic family form as the most common type of household structure and the dominant idiom of its social relations; and it did this because of, not despite, the prosperity that resulted from modernization and integration into the nation-state. Modernity, in effect, enabled it to afford tradition. An ideal which many had, for centuries, been too poor to embody became translated into a common reality – yet unintentionally, without the inhabitants' awareness, not in any self-conscious spirit of tourist-pleasing folklorism.

The community in question is the village to which Rogers gives the pseudonym Ste Foy. It lies in the Aveyron/Rouergue region, somewhere to the south of Rodez – a position that the inhabitants punningly think of as 'Midi moins le quart': three-quarters Mediterranean, or alternatively 'a quarter to noon' (47). Ste Foy comprises some 800 souls, divided between the *bourg* and outlying hamlets and isolated farms. Its inhabitants refer to their community as 'holding on' numerically, and its population in the 1980s was indeed, so far as is known, 80 per cent of the maximum that it reached in the nineteenth century (59). Ste Foy is eccentric in being able thus to hold on. 'It stands in marked contrast, not only with the severely depopulated villages in the valleys just to its south, but to a number of smaller communities in its immediate area, which [as in Gagliano] have declined dramatically with the exodus of their young people over the decades since World War II' (9–10). There has been very little immigration this century (16); the stability is therefore remarkable.

In recent decades Ste Foyans have enjoyed access to a range of quasi-urban services such as an electrician's shop and a sports club, garages and cafés. Nearly all the inhabitants live in new or renovated homes and own coffee-grinders, dishwashers, freezers and television sets. Everyone has, at the least, access to a car, and all children gain at least some secondary education (58).

The background to this prosperity is, however, presented as a long history of poverty and seclusion (59) – an apparent local confirmation of everything Weber that wrote about provincial France as a whole.

> None of the royal roads or major waterways built under the Old Regime crossed [the Aveyron], and neither do any of the major train lines or highways built since the Revolution. Its terrain and poor soils and its weakly developed internal transportation networks . . . long kept it relatively autarkic, dominated by barely subsistence agriculture . . . During the nineteenth century the Aveyron was considered a punishment post for French administrators, at least one of whom found its population comparable to James Fennimore Cooper's Mohicans in terms of its savagery . . . [Cf. Balzac's *Les Paysans*, 1844.] State attempts to replace local patois with standard French failed utterly for close to a century; only beginning with the generations born since World War II have all Aveyronnais spoken French as their first language. (48)

Ste Foy's region, the Ségala, was far from being relatively advantaged within this unpromising area. Ste Foy therefore began the post-war era of 'thirty glorious years' of economic development as poorer, more nearly isolated, and closer to a 'subsistence' economy than the French average (24). Yet by the time that Rogers began her field work, in 1975, the settlement had caught up and become 'a very prosperous community, thoroughly integrated into national and international markets and enjoying a standard of living comparable to that now found anywhere in France' (24) – and higher than that of many of its close neighbours.

This transformation has not been achieved by industrialization of any predictable kind. Like most in its area, Ste Foy remains a predominantly agricultural community. And two kinds of agricultural change introduced since the Second World War are above all responsible for its modern prosperity (60). The first is technological: tractors became more widespread and could be used for the permanent clearance of otherwise ineradicable shrub; so did the means of mechanically draining humid soils. Far more pasture and arable land thus became available. More significant, though, was the other major change: a shift to market-orientated agriculture, and above all to the provision of ewes' milk under lucrative contract to the Roquefort cheese firms.

The village of Roquefort, 50 kilometres from Ste Foy in the south-eastern Rouergue, has been famed for its ewes' cheese since at least the close of the Middle Ages. In the post-war period, technical advances that facilitated the safer transportation of this fragile cheese, together with governmental encouragement of exports and the Roquefort firms' aggressive promotion of international markets, combined to raise the price of ewes' milk to three times that of cows'. More and more Ségala farmers were prompted to turn to sheep raising, a strategy that required little capital investment. By 1975, then, ewes' milk was the main source of revenue for most Ste Foyan farmers (61–3). Not that they abandoned other options: everyone continues to raise cattle, pigs and poultry, and to grow the field crops that feed livestock. Most farms also sell milk lamb – young lamb fed only on ewes' milk and one of the highest-priced meats in French markets (65 with n.11). But it is indisputably Roquefort that has financed Ste Foy's post-war prosperity: a classic case overall of the impact on a Mediterranean community of directed trade in a luxury foodstuff (IX.4).

Modernization in the sense of integration into national and international markets has therefore been achieved, less by dramatic change than by the generalization and intensification of long-established practice: sheep and cattle husbandry with production for the market. The social consequences of prosperity seem to have been comparably embedded in the past.

Ste Foyans are apparently preoccupied with household structure (74). They see themselves as defined in terms of their families and family organization. Their ideal is a version of that type of extended family, the stem family (*famille souche*) classically identified by Le Play (1871), historically widespread in many areas of France, particularly the centre and south, as well as in Spain, Portugal and Italy (especially Tuscany), and certain parts of Ireland and Austria. This stem-family organization can be documented in the area of Ste Foy since 1690 and is doubtless older (133). The family farm, the *ostal* or house, is, in principle, passed from father to eldest son in a continuous male line. At any one time it will stereotypically include a parental couple, their heir and his wife and children, and the unmarried siblings of the owner and his son. If daughters and non-inheriting sons marry, they forfeit their right to membership of the *ostal* and must move out.

> It has frequently been argued by historians of the European family that this type of household structure – with its rather rigid and elaborated series of hierarchies based on age, sex, birth order, and marital status – necessarily gives way under the pressures of 'modernization' to the simpler and more individualist nuclear household . . . In rural France in particular, the ostal system flies in the face of [the Napoleonic] code . . . mandating egalitarian inheritance . . . a dominant French cultural code . . . whereby close relations between parents and their adult children are expected and desirable, but their coresidence is not; and French agricultural policies instituted in the 1960s . . . as part of attempts to modernize French agriculture by extricating it from the influence of older generations. (68–9)

Confronted by all this, the *ostal* system should have withered. Ste Foyans themselves think that it has (31). They are perplexed by the archival revelations of their demographer-anthropologist (143). In nineteenth-century Ste Foy the number of three-generation stem-family households in the hinterland of the *bourg* never surpassed 15 per cent of all households; by 1975 it had reached 45 per cent. Of course, demographic factors such as increasing life expectancy and falling age at marriage need to be brought into the reckoning. None the less, the broad contrast between nineteenth- and twentieth-century levels of adherence to the full *ostal* cycle is impressive. The period of increasing prosperity that followed World War II clearly did not coincide with any weakening of the system. Rather, the prosperity enabled families to adhere to it more rigorously. So too did political integration: state-sponsored insurance, credits and subsidies have all helped prevent *ostals* from slipping out of family control (150). *Ostals* are therefore better able to support marginally productive or non-productive members (147); they can more readily absorb the wife and children of the heir whenever that heir is ready to marry. The greater availability of secondary education has also enhanced the distinction between heirs and their younger siblings. Heirs are typically removed from school at the minimum age to work on the *ostal* and are thus deprived of the qualifications that would open alternative employment to them.

Le Play nostalgically supposed that the stem family promoted social stability. Yet it is important to note, finally, that this reinforcement of tradition has been not been achieved without friction. For example, in the period 1960–75 nubile women reacted sharply and tangibly to the enhanced gender inequality that lies at the heart of the *ostal* system: they emigrated – leaving behind a cohort of bachelor farm owners (155).

Rogers's monograph yields a view of one striking, even dramatic, moment in the secular interplay of capital and province (or centre and periphery), integration and diversity, tradition and modernity – an interplay so complex and unexpected in its recent outcomes that neither sociology nor ethnography have quite found the vocabulary to describe it. We gain a contemporary insider's view of how tradition may be reasserted and continuity prolonged, not in any archaizing spirit, but in response to the most profound economic change that the community is likely ever to have faced. And, thanks to the coupling of ethnographic observation and archival demographic research, we can also gauge the parameters of transformation over more than a century – which is some basis for imaginative extrapolation, not into an immobile past, but rather into what may have been the recurrent way in which widespread change has been translated by local conditions.

We turn to a second example of a historical ethnography that may show us ecologies preserving their identity without being set apart from history. In a manner that has gradually assumed classic status, Lison-Tolosana's *Belmonte de los Caballeros* (1966) shows anthropologists how the use of unusually rich local archival evidence from as far back as the twelfth century can enrich and develop the interpretation of evidence gathered in the field. By incorporating history into anthropology it too avoids the dangers of presenting an apparently static picture, the historical applicability of which is always open to question. Here as in Rogers's work, secular change is no longer an unknown and supposedly remote quantity, the hidden enemy of anthropological analysis. The experience of such change is, rather, anchored in, and to a great extent explained by, a sociology organized in terms of the generation rather than class or rank.

Belmonte de los Caballeros is the name that Lison-Tolosana gives to the Spanish settlement (of some 1,300 inhabitants) in which he was born, and in which he conducted field work during the years 1958–60, the heyday of the Fascist regime. The economy is overwhelmingly agrarian, and intimately bound up with two very ancient microecologies between which Belmonte's main street forms a neat symbolic frontier. To the north-east, beneath the slopes of a range of chalk mountains, there lies 'a great terrace of boulders and reddish soil where the vines, cereals and almond trees grow'; towards the south-west 'there stretches a broad plain broken up into a multitude of small green or yellow plots inter-sected with hundreds of veins injecting water everywhere' – the *huerta* or irri-gated land (1). Irrigation has been practised on it since the later Middle Ages and perhaps earlier.

Belmonte lies in the heart of the middle Ebro valley. It is the one area of agricultural settlement in the locality. Those who work the surrounding fields all live in Belmonte: there are no scattered farmsteads. Yet Belmonte's layout has nothing in common with the numerous hill-top settlements to be found else-where in Aragon whose nucleus is a church tower, a castle or fortified manor house perched on the highest point. 'No house can claim the privileges of overlordship or boast a coat of arms. In fact there is no nucleus, unless it is the geometric centre of the town occupied by the parish church' (5). By the first half of the sixteenth century Belmonte was under the direct jurisdiction of the Crown. That is why no local landlord was ever in a position to dominate it. This link with the centre of political power finds a modern counterpart in ease of communications with the provincial capital, Zaragoza. Belmonte is only a two-hour bus journey away, and more than a dozen of its inhabitants commute to jobs there. Men visit the banks and buy farming implements; women go to buy clothes and household goods.

Belmonte is therefore hardly remote and isolated. Yet, like Ste Foy, it is exemplary in that the cosmopolitan influence is absent to a remarkable degree from many of the domains of urban life that Lison-Tolosana describes. What is primarily striking is the vast area of social life that is 'dogged by tabus' that are local in character, unlikely to have been derived from those of the city (179). The life of honour for one thing, the *vida de honor* – to which we return in the next chapter – embraces how much should be spent on a wedding, how one should maintain one's point of view in an argument whatever its manifest weaknesses, the age at which flirtation with the prettiest girls is permissible at a dance, attendance at bull fights, choice between the two cinemas regardless of the film being shown – and much else besides.

Belmonte society is heavily stratified, and stratified virtually exclusively accord-ing to landed wealth. The working of the land dominates conversation every-where, and at all levels, marking the sense of inferiority that nearly all inhabitants feel when comparing themselves with city-dwellers.

> If the schoolmaster tells them that their son 'would make a good student', they spare no effort or sacrifice so that he can study the *bachillerato* and get a position in the city or at least *no ser del campo* (not be of the country) . . . They do not say *no trabajar en el campo* (not to work in the country), '*no estar en el campo*' (not to be in the country), or '*no pertenecer al campo*' (not to belong to the country), but

> '*ser del campo*' (to be of the country) . . . By saying '*ser del campo*' . . . they are
> assuming that the cultivation of the land affects an individual's personality in such
> a way that this quality can be expressed grammatically in the same way as being
> man or being a Spaniard. (17–18)

Within Belmonte society, an individual is usually assigned to a social class – that of the *peones* (poor), *pudientes* (rich and powerful), *ricos-ricos* and the like – according to how much land he possesses. At one extreme *ricos-ricos* will have more than fifteen hectares; at the other a man 'hasn't got anywhere to fall dead in' (81). Land, Lison-Tolosana tells us, measures social status, and social status gives the measure of land (82). Moreover, he is able to chart the precise ways in which it has done so over the last four centuries by recourse to the minutes of the Town Council, where many the same categories as those of today are implied in, for example, the records of burial.

These economic groupings define the limits of the individual's social world: they designate with whom he may *tratar* (have dealings or social contact) and exactly how he should comport himself.

> Leisure hours, in the case of married men, are shared with people of the same
> position; the groups of café cronies are the most revealing. Each one 'knows what
> appertains to him', whom he can have anything to do with, treat to or accept a
> beer or a glass of brandy from. When anyone from an inferior economic group
> butts in on a discussion in which only *pudientes* are taking part, they remark 'he
> doesn't know where he belongs'. (90–1)

That exclusivity is reflected in the history of the Belmonte Council's political response to national events. Over a period of little more than a century, from 1812 to 1936, Spanish history includes thirteen important revolts against the government; numerous *pronunciamentos*; a variety of political regimes ranging from democracy to absolute monarchy, republic to dictatorship; a profusion of political parties to the point of anarchy; anticlerical violence and strikes. Yet for all that the Council minutes make no mention of any such national events before 1856, when the Council for the first time describes itself as 'constitutional'. Thereafter, regular alternations of membership (the same names recurring in the minutes) and enthusiastic but vague acclamations reflect the many changes of government. But none of the various forms of government introduced – except perhaps the traditional monarchy – seems to have meant very much to the inhabitants. So long as the Council endorsed a political style more or less in keeping with that of the capital, no one in Belmonte concerned themselves in the least with its deliberations.

The singular merit of Lison-Tolosana's analysis is that it is related to generational divisions within Belmonte society. That broad indifference to politics is most noticeable among what he calls the 'declining' and the 'controlling' generations. Like *curiales* of late Roman cities, outgoing councillors have the gravest difficulty in finding new candidates. A father habitually tells his son that 'you can't hope for any good from politics' (233). Such advice comes from those who fought in the Civil War, who were thus aged between 39 and 54 in 1961, and who monopolize public office: they form the controlling generation. Those aged between 55 and 70 in 1961 are the declining generation (181). They remember the bitter local antagonism of the republican period without ever having had any clear understanding of the propaganda in which both sides sought to immerse them. They have learned to be contemptuous of politicians. The emerging generation is, however, different. A new political attitude is discernible among those aged between 20 and 38 in 1961. A number of them had united to propose their own councillor. They wanted a representative in power who would support the cultural and recreational programme which they were developing under the guidance of their parish priest. Their stance remained, in general terms, relatively apolitical. But, in comparison with their elders in Belmonte, they were far more ready to criticize the Fascist government, and if political parties had then existed they might well have demonstrated an unambiguous alignment.

The emergent generation can thus be seen as breaking the mould of the 'traditional' Belmonte – 'tradition' here comprising those aspects of community life, whether economic, social or political, that can most easily be interpreted in the light of the local historical record over the last three centuries. In that sense the emergent generation is synonymous with 'modernity' – with technical innovation, broadening horizons, chafing under old customary constraints. Paradoxically though, and crucially in the present context, it is not the generation which has witnessed the most profound of the changes that fall under such headings.

> For the 'declining' generation, the town they knew in their adolescence has changed enormously. There was no electric light, no telephone, not even a reservoir of drinking water. Newspapers were unknown. Not many men and very few women learned to read and write. The education acquired during schooldays was minimal . . . Farming methods were purely Roman; there was no machinery of any kind. A stage coach linked the town to the city, but the highway was in such a state that in winter it was an adventure to take the road. No-one thought of visiting other cities. (182)

In so many respects the Civil War marked a watershed. An almost invariable reply to Lison-Tolosana's questions during his field work was of the form, 'before [1936–9] it used to be like that; nowadays we do so-and-so' (353). Yet what is most striking, and illuminating for the wider Mediterranean history of how microecologies have reacted to violent change, is the way the declining and controlling generations' experience of the transition from 'before' to 'after' was shaped by traditional aspects of Belmonte society.

The resilience of the old order was not merely a reflection of the Fascists' victory in the Civil War. In the period since that War there have been technical improvements (notably, again, the advent of the tractor). There has been accelerated economic growth: wheat production rose from 700,000 kg in 1936 to 2 million kg in 1959. There have been increases in the cost of living – but also in its standard, so that Belmonte, like Ste Foy, could be rated significantly above the average for agricultural districts. There has been emigration, as improved transport and the experience of distant posting in the Civil War combined to broaden horizons; and there has been a recasting of the occupational structure in response to the altered opportunities that followed from technical innovation. The important point, however, is the degree to which all these changes could be absorbed into the established patterns of Belmonte life. The slow acceptance of modernization was, as we noted above (VII.7) dominated by those of the highest social strata: no subversion involved there. And customary social pressures were important too:

The pattern of all innovation in agricultural methods and implements has followed approximately the same lines. A *pudiente* decides to apply new techniques in his fields; the reaction of others is generally negative and disposed to demonstrate the greater efficiency of the traditional methods. They say of the innovator who fails in his experiments that *ha hecho la risa* (he has made a laughing-stock of himself). The fear of incurring laughter may hinder the development of new methods, but at the same time it prompts a scrupulous study of any innovation before it is introduced. If the change proves successful it is quickly adopted, and acceptance implies its immediate and necessary application, for the contrary would mean *hacer el ridículo* (to make a fool of oneself). It is at these points that the economy, attitudes, and values converge and influence each other. (137)

The pace of innovation has clearly been such that old established frames of reference are, as we should expect, modified at a quite leisurely rate. What Lison-Tolosana appropriately calls an 'ecological' conception of time – though one also surrounded by a religious aura because of its relation to the cycle of Church festivals (X.3) – was, in the period of his field work, giving way to something rather different: a notion of time too flexible to be readily specified and owing little to the tasks of the field. Yet the transition was a slow one, only just observable when Lison-Tolosana was working in Belmonte. Those who subsequently brought it to prominence were the emerging generation of 1961, the ones who had most contact with the city, who have most often rejected parental authority and example, in the choice of a wife as much as in the choice of a profession.

The exemplary value of Lison-Tolosana's account is precisely that no aspect of Belmonte society is merely presumed to have remained unaltered over several centuries: clear supporting historical evidence is sought. Continuities are therefore demonstrated, not asserted. Anthropology and history, no longer the clearly distinguishable representatives of the eternal order and the continuum of change, are not kept in separate analytical compartments. There is no presupposition that certain anthropological topics automatically lead us back into the *longue durée*. The Civil War period certainly marks a point of transition, the beginning of a period of accelerating change; yet there is no suggestion that the world before that period was unchanging. Moreover, the use of the generation as a heuristic category, rather than a mere biological fact, enables Lison-Tolosana to be precise about who has experienced which form of modernization, when they did so, to what extent each group has adhered to customary procedures, and what events in particular seem to have enforced changes of attitude. We therefore know where we should look within his account for some general inkling of a still more distant past than his records can reveal: not to the emerging generation but to the one that preceded it – which is, in effect, the last generation of Mediterranean history.

The standards set by Lison-Tolosana for a historically aware Mediterranean ethnography have seldom been matched. But there is at least one anthropologist of Spain whose work can, in this particular context, immediately be set alongside *Belmonte*. The subtitle of Ruth Behar's monograph, *Santa María del Monte: The Presence of the Past in a Spanish Village* (1986), gives this section its title. Santa María is a small village in León, in the foothills of the Cantabrian mountains. Therefore her area of study falls outside any comfortable definition of the

Mediterranean part of the peninsula. Her methods and her broad conclusions deserve airing here, however, because of the processes and patterns to which they alert us.

Santa María initially shows a similar mixture of isolation and integration to that of Belmonte. It is situated only 300 metres from a highway along which buses run twice daily to the provincial capital, a mere forty minutes' journey away. On the other hand its neighbouring villages take almost an hour's walk to reach. And, when Behar arrived in the village at the start of her field work in 1978, she and her husband were the first Americans that the inhabitants had seen there.

The field work was spread over several visits between 1978 and 1981. In 1984 Behar returned briefly to the village, in time for her impressions of it then to be recorded in an epilogue to her book. The precise dates are important for understanding how Behar came to write this particular book rather than one of a different stamp. If she had conducted her fieldwork in the sixties or early seventies, she observes (13), she would have been much more inclined to follow anthropological fashion, and would have emphasized the short term and the mighty changes that it embraced, such as migration and agricultural mechanization. There would have been little thought for 'the presence of the past'. 'Arriving later, during the calm following the storm, a different picture came into view' – the one recorded in the book that we have. The result of that return in 1984 was different again.

Although Behar does not herself sum it up this way, it seems that the village's history could (in 1984, at least) have been well captured in Braudellian terms. There were three more or less distinct periods in that history, to each of which a different *durée* corresponded – though not, of course, in an entirely straight-forward manner.

The short *durée* seemed to preponderate in 1984. Agriculture was by then almost wholly mechanized and there were far more tractors about than there had been only a few years before. On the other side of the nearby motorway a summer resort for visitors was now complete. Thus, in the village street there were, quite unwontedly, a number of strangers. The whole environment, too, had altered unmistakably. A government-sponsored consolidation of the several tiny scattered plots of land that each indigenous family owned had recently been completed. With fields therefore having become much larger, the countryside looked more open. The immediate impression was that the old order had gone: the past was no longer present.

To recover it, we have to move back to the second of those three periods, comparable to that of Belmonte's controlling generation. In this period it was the *moyenne durée*, the medium term, that created the strongest impression. Change was occurring, but not so rapidly as it would a few years later. While Behar was doing her field work, at the end of the 1970s, sewers were constructed in the village and lavatories began to be installed – many of them even before they could be connected to the system, so that they were initially no more than symbols of status. Also, the nucleus of the holiday resort was evident, and the consolidation of family holdings was beginning. It is not entirely artificial to see these changes, less as inaugurating the more recent period described above than as part of the preceding phase. That phase was coming to an end during Behar's field work and was definitely over by the time of her 1984 visit.

To the question of when it had begun there are several answers. From the point of view of demography it started in the late nineteenth century, when the population expanded dramatically. Collectively, the villagers of course remember only the later phases of this increase. For them, as for the inhabitants of Belmonte, the world began to change only at the time of the Civil War. Petrol became available; and, less predictably, there was a change in the customary implement for harvesting. And yet, as Behar writes, beneath these changes 'lay the more solid substratum of a deeper, enduring pattern of life' (12). That sounds like Braudel and Tillion. But whereas their geological metaphors masked little more than a declaration of faith, Behar's combination of ethnographic and historical evidence brings out fully the good sense of her assertion.

The third of those three periods that we identified therefore does not end wherever the second began. Rather, it overlaps it. Indeed in many respects the end of the two periods virtually coincides. And, because of its 'enduring pattern', the third period is characterized by *longues durées*. After all, that change in harvesting implement involved the abandonment of the sickle in favour of nothing more modern than the scythe, and most villagers were reluctant to make it until the end of the 1930s. Again, only around the years of Behar's field work did the typical village house cease to be a mud-walled structure in which the storage of grain and the shelter of animals was clearly of more central importance than human habitation. But the chief instance of such continuity in the village during these overlapping phases of its history was of a different order, and it determined the whole ethos of the community. It is the exceptional survival of agrarian communalism, with its open fields and common herds, its 'web of use-rights' in Behar's description, and of the political autonomy and communal self-regulation represented by the village *concejo* or council.

Survival is for once an appropriate term here. In most parts of Spain outside León, the culture of the common fields had, by the beginning of this century if not earlier, succumbed to a variety of pressures, political, legal and demographic. But in villages like Santa María it continued without great modification until the consolidation of dispersed smallholdings began to weaken the need for it. That is certainly survival – but it is not that of a custom supposedly unchanged for no better reason than the backwardness of its adherents. It represents an active and deliberate response to adverse influences. The response is evident at the political level in the history of the village council, which over the centuries has defended the autonomy, approximate equality and communal rights of the inhabitants against prosperous farmers, rural seigneurs and bureaucrats (cf. VII.5–6). Such continuity as emerges in the *longue durée* has had to be vigorously maintained at every turn. Again, as in Ste Foy, it is a dynamic rather than a static phenomenon. Indeed, the true continuity lies not so much in communal village institutions as in the attitude to powerful outsiders that the durability of those institutions embodies.

'How must the world have been in the past', a villager says of the period before the Civil War, much as did Lison-Tolosana's informants: 'it seems it was standing still . . .' (21). Behar can explain the perception – it arises mainly from the discontinuities bound up with the mechanizing of agriculture – but she is far from endorsing it. The *longues durées* that she unveils have been inseparable from highly significant changes that preclude all talk of standing still – in the political environment, for instance with the municipal reforms of the 1830s; in the natural environment, arising especially from woodland clearances; and in the favoured agricultural regime, for instance with the introduction of the potato in the nineteenth century. Particularly in the framing of local legislation by the *concejo*, the past has been continually reformulated to meet current requirements. Its continued 'presence' has been the product of will rather than inertia.

4. UPSTREAMING

'Upstreaming' was coined by the historian of Native Americans, William Fenton, as a term for the interpretation of the past using very recent evidence. The technique rests on three premises: first, that major cultural patterns are often stable over long periods; second, that it is still valid practice to proceed from the known to the unknown; and third, that a good test of our beliefs about the past is to measure them against a general social anthropology (Fenton 1949, 236; cf. Galt 1991b, 304–5). That is more or less what we have been attempting in this chapter, although we have laid just as much stress on the ways in which modern societies have experienced change as on the stability of their cultures. It is an approach also recommended, though using a different metaphor, by Marc Bloch, whom we quoted in the second epigraph to this Part of the book: winding the film backwards from the final, clearest, frame.

The French ethnography of Rogers and the two Spanish examples provided by Lison-Tolosana and Behar show the sort of qualitative glimpse into the remoter past of which anthropology may be capable – if both anthropologists and historians treat the anthropological data with sensitivity. Other Mediterranean monographs have of course shown themselves potentially useful in this way (see Bibliographical Essay), although to set out their lessons for the historian at the necessary level of detail would take disproportionate space here. Between them, we suggest, they would contribute something to a portrait of Mediterranean society in its terminal phase – the phase, that is, in which history *of* the Mediterranean ceases to be appropriate. Yet these examples also help us look back. And in showing how microecologies can to a surprising degree absorb the most powerful agents of modernity, they also, we believe, validate our earlier picture of microecologies under stress.

CHAPTER XII

'I ALSO HAVE A MOUSTACHE': ANTHROPOLOGY AND MEDITERRANEAN UNITY

1. GRANDS FAITS MÉDITERRANÉENS?

The previous chapter presented anthropological reports from the very recent past indeed. But there is nothing new about Mediterranean anthropology. In a sense, the ethnography of this minutely divided cultural domain dates from Herodotus. Less remotely, ethnographic evidence from the Mediterranean region attracted the attention of several figures recognized as founding fathers of social anthropology as a modern discipline: Maine, Westermarck, Fustel de Coulanges, Robertson Smith, Frazer, Durkheim (J. Davis 1977, 1). Mediterranean evidence has moreover contributed substantially to the development of general anthropological theory (1977, 2, *pace* Herzfeld 1987b, 5), not least because of colonial ties. Take for example the lasting exemplary value of the Kabyle of Algeria, in works ranging from Durkheim's *Division of Labour in Society* (1933), first published in 1893, to Bourdieu's elaboration of a 'theory of practice' (1977). Or, again, recall the stimulus that the ethnography of Greece has provided to Herzfeld's project of a 'reflexive' anthropology in which the practice of ethnography becomes a subject for enquiry in its own right.

Despite the quantity of publications now devoted to it, Mediterranean anthropology remains in many ways a still young and uncertain branch of the discipline. 'Anthropology *in* the Mediterranean area is nothing new . . . But an anthropology *of* the Mediterranean area which includes both Christian and Muslim sides is new and controversial' (Gilmore 1982, 175). We shall not dissent from that characterization, in the terms that we ourselves settled on (independently) and used from Chapter I on with regard of course to history. Nor, some time after the publication of Gilmore's compendious survey, and with the continuing academic predominance of anthropology *in* the region, is there much cause to doubt that anthropology genuinely *of* the region remains difficult and controversial.

There is one clear reason for that. No agreement has been reached on the crucial question of what gives Mediterranean anthropology its credentials, of what (if anything) makes it a discrete and coherent subject of study. A rather too confident beginning was made on this front in 1927, when Maunier, a pupil of Marcel Mauss, published his account of the Kabyle *taoussa*, a system of exchange, indebtedness and competition. Upon finding (as he thought) similar institutions in Egypt, Provence and Morocco, he proclaimed the discovery of *un grand fait méditerranéen*. Theorizing about anthropology *of* the Mediterranean had not risen much above this level of sophistication in the 1960s, when it was still necessary to write, perhaps only half in jest: 'the fact that, on being provoked, a Greek Cypriot, a Bedouin and a Berber may answer "I also have a moustache" as the least common denominator of equality between all males, does not necessarily point to affinities between their cultures' (Peristiany 1965, 9).

Anthropology *of* the Mediterranean needs a more secure conception of what it is that Mediterranean unity and distinctiveness might consist in. Various professional attempts to develop one have been discussed by Davis (1977, 11–15) and Gilmore (1982, 175–84). We need not review them here; it is simply worth noting their frequent reliance on just the sort of environmental and historical commonplaces that we have tried either to dispel or to substantiate in earlier chapters. Pitkin (1963), to take one of the earliest syntheses, talks (rightly) of the interdigitation of mountain, valley and sea, but does so at a level of utter abstraction and with no element of comparativism. Gilmore proposes simplistically that the unique combination of climate and topography in the region has posed identical problems for all those inhabiting it, and that they have responded in like ways (1982, 178). Davis bases his assumption that 'some anthropological meaning can be given to the category "mediterranean"' on the fact that those living round the sea 'have been trading and talking, conquering and converting, marrying and migrating for six or seven thousand years' – connectivity in other words, although he also writes that 'it is too early to say what sort of an entity [the Mediterranean] might be' (1977, 13, 11). Apart from such familiar ecologizing and interactionist approaches – to which social anthropology has added nothing – a source of Mediterranean unity has also sometimes been found on a more theoretical plane: in the region's 'peripheral' status within the capitalist world economy (Gilmore 1982, 182–4). Otherwise there remains only the search for Mediterranean-wide peculiarities that would mark the region out as a 'culture area' (Magnarella 1992). And this search, in essence, is a hardly more sophisticated version of Maunier's project – 'a certain kind of agriculture, a certain respect for towns, a climate, a type of plough and a couple of syndromes', as Davis (1977, 12–13) has well delineated it. In sum, anthropology *of* the Mediterranean has so far produced no unified and distinctive theory of its own about the unity and distinctiveness of its subject: it can describe and compare but it cannot yet explain – at least not in specifically anthropological terms.

Small wonder, then, that the whole notion of Mediterranean anthropology as a valid sub-division of the subject has fallen under hostile scrutiny. In Chapter I.3 we have already registered the case made against it by Herzfeld (1987b); another vocal critic is Pina-Cabral (1989). The sin of 'Mediterraneanism', mainly as these two present it, similar to Orientalism, can be summarized under three headings. First, it involves *exoticizing*: the label 'Mediterranean' serves the interests of anthropologists studying southern Europe because they feel vulnerable to the charge of operating too close to home for discomfort – for the culture shock that is the supposed beginning of ethnographic wisdom. These anthropologists therefore have to defamiliarize their subjects, denying them their Europeanness, and thereby linking them with the less controversially 'exotic' Middle East (cf. Just 1978). In order to create for themselves a respectable and distinct academic identity, and to justify their emphasis on field work in small and isolated communities, they emphasize all that is apparently archaic, culturally and economically primitive in southern Europe, implicitly contrasting (northern) European diversity and modernity with the inferior, atomized uniformities of the south (cf. Llobera 1986). The second element in Mediterraneanism is thus *homogenizing*: the discipline has to be validated by exaggerating the uniformity of its chosen area, usually by recourse to vaguely defined cultural traits. But this homogeneity is assumed *a priori* rather than demonstrated; close and uncommitted inspection of the ethnography fails to reveal it. The assumption of homogeneity, thirdly, determines the *restricted comparativism* that is typical of Mediterraneanists. *A priori*, comparison across the sea, between Christendom and Islam, is essential – whether relevant to the matter in hand or not. Other directions for comparison (European or Atlantic), other units of research, smaller perhaps than the Mediterranean region and irrespective of its presumed boundaries, become neglected:

> Are the Algarve mountaineers more like Moroccans than like [Portuguese] *minhotos*? Are Andalusians more like Tunisians than like *gallegos*? Are the Pisticcesi more like Libyans than like Piedmontese? . . . the obvious task at hand is to compare societies in adjoining linguistic, religious, economic, and historical spaces and then move on to slightly more embracing comparisons. (Pina-Cabral 1989, 399, 404)

Indeed; and we hope already to have shown that, following the grain of the evidence as Pina-Cabral recommends, proceeding outward from the smallest units of human geography, the historian rapidly reaches Mediterranean horizons (and, indeed, extra-Mediterranean ones; see Volume 2). For the region is, we have argued, a genuine unit of study, despite revealing numerous interdependencies and parallels with neighbouring worlds, and despite lacking that social homogeneity by which devotees of culture areas set such store. It bears re-emphasis that the region's unity and distinctiveness must be conceived in relative, not absolute, terms: neat frontiers, enclosing blatant uniformities, are hardly to be expected. We might add that it is in the nature of any human science to defamiliarize its field of enquiry – as we have attempted to do with our microecological model – and to operate with makeshift heuristic categories that inevitably have deep (if obscure) political and social roots. We might further add that the game of identifying these roots can be played by both parties to the discussion of the categories' validity. Pina-Cabral's evident desire to detach the comparative study of southern Europe from that of the Islamic Mediterranean might for instance, with some justification, be interpreted as a species of 'Orientalism'.

The debate about Mediterranean anthropology cannot of course be settled at this level of generality, by accusation and counter-accusation. It must be more precisely focused. Gilmore (1982) musters an array of familiar anthropological topics for the sort of detailed and wide-ranging comparison that might eventually tell us how far, and in what way, the region is unified and distinct. Of these topics – gender relations, the evil eye, class conflict, patronage, and so forth – we shall, for the remainder of the chapter, consider the one that prompted the remark about provocation and moustaches quoted above. We select it because it has been seen as an example of Mediterraneanism at its worst, and so enables us to test the arguments of the 'anti-Mediterraneanists' where they feel most confident; because it is the heading under which discussion of the region is, as we write, the most lively – history and the other social sciences yielding little of comparable vigour (cf. I.3, II.3); and finally, because it brings us back full circle to that history of ideas about the region with which we began in Chapter I and thus makes a fitting conclusion to the volume.

2. MEDITERRANEAN VALUES?

Introducing the collection of papers that initially did most to incite debate on this topic, Peristiany wrote: 'more convincingly, perhaps, than any recourse to past history, the essays contained in this volume reveal the continuity and persistence of Mediterranean modes of thought' (1965a, 9). That ringing declaration of 'the presence of the past' takes us back to the subject of the previous chapter, and invites us to consider honour and shame first of all in historical terms. There is certainly a history to be written of ideas about honour, despite numerous foreseeable problems with the nature of the sources and with attendant problems of definition and comparison over a very long period. The history would have to include all those honourable exemplars that immediately come to mind when the word is mentioned: Homeric heroes, Roman patricians, medieval knights, Renaissance courtiers, the protagonists of the Spanish Baroque stage, Romantic duellists. We shall invoke particular fragments of this history at the end of the chapter. But, for the rest, we shall be content with the ethnographic present, or something near it, and turn from continuity, the subject of Chapter XI, to our other two preoccupations: unity and distinctiveness.

The title of the Peristiany collection was *Honour and Shame: The Values of Mediterranean Society*. It suggested not only the presumed centrality of those values to the peoples under consideration, but also, by invoking 'Mediterranean society' in the singular, the possibility of generalizing about the whole region and differentiating it from its neighbours. In many cultures, from Iceland to Japan, there are social values that can be understood in terms of honour and shame. Perhaps, Peristiany wrote, 'as all societies evaluate conduct by comparing it to ideal standards of action, all societies have their own forms of honour and shame' (1965a, 10). But some societies use these forms of evaluation with greater frequency and articulacy than do others. 'The Mediterranean peoples discussed in these papers are *constantly* called upon to use the concepts of honour and shame in order to assess their own conduct and that of their fellows' (10, our italics). That frequency of recourse is implicitly taken to show that Mediterranean peoples are distinct from others as well as forming some kind of unity in themselves. The essays in the Peristiany volume did not carry intra- and extra-regional comparison any further, however. Wisely at that stage of the investigation, they preferred ethnographic particulars from a small number of circum-Mediterranean societies. After much piecemeal consideration, it was left to a more recent collection of papers, deliberately conceived as a sequel to Peristiany's, to resume in a more sustained and explicit way, if with rather less confidence, the themes of the homogeneity and particularity of the region. The collection edited by Gilmore, *Honor and Shame and the Unity of the Mediterranean* (1987), shows the stage that the discussion had reached after more than two decades. Subsequently, there have appeared several collections that ranged far more widely than their predecessors. One (Peristiany and Pitt-Rivers 1992) brought into play the notion of grace, with which honour was shown to be intimate in various ways; another (Fiume 1989) brought together historical and anthropological contributions; a third (Gautheron 1991) included investigations of the meaning of honour in contemporary northern Europe. Beside a stream of articles, a monograph has also been produced (F. H. Stewart 1994) which at last begins the task of systematic comparison with non-Mediterranean ideas of honour, from historical, literary and legal sources, as well as from ethnography. This is the point at which to take stock of the debate – where the major themes have been fully aired and much detail accumulated, but (it must be said) no consensus reached about any of them.

Our contribution might bring such consensus a little nearer. The purpose of this chapter is not, of course, to advance enquiry in strictly ethnographic terms; we have no revelatory field work of our own to report. But we do hope to grasp and sum up as wide an array of anthropological evidence as we can, to see what implications that evidence might have for our view of Mediterranean micro-ecologies, and, at the end, to add an unusual historical dimension to the debate.

Following the practice of earlier chapters we shall begin with some detailed examples. These establish the dimensions of the topic, and a working definition of it can be allowed to emerge from them. They may also establish a *prima facie* case for considering the Mediterranean a region in which honour and shame are – to a marked though not a unique extent – the dominant values of popular morality. We shall then have to see whether the case can be sustained, and what its success or failure has to tell us about the longer-term history of Mediterranean social values.

3. Honour and Shame I

Both the classic status of Campbell's (1964) monograph and its title – *Honour, Family, and Patronage* – make it the obvious place from which to draw some introductory data if we are looking for a Mediterranean community that has had honour as its ruling value, its daily point of reference in matters both trivial and momentous. Its exemplary value for the *historian* is not diminished by the fact that the monograph has become a historical document. This not just because Campbell analyses the results of field work conducted in 1954 and 1955 (1964, vi, 7), but also because according to a more recent report on a neighbouring culture, the Sarakatsani 'seem to have vanished almost entirely from the Greek scene' (Winnifrith 1987, 12). Simply for consistency with the other examples that follow we shall, however, preserve them in the ethnographic present.

The Sarakatsani are Greek transhumant shepherds who spend the summer with their flocks in the central Zagori mountains and number in all about 4,000 souls. The theme that we are pursuing emerges very early on in Campbell's book: 'Sarakatsani are deeply concerned about three things; sheep, children . . . and honour' (1964, 19). In the more detailed discussion that constitutes the penultimate section of the book, however, a slightly different formulation is used. Here, the overriding value is that described as 'social prestige' (*goetro*) (265). Prestige has to be competed for, but the competition takes place primarily at a symbolic level. This is because, while the Sarakatsani are by no means all equal in wealth, no family is materially powerful enough to achieve prominence solely through the use of force. Social rank must be earned; it cannot be enforced.

Recognition must be won through the closest possible conformity to certain ideals. That is what concerns the Sarakatsani in every kind of public encounter. One's prestige or 'name' falls under a scrutiny that is always curious and usually hostile.

Prestige, as Campbell presents it, has several ingredients. Of these, the fundamental one is *time*, which Campbell here translates as honour (268). Honour of this kind is conferred by the community in acknowledgement of the excellence of an individual or family. It is also more broadly applicable to the market value of an object or a service, and hence it expresses the general idea of worth, whether moral or monetary. Honour is typically threatened when a person or family is insulted, when there is violence or killing, when a woman is seduced or raped, when a betrothal is broken (268–9). To be honourable is, then, to be seen to be untouched by such threats, either because other members of the community feel constrained to avoid making them, or because, once made, they are speedily and successfully answered.

The honourable man, who achieves this sort of integrity, must display certain qualities, and he will have a certain more or less predictable history. Indeed, it is possible to specify the appearance and behaviour appropriate to each of the three stages of a life lived honourably. The ideal young unmarried adult shepherd will be physically unblemished, tall, slim, agile, with an open, regular physiognomy. He will be resolute, courageous and assertive. As yet unsullied by the sexuality of women and unburdened by responsibility for a family, he should dedicate himself unstintingly to the maintenance of his own and his family's honour, sensitive to any insult, ready to answer any challenge – and, if necessary, to die in the process. On marriage, however, he loses some of his independence, his freedom single-mindedly to enact the moral ideal. His overriding duty is now to protect his new family and his flock. For their sake he may have to make compromises with pride and conscience. He must be clever, far-sighted, guileful, and will lie if he has to. Thinking of his family, he can no longer be as sensitive to insults, for a violent response now brings the risk of leaving his household without a head, his wife and children unprotected. None the less, he remains a man of honour. He displays manliness, *andrismos*. He is *barbatos*, well endowed with testicles. He must strut about as if his family concerns are of the greatest importance. His conversation is sharp, monosyllabic, designed more to assert than to communicate. Only in old age are these demands relaxed. The man who has handed over control of affairs to his eldest son will maintain a quiet dignity. His whole life up to this time has established his reputation and claim to pride. So only extreme insults will now provoke him, and these should be rare; insulting an old man dishonours the aggressor rather than, as would be the case with someone younger, the victim.

For women too there are three stages of adult life to which different sets of ideals respectively attach. In general it can be said that, although women have their own honour, it is not for them to guard it; that is a man's task. Rather, the overriding quality required of them is *ntrope*, shame – and, in particular, sexual shame. Internally this amounts to a revulsion from sexual activity. Externally, in dress and comportment, it should manifest itself as a denial of the physical attributes of the female sex. It hardly needs stressing, then, that the unmarried girl should be a virgin – and acknowledged as such. She is secluded from the outside world as far as possible. Everything is done to disguise the power of her sexuality, through which her personal honour and that of her family are at their most vulnerable. 'The shame which is felt at the exposure of the body, even when no other person is present, means that undergarments are not changed for long periods and the body between the neck and the ankles is never washed' (287). The married woman, like the married man, cannot pursue the ideal to quite the same extent. She cannot remain entirely secluded. But her demeanour must be as virginal as before. She should appear modest and serious, revealing none but conventional emotions. Even in childbirth she (or her relatives) must silence her groans and screams. Indiscipline in matters of public scrutiny would after all suggest a similar failing in private – that is, a lack of sexual modesty. The most intimate part of her private life – sexual relations with her husband – must exhibit the same iron restraint. Copulation should take place in complete dark; she should remain motionless.

It is by her husband's family that the married woman is chiefly judged. She will respect her husband's authority yet be prepared to shame him into action should he respond inadequately to a slur on his honour. She should have sons, but also a daughter. And their respective senses of honour and shame will, through the combined effects of heredity and education, reflect her own worth. The severity of the constraints imposed by custom on the maiden and the mother can be measured by noticing some of the ways in which they are relaxed for the older woman, in the period between her eldest son's marriage and her death. She may go out to the shops. She may stop to pass the time of day with unrelated men in the streets. But only when her husband dies or she reaches the age of sixty will her sexuality be considered a spent force, no longer a threat.

These are the ideals appropriate to each of the three stages of life that follow upon the beginning of adolescence. To what extent are they actually attainable? Few physically weak children survive childbirth, so that most are strong enough to perform the duties required of them. The values of honour and shame are instilled in the young through constant example and exhortation. They become animated by *egoismos* – a word meaning self-regard, but which might suitably be translated as an obsessive concern with others' evaluation of oneself. The consequences of failure in the competition for prestige are so serious that the large majority of families strive to behave honourably. The gap that we might expect between ideal and attainment appears remarkably narrow.

The result is a community whose actual moral geography is easily mapped. Most families are assumed to be – and to that extent therefore are – more or less equal in worth. These are the ones who must be sensitive to every hint of insult. Of course, there are individuals who have lost their honour irremediably, for some venial indiscretion. There are also families who, whatever the individual manliness or modesty of their members, are indelibly dishonoured. They are likely to be – though are not inevitably – poor. At the other extreme, there are some families who rise above the pressures of the ideal because their wealth and ancestry makes their honour so robust that they can if necessary flout the code and yet suffer no lasting shame.

Indeed, the primary material correlate of honour among the Sarakatsani seems to be wealth – wealth in relatives, simple weight of numbers, which enhances the response to a challenge; wealth in livestock, which enables the family to be independent and generous with its hospitality, to provide substantial dowries for its daughters and gain prestigious marriages for its sons. Honour is further correlated with quality of lineage. That quality will have derived from the wealth and prestige of certain ancestors, but to the Sarakatsani honour is to be found literally in the blood that defines family relationships and 'takes fire' at insult (185).

The central position accorded to honour and shame in the Sarakatsan scheme of values must be related, first, to the solidarity of the family and, second, to the hostility continually evinced between families unconnected by kinship or marriage. 'Whatever is done or suffered by one member [of a family] equally affects the honour and shame of the others' (319). Men defend (perhaps to the death) each other's honour and the honour of their women. Women defend their own modesty by muting their sexuality, and they uphold the honour of their men by complementing the men's assertiveness with their own delicate sense of shame.

The family is autonomous as well as solid within itself. Inevitably its members must often co-operate with kinsmen or affines in the management of flocks. And on the rare occasion that the honour of the whole community of Sarakatsani is at stake in some exchange or tussle with outsiders, then men who are not related may make common cause. But no such alliance compromises the essential principle that the interests of unrelated families are seen as inevitably opposed (192). One family's advantage must be another's loss: it is a zero-sum game.

We cannot say that this kind of atomistic social structure *causes* the preoccupation with familial honour that we have just outlined. But the need that individuals and families clearly feel constantly to be on their guard against outsiders, and the fact that the majority of families are roughly equal in wealth and can achieve superiority over one another only in terms of prestige, certainly makes the concern with honour more intelligible. The defence of honour, seen not as a set of ideals but rather as an everyday requirement, acquires its centrality to social behaviour from the unremitting hostility and suspicion that exists between those not tied by blood or marriage. The hostility can be interpreted as having been canalized into symbolic forms to avoid a Hobbesian war of all against all (264, 320).

At no point is this '*moral* familism' (contrast Banfield 1958) more at risk than from the sexuality of women. A broken betrothal is a deep insult that demands retaliation. The penalty for rape exacted by the woman's kinsmen should be death. Since women are seen as creatures of pure sensuality, weak in self-discipline, they may well also be caught in fornication or adultery. In these cases, the woman has herself dishonoured the family in the grossest fashion. She has shamed all of them by betraying their corporate solidarity. She will transmit her dishonour to her children: it will be in their blood as it is now in hers. Ideally, therefore, she should be put to death. Her lover should be attacked by the men of the family only after that has been done. Since the Second World War, however, policemen are more numerous and efficient than they used to be – and in any case hardly need subtle powers of detection to discover who has been involved in what is likely to have been a public affair. Thus, in practice, murder for the sake of honour is an extreme rarity. Considerable care is taken that knives are drawn in front of disinterested witnesses who can be relied upon to restrain the combatants.

The topic of honour killings is a suitably extreme point at which to leave the example of Campbell's Sarakatsani for the moment. Rather than attempt to generalize about this Greek evidence (to the extent that the Sarakatsani are Greek!), we can more usefully set alongside it data from another, contrasting area on the Mediterranean's southern shore.

Lila Abu-Lughod's *Veiled Sentiments: Honor and Poetry in a Bedouin Society* (1986) is one of the most extensive monographic treatments of the place of honour in a Mediterranean society since Campbell's *Honour, Family and Patronage*. It therefore offers an admirable source for comparisons with Campbell's data. Abu-Lughod conducted her field work between 1978 and 1980 among one of the bedouin tribes known collectively as the Awlad 'Ali who inhabit the Western Desert that stretches along the Egyptian littoral from Alexandria to the Libyan border. Like the Sarakatsani, they have been pastoralists, but they last migrated to desert pastures with their sheep and camels in 1971 and have since developed a thoroughly mixed economy that can embrace urban investment (8). They have also, it is no surprise to learn, mostly exchanged their tents for houses of stone and mud.

As is to be expected, there are some fundamental differences between this society and that of Campbell's Sarakatsani. The latter were Greek Orthodox Christians; the group with whom Abu-Lughod lived are devout Muslims. The Sarakatsani were monogamous; the Awlad 'Ali are polygynous. The basic institution of Sarakatsan society was the elementary family; outside it, the range of kin (bilaterally extended) with whom an individual had effective relations was very limited. By contrast the bedouin households of the community in which Abu-Lughod lived ranged in size from three to twenty-five (5–6), and seem generally larger than the few households of which Campbell gives details (1964, Appendix I). More importantly, the bedouin view kinship in terms of agnation or lineage, of descent from a common patrilineal ancestor. Their residential communities derive from the tent camps in which they used to live, and most of these camps take their name from the lineage or group of agnates who form its core. A community may well include affinal or distant kin as well as unrelated client families. But the patriline provides the dominant idiom in which social relationships are conceived. And it is consistent with this that the size of the effective kindred with which a member of the Awlad 'Ali deals is much larger than that of a Sarakatsani. The bedouin social world is not nearly as fragmented.

Against these profound differences can, however, be set some striking similarities. Of these, the main one has already been hinted at: the importance, in a quite literal sense, of blood. 'Blood is the authenticator of origin or pedigree and as such is critical to Bedouin identity . . . A person's nature and worth are closely tied to the worthiness of his or her stock' (L. Abu Lughod 1986, 45). As with the Sarakatsani, ethical character is thus to a considerable extent perceived as inherited. A second similarity: 'the social world . . . is bifurcated into kin versus strangers/outsiders . . . individuals identify with everyone else who shares the same blood' (51, cf. 20). The final pair of relevant similarities follow from these two. First, 'Bedouins value a constellation of qualities that could be captured by the umbrella phrase "the honor code"' (45). And, second, in keeping with the importance of the bloodline and of the moral qualities that membership of it confers,

one family member's shameful acts bring dishonor on the rest of the family, just as everyone benefits from the glories of a common agnate or patrilineal ancestor. The rationale for both vengeance for homicides and honor killings (in practice extremely rare) is that an affront to one individual or a shameful act by one person affects the whole group, not just the individual. (65–6)

In almost all particulars those lines could have come from Campbell's mono-graph. What then is this constellation of moral qualities that constitutes the 'honour code'? With the Sarakatsani, the basis for moral evaluation – the attri-bution of honour – was a certain physical and moral integrity. Abu-Lughod has little to say about bodily perfection but refers instead (as Campbell does occasionally) to a fundamental ideal of autonomy. 'Autonomy or freedom is the standard by which status is measured and social hierarchy determined' (79). As with the Sarakatsani, the ruling value is to be related to an ideal of equality. Men, families and lineages are presumed equal in honour unless they have markedly risen above or fallen below the majority. And in material terms this can be seen to reflect the difficulty of amassing extreme wealth (at least before the cash economy produced new opportunities) in a land of frequent drought and general precariousness of resources (1986, 70; cf. J. K. Campbell 1964, 265, 316). In the eyes of these bedouin, precedence is achieved solely through moral excellence. Wealth may be a good predictor of who will be found to have excelled – but it is in no wise infallible. *Asl*, ancestry or nobility, is, on the other hand, an important component in 'the honour code'. In the term usually trans-lated as honour – that is, *sharaf* – are implied a cluster of values that a morally excellent man is likely to have inherited: generosity, honesty, sincerity and keep-ing one's word, loyalty to friends. Still more important than these (which have a markedly warmer tone than some of the values of the agonistic Sarakatsani) are the qualities associated with *hurr*, being free. Freedom is won – and here we detect a clearer echo of a Greek refrain – through assertiveness, fearlessness, pride, potency, self-control.

Whereas the honour of the most powerful Sarakatsani families was virtually impregnable and they therefore did not need to be as careful of their reputa-tion as most, those at the summit of the bedouin hierarchy must be supremely punctilious in maintaining their autonomy, for greater honour brings greater responsibility. At every level of bedouin social organization – between one tribe and another, within a lineage, within a single household – the powerful owe protection and even respect to the weak, whether they be unrelated clients, needy relatives, the insane, women, youths or children. These are their dependants upon whose esteem their reputation in large measure depends. They must not be tyrannized over: they respond to authority rather than mere power. More than that, they have their own kind of honour and autonomy.

The bedouin value to be associated with honour is translated by Abu-Lughod, not principally as shame, but rather as modesty or shyness: *hasham*. This is the ideal appropriate to women, but it is not peculiar to them; it is attributable to all who are in a position of dependence. Their problem is to reconcile their lowly status with their claim to respect as bedouin. They may well possess *asl*, a noble pedigree. But they cannot realize the full potential of those with *asl* because they are not autonomous. The 'code' of modesty provides a solution to the problem, because modesty is displayed voluntarily rather than under compulsion from superiors. It involves cultivated feelings of shame and acts of deference that arise from those feelings.

Bedouin ideals encourage in the subordinate many of the same virtues as are appropriate to the independent. In certain contexts a subordinate should be wilful, tough, assertive, enterprising, generous to guests, and so forth. The point is that those contexts are the ones in which he or (more likely) she is dealing with social equals. When faced with those upon whom he or she is dependent, a subordinate can no longer strive for honour in the fullest – that is, the autonomous, male – sense. Thus a young man *tahashsham* (or displays shame in front of) his father, male agnates of his father's generation, and his own older brothers. Women *tahashsham* some older women and most older men unless they are of client status.

As far as women are specifically concerned, they should generally dress modestly, which includes veiling the face. They should also – as should Sarakatsan women – conceal their natural needs and passions. In front of a superior, a woman should assume a rigid posture, remain silent unless called upon, and not look the superior in the eyes. More generally, she should avoid all contact with superiors unless absolutely necessary. Since she will do that voluntarily, the bedouin consider the separation of the women's world from that of the men to be the response of the weak to the powerful, not the product of male exclusivity. On the other hand, bedouin esteem all things feminine so lowly that there is perhaps also a sense in which women should be kept at a distance by men, socially as well as physically.

Women are prevented from the achievement of full honour not only by their weakness (and hence inability to reach autonomy) but by their 'closeness to nature'. There are clearly forces within women that they cannot control. Menstruation is one obvious sign of this, sexuality another. In sexual activity – that inevitably involves a submission to men – as well as in the ensuing pregnancy, women manifestly have no mastery over their bodies. It is clearly essential, however, that the effects of this loss of mastery should be minimized. The code of honour requires as much self-control as an individual can muster. And this control is more than ever desirable when sexuality is its object. Love or sexual desire can lead men to dependence on women and thus to dishonour.

On a broader front, sexuality is seen as a potential threat to the entire social order. Even an arranged marriage, though obviously necessary for the perpetuation of that order, can actually undermine it since it may bring together a man and woman who are unrelated and hence compromise the solidity of the lineage. That is why the preferred marriage for these bedouin, as for so many other Middle Eastern societies, is to a patrilateral parallel cousin, which 'subsumes the marriage bond under the prior and more legitimate bond of kinship' (L. Abu-Lughod 1986, 145) – that is, keeps the matter literally within the family, and also within range of the men who remain morally responsible for her behaviour when she is married – father, brothers, uncles (Holy 1989, 120–27; Section 7 below). Even with this recourse, however, the woman must move from one domestic group to another. Although she remains emphatically a member of her own patriline, her blood relatives' control over her must be shared with that of her husband and his immediate kin. For the husband, meanwhile, his new wife gives him a new domain of authority that is essentially his own and less that of his agnates. 'Among the Awlad 'Ali the groom's father and elder paternal uncles are never among the men firing rifles to celebrate the engagement or marriage of a son or nephew' (L. Abu-Lughod 1986, 147). Custom reflects the perception that the separate sphere which the new husband is making for himself compromises their authority within the lineage.

There are several means of limiting the moral harm of which women, through their sexuality, are supposed capable (148–50). Cousin marriage is one of these;

the modesty code can be interpreted as another. Women have to mute that in themselves which poses the most direct and difficult challenge to the whole social system. Thus, with the Awlad 'Ali as with the Sarakatsani, female virtue is centred on the denial of reproductive capacity. Through shame, it is always open to a woman to discipline and redeem her sexuality. She must be virgin at marriage: uncertain paternity would make the patriline disintegrate. She should cry when someone comes to ask for her hand. After marriage, she must studiously deny all sexual interests in front of those on whom she depends, and avoid men who are not kin. Thereby, a bedouin woman not only disguises her sexuality, but also expresses deference to those who can (as men, as less tied to nature) better exemplify the ideals of honour. The clearest way in which she does this is through manipulating her black veil.

Veiling has its own code, and deference is the key to it. Whether one veils, and how much of the face one covers, depends on the social context. Girls only begin veiling at marriage, when they are presumed to begin sexual activity (and when they start to wear a red belt), and they cease veiling if and when they enter widowhood. Women may veil at embarrassing references to sexuality, whoever is present. But usually they are selective in the company of men. As might now be predicted, they reserve veiling for those who have authority over them or greater social responsibility in general: fathers, elder relatives, elder brothers if they have assumed the leadership of the household, older non-kinsmen (providing they are not of lower social standing), older strangers (providing they are bedouin). In these last two instances they are perhaps demonstrating not only their deference to those with responsibility, but also their identification with the honour of their whole kin group: by veiling even when kin are absent they demonstrate the modesty which is an essential component of the absentees' prestige.

There we can end our second detailed example. We can now, more rapidly, look at some other areas – from the western Mediterranean to complement those eastern examples, and from work on societies in which the current emphasis is upon agriculture to balance the preceding studies of pastoral economies. The basis for selection remains arbitrarily confined to monographic treatments, the scale of which gives some indication of the significance of the topic.

4. HONOUR AND SHAME II

For a Spanish example, there are a number of treatments to hand, not least the one which inaugurated the post-war development of Mediterranean ethnography in English, Pitt-Rivers's *People of the Sierra* (1971, first edition 1954), describing the inhabitants of a 'small town' ('Alcalà', a pseudonym for Grazalema) in the Sierra de Cádiz, Andalusia. Here, as Pitt-Rivers elsewhere has it, questions of honour 'loom large both in theoretical discussions regarding the propriety of conduct and also in the daily idiom of social intercourse' (1977, 18). But, as an alternative to pursuit of the detail offered in support of that discussion – reminiscent of Campbell's in the reported emphasis on boastful manliness (*hombría*) and the sexual shame (*vergüenza*) appropriate to women – we can return to the ethnography on which we have already drawn in Chapter XI (and VII.7), Lison-Tolosana's *Belmonte de los Caballeros* (1966). Here, as in Greece and Andalusia, 'prestige' is again found to be the overarching personal quality which men and women should strive to acquire. Prestige can have an intellectual sense that is highly regarded in this community, such as we have not found elsewhere. Status, in other words, can derive from acknowledged intelligence. Prestige can also come from age – but, as we might now expect, only if the old man's conduct has been irreproachable. The most important way in which prestige is acquired is through the practice of 'moral virtues' – and all the moral virtues are summed up in one word: *honradez* (108).

The components of honour as prestige are not entirely surprising either – although it is salutary to record that, as Pitt-Rivers also notes (1977, 20), honour and shame (*honradez, vergüenza*) do not constitute a polarity which can instantly be referred to another one such as male/female or autonomy/dependence. Rather, the man who *is* honourable also *has* shame – an acute sense of the possibility of dishonour – even though *vergüenza* can be used 'in popular speech' as a measure of the absence of *honradez* and is to that limited extent its opposite (Lison-Tolosana 1966, 314). The man of honour is 'nothing less than a whole man'. He is ready to defend his own interests and opinions and also those of his family – whatever the rights and wrongs or the truth of the matter. He is hard-working, magnanimous, competitive – those adjectives that are starting to sound familiar in this context. Although wealth is not seen as a prerequisite of personal excellence, greater prestige clearly attaches to those with greater property (cf. J. Davis 1977, 96–8). As for women, 'feminine *honradez* demands special qualities': the ability to look after the house and its finances properly and make sure that the children are well dressed. 'Contrary to men, who are required . . . to seek for themselves individual pre-eminence, women must assert themselves by creating an aura of modesty and silence' (Lison-Tolosana 1966, 331). When a woman is said to have 'lost her *honra*', the cause is almost always sexual: a girl has lost her virginity, a married woman her chastity. A woman 'must stay on the alert all the time, ready for any attempt on her virtue' (332). Those who succumb too easily to the Don Juans in the community may well leave the *pueblo*, unable to endure the resultant opprobrium. Those who are raped should find their husbands or other male kinsmen ready to kill the assailant.

To Italy. On the basis of a study of four widely-separated settlements, in the north as well as the *mezzogiorno* and Sicily, Bell (1979, 1) is ready to include *onore* as one of the four words that 'capture the essence of the Italian peasant's response to life' (the others being *fortuna, famiglia* and *campanilismo*). *Onore* denotes the ability of a man to be a man in the fullest sense, to father children, especially boys, to meet his obligations, to protect the chastity of his wife and the virginity of his daughters. It is inherited rather than acquired – yet is not easily passed on. '*Onore* always existed in some dim past; it turned the present into a contest for preservation. A family lacking honor might indeed act with dignity, but the resulting *onore* would not be recognized before the generation of its grandchildren's children' (31).

Another study, of Sicily, offers a picture that, while broadly similar to Bell's, is particularly reminiscent of Campbell's data on the Sarakatsani. In Villamaura, on the western part of the island, the nuclear family is the basic unit of local society and disputes between one family and another over the allocation of resources occur quite frequently because collective honour is at stake.

One's virtue, dignity, morality and status constitute one's honour. To be rich in these qualities presupposes personal autonomy – the freedom and capacity to act ...honor implies a quick response to offence, intolerance of any encroachment upon one's person or patrimony or the person or patrimony of others to whom one is loyal. (Schneider and Schneider 1976, 86)

Those to whom one is loyal are primarily one's own immediate family. A man should be a good father to them, seeing his daughters well married and his sons securely employed. 'Above all, he must promote and defend the chastity of the women in his family' (89). Female sexuality has to be carefully controlled. Young girls must learn the values of restraint and should be kept in semi-seclusion. Loss of virginity means the 'failure of the family' – for reasons close to those given by Abu-Lughod. The woman is suspected of complicity in the loss, and therefore of treasonably subverting the interests of the family to which she owes allegiance. The solidarity of the family, its ability to control its weaker members, and finally the honour and dignity of its menfolk, are thus all brought into question.

The agonistic tone of life among the Sarakatsani is recalled by a monograph dealing with a Moroccan society (Jamous 1981). Among the Iqar'iyen, a Berber-speaking group from the eastern Rif, honour and *baraka* (divine blessing) 'define the encompassing ideology of Iqar'iyen society and are embedded in its social structure, whose coherence they alone render comprehensible'. Here, the analysis of honour is summarized by two apparently paradoxical propositions:

1. Honor consists in the exercise of authority over domains that are 'forbidden' or *haram* (territory in the case of segmentary groups; land and wife for each head of household, and in the transgression of the integrity of the forbidden domain of others by means of what we shall call exchanges of violence. 2. Exchanges of violence assume different forms: contests of oratory, conspicuous expenditure, killing and physical violence. (Jamous 1992, 168, translating 1981, 6)

The man of honour, *ariaz*, possesses land; he is therefore autonomous, not dependent – unlike his clients, sons and womenfolk (cf. L. Abu-Lughod 1986, 79). He 'must obtain fidelity and chastity from his wife or wives; exemplary conduct and premarital chastity from his daughters; obedience without argument in family matters from his sons (Jamous 1992, 169). Conflicts inevitably arise but they must be kept hidden; otherwise an outsider might draw public attention to them, and that would require a response. The outsider's comment transgresses the forbidden domain. It is, in its way, as aggressive and invasive as theft, sexual predation or homicide.

Such punctilious concern with reciprocal violence contrasts with the correlates of honour that emerge from Abu Zahra's study, *Sidi Ameur: a Tunisian Village* (1982). Here it is the one who moves into another's domain who is vulnerable. It is therefore a manifestation of prestige to be able to make few visits while yet receiving many. An honourable reputation (*'ard*) is earned through possessing wealth and using it to help others – in the spirit of kindness and gentleness. None the less, on social occasions men compete in the display of wealth, influence and propriety, and they cannot do this 'unless they possess the quality of manliness, which does not exist unless they are born of a legitimate union', and that legitimacy is of course guaranteed by the honour of women – 'not only because their behaviour may lead to the birth of illegitimate sons but also because it is the expression of the power and influence of the males of the family' (117).

In these two sections headed 'Honour and Shame' we have looked in some detail at the functioning of honour, shame and related concepts in a Greek and a bedouin society, and more briefly in parts of Spain, Italy, Sicily, Morocco and Tunisia: a mixture of Christian and Islamic examples, a variety of economies. With each of them, honour has been seen as important enough to warrant a monograph or a substantial part of one: we have not so far presented any material derived from articles. Before we try to generalize about what they have to tell us, there is, however, an omission to be repaired.

5. Honour in the City

The preceding sample must not be allowed to create the impression that honour and shame are the values of only the supposed 'backwoods' of the Mediterranean region. There is an growing body of evidence from larger settlements that can be called on to counteract the bias of so much Mediterranean ethnography towards rural communities. 'Honour and shame [it has been well said] are the constant preoccupation of individuals in small scale, exclusive societies where face to face personal, as opposed to anonymous, relations are of paramount importance' (Peristiany 1965a, 11). That should be as true of the quarter or neighbourhood within the big city as of the village or desert camp.

> The *popolino*, Tom, not *i grandi signori* – they have their honor – but the *popolino* of here, and of places like Forcella; you know how we are made? Tonight, today, I have some money, so I offer you to eat. But tomorrow if I'm broke, and I and my family have to eat, I'll try to rob you and trick you. I'll send you a letter in America and tell you my son is dying, and I need money terribly and of course, as a *grande signore* you'll respond. (Belmonte 1983, 279)

The *signori* have their honour, a proletarian does not – at least according to that informant for a study of a slum area of Naples. Poverty and dishonour often go together, as we have already seen. Yet a sense of honour is also quite compatible with the necessary alternation of hospitality and deception that the informant describes. And his forecast appeal to the anthropologist as *grande signore* or patron would by no means be out of place in our earlier ethnographies. More recent accounts of the working-class culture of contemporary Naples has certainly found 'certain continuities' to be evident between that culture and the 'village' norms that we have surveyed 'with regard to the concern with controlling women's sexuality and the importance of female chastity for male social reputation' (Goddard 1987, 178; cf. Goddard 1996). Pre-marital sex may no longer be as severely stigmatized as it would have been in the 1960s or 1970s: but, among the *popolino*, concern for honour and respect remains (I. Pardo 1996, 41).

There are a number of studies that can be set alongside such reports, on substantial settlements of varying kinds. Some of them are by no means new. It is worth recalling that Lison-Tolosana's Belmonte de los Caballeros was, at the time of his field work, 'a small town of some 1,300 people' (1966, 1). Villamaura in Sicily, the focus of the Schneiders' ethnography, was a settlement of about 7,500 (1976, 14). No dearth of honourable – and dishonourable – sentiments and actions in either of those two settings. Pitt-Rivers's Alcalà, and two of the four Italian settlements analysed by Bell (1979) – Castel San Giorgio in Campania and Rogliano in Calabria – could also be described as small towns.

Davis's Pisticci in the Basilicata region (in the very instep of the Italian boot) provides a most striking instance of the value placed on honour in an urban setting. Pisticci had a population of more than 12,800 in 1961 (1973, 2). This, paradoxically, was where honour was to be found.

> It would be difficult to over-emphasize the importance which Pisticcesi attach to the town, and more particularly to the social sanctions which are exercised within it. People who live in the country are morally suspect just because their every movement cannot be known, because it is not known what they eat, what they buy, whom they talk to. (10)

A man gains greater recognition, and therefore has a more secure existence, where there are more people round about to observe him. The honour – especially the sexual honour – of his women will be much easier to preserve as well. 'It is maintained that women, however demure they may be in town, become uninhibited and lascivious when they leave the built-up area.' In the sparsely populated *contado*, away from public scrutiny, there is nobody to restrain them. So much for the anonymity of urban life.

Preference for the city is not inevitably diminished by economic innovations of the sort that might be expected to disrupt the patterns of family and household upon which honour depends. In Garre, Sicily, about which Giovannini reports (1985, 1987), a clothing factory was opened in 1966 that employed a quarter of the adult women aged between eighteen and fifty-four. This employment might be thought to have weakened male control since it took the women away from the home – their customary, honourable, arena – and out into the wider, industrial economy, so potentially threatening to virtue. Honour and virtue were, however, saved. The men in effect accommodated the shift of work place by designating it a mere extension of the household, since clothing was already part of the women's domestic sphere and since the jobs were found for them through the 'usual channels' of kinship and patronage networks.

Hirschon's (1989) account of Greek refugees from Asia Minor living in Piraeus, a much larger city, during the early 1970s (when the military dictatorship was at its most repressive) places honour firmly at the centre of the local set of values. It also shows another way in which concern for it is compatible with entering the market economy. Although the honour of men is again seen as vulnerable to female sexuality, distinctions of gender are not so marked in this context of suburban poverty. Women have to go out to work. But their choice of work place is deeply affected by considerations of honour – which, as among the Awlad 'Ali, can be construed in terms of integrity and autonomy: the ideal is 'to have no one over your head'. That is why small family businesses proliferate: a man should be his own boss. That is also why women prefer low-paid factory jobs to house cleaning. House cleaning may be better paid, but in the course of it a woman's dependence is manifest at every turn. One takes orders in a factory, certainly, but one can walk away from the job each evening (1989, 84, 102, 105, 149).

Among the fullest accounts that we have of honour and shame in a major city is Wikan's *Life among the Poor in Cairo* (1980, cf. her 1984), the reflection of field work conducted intermittently between 1969 and 1982. In Cairo, shame (*'eb*) is a word that is constantly heard on the back streets. The types of action to which it is applied 'range from trifling misdeeds or accidents, such as insulting a guest, gossiping, stealing and miserly behaviour, to acts judged horribly immoral, such as homosexuality, female adultery or loss of virginity before marriage' (1984, 636). The community is so quick to cry *'eb*, it is thought, that no one has any freedom of action. Popular evaluation must be anticipated in every sphere of conduct. Here, there are not the two camps of the honourable and the dishonoured or shamed that have been made familiar from other ethnographies. All have been subjected to calls of 'shame' at some time or another. Honour does seem to be used as a term for an individual's moral worth but only in its sexual aspect. When a girl was sexually molested by a man, he was said to have 'taken her honour'. On the other hand, approbation for the person who behaves (as the ethnographer would say) honourably is expressed in terms of goodness, generosity, kind-heartedness and love. And when they claim status or precedence, 'people scream . . . "I am better than you!" Not "I have more honour than you". And this is so whether superiority is claimed on moral or on material grounds . . .' (637).

6. Pattern and Depth

Even on this limited sample of the evidence, some recurrent features begin to emerge. We can see that, in these cultures, honour is a measure of an individual's or family group's moral and social worth that has to be both sensed by those who struggle to maintain it and also validated by public estimation. In matters of honour, as they have here been presented, the distinction between private sentiment and public response, between subjective and objective aspects of the phenomenon, is continually being blurred (F. H. Stewart 1994, ch. 2). As Pitt-Rivers has it, 'honour felt becomes honour claimed and honour claimed becomes honour paid' – that is, in an ideally harmonious society (1977, 2). To approach this ideal, the closest possible conformity is usually required to local ideals of behaviour – for women, it seems, sexual behaviour in particular. Autonomy, wealth in both material and human resources, integrity, self-control, protective-ness, readiness to respond to insult: these are terms that we have heard again and again on the male side. Deference, modesty, concealment, shame: these are frequently appropriate for the honourable (or shameful) woman.

An essential point is that attributions of honour are gender-specific: differing norms are required of men and women. A seduced woman is always shamed, her seducer may well gain in honour (although among the Sarakatsani, it will be remembered (J. K. Campbell 1964, 280), pre-marital chastity is expected of *both* sexes). Not only that, but the seduced woman's whole family is shamed or dishonoured by the violation. Honour involves the collectivity (usually the family) in the faults or triumphs of an individual (very often the errant woman). A second essential point: attributions of honour are opposed to universals, not only with regard to the sexes but also with regard to social groups. One behaves differently towards different categories of person. An outsider (whether to country, village, or household), a shameless or dishonoured insider, an insider of superior status – each requires a different response and different degree of sensitivity to opinion or insult. Despite recurrent features, the precise meaning of honour, the exact range of honourable behaviour, is specific to group and locale – as fragmented, in that sense, as Mediterranean ecologies.

We shall not press this summary any further for the moment. These are concepts that it is extremely hard to bring into focus. Much effort has been expended, not entirely fruitfully, on the questions of what honour *is* (F. H. Stewart 1994), whether it has a 'general structure' (Pitt-Rivers 1977), what are its 'vectors' (Gilmore 1982) – none of which responds sufficiently to the complexities of the matter that even a smattering of ethnography makes plain. The point of our detailed examples was not to yield another definition of honour in general or Mediterranean honour in particular. Rather, we have taken instances of the term's varying application, its changing idioms around the Mediterranean shore, in order to raise the question of whether notions of honour and shame can be found right across the region.

An answer to that question, however provisional, would of course require a monograph to itself. Statements of the order 'in culture X, honour means A' are no use: conviction can only be carried by the details. Nor can any rapid muster of a few books and articles on the topic claim to be representative. Abu-Lughod's bedouin cannot stand for all bedouin; Campbell's Sarakatsani, now sedentarized and culturally invisible, are in a sense no longer even representative of themselves. Ethnographic writings separated in date of publication by up to several decades are no real guide to the degree of cultural similarity evinced by even the few isolated points on the map which they explore. Only comprehensive coverage and exhaustive comparison will really do, and we may be forgiven for not essaying that – a project which no anthropologist has satisfactorily accomplished. Instead, we shall have to be content with some brief generalizations, less about the field data than about the literature on them.

First, we can derive some encouragement from the confidence displayed by a few anthropologists. Even Davis, sceptical about the possibility of defining and characterizing the region, nevertheless asserts, in his discussion of stratification, that honour is the most important way in which material differences are socially construed in the Mediterranean (1977, 89). Others are bolder. In an essay to which we shall return, Blok (1981) writes happily of 'the Mediterranean code of honour', as if its fundamentally uniform character and pan-Mediterranean diffusion could be taken for granted. Gilmore introduces the collection, *Honor and Shame and the Unity of the Mediterranean* (1987), sure that most (though, as we shall see, not all) of his contributors do indeed see the first part of their title as endorsing the second; and he writes of the distinctive thread running through the literature of the subject – 'the organic connection between sexuality and economic criteria in the evaluation of moral character' (1987a, 3–7). The obsessive, even neurotic, masculinity so often required of the honourable man (at least in Christian countries) is related to the strength of the mother–son bond in the characteristic Mediterranean family, where the husband may be absent for long periods on distant fragmented holdings (11–13). In her contribution to Gilmore's collection (1987), and more extensively in a monograph (1991), Delaney proposes, as the 'genetic code' for the various phenotypes to which the

Mediterranean social environment gives rise, a single theory of sexuality and procreation: 'monogenesis' (God the Creator correlated with man the sower of seed on land and in woman).

On what do such confident generalizations rest? We can point, secondly, to the profusion of reports concerning cultures all round the Mediterranean in which values reported as approximating to honour and shame are upheld at some level (cf. Bibliographical Essay). Sheer weight of numbers will hardly carry the day; but it counts for something. Of course the ethnographies vary in date of publication, so that like is not necessarily being compared with like. They also vary in the amount of detail offered. Anthropologists do not always make it clear whether the sense of honour that they attribute to their subjects is evinced in overheard conversation, in disclosure to the anthropologist (which may have a rather different tone), in observable action, or in imputed ideology. What words are used, in whose company, and how often? How closely and effectively is the chastity of women actually preserved? How often is violence threatened or exercised in response to perceived insult? How deeply does the anthropologist have to probe to uncover indigenous ethics? Answers to such questions are seldom clearly given. The cumulative testimony is nevertheless impressive: no other topic of contemporary anthropological concern has produced so much evidence that so strongly suggests a high degree of Mediterranean unity.

The wide geographical distribution of the reports is impressive, too. That may be shown by searching for Mediterranean communities in which such values might have been expected, but are in fact strikingly absent from discourse and practice. The results of the search are relatively meagre. Davis asserts that 'only central Italy has not produced reports of honour' – in the sense in which he has just defined it, as the means by which differences in wealth are construed (1977, 90). But both the examples that he mentions include prestige and respect as objects of inter-familial or political competition, and these terms are far from alien to the vocabulary of honour (Silverman 1966; Wade 1971). Perhaps it is not central Italy that should be singled out. Mediterranean France may provide more striking exceptions, as Rogers's monograph (1991), discussed in Chapter XI, shows: among Ste Foyans, the values associated with honour and shame were apparently not among those paradoxically reinvigorated by industrialization. On the other hand, in an older study of a French community, this one in the Alps, the moral stratification discovered is assimilated to the Mediterranean pattern, albeit not to its most competitive variety (Hutson 1971, 48).

Other areas show, less the absence of a sense of honour, than its obsolescence. In 'Fuenmayor' for instance, the pseudonym for the 'agro-town' in Andalusia which Gilmore investigated, *honor* or *honora* are thought archaic terms. On being asked about them, a local informant is more likely to mention the plays of Lope de Vega than any contemporary mores (1987b, 93). By contrast *vergüenza*, shame, remains a powerful guide to conduct. The same could be said, however, of Belmonte de los Caballeros: the word *honor* may be archaic, but it has numerous substitutes and shame is once again a ruling value (Lison-Tolosana 1966, 314). Among the Cairo poor, *'eb* (shame) 'is such a vital word that there is not a toddler who does not understand what it means', even though no child or adult would speak of 'honour' unselfconsciously; instead they would characterize the ideal male as good, generous or kind-hearted (Wikan 1984, 636–7). In the Fucino basin of the Abruzzo, in central Italy, studied by White, honour is also seen as a 'historic curiosity' (1980, 78–80). Nobody uses the word – although the implication is that they once did. Within such reports as these, we may detect an echo of the theme of *Christ Stopped at Eboli* enunciated in the passage quoted in XI.2. The old code (it is tempting to say) has ceased to be honoured, although we should be chary of generalizing about exactly how it has declined in significance. It seems that things were ordered differently in the past. Even if this was not actually so, if the anthropologist's informants are purveying (to themselves as much as anyone else) a consoling myth, the idea that their society once lived according to the dictates of honour is itself some testimony to the hold that the concept has over them. It, rather than any other value, provides them with a measure of moral decline.

The overall picture of the Mediterranean obviously includes many more blank spaces than is suggested by these few examples of partial obsolescence. There are presumably numerous larger settlements in which the aristocratic or bourgeois conceptions of honour attested by historical sources are no longer apparent to the ethnographer. There must be yet more numerous areas in which a sense of honour has no place at all. Greater precision is difficult: the absence of honour is not a topic on which historians or sociologists of the modern Mediterranean are prone to comment; and, as we have noted, anthropologists have until recently tended to concentrate their studies on the disenfranchised: villagers more than city-dwellers, poor rather than rich (though cf. McDonogh 1986; Marcus 1983). The decline or disappearance of honour has thus received little attention. It is relatively easy to guess what honour and shame are incompatible with in the post-modern, post-industrial world – impersonal bureaucracy, contractual and market relationships, universalizing codes of conduct, the cult of the authentic self, the sexual revolution, mass communications, growing literacy, rapid political change and so on. It is a much harder task to show in what way any of these actually *caused* honour's demise (cf. Dodd 1973, 46–54).

Fortunately, that does not matter here. The blank spaces on the map of honour are quite consistent with the sort of Mediterranean unity that we are provisionally sketching. It is enough for present purposes – and for the historical argument to which we come in the final section below – that honour and shame be widespread *'non-aristocratic'* values in virtually all circum-Mediterranean countries.

Not only are they widespread. The implication of the more recent ethnography (and our third general assertion) is that, in the Mediterranean, the values of honour and shame have what we might, extending the metaphor, call depth. That is, they are more than notions to which only lip-service is paid: they exercise a profound hold over the conduct of daily life, 'intersecting' with other cultural and religious values. Examples are readily forthcoming from works already cited. We could instance the way in which the Sarakatsani reduced the contradictions between their sense of honour and their devotion to Christianity by projecting the sins of Adam – sensuality and envy – onto the Devil, thus freeing themselves of the sense of personal guilt that would otherwise inhibit or tarnish honourable behaviour (J. K. Campbell 1965). Another example would be the ideology embodied in *ghinnawas*, 'little songs' sung in private by Abu-Lughod's bedouin, in which they admit, albeit in a formalized way, precisely those sentiments that the code of honour normally forces them to deny or disguise (1986, 206–7). A third instance of depth would be the intimate connections between honour and *baraka* (blessedness) revealed by Jamous (1981). We could also go on to show how honour 'reaches out' into the wider worlds of politics, not just in the exercise of patronage or the diplomatic exchanges of nation-states, but also, for example, in the unusual impact of tribal honour on politics in Libya, where bureaucratic institutions have in theory been abolished and where, in 1982, one tribe therefore claimed blood money from Qadaffi's government for its members killed fighting in Chad (J. Davis 1987a, 1987b).

The attachment to honour might seem to be displayed at its most profound in the murder for honour's sake – the response to grave insult, the prosecution of feud or vendetta, and especially the punishment of female adultery or fornication. Yet reliable statistics of this are hard to come by, and Mediterranean-wide generalization is therefore correspondingly unwise (Kressel 1981; Safilios-Rothschild 1969; Makris 1992). Those committing a crime of honour are often not prosecuted, or not prosecuted under that description: police turn a blind eye; official records are ambiguously phrased. On the other hand, the relative leniency towards honour crimes displayed by some Mediterranean legal systems may lead defendants falsely to claim honour as a motive, and so bias the statistics in the other direction. Accurate balance sheets are thus impossible, and the few ethnographic enquiries that we have are really no substitute. Overall, however, it may be estimated that serious honour crimes have for some time been comparatively rare – partly for the reason already apparent from earlier examples (one takes care to reach for a weapon only when there are others around to offer restraint) and partly because of the accessibility of alternatives, such as divorce for unchaste wives (J. Davis 1989).

Paradoxically, a better measure of honour's 'depth' than the dramas surrounding homicide can be had from the obsession with apparent trivia in which it is often expressed. Crises of sexual morality do not occur every day: other provocations to ethical appraisal do.

> It is hard to conceal much from neighbours . . . People can observe and comment on how much food is bought and consumed . . . Washed linen is dried in front of the house, in the street, and it is easy to tell not only how often clothes, sheets and so on are washed, but also what condition they are in . . . Who goes out, how often and in what clothes; how often girls change their clothes, and whether they go to their announced destination by the shortest routes – all these things are quickly noted, and conclusions drawn about the conduct of the family . . .

As in Pisticci, so (we would add) elsewhere, ' . . . it would be difficult to exaggerate the minuteness of the observation and the fineness of the moral allusion' (J. Davis 1970a, 72; cf. 1977, 99). That is how honour's depth as a value, its tenacious hold on everyday conduct, is most fully revealed.

The final point to be made under this heading of 'pattern and depth' is that, whether homicide or gossip is involved, immense local variation must be expected. No *one* set of precepts has gained Mediterranean-wide acceptance. The purpose of providing so much ethnographic detail earlier on was, we said, to give the flavour of the topic. But it was also to bring out the mixture of similarities and differences – the differences which resemble one another – that altering the focus from one location to another always entails. Perhaps it is best to think of the particular bundle of attributes associated with honour and shame in any given Mediterranean society as a member of a 'family resemblance group' or 'polythetic class': no one attribute is necessarily common to all members (i.e. Mediterranean-wide), but each member shares a number of attributes with many other members (Needham 1975).

Thus in some Mediterranean societies people are garrulous on the matter of honour but less inclined to let it govern their actions. Others are animated by the notion but scarcely mention it. Some cultures recognize a concept translatable as honour but not one that can be construed as shame. Others, as we have seen, do the reverse – to the needless consternation of those who want to view 'honour-and-shame' as a virtual syndrome. Some cultures have sex-specific ideals – honour for men, shame for women. Others (*pace* Wikan 1984) admit the existence of female honour. Some groups, notably the Sarakatsani but also the Glendiots of Crete (Herzfeld 1985) and the Kabyle of Algeria (Bourdieu 1977), emphasize the agonistic, reactive side of the honourable life – in which failure to respond to the merest hint of insult is itself a dishonour (F. H. Stewart 1994, ch. 5). Others equate it with gentler virtues, such as offering as much hospitality as one can afford, 'honouring' commitments, or receiving numerous visitors. Several of the societies that we have looked at are professedly egalitarian in their ascription of honour; in others, the correlation of honour with wealth is not only close but acknowledged as such, and, at the extreme, derives from the leisure that comes with wealth rather than the hard manual labour that is the lot of poorer families (cf. Gilsenan 1977, 169). Pitt-Rivers (1977) detected this difference, and attempted to make it the foundation for a sociology of honour which distinguished 'honour-as-virtue' – gentle, characteristic of poor egalitarian societies – from 'honour-as-precedence' – a quality evinced by the powerful in stratified societies (compare F. H. Stewart 1994, chs. 4–5 for a similar distinction between 'horizontal' and 'vertical' honour). It seems clear, however, that, of those Mediterranean communities which value honour, most uphold an ideal embodying some mixture of the hierarchical and the egalitarian.

Such variation in content from one locale to another is matched by variation in time, often over a quite short period. In Ambéli, the 'dying village community' in the Euboea that du Boulay studied in the later 1960s, honour/prestige used to be demonstrated

> in terms of physical confrontation and a continual reaffirmation of verbal, physical, or economic superiority; now [*c*.1970] it is . . . revealed primarily in the application, sincerity, and efficiency with which a man dedicates himself to the task of promoting the fortunes of his family in the life and values of the modern world. The older expressions of the search for reputation are, however, not entirely lost . . . (du Boulay 1974, 111)

We should not imagine that accretions or transformations of this order occurred only once, when the immutably 'traditional' yielded to the restlessly 'modern'. Rather, as we argued in the preceding chapter, accounts such as du Boulay's may well be exemplary of changes that have occurred throughout the Mediterranean past. Even in one small village – its social and economic configuration, its connectivity with a wider world always evolving – the meaning of honour changes over time.

Variations of this degree, whether in place or time, will usually produce significant counter-examples to any generalization. The common feature of almost all reports of Mediterranean honour is, for instance, a focus on the sexuality of women, as fundamental to their own honour or shame, and also as the point at which the honour of the family or patriline is most vulnerable and most in need of protection. Young women should be virgins, married ones should be chaste. Both should be secluded from the public arena, where corporate family honour is most at risk. And yet, of course, one comes across Mediterranean communities in which questions of honour are not much focused on women's virtue (J. Davis 1987a, 26); where virginity at marriage is not absolutely essential as long as it has previously been lost to the future husband (du Boulay 1974, 115) or is compensated for by other virtues such as generosity (du Boulay 1976, 406 n.2); and where, as we have seen, wives commonly have to work outside the household. This means that it is exceedingly hard to propose operational definitions of Mediterranean honour: indicators that are passably objective, such as illegitimacy rates as measures of pre-marital chastity, can be very misleading.

Counter-examples to any generalization are, then, inevitable; but they are not inevitably damaging. Local variation should be the constituent, not the enemy, of the comparative analysis. We were not hoping to find simple ethical homogeneity. Honour arises after all from local evaluation, the constant intercourse of a 'face-to-face' society – in the village, on the mountainside, or in the urban slum (Davis 1987a, 23).

For all this diversity, recurrent features do emerge – from the profusion of specific reports to which we have referred, from the less numerous but no less weighty studies that show the 'depth' of the values in question, and even from the competing general theories of some anthropologists. Moreover, the fact that general theories, however inadequate, can be attempted at all does not merely reflect sophisticated comparative technique. Mediterranean peoples have themselves eased the anthropologist's task. The connectivity that we have identified as a distinguishing feature of microregions (Chapter V), together with the degree of mobility evinced by so many groups within the region (IX.5–6), ought to have promoted the mutual influence of local cultures even some distance from one another. It ought to have blurred distinctions between local forms of personal evaluation, reducing the range and number of idiosyncrasies. Is it entirely premature to suppose that it may actually have done this?

A provisional conclusion to the present phase of the enquiry could be, then, that honour and shame reveal just the sort of loose unity that we might have hoped to find: one in which, right across the Mediterranean, on whatever axis we choose to make comparisons, and despite other profound contrasts of faith or political structure, the differences which resemble are continually striking. Most of the individual local vocabularies and dramas of evaluation recognizably belong to one single family.

7. DISTINCTIVENESS

Unity, then, to a considerable extent; a unity that is nowhere tight or smooth, and that is always subject to qualification. What of distinctiveness? In what ways – if any – does the study of honour and shame help to bring out Mediterranean boundaries, or establish criteria for differentiating this region from others,

especially its European, African and Middle Eastern neighbours? As so often
with our project, any attempt to address such fundamental questions encounters
huge problems, both empirical and conceptual.

The empirical problem is easily specified. Anthropological study of honour
and shame began in the Mediterranean, and in no other area, with the possible
exception of the Indian subcontinent, has it been so abundantly pursued. Therefore it is hard to find substantial and accessible bodies of reports with which the
Mediterranean literature can be systematically compared. That lack of a corpus
of reports is important: not even the most ardent Mediterraneanist will claim
that the Mediterranean constellation of ideas about honour and shame is unique;
we must clearly expect to find numerous analogues of it elsewhere. The question
is whether those analogues cluster in a significant fashion – predominate in a
recognized area, however roughly bounded. Isolated instances are not important, particularly if they are to be found among communities with strong cultural
or demographic links with Mediterranean lands, for example in the Caribbean
or in Latin American societies (P. J. Wilson 1969; Horowitz 1983).

An example of how to proceed has long been available. In his classic essay
of 1925, *The Gift*, Marcel Mauss adverted briefly to notions of honour among
the North American Indians and the peoples of Melanesia and Polynesia (1969,
35–6), implying the potentially vast dimensions of the subject and the desirability of really far-flung comparison. Mauss's breadth of enquiry has not been
approached since, least of all by ethnographers primarily interested in the Mediterranean. Stewart (1994, ch. 12) has contrasted bedouin honour with what he
takes to be the more usual European varieties, and he includes some valuable
discussion of the place of honour in the legal systems of northern Europe. Yet,
as he acknowledges (2), 'comparative work on honor has scarcely begun'. Indicative of the state of play is the fact that the Gilmore collection (1987), despite
its title and emphasis, includes only a single comparative discussion of extra-
Mediterranean evidence, by Asano-Tamanoi. That paper's strategy of juxtaposing evidence from villages in Catalonia and Japan is, moreover, hailed by another
contributor to the volume as innovative (S. Brandes 1987, 124). Yet its conclusions are far from startling. Unlike in Catalonia, shame and honour in Japan do
not attach to particular men and women, but rather to the continuity of the
household and the family name: sexuality and aggression have very little to do
with it. We learn, then, that in this as in other respects Spanish and Japanese
village cultures differ; but, because of the understandably restricted nature of the
project, we have not gained any clearer idea of whether or not Mediterranean
values are globally distinctive.

If this lack of accessible ethnographies were made good, the main problem
would of course still not have been solved. In making comparisons across the
globe, there can be no ready agreement on what are to count as similarities and
differences. At the extreme, we do not know how to place our subject within the
larger context of the anthropology of personal evaluation. Older distinctions
between shame cultures and guilt cultures no longer seem fruitful (Lebra 1971;
Peristiany and Pitt-Rivers 1992, 6–8; Cairns 1993, 27–47); we have no theoretical
framework within which to locate the differences between honour and shame
and other 'prestige structures', such as that expressed in a caste system (Ortner
and Whitehead 1981, 15). Closer to home, conceptually speaking, there are no
criteria to enable us to decide whether, for instance, Polynesian *mana*, or indeed

any other indigenous category, really can be partially translated as honour, as some have proposed (Pitt-Rivers 1977, x–xi; Ortner 1981, 377). When comparative work suggests similarities between the Mediterranean and some other culture, we have to reckon with the possibility that the analysis of honour and shame in Polynesia (or wherever) may have been so coloured by prior reading of Peristiany et al. as to weaken the force of any independent comparison. Because the study of honour and shame was first elaborated using Mediterranean evidence, similarities between the Mediterranean and elsewhere may be overestimated and important divergences obscured. If, on the other hand, we try to compensate for that by recalling just how much variation there is *within* the Mediterranean, it becomes very hard to settle on a yardstick by which the values of another area could be judged either similar or significantly different. Suppose that intra-Mediterranean notions of honour, as suggested earlier, constitute a 'family resemblance group'; it would then be well to bear in mind how urgently we have been warned that adopting this form of classification renders comparative studies 'more daunting and perhaps even unfeasible' (Needham 1975, 358).

To illustrate some of these conceptual difficulties, we can take the example of the Indian subcontinent. The equivalents of honour and shame in its 'purdah zone' have been usefully surveyed by Mandelbaum (1988). That zone, characterized above all by the modesty, seclusion, and finely coded veiling of women, embraces Pakistan and the north Indian states of Punjab, Rajasthan, Haryana and Uttar Pradesh, together with adjoining parts of Madhya Pradesh, Kashmir and Himachal Pradesh (1988, 27). Within this area, among Hindus as well as Muslims, *izzat*, an Arabic and Persian word that ethnographers usually translate as honour, is 'often heard in men's talk, particularly when the talk is about conflict, rivalry, and struggle . . . it takes in the zealously sought qualities of prestige and status, rank and esteem, respect and self-respect' (20–1). *Izzat* is both a personal and a corporate attribute. Its primary bearers are male, but women may also be said to have – or lose – it. Its antithesis, *sharm* (shame), is usually to be avoided as diligently as *izzat* is to be sought, although *sharm* is sometimes used in a positive sense as well. The amount of honour that a family may attain is roughly, but only roughly, correlated with wealth and, in Hindu communities, with caste: 'a family of a low group may gain high regard both among its peers and more widely in its locality; one of high caste rank may come to be disdained by all' (23). Male honour, not surprisingly, is especially vulnerable to the sexual misdemeanours of women. One indiscretion blights not only the woman's life but the reputation of all her menfolk.

The meaning of *izzat* changes over time: that which was traditionally earned by completing the pilgrimage to Mecca may nowadays accrue from gaining a medical degree (23). It also, inevitably, varies from region to region within the purdah zone, being upheld most stringently and agonistically in the north-west (27). ('Thank Allah, I have many enemies', one elder of the Pukhtun of Swat said to his ethnographer (Lindholm 1982, 15).) *Izzat* varies further with economic class: poorer women are, of necessity, generally the more publicly visible; townswomen are more visible than villagers (Mandelbaum 1988, 36); and, for both, an elastic definition of the household may be in order.

The deepest source of variation in the meaning of *izzat* is, however, religion. The influence of Islam on north Indian Hindu practices and concepts has been as considerable as it is hard to specify; without the overwhelming presence of

Islam in the north, Hindus there would perhaps be little concerned with *izzat* or its equivalents. For all that, the two religious cultures now evince contrasting versions of purdah. Whereas in popular Muslim belief the close seclusion of women is a fundamental precept, ordained in the Koran, Hindus do not see purdah as an integral part of their religion. 'It is more a matter of social concern for family and caste-group . . . mandates for purdah in Hindu holy writ are not commonly invoked' (87–8). Hindu communities are more likely to practice village exogamy than are Muslim ones; and marriage between the children of brothers, so often preferred by Muslims, falls within Hindu incest prohibitions (30, 92). That difference entails further differences in the minutiae of veiling codes. Muslim women do not on the whole have to show their distance from, and deference to, their own or their children's affines as Hindus must. Hindu men of the purdah zone appear more sensitive to threats to their honour from within the household than outside it, from junior wives and their blood relatives for example; so they are more insistent upon veiling within the home than their Muslim counterparts. On the other hand, Hindu women are less confined to their own quarters of the house by comparison with Muslims, and are far less likely to wear the all-enveloping *burka* when out of doors. Muslim veiling emphasizes less the dichotomy between affinal and consanguineal kin (which endogamy tends to erase) than the distinction between the family inner circle of kin and close friends and all others; outsiders pose the greater threat to familial prestige (80–3, 96–7).

What is a student of the Mediterranean to make of such data? The purdah zone, on Mandelbaum's definition, looks like a relatively discrete entity – an entity of comparable scale and cohesion to the Mediterranean as we have been trying to present it. Of course, like those of the Mediterranean, its frontiers must not be drawn at all sharply:

> There is no abrupt shift from a purdah to a non-purdah region, but rather a gradual transition through the intervening regions to the quite different gender relations of South India . . . In the south as in the north, women are required to conduct themselves with alert modesty outdoors and to show proper respect to elders within the home. But the symbolic displays of modesty and respect are generally less stringent and constant, and concern about them is less central to society and culture . . . while the competition for personal and group status is generally keen, it is cast in different terms than izzat, with greater stress on ritual pollution and purity. (3, 128)

That is exactly the sort of difference that we might expect to find when comparing the Mediterranean with its neighbours. And equally distinct changes in gender relations and prestige systems can also be detected when moving eastward (130, cf. Ortner 1981, 398–9). Only in one direction – though that is, of course, a vast enough exception – to the west, is there an apparent continuum between Muslim areas of the purdah zone and the Mediterranean and Middle East: Mandelbaum comments on the similarities in the comportment of Muslim women in Cox's Bazaar, near the boundary between Burma and Bangladesh, Casablanca, and San'a, the capital of North Yemen (Mandelbaum 1988, 102–3; cf. Pastner 1972, 251).

How can this zone, distinct enough from its neighbours in several directions, best be summed up? In outline, its notions of honour and shame are clearly very close to those encountered round the Mediterranean – and not only because in each area there are considerable numbers of Muslims and large areas irradiated by Islamic culture. We might then conclude that there is nothing special about Mediterranean honour: here, in India, is another area big enough and similar enough in its system of personal evaluation to dispel any idea of Mediterranean uniqueness. Indeed, on an extreme but not implausible view, both Mediterranean and Indian honour might figure simply as 'local' refractions of a more general Islamic notion. Against such a sweeping and unfocused interpretation of cultural geography we might, however, argue just as forcefully that it is a symptom of Mediterraneanist bias, rather than a sign of similarity, to translate *izzat* and *sharm* as honour and shame. Do not the quite different linguistic, religious and cultural contexts of those terms in north India – contexts merely hinted at in the foregoing references to caste and Hinduism – show the need for a more circumspect approach? Again, how much analytical weight should be given to apparently un-Mediterranean aspects of the purdah zone – for example the benefits to family solidarity thought by some caste groups to accrue from sexual relations between a woman and her husband's younger brother; or, again, a local peculiarity in the modesty code which permits a woman to breast-feed her child in the presence of any man, the claims of motherhood negating the shame of exposure (Mandelbaum 1988, 15, 75)? It is as if we are comparing two paintings and do not know to which aspect of them we should give prominence. Palette and subject matter are extremely close; style and iconography derive from closely linked traditions; only when we draw near to the surface of the canvas do the peculiarities become unmistakable. How profoundly alike then, in respect of their prestige structures, are the Mediterranean and the Indian subcontinent? A question we still do not know how to answer.

For all this uncertainty, some preliminary conclusions can be drawn about the comparison of Mediterranean honour with the prestige systems of its neighbours. There could after all be no clearer contrast between the Mediterranean, with its numerous reports of honour and shame as matters of profound and daily concern among all classes, and northern Europe. In the north, the language of honour now almost always sounds archaic and seems largely restricted to the gang, club or regiment; crimes of honour, though more commonly acknowledged in law than is often supposed (F. H. Stewart 1994, 76 n.6), hardly resonate in popular morality; and, in contrast to Mediterranean legal systems, the truth of what one person says about another is usually an adequate defence against the charge of defamation (14 n.22). We cannot yet explain this contrast between the Mediterranean and the north, any more than we can explain the blank spaces on the map of Mediterranean honour (Section 6 above); it is stark none the less.

In the other direction in which extra-Mediterranean comparisons should principally be launched, the Islamic Middle East (along with parts of sub-Saharan Africa) the broad picture, as the evidence mustered by Mandelbaum has begun to show, is completely different. We argued in our first chapter that the Middle East was hard to define and could easily be conceptually redivided. Yet, so far as value systems are concerned, there is no compelling distinction to be made between Mediterranean and non-Mediterranean: the ethnographies of Iraq, Iran, the Arabian peninsula, Somaliland, the Sudan, the Indian subcontinent – all yield accounts of the meanings and functions of honour that are undeniably akin to those of Mediterranean anthropologists. Something more is involved than an anthropological equivalent of Braudel's (1972a, ch. 3) 'greater Mediterranean'. To seek out frontiers in this easterly direction – even frontiers of the 'fuzziest' kind – would seem a hopeless task.

Sometimes, indeed, the geographical divisions suggested by focusing on one particular aspect of the subject are consistent neither with the unity of the Mediterranean nor with that of Islam. Take for example the question of which men are most dishonoured by the shameful misdemeanours of a married woman, and thus bear primary responsibility for punishing them: those of the family into which she has married (especially of course her husband) or those of her family of origin (father, uncles, brothers). That question is of some significance for the type of marriage that is likely to be preferred for her. Cultures in which she remains under the moral authority of her natal family are more inclined to favour endogamy, particularly to the father's brother's son (on which compare Abu-Lughod 1986, 145, discussed earlier). Endogamy avoids relinquishing a woman to another family, where her potentially damaging conduct is less readily controlled. So at least it has been argued (Holy 1989, 120–7, with references), although the argument takes no account of those who, like the Iqar'iyen reported on by Jamous (1981), see exogamy almost as an aggressive way of challenging the honour of another family while cavalierly putting one's own at risk (see also Tillion 1983, 98–9).

Whatever the aptness of this interpretation of patrilateral cousin marriage, the regional contrasts that emerge are arresting. In the northern, Christian, Mediterranean it is *on the whole* the husband and his family who are responsible for the misbehaviour of their in-marrying women – even if in some areas they share that responsibility with the men of natal families. 'The naming system whereby a woman adopts the name of her husband upon marriage expresses symbolically the transfer of control from her father and brothers, whose name she bore before marriage, to her husband, whose name she now bears' (Holy 1989, 121). In Islamic Mediterranean lands by contrast, for instance (as we saw) among Abu-Lughod's bedouin, the men of the married woman's family of origin retain primary moral guardianship over her. They may signal that by ignoring her wedding, thus denying that the ceremony involves any symbolic transfer between agnates and affines (122–3). North and south in the Mediterranean look rather different from each other in this respect. But this is not because the south is better seen as part of the wider Islamic Middle East. So far as can be told from the few ethnographies that are explicit about such matters, the 'southern pattern' is not entirely typical of Islam. In parts of Turkey, and eastward into the Middle East – Iran, Afghanistan, the Black Sea, the Hindu Kush – the pattern found in the Christian Mediterranean is more common: control of a married woman again rests with her husband and his agnates (121 with n.7, 126; Delaney 1991, 101; Muhawi 1989, 266).

Such geographical generalizations are extremely fragile: al-Khayyat's discussion of Iraqi women provides just one counter-example to it (1990, 2). Yet what is important is not the divergence between north and south just sketched, or the similarity between the north and some of the non-Mediterranean Middle East, or the possibility that Middle Eastern variations reflect differences between Arab and non-Arab (Meeker 1976, 390). The point, rather, is that the map of honour can be drawn and redrawn in a number of complex ways. Anthropology gives us no single authoritative or overriding interpretation on the matters of unity and distinctiveness. On the contrary, the evidence implies a variety of anthropological geographies. At a high level of generality, the Mediterranean can hardly be distinguished from the remainder of the Middle East. Yet when the ethnographies are made to respond to one specific question about male responsibility, what emerges is not only a divergence between north and south, but also a contrast, of sorts, between the Islamic Mediterranean and at least some parts of the wider Middle East. It is not therefore entirely pointless to ask whether the Mediterranean has any external frontiers, any broad 'marcher' territory in which the predominant pattern may begin perceptibly to change into something else.

Whether we can reasonably expect the available ethnography to yield an answer is quite another matter: its unevenness in quality and coverage is forbidding. Yet, for instance, as one moves through the Iberian ethnographies towards the Atlantic part of the peninsula, the cultural centrality of the honour code perceptibly diminishes, and we seem to be crossing the boundary between Mediterranean Europe and the north. In Behar's Santa María del Monte, to revert to a non-Mediterranean example offered in the preceding chapter, its irrelevance is specifically noted (1986, 15–16). In Fontelas, the hamlet in northern Portugal on which O'Neill focuses, 'the concept of honour and shame is entirely inapplicable . . . Compared with other communities in the mainstream of Mediterranean ethnography, Fontelas is really on another planet' – not least because its illegitimacy ratios approach 75 per cent (1987, 16). The contrast with the cluster of settlements in south-east (Mediterranean) Portugal, classically analysed by Cutileiro (1971), is marked.

No such clarity is immediately attainable in other corners of the region. It may be that, as one moves northward and westward in the Balkans from Greek into Slavic cultures, that Mediterranean-type values become less frequent. In Montenegro, as demonstrated both ethnographically and historically by Boehm, 'the moral system still centers on the concept of *obraz*, literally "cheek", which is very similar to "honor" terms all around the Mediterranean' (1980, 8; cf. 1983, 73, 83, 86, 90). In Skopska Crna Gora, the rural area of 'Yugoslav' Macedonia described by Rheubottom (1985), on the other hand, though all social interaction is profoundly suspicious and agonistic, no comparable values seem to have been cherished. We cannot, of course, generalize about the geography of value systems in south-eastern Europe from two ethnographies: more field work is clearly needed. Political conditions in and around the former Yugoslavia at the close of the twentieth century are hardly likely to hasten it, however; and in the meanwhile the possibility that there is a Balkan frontier zone to the Mediterranean in this respect must remain open.

Turkish evidence is perhaps similarly ambiguous, as can again be illustrated by reference to two ethnographies. The village in the central Anatolian steppe (to which its anthropologist, Delaney, gives the pseudonym Gökler) evinces conceptions of honour that are readily assimilable to those of Mediterranean cultures (Delaney 1987, 1991). By contrast, in Of, the Black Sea district studied by Meeker (1976), honour, *seref* (Arabic *sharaf*), is most commonly predicated of events or persons of great national or Islamic importance. The ordinary villager partakes of it in that he is a member of the community which the men or events with *seref* represent. Also, when he undertakes some task of national or religious importance, such as military service or going on pilgrimage, his own acts and person acquire an aspect of *seref*. Lastly he partakes of the honour of his clan, in comparison with which the *seref* accruing from his own acts will be insignificant. The revenge of insults, the daily assertion of honour, is attributed not to the ordinary villager but to the 'aghas', moral leaders of a sort, dominant figures in large and honourable clans, who are the most attentive to their clan's genealogy and history and the most sensitive to any scandal that could besmirch the clan's name. All rather different from the bulk of our earlier Mediterranean examples. Only when the analysis turns to *namus*, sexual honour, an honour 'tied to the chastity of specific women' (260), are more familiar notes struck. Does this partial contrast between Of and 'Gökler' simply reflect the differing importance of clan organization in each of the two settlements, or does it hint more broadly at another northern frontier to the Mediterranean? Once again, the question must remain open.

There are other ethnographies, in the same vein as those Balkan and Turkish comparisons, that could be explored in this connection. We could instance the apparently peculiarly legalistic approach to the settlement of questions of honour found among those Sinai bedouin whom Stewart (1994) uses to show the difference between European and Middle Eastern honour, but who might equally well stand in contrast to Abu-Lughod's (1986) more comfortably Mediterranean bedouin. Or we could point out the strikingly relaxed attitude to sexual misdemeanour which, in contrast to her field experience in Cairo, Wikan (1984) finds in Sohar, Oman:

> the substance of 'honour' in Oman, what people have to do and be to think well of themselves, is strikingly different from what is reported from much of the Mediterranean and the Middle East – so strikingly indeed that, had the Omanis not been a Middle Eastern people who denounce sexual immorality in *females* as the utmost shame, it would probably not have occurred to me to try to analyse their behaviour in terms of honour. (647; though cf. Kressel and Wikan 1988)

There is no need to multiply such instances. The map of possible Mediterranean frontier zones to which they might contribute a little detail will long be incomplete. Also, it will always be controversial. This is partly because of the methodological difficulties rehearsed earlier: first, of defining the Mediterranean norm and second, *a fortiori*, of deciding what is significantly different from it. But another reason is that any cultural map based on the work of ethnographers leaves itself open to the charge that it ignores historical change, and presents a misleading picture of the relation between the Mediterranean and its neighbours – its northern neighbours especially.

> Much of southern Europe has in recent centuries changed far more slowly than the rest of the continent. It is therefore in many ways more reasonable to compare, say, Andalusian or Sicilian villages of the first half of the twentieth century with English or German villages of two centuries earlier, rather than with English or German villagers who were their contemporaries. (F. H. Stewart 1994, 76–7)

We would not endorse any interpretation which has Mediterranean Europe since the nineteenth century simply as a static relic of an earlier age. None the less, what is likely to have been the prior decline of honour as a leading value in the north certainly presents the ethnographer with a far more extreme contrast between north and south than would have been apparent in, say, the seventeenth century.

Now the purpose of this chapter has been to see what sort of case could be made for Mediterranean unity and distinctiveness simply on the basis of modern anthropology, because anthropology is the discipline in which contemporary discussion of the region's integrity is probably at its liveliest. We have done that in a way which is more descriptive than explanatory, although the detailed examples reviewed earlier each sought to place concern for honour in its local social context. And we have naturally done it by looking more at the present than at history. Our comparisons have all been roughly synchronic, founded in an (admittedly somewhat elastic) 'ethnographic present'. It was never our intention to suggest that the resulting picture would necessarily be *historically* valid as well, a rather grander version of the other exemplary vignettes assembled in Chapter XI. Only at the beginning of the present chapter have we referred to the long-term history of honour, from Homeric heroes to Prussian duellists.

There are powerful reasons for leaving the matter there. To find a satisfying explanation for honour is not likely to be an easy task. At least part of its explanation is presumably to be found in its history. And to deal adequately with that history would require cultural, philological, and legal investigation on a daunting scale. Few guides to such vast territory exist: we have no adequate surveys of the history of honour in any of the countries that we might wish to consider. Embarking on even a superficial comparative account would moreover take us unconscionably far from our microecological focus at this stage. And it would anticipate some of the topics, tangential to honour and shame, which will appear in Volume 2 under the heading of Mediterranean demography – topics such as rates of illegitimacy, the age at marriage and the structure of the family. On the other hand, it may be that only some appeal from anthropology to history can begin to resolve the ambiguities of the ethnographic evidence, especially as that evidence concerns the possible distinctiveness of the Mediterranean. We need also to address the accusation of the anti-Mediterraneanists that Mediterranean anthropology rests in part on a suppression of history (Herzfeld 1987b, 11–12). In so doing, we can, finally, bring out the contribution that anthropologists have actually made, both directly and indirectly, to the writing of a history of honour in Europe and the Middle East.

8. ORIGINS

Bernard Mandeville's *An Enquiry into the Origins of Honour* appeared in 1732. Early on in its First Dialogue, the multiplicity of meanings of the concept is given as a reason for not trying to trace those origins. Modern anthropologists have been undeterred. Their direct contribution to the history of honour has been to acknowledge that the notion is not an inevitable by-product of human social evolution – that its appearance requires historical explanation. We need not review in any detail the various theories on offer. It is more pertinent to note how often the origin suggested is specifically Mediterranean (for more generalized accounts cf. Ortner 1978, 1981; Cucchiari 1981). We can register the theories' common features, and enquire whether they have anything to contribute to our own understanding of the long-term distinctiveness of the area.

Most of the theories are speculative reconstructions of a very distant, indeed prehistoric, past. In different ways, Tillion and Pitt-Rivers associate the origin of family honour in the Mediterranean, an honour grounded above all in the control of female sexuality, with the substitution of endogamy for the exchange of women between groups; and they explain that substitution in turn by reference to social changes in the eastern Mediterranean at the beginning of the Neolithic period. Tillion (1983, 74) gives more emphasis to a population expansion that supposedly released communities from the obligation to create political alliances through out-marriage; Pitt-Rivers is more impressed by the increased social stratification that accompanied the emergence of civilization, and that engendered 'a competition in which the winners are those who keep their daughters' (1977, 160). We have already, in Chapters V and VII–IX, given reasons for doubting interpretations of this kind: interpretations which depend on pivotal moments of transition from one age to another, whether these be 'the emergence of civilization', 'the decline of the ancient economy', a technological change, or some far-reaching catastrophe.

Another type of account, though still speculative, is more congenial: it locates the origins of honour in the competition for scarce resources. For Jane Schneider (1971), honour emerged spontaneously from an ancient pastoral way of life, cementing the loyalty of menfolk, making women a valuable – and hence jealously hoarded – currency in the building up of large families: 'In the absence of the state, pastoral communities, and agricultural communities in their midst, developed their own means of social control – the codes of honor and shame – which were adapted to the intense conflict that external pressures had created within them, and between them' (1971, 3). A similar hypothesis is to be found accompanying Blok's revelation of 'a key to the Mediterranean code of honour' (1981), already cited in Chapter IX.5–6. This code is again seen as an originally pastoral code, predicated upon virility and physical strength – both of them essential to safeguarding the patrimony, of which women are the most precious and vulnerable part.

The state is significant for its impact rather than its absence in another attempt at a theory of origins. The Schneiders, Jane and Peter (1976, 94–8), modify Jane Schneider's earlier discussion of pastoralism with the suggestion that honour reflects the divisive pressure on local patrimonies exerted by ancient centralizing empires, the two world religions that enhanced women's power of inheritance, and the slave trade in women. So for Jane Schneider honour is first a response to 'stateless' competition, then a defence against the incursions of the state (cf. Ortner 1978, 31).

Whether anything can be usefully said about, or learned from, abstractions such as 'the state' in ancient times; whether enslavement was the stressor that provoked the ideological response of female shame or some such value – all this is surely doubtful. Since honour antedates the expansion of Christianity and Islam and has not by any means always been in conflict with them, they cannot be used as primary causes either (compare Delaney's (1991) rather different understanding of the symbolic role of monotheism, noted earlier). The invocation of an aboriginal pastoral society is equally suspect. Pastoralism cannot be seen as prior to agriculture, either conceptually or historically (III.6). All theories of this kind remain on the level of 'just so stories', fascinating certainly, yet on a par as convincingly evidenced history with Freud's *Totem and Taboo*.

Two less speculative accounts deserve notice, finally. They are very different from one another in scale and purpose; yet they can be yoked together here because both suggest origins of Mediterranean honour that are firmly within the historical period rather than the impenetrable depths of the Stone Age, and both can adduce evidence in their support.

Concerned specifically with the modern history of the Italian *mezzogiorno*, Davis (1992a) traces the origins of the ideal of *civiltà contadina* in its aspect of *onore* to the profound tenurial changes of the Napoleonic age. In a period of rising population and industrial growth, the vocabulary of honour provided the small rural proprietor with a symbolic means of demonstrating control over resources and of integrity and independence in the face of social superiors. So for the first time in Italy – in 1814 – honour, which had, for the most part, previously been the preserve of their superiors became, among *contadini*, the basis for a social stratification based ultimately upon wealth.

Herzfeld also focuses on the nineteenth century as the period in which the honour of Mediterranean countrymen familiar to the modern ethnographer became generalized. He takes his cue from a theory already cited:

> It is the state, according to Anton Blok (1981) . . . that usurped the code of honour in the northern and western parts of Europe . . . In the Mediterranean lands, so his essentially survivalist argument runs, the code remained relatively unaffected, a testimony to older values and virtues. But since the Mediterranean state bureaucracies were largely modelled on Great Power prototypes, we could just as easily assume that the ideology was transferred back to the Mediterranean as a component of these new structures. It was the rise of bourgeois nationalism in northern and western Europe, after all, that elevated the medieval chivalric code to the status of a general morality . . . (1987b, 11)

By implication, the rise of nationalism and the nation-state in the Mediterranean might have had a similar effect, generalizing a code that had previously been restricted to the elite. In their very different ways, then, both Davis and Herzfeld characterize the history of honour in terms of diffusion down the social hierarchy.

Unlike their speculative counterparts, both of the last two hypotheses are testable, and in a moment we shall look at some evidence that bears on them. But it is *prima facie* unlikely that the origins of honour as a popular value in the Mediterranean could be attributed to any one factor, be it a relatively circumscribed one like the Napoleonic land reforms or something as grand as the rise of bourgeois nationalism (incidentally, just the sort of explanatory cliché that Herzfeld so condemns in the writings of Mediterranean anthropologists). Everything that we have concluded in the foregoing chapters inclines us to suppose that ideas of honour have evolved in the Mediterranean under a wide variety of stimuli, radiating outward both geographically and socially from numerous different centres inside and outside the Mediterranean – the pre-classical Semitic Levant, Greek colonizing city-states, early Islamic Arabia, the courts of medieval France and Renaissance Italy, and so on. To select just one factor in all this complexity will yield a picture as unreal as any speculations about prehistory. The search for *the* origin of honour is misconceived. It is also unhelpful: what we want to know is not so much why a sense of honour arose in the Mediterranean as why it has stayed there. We need to account for its durability, not just its creation.

Demolition is not our primary concern in rehearsing these theories. It is more useful to draw out their recurrent features. Note how often honour is given a

broadly *ecological* explanation, in terms of husbanding, defending or appropriating scarce resources – not least, in a world of often low populations and fragile
lineages, the scarce resource constituted by women (IX.5–6). To add a further
example: for Lindholm (1996, 20), honour is a necessity 'in a world of uncertainty, where a man's reputation is his only guarantee of esteem'; it is adaptive to
the competitive, egalitarian world of the bedouin, whose values he sees as having
dominated Middle Eastern history since well before the rise of Islam. Lindholm
thereby aligns himself with those who discern honour's origins in pastoralism.
But his approach can and must be given wider application. For note how often
honour arises from, or mediates, dealings with a wider and more varied political and economic world: the world of agriculture, of cities, of the state, of
religious authority. It is from those features that we take our cue. Rather than
offer yet another theory of origins, we suggest that honour and shame might
suitably be interpreted as the values of Mediterranean microecologies. To put it
that way is not to substitute a functional explanation for a genetic one: honour
and shame come with too heavy a freight of history to be narrowly related to
the possibly ephemeral concerns of any one period or area. Nor do we want to
assign explanatory primacy either to the microecologies or to the values. Rather,
we envisage the whole cultural history of the codes of honour and shame as one
more facet in the complex picture of the microecology that earlier chapters have
attempted to build up. These values at once express and help create the continuing identity of those exploiting the microecologies as they mutate and
interact. (In that sense the discussion of them does, after all, belong with the
demonstration of how microregions persist that was attempted in Chapter XI.)
A concern for honour, *itself* often seen as a finite symbolic resource, reflects
something of the unpredictability and perceived scarcity of Mediterranean resources in general, and the fraught balancing of autonomy and co-operation that
their management necessitates. Also, honour is both highly local in content and
(seemingly) universal in significance. It is analogous to the way in which, we
have been arguing, the Mediterranean world works as a gigantic set of microecologies, with no significant intermediate level between the very small and the
very large.

We can hardly produce direct evidence of the postulated 'fit' between values
and ecology: our case has to be a cumulative yet impressionistic one, based on
the overall impression created by the whole volume. But if there is any validity in
this conception, a resolution of the problem of Mediterranean distinctiveness
may additionally be to hand. For that distinctiveness could now be said to lie in
the very closeness of the fit. Although similar codes of honour and shame are
found right across the Middle East and Mediterranean boundaries are exceedingly hard to specify, nowhere else, perhaps, outside the Mediterranean is the
human geography so strikingly paralleled in systems of value.

How can we support that conjecture? First, we can refer the case studies in
the anthropology of honour presented at the start of this chapter back to the
descriptions of exemplary microecologies given in Chapter III, where individuals
are seen minimizing risks by moving flexibly along a spectrum of resources
in order to achieve as much independence as they can – in competition with,
but also intimately connected to, a wider cultural and economic environment.
We can also adduce the profound connectivity between microecologies that was
the theme of several subsequent chapters, and relate that to the centrality of

the distinction between kin and non-kin, insider and outsider, that is so often implicated in the concern for honour and shame.

Finally, we can show that Mediterranean honour has a history appropriate to its involvement in the microecology – a history that reaches considerably further back than the Napoleonic period. We contended earlier that this was not the place in which even to outline such a topic; but there is one aspect of it that cannot entirely be confined to sample references in the Bibliographical Essay, and that is the history of honour among those most closely concerned with managing the Mediterranean environment: small-scale producers, artisans and traders – non-aristocratic honour, in other words. This, incidentally, is where anthropologists have made their most valuable, if indirect, contribution to an understanding of the history of values in the Mediterranean region: not by proposing theories of origins so much as by inspiring historical studies of anthropological topics. In studies of honour's history, the works of Campbell and Pitt-Rivers grace many a bibliography.

9. History

We leave aside (or in some cases postpone to Volume 2) what might, sometimes controversially, be taken as oblique evidence of the history of honour: women's seclusion and public veiling, their opportunities for extra-domestic employment; and, for both sexes, age at marriage, illegitimacy rates, recorded impressions of levels of sexual pudicity, the history of feuding, duels and public violence generally. A report based on these would not be sufficient to refute the claim occasionally made by anthropologists (cf. J. Davis 1992a) that the history of *non-aristocratic* honour, as a local expression of social differences, really begins only in quite modern times. Of course, in almost every Mediterranean society, from ancient times onward, *aristocracies* have denied that groups below them in the hierarchy may claim honour as they themselves do. These groups, defined by occupation or wealth, are often regarded (to generalize the Roman legal term) as 'infamous'. But members of them may none the less assert an honour of their own. And enough of their assertions are registered in surviving documents for us to glimpse, at least occasionally, some remote forerunners of the honour communities that ethnographers describe.

Probably the oldest Mediterranean evidence is that of Hesiod's *Works and Days*, written some time in the decades around 700 B.C. Whatever his own background, Hesiod seems to offer very much an insider's view of the world of the small, but not necessarily impoverished, farmer in the Boeotia of his time (Millett 1984). 'The honourable farmer will not win the same kind of honour as a hero; but shame, no less than the fear of divine punishment, will restrain him from injustice, and he will display an *areté*, an excellence, of his own' (Lloyd-Jones 1990, 260; cf. Cairns 1993, 148–56). The same might perhaps be said of the less well-off citizen of a Greek city-state in the age of Aristotle (Dover 1974, 226–38).

Perhaps Islam is the area in which the greatest continuity of 'low-level' honour may be conjectured – a rough continuity running from the all-embracing tribal honour of the inhabitants of pre-Islamic Arabia (Farès 1932) to the remarkably similar notions reported among modern bedouin (L. Abu-Lughod

1986; though cf. F. H. Stewart 1994, 103). But the stages between ancient and modern are generally hard to document (cf. Guichard 1977). The 989th of the *Thousand and One Nights* is the story of a cobbler who cared for his honour. Archives such as the Geniza of the Jewish community in medieval Muslim Cairo contain numerous references to the concept (though rarely to shame) and these references have come from the pens of both the prosperous merchants and the poor (Goitein 1967–88, 5.199–204; cf. Stillman 1974, 198): 'my honor is worth something to me', protests a poor, semi-educated woman shackled to a grasping husband. Women can also sometimes be found defending their honour in Sharia courts of the early Ottoman period (Jennings 1975, 62). Yet more substantial documentation is needed – for which we have to look elsewhere. The Byzantine corner of the Mediterranean yields little explicit evidence apart from snide references to honour-seeking artisans (Magdalino 1984, 60). So we must look to Europe.

In particular, we must look to European legal records, far more thoroughly investigated than their Middle Eastern counterparts. These are of course removed several times from the everyday assertions and attributions of honour that quite deliberately avoid resort to litigation, and that anthropologists can observe directly – even though, as we have seen, in their monographs they are often curiously reticent about who says and does what. The slight compensation for the abstraction of the legal record from the quotidian is that plaintiffs may feel called upon to use the moral rhetoric appropriate to their station: they parade the values which they would like to be seen as upholding. Here we can only sample these sources, moving from the modern period tentatively backward in time, in order to see how long-term a history it is possible to sketch.

Everyone, said a poor farmer of Verja in Andalusia during a court case of 1735, had some honour, except perhaps the Gypsies (James Casey 1983, 195). A man's reputation could be undermined by failure to control his household, a married woman's by leaving the house – unless she were going to Mass. Not that such persons always upheld their honour: even in adultery cases, discretion may have seemed the better part of masculinity. But the hold of recognizable ideals is amply attested. In the courts of seventeenth- to eighteenth-century Piedmont 'reference to honour was . . . constant', not least among servants and artisans; 'witnesses . . . measured their own and others' conduct in terms of honorability' (Cavallo and Cerutti 1990, 75). Naturally, we should not assume that concern for honour at this level is always going to be a particularly Mediterranean thing: damage or potential damage to reputation, slurs on one's *honnêteté*, were the commonest reason for making official complaint to a *commissaire* among the poor of eighteenth-century Paris (Garrioch 1986, 37), whereas in contemporary Languedoc the dented honour of common folk justified no recourse to officialdom (Castan 1974, 260–1). But the evidence is too disparate in date and quality to make sustained comparison of Mediterranean and non-Mediterranean possible: here, the historian certainly has no advantage over the anthropologist.

To move back in time: in 1641 (Farr 1988) a master shoemaker of Dijon complained to the court that a gardener had so slandered him that his honour was engaged. Such a man 'possessed honour even if the upper classes failed to acknowledge it' (179). His artisan colleagues were also clearly vulnerable through the indiscretions of their women. (Ferrante (1989) reports analogous cases from contemporary Bologna.) Innkeepers, apothecaries, prostitutes, barbers, butchers and coppersmiths were equally zealous in defending their honour before papal magistrates or the tribunal of the Governor in High Renaissance Rome (Burke 1987, ch. 8; Cohen and Cohen 1993; cf. E. Cohen 1992). There, as earlier still in Venice, family honour was easily diminished by female fornication: when the daughter of a school teacher was seduced in 1345, it was her father's reputation for which the Avogadori of the Commune showed primary concern (Ruggiero 1985).

All over Europe in later medieval to early modern times, it seems, quite humble people were jealous of their honour. German agriculturalists fought duels about what might be construed as affairs of honour. In cities such as Augsburg, during the Reformation, a serving woman might hire an assassin to avenge the slight to her honour involved in a broken promise of marriage (Roper 1994, 66). In France, German-speaking Switzerland and the Low Countries, villagers evinced developed and articulate notions of personal reputation (F. H. Stewart 1994, 130–1). Moreover, we should not assume that their doing so aroused the anger or anxiety of social superiors. In Renaissance Florence, very substantial donations and bequests came the way of charities that provided dowries for impoverished girls, so enabling them to make honourable marriages, or that gave temporary relief to the 'shame-faced' – that is, respectable persons fallen on hard times who would be dishonoured by begging. The flourishing of these charities shows that 'even if the codes of honour and shame were not democratized, wealthy Florentines wished to emphasize their applicability and urgency at every level of the social hierarchy' (Gavitt 1990, 134; Spicciani 1981; cf. Ferrante 1990).

Some observers have detected differences between the Mediterranean and northern Europe in popular notions of honour during this earlier period: in some English court cases, far less emphasis is for instance placed on the sensitivity of the whole family's honour to the behaviour of its members (Ingram 1987, 310); very few cuckolds appear in cases of defamation heard by the church courts in Elizabethan York (Sharpe n. d.; contrast Gowing 1994, 1996 on London). In early modern Muscovy, the honour of women – women of every status, even slaves – seems to have been more generously protected in law than was that of men (Kollmann 1991). Local idioms indeed emerge that seem far removed from Mediterranean norms: for example, among fifteenth-century Parisian 'pardon tellers' (trying, in the court of the king himself, to exonerate themselves of murder), pulling hair and knocking hats off seem to be recurrent means of attempting to damage poor people's reputation (N. Z. Davis 1987, 38–40, 96–101). But all such comparisons between Mediterranean and non-Mediterranean are hazardous in the extreme, and our argument at this stage does not depend on our being able to draw them. For we do not propose that there has always been a *distinctively Mediterranean* non-aristocratic honour: the point is simply that such honour is far better attested in the region's past than a number of students of honour – historians, literary scholars and anthropologists – have maintained.

How far back can the story be taken in Europe? Certainly to the villages of Catalonia in the later twelfth century (T. N. Bisson 1998, 127–34). There, as in early fourteenth-century Montaillou, notions of dishonour, and above all shame, were 'at the centre of rural morals' (Le Roy Ladurie 1975, 294). Possibly back to Hesiod's Boeotia, with which we began.

Altogether, then, a case – inevitably patchy and incomplete – can be made for there having been a non-aristocratic honour, an honour of those most immediately concerned with the 'decision-making under uncertainty' that characterizes the Mediterranean microecology. Its history can be traced over a number of centuries, if not into Braudel's 'mists of time', then certainly into the later Middle Ages and possibly into Antiquity.

10. Conclusion: The Case for Mediterraneanism

Introducing the subject of this chapter, we wrote that an examination of it would enable us to test the arguments of the anti-Mediterraneanists such as Herzfeld and Pina-Cabral at the point where they are most confident. For them, nothing so well encapsulates the Mediterraneanist desire to make the region seem backward and exotic as the attribution of honour and shame to Mediterranean peoples.

> By concentrating the weight of its attention on these values, Mediterraneanist anthropology suggests a pervasive archaism. This reinforces the hierarchical relationship between nation-state and village studies . . . The nation-state – by its own reckoning, the ultimate symbol and embodiment of modernity – serves as a touchstone against which Mediterranean society and culture acquire their distinctive characteristics, their fundamental otherness, and above all their removal to a more primitive age. (Herzfeld 1987b, 11)

The anti-Mediterraneanist polemic against honour and shame assumes the overall shape of four not entirely compatible assertions:

First, Mediterranean peoples share these values with their northern neighbours, at the level of nation-state politics and diplomacy, if not at that of popular morality (1987b, 12, 15); Mediterranean anthropologists have simply not been sufficiently wide-ranging in their comparisons (Pina-Cabral 1989, 402).

Secondly, Mediterranean peoples do not primarily uphold the values of honour and shame. These have been attributed to them in order that they may seem sufficiently different from Europeans to merit field work (the implication of the above extract from Herzfeld and his 1987a, 76; Just (1978) is a blunter reading of the charge, adding the suggestion (89) that honour is not coincidentally a nebulous concept, so that its ascription to Mediterranean communities is hard to challenge). Honour and shame even define the Mediterranean, which can then, with blithe circularity, be used to interpret the value systems of its inhabitants.

Thirdly, to the extent that they *do* live by such values, 'honour' and 'shame' are very inadequate glosses on the immense variety of local idioms in which the values are expressed (Herzfeld 1980).

Fourthly, a concomitant of the glossing of that heterogeneity with just two monolithic terms is that far too much explanatory power is attributed to them. In the name of supposedly 'traditional values', the variously contested, labile 'discourses' of gender and class politics are ignored or even suppressed; yet it is precisely these politics, in which men are usually the masters, that actually determine the ideals described by ethnographers (Lever 1986). Analysis of honour and shame should be superseded by that of 'hegemonic masculinity' (Cornwall and Lindisfarne 1994, especially Lindisfarne 1994).

To the first assertion we might reply that, within the limits set by the availability of evidence, we have tried to be as comparative as anti-Mediterraneanism recommends. The second assertion is surely refuted by the substantial body of ethnography presented in this chapter. A good portion of this ethnography is provided by indigenous scholars; they are presumably (to suggest otherwise would surely be patronizing) untainted by the none-too-subtle political agenda of their Anglo-American colleagues and therefore sufficiently reliable. The message is that honour and shame are indeed deeply held values right across the region: they have not been foisted upon it by anthropological imperialists. Thirdly, while it can readily be agreed that the translation of local evaluative terms is never simple (cf. J. K. Campbell 1983, 206 n.2), the consensus that honour and shame are not wholly misleading glosses seems overwhelming. Even Herzfeld is content to demonstrate unmistakable similarities between Greek and Italian evidence, and is able to represent the ethical values of three otherwise distinct Greek cultures as 'points on a continuum', differing behavioural norms 'within a common terminological tradition' (1980, 348). He also, despite nominalist protestations, seems intent on operationally defining honour in terms of hospitality (1987a).

On the final count, we must plead that our discussion, though lengthy, is deliberately narrow in purpose and focus. As part of our primarily historical enquiry into Mediterranean unity, it has seemed task enough to draw inevitably crude comparisons using accounts of honour ranging from Japan to Portugal, without also exploring the tangled web of underlying political and ideological patterns. We have not, for instance, attempted to engage with the full agenda of feminist anthropological theory.

Debate can pause there, although it can hardly be expected to end. The Mediterranean is rather like a member of that class of ethical terms which was defined by the philosopher W. B. Gallie (1956). It is an 'essentially contested concept': no definition can fail to be controversial. As we have argued throughout, the region is only loosely unified, distinguishable from its neighbours to degrees that vary with time, geographical direction and topic. Its boundaries are not of the sort to be drawn easily on a map. Its continuities are best thought of as continuities of form or pattern, within which all is mutability.

In this volume we have mostly been concerned to begin with the microecology and work outward from there, from the smallest unit of analysis. But the study of honour and shame can be seen as a transitional phase in the overall argument. The direct evidence for non-aristocratic honour just assembled will be complemented, in Volume 2, by the indirect evidence of demographic history. More generally, the far-flung cultural comparisons of the present chapter anticipate the view of the Mediterranean from the 'outside in' that will be adopted in several other parts of the successor tome.

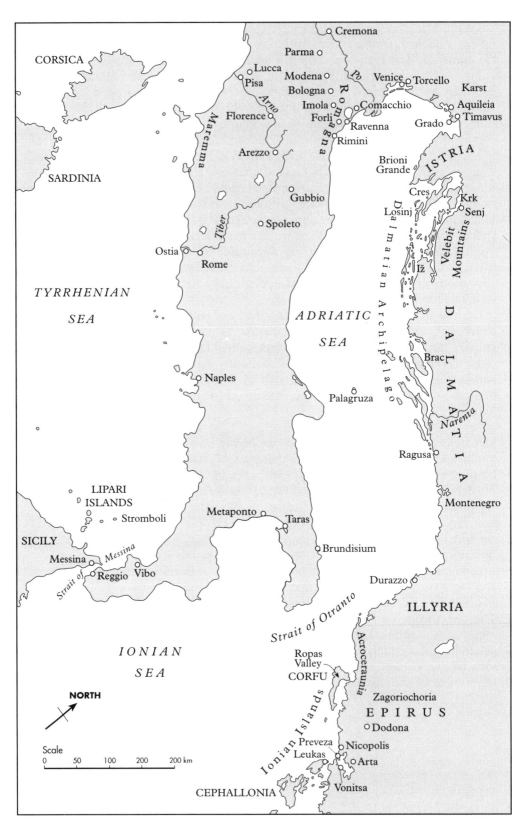

Map 29 The Adriatic region

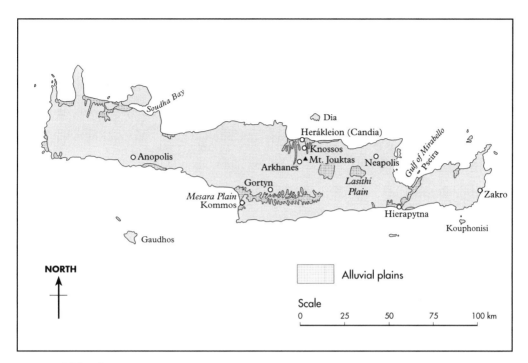

Map 30A Crete

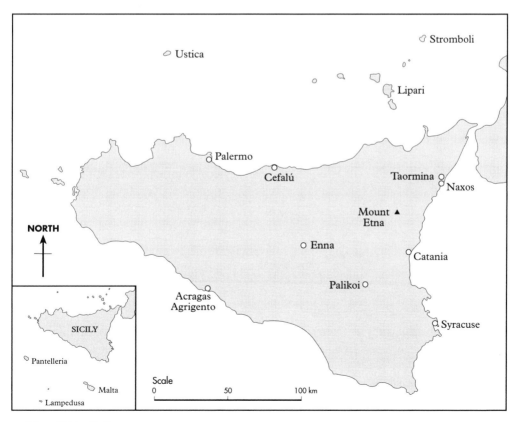

Map 30B Sicily

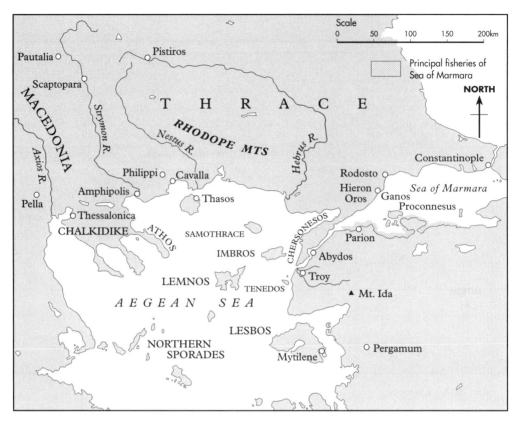

Map 31A The Hellespontine region

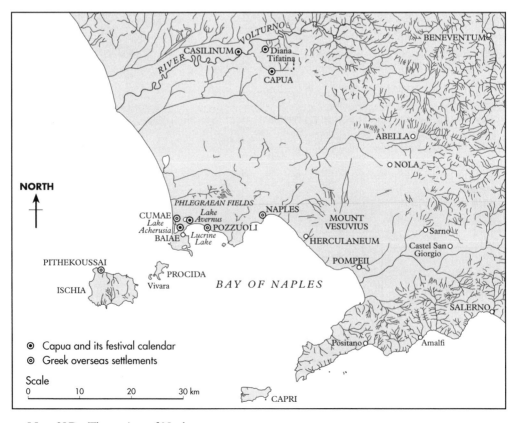

Map 31B The region of Naples

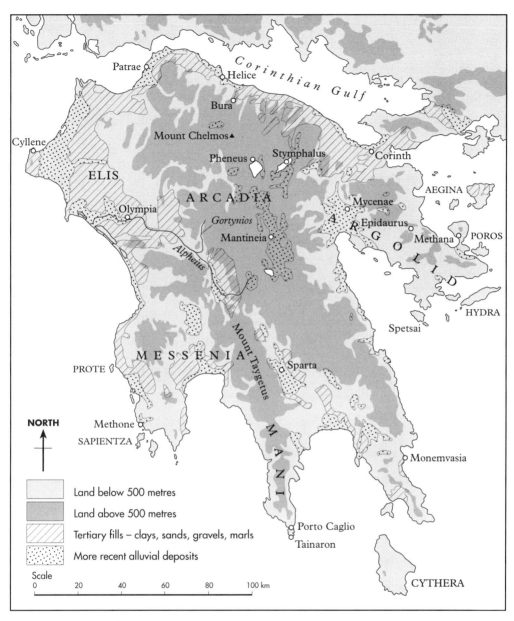

Map 32 The Peloponnese

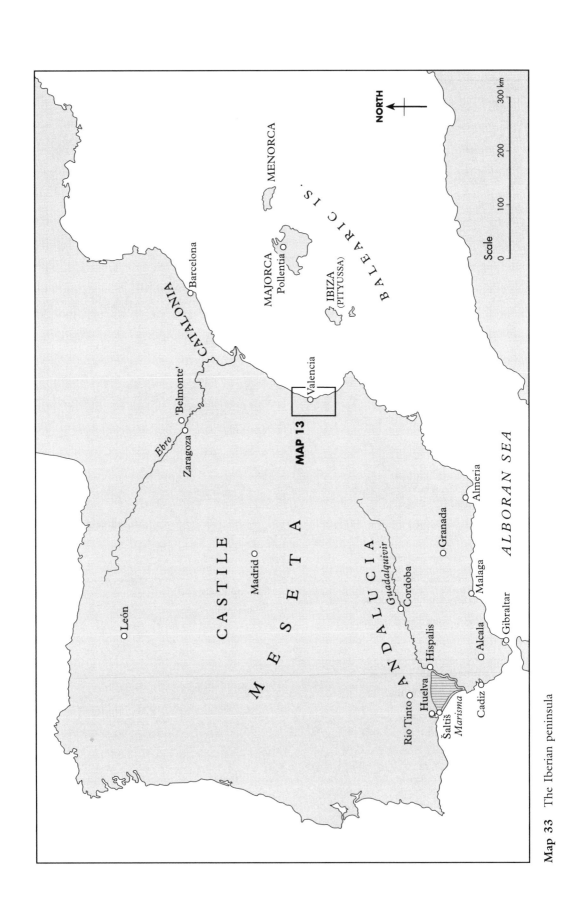

Map 33 The Iberian peninsula

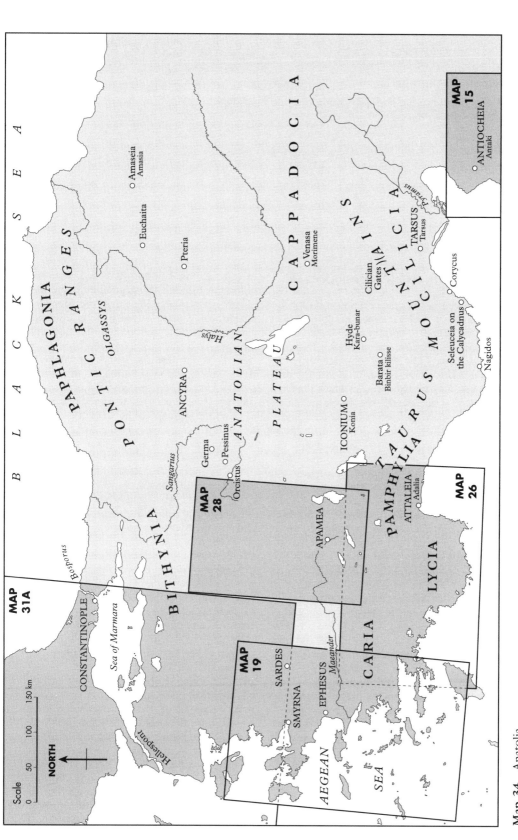

Map 34   Anatolia

A GEOGRAPHICAL EXPRESSION

1. WHAT IS THE MEDITERRANEAN?

The origins of the unified designation for the sea itself are well examined in Burr (1952) *Nostrum Mare: Ursprung und Geschichte der Namen des Mittelmeeres und seiner Teilmeere im Altertum*. The world of maritime communications of the first half of the first millennium B.C. is the context in which the term *koine* came to refer to the whole milieu of cultural, social and economic interchanges. See Braun (1982) 'The Greeks in the Near East', and Purcell (1990a) 'Mobility and the Polis'. For the term *Great Sea*, Burr (1952) 80–5. For the early origin of the navigational devices of the *periplous* (in the fourth-century text, with fifth-century antecedents, known as Pseudo-Scylax) see Peretti (1979) *Il periplo di Scilace: studio sul primo portolano del Mediterraneo*, making (11) the distinction that we have used between empirical and learned geographies. See also Dilke (1985) *Greek and Roman Maps*, 130–44; for the Mediterranean as a list of harbours, Strabo, *Geography*, 1.1.21 (but cf. IX.7). On the literary background of the ancient windrose, Kaibel (1885) 'Antike Windrosen'. See also Murray (1995) 'Ancient sailing winds in the eastern Mediterranean: the case for Cyprus'. Obrist (1997) 'Wind diagrams and medieval cosmology', is now essential for understanding the important contribution made to medieval conceptions of space by the legacy of ancient wind theories.

That the perceptions which we discuss really amount to a proper conception of the Mediterranean in Antiquity is doubted in the important and interesting paper of Shavit (1988) 'The Mediterranean world and "Mediterraneanism": the origins, meaning, and application of a geo-cultural notion in Israel'. In what follows, we shall not engage directly and explicitly with his argument that 'the Mediterranean world' must be construed as a united and uniform entity for the term to have any meaning, and that this world has been *solely* created 'at the historian's and geographer's desks and in the imagination of artists and men of letters' (98) chiefly in the nineteenth century. Our (implicitly) attempted refutation of that argument spans the whole book; and we do not seek to uncover the cultural unity and uniformity that Shavit takes to be the essential characteristics of such a world. We prefer to endorse his rather different definition of unity in systemic terms (98–9): 'unity . . . is achieved when and where continuous and stable patterns of interdependence exist, and this interdependence extends to a range of components. It must be more intensive, stronger and more effective than the mutual dependence existing between the component parts of the particular system and other cultural systems . . .' We hope to show that the Mediterranean has variously satisfied that criterion in prehistoric, ancient, and medieval times.

Even at the learned level, the evidence of the normal parlance of geographers, historians and literary authors in general seems to confirm that there was indeed a consciousness of the unity of the area over a very long period, while the increasingly well-understood subject of cognitive geography enables us to perceive the likely character of more widely diffused perceptions. Janni (1984) *La mappa e il periplo: cartografia antica e spazio odologico*, is the most relevant study in this area. For an attempt to apply the techniques of cognitive geography and Janni's idea of 'hodological space' to Roman ideas of the parts of the Italian peninsula that Rome conquered in the middle Republic, see Purcell (1990b) 'The creation of provincial landscape: the Roman impact on Cisalpine Gaul'. The idea of the Mediterranean as a river – connected to the other watercourses of the world-ocean, to the features that *we* think of as rivers, and to the strange underground waters of mythology – is discussed further in Volume 2. For the related geographical concept of 'oppositeness', fundamental to the ancient Mediterranean sense of topography, as in the notion of *peraia*, see especially Dilke (1985) 74–5 (also V.2). For coastwise trade as riverine see V.3. For background, Downs and Stea (1973) *Image and Environment: Cognitive Mapping and Spatial Behaviour*, (1977) *Maps in Mind: Reflections on Cognitive Mapping*; Buttimer and Seamon (1980) *The Human Experience of Space and Place*. Application to other navigational systems: Frake (1985) 'Cognitive maps of time and tide'; and A. Gell (1985) 'How to read a map: remarks on the practical logic of navigation'. Compare Helms (1988) *Ulysses' Sail*. On problems of prehistoric navigation, Broodbank (1993) 'Ulysses without sails: trade, distance, knowledge and power in the early Cyclades'; Cline (1994) *Sailing the Wine-Dark Sea*. For an older approach to the science of navigation see E. G. R. Taylor (1956) *The Haven-Finding Art*.

For Greek ideas of 'Our Sea', Burr (1952) 106–7; compare Rougé (1981) *Ships and Fleets of the Ancient Mediterranean*, 41–5. Agathemerus the ancient geographer in fact distinguished *twenty-one* Mediterraneans. Much has been written about the conceptual sub-division of the world in Antiquity. On the 'Far West' see P. Fabre (1981) *Les Grecs et la connaissance de l'occident*. For the Romans, Nicolet (1988) *L'inventaire du monde*, is now fundamental. Some wrong approaches to the Greek precursors are discussed in Prontera (1981) 'A proposito del libro di Pédech sulla geografia dei Greci'. For a general context see Cordano (1993) *La geografia degli antichi*.

On Rome as a Mediterranean empire see also Garnsey and Saller (1987) *The Roman Empire: Economy, Society, and Culture*, 5–19; and Rubin (1986) 'The Mediterranean and the dilemma of the Roman Empire in late Antiquity'. For some possible links between mapmaking and political power in the late Republic and early Empire see Wiseman (1987) 'Julius Caesar and the Hereford world map'. Further II.1, V.3.

For the subject of cartography as political expression as a whole, Harley and Woodward (1987–) *The History of Cartography*, is proving fundamental. Compare also Buisseret (1992) *Monarchs, Ministers and Maps: The Emergence of Cartography as a Tool of Government in Early Modern Europe*.

On medieval maps, Wiseman (1987) again; E. G. R. Taylor (1956); Delatte (1947, 1958) *Les portolans grecs*; Kahane, Kahane and Bremner (1967) *Glossario degli antichi portolani italiani*; Kretschmer (1909) *Die italienischen Portolane des Mittelalters* (a landmark in the scholarship of its subject); Mollat du Jourdin et al. (1984) *Portulans: Sea Charts of the Early Explorers* (note 11: 'empiricism and experience prevail where formerly the conceptual dominated'); Udovitch (1978) 'Time, the sea and society: duration of commercial voyages on the southern shores of the Mediterranean during the High Middle Ages'; Randles (1980) *De la terre plate au globe terrestre: une mutation épistémologique rapide, 1480–1520*; Dalché (1995), *Carte marine et portulan au XIIe siècle*; and especially T. Campbell (1987) 'Portolan charts from the late thirteenth century to 1500'. This last account rightly rejects the idea of an origin for the portolan in the *learned* geography of Antiquity, and associates it rather with practical navigational skills. Such skills too are ancient: see for example Peretti (1979); note also the diagrammatic representation of distances from Delos and Rhodes in the *Stadiasmus Maris Magni* (on which see Dilke (1985) 140).

For zones of coherent practice in nautical craftsmanship, which together, through overlap and mutual influence, make up a further way in which the unity of the region has been *conceived*, Bonino (1978) *Archeologia e tradizione navale tra la Romagna e il Po*; McGrail and Kentley (1985) *Sewn plank boats*; Lixa Filgueras (1988) *Local Boats*; Heers (1958) 'Types de navire et spécialisation des trafics en Méditerranée à la fin du moyen âge'; Pryor (1988) *Geography, Technology, and War: Studies in the Maritime History of the Mediterranean, 649–1571*, ch. 2. Matvejević (1991) *Mediterraneo: un nuovo breviario*, is in part a sustained meditation on the history of Mediterranean nautical vocabulary. For the Mediterranean *koine* of such vocabulary see V.2. Also BE V.3.

On associated harbour technology, see for instance Raban (1985) *Harbour Archaeology*; Rickman and Raban (1988) 'The archaeology and history of Roman ports'; Blackman (1988b) 'Bollards and men'; Gertwagen (1988) 'The Venetian port of Candia' (BE IX.7).

The 'Odyssean' Mediterranean: fundamental to our argument about the nature of the Mediterranean is the relative ease of transportation by sea. Purcell (1990a) 'Mobility and the Polis', includes some reflections on an opposing view: that ancient societies shunned the sea. Compare Holland Rose (1933) *The Mediterranean in the Ancient World*, 1–32, making a vigorous case, principally on the foundation of the *Odyssey*, for envisaging this sea rather as 'a nursery for navigation'. Some medieval *testimonia*: Deluz (1987) 'Pèlerins et voyageurs face à la mer (XIIe–XVIe siècles)'. The classic statement of the 'fluidity' of ancient sea-communications, based on a deduction from Diocletian's Edict of Maximum Prices (A.D. 301) about the very high relative cost of land transport in Antiquity, is A. H. M. Jones (1964) *The Later Roman Empire*, 841–2. See further V.4, IX.4. Here it should be firmly stated that our remarks on ease of communication and transportation (later amplified under the sign of 'connectivity') must be understood as *relative*. The Mediterranean is a dangerous, unpredictable, stormy and violent body of water, and has been deservedly feared throughout history. Generalization about the efficiency of connections across it hides innumerable wrecks and enormous human misery. That communications between Aegean islands were 'easy' enough for early cultural development to be greatly facilitated (Renfrew and Wagstaff (1982) *An Island Polity: The Archaeology of Exploitation in Melos*) in a sea renowned for its dangerous unpredictability (Slot (1982) *Archipelagus Turbatus*, 20) is an exemplary paradox to be constantly borne in mind (VI.11; IX.3–4). That people have persevered is ample testimony to the underlying importance of the sea; but sailing on it has seldom been undertaken without precautions or trepidation.

On the modern physical geography of the Mediterranean still basic in many ways is Philippson (1904) *Das Mittelmeergebiet: seine geographische und kulturelle Eigenart*. The traditions to which that work should be related – the history, that is, of geographical conceptions of the Mediterranean subsequent to those of the ancient writers already cited – deserve fuller investigation; but a synoptic work on this topic seems yet to be written. See again, provisionally, T. Campbell (1987) and the other works noticed above on the medieval European cartographic tradition. Also J. K. Wright (1965) *The Geographical Lore of the Time of the Crusades*, a dense and valuable survey; Kimble (1938) *Geography in the Middle Ages*; and further references in bibliographies to chs. 6 and 9 of Fernández-Armesto (1987) *Before Columbus*.

The Muslim coasts of the medieval Mediterranean are excellently served by Miquel (1967–88) *La géographie humaine du monde musulmane jusqu'au milieu du XIe siècle*. See 2.377–9, 532, on the tradition of seeing the region as a unity and on its rival currents of thought. Also, conveniently, Miquel (1980) 'Origine et carte des mers dans la géographie arabe'. The ancient Arabic term for the Mediterranean is 'The Sea of the Romans [meaning Greeks]', first used especially of the eastern Mediterranean and gradually extended westwards in scope; see *EI*, 'Bahr al-Rūm', and Lewicki (1965) 'L'apport des sources arabes médiévales (IXe–Xe siècles) à la connaissance de l'Europe centrale et orientale', 464–6. For the Byzantine perspective, the entry 'Mediterranean sea' in *ODB* confirms that the inhabitants of the eastern empire had names for only the parts of the sea; they did not generally refer to it as a whole.

The apparent relative lack of learned interest in the Mediterranean as a distinct 'geographical expression' in the early modern period can be gauged from de Dainville (1940) *La géographie des humanistes*. Compare, though, the cartographic history (in the post-modern manner) included in Matvejević (1991) *Mediterraneo: un nuovo breviario*. The two volumes of E. G. R. Taylor – (1930) *Tudor Geography, 1485–1583*, and (1934) *Later Tudor and Early Stuart Geography, 1583–1650* – are also of more than local interest. Modern thinking about the Mediterranean has its roots in the works of the great geographers of the nineteenth century. See generally Dickinson and Howarth (1933) *The Making of Geography*; R. E. Dickinson (1969) *The Makers of Modern Geography*.

The Mediterranean makes some appearance as a discrete subject in the writings of Carl Ritter (1779–1859). R. E. Dickinson (1969) ch. 3, provides a useful introduction; for a fuller account see Beck (1979) *Carl Ritter: Genius der Geographie*; also Shavit (1988) 102–3. More significant in this context is Friedrich Ratzel (1844–1904), whose interest in the Mediterranean as a region began with an exploration of its zoology. See Dickinson (1969) ch. 5; Steinmetzler (1956) *Die Anthropogeographie Friedrich Ratzels und ihre ideengeschichtlichen Wurzeln*; Wanklyn (1961) *Friedrich Ratzel: A Biographical Memoir and Bibliography*. Ratzel's anthropogeography, his version of environmental determinism, yielded an idea which in his own time was to add intellectual legitimacy to German imperial expansionism and was to have a greater posthumous significance – the idea of *Lebensraum*. For a Marxist analysis of Ratzel's contribution to social Darwinism and German imperial expansion, see Peet (1985) 'The social origins of environmental determinism'.

This is the background against which to locate Alfred Philippson (1864–1955): R. E. Dickinson (1969) 142–4. Philippson's (1939) *Das Byzantinische Reich als geographische Erscheinung*, reveals a neglected aspect of his historical scholarship. His geography of Greece (1950–9) *Die griechischen Landschaften*, the product of extensive travel and intimate local knowledge, still repays reading. On all these figures further bibliography can be had from *Deutsches Literatur-Lexikon*. The work of Semple (1932) *The Geography of the Mediterranean Region: Its Relation to Ancient History*, which we quote in II.1, also belongs here. Buttimer (1971) *Society and Milieu in the French Geographic Tradition*, brings out the connections between German and French thought, important for understanding the intellectual parentage of Braudel (see further BE II.2). Peet (1985) shows how Semple introduced Ratzel's ideas into American geography while trying to soften their political implications.

Among more recent surveys we should first mention Birot (1964) *La Méditerranée et le moyen Orient*, which remains the major modern synthesis. For a comparable historical geography, although of only part of the region, see Delano Smith (1979) *Western Mediterranean Europe*. Girgis (1987) *Mediterranean Africa*, is a far more rudimentary handbook. Cary (1949) *The Geographic Background of Greek and Roman History*, is still the most widely known synopsis from a classical scholar. Among a substantial number of

less original monographs we may note: East (1940) *Mediterranean Problems*; D. S. Walker (1962) *The Mediterranean Lands*; Branigan and Jarrett (1969) *The Mediterranean Lands*; Stanley (1972) *The Mediterranean Sea*; Isnard (1973) *Pays et paysages méditerranéens*; Beckinsale and Beckinsale (1975) *Southern Europe: A Systematic Geographical Study*; Dufourcq (1975) *La vie quotidienne dans les pays méditerranéens*. Among geographical journals we should mention the relatively long-established *Méditerranée: revue géographique des pays méditerranéens* (1960); see especially vol. 79 (1994) including an issue on 'l'arc méditerranéen en question', the arc being that formed by the sea's north-western coastal nations.

Climate: a useful survey is to be found in Amouretti (1986) *Le pain et l'huile*, 17–28. See also the avowedly Braudellian introduction to the topic in Pryor (1988) *Geography, Technology, and War*. For interannual variation some figures in Garnsey (1988a) *Famine and Food Supply in the Graeco-Roman World*, 8–18. For an instance of the difficulty of determining the boundary of the Mediterranean in this respect, Crumley (1987) 'Historical ecology', on Burgundy. See further BE V.4. We return to the climatic history of the Mediterranean in Volume 2.

On the Platonic image with which we began of Mediterranean peoples as frogs round a pond, we add only that it was turned by the pagan Celsus into a derogatory description of early Christian communities. See Origen, *Against Celsus*, 4.23.

2. COLLECTIVITIES AND SUBDIVISIONS I: THE CHALLENGE OF THE CONTINENTS

A time when the Cold War is over, and when 'the idea of Europe' as a political entity is more widely and vociferously debated than ever before, may be an appropriate one for a sceptical enquiry into the usefulness of Europe as a historiographical demarcation. Encouragement may be drawn from an unexpected quarter: Herodotus (*Histories*, 4.45). As an inheritor of the more unifying world-view that had been evolved by the Ionian Greeks of western Asia Minor, he was puzzled why three distinct names (equivalent to Europe, Africa, and Asia) should have been given to what is really a single landmass. Yet even Herodotus

– 'the father of history' – felt that he had to go on using the tripartite division which custom had made familiar. In contrast, Braudel's unexpectedly Eurocentric notion of the 'three great peninsulas', Spain, Italy, Greece, seems deliberately to perpetuate exactly the sort of category that his work is generally devoted to challenging (1972a, 162–7).

For a systematic survey of the use of the term 'Europe' from the fifth to the end of the eleventh century, see J. Fischer (1957) *Oriens-Occidens-Europa*. A brief but useful account of the emergence of 'the idea of Europe' from that of Latin Christendom in the later medieval period, and something of its subsequent fate as both a political and a geographical expression, is offered by Hay (1968) *Europe: The Emergence of an Idea*, and, more vividly, by Hale (1993) *The Civilization of Europe in the Renaissance*, ch. 1. See also the lively introduction to N. Davies (1996) *Europe: A History*. For more thorough scrutiny of particular phases of the idea, see *Past and Present* 137 (1992) special issue, *The Cultural and Political Construction of Europe*, especially the contributions by Leyser, 'Concepts of Europe in the Early and High Middle Ages' (25–47) and S. Woolf, 'The construction of a European world-view in the revolutionary–Napoleonic years' (72–101). See also Cuisenier (1979) *Europe as a Culture Area*; and Chabod (1964) *Storia dell'Idea d'Europa*.

On Christendom, Herrin (1987) *The Formation of Christendom*, offers a detailed narrative of the political and ecclesiastical events from which the idea arose during the early Middle Ages. Brown (1996) *The Rise of Western Christendom*, offers a characteristically vivid narrative of the Christianizing of Atlantic Europe.

Europe as a distinct historiographical subject emerges much later than 'the idea' – during the eighteenth-century Enlightenment and the Romantic movement, for example with Montesquieu, Voltaire and Guizot. And the regular addition to this mainstream of historical writing (which mostly confined itself to western Europe) of scholarly work on Scandinavia, eastern Europe or Russia is an even more recent phenomenon. For the young Leopold von Ranke, for instance, the Europe of the 'Romano-Germanic peoples' was the intelligible unit of study (as it was later to be for Arnold Toynbee in his (1934–61) *A Study of History*). Note the title of Ranke (1824) *Geschichte der Romanischen und Germanischen Völker von 1494 bis 1514* [*History of the Latin and Germanic Peoples* . . .]. On the question of whether Europe really is an intelligible unit of study, cf. Halecki (1950) *The Limits and Divisions of European History*; and Okey (1992) 'Central Europe/Eastern Europe: behind the definitions'. Compare the separation of Romano-Germanic West from Slavic East in the analysis of P. Anderson (1974) *Passages from Antiquity to Feudalism*. G. R. Elton (1985) 'Europe and the Reformation', is a stimulating essay on the forces promoting, respectively, unity and fragmentation on the continent – on both sides, medieval and modern, of the 'great divide' that Elton discerns in the Reformation. Notable in the present context is his definition of modern, self-conscious, Europe (between the Reformation and 1945). He sees it in terms (i) of the international order of mutually suspicious nation-states, (ii) of the vitality of capitalism, waning as one proceeds away from Britain, France and Germany in any direction, and (iii) of a world of ideas dominated by the natural sciences and historicism. N. Davies (1996) *Europe: A History*, is a sustained, witty and effective plea for a vision of the past that gives full weight to eastern Europe. For a prehistorian's view see Rowlands (1987) 'The concept of Europe in prehistory'; Randsborg (1992) 'Barbarians, classical Antiquity and the rise of western Europe: an archaeological essay'. The creation of a predominantly Latin Christian Europe through internal colonization during the period *c*.950–1350 is the theme of an excellent interpretative survey by Bartlett (1993) *The Making of Europe*.

We can note here that attempts by anthropologists to reassert the integrity of Europe as a field of study do not rest on new or powerful conceptual foundations: increased economic interdependence and information exchange between European states, at a time, however, when all such contacts, worldwide, are also becoming more intense (Goddard et al. (1994) *The Anthropology of Europe*, 24–7, 86 with references).

The European Miracle: Crone (1989) *Pre-industrial Societies*, offers a valuable select bibliography and a brief statement (149–50) of the Romantic theme of unity in diversity – a theme that had been enunciated by Guizot's lectures at the Sorbonne in the 1820s. See also E. L. Jones (1981) *The European Miracle: Environments, Economies and Geo-Politics in the History of Europe and Asia*; Gellner

(1988) *Plough, Sword and Book: The Structure of Human History*. Goody (1996) *The East in the West*, tellingly challenges many earlier sociological explanations of the presumed 'uniqueness of the West'. For some medieval anticipations of this theme of European superiority see Leyser (1992) 'Concepts of Europe in the early and high Middle Ages', 34, 37–8. For the effects of Eurocentrism on the historiography of technology see Chapter VII. On Guizot's thought D. Johnson (1963) *Guizot*.

Early Islamic geographical traditions and perceptions (of the Mediterranean and elsewhere) can be traced through Miquel (1967–88) *La géographie humaine du monde musulmane*. Some medieval European perceptions are recorded by Southern (1962) *Western Views of Islam in the Middle Ages*. On the political 'Orientalism' that has had a considerable part to play in the definition of the modern Middle East, see Said (1978) *Orientalism*, and, as a sample of the debate which that book provoked, Lewis and Said (1982) 'Orientalism: an exchange'. Also pertinent is Kabbani (1986) *Europe's Myths of Orient*. For a review of the whole controversy Freitag (1997) 'The critique of orientalism'.

A comparable analysis of the political presuppositions of what the author defines as 'Mediterraneanism' has been offered by, among others, Herzfeld (1987b) *Anthropology through the Looking-Glass* (see further XII.1). Note also the attempt (in effect) to redress the balance, by emphasizing the 'oriental', particularly Phoenician and Egyptian, component in early classical civilization, in the multi-volume polemic of Bernal (1987–) *Black Athena*, adumbrated in Bernal (1989) 'First by land, then by sea'; compare Lefkowitz and Rogers (1996) *Black Athena Revisited*. European Orientalism and Mediterraneanism finds a counterpart in the indigenous Mediterraneanism of some of the countries of the sea's coastlands today: see Shavit (1988) for the Israeli perspective; and for the Egyptian, Hourani (1962) *Arabic Thought in the Liberal Age, 1797–1939*, especially 324–40 on the liberal views of Taha Husayn (born 1889) who envisaged Egypt as part of a Mediterranean, classical West.

Modern western scholarly definitions of the Middle East can be sampled in: Patai (1952) 'The Middle East as a culture area'; Keddi (1973) 'Is there a Middle East?'; Lewis and Holt (1962) *Historians of the Middle East*,

1–3; and B. Lewis (1988–9) 'The map of the Middle East', stressing the discontinuities of Middle Eastern history and the ultimate meaninglessness of the term. How much is excluded from conventional general histories, implicitly written from the standpoint of empires based on the plains, is suggested by the projected work announced by Fowden (1990a) 'Religious developments in late Roman Lycia', 347 n.10: *The Mountain Crescent: Missing Dimensions of Middle Eastern History*.

Anthropological approaches: Eickelman (1998) *The Middle East*, in this, the third, edition of the book, adding the former Soviet Central Asia to his purview, and thus admitting contingent political frontiers into his definition of the region; Gulick (1983) *The Middle East: An Anthropological Perspective*, which is unusual in including a systematic examination of proposed boundaries as well as defining characteristics. Contrast the crisis of confidence in all such definitions that has been wrought by post-modernist anthropology, and that is described, with admirable scepticism, in Lindholm (1995) 'The new Middle Eastern ethnography'. (Lindholm's (1996) *The Islamic Middle East*, seems a reversion to an older tradition of searching for shared cultural traits.) The views of geographers: Beaumont et al. (1976) *The Middle East: A Geographical Study*; Wagstaff (1985) *The Evolution of Middle Eastern Landscapes: An Outline to A.D. 1840*. The feasibility of separating the Mediterranean territory of Islam from the rest is asserted by a collaborative research project sponsored by the European Science Foundation under the title 'Individual and society in the Muslim Mediterranean world'; its first *Newsletter* was published in January 1997.

The general question of bounding the Mediterranean will form a principal theme of Volume 2. For 'all-pervasive religiosity' (ecologically construed) as a way of defining the Mediterranean, rather than the Middle East, see Chapter X.

3. COLLECTIVITIES AND SUBDIVISIONS II: THE MEDITERRANEAN DISINTEGRATED

On *klimata*, beside Nicolet (1988) cited in the text, see J. K. Wright (1965) *The Geographical Lore of the Time of the Crusades*; for medieval Arab traditions, Harley and Woodward (1987–) *The History of Cartography*, 2.102,

146–8, and Miquel (1967–88) *La géographie humaine du monde musulmane*, 1.12; 2.56–60.

Human and physical geography as currently practised: compare section on modern physical geography above. To our knowledge, there has been no detailed and authoritative geographical survey of even half the Mediterranean since that of J. M. Houston (1964) *The Western Mediterranean World: An Introduction to its Regional Landscapes*; though cf. Margalef (1985) *Western Mediterranean*, for some more recent oceanography. On the whole, however, geographers apparently lost interest in the Mediterranean just as historical concern with it quickened.

Political science and economics – a sample from a large body of writings: Pinkele and Pollis (1983) *The Contemporary Mediterranean World*; Luciani (1984) *The Mediterranean Region: Economic Interdependence and the Future of Society*; A. Williams (1984) *Southern Europe Transformed: Political and Economic Change in Greece, Italy, Portugal, and Spain*; Nachmani (1987) *Israel, Turkey, and Greece: Uneasy Relations in the Eastern Mediterranean*; Chipman (1988) *NATO's Southern Allies: Internal and External Challenges*; R. O'Neill (1988) *Prospects for Security in the Mediterranean*.

Ecological concerns: Grenon and Batisse (1989) *Futures for the Mediterranean Basin: 'The Blue Plan'*; Haas (1990) *Saving the Mediterranean: The Politics of International Environmental Cooperation*. For an appeal to some stock images (as well as to Braudel) see Boxer (1983) 'Environment and regional identity'.

The tradition of popular writing, which perhaps does more to preserve the Mediterranean as a unified subject than do many academic disciplines, has, paradoxically, often proved less reliant on cliché and predictable quotation: Attenborough (1987) *The First Eden*, and Arenson (1990) *The Encircled Sea*, between them cover a wide variety of topics, including the geological and faunal history of the region, as well as an outline of its political and economic history, and both have some vivid illustrations. Fox (1991) *The Inner Sea: The Mediterranean and its People*, is less stimulating: a country-by-country combination of potted historical background and interviews with notable local figures.

Political frontiers: Febvre (1973a) '*Frontière*: the word and the concept', remains funda-

mental. Examples of the complexity of Mediterranean or near-Mediterranean frontiers in their relation to politics, society and environment: Whittaker (1983a) 'Trade and frontiers of the Roman empire', foreshadowing Whittaker (1994) *Frontiers of the Roman Empire*; Elton (1996) *Frontiers of the Roman Empire*; various contributions to Bartlett and MacKay (1989) *Medieval Frontier Societies*; Hess (1978) *The Forgotten Frontier: A History of the Sixteenth-Century Ibero-African Frontier* (hostile to notions of Mediterranean unity; cf. Faroqhi (1990–1) 'In search of Ottoman history'); P. Sahlins (1989) *Boundaries: The Making of France and Spain in the Pyrenees*, showing how villages either side of the frontier created by the Treaty of the Pyrenees of 1659 were in some respects brought closer together by their political separation, despite divergent national sentiments. Braudel (1988–90) *The Identity of France*, vol. 1, chs. 9–10, uses frontiers as a test case. An anthropological investigation of two adjacent Alpine villages, both formally part of Italy yet one of them German in allegiance, shows how far cultural frontiers may affect areas of homogeneous ecology: Cole and Wolf (1974) *The Hidden Frontier: Ecology and Ethnicity in an Alpine Valley*. On the most significant of Mediterranean frontiers, and some possible geographical explanations of it, see the brief but thoughtful essay by Issawi (1981a) 'The Christian–Muslim frontier in the Mediterranean: a history of two peninsulas'.

Our allusion to the 'anomaly' of Muslim Spain is intended to recall the great debate within modern Spanish historiography about the contribution of Islam to Spanish history in the long run (cf. VII.2 for some of its continuing repercussions). This debate can be sampled in Castro (1971) *The Spaniards*, and Sánchez-Albornoz (1975) *Spain: A Historical Enigma*. Glick (1979) *Islamic and Christian Spain in the Early Middle Ages*, offers some corrective. The medieval origins of the debate are amply treated by Linehan (1993) *History and the Historians of Medieval Spain*.

Mediterranean empires (VII.6): *Les Phéniciens et le monde méditerranéen* (1986), an exhibition catalogue that provides a useful conspectus; Niemeyer (1982) *Phönizier im Westen*; Aubet (1993) *The Phoenicians and the West*; Pippidi (1976) *Assimilation et résistance à la culture gréco-romaine dans le monde ancien*; Nicolet (1977–8) *Rome et la conquête du monde méditerranéen*; Garnsey and Saller (1987) *The Roman Empire*, ch. 1; Sartre and Tranoy (1990) *La Méditerranée antique*, raising the question of how far the sea has divided rather than united. C. Mango (1980) *Byzantium*, on the question of the 'Greekness' of the Byzantine Empire; Fernández-Armesto (1987) *Before Columbus*, for a general survey of medieval Mediterranean empires. The equal significance of the Fertile Crescent for ancient empire-builders is forcefully argued by Fowden (1993) *Empire to Commonwealth*; see also Z. Rubin (1986) 'The Mediterranean and the dilemma of the Roman empire'.

Trevor-Roper (1972) 'Fernand Braudel, the *Annales*, and the Mediterranean', is one of those who have spoken, in interesting terminology from the cognitive geographer's point of view, of the various powers who have regarded the Mediterranean as their lake. This has been a common perspective on ancient history, thanks no doubt to Thucydides (*History*, 1.6; cf. Herodotus, *Histories*, 3.122). See Myres (1906) 'On the list of "Thalassocracies" in Eusebius'; and Momigliano (1960) 'Sea-power in Greek thought'. Prehistorians have applied the idea to various seaborne cultural collectivities; for an instance see Sandars (1978) *The Sea Peoples*. On Roman sea power, Holland Rose (1933) *The Mediterranean in the Ancient World*; Starr (1982) *The Roman Empire*; Reddé (1986) *Mare Nostrum*; Rickman (1996) 'Mare nostrum'. Reddé argues

(660) that sea power was 'une composante essentielle, non un luxe inutile' for the Roman Empire. A. R. Lewis (1951) *Naval Power and Trade in the Mediterranean A.D. 500–1100*, is an example of the writing of Mediterranean history in terms of one thalassocracy after another. See also the brief outline in Mollat du Jourdin (1993) *Europe and the Sea*. On the Spanish medieval thalassocracies, Hillgarth (1975) *The Problem of a Catalan Mediterranean Empire, 1229–1327*, with further bibliography.

For the role of redistribution in prehistoric state-formation, Renfrew (1972) *The Emergence of Civilization: The Cyclades and the Aegean in the Third Millennium B.C.*, remains classic; but see the discussion in van Andel and Runnels (1988) 'An essay on the "emergence of civilization" in the Aegean world'; Runnels and van Andel (1988) 'Trade and the origins of agriculture in the eastern Mediterranean', and VII.4. Under the sign of interactionism, Sherratt (1995a) 'Reviving the grand narrative: archaeology and long-term change', also revives long-distance trade as the motor of prehistory in general. Compare the differentiation of Mediterranean from northern Europe in the diffusion of farming in Whittle (1985) *Neolithic Europe*, and G. W. W. Barker (1985) *Prehistoric Farming in Europe*. See also Guilaine (1994), *La mer partagée: la Méditerranée avant l'écriture*, its stance revealed in its title.

BIBLIOGRAPHICAL ESSAY TO CHAPTER II

A HISTORIAN'S MEDITERRANEAN

Mediterranean landscape and environment: for the identification of the Mediterranean region with the agriculture of olive and vine see BE I.1, with VI.9; for mountain environments see III.6, V.4.

1. THE IMAGINARY SEA

The scholarly disciplines of classics and ancient history have played a large part in producing some of the more influential synoptic accounts of Mediterranean history. A notable, though heavily deterministic, work, is Semple (1932) *The Geography of the Mediterranean Region: Its Relation to Ancient History*, with its quasi-Braudellian epigraph from Ecclesiastes ('One generation passeth away and another generation cometh, but the earth abideth for ever'). For the intellectual and political background to Semple's work in nineteenth-century German geography, see Semple (1911) *Influences of Geographic Environment on the Basis of Ratzel's System of Anthropo-geography*; Peet (1985) 'The social origins of environmental determinism' (I.1).

Newbigin (1924) *The Mediterranean Lands*, 5–6, explicitly links her studying Mediterranean geography to the task of understanding the classical world. On the whole, those classicists who could have produced syntheses have left their work in essay form, even where the essays have been collected in volumes devoted to certain themes. Myres (1953) *Geographic History in Greek Lands*, is a case in point, although the blend of physical anthropology, archaeology, geology and geography in Myres's intellectual formation has yielded an interpretation of ancient

Mediterranean unity that deserves wider appreciation. See also Myres (1943) *Mediterranean Culture*. For background, and some idea of the curious physical determinism that Myres occasionally espoused (for instance, the notion that round-headed people wear round hats) see Dunbabin (1955) 'Sir John Myres 1869–1954'. The voluminous output of Louis Robert, mostly written with his wife Jeanne, are a still more recent example (see below).

The 'Romantic Mediterranean': we touch on too many authors and texts to supply all relevant references, some of which are to be had from Shavit (1988) 'The Mediterranean world and "Mediterraneanism"'. The epigraph to the whole book that we take from Cyril Connolly may stand, in its 'inverted Romanticism', as a testimony to the force of the tradition against which it reacts – on which note the salutary brief remarks of Jameson et al. (1994) *A Greek Countryside: The Southern Argolid from Prehistory to the Present Day*, 1–5. Among recent scholarly exemplars of 'Romantic Mediterraneanism' we may note here (rather than in the text) the author quoted most extensively by Shavit (1988, 108–11) who perhaps belongs in the tradition of Myres and Robert, the Jewish scholar-archaeologist-traveller Nahum Slouschz (1872–1966). Slouschz's *The Book of the Seas* was published in Hebrew in 1948, the year before the first appearance of Braudel's *Mediterranean*, the Romanticism of which it apparently quite strikingly anticipates. See also, for some context, Shavit (1987) *The New Hebrew Nation*, 49, 178. One further instance (a fine one) of Romantically charged writing:

'the traveller who drives along the coastline of the Mediterranean, always aware of the grey band of mountains to the North, massive forerunners of the Alps, that dwarf the plains covered with vineyards and the porphyry escarpments heavy with the scent of cistus . . .' (P. Brown (1982b) '*Mohammed and Charlemagne* by Henri Pirenne', 74).

In general we have here profited from: Jenkyns (1980) *The Victorians and Ancient Greece*; F. M. Turner (1981) *The Greek Heritage in Victorian Britain*; Lloyd-Jones (1982) *Blood for the Ghosts*; Dover (1992) *Perceptions of the Ancient Greeks*. We may note only in passing an aspect of Mediterraneanism that involves a bogus physical anthropology: the belief that there was an ur-Mediterranean race whose last representatives can still be identified. For this see Bradley (1912) *Malta and the Mediterranean Race*.

On Cyriaco of Ancona: Ashmole (1959) 'Cyriac of Ancona'; Weiss (1965) *The Renaissance Discovery of Classical Antiquity*; Stoneman (1987) *Land of Lost Gods: The Search for Classical Greece*, ch. 2.

The interconnection of scholarship and Romantic travel: responding in late Victorian Oxford to the mood of German antiquarian geography, travelling with a text of Dante and observing the Sabbath, the learned Tozer, a forerunner of Myres, constituted 'the last and not the least distinguished of the classical tourists', according to W. W. Jackson (1916) 'H. F. Tozer' (obituary). He exemplifies the way in which archaeological and historical scholarship grew out of the tradition of Romantic travel. Cf. Tozer (1882) *Lectures on the Geography of Greece*.

On Hogarth: see Lock (1990) 'D. G. Hogarth (1862–1927)'. Hogarth was concerned with the application to the Levant of his day of the theories connecting race and environment that appear in Herodotus and to which we allude at the beginning of II.1 (cf. Hogarth (1906) 'Geographical conditions affecting population in the east Mediterranean lands'). We return to Sir William Ramsay in Chapter X.

On Louis Robert (1904–1985): see Pouilloux (1986) 'Notice sur la vie et les travaux de Louis Robert'. Robert's Romanticism is well brought out on 360, quoting Robert's *ipsissima verba* of 1984:

il resta un homme de la terre à qui les géographes, le 'grand Vidal de la Blache surtout' [on whom see below, Section 3], comme il disait, avaient enseigné à comprendre les paysages . . . par delà la mer, la mer lentement traversée, il découvrait la Méditerranée, ses terres, ses eaux et sa lumiére, l'architecture des formes sèches et pures, les acropoles rocheuses où danse la chaleur de midi, sièges de cités, de la foule des minuscules états grecs avec l'horizon des garrigues et des forêts de pins sur les montagnes frontières . . .

The Mediterranean was taken by the Romantics as an illustration of the canon of classical literature (contrast our quotation from Disraeli in the text of the chapter with that following the next paragraph below). In modern scholarship, we take this opportunity to note, the opposite case is often made. Stern doubts are expressed as to the autopsy of classical authors – to the effect, for instance, that the landscape of exile in the poems of Ovid purporting to be written from the Danube region represents only an imaginative *mise-en-scène* (cf. Fitton-Brown (1985) 'The unreality of Ovid's Tomitan exile'). Similarly, the naive belief that the modern folkways which entranced the Romantics actually illustrate ancient realities is increasingly questioned (cf. Halstead (1987) 'Traditional and ancient rural economy in Mediterranean Europe: plus ça change?', and Chapters III, VI, X, XI below).

Mediterranean history will always depend heavily on travellers' accounts. See Goudie (1987) 'History and archaeology: the growth of a relationship'; Pemble (1987) *The Mediterranean Passion: Victorians and Edwardians in the South*; Constantine (1984) *Early Greek Travellers and the Hellenic Ideal*; Stoneman (1987) *Land of Lost Gods*; Vryonis (1980) 'Travelers as a source for the societies of the Middle East, 900–1600', for the Byzantine–Muslim world (and some remarks on Friar Felix whom we cite in the chapter). Some useful general remarks by Beard (1985) 'British travel writing in the seventeenth and eighteenth centuries', with bibliography for Italy. For more detail, especially of manuscript accounts, Black (1992) *The British Abroad: The Grand Tour in the Eighteenth Century*; the quotation on 278–9 from the record of his Italian travels left by George Carpenter shows a perhaps unusual scepticism about the supposed continuity of Mediterranean life, but none the less exemplifies the instinct to compare ancient and modern that would be characteristic of Romanticism:

I took a great deal of pleasure in comparing the descriptions that are given us by the ancient authors of particular places ... with what they are at present. I found that time had made such vast alterations in landscapes that it was not easy to know them by the description.

On travel as source of power, considered from a theoretical point of view, some thoughts in Helms (1988) *Ulysses' Sail*, especially ch. 5.

For one striking outcome of this tradition in the art and literature of Europe between *c.*1750 and *c.*1950, see Aldrich (1993) *The Seduction of the Mediterranean: Writing, Art and Homosexual Fantasy.* (Compare, for ancient Greek literature, the rather humourless but enormously full account of erotic maritime imagery in Murgatroyd (1995) 'The sea of love'.) For less heated effects on the popular literature of the Mediterranean, we may refer to Ludwig (1929) *On Mediterranean Shores;* Bradford (1964) *Ulysses Found;* and Carrington (1971) *The Mediterranean: Cradle of Western Culture;* as well as to their successors already noted, such as Attenborough (1987), Arenson (1990) and Matvejević (1991). Given the scale of movement across and within the boundaries of the Mediterranean region (Chapters V and IX) the texts generated by those movements can hardly be ignored by the Mediterranean historian, who has, after all, also been formed by the tradition which they represent.

To our allusion in the text to Eliot's Phlebas in *The Waste Land* we add here an often-quoted word from Dr Johnson:

the grand object of travelling is to see the shores of the Mediterranean. On those shores were the four great Empires of the world; the Assyrian, the Persian, the Grecian, and the Roman. – All our religion, almost all our law, almost all our arts, almost all that sets us above savages, has come to us from the shores of the Mediterranean. (Boswell (1936) *Life of Johnson*, 3.36)

Johnson, along with a number of more recent authors associated with the region, is quoted in a version of the Grand Tourist narrative that reasserts the unity of the region: Theroux's (1995) *The Pillars of Hercules,* an account of a trip, by land, around the Mediterranean coast from Gibraltar to Ceuta that offers (*à la* Cyril Connolly) a jaundiced, *fin de siècle* inversion of Romantic Mediterraneanism.

2. FOUR MEN IN A BOAT

On Rostovtzeff see above all Momigliano (1969a) 'M. I. Rostovtzeff'; G. W. Bowersock (1974) '*The Social and Economic History of the Roman Empire* by Michael Ivanovitch Rostovtzeff'; Wes (1990) *Michael Rostovtzeff, Historian in Exile: Russian Roots in an American Context.* Salmeri (1998) 'Per una lettura dei capitoli V–VII della *Storia economica e sociale dell'impero romano* di M. Rostovtzeff', is a highly sophisticated analysis and an account of the historiographical context. Rostovtzeff envisaged the Mediterranean as united by trade in a network based around such centres as Rhodes or Delos: (1941) *The Social and Economic History of the Hellenistic World,* 1256–8. This network could be explicitly compared with the Hansa of the late Middle Ages (1941, 1268). It reached its peak under Rome, only to decline: (1957) *The Social and Economic History of the Roman Empire,* 470. For a more recent conception of the Mediterranean as the formative core of the Roman empire see Garnsey and Saller (1987) *The Roman Empire,* 5–19. For renewed appreciation of Rostovtzeff's vision of the ancient Roman economy, and a brief comparison between him and Braudel, see Carandini (1986) 'Il mondo della tarda antichità visto attraverso le merci', especially 15; and, for the background to Carandini's ideas, the review-article by Wickham (1988a) 'Marx, Sherlock Holmes, and late Roman commerce'; further V.4.

On Pirenne, see Lyon (1974) *Henri Pirenne;* with the subtle appreciation by P. Brown (1982b) '*Mohammed and Charlemagne* by Henri Pirenne', 79: 'Pirenne for the Middle Ages; Rostovtseff for the ancient world: each in his way was a great European *bourgeois,* studying with deep commitment the fate of civilizations based on cities.' Also see Hodges and Whitehouse (1983) *Mohammed, Charlemagne and the Origins of Europe* – reflecting in their title Pirenne's own (1939) *Mohammed and Charlemagne.* More generally, Despy and Verhulst (1986) *La fortune historiographique des thèses d'Henri Pirenne.* Further discussion and bibliography in V.5.

On Goitein see his own (1975) 'The life story of a scholar'; the foreword (ix–xviii) by Udovitch, and the epilogue by the author himself (496–502) to Goitein (1967–88) *A Mediterranean Society,* vol. 5: *The Individual.* Gil (1986) 'Shlomo Dov Goitein,

1900–1985: a Mediterranean scholar', is a brief but useful obituary. Some idea of the qualities of Goitein's work can also be found in his (1966a) *Studies in Islamic History and Institutions*.

3. THE END OF THE MEDITERRANEAN

The bibliography on Braudel is now vast; we mention only what has proved most useful in the present context. The best point of entry into Braudel's thought is his collection of essays (1980) translated as *On History*, especially Part 2, 'History and the Other Human Sciences'. For briefer reflections on Mediterranean history and its environment than Part 1 of *The Mediterranean*, see the popular illustrated account that Braudel edited (1977b), *La Méditerranée: l'espace et l'histoire*. Braudel's last thoughts on the Mediterranean (as on the two other main subjects of his writings) can be found in Braudel et al. (1986) *Une leçon d'histoire de Fernand Braudel . . . 18, 19 et 20 Octobre, 1985*, the transcript of a colloquium in which Braudel introduced and responded to discussion of his work by an international panel of scholars. (Braudel died just over a month later, on 28 November.) His final *published* monographic words on *la longue durée* are to be read in his (1988–90) *The Identity of France*, vol. 2 (*People and Production*) 678–9, though note also our description of the manuscript volume discussed in the text, and Braudel (1986), 'Fernand Braudel, l'antiquité et l'histoire', 18, his last interview, in which his powers seem undiminished and his wit coruscating.

The essential parts of the symposium on him and the *Annales* school in *Journal of Modern History*, vol. 44, are Braudel's (1972b) 'Personal testimony', and the discussion by Hexter, reprinted in his (1979) *On Historians*. We have already noted Trevor-Roper (1972). There is a useful collection of references to articles on Braudel, both hostile and friendly, in Harsgor (1986) 'Braudel's sea revisited' (itself a useful discussion of *The Mediterranean* in the sixteenth century). For a sample brief attack see Gress (1983) 'The pride and prejudice of Fernand Braudel'.

In the context of our remarks in Section 1 about the historiography of Europe, Aymard (1987) 'Fernand Braudel, the Mediterranean, and Europe', is also of interest. Aymard quotes *The Mediterranean* (1972a, 188): 'The

Mediterranean, by its profound influence over Southern Europe, has contributed in no small measure to prevent the unity of that Europe which it has attracted towards its shores and then divided to its own advantage'.

S. Clark (1985) 'The *Annales* historians', is a useful introduction to the historiographical movement from which Braudel sprang. There are trenchant observations in M. Bentley (1997) 'Introduction: approaches to modernity: western historiography since the Enlightenment', 464–73, and Huppert (1997) 'The *Annales* experiment', who provides a stimulating balance-sheet on the house journal. Burke (1990) *The French Historical Revolution: The 'Annales' School, 1929–89*, is now, however, the basic guide. More detail may be found in Stoianovich (1976) *French Historical Method: The Annales Paradigm*. On the tension between the poetic and scientific strains in *Annaliste* writing, see Carrard (1992) *Poetics of the New History: French Historical Discourse from Braudel to Chartier*, registering naive surprise at the extent to which the authors discussed use figurative language to convey a history that aspires to objectivity. A larger plot connecting all three parts of *The Mediterranean* is discerned by Ricoeur (1984–8), *Time and Narrative*, esp. vol. 1, ch. 6. For wider intellectual background, see H. S. Hughes (1966) *The Obstructed Path: French Social Thought in the Years of Desperation, 1930–1960*, especially ch. 2. Fink (1989) *Marc Bloch: A Life in History*, also contains much valuable history of the *Annales* school, based on manuscript sources. See also Burguière (1979) 'Histoire d'une histoire; la naissance des *Annales*'; and Carbonell and Livet (1983) *Au berceau des Annales*. The major discussion of Braudel's method is Kinser (1981) '*Annaliste* paradigm? The geohistorical structuralism of Fernand Braudel'. Cf. Perrot (1981) 'Le présent et la durée dans l'oeuvre de Fernand Braudel'. On different planes of temporality, it is of interest to compare Braudel's conception with that in Giddens (1981) *A Contemporary Critique of Historical Materialism*. There is, too, a likely connection between Braudel's *longue durée* and the concept of 'perdurance' advocated by the historian of the family, Peter Laslett. See the latter's (1977) *Family Life and Illicit Love in Earlier Generations*, 3–4. See also Santamaria and Bailey (1984) 'A note on Braudel's structure as duration'. On the history of *mentalités*, one component of the

Annales paradigm to which Braudel devoted relatively scant attention, see Burke (1990) 73–4, 115; Vovelle (1990) *Ideologies and Mentalities*; Gismondi (1985) ' "The gift of theory": a critique of the *histoire des mentalités*'; and the distinguished consideration of the presumed radical 'otherness' of modes of thought by G. E. R. Lloyd (1990) *Mentalities Demystified*.

Ghosh (1997), 'The Conception of Gibbon's *History*', 271–2, draws attention to the fact that, like all modern historians who deal in a hierarchy of causes, Braudel is anticipated by Gibbon in his *Essai sur l'étude de la littérature* of 1758–61, where he distinguishes 'determinate, but general causes', such as religion, from 'particular causes'.

Braudel's biography: Gemelli (1995) *Fernand Braudel*, gives some idea of what a full intellectual biography of Braudel will eventually look like and gives much space to the institutions with which he has been associated. Daix (1995) *Braudel*, is a little narrower in scope but perhaps more vivid. Braudel's son, P. Braudel (1992) 'Les origines intellectuelles de Fernand Braudel', offers a brief account of the formative years.

The precursors: on Febvre, see Mann (1971) *Lucien Febvre: la pensée vivante d'un historien*, and Peter Burke's introduction (ix–xvi) to a collection of Febvre's articles in translation (1973b) *A New Kind of History*. Among Febvre's own writings see especially (1925) *A Geographical Introduction to History*, in which the list of topics treated closely foreshadows those discussed in Part 1 of Braudel's (1972a) *The Mediterranean*. On Bloch see Fink (1989) *Marc Bloch* (with much useful information on Febvre also) and, for wider intellectual context, Atsma and Burguière (1990) *Marc Bloch aujourd'hui: histoire comparée et sciences sociales*; Friedman (1997) *Marc Bloch, Sociology and Geography*. There is no accessible and satisfactory study of Vidal. But see Buttimer (1971) *Society and Milieu in the French Geographic Tradition*; Lewthwaite (1988) 'Trial by durée: a review of historical-geographical concepts relevant to the archaeology of settlement on Corsica and Sardinia', 163–8; also the brief encyclopedia entry, *IESS*, 'Vidal de la Blache, Paul'. For the wider context of the links between geography and historiography, Baker (1984) 'Reflections on the relations of historical geography and the *Annales* school of history'. In the present context a suitable introduction to Vidal's writings is (1928) *The Personality of France*, with its substantial chapter on the country's 'physiognomy'.

Braudel's indebtedness to Alfred Philippson is recorded in (1972a) *The Mediterranean*, 2.1273, and confirmed in Braudel (1986) 'Fernand Braudel, l'antiquité et l'histoire', 18. On (1972a) 2.1275–6, he also refers to Ludwig (1929) *On Mediterranean Shores*, a work which Goitein (1967–88, 5.498) also recalls having been impressed by at an early stage. Ludwig's treatment of the Mediterranean region as a virtual personality aligns him with the tradition of Vidal. Something of Pirenne's significance for Braudel (see 1972a, 1273) may derive from Pirenne's (1929) *Histoire de Belgique*, vol. 1, for the early volumes of which he had to find a way of defining his subject other than through recourse to national boundaries. Belgium therefore had to be treated as a distinctive region, regardless of the divisions that ran across it, in something of the same way as Braudel would treat the sixteenth-century Mediterranean. See also, for historical background, Lyon (1980) 'Henri Pirenne and the origins of *Annales* history', 69–84.

It is of interest to follow the fortunes of the *Annales* paradigm as it has been adopted by other disciplines – at precisely the time that its influence is perhaps waning among historians. On the historiographical reception see Gemelli (1995) *Fernand Braudel*, 171–244. For archaeology, see for example Bintliff (1991) *The 'Annales' School and Archaeology*; Knapp (1992) *Archaeology, 'Annales', and Ethnohistory*, in which see esp. Sherratt (1992), 'What can archaeologists learn from Annalistes?', to which the answer is essentially: style and imaginative breadth; see also his (1995a) 'Reviving the grand narrative: archaeology and long-term change'. Despite the argument of these, and despite the specific example of Barker et al. (1995) *A Mediterranean Valley: Landscape Archaeology and 'Annales' History in the Biferno Valley*, it remains unclear what Braudel has to offer archaeologists beyond encouragement to relate, in their analyses, the long term to the short term. Note also Greene (1986) *The Archaeology of the Roman Economy*, 1.

Those seemingly most directly indebted to Braudel, of the 'Fernand Braudel Center for the Study of Economies, Historical Systems, and Civilizations' at the State University of New York at Binghampton, have in fact pursued global economic history rather than geo-history of a Braudellian kind, and they do not approach the *longue durée* in quite the same spirit as Braudel does. See the major work of their director, Wallerstein (1974–) *The Modern World-System*. Compare Braudel's remarks on Wallerstein in his (1981–4) *Civilization and Capitalism*, vol. 3, ch. 1. Still further removed from the Braudellian approach is the chronological corrective to Wallerstein offered by J. L. Abu-Lughod (1989) *Before European Hegemony*; cf. Moore (1993) 'World history', on both her and Wallerstein. Dietler (1995) 'The cup of Gyptis: rethinking the colonial encounter in early-Iron-Age western Europe and the relevance of world-systems models', is a critique of Wallerstein's core–periphery dichotomy, by way of an account of its origins in the very colonialism it sets out to analyse, that should be important to historians as well as archaeologists. Also Gunder Frank and Gills (1993) *The World System: Five Hundred Years or Five Thousand?*.

The various directions that French historiography has taken in the closing decades of the twentieth century – towards the small-scale and rural, the history of *mentalités*, cultural history – can be gauged from Burke (1990) *The French Historical Revolution*, ch. 4.

For regional history of a Braudellian cast and scope and, perhaps, for the closest descendents of *The Mediterranean*, one must turn right away from Europe and the Middle East. Spate's history of the Pacific, though chronological in organization, certainly invites comparison with Braudel's work in its scope: Spate (1979–89) *The Pacific since Magellan*. See also the same author's (1978) 'The Pacific as an artefact'. For a different region that is again focused on and defined by a stretch of water, see Watts (1987) *The West Indies: Patterns of Development, Culture and Environmental Change since 1492*, favouring a much more ecological approach but still Braudellian in inspiration. Chaudhuri (1985) *Trade and Civilization in the Indian Ocean from the Rise of Islam to 1750*, and (1990) *Asia before Europe: Economy and Civilisation of the Indian Ocean from the Rise of Islam to 1750*, has magisterially examined the economic life and culture of the regions around his chosen sea in a manner strongly influenced by Braudel (1981–4) – as also by Cantorian set theory.

4. MEDITERRANEAN HISTORY

Reflex quotations of Braudel are too numerous to document; he has been popular among specialists in the ancient world since the translation of *The Mediterranean* appeared in 1972.

Meanwhile, to revert to a distinction drawn at the outset of Chapter I, work on the Mediterranean has remained more usually history *in*, rather than *of*, the region. Journals devoted to Mediterranean studies provide the best evidence of this, often despite their titles and declared editorial intentions.

Thus, for instance, *Mediterranean Archaeology: The Australia and New Zealand Journal for the Archaeology of the Mediterranean World* (1988–) claims to be responding to the need for an international journal that treats the Mediterranean region as an entity. The first studies included, though of importance within their fields, made little attempt to fulfil this implied brief. The *Mediterranean Historical Review* (1986–), its inauguration predicated upon the 'structural unity and coherence of the region' ('Foreword' by Ben-Ami, vol. 1, 5), has been more successful in dealing with, and sometimes questioning the validity of, history of the region as a whole. *The Journal of Mediterranean Archaeology* also began in 1988 with a preamble by its editor, Knapp, that spoke, in Braudellian terms (vol. 1, 4) of the Mediterranean as an archaeological and geographic entity. Compare, among others, the *Journal of Mediterranean Anthropology and Archaeology* (1981–), the *Journal of Mediterranean Studies* (1991–), *Al-Masâq: Studia Arabo-Islamica Mediterranea* (1988–) (subtitle later changed to *Islam and the Medieval Mediterranean*), and the older *Mediterranean Studies* (1978–).

W. H. McNeill's (1986) criticism of Braudel ('Fernand Braudel'): for a striking example of the perils of synchronic social and economic history, studied without reference to events, see the discussion of the fish-resources of the Sea of Marmara in VI.6. McNeill's interpretation is explicitly evolutionist; as will be clear from Chapter VII, we distance ourselves from the notion that what is missed in omitting conscious behaviour is mainly the history of 'the genesis of new skills and ideas'. For a more balanced (and witty) appraisal of the tendency in much recent historical writing – *Annaliste* and other – to belittle the importance of events and conscious ideas in the past, see Himmelfarb (1987) *The New History and the Old*.

We allude to 'fuzzy sets', a mathematical approach to those social or physical phenomena that can only vaguely be specified. See Wang and Chang (1980) *Fuzzy Sets*; Smithson (1987) *Fuzzy Set Analysis for Behavioral and Social Sciences*; Novák (1989) *Fuzzy Sets and their Applications*. Far more detail of Mediterranean history would need to be available before the mathematics could be usefully applied to any of the problems that we address. (Compare, however, Naveh (1990) 'Ancient man's impact on the Mediterranean landscape in Israel' (VIII.3), and the invocation of set theory to justify a comparable unit of study in Chaudhuri (1990) *Asia before Europe*.) The development of these techniques shows at least that the precise modelling of vague phenomena, which is what we attempt in our own way in subsequent chapters, is not an entirely eccentric pursuit. Another approach that we are prevented from using through lack of evidence is systems analysis. Compare Huggett (1980) *Systems Analysis in Geography*; Ellen (1982) *Environment, Subsistence and System: The Ecology of Small-Scale Social Formations*, ch. 8; Shavit (1988) 98–9, quoted in Section 1 above.

Continuity: its different historical kinds – in time, space, and function – are usefully distinguished, though with respect to German folk-lore, by Bausinger (1969) 'Zur Algebra der Kontinuität'; see also Gerschenkron (1968) *Continuity in History and Other Essays*, 11–39; Golden and Toohey (1997) *Inventing Ancient Culture: Historicism, Periodization, and the Ancient World*.

Environmental determinism: beside Ellen (1982) ch. 1, we shall cite only the somewhat damaging empirical critique in Hallpike (1986) *The Principles of Social Evolution*, a detailed examination of cultural and structural differences between adjacent African societies living in similar environments, and a work that encourages a return to the possibilism advocated by Febvre (1925) *A Geographical Introduction to History*, 225 (on which, Ellen (1982) ch. 2). Note also Goudie (1987) 'History and archaeology: the growth of a relationship', 15–18, for some remarks on climatic determinism. For the historical pedigree of such approaches, Glacken (1967) *Traces on the Rhodian Shore: Nature and Culture in Western Thought from Ancient Times to the End of the Eighteenth Century*, remains fundamental.

For an attempt at a behaviourist analysis of a Mediterranean society an example (dealing with ancient Greek religion) is at hand in Burkert (1983) *Homo Necans: The Anthropology of Ancient Greek Sacrificial Ritual and Myth*.

5. HISTORICAL ECOLOGY

Human ecology: for general orientation McIntosh (1985) *The Background of Ecology: Concept and Theory*, and Bramwell (1989) *Ecology in the Twentieth Century: A History*, revealing the various political forms that ecological concern has taken. A pioneering work was Eyre and Jones (1966) *Geography as Human Ecology*, whence the title of Butzer (1982) *Archaeology as Human Ecology*. A major general work on the human aspect of the discipline: Hawley (1986) *Human Ecology: A Theoretical Essay*. See further, the sophisticated presentation of Carlstein (1982) *Time Resources, Society and Ecology*. We also draw on Guilaine (1976) *Les premiers bergers et paysans de l'occident méditerranéen*. Ellen (1982) contains useful introductions to such ecological matters as microenvironments, carrying capacity and energy flows. Like Sallares (1991) *The Ecology of the Ancient Greek World*, briefly discussed in the chapter, it has an ample bibliography. Current work can be sampled in, for instance, *Human Ecology: An Interdisciplinary Journal* (1972–). B. D. Shaw (1986) 'Autonomy and tribute: mountain and plain in Mauretania Tingitana', 66–7, also for perspectives in Mediterranean ecological history. We note, however, Ellen's comment (1982, 275): 'ecology itself cannot answer all the questions we might wish to ask, it cannot even pose them.' We hope in this book to have adequately heeded the warning delivered by Stuart Piggott against a (pre)history 'inhabited not by human beings . . . but by the pale phantoms of modern theory, who do not live, but just cower in ecological niches, get caught in catchment areas, and are entangled in redistributive systems' (1985, 146).

Theoretical developments since the 1930s – cultural ecology, neofunctionalism, processual ecology – are incisively categorized and appraised in Orlove (1980) 'Ecological anthropology'. See also Moran (1984) *The Ecosystem Concept in Anthropology*. For the 'new ecological economic history' see VI.1 with BE. The work of Rappaport (1984, first published 1968) *Pigs for the Ancestors*, is subjected to brief critical review by J. N. Anderson (1973) 'Ecological anthropology and anthropological ecology', a useful survey of the whole field, at 199–200. On the lack of detailed information about palaeozoology or botany in the region see Randsborg (1991) *The First Millennium A.D. in Europe and the Mediterranean: An Archaeological Essay*, 30–9; Sallares (1991) 2, 69. An outstanding attempt to capture the *longue durée* in food production and consumption in a relatively restricted area, under the banner of the 'food system concept', is LaBianca (1990) *Sedentarization and Nomadization: Food System Cycles at Hesban and Vicinity in Transjordan* (cf. VI.1, VII.4). It is significant, however, that the explanation for secular change in those cycles still has to be couched in terms of independent variables such as 'the intrusive state', tribalism and so forth. There is no genuinely ecological interpretation of all relevant factors. Indeed, refuge is sometimes taken in a modified possibilism (cf. 54).

Archaeology and anthropology combine in Hodges and Whitehouse (1983) *Mohammed, Charlemagne and the Origins of Europe*. See Bintliff (1984) *European Social Evolution*. Also Renfrew (1982a) *Towards an Archaeology of Mind*. (Compare Rappaport (1979) *Ecology, Meaning and Religion*, and the collection of essays by the anthropologist Bateson (1987) *Steps to an Ecology of Mind*.) Renfrew (1985) *The Archaeology of Cult: The Sanctuary of Phylakopi*, chs 1, 10. For salutary scepticism about the use of ethnographic parallels in explaining archaeological data see Leach (1973) 'Concluding remarks'. For attacks, however, from within the archaeological community, on the less rigorously 'scientific' approaches that involve rapprochement with the humanities, see Binford (1988) 'Data, relativism and archaeological science', opposing 'archaeological theology'. Compare Hodder (1988) 'Archaeology and theory'.

An attractive plea for distinguishing the social from the ecological aspects of economic production, and for not *reducing* the social to the ecological, is made by Ingold (1981) 'The hunter and his spear: notes on the cultural mediation of social and ecological systems'. We may guess that, in the end, it will prove easier for essentially *cultural* theories to include and explain the subject matter of the *scientistic* tradition, than it will be for the latter to comprehend – in the strict sense – the cultural approach. For other sceptical comments on the possibilities and limitations of historical human ecology, both dealing with an area where such an approach might have seemed very promising, see Netting (1981) *Balancing on an Alp: Ecological Change and Continuity in a Swiss Mountain Community*, preface and ch. 11; Cole and Wolf (1974) *The Hidden Frontier*, explicitly challenging (284) the usefulness of ecological theory in explaining the cultural divergences within the single environmentally uniform area that they describe. Viazzo (1989) *Upland Communities: Environment, Population and Social Structure in the Alps since the Sixteenth Century*, provides a broader view of early modern Alpine demography in its relation to the environment and calls into question any simplistic use of an ecosystemic approach (cf. III.6 below).

BIBLIOGRAPHICAL ESSAY TO CHAPTER III
FOUR DEFINITE PLACES

Our choice of definite places has been facilitated by the growing number of detailed surveys of Mediterranean microecologies. Within the limits set by the need to achieve some degree of geographical 'spread', the selection was arbitrary. It would have been equally possible to illustrate the Mediterranean phenomena of sub-dividedness, diversity and interaction with detail derived from such studies as: Goodman (1983) *State and Society in Roman Galilee, A.D. 132–212*; Pringle (1986) *The Red Tower (al-Burj al-Ahmar): Settlement in the Plain of Sharon at the Time of the Crusaders and Mamluks, A.D. 1099–1516*; Bryer (1986a) 'Rural society in Matzouka'; Molinier (1976) *Ardèche*; Favory and Fiches (1994) *Les campagnes de la France méditerranéenne dans l'antiquité et le haut moyen âge: études microrégionales*; Barker et al. (1995) *A Mediterranean Valley: Landscape Archaeology and 'Annales' History in the Biferno Valley*; Wickham (1988b) *The Mountains and the City: The Tuscan Appennines in the Early Middle Ages*; Jameson et al. (1994) *A Greek Countryside: The Southern Argolid from Prehistory to the Present Day*; Chapman, Shiel and Batović (1996) *The Changing Face of Dalmatia*; J. L. Davis (1991) 'Contributions to a Mediterranean rural archaeology: historical case studies from the Ottoman Cyclades'.

In this Second Part of the book our aim, following these and other studies, is to begin to seek patterns in the description of the Mediterranean and its land- and seascapes. The major task of historical explanation of the patterns and how they relate to other historical disciplines is undertaken in the four chapters of Part Three.

1. THE BIQA

We have drawn above all on the excellent study of Marfoe (1979) 'The integrative transformation: patterns of sociopolitical organisation in southern Syria'; see also, for the historical dimension, the same author's dissertation (1978) *Between Qadesh and Kumidi: A History of Frontier Settlement and Land Use in the Biqa, Lebanon*; Pairman-Brown (1969) *The Lebanon and Phoenicia*, 71–2, for the irrigation of Baalbek; Ghadban (1987) 'Observations sur le statut des terres et l'organisation des villages dans le Beqa hellénistique et romaine', especially 224–7 for the Paradeisos at El Qa'. For the Roman institutional geography see Millar (1990) 'The Roman *coloniae* of the Near East: a study of cultural relations', 10–23, and Millar (1993) *The Roman Near East*, chs. 3, 8. Hachmann (1989) 'Kâmid el-Lôz 1963–1981: German excavations in Lebanon part I', especially 17–25, offers a bibliography of the more recent archaeology and a summary of the historical geography. For the wider, and more recent, context: Khalaf (1979) *Persistence and Change in Nineteenth Century Lebanon*, on the impact of early modernization; Touma (1986) *Paysans et institutions féodales chez les Druses et les Maronites du Liban*. The literature on late twentieth-century conflict in the region, to which we no more than allude in the chapter, is extremely large and variable in quality. One useful and accessible political analysis, with a wide-ranging historical summary, remains that of Salibi (1988) *A House of Many Mansions: The History of Lebanon Reconsidered*.

2. SOUTH ETRURIA

The best general account remains Potter (1979) *The Changing Landscape of South Etruria*, with full bibliography. It should be read alongside Toubert (1973) *Les structures du Latium médiéval*, especially 135–98.

For more recent summaries of the south Etruria archaeological field survey, on which we have also drawn, Potter (1987) *Roman Italy*; Hodges, and White-house (1983) *Mohammed, Charlemagne and the Origins of Europe*, 36–48; Greene (1986) *The Archaeology of the Roman Economy*, ch. 5; Greenhalgh (1989) *The Survival of Roman Antiquities in the Middle Ages*, 17ff.

Bietti Sestieri (1980) 'Cenni sull'ambiente naturale', and Ampolo (1980) 'Le condizioni materiali della produzione', each offer useful surveys for the ancient historian. See also Quilici (1979) *Roma primitiva e le origini della civiltà laziale*; Colonna (1988) *Etruria meridionale: conoscenza, conservazione, fruizione*, especially 39–50. For details of alluviation, see Cherkauer (1976) 'The stratigraphy and chronology of the River Treia alluvial deposits'; Fentress et al. (1983) 'Excavations at Fosso della Crescenza, 1962', 70–2; further, VIII.3. For pastoralism see also G. W. W. Barker (1976) 'Animal husbandry at Narce'. A detailed comparison with another Italian survey, of the Biferno Valley, Molise, can be had from Barker et al. (1995) *A Mediterranean Valley*. For wide-ranging summary of such surveys: S. L. Dyson (1982) 'Archaeological survey in the Mediterranean basin: a review of recent research'; Barker and Lloyd (1991) *Roman Landscapes: Archaeological Survey in the Mediterranean Region*. On secular changes in the strength of the gravitational force exerted by Rome see Potter (1991) 'Towns and territories in southern Etruria'. This is also the theme of the regional study of Morley (1996) *Metropolis and Hinterland: The City of Rome and the Italian Economy*. For human responses to this landscape, and in particular to its hydrology, Purcell (1996b) 'Rome and the management of water'.

3. THE GREEN MOUNTAIN, CYRENAICA

Our starting-point is D. L. Johnson (1973) *Jabal al-Akhdar, Cyrenaica: An Historical Geography of Settlement and Livelihood*, summarized for comparative purposes in LaBianca (1990) *Sedentarization and Nomadization*, 46–9. General geographic background: Girgis (1987) *Mediterranean Africa*. For the tectonic structure of the region, Bousquet and Péchoux (1983) 'Le Djebel Akhdar (Cyrénaïque, Libye): évolution morphostructurale', discussing the microfragmentation of a subduction zone. For pastoralism see Behnke (1980) *The Herders of Cyrenaica: Ecology, Economy, and Kinship among the Bedouin of Eastern Libya*. Ancient Cyrenaica: Barker, Lloyd and Reynolds (1985) *Cyrenaica in Antiquity*; Laronde (1987) *Cyrène et la Libye héllénistique – Libykai historiai – de l'époque républicaine au principat d'Auguste*, (1990) 'Greeks and Libyans in Cyrenaica', (1996b) 'L'exploitation de la chôra cyrénéenne'. On the fragility of the surplus achieved and the growing dependence of some areas of Cyrene on imported goods see Fulford (1984) 'Berenice and the economy of Cyrenaica'; Kennet (1994) 'Pottery as evidence for trade in medieval Cyrenaica'. On the importance of Saharan links, Stucchi (1989) 'Problems concerning the coming of the Greeks to Cyrenaica and their relations with their neighbours'. Compare Brett (1969) 'Ifrîqya as a market for Saharan trade from the tenth to the twelfth century A. D.', for an almost adjacent area in the Middle Ages. Applebaum (1979) *Jews and Greeks in Ancient Cyrene*, 1–7, 16, for bibliography on *silphion*. For Synesius, Roques (1987) *Synésios de Cyrène et la Cyrénaïque du Bas-Empire*; and, with some further bibliography, Liebeschuetz (1990) *Barbarians and Bishops: Army, Church and State in the Age of Arcadius and Chrysostom*, ch. 23. The journal *Libyan Studies* (1979–) is essential for the latest archaeology. On the Hilali invasion, a warning note was sounded by Poncet (1967) 'Le mythe de la catastrophe hilalienne'. Compare, from the same year, Goitein (1967–88) *A Mediterranean Society*, vol. 1, 32. The writings of Cahen on the subject have, however, been the most influential: (1968) 'Quelques mots sur les Hilaliens et le nomadisme', and (1973) 'Nomades et sédentaires dans le monde musulman du milieu du moyen âge'. For further ethnography see the classic Evans-Pritchard (1949) *The Sanusi of Cyrenaica*; and, for the ethnography of an adjacent region, the Egyptian Western Desert, see XII.3.

4. Melos

The obvious starting point is Renfrew and Wagstaff (1982) *An Island Polity: The Archaeology of Exploitation in Melos*; note some important statistical corrections in Sanders (1984) 'Reassessing ancient populations'. Cherry et al. (1991) *Landscape Archaeology as Long-Term History. Northern Keos*, is a parallel study of another Aegean island, less ambitious in its spatial extent, but equally inclusive chronologically: see the review of Purcell (1995a) 'Field survey of an asteroid', questioning the degree of isolation of these islands. The Southern Argolid survey on the adjacent mainland provides another very instructive set of comparisons: Jameson et al. (1994) *A Greek Countryside: The Southern Argolid from Prehistory to the Present Day*. See also Mee and Forbes (1997) *A Rough and Rocky Place: The Landscape and Settlement History of the Methana Peninsula*; Halstead and Jones (1989) 'Agrarian ecology in the Greek island: time stress, scale and risk'; J. D. Evans (1977) 'Island archaeology in the Mediterranean'; Rackham (1990a) 'Ancient landscapes'.

5. 'La trame du monde'

Some insight into the character and context of our opening quotation from Momigliano may be derived from Murray (1991) 'Arnaldo Momigliano in England'.

The diversity of the Mediterranean landscape already had a place in Greek geography. Strabo commented on the *poikilmata*, details of design or decoration, with which the chorographer's map must be filled (*Geography*, 2.5.17, immediately following the description of the topographic primacy of the sea which we used as an epigraph to Part One). The modern appreciation of Mediterranean microtopography may be traced to the proto-Romantic predilection for the picturesque. Nineteenth-century natural science reinforced the tendency which began with visually alert travellers; and the two strands may be seen together in the unusual case of the Colosseum and its botany (Deakin (1855) *Flora of the Colosseum*; outrage at the destruction of this habitat in antiquarian frenzy after 1871: Gregorovius (1911) *Roman Journals*, 402).

That the contribution of microregional analysis to the understanding of the Mediter-ranean lands is now generally accepted is above all the consequence of the minute researches, often in tandem, of archaeologists and ethnographers studying whole landscapes: Malone et al. (1994) *Territory, Time and State*, on the Gubbio basin of the central Apennines, is a characteristic example. Further bibliography of this and other fruitful results of this scholarship will be found in VI.1 below. For examples from Greece, Forbes (1982) *Strategies and Soils*, 37, cf. 78–106; Rackham and Moody (1997) *The Making of the Cretan Landscape*, 36; also on Crete, Brulé (1978) *La piraterie*, 143: 'en symbiose avec les données climatiques, cette compartimentation . . . a donné naissance à des microclimats qui se trouvent parfois en violente opposition'. Italian cases, Pelosi (1991) 'Dinamiche territoriali del VII secolo a.C. nell'area Sirite-Metapontina', 74; Bottini (1992) 'La Magna Grecia in epoca preromana', 11: 'the history of Greek southern Italy is a mosaic of micro-histories.' For Spain, see the discussions of the essentially microregional archaeology of the 'hydraulic landscape' in VII.2.

Anglo-Saxon historians have perhaps been more used to the other end of the spectrum, as represented by the generalized cultural history of generic landscapes, e.g. Schama (1995) *Landscape and Memory*. Starting from the fragmentation of Mediterranean France, however, the geographical tendency in French historiography has extended the emphasis on diversity to cover the country as a whole: as is to be found in some of Braudel's last published writings, notably (1988–90) *The Identity of France*, vol. 1, Part 1, 'The diversity of France'; or vol. 2, 669. Medeiros (1988) 'Espaces ruraux et dynamiques sociales en Europe du Sud', also emphasizes fragmentation, but adds a further dimension: that of variation in the degree of fragmentation. Equally axiomatic is the mosaic-like texture of the Levant: see for instance Coon (1958) *Caravan: The Story of the Middle East*.

Our claim that fragmentation is a key to Mediterranean history is substantiated over the remainder of the volume. The essential ingredient is the relationship between topographical diversity and the landscape of production, which is discussed in Chapter VI. The physical frameworks of the diversity are of obvious importance to the historian, as Chapter VIII attempts to show, while continuing to assert, against deterministic theories, that it is changing human responses that give the staccato landscape of the Mediterranean its pattern. As for the paradox that the kaleidoscopic mosaic of the Mediterranean is distinguished by the structures which overcome the fragmentation, and above all by maritime communications, full treatment will be found in Chapters V and IX. The comparison in respect of this unique combination of fragmentation and connectivity between the Mediterranean and its neighbours we reserve for Volume 2.

Some of the difficulties of operating with conceptual divisions of the Mediterranean region intermediate in size between the whole and its component microecologies are illustrated in, for example, C. Mango (1984) 'Chypre, carrefour du monde Byzantin', showing how Cyprus's status as an important crossroads was not inherent in its geographical position but dependent on surrounding political and commercial patterns; see also Goitein (1966b) 'Medieval Tunisia: the hub of the Mediterranean'; J. Richard (1977) 'The eastern Mediterranean and its relations with its hinterland, eleventh to fifteenth centuries'. 'Hubs' are not determined by geography but by their place in the overall 'system' which may well change from one period to another as the component microecologies alter.

The essential mutability of the human landscape, which we shall be stressing throughout this work, is the subject of Burnouf et al. (1996) *La dynamique des paysages protohistoriques, antiques, médiévaux et modernes*. See also Wagstaff (1975) 'A note on settlement numbers in ancient Greece', arguing against notions that there might have been a steady optimal number of settlements. Bresc (1986b) *Un monde méditerranéen*, 95–6, cf. 102, instructively discusses environmental disequilibria in Sicily (further VIII.6).

6. MOUNTAINS AND PASTURES

Braudel on mountain society: we may recall Hexter's wry conclusion having scrutinized Braudel's discussion in (1972a) *The Mediterranean*: 'in sum, on the face of the evidence, mountains that house incomplete forms of civilization house them, and mountains that don't, don't' (Hexter 1979, 'Fernand Braudel', 112). Compare Febvre (1925) *A Geographical Introduction to History*, 194–200.

Further, in addition to those works cited in the text, see de Planhol (1966) 'Aspects of mountain life in Anatolia and Iran'; and for comparative perspective, showing mountain environments to be zones of communication and transition, Beaver and Purrington (1984) *Cultural Adaptation to Mountain Environments*; Bergier (1989) *Montagnes, fleuves, forêts dans l'histoire*, especially, in this context, the contributions of Jameson, 'Mountains and the Greek city states', and Toch, 'Peasants of the mountains, peasants of the valleys and medieval state building: the case of the Alps'. Another relevant small collection of papers is G. Fabre (n.d.) *La montagne dans l'antiquité*. Especially useful for the question of marginality, Leveau (n.d.) 'L'occupation du sol dans les montagnes méditerranéennes pendant l'antiquité: apport de l'archéologie des paysages à la connaissance historique'. B. D. Shaw (1986) 'Autonomy and tribute: mountain and plain in Mauretania Tingitana', deserves to be seen as a classic statement about the relations between mountains and lowlands. J. R. McNeill (1992) *The Mountains of the Mediterranean World*, is most concerned with deforestation and soil erosion in the early modern period; cf. Chapter VIII. For mountain environments and religious practice see X.2 below.

Pastoralism: in this discussion we have been principally interested in the broad question of whether a microregional analysis can reasonably be extended across all Mediterranean environments. Mountains provide simply the strongest case in an argument which has forcefully maintained a dualistic perspective on Mediterranean production. Against that dualism, we advocate an approach which enables all productive environments to be assessed side by side. The literature on pastoralism is enormous, and we have done no more than to cite some noteworthy contributions to our part of the debate. In VI.7 and its BE we say more on animal husbandry as part of the repertoire of Mediterranean productive strategies, and on problems connected with seeing it in that light.

It is appropriate to set at the head of the bibliography Braudel (1972a) *The Mediterranean*, 85–102, a useful geographical survey of nomadism and transhumance in the sixteenth century, rightly stressing the historical and political contexts in which large-scale pastoralism such as that of the Castilian *Mesta* has to be understood, but giving too little attention to less ambitious husbandry and to its close links with agriculture. (In his (1988–90) *The Identity of France*, 2.305–8, he shows a lesser grasp of earlier periods, repeating clichés about French transhumance being 'as old as the world'.) More convincing as a general survey, and adducing a wider range of evidence, is Delano Smith (1979) *Western Mediterranean Europe: A Historical Geography of Italy, Spain and Southern France since the Neolithic*, ch. 7, bringing out the full but highly variable interdependence of arable and pastoral in her region and (231) clearly distinguishing between short- and long-distance transhumance. An example from medieval northern Europe: Biddick (1989) *The Other Economy: Pastoral Husbandry on a Medieval Estate*. LaBianca (1990) *Sedentarization and Nomadization: Food System Cycles at Hesban and Vicinity in Transjordan*, gives full weight to the continuum of pastoralism and agriculture in the Levant. Compare Briant (1982a) *État et pasteurs au Moyen-Orient ancien*, and Aurenche and Desfarges (1983) 'Travaux d'ethnoarchéologie en Syrie et en Jordanie'.

On interdependence, the major synoptic analysis is Khazanov (1984) *Nomads and the Outside World*. But also instructive is the earlier collection of essays by anthropologists, Nelson (1974) *The Desert and the Sown: Nomads in the Wider Society*. See also Koster and Koster (1976) 'Competition or symbiosis?: Pastoral adaptive strategies in the southern Argolid'.

On the question of continuity: the necessity of relating the varieties of pastoralism to patterns of field management, cultivation and settlement has been valuably brought out by Halstead in a number of papers: see especially (1987) 'Traditional and ancient rural economy in Mediterranean Europe: plus ça change?', and Halstead and Jones (1989) 'Agrarian ecology in the Greek island: time stress, scale and risk'. On the variety, yet broad continuity, of pastoral–arable interactions (and agrarian relations in general) from proto-historic times to the nineteenth century in one particular area, see Whittaker (1978) 'Land and labour in North Africa', especially 350. The difficulties attendant upon any narrowly ecological approach to the subject are well shown in Dyson-Hudson and Dyson-Hudson (1980) 'Nomadic pastoralism'. Compare the theoretically dense Carlstein (1982) *Time Resources, Society and Ecology*, ch. 4. The

papers in *World Archaeology* (1983) 15 (1), special issue on *Transhumance and Pastoralism*, present hypotheses on prehistoric Mediterranean pastoralism: see also Sherratt (1983) 'The secondary exploitation of animals in the Old World'; D. R. Harris (1996) *The Origins and Spread of Agriculture and Pastoralism*; K. W. Russell (1988) *After Eden*, 159–60.

Roman Italy has been an especially controversial case. Gabba and Pasquinucci (1979) *Struture agrarie e allevamento transumante nell'Italia romana*, argued forcefully that large-scale, long-distance horizontal transhumance is a *structure* of Italian history, environmentally determined; cf. Gabba (1985) 'Transumanza nell'Italia romana', with the remarks of Clementi (1985), 392–8; Gabba (1990) 'La transumanza nell'economia italico-romana'. For an overview, Frayn (1984) *Sheep-Rearing and the Wool-Trade in Italy during the Roman Period*. The argument was based in part on the coincidence that apparently the same regions, and even the same drove-roads, were used for large-scale transhumance in the early modern period. The valuable collection of Whittaker (1988) *Pastoral Economies in Classical Antiquity* (see the review-article of Kehoe (1990) 'Pastoralism and agriculture') emphasized, however, that pastoralism on any scale, and particularly long-distance transhumance, cannot simply be predicated upon a description of aspects of the physical environment, even mountains. Only the smaller-scale pastoral enterprises which are closely integrated with other systems of production may be regarded as a feature of the *longue durée* (on these, see VI.6). The authoritative paper contributed to the Whittaker volume by Garnsey (1988b) 'Mountain economies in southern Europe', rightly insists that these enterprises are normal in Mediterranean production, and that the effort involved in their extension into the less accessible, more marginal, fastnesses of forest and upland makes such episodes unusual, specialized, and short-lived. There is nothing odd about the lapsing and repetition of phases of intensification (cf. VII.4). And that they can take different forms is suggested by the research of Davite and Moreno (1996) 'Des "saltus" aux "alpes" dans les Appenins du Nord', showing the novelty of the pastoral system introduced with the Lombards – wooded meadow with occasional very short-term arable intrusions.

On specialized transhumance in southern Italy, Marino (1988) *Pastoral Economics in* the *Kingdom of Naples* is particularly to be recommended; see also Narciso (1991) *La cultura della transumanza*. Blanks (1995) 'Transhumance in the Middle Ages: the Eastern Pyrenees', shows how, in the upper Foix, the growing market for wool generated not improved opportunities for local pastoralists but a large-scale transhumance run especially by Cistercian monasteries, of a kind that was directly inimical to the concerns of smallholders. For Castile, Lewthwaite (1981) 'Plain tales from the hills'. For the Levant, Sartre (n.d.) 'Transhumance, économie et société de montagne en Syrie du sud'. On pastoralism in the Greek world and the absence of transhumance, Georgoudi (1974) 'La transhumance dans la Grèce ancienne'; Hodkinson (1988) 'Animal husbandry in the Greek polis', 57, on why ancient Greece did not develop highly specialized systems. Cherry (1988) 'Pastoralism and the role of animals in the pre- and protohistoric economies of the Aegean', 25–6, for elite investment in animals. On Crete, Rackham and Moody (1997) *The Making of the Cretan Landscape*, 159–64, on shepherding, with particular reference to transhumance.

For the ancient prejudice that nomads are the enemies of civilization (equated with agriculture) B. D. Shaw (1982–3) ' "Eaters of flesh, drinkers of milk": the ancient Mediterranean ideology of the pastoral nomad'; also, briefly, Sallares (1991) *The Ecology of the Ancient Greek World*, 36. For the Byzantine outlook, Ahrweiler (1998) 'Byzantine concepts of the foreigner: the case of the nomads'. For a twentieth-century exemplification of the prejudice, attributing considerable destructiveness of agriculture to nomads of the North African desert, Frend (1955) 'North Africa and Europe in the early Middle Ages'. It is disheartening to see that some archaeologists have continued to employ the clear-cut dyadic opposition of pastoralist and agriculturalist while at the same time patiently amassing information that demonstrates its invalidity from the very beginning of the archaeological record: cf. Bar-Yosef and Khazanov (1992) *Pastoralism in the Levant: Archaeological Materials in Anthropological Perspective*. The geographical tradition of schematically separating nomadic pastoralists from settled animal husbandry on one hand and agriculture on the other owes much to de Planhol (1968) *Les fondements géographiques de l'histoire de l'Islam*. Contrast Cahen (1973) 'Nomades et

sédentaires', and above all Mohammed (1978) 'The nomadic and the sedentary: polar complementaries – not polar opposites'.

For late Antiquity and the early Middle Ages see esp. Wickham (1983–5) 'Pastoralism and underdevelopment in the Middle Ages'; Donner (1989) 'The Role of nomads in the Near East in late Antiquity (400–800 C.E.)', with a welcome emphasis not only on how nomads have needed settled neighbours, but also on how the economy of settled peoples has been affected by the proximity of nomads. Medieval Anatolia offers a particularly rewarding set of examples. The arrival of bands of Türkmen nomads dislocated the existing population, but a symbiosis was the more readily achieved both because the newcomers were themselves partly agricultural anyway, and because the everyday pastoral enterprises of their new home provided a niche within the existing economy in which they might establish themselves: Hopwood (1991) 'Nomads or bandits? The pastoralist/sedentarist interface in Anatolia'. Compare Zachariadou (1983) *Trade and Crusade*, 163 n.684, on the sound equilibrium quickly established in the Menteshe emirates of Ionia and Lydia between former nomads and agriculturalists.

For the ebb and flow of pastoralism as a significant sector of the rural economy in the Middle Ages proper, beyond the works cited in the text, we mention only three discussions: Jameson et al. (1994) *A Greek Countryside*, 298–301, with a summary of pastoral interventions and a valuable discussion of the demographic effects of transhumance; Le Roy Ladurie (1975) *Montaillou*, 108–96; and (again) LaBianca (1990) *Sedentarization and Nomadization*, although its chronology is open to question: see Whittow (n.d.) 'Pastoralism and underdevelopment in the early medieval Near East', and compare Vryonis (1975) 'Nomadization and Islamization in Asia Minor'. As an example of a complex explanatory setting for the intensification of production into the mountain margins, see the interesting argument of J. R. McNeill (1992) *The Mountains of the Mediterranean World*, 352, with VIII.5. See also the brief remarks in Harvey (1989) *Economic Expansion in the Byzantine Empire 900–1200*, 149–57.

A more modern comparison: N. N. Lewis (1987) *Nomads and Settlers in Syria and Jordan 1800–1900*. And for the religious dimension of pastoralism X.3.

In the study of the minute interactions and small-scale movements which we have emphasized in summing up the *longue durée* in Mediterranean pastoralism, the way forward seems to lie with ethnoarchaeology – examination of the material deposits of modern societies which can then be used to interpret the archaeological record. See Barker and Grant (1991) 'Ancient and modern pastoralism in Central Italy: an interdisciplinary study in the Cicolano mountains', with some further bibliography, and VI.2 below.

ECOLOGY AND THE LARGER SETTLEMENT

On some of the topics alluded to or discussed in this chapter, the secondary sources to which reference might be expected are too voluminous to list. On other topics very little has been written and the major references are those included in the text. What follows is therefore even more highly selective in scope than has been the case in the preceding bibliographical essays.

1. AN URBAN TRADITION

We shall not attempt even a short list of works on the cities named at the beginning of the section. Indeed, our contention is precisely that Mediterranean history should *not* be read in this way. Compare Caro Baroja (1963) 'The city and the country: reflections on some ancient commonplaces'. Also the surprisingly still influential sketch by Pitkin (1963) 'Mediterranean Europe', making large claims for the essentially urban orientation of his subject. On some of the failings of city histories produced by ancient historians see Finley (1985b) *Ancient History: Evidence and Models*, ch. 4. Some of the problems inherent in the genre are explicitly addressed, and to some extent resolved, by Fernández-Armesto (1991) *Barcelona: A Thousand Years of the City's Past*.

On 'levels of urbanization' in Antiquity: Garnsey and Saller (1987) *The Roman Empire*; Pounds (1969) 'The urbanization of the classical world'. A medieval regional comparison: S. R. Epstein (1992) *An Island for Itself: Economic Development and Social Change in Late Medieval Sicily*. An instance of the problems involved in trying to assess medieval levels of urbanization is provided by Britnell (1991)

'The towns of England and northern Italy in the early fourteenth century'. For the Muslim as well as the Christian side of the Mediterranean during the Middle Ages, a modern outline of urban history can be gained from Fossier (1982–3) *Le moyen âge*. See also, although it relies heavily on a relatively small selection of secondary sources, Bairoch (1988) *Cities and Economic Development: From the Dawn of History to the Present*. Hohenberg and Lees (1985) *The Making of Urban Europe 1000–1950*, is less detailed and helpful. Recourse can also be had to 'national' urban histories such as Duby (1980–5) *Histoire de la France urbaine*.

On the *relative* (if hard to specify) continuity of urban history from Antiquity to the early Middle Ages in much of the Mediterranean region, see for example: B. Ward-Perkins (1984) *From Classical Antiquity to the Middle Ages: Urban Public Building in Northern and Central Italy, A.D. 300–850*; Barley (1977) *European Towns: Their Archaeology and Early History*; Hodges and Hobley (1988) *The Rebirth of Towns in the West A.D. 700–1050*, more up-to-date but also more narrowly focused than Barley; Christie and Loseby (1996) *Towns in Transition*, more wide-ranging, indeed trans-Mediterranean; Hendy (1985) *Studies in the Byzantine Monetary Economy*, for the Balkans and Anatolia; Kennedy (1985a) 'From *Polis* to *Madina*: urban change in late Antiquity and early Islamic Syria', with the modifications of B. Ward-Perkins (1996) 'Urban survival and urban transformation in the eastern Mediterranean'; Ashtor (1976) *A Social and Economic History of the Near East in the Middle Ages* – which is no substitute for the kind of synthesis that European medievalists enjoy in Nicholas (1997a and b) *The Growth of the Medieval City* and *The Later Medieval City*.

The urban vision of the 'four men in a boat': Momigliano (1969b) 'M. I. Rostovtzeff', 97–8, comments wittily on the formative character for his subject of the Russian agrarian economy. As for Pirenne, it will be sufficient to refer here to his (1925) *Medieval Cities: Their Origins and the Revival of Trade*, in which towns appear not only (as the title forewarns) as direct reflections of the vitality of long-distance commerce, but also as virtually autonomous agents of transformation in medieval society and culture (final chapter, 'Cities and civilization'). In this connection, Pirenne's ideas are appraised by Verhulst (1989) 'The origins of towns in the Low Countries and the Pirenne thesis'. (On the Pirenne Thesis see further V.5) Braudel's final published thoughts on towns, in his (1988–90) *The Identity of France*, suggest no great change of stance. Towns have 'sometimes enlivened and sometimes blocked' French history (2.415). Clearly separable from other kinds of settlement, they are allocated an independent role in the formation of the *longue durée*.

For the context of these ideas in the history of economic and social thought, see above all the excellent survey by Langton and Hoppe (1983) *Town and Country in the Development of Early Modern Western Europe*. See 5 for Marx, 6–8 for Pirenne. Merrington (1978) 'Town and country in the transition to capitalism', quotes texts from the pertinent eighteenth-century background and (175–9) the major discussions in Marx's writings of the division of labour between town and country as the motor of change in civil society. The classic essay, *The City*, by Max Weber, originally published in 1921 and finally to appear in his posthumous (1968) *Economy and Society*, vol. 3, ch. 16, is most accessible in the translation of 1958. For the interpretation of cities in Antiquity offered by such figures, the trenchant survey by Finley (1981a) 'The ancient city: from Fustel de Coulanges to Max Weber and beyond', remains fundamental.

On the 'ruralization' of history, there are salutary paragraphs questioning the historical validity of the etymological link between civilization and cities in Hallpike (1986) *The Principles of Social Evolution*, 258–60.

2. Definitions

Some functional definitions offered by geographers and historians: Hodges (1982a) *Dark Age Economics: The Origins of Towns and Trade A.D. 600–1000*, 20–5 (a convenient brief review). See also Berry (1972) *City Classification Handbook*; Lefebvre (1970) *La révolution urbaine* (its 333 urban variables noted by Finley (1981) 'The ancient city'); Scargill (1979) *The Form of Cities*; D. Clark (1982) *Urban Geography*, London; H. Carter (1983) *An Introduction to Urban Historical Geography*; Ucko, Tringham and Dimbleby (1972) *Man, Settlement and Urbanism*. The conclusion early reached by de Vries (1984) *European Urbanization 1500–1800*, 11, is notable: 'all . . . of these criteria are continuums, so that one must draw a line at some point dividing cities from non-cities. This cannot help but be arbitrary.'

The work of early medievalists is (or should be) of more than local interest in this respect: in no other post-classical period does the question 'what is a town?', or perhaps, better, since the decline of urbanism is a main issue, the question 'when is a town not a town?' loom so inevitably large. The contributors to Christie and Loseby (1996) *Towns in Transition*, who are most forcefully aware of the indissolubility of town and countryside and the need to study both 'urban' and 'rural' evidence simultaneously are, unfortunately, not Mediterranean in focus. B. Ward-Perkins (1997) 'Continuitists, catastrophists, and the towns of post-Roman northern Italy', is an entertaining analysis of the disciplinary and ethnic preconceptions informing historians' and archaeologists' definitions of Dark Age urban life.

The criterion of size: the classic work of Mols (1954–6) *Introduction à la démographie des villes d'Europe du XIVe au XVIIIe siècle*, adopts a threshold of 4,000 inhabitants as a practical definition. Bairoch, Batou and Chièvre (1988) *La population des villes européennes . . . 800–1500*, uses a threshold of 5,000. De Vries (1984) confines his study to settlements of at least 10,000 because historical evidence of smaller cities is too scanty (22).

Other criteria: ancient architectural expectations, along with the religious and cultural definitions favoured by some classics of historiography and sociology, are deftly summarized by Finley (1981a) 'The ancient city'.

Finley also comments on the impossibility of establishing transcultural criteria. Such 'qualitative models' of what makes urban life distinctively urban are reviewed by Gulick (1973) 'Urban anthropology', 984–95. Among these models see especially two classics: Redfield (1956) *Peasant Society and Culture*; and Sjoberg (1960) *The Preindustrial City*. Also, again, Weber (1958) *The City*.

Among modern demographic studies, 'a clear empirical understanding of the specificity of urban behavior' is for example attempted by Reher (1990) *Town and Country in Pre-industrial Spain: Cuenca, 1550–1870*, quotation from 4. On the 'urban graveyard effect', the negative growth rates taken to be characteristic of urban populations, see Sharlin (1978) 'Natural decrease in early modern cities'; Reher (1990) 59; de Vries (1984) *European Urbanization*, 179–82, both with further bibliography; Finlay (1981) *Population and Metropolis: The Demography of London 1580–1650*; compare also Landers (1993) *Death and the Metropolis*, on the demography of eighteenth-century London. Higounet-Nadal (1978) *Périgueux aux XIVe et XVe siècles*, 214, offers an extreme instance of a settlement that is 'kept going' by immigration (IX.5).

A classic in the ever-growing literature of attempts to depict a peculiarly urban psychology is Wirth (1938) 'Urbanism as a way of life'. For other sociological approaches, Saunders (1986) *Social Theory and the Urban Question*, offers a convenient if now slightly dated review.

It will be clear throughout that we have not derived much stimulus from explorations of the 'social construction of space' by geographers, whether of 'modern' or 'post-modern' temper. Cf. Duncan (1996) *BodySpace*; Benko and Strohmayer (1997) *Space and Social Theory: Interpreting Modernity and Postmodernity*. Even widely admired classics of an earlier generation such as Lefebvre's (1991, first published 1974) *The Production of Space*, fail to offer any empirical support for assertions about the special space 'produced' in towns – cf. 101, 235 – which makes the work less useful here even than his (1970) with its self-defeatingly immense catalogue of variables. Lefebvre and Régulier's brief (1996) 'Rhythmanalysis of Mediterranean cities', promises much in its title but fails to offer any basis for contrasting Mediterranean from Atlantic cities beyond historiographical clichés

about 'ritual' as against 'contractual' forms of association, and the like. Hillier and Hanson (1984) *The Social Logic of Space*, differentiate between small and large towns but not between towns and villages.

Granting that space is never culturally neutral does not forbid our microecological conception of the links between different parts of 'urban space' or between 'urban' and 'non-urban' space. On the other hand, our emphasis on the fragility and multiplicity of settlement ecologies might be seen as echoing one general thrust of post-modernism without committing us to its relativistic epistemology.

Mutability of Mediterranean settlements: the ancient concepts of synoicism and dioicism are usefully applied to a later period by Bryer (1986b) 'The structure of the late Byzantine town: *dioikismos* and the *mesoi*'. The classic study of such matters is Hodkinson and Hodkinson (1981) 'Mantinea and the Mantinike: settlement and society in a Greek polis', whence our example in the text. See also Cavanagh (1991) 'Surveys, cities and synoicism', for a range of archaeological instances. The title of Demand (1990) *Urban Relocation in Archaic and Classical Greece: Flight and Consolidation*, indicates its convincing argument that early Greek shifts of site were politically rather than environmentally inspired.

We note that for Rendeli (1993) *Città aperte: ambiente e paesaggio rurale organizzato nell'Etruria meridionale costiera durante l'età orientalizzante e arcaica*, the urban network of his period is a more fluid one than historians of the contemporary Greek polis usually admit, hence the 'open cities' of his title.

3. THE URBAN VARIABLE

Thesis: for Pirenne see section 1 above.

Antithesis: the most useful collection on the 'Brenner debate', which we take as exemplary, is Aston and Philpin (1985) *The Brenner Debate: Agrarian Class Structure and Economic Development in Pre-industrial Europe*. This includes a reprint of the paper that originated the controversy, Brenner (1982) 'The agrarian roots of European capitalism'. See also the valuable summary of the various arguments in Langton and Hoppe (1983) *Town and Country*, 17–35. Brenner's leading ideas are submitted to rigorous empirical scrutiny by S. R. Epstein (1992) *An Island for Itself*. The argument there is foreshadowed in Epstein (1991) 'Cities, regions and the late medieval crisis: Sicily and Tuscany compared'. On proto-industrialization see the special issue of the journal *Continuity and Change* (1993) vol. 8.2.

Synthesis: we follow the classic essay by Abrams (1978) 'Towns and economic growth: some theories and problems'. See also the works cited by Langton and Hoppe (1983) 40, with the excellent conspectus of Holton (1986) *Cities, Capitalism, and Civilization*. That settlements of widely varying sizes should still be seen, for ecological purposes, as lying on a continuum is one important theme in Hall and Kenward (1994) *Urban–Rural Connections: Perspectives from Environmental Archaeology*; cf. p. v.

4. TYPES AND THEORIES

Besides the references in the text, see again Finley (1981a) 'The ancient city', and Section 5 below for the typology of Greek and Roman settlements; Rich and Wallace-Hadrill (1991) *City and Country in the Ancient World*; S. L. Dyson (1992) *Community and Society in Roman Italy*, for the smaller settlements; Ennen (1987) *Die Europäische Stadt des Mittelalters*; Miskimin, Herlihy and Udovitch (1977) *The Medieval City*; Hohenberg and Lees (1985) *The Making of Urban Europe*. The most extensive debate over typology has concerned the Islamic city. Apart from references in text, see Hourani and Stern (1969) *The Islamic City*; Eickelman (1974) 'Is there an Islamic city? The making of a quarter in a Moroccan town'; J. L. Abu-Lughod (1987) 'The Islamic city: historic myth, Islamic essence, and contemporary relevance'; Goitein (1967–88) *A Mediterranean Society*, vol. 4, ch. ix, A, 1, for the form of Islamic cities as reflected in the Cairo Geniza. Barceló (1992) '¿Por qué los historiadores académicos preferien hablar de islamización en vez de hablar de campesinos?' exemplifies the resemblance between ancient and Islamic towns in their relationship to the countryside.

Central place theory: the original exposition was Christaller (1966) *Central Places in Southern Germany*. Sites were observed to achieve the most efficient spatial relationship to one another by being distributed in a hexagonal pattern. For useful summaries of the theory, its predictions and assumptions, see B. J. L. Berry

(1967) *The Geography of Market Centers and Retail Distribution*; C. A. Smith (1976) 'Regional economic systems: linking geographical models and economic problems'. Smith's modifications of the original theory are summarized and appraised (with bibliography) in Hodges (1988) *Primitive and Peasant Markets*, 17–25. See also Hohenberg and Lees (1985) *The Making of Urban Europe*. For both central place and rank-size distribution, Haggett, Cliff and Frey (1977) *Locational Analysis in Human Geography*, 110–53, and Bairoch (1988) *Cities and Economic Development*, ch. 9.

The relevance to pre-modern societies of such an approach was challenged by Clarke (1977) 'Introduction'. Attempts have none the less been made to apply the theory to ancient settlement patterns: Hodder and Hassall (1971) 'The non-random spacing of Romano-British walled towns'; Leveau (1983) 'La ville antique et l'organisation de l'espace rural: villa, *ville, village*', 924 (on the distribution of villas in Roman Mauretania); Grant (1986) *Central Places, Archaeology and History*; Randsborg (1991) *The First Millennium A.D. in Europe and the Mediterranean: An Archaeological Essay*, 90–4, with further references. A different approach, derived from Graph Theory and network analysis, is essayed by Sanders and Whitbread (1990) 'Central places and major roads in the Peloponnese', and is referred to again in V.1 below.

Rank-size distribution: brief summaries, bringing out the connection with central place theory: Wrigley (1991) 'City and country in the past: a sharp divide or a continuum?', 109–10; Hodges (1988) *Primitive and Peasant Markets*, 27–8. See also H. W. Richardson (1973) 'Theory of the distribution of city sizes: review and prospects'. The major historical analyses that we have found most useful and stimulating are de Vries (1984) *European Urbanization 1500–1800*, especially chs. 2 and 6 (the latter with full bibliography) and van der Woude et al. (1990) *Urbanization in History*, particularly the papers by Smith, 'Types of city-size distributions: a comparative analysis' (20–42) and de Vries, 'Problems in the measurement, description, and analysis of historical urbanization' (43–60). See also Schmal (1981) *Patterns of European Urbanization since 1500*. The pioneering attempt to apply rank-size theories to medieval Europe was that of J. Russell (1972) *Medieval Regions and their Cities*. It has not been generally reckoned a success, partly because it is based on inadequate data, partly because of its eccentric analytical techniques. See Britnell (1991) 'The towns of England and northern Italy', and de Vries (1984) *European Urbanization*, 42–3. With regard to the cities of ancient Roman Italy, the difficulties are exemplified in Morley (1996) *Metropolis and Hinterland*, 181–3. See also his (1997) 'Cities in context: urban systems in Roman Italy'. S. R. Epstein (1992) *An Island for Itself*, 150–7, applies 'Smithian' rank-size theory to later medieval Sicily and finds (unsurprisingly, we would add) 'rapid changes in size and ranking' and a 'fluid and complex structure' (157).

5. CONSUMPTION

We begin the section with Werner Sombart, whose (1916–27) *Der Moderne Kapitalismus*, vol. 1, has provided the most influential and most frequently quoted formulation of the the theory of the 'consumption city'. But it should be stressed that there are other formulations, both earlier and later, and that in the chapter we omit consideration of their subtleties. See especially Sjoberg (1960) *The Preindustrial City*. For summaries see Finley (1981a) 'The ancient city', offering his own glosses (note also Finley (1985a) *The Ancient Economy*, 125, and the further thoughts on 191–6); Bruhns (1985) 'De Werner Sombart à Max Weber et Moses Finley: la typologie de la ville antique et la question de la ville de consommation', usefully bringing out the evolution of Weber's views and the limited extent to which he was interested in the city *per se*; compare Capogrossi Colognesi (1995) 'The limits of the ancient city and the evolution of the medieval city in the thought of Max Weber', stressing the contradictions that eventually emerged in Weber's typology of cities. For the larger story Love (1991) *Antiquity and Capitalism: Max Weber and the Sociological Foundations of Roman Civilization*. Whittaker (1990) 'The consumer city revisited: the *vicus* and the city', and (1995) 'Do theories of the ancient city matter?', with full bibliography, defends Weber's against alternative theories. On Sombart's version of the subject see also the stimulating remarks of Hopkins (1978a) 'Economic growth and towns in classical Antiquity', 72–5: 'were ancient cities consumer cities? The answer must be yes.' The continuing hold of Sombart is

well reflected in the optimistic title of Parkins (1997) *Roman Urbanism: Beyond the Consumer City*, and by the studied omission of reference to consumption from the title of Parkins and Smith (1998) *Trade, Traders and the Ancient City*, though the Sombartian model is still debated in several contributions.

On Weberian ideal types: Finley (1981a) 12–15, Hopkins (1978a) 72–3. Weber's own thoughts are most accessible in the translated collection of his writings: (1949) *The Methodology of the Social Sciences*, 89–105. See also the comprehensive appraisal in McKinney (1966) *Constructive Typology and Social Theory*.

Constantinople and Madrid as consumer cities: Hendy (1985) *Studies in the Byzantine Monetary Economy*, 51, 561; Durliat (1990) *De la ville antique à la ville byzantine: le problème des subsistances*; C. Mango (1985) *Le développement urbain de Constantinople (IVe–VIIe siècles)* ch. 4; Mango and Dagron (1995) *Constantinople and its Hinterland*; Koder (1993) *Gemüse in Byzanz: Die Versorgung Konstantinopels mit Frischgemüse*; Teall (1959) 'The grain supply of the Byzantine empire 330–1025'. (It was complained that Constantinople grew fat while other cities sweated to feed it.) Ringrose (1983) *Madrid and the Spanish Economy, 1560–1850*, 314. For wider context, Clark and Lepetit (1996) *Capital Cities and their Hinterlands in Early Modern Europe*; S. L. Kaplan (1984) *Provisioning Paris: Merchants and Millers in the Grain and Flour Trade during the Eighteenth Century*. What is needed, where the archives permit, is the equivalent for some medieval Mediterranean centres of Campbell et al. (1993) on medieval London, *A Medieval Capital and its Grain Supply*.

On economic production in ancient cities, see again the perhaps too critical comments of Whittaker (1990) 'The consumer city revisited', with (1995) 'Do theories of the ancient city matter?', salutary on the extent to which evidence of profit-making by civic elites offers any genuine challenge to the Weber–Sombart ideal type. Contrast Carandini (1981) 'Sviluppo e crisi delle manifatture rurali e urbane', 255–60; Parkins (1997) *Roman Urbanism: Beyond the Consumer City*. For the sociological context, A. Wallace-Hadrill (1991) 'Elites and trade in the Roman town', although his medieval and modern Italian evidence, briefly adduced for the sake of comparison, tends to contradict his quasi-Weberian distinction between ancient and medieval towns. That commodity production in cities should be found to be petty in scale does not prove that it was insignificant in aggregate. And Whittaker himself shows how, if the enquiry is broadened to include *vici* (ancient small towns), evidence of specialist artisan centres becomes a good deal more ample. Hopkins (1980) 'Taxes and trade in the Roman empire', and (1983a) 'Models, ships and staples', has argued for a high level of trade in ancient Roman cities, partly so that citizens could earn money to pay taxes, and hence for the economic significance of cities as providers of markets and as centres of production for export (cf. V.4). The somewhat abstract and speculative modelling involved has not, of course, escaped criticism or modification from others. See, for example, Garnsey and Saller (1987) *The Roman Empire*, 46–51; Duncan-Jones (1990) *Structure and Scale in the Roman Economy*, chs. 3 and 12; but there is also growing empirical confirmation of Hopkins's ideas. It comes, first, from estimates of the degree to which the Roman world was monetized and thus paid taxes in coinage rather than in kind (taxation in kind requiring no production for export). Howgego (1992) 'The supply and use of money in the Roman world 200 B.C. to A.D. 300', gives a comprehensive survey and bibliography. Note the conclusion at 30: 'money was the dominant means of exchange for goods, at least in the cities'. Confirmation of Hopkins's models comes above all from the archaeology of the dispersed rural occupation sites that seem to have been very common in the ancient Mediterranean. J. Lloyd (1991) 'Forms of rural settlement in the early Roman empire', 238:

> it would seem increasingly difficult to retain the view . . . that the typical Roman town was a collection of amenities for the rich and their retainers, sucking in wealth from the countryside and returning to it very little. The sheer quantity of sites in the remoter countryside with centrally manufactured objects . . . suggests a more vigorous economic role for the town and the large village, in trade and quite possibly in manufacture too.

Compare Snodgrass (1990) 'Survey archaeology and the rural landscape of the Greek city'; III.2 above for dispersed settlement in south Etruria during Antiquity.

On the possible commercial involvement of the Roman upper classes see again Hopkins (1983a) 'Models, ships and staples', and Whittaker (1990) 'The consumer city revisited'; also Garnsey and Saller (1987) *The Roman Empire*, 47–8, with their further references. Osborne (1991a) 'Pride and prejudice, sense and subsistence: exchange and society in the Greek city', argues that 'the economic relationship between town and country should be understood as much in terms of the need of wealthy landowners for cash as of the need of landless town residents for food' (120), an interpretation which maintains the original model's emphasis on major consumers, but suggests a more sophisticated analysis of their needs, and also brings them into a far more wide-ranging contact with civic markets.

This section, and especially its closing remarks, owe much to Wrigley (1978b) 'Parasite or stimulus: the town in a pre-industrial economy'.

6. Settlement Ecology

Gottmann (1984) *Orbits: The Ancient Mediterranean Tradition of Urban Networks*, 14, offers an answer the question 'Why did the tradition of large, far-flung networks of cities originate [in the Mediterranean]? . . . Could this have been caused by the challenge of a difficult physical environment, with an uncertain rainfall, a mountainous topography, high seismicity, few good soils, a difficult sea?' Our own view is that these characteristics – albeit much less pessimistically assessed – are indeed strongly implicated in the formation of large, far-flung *networks*. But 'urban' does not seem to us to be the right word to describe them (IX.7).

Processes of microecological interaction within settlements: beyond what is mentioned in the text too little work has been done here, at least so far as Antiquity and the Middle Ages are concerned, for us to do more than advert to the potential of the topic. Some of the most promising studies have concerned medieval and Renaissance Italy. Cf. Heers (1977) *Family Clans in the Middle Ages*, and S. K. Cohn, Jr. (1980) *The Laboring Classes in Renaissance Florence*, although his chapter headed 'The ecology of the Renaissance city' delivers less than it promises; Owen Hughes (1977) 'Kinsmen and neighbours in medieval Genoa'. Work on 'the Islamic city' has touched on the themes of territoriality and neighbourhood; see again Eickelman (1974) 'Is there an Islamic city?', and J. L.

Abu-Lughod (1987) 'The Islamic city'. But there is a distinct lack of Mediterranean historical monographs to compare with e.g. Boulton (1987) *Neighbourhood and Society: A London Suburb in the Seventeenth Century*, or Garrioch (1986) *Neighbourhood and Community in Paris, 1740–1790*.

Rus in urbe: Purcell (1987b) 'Town in country and country in town'; for Rome's *disabitato* in the Middle Ages, Krautheimer (1980) *Rome: Profile of a City, 312–1308*; Hubert (1990) *Espace urbain et habitat à Rome*. On agriculture within the walls of ancient Pompeii, Jashemski (1979a) *The Gardens of Pompeii*, chs. 11–12, 14; Harvey (1989) *Economic Expansion in the Byzantine Empire*, 200–2; Bryer (1986b) 'The structure of the late Byzantine town'. More generally, on this and on urban farmers, Delano Smith (1979) *Western Mediterranean Europe*, ch. 4; on urban farmers in Antiquity, see also Garnsey (1979) 'Where did Italian peasants live?'

Suburbs: for the ancient world Purcell (1987a) 'Tomb and suburb'; Dagron (1979) 'Entre village et cité: la bourgade rurale des IVe–VIIe siècles en Orient'. For northern medieval cities Nicholas (1997a) *The Growth of the Medieval City*, ch. 6, and (1997b) *The Later Medieval City*, ch. 3, for some orientation.

Firewood for large settlements: see further Delano Smith (1979) *Western Mediterranean Europe*, 298–307; Meiggs (1982) *Trees and Timber in the Ancient Mediterranean World*, chs. 7–8, for the wood supplies of classical Athens and Rome; Olson (1991) 'Firewood and charcoal in classical Athens'; Bechmann (1990) *Trees and Man: The Forest in the Middle Ages*, ch. 6; Dunn (1992) 'The exploitation and control of woodland and scrubland in the Byzantine world', especially 257–9; and for a comparison with eighteenth-century Paris, Braudel (1988–90) *The Identity of France*, 2.479; also VI.4 below.

The arresting and theoretically dense archaeological-historical study of Fletcher (1995) *The Limits of Settlement Growth*, concerns the 'urban fabric' in its material aspects and has only rudimentary comments on the role of the supply base.

7. AUTARKY

Food supplies of Rome: see further Fulford (1987) 'Economic interdependence among urban communities of the Roman Mediter-ranean', 66–71; Sirks (1991) *Food for Rome*. On the trade in staples under the Roman Empire, Herz (1988) *Studien zur römischen Wirtschaftgesetzgebung: die Lebensmittelver-sorgung*. Compare Revel (1979) 'A capital city's privileges: food supplies in early-modern Rome'. Cf. Laiou (1967) 'The provisioning of Constantinople during the winter of 1306–7'; Mango and Dagron (1995) *Constantinople and its Hinterland*.

Civic responses to food shortage: there has been surprisingly little comparative work. See, however, Garnsey (1988a) *Famine and Food Supply in the Graeco-Roman World: Responses to Risk and Crisis*; and Garnsey and Morris (1989) 'Risk and the polis: the evolution of institutionalized responses to food supply problems in the ancient Greek state'. For hints that imports of grain were not wholly irregular, Mitchell (1993) *Anatolia*, 1.244, 247. On the near total absence of movements of grain from the nautical archaeological record of Antiquity see A. J. Parker (1984) 'Ship-wrecks and ancient trade in the Mediterra-nean'; cf. Parker (1992a) *Ancient Shipwrecks*, with BE IX.4. For the Middle Ages, Pounds (1974) *An Economic History of Medieval Europe*, 269–72, a most useful brief section on the food supply of various medieval European cities; also Nicholas (1997a) *The Growth of the Medieval City*, 176–8. For further bibliography, see Murphy (1998) 'Feeding medieval cities', esp. n.3. Lucas (1930) 'The great European famine of 1315, 1316, and 1317', sorely needs replacement, and has little on governmental response. Curschmann (1900) *Hungersnöte im Mittelalter*, remains an essential reference work. For some further bibliography on later medieval famines see Day (1987) *The Medieval Market Economy*, 220. It is a pity that Jordan (1996) *The Great Famine*, does not venture much beyond its subtitle: *Northern Europe in the Early Four-teenth Century*.

More wide-ranging study, along the lines of Peyer (1950) *Zur Getreidepolitik ober-italienischer Städte im 13. Jahrhundert*, is re-quired. See, however, Abulafia (1983a) 'Sul commercio del grano siciliano nel tardo Duecento', on the imports of Siena, Pisa, and other Italian cities. Thiriet (1981) 'Les routes maritimes dans l'Adriatique', shows that Ven-ice was dependent on 'blé de mer' for five to six months of the year, and Ragusa for ten, cf. Aymard (1966) *Venise, Raguse et le commerce du blé*. Reyerson (1995) *Society, Law and*

Trade in Medieval Montpellier, is also relevant to cereal and textile trades. Compare the dependence of much of North Africa, especially Tunisia, on Sicilian grain in the twelfth and thirteenth centuries that is revealed in the *fatwa* reported by Udovitch (1993) 'Muslims and Jews in the world of Frederic II', 91. Ashtor (1984) 'The wheat supply of the Mamlûk kingdom', stresses that grain was imported to later medieval Syria and Egypt, mainly from Sicily, in years of 'normal' Nile levels and harvest, perhaps because Sicilian grain was cheaper. Cf. Lapidus (1969) 'The grain economy of Mamluk Egypt'; Shoshan (1980) 'Grain riots and the moral economy: Cairo, 1350–1517'. As for Sicily, S. R. Epstein (1992) *An Island for Itself*, 145–50, presents a picture remarkably similar to Garnsey's: very low incidence of dearth, shortages often not very serious. Cf. BE VI.8.

More wide-ranging comparisons: Newman (1990) *Hunger in History: Food Shortage, Poverty, and Deprivation*.

The ideal and practice of autarky: A. H. M. Jones (1964) *The Later Roman Empire*, 2.844–5; Finley (1985a) *The Ancient Economy*, 125; Hopkins (1983a) 'Models, ships and staples', 105: 'very few Roman cities, located on river bank or sea-coast, grew in population significantly beyond the supportive capacity of their immediate hinterland'. Contrast Fulford (1987) 'Economic interdependence', 58: 'the degree of dependence of other communities [than Rome] on food supplies obtained from beyond their immediate hinterland is far from clear'. The leading ancient discussions of the ideal are Plato, *Republic*, 370E–371A; Aristotle, *Politics*, 1327a25–31. On von Thünen there is a useful brief introduction in *IESS*, 'Thünen, Johann Heinrich von'.

The most frequently cited ancient source for the difficulties of supplying the ancient city from beyond its hinterland is the fourth-century Gregory Nazianzen, *Oration* 43.34–5. This reveals the plight of Caesarea of Cappadocia (Kayseri) an inland city. According to Gregory, since the city lay inland and was not in a position to take advantage of the relative cheapness of water-borne transport, it could neither import food when it was lacking nor export a surplus. We should, however, remember that Gregory was describing, in highly charged rhetoric, the circumstances of a terrible famine; and that he was not generalizing across the whole of the late Roman world. On the other hand, it would

be a mistake to assume that Gregory's comments can be taken to apply only to the ancient world and that, say, later medieval inland cities would be more nearly able to afford the transport costs of overland trade. The transport costs of Antiquity, so far as they can now be established, were those of almost any pre-modern, pre-railway, society: see Hopkins (1983a) 'Models, ships and staples'; V.4; IX.4.

For some indication of the contribution that analysis of archaeologically recovered cereal grain could make to the debate on where a settlement found – and processed – its supplies, see Millett (1991) 'Roman towns and their territories: an archaeological perspective', esp. 184–5. The medieval archaeology of such matters is comparatively meagre, though cf. Hall and Kenward (1994) *Urban–Rural Connections*.

8. Dispersed Hinterlands

The principal references are all in the text. But on Córdoba see also Edwards (1987) '"Development" and "underdevelopment" in the western Mediterranean: the case of Córdoba and its region in the late fifteenth and early sixteenth centuries'. For the Italian cities P. Jones (1997) *The Italian City-State*, is indispensable context, although we would not accept some of the ideas underlying the detail (cf. BE V.4).

On Amalfi: Citarella (1968) 'Patterns in medieval trade: the commerce of Amalfi before the Crusades'; Balard (1976) 'Amalfi et Byzance (Xe–XIIe siècles)'. For the legendary origin of Amalfi in a shipwreck of voyagers to Constantinople, interestingly placed not in ancient times but as late as the fourth century, Manacorda (1979) 'Le urne di Amalfi non sono amalfitane'. Cahen (1953–4) 'Un texte peu connu relatif au commerce d'Amalfi au Xe siècle', presents a description of a riot at Cairo on 29 May A.D. 996 in which, it was alleged, 160 Amalfitan traders had perished. The Fatimid government had probably made it easier over the previous decades for Amalfitans and other Italians who had been used to dealing with their earlier dominion in the Maghreb to expand operations into their new territories in Egypt; the government took interestingly violent punitive measures against the malefactors.

On Genoa, Milanese (1987) *Scavi nell'oppidum preromano di Genova*, shows that it had already been involved in an 'économie du littoral' in the fifth century B.C.; see also

Cristofani (1985) *Il commercio etrusco arcaico*; Milanese and Mannoni (1986) 'Gli Etruschi a Genova e il commercio Mediterraneo'. For the Byzantine period Origone (1992) *Bisanzio e Genova*, 18–23. Wider context – and early medieval evidence: S. A. Epstein (1996) *Genoa and the Genoese 958–1528*. The few documents bearing on Genoa in the century preceding the First Crusade are assembled by Airaldi (1983) 'Groping in the dark: the emergence of Genoa in the early Middle Ages'. See also P. Jones (1997) *The Italian City-State*, 106–7.

Pisa: Herlihy (1958a) *Pisa in the Early Renaissance*, chs. 2, 8. Compare Caferro (1994) 'City and countryside in Siena in the second half of the fourteenth century', with wider bibliography.

For the examples taken from early modern Anatolia, see also McGowan (1981) *Economic Life in Ottoman Europe*, ch. 1 on Ottoman policies for provisioning Istanbul, and cf. Mitchell (1993) *Anatolia*, vol. 1, ch. 14, often usefully juxtaposing ancient and Ottoman sources.

BIBLIOGRAPHICAL ESSAY TO CHAPTER V

CONNECTIVITY

1. LINES OF SOUND AND LINES OF SIGHT

For a good deal that is touched on here see further Chapter IX. Principal references are in the text of this chapter. On auditory landscapes, see, however, A. Gell (1995) 'The language of the forest'.

Connectivity: our own informal definition should be distinguished from that of the topologists and geographers, conveniently summarized in Haggett et al. (1977) *Locational Analysis in Human Geography*, 315, and in Sanders and Whitbread (1990) 'Central places and major roads in the Peloponnese', 334–8, both with further references.

Routes: our concern is not with mapping routes in the conventional manner but rather with indicating the processes, only some of them environmental, by which they formed or altered. Our starting point has been Braudel (1972a) *The Mediterranean*, 276–312, though see also 103–38 on the seas within the Mediterranean. Note particularly 277 on the through route that seems not to engage with the settlement or economy of its immediate environs, 282 on communications as 'the infrastructure of all coherent history', and 295 on the patterns of relationship between the volumes of land- and sea-borne commerce. See also Braudel (1981–4) *Civilization and Capitalism*, 1.415–30, on pre-modern, almost invisible roads: those distinguishable from the surrounding countryside only by the regularity of movement along them, and determined more by the location of services for travellers than by any natural features, (1988–90) *The Identity of France*, 1.110–15, on obstacles to communication, vol. 2, ch. 12, and especially 461, distinguishing 'high' from 'low' routes, commercial arteries and veins from capillaries, the volume of goods carried on the latter being both the greater and the more stable. This distinction is analogous to that between shipping lanes and all-round maritime connectivity explored in Sections 2 and 3 of our chapter.

The problems of the history of land-transportation in the Mediterranean fit exactly to a pattern which we shall have cause to discuss more than once (VII.7; VIII.1). First a charismatic and exciting book with a big idea: Lefebvre des Noettes (1931) *L'attelage, le cheval de selle*; then caution and criticism which fails to counter the reception of the new orthodoxy: Sion (1935) 'Quelques problèmes de transport dans l'antiquité'; eventually, careful work based in part on unassailable new evidence: Raepsaet (1979) 'La faiblesse de l'attelage antique; le fin d'un mythe?'; Raepsaet (1982) 'Attelages antiques du nord de la Gaule: les systèmes de traction par équides'. Is it too much to hope that the myth of crippling weakness in ancient harnessing capabilities has now been finally refuted? Masschaele (1993) 'Transport costs in medieval England', shows that costs were much lower than progressivist orthodoxy suspected, thanks to improvements to infrastructure. There are interesting implications for the Roman world, for which see also Greene (1986) *The Archaeology of the Roman Economy*, ch. 2 (further IX.4).

For pack-animals, LeGall (1994) 'Un mode de transport méconnu: les animaux de bât'. On horses, see Vigneron (1968) *Le cheval dans l'antiquité gréco-romaine*; Anthony and Brown (1991) 'The origins of horseback riding'. Law (1976) 'Horses, firearms and political power in pre-colonial West Africa', 132, presents an instructive case of the historical ecology of the horse: except in the fodder-rich, transport-easy Niger delta 'west African kings were able to mobilize [by slave-sales] the purchasing power needed to import military supplies, whether horses or firearms; but they had more difficulty in finding the labour to maintain the horses'. The special case of the camel was famously discussed by Bulliet (1992) *The Camel and the Wheel*; but note the reconsiderations of Russell (1988) *After Eden*, and Irwin (1984) *The Camel*, 159–60, arguing for a relatively late date for the formation of pastoral strategies involving camels, and their independence of adaptation to the margin; see also Gauthier-Pilters and Dagg (1981) *The Camel*, and the remarkable, acute study by B. D. Shaw (1979) 'The camel in Roman North Africa and the Sahara: history, biology and human economy'.

On road and river transportation, the early evidence is collected by Piggott (1983) *The Earliest Wheeled Transport*; Greene (1986) *Archaeology of the Roman economy*, 36–43; Korres (1992) *Vom Penteli zum Parthenon*; Burford (1960) 'Heavy transport in classical Greece'; Tarr (1969) *The History of the Carriage*. For the Middle Ages, see Lopez (1956) 'The evolution of land transport in the Middle Ages'; Leighton (1972) *Transport and Communication in Early Medieval Europe, A.D. 500–1100*; Pounds (1974) *An Economic History of Medieval Europe*, 386–93, with further references; or Melis (1985) *I trasporti e le communicazioni nel medioevo*.

What are needed for the Mediterranean are regional studies of the overall characteristics of routes. Goitein (1967–88) *A Mediterranean Society*, vol. 1, ch. 4, includes many illuminating details. The characteristics of routes in the Mediterranean are specific to the configuration of microregions at any given period. They will therefore be both mutable and local. An extraordinarily well-preserved network of ancient roads across a classically small cluster of microregions in the Akamas peninsula of western Cyprus is studied by Bekker Nielsen (1995) 'The road network'. Tzedakis (1989) 'Les routes minoennes', examines another, even older, landscape of communications, in eastern Crete, although it distinguishes administrative and security functions from economic ones too sharply. For Cretan roads in general, compare Rackham

and Moody (1997) *The Making of the Cretan Landscape*, 154–8. Kase (1991) *The Great Isthmus Corridor Route*, is an unusually detailed analysis of a collection of paths which variously instantiated a more general line of communications in central Greece, set against the background of a percipient account of the physical landscape. A medieval case is revealed in the prominence of local roads in the Mount Athos archives which document the villages of western Chalcidice: Lefort (1991) 'L'organisation de l'espace rurale'. Bautier (1991) *Sur l'histoire économique de la France médiévale: La route, le fleuve, la foire*, a collection of reprinted studies showing the lack of 'fit' between between medieval French roads and both their Roman predecessors and pilgrim routes, suggests something of what can be attempted at 'national' level. Compare French (1981) *Roads and Milestones of Asia Minor*, 1: *The Pilgrims' Road*; Mitchell (1993) *Anatolia*, 1.124–36; Hild (1977) *Das byzantinische Strassensystem in Kappadokien*, shows some of the weaknesses of a traditional approach: the absence of comparisons to bring out regional peculiarities, the presentation of a static picture, the lack of geographical detail, and the concomitant assumption that routes can be mapped by joining archaeological sites with straight lines. For the routes of the medieval Atlantic Maghreb as delineated by the early Arab geographers, Siraj (1995) *L'image de la Tigitanie*, parts 2–3.

For further examples on the ways in which ties of perception become enshrined in the toponyms of the Mediterranean, see Kahane and Kahane (1971) 'From landmark to toponym', drawing on the evidence of the fifteenth-century Italian portolans.

2. Extended Archipelagos: The Connectivity of the Maritime

Gateway settlements: further historical studies that bear on the phenomenon include: Ducellier (1981) *La façade maritime de l'Albanie au moyen âge: Durazzo et Valona du XIe au XVe siècle*; and Milanese and Mannoni (1986) 'Gli Etruschi a Genova e il commercio Mediterraneo'. Beach-head settlements: Tucciarone (1991) *I Saraceni nel Ducato di Gaeta*. Rickman (1985) 'Towards a study of Roman ports', stresses the usefulness of the British Admiralty Handbooks for the study of ancient ports. It is interesting to reflect that this usefulness derives directly from the fact that imperial Britain inherited the preoccupations and responses of the maritime milieu in which the ports of Antiquity had their origin. For the whole idea of the maritime milieu, usefully known in the literature of classical archaeology as a *koine*, see Purcell (1990a) 'Mobility and the polis'. On the convenience of ancient sea-travel add Rougé (1984) 'Le confort des passagers à bord des navires antiques'. For the Islamic world, Hourani (1963) *Arab seafaring*, although orientated to the Indian Ocean and perhaps too cautious about techniques, provides instructive parallels. (Further BE IX.7.)

Examples of the significance of islands for the commerce associated with sea-lanes in the Middle Ages: Thiriet (1953) 'Venise et l'occupation de Ténédos au XIV siècle'; Abulafia (1994) *A Mediterranean Emporium: The Catalan Kingdom of Majorca*; Malamut (1988) *Les îles de l'empire byzantin (VIIIe–XIIe siècles)*. For the earlier periods, see for example Schallin (1993) *Islands under Influence*; Brun (1996) *Les archipels égéens dans l'antiquité grecque*. A good and early example of a maritime hinterland is offered by Lolos (1995) 'Late Cypro-Mycenaean seafaring: new evidence from sites in the Saronic and Argolic Gulfs'. For Cretan offshore islands and their unexpected importance, Rackham and Moody (1997) *The Making of the Cretan Landscape*, 202–8. The tendency to over-emphasize island isolation, in order to apply the theories of insular biogeography to social and economic history, is well presented by Patton (1996) *Islands in Time*. For the interactionist alternative, see Waldren (1985) *The Deya Conference of Prehistory: Early Settlement in the Western Mediterranean Islands*, or, briefly, Purcell (1995a) 'Field survey of an asteroid'. But the very sensible account of Febvre (1925) *A Geographical Introduction to History*, 219, may also be recommended. See also VI.11.

One further indirect measure of the 'higher connectivity' of the maritime deserves mention here: the evidence of linguistic borrowing. Particular sets of navigational and mercantile terms can, at various stages, be discerned radiating outward from centres of influence to achieve something approaching Mediterranean-wide currency. Byzantium could not, we suggest in the chapter, have achieved a genuine thalassocracy in the early Middle Ages; but it did perhaps manage the linguistic equivalent, contributing over fifty loan-words

to the vocabulary of western Mediterranean navigation. On this see Kahane and Kahane (1970–6) 'Abendland und Byzanz: Sprache', 408–22. For the centres of influence within Islam, Pellegrini (1978) 'La terminologia marinara di origine araba in italiano e nelle lingue europee'. See also Yajima (1986) *Arwad Island: A Case Study of Maritime Culture on the Syrian Coast*. In the later Middle Ages, Venice and Genoa became centres from which lexemes radiated, especially eastward. The major work in this field remains Kahane, Kahane and Tietze (1958) *The Lingua Franca in the Levant: Turkish Nautical Terms of Italian and Greek Origin*, which documents the Mediterranean-wide distribution of the origins of 878 nautical terms in pre-modern Turkish (thirteenth to eighteenth centuries) thereby hoping to demonstrate the 'linguistic-cultural unity of the Mediterranean' (vii). See especially 227 on the way in which the Italian *fortuna*, meaning primarily 'ill fortune' developed into the word for 'storm' (at sea) in some ten circum-Mediterranean languages. The major reference work: the *glossaire nautique* of Augustin Jal was first published in 1848; as we write its second edition has reached the letter K: Jal (1988–) *Nouveau glossaire nautique*.

3. SHIPPING LANES

As will be plain from references in the text, the whole section is greatly indebted to Pryor (1988) *Geography, Technology, and War: Studies in the Maritime History of the Mediterranean 649–1571*, which we have read in conjunction with Udovitch (1978) 'Time, the sea and society: duration of commercial voyages on the southern shores of the Mediterranean during the high Middle Ages'; Lewicki (1978) 'Les voies maritimes de la Méditerranée dans le haut moyen âge d'après les sources arabes'; and Braudel (1972a) *The Mediterranean*, 103–38. Vidal de la Blache (1896) 'Les voies de commerce dans la géographie de Ptolémée', made an early, grand attempt at the representation of redistribution through the delineation of sources of commodities and trade routes. For the classical world cf. Charlesworth (1926) *Trade-Routes and Commerce of the Roman Empire*, but contrast Braemer (1998) 'Eléments naturels', on winds and currents; Arnaud (1998) 'La navigation hauturière', on direct routes across open sea.

Cabotage: Udovitch (1978) valuably stresses the small size of many Mediterranean ships and the importance of coastwise sailing as against open-sea passages (especially 544, on how ships that seemed to have passed into the open sea may well just have been taking advantage of higher coastal reference points, and 551). A. J. Parker (1996) 'Sea transport and trade in the ancient Mediterranean', is a helpful survey; L. Casson (1971) *Ships and Seamanship in the Ancient World*, offers a classification of the numerous types of boat attested; Rougé (1966b) *Recherches sur l'organisation du commerce maritime en Méditerranée sous l'empire romain*, 173–4, also argues for the importance of *cabotage* in Antiquity, while Broodbank (1993) 'Ulysses without sails: trade, distance, knowledge and power in the early Cyclades', takes the story back to prehistory.

On the tiny, but eloquent, island site of Aghios Petros in the northern Sporades, Efstratiou (1985) *Agios Petros: A Neolithic Site in the Northern Sporades: Aegean Relationships during the Neolithic of the Fifth Millennium B.C.* A wider horizon is offered by Korfmann (1988) 'East–west connections throughout the Mediterranean in the early Neolithic period'. See also E. M. Melas (1985) *The Islands of Karpathos, Saros and Kasos in the Neolithic and Bronze Ages*. Balard (1974) 'Escales génoises sur les routes de l'Orient méditerranéen au XIVe siècle', brings out the problem of the bias of the documentary sources towards the larger ports that had a legal or administrative identity; that bias renders the lesser ports hard for the historian to 'see' (cf. IX.7). See also Cahen (1978) 'Ports et chantiers navals dans le monde méditerranéen musulman jusqu'aux Croisades'; Ahrweiler (1978) 'Les ports byzantins (VIIe–IXe siècles)', Goitein (1967–88) *A Mediterranean Society*, 1.211–14, 318–21. For the importance of *cabotage* in the medieval wine trade Zug Tucci (1978) 'Un aspetto trascurato del commercio medievale del vino', 320.

On the sailing season, see Pryor (1988) 1–3, 87–9; Duncan-Jones (1990) *Structure and Scale in the Roman Economy*, 10–11; Claude (1985–7a) *Der Handel im westlichen Mittelmeer während des Frühmittelalters*, 31–4; Udovitch (1978) 530–3; Goitein (1967–88) *A Mediterranean Society*, 1.316–17; S. A. Epstein (1988) 'Labour in thirteenth-century Genoa', 125; also Byrne (1930) *Genoese Shipping in the Twelfth and Thirteenth*

Centuries. On *mare clausum* and winter sailing in Antiquity, Rougé (1952) 'La navigation hivernale sous l'empire romain'. All estimates are likely to be revised in the light of the Elephantine Palimpsest (see the following section), attesting year-round navigation in the eastern Mediterranean of the early fifth century B.C. except for January and February. A striking medieval example of how expectations of a winter standstill might be contradicted is provided, from a ninth-century Arabic chronicler, by Conrad (1992) 'The conquest of Arwâd: a source-critical study in the historiography of the early medieval Near East', 366–8; contrast Ashburner (1909) *The Rhodian Sea Law*, cxlii–cxliii. Randsborg (1991) *The First Millennium in Europe and the Mediterranean*, 125, suggests, somewhat boldly, that the number of ancient Mediterranean shipwrecks (BE IX.4) is an indication of the extent to which goods were transported 'at times of the year with poor weather because of the considerable pressure on the economic systems for provisions'.

On ships and their history, see Greenhill (1976) *Archaeology of the Boat*, Morrison (1980) *Long Ships and Round Ships: Warfare and Trade in the Mediterranean 3000 B.C.–A.D. 500*; McGrail (1981) *Rafts, Boats and Ships from Prehistoric Times to the Medieval Era*. The treatment of marine technology in Pryor (1988) 25–86, is especially helpful. At 33–5, for instance, he argues that 'early medieval round ships conceded as much ground in leeway as they gained through their ability to point to the wind', cf. 51, and Adam (1976) 'Conclusions sur les développements des techniques nautiques médiévales'. See also Christides (1988) 'Naval history and naval technology in medieval times: the need for interdisciplinary studies'. For later medieval nautical technology and technique, Goitein (1967–88) *A Mediterranean Society*, 1.325; cf. 1.213 on the mixture and overlapping of long- and short-distance routes in the Muslim Mediterranean; Ashtor (1992) *Technology, Industry and Trade: The Levant versus Europe, 1250–1500*. Kreutz (1976) 'Ships, shipping and the implication of change in the early medieval Mediterrranean', shows that change in shipbuilding technique was normal and gradual, although, in the eighth and ninth centuries, the special requirements of all-weather raiding promoted skeleton-first building and the lateen. On her view, however, the faster technique, involving less skill, was a dubious advance – simply a foundation for future improvement; the main revolution lay in the introduction of North Sea techniques in the late Middle Ages. Lane (1986) 'Technology and productivity in seaborne transportation', 238–40, discusses the relation between technology and productivity in seaborne transportation. He argues that the efficiency gains, especially in labour costs, of what he calls the Medieval Nautical Revolution were offset even after 1250 by the continuing high cost of security. The older view that the compass made a dramatic difference to navigation will be found in E. G. R. Taylor (1956) *The Haven-Finding Art*, and Lane (1963) 'The economic meaning of the invention of the compass'. For star-navigation and night sailing in Antiquity, Rutherfurd-Dyer (1983) 'Homer's wine-dark sea'.

4. ECONOMIES COMPARED

We allude to the usual outline economic history of the ancient and medieval Mediterranean, and in particular to the great commercial empires of the later Middle Ages. An adequate bibliography on all this would, of course, be enormous, and hardly necessary to sustain a brief allusion. We come to the economy of the Roman Empire in a moment. For the Middle Ages it will be enough here (cf. BE IX.1) to point to the references in Pryor (1988) ch. 6; to Abu-Lughod (1989) *Before European Hegemony*, chs 4 and 7, with very useful bibliographies; to P. Jones (1997) *The Italian City-State*, chs 1, 3, of much wider geographical implication than its title, for the 'commercial revolution', on which the basic introduction remains Lopez (1976) *The Commercial Revolution of the Middle Ages 950–1350*; Lopez (1987) 'The trade of medieval Europe: the South', and Abulafia (1987) 'Asia, Africa and the trade of medieval Europe'.

At the other extreme, we touch on the lowest common denominators of economic history: H. Forbes (1982) *Strategies and Soils: Technology, Production, and Environment in the Peninsula of Methana, Greece*, 356–75, for systematic overproduction as a safeguard against future dearth; cf. Halstead (1990a) 'Waste not, want not: traditional responses to crop failure in Greece', 152. Gallant (1991) *Risk and Survival in Ancient Greece*, ch. 3. For low-level exchange between communities lacking a common language, in North Africa, Parise (1978) ' "Baratto silenzioso" fra punici e libi'. For a later example of the sort of local trade that deserves much further archival study, see Ducellier (1981) *La façade maritime de l'Albanie au moyen âge*; and, for the pre-Ottoman Islamic world, Lutfi (1985) *Al-Quds al-Mamlûkiyya: A History of Mamlûk Jerusalem based on the Haram Documents*. Something of the range, and distant origins, of the goods that a humbler figure might be able to sell can be gleaned from comparative material: e.g. Spufford (1984) *The Great Reclothing of Rural England: Petty Chapmen and their Wares in the Seventeenth Century*, chs 1, 6; Métral (1996) 'Du commerce itinérant à l'import-export'. Further, Chapters VI, IX.

The argument that local and interannual climatic and crop-yield variability generated trade in commodities is deployed by Hopkins, in e.g. (1978a) 'Economic growth and towns in classical Antiquity', 48, and (1983a) 'Models, ships and staples', 90.

It is, indeed, Hopkins who has most effectively and interestingly challenged the orthodoxy established by A. H. M. Jones (1964) *The Later Roman Empire*, and Finley (1985a) *The Ancient Economy* (and still well-represented by P. Jones (1997) *The Italian City-State*, ch. 1). The most authoritative reply to Finley's minimalist position is, however, generally regarded as being Frederiksen (1975) 'Theory, evidence and the ancient economy'. Apart from Hopkins's two papers cited in the previous paragraph, see Hopkins (1980) 'Taxes and trade in the Roman empire', on the trade perhaps generated by the state's monetary tax demands; cf. BE IV.5. On elite involvement in trade see A. Wallace-Hadrill (1991) 'Elites and trade in the Roman town', with ample bibliography and our references in BE IV.5. On the diffusion around the region of cheap goods such as cooking and table wares, suggestive of Mediterranean-wide trade in staples in Antiquity, Fulford (1987) 'Economic interdependence among urban communities of the Roman Mediterranean'; Tortorella (1986) 'La ceramica fine di mensa Africana dal IV al VII secolo d.C.' The degree of interdependence and the high volumes and complexity of 'international' trade that has been discerned in ancient economies by scholars at the close of the twentieth century can be gauged from Parkins and Smith (1998)

Trade, Traders and the Ancient City. It *may* be, as argued by Wickham (1988a) 'Marx, Sherlock Holmes, and late Roman commerce', section IV, that only the state could provide the infrastructure necessary for a region such as North Africa to gain the commercial advantage that could result in the integration of those zones. But if private traders 'piggy-backed' off state infrastructure, it could equally be said that that very same infrastrucure pre-supposed the existence of a multiplicity of available private traders who could be enlisted. See Paterson (1998) 'Trade and traders in the Roman world', esp. 157, in an analysis we generally find very congenial (IX.4).

The similarities between the ancient economy thus 'revised' upwards in sophistication and that of later centuries is most forcefully emphasized by Carandini and his associates. Wickham (1988a) is a sympathetic introduction. Cf. Carandini (1986) 'Il mondo della tarda antichità visto attraverso le merci'. Contrast the sceptical comparative use made of Braudel in, for instance, Whittaker (1990) 'The consumer city revisited', 111–12 (see also his (1988) 'Trade and the aristocracy in the Roman empire'): references to Braudel (1972a) *The Mediterranean*, are used to cast doubt on Hopkins's model of the economics of the ancient city. Braudel comments (425) that 60 or 70 per cent of the gross product of the Mediterranean never reached the market. This makes the region in the early modern period sound rather like the Jones–Finley conception of the ancient Mediterranean. Yet the rest of Braudel's monograph also, of course, demonstrates that such a substantial non-market sector was entirely compatible with vigorous long-distance commerce in staples, indeed with nascent merchant capitalism. The ancient economy could perhaps be imagined in terms of a similar conjunction. For examples of the great later medieval western entrepreneurs who have too often unbalanced comparisons of this kind, Lopez (1933) *Genova marinara nel Duecento: Benedetto Zaccaria, ammiraglio e mercante*; Origo (1979) *The Merchant of Prato: Francesco di Marco Datini, 1335–1410*; P. Jones (1997) *The Italian City-State*, 197–200. Contrast the figures passed in review by Lopez (1987) 'The trade of medieval Europe', 366–70.

Finally on the historiography of primit-ivism/minimalism as a species of Orientalism, contrasting a varied modernity with an undifferentiated distant past, see Macfarlane (1994) 'History and anthropology'.

5. The Early Medieval Depression

As before, principal specific references are in the text. Although no one work covers the 'Pirenne period' in quite the way that we do here, there is a sizeable literature surrounding many of the topics that we touch on – not the least part of which is generated by continuing debate on the Pirenne thesis. In what follows, we limit ourselves to the more recent and more wide-ranging publications that can serve as a guide to fuller bibliography.

The agreed picture of the late Antique economy: shipwreck evidence may be sampled in A. J. Parker (1984) 'Shipwrecks and ancient trade in the Mediterranean', but the standard reference work is Parker (1992a) *Ancient Shipwrecks of the Mediterranean* (IX.4). B. Ward-Perkins (forthcoming) 'Specialized production and exchange', will be an extremely valuable survey, of the latest archaeology especially, suggesting, within an overall story of decline, the complexity of the possible causes, and, with all due regard to the limitations of the evidence, proposing a shift in the geography of sophisticated economic life southwards and eastwards. Loseby (forthcoming b) 'The Mediterranean economy', will continue the story, emphasizing (to a far greater extent than would we) collapse and crisis in the mid to late seventh century, a product of the simultaneous waning of state mechanisms of supply and falling demand. The major collections of essays, over which the shadow of Pirenne looms large: Hodges and Bowden (1998) *The Sixth Century: Production, Distribution and Demand*; Wickham and Hansen (forthcoming) *The Long Eighth Century*. For the preceding period Garnsey and Whittaker (1998) 'Trade, industry and the urban economy'.

Interim syntheses of the archaeological (primarily ceramic) evidence for exchange up to the seventh century, Panella (1986) 'Le merci: produzione, itinerari e destini'; Wickham (1998) 'Overview: production, distribution and demand [sixth-century]', (forthcoming) 'Trade and exchange, 550–750: the view from the West'; Citter et al. (1996) 'Commerci nel Mediterraneo occidentale nell'alto medioevo'.

The challenges and complexities of the ceramic evidence are well illustrated by Reynolds (1995) *Trade in the Western Mediterranean, A.D. 400–700.*

An important caveat is entered by Whittaker (1983b) 'Late Roman trade and traders', 178: 'we must beware of supposing that a reduction in long-distance trade, as may have happened [in late Antiquity] is a symptom of absolute decline.'

On demand, Bridbury (1969) 'The Dark Ages', can now be compared with Lewit (1991) *Agricultural Production in the Roman Economy A.D. 200–400*, arguing for the vigorous persistence of agriculture virtually right across the late Empire. See also Gunderson (1976) 'Economic change and the demise of the Roman empire'; and Moreland (1994) 'Wilderness, wasteland, depopulation and the end of the Roman empire?', both challenging theories of decline based on depopulation.

Civic life – with which we are not specifically concerned, seeing the demand for goods as shifting across a spectrum that included both 'urban' and 'rural' settings in Antiquity just as much as in the early Middle Ages (IV.5): a useful synopsis in Cameron (1993) *The Mediterranean World in Late Antiquity A.D. 395–600*, ch. 7. Barnish (1989) 'The transformation of classical cities and the Pirenne debate', is an extremely wide-ranging and detailed survey. More recent work: Christie and Loseby (1996) *Towns in Transition: Urban Evolution in Late Antiquity and the Early Middle Ages*; Brogiolo (1996) *Città altomedievali nel mediterraneo occidentale.*

The 'core' Pirenne period (roughly seventh to ninth centuries): some bibliography on Pirenne himself and on the general discussion of his ideas was given in BE II. Collections of work on Pirenne and the problem of the Dark Age caesura: Havighurst (1958) *The Pirenne Thesis: Analysis, Criticism and Revision*; Hübinger (1968) *Bedeutung und Rolle des Islams beim Übergang von Altertum zum Mittelalter*. But the most accessible examination of the history and archaeology of the early medieval depression remains Hodges and Whitehouse (1983) *Mohammed, Charlemagne and the Origins of Europe*. Its somewhat simplistic analysis of the causes of Carolingian economic and cultural success (assigned, *à la* Pirenne, to long-distance trading links) has not, however, found favour. See, as a sample review, that by B. Ward-Perkins (1986); also various local elaborations of the theme of

collapsing demand by Hodges, e.g. (1990) 'Rewriting the rural history of early medieval Italy'. Randsborg (1991) *The First Millennium A.D. in Europe and the Mediterranean: An Archaeological Essay*, ch. 6: 'Production and exchange', is disappointingly unfocused. Barnish (1989) 'The transformation of classical cities and the Pirenne debate', unfortunately devotes only its final section (396–400) to commerce, and is more concerned with the decline of ancient centres than with the rise of early medieval ones. Z. Rubin (1986) 'The Mediterranean and the dilemma of the Roman empire in late Antiquity', makes an unusual contribution to the debate inspired by Pirenne on when and how the Mediterranean unity fostered by the Roman Empire came to an end. The growing interdependence of Byzantium and Sassanian Iran is seen as shifting the centre of gravity of the late Roman world eastwards and as creating a vacuum in the western Mediterranean. An immense and somewhat indigestible accumulation of learning on the whole 'Pirenne period', from early Byzantium to Viking Ireland, is to be found in Düwel et al. (1985–7) *Untersuchungen zu Handel und Verkehr der vor- und frühgeschichtlichen Zeit in Mittel- und Nordeuropa.*

For our purposes the most stimulating relevant discussions, which do not take too pessimistic a view of the possibilities of continued connectivity, have been Kreutz (1976) 'Ships, shipping, and the implications of change in the early medieval Mediterranean'; Udovitch (1978) 'Time, the sea and society'; and Doehaerd (1978) *The Early Middle Ages in the West: Economy and Society.*

On thalassocracy and naval hostilities in the period, see also Fahmy (1966), *Muslim Sea-Power in the Eastern Mediterranean from the Seventh to the Tenth Century A.D.*; Eickhoff (1966) *Seekrieg und Seepolitik zwischen Islam und Abendland: das Mittelmeer unter Byzantinischer und Arabischer Hegemonie (650–1040)*; J. Haywood (1991) *Dark Age Naval Power: A Re-assessment of Frankish and Anglo-Saxon Seafaring Activity*; Ahrweiler (1966) *Byzance et la mer: la marine de guerre, la politique et les institutions maritimes de Byzance aux VIIe–XVe siècles*; A. R. Lewis (1951) *Naval Power and Trade in the Mediterranean, A.D. 500–1100*, to be used with caution; Gabrieli (1964) 'Greeks and Arabs in the central Mediterranean area'. On the historiographical question of natural seafarers and natural landlubbers, Rougé (1981) *Ships and Fleets of the Ancient Mediterranean*; ch. 1 provides a generally optimistic account, stressing the vanity of supposing some peoples constitutionally good sailors and others not, and attacking the technological determinism of Major Lefebvre des Noettes. Also Purcell (1996a) 'The ports of Rome: evolution of a *façade maritime*'. For the *longue durée* of Semitic precursors of the supposed Arab 're-jection' of the Mediterranean, Linder (1996) 'Human apprehension of the sea'.

The international and interreligious character of trade in the period: well brought out by Kreutz (1976) 89–93. Lombard (1948) 'Mahomet et Charlemagne: le problème éco-nomique', is the much-discussed and criti-cized classic that occupies the background to subsequent debate. See further the section on Byzantium below. On later Muslim juristic attitudes to travel to the land of the infidels for the purpose of such trade, see B. Lewis (1992) 'Legal and historical reflections on the position of Muslim populations under non-Muslim rule', 7; Udovitch (1993) 'Muslims and Jews in the world of Frederic II', 91.

Piracy and the economy: Ashtor (1970) 'Quelques observations d'un orientaliste sur la thèse de Pirenne'; Ashtor (1976) *A Social and Economic History of the Near East in the Middle Ages*, 103–4, overestimates the dam-age done by Byzantine and Muslim raiders in the eighth and ninth centuries and the extent to which they could afford to disrupt the sources of their livelihood. To us, Udovitch (1978) 'Time, the sea and society', again offers a more congenial perspective. Com-parison with near-contemporary Viking raids would be instructive. For the repeated raids on such northern trading emporia as Dorestad in Francia and Hamwih (Saxon Southamp-ton) see the convenient summary in Sawyer (1982) *Kings and Vikings: Scandinavia and Europe A.D. 700–1100*, ch. 6. Cf. Sawyer (1971) *The Age of the Vikings*, ch. 8, espe-cially 192, on Baltic piracy, profitable only if there was wealth to be plundered, and if there were markets available in which plundered luxuries could be exchanged for necessities. For the wider view of Mediterranean piracy and its relation to other economic activity, compare Ormerod (1924) *Piracy in the An-cient World*, a remarkably wide-ranging work, which remains an excellent introduction to its subject. Other helpful studies of ancient piracy include Gianfrotta (1981) 'Commerci

e pirateria: prime testimonianze archeologiche sottomarine'; Giuffrida Gentile (1983) *La pirateria tirrenica: momenti e fortuna*; Clavel-Lévecque (1978) 'Brigandage et piraterie'; and Garlan (1978) 'Signification historique de la piraterie grecque'. For the later period, compare Goitein (1967–88) *A Mediterranean Society*, 1.327–33; Burns (1980) 'Piracy as an Islamic–Christian interface in the thirteenth century'. On wrecking Rougé (1966a) 'Le droit de naufrage et ses limitations'. Cf. IX.6.

6. Connectivity Maintained?

The evolving nature of the archaeological evidence: B. Ward-Perkins (forthcoming) 'Specialized production and exchange', and also A. R. Lewis (1978) 'Mediterranean mari-time commerce, A.D. 300–1100', 3, drama-tizing the change in terms of a 'container revolution' (IX.4). This is too charged a way of indicating a far more gradual shift from amphorae to barrels: Arthur (1993) 'Early medieval amphorae, the duchy of Naples and the food supply of Rome', 241 n.39, shows that the change began in Roman times (for barrels in Antiquity see also Vandermersch (1994) *Vins et amphores de Grande Grèce et de Sicile*, 16) and that it lasted, in the Byzantine and Islamic Mediterranean, until the end of the Middle Ages.

Coinage: much discussion has focused on the role of Muslim coinage in commercial relations between Islam and Europe, less on what the few individual finds can tell us about possible networks of exchange. See Ehrenkreutz (1972) 'Another orientalist's re-marks concerning the Pirenne thesis', 95 n.4; Cahen (1965) 'Quelques problèmes con-cernant l'expansion économique musulmane au haut moyen âge', modified in (1980) 'Commercial relations between the Near East and western Europe from the VIIth to the XIth century'; and, for the West, Hendy (1988) 'From public to private: the western barbarian coinages as a mirror of the disinteg-ration of late Roman state structures'. On the paucity of numismatic evidence for trade betwen Islam and the West see Lopez (1965) 'L'importanza del mondo Islamico nella vita economica Europea', 442, 531. On the de-cline of copper coinage, in western Europe and Byzantium though not the Muslim Mid-dle East, see Haldon (1990) *Byzantium in the Seventh Century*, 117–20; Whittow (1990) 'Ruling the late Roman and early Byzantine city', 19–20, with bibliography at n.37; B. Ward-Perkins (1996) 'Urban survival and urban transformation in the eastern Mediterranean', 144–5.

Textual evidence for connectivity: Malamut (1993) *Sur la route des saints byzantins*, is an excellent source of itineraries; see 243–65 for other pertinent examples than those mentioned in the chapter.

The Radhanites have elicited a large number of discussions: Ashtor (1985) 'Recent research on Levantine trade', 362–3, offers summaries and bibliography. See also Gil (1974) 'The Radhanite merchants and the land of Radhan'; Ashtor (1970) 'Quelques observations d'un orientaliste sur la thèse de Pirenne', 182–8 (1976) *A Social and Economic History of the Near East in the Middle Ages*, 105–6, (1977a) 'Aperçus sur les Râdhânites'. Abulafia (1987) 'Asia, Africa and the trade of medieval Europe', 415–18; Lewicki (1978) 'Les voies maritimes de la Méditerranée dans le haut moyen âge d'après les sources arabes', 450–52.

The Corbey grant and the commerce of Marseille: our primary guides have been Loseby (1992) 'Marseille: a late antique success story?', for the immediate written and archaeological evidence, amplified in Loseby (1998) and (forthcoming) 'Marseille and the Pirenne Thesis' (in two parts), and Wood (1994) *The Merovingian Kingdoms 450–751*, for the wider economic and political setting. But see also Düwel et al. (1985–7) *Untersuchungen zu Handel und Verkehr der vor- und frühgeschichtlichen Zeit in Mittel- und Nordeuropa*, vol. 3: *Der Handel des frühen Mittelalters*, especially Claude (1985–7b) 'Aspekte des Binnenhandels im Merowingerreich auf Grund der Schriftquellen', at 79–81 for tolls. Still worth consulting are two older works: Ganshof (1938) 'Notes sur les ports de Provence du VIIIe au Xe siècle', and Pernoud's contribution to Busquet and Pernoud (1949) *Histoire du commerce de Marseille*.

The early Italian emporia: for general context and archaeological background see B. Ward-Perkins (1988) 'The towns of northern Italy: rebirth or renewal?'. Schmiedt (1978) 'I porti italiani nell'alto medioevo', offers a catalogue of minor centres neglected in the more usual history of the 'commercial revolution'; see especially 244–9, on the continuous history of a number of small centres throughout the early Middle Ages; cf. von Falkenhausen (1989) 'Réseaux routiers et ports dans l'Italie méridionale Byzantine (VIe–XIe s.)'. The paucity of modern excavations of the Italian emporia, which might between them hold the key to a better understanding of the whole Mediterranean economy in the Pirenne period, is lamented by Hodges (1994) 'In the shadow of Pirenne: San Vincenzo al Volturno and the revival of Mediterranean commerce', 124–5; cf. Balzaretti (1996) 'Cities, emporia and monasteries: local economies in the Po valley, *c.* A.D. 700–875'. For the South see also Citarella (1993) 'Merchants, markets and merchandise in southern Italy in the high Middle Ages'. For the political setting Wickham (1981) *Early Medieval Italy: Central Power and Local Society 400–1000*; and T. S. Brown (1984) *Gentlemen and Officers: Imperial Administration and Aristocratic Power in Byzantine Italy A.D. 554–800*.

On Venice: Ammerman et al. (1992) 'New evidence on the origins of Venice', tells us nothing about exchange but offers well-dated evidence for human occupation – at a greater level of sophistication then the early written evidence would suggest – from the sixth century. Cf. Ammerman et al. (1995) 'More on the origins of Venice', for the Piazza San Marco. The subsequent progress of such excavations can be followed in the periodical *Quaderni di Archeologia del Veneto*. For that written evidence, see Luzzato (1961) *Storia economica di Venezia dall'XI al XVI secolo*, 3–6; Carile and Fedalto (1978) *Le origini di Venezia*; Ortalli (1993) 'Il mercante e lo stato: strutture della Venezia altomedievale'.

On Naples: Arthur (1985) 'Notes on the economy of a Dark Age city'; Whitehouse (1988) 'Rome and Naples: survival and revival in central and southern Italy'. For the political and economic context, Kreutz (1991) *Before the Normans: Southern Italy in the Ninth and Tenth Centuries*.

The Adriatic: our depiction owes much to Ferluga (1987) 'Navigation et commerce dans l'Adriatique aux VIIe et VIIIe siècle'; see also his (1993) 'Mercati e mercanti fra Mar Nero e Adriatico: il commercio nei Balcani dal VII all'XI secolo'.

Byzantium: Lilie (1976) *Die byzantinische Reaktion auf die Ausbreitung der Araber*, 266–85, musters what little evidence there is for long-distance trade in the seventh and eighth centuries, especially trade with Islam; see also McCormick (1995) 'Byzantium and the West, 700–900', 357–9. On links with Islam: Canard (1964) 'Les relations politiques et sociales entre Byzance et les Arabes', 48–50, for the eighth century, with Teall (1959) 'The grain supply of the Byzantine empire', 104, 137. Treadgold (1988) *The Byzantine Revival 780–842*, 36–43, 164–5, 364–5, is a useful outline. On the continued prosperity of some parts of Syria, Palestine and Jordan through the seventh century and beyond, into the early Islamic period, with all that that might imply for the history of demand around the eastern Mediterranean, see most assertively Whittow (1990) 'Ruling the late Roman and early Byzantine city', 13–20; Canivet and Rey-Coquais (1992) *La Syrie de Byzance à l'Islam VIIe–VIIIe siècles*, parts 3 and 4; King and Cameron (1994) *The Byzantine and Early Islamic Near East II: Land Use and Settlement Patterns*. Also Kennedy (1985a) 'From *Polis* to *Madina*: urban change in late antique and early Islamic Syria', though alongside it, B. Ward-Perkins (1996) 'Urban survival and transformation in the eastern Mediterranean', and Kennedy (1985b) 'The last century of Byzantine Syria: a reinterpretation', stressing the decline of coastal cities well before the arrival of Muslim conquerors. See, however, Foss (1997) 'Syria in transition', for some different interpretations of the archaeology. Angold (1985) 'The shaping of the medieval Byzantine "city"', perhaps taking too pessimistic a view of the dating of both decline and recovery. For networks of exchange up to the seventh century, *Hommes et richesses dans l'empire byzantin* (1989), especially Abadie-Reynal, 'Céramique et commerce dans le bassin égéen du IVe au

VIIe siècle', and Panella (1989a) 'Gli scambi nel Mediterraneo occidentale dal IV al VII secolo'. Haldon (1994) 'Quelques remarques sur l'économie byzantine de 600 à 1100', is a useful conspectus, especially of the morphology of cities. References given above at the beginning of Section 5 are also of course highly relevant.

On the state administration and taxation of commerce in the period, see Hendy (1985) *Studies in the Byzantine Monetary Economy*, 174, 592, 626–7, with Oikonomides (1986) 'Silk trade and production in Byzantium from the sixth to the ninth century' (IX.3).

Islam: Bridbury (1969) 'The Dark Ages', importantly stresses that Mediterranean trade was simply diverted, rather than extinguished, by the rise of Islam. For the viewpoint from the Muslim side, Ashtor (1976) *A Social and Economic History of the Near East*; Abulafia (1987) 'Asia, Africa and the trade of medieval Europe', 411–19; Lombard (1975) *The Golden Age of Islam*, part 3. For the vigour of the Umayyad economy Watson (1983) *Agricultural Innovation in the Early Islamic World* (though cf. VII.3).

For an example of what happened during this period in an area physically close to the Mediterranean, microfragmented, but lacking the sort of connectivity we have described, W. E. Berry (1987) 'Southern Burgundy in late Antiquity and the early Middle Ages', esp. 578: 'no one area could sustain a population high enough to enable its central place to develop to the point where it could sustain a market economy'.

BIBLIOGRAPHICAL ESSAY TO CHAPTER VI

IMPERATIVES OF SURVIVAL: DIVERSIFY, STORE, REDISTRIBUTE

1. THE HISTORY OF MEDITERRANEAN FOOD SYSTEMS

For a résumé (with some bibliography) of the 'new ecological economic history', which includes the work by Rappaport that we have already had occasion to cite (II.5), see LaBianca (1990) *Sedentarization and Nomadization*, 4–9. Compare the useful account of the 'behavioural ecology' of prehistoric food production on the dry margins of the Mediterranean in K. W. Russell (1988) *After Eden*. On the necessity of comparative history in a Mediterranean context, B. D. Shaw (1991) 'The noblest monuments and the smallest things: wells, walls and aqueducts in the making of Roman Africa'; Gallant (1991) *Risk and Survival in Ancient Greece*, 1–5. Traina (1994) 'Paesaggi tardoantichi: alcuni problemi', 85, proclaims the necessity of ancient-medieval comparisons, and makes (96) a subtle statement of the paradox of 'discontinuous continuity' between the two. Lock (1995) *The Franks in the Aegean*, 240–2, despairs of the intractability of the economic evidence for the Frankish Aegean. It is precisely to cases like this that a comparative approach has most to offer.

2. THE NEW ECOLOGICAL ECONOMIC HISTORY

Garnsey (1988a) *Famine and Food Supply*, 93–4, described the novelty of the ethnoarchaeological technique and contrasted it with earlier approaches. In the same spirit, O. Murray (1992) 'The ecology and agrarian history of ancient Greece'. It is among specialists in Greek history that there has been most reluctance to accept the new approach. Osborne (1996a) '*Classical Landscape* revisited', offers an illuminating account of how the evolving debate around the ethnoarchaeological perspective has promoted reconsideration of economic history. Some interesting points are advanced (both consciously and unwittingly) by the contributors to the debate (essentially between text-based and ethnoarchaeological perspectives) printed in B. Wells (1992) *Agriculture in Ancient Greece*, especially 167–73. The same controversies are presented in two review-articles by Cartledge (1993) 'Classical Greek agriculture: recent work and alternative views' (favouring Burford (1993) *Land and Labor in the Greek World*, as against Isager and Skydsgaard (1992) *Ancient Greek Agriculture*) and Cartledge (1995) 'Classical Greek agriculture II: two more alternative views', noting that both Jameson et al. (1994) *A Greek Countryside*, and Hanson (1995) *The Other Greeks*, adhere to the 'new or alternative model of ancient Greek agriculture'. Familiar to Mediterranean historians and archaeologists of almost all other periods, and to those working on the first millennium B.C. everywhere except in the Aegean, an ecological and ethnoarchaeological approach to primary production no longer deserves to be labelled as either new or alternative. Compare, however, the studies collected in Kardulias and Shutes (1997) *Aegean Strategies*.

A holistic approach to the Mediterranean past founded on archaeology, especially that of the productive landscape, was outlined and advocated by S. C. Humphreys (1967) 'Archaeology and the economic and social history of classical Greece' (and described as an unrealizable vision by Cartledge (1976) 'Seismicity and Spartan society'). Her vision was fulfilled over the next thirty years. Two important surveys of progress in landscape archaeology: Bintliff and Snodgrass (1988) 'Mediterranean survey and the city'; G. W. W. Barker (1997) 'Writing landscape: archaeology and history'. For survey in Greece, see also Alcock et al. (1994) 'Intensive survey, agricultural practice and the classical landscape of Greece'; Fotiadis (1995) 'Modernity and the past-still-present: politics of time in the birth of regional archaeological projects in Greece'.

Johns (1988) 'Sistemi socio-economici, ricognizione a scala regionale e campionamento ad uso probabilistico', was a polemic that provoked interesting reactions. These included Bazzana and Noyé (1988) 'Du "bon usage" de l'archéologie extensive: une réponse en forme de bilan', which drew a schematic distinction between (on one hand) British and Italian survey archaeology, with its ancestry in prehistoric and classical archaeology, and with its geographical methodology, directed at the study of production, and (on the other hand) the French and Spanish approach to landscape research, with its ties to archival medieval history, and its tendency to reify the names found in such evidence, in its preoccupation with 'peuplement'. It should be stressed, with these authors, that the archaeology of the medieval Mediterranean does indeed, by comparison with that of earlier periods, seem to be less well suited to the methods of field survey – which is generating an imbalance of available evidence.

Helpful general statements from the classical end are to be found in Cherry et al. (1991) *Landscape Archaeology as Long-Term History: Northern Keos*, 13–20; Barker and Lloyd (1991) *Roman Landscapes*, 1–17; Barker et al. (1995) *A Mediterranean Valley: Landscape Archaeology and 'Annales' History in the Biferno Valley*, 5–9. For some other examples, see the opening of BE III. It was the early work of the British School at Rome on the landscape of south Etruria (compare III.2) that provided the original model for much British effort in this field.

Hamish Forbes was the pioneer of the ethnoarchaeological interpretation of Mediterranean food-systems: H. Forbes (1992) 'The ethnoarchaeological approach to ancient Greek agriculture'. The starting point, however, is his dissertation (1982) *Strategies and Soils: Technology, Production and Environment in the Peninsula of Methana*. On risk control, see especially: 324–55 (land fragmentation and risk-reduction), 356–76 (production strategies), 377–91 (storage), 411–35 (conclusions on hazard and resilience and the working of a system to produce both stability and efficiency). The project to combine archaeological surface survey of the Aegean island of Melos with a complete investigation of the island's history, social, economic and political, provided another decisive model: Renfrew and Wagstaff (1982) *An Island Polity*, especially Renfrew (1982b) 'Polity and power: interaction, intensification and exploitation'; Wagstaff et al. (1982) 'Alternative subsistence strategies'. Hence our choice of Melos as a 'definite place' (III.4). Much has been added by the very helpful range of articles of Paul Halstead: see especially (1989) 'The economy has a normal surplus: economic stability and social change among early farming communities of Thessaly', and (1990a) 'Waste not, want not: traditional responses to crop failure in Greece'. A further landmark was the volume edited by Halstead and O'Shea (1989) *Bad Year Economics: Cultural Responses to Risk and Uncertainty*, especially the remarks by the editors, 1–7 and 123–6. Most of these accounts also treat the underlying causes of risk, on which see, in addition, Ruschenbusch (1988) 'Getreideerträge in Griechenland in der Zeit von 1921 bis 1938 n. Chr. als Maßstab für die Antike'. Methodological caution: Halstead (1987) 'Traditional and ancient rural economy in Mediterranean Europe'; Ammerman (1985) 'Modern land-use versus the past: a case-study from Calabria'.

For diversification, Jameson et al. (1994) *A Greek Countryside*, 260–324, 'using the resources of the land and sea', and especially 322–4. A nineteenth-century example: Petrusewicz (1996) *Latifundium*, 6: the Barracco estate in Calabria was 'complex and diversified in both production and administration, with a whole mosaic of tenancy forms, a multiple-crop system [on which cf. 116–17] . . . and a great variety of farming techniques . . . as well as a complex web of markets'.

For the interest and complexity of harvesting techniques and storage-behaviour, Sigaut (1988) 'A method for identifying grain storage techniques', provides a very stimulating and helpful introduction; compare Forbes and Foxhall (1995) 'Ethnoarchaeology and storage in the ancient Mediterranean: beyond risk and survival?'; Smyth (1989) 'Domestic storage behavior in Mesoamerica'. Definitions and discussion of the notion of social storage (to which we return, in the context of the social connotations of choice of agricultural strategy: VII.4) are to be found at Halstead and O'Shea (1982) 'A friend in need is a friend indeed: social storage and the origins of social ranking'; O'Shea (1981) 'Coping with scarcity: exchange and social storage', 167–83. Examples of the application of the idea to the prehistoric Mediterranean include Halstead (1981a) 'From determinism to uncertainty: social storage and the rise of the Minoan palace'; Webb and Frankel (1994) 'Making an impression: storage and surplus finance in late Bronze Age Cyprus'; and the discussions reported by Farnoux (1996) 'Les magasins à vivres (IIe et Ie millénaires): bilan de la journée d'étude'. On an important related topic, Foxhall (1998b) 'Snapping up the unconsidered trifles: the use of agricultural residues in Greek and Roman farming'.

The ecological/archaeological approach has not tended to favour historical minimalism (cf. V.4): Jameson et al. (1994) *A Greek Countryside*, 280–4, feels able to give an 'optimistic' account of ancient Greek agriculture. Pleket (1993) 'Agriculture in the Roman Empire in comparative perspective', uses the new findings to excellent effect against minimalist claims, as does Spurr (1986) *Arable Cultivation in Roman Italy*, an early application of ethnoarchaeology to Roman agriculture. The idea that production of a basic surplus for redistribution functions as a risk-buffering strategy is treated by Butzer et al. (1982) 'Medieval Muslim communities'. It is an instructive weakness of Gallant (1991) *Risk and Survival in Ancient Greece*, that he has difficulty in reconciling an essentially minimalistic view of ancient production with the ethnoarchaeological perspective.

3. UNDERSTANDING THE MARGINAL

On the tendency to undervalue the marginal and to prefer the cultivated, visible in economic practice from the tenth century,

Fumagalli (1992) *L'uomo e l'ambiente*, 99–101, who calls it *la scelta ambientale* (environmental choice). On the old questions of fallowing, weeding and fertilizer, Sigaut (1975) *L'agriculture et le feu*, 131–3, is highly illuminating.

A classic article on 'waste', Forbes (1996) 'The uses of the uncultivated landscape in modern Greece', 69, emphasizes that 'uncultivated' does not mean 'unproductive'. It is worth listing the themes examined in this survey in some detail: 70 on variety of uncultivated environments; 72 for the difficulty of defining the uncultivated given long-fallow merging into set-aside; 72–3 for wild lowlands (75 on problems of ownership of these, with grants of pasture and wood rights in the epigraphic evidence); 77–8 the genetic resource for grafting (pears and olives, link with pocket terraces); 79–84 for construction materials, including reeds; 84–8 fuel; 88–90 resin, dyestuffs, astringents etc.; 90–2 plant-food and game; 92–3 pastoralism and apiculture. Gathering in general: in ancient Italy, J. K. Evans (1980) 'Plebs rustica', 138–9; Frayn (1975) 'Wild and cultivated plants: a note on the peasant economy of Roman Italy'; Duby (1974) *The Early Growth of the European Economy*, 16–17; Gallant (1991) *Risk and Survival in Ancient Greece*, 115–21. Pollard (1997) *Marginal Europe*, and Thirsk (1997) *Alternative Agriculture*, deal with non-staple production in early modern and modern times; Groenman-van Waateringe (1996) 'Wasteland: buffer in the medieval economy', is also concerned with northern Europe.

There has been very little investigation of social responses to seasonal patterns of diet and of nutritional glut and shortage in Mediterranean history: suggestive examples, mainly from West African ethnography, may be found in De Garine and Koppert (1990) 'Social adaptation to season and uncertainty in food supply'. See however Camporesi (1989) *Bread of Dreams*. For food crisis in Mediterranean history, see also IV.7 and VII.5–6.

4. THE INTEGRATED MEDITERRANEAN FOREST

The general accounts of Meiggs (1982) *Trees and Timber*, for Antiquity and Bechmann (1990) *Trees and Man*, for the Middle Ages (though somewhat further north in its centre of gravity) are the starting points for understanding pre-modern woodland ecologies.

The *Settimane di Spoleto* volume *L'ambiente vegetale* (vol. 37, 1990) also has many helpful discussions for the early medieval period. On *garrigues* as margins Barbero and Quézel (1983) 'La végétation de la Grèce et l'action de l'homme', 69–70; Rackham (1983) 'Observations on the historical ecology of Boeotia'; on maquis as climax, also Quézel (1981) 'Floristic composition and phytosociological structure of sclerophyllous matorral'. The relationship between woodlands and scrublands is discussed further, with additional bibliography, below, VIII.5. See also Rackham (1982) 'Land-use and the native vegetation of Greece', (1990a) 'Ancient landscapes'; and Rackham and Moody (1997) *The Making of the Cretan Landscape*. The studies collected in Béal (ed.) (1995) *L'arbre et la forêt: le bois dans l'antiquité*, are mainly concerned with non-Mediterranean woodlands. For the cultural response to forest in general, Schama (1995) *Landscape and Memory*, ch. 2.

On the fruits of forest trees, Lewthwaite (1982) 'Acorns for the ancestors'; Mason (1995) 'Acornutopia?', cf. Usai (1969) *Il pane di ghiande e la geofagia in Sardegna*. Chestnuts: Toubert (1973) *Les structures du Latium médiéval*, 266; Pitte (1986) *Terres de castanide*; Quaini (1975) 'Per lo studio dei caratteri originali del paesaggio agrario della Liguria pre-industriale', 468–9. A good case study of the uses of oak and chestnut forest in the early Middle Ages, Galetti (1988) 'Bosco e spazi incolti nel territorio piacentino durante l'alto medioevo'. On the unjustly neglected subject of apiculture, J. E. Jones (1976) 'Hives and honey of Hymettus: beekeeping in ancient Greece'; Crane (1983) *Archaeology of Beekeeping*.

General accounts of forest as margin: Lewthwaite (1982) 'Acorns for the ancestors', 220, with bibliography, seeing systems of margins clearance for cereals as 'an adaptation to social rather than ecological marginality'; M. Bailey (1989) *A Marginal Economy? East Anglian Breckland in the Later Middle Ages*, on medieval Breckland, not Mediterranean of course, but helpful on the nature of margins in medieval agriculture. For a definition of 'swidden' farming, see Tvengsberg (1995) 'Rye and swidden cultivation', 131: 'the cultivation of human foodplants in the ashes of burnt forest land'. Spencer (1996) '*To Pyrrhaiōn Oros to pityōdes*', includes an interesting demonstration that the village/estate centres listed on late Roman docu-

ments from Lesbos did take an active interest in the forest of the central mountains of the island.

On the maintenance of supplies of wood for fuel and construction through forest-management, Meiggs (1982) *Trees and Timber*, 260–70; Frenzel (1994) *Evaluation of Land-Surfaces Cleared from Forests*; Dunn (1992) 'The exploitation and control of woodland and scrubland in the Byzantine world'; Wickham (1990) 'European forests in the early Middle Ages'. For the effectiveness of forest law in preserving forests in medieval Lazio, Toubert (1973) *Les structures du Latium médiéval*. Combustion: Wertime (1983) 'The furnace and the goat', with Rackham (1996) 'Ecology and pseudo-ecology', 29–30; sugar boiling: von Wartburg (1995) 'Desing [*sic*] and technology of the medieval refineries of the sugar cane in Cyprus', 104; Olson (1991) 'Firewood and charcoal in classical Athens'. There is some further discussion of the demands of Mediterranean cities for fuel in IV.6 above. Construction: Meiggs (1982) *Trees and Timber*, 116–53, and Lombard (1959) 'Le bois dans la Méditerranée musulmane', deal with the particular case of ship-timber, which links (as the Greek and Roman tradition clearly perceived) the marginal forest with the world of seafaring in a close conceptual tie. Pasquali (1988) 'Il bosco litoraneo nel medioevo, da Rimini al delta del Po', makes the interesting point that the numerous early medieval monasteries which occupied the shifting coastal wet woodland belt of the Romagna were the heirs of the Roman emperors' estates for maintaining the timber supply of the Ravenna fleet. On pitch, see Béal (1995) 'Le massif forestier de la Sila et la poix de Bruttium d'après les textes antiques'.

5. THE UNDERESTIMATED MEDITERRANEAN WETLAND

Its prehistoric importance: Delano Smith (1979) *Western Mediterranean Europe*, 290–1; for the dietary role of marsh-plants, Darby et al. (1977) *Food: The Gift of Osiris*, 619–52; cf. D. J. Crawford (1979) 'Food: tradition and change in Hellenistic Egypt', 136–7; Diodorus Siculus, *Historical Library*, 1.80.5–6.

For the Iberian cases, we may cite the long-vanished attitudes of W. J. Buck, a classic shoot-it-first ornithologist and egg-collector who breakfasted on avocets' eggs, noted the feral camels of the Seville marisma, and recorded diary-entries such as 'shot a hen-harrier . . . and knocked over my last bottle of Bass': (1893) *Wild Spain: Records of Sport*, ch. 8: it is on such material that even recent Mediterranean environmental history must draw, since so much has vanished in the last century. For the Marjals, Pardo (1942) *La Albufera de Valencia*, and for the present situation, Docavo Alberti (1985a) 'La Albufera de Valencia y son entorno'; Dobby (1936) 'The Ebro delta', 455–69, and Docavo Alberti (1985b) 'El Delta del Ebro'.

An honourable exception to the scholarly neglect of the Mediterranean wetland is the oeuvre of Giusto Traina, especially (1988) *Paludi e bonifiche del mondo antico*; see in particular 77 and 108, with 101–8 on the question of whether the wetland economy can be considered as a 'subsistence economy'; 109–32 on reclamation and its *mentalité*, also (1990) *Ambiente e paesaggi di Roma antica*. For the complexity of use of the wooded marshes of the Po delta, see the excellent study of Bacchi (1988) 'Il bosco e l'acqua. Uso dell'incolto e colonizzazione agraria nel territorio ferrarese (secoli XI–XIII)', 188: 'possediamenti fondiari più di acque che di terre asciutte; e più di boscaglie, di canneti o di vegetazione palustre che di arativi' ('property holdings whose surface was more water than dry land, and which comprised thickets, reedbeds and marshplants more than they did ploughland'). Life was not attractive, but the resources were much in demand; and continuous reclamation was part of the exploitation.

Good illustrative material is to be found in Attenborough (1987) *The First Eden*, 220–9. Anatolian examples: Robert (1982) 'Documents de l'Asie Mineure XXI: au nord de Sardes, Lycophron et le marais d'Echidna, Strabon et le lac Koloe', (1983) 'Documents de l'Asie Mineure XXIII: Sardes et les roseaux du lac Koloe', with particular emphasis on the economy of the reed-bed, and vivid nineteenth-century texts illustrating its richness in fish and fowl; Lake Copais, Lauffer (1985) 'Problèmes de Copaïs, solutions et énigmes', and (1986) *Kopaïs: Untersuchungen zur historischen Landeskunde Mittelgriechenlands*; cf. Fossey (1979) 'The cities of the Kopaïs in the Roman period'. For Roman villas as improved wetlands, Purcell (1996b) 'Rome and the management of water'. On sugar-cane as a wetland crop on Cyprus, Zacour and Hazard (1985) *The Impact of the Crusades*, 277.

Routes d'étangs: Laven (1989) 'The Venetian rivers in the sixteenth century', for the 'Seven Seas' (*septem maria*) which provided a safe route along the Adriatic coast from Aquileia to Ravenna through the Venetian lagoons and their continuations. Such places have based their social and economic organization on the boat from prehistoric times: Trump (1980) *The Prehistory of the Mediterranean*, 21, 43–7, 80.

6. 'These Places Feed Many Pickling-Fish . . .'

The fisheries of the Mediterranean, little discussed by historians, have been rather misunderstood. Analyses of their twentieth-century history make a convenient starting point, such as Margalef (1985) *Western Mediterranean*, or the general geographies: Parain (1936) *La Méditerranée*; J. M. Houston (1964) *The Western Mediterranean World*; Delano Smith (1979) *Western Mediterranean Europe*; or Beckinsale and Beckinsale (1975) *Southern Europe*, 17–19, for the oceanographic conditions and their variability, drawing attention to the *Poseidonia* 'meadows'; 19–22 for modern fisheries. General historical accounts also in *Navigation et gens de mer en Méditerranée de la préhistoire à nos jours* (1980); Brinkhuizen and Clason (1986) *Fish and Archaeology*. Acheson (1981) 'Anthropology of fishing', stresses the unpredictable returns and the possibility of glut, and the dependency of the fisherman.

For Antiquity Gallant (1985) *A Fisherman's Tale*, is now standard, but committed, as we argue, to an unhelpfully minimalist assessment. Shoaling fish were more important than he allows, especially in the Black Sea and its approaches. Here Gallant makes an interesting mistake, assessing the Marmara catch on the basis of Turkish records which begin after the Treaty of Lausanne exchanges deprived the area of most of its (Greek-speaking) fisherfolk, so that the unimpressive totals are hardly surprising. Before 1922 more than 10,000 kg of mackerel were taken each year in the area using traditional methods: T. Lefebvre [1929], 'La pêche en Turquie', derived from Devecian (1928) *Pêche et pêcheries en Turquie*: a salutary reminder of the importance of political *événements* in the synchronic study of Mediterranean history. For Propontic techniques introduced by the departing fisherfolk to the

Gulfs of Pagasae and of Ambracia, see Guest-Papamanoli (1986) 'Une pêche au guet: le taliani. Origines et distribution géographique'. Gallant also misrepresents Faber (1883) *The Fisheries of the Adriatic*, actually a lavish and laudatory account of fisheries in the then Austrian Adriatic. See also Purcell (1995b) 'Eating fish: the paradoxes of seafood'.

For the anchovy-catch in Pontus cf. also Bryer and Winfield (1985) *The Byzantine Monuments and Topography of the Pontus*, 5, with Strabo, *Geography*, 12.3.19 (cf. 12.3.11 on the fixed traps for pelamyds at Sinope which were one of the sights of the city). Fishing administered in 260 districts in the neighbourhood of Parion in Ottoman times: Robert (1955) 'Inscriptions des Dardanelles'. The commercial interests of the Roman entrepreneurs of the late Republic in the fisheries of this city are attested by the fishing association described in Frisch (1983) *Die Inschriften von Parion*, no. 5. For the Middle Ages, Dagron (1995) 'Poissons, pêcheurs et poissonniers de Constantinople'; note 73: 'un des rares endroits au monde où il est justifié d'assimiler en droit les fonds marins à la propriété foncière, en rhétorique les pêcheurs à des laboureurs de la mer, et dans la vie quotidienne le poisson au pain'. Originally regulated by custom, Constantinople's fisheries were subject to new legal rulings under the Emperor Leo VI.

On lagoon fisheries, see Paskoff et al. (1991) 'Le litoral de la Tunisie dans l'antiquité'; for Egypt, Brewer and Friedman (1989) *Fish and Fishing in Ancient Egypt*. Yields: in general, Margalef (1985) *Western Mediterranean*, 15–16. For the Adriatic, Beckinsale and Beckinsale (1975) *Southern Europe*, 18; Valencia: Pardo (1942) *La Albufera de Valencia*, 161–76 and 180–213; Tunisia: Parain (1936) *La Méditerranée*, 58. On the important fisheries of the lagoons of Provence, Bresc (1986a) 'Pêche et coraillage aux derniers siècles du moyen âge: Sicile et Provence orientale'; Brien-Poitevin (1996) 'Consommations des coquillages marins en Provence'.

For the medieval Mediterranean, see Zug Tucci (1985) 'Il mondo medioevale dei pesci', and for a particular example, Pini (1976) 'Pesci, pescivendoli e mercanti di pesce in Bologna medievale'. For the medieval *madragues* in Sicily, Bresc (1986b) *Un monde méditerranéen*, 261–2, stressing also freshwater fish and eels; note also Abulafia (1983b)

'The Crown and the economy under Roger II and his successors', showing that these practices were already known in the eleventh century. On the value of control of the fishing-port of Castellamare in the Middle Ages, see Abulafia (1981) 'Southern Italy and the Florentine economy', 380 with n.14. Our example of Lake Bolsena is from Lamonelli (1990) 'I lavori alla peschiera del Marta'. Trexler (1974) 'Measures against water pollution in fifteenth century Florence' for freshwater trout in medieval Tuscany: the problem of the ratio of labour expenditure to nutritional gain was solved in this case by the use of poisoning. Squatriti (1995) 'Water, nature and culture in early medieval Lucca', 37–8, discusses the 'marsh-abbey' of Sesto near Lucca, control of the Bientina and Fucecchio depressions and their crucial fisheries. See also Mane (1983) *Calendriers et techniques agricoles*, 269. Freshwater fish in the Levant: Safrai (1994) *The Economy of Roman Palestine*.

Pickling: the pioneering account of Corcoran (1957) *The Roman Fishing Industry of the Late Republic and Early Empire*, is now supplemented by the researches into the archaeological remains of the pickling-works by Ponsich and Tarradell (1965) *Garum et industries de salaison dans la Méditerranée occidentale*; cf. Edmondson (1987) *Two Industries in Roman Lusitania: Mining and Garum Production*. An excellent account of the trade in these products: Curtis (1991) *Garum and Salsamenta: Production and Commerce in Materia Medica*.

Salt: Adshead (1992) *Salt and Civilisation*; cf. Tora (1993) *Salt Production Techniques in Ancient China*; Mollat (1968) *Le rôle du sel dans l'histoire*. The ancient data are collected by Moinier (1986) 'Lecture moderne de Pline l'Ancien: communication sur la production et consommation de sel de mer'; see also Küthmann (1966) 'Salz zum Würzen?', 407, and the specific studies of A. Giovannini (1985) 'Le sel et la fortune de Rome'; Baladié (1994) 'Le sel dans l'antiquité sur la côte nord de la mer Noire'; and Vandenabeele (1991) 'Salt on Cyprus in Antiquity'. For the Middle Ages, Hocquet (1978) *Le sel et la fortune de Venise*, the study which inspired Giovannini's argument that salt was central among the economic advantages of early Rome. Also Hocquet (1985) *Le sel et le pouvoir*, and, for Sardinian salt, Bautier (1992) *Commerce méditerranéen et banquiers italiens au moyen âge*.

Fowling: di Lusignano (1573) *Chorograffia et breve historia universale dell'isola di Cipro*, 88r:

The island also produces – or rather, there comes to it from outside – in the months of October, September and even August, a huge quantity of little birds, and because these come at vintage time, they call them vine-birds, and eating grapes and lentisc seed and other things, they get so fat that you can hardly see their bones. They catch a large number of these in different parts of the island, and the catching is let out for hire or for a rent by the owners of the land, at a rate of nine ducats for a thousand birds; they keep accounts, and send them off to Venice in their thousands. They are prepared thus: they strike them a light blow so as not to disfigure them and put them in jars, pouring in strong vinegar. Like this they keep until Easter, or sometimes for a whole year, but when they are fresh their flavour is much better, and the person who eats half-a-dozen is completely stuffed and has no more appetite. When I went to Italy, the captain of my ship, the *Vianolà*, told me that he had 80,000 on board, as well as everything else; the ships get five or six ducats for each and that is not even for retail: they are bought as presents for friends and patrons.

Compare Pliny, *Natural History*, 10.23, on hawking at Amphipolis; Toubert (1973) *Les structures du Latium médiéval*, 267 n.1 (Circeo); Robert (1983) 'Documents de l'Asie Mineure XXIII: Sardes et les roseaux du lac Koloe'.

Hunting: Lee and De Vore (1968) *Man the Hunter*; for attitudes to this in general: Traina (1986) 'Paesaggio e decadenza; la palude nella trasformazione del mondo antico'; cf. B. D. Shaw (1982–3) ' "Eaters of Flesh, Drinkers of Milk": the ancient Mediterranean ideology of the pastoral nomad'.

7. THE MOVEABLE MICROREGION: MEDITERRANEAN ANIMAL HUSBANDRY

In general: Boyazoglou and Flamant (1992) 'Mediterranean systems of animal production'; Maggi et al. (1990) *Archeologia della pastorizia nell'Europa meridionale*.

Perhaps the most complete and interesting statement of the view presented here (and cf. III.6) is Hodkinson (1988) 'Animal husbandry in the Greek polis', 60–2 on risk-avoidance, 42 on complementary fodder-crop, stubble-grazing and wild grazing, 45 on the fodder-crop/olive grove association, 51 on manuring, and in particular the discussions of

the logic of production – how other considerations may affect the calculus of how best to achieve subsistence – at 59–61; and 65 for how producers cope with glut, using animals as an opportunistic 'cash crop'. For the ethnological perspective, Halstead (1981b) 'Counting sheep in Neolithic and Bronze Age Greece', (1987) 'Traditional and ancient rural economy in Mediterranean Europe', and (1990a) 'Waste not, want not: traditional responses to crop failure in Greece', 149–52, for investment of surplus as 'animal capital', cf. also Halstead (1993) 'Banking on livestock: indirect storage in Greek agriculture'. Also Cherry (1988) 'Pastoralism and the role of animals in the pre- and protohistoric economies of the Aegean', 21–2. For the social implications, Cherry mainly follows Sherratt (1983) 'The secondary exploitation of animals in the Old World', and (1981) 'Plough and pastoralism' – as do Bogucki (1993) 'Animal traction and household economies in neolithic Europe' (seeing cattle as 'self-regenerating productive assets'), and Pullen (1992) 'Ox and plow in the early Bronze Age Aegean', all three making perceptive suggestions about the possible social consequences of adaptations of animal husbandry.

For a general application of this ethno-archaeological treatment of animal husbandry to the ancient Mediterranean: Garnsey (1988b) 'Mountain economies in southern Europe', esp. 206–7. Columeau (1996) 'Pratiques cultuelles et spécialisation pastorale autour de l'Étang de Berre', who advocates a microregional rather than a site-centred archaeology, draws attention to the visible differences in ancient pastoral practice between the areas abutting on the largely extensive pastoral landscape of the Crau, and those whose intensive animal husbandry was oriented towards the market of Massalia. Cf. Petrusewicz (1996) *Latifundium*, 12, for the mixture of cereals and pastoral enterprises, on a great Calabrian estate in the nineteenth century. Ridgway (1997) 'Nestor's cup and the Etruscans', uses finds of ceremonial cheese-graters to show how cheese consumption was integrated with the central symbolic wine consumption of the early first millennium B.C. Our 'definite places' provided further examples: husbandry in Biqa for risk-avoidance (III.1), very varied interactions of husbandry in south Etruria (III.2), and the different ecological zones of the Jebel Akhdar (III.3).

This view of the integratedness of husbandry with a wider range of productive techniques has not found universal acceptance: Skydsgaard (1988) 'Transhumance in ancient Greece', finds it incompatible with the pre-conceptions of the ancient literary texts; while a strong view of the physical constraints on animal husbandry (limited meadowland, rare fodder-crops, absence of ley) persists in Sallares (1991) *The Ecology of the Ancient Greek World*, 382–6, arguing a minimalist case for overall productivity in ancient Attica, and therefore wishing to play down the contribution of manure to cereal cultivation. He cites (499) Ellen Semple 'that deservedly most famous environmental determinist': (1922) 'The influ-ence of geographical conditions upon ancient Mediterranean stock-raising'; cf. Peet (1985) 'Social origins of environmental determinism', 317–24; Cherry (1988) 12–14; Hodkinson (1988) 50; Garnsey (1988b) 203. Ancient authors and environmental determinists alike incline to the view that animal husbandry requires specialized environments which are always scarce in Mediterranean conditions, and which are better used for arable production if the human population increases. Thus low population aggregates are commonly linked with high consumption of animal products – in the Greek Dark Age, for instance. Rising populations are thought to entail a reduction in the importance of husbandry. Cf. Sallares (1991) 309–13, with 375, also committed to an underpopulated Dark Age followed by a demographic boom. Against, Cherry (1988) 26–30, clearly rightly: Mediterranean hus-bandry normally makes productive use of land-scapes and labour resources that are of little significance for other forms of production, and its products frequently have an exchange value which makes the calculation of whether it is better to grow wheat for domestic con-sumption or use the bottomland for high-quality pasture less straightforward, even in conditions of high population. On fodder, H. Forbes (1998) 'European agriculture viewed bottom-side upwards'.

Competition of humans and animals: see also Jongman (1988a) 'Adding it up', and again (1988b) *Economy and Society of Pompeii*; *contra* Purcell (1990c) 'The economy of an ancient town', citing Marino (1988) *Pastoral Economics in the Kingdom of Naples*, still the best account of the very complex accommoda-tion that is possible between arable strategies and even very highly developed long-distance pastoralism (III.6). For ancient Italy, Capogrossi Colognesi (1982) *L'agricoltura romana*, xii, on *ager compascuus* (shared pas-

ture) as an integral part of the economy of the centuriated landscape. But for the most part Italian historians and archaeologists have not been tempted to see animal husbandry and cultivation as mutually exclusive: the debate here is rather about the modalities and continuities of long-distance transhumance, which is a rather different question. See also G. W. W. Barker (1989) 'The archaeology of the Italian shepherd'; Barker and Grant (1991) 'Ancient and modern pastoralism in central Italy'.

Animal husbandry and vegetation cover: Le Houerou (1981) 'Impact of man and his animals on Mediterranean vegetation'. See also Dell et al. (1986) *Resilience in Mediterranean-Type Ecosystems*. Compare Thornes (1987) 'Palaeo-ecology of erosion', 54: 'the all or none approach to vegetation cover [is] clearly inadequate.' For goats, Rackham (1983) 'Observations on the historical ecology of Boeotia'. For ruthless exploitation of the Sicilian forest lands in the fifteenth century, Bresc (1986b) *Un monde méditerranéen: éco-nomie et société en Sicile, 1300–1450*, 95–8 (cf. 102 on the overall impact of humans on the ecosystem). On the question of why for-est pastoralism has been despised, B. D. Shaw (1982–3) '"Eaters of flesh, drinkers of milk"'.

8. Cereals and the Dry Margin

On dry-farming as part of the orthodox repertoire of determinative Mediterranean phenomena see Semple (1932) *The Geogra-phy of the Mediterranean Region*, 385–8; as a feature of standard handbooks, K. D. White (1970) *Roman Farming*, 173–4; for newer views, Forbes (1976) 'The thrice-ploughed field'; Halstead (1987) 'Traditional and an-cient rural economy'; Gallant (1991) *Risk and Survival in Ancient Greece*, 52–6, on fallow.

For the early history of cereals, Charles (1984) 'Introductory remarks on the cereals'; Sherratt (1980) 'Water, soil and seasonality in early cereal cultivation'. For attempts to identify the conditions under which cereal-centred production originated, and what follows from the identification, see Sherratt (1997c) 'Climatic cycles and behavioural re-volutions'; Diamond (1997) *Guns, Germs and Steel*.

For the dietary role of cereals: Allbaugh (1953) *Crete*, with the sensible critique of Gallant (1991) *Risk and Survival in An-cient Greece*, 63–4, drawing attention to the difficulties facing a field-worker with preconceptions about the inefficiency of traditional agriculture, in the circumstances of post-war dearth, which included the incentive to misinform outsiders.

Instructively, the evidence for Greece in the late Neolithic suggests that dry, open countryside provided a very helpful resource for an expanding population, but did so through the opportunities it offered for the expansion of animal husbandry, beyond the favoured watery environments where agriculture was practicable: M. Johnson (1996) 'Water, animals and agricultural technology: a study of settlement patterns and economic change in neolithic southern Greece'.

Coexistence of different cereals: for *triticum vulgare* and barley, see Forbes and Foxhall (1982) 'Sitometreia: the role of grain as a staple food in classical Antiquity'. The coexistence of barley and wheat in Roman Sicily was the brilliant deduction of Mazzarino (1961) 'In margine alle "Verrine"'; cf. Gallo (1983) 'Alimentazione e classi sociali: una nota sull'orzo e frumento in Grecia', (1992) 'La Sicilia occidentale e l'approvvigionamento cerealicolo di Roma'. [Aristotle] *On Wonderful Reports*, 82, noted that at Enna in Sicily they grew characteristic native wheat, characteristic imported wheat, and a third kind found nowhere else. More generally, see Sallares (1991) *The Ecology of the Ancient Greek World*, 313–89, with excellent bibliography; Spurr (1986) *Arable Cultivation*; Scheidel (1994) 'Grain cultivation in the economy of Roman Italy'; and the very sophisticated account of Valensi (1985) *Tunisian Peasants in the Eighteenth and Nineteenth Centuries*, 125–7. Two cases of the range of products possible from cereal 'staples': Braun (1995) 'Barley cakes and emmer bread'; Bolens (1980) 'Pain quotidien et pain de disette dans l'Espagne musulmane'. For cereals and oil as associates in early Greece, Amouretti (1986) *Le pain et l'huile*; on the independence of cereals of early medieval Italian society, Montanari (1985a) 'Il cibo dei contadini', (1985b) 'Tecniche e rapporti di produzione: le rese cerealicole dal IX al XIV secolo'. The saga of *Triticum durum*: Rickman (1980) *Corn Supply of Ancient Rome*, 6–7.

Other introductions: for rice, see Marinone (1992) *Il riso nell'antichità greca*; for the connection with drainage, Dixon (1969) 'Cereals in ancient Egypt', 137; sorghum: Watson (1983) *Agricultural Innovation in the Early Islamic World*, 9–14, 81–2; maize:

Hémardinquer (1973) 'Les débuts du maïs'; for its confusing nomenclature, Darby et al. (1977) *Gift of Osiris*, 460; *grano saraceno*: Spurr (1986) *Arable Cultivation*, 60–1.

Legumes: Spurr (1986) *Arable Cultivation*, 103–16; Garnsey (1988a) *Famine and Food Supply*, 52–5; Zohary and Hopf (1988) *Domestication of Plants in the Old World*, 83–112. Sarpaki (1992) 'The paleoethnobotanical approach: the Mediterranean triad, or is it a quartet?' On beans, see also Garnsey (1992) 'La fève: substance et symbole'; Hodkinson (1988) 'Animal husbandry in the Greek polis', 43–5; For the Keftiu[=Cretan]-bean, imported or introduced into second millennium B.C. Egypt, see Warren (1995) 'Minoan Crete and pharaonic Egypt'.

Other complementary staples: for chestnuts, see Pitte (1986) *Terres de castanide*; Toubert (1973) *Latium médiéval*, 191–2; Quaini (1975) 'Per lo studio dei caratteri originali del paesaggio agrario della Liguria preindustriale', at 468–9. Acorns: see Section 4 above.

After the harvest: for the intervention of saints in the distribution of staples in cities, and its interest for the economic historian, see Lemerle (1979a) *Les plus anciens recueils des miracles de Saint Démétrius et la pénétration des Slaves dans les Balkans*, 73. For similar circumstances in the Life of St Benedict of Aniane, Montanari (1985a) 'Il cibo dei contadini'. Other illustrations of the importance of the control of stored cereals: Gauthier (1987) 'Nouvelles récoltes et grain nouveau: à propos d'une inscription de Gazôros' (a landlord has grain in store which he generously releases at low prices in the months of difficulty before the new harvest); Cassiodorus, *Variae*, 10.27, gives details of warehousing at Ticinum, Dertona, Tarvisium and Tridentum and provisions for release of grain at low prices, cf. 12.27; also Gargola (1992) 'Grain distribution and the revenue of the Temple of Hera on Samos' (late third–early second centuries B.C.).

Cereal-storage: a most thought-provoking survey in Sigaut (1988) 'A method for identifying grain storage techniques and its application for European agricultural history'. Storage together of a great range of products in Greek Bronze Age contexts: G. Jones (1987) 'Agricultural practice in Greek prehistory'.

For sealed underground storage, Andrews (1982) 'Underground grain storage in central Italy', for the instructive remains of medieval *pozzi*; note also Buckland (1991) 'Granaries, stores and insects', 77, on the effectiveness of this technique against insect damage, which has been known to destroy as much as 5 per cent of a crop. At Herculaneum, 12 per cent infestation of cereals with parasites was found: Pagano (1994) 'Commercio e consumo di grano a Ercolano', 142. For Roman storage, Rickman (1971) *Roman Granaries and Store Buildings*; Purcell (1995c) 'The Roman *villa* and the landscape of production'; also Amouretti (1985) 'La transformation des céréales dans les villes'. Note the *lex Iulia de annona*, which on the evidence of the *Lex Irnitana* forbade hoarding.

Redistribution and the support of agglomerations (with BE IV.6–7): Pritchett (1991) 'Spanositia and the problem of the grain route', on the profits of war and the Athenian grain trade; L. Casson (1954) 'The grain trade of the Hellenistic world'; Rathbone (1983) 'The grain trade and grain shortage in the Hellenistic East'; Durliat (1995) 'L'approvisonnement de Constantinople'; Magdalino (1995) 'The grain-supply of Constantinople, ninth–twelfth centuries'.

For an interesting case of tithes in grain, showing that Venetian collectors in December 1700 managed to collect from the whole north-east Peloponnese only about 41,782 kg of grain (about enough to supply 114 men for a year on ancient standard rations): S. Davies (1994) 'Tithe-collection in the Venetian Peloponnese'. On the question of yields, J. K. Evans (1981) 'Wheat production and its social consequences in the Roman world', is a particularly pessimistic account; also Sallares (1991) *The Ecology of the Ancient Greek World*, 372–89; contrast Spurr (1986) *Arable Cultivation*, 82–8; Montanari (1985b) 'Tecniche e rapporti di produzione', for Italy. For surprisingly high yields, 1 tonne/ha or 5–6-fold, Issawi (1980) *Economic History of Turkey 1800–1914*, 214–5. A papyrus from the seventh-century Negev gives a series of very precise wheat and barley yields. These are around seven- to eightfold in conditions of mineral-rich wadi-floor opportunistic production: Mayerson (1984) 'Wheat in the Roman world: an addendum'.

9. Adjustable Agriculture: The Case of the Tree-Crop

The best *mise-au-point* on the debate on Mediterranean arboriculture in general is Amouretti and Brun (1993) *La production du vin et de l'huile en Méditerranée*. Cf. also Heltzer (1993) 'Olive oil and wine production in Phoenicia and the Mediterranean trade'; Bolens (1993) 'Al-Andalous: la vigne et l'olivier, un secteur de pointe'. In an impassioned argument, Hanson (1995) *The Other Greeks: The Family Farm and the Agrarian Roots of Western Civilization*, overstates the connection between arboriculture and a certain sort of agrarian regime, the citizen plot. In Mediterranean conditions arboriculture has often been a crop in the portfolio of the very wealthy. Like fishing and hunting, Mediterranean arboriculture is reflected in the Italian but not in the French medieval calendar-scenes: Mane (1983) *Calendriers et techniques agricoles*, 266–7.

Oleiculture: see Vernet (1997) *L'homme et la forêt méditerranéenne*, 124, for attestation of the olive for the first time in southern France as part of the lentisc association of the natural shrublands before cultivation. Blitzer (1993) 'Olive cultivation and oil production in Minoan Crete', has now established against sceptics a serious role for the olive in the economies whose products were collected in the great palaces: see also Melena (1983) 'Olive oil and other sorts of oil in the Cretan tablets'. Foxhall (forthcoming) *Olive-Cultivation*, will be authoritative for the Greek and Roman worlds; see also Amouretti (1986) *Le pain et l'huile*; Hadjisavvas (1992) *Olive Oil Processing in Cyprus: From the Bronze Age to the Byzantine Period*; Mattingly (1996) 'First fruit?' Sallares (1991) *The Ecology of the Ancient Greek World*, 304–9, to enhance a primitivist vision of Attic agriculture, argues for the insignificance of the Athenian olive harvest: the inadequacies of other forms of production explain the relatively high Athenian grain-rations, in spite of the logic of diversification. But Sallares's figures for the relative cost of labour (extra harvest labour as 80 per cent of the total investment in production) need to be set against the fact of the very low overall cost. For De Martino (1990) 'Economia dell'oliveto nell'Italia romana', 343–4, early nineteenth-century evidence from Venafro suggests expected returns of six times the cost of cultivation; cf. 345 on the very low labour costs. Post-classical: Grieco (1993) 'Olive tree cultivation and the alimentary use of olive oil in late medieval Italy'. North Syria: Tchalenko (1953–8) *Villages antiques de la*

Syrie du nord. North Africa: Frend (1955) 'North Africa and Europe in the early Middle Ages'; for Tunisia, Hitchner (1988) 'The Kasserine archaeological Survey, 1982–86'.

Viticulture: on the plant, its habitat, and its domestication, see Rivera Nuñez and Walker (1989) 'A review of palaeobotanical findings of early *Vitis* in the Mediterranean and of the origins of cultivated grape-vines'; Olmo (1995) 'The origin and domestication of the Vinifera grape'; Zohary (1995) 'The domestication of the grapevine *Vitis vinifera L.* in the Near East'. A general survey: Sherratt (1995b) 'Alcohol and its alternatives: symbol and substance in pre-industrial cultures'.

The classic work on the history of viticulture remains Dion (1959) *L'histoire de la vigne et du vin en France*, important for its clarity of vision on the whole nature of viticulture. Significantly, the third number of the *Annales* in its second year was devoted to the vine and wine: Febvre (1947) 'Vignes, vins, et vignerons', and Isnard (1947) 'Vigne et colonisation en Algérie', may be cited. Modern syntheses listed by (and including) Unwin (1991) *Wine and the Vine*, do not represent a significant advance. The study of Greek viticulture has been retarded by slow publication of the amphorae which are so essential a diagnostic of exchanges. See, however, Amouretti (1992) 'Oléiculture et viticulture dans la Grèce antique'; Saprykin (1994) *Ancient Farms and Land Plots in the Khora of Khersonesos Taurike*; Hanson (1992) 'Practical aspects of grape-growing and the ideology of Greek viticulture'; and – a wonderful example of how whole chapters of ancient economic history are waiting to be written from evidence which requires patient and imaginative reconstruction – Vandermersch (1994) *Vins et amphores de Grande Grèce et de Sicile*, with its 'prequel', Vandermersch (1996) 'Vigne, vin et économie dans l'Italie du sud grecque à l'époque archaïque', very valuable in linking Greek overseas settlement with the spread of export-viticulture. For the comparable case of Thasos, see Salviat (1986) 'Le vin de Thasos'; Garlan (1988) *Vin et amphores de Thasos*; Avram (1988) 'Zu den Handelsbeziehungen zwischen Histria und die Insel Thasos im Lichte der Amphorenstempel'. For the Bronze Age Aegean, see Palmer (1994) *Wine in the Mycenaean Palace Economy*; for Egypt: Darby et al. (1977) *Food: The Gift of*

Osiris, 597–607; Empereur (1993) 'La production viticole dans l'Égypte ptolémaïque et romaine'. For Rome: Ampolo (1980) 'Le condizioni naturali della produzione: agricoltura e paesaggio agrario'; Panella and Tchernia (1994) 'Produits agricoles transportés en amphores: l'huile et surtout le vin'. The most important contribution on Roman viticulture, which is in many ways the core of the subject, remains the classic study of Tchernia (1986) *Vin de l'Italie romaine*. For Crete, Chaniotis (1988) 'Vinum Creticum excellens: zum Weinhandel Kretas', and especially Marangou-Lerat (1995) *Le vin et les amphores de Crète*, 155–63, setting the abundance of ancient production in a helpfully wide historical context with Venetian comparisons.

Byzantium: Mayerson (1985) 'The wine and vineyards of Gaza in the Byzantine period'. Bibliography for the Christian Mediterranean in the Middle Ages and early modern period respectively will be found in the excellent articles of Zug Tucci (1978) 'Un aspetto trascurato del commercio medievale del vino', and R. C. Davis (1997) 'Venetian shipbuilders and the fountain of wine'.

The Islamic world: Heine (1982) *Weinstudien: Untersuchungen zu Anbau, Produktion und Konsum des Weins im arabisch-islamischen Mittelalter*; Bolens (1990b) 'La viticulture d'après les traités d'agronomie andalous' (referring to massive popular consumption of *jamhuri*, a concentrated fermented must).

10. THE MEDITERRANEAN GARDEN

G. Jones (1987) 'Agricultural practice in Greek prehistory', a study of weed species, suggests much more garden cultivation than usually supposed in the Bronze Age Aegean: the question is, how long did this last? See Forbes (1982) *Strategies and Soils*, 312–23, for polycropping. For Aetolia and the garden/pastoralist mix, Bommeljé and Doorn (1987) *Aetolia and the Aetolians*; similar arguments in Andreolli (1990) 'Il ruolo dell'orticoltura e della frutticoltura nelle campagne dell'alto medioevo'.

Fragmentation: J. W. Bentley (1990) 'Wouldn't you like all your land in one place?', with earlier bibliography; cf. 53 for the close link with intensive agriculture in which reduced productivity per unit labour is an acceptable choice if productivity per unit land is increased. He questions, however, the connection with partible inheritance practices. See also Bentley (1987) 'Economic and ecological approaches to land fragmentation; in defense of a much maligned phenomenon', quoting agricultural policy documents of 1960 which call it as pernicious as prostitution or blackmail.

Peri-urban horticulture: Bresc (1972) 'Les jardins de Palerme 1290–1460'. For Campania, Delille (1985) *Famille et propriété*; for Roman examples, Carandini (1985) 'Orti e frutteti intorno a Roma'; Jashemski (1979a) *Gardens of Pompeii*; Kolendo (1994) 'Praedia suburbana e la loro redditività'. Compare, for Rome in the Middle Ages, Castagnetti (1990) 'La "Campanea" e i beni communi'. Koder (1995) 'Fresh vegetables for the capital', and (1993) *Gemüse in Byzanz*, effectively uses the evidence of the *Geoponika* to fill in a gap in the other evidence. Note that as with hunting, fishing and arboriculture, vegetable-growing is found in the Italian but not in the French calendar scenes: Mane (1983) *Calendriers et techniques agricoles*, 269–70.

11. THE CASE OF THE SMALLER MEDITERRANEAN ISLAND

Cf. III.4, V.2, IX.3–4. Particularly helpful studies of the Greek archipelago in the late medieval and early modern periods include: Slot (1982) *Archipelagus Turbatus*; J. L. Davis (1991) 'Contributions to a Mediterranean rural archaeology: historical case-studies from the Ottoman Cyclades', (1992) 'The islands of the Aegean'; Kolodny (1974) *La population des îles de Grèce*, 22–3. Compare the ecological study of Halstead and Jones (1989) 'Agrarian ecology in the Greek islands: time-stress, scale and risk' (particularly concerned with Karpathos and Amorgos), and (also concerned with Amorgos) Rougemont (1990) 'Géographie historique des Cyclades: l'homme et le milieu dans l'Archipel'. Also Berthier (1969) *Un épisode de l'histoire de la canne à sucre*, reviewed by Salmi-Bianchi (1969). Sallares (1991) *The Ecology of the Ancient Greek World*, 38–41, 235, 402–3. Rackham (1990b) 'Observations on the historical ecology of Santorini'.

On the question of insularity: MacArthur and Wilson (1967) *Theory of Island Biogeography*; J. D. Evans (1977) 'Island archaeology in the Mediterranean'; Patton (1996) *Islands in Time: Island Sociogeography and Mediterranean Prehistory*. Against such strong views of the isolation of Mediterranean islands, Purcell (1995a) 'Field survey of an asteroid'.

Island viticulture: for the high-quality wine of Chios, Sarikakis (1986) 'Commercial relations between Chios and other Greek cities in Antiquity'. Clinkenbeard (1982) 'Lesbian wine and storage amphoras: a progress report on identification', (1986) 'Lesbian and Thasian wine amphoras: questions concerning collaboration'.

For the very intensive agriculture of Delos, Brunet (1990a) 'Contribution à l'histoire rurale de Délos aux époques classique et héllénistique', also (1990b) 'Terrasses de cultures antiques: l'exemple de Délos, Cyclades'; Kent (1948) 'The temple-estates of Delos, Rheneia and Mykonos'; Reger (1994a) *Regionalism and Change in the Economy of Independent Delos*; Boussac and Rougemont (1993) 'Observation sur le territoire des cités d'Amorgos'. For islands specializing in the production of cheap pottery: on Pantelleria, Peacock (1982) *Pottery in the Roman World: An Ethnoarchaeological Approach*, 79–80, cf. Bresc (1971) 'Pantelleria entre l'Islam et la chrétienté'.

For the cash-crop economy of islands, J. L. Davis (1991) 'Contributions to Mediterranean rural archaeology: historical case-studies from the Ottoman Cyclades'. The symbiosis between the Ionian islands and the area of the Gulf of Ambracia is described by H. Holland (1815) *Travels in the Ionian Isles, Albania, Thessaly, Macedonia*, 62–3; Goodisson (1822) *Historical and Topographical Essay upon the Islands of Corfu*, 58 (cf. 111), gives approximate numbers of migrant workers – 600 from Lefkada; 500 from Ithaca.

For 'colonial' exploitation in medieval and early modern islands: for Sicily, Bresc (1986) *Un monde méditerranéen*; S. R. Epstein (1992) *An Island for Itself*. J.-P. Richard (1985) 'Agriculture in the Latin empire of Constantinople', especially on the selective growing of cash crops in 'colonial' Crete (prohibition on cultivation of Lasithi and Anopolis plains, 1364–1463). Cyprus: Maier and Karageorghis (1984) *Paphos*, 326–41. Chaouache (1964) 'Les structures économiques de la Byzacène'. For agriculture, see also Kolodny (1974) *La population des îles de Grèce*, 159–62. The precariousness and negative effects of cash-crop extraction (especially sugar-cane) is stressed by Braudel (1972a) *The Mediterranean*, 151–8.

BIBLIOGRAPHICAL ESSAY TO CHAPTER VII
TECHNOLOGY AND AGRARIAN CHANGE

1. WORKING THE SOIL

The much-cited study of Haudricourt and Delamarre (1955) *L'homme et la charrue*, was the classic statement of the theory of the 'plough-revolution' in the historical period. A late statement of a related position: L. T. White (1980) 'Technological development in the transition from Antiquity to the Middle Ages'. Compare the bibliography on the medieval 'agricultural revolution' in general in Section 7 below. General accounts include Bentzien (1969) *Haken und Pflug*; Beck et al. (1980) *Untersuchungen zur eisenzeitlichen und frühmittelalterlicher Flur in Mitteleuropa und ihrer Nutzung*; for traction, Langdon (1986) *Horses, Oxen and Technological Innovation*.

Against the idea of a 'plough-revolution', see especially the judicious, up-to-date survey of Raepsaet (1995) 'Les prémices de la mécanisation agricole', on medieval agricultural innovation and especially the plough, claiming particular importance for the Rhine–Seine area. M. Kaplan (1992) *Les hommes et la terre à Byzance du VIe au XIe siècle*, 50, for the advantages of the light plough in Mediterranean environments.

The application of technological determinism in prehistoric archaeology is not surprising given the history of the discipline and its close dependence on artefact studies; but the contributions of Sherratt (1981) 'Plough and pastoralism', and (1983) 'The secondary exploitation of animals in the Old World', have greatly illuminated the debate. Further thoughts in Sherratt (1997a) 'The evolution of the plough in temperate Europe'. For additional bibliography Bogucki (1993) 'Animal

traction and household economies in neolithic Europe'.

On the history of the plough in the classical world, see Amouretti (1976) 'Les instruments aratoires dans la Grèce archaïque'; Spurr (1986) *Arable Cultivation in Roman Italy*; K. D. White (1970) *Roman Farming*; and Forni (1980a) 'Il *plaumaratum* di Plinio', for the Roman imperial wheeled plough and its specific geographical context (Aquileia). Forni (1989) 'Progrediti strumenti agricoli a fondamento della ricca economia lombarda in età romana imperiale', makes technology responsible for the abundance extravagantly praised by Bonvesin della Riva, *De magnalibus Mediolani*. A further instance of topographical fragmentation of technical progress, from Corsica, shows the coexistence of parallel levels of technological complexity: Casanova (1993) 'Types de pressoirs et types de production'. This capricious distribution was a common feature of the history of technological change in Antiquity. Brunner (1995) 'Continuity and discontinuity of Roman agricultural knowledge in the early Middle Ages', for scythes, ploughs and manure, from Antiquity to the Middle Ages mainly in northern Europe, usefully stresses gradual change, creative adaptation and the priority of 'social relations' in explaining history of technology. For Sherratt's more recent views on the early history of the plough, see his (1997d) 'Changing perspectives on European prehistory'.

On tools and basic equipment, see Comet (1992) *Le paysan et son outil*; Pesez (1991) 'Outils et techniques agricoles du monde médiéval'. For the eastern Mediterranean, Bryer (1986c) 'Byzantine agricultural implements'; compare Bryer (1982) 'The question of Byzantine mines', 138, for the high value and scarcity of iron tools in parts of the Byzantine Empire. See also Kazhdan (1994) 'One more agrarian history of Byzantium', 77. For the continuity in tools in medieval Egypt, Rabie (1981) 'Some technical aspects of agriculture in medieval Egypt', 63. Amouretti (1986) *Le pain et l'huile*, 79–110, is helpful on the essential simplicity of Mediterranean agricultural equipment. For the famous apparent exception of the Gallo-Roman mechanical reaper, the *vallus*, see Sigaut (1988) 'A method for identifying grain storage techniques', 20: 'so the invention itself is no longer an isolated stroke of genius, since it can be seen as the "mechanization" of a traditional technique, that of stripping off the grains'. In this important discussion, Sigaut also argues for the central significance of the widespread introduction of the reaping sickle, a low-technology change which accompanied the use of sheaves. The change made it possible to dispense with bags and baskets, but required animal transport, as well as immediate threshing (and winnowing) using animals which consumed the straw; it increased the demand for bulk storage, and was usually linked with a male labour force. This set of changes is (for example) found with the introduction of Roman cerealiculture. On the importance of tools for clearance of scrub and woodland, note that the Villanovan bronzesmith's hoard found at Bologna in the nineteenth century, and datable to between the tenth and seventh centuries B.C., comprised 14,838 pieces of bronze and 3 of iron, including 349 scythes, sickles and similar bladed tools: Bentini (1995) 'Per una storia della economia agricola di Bologna Villanoviana: gli strumenti agricoli del deposito di S. Francesco'.

The terraced landscape

> L'arbor che sovr'un colle o'n piagga assiede
> Ben cerchi, e gradi, e se da quella il senta
> Ch'alle radici sue sostenga oltraggio
> Con poca riga che piu in altro muova
> La svolga altronde, o, lui circonde in giro
> A gusa di castel di sterpi e sassi.
>   L. Alamanni, *La coltivazione*,
>   Padua, 1546, L. 1.6

The general accounts of the Mediterranean terrace by Blanchemanche (1986) *Les terrasses de culture*, and (1990) *Bâtisseurs de paysages*, are excellent on the technical details, but not very inclined to ask questions about the driving-force behind the investment of labour

and capital; see also Amboise et al. (1989) *Paysages de terrasses*. Comparative accounts: Wagstaff (1992) 'Agricultural terraces: the Vasilikos valley, Cyprus'; Moody and Grove (1990) 'Terraces and enclosure walls in the Cretan landscape', with Rackham and Moody (1997) *The Making of the Cretan Landscape*, 140–45; de Reparaz (1990) 'Culture en terrasses, expression de la petite paysannerie'. Ancient Greek terraces are presented by Rackham and Moody (1992) 'Terraces', and Lohmann (1992) 'Agriculture and country life'; Foxhall (1996) 'Feeling the earth move', dissents. Italian cases: Quilici Gigli (1995) 'Bonifica agraria'. Forbes (1982) *Strategies and Soils*, 200, notes that 'soil moisture and its control are the single most important factor in tillage practices on Methana', through reducing moisture loss and increasing absorption (204).

2. THE IRRIGATED LANDSCAPE

In composing this *mise-au-point* we have been very struck by the general lack of information and interest that economic historians have shown in the subject; see however Schüle (1968) 'Feldbewasserung in Alteuropa'.

The nature of Mediterranean irrigation

Winter run-off cultivation: the use of dams to control flash-flooding is documented by N. A. F. Smith (1971) *History of Dams*, Calvet and Geyer (1992) *Barrages antiques de Syrie*; and Garbrecht (1984) 'Talsperren im östlichen Mittelmeerraum', for the period before 600 B.C. Other examples in Castellani (1993) 'Evidence for hydrogeological planning in ancient Cappadocia', and Zangger (1992a) *Flood from Heaven*, 81–5. Floodwater farming in general: Barker and Jones (1982) *The UNESCO Libyan Valleys Survey 1979–1981: Palaeoeconomy and Environmental Archaeology in the Pre-desert*; Hodge (1992) *Roman Aqueducts and Water-Supply*, 250–52. On North Africa in Antiquity, Birebent (1964) *Aquae Romanae*; B. D. Shaw (1984a) 'Water and society', describing the Roman effort as a 'magnificent failure' (*contra* Euzennat (1992) 'L'hydraulique dans l'Afrique romaine'); Shaw (1991) 'Wells, walls and aqueducts'. The best known ancient case, thanks to a detailed regulatory inscription, is Lamasba in Algeria: Shaw (1982) 'Lamasba', note especially 93 for emphasis on microenvironments. The sophistication is well displayed by Meuret (1996) 'Le règlement de *Lamasba*'.

Management of perennial streams: for some general reflections, see Farrington (1980) 'The archaeology of irrigation canals, with special reference to Peru'. On the origins of Egyptian hydraulic culture, Butzer (1976) *Early Hydraulic Civilization in Egypt*, but see Luft (1994) 'L'irrigation au Moyen Empire'; for Egypt in the Hellenistic and Roman period, see the excellent account of Bonneau (1993) *Le régime administratif de l'eau du Nil dans l'Égypte grecque, romaine et byzantine*, (1994) 'Usage et usages de l'eau dans l'Égypte ptolémaïque et romaine'; Menu (1994) *Problèmes institutionnels de l'eau*. For Nile irrigation and its intensification, Bagnall (1993) *Egypt in Late Antiquity*, 17–18, 311–13. On Mesopotamia, R. McC. Adams (1974) 'Historic patterns of Mesopotamian irrigation agriculture'; and the two volumes of the *Bulletin on Sumerian Agriculture* on 'Irrigation and cultivation in Mesopotamia', 4 and 5 (1988–90); also Geyer (1990) *Techniques*, 63–254, on the Euphrates. For the Orontes, Weulersse (1940a) *L'Oronte*.

For the Valencian *huerta*, see Glick (1970) *Irrigation and Society*; more generally, Glick (1995) *From Muslim Fortress to Christian Castle*, 65–91. For the earlier periods, see Butzer et al. (1985) 'Irrigation agrosystems in eastern Spain: Roman or Islamic origins?', criticized for its stress on continuities, deriving from its 4,000 year perspective, by Glick (1995) 64.

On *norias*, useful material is to be found in Balty (1987) 'Problèmes de l'eau à Apamée de Syrie'; Glick (1995) 82–3; Zaqzouq (1990) 'Les Norias: anciens moyens d'irrigation les plus importants dans la région de Hama'; and Girard et al. (1990) 'Les Norias hydrauliques du moyen-Oronte'.

Groundwater and its management: for the special case of oases, see Trousset (1986) 'Les oasis présahariennes dans l'antiquité: partage de l'eau et division du temps'; and Bousquet and Reddé (1994) 'Les installations hydrauliques et les parcellaires dans la région de Tell Douch (Égypte) à l'époque romaine', for the very untypical natural artesian springs of the Khargeh oasis. On *qanawat*, English (1968) 'Qanats'; Glick (1970) *Irrigation and Society in Medieval Valencia*, (1995) *From Muslim Fortress to Christian Castle*, 77–8; D. R. Hill (1980) *Islamic Technology*; Watson (1983) *Agricultural Innovation in the Early*

Islamic World; Hodge (1992) *Roman Aqueducts*, 20–4. Lombard (1991) 'Du rhythme naturel au rhythme humain: vie et mort d'une technique traditionelle, le *qanât*', shows how falling water-tables and the decay of the structure gradually make this form of water-supply more and more of a burden to the communities which depend on it. Mountain irrigations: Netting (1974a) 'The system nobody knows: village irrigation in the Swiss Alps'.

The underrated irrigations of the ancient Mediterranean

The scantiness of the evidence collected in the frequently-cited article by C. Knapp (1919–20) 'Irrigation among the Greeks and Romans', reflects the author's competence (and the popular nature of the periodical) rather than the importance of the theme.

Historians of technology are apt to discount the possibility of 're-inventing the wheel'. A study of the Islamic hydraulic landscape of a valley in the province of Almeria in Spain notes with surprise how the river-bed catchments here are identical in technique to those of pre-Columbian Peru 'par un curieux phénomène de convergence' (Bertrand and Cressier (1985) 'Irrigation et aménagement du terroir dans la vallée de l'Andarax (Almeria)', 123).

Gallant (1991) *Risk and Survival in Ancient Greece*, 56–7, plays down the importance of ancient Greek irrigation; on dry and irrigated farming see also Burford (1993) *Land and Labor in the Greek World*, 109. Hydraulic technology in ancient Greece: Wörrle (1981) 'Wasserrecht und -verwaltung'; for the interesting case of the Acharnae aqueduct; Vanderpool (1965) 'Acharnian Aqueduct', inclining as usual to interpret it as urban supply although it seems much more likely that the 'Community of the Acharnae Pipeline' is a collectivity of agricultural users (cf. Euripides, *Medea*, 824–42, on the Kephisos). Cistern and watercourse irrigation was linked with intensification around Roman-period villas on the Mesara plain in Crete: Sanders (1976) 'Settlement in the Hellenistic and Roman periods on the Plain of the Mesara, Crete'. A valley-dam near Alyzeia in Acarnania, probably of the fourth century B.C., was certainly for irrigation as well as flash-flood control, and closely resembles the prescription of Plato's *Laws*: W. M. Murray (1984) 'The ancient dam of the Mytikas valley'. The example of Copais: Argoud (1987)

'Eau et agriculture', citing *Iliad*, 21.257–62; Lauffer (1986) *Kopais: Untersuchungen zur historischen Landeskunde Mittelgriechenlands*; Fossey (1979) 'The cities of the Kopais in the Roman period'; Knauss (1990b) *Wasserbau und Geschichte: Minysche Epoche–Bayerische Zeit*. For irrigation-heroes cf. X.2 below.

Italian cases: Violante (1989) 'Suolo e paesaggio agrario', stresses fear of drought, overemphasizing 'l'agricoltura asciutta' (cf. VI.8 for dry farming). For pre-medieval Italian water-management, Hodge (1992) *Roman Aqueducts and Water-Supply*, is now the starting point for this, as for most other aspects of Roman water-supply and consumption: see 246–53 with earlier bibliography. This sensible brief account laments the neglect of the subject, and classifies irrigation as a 'special use' of water. Allowing, on the basis of Roman water-law and the literary texts, that irrigation was normal, he strongly emphasizes gravity-fed systems, adhering to the view that 'there was no mechanical irrigation in Italy' because of the small size of farms (following K. D. White (1970) *Roman Farming*, 157: an all-too-familiar instance of what happens when the history of the social relations of production are subordinated completely to the history of techniques). On mixed provision of horticultural and urban water in Roman aqueducts, Purcell (1996b) 'Rome and the management of water'; Hodge (1992) 249–50, on the Aqua Crabra, a managed natural stream of the periphery of Rome. On *cuniculi*, Riera (1994) *Utilitas necessaria*, esp. 419–73, 'Gli emissari e drenaggi'. Quilici Gigli (n.d.) 'Antiche opere di bonifica idraulica nella zona Pontina settentrionale', stresses their varied function, and argues for a connection with the establishment of the Roman agrarian landscape in the late fourth century; cf. (1983) 'Sistemi di cunicoli tra Velletri e Cisterna', also (1997) *Uomo acqua e paesaggio*. Attema (1993) *An Archaeological Survey in the Pontine Region*, 65–76, has an excellent survey of the debate, but opts for an archaic date for the transformation of the landscape. Hydraulic aspects of the Roman provincial landscape: Leveau (1994) 'Dal paesaggio naturale al paesaggio coltivato. Dati archeologici relativi ai grandi lavori agricoli in età romana: il drenaggio dei paludi nella Bassa Provenza', on the reclamation of the 'paluns' or marshy *polje* of the limestone landscape of Provence.

The cistern as an adjunct of the villa may be seen as analogous to the villa's role as a centre for storage: Purcell (1995c) 'The Roman *villa* and the landscape of production'. Examples: Thomas and Wilson (1994) 'Water supply for Roman farms in Latium and south Etruria'; cf. Butzer et al. (1985) 'Irrigation agrosystems in eastern Spain', 498, on the interest of Roman tank- and cistern-fed micro-irrigations. The question of Roman precursors for the hydraulic landscape of Islamic south-eastern Spain: Bazzana (1992) *Maisons d'al-Andalus*, 33, on the concentrated pockets of Roman occupation in the *huerta* of Valencia; 385, giving a very conventional picture of late-Roman hiatus: contrast the picture of complex interaction presented by Reynolds (1995) *Trade in the Western Mediterranean*.

Why big and expensive water-projects are rare

The intellectual affiliations of Wittfogel (1957) *Oriental Despotism*, are discussed by Peet (1985) 'The social origins of environmental determinism'. Archaeological discussions include Scarborough (1991) 'Water management adaptations in non-industrial complex societies: an archaeological perspective'; Spooner (1974) 'Irrigation and society: the Iranian plateau'; and Sherratt (1980) 'Water, soil and seasonality in early cereal cultivation'. A medieval example, exploring the relationship between drainage imperatives, collective responsibility, smallholding and community, and stressing the close associations of drainage and irrigation, and of irrigated meadows and intensive horticulture: Squatriti (1995) 'Water, nature and culture in early medieval Lucca'. See more generally his (1998) *Water and Society in Early Medieval Italy*, ch. 3.

Among the not very extensive contibutions from social anthropology and human ecology, both Geertz (1972) 'The wet and the dry', and Varisco (1983) '*Sayl* and *ghayl*: the ecology of water allocation in Yemen', investigate the contrast between state control and 'tribal' individual rights; both also schematically link the former with abundance, whether short-lived (flash-flood management) or perennial (as in Bali) and the latter with the uncertainties of variable sources in an unpredictable environment. Bédoucha (1993) 'The watch and the waterclock; technological choices/social choices', is very helpful on the consequences of technological change in irrigation. For negative consequences of changes in the hydraulic landscape, such as salinization, see N. A. F. Smith (1971) *History of Dams*,

39–43, (1976) *Man and Water*, ch. 16, on the 'vicious spiral' of water technology; cf. Popp (1986) 'L'agriculture irriguée dans la Vallée de Sous (Maroc): formes et conflits d'utilisation d'eau'. For other bibliography on ancient ecological disaster, see BE VIII.

Social consequences of irrigation in Spain and the Maghreb: for co-operation and local systems, Glick (1970) *Irrigation and Society*, and (1995) *From Muslim Fortress to Christian Castle*, are still instructive. Segura Graíño (1992) *Los regadíos hispanos en la Edad Media*, is an excellent introduction to the question of irrigation in medieval Spain. A model archaeological study of a microregion in this area is Butzer et al. (1982) 'Medieval Muslim communities'. Bazzana et al. (1987) 'L'hydraulique agricole dans al-Andalus: données textuelles et archéologiques'. See also Bolens (1989) 'L'irrigation en al-Andalus'. But the subject is ideologically charged. At the beginning of the twentieth century, in his masterly descriptive treatise on irrigation, Jean Brunhes, a pupil of Vidal de la Blache (II.2 with BE), stressed that social organization was a better way of achieving irrigation than massive construction projects, in a misleading dichotomy which we have already noticed: (1902) *L'irrigation, ses conditions géographiques, ses modes, et son organisation dans la Péninsule Ibérique et dans l'Afrique du Nord*, 141). And he cited the Spanish pride in this co-operative social behaviour (Costa (1898) *Colectivismo agrario en España*) which is still to be felt in the scholarship of the end of the twentieth century.

Watermills

Bloch's classic (1935) 'Avènement et conquêtes du moulin à eau', is most accessible in his (1967) *Land and Work in Mediaeval Europe*, 136–68. Cf. Squatriti (1997) '"Advent and Conquests" of the water mill in Italy'. From Antiquity, at least thirty instances are known archaeologically: see K. D. White (1984) *Greek and Roman Technology*, 126–201; Landels (1978) *Engineering in the Ancient World*, 66–75; Wikander (1991) 'Water mills and aqueducts'; Hodge (1992) *Roman Aqueducts and Water-Supply*, 254–57, the last two with full bibliography. A further example: Schioler (1989) 'The watermills at the Crocodile River: a turbine mill dated to 345–380 A.D.' It has been established that the date of the Barbégal complex is too early

to fit the hypothesis that it was built as a result of the decline of the slave-system: Leveau (1995) 'Les moulins de Barbégal'; cf. Leveau (1996) 'The Barbégal water mill in its environment: archaeology and the economic and social history of Antiquity'.

For the Middle Ages: Squatriti (1998) *Water and Society in Early Medieval Italy*, ch. 5; Holt (1988) *Mills of Medieval England*; and, on wind power, Hills (1994) *Power from Wind: A History of Windmill Technology*; Wickham (1988b) *The Mountain and the City*, 165–6, with bibliography on Italian mills. Glick (1995) *From Muslim Fortress to Christian Castle*, is also suggestive. Cresswell (1993) 'Of mills and waterwheels: the hidden parameters of technological choice', is good on the technical side but somewhat out of date on the history. See also Aguade Nieto (1988) *De la sociedad arcáica a la sociedad campesina en las Asturias medieval*, 147–94; Lagardère (1993) *Campagnes et paysans d'al-Andalus*, 286–357, esp. 295 on flour bought up from rural mills by courtiers. Lock (1995) *The Franks in the Aegean*, 248, estimates that ownership of a mill could yield the equivalent of some twenty substantial rents. Squatriti (1995) 'Water, nature and culture in early medieval Lucca', 36, for the link in the plains of the western Mediterranean between mills, fisheries and irrigated gardens. Wickham (1988b), 165–6, notes the vulnerability of mills to stream-erosion.

3. On the Diversity of Cultivated Plants

Newly domesticated and selectively bred plant and animal species are examples of technical innovation too. Their importance was recognized by Febvre (1940) 'Les surprises d'Hérodote, ou les acquisitions de l'agriculture méditerranéenne', and is urged by Sallares (1991) *The Ecology of the Ancient Greek World*, 13–14. It is not, however, useful to transfer to the biological sphere the language and ideas of mechanical determinism. Indeed, the universal, gradual, imperceptible nature of biological innovation offers an important analogy for the real social processes involved in other technical improvement. The most important argument is that of A. W. Johnson (1972) 'Individuality and experimentation', which should be set against the role of the Mediterranean lands as a 'Vavilov centre' of genetic variety (already adumbrated by Febvre 1940) which is discussed below in VIII.5: cf. Kloppenburg (1988) *First the Seed*; Hawkes (1983) *Diversity of Crop Plants*. For unconscious selection of cultivated species, see also Amouretti (1976) 'Les instruments aratoires dans la Grèce archaïque', 25–72. Basic information on domestication: Zohary and Hopf (1988) *Domestication of Plants in the Old World*.

The discussion has centred on the Islamic world. The treatments by Ashtor (1976) *A Social and Economic History of the Near East in the Middle Ages*, and Watson (1981) 'Towards denser and more continuous settlement', are sophisticated on agricultural change, but somewhat inclined to use the progressivist language of the history of inventions. This is also the spirit of the substantial contribution of Watson (1983) *Agricultural Innovation in the Early Islamic World*, on which see Aubaile-Sallenave (1984) 'L'agriculture musulmane aux premiers temps de la conquête: apports et emprunts, à propos de *Agricultural Innovation in the Early Islamic World* de Andrew M. Watson'. Hostile to extreme views of the novelty of Islamic agronomy, Zakri (1990) 'Pratiques hydro-agricoles traditionelles d'après les manuscrits arabes d'agronomie à la période médiévale dans le monde musulman', 38, discusses the strong connections with the Roman and Byzantine agronomic tradition in the Levant of the Islamic literature, via Costus's *Book of Greek Agriculture* of the fifth century; cf. Bolens (1981) *Agronomes andalous*. Against Watson's view of a 'Muslim green revolution' as far as Mesopotamia and the Iranian plateau are concerned, arguing for a Sassanian zenith for productivity there, Christensen (1993) *Decline of Iranshahr*, 71–2; and against the general view of an Islamic super-economy, see the judicious account of Butzer (1994) 'The Islamic traditions of agroecology', 42 n.5.

For specialized crops of the Hellenistic and Roman periods: D. J. Crawford (1979) 'Food: tradition and change in Hellenistic Egypt', (1989) 'Agriculture'. On Roman elite interests in exotica, showy and recreational but not economically disinterested, Purcell (1995c) 'The Roman *villa* and the landscape of production'. For the fortunes of particular crops: citron, attested in Roman Campania (*pace* Watson), Jashemski (1979a) *The Gardens of Pompeii*, 240, 285, 295; opium poppy, Merlin (1984) *On the Trail of the Ancient*

Opium Poppy. On *silphion* see III.3 above. For *Triticum durum* in Antiquity, Sallares (1991) *The Ecology of the Ancient Greek World*; Spurr (1986) *Arable Cultivation in Roman Italy*.

For sugar-cane, Lagardère (1993) *Campagnes et paysans d'al-Andalus*, 361–90; Malpica (1995) *Paisajes del Azúcar*, and von Wartburg (1995) 'Desing [*sic*] and technology of the mediaeval refineries of the sugar cane in Cyprus. A case of estudy [*sic*] in industrial archaeology', who argues against deterministic explanations for this enterprise based on mill-technology.

4. ABATEMENT AND INTENSIFICATION

How much better is what kind of more?

On decision-making and planning: Carlstein (1982) *Time Resources, Society and Ecology*, and Halstead and Jones (1989) 'Agrarian ecology in the Greek islands: time stress, scale and risk'.

For abatement in general, see Cameron and Tomka (1993) *Abandonment of Settlements and Regions: Ethnoarchaeological and Archaeological Approaches*; Tainter (1988) *Collapse of Complex Societies*. Creighton and Segui (1998) 'The ethnoarchaeology of abandonment and post-abandonment behaviour in pastoral sites', show how difficult the interpretation of the archaeology of abatement is likely to be. Antoniadis Bibicou (1965) 'Villages désertés en Grèce: un bilan provisoire'.

Uncultivated land: for evidence from the field, see Gilman and Thornes (1985) *Land Use and Prehistory in South East Spain*; Chapman (1990) *Emerging Complexity*. The landscape of the southern Argolid is amenable to analysis in terms of intensification and abatement: Jameson et al. (1994) *A Greek Countryside*, 325–414: '50,000 years of co-evolution of landscape and human settlement'. Abatement because of shortage of population in nineteenth-century Greece: W. J. Woodhouse (1897) *Aetolia*, 12; on the abandoned rural lots or *debbi* of Liguria, Sereni (1955) *Comunità rurali nell'Italia antica*, 539.

Crisis or abatement? See Watson (1983) *Agricultural Innovation in the Early Islamic World*, 139–46, for crisis as it is often portrayed. An excellent example of a crisis reconsidered: Patterson (1987) 'Crisis? what crisis? Rural change and urban development in early imperial Appennine Italy'. For demographic mobility, cf. IX.5–6.

Demography, intensification and abatement

For declining urban and rural populations in early fourteenth-century Tuscany, see Herlihy (1967) *Medieval and Renaissance Pistoia*, 64–6; and in Provence, Baratier (1961) *La démographie provençale*, 80–1. The basis of many misleading demographic arguments in Mediterranean history is site-counting (for an example, Snodgrass (1979) *Archaic Greece*). I. Morris (1987) *Burial and Ancient Society*, makes the basic point that numbers of incidental sites reflect social organization at least as much as they reflect demographic realities (compare our remarks in Section 6). This argument is also often used to establish demographic decline in the 'Dark Ages': see below for discussion of the Italian evidence. On the correlation of demography with other factors in Antiquity, Duncan-Jones (1980) 'Demographic change and economic progress under the Roman Empire'. See also Netting (1974b) 'Agrarian ecology', 24–8, on shifting cultivation; 36–42, for present intensification as a systemic change, discussing coercion. Gallant (1991) *Risk and Survival in Ancient Greece*, 194–6, shows how elite actions result in pauperization.

Connectivity as intensification: see Runnels and van Andel (1988) 'Trade and the origins of agriculture in the eastern Mediterranean', with discussion; Tangri (1989) 'On trade and assimilation in European agricultural origins'; Runnels (1989) 'Trade models in the study of agricultural origins and dispersals'; Dickson (1989) 'Out of Utopia: Runnels' and van Andel's non-equilibrium growth model of the origins of agriculture'. Gallant (1991) *Risk and Survival in Ancient Greece*, 143–69, for exchange as protection against risk, cf. Halstead (1989) 'The economy has a normal surplus'. A very suggestive account of the abutment of zones characterized by different degrees of redistributive engagement, charted by their dietary expression: Lombardo (1995) 'Food and "frontier" in the Greek colonies of southern Italy'.

The adaptability of labour

Women's labour: Varro, *Country Matters*, 2.10.9, with Scheidel (1995) 'The most silent women of Greece and Rome: rural labour

and women's life in the ancient world'; Bennett (1987) *Women in the Medieval English Countryside*; Hanawalt (1986) *Women and Work in Pre-industrial Europe*; Herlihy (1990) *Opera Muliebria: Women and Work in Medieval Europe* (disappointing). Also Sallares (1991) *The Ecology of the Ancient Greek World*, 431 n.50; Sigaut (1988) 'A method for identifying grain storage techniques', on differential gender roles in harvesting. Also note Forbes (1982) *Strategies and Soils*, 290–311, on decisions in household labour allocation.

Late Antique and early medieval Italy: see Potter (1978) 'Population hiatus and continuity: the case of the South Etruria Survey'; Wickham (1979) 'Historical and topographical notes on early mediaeval south Etruria' (III.2); Christie (1996) 'Barren fields: landscapes and settlements in late Roman and post-Roman Italy'. Fumagalli (1994) *Landscapes of Fear*, sees reoccupation of land in Italy in the Middle Ages as a piecemeal process continuing over centuries rather than a sudden turning-point. Cf. also Moreland (1992) 'Restoring the dialectic: settlement patterns and documents in medieval central Italy'; Traina (1994) 'Paesaggi tardoantichi: alcuni problemi'; Moreland (1993) 'Excavations at Casale San Donato, Castelnuovo di Farfa (RI), Lazio, 1992', presenting a site in Sabinum the material of which would be largely resistant to field-survey, with a villa of the imperial period about 100 metres from a farm of the sixth to eighth centuries. Similarly unsettling conclusions result from the comparison of Aetolian villages: Vroom (1998) 'Early modern archaeology in central Greece'.

5. ANATOMY OF THE MEDITERRANEAN COUNTRYMAN

For the reality of Romanov Russia and its differences from the literary image, see Pallot and Shaw (1990) *Landscape and Settlement in Romanov Russia, 1613–1917*. Note the finding of Blum (1982) 'Fiction and the European peasantry: the realist novel as a historical source', 127, that novelists of nine different nationalities 'all delineate a clearly identifiable type of European peasant, with essentially the same characteristics and behavior patterns that transcended national boundaries'; cf. Aydelotte (1948) 'The England of Marx and Mill as reflected in fiction', on the dilettantism of attempting to tell the social history of a period by quotations from its novels. Over-wrought, literary language is used, however, to striking effect by Camporesi (1989) *Bread of Dreams*.

Forbes (1982) *Strategies and Soils*, 17–23, addresses the difficulty of applying widely held concepts of 'peasant' to Greek country people, but accepting the definition of Macfarlane (1978) *The Origins of English Individualism*, to the extent that the Methana household is a social and economic unit in which farm labour is family labour, and *autoconsommation* rather than production either for a market or for an elite is normal: but note, at 197, his emphasis on the 'dynamic (and often uncomfortable) juxtaposition and balance of both subsistence oriented and cash generating pursuits engaged in by peasant householders', after the description of Wolf (1966) *Peasants*. Other accounts from the vast literature include: Durrenberger (1984) *Chayanov, Peasants and Economic Anthropology*; Donham (1981) 'Beyond the domestic mode of production'. Against the term and its implications: Hill (1986) 'Why country people are not peasants'; Macfarlane (1984) 'The myth of the peasantry: family and economy in a northern parish', and the excellent arguments of Banaji (1992) 'Historical arguments for a "logic of deployment" in "pre-capitalist" agriculture', and (1997) 'Modernizing the history of rural labour: an unwritten agenda'. Scott (1998) *The Peasantries of Europe*, is a very helpful comparative contribution.

Briant (1982b) *Rois, tributs et paysans*, presents the evidence for the ancient Levant. De Ste Croix (1981) *The Class Struggle in the Ancient Greek World*, 219, addresses the difficulties of using the term 'peasant' for Antiquity. On the Roman world, Garnsey (1988a) *Famine and Food Supply*, ch. 4: 'Subsistence and survival: the peasantry', compare (1975–6) 'Peasants in ancient Roman society'; De Neeve (1984) *Peasants in Peril: Location and Economy in Italy in the Second Century B.C.* Transitions to the Middle Ages: Hodges (1988) *Primitive and Peasant Markets*, on which see the review of Stopford (1992) 'After Dark Age economics'. For Byzantium, M. Kaplan (1986) 'L'économie paysanne dans l'Empire Byzantin du Ve au Xe siècle', (1992) *Les hommes et la terre à Byzance*, and for the later period, Laiou (Laiou-Thomadakis) (1977) *Peasant Society in the Late Byzantine Empire*. Dalton (1974) 'How exactly are peas-ants exploited?', for the view that appropriation of surpluses cannot be enough to define exploitation. J. L. Davis (1991) 'Contributions to Mediterranean rural archaeology: historical case-studies from the Ottoman Cyclades', on the independence of production strategy from capacity, population or demand.

A critique of 'subsistence'

A standard account: Clark and Haswell (1969) *The Economics of Subsistence Agriculture*. Rotberg and Rabb (1983) *Hunger and History*, on the difficulty of defining subsistence minima and productive maxima, cf. Sen (1972) *On Economic Inequality*; Foxhall (1990a) 'The dependent tenant', 113, argues against schematic separations between primitive subsistence practices and modernizing market-orientated ones. On social as against environmental causes for rural poverty, Taussig (1982) 'Peasant economics and the development of agriculture in the Cauca valley, Colombia'; Gallant (1991) *Risk and Survival in Ancient Greece*; and, for nutritional aspects, Camporesi (1989) *Bread of Dreams*. Adam (1987) 'Poissons, marins, pauvres, et démographie', finds it astonishing that the poor managed to survive.

Discussion of the notion of surplus: Pearson (1957) 'The economy has no surplus'; Dalton (1960) 'A note of clarification on economic surplus', (1963) 'Economic surplus, once again'; Halstead (1989) 'The economy has a normal surplus'. Also De Ste Croix (1981) *The Class Struggle in the Ancient Greek World*, 221–2.

For the inadequacy of the traditional language of agricultural history to the sophistication of producers' responses, Banaji (1992) 'Historical arguments for a "logic of deployment" in "pre-capitalist" agriculture'.

Self-determination?

Davis and Sutton (1995) 'Response to A. J. Ammerman', speak up for the struggle of the Mediterranean farmer, and stress economic change and migration; cf. Halstead (1987) 'Traditional and ancient rural economy in Mediterranean Europe'; Sutton (1988) 'What is a village in a nation of migrants?'; Forbes (1993) 'Ethnoarchaeology and the place of the olive'. Against timeless stability: Herzfeld (1987b) *Anthropology through the Looking-Glass*; Fotiadis (1995) 'Modernity and the past-still-present: politics of time in the birth of regional archaeological projects in Greece', with Chapter XI below.

A sophisticated statement of the inter-relationship between *autoconsommation* and *commercialisation* is to be found in Aymard (1983) 'Autoconsommation et marchés'. A sensitive and percipient recent survey, for Antiquity, is Garnsey (1988a) *Famine and Food Supply*, ch. 4, but this too takes peasants and subsistence as a starting point: see the observant review of B. D. Shaw (1989) 'Our daily bread', esp. 206–7. On Byzantium, M. Kaplan (1986) 'L'économie paysanne dans l'Empire Byzantin'; Svoronos (1956) 'Sur quelques formes de la vie rurale à Byzance: petite et grande exploitation'. We find generalizing about the whole Byzantine *koine* unrewarding, especially since it covered both Mediterranean and continental environments. A comparison of the differences between the two would be instructive. For later evidence, cf. Walter and Schofield (1989) *Famine, Disease and the Social Order*.

The reconsideration of Tchalenko's work in north Syria is to be found in Tate (1992a) *Les campagnes de la Syrie du nord*; Sodini et al. (1980) 'Déhès (Syrie du nord) campagnes I–III (1976–8): recherches sur l'habitat rural', 294–301, and Tate (1989) 'Les campagnes de la Syrie du nord à l'époque proto-Byzantine'. See also the survey papers by Foss (1995) 'The Near Eastern countryside in late Antiquity', 213–23, and (1997) 'Syria in transition', 198–204.

Immemorial stability?

On the social aspects of risk-avoidance, and the tension between household resource-management and that of a community run on either co-operative or exploitative lines, see for instance, on life-cycle, Gallant (1991) *Risk and Survival in Ancient Greece*; on the relationship between the construction of kinship and inheritance in an ecologically diverse environment, Goody (1986) *Production and Reproduction: A Comparative Study of the Domestic Domain*; for tenancy, Foxhall (1990a) 'The dependent tenant'. See also Douglas (1985) *Risk Acceptability according to the Social Sciences*. For more exploitative social systems, Foxhall cites the interesting study of Taussig (1982) 'Peasant economics and the development of agriculture in the Cauca Valley, Colombia'; see also the elegant

argument of Gallant (1989) 'Crisis and response: risk-buffering behavior in Hellen-istic Greek communities': the replacement of household-based storage strategies with central community-based ones widened the gap separating primary producers from the elite. For debt as an instrument of control of labour, De Ste Croix (1981) *The Class Struggle in the Ancient Greek World*, 162–70, 238–40. A selection from the debate about these issues in the contemporary world: Wilkinson (1973) *Poverty and Progress*, attacked by Mokyr (1990) *The Lever of Riches*, 192; Hill (1986) *Development Economics on Trial*, against the notion of peasants, criticized by Hodges (1988) *Primitive and Peasant Markets*.

On adaptability in general (in addition to the material on 'ecological history of production' in BE VI.2) see Fumagalli (1992) *L'uomo e l'ambiente*, 19–23; Gallant (1991) *Risk and Survival in Ancient Greece*, 34–59, identifying diversification, intercropping, fragmentation, sowing rates and seedbed preparation as the principal variables; Forbes (1989) 'Of grandfathers and grand theories'; Halstead and O'Shea (1989) 'Introduction', on diversification, mobility and storage; and Sallares (1991) *The Ecology of the Ancient Greek World*, 343–6.

6. Colonizations and Allotments: The Unreason of Far-Flung Power

The effect of distance

For the idea of decentralization, see Bolens (1981) *Agronomes andalous du moyen âge*.

The Mediterranean latifundium

Capogrossi Colognesi (1982) *L'agricoltura romana*, vii, speaks of the latifundium as a will-o'-the-wisp ['una fata morgana: il latifondo'] and argues (xxxiii), as we would, for the coexistence of villas and small property. Capogrossi Colognesi (1986) 'Grandi proprietari contadini e coloni nell'Italia romana', 355, however takes the view that latifundism is characterized by a distance from markets. For the fragmented portfolio, Foxhall (1990) 'The dependent tenant', 100: 'good quality irrigable land is exploited in small units even when it is owned in large units.' On extensification, Halstead (1992a) 'Agriculture in the Bronze Age Aegean: towards a model of palatial economy'. Cf. III.4. On the vital question of connectivity, Vera (1983) 'Strutture agrarie e strutture patrimoniali nella tarda antichità: l'aristocrazia romana fra agricoltura e commercio'. For Egypt, Bowman (1986) *Egypt after the Pharaohs*, 90–107, and for the surprising mutability of estate-status, Bowman (1985) 'Land-holding in the Hermopolite nome'. Remarkable for the breadth of its vision but sadly brief, Atkinson (1972) 'A Hellenistic land-conveyance' (on the estate of Mnesimachus in the plain of Sardis), proposing a continuum in agrarian history across much of Antiquity.

Literature on the later history of latifundia includes: *Du Latifundium au Latifondo: un héritage de Rome, une création médiévale ou moderne?* (1995); Edelman (1992) *The Logic of the Latifundio: The Large Estates of Northwestern Costa Rica since the Late Nineteenth Century*; Barresi (1981) *La scomparsa del latifondo: crisi, declino e trasformazione di una società tradizionale*; Arlacchi (1983) *Mafia, Peasants and Great Estates: Society in Traditional Calabria*; and Petrusewicz (1996) *Latifundium*: see 12, with 130–43, for the mix of self-sufficiency and flexible market engagement, 13 for variety of methods of labour control, and 16 n.41 for non-economic goals.

The ecological and ethnoarchaeological approaches help to outflank the so far relatively unproductive debate on Mediterranean feudalism, on which see Haldon (1989) 'The feudalism debate once more: the case of Byzantium'; Banaji (1975–6) 'The peasantry in the feudal mode of production'; *Structures féodales et féodalisme dans l'Occident méditerranéen* (1980), with the review by Wickham (1982); Wickham (1984) 'The other transition: from the ancient world to feudalism'. It is more instructive to study the various institutions of a more or less feudal kind attested from time to time in the Mediterranean lands from the viewpoint of Mediterranean production, in comparison with other forms of power in the landscape, than to analyse their institutional resemblance to what is found in northern Europe.

The ecology of colonization

B. D. Shaw (1989) 'Our daily bread', cites works on 'colonial' exploitation. For the setting, *Zones cotières et plaines littorales dans le monde méditerranéen médiéval: défense, peuplement et mise en valeur* (1996). Precedents include the Egyptian subjugation of Palestine in the second millennium B.C.: Wengrow (1996) 'Egyptian taskmasters and heavy burdens: highland exploitation and the collared-rim pithoi of the Bronze/Iron Age Levant' – the economy reconsidered as colonial in the last phase of Ramesside dominion. For the gradual occupation of the agrarian resources of the Delta as late as the 22nd–26th dynasties, Meeks (1979) 'Les Donations aux temples d'Égypte'. Other Levantine examples, Briant (1982a) *État et pasteurs au Moyen-Orient ancien*.

The movements and settlements of the second quarter of the first millennium across the Mediterranean included Phoenicians as well as Greeks: Niemeyer (1990) 'The Phoenicians in the Mediterranean: a non-Greek model for expansion and settlement in Antiquity'. For Greek settlement in the western Mediterranean, see the essay of Morel (1984) 'Greek colonisation in Italy and the West'. A useful collection of different points of view in Descoeudres (1990) *Greek Colonists and Native Populations*. Somewhat too sceptical historically, but pioneering in its interest in the exploitative side of Greek overseas settlement, is Dougherty (1993) *The Poetics of Colonization*. See also Osborne (1998) 'Early Greek colonization? The nature of Greek settlement in the West'.

An excellent balance-sheet on the debate about Roman agriculture, between immobilism and agricultural revolution: Pleket (1993) 'Agriculture in the Roman empire in comparative perspective'. For the villa system and its relationship to allotted landscapes, Purcell (1995c) 'The Roman *villa* and the landscape of production'. Labud (1995) *Ricerche archeologico-ambientali dell'Istria settentrionale: la valle del fiume Risano*, on the interestingly dramatic onset of the Roman villa-landscape in Istria. On the important question of state land, Capogrossi Colognesi (1986) 'Grandi proprietari contadini e coloni nell'Italia romana (I–III d.C.)', 330ff; Capogrossi Colognesi (1981a) 'Alcuni aspetti dell'organizzazione fondiaria romana nella tarda repubblica e nel principato'. For the related question of the management of Roman imperial land, Kehoe (1988) *The Economics of Agriculture on Roman Imperial Estates in North Africa*; the Byzantine sequel is discussed by Kazhdan (1993) 'State, feudal and private economy in Byzantium', but see the 'response' of M. Kaplan (1994) 'Réponse à A. P. Kazhdan'. On Antiquity in general, De Ste Croix (1981) *The Class Struggle in the Ancient Greek World*, 231–7.

Some considerations of production under medieval imperialism: Ashtor (1977b) 'Levantine sugar industry in the later Middle Ages – an example of technological decline'; Jacoby (1994b) 'La production du sucre en Crète vénitienne: l'échec d'une entreprise économique', shows how climatic marginality for the crop combined with Cypriote competition to extinguish this attempt at plantation exploitation. On Venetian interventionism see also Rackham and Moody (1997) *The Making of the Cretan Landscape*, 76–82, for encouragement of wheat, through the discouragement of vines – which resulted in increases in olive production. Political interference in local intraregional redistribution of cereals promoted only diversification.

7. THE RECEPTION OF INNOVATION AND THE HISTORY OF TECHNOLOGY

Reflections on the history of technology

Febvre (1935) 'Réflexions sur l'histoire des techniques', 661, had already stated: 'l'activité technique ne saurait s'isoler des autres activités humaines.' Cf. Lemonnier (1993) 'Introduction'; Pfaffenberger (1992) 'Social anthropology of technology', against the 'standard view' of a unilinear progression from tools to complex machines, but curiously tentative and perhaps too holistic in his conception of a technical system. Cf. Haudricourt (1987) *La technologie, science humaine: recherches d'histoire et d'ethnologie des techniques*. The definition which we have quoted in the text embraces most human experience, and is perhaps too inclusive to make it easy to characterize technical *change* or to relate it, as we should prefer, to the catalytic impetus offered by the shock of broadly colonial settlements or the opportunistic imposition by the powerful or the state of a determined increase in production.

Frederiksen (1980) 'Plinio il Vecchio e l'agricoltura in età imperiale romana', 97: 'il mondo era vario e immenso, e la scienza era difettuosa' ('the world was varied and vast; technical knowledge was unreliable'). Frederiksen argues that, because of the problems of dissemination in a complex Mediterranean world, we should not exaggerate the contribution of singular innovation of

the kind discussed in authors like the elder Pliny (cf. Sigaut 1988 on the *vallus*, above, Section 1). Cf. Fox (ed.) (1996) *Technological Change: Methods and Themes in the History of Technology*; L. T. White (1980) 'Technological development in the transition from Antiquity to the Middle Ages'; Greene (1994) 'Technology and innovation in context: the Roman background to medieval and later developments', 39. For Harvey (1989) *Economic Expansion in the Byzantine Empire*, 120ff, Byzantium can be seen as a continuation of the low-technology ancient world.

The autonomy of the discipline is proclaimed in D. R. Hill (1984) *A History of Engineering in Classical and Medieval Times*, Preface. His work has greatly illuminated the learned tradition of technological literature in medieval Islam. McNeil (1989) *An Encyclopaedia of the History of Technology*, is a classic example of mechanomania.

The historiography of ancient technology : the accounts of Finley (1965) 'Technological innovation and economic progress in the ancient world', and Reece (1969) 'Technological weakness of the ancient world', are essentially progressivist. This approach has had a deleterious effect on the study of ancient technology. It is instructive to compare Crombie (1963) *Scientific Change: Historical Studies in the Intellectual, Social and Technical Conditions for Scientific Discovery and Technical Invention from Antiquity to the Present*, with its successor-volume, Fox (ed.) (1996) *Technological Change: Methods and Themes in the History of Technology*. The first includes important and influential accounts of ancient technology; the latter has very little time for Antiquity. Ancient cultural and economic historians have succeeded in writing their period out of this debate, when it is actually of the greatest importance for it; whereas the legacy of Lynn White ensures a prominence for the Middle Ages despite widespread dissent from almost every aspect of his work – see B. Hall (1996) 'Lynn White's *Medieval Technology and Social Change* after thirty years'; and Holt (1996) 'Medieval technology and the historians: the evidence for the mill'. And the historiography of medieval technology retains an almost exclusively north-western European focus: the nature of technical innovation in a Mediterranean context has yet to find substantial analysis. Yet had ancient and Mediterranean examples been more systematically included in the study of this subject, recognition of the importance of reiterated piecemeal innovation in a household context would undoubtedly have been achieved more rapidly.

A rather different view of Greek technology was taken by Vernant (1983) *Myth and Thought among the Greeks*, 279–301: 'Some remarks on the forms and limitations of technical thought among the Greeks'; cf. D. Lee (1973a and 1973b) 'Science, philosophy and technology in the Greco-Roman world', for a similar approach to the *mentalités*. Landels (1978) *Engineering in the Ancient World*, more limited in scope, has a useful consideration of the real gain in efficiency of each invention; K. D. White (1984) *Greek and Roman Technology*, offers a thorough survey. Thoughtful opinions from outside ancient history and archaeology (and some eccentric views) are to be found in Mokyr (1990) *The Lever of Riches*, 193–208. A more contextual approach to innovation, with interesting observations on the control of labour, Torelli (1980) 'Innovazioni nelle techniche edilizie romane', links Roman construction technique and slave labour. Cf. Raepsaet (1994) 'Le renouveau de l'histoire des techniques: quelques jalons récents', 325, percipient on the tradition represented by Landels: 'leur intérêt est incontestable mais plus documentaire que véritablement historique.' Mokyr (1990) *The Lever of Riches*, 199–201, accepts religion as a brake on ancient technology; *contra*, D. Lee (1973a) 'Science, philosophy and technology in the Greco-Roman world, I', 69; and the decisive statement of Scheid (1989) '*Lucus, nemus*: qu'est-ce qu'un bois sacré?', 18 n.29.

Receptivity, rationality and development

Questions of receptivity to ideas are receiving more attention. Early examples include Bloch 'Technical change as a problem of collective psychology' (first published 1948), and 'Mediaeval "inventions"' (first published 1935), in Bloch (1967) *Land and Work in Mediaeval Europe*, 124–35, 169–85. Also on the Middle Ages, Le Roy Ladurie (1966) *Les paysans de Languedoc*, 76–90 (on ploughs etc.). On the lack of widespread dissemination of the technological innovations of the Arab tradition, D. R. Hill (1984) *A History of Engineering in Classical and Medieval Times*,

146–52. Some generalities about modern times can be found in Iftikhar and Ruttan (1988) *Generation and Diffusion of Agricultural Innovations: The Role of Institutional Factors*, and the important volume of Bailey (1973) *Debate and Compromise: The Politics of Innovation*; a useful case study along these lines, Layton (1973) 'Social systems theory and a village community in France'. Gilsenan (1996) *Lords of the Lebanese Marches*, is in part a case study of the 'capitalist' innovations of which seemingly 'feudal' local bosses may be capable. Mokyr (1990) *The Lever of Riches*, 162–5, addresses the useful concept of 'path-dependency', the idea that technical change depends principally on its own past. Note also Elster (1983) *Explaining Technical Change*; L. Brown (1981) *Innovation Diffusion: A New Perspective*.

For the diversity of activities of the 'learned' countryman: Garnsey (1980) 'Non-slave labour in the Roman world', 36–7; J. K. Evans (1980) 'Plebs rustica: the peasantry of classical Italy'; Forbes (1982), *Strategies and Soils*, 200–29, on agrarian technology, quoting the definition of *IESS*, 'The study of technology', 585, that rural technology should be seen as a 'flexible repertoire of skills, knowledge and methods of obtaining desired results and avoiding failures under varying circumstances'. Compare Nouschi (1983) 'Les savoirs dans les pays méditerranéens: conservations, transmissions et acquisitions'. The important article of Mattingly (1997) 'Olive presses in Roman Africa: technical innovation or stagnation?' links the adoption of differing technologies to different strategies in the processing and marketing of the end-product. Note especially 594: 'there appear to be rational explanations as to why . . . the olive producers acted as they did, and it would be incorrect to describe the resultant situation as technological stagnation. Rather it demonstrates a remarkable level of local innovation obviating the need for technology transfer from outside'. An example of the techniques that really matter: Sigaut (1991) 'Les techniques de récolte des grains'. Lemonnier (1993) 'Introduction', notes that 'the perception of risk itself is encoded in social institutions', quoting Douglas (1985) *Risk Acceptability according to the Social Sciences*. Geertz (1963) *Agricultural Involution*, stressed the role played in agrarian change by the country person's systems of ethics. See his revised views on the subject in Geertz

(1984) 'Cultural and social change: the Indonesian case'. For social aspects of the 'secondary products revolution' compare Goody (1986) *Production and Reproduction*.

On the question of rationality, see Carandini (1983) 'Columella's vineyard and the rationality of the Roman economy', for an acute argument that the alleged irrationality and incompetence of Columella's notorious account is perfectly explicable in contemporary terms; Rathbone (1991) *Economic Rationalism and Rural Society in Third-Century Egypt*, with the review of Kehoe (1993). Rathbone (1994) 'More (or less?) economic rationalism in Roman agriculture', reviewing Kehoe (1992) *Management and Investment on Estates in Roman Egypt during the Early Empire*, 436, is illuminating on the Finleyan adaptation of the Weberian explanation of the development of modern economies. An excellent, balanced account of the debate on bookkeeping is to be found in Macve (1985) 'Some glosses on "Greek and Roman accounting"', radically modifying the deterministic claims of those who proclaim a thirteenth-century revolution. See also Mickwitz (1937) 'Economic rationalism in Graeco-Roman agriculture'; De Ste Croix (1956) 'Greek and Roman accounting'. For sensible reconsideration of the contribution of accounting techniques to economic change in the later Middle Ages, Yamey (1975) 'Notes on double-entry bookkeeping and economic progress'; also, cautiously, Lane (1977) 'Double-entry bookkeeping and resident merchants'. Cf. Lane (1986) 'Technology and productivity in seaborne transportation'.

The post-classical world offers some revealing instances of receptivity. Braunstein (1983) 'Innovations in mining and metal-production in Europe in the late Middle Ages', showed how complex were the interrelationships between innovatory theory and economic practice in a case where the evidence is sufficient to see the process in some detail. Lopez (1945) 'Silk industry in the Byzantine empire', analyses how the high status of the Byzantine silk industry and its practitioners led to great secrecy about techniques and hence only very slow dissemination; also Ashtor (1989) 'The factors of technological and industrial progress in the late Middle Ages', sensible on the complexity of the question, and also (16–19) helpful on the contribution of the mobility of skilled workers. For socio-political considerations, Goody (1971) *Technology, Tradition and the State in Africa*, with Law (1976)

'Horses, firearms and political power in pre-colonial West Africa'. Much helpful material on reception of technology in the period since the Renaissance can be had in J. A. Davis (1982) 'Innovation and technology in the Mediterranean countries, XIVth–XXth centuries', reviewing the conference published as Aymard (1983) *Les Savoirs dans les pays méditerranéens: XVIe–XXe siècles*. Compare Cipolla (1993) *Before the Industrial Revolution*, ch. 6, and (1972) 'The diffusion of innovations in early modern Europe', on receptivity to ideas and movement of experts.

On the systemic model of technological change, compare Picon (1996) 'Towards a history of technological thought', arguing (41), against the Weberian separation of means-rationality and objective-rationality, that the two are indissolubly related. It is striking that here (43) the ancient location of technological creativity is thought to be the inventor in the service of a prince, as opposed to the more widely disseminated milieu of inventiveness from the eighteenth century on. This is, no doubt, how early modern thinkers conceived of Antiquity, but it is ironic that more modern historians have used the *absence* of such high-profile patronage, and the relegation of technological enquiry to a humdrum and unglamorous practical milieu, as arguments for the backwardness of the ancient world!

Revolutions and evolutions

Population is another theme which will receive fuller treatment in Volume 2, but see also Chapter IX of the present volume. General accounts include Grigg (1980) *Population Growth and Agrarian Change: An Historical Perspective*, (1982) *The Dynamics of Agricultural Change: The Historical Experience*, (1992) *The Transformation of Agriculture in the West*; and Spooner (1973) *Population Growth: Anthropological Implications*. There is a helpful survey of demographic explanations in R. M. Smith (1991) 'Demographic developments in rural England, 1300–48: a survey'.

The original contributions of Boserup (1965) *The Conditions of Agricultural Growth*, and (1981) *Population and Technology* (which, like Richards (1985) *Indigenous Agricultural Revolution*, avoid ethnocentrism), are reviewed and assessed by Grigg (1979) 'Esther Boserup's theory of agrarian change: a critical review', (1980) 'Population pressure and agrarian change'. See also Lopez (1976) *The Commercial Revolution of the Middle Ages*, ch. 2, and Mokyr (1990) *The Lever of Riches*, 190–2. Contrast Ammerman and Cavalli-Sforza (1973) 'A population model for the diffusion of early farming in Europe', emphasizing demographic pressure. Cf. Ammerman and Cavalli-Sforza (1984) *Neolithic Transition*, also Renfrew (1987) *Archaeology and Language*, 126–31, 153–9. The Mediterranean rather complicates this stately model. Further support from Dickson (1989) 'Out of Utopia: Runnels' and van Andel's non-equilibrium growth model of the origins of agriculture'. The position is closely linked to the 'wave of advance' theory of cultural diffusion in prehistory.

Shadows of the industrial revolution: for the term 'pre-industrial' itself, so close in flavour to the much-quoted misleading text from Hume, see Crone (1989) *Pre-industrial Societies*, 1–2. Cf. Cipolla (1993) *Before the Industrial Revolution*, 276–9, recognizing the primacy of social and cultural transformations in the 'industrial revolution' over technical ones, but very committed to the long ascent of Europe – and to a very American gloom

about the 'agony of Europe' which has followed. Sigaut and Fournier (1991) 'La préparation alimentaire des céréales: fil directeur dans l'histoire technique et économique de l'Europe' (note the implications of their title), speak (9) of ancient slavery as causing a 'véritable révolution industrielle' (cf. IX.6). Gimpel (1992) *The Medieval Machine: The Industrial Revolution of the Middle Ages*, is an instance of a progressivist interest in paths towards the (or an) industrial revolution. E. L. Jones (1981) *The European Miracle*, advocates 'technological drift' as an explanation rather than sudden change.

For the medieval 'agricultural revolution', the principal accounts still include L. T. White (1962) *Medieval Technology and Social Change*; Duby (1968) *Rural Economy and Country Life in the Medieval West*, (1974) *The Early Growth of the European Economy: Warriors and Peasants from the Seventh to the Twelfth Century*. A useful summary of the contrary case can be found in Verhulst (1990) 'The "agricultural revolution" of the Middle Ages reconsidered'. See also Cooter (1978) 'Ecological dimensions of medieval agrarian systems', who, against the approach of White and Duby, asserts the historical importance of effects like 'feudal coercion'.

BIBLIOGRAPHICAL ESSAY TO CHAPTER VIII
MEDITERRANEAN CATASTROPHES

1. ON THE HISTORY OF CATASTROPHE

Historia naturalis

For the meaning and significance of the term, Beagon (1992) *Roman Nature*; R. K. French (1994) *Ancient Natural History*; Siebert (1996) *Nature et paysage dans la pensée et l'environnement des civilisations antiques*. The catastrophe theory of the ancients continues to fascinate: see in general Dundes (1988) *The Flood Myth*. Knauss (1992) 'Die griechische Sintflut in Legende und Wirklichkeit', offers a location for Deucalion's flood. Zangger (1992a) *Flood from Heaven*, locates the fabulous city and intricate landscape of Plato's Atlantis *mythos* in the much-abused Scamander plain. Geoarchaeology is unlikely to illustrate Plato's *mythopoeia*. For an example of the problems which may be encountered in incautiously blending the presentation of large themes in geological history with historical narrative, Rupke (1996) 'Eurocentric ideology of continental drift'.

The humour of blaming the past

For the context in intellectual history since the Enlightenment of the ways of thinking which we are describing, a helpful overview is Glacken (1967) *Traces on the Rhodian Shore*. Another *aperçu* by Hume in *On the Populousness of Ancient Nations* (*Essays Moral, Political and Literary*, 11) illustrates the bizarre legacy for historians of the eighteenth-century debate on modernity. His remark that he knew of no classical literary text which ascribed the rise of a city to a manufacture, has been quoted and requoted to a remarkable degree. The observation was acute and rhetorically apposite for a progressivist tract. From the historical point of view, many features of the ancient economy are however more arresting than the absence of the economic and social factors which generated the great cities of modern Britain (IV.5). Insistent, approving, reproduction of this remark dates the conceptual framework of the writer.

Historical environmentalism, as opposed to the history of the environment, is represented by a number of studies which enthusiastically adopt the idea of catastrophe and the habit of apportioning blame to past cultures. Medieval ecological disaster is presented by Fumagalli (1992) *L'uomo e l'ambiente*, and (1994) *Landscapes of Fear: Perceptions of Nature and the City in the Middle Ages*. See also Richter (1991) 'Mensch und Umwalt', and Weeber (1990) *Smog über Attika*. Fedeli (1990) *Natura violata*, has a more interesting theme: Greek and Roman conceptions of damage to nature. Hughes (1994) *Pan's Travail*, however, is just the sort of retrojection of the clichés of modern environmentalism that we want to banish from Mediterranean historiography. Compare Hughes (1975) *Ecology in Ancient Civilizations*. A more serious account is to be found in Butlin and Roberts (1995) *Ecological Relations in Historical Times*. We wholeheartedly applaud the terse statement of principles for the study of this subject in Rackham (1996) 'Ecology and pseudo-ecology', 17: 'there is something about landscape-history peculiarly productive of factoids'. Rackham and Moody (1997) *The Making of the Cretan Landscape*, 9–10, have trenchant remarks on Ruined Landscape theory and methodology in environmental history.

On determinism, we note that the helpful account of Peet (1985) 'The social origins of environmental determinism', cites an early work by Wittfogel – of 'oriental despotism' fame – (1929) 'Geopolitik, geographischer Materialismus und Marxismus'.

The vulgar applications of Darwinism in the late nineteenth and twentieth centuries added an evolutionist perspective which in its cruder forms offers an easy target for criticism: see Blaas (1978) *Continuity and Anachronism*; Greta Jones (1980) *Social Darwinism and English Thought*. One legacy is the strange combination of the language of morals with that of biology: for instance: 'in yielding to parasitism [Rome] forfeited at the same time the predatory vitalities that made it possible' (Mumford (1961) *The City in History*, 267); for another example of the parasitological metaphor, W. H. McNeill (1980) *The Human Condition*. Scientists writing on geomorphology, demography or sociology often use a less extreme version of this language in historical overviews or introductions. It is regrettable that, when they write about the Mediterranean world, they should lend their authority not just to the fruits of their own researches, but to this kind of history, which would otherwise be simply a quaint survival of another age.

Humanity and Nature: dissolving the dichotomy

A different way of achieving this from the one adumbrated in the chapter is to apply the much more sophisticated evolutionary biology of the late twentieth century to the explanation of history, in the manner of Colinvaux (1980) *The Fates of Nations: A Biological Theory of History*. The evolutionary analogy for technological progress is discussed by Mokyr (1990) *The Lever of Riches*, 273–299, with some interesting observations on Cardwell's Law and the usefulness of political fragmentation in promoting fertile diversity, which has some relevance to the fragmentation of the Mediterranean; or again Mokyr (1996) 'Evolution and technical change: a new metaphor for economic history?', especially 78–82, with the remarks of Fox (1996) 'Introduction: methods and themes in the history of technology', 6–7, observing that the analogy helps show how diversity and

wasteful prodigality are preconditions for creativity rather than symptoms of economic inefficiency. Compare the overtly selectivist/evolutionist account of Redding (1993) 'Subsistence security as a selective practice favoring increasing cultural complexity', and, also very interested in the evolutionary analogy, Greene (1994) 'Technology and innovation in context'.

Mokyr (1990) *The Lever of Riches*, 15, shrugs off the accusation of Whiggishness as if it were a quite insignificant problem; but see 16 on the exceptional nature of progressive societies. Some archaeological theorists have seen in more modern biology a possible bridge between the divergent tendencies in modern archaeology towards – to put it crudely – the methods of the sciences on the one hand and those of the humanities on the other (Bintliff (1984) 'Introduction'). Sherratt (1995a) 'Reviving the grand narrative', offers a stimulating case for maintaining and extending the progressivist approach. We cannot, however, agree that it is 'the task of archaeology . . . and the social sciences in general . . . both to chart these processes of growing uniformity and to recover the locally unique patterns and structures that they overwhelmed' (24–5). This is the traditional technique of identifying a feature of the present – in this case the alleged tendency towards global cultural uniformity – and choosing to study those bits of the past which might be thought to have given rise to it, in an unquestioning spirit of progressivism. Cf. V.4.

2. An Unstable World

An excellent synthesis from a geomorphological point of view is to be found in *La mobilité des paysages méditerranéens* (1984). Selli et al. (1985) *Geological Evolution of the Mediterranean Basin*, is helpful on the structural background. The very well conceived Higgins and Higgins (1996) *A Geological Companion to Greece and the Aegean*, is an excellent example of the potential for making Mediterranean geology accessible to the non-specialist.

Structure and landscape

On the impact of volcanoes in general, see Grayson and Sheets (1979) *Volcanic Activity and Human Ecology*, 83–124, and Albore

Livadie and Widemann (1990) *Volcanologie et archéologie*. Discussions of Thera/Santorini include Nixon (1985) 'The eruption of Thera'; Manning (1988) 'The Bronze Age Eruption of Thera'; Hardy (1990) *Thera and the Aegean World III*; and Forsyth (1996) 'The pre-eruption shapes of Bronze Age Thera: a new model' (note however the dendrochronological evidence for a date rather earlier than the previous orthodoxy). A sceptical account: Lohmann (1998) 'Die Santorin-Katastrophe'. For Vesuvius in the history of Campania, Frederiksen (1984) *Campania*, 4–13; Tchernia (1986) *Vin de l'Italie romaine*, 230–2, discusses possible effects on Italian wine-production; see also Albore Livadie (1986) *Tremblements de terre*.

The pioneer of historical seismology in the Mediterranean is Nicholas Ambraseys, whose articles established this branch of the discipline: (1970) 'Some characteristic features of the Anatolian fault zone', (1971) 'Value of historical records of earthquakes', (1975) 'Studies in historical seismicity and tectonics', (1978) 'Middle East: a reappraisal of the seismicity'. Two pioneering studies may also be recommended: Bousquet et al. (1981) 'Séismes et géomorphologie'; Bousquet et al. (1984) 'Nature, répartition et histoire du risque sismique dans l'aire méditerranéenne'. Some very helpful collections of studies have been devoted to this subject: Helly and Pollino (1984) *Tremblements de terre: histoire et archéologie*; Albore Livadie (1986) *Tremblements de terre*; Guidoboni (1989) *I terremoti prima del Mille*; and Stiros and Jones (1996) *Archaeoseismology*. General accounts: Pauly-Wissowa, 4 Suppl. 'Erdbebungforschung'; *RAC*, 'Erdbebung'. See *Archäologie und Seismologie* (1995) for the Vesuvian area. On Byzantine earthquakes, Ducellier (1980) 'Les séismes en Méditerranée orientale'. Note also Helly (1998) 'La sismicité est-elle un objet d'étude pour les archéologues?'

J. P. Brown (1969) *Lebanon and Phoenicia*, 113–39, is a model presentation of the sources for the earthquake-history of a region. For the impact of an early modern earthquake, Kendrick (1956) *Lisbon Earthquake*; for ancient cases, Cartledge (1976) 'Seismicity and Spartan society'; Andreau (1973) 'Histoire des séismes et histoire économique: le tremblement de terre de Pompéi (62 ap. J.-C.)'. For religious responses to tectonic activity, Dagron (1981) 'Quand la terre

tremble'; and our own remarks in X.2 below. Helpful presentation of the question of the impact of earthquakes on the landscape is to be found in Bousquet et al. (1983) 'Temps historiques et évolution des paysages égéens', and for the effect on the human understanding of landscape, Bousquet et al. (1984).

La tyrannie de la pente

Introducing the geomorphology of karst and its significance: *Milieux calcaires et politique hydraulique* (1991); Salomon and Maire (1992) *Karst et évolutions climatiques*; P. W. Williams (1993) *Karst terrains*. Cvijić (1960) *Géographie des terrains calcaires*, is something of a classic; see also Dufaure and Vaudour (1984) 'Aspects des grands karsts méditerranéens'. For ambitious claims for the cultural influence of Mediterranean landscape, see Crouch (1993) *Water Management in Ancient Greek Cities*. Cf. Rackham and Moody (1997) *The Making of the Cretan Landscape*, 27–8, for Cretan upland plains.

Effects of precipitation on geomorphology, and response to run-off of different land-surfaces: Delano Smith (1979) *Western Mediterranean Europe*, 276–81; also Bousquet et al. (1983) 'Temps historiques et évolution des paysages égéens', and Neboit et al. (1984b) 'Les travaux et les jours de l'érosion méditerranéenne', esp. 303–5 on 'torrentialité'; Neboit et al. (1984a) 'Facteurs naturels et humains dans la morphogenèse méditerranéenne', where there is also a good general account of soil-erosion; compare van Andel and Zangger (1990b) 'Land-use and soil erosion'; and Bell and Boardman (1992) *Past and Present Soil Erosion*. Thornes (1987) 'Palaeo-ecology of Erosion', is also helpful; for the effects of predominantly pastoral production, cf. Thornes (1988) 'Erosional equilibria under grazing'. Zangger (1992b) 'Prehistoric and historic soils in Greece', postulates catastrophe at the end of the Neolithic; cf. Zangger (1992c) 'Neolithic to present soil-erosion in Greece'. Neboit (1984) 'Erosion des sols et colonisation grecque', investigates the environmental effects of major examples of allotted resettlement (cf. VII.6). Compare Neboit et al. (1984b); Neboit-Guilhot (1990) 'Les mouvements de terrain en Basilicate'. On the formation of various kinds of degraded 'badland' topography, Fantechi and Margaris (1986) *Desertification in Europe*; Bryan and Yair (1982) *Badlands Geomorphology*. Bailey et al. (1990) 'The "older fill" of the Voidomatis valley', consider the whole nexus, erosion–deforestation–deposition, with examples from north-west Greece, and identify an eleventh-century A.D. terrace possibly caused by a period of over-grazing; cf. Bommeljé and Doorn (1983) *The Strouza Valley Project*.

The normality of flood

Ashtor (1976) *A Social and Economic History of the Near East in the Middle Ages*, 51–8, discusses the effects of run-off on soil erosion; compare Hendy (1985) *Studies in the Byzantine Monetary Economy*, 58–68. Historical study of flood-records is instructive: for an example concerning a perennial river, Pichard (1995) 'Les crues sur le bas Rhône de 1500 à nos jours. Pour une histoire hydro-climatique'. At Nîmes, comparable records illustrate flash-flooding, attesting particularly bad episodes in 1988, 1915, 1859, 1577, and 1399 (G. Fabre (1990–2) 'La catastrophe hydrologique'). For the variety of conditions in the valleys of perennial rivers, Petts (1990) 'Forested river corridors, a lost resource'.

The problem of sea-level: post-glacial changes are conveniently presented and explained by Lambeck (1996) 'Sea-level change and shoreline evolution: Aegean Greece since the Upper Palaeolithic'. See also Flemming (1996) 'Sea level, neotectonics and changes in coastal settlements: threat and response'. Among general studies, Blackman (1973) *Marine Archaeology*, Gamble and Yorke (1978) *Progress in Underwater Science*; Flemming and Masters (1983) *Quaternary Coastlines and Marine Archaeology*, have been important. Collections of instructive case studies: *Déplacements des lignes de rivage en Méditerranée* (1987); Raban (1988) *Archaeology of Coastal Changes*; Psychoyos (1988) *Déplacements de la ligne de rivage et sites archéologiques dans les régions cotières de la Mer Égée au néolithique et à l'Âge de Bronze*, stressing numbers of prehistoric coastal settlements in the Aegean. Rackham and Moody (1997) *The Making of the Cretan Landscape*, 195, for the interesting case of Crete. For the future, Leftic et al. (1992) *Climatic Change and the Mediterranean: Environmental and Societal Impacts of Climatic Change and Sea-Level Rise in the Mediterranean Region*.

For oscillations in the eustatic curve, see Fairbridge (1976) 'Shellfish-eating pre-ceramic Indians in coastal Brazil'; Fairbridge (1972) 'Quaternary sedimentation in the Mediterranean region controlled by tectonics, paleoclimates and sea-level'; Kraft et al. (1982) 'Geology and paleogeographic reconstructions of the region of Troy', 17–19.

On tectonic changes in sea-level, see Flemming (1972) 'Eustatic and tectonic factors in the relative vertical displacement of the Aegean coast'; other cases in the two studies by Bousquet et al. (1983) 'Temps historiques et évolution des paysages égéens', (1987) 'Ports antiques et lignes de rivage égéennes'. See also Jameson et al. (1994) *A Greek Countryside*, 194–213, for the interesting balance of transgression and progradation in the coastlines of the southern Argolid. Examples from the western Mediterranean are discussed by Pirazzoli (1988) 'Sea-level changes', and (1976) 'Sea level variations in the north-west Mediterranean during Roman times'. Important fieldwork was published in Schmiedt (1972) *Il livello antico del Mar Tirreno*. Archaeological context is analysed in Kraft et al. (1985) 'Geological studies of coastal change applied to archaeological settings'.

Recent coastal changes due to sedimentation are discussed in general by G. Evans (1973) 'Recent coastal sedimentation: a review': see especially 93–6 on the Seyhan delta in Cilicia. On deltas, Dupré (1987) 'Évolution de la ligne de rivage à l'embouchure de l'Èbre'; R. J. Russell (1942) 'Geomorphology of the Rhone delta'. Loss of anchorages and havens is assessed by Hoffman and Schulz (1988) 'Coastline shifts and holocene stratigraphy on the Mediterranean coast of Andalucia', for the south coast of Spain, deeply indented at the time of Phoenician settlement; Zangger (1991) 'Vanished landscapes of Dimini Bay and Lake Lerna', for the southern Argolid. Introducing a very promising project combining archaeological and geomorphological methods: Lambrianides et al. (1996) 'The Madra Çay Delta archaeological project'. Studying a small delta in Provence, Leveau and Provansal (1991) 'Construction deltaïque et histoire des systèmes agricoles', 130–1, show that there appears to be no easy match between delta sediments and agrarian history, rather as the proponents of catastrophe theory predict.

3. ALLUVIAL CATASTROPHE AND ITS CAUSES

The Greek discovery of anthropogene process

For the history of geomorphological thought, Oldroyd (1996) *Thinking about the Earth: A History of Ideas in Geology*. Chorley et al. (1964) *The History of the Study of Landforms or the Development of Geomorphology*, is a less sensitive account. On non-geomorphological ways of thinking about landforms, Tuan (1968) *The Hydrological Cycle and the Wisdom of God*, for the 'perennial debate on the origin of rivers'. Buxton (1994) *Imaginary Greece*, ch. 6, is particularly rich on the 'otherness' of the mountain, its association with the time of origins, its role as the abode of the divine, and as a place for the reversal of norms; this account is equally helpful on perhaps surprisingly positive ancient attitudes to the sea, and on the process by which landforms and landscapes were 'constructed', above all in tragedy: they were highly flexible according to the user's perspective. See also Siebert (1996) *Nature et paysage dans la pensée et l'environnement des civilisations antiques*.

Herodotus's examples have been the object of much scholarly attention. For the Scamander, see Rapp and Gifford (1982) *Troy: The Archaeological Geology*; and on the Maeander, Eisma (1978) 'Stream deposition and erosion by the eastern shore of the Aegean'; Marchese (1986) *Lower Maeander Flood-Plain*. Alluviation confined in a narrow trough naturally produces dramatic shore-line changes.

From Curtius to Vita-Finzi and his heirs

Vita-Finzi (1969) *Mediterranean Valleys*, was foreshadowed by (1966) 'The new Elysian fields', compare his (1972) 'Supply of fluvial sediment to the Mediterranean during the last 2,000 years'. Discussion followed in the collections of Davidson and Shackley (1976) *Geoarchaeology*; Brothwell and Dimbleby (1981) *Environmental Aspects of Coast and Islands*; and Bintliff and Van Zeist (1982) *Palaeoclimates, Palaeoenvironments and Human Communities*. Some, such as Hutchinson (1969) 'Erosion and land-use: the influence of agriculture on the Epirus region', adapted the new technique to the argument *against* catastrophic change. But for the great majority of those who became interested in the historical and archaeological implications of Vita-Finzi's work, the drama of a really good historical *bouleversement* proved too enticing.

The debate of the 1980s on the causes and effects of alluviation owed a great deal to the work of John Bintliff: (1976a) 'Sediments and settlements in southern Greece', (1981) 'Archaeology and the Holocene evolution of coastal plains', (1982) 'Palaeoclimatic modelling of environmental changes in the eastern Mediterranean', esp. 512–8, and his (1977a) 'New approaches to human geography: prehistoric Greece, a case study', (1976b) 'The plain of Macedon and the Neolithic site of Nea Nikomedeia'. Support for the model from Provence: Ballais and Crambes (1992) 'Morphogenèse holocène, géosystèmes et anthropisation sur la Montagne Sainte-Victoire'. A recent re-evaluation of his own oeuvre and of the history of the subject: Bintliff (1992) 'Erosion in the Mediterranean lands: a reconsideration of pattern, process and methodology'.

Pausanias was right

For general reflections on anthropogene versus physical causation, Van der Leeuw (1994) 'Social and environmental change'. See also Neboit (1980) 'Morphogenèse et occupation humaine dans l'antiquité', and Brückner (1986) 'Man's impact on the evolution of the physical environment in the Mediterranean'. Brückner (1990) 'Changes in the Mediterranean ecosystem during Antiquity'; and Zangger (1992b) 'Prehistoric and historic soils in Greece', offer interpretations of Mediterranean soil-history. Van Zuidam (1975) 'Geomorphology and archaeology. Evidence of interaction at historical sites in the Zaragoza region', is historically simplistic. Rackham and Moody (1997), *The Making of the Cretan Landscape*, 18–24, on erosion and deposition, do not favour anthropogene causation and prefer to reinstate dramatic but randomly spaced events in meteorological history. Naveh (1990) 'Ancient man's impact on the Mediterranean landscape in Israel', recommends the employment in this field of fuzzy set theory (compare our own brief discussion, II.4) and multivariate equations.

Against explanation of the Younger Fill in physical terms: Wagstaff (1985) *The Evolution of Middle Eastern Landscapes*, 214–32, a useful essay; also Wagstaff (1981) 'Buried assumptions: some problems in the interpretation of the "Younger Fill"'. Equally hostile to the Vita-Finzi/Bintliff model, Davidson (1980) 'Erosion in Greece in the first and second millennia B.C.' Brückner (1986) argued effectively against climatic causation, and presented a convenient round-up of evidence from several different parts of the Mediterranean. In North Africa, alluviation has been studied by Bourgou and Oueslati (1987) 'Les dépôts historiques de la vallée du Kébir-Miliane'; for an authoritative account of coastal change at the mouth of the Bagradas, Chelbi et al. (1995) 'La baie d'Utique et son évolution depuis l'antiquité'.

The Argolid: Pope and van Andel (1984) 'Late quaternary alluviation and soil-formation in the southern Argolid'; Jameson et al. (1994) *A Greek Countryside*, 172–94; van Andel et al. (1986) 'Five thousand years of land use and abuse in the southern Argolid', 103–28.

4. SEDIMENTS AND HISTORY: THE PROBLEMS DISPLAYED

The normality of alluviation: the general problems of understanding Mediterranean stream process are propounded by Wagstaff (1981) 'Buried assumptions', and by Pope and van Andel (1984) 'Late quaternary alluviation and soil-formation in the southern Argolid', 290; cf. R. J. Russell (1954) 'Alluvial morphology of Anatolian rivers'. Among helpful general accounts of the subject, see also Möller et al. (1989) *Historical Change of Large Alluvial Rivers*, and Lewin et al. (1995) *Mediterranean Quaternary River Environments*. An excellent general account of the subject in A. G. Brown (1997) *Alluvial Geoarchaeology* (for the Mediterranean, 237–48).

Case studies and examples include the authoritative interpretation of the sedimentological history of south Etruria (III.2): Brown and Ellis (1995) 'People, climate and alluviation'; note especially 67–8 on the factors causing variability in the sediments from valley to valley. For the Jucar valley, Butzer et al. (1983) 'Urban geo-archaeology in mediaeval Alzira'; cf. Gilman and Thornes (1985) *Land Use and Prehistory*. Our material from the north-west Peloponnese is derived from Raphael (1978) 'The erosional history of the Plain of Elis'; for the historical geography of the area, cf. Baladié (1980) *Péloponnèse de Strabon*, 61–4, 88–92. For late Antique north-

ern Italy, Dall'Aglio (1997) 'Il "diluvium di Paolo Diacono"'.

Finally, for the demonstration that alluvial events suggesting the correlation of environmental change with social, economic or political history can be described mathematically by catastrophe theory, as parts of much more complex systems, Burrin and Scaife (1988) 'Environmental thresholds, catastrophe theory, and landscape sensitivity: their relevance to the impact of man on valley alluviations'.

5. ECOLOGY IN AN UNSTABLE ENVIRONMENT: THE HISTORY OF VEGETATION

Fire and ecology: on human effects on Mediterranean vegetation in general, we may cite Naveh and Vernet (1991) 'Palaeohistory of Mediterranean biota'; and Pignatti (1983) 'Human impact on the vegetation of the Mediterranean'. Rackham and Moody (1997) *The Making of the Cretan Landscape*, 109–22, makes an admirable introduction to Mediterranean vegetation, suitably cautious about attempting Mediterranean-wide classifications. For the necessity of including human activity in the study of Mediterranean biology, Naveh and Kutiel (1990) 'Changes in the Mediterranean vegetation of Israel', 288–9, asserting that the study of ideal climax vegetations which does not include human ecology is now obsolete in the Mediterranean; cf. Sallares (1991) *The Ecology of the Ancient Greek World*, 3–11.

The specific question of fire is addressed in Trabaud (1991) 'Is fire an agent favouring plant invasions?'; Trabaud and Lepart (1981) 'Diversity and stability in garrigue ecosystems after fire', and Trabaud (1981) 'Man and fire'. Homer's wildfire similes – *Iliad*, 14.396–7, 20.490–4 – are discussed by Meiggs (1982) *Trees and Timber*, 107; also 374–6 on other evidence for wildfire in Antiquity. Gödde (1976) 'Données climatiques et risques d'incendie', presents the evidence from modern fires in Provence; cf. Ballais (1993–5) 'L'érosion consécutive à l'incendie d'août 1989 sur la montagne Saint-Victoire', showing that, despite quite rapid recovery, the environment remains fragile. Recovery after destruction: Delano Smith (1979) *Western Mediterranean Europe*, 295–6, and Le Houerou (1987) 'Vegetation wildfires in the Mediterranean Basin: evolution and trends'.

Kloppenburg (1988) *First the Seed*, is primarily concerned with the political control of germplasm, the genetic information encoded in the seed, in the more recent periods when it has become apparent as a resource. But his work has much of interest for the history of the world before this commoditization of genetic material took place. Cf. Hawkes (1983) *Diversity of Crop Plants*. Harlan worked on centres of genetic diversity on a microregional level in Turkey: (1951) 'Anatomy of gene centers'; also, on a global scale, Crosby (1986) *Ecological Imperialism*. Mediterranean species have been much more successful in invading other similar ecologies elsewhere than the Mediterranean itself has been vulnerable to such invasions in recent times (with the partial exception of summer-wet habitats): Blumler (1995) 'Invasion and transformation of California's valley grassland', 310. The same author (324) argues that 'the spectacular success of (true) Mediterranean species is undoubtedly due in part to co-evolution with agropastoralism', and wryly suggests (325) that 'the superior adaptation of vigorous annuals [the cereals] to winter-wet, summer-dry environments may have allowed these plants to domesticate humans in an agricultural relationship, eventually allowing these plants to be transferred overseas – a case of long-time, long-distance dispersal!'

Mediterranean forest history: two basic monographs are Bechmann (1990) *Trees and Man*, on the Middle Ages, referring primarily to north-west Europe but with some material relevant to the Mediterranean lands, and a helpful approach; and, for Antiquity, but taking a very wide range of comparative evidence, Meiggs (1982) *Trees and Timber*, esp. 13–48 and 371–403. An important collection of papers: Bell and Limbrey (1982) *Woodland Ecology*.

The French scholarly tradition behind Bechmann includes Kuhnholtz-Lordat (1939) *La terre incendiée*, which considered it possible to attain a balance between pastoral activities and forest maintenance, and Higounet (1966) 'Les forêts de l'Europe occidentale', consciously complementing M. Lombard (1959) 'Le bois dans la méditerranée musulmane', and like him generalizing on a scale which far transcends the microregional. He therefore believes in the possibility of general catastrophe for the Mediterranean forest, but also attributes recovery after the

classical period to a move towards a climatic optimum in the years 500–1200. The *foresta* (the replacement of the name *silva* is significant, one of the first attestations of *foresta* being at Bobbio in A.D. 774) was a more marginal space, a frontier. A more recent general account than Higounet's: Barbero and Quézel (1983) 'La végétation de la Grèce'. For the vastly better informed accounts made possible by the development of the techniques of anthracology, Chabal (1997) *Forêts et sociétés en Languedoc*; Vernet (1997) *L'homme et la forêt méditerranéenne*.

Deforestation: the classic statement is Thirgood (1981) *Man and the Mediterranean Forest*; see 5 on the simplicity of ecosystems. The personal passion which Thirgood, as a forester, derived from his first-hand experience in the forestry of Cyprus is sympathetic and persuasive. He took care to avoid a romanticized, touristic notion of the present state of the area, but his admirably principled indignation still echoes the impressionistic judgements of an earlier age of study in the Mediterranean. Compare popular statements of the same view in Parain (1936) *La Méditerranée: les hommes et leurs travaux*, 39–43, and Attenborough (1987) *The First Eden*, 165–173; also Hughes (1983) 'How the ancients viewed deforestation', and (1994) *Pan's Travail*, 73–90. For an extreme combination of views, Hughes and Thirgood (1982) 'Deforestation in ancient Greece and Rome: a cause of collapse'. Contrast Rackham (1996) 'Ecology and pseudo-ecology', 28–9; Fedeli (1990) *Natura violata*, 72–80. Religious response: Jordan and Perlin (1984) 'On the protection of sacred groves'. For the need to distinguish types of forest-habitat, and to note that some environments are just not suited to forest, Raynal (1977) 'Milieux forestiers réels, potentiels et illusoires'.

With regard to the interpretation of Plato, Rackham (1996) 'Ecology and pseudo-ecology', 22, 33–4. For a more environmentalist interpretation of the *Critias* passage, compare Westra and Robinson (1997) *The Greeks and the Environment*, 73–80. Even late Antique Attica retained forest resources: Fowden (1988) 'City and mountain in late Roman Attica'.

Meiggs (1982) *Trees and Timber*, 399–403, holds that the nineteenth century saw a decisive change in the danger posed to Mediterranean forests by human activity; cf. 371–403 for the less disastrous pre-modern past. Other modifications of the orthodoxy on deforestation are to be found in various articles by Rackham: (1982) 'Land-use and the native vegetation of Greece', (1983) 'Observations on Boeotia', (1990a) 'Ancient landscapes', and (1996) 'Ecology and pseudo-ecology'. A relatively recent date for deforestation in southeast Spain is proposed by Gilman and Thornes (1985) *Land Use and Prehistory*, 11–15.

For damage caused by intensification, in the case of sugar-boiling, see Berthier (1969) *Un épisode de l'histoire de la canne à sucre*, and other studies cited in BE VII.3. Braudel (1972a) *The Mediterranean*, 155, describes the example of Madeira. Fuel consumption by centres of population is discussed by Delano Smith (1979) *Western Mediterranean Europe*, 298–307; Meiggs (1982) *Trees and Timber*, 257–8; Bechmann (1990) *Trees and Man*, 140–51: see also our own remarks in IV.6. For the use of olive-pulp from pressing

to fire the kilns that baked the amphorae in which the olive oil was exported, see W. Smith (1998) 'Fuel for thought: archaeobotanical evidence for the use of alternatives to fuel in late Antique North Africa'. On dung, S. Anderson and Ertug-Yaras (1998) 'Fuel, fodder and faeces'. Lock (1995) *The Franks in the Aegean*, 249–50, discusses forest management in the Frankish Aegean, and makes a good sequel to Dunn (1992) 'The exploitation and control of woodland and scrubland in the Byzantine world', an account opposed both to primitivism and to Lombard, arguing that there was no major long-term depletion of forest resources. Also against Lombard: Fahmy (1966) *Muslim Sea-Power*, 143–7.

The anthracological study of material from excavations in Mediterranean France and Spain is excellently presented in Chabal (1997) *Forêts et sociétés en Languedoc*, and Vernet (1997) *L'homme et la forêt méditerranéenne*.

BIBLIOGRAPHICAL ESSAY TO CHAPTER IX

MOBILITY OF GOODS AND PEOPLE

1. INESCAPABLE REDISTRIBUTION

We have argued that *redistributive engagement* (the degree of participation in the networks of exchange and supplementary supply, VI.2) is one of the ways of coping with risk which may be regarded as diagnostic of a Mediterranean microregion's character. The term 'redistribution' itself, for all its overtones of egalitarian sharing, is intended merely as a discreetly agnostic shorthand for all the processes by which goods change hands, of which the more commercial forms of exchange are only a subset. It is for that reason that the term has commended itself to prehistoric archaeologists, such as Rowlands (1984) 'Conceptualizing the European Bronze and Early Iron Ages', or Sherratt (1982) 'Mobile resources: settlement and exchange in early agricultural Europe'. Behind such inclusive terminology, of course, lies the economic anthropology of Karl Polanyi (on whom see Humphreys (1969) 'History, economics and anthropology: the work of Karl Polanyi'; also M. Sahlins (1974) *Stone-Age Economics*). Sherratt and Sherratt (1991) 'From luxuries to commodities: the nature of Mediterranean Bronze Age trading systems', 366, cf. 376, reject the concept of 'redistribution', preferring a present-centred analysis in terms of Hicksian market-forces to the anthropological approach. For all that, the 'substantivist' position retains its appeal: J. Davis (1992b) *Exchange*, considering the 'embeddedness' and symbolizing aspects of all market transactions, mounts a vigorous attack on economic formalism; cf. Maucourant (1996) 'Une analyse économique de la redistribution est-elle possible? Éléments de comparaison entre la

"New Institutional Economics" et l'approche substantive'. It is emphatically endorsed by the present study. For the continuing formalist/substantivist debate, see Meikle (1995a) 'Modernism, economics and the ancient economy', (1995b) *Aristotle's Economic Thought*; Silver (1985) *Economic Structures of the Ancient Near East*, (1995) *Economic Structures of Antiquity*. Pleket (1993) 'Agriculture in the Roman Empire in comparative perspective', squares the circle in suggesting the coexistence, with primitive conditions, of pockets of more sophisticated (even capitalistic) economy.

The indeterminacy of apparently 'natural regions' (cf. V.1–2) is central to our argument. In the context of seaborne exchanges, an eloquent example is offered by the Aegean Sea. Lock (1995) *The Franks in the Aegean*, 12, addresses, inconclusively, the problem of deciding whether or not the medieval Aegean can be described as wealthy. This is a question which will remain insoluble if the cluster of regions and connectivities which makes up the Aegean, with its archipelagos and coastlands, is considered in isolation, as Lock himself sees (253) when he explores the role of the Aegean as a transit centre for eastern produce. Cf. Zachariadou (1977) 'Prix et marchés de céréales en Romanie', 291–2.

The papers collected in Appadurai (1986) *The Social Life of Things*, illustrate our concern for the 'cultural construction' of commodities. Other work in this tradition which offers valuable parallels for earlier Mediterranean history include Brewer and Staves (1996) *Early Modern Conceptions of Property*, Brewer and Porter (1993) *Consumption and the World of Goods*, and Brewer and Bermingham (1995) *The Consumption of Culture 1600–1800*.

Paterson (1998) 'Trade and traders in the ancient world: scale, structure and organization', 164–6, presents the ebbing and flowing of economic fortunes in a way entirely compatible with 'intensification and abatement' theory (VII.4).

It is neither feasible nor desirable to give here even an outline bibliography of Mediterranean commerce. This chapter presupposes knowledge of the familiar discussions of medieval commercial history, some bibliography for which appears in the BE V.4. The main agendas of scholarship on the trade of the medieval Mediterranean have been rather different from ours. In advocating more general familiarity with the works listed below – those which have been especially helpful to us, and which are for the most part concerned with earlier periods – we hope to encourage an illuminating interdisciplinarity.

The interdependence which can now be demonstrated in Mediterranean prehistory poses particular challenges to interpretation, and above all to an unreflective progressivism. Arresting scholarship in this field may be sampled in the collected studies of Laffineur and Basch (1991) *Thalassa: l'Egée préhistorique et la mer*, and Karageorghis and Michaelides (1995) *Cyprus and the Sea*. The Bronze Age Aegean is conveniently surveyed in O. Dickinson (1992) *The Aegean Bronze Age*, ch. 7: 'Trade, exchange and foreign contact'. T. Smith (1987) *Mycenaean Trade and Interaction in the West Central Mediterranean, 1600 B.C.–1000 B.C.*, and Gillis et al. (1995) *Trade and Production in Premonetary Greece: Aspects of Trade*, are also important contributions. The modalities of connectivity are explored by R. E. Jones and Vagnetti (1991) 'Traders and craftsmen in the central Mediterranean', and Cline (1994) *Sailing the Wine-Dark Sea: International Trade and the Late Bronze Age Aegean*; compare Ross Holloway (1990) '*Koine* and commerce in the Sicilian Bronze Age'. Karageorghis (1993) 'Le commerce chypriote avec l'occident au bronze récent', presents the Iria wreck, carrying Cypriot pottery and perhaps on the way to Tiryns in the Argolid about 1200 B.C.

For the nature of redistribution in the ninth and eighth centuries, and Hesiod's father: Mele (1979) *Il commercio greco arcaico: prexis ed emporie*; I. Morris (1986) 'Gift and commodity in archaic Greece', (1989) 'Circulation, deposition and the formation of the Greek Iron Age'; Foxhall (1998a) 'Cargoes of the

heart's desire: the character of trade in the archaic Mediterranean world'. On the redistributive context of Greek overseas settlements, see Popham and Lemos (1995) 'A Euboean warrior-trader', and Docter and Niemeyer (1994) 'Pithekoussai: the Carthaginian connection. On the archaeological evidence of Eubeo-Phoenician partnership in the 8th and 7th centuries B.C.' The origins of piracy are discussed by Giuffrida Gentile (1983) *La pirateria tirrenica, momenti e fortuna*; compare Hackens (1988) *Navies and Commerce of the Greeks, the Carthaginians and the Etruscans in the Tyrrhenian Sea*.

The problems of Roman economic history receive an excellent recent survey in Garnsey and Saller (1987) *The Roman Empire*, ch. 5. Texts about commerce are collected by Meijer and van Nijf (1992) *Trade, Transport and Society in the Ancient World*. Fulford (1987) 'Economic interdependence among urban communities of the Roman Mediterranean', addresses the question of levels of connectivity. See also Hackens and Miró (1990) *Le commerce maritime romain en Méditerranée occidentale*; Lewit (1991) *Agricultural Production in the Roman Economy*; Paterson (1998) 'Trade and traders in the Roman world: scale, structure and organization'. Further BE V.4.

For late Antiquity and the early Byzantine world, Panella (1989a) 'Gli scambi nel Mediterraneo occidentale dal IV al VII secolo dal punto di vista di alcune "merci"'; Reynolds (1995) *Trade in the Western Mediterranean A.D. 400–A.D. 700*. On commerce in the Islamic Mediterranean, in addition to the works cited in BE V.5, note Constable (1994) *Trade and Traders in Muslim Spain*. For the western Mediterranean in the later Middle Ages, see e.g. Bautier (1992) *Commerce méditerranéen et banquiers italiens au moyen âge*.

2. ANIMAL, VEGETABLE AND . . .

Heavy commodities in search of a category

Some particular studies of the mineral resources of islands include: Salmeri (1992) 'Miniere di zolfo in Sicilia ed in Grecia in età imperiale', for Sicilian sulphur; Hasluck (1909–10) 'Terra Lemnia'; J. B. Ward-Perkins (1992) *Marble in Antiquity*, on Proconnesian marble; Renfrew and Wagstaff (1982) *An Island Polity*, 182–221, on Melian obsidian; and Cherry et al. (1991) *Landscape Archaeology as Long-Term History: Northern Keos in* the Cycladic Islands from Earliest Settlements until Modern Times, 299–303, for Cean ruddle (a red dyestuff).

The issue of World Archaeology for October 1984 is devoted to the archaeology of mines and quarries. On the timber trade, Meiggs (1982) Trees and Timber in the Ancient Mediterranean World; Lombard (1959) 'Le bois dans la Méditerranée musulmane' (and cf. VIII.5). For marble, Sodini (1989) 'Le commerce des marbres à l'époque protobyzantine'. A special case: Ashtor and Cevidalli (1983) 'Levantine alkali ashes and European industries'. Trade in terracotta revetments is discussed by Rico (1995) 'La diffusion par mer des matériaux de construction en terre cuite: un aspect mal connu du commerce antique en Méditerranée occidentale'.

The elder Pliny, Natural History, 34.9–11, specifies that the fame of Delian bronze derived from the 'market frequented by the whole world', and that Aeginetan bronze was not derived from local ores. The evidence for travelling metallurgists is presented by Galili et al. (1986) 'Bronze Age ship's cargo of copper and tin'; cf. Lambrou-Philippson (1995) 'Smiths on board late Bronze Age ships'. For travelling craftsmen (demiourgoi) see Zaccagnini (1983) 'Patterns of mobility among ancient Near Eastern craftsmen'; Purcell (1990a) 'Mobility and the polis'; and C. J. Smith (1998) 'Traders and artisans in archaic central Italy', who gives a radical reassessment of the importance of mobile craftsment to social change in archaic Italy. Evidence for Levantine goldsmiths on Crete is presented by Boardman (1967) 'The Khaniale Tekke tombs II'; cf., more generally, Treister (1995) 'North Syrian metalworkers in archaic Greek settlements'. Hoffman (1997) Imports and Immigrants: Near Eastern Contacts with Iron Age Crete, gives a cautious general response to these data.

Light from prehistory

See generally Sorensen and Thomas (1989) The Bronze Age–Iron Age Transition in Europe, and Wertime and Muhly (1980) The Coming of the Age of Iron. Estimations of the role of metals in Mediterranean exchanges in the late Bronze Age have changed dramatically as the result of archaeological discoveries, especially on Sardinia: Lo Schiavo (1986) 'Sardinian metallurgy: the archaeological background'. Connections became apparent with

the late Mycenaean world: Balmuth (1987) Studies in Sardinian Archaeology III: Nuragic Sardinia and the Mycenaean World; Bietti Sestieri (1988) 'The "Mycenaean Connection" and its impact on the central Mediterranean societies'; also with Cyprus: Muhly et al. (1988) 'Cyprus, Crete and Sardinia: copper oxhide ingots and the metals trade'. This was the foundation for the far-reaching hypotheses about power-relations formulated in A. B. Knapp (1986) Copper Production and Divine Protection: Archaeology, Ideology and Social Complexity on Bronze Age Cyprus, and (1990) 'Ethnicity, entrepreneurship and exchange: Mediterranean inter-island relations in the Late Bronze Age'. Giardino (1992) 'Nuragic Sardinia and the Mediterranean: metallurgy and maritime traffic', and (1995) Il Mediterraneo occidentale fra XIV ed VII secolo a.C.: cerchie minerarie e metallurgiche, give further detail on Sardinia. See also the useful résumé of Ridgway and Serra Ridgway (1992) 'Sardinia and history'. For the finds from Punta d'Alaca we rely on the brief report in Archeo: attualità del passato, February 1996, 14. Another promising direction for study is the comparison of Mediterranean trade with that apparent from the copious documentary evidence of Mesopatamia and its extensive penumbra. A mise-au-point can be found in Kuhrt (1998) 'The Old Assyrian merchants', presenting an ambitious picture of exchange in metal and woollen textiles between Kanesh on the Anatolian Plateau and Mesopotamia, but not progressing far beyond the rhetoric of organizational sophistication. In neither area is the systemic impact of such exchanges on the relations of production yet clear, relatively large though the exchanges are in scale. And comprehension has not been aided by the prevalance of enthusiastic economic anachronism among those who have attempted to generalize about the nature of the economics of Fertile Crescent societies.

The scientific investigation of the provenance of metal ingots has played an important part in this rapidly changing picture: Stos-Gale and Gale (1992) 'New light on the provenience of the copper oxhide ingots found on Sardinia'. Budd et al. (1995) 'Oxhide ingots, recycling and the Mediterranean metals trade', a contribution to the debate on the limits of provenancing, interestingly suggests that the ingots are not the product of primary smelting but the form in which recycled metal was passed on in a complex redistributive economy. For continuity of marks on ox-hide ingots, see Galili et al. (1986) 'Bronze Age ship's cargo of copper and tin'; Gale et al. (1985) 'Alloy types and copper sources of Anatolian copper alloy artefacts', for copper sources in Anatolia, regarding seaborne distribution as certain. Muhly et al. (1985) 'Iron in Anatolia and the nature of the Hittite iron industry', give the evidence for wide distribution and early sophistication of ironworking, possibly associated with the Hittite state. See also Muhly (1996) 'The significance of metals in the late Bronze Age economy of Cyprus'.

Metal in the Greek and Roman Mediterranean

General accounts, with good coverage of metallurgical technicalities, are Healy (1978) *Mining and Metallurgy in the Ancient World*, and Shepherd (1993) *Ancient Mining*; also Treister (1996) *The Role of Metals in Ancient Greek History*. On specific metals, see Penhallurick (1986) *Tin in Antiquity*; Waldron (1983) *Lead and Lead Poisoning in Antiquity*.

For the association of Euboea, the acquisition and processing of metals and the change in scale of Greek overseas settlement in the eighth century: Bakhuizen (1976) *Chalcis in Euboea, Iron and Chalcidians Abroad*, and (1977) 'Greek steel'. A series of studies illuminates the prominence of the metalliferous north Aegean in the processes of overseas settlement in the seventh and sixth centuries B.C.: Snodgrass (1995) 'The Euboeans in Macedonia: a new precedent for westward expansion'. Papadopoulos (1996) 'Euboians in Macedonia: a closer look', argued, however, that Chalkidike was named for its bronze-working and not because of connection with Chalkis. In general, see Boruchovič (1988) 'Die ägäische Kolonisation'; and for silver in Thrace, Graham (1978) 'The foundation of Thasos'. The continuum of settlement-practice between the Aegean and the more geographically distant parts of the Mediterranean argues in favour of the interpretation of metallurgically orientated settlement as 'the continuation of local intensification by other means', and against that which sees it in terms of 'colonization'.

Curtis (1988) *Bronzeworking Centres of Western Asia, c. 1000 B.C.–539 B.C.*, is useful on the Levantine metalworking tradition; cf. Markoe (1985) *Phoenician Bronze and*

Silver Bowls. The combination of Greek and Phoenician enterprise in the western Mediterranean is discussed by Gill (1988) 'Silver anchors and cargoes of oil', with Shefton (1982) 'Greeks and Greek imports in the south of the Iberian peninsula: the archaeological evidence', on the possibility that Attic pottery traces Phoenician distribution of Attic olive oil in return for Tartessian silver; it is also considered by Docter and Niemeyer (1995) 'Pithekoussai: the Carthaginian connection'.

The best-known metalworking area of ancient Greece is the silver-producing district of Laurion in Attica, on which see Conophagos (1980) *Le Laurium antique et la technique grecque de la production de l'argent*. For Roman mines in Spain, see Domergue (1990) *Les mines de la péninsule Ibérique dans l'antiquité romaine*; G. D. B. Jones (1980) 'The Roman mines at Rio Tinto'.

After the Iron Age?

Vryonis (1962) 'The question of the Byzantine mines', raised the interesting and eloquent problem of the discontinuities in exploitation of Anatolian metal resources. For the abundance and wide distribution of those resources, see the useful summary of De Jesus (1978) 'Metal resources in ancient Anatolia'; also Gale et al. (1985) 'Alloy types and copper sources of Anatolian copper alloy artefacts'. Bryer (1982) 'The question of Byzantine mines', 138, argues that fuel was sometimes (as in the ironsands of the Pontic coast) more of a limiting factor in the availability of iron than the ore. For the special status and occasional exploitation of metals, compare Cassiodorus's *Variae*, 3.25, describing a special request for iron from Dalmatia; or 9.3 on gold-mining in Bruttium. For silver in Anatolia, Aslıhan Yener (1992) 'Byzantine silver mines: an archaeo-metallurgy project in Turkey', on Bolkardağ and especially Gümüşköy between Tyana and the Cilician Gates.

For metals in the medieval Mediterranean: in general see Lombard (1974) *Les métaux dans l'ancien monde du Ve au XIe siècle*; compare Braunstein (1983) 'Innovations in mining and metal-production in Europe in the late Middle Ages', and Benoît and Braunstein (1983) *Mines, carrières et métallurgie dans la France médiévale*; Ashtor (1983c) *Levant Trade in the Later Middle Ages*, 440–2; Nef (1987) 'Mining and metallurgy in medieval civilisation'. For the bullion famine of the fifteenth century, Day (1987) *The Medieval Market Economy*, ch. 1.

3. The Problem of Mediterranean Textiles

Inedible crops

Sea-wool ('marine *byssus*') is the product of the mollusc *Pinna nobilis*, the fan mussel (Lauffer (1971) *Diokletians Preisedikt*, 264 at 19.14); its use in the Islamic world is discussed by Serjeant (1972) *Islamic Textiles: Materials for a History up to the Mongol Conquest*, 60, and Goitein (1961) 'The main industries of the Mediterranean as reflected in the records of the Cairo Geniza', 180.

For the technical details of wool production, Ryder (1993) 'Sheep and goat husbandry with particular reference to textile fibre and milk production'; also Frayn (1984) *Sheep-Rearing and Wool-Production in Roman Italy*. For the flax of al-Andalus, see Lagardère (1993) *Campagnes et paysans d'al-Andalus*, 413–39. On flax, see also VI.8, 11 above; and on leather Goitein (1961) 189–91. For textiles in the prehistoric world, see E. J. W. Barber (1991) *Prehistoric Textiles: The Development of Cloth in the Neolithic and Bronze Ages with special reference to the Aegean*; compare what we have said (VII. 1) about the 'secondary products revolution' described by Sherratt.

The nature of textile redistribution

Reyerson (1995) *Society, Law, and Trade in Medieval Montpellier*; Schneider (1978) 'Peacocks and penguins: the political economy of European cloth and colours'. There is a useful discussion of *thésaurisation* in Lombard (1978) *Les textiles dans le monde musulman*; Millar (1977) *The Emperor in the Roman World*, 135, 137, 144, has examples from imperial Rome. A general picture of textiles in Byzantine trade is to be found in Laiou (1981–2) 'The Byzantine economy in the Mediterranean trade system'. Byzantine silk, and its complex cultural setting, are examined at length by Liu (1996) *Silk and Religion*; economic aspects are set out by Lopez (1945) 'Silk industry in the Byzantine empire', and more recently by Oikonomides (1986) 'Silk trade and production in Byzantium from

the sixth to the ninth century: the seals of Kommerkiarioi', resumed in (1989) 'Commerce et production de la soie à Byzance'. Also on silk see Guillou (1974) 'Production and profits in the Byzantine province of Italy'; but note the corrections of Muthesius (1997) *Byzantine Silk Weaving*.

Pacemakers of industrial progress?

Bridbury (1982) *Medieval English Clothmaking*, 68, cf. 101, also argues that the supposed revolution of the spinning-wheel was in fact a more gradual process of change. Figures on the scale of late medieval production are quoted conveniently in Lopez and Raymond (1955) *Medieval Trade in the Mediterranean World*, 71; cf. 74 for the comparable scale of manufacturing in fourteenth-century Fez. Figures for the fifteenth and sixteenth centuries are selected in Cipolla (1993) *Before the Industrial Revolution*, 103–6, 242–3.

There is a copious literature on medieval textiles, from which we select some of what seems most relevant to the Mediterranean comparisons. Work on the English medieval cloth trade has brought some widely applicable insights: T. H. Lloyd (1977) *The English Wool Trade in the Middle Ages*; Spufford (1984) *The Great Reclothing of Rural England*, for cheap clothing and itinerant vendors. For the Continent, a brief survey in Pounds (1973) *An Historical Geography of Europe 450 B.C.–A.D. 1330*, 213–4, 386–94; and for the Mediterranean itself, Lopez and Raymond (1955) *Medieval Trade in the Mediterranean World*, with Riu (1983) 'The woollen industry in Catalonia in the later Middle Ages'; Gervers (1983) 'Medieval garments in the Mediterranean world'. For competition between local centres and the export trade in wool from southern Spain, see Edwards (1987) '"Development" and "underdevelopment" in the western Mediterranean: the case of Córdoba and its region in the late fifteenth and early sixteenth centuries', 21.

On Islamic textiles, Lombard (1978) *Les textiles dans le monde musulman*, remains basic, but see the useful response of Chapoutot-Remadi (1980) 'Réflexions sur l'industrie textile dans le monde musulman', also stressing the role of the state in flax-growing and linen-manufacture (cf. Section 4 below). Also Goitein (1961) 'The main industries of the Mediterranean as reflected in the records of the Cairo Geniza', 172–83, and Serjeant (1972) *Islamic Textiles: Materials for a History up to the Mongol Conquest.* The large-scale commerce of thirteenth-century Anatolia included wool: Cahen (1953–4) 'Un texte peu connu relatif au commerce d'Amalfi au Xe siècle'. Much of the work done on the Islamic world has been descriptive rather than analytical; an exception is Frantz-Murphy (1986) *The Agrarian Administration of Egypt.* The problem is the explanation of expansion and decline. Mazzaoui (1981) *The Italian Cotton Industry in the Later Middle Ages 1100–1600*, notes the importance of the labour supply which made possible an industry on a scale large enough to promote standardization and to reach mass markets. J. L. Abu-Lughod (1989) *Before European Hegemony: The World System A.D. 1250–1350*, 233–6, links the collapse of Levantine manufactures with the growth of the European 'world-system', a form of explanation about which we have considerable reservations.

There has been virtually no systematic comparison of textile production and distribution in the ancient world with that in either medieval Italy and north-western Europe or in the still more directly comparable Islamic Mediterranean. The evidence is very scattered, and some scholars have based their accounts on its inadequacies. For Roman textile production, A. H. M. Jones (1960) 'The cloth industry under the Roman empire', is the starting point, and Egypt once again has a prominent place in the discussion: see Wipszycka (1965) *L'industrie textile dans l'Égypte romaine*, and Dunand (1979) 'L'artisanat du textile dans l'Égypte lagide'; Bagnall (1993) *Egypt in Late Antiquity*, 23–33. For Anatolia: Labarre and Le Dinahet (1996) 'Les métiers du textile'. Archaeological evidence of textile processing at Pompeii is presented by Moeller (1976) *The Wool Trade of Ancient Pompeii* (with the critical comments of Jongman (1988b) *The Economy and Society of Pompeii*, 155–86). Excavation has revealed what appears to be a woollen textile industry of noteworthy scale where it had not been suspected before, in the central Greek city of Eretria in the Roman period (Blackman (1998a) 'Archaeology in Greece 1997–8', 62–4). Other aspects of textile production in Roman Italy are discussed by Frayn (1984) *Sheep-Rearing and the Wool Trade in Italy during the Roman Period*; for the same area

in other conditions, see Marino (1988) *Pastoral Economics in the Kingdom of Naples.*

Lombard (1978) *Les textiles dans le monde musulman*, 47, takes Gallienus's insouciance seriously and uses it as evidence for the importance of the trade to the Roman state. He might have added Gallienus's supposed reaction to Gallic recession: 'is the republic really secure without Atrebatic cloaks?' This is a beautiful illustration of the dangers of using anecdotal sources.

Historically, the most important of the ancillary products for textile production has been alum: Nenci (1982) 'L'allume di Focea'; Cahen (1963) 'L'alun avant Phocée: un chapitre d'histoire économique islamo-chrétienne au temps des Croisades', traces the trade back to the tenth century and presents a document of 1192 illustrating the importance at that epoch of Egyptian alum exports. Bryer (1982) 'The question of Byzantine mines', 146–9, on Pontic sources, wrongly suggests that alum (attested, for instance, as a commodity by the Zarai Customs Regulation of A.D. 202, Table 2) was not of great significance to ancient textile manufacture. Other ancillary products include tragacanth, the importance of which for the textile manufacture of Miletus is examined by Robert (1980) *A travers l'Asie mineure*, 342–50. A theme that is worth exploring in the Mediterranean textile trade is the contribution of processing to the increase of value through adulteration and its redress. A parallel from Central Asia is suggestive:

> It was normal practice, when buying wool from Mongols, to add to its weight by sprinkling it with water to which a little sugar had been added to make it sticky. Fine dust, sifted out of sand and clay, could then be stirred into the sticky wool. This added a labour cost and an extra transport cost to the price of the wool, but it widened the gambling margin in trade. A wool merchant had to be a man who could pluck a handful of wool out of a bale and guess, within narrow limits, the percentage of adulteration. He had then, before buying, to make a mental calculation: would he, before selling again, be able to add a little more dust, or would he have to shake a little out?' (Lattimore (1940) *Inner Asian Frontiers of China*, 14–15)

Tinnis: a case study

Our account is indebted to the excellent presentation by Lombard (1978) *Les textiles dans le monde musulman*, 151–74.

4. Problems with High Commerce: Variety, Specialization and Choice

Oddly, the debate about the origins and nature of commercial exchange has had much greater prominence among ancient historians (Hopkins (1983b) 'Introduction') than among their medieval or Islamic colleagues – perhaps because the much more copious evidence available to the latter has made it possible to avoid asking fundamental questions. With respect to these later stages of Mediterranean history there is still much emphasis on the 'sources of commodities and trade-routes view', which was most notably represented for the classical world by Charlesworth (1926) *Trade-Routes and Commerce of the Roman Empire* (an earlier, grand attempt at the same kind of representation: Vidal de la Blache (1896) 'Les voies de commerce dans la géographie de Ptolémée'). The approach has since been used to good effect by the French school, influencing Braudel himself and Maurice Lombard. It is clear that, as in the discussion of primary production, there is a tacit or explicit belief that these modern-sounding elements can be legitimately predicated of the medieval period and rejected for the ancient; thereby making it useless to compare the two, and necessary to erect various barriers to separate the domains.

High and low commerce indissolubly linked

Crone (1987) *Meccan Trade and the Rise of Islam*, and Peters (1988) 'The commerce of Mecca before Islam', both argue that the prosperity of Mecca was ordinary local redistribution and not high-value high-status exchange. Cf. Simon (1989) *Meccan Trade and Islam: Problems of Origin and Structure*.

Coastwise *cabotage*: cf. BE V.3.

Shipwrecks and the normality of the mixed cargo

Charlesworth, like Rostovtseff, was before his time in his use of the archaeological data then available, and it has been a pity that the obvious methodological flaws of such modernizing accounts have made it possible for more recent theorists to belittle the material evidence (sometimes very cheaply). Ilsley (1996) *An Indexed Bibliography of Underwater Archaeology*, is an invaluable resource for this topic. A good illustrated introduction: Gianfrotta and Pomey (1980) *Archeologia subacquea: storia, techniche, scoperte e relitti*. Gibbins (1991) 'Archaeology in deep water: a preliminary view', 164–8, for new developments in deep-water archaeology. An overview of the subject is to be found in A. J. Parker (1992b) 'Cargoes, containers and storage: the ancient Mediterranean'.

The basic account remains the invaluable survey of 1259 wrecks in A. J. Parker (1992a) *Ancient Shipwrecks of the Mediterranean and the Roman Provinces*, which has full bibliography. To give an idea of the contribution made by this material there seems no better way than to list twenty-one of the best-known and most striking wrecks excavated over the last few decades. We have largely drawn directly from Parker, citing only his catalogue number and the date of first major publication of the wreck.

Panella (1981) 'La distribuzione e i mercati', was a pioneering study of the 'piggy-back' cargo effect; see also McGrail (1989) 'The shipment of traded goods and of ballast in Antiquity'.

The problem of pottery: see Osborne (1996b) 'Pots, trade and the archaic Greek economy', for an example of directed trade from the archaic period. The case of the distinctive Etruscan ware *bucchero* is examined by Bonghi Jovino (1993) *Produzione artigianale ed esportazione nel mondo antico: il bucchero etrusco*; Gill (1994) 'Positivism, pots and long-distance trade', is a sample of the long-running debate on the relative value of ancient pottery. Kreuzer (1994) 'Überlegungen zum Handel mit bemalter Keramik im 6. Jahrhundert v. Chr. unter besonderer Berücksichtigung des Heraion von Samos', discusses the Attic black-figured pottery at the sanctuary of Hera on the island of Samos, and constructs a sophisticated explanation of how it got there. Another revealing by-product of the pottery trade is the ceramics from Muslim centres of production incorporated in medieval Italian churches: Abulafia (1985b) 'The Pisan *bacini* and the medieval Mediterranean economy'.

The problem of the history of the amphora

A very selective bibliography of a vast subject includes Giardina and Schiavone (1981) *Società romana e produzione schiavistica*, vol. 2: *Merci, mercati e scambi nel Mediterraneo*,

Table 7 A conspectus of Mediterranean shipwrecks

Ulu Burun (1984) Parker 1193: probably about 1325 B.C.	6 tons of copper in 200 ox-hide ingots; 100 'Canaanite' amphorae with varied high-value contents.
Cape Gelidoniya A (1967) Parker 208: 1200–1150 B.C.	60 copper ox-hide ingots, metal-working equipment, glass.
Haifa: Galili et al. (1986).	Bronze Age seaborne metallurgists.
Cap d'Antibes (1956) Parker 183: mid-sixth century B.C.	About 600 Etruscan wine amphorae.
Porticello (1987) Parker 879: end of fifth century B.C.	Attic lead ingots, wine amphorae from the Bosporus/Sea of Marmara area, and statues.
El Sec (1972) Parker 1058: 360–340 B.C.	Great diversity of amphorae (Black Sea, Punic Africa, Aegean); large quantities of finished bronze utensils; fine Attic painted pottery.
Kyrenia (1973) Parker 563: 310–300 B.C.	404 amphorae from Aegean islands and Palestine, 343 from Rhodes; 10,000 almonds in sacks; a large load of perishable material, probably cloth. A replica with 9 tons of cargo sailed from Paphos to Piraeus in 3 weeks, and reached a maximum speed of 12 knots, proving surprisingly good at sailing close to the wind.
Secca di Capistello (1978) Parker 1065: 300–280 B.C.	At least 100 'Graeco-Italic' amphorae.
Grand-Congloué A (1961) Parker 472: 210–180 B.C.	400 Graeco-Italic, and some Aegean, wine amphorae in two sizes, and about 7,000 pieces of black-glaze pottery. A pioneering excavation, marred by the hostilities between divers and archaeologists.
Capo Graziano A (1985) Parker 233: mid-second century B.C.	1,000–3,000 wine amphorae transitional between Graeco-Italic and Dressel I.
Baie de la Cavalière (1978) Parker 282: end of second century B.C.	Particularly notable for the variety of its cargo, indicating connections with Africa, south Italy and Spain, as well as the quarters of prepared meat which may have been taken on at Genoa and ballast from the Antibes area.
Colonía de Sant Jordí (1980) Parker 326: about 100 B.C.	Two sizes of olive, salt pork, almonds, several sorts of wine-amphora.
Albenga (1961) Parker 28: 100–80 B.C.	Wine-amphorae and black-glaze pottery: one of the pioneering examples of underwater archaeology.
Madrague de Giens (1978) Parker 616: 70–50 B.C.	400 tonnes of cargo, mostly amphorae of which the greater part are marked as belonging to P. Vevius Papus, wine amphorae from south Latium, probably Caecuban, alongside some black-glaze pottery: the largest ancient wreck yet excavated.
Petit Congloué (1985) Parker 806: around A.D. 50.	Notable as an example of a 'tanker' containing 15 2,000-litre *dolia*.
Culip D (1985) Parker 347: A.D. 70–80.	Several thousand pieces of table-pottery from Baetica and south Gaul; several dozen Dressel 20 olive-oil amphorae perhaps re-used.

Table 7 (*cont.*)

'Isis' (1990) Parker 517: end of fourth century A.D.	Amphorae: notable for being in 818 m of water between Sicily and Sardinia.
Mateille A (1981) Parker 682: A.D. 400–25.	Numerous amphorae and iron ingots.
Saint Gervais B (1983) Parker 1001: later seventh century (cf. V.6).	Rare example of cargo of wheat: *Triticum turgidum*, rivet wheat, probably destined for consumption in south Gallic cities such as Arles; also amphorae of pitch.
Yassi Ada A (1971) Parker 1239: soon after A.D. 626 (cf. V.6).	900 Byzantine amphorae, re-used for a variety of agricultural produce including lentils and olive oil, weighing at least 37 tons.
Serçe Liman (1978) Parker 1070: about A.D. 1025 (cf. V.3).	3 tons of glass and glass cullet, wine amphorae.

which was something of a turning-point at the time, and remains an important collection: see especially Manacorda (1981) 'Produzione agricola, produzione ceramica e proprietari nell'*ager Cosanus* nel I a.C.'; Panella (1981) 'La distribuzione e i mercati'; and Morel (1981) 'La produzione della ceramica campana: aspetti economici e sociali'.

Peacock (1982) *Pottery in the Roman World*, is a pioneering and fundamental study drawing on ethnographic parallels. Early ethnoarchaeological observations on the mechanics of packaging are to be found in S. Casson (1938) 'The modern pottery trade in the Aegean', and (1952) 'The modern pottery trade in the Aegean: further notes'; later observations in the same field in Blitzer (1990) 'Koroneïka: storage jar production and trade'. Whitbread (1995) *Greek Transport Amphorae*, 11–12, discusses the case of Thasos.

On the period of origins, Leonard (1995) '"Canaanite jars" and the Late Bronze Age Aegeo-Levantine wine trade', 233–54, sees no reason to postulate a developed specialized trade, since the jars were multipurpose. A lucid presentation of the transport amphorae of fifth-century B.C. Chios can be found in Lawall (1998) 'Ceramics and positivism revisited: Greek transport amphorae and history'. See Rodero (1995) *Las anforas preromans en Andalusia*, for the various containers for the distribution of fish-pickles in southern Spain from the seventh to the second centuries B.C.

For the Roman period, the heyday of the amphora as a container, Empereur and Picon (1989) 'Les régions de production d'amphores impériales en Méditerranée orientale'; Panella (1989b) 'Le anfore italiche del II secolo d.C.'; Zevi (1989) 'Introduzione'; Carandini (1989) 'L'economia italica fra tarda repubblica e medio Impero considerata dal punto di vista di una merce: il vino'; Tchernia (1989) 'Encore sur les modèles économiques et les amphores'; Empereur and Garlan (1986) *Recherches sur les amphores grecques*. For a full treatment of the amphorae of the Laecanii, Bezeczky (1998) *The Laecanius Amphora Stamps*. For late Antiquity and afterwards, Abadie-Reynal (1989) 'Céramique et commerce dans le bassin égéen du IVe au VIIe siècle'; Arthur (1986) 'Amphorae and the Byzantine world'; Keay (1984) *Late Roman Amphorae in the Western Mediterranean*.

Tomber (1993) 'Quantitative approaches to the investigation of long-distance exchange', argues (in the context of late Antique amphorae) that more complex statistical analyses of amphora data do not support some of the pessimistic conclusions which earlier studies drew from the decline of particular amphora types. Thus, for example (159), African exports do seem to have declined with the abandonment of the *annona* and its privileged link with Rome; but a Mediterranean-wide survey reveals a much more varied pattern which is to be linked with local competition. The Mediterranean presented here is indeed one in which, for primary cargoes at least, when one went to sea all coasts and harbours were potential destinations and distance across the friction-free medium was not a major limiting factor.

For containers in the Middle Ages Zug Tucci (1978) 'Un aspetto trascurato del commercio medievale del vino', is crucial. She also raises questions about the economics of packaging in relation to customs-dues and profit margins analogous to those about wool-processing mentioned earlier.

Intensification, technology and directed trade

For Antiquity, the volume Andreau et al. (1994) *Les échanges dans l'antiquité: le rôle de l'état*, is an important contribution. See also the critique of Maucourant (1996) 'Une analyse économique de la redistribution est-elle possible? Éléments de comparaison entre la "New Insitutional Economics" et l'approche substantive', with helpful bibliography.

On systems of redeployment: Garnsey and Morris (1989) 'Risk and the polis: the evolution of institutionalized responses to food-supply problems in the ancient Greek state'; Hopkins (1980) 'Taxes and trade in the Roman empire'. Whitby (1998) 'The grain trade of Attica in the fourth century B.C.', emphasizes the ways in which the state's estimates reflected an uncertain and unpredictable supply. For Roman customs-duties (*portoria*) see Laet (1949) *Portorium*; Badian (1972) *Publicans and Sinners*, 61–2; with the new customs-dossier from Ephesus, *SEG*, 39.1180. An interpretation identifying continuities in the social location of trade between Antiquity and the early Middle Ages is offered by Whittaker (1983b) 'Late Roman trade and traders'. See also Antoniadis Bibicou (1966) 'Vocabulaire maritime et puissance navale'; Wickham (1988a) 'Marx, Sherlock Holmes, and late Roman commerce'.

The movement of cereals was discussed in VI.8. In addition to the studies cited there, see Marasco (1988) *Economia, commerci e politica nel Mediterraneo fra il 3 e il 2 s. a.C.*, on the centrality of Hellenistic Delos to the grain-distribution network of the time; also Gauthier (1979) '*EXAGŌGĒ SITOU*: Samothrace, Hippomédon et les Lagides'. Contrast the account of Reger (1994a) *Regionalism and Change in the Economy of Independent Delos*.

Our knowledge of ancient shipping prices (not costs) derives from Diocletian's Price Edict; Lauffer (1971) *Diokletians Preisedikt*, section 37, is the essential full publication and discussion of this document (but cf. also Graser (1940) 'The Edict of Diocletian on maximum prices'). See the discussion of Duncan-Jones (1982) *The Economy of the Ro-man Empire: Quantitative Studies*, appendix, with reference to the famous calculation of A. H. M. Jones of relative costs of land and sea transport. Duncan-Jones (1990) *Structure and Scale in the Roman Economy*, 7–29 and 48–58, continues to take a pessimistic line on sailing conditions (cf. V.3). The proposition about tax-generated trade is that of Hopkins (1980) 'Taxes and trade in the Roman empire' (see BE IV.5). Brun (1997) 'Du fromage de Cythnos au marbre de Paros', is a useful account of problems in attributing origin, rarity, and standards. He argues that the tariffing of customs regulations played an important part in the classification of commodities. Low-value trade needs stressing here. A dramatic change in Italy, the *rivoluzione dei noli* (Pini (1989) *Vite e vino*, 173) by which shippers suddenly began to calibrate tariffs by value, rather than at fixed rates, allowed much more redistribution of lower-value goods in the later Middle Ages than immediately previously.

5. THE ULTIMATE RESOURCE

The basic account of the importance of population in early Greek history is that of Snodgrass (1979) *Archaic Greece*, esp. 22–5, but see the brief criticisms of Manville (1982) 'Geometric graves and the eighth century "population boom" in Attica'. Also I. Morris (1992) *Death-Ritual and Social Structure in Classical Antiquity*, and (1987) *Burial and Ancient Society: The Rise of the Greek City-State*.

Who was your mother's maternal grandmother?

On the neglected question of the historical importance of the demography of female mobility, see Ketzer and Brettell (1987) 'Advances in Italian and Iberian family history'. Jennings (1975) 'Women in early 17th century Ottoman judicial records: the Sharia court of Anatolian Kayseri', discusses how court records document a strikingly high degree of male mobility, because of the problems caused by leaving women family members for five, ten or twenty years.

Why islands have large populations

Kolodny (1974) *La population des îles de Grèce*, is the fundamental study. For high populations in the history of the Cyclades, note the correction to Wagstaff and Cherry (1982) 'Settlement and population change', by Sanders (1984) 'Reassessing ancient populations', reducing the minimum land for the support of 5,000 people from 61.5 km² to 9.5 km²! Rackham and Moody (1997) *The Making of the Cretan Landscape*, 208, are puzzled by the high and dense population of some of the Cretan islets, especially Kouphonisi, which has a large Roman settlement (206), Gaudhos (as revealed in the tithes paid to Apollo at Gortyn) and Dia. The explanation which they themselves advance for the contribution of Dia to the network of maritime communications also seems a more promising explanation of the demography than one centred on the islands' own productive capacities, such as the murex of Kouphonisi.

Early island-sites in the western Mediterranean attest high populations. For the site at I Faraglioni on Ustica, see Ross Holloway (1991) *Archaeology of Ancient Sicily*, 31–42; cf. Ross Holloway and Lukesch (1991) 'Ustica 1990', and subsequent reports in the same journal, *Archäologischer Anzeiger*; Said-Zammit (1997) *Population, Landuse and Settlement on Punic Malta*, provides a helpful survey of the whole population-history of the island. For the Balearics, Chapman and Grant (1997) 'Prehistoric subsistence and monuments in Mallorca'. For the founding of consolidated cities on islands (synoicism) Demand (1990) *Urban Relocation in Archaic and Classical Greece*, with BE IV.2; also Hornblower (1982) *Mausolus*, 78–105.

Arrivals: in Homer (*Odyssey*, 12.134–5) occupation of the pastoral resources of the island Thrinakie by the Daughters of the Sun is termed *apoikesis*, 'overseas settlement'. The opportunistic exploitation of island resources and the systematic mobility of populations are structurally linked. For the first inhabitants of Mediterranean islands, see Cherry (1990) 'The colonisation of the Mediterranean islands: a review of recent research'; Gomez Bellard (1995) 'The first colonisation of Ibiza and Formentera'; Broodbank and Strasser (1991) 'Migrant farmers and the Neolithic colonization of Crete'. Compare also BE VI.11.

Sequent occupance: see Carter (1977) 'Brač island, Dalmatia: a case for sequent occup-

ance?', for the normality of ethnic confusion; cf. Diodorus Siculus, *Historical Library*, 5.16, on Pityoussa (Ibiza), praised for its harbours, its tracts of level cultivable ground (*pedia*), quality of houses, and wool, in terms rather like those he applied to Malta; 'barbarians of every variety have settled it, though Phoenicians predominate'. Luttrell (1989) 'The Latins and life on the smaller Aegean islands, 1204–53', is gloomy and judgemental, with a strong emphasis on shifting population. See also Conrad (1992) 'The conquest of Arwâd', arguing for the demographic interdependence of the island population with the local mainland: compare Yajima (1986) *Arwad Island: A Case Study of Maritime Culture on the Syrian Coast*. Slot (1991) 'The Frankish archipelago', presents a 1670 tax-register for Naxos, Paros, Syros, Santorini, Milos, Andros (VII.6). The role of Frankish landlords in settling new cultivators, including the Albanians of Andros, is especially notable. On Cyprus: Loukopoulou and Raptou (1996) 'Mobilité et migration dans la Chypre antique'. For the diverse origins of modern Cretans, Rackham and Moody (1997) *The Making of the Cretan Landscape*, 88–9, and for Cretan demographic links in Antiquity, Brulé (1990) 'Enquête démographique sur la famille grecque antique'. The islands naturally served as refuges in times of trouble: Vacalopoulos (1980) 'The flight of the inhabitants of Greece to the Aegean islands'.

Depopulation: for the violence of the islands' depopulation, see Kolodny (1974) *La population des îles de Grèce*, 149–57; cf. Étienne (1984) 'Astu et polis à Ténos', suggesting resettlement after mid-fourth-century rupture. Cf. Diodorus, *Historical Library*, 31.45, for the depredations of Cretan pirates.

6. ORGANIZED MOBILITY

For mobility in ancient Greece, Purcell (1990a) 'Mobility and the *polis*'; Pritchett (1991) 'Spanositia and the problem of the grain route'; Osborne (1991b) 'The potential mobility of human populations'. Hoffman (1997) *Imports and Immigrants*, 153–90 and 247–60, offers a very cautious interpretation of the Cretan evidence for immigration in the Geometric and Archaic periods. Chevallier (1988) *Voyages et déplacements dans l'empire romain*, presents the Roman evidence. General accounts of medieval mobility include

Malamut (1993) *Sur la route des saints byzantins*; de Rachewiltz and Riedmann (1995) *Kommunikation und Mobilität im Mittelalter*; and two particular instances, Reyerson (1979) 'Patterns of population attraction and mobility: the case of Montpellier, 1293–1348'; Segura Graíño (1994) *Caminos y caminantes por las tierras del Madrid medieval*. With the latter compare Reher (1990) *Town and Country in Pre-industrial Spain*.

Theoretical discussions of migration include Mangin (1970) *Peasants in Cities: Readings in the Anthropology of Urbanization*; Kearney (1986) 'From the invisible hand to visible feet: anthropological studies of migration and development', on modernization theory versus dependency theory (XI.2): the colonial encounter leads to dependency, and this in turn to urbanization. An interesting study of mobility and community in modern Greece, Sutton (1988) 'What is a village in a nation of migrants?' A restatement of the older 'migratory' view: Arenson (1990) *The Encircled Sea*, 149–66. Movements in general are analysed in Adams and McNeill (1978) *Human Migration: Patterns and Policies*; Standing (1980–1) 'Migration and modes of exploitation: social origins of immobility and mobility'. On migration, see also Angelomatis-Tsougarakis (1990) *The Eve of the Greek Revival*, 71–6; Pooley and Whyte (1991) *Migrants, Emigrants and Immigrants*.

Among historical studies of emigration we may cite A. J. N. Wilson (1966) *Emigration from Italy in the Republican Age of Rome*, and the collections Sordi (1994) *Emigrazione e immigrazione nel mondo antico*, and Sordi (1995) *Coercizione e mobilità umana nel mondo antico*. Inward movements towards the Mediterranean are the theme of Ashtor (1972) 'Migrations de l'Irak vers les pays méditerranéens'. Braudel (1972a) *The Mediterranean*, 158–61, discusses the example of sixteenth-century Corsica. More generally: Comba (1984) 'Emigrare nel medioevo: aspetti economico-sociali della mobilità geografica nei secoli XI–XVI'. Cf. S. R. Epstein (1992) *An Island for Itself*, 70–1, for Sicily. The history of Mediterranean diasporas is also very germane to this subject: Trombley (1994) 'Religious transition in sixth century Syria', 155–6 and n.12, presents evidence from Corycus in Cilicia on a Syrian exodus of the sixth century. Cf. Ahrweiler and Laiou (1998) *Studies on the Internal Diaspora of the Byzantine Empire*.

Such movements have very often been connected directly or indirectly with the procurement of military manpower. That was certainly true of mass transferrals of population in the Levant in the first millennium B.C.: Postgate (1974) *Taxation and Conscription in the Assyrian Empire*; Oded (1979) *Mass Deportations and Deportees in the Neo-Assyrian Empire*. Heurgon (1957) *Trois études sur le 'ver sacrum'*, presents the interesting case of a ritual in pre-Roman Italy associating the military *razzia* with the constructed folk-memory of nomadic migration. For later periods, McCormick (1998) 'The imperial edge: Italo-Byzantine identity, movement and integration, A.D. 650–950', and Charanis (1961) 'The transfer of populations as a policy in the Byzantine empire'; and on *devshirme* Vryonis (1956) 'Isidore Glebas and the Turkish *devshirme*', showing that the practice was already a source of anxious misery to the people of Thessalonica in 1395. Zachariadou (1987) 'Notes sur la population de l'Asie Mineure Turque au XIVe siècle', explores how mercenary recruitment within the Menteshe Emirates was conducted by outsiders with permission from the emir; the rulers were thus simply new bosses for a pre-existing manpower resource. Genoa brokered the movement from the Crimea to the armies of Egypt of decisive quantities of slave manpower for military uses: Ehrenkreutz (1981) 'Strategic implications of the slave trade between Genoa and Mamluk Egypt in the second half of the thirteenth century'.

The *condottiere*: an early example is described by Popham and Lemos (1995) 'A Euboean warrior-trader'. The context of some movements of this kind and their cultural reception is described well by Malkin (1994) *Myth and Territory in the Spartan Mediterranean*. Another interesting case of an Archaic mercenary is Hylaeus of Phocaea on Lemnos (about 515 B.C.: Heurgon (1982) 'A propos de l'inscription tyrrhénienne de Lemnos'). Polybius, *History*, 2.5–7, describes the wanderings of a group of mercenaries in terms very reminiscent of the escapades of the Catalan Grand Company.

A rather different epiphenomenon of mobility was the encouragement of the resident foreigner: for Athens, see Whitehead (1977) *The Ideology of the Athenian Metic*; McKechnie (1989) *Outsiders in the Greek Cities in the Fourth Century B.C.*; cf. Gauthier (1975) *Symbola: les étrangers et la justice dans les cités grecques.* For Rome, see Sherwin-White (1973) *The Roman Citizenship*; for Constantinople, Lopez (1974) *Foreigners in Byzantium*; Balard (1991) 'L'organisation des colonies étrangères dans l'empire byzantin'. Seibert (1979) *Die politischen Flüchtlinge und Verbannten in der griechischen Geschichte*, for the ideology of exile; Purcell (1990a) 'Mobility and the polis'. In this context we recall the prominence of the 'emigration of disloyalty', the changing of sides by soldiers or civilians even in ideologically antagonistic settings. See, for instance, Bennassar and Bennassar (1989) *Les chrétiens d'Allah: l'histoire extraordinaire des renégats, XVIe et XVIIe siècles.*

Pirates and brigands

Ormerod (1924) *Piracy in the Ancient World*, a remarkably wide-ranging work, remains an excellent introduction to its subject. States founded on the management of piracy included the Aetolian league and the Illyrians: Benecke (1934) *Die Seepolitik der Aitoler*, Larsen (1968) *Greek Federal States, their Institutions and History*, 195–215, at 210–12; cf. Dell (1967) 'The origin and development of Illyrian piracy'. On the parallel case of the Uskoks, see Anselmi (1991) *Adriatico*. Tenenti (1967) *Piracy and the Decline of Venice 1580–1615*, shows that at any one time there were only about 1,000 Uskoks – whose name, importantly, means 'fugitive'. For pirate-communities, see Avidov (1997) 'Were the Cilicians a nation of pirates?'

Other helpful studies of ancient piracy are listed in BE V.5. Rackham and Moody (1997) *The Making of the Cretan Landscape*, 197–9, make a particularly helpful suggestion about the recolonization of pirate landscapes. Instead of a decisive turning away from the sea in such episodes, it is better to envisage an irregular oscillation analogous to other shifts in the configuration of exploitation. For booty, Pritchett (1991) 'Profits of war', 439–45. For island reactions to pirates, Reger (1994a) *Regionalism and Change in the Economy of Independent Delos*, 261–4, (1994b) 'The political history of the Kyklades'; Ducrey (1983) 'Les Cyclades à l'époque hellénistique: la piraterie symptôme d'un malaise économique et social'.

On banditry, following in the tradition of the classic Hobsbawm (1960) *Bandits*, Briant (1976) 'Brigandage, dissidence et conquête en Asie achéménide et hellénistique'; B. D. Shaw (1984b) 'Bandits in the Roman empire'; and Hopwood (1989) 'Bandits, elites and rural order'. Shaw (1990) 'Bandit highlands and lowland peace: the mountains of Isauria-Cilicia', studies the relationship of banditry to mountain environment in Anatolia. Cf. van Hoof (1988) 'Ancient robbers: reflections behind the facts'. For the early modern period, Braudel (1972a) *The Mediterranean*, 734–49, and with more recent examples, Gallant (1988) 'Greek bandits: lone wolves or a family affair?'; Barkey (1994) *Bandits and Bureaucrats: The Ottoman Route to State Centralization*, and Sant Cassia (1993) 'Banditry, myth, and terror in Cyprus and other Mediterranean societies'.

Understanding Mediterranean slavery

Slavery is so complex a phenomenon that it is perhaps not particularly surprising that only limited attention has been given to its role as a redistributor of population and to its significance within the demographic structure of a population. We cannot even begin to give here a bibliography of Mediterranean slavery. What we do urge is that scholars should at least consider possible structural similarities between ancient slavery and the medieval systems which are at least contiguous with it, and may derive from it, as well as focusing on the much more thoroughly explored comparison with early modern slavery in the Americas. A good starting point on ancient slavery is Hopkins (1978b) *Conquerors and Slaves*, concerned principally with the last two centuries B.C.; for the trade as such, W. V. Harris (1980) 'Towards a study of the Roman slave trade'.

The standard account of medieval Mediterranean slavery is Verlinden (1977) *L'esclavage dans l'Europe médiévale*, a work which collects material admirably, though it lacks the explanatory and interpretative dimension. There is also useful material in Dufourcq (1975) *La vie quotidienne dans les ports méditerranéens au moyen âge*; for the demographic effects of medieval slavery, Heers (1981) *Esclaves et domestiques au moyen âge dans le monde Méditerranéen*. See also Annequin and Léveque (1991) *Le monde méditerranéen et l'esclavage*; Bonnassie (1991) *From Slavery to*

Feudalism in South-Western Europe, and in general D. B. Davis (1966) *The Problem of Slavery in Western Culture*. On voluntary slavery in the Roman world Ramin and Veyne (1981) 'Droit romain et société: les hommes libres qui passent pour esclaves et l'esclavage volontaire'; and in the Middle Ages, Stuard (1986) 'To town to serve: urban domestic slavery in medieval Ragusa'. Stuard (1995) 'Ancillary evidence for the decline of medieval slavery', is an important treatment of female slavery: see also Phillips (1985) *Slavery from Roman Times to the Early Transatlantic Trade*, 73–4. See Avril and Gaborit (1967) 'L'*Itinerarium Bernardi monachi*', 280–1, for Muslim toeholds in Italy and the slave trade. For the Byzantine Aegean, Lemerle (1979a) *Les plus anciens recueils des miracles de Saint Démétrius et la pénétration des Slaves dans les Balkans*, 191–2. In A.D. 741–75 Constantine V ransomed with silk vestments 2,500 Christian prisoners taken from Imbros, Tenedos and Samothrace (Nicephorus, *Short History*, 86, ed. Mango (1990) 162).

7. PLACES OF REDISTRIBUTION

Harbourlessness and the epiphenomenal port

For Mediterranean ports, see Rickman (1985) 'Towards a study of Roman ports', (1988) 'The archaeology and history of Roman ports', (1991) 'Problems of transport and development of ports'. Houston (1988) 'Ports in perspective: some comparative materials on Roman merchant ships and ports'; Purcell (1996a) 'The ports of Rome: evolution of a *façade maritime*'. The statement of Pounds (1973) *An Historical Geography of Europe*, 132, that 'the rise of Rome owed little to its navigable communication with the sea' is extraordinary. For the ports of south Etruria, see also BE III.2.

Bibliography on the theory of gateway settlements includes Hirth (1978) 'Inter-regional trade and the formation of prehistoric gateway-communities'; Polanyi, Arensberg and Pearson (1957) *Trade and Market in the Early Empires: Economies in History and Theory*; Polanyi (1963) 'Ports of trade in early societies'; Revere (1957) '"No man's coast": ports of trade in the east Mediterranean'. Application of the theory to the Middle Ages

can be found in Hodges (1982b) 'The evolution of gateway settlements: their socio-economic implications'. For the parallel of the medieval *fondaco*: Lopez (1949) 'Du marché temporaire à la colonie permanente: l'évolution de la politique commerciale au moyen âge'. For Roman traders at Narona, Wilkes (1969) *Dalmatia*, 35; Sherwin-White (1973) *The Roman Citizenship*, 225–6. On the medieval commerce of the area, Stuard (1995) 'Ancillary evidence for the decline of mediaeval slavery', 16. Also BE V.2.

Haggis (1996) 'The port of Tholos in eastern Crete', presents another Cretan example of the sudden engagement of settlements with the milieu of redistribution. Genoa is a case on a rather different scale (BE IV.8). It is important in general to set the vicissitudes of the gateway settlement in a wider context. In the case of the Greek overseas settlement of Taras its independent neighbours developed an involvement in the milieu of redistribution in parallel with rather than because of the links of the Greek city: Lamboley (1996) *Recherches sur les Messapiens*, 468: 'la fondation de Tarente ne conditionne pas l'évolution des échanges entre Grecs et Messapiens, elle confirme simplement que la colonisation grecque s'inscrit dans un mouvement d'intensification des échanges entre le monde égéen et l'Occident'.

The instability of the *façade maritime* is illustrated by Sodini (1993) 'La contribution de l'archéologie à la connaissance du monde byzantine (IVe–VIIe siècles)', 174; or by examples on which we have touched in Chapter III: Orvietani Busch (1995) 'Northern Tuscan ports', or Buzaian and Lloyd (1996) 'Early urbanism in Cyrenaica: new evidence from Euesperides'. Goffman (1990) *Izmir and the Levantine World, 1550–1650*, describes the mushroom growth of Smyrna in the seventeenth century (cf. IV.2). The striking example of the island-city of Aradus is discussed by Weulersse (1940b) *Le pays des Alaouites*, 180–3; also Yajima (1986) *Arwad Island* (for the ancient city and its *peraia*, see Grainger (1990) *The Cities of Seleucid Syria*, 16–18, 27–30; also Frost (1995) 'Harbours and proto-harbours'). Microregions persist but their outlets and foci come and go: Goy (1985) *Chioggia and the Villages of the Venetian Lagoon*.

These instabilities are instantiated in the ancient Greek Mediterranean. Thus Morgan (forthcoming) 'Ethne, ethnicity and early Greek states': 'there is no point in their history when Greeks were not on the move, and taking our lead from Greek historians' discussion of their own past, we rationalize this as movement in terms such as colonization, refuge, or urban relocation'. Osborne (1998) 'Early Greek colonization? The nature of Greek settlement in the west', is also sceptical about the usefulness of the traditional category 'colonization'. The texts inscribed on lead which reveal the cosmopolitan nature of early Greek exchanges are *SEG* 26 (1976–7), 845; 37 (1987), 665 and 838; 38 (1988), 1036. On ethnic mixing in a nodal centre of another period, Reinert (1998) 'The Muslim presence in Constantinople, 9th–15th centuries: some preliminary observations'; also generally Ahrweiler and Laiou (1998) *Studies on the Internal Diaspora of the Byzantine Empire*. Medieval Acre is a textbook example. Here a congeries of trading communities and fragmented markets existed within the space of the city in a manner strongly reminiscent of ancient Naucratis, as described by Herodotus: Jacoby (1989) 'L'évolution urbaine et la fonction méditerranéenne d'Acre'. Balard (1988) 'Les formes militaires de la colonisation génoise (XIIIe–XVe siècles)', argues that Chios was the only true settled 'colony' of the Genoese. Other places were beachhead settlements, essentially what the Greeks would have called emporia.

The question of the nature of the interaction between different kinds of economy or ecology is debated in I. Morris (1994) *Ancient Histories and Modern Archaeologies*, and in the heated exchange between Sherratt (1995c) '*Fata morgana*: illusion and reality in "Greek–barbarian relations"', and Arafat and Morgan (1995) 'A reply to Andrew Sherratt'. Morel (1991) 'La romanisation du Samnium et de la Lucanie', discusses the involvement of 'pre-Roman modes of production' in the contacts of the Italic peoples with the wider world of Mediterranean commerce. On communications and settlement: Runnels and van Andel (1987) 'The evolution of settlement in the southern Argolid, Greece: an economic explanation', 322–30; Acheson (1997) 'Does the economic explanation work? Settlement, agriculture and erosion in the territory of Halieis', argues that the causal sequence, 'access to external markets leads to increase in site-density and probably population, and in turn to environmental change', can be challenged on grounds of local microdiversity.

The emporion *and the colony*

The starting point is the volume Bresson and Rouillard (1993) *L'Emporion*, and especially the papers by Zaccagnini (1993) 'In margine all'*emporion*: modelli di scambio nelle economie del Vicino Oriente antico'; Perreault (1993) 'Les *emporia* grecs du levant: mythe ou réalité?'; and Bresson (1993) 'Les cités grecques et leurs *emporia*'. Medieval equivalents: Lopez (1949) 'Du marché temporaire à la colonie permanente'. On the ancient notion of *emporie*, Casevitz (1993) '*Emporion*: emplois classiques et histoire du mot'; Mele (1979) *Il commercio greco arcaico: prexis ed emporie*, discusses its place in the premonetary economy of archaic Greece. For Strabo's usage, Rouillard (1983) '*L'emporion* chez Strabon'. This approach is unashamed of the language of commerce: 'l'emporion est lié par nature au développement d'un impérialisme marchand': Lévêque (1993) 'La richesse foisonnante de l'emporion', 230; contrast Cawkwell (1992) 'Early colonisation', on colonization as the 'cure . . . of the epidemic woes of climatic disaster . . . commerce made colonisation unnecesssary.'

A remarkable case of an inland *emporion* between the upper Hebrus plain and the inner fastnesses of the Balkans is published by Velkov and Domaradzka (1994) 'Kotys I (383/2–359 av. J.-C.) et l'*emporion* Pistiros de Thrace'. Accounts of inland markets, offering possible parallels for a site like this, are to be found in Anderson and Latham (1986) *The Market in History*; see also the brief account of Hodges (1988) *Primitive and Peasant Markets*. Peripheral markets in Bosnia did not promote interethnic contact: Lockwood (1975) *European Moslems: Economy and Ethnicity in Western Bosnia*, alas now something of a period piece. Fanselow (1990) 'The bazaar economy or how bizarre is the bazaar really?', emphasizes the issues of diversification and rationality, and of information, standardization and quality control. The complexity and lability of market-geography is illustrated by the Barracco estate in Calabria: 'complex and diversified in both production and administration, with a whole mosaic of tenancy forms, a mutliple-crop system [on which cf. 116–17] . . . and a great variety of farming techniques . . . as well as a complex web of markets': Petrusewicz (1996) *Latifundium*, 6. Fairs are a further, still more flexible and fluid alternative form of market. On Roman fairs there are useful accounts in de Ligt (1993) *Fairs and Markets in the Roman Empire* (compare MacMullen (1970) 'Market-days in the Roman empire'; Frayn (1993) *Markets and Fairs in Roman Italy*) and B. D. Shaw (1981) 'Rural markets in North Africa and the political economy of the Roman Empire'. For the Middle Ages, Bautier (1991) *Sur l'histoire économique de la France médiévale: la route, le fleuve, la foire*, also relevant to river transportation, and for the Islamic world, Faroqhi (1978) 'The early history of the Balkan fairs'.

BIBLIOGRAPHICAL ESSAY TO CHAPTER X
'TERRITORIES OF GRACE'

Our title, 'Territories of Grace', is borrowed from Christian (1989) *Person and God in a Spanish Valley*, 44.

1. RELIGION AND THE PHYSICAL ENVIRONMENT

The landscape of cult has formed a theme in human geography (see, for example, Johnston and Smith (1994) *The Dictionary of Human Geography*, s.v. 'Geography of Religion'; Park (1994) *Sacred Worlds*), and in archaeology, especially that of prehistoric and New World societies. If relatively little *historical* work appears to have been done on the subject, it is perhaps because the principal interests of historians of religion who cover the traditions relevant to the Mediterranean have often lain in more abstract quarters. For an innovative conference on a connected theme see Boesch Gajano and Scaraffia (1990) *Luoghi sacri e spazi della santità*; also Carmichael et al. (1994) *Sacred Sites, Sacred Places*. We have not found any attempt to approach the subject *in extenso* from the points of view which we adopt: see however the suggestive remarks of Fowden (1990a) 'Religious developments in late Roman Lycia', 344–5, addressing the challenge of a microregional approach to Mediterranean religious history, and promising further work on it; also the ambitious collection of materials on the religious topography of central Anatolia in Mitchell (1993) *Anatolia: Land, Men and Gods in Asia Minor*, vol. 2. The combination there of landscapes of unusual fragmentation (even by Mediterranean standards) with an extremely disturbed social history and with relatively abundant documentary evidence has given Anatolia a special position in the history of this subject, as will be seen from the survey which follows.

Interest in the patterns of Mediterranean religion discernible in the landscape, and the perception that modern practice appeared closely to resemble what was known of the distant past, arose from the better understanding of ancient religion which was acquired from the third quarter of the nineteenth century onwards, the systematic exploration of the remoter parts of the Mediterranean lands, and the new interest in popular culture, especially from the folkloric and ethnographic standpoints. The very imperfect knowledge of ancient religion shown by travellers and expatriate residents with political agendas (II.1), such as W. B. Barker (1853) *Lares and Penates* (compare the intelligent but unsophisticated view of Lenormant (1883) *À travers l'Apulie et la Lucanie*), are representative of the period before the quickening of serious research. Barker's fascinating account of Cilicia takes its title from a deposit of terracotta *ex voto* offerings found by accident at Tarsus, which he interpreted as the tutelary deities of the whole region, thereby committing two instructive errors: he was quite ignorant of all aspects of ancient religion not immediately described by the mainstream literary texts, and he assumed that every random survival revealed by archaeology was likely to have a central and unique historical importance.

That second fallacy (not entirely extinct among historians today) reminds us how much of our knowledge of this field is owed to systematic archaeology, which began at the same period and formed part of the justification for a more thorough exploration of the

Mediterranean. It was travellers at the end of the century such as (above all) Ramsay, who began to come to terms with the tremendous cultural complexity of the Near East: (1890) *A Historical Geography of Asia Minor*, (1908) *Pauline and Other Studies*; Ramsay and Bell (1909) *The Thousand and One Churches*. The rather simple ideas of survival and continuity critically discussed in the chapter were deployed for this task. The (posthumous) work of Hasluck (1929) *Christianity and Islam under the Sultans*, vol. 2, belongs in the same tradition. In (1914–16) 'Stone cults', and (1913–14) 'Ambiguous sanctuaries', Hasluck was, however, conscious that the veneration of significant stones, whether natural or wrought, is a matter of continuous re-creation rather than continuity or survival (cf. Halliday (1910–11) 'Cenotaphs and sacred localities', also from the circle of the British School at Athens). Hasluck, indeed, wrote with exasperated aposiopesis in a letter of 20 October 1915 (1926, *Letters on Religion and Folklore*, 13): 'everyone is so eager to believe in picturesque survivals: i.e. that every cult in a given radius *must* be a survival of every other in that radius. This is, well –'.

Had Hasluck not died prematurely there might have been a quicker application of the promising start made a generation earlier by Robertson Smith in (1889, 2nd edn 1894) *Lectures on the Religion of the Semites*, a landmark in the study of Mediterranean religion (see Beidelman (1974) *W. Robertson Smith and the Social Study of Religion*). The valuable account of Goldziher (1971) *Muslim Studies* (see especially 'The veneration of saints': 2.255–341) shares Robertson Smith's views of pagan-Islamic continuity. The later observations of Sir James Frazer (1906) *Adonis, Attis, Osiris*, were far less original than the work of Robertson Smith, and his contribution to the history of Mediteranean religion is slight, for all that his own work was founded on the elucidation of the Greek and Roman evidence (Ovid and Pausanias, for instance) through the comparative method.

The investigation of actual practice continued, but without great methodological or interpretative sophistication. A classic instance is the compendious Lawson (1910) *Modern Greek Folklore and Ancient Greek Religion*, in a tradition which proved long-lasting: for instance Ashby (1929) *Some Italian Scenes and Festivals*, or Kriss and Kriss-Heinrich (1955) *Peregrinatio Neohellenica*, and their

(1960–2) *Volksglaube in Bereich des Islam*, for the Islamic world – the comparison of the two traditions implicit in their oeuvre is noteworthy. While providing good surveys of fast-changing traditional religion, these works and the many like them did not represent an intellectual advance. Cf. BE XI.2.

Two approaches combined in the second half of the twentieth century to transform the study of the religious history of the Mediterranean. The first, starting where Robertson Smith and Frazer left off, is that of the social anthropologist. The pioneering work of Robert Hertz, before his untimely death in the First World War, included the famous article on the Alpine cult of St Besse which we cite in Section 5 (see further Evans-Pritchard (1960) 'Introduction'). Two particularly helpful accounts of Mediterranean religion in this context are the studies collected by Pitt-Rivers (1963) *Mediterranean Countrymen*, and (1977) *The Fate of Shechem*. This approach has, as we shall see, made especially important contributions to our understanding of pilgrimage. Compare Chapters XI and XII. See too the general survey of Nolan (1990) 'Shrine locations: ideals and realities in continental Europe'. As the influence of social anthropology on archaeology and ancient history has grown, so there has been a renewal of interest in the spatial dimensions of social history, including religion; the works of Alcock (1993) *Graecia Capta: The Landscapes of Roman Greece*, ch. 5: 'The sacred landscape', and Alcock and Osborne (1994) *Placing the Gods*, are good examples.

For the impact of 'modern' and 'postmodern' geographical thought on the conceptualizing of space in the social sciences, cf. works cited in BE IV.2.

Dillon (1997a) 'The ecology of the Greek sanctuary', counters extreme views, but displays little sense of the problems in current debate and little general argument. One of the most influential works in this area was De Polignac (1984) *La naissance de la cité grecque*; cf. (1994) 'Mediation, competition and sovereignty', and Morgan (1994) 'The evolution of a sacral "landscape"'; also D'Onofrio (1995) 'Santuari "rurali" e dinamiche insediative in Attica fra il protogeometrico e l'orientilizzante (1050–600 a.C.)', or G. R. H. Wright (1992) 'The Cypriot rural sanctuary: an illuminating document in comparative religion' – rather inclined towards older ideas of cultic continuity. For the Cretan religious landscape, Rackham and Moody (1997) *The Making of the Cretan Landscape*, 179–88, at 187. It is landscape-wide archaeology, foreshadowed by the topo-graphical researches of the age of Ramsay, and continued through the painstaking study of epigraphy, which has made the second great contribution to the understanding of the spatial dimension of cult in the past.

The awakening of interest in the social background of the religious changes of late Antiquity, of which, too, Fowden (1990a) 'Religious developments in late Roman Lycia', is an instance, is another very fruitful strand in the history of the subject, partly because of the richness of the evidence, which allows us to perceive the setting of religious life in a credible landscape, and partly because the emphasis of the study of such a period must naturally be on explaining change rather than postulating survival: cf. Trombley (1993–4) *Hellenic Religion and Christianization*, 1.98–9 n.4, fiercely attacking the survivalism of Lawson (1910) *Modern Greek Folklore and Ancient Greek Religion*. On the particular question of the transformation of paganism, see Gregory (1986) 'The survival of pagan-ism in Christian Greece: a critical essay', for Greece; for the West, and Gaul in particular, Pietri (1990) 'Loca sancta: la géographie de la sainteté dans l'hagiographie gauloise (IVe-VIe s.)'. Also Fowden (1978) 'Bishops and temples in the eastern Roman empire, A.D. 320–453'; Frantz (1965) 'From pagan-ism to Christianity in the temples of Athens'; Trombley (1985a) 'Paganism in the Greek world at the end of Antiquity: the case of rural Anatolia and Greece'. An ethnographer's general view (on his anti-Mediterraneanism cf. Chapter XI): Pina-Cabral (1992a) 'The gods of the Gentiles are demons: the prob-lem of pagan survivals in European culture'. Also Mitchell (1993) *Anatolia: Land, Men and Gods in Asia Minor*, 2.53–108.

Markus (1990) *The End of Ancient Christi-anity*, ch. 10: 'Holy places and holy people', perceives a discontinuity in the Christian acquisition of holy places; they had in com-mon with pre-Christian cults the fact of being places, but Markus emphasizes (155) the inter-pretative, historical dimension as much as their being sacred localities. See further on this important and fruitful argument Taylor (1993) *Christians and the Holy Places*, 318–41; Markus (1994) 'How on earth could places become holy?'; and, taking a rather different view, Wilken (1992) *The Land called Holy*, 88–93. See Fowden (1990b) 'The Athenian Agora and the progress of Christianity', 500, on the way in which crucial geographical loca-tions reinforced messages of monks and later dervishes. Compare also Section 5 below.

It is striking that so little attention has been accorded to the geography of cult in the Mediterranean in more recent periods, be-tween late Antiquity and the recent times covered by the ethnographic studies to which we have already alluded. The emphasis has been placed more on the sociology of sanc-tity (who became a saint), the societal role of saints, and the analysis of miracle collections. Cf. S. Wilson (1983) *Saints and their Cults*, still not unrepresentative. A model of what can be done, in the British tradition of landscape-history, is R. Morris (1989) *Churches in the Landscape*.

2. A PERILOUS ENVIRONMENT

For the perceived dangers of the environment see in general C. Stewart (1991) *Demons and the Devil: Moral Imagination in Modern Greek Culture*; for a more northerly comparison, Horden (1992) 'Disease, dragons and saints'. Further bibliography on eschatological inter-pretation of landscape is to be found below under Section 4. Among noteworthy con-tributions of human geography to this field, we should mention in particular Tuan (1974) *Topophilia: A Study of Environmental Percep-tion, Attitudes, and Values*, developing the ideas of Scully (1962) *The Earth, the Temple and the Gods*, which attempted to examine the relationship of ancient Greek shrines to the local landforms as seen from a variety of viewpoints; if his interpretations may some-times seem fanciful and are seldom so obvi-ous as to be considered proven, they are not absurd (V.1). Agnew and Duncan (1989) *The Power of Place: Bringing together Geographical and Sociological Imaginations*, for example 1, plead persuasively for a reintegration of local-ity with other aspects of sociological research. Cosgrove (1988) 'The geometry of landscape: practical and speculative arts in sixteenth century Venetian land-territories', represents an attempt in the same spirit, in this case related to the entire conceptual landscape, an idea which has considerable usefulness for the question of a distinctively religious landscape, the more so since his approach tends towards visual evocations.

Holy waters

There is still no general account of what one might label 'conceptual hydrology' for the Mediterranean, though it plays a large part in the religious geography of Hindu thought and modern work on it. The Islamic world has had more systematic treatment than the ancient or Christian: Robertson Smith (1889) *Lectures on the Religion of the Semites*, 165–84, and Goldziher (1971) *Muslim Studies*, stand out. River-cults are the theme of Brewster (1997) *The River Gods of Greece*; some other reflections on rivers in Purcell (1990b) 'The creation of provincial landscape'; for Roman attitudes to water in general, compare Purcell (1996b) 'Rome and the management of water'. For inland cults of Neptune in Roman North Africa, perhaps connected with irrigation, Petitmergin (1967) 'Inscriptions de la région de Milev'. Discussions of the ambiguous associations of springs, especially hot ones, is to be found in Dunbabin (1989) '*Baiarum grata voluptas*: pleasures and dangers of the baths'; cf. Rousselle (1990) *Croire et guérir: la foi en Gaule dans l'antiquité tardive*; also Chevallier (1992) *Les eaux thermales et les cultes des eaux en Gaule et dans les provinces voisines*, for regional studies of water cults. For an example from the volcanic Lipari islands, Bernabò Brea (1994) 'La source thermale de S. Calogero (Lipari)'. On *agiasmata* see Trombley (1993–4) *Hellenic Religion and Christianization*, 1.1–6, largely superseded by the much more broadly conceived study of local cults in a microregional landscape of Mitchell (1993) *Anatolia*, vol. 2. For the preceding period see Debord (1982) *Aspects sociaux et économiques de la vie religieuse dans l'Anatolie gréco-romaine*.

High places

High places in the Aegean Bronze Age are a major focus of debate: Rutkowski (1986) *Cult Places in the Aegean*, 11–12, 73–96; and on the Cretan cases, Peatfield (1983) 'The topography of Minoan peak sanctuaries', (1992) 'Rural ritual in Bronze Age Crete: the peak sanctuary at Atsipadhes'. Mount Juktas is a prominent example. Rackham and Moody (1997) *The Making of the Cretan Landscape*, 179, discuss the visibility of high-place sanctuaries and aspects of their territories. For

the Levant, D. Levi (1981) 'Features and continuity of Cretan peak-cults'; a striking example of a high-place pilgrimage centre on a crater-rim, from central Anatolia: Schirmer (1995) 'Archaeology in Turkey'. For a modern case in Provence, Vidal-Naquet (1992) 'Genèse d'un haut-lieu', 7–16. The account of Schmidt (1939) *Heilige Berge Griechenlands*, is not very profound. R. C. T. Parker (1996) *Athenian Religion: A History*, 29–33, has some very suggestive remarks about archaic mountain sanctuaries with good parallels elsewhere in the Greek world, and discussion of M. K. Langdon (1976) *Sanctuary of Zeus on Mt. Hymettus*. For the evidence of Jacob of Serugh on cults of hill-top and valley-bottom, Bowersock (1990) *Hellenism in Late Antiquity*, 37. Mountains in general have their own religious landscapes: ancient Greek cases in Jost (n.d.) 'La vie religieuse dans les montagnes d'Arcadie'; and Buxton (1994) *Imaginary Greece*, ch. 6: 'Landscape'. For Elijah and mountains, Megas (1958) *Greek Calendar Customs*, 142–4, to which the summary by Vryonis (1988) 'The Byzantine legacy in folk life and tradition in the Balkans', 122–4, adds little.

Woodland religion

Sacred groves in the ancient world have been excellently treated in the collection ed. de Cazenove and Scheid (1989) *Les bois sacrés*. For forest zones and their religious status in the Middle Ages, Bechmann (1990) *Trees and Man*, 327–41. On tree cult also Birge (1994) 'Trees in the landscape of Pausanias' *Periegesis*'; Meiggs (1982) *Trees and Timber*, 378; Trombley (1993–4) *Hellenic Religion and Christianization*, 1.156–8. Much background to our remarks on this subject will be found in VIII.5.

Cults and the underworld

The cave-sanctuaries of Crete are discussed by Rutkowski (1986) *Cult Places in the Aegean*, 226, cf. 9–11 and 47–67. On evocations of awesome caves in ancient art, Lavagne (1988) *Operosa antra*. Biamonte (1997) 'Uno *spelaeum* mitraico', 34–6, has pertinent remarks on striking landscapes, water, and the location of Mithraic caves. Among other instances of the sanctity of caves and rocks we may cite the link that, in Muslim popular thought, such places have to Ali (to whom the site of Persepolis was sacred). He created a gorge near Hammam Lif in Algeria; at Mount Janshan near Aleppo, his cult replaces Marat Marutha; see Yaqut, quoted by Miquel (1967–88) *La géographie humaine du monde musulman*, 2.300–1. J. E. Taylor (1993) *Christians and the Holy Places*, 157–79, presents the multiple meanings of caves in the pagan, Jewish and Christian traditions.

Lawson (1910) *Modern Greek Folklore and Ancient Greek Religion*, 280–3, discusses dragons and other monsters of rocks and caves. On cave-sanctuaries of St Michael, Angelillis (1955) *Il santuario del Gargano e il culto de S. Michele*; Otranto and Carletti (1990) *Il santuario di S. Michele Archangelo sul Gargano*; Petrucci (1963) 'Aspetti del culto e dei pellegrinagi di S. Michele arcangelo sul Monte Gargano'. The treatment of the insane in the Lebanon is discussed by Katchadourian (1984) 'The historical background of psychiatry in Lebanon', 547–8; cf. Howell (1970) 'Health rituals at a Lebanese shrine'.

Dangerous weather

For the relationship between the Attic cult of Zeus Hymettius and pluviality, M. K. Langdon (1976) *Sanctuary of Zeus on Mt. Hymettus*; cf. Fowden (1988) 'City and mountain', 48–5; R. C. T. Parker (1996) *Athenian Religion: A History*, 29–33. On weather divination see Flint (1991) *The Rise of Magic in Early Medieval Europe*, 191–3 (cf. 109, 111). We return to this topic of 'ethnometeorology' in Volume 2.

Locusts, sand-dunes and lava: protecting the microregion

Herakles as drainage-hero is examined by Knauss (1990a) 'Der Graben des Herakles in Becken von Pheneus und die Vertreibung der Stymphalischen Vögel'. Saints credited with changes to the landscape are discussed by Lane Fox (1986) *Pagans and Christians*, 531–2. Cf. Horden (1992) 'Disease, dragons and saints', for the link between monster, miracle and benefactor. For earthquake-religion, Dagron (1981) 'Quand la terre tremble'; Guidoboni (1989) 'Sismicità e disastri sismici: il lungo periodo e i punti di vista'.

Controlling the periphery: the case of water

The cult at Aphaca and its treatment in scholarship are presented by Soyez (1977) *Byblos et la fête des Adonies*; general survey of ancient attitudes to water in Ginouvés et al. (1994) *L'eau, la santé et la maladie dans le monde grec*; Tölle-Kastenbein (1990) *Antike Wasserkultur*, esp. ch. 1. The connection of water with the uncontrolled periphery is made by Gose (1993) 'Segmentary state formation and the ritual control of water under the Incas', 482, applied to Rome by Purcell (1996b) 'Rome and the management of water: environment, culture and power'. Note also Tuan (1968) *The Hydrological Cycle and the Wisdom of God*. In an uncharacteristically materialist spirit, Momigliano (1976), reviewing T. D. Barnes *Tertullian: A Historical and Literary Study* (1971), advanced the view that Tertullian's preoccupation with holy water in *On Baptism* was a reflection of the physical circumstances of his Maghreb background (compare now Cramer (1993) *Baptism and Change in the Early Middle Ages*). Lansing (1991) *Priests and Programmers*, offers a suggestive account of religious aspects of water-technology in Bali. For rivers, Aelian, *True History*, 2.83, is a basic text: see now Brewster (1997) *River Gods of Greece*.

3. THE SACRALIZED ECONOMY

The religion of the productive landscape

Among types of production which do not aim at supplying nutritional needs directly, but which resemble the other activities of the microregion, we have stressed salt: for our Cypriot example, see Vandenabeele (1991) 'Salt on Cyprus in Antiquity'; and Yon (1992) 'The goddess of the salt lake'. For the religion of metallurgy, see IX.2: and, for another Cypriot case, A. B. Knapp (1986) *Copper Production and Divine Protection: Archaeology, Ideology and Social Complexity on Bronze Age Cyprus*. The strange case of Lemnian earth was first systematically studied by Hasluck (1909–10) 'Terra Lemnia'; Raby (1995) 'Terra Lemnia and the potteries of the Golden Horn: an antique revival under Ottoman auspices', argued that there was more learned revival than continuity of observance in the veneration of this resource in the early modern period. For the productive associations of the Athenian ephebic oath, cf. Osborne

(1987) *Classical Landscape with Figures*, and Merkelbach (1972) 'Aglauros'. For *georgos* in patristic exegesis, see *RAC*, 'Erde', 1161–3.

The religion of the extractive landscape

On the religion of agriculture, Isager and Skydsgaard (1992) *Ancient Greek Agriculture*, 157–98. On the rather neglected subject of temple economies in Roman Italy, the classic account is Bodei Giglioni (1977) 'Pecunia fanatica: l'incidenza economica dei templi laziali'; see also Carlsen (1994) '*CIL* X 8217 and the question of temple land in Roman Italy'. For precursors among the *apoikiai* of Magna Graecia, Ampolo (1992) 'The economics of the sanctuaries of southern Italy and Sicily', and for the animals owned by temples, Isager (1992) 'Sacred animals in classical and Hellenistic Greece'. The older accounts of the temple-states of Anatolia by Rostovtseff (1941) *The Social and Economic History of the Hellenistic World*, 503–7, with nn.279–83, and Broughton (1938) 'Roman Asia Minor', 640–6 and 676–84, are still useful; compare also Zawadzki (1952–3) 'Quelques remarques sur l'étendue et l'accroissement des domaines des grands temples en Asie mineure'; Virgilio (1981) *Il 'tempio-stato' di Pessinunte*; Isager (1990) 'Kings and gods in the Seleucid Empire: a question of landed property in Asia Minor'. For the monastic successors to such estates, see Trombley (1985b) 'Monastic foundations in sixth century Anatolia and their role in the social and economic life of the countryside'. This is an area which richly deserves further examination, particularly in comparison with the economy of cult-centres in the earlier periods and in the Levant and Fertile Crescent. For the religious implications of the classification of terrains, which has also frequently been connected with the processes of allotment and the regime of property, see briefly Hegyi (1976) *'Temene hiera kai temene demosia'*, discussing sacred and public land in ancient Greece.

The metallurgical importance of early Greek sanctuaries: see IX.2; cf. Risberg (1992) 'Metal working in Greek sanctuaries'. For the accumulation of precious materials in cult-places, see Baratte (1992) 'Les trésors des temples dans le monde romain: une expression particulière de la piété'; M. M. Mango (1992) 'The monetary value of silver revetments and objects belonging to churches, A.D. 300–700':

the very large quantities of silver involved, it can be argued, were depleted but replenished, and therefore not withdrawn from economic functioning. On this theme also Caillet (1996) 'Le trésor de l'antiquité à l'époque romane: bases de la recherche actuelle et éléments de problématique'; Baratte (1996) 'L'argent et la foi: réflexions sur les trésors de temple'.

On religious aspects of Hellenic overseas settlement, the basic work is Malkin (1987) *Religion and Colonization in Ancient Greece*. Lamboley (1996) *Recherches sur les Messapiens*, 469, describes the introduction into Messapia of cults of 'colonial'-style fertility and of harbours, when, during the fourth century B.C., the region became increasingly engaged in maritime networks. Edlund (1984) 'Sacred and secular: evidence of rural shrines and industry among Greeks and Etruscans', identifies a difference between them which she attributes to the differing role of the city: in a sense this is true, but the difference is rather that between sanctuaries orientated towards production in the 'colonial' landscape of the *chorai* of the Greek cities on the one hand, and those promoting federal-style relationships between groups of cities in Etruria on the other; see also Edlund (1985) 'Man, nature and the Gods: a study of rural sanctuaries in Etruria and Magna Graecia from the seventh to the fourth century B.C.' On cereals in this context, Martin (1990) 'Greek goddesses and grain'. For religion and pastoralism, including rural sanctuaries (e.g. of St Michael), in a later period, Marino (1988) *Pastoral Economics in the Kingdom of Naples*, 40, cf. 44.

Festivals and fairs

For markets and fairs in the ancient world, see BE IX.7. For Scaptopara, Hallof (1994) 'Die Inschrift von Skaptopara: neue Dokumente und neue Lesungen'; also Herrmann (1990) *Hilferufe aus römischen Provinzen*. Much of the very eloquent evidence of the tenacity of the commercial and religious *panegyris* in the Greek world from ancient times through the Byzantine world and the Ottoman Empire to the present day is collected by Vryonis (1981) 'The *panegyris* of the Byzantine saint'. The shrine of St Thecla at Seleucia on the Calycadnus is one of the most conspicuous examples: Dagron (1978) *Vie et miracles de Ste Thècle*; see also Kazhdan and Constable (1982) *People and Power in Byzantium*, 236, and Kennedy (1985a) 'From *Polis* to

Madina: urban change in late Antique and early Islamic Syria', 24–5, also discussing the fair of St Sergius at Resafa. For the fair of Saint-Gilles, Wolff (1988) 'The French city of the Mediterranean Midi', 23–4. For a modern example of a *panegyris*, Campbell (1964) *Honour, Family and Patronage*, 115. See also Eickelman (1976) *Moroccan Islam: Tradition and Society in a Pilgrimage Center*, showing maraboutic notables acting as guarantors of the peace of the market.

The religion of the epiphenomenal town

Social anthropologists proclaim the importance of Mediterranean rural religion: Christian (1981a) *Local Religion in Sixteenth Century Spain* (compare the further development of the case for the importance of Spanish local cults in the same author's (1981b) *Apparitions in Late Medieval and Renaissance Spain*); on the need to turn aside from received notions of 'popular religion' in this context, McManners (1982) *Popular Religion in Seventeenth and Eighteenth Century France*. For Chittolini (1990) 'Civic religion and the countryside in late medieval Italy', religion expresses the links between city and its territory. Christian centres generated new settlements, not all of which flourished: for Theopolis in the Maritime Alps, Barnish (1989) 'The transformation of classical cities and the Pirenne debate', 389 n.36; on the complex settlement connected with the monastery of San Vincenzo al Volturno, Hodges (1997) *Light in the Dark Ages*. For *domuscultae* in the neighbourhood of Rome: Christie (1991) *Three South Etrurian Churches*, 356–9. Indian parallels: B. L. Smith and Reynolds (1987) *The City as a Sacred Centre: Essays on Six Asian Contexts*.

Haldon (1990) *Byzantium in the Seventh Century*, 117, dicusses the *panegyris* in the Byzantine city, perhaps overstating the stagnation of the remainder of the year. Ancient historians and archaeologists have turned increasingly to the village as an object of study. See for instance Calbi (1993) *Epigrafia del Villagio*. On the *kome*, Hansen and Raaflaub (1995) *Studies in the Ancient Greek Polis*, 45–81. The distribution of votive offerings in ancient Greece and Italy is briefly compared by Alcock (1993) *Graecia Capta*, 208–10. Corsaro (1983) 'Le forme di dipendenza nella *chora* del re e in quella cittadina dell'Asia Minore ellenistica', as discussed in VII.6, distinguishes the settlement patterns of temple-states in Anatolia from those of city territories. Comparative attention to the realities of religious practice in Mediterranean cities and villages in the Middle Ages, rather than church history on the grand scale, is badly needed. See however M. Rubin (1992) 'Religious culture in town and country'.

On a special case of religious continuities and revivals, Purcell (1992) 'The city of Rome'. The religion of the ancient city of Rome is helpfully discussed in Beard et al. (1998) *Religions of Rome*, 167–210; for the unexpected observance of Rome as a complex sacral space by its Jewish inhabitants too, di Segni (1990) 'Spazi sacri e spazi maledetti nella Roma ebraica'.

On the religious space of medieval Mediterranean cities: Seiber (1977) *The Urban Saint in Early Byzantine Social History*; C. Mango (1980) *Byzantium: The Empire of New Rome*, ch. 5. Dagron (1977) 'Le christianisme dans la ville byzantine', has a nuancé study of the place of religion in moulding the Byzantine city; for the West, Picard (1981) 'Conscience urbaine et culte des saints'; Picard (1986–9) *Topographie chrétienne des cités de la Gaule*; also Edwards (1982) *Christian Córdoba: The City and its Region in the Late Middle Ages*; and P. Brown (1981) *The Cult of the Saints*. See, however, the rather different views of Février (1974) 'Permanence et héritages de l'antiquité dans la topographie des villes de l'occident durant le haut moyen âge'; Krautheimer (1980) *Rome: Profile of a City*, or Vieillard (1942) *Recherches sur les origines de la Rome chrétienne*. For inscriptions as charms Hasluck (1914–16) 'Stone cults', 73–4; also C. Mango (1963) 'Antique statuary and the Byzantine beholder'.

4. THE RELIGION OF MOBILITY

The mysteries of Euploia

For the abstract Euploia, among the various pre-Christian protectors of seafarers, see Miranda (1989) 'Osservazioni sul culto di Euploia'; Purcell (1993) 'Continuity and change: the Mediterranean from Antiquity to the present'. We have drawn our illustrations of the cult from the lesser-known sites where inscriptions or graffiti attest the significance of the place to the geography of communications. For Prote in the Middle Ages: Balard (1974) 'Escales génoises sur les routes de l'Orient Méditerranéen au XIVe siècle'. The inscriptions of the typically remote seafarers' sanctuaries are published as follows: Syros: *IG*, XII/5.712.25–30; Prote: *IG*, V/1.1538–56, cf. Thucydides, *History*, 4.13.3; Aliki: *IG*, XII/8.581ff; Vieste: Russi (1989) 'La grotta con iscrizioni sull'isolotto del Faro di Vieste'; for Albanian Grammata, Hammond (1967) *Epirus*. Meinardus (1973) 'Testimonies to the economic vitality of Balat, the mediaeval Miletus', argues that even in much more mundane locations, ancient or medieval ship-graffiti are not casual, but record significant journeys such as pilgrimage or Hajj. Susini (1963–4) 'Supplemento epigrafico di Caso, Scarpanto, Saro, Calchi, Alinnia e Tilo', is a useful account of navigation-sanctuaries in relation to routes and landfalls in the southeast Aegean. It should be noted that the remoteness of the examples cited, in the Aegean and elsewhere, reflects in part the accidents of the evidence's survival. Such cults were important in the major nodes too, where their traces have often wholly disappeared.

The positive religious dimension of attitudes to the Mediterranean: Buxton (1994) *Imaginary Greece*, ch. 6, 'Landscape'. Malkin (1994) *Myth and Territory in the Spartan Mediterranean*, shows how concepts of space and territory could be shaped by myth and ritual.

A prehistoric case of the connection between cult and the geography of communications is presented by Stoddart et al. (1993) 'Cult in an island society: prehistoric Malta in the Tarxien period'.

For the religion of exchange: Laiou (1990) 'Händler und Kaufleute auf dem Jahrmarkt'; Laiou (1980) 'Saints and society in the Byzantine empire', 97–8, on monks' travels in the fourteenth century, and especially those of St Sabas; Malamut (1993) *Sur la route des saints byzantins*. St Julian of Rimini, *c*.961–73, is another good case of the commoditization of relics: Geary (1978) *Furta Sacra: Thefts of Relics in the Central Middle Ages*. Frugoni (1991) 'The city and the "new" saints', 73 and 81–2, has some cases of the religion of connectivity in the medieval Christian West. Note also Aasved (1996) 'The sirens and cargo cults', for another possible evocation in cult of the world of redistribution.

The imposition on the visible world of a supernatural template, and the formation of an alternative topography based on the points at which the hidden dimensions of cosmology – and above all the eschatological ones – impinge on the more directly experienced world, has been the object of excellent work by scholars studying medieval Christianity: see Gurevitch (1988) *Medieval Popular Culture: Problems of Belief and Perception*, 130–44; LeGoff (1984) 'The learned and popular dimensions of journeys in the Otherworld in the Middle Ages'. Cf. Gatto (1979) 'Le voyage au paradis: la christianisation des traditions folkloriques au moyen âge'; Boesch Gajano (1988) 'Agiografia e geografia nei dialoghi di Gregorio Magno', 209–20, on 'lo spazio come strumento e oggetto della santità'; Carozzi (1983) 'La géographic de l'au-delà et sa signification', and (1994) *Le voyage de l'âme dans l'au-delà d'après la littérature latine (Ve–XIII siècles)*; M. Himmelfarb (1983) *Tours of Hell*. For bridges as sacred spots, because of their strong eschatological significance, L. A. Holland (1961) *Janus and the Bridge*; Dinzelbacher (1990) 'Il ponte come luogo sacro nella realtà e nell'immaginario'. For navigation and cosmology, see for instance Dagron (1990a) 'Das Firmament soll christlich werden: zu zwei Seefahrtkalendern des 10. Jahrhunderts'; and note also Kosmas Indikopleustes's attempt to reclaim cosmology from pre-Christian knowledge by using systematic geography to prove that the earth was flat.

Material on this theme for the ancient world still awaits synthesis and interpretation. Meanwhile, cf. Gabba (1981) 'True history and false history'. On Delos and earthquakes, Traina (1989) 'Tracce di un'immagine: il terremoto fra prodigio e fenomeno', with VIII.2. Chirassi Colombo (1975) 'Acculturation et cultes thérapeutiques', sets the striking spread of healing cults in the later classical and Hellenistic and Roman periods in the context of incorporation into a steadily widening cultural *koine*. For Leuke, see Hedreen (1991) 'The cult of Achilles in the Euxine'.

Unconscious pilgrims

Medieval pilgrimage was formerly subjected to the rationalizing and politicizing approach which still dominated the study of much Anglophone historiography of the ancient world until the third quarter of the twentieth century. That approach was already rejected by Febvre (1925) *A Geographical Introduction to History*, 330–4.

The works of Turner and Turner (1978) *Image and Pilgrimage in Christian Culture*, and Turner (1974) *Dramas, Fields, and Metaphors*, remain fundamental. Eade and Sallnow (1991) *Contesting the Sacred*, reinstates the spatial element in understanding this social phenomenon and stresses the way that pilgrimage-geography involves imitations, duplications and hierarchies of lesser and greater centres: a sensible appraisal in Coleman and Elsner (1995) *Pilgrimage Past and Present*, 208. Archaeological evidence is evaluated in Graham-Campbell (1994) *The Archaeology of Pilgrimage*.

An instructive ethnography of Tenos, an insular pilgrimage site of paradoxical national centrality: Dubisch (1990) 'Pilgrimage and popular religion at a Greek holy shrine', (1995) *In a Different Place: Pilgrimage, Gender, and Politics at a Greek Island Shrine*.

Among a huge bibliography on medieval Christian pilgrimage, Sumption (1975) *Pilgrimage: An Image of Medieval Religion*, is a basic general account; see also R. Barber (1991) *Pilgrimages*; and Maraval (1985) *Lieux saints et pèlerinages d'Orient*. Bull (1993) *Knightly Piety and the Lay Response to the First Crusade*, 217, shows how high-profile pilgrimage was an epiphenomenon of ordinary and more local mobilities. Simek (1996) *Heaven and Earth in the Middle Ages*, 73–81, demonstrates the link between the geography of pilgrimage and the cosmic order. On holy cities, Haverkamp (1987) '"Heilige Städte" im hohen Mittelalter'.

For the origins of Christian pilgrimage, J. E. Taylor (1993) *Christians and the Holy Places*, 306–18. MacCormack (1990) '"Loca sancta": the organization of sacred topography in late Antiquity', is important for its treatment of the dimension of time. The geographical assumptions of early Christian pilgrim-literature are presented by Heim (1986) 'L'expérience mystique des pèlerins occidentaux'; Maraval (1984) 'Le temps du pèlerin', and Hunt (1982) *Holy Land Pilgrimage in the Later Roman Empire*.

For the classical precursors, Coleman and Elsner (1995) *Pilgrimage Past and Present: Sacred Travel and Sacred Space in the World Religions*, 10–29; Elsner (1997) 'Hagiographic geography'. Dillon (1997b) *Pilgrims and Pilgrimage in Ancient Greece*, takes for granted the existence of pilgrimage directly comparable to that of the Christian Middle Ages and offers no theoretical discussion. Much to be preferred is the trenchant account of Rutherford (1995) 'Theoric crisis:

the dangers of pilgrimage in Greek religion and society'. Wilken (1992) *A Land called Holy*, 101–8, presents a broad comparison between pagan, Jewish and Christian pilgrimage. The connection between the journeys of emperors and pilgrimage is explicitly made by Holum (1990) 'Hadrian and St Helena: imperial travel and the origins of Christian Holy Land pilgrimage'. For imperial mobility, a significant aspect of the nature of the Roman state, Hanfmann (1986) *Itinera Principum: Geschichte und Typologie der Kaiserreisen im Römischen Reich*; Millar (1977) *The Emperor in the Roman World*.

For the Islamic world, Eickelman and Piscatori (1990) *Muslim Travellers: Pilgrimage, Migration and the Religious Imagination*. Petersen (1994) 'The archaeology of the Syrian and Iraqi Hajj', argues against Crone (1987) *Meccan Trade and the Rise of Islam*, that there was a convergence of commercial and religious mobility in the medieval Hajj.

5. CONCLUSION: THE RELIGION OF BOUNDARY AND BELONGING

Competing centralities

The cult of St Besse is particularly apt for our purpose since it is not only a representative example of a landscape-based observance articulated on several different scales, but in addition the subject of the classic study by Hertz (BE to Section 1 above): Hertz (1913) 'Saint Besse, étude d'un culte alpestre'. Cf. Werbner (1977) *Regional Cults*, for the recognition of the importance of cults of intermediate scale. The evidence for the religious territory of Capua in the fourth century which we describe derives from an inscribed calendar: *CIL*, 10.3792 = *ILS*, 4918. Bowersock (1990) *Hellenism in Late Antiquity*, 1–3, takes the notice about the estate of the Daeira temple literally, but cf. Mitchell (1993) *Anatolia: Land, Men and Gods in Asia Minor*, 2.118, rightly stressing the oddity of this hegemonial claim and linking it to memory of the paraepiscopal structures which Maximin and Julian had tried to create (cf. 2.90–7).

The religion of economic neutrality

Further examples of the structures described in the text include the sacral guarantee which served Mycenaean palaces as centres of storage and redistribution: Kilian (1987) 'Zur Funktion der mykenischen Residenzen auf dem griechischen Festland'. For water and sacred neutrality, B. D. Shaw (1984a) 'Water and society in the ancient Maghrib: technology, property and development'. For *asylia*, Rigsby (1996) *Asylia: Territorial Inviolability in the Hellenistic World*; Sinn (1990) 'Das Heraion von Perachora: eine sakrale Schutzzone in der korinthischen Peraia'. Sinn (1996) 'The influence of Greek sanctuaries on the consolidation of economic power', an important contribution, develops the treatment of the economic significance of sacred neutrality at greater length. De Polignac (1984) *La naissance de la cité grecque*, (1994) 'Mediation, competition and sovereignty: the evolution of rural sanctuaries in Geometric Greece', on sanctuaries and boundaries.

The religion of Greek overseas settlement is the subject of Malkin (1987) *Religion and Colonization in Ancient Greece*; on the cult of Delian Apollo at Sicilian Naxos, see also Brugnone (1980) 'Annotazioni sull'Apollo Archegete di Nasso'.

Territories of grace?

See Tambiah (1990) *Magic, Science, Religion and the Scope of Rationality*, 106–7, on the Melanesian sense of participation in a mythic landscape; also Tambiah (1982) *Do Kamo: Person and Myth in a Melanesian Village*; and on the equivalent in Moroccan maraboutism, Crapanzano (1973) *The Hamadsha*; cf. Eck (1981) 'India's *tirthas*: crossings in sacred geography', on 'sacramental natural ontology'.

Mystic links with Zamzam as a popular belief, Dermenghem (1954) *Le culte des saints dans l'Islam maghrébin*, 144–5; compare the evocation of Mecca in the strange landscape of the Anatolian plateau discussed in Section 3. The creation of hadiths attributing to the Prophet a clairvoyant sense of the importance of various localities, especially in the Maghreb, is a further response to the need to disseminate religious focality beyond unique Holy Places: Goldziher (1971), *Muslim Studies*, 125. Hirsch (1995) 'Landscape: between place and space', has some helpful general orientations.

On cosmological centrality and the notion of the 'navel of the earth', Mueller (1961) *Die heilige Stadt: Roma quadrata, himmlisches Jerusalem und die Mythe vom Weltnabel*, cf. Downey (1961) *A History of Antioch in Syria*, 169–84, on the Antiochene *omphalos*; Scotoni (1992) 'L'Umbilicus Italiae secondo Varrone'; P. W. L. Walker (1990) *Holy City, Holy Places: Christian Attitudes to Jerusalem and the Holy Land in the Fourth Century*.

P. Brown (1995) *Authority and the Sacred*, 7–16, on the changes in the conception of the *mundus* with the arrival of widespread Christianity. Cf. Maraval (1984) 'Le temps du pèlerin'; Turner and Turner (1978) *Image and Pilgrimage*, 233, see pilgrimage as a complex of behaviour characteristic of the Holy Land which was deracinated by the expansion of Islam, and transferred to Christian Europe. For the Mediterranean as the vehicle of religious conflict, Burns (1980) 'Piracy as an Islamic–Christian interface in the thirteenth century'.

'MISTS OF TIME': ANTHROPOLOGY AND CONTINUITY

For general orientation and extensive bibliography on the social anthropology of the Mediterranean and its potential contribution to our themes of continuity, unity, and distinctiveness see above all the critical survey in J. Davis (1977) *People of the Mediterranean: An Essay in Comparative Social Anthropology*, entering a plea (as its title suggests) for more comparative work (to include cities) and also for a greater historical awareness. The review article of Gilmore (1982) 'Anthropology of the Mediterranean Area', expands Davis's bibliography, and discusses a wide range of themes and approaches (though see only 181, 188–9 on history). Still worth consulting are the brief surveys in Boissevain and Blok (1974) *Two Essays on Mediterranean Societies*. Kayser (1986) *Les sociétés rurales de la Méditerranée: un recueil de textes anthropologiques anglo-amercains*, remains a useful introductory anthology. For more recent ways in which the validity of Mediterranean social anthropology as a sub-division of the discipline has been contested, see Chapter XII.

On larger settlements than those that anthropologists have so often chosen to study, see Kenny and Kertzer (1983) *Urban Life in Mediterranean Europe: Anthropological Perspectives*, and Eickelman (1998) *The Middle East and Central Asia*, chs 5, 9. Among monographic instances of 'urban anthropology', see for example Wikan (1980) *Life Among the Poor in Cairo*; McDonogh (1986) *Good Families of Barcelona*; Hirschon (1989) *Heirs of the Greek Catastrophe: The Social Life of Asia Minor Refugees in Piraeus* (XII.5).

The history of anthropology in the Mediterranean, of considerable importance to an understanding of its contemporary character, has not yet been written in more than piecemeal fashion. Beginning in the 1950s, it is a story often told from a predominantly Anglophone viewpoint, with Pitt-Rivers and Campbell as protagonists (Gilmore (1982) 'Anthropology of the Mediterranean Area', 175). This gives too little weight to the older history of French and Spanish colonially based ethnography in North Africa, of the great nineteenth-century scholar-travellers such as Edward Lane, of twentieth-century figures active in the inter-war years such as Gerald Brenan, of the wider tradition maintained by southern European ethnographers (such as Julio Caro Baroja and Ernesto de Martino) working in their own countries, and (not least) of the pioneering monograph of Charlotte Gower Chapman, *Milocca: A Sicilian Village*, not published until 1973, but based on field work undertaken as early as 1928–9. See Eickelman (1998) *The Middle East and Central Asia*, ch. 2; J. Davis (1977) *People of the Mediterranean: An Essay in Comparative Social Anthropology*, 1–4; Driessen (1981) 'Anthropologists in Andalusia: the use of comparison and history', 452; Pina-Cabral and Campbell (1992) *Europe Observed*, chs 1, 9; Hauschild (1992) 'Making history in southern Italy', esp. 39 n.1. For a critical overview, emphasizing the artificiality of the Mediterranean as an area of speciality, and attempting (sometimes rather patronizingly, cf. 5 n.6) to bring out the assumptions and paradigms of the enterprise, Goddard et al. (1994) *The*

Anthropology of Europe, 4–23. See further the opening of Chapter XII below.

As for the various ecological approaches within anthropology, see II.5, VI.1–2.

1. SURVIVALS REVISITED

Braudel and his Romantic precursors: on the immunity to change of local economies in pre-1914 France see Braudel's (1988–90) *The Identity of France*, 2.496–500, citing E. Weber (1977) *Peasants into Frenchmen*. We return to that in Section 2 of the chapter and below; we note here a Romantic contemporary of Braudel, already named in BE II.1: Nahum Slouschz; Braudel as quoted in the chapter is anticipated by a year in passages like the following (quoted by Shavit (1988) 'The Mediterranean world and "Mediterraneanism"', 109):

> He who reads the Provençal poetry of Frédéric Mistral discovers that the main difference between his conception of nature and love of life and the majority of the Homeric idylls . . . is only one of time. The sounds, the perceptions, the sentiments are the same.

On the supposed resistance of an area within the Mediterranean region to changes attempted by colonial outsiders, the classic statement is perhaps Lampedusa's great novel, *The Leopard* (first published 1958). Before Braudel, the phrase 'mists of time' had been used by for instance Marc Bloch (1966) *French Rural History: An Essay on its Basic Characteristics*, 247.

The historical uses of anthropological data: it should be remembered first that late nineteenth- and early twentieth-century anthropology, thanks to its evolutionism, was firmly historically minded, and that earlier generations of historians this century have been quite accustomed to admit ethnography, for example that of Frazer or of Chadwick, to their library shelves (cf. C. N. L. Brooke (1989) *The Medieval Idea of Marriage*, 9 n.11). K. Thomas (1963) 'History and anthropology', is a fundamental plea for historians to use ethnography to help them visualize the past. Goodman (1997) 'History and anthropology', stresses the theoretical stimulation to be derived from history's opening up to anthropology, which he conceives as a 'gateway' discipline. Compare though the various warnings sounded by Finley (1987) 'Anthropology and the classics', and Golden (1992) 'The uses of cross-cultural comparison in ancient social history'. See also BE VI.1. More recent statements by historians include brief but incisive essays in the *Journal of Interdisciplinary History* 12 (1981) 227–78 ('Anthropology and history in the 1980s'). But compare the limited space felt to be needed for anthropological reference in Burke (1991) *New Perspectives on Historical Writing*; see G. Levi's contribution, 'On microhistory', 98–105.

2. BALANCED ARCADIAS

Anthropologists' changing attitudes to history: for some context, Evans-Pritchard (1981) *A History of Anthropological Thought*.

A chronologically arranged sample of general discussions of the disciplines' past and prospective interactions, mostly from an anthropological perspective: Schapera (1962) 'Should anthropologists be historians?'; I. M. Lewis (1968) *History and Social Anthropology*; J. Davis (1980) 'Social anthropology and the consumption of history' (review article); Driessen (1981) 'Anthropologists in Andalusia: the use of comparison and history'; M. Sahlins (1983) 'Other times, other customs: the anthropology of history'; Lévi-Strauss (1983) 'Histoire et ethnologie'; Kertzer (1984) 'Anthropology and family history'; Rutman (1986) 'History and anthropology: Clio's dalliances'; Silverman (1986) 'Anthropology and history: understanding the boundaries'; B. S. Cohn (1988) *An Anthropologist among the Historians and Other Essays*, chs 1–3; Tonkin et al. (1989) *History and Ethnicity*; Geertz (1990) 'History and anthropology'; Hastrup (1992) *Other Histories*. The thematically organized issues of the journal *History and Anthropology* (1984–) are well worth pursuing.

On a more extended scale, N. Thomas (1989) *Out of Time: History and Evolution in Anthropological Discourse*, discusses Radcliffe-Brown's view of history in ch. 2, and the subtle exclusion of history from ethnography even by some (e.g. Geertz) who profess to be open to it. Cf. also Fabian (1983) *Time and the Other: How Anthropology Makes its Object*.

It is notable how much space is given to discussion of history in a volume concerned with the theory and the problems of anthropological field work in (mostly) Mediterranean settings: Pina-Cabral and Campbell (1992) *Europe Observed*; see esp. chs. 4, 5, 6, 10.

For an understanding of Levi's perception of Gagliano, some attention to the economic history of the area, and indeed to the whole 'southern question', is obviously important: see among numerous discussions S. R. Epstein (1992) *An Island for Itself: Economic Development and Social Change in Late Medieval Sicily*, exonerating his own period and blaming the early modern one for the differences between north and south; Chubb (1982) *Patronage, Power, and Poverty in Southern Italy: A Tale of Two Cities*, 14–18, for a useful brief survey; Marino (1988) *Pastoral Economics in the Kingdom of Naples*; Mantelli (1985) 'Industrialization in southern Italy before and after unification'. The full economic context can be derived from Zamagni (1993) *The Economic History of Italy 1860–1990*, esp. ch. 8 for the Fascist agricultural policies that are essential to an understanding of the world that Levi depicts. On Levi himself there is a substantial literature, as well as a Foundation bearing his name. See e.g. King and Killingbeck (1989) 'Carlo Levi, the mezzogiorno and emigration', for further references and a comparison between emigration patterns in Levi's time and those of post-war decades; the authors perhaps tend, however, to overestimate Gagliano's isolation, even in the Fascist period.

The modern Mediterranean: see references in BE I.3, on strategic thought and economics; general references on urbanization given in BE IV.1 are also relevant.

What follows are some additional discussions – a list that makes no claim to be representative: E. C. Clark (1974) 'The Ottoman industrial revolution'; Black and Brown (1992) *Modernization in the Middle East: The Ottoman Empire and its Afro-Asian Successors*; Girgis (1987) *Mediterranean Africa*; Valensi (1985) *Tunisian Peasants in the Eighteenth and Nineteenth Centuries*; Lewis and Hudson (1985) *Uneven Development in Southern Europe: Studies of Accumulation, Class, Migration and the State*; Pridham (1984) *The New Mediterranean Democracies: Regime Transition in Spain, Greece and Portugal*; Payne (1986) 'The concept of "southern Europe" and political development'; Medeiros (1988) 'Espaces ruraux et dynamiques sociales en Europe du sud'; Van Nieuwenhuijze (1972) *Emigration and Agriculture in the Mediterranean Basin*; Leontidou (1990) *The Mediterranean City in Transition: Social*

Change and Urban Development, actually a study of Athens, 1948–81; Tortella (1994) 'Patterns of economic retardation and recovery in south-western Europe in the nineteenth and twentieth centuries'; Alpher (1986) *Nationalism and Modernity: a Mediterranean Perspective*. Argyrou (1996) *Tradition and Modernity in the Mediterranean*, actually a study of the symbolism of weddings, makes the important point that talk of modernity can be a means of justifying social behaviour (a 'legitimizing discourse'), and must thus be part of the ethnographer's (and historian's) field of study and not just a category imposed on that field from the outside.

On general theories of economic and social modernization see: Eisenstadt (1987) *Patterns of Modernity*; Tipps (1973) 'Modernization theory and the comparative study of societies: a critical perspective'; Roxborough (1988) 'Modernization theory revisited' (review article).

Modernization theory as applied to the Mediterranean: Schneider et al. (1972) 'Modernization and development: the role of regional elites and noncorporate groups in the European Mediterranean', with the response of Pi-Sunyer (1974) 'Elites and noncorporate groups in the European Mediterranean: a reconsideration of the Catalan case'. For some anthropological studies of modernizing communities, see below under Section 3.

Development and dependency theory and the Mediterranean: see for example Arrighi (1985) *Semiperipheral development: The Politics of Southern Europe in the Twentieth Century*.

The cautionary example of rural France: E. Weber (1977) *Peasants into Frenchmen: The Modernization of Rural France 1870–1914*, now needs to be read in the light of the following. First, some reviews and review articles: Goldsmith (1979) 'The agrarian history of pre-industrial France: where do we go from here?'; Berenson (1979) 'The modernization of rural France'; Margadant (1984) 'Tradition and modernity in rural France during the nineteenth century', esp. 679–81. Relevant monographs include Price (1983) *The Modernization of Rural France: Communications Networks and Agricultural Market Structures in Nineteenth-Century France*, giving more weight to continuities across the century than its title would suggest. McPhee

(1992) *A Social History of France 1780–1880*, esp. 221–2 on Weber, is a useful survey. For the preceding period, P. T. Hoffman (1996) *Growth in a Traditional Society: The French Countryside, 1450–1815*. For the cultural context of seemingly archaic magical beliefs and practices, add Devlin (1987) *The Superstitious Mind: French Peasants and the Supernatural in the Nineteenth Century*, to the ethnography mentioned in Chapter X. It is worth including here, to distinguish our own approach more fully, some examples of the kinds of continuity that we have *not* been looking for. Most to be avoided is the simple juxtaposition of ancient and very modern evidence, with the presumption of some sort of continuity between them, as in Walcot (1970) *Greek Peasants Ancient and Modern: A Comparison of Social and Moral Values*, who like Braudel envisages groups essentially uncontaminated by the civilizations of Christianity or Islam that have preserved very old values. (For a more subtle blending of ancient and ethnographic evidences on related matters cf. Millett (1984) 'Hesiod and his world'.) Walcot's strategy is replicated by D. Morris (1977) *Manwatching*, 53–5, 68–9, on gestures (the head toss and the chin flick) whose regional specificity is thought to be traceable back to ancient Greek colonization. Golden (1992) 'The uses of cross-cultural comparison in ancient social history', already cited here, is salutary. Further, BE X.1.

Also to be avoided are the bland geographical generalizations of the 'culture area' approach, which claims to identify regions bounded by natural frontiers that retain their character (loosely defined) despite changes of technology or inhabitant: see classically Kroeber (1939) *Cultural and Natural Areas of Native North America*. Cf. Patai (1952) 'The Middle East as a culture area', and Magnarella (1992) 'Conceptualizing the circum-Mediterranean for purposes of social scientific research', for an insufficiently critical review of Mediterranean applications of the approach.

What we need are many more instances of practices or beliefs whose slowly evolving (let us say, rather than 'unchanging') profile can be documented over a substantial period – instances such as those provided by Alexiou's (1974) *The Ritual Lament in Greek Tradition*, ranging from the Homeric world to what she perhaps unfortunately calls 'modern survivals' (X.1); or by the study reported in

J. Davis (1977) *People of the Mediterranean*, 251–2: Levy (1956) 'Property distribution by lot in present day Greece', which custom *may* have a history going back two millennia.

3. THE PRESENCE OF THE PAST

In addition to the works cited and discussed in the text, see J. Davis (1977) *People of the Mediterranean*, ch. 2, on the economy, for some further references.

Some examples of ethnographic studies of modernization in small communities – on which a more extensive discussion might well have drawn: Bourdieu (1979) *Algeria 1960*; Miller (1984) *Imlil: A Moroccan Mountain Community in Change*; J. Davis (1973) *Land and Family in Pisticci*, ch. 9; Galt (1991b) *Far from the Church Bells: Settlement and Society in an Apulian Town*; Barrett (1974) *Benabarre: The Modernization of a Spanish Village*; S. H. Brandes (1975) *Migration, Kinship and Community: Tradition and Transition in a Spanish Village*.

The Alps are one area, from the extreme boundary of the Mediterranean region, in which the conjunction of ethnography and demographic history has been particularly fruitful, and we shall need to return to it (in Volume 2) in our general discussion of Mediterranean demography. We have already in BE I.3 had occasion to refer to Cole and Wolf (1974) *The Hidden Frontier: Ecology and Ethnicity in an Alpine Valley*, which effectively challenges the possibility of an ecological explanation of differences between the two sides of a quite distinctive cultural frontier in the South Tyrol that, rather, substantially reflects the political geography of early medieval colonizing. Netting (1981) *Balancing on an Alp: Ecological Change and Continuity in a Swiss Mountain Community*, by contrast, seems to admit a far greater degree of environmental determinism in its characterization of life in Törbel, a village in the Swiss canton of Valais. The whole field is set in historical and environmental context by Viazzo (1989) *Upland Communities*, on which we have also drawn already, in III.6.

The works of Michael Herzfeld offer an arresting variety of insights in an area, which it should be noted, is not quite the same as ours here: that is, modern Mediterranean inhabitants' own various and often competing senses of their history, as reflected in ideology, lore and symbolism: see his (1985) *The Poetics of Manhood: Contest and Identity in a Cretan Mountain Village*, and (1991) *A Place in History: Social and Monumental Time in a Cretan Town*. Hastrup (1992) *Other Histories*, also contains a number of contributions pertinent to this theme of 'ethnohistory'.

The France of S. C. Rogers (1991) *Shaping Modern Times in Rural France: The Transformation and Reproduction of an Aveyronnais Community*: for wider context see Moulin (1991) *Peasantry and Society in France since 1789*, chs. 4 ('Towards a separate world: 1914–50') and 5 ('A spectacular transformation: 1950 to the present'). Note 162: 'the structures of material life [in the 1950s]

appeared timeless.' On the theory and distribution of the stem family, see Wall (1983) 'Introduction', 18–28 on Le Play, and Verdon (1979) 'The stem family: towards a general theory'. Collomp's studies of families in Haute-Provence also form part of the context of Rogers's work; see esp. his 1983 monograph, *La maison du père: famille et village en Haute-Provence aux XVIIe et XVIIIe siècles*. It should be noted, too, that industrialization of a different kind, in an earlier period, and outside the Mediterranean, has been interpreted as reinvigorating the stem family: M. Anderson (1971) *Family Structure in Nineteenth-Century Lancashire*. On Le Play generally see M. Z. Brooke (1970) *Le Play: Engineer and Social Scientist*.

'I ALSO HAVE A MOUSTACHE': ANTHROPOLOGY AND MEDITERRANEAN UNITY

1. GRANDS FAITS MÉDITERRANÉENS?

For discussions of the unity of the Mediterranean area other than those cited in the chapter, see Boissevain (1974) 'Uniformity and diversity in the Mediterranean: an essay in interpretation', and Boissevain (1979) 'Towards a social anthropology of the Mediterranean'. A sample of the least plausible accounts of cultural stereotypes: Pitkin (1963) 'Mediterranean Europe'; Quigley (1973) 'Mexican national character and circum-Mediterranean personality structure'; and Gaines and Farmer (1986) 'Visible saints: social cynosures and dysphoria in the Mediterranean tradition'.

The attack on 'Mediterraneanism': other writings by Herzfeld, besides his (1987b) *Anthropology through the Looking-Glass*, remain highly pertinent: (1980) 'Honour and shame: problems in the comparative analysis of moral systems', (1984) 'The horns of the Mediterraneanist dilemma'. See further Fernandez (1983) 'Consciousness and class in southern Spain'; Sant Cassia (1991) 'Authors in search of a character: personhood, agency and identity in the Mediterranean'; Goddard et al. (1994) *The Anthropology of Europe*, chs. 1, 3.

On the 'culture area' approach referred to, see also BE XI.2, and the stringent comments of Pina-Cabral (1989) 'The Mediterranean as a category of regional comparison: a critical view'.

On the difficulties, conceptual and practical, of Mediterranean field work, see J. Davis (1977) *People of the Mediterranean*, 6–7; Just (1978) 'Some problems for Mediterranean anthropology'; Llobera (1986) 'Fieldwork in southwestern Europe: anthropological panacea or epistemological straitjacket?'; and Pina-Cabral (1992b) 'Against translation: the role of the researcher in the production of ethnographic knowledge', 3–10.

On the history of anthropology in the Mediterranean, to which we advert in the chapter's introduction, see the opening of BE XI.

2. MEDITERRANEAN VALUES?

The indispensable starting point for both the history and the ethnography of honour codes remains: Peristiany (ed.) (1965) *Honour and Shame: The Values of Mediterranean Society*. This collection is not superseded by Gilmore (1987) *Honor and Shame and the Unity of the Mediterranean*, which naturally has a more up-to-date set of references but is surprisingly unsystematic in its coverage and avoids sustained extra-Mediterranean comparisons. Nor are the other volumes referred to in Section 2 of the chapter effective substitutes. Entry into the ample bibliography on this subject is, however, well provided in their footnotes; below, therefore, we offer amplification on only a few topics, nearly all the works that we have found essential being cited in our text. Eickelman (1998) *The Middle East*, 195–9, is a disappointingly brief conspectus.

3–4. HONOUR AND SHAME I–II

On J. K. Campbell and the ethnography of modern Greece: see also Campbell (1983)

'Traditional values and continuities in Greek society', (1965) 'Honour and the devil', in some respects a digest of (1964) *Honour, Family, and Patronage*, and (1992) 'Fieldwork among the Sarakatsani, 1954–55'.

L. Abu-Lughod's formal ethnography, (1986) *Veiled Sentiments*, can be supplemented by her deliberately less analytical (1993) *Writing Women's Worlds: Bedouin Stories*, ch. 5. (On the post-modern turn that such an approach represents, see Lindholm (1995) 'The new Middle Eastern ethnography'.) See also Eickelman (1998) *The Middle East*, 241–5, for a summary of *Veiled Sentiments*.

Familism, moral and amoral: we allude to Banfield (1958) *The Moral Basis of a Backward Society*, a noted but now uncreditworthy ethnographic account of the supposedly family-centred ethos and lack of wider forms of association or co-operation in southern Italian society: in a phrase, of *amoral familism*. See the critical discussions by J. Davis (1970b) 'Morals and backwardness', and du Boulay and Williams (1987) 'Amoral familism and the image of limited good'.

6. PATTERN AND DEPTH

Some pertinent reports not discussed in the text: Antoun (1968) 'On the modesty of women in Arab Muslim villages: a study in the accommodation of traditions', on the parallels and differences between local custom and Koranic ethics in a village in Jordan, with a concluding attempt to sketch the logic of the beliefs underlying the seclusion of women and the centrality of that seclusion to male honour. The case histories in this account do not seem to us to be invalidated by the philological 'Reply' to the paper from N. M. Abu Zahra (1970); cf. Antoun's rejoinder (1970) to that 'Reply'. See further Kressel (1992) 'Shame and gender', comparing gender segregation, and its accommodation of the need for female labour, among bedouin in both Ramla, Israel, and the Negev Highlands. For North Africa we have also profited from the brief discussion in Rosen (1984) *Bargaining for Reality*, 66–7, and from MacLeod (1991) *Accommodating Protest: Working Women, the New Veiling, and Change in Cairo*, on the perceived vulnerability of family honour to the public exposure of lower-middle-class working women; for Greece, from Friedl's classic ethnography of a village (1962) *Vasilika*, 85–

7; from Pitkin's evocative, though perhaps sentimental (1985) *The House that Giacomo Built: History of an Italian Family, 1898–1978*, in which shame is a recurrent and powerful theme. Also: Boissevain (1969) *Hal-Farrug: A Village in Malta*, discussing reputation and fame/face; Lisón Arcal (1986) *Cultura e identitad en la provincia de Huesca: una perspectiva desde la antropología social*, 111–54; Gilsenan (1996) *Lords of the Lebanese Marches*. On a wider front, for the role of dishonour in the initiation and prosecution of feud or vendetta, as well as some valuable ethnography of Albania, Black-Michaud (1975) *Cohesive Force*, esp. ch. 4; compare also Makris (1992) 'Ethnography, history and collective representations: studying vendetta in Crete', and the substantial historical monograph of S. Wilson (1988) *Feuding, Conflict and Banditry in Nineteenth-Century Corsica*, ch. 4.

7. DISTINCTIVENESS

The decline of honour in modern Western society: the classic discussion, giving some weight to diminishing sensitivity to, and legal redress against, insult, is Berger (1970) 'On the obsolescence of the concept of honour', which reappears, slightly modified, in Berger, Berger and Kellner (1973) *The Homeless Mind*, 83–96; yet Berger redescribes rather than explains. Pitt-Rivers (1991) 'La maladie de l'honneur', essays the bold argument that, in the modern Western world, honour is not so much obsolete as camouflaged, cf. his encyclopedia article, *IESS*, 'Honor', 510.

Whereas there is little to mention here concerning honour, shame has been more copiously – though perhaps not better – served. See among a large socio-psychological literature Kaufman (1989) *The Psychology of Shame*; Braithwaite (1989) *Crime, Shame and Reintegration*. Philosophers too have been attracted: G. Taylor (1985) *Pride, Shame and Guilt*; Casey (1990) *Pagan Virtue*, 83–99; B. Williams (1993) *Shame and Necessity*, ch. 4.

Extra-Mediterranean comparisons in other directions: Gilmore (1990) *Manhood in the Making: Cultural Concepts of Masculinity*, offers what might have been an extremely illuminating comparison between circum-Mediterranean ideas of honour (ch. 2) and concepts of personal worth elsewhwere (e.g. 73–4 on Micronesia, 131–2 on East Africa);

but the analysis is conducted at too great a level of generality, and is too uncritical of its source material, to yield helpful results.

The Portuguese direction: Pina-Cabral (1986) *Sons of Adam, Daughters of Eve: The Peasant Worldview of the Alto Minho*, 155–6, on respect and prestige. Cutileiro (1971) *A Portuguese Rural Society*, a study of six settlements in south-eastern (Mediterranean) Portugal close to the Spanish border (ch. 8 on the potential threat posed by a wife to her husband's honour, ch. 13 on the relentlessness of neighbourhood scrutiny and on shame). Brettell (1986) *Men who Migrate, Women who Wait: Population and History in a Portuguese Parish*, esp. 213 on the absence of effective local preoccupation with honour or shame.

On the, in some respects, apparently quasi-Mediterranean value of honour among a tribe of the Durrani Pashtuns of north-central – Afghan – Turkestan in the early 1970s (before the Soviet invasion) see Tapper (1991) *Bartered Brides: Politics, Gender and Marriage in an Afghan Tribal Society*, 103–7, and ch. 10.

Non-Mediterranean Middle Eastern honour: Kocturk (1992) *A Matter of Honour: Experiences of Turkish Women Immigrants* (note 127: 'honour is all we have'). The Arabian peninsula: the best and fullest ethnography is Dresch (1989) *Tribes, Government, and History in Yemen*, esp. chs 2, 3, with a welcome explicitness about how and when the terms variously corresponding to honour and shame are used in actual conversation. See also 70 n.5, 72 n.18, for some helpful comparisons across the remainder of the Middle East and the Mediterranean. Bruck (1996) 'Being worthy of protection: the dialectics of gender attributes in Yemen', brings an unusual perspective to discussions of gender and honour: the quasi-feminine moral standing of groups of men such as the handicapped and the service classes.

The direction of the Sudan: Boddy (1989) *Wombs and Alien Spirits: Women, Men, and the 'Zâr' Cult in Northern Sudan*, 53; Nordenstam (1968) *Sudanese Ethics*, ch. 8; Barclay (1964) *Buurri al Lamaab: A Suburban Village in the Sudan*, 51–4, on offences against family honour, arising for the most part from the behaviour of women. Contrast the far more relaxed gender ideals and sexual mores described in Hallpike (1972) *The Konso of Ethiopia: A Study of the Values of a Cushitic People* (for example 150–3).

The Far East: Hu (1944) 'The Chinese concept of face', analyses the components of prestige – *mien-tzu* (success/ostentation) and *lien* (integrity/decency) – in ways that may remind us of some Mediterranean accounts. A. L. Epstein (1984) *The Experience of Shame in Melanesia*.

9. History

A concern for the history of honour was manifest right from the beginning of its ethnography (cf. XI.1 for the different fate of other topics within the social anthropology of the Mediterranean).

To look first at the main volumes of essays: see the contribution of Caro Baroja to the 1965 Peristiany collection, 'Honour and shame: a historical account of several conflicts'; and the historico-philosophical discussions of Pitt-Rivers: (1968) 'Honor', (1977) *The Fate of Shechem*, ch. 1, (1997) 'Honour'. The historical dimension is prominent again in Gautheron (1991) *L'honneur*; in Peristiany and Pitt-Rivers (1992) *Honor and Grace*; and, above all, in Fiume (1989) *Onore e storia nelle società mediterranee*.

Only occasionally, however, have anthropologists of honour brought history into fruitful relation with field work. We have reviewed some of the failures and the modest successes in Section 8. Apart from Schneider and Schneider (1976) *Culture and Political Economy in Western Sicily*, the only monograph to include much more than pseudo-historical speculation is one to whose excellence we drew attention in the preceding chapter: Lisón-Tolosana (1966) *Belmonte de los Caballeros* – see 331–2, reaching back to an archiepiscopal visitation of 1690.

The historical account of honour that emerges from such work is inevitably patchy, interrupted. There has been no adequate survey of the history (or even the historiography) of honour from either an anthropological or an historical point of view. Serious analytic study has on the whole been either *literary* or *juristic*. The focus of literary study has been Renaissance and Baroque drama (especially that of Spain); the most significant juristic accounts have come from German scholars. An *historical* treatment has been promised by Mervyn James, author of the exemplary and influential (1978) *English Politics and the Concept of Honour, 1485–1642*; there is apparently no interim conspectus. (See, however,

O. Patterson (1982) *Slavery and Social Death*, 79–97, for a wide-ranging comparative essay on the honour of slave-owning.) The closest that we have to a history of honour from the hand of an anthropologist is F. H. Stewart (1994) *Honor*. The history there invoked is, however, incidental to the book's main comparative and analytic thrust and has to be sought out. See esp. 55–8, 67–8, on Roman honour, Appendix 2 on medieval Iceland, and 34–46 for a sketch of a broad evolution from a medieval 'exterior' definition of the term – as reputation – to a more interiorized Renaissance sense – of honour as virtue. We could not wholly endorse that sketch, in part for the reason set out in the chapter – the rough continuity of *non*-aristocratic honour in much of Mediterranean history – and in part because the sketch derives from unreliable historical accounts, as well as from literary evidence whose bearing on 'real life' is inevitably obscure. Stewart's account is pioneering and admirable none the less. It also provides such a full list of the juristic, the literary, and the (relatively meagre) historical corpus of studies that we may be dispensed from repeating any of it here. We can merely supplement that bibliography with some references to historical works that we have found helpful and that are not already cited in our chapter; they begin to counteract Stewart's unavoidable leaning towards legal and literary sources, and the value systems that they describe may have exerted some influence on non-aristocratic traditions (though we cannot possibly be precise about when or how).

Classical Antiquity – Greece: N. R. Fisher (1992) *Hybris: A Study in the Values of Honour and Shame in Ancient Greece*. Walcot (1970) *Greek Peasants Ancient and Modern*, makes too much of similarities between ancient and ethnographic evidence (XI.2). Cf. D. Cohen (1991a) *Law, Sexuality, and Society: The Enforcement of Morals in Classical Athens*, and Cohen (1995) *Law, Violence and Community in Classical Athens*, in both of which ethnographic parallels sometimes loom so large as nearly to obliterate the ancient evidence about honour. Cohen has his critics, although even among some of them, it is encouraging to find, honour and shame are prominent, if under modified definitions: cf. Hindley and Cohen (1991) 'Debate: law, society and homosexuality in classical Athens'. Contrast Golden (1992) 'The uses of cross-cultural comparison in ancient social history';

Herman (1996) 'Ancient Athens and the values of Mediterranean society', exaggerating the incompatibility of a sense of honour and resort to law courts, as early modern examples (listed below) demonstrate.

Rome: MacMullen (1980) 'Roman elite motivation: three questions'; Cohen (1991b) 'The Augustan law on adultery: the social and cultural context'; Saller (1994) *Patriarchy, Property and Death in the Roman Family*, esp. 93–4, 134–53, bringing out the way in which the sense of honour can be *interpreted* as central to relations within the Roman household, even if the Latin vocabulary of it remains variable or unclear. Lendon (1997) *Empire of Honour: The Art of Government in the Roman World*, tries to explain too much in terms of his subject.

From late Antiquity, the most tantalizing piece of evidence is the edict issued in 326 by the Emperor Constantine (*Theodosian Code*, 9.24.1) prescribing the direst punishments for those involved in bride theft or abduction marriage, including the abducted girl herself and her parents if they later acquiesce in her marriage to the abductor. This law has been very satisfyingly interpreted by Evans-Grubbs (1989) 'Abduction marriage in Antiquity', in terms of the concern for family honour revealed by modern ethnographic accounts of bride theft. On later abduction marriages, see further Laiou (1993) 'Sex, consent, and coercion in Byzantium'. For late Antiquity generally, see also the occasional references to honour in B. D. Shaw (1987) 'The family in late Antiquity: the experience of Augustine'.

For an implausible application of the standard literature of Mediterranean honour to the world implied in the Gospels, see Esler (1994) *The First Christians in their Social Worlds*, 25–9.

For honour in Jewish, especially Talmudic, thought, see *EJ*, 'Honor'.

For Byzantium, the only noteworthy studies are Dagron (1990b) 'L'homme sans honneur ou le saint scandaleux', on the supposed decline of honour in Byzantium; and Magdalino (1989) 'Honour among Romaioi: the framework of social values in the world of Digenes Akrites and Kekaumenos' – although there are also a number of incidental references to honour and shame in Laiou (1993) 'Sex, consent, and coercion in Byzantium'. Not only the evidence cited by Magdalino and Laiou, but his own material too, seem to refute

Dagron's assertion that there is no continuity in this respect between Antiquity and the middle Byzantine period. Dagron concentrates on the deliberately dishonourable behaviour of holy fools and the castigation of vainglory in Byzantine ecclesiatical thought; and these both might attest the persistence, not the decline, of some notion of honour.

The medieval West: two studies of the evolution of knightly values – Jaeger (1985) *The Origins of Courtliness: Civilizing Trends and the Formation of Courtly Ideals, 939–1210*; and, giving far more attention to honour, Scaglione (1991) *Knights at Court: Courtliness, Chivalry and Courtesy from Ottonian Germany to the Italian Renaissance*. Dillard (1984) *Daughters of the Reconquest: Women in Castilian Town Society, 1100–1300*, esp. chs. 7–8.

Cantarella (1991) 'Homicides of honor: the development of Italian adultery law over two millennia', sets out, perhaps too ambitiously, 'to demonstrate the survival of an ideology [of family honour] that remained unchanged through the centuries in spite of political vicissitudes and social and economic change' (236) by means of an analysis of the Roman law tradition in late Antiquity, the Renaissance and more recent times. *Unchanged* is surely too strong an epithet.

On medieval Iceland, add to the references given by F. H. Stewart (1994) *Honor*, Appendix 2, Hastrup (1985) *Culture and History in Medieval Iceland*.

On Renaissance Florence: Klapisch-Zuber (1986) 'Women servants in Florence during the fourteenth and fifteenth centuries'; Kuehn (1991) *Law, Family, and Women: Toward a Legal Anthropology of Renaissance Italy*, ch. 4: 'Honor and conflict in a fifteenth-century Florentine family'.

Some suggestive accounts, primarily dealing with periods later than our main focus: Wiesner (1993) *Women and Gender in Early Modern Europe*, stressing throughout the interdependence of female labour opportunities and conceptions of male honour. For the English comparison, besides references in the text see also Mendelson and Crawford (1998) *Women in Early Modern England*, ch. 12; Neuschel (1989) *Word of Honor: Interpreting Noble Culture in Sixteenth-Century France*; Kiernan (1988) *The Duel in European History: Honour and the Reign of Aristocracy*, and Nye (1993) *Masculinity and Male Codes of Honor in Modern France*, two useful syntheses each with a broad sociological dimension; see also Reddy (1997) *The Invisible Code: Honor and Sentiment in Postrevolutionary France 1814–1848*. Kertzer (1993) *Sacrificed for Honor: Italian Infant Abandonment and the Politics of Reproductive Control*, concerns the forcible removal by priests, midwives, and police (all obsessed with female honour) of babies born to single mothers in nineteenth-century Italy. Note too Dinges (1989) 'Die Ehre als Thema der Stadtgeschichte: eine Semantik im Übergang vom Ancien Régime zur Moderne'.

CONSOLIDATED BIBLIOGRAPHY

Aasved, M. J. (1996) 'The sirens and cargo cults', *CW* 89, 383–92.

Abadie-Reynal, C. (1989) 'Céramique et commerce dans le bassin égéen du IVe au VIIe siècle', in *Hommes et richesses*, 143–59.

Abou-Zaid, A. M. (1963) 'Migrant labour and social structure in Kharga Oasis', in Pitt-Rivers, 41–53.

Abrams, P. (1978) 'Towns and economic growth: some theories and problems', in Abrams and Wrigley, 9–33.

Abrams, P. and Wrigley, E. A. (eds) (1978) *Towns in Societies: Essays in Economic History and Historical Sociology*, Cambridge.

Abu Zahra, N. (1982) *Sidi Ameur: A Tunisian Village*, London.

Abu Zahra, N. (1970) 'On the modesty of women in Arab Muslim villages: a reply', *AmAnth* 72, 1079–88.

Abulafia, D. (1977) *The Two Italies: Economic Relations between the Norman Kingdom of Sicily and the Northern Communes*, Cambridge.

Abulafia, D. (1981) 'Southern Italy and the Florentine economy, 1265–1370', *EcHR* 33, 377–88.

Abulafia, D. (1983a) 'Sul commercio del grano siciliano nel tardo Duecento', in *La società mediterranea all'epoca del Vespro . . . XI Congresso di storia della Corona d'Aragona*, vol. 2: *Communicazioni*, Palermo, 5–22.

Abulafia, D. (1983b) 'The Crown and the economy under Roger II and his successors', *DOP* 37, 1–14.

Abulafia, D. (1985a) 'The Norman kingdom of Africa and the Norman expeditions to Majorca and the Muslim Mediterranean', in R. Allen Brown (ed.) *Anglo-Norman Studies VII*, Woodbridge, 26–49.

Abulafia, D. (1985b) 'The Pisan *bacini* and the medieval Mediterranean economy: a historian's viewpoint', in Malone and Stoddart, 287–302.

Abulafia, D. (1987) 'Asia, Africa and the trade of medieval Europe', in Postan and Miller, 402–73, 905–11.

Abulafia, D. (1991) 'The problem of the Kingdom of Majorca (1229/76–1343) 2: economic identity', *MHR* 6, 35–61.

Abulafia, D. (1994) *A Mediterranean Emporium: The Catalan Kingdom of Majorca*, Cambridge.

Abu-Lughod, J. L. (1969) 'Varieties of urban experience: contrast, coexistence and coalescence in Cairo', in I. M. Lapidus (ed.) *Middle Eastern Cities*, Berkeley, 159–87.

Abu-Lughod, J. L. (1987) 'The Islamic city: historic myth, Islamic essence, and contemporary relevance', *IJMES* 19, 155–76.

Abu-Lughod, J. L. (1989) *Before European Hegemony: The World System A.D. 1250–1350*, New York and Oxford.

Abu-Lughod, L. (1986) *Veiled Sentiments: Honor and Poetry in a Bedouin Society*, Berkeley, Los Angeles and London.

Abu-Lughod, L. (1993) *Writing Women's Worlds: Bedouin Stories*, Berkeley, Los Angeles, and Oxford.

Acheson, J. M. (1981) 'Anthropology of fishing', *ARA* 10, 273–316.

Acheson, P. E. (1997) 'Does the economic explanation work? Settlement, agriculture and erosion in the territory of Halieis in the late Classical and early Hellenistic period', *JMA* 10, 165–90.

Adam, P. (1976) 'Conclusions sur les développements des techniques nautiques médiévales', *RHES* 54, 560–7.

Adam, P. (1987) 'Poissons, marins, pauvres, et démographie: problèmes de méthode démographique', in Dubois, Hocquet and Vauchez, 2.243–50.

Adams, R. McC. (1974) 'Historic patterns of Mesopotamian irrigation agriculture', in Downing and Gibson, 1–6.

Adams, R. S. and McNeill, W. H. (1978) *Human Migration: Patterns and Policies*, Bloomington.

Adas, M. (1989) *Machines as the Measure of Man*, Ithaca.

Adroher, A. M., Pons, A., Brun, E. and Ruiz de Arbulo, J. (1993) 'El yacimiento de Mas Castellar de Pontós y el comercio del cereal ibérico en la zona de *Emporion* y *Rhode*', *AEA* 66, 31–70.

Adshead, S. A. M. (1992) *Salt and Civilisation*, New York.

Agnew, J. A. and Duncan, J. S. (1989) *The Power of Place: Bringing Together Geographical and Sociological Imaginations*, London.

Aguade Nieto, S. (1988) *De la sociedad arcáica a la sociedad campesina en las Asturias medieval*, Alcala de Henares.

Ahrweiler, H., Glykatzi- (1958) 'Politique agraire des empereurs de Nicée', *Byzantion* 28, 57–66.

Ahrweiler, H. (1966) *Byzance et la mer: la marine de guerre, la politique et les institutions maritimes de Byzance aux VIIe–XVe siècles*, Paris.

Ahrweiler, H. (1978) 'Les ports byzantins (VIIe–IXe siècles)', *SS* 25, 259–83.

Ahrweiler, H. (1998) 'Byzantine concepts of the foreigner: the case of the nomads', in Ahrweiler and Laiou, 1–16.

Ahrweiler, H. and Laiou, A. E. (eds) (1998) *Studies on the Internal Diaspora of the Byzantine Empire*, Washington DC.

Airaldi, G. (1983) 'Groping in the dark: the emergence of Genoa in the early Middle Ages', in *Miscellanea di studi storici II*, Collana storica di fonti e studi 38, Genoa, 7–17.

Albore Livadie, C. (ed.) (1986) *Tremblements de terre, éruptions volcaniques et vie des hommes dans la Campanie antique*, Naples.

Albore Livadie, C. and Widemann, F. (eds) (1990) *Volcanologie et archéologie: Actes des ateliers européens . . . Ravello*, Strasbourg.

Alcock, S. E. (1993) *Graecia Capta: The Landscapes of Roman Greece*, Cambridge.

Alcock, S. E. (1994) 'Minding the gap in Hellenistic and Roman Greece', in Alcock and Osborne, 247–61.

Alcock, S. E., Cherry, J. F. and Davis, J. L. (1994) 'Intensive survey, agricultural practice and the classical landscape of Greece', in I. Morris, 137–70.

Alcock, S. E. and Osborne, R. (eds) (1994) *Placing the Gods: Sanctuaries and Sacred Space in Ancient Greece*, Oxford.

Aldrich, R. (1993) *The Seduction of the Mediterranean: Writing, Art and Homosexual Fantasy*, London.

Alexandrescu-Drersca, M.-M. (1987) 'Le rôle des esclaves en Romanie Turque au XVe siècle', *BF* 11, 15–28.

Alexiou, M. (1974) *The Ritual Lament in Greek Tradition*, Cambridge.

al-Khayyat, S. (1990) *Honour and Shame: Women in Modern Iraq*, London.

Allaya, A. et al. (1984) *Alimentation et agriculture en Méditerranée: auto-suffisance et dépendance*, Montpellier.

Allbaugh, L. G. (1953) *Crete: A Case Study of an Underdeveloped Area*, Princeton NJ.

Alpher, J. (1986) *Nationalism and Modernity: A Mediterranean Perspective*, New York and London.

Ambert, P. (1987) 'Modifications historiques des paysages litoraux en Languedoc central: état actuel des connaissances', in *Déplacements des lignes de rivage*, 35–43.

Amboise, R. et al. (1989) *Paysages de terrasses*, Aix-en-Provence.

Ambraseys, N. N. (1970) 'Some characteristic features of the Anatolian fault zone', *Tectonophysics* 9, 143–65.

Ambraseys, N. N. (1971) 'Value of historical records of earthquakes', *Nature* 232, 375–9.

Ambraseys, N. N. (1975) 'Studies in historical seismicity and tectonics', *Geodynamics Today* 1, 7–16.

Ambraseys, N. N. (1978) 'Middle East: a reappraisal of the seismicity', *QJEG* 11.1, 19–32.

Amidon, P. R. (1990) *The 'Panarion' of St. Epiphanius, Bishop of Salamis: Selected Passages*, New York and Oxford.

Ammerman, A. J. (1985) 'Modern land-use versus the past: a case-study from Calabria', in C. Malone and S. Stoddart (eds) *Papers in Italian Archaeology, The Cambridge Conference Part I: The Human Landscape*, BAR 243, Oxford, 27–40.

Ammerman A. J. and Cavalli-Sforza, L. L. (1973) 'A population model for the diffusion of early farming in Europe', in Renfrew, 343–57.

Ammerman A. J. and Cavalli-Sforza, L. L. (1984) *The Neolithic Transition and the Genetics of Populations in Europe*, Princeton NJ.

Ammerman, A. J., De Min, M. and Housley, R. (1992) 'New evidence on the origins of Venice', *Antiquity* 66, 913–16.

Ammerman, A. J., De Min, M., Housley, R. and McClennen, C. E. (1995) 'More on the origins of Venice', *Antiquity* 69, 501–10.

Amouretti, M.-Cl. (1976) 'Les instruments aratoires dans la Grèce archaïque', *DHA*, 2.25–72.

Amouretti, M.-Cl. (1985) 'La transformation des céréales dans les villes, un indicateur méconnu de la personalité urbaine: l'exemple d'Athènes à l'époque classique', in *Les origines des richesses dépensées dans la ville antique*, Aix-en-Provence, 133–46.

Amouretti, M.-Cl. (1986) *Le pain et l'huile dans la Grèce antique: de l'araire au moulin*, Paris.

Amouretti, M.-Cl. (1988) 'La viticulture antique: contraintes et choix techniques', *REA* 90, 5–17.

Amouretti, M.-Cl. (1990) 'Vin, vinaigre, piquette dans l'antiquité', in G. Garrier (ed.) *Le vin des historiens: Actes du 1er symposium 'Vin et histoire'*, Suze-la-Rousse, 75–87.

Amouretti, M.-Cl. (1991) 'Les rhythmes agraires dans la Grèce antique', in Cauvin, 119–26.

Amouretti, M.-Cl. (1992) 'Oléiculture et viticulture dans la Grèce antique', in B. Wells, 77–86.

Amouretti, M.-Cl. (1994) 'L'agriculture de la Grèce antique: bilan de recherches de la dernière décennie', *Topoi* 4.1, 64–94.

Amouretti, M.-Cl. and Brun, J.-P. (eds) (1993) *La production du vin et de l'huile en Méditerranée . . . Actes du Symposium international organisé par le Centre Camille Jullian . . . (Aix-en-Provence et Toulon, 20–22 novembre 1991)*, Paris.

Amouretti, M.-Cl. and Comet, G. (eds) (1993a) *Des hommes et des plantes: plantes méditerranéennes, vocabulaire et usages anciens: table ronde, Aix-en-Provence, mai 1992*, Aix-en-Provence.

Amouretti, M.-Cl. and Comet, G. (eds) (1993b) *Hommes et techniques de l'antiquité à la renaissance*, Paris.

Amouretti, M.-Cl. and Villard, P. (eds) (1994) *Eukrata: mélanges offerts à Claude Vatin*, Aix-en-Provence.

Amphores romaines et histoire économique: dix ans de recherche (1989), Rome.

Ampolo, C. (1980) 'Le condizioni materiali della produzione: agricoltura e paesaggio agrario', *Dd'A*, new series 2 (*La formazione della città nel Lazio*), 15–46.

Ampolo, C. (1992) 'The economics of the sanctuaries of southern Italy and Sicily', in Linders and Alroth, 25–8.

Anderson, B. L. and Latham, A. J. H. (1986) *The Market in History*, London.

Anderson, J. N. (1973) 'Ecological anthropology and anthropological ecology', in J. J. Honigmann (ed.) *Handbook of Social and Cultural Anthropology*, Chicago, 179–239.

Anderson, M. (1971) *Family Structure in Nineteenth-Century Lancashire*, Cambridge.

Anderson, P. (1974) *Passages from Antiquity to Feudalism*, London.

Anderson, S. and Ertug-Yaras, F. (1998) 'Fuel, fodder and faeces: an ethnographic and botanical study of dung fuel use in central Anatolia', *Environmental Archaeology* 1, 99–110.

Andreau, J. (1973) 'Histoire des séismes et histoire économique: le tremblement de terre de Pompéi (62 ap. J.-C.)', *Annales*, 369–95.

Andreau, J., Briant, P., and Descat, R. (eds) (1994) *Les échanges dans l'antiquité: le rôle de l'état*, Saint Bertrand de Comminges.

Andreolli, B. (1990) 'Il ruolo dell'orticoltura e della frutticoltura nelle campagne dell'alto medioevo', *SS* 37, 175–211.

Andreolli, B., Fumagalli, V. and Montanari, M. (eds) (1985) *Le campagne italiane prima e dopo il Mille: una società in transformazione*, Bologna.

Andreolli, B. and Montanari, M. (eds) (1988) *Il Bosco nel Medioevo*, Bologna.

Andrews, D. (1982) 'Underground grain storage in central Italy', in D. Andrews, J. Osborne and D. Whitehouse (eds) *Medieval Lazio: Studies in Architecture, Painting and Ceramics*, *BAR* 125, Oxford, 123–36.

Andrews, T. K. and Tykot, R. H. (eds) (1986) (1992) *Sardinia in the Mediterranean: A Footprint in the Sea. Studies in Sardinian Archaeology presented to Miriam S. Balmuth*, Sheffield.

Angeli, C. (1989) 'Messa a coltura e allivellamento di terre vescovili lucchesi nella "Cerbaiola" (1068–72) al tempo del vescovo Anselmo I da Buggio', *RIL* 123, 45–57.

Angelillis, G. (1955) *Il santuario del Gargano e il culto di S. Michele nel mondo*, Foggia.

Angelomatis-Tsougarakis, H. (1990) *The Eve of the Greek Revival: British Travellers' Perceptions of Early Nineteenth-Century Greece*, London.

Angold, M. (1985) 'The shaping of the medieval Byzantine "city"', *BF* 10, 1–37.

Annequin J. and Léveque, P. (1991) *Le monde méditerranéen et l'esclavage*, Paris.

Ansell, D. J., Bishop, C. and Upton, M. (1984) *Part-Time Farming in Cyprus*, Reading.

Anselmi, S. (1991) *Adriatico: studi di storia, secoli XIV–XIX*, Ancona.

Anthony, D. and Brown, D. (1991) 'The origins of horseback riding', *Antiquity* 65, 22–38.

Antoniadis Bibicou, H. (1965) 'Villages désertés en Grèce: un bilan provisoire', in *Villages désertés et histoire économique*, Paris, 343–417.

Antoniadis Bibicou, H. (1966) 'Vocabulaire maritime et puissance navale en Méditerranée orientale au moyen âge, d'après quelques texts grecs', in Antoniadis Bibicou, *Études d'histoire maritime de Byzance: à propos du thème des Caravisiens*, Paris, 151–73.

Antoun, R. (1968) 'On the modesty of women in Arab Muslim villages: a study in the accommodation of traditions', *AmAnth* 70, 671–97.

Antoun, R. (1970) reply to Abu Zahra (1970), *AmAnth* 72, 1088–92.

APOIKIA: scritti in onore di Giorgio Buchner (*AION* 1, 1994 [1995]), Naples.

Appadurai, A. (ed.) (1986) *The Social Life of Things: Commodities in Cultural Perspective*, Cambridge.

Applebaum, S. (1979) *Jews and Greeks in Ancient Cyrene*, Leiden.

Arafat, K. and Morgan, C. (1994) 'Athens, Etruria and the Heuneburg: mutual misconceptions in the study of Greek–barbarian relations', in I. Morris, 108–34.

Arafat, K. and Morgan, C. (1995) 'A reply to Andrew Sherratt', *CAJ* 5.1, 148–51.

Arbel, B. (1989) 'The Cypriot nobility from the fourteenth to the sixteenth century: a new interpretation, *MHR* 4 , 175–97.

Arbos, P. (1923) 'The geography of pastoral life', *Geographical Review* 13, 539–75.

Arcangeli, F., David, P. and Dosi, G. (eds) (1993) *The Frontiers of Innovation Diffusion*, 3 vols, Oxford.

Archäologie und Seismologie: la regione vesuviana dal 62 a 79 d.C. (1995), Munich.

Arenson, S. (1990) *The Encircled Sea: The Mediterranean Maritime Civilisation*, London.

Argoud, G. (1987) 'Eau et agriculture en Grèce', in Louis, Métral and Métral, 25–43.

Argoud, G. (ed.) (1992) *L'eau et les hommes en Méditerranée et en Mer Noire dans l'antiquité de l'époque mycénienne au règne de Justinien: Actes du Congrès international, Athènes . . . 1988*, Athens.

Argyrou, V. (1996) *Tradition and Modernity in the Mediterranean: The Wedding as Symbolic Struggle*, Cambridge.

Arlacchi, P. (1983) *Mafia, Peasants and Great Estates: Society in Traditional Calabria*, Cambridge, originally Bologna (1980).

Arnaud, P. (1998) 'La navigation hauturière en Méditerranée antique d'après les données des géographes anciens: quelques exemples', in Rieth, 75–87.

Arnold, T. (1840) *The History of the Peloponnesian War by Thucydides*, vol. 1, Oxford.

Arrighi, G. (1985) *Semiperipheral Development: The Politics of Southern Europe in the Twentieth Century*, Beverly Hills, London and New Delhi.

Arthur, P. (1985) 'Notes on the economy of a dark age city', in Malone and Stoddart, 247–59.

Arthur, P. (1986) 'Amphorae and the Byzantine world', in Empereur and Garlan, 655–60.

Arthur, P. (1991) *Romans in Northern Campania: Settlement and Land-Use around the Massico and the Garigliano Basin*, London.

Arthur, P. (1993) 'Early medieval amphorae, the Duchy of Naples and the food supply of Rome, *PBSR* 61, 231–44.

Arthur, P. and Oren, E. D. (1998) 'The North Sinai survey and the evidence of transport amphorae for Roman and Byzantine trading patterns', *JRA* 11, 193–212.

Arthur, P. and Patterson, J. (1994) 'Ceramics and early medieval central and southern Italy: "a potted history"', in Francovich and Noyé, 409–41.

Asano-Tamanoi, M. (1987) 'Shame, family, and state in Catalonia and Japan', in Gilmore (ed.), 104–20.

Ashburner, W. (ed.) (1909) *Nomos Rhodion Nautikos: The Rhodian Sea Law*, Oxford.

Ashby, T. (1929) *Some Italian Scenes and Festivals*, London.

Ashmole, B. (1959) 'Cyriac of Ancona', *PBA* 45, 25–41.

Ashtor, E. (1970) 'Quelques observations d'un orientaliste sur la thèse de Pirenne', *JESHO* 13, 166–94.

Ashtor, E. (1971) *Les métaux précieux et la balance des payements du Proche-Orient à la basse époque*, Paris.

Ashtor, E. (1972) 'Un mouvement migratoire au haut moyen âge: migrations de l'Irak vers les pays méditerranéens', *Annales*, 185–214.

Ashtor, E. (1976) *A Social and Economic History of the Near East in the Middle Ages*, London.

Ashtor, E. (1977a) 'Aperçus sur les Rådhânites', *Revue suisse d'histoire* 27, 245–75.

Ashtor, E. (1977b) 'Levantine sugar industry in the later Middle Ages: an example of technological decline', *Israel Oriental Studies* 7, 226–80 (repr. in Ashtor 1992).

Ashtor, E. (1978) *The Medieval Near East: Social and Economic History*, Variorum, London.

Ashtor, E. (1983a) 'L'ascendant technologique de l'occident médiévale', *Revue suisse d'histoire* 33, 385–413 (repr. in Ashtor 1992).

Ashtor, E. (1983b) 'Le proche Orient au Bas-Moyen-Age: une région sous-dévélopée', in A. Guarducci (ed.) *Sviluppo e sottosviluppo in Europa e fuori l'Europa dal secolo XIII alla rivoluzione industriale*, 375–433 (repr. in Ashtor 1992).

Ashtor, E. (1983c) *Levant Trade in the Later Middle Ages*, Princeton NJ.

Ashtor, E. (1984) 'The wheat supply of the Mamlûk kingdom', *Asian and African Studies* 18, 283–95.

Ashtor, E. (1985) 'Recent research on Levantine trade', *JEEH* 14, 361–85.

Ashtor, E. (1986) *East–West Trade in the Medieval Mediterranean*, ed. B. Z. Kedar, Variorum, London.

Ashtor, E. (1989) 'The factors of technological and industrial progress in the late Middle Ages', *JEEH* 18, 7–36 (repr. Ashtor 1992).

Ashtor, E. (1992) *Technology, Industry and Trade: The Levant versus Europe, 1250–1500*, ed. B. Z. Kedar, Variorum, Aldershot.

Ashtor, E. and Cevidalli, G. (1983) 'Levantine alkali ashes and European industries', *JEEH* 12, 475–522 (repr. Ashtor 1992).

Aslıhan Yener, K. (1992) 'Byzantine silver mines: an archaeometallurgy project in Turkey', in Boyd and Mango, 155–68.

Aston, T. H. and Philpin, C. H. E. (eds) (1985) *The Brenner Debate: Agrarian Class Structure and Economic Development in Pre-industrial Europe*, Cambridge.

Atkinson, K. M. T. (1972) 'A Hellenistic land-conveyance', *Historia* 21, 45–74.

Atsma, H. and Burguière, A. (eds) (1990) *Marc Bloch aujourd'hui: histoire comparée et sciences sociales*, Paris.

Attema, P. (1993) *An Archaeological Survey in the Pontine Region: A Contribution to the Early Settlement History of South Lazio 900–100 B.C.*, Groningen.

Attenborough, D. (1987) *The First Eden: The Mediterranean World and Man*, London.

Atti del Convegno Internazionale 'I parchi costieri mediterranei 1973', Salerno.

Aubaile-Sallenave, F. (1984) 'L'agriculture musulmane aux premiers temps de la conquête: apports et emprunts, à propos de *Agricultural Innovation in the Early Islamic World* de Andrew M. Watson', *Journal d'agriculture traditionelle et de botanique appliqué* 31, 245–56.

Aubet, M. E. (1993) *The Phoenicians and the West: Politics, Colonies and Trade*, Cambridge.

Aurenche, O. and Desfarges, P. (1983) 'Travaux d'ethnoarchéologie en Syrie et en Jordanie, rapports préliminaires', *Syria* 60, 147–85.

Austin, M. M. (1970) *Greece and Egypt in the Archaic Age*, Cambridge.

Auzépy, M.-F. (1993) 'De Philarète, de sa famille, et de certains monastères de Constantinople', in C. Jolivet-Lévy, M. Kaplan and J.-P. Sodini (eds) *Les saints et leur sanctuaire: textes, images et monuments*, Paris, 117–35.

Avidov, A. (1997) 'Were the Cilicians a nation of pirates?', *MHR* 12, 5–55.

Avram, A. (1988) 'Zu den Handelsbeziehungen zwischen Histria und die Insel Thasos im Lichte der Amphorenstempel', *Klio* 70, 404–11.

Avril, F. and Gaborit, J.-R. (1967) 'L'*Itinerarium Bernardi monachi*', *MAH* 79, 269–98.

Aydelotte, W. O. (1948) 'The England of Marx and Mill as reflected in fiction', *JEH* Suppl. 8, 42–58.

Aymard, M. (1966) *Venise, Raguse et le commerce du blé pendant la seconde moitié du XVIe siècle*, Paris.

Aymard, M. (1983) 'Autoconsommation et marchés: Chayanov, Labrousse ou Le Roy Ladurie?', *Annales*, 1392–1410.

Aymard, M. (1987) 'Fernand Braudel, the Mediterranean, and Europe', *MHR* 2, 102–14.

Aymard, M. (ed.) (1983) *Les Savoirs dans les pays méditerranéens, XVIe–XXe siècles: conservations, transmissions et acquisitions, Actes des journées d'études . . .*, Nice.

Babinger, F. (1957) *Die Aufzeichnungen des Genuesen Iacopo de Promontorio-de Campis über den Osmanenstaat um 1475*, Munich.

Bacchi, T. (1988) 'Il bosco e l'acqua: uso dell'incolto e colonizzazione agraria nel territorio ferrarese (secoli XI–XIII)', in Andreolli and Montanari, 185–98.

Badian, E. (1972) (second edn 1983) *Publicans and Sinners*, Ithaca.

Baehrel, R. (1961) *Une croissance: la basse Provence rurale*, Paris.

Bagnall, R. S. (1993) *Egypt in Late Antiquity*, Princeton NJ.

Bailey, F. G. (ed.) (1971) *Gifts and Poison: The Politics of Reputation*, Oxford.

Bailey, F. G. (ed.) (1973) *Debate and Compromise: The Politics of Innovation*, Oxford.

Bailey, G. N., Lewin, J., Macklin, M. G. and Woodward, J. C. (1990) 'The "Older Fill" of the Voidomatis Valley, northwest Greece and its relationship to the palaeolithic archaeology and glacial history of the region', *JAS* 17, 145–50.

Bailey, M. (1989) *A Marginal Economy? East Anglian Breckland in the Later Middle Ages*, Cambridge.

Bairoch, P. (1988) *Cities and Economic Development: From the Dawn of History to the Present*, London.

Bairoch, P. (1990) 'The impact of crop yields, agricultural productivity, and transport costs on urban growth between 1800 and 1910', in van der Woude, Hayami and de Vries, 135–51.

Bairoch, P., Batou, J. and Chièvre, P. (1988) *La population des villes européennes: banque de données et analyse sommaire des résultats, 800–1500*, Geneva.

Baker, A. R. H. (1984) 'Reflections on the relations of historical geography and the *Annales* school of history', in A. R. H. Baker and D. Gregory (eds) *Explorations in Historical Geography: Interpretative Essays*, Cambridge, 1–27.

Bakhuizen, S. C. (1976) *Chalcis in Euboea: Iron and Chalcidians Abroad, Chalcidian Studies III*, Leiden.

Bakhuizen, S. C. (1977) 'Greek steel', *WA* 9.2, 220–34.

Baladié, R. (1980) *Le Péloponnèse de Strabon*, Paris.

Baladié, R. (1994) 'Le sel dans l'antiquité sur la côte nord de la mer Noire', *Il Mar Nero* 1, 145–66.

Balard, M. (1974) 'Escales génoises sur les routes de l'Orient Méditerranéen au XIVe siècle', in *Les Grandes Escales, Recueils de la Société Jean Bodin* 32, vol. 1: *Antiquité et moyen-âge*, Brussels, 243–64.

Balard, M. (1976) 'Amalfi et Byzance (Xe–XIIe siècles)', *Travaux et Mémoires* 6, 85–95.

Balard, M. (1987) 'Les orientaux à Caffa au XVe siècle', *BF* 11, 223–38.

Balard, M. (1988) 'Les formes militaires de la colonisation génoise (XIIIe–XVe siècles)', in Bazzana, 67–78.

Balard, M. (1991) 'L'organisation des colonies étrangères dans l'empire byzantin (XIIe–XVe siècle)', in Kravari, Lefort and Morrisson, 261–76.

Ballais, J. L. and Crambes, A. (1992) 'Morphogenèse holocène, géosystèmes et anthropisation sur la Montagne Sainte-Victoire', *Méditerranée* 1.2, 29–42.

Ballais, J.-M. (1993–5) 'L'érosion consécutive à l'incendie d'août 1989 sur la montagne Saint-Victoire: trois années d'observations (1989–92)', *BAGF* 70, 423–37.

Balmuth, M. (ed.) (1987) *Studies in Sardinian Archaeology III: Nuragic Sardinia and the Mycenaean World*, *BAR* 387, Oxford.

Balmuth, M. (ed.) (1997) *Encounters and Transformations: The Archaeology of Iberia in Transition*, Sheffield.

Balty, J.-Ch. (1987) 'Problèmes de l'eau à Apamée de Syrie', in Louis, Métral and Métral, 9–23.

Balzaretti, R. (1996) 'Cities, emporia and monasteries: local economies in the Po valley, *c*. A.D. 700–875', in Christie and Loseby, 213–34.

Banaji, J. (1975–6) 'The peasantry in the feudal mode of production', *JPS* 3, 299–320.

Banaji, J. (1992) 'Historical arguments for a "logic of deployment" in "pre-capitalist" agriculture', *Journal of Historical Sociology* 5, 379–91.

Banaji, J. (1997) 'Modernizing the history of rural labour: an unwritten agenda', in M. Bentley (1997b), 88–102.

Banfield, E. C. (1958) *The Moral Basis of a Backward Society*, Glencoe IL and Chicago.

Baratier, E. (1961) *La démographie provençale du XIIIe au XVIe siècle*, Paris.

Baratte, F. (1992) 'Les trésors des temples dans le monde romain: une expression particulière de la piété', in Boyd and Mango, 111–22.

Baratte, F. (1996) 'L'argent et la foi: réflexions sur les trésors de temple', in Caillet and Bazin, 19–34.

Barber, E. J. W. (1991) *Prehistoric Textiles: The Development of Cloth in the Neolithic and Bronze Ages with special reference to the Aegean*, Princeton NJ.

Barber, R. (1991) *Pilgrimages*, Woodbridge.

Barbero, M., Bonin, G., Loisel, R. and Quézel, P. (1990) 'Changes and disturbance of forest ecosystems caused by human activities in the western part of the Mediterranean basin', *Vegetatio* 87, 151–73.

Barbero, M. and Quézel, P. (1983) 'La végétation de la Grèce et l'action de l'homme', *Méditerranée* 2, 65–70.

Barceló, M. (1988) 'La arqueología extensiva y el estudio de la creación del espacio rural', in Barceló and Kirchner, 195–274.

Barceló, M. (1992) '¿Por qué los historiadores académicos preferien hablar de islamízación en vez de hablar de campesinos?' *AM* 19, 63–74.

Barceló, M. and Kirchner, H. (eds) (1988) *Arqueología medieval, en las afueras del 'medievalismo'*, Barcelona.

Barclay, H. B. (1964) *Buurri al Lamaab: A Suburban Village in the Sudan*, Ithaca.

Barker, G. W. W. (1975) 'Prehistoric territories and economies in central Italy', in E. S. Higgs (ed.) *Palaeoeconomy*, Cambridge, 111–75.

Barker, G. W. W. (1976) 'Animal husbandry at Narce', in Potter, 295–307.

Barker, G. W. W. (1985) *Prehistoric Farming in Europe*, Cambridge.

Barker, G. W. W. (1989) 'The archaeology of the Italian shepherd', *PCPS* 215, 1–19.

Barker, G. W. W. (1997) 'Writing landscape: archaeology and history', *Topoi* 7, 267–81.

Barker, G. W. W. and Grant, A. (eds) (1991) 'Ancient and modern pastoralism in central Italy: an interdisciplinary study in the Cicolano Mountains', *PBSR* 59, 15–88.

Barker G. W. W. and Jones, G. D. B. (1982) *The UNESCO Libyan Valleys Survey 1979–1981: Palaeoeconomy and Environmental Archaeology in the Pre-Desert*, London.

Barker, G. W. W. and Lloyd, J. (eds) (1991) *Roman Landscapes: Archaeological Survey in the Mediterranean Region* (archaeological monographs of the British School at Rome 2), London.

Barker, G. W. W. et al. (1995) *A Mediterranean Valley: Landscape Archaeology and 'Annales' History in the Biferno Valley*, Leicester.

Barker, G. W. W., Lloyd, J. and Reynolds, J. (eds) (1985) *Cyrenaica in Antiquity*, BAR 236, Oxford.

Barker, W. B. (1853) *Lares and Penates: or Cilicia and its Governors, being a short historical account of that province from the earliest times to the present day together with a description of some household gods of the ancient Cilicians*, ed. W. F. Ainsworth, London.

Barkey, K. (1994) *Bandits and Bureaucrats: The Ottoman Route to State Centralization*, Ithaca and London.

Barley, M. W. (ed.) (1977) *European Towns: Their Archaeology and early History*, London.

Barnish, S. J. B. (1987) 'Pigs, plebeians and potentes', *PBSR* 55, 157–85.

Barnish, S. J. B. (1989) 'The transformation of classical cities and the Pirenne debate' (review article), *JRA* 2, 385–400.

Barresi, V. (1981) *La scomparsa del latifondo: crisi, declino e trasformazione di una società tradizionale*, Cosenza.

Barrett, R. (1974) *Benabarre: The Modernization of a Spanish Village*, New York.

Bartlett, R. (1993) *The Making of Europe: Conquest, Colonization and Cultural Change 950–1350*, Harmondsworth.

Bartlett, R. and MacKay, A. (eds) (1989) *Medieval Frontier Societies*, Oxford.

Bar-Yosef, O. and Khazanov, A. (eds) (1992) *Pastoralism in the Levant: Archaeological Materials in Anthropological Perspective*, Madison WI.

Bas, C., Macpherson, E. and Sarda, F. (1985) 'Fishes and fishermen: the exploitable trophic levels', in Margalef, 296–316.

Bass, G. F. and van Doorninck, F. H. (eds) (1982) *Yassi Ada: A Seventh-Century Byzantine Shipwreck*, College Station Nautical Archaeology Series 1, vol. 1, Texas.

Bateson, G. (1987) *Steps to an Ecology of Mind*, 2nd edn, London.

Bausinger, H. (1969) 'Zur Algebra der Kontinuität', in H. Bausinger and W. Brückner (eds) *Kontinuität? Geschichtlichkeit und Dauer als volkskundliches Problem*, Berlin, 9–30.

Bautier, R.-H. (1991) *Sur l'histoire économique de la France médiévale: la route, le fleuve, la foire*, Variorum, Aldershot and Brookfield VT.

Bautier, R.-H. (1992) *Commerce méditerranéen et banquiers italiens au moyen âge*, Variorum, Aldershot.

Bazzana, A. (1992) *Maisons d'al-Andalus: habitat médiéval et structures du peuplement dans l'Espagne orientale*, Madrid.

Bazzana, A. (ed.) (1988) *Castrum III: guerre, fortification et habitat dans le monde méditerranéen au moyen âge*, Rome and Madrid.

Bazzana, A., Guichard, P. and Montmessin, Y. (1987) 'L'hydraulique agricole dans al-Andalus: données textuelles et archéologiques', in Louis, Métral and Métral, 57–76.

Bazzana, A. and Noyé, G. (1988) 'Du "bon usage" de l'archéologie extensive: une réponse en forme de bilan', in Noyé, 544–62.

Bazzana, A. and Trauth, N. (1997) 'L'Île de Saltés (Huelva): la ville islamique, centre d'une métallurgie de concentration au moyen âge', *CRAI*, 47–74.

Beagon, M. (1992) *Roman Nature: The Thought of Pliny the Elder*, Oxford.

Béal, J.-C. (1995) 'Le massif forestier de la Sila et la poix de Bruttium d'après les textes antiques', in Béal (1995b), 11–25.

Béal, J.-C. (ed.) (1995) *L'arbre et la forêt: le bois dans l'antiquité*, Paris.

Beard, M. (1985) 'Appendix IV: a comparative example: British travel writing in the seventeenth and eighteenth centuries', *PBSR* 53, 161–2.

Beard, M., North, J. and Price, S. R. F. (1998) *Religions of Rome*, Cambridge.

Beardsley, R. K. (1959) *Village Japan*, Chicago.

Beaumont, P., Blake, G. H. and Wagstaff, J. M. (1976) *The Middle East: A Geographical Study*, New York.

Beaver, P. D. and Purrington, B. L. (eds) (1984) *Cultural Adaptation to Mountain Environments*, Athens GA.

Bechmann, R. (1990) *Trees and Man: The Forest in the Middle Ages*, first published 1984, New York.

Beck, H. (1979) *Carl Ritter: Genius der Geographie*, Berlin.

Beck, H., Denecke, D. and Jankuhn, H. (eds) (1980) *Untersuchungen zur eisenzeitlichen und frühmittelalterlicher Flur in Mitteleuropa und ihrer Nutzung*, Göttingen.

Beckinsale, M. and Beckinsale, R. (1975) *Southern Europe: A Systematic Geographical Study*, New York.

Bédoucha, G. (1993) 'The watch and the waterclock: technological choices/social choices', in Lemonnier, 77–107.

Behar, R. (1986) *Santa María del Monte: The Presence of the Past in a Spanish Village*, Princeton NJ.

Behnke, R. H., Jr. (1980) *The Herders of Cyrenaica: Ecology, Economy, and Kinship among the Bedouin of Eastern Libya*, Illinois Studies in Anthropology 12, Urbana IL.

Beidelman, T. O. (1974) *W. Robertson Smith and the Social Study of Religion*, Chicago.

Bekker, I. (ed.) (1838) Theophanes Continuatus, *Chronographia*, Bonn.

Bekker Nielsen, T. (1995) 'The road network', in Fejfer, 87–132.

Bell, G. (1907) (repr. 1985) *The Desert and the Sown*, London.

Bell, M. and Boardman, J. (eds) (1992) *Past and Present Soil Erosion: Archaeological and Geographical Perspectives*, Oxford.

Bell, M. and Limbrey, S. (eds) (1982) *Archaeological Aspects of Woodland Ecology*, BAR 146, Oxford.

Bell, R. M. (1979) *Fate and Honor, Family and Village: Demographic and Cultural Change in Rural Italy since 1800*, Chicago.

Belmonte, T. (1983) 'The contradictions of social life in subproletarian Naples', in Kenny and Kertzer, 273–81.

Beloch, K.-J. (1886) *Die Bevölkerung der griechisch-römischen Welt*, Leipzig.

Benecke, H. (1934) *Die Seepolitik der Aitoler*, dissertation, Hamburg.

Benko, G. and U. Strohmayer (eds) (1997) *Space and Social Theory: Interpreting Modernity and Postmodernity*, Oxford and Malden MA.

Bennassar, B. and Bennassar, L. (1989) *Les chrétiens d'Allah: l'histoire extraordinaire des renégats, XVIe et XVIIe siècles*, Paris.

Bennett, J. M. (1987) *Women in the Medieval English Countryside: Gender and Household in Brigstock before the Plague*, Oxford.

Benoit, P. and Braunstein, P. (1983) *Mines, carrières et métallurgie dans la France médiévale*, Paris.

Bensch, S. (1994) 'From prizes of war to domestic merchandise: the changing face of slavery in Catalonia and Aragon, 1000–1300', *Viator* 25, 63–91.

Bentini, L. (1995) 'Per una storia della economia agricola di Bologna Villanoviana: gli strumenti agricoli del deposito di S. Francesco', in Quilici and Quilici Gigli (1995a), 31–40.

Bentley, J. W. (1987) 'Economic and ecological approaches to land fragmentation: in defense of a much maligned phenomenon', *ARA* 16, 31–67.

Bentley, J. W. (1990) 'Wouldn't you like all your land in one place? Land fragmentation in north western Portugal', *Human Ecology* 18, 51–79.

Bentley, M. (1997) 'Introduction: approaches to modernity: western historiography since the Enlightenment', in Bentley (ed.), 395–506.

Bentley, M. (ed.) (1997) *Companion to Historiography*, London.

Bentzien, U. (1969) *Haken und Pflug*, Berlin.

Berenson, E. (1979) 'The modernization of rural France', *JEEH* 8, 209–15.

Berger, P. (1970) 'On the obsolescence of the concept of honour', *Archives européennes de sociologie* 11, 339–47.

Berger, P., Berger, B. and Kellner, H. (1973) *The Homeless Mind: Modernization and Consciousness*, New York.

Bergier, J.-F. (ed.) (1989) *Montagnes, fleuves, forêts dans l'histoire: barrières ou lignes de convergence? . . . travaux présentés au XVIe Congrès International des Sciences Historiques, Stuttgart, août 1985*, St Katharinen.

Bernabò Brea, B. (1994) 'La source thermale de S. Calogero (Lipari)', in Ginouvés, 169–81.

Bernal, M. (1987–) *Black Athena: The Afroasiatic Roots of Classical Civilization*, London.

Bernal, M. (1989) 'First by land, then by sea: thoughts about the social formation of the Mediterranean and Greece', in E. D. Genovese and L. Hochberg (eds) *Geographic Perspectives in History*, Oxford and New York, 3–33.

Berry, B. J. L. (1967) *The Geography of Market Centers and Retail Distribution*, Englewood Cliffs NJ.

Berry, B. J. L. (1972) *City Classification Handbook*, New York.

Berry, W. E. (1987) 'Southern Burgundy in late Antiquity and the early Middle Ages', in Crumley and Marquardt, 447–607.

Berthier, P. (1969) *Un épisode de l'histoire de la canne à sucre*, Rabat.

Bertrand, M. and Cressier, P. (1985) 'Irrigation et aménagement du terroir dans la vallée de l'Andarax (Almeria): les réseaux anciens de Ragol', *MCV* 21, 113–35.

Bezecky, T. (1995) 'Amphorae and amphora stamps from the Laecanius workshop', *JRA* 8, 41–64.

Bezeczky, T. (1998) *The Laecanius Amphora Stamps and Villas of Brijun*, Vienna.

Biamonte, G. (1997) 'Uno *spelaeum* mitraico nel territorio dell'antica Visentium', *Studi e Materiali per la Storia delle Religioni* 63, 23–36.

Biddick, K. (1989) *The Other Economy: Pastoral Husbandry on a Medieval Estate*, London.

Bietti Sestieri, A.-M. (1980) 'Cenni sull'ambiente naturale', *Dd'A*, new series 2 (*La formazione della città nel Lazio*), 5–14.

Bietti Sestieri, A.-M. (1988) 'The "Mycenaean Connection" and its impact on the central Mediterranean societies', *Dd'A*, new series 6, 23–51.

Biller, P. (1997) 'Popular religion in the central and later Middle Ages', in M. Bentley (1997b), 221–47.

Binford, L. (1988) 'Data, relativism and archaeological science', *Man* 22, 391–404.

Bintliff, J. L. (1976a) 'Sediments and settlements in southern Greece', in Davidson and Shackley, 267–75.

Bintliff, J. L. (1976b) 'The plain of Macedon and the Neolithic site of Nea Nikomedeia', *PPS* 42, 241–262.

Bintliff, J. L. (1977a) 'New approaches to human geography: prehistoric Greece, a case study', in F. W. Carter (ed.), 59–114.

Bintliff, J. L. (1977b) *Natural Environment and Human Settlement in Prehistoric Greece*, *BAR* 28 (i–ii), Oxford.

Bintliff, J. L. (1981) 'Archaeology and the Holocene evolution of coastal plains in the Aegean and circum-Mediterranean', in Brothwell and Dimbleby, 11–31.

Bintliff, J. L. (1982) 'Palaeoclimatic modelling of environmental changes in the eastern Mediterranean region since the last glaciation', in Bintliff and Van Zeist, 485–527.

Bintliff, J. L. (1984) 'Introduction', in Bintliff (ed.) *European Social Evolution: Archaeological Perpsectives*, Bradford, 13–40.

Bintliff, J. L. (1990) 'Territorial behaviour and the natural history of the Greek Polis', in E. Olshausen and H. Sonnabend (eds) *Stuttgarter Kolloquium zur historischen Geographie des Altertums* 4, 207–49.

Bintliff, J. L. (1992) 'Erosion in the Mediterranean lands: a reconsideration of pattern, process and methodology', in Bell and Boardman, 125–32.

Bintliff, J. L. (1996) 'The Frankish countryside in central Greece: the evidence from archaeological field survey', in P. Lock and G. D. R. Sanders (eds) *The Archaeology of Medieval Greece*, Oxford, 1–18.

Bintliff, J. (1998) 'Catastrophe, chaos and complexity: the death, decay, and rebirth of towns from antiquity to today', in Olshausen and Sonnabend.

Bintliff, J. L. (ed.) (1991) *The 'Annales' School and Archaeology*, Leicester and London.

Bintliff, J. L., Davidson, D. A. and Grant, E. G. (eds) (1988) *Conceptual Issues in Environmental Archaeology*, Edinburgh.

Bintliff, J. L. and Snodgrass, A. (1988) 'Mediterranean survey and the city', *Antiquity* 62, 57–71.

Bintliff, J. L. and Van Zeist, W. (eds) (1982) *Palaeoclimates, Palaeoenvironments and Human Communities in the Eastern Mediterranean Region in Later Prehistory*, BAR 133, Oxford.

Birebent, J. (1964) *Aquae Romanae: recherches d'hydraulique romaine dans l'est algérien*, Algiers.

Birge, D. (1994) 'Trees in the landscape of Pausanias' *Periegesis*', in Alcock and Osborne, 231–45.

Birot, P. (1964) *La Méditerranée et le moyen Orient* (1st edn co-author J. Dresch, Paris 1953–6), 2nd edn in collaboration with P. Gabert, vol. 1, Paris.

Bisson, J. (1975) 'Permanence ou reflux de l'emprise citadine: conséquences sur l'aménagement des campagnes: l'exemple de Majorque et Minorque (Baléares, Espagne)', in *I paesaggi rurali europei*, 1–47.

Bisson, T. N. (1998) *Tormented Voices*, Cambridge MA.

Blaas, P. B. M. (1978) *Continuity and Anachronism: Parliamentary and Constitutional Development in Whig Historiography and in the Anti-Whig Reaction between 1890 and 1930*, The Hague and London.

Black, C. E. and Brown, L. C. (eds) (1992) *Modernization in the Middle East: The Ottoman Empire and its Afro-Asian Successors*, Princeton NJ.

Black, J. (1992) *The British Abroad: The Grand Tour in the Eighteenth Century*, Stroud and New York.

Blackman, D. J. (1997) 'Archaeology in Greece 1996–7', *JHS Archaeological Reports* 43, 1–143.

Blackman, D. J. (1998a) 'Archaeology in Greece 1997–8', *JHS Archaeological Reports* 44, 1–128.

Blackman, D. J. (1988b) 'Bollards and men', *MHR* 3, 7–20; also in Malkin and Hohlfelder, 7–20.

Blackman, D. J. (ed.) (1973) *Marine Archaeology*, London.

Black-Michaud, J. (1975) *Cohesive Force: Feud in the Mediterranean and the Middle East* (paperback edition entitled *Feuding Societies*), Oxford.

Blanchemanche, P. (1986) *Les terrasses de culture des régions méditerranéennes: terrassement, épierrement et dérivation des eaux en agriculture, XIIe–XIXe siècle. Étude ethnohistorique*, Paris.

Blanchemanche, P. (1990) *Bâtisseurs de paysages: terrassement, épierrement et petite hydraulique agricoles en Europe, XVIIe–XIXe siècle*, Paris.

Blanks, D. R. (1995) 'Transhumance in the Middle Ages: the eastern Pyrenees', *JPS* 23, 64–87.

Blitzer, H. (1990) 'Koroneïka: storage jar production and trade', *Hesperia* 59, 675–711.

Blitzer, H. (1993) 'Olive cultivation and oil production in Minoan Crete', in Amouretti and Brun, 163–76.

Bloch, M. (1935) 'Avènement et conquêtes du moulin à eau', *Annales*, 538–63 (repr. in Bloch (1967), 136–68).

Bloch, M. (1954) *The Historian's Craft*, Manchester.

Bloch, M. (1962) *Feudal Society*, 2nd edn, 2 vols, London.

Bloch, M. (1966) *French Rural History: An Essay on its Basic Characteristics*, London.

Bloch, M. (1967) *Land and Work in Mediaeval Europe: Selected Papers*, London

Blok, A. (1981) 'Rams and billy-goats: a key to the Mediterranean code of honour', *Man* 16, 427–40.

Blum, J. (1982) 'Fiction and the European peasantry: the realist novel as a historical source', *PAPS* 126.2, 122–9.

Blumler, M. A. (1995) 'Invasion and transformation of California's valley grassland: a Mediterranean analogue ecosystem', in Butlin and Roberts, 308–32.

Boardman, J. (1967) 'The Khaniale Tekke tombs II', *ABSA* 62, 57–67.

Boddy, J. (1989) *Wombs and Alien Spirits: Women, Men, and the 'Zâr' Cult in Northern Sudan*, Madison WI.

Bodei Giglioni, G. (1977) 'Pecunia fanatica: l'incidenza economica dei templi laziali', *RSI* 89, 33–76.

Boehm, C. (1980) 'Exposing the moral self in Montenegro: the use of natural definitions to keep ethnography descriptive', *American Ethnologist* 7, 1–26.

Boehm, C. (1983) *Montenegrin Social Organization and Values: Political Ethnography of a Refuge Area Tribal Adaptation*, New York.

Boesch Gajano, S. (1988) 'Agiografia e geografia nei dialoghi di Gregorio Magno', in S. Pricoco (ed.) *Storia della Sicilia e tradizione agiografica nella tarda antichità*, Catania, 209–20.

Boesch Gajano, S. and Scaraffia, L. (eds) (1990) *Luoghi sacri e spazi della santità*, Turin.

Bogucki, P. (1993) 'Animal traction and household economies in neolithic Europe', *Antiquity* 67, 492–503.

Böhlig, G. (ed.) (1975) *Die Einnahme Thessalonikes durch die Araber im Jahre 904* (John Cameniates, *De expugnatione Thessalonicae*), Graz.

Boissevain, J. (1969) *Hal-Farrug: A Village in Malta*, New York.

Boissevain, J. (1974) 'Uniformity and diversity in the Mediterranean: an essay in interpretation', in J. Boissevain and A. Blok, *Two Essays on Mediterranean Societies*, Papers on European and Mediterranean Societies no. 1, Anthropological-Sociological Center, University of Amsterdam, Amsterdam, 13–29.

Boissevain, J. (1979) 'Towards a social anthropology of the Mediterranean', *Current Anthropology* 20, 81–93.

Bolens, L. (1980) 'Pain quotidien et pain de disette dans l'Espagne musulmane', *Annales*, 462–76.

Bolens, L. (1981) *Agronomes andalous du moyen âge*, Geneva.

Bolens, L. (1989) 'L'irrigation en al-Andalus: une société en mutation, analyse des sources juridiques (les "nawâzil" d'al-Wansharîsî)', in *El agua en zonas áridas: arqueología e historia . . . Instituto de Estudios Almerienses*, Almeria, 71–87 (repr. in Bolens 1990a).

Bolens, L. (1990a) *L'Andalousie du quotidien au sacré XIe–XIIIe siècles*, Variorum, Aldershot.

Bolens, L. (1990b) 'La viticulture d'après les traités d'agronomie andalous (XIe–XIIe s.)', in Bolens (1990a), no. V, 1–7.

Bolens, L. (1990c) 'Le haricot vert en Andalousie et en Méditerranée médiévales (phaseolus, dolichos, lûbiâ, judía)', *Al-Qantara* 8, 65–86 (repr. in Bolens 1990a).

Bolens, L. (1993) 'Al-Andalous: la vigne et l'olivier, un secteur de pointe XIe–XIIIe siècle', in Amouretti and Brun, 423–38.

Bommeljé, L. S. and Doorn, P. K. (eds) (1983) *The Strouza Valley Project*, Utrecht.

Bommeljé, L. S. and Doorn, P. K. (eds) (1987) *Aetolia and the Aetolians*, Utrecht.

Bonamici, M. (1995) [1996] 'Contributo alle rotte arcaiche nell'alto Tirreno', *Studi Etruschi* 61, 3–43.

Bonghi Jovino, M. (ed.) (1993) *Produzione artigianale ed esportazione nel mondo antico: il bucchero etrusco: Atti del Colloquio Internazionale, Milano, 10-11 maggio 1990*, Milan.

Bonifay, M., Carre, M.-B., and Rigoir, Y. (1998) *Fouilles à Marseille: les mobiliers, Ier–VIIe siècles ap. J.C.*, Paris and Lattes.

Bonifay, M. and Piéri, D. (1995) 'Amphores du Ve au VIIe siècle à Marseille: nouvelles donnés sur la typologie et le contenu', *JRA* 8, 94–120.

Bonino, M. (1978) *Archeologia e tradizione navale tra la Romagna e il Po*, Ravenna.

Bonnassie, P. (1991) *From Slavery to Feudalism in South-Western Europe*, Cambridge.

Bonneau, D. (1993) *Le régime administratif de l'eau du Nil dans l'Égypte grecque, romaine et byzantine*, Leiden.

Bonneau, D. (1994) 'Usage et usages de l'eau dans l'Égypte ptolémaïque et romaine', in Menu, 47–71

Bonnet, C. and Jourdain-Annequin, C. (eds) (1992) *Héraclès, d'une rive à l'autre de la Méditerranée, bilan et perspectives*, Brussels.

Boruchovič, V. (1988) 'Die ägäische Kolonisation', *Klio* 70, 86–144.

Boserup, E. (1965) *The Conditions of Agricultural Growth: The Economics of Agrarian Change under Population Pressure*, London.

Boserup, E. (1981) *Population and Technology*, Oxford.

Boswell, J. (1936) *Boswell's Life of Johnson*, ed. G. B. Hill, revised L. F. Powell, 4 vols, Oxford.

Bottema, S., Entjes-Nieborg, G. and van Zeist, W. (eds) (1990) *Man's Role in the Shaping of the Eastern Mediterranean Landscape: Proceedings of the INQUA/BAI Symposium on the Impact of Ancient Man on the Landscape of the Eastern Mediterranean Region and the Near East, Groningen . . . 1989*, Rotterdam.

Bottini, A. (1992) 'La Magna Grecia in epoca preromana', *Dd'A*, new series 3.10, 11–20.

Boulton, J. (1987) *Neighbourhood and Society: A London Suburb in the Seventeenth Century*, Cambridge.

Bounni, A. (1997) 'La permanence des lieux de culte en Syrie: l'exemple du site de Qadboun', *Topoi* 7, 777–89.

Bourdieu, P. (1977) *Outline of a Theory of Practice*, Cambridge.

Bourdieu, P. (1979) *Algeria 1960*, Cambridge.

Bourgou, M. and Oueslati, A . (1987) 'Les dépôts historiques de la vallée du Kébir-Miliane (nord-est de la Tunisie)', *Méditerranée* 3.1 , 43–9.

Bousquet, B. (1984) 'Conclusion: les sociétés antiques et le géosystème méditerranéen', *BAGF* 499, 69–72.

Bousquet, B. and Péchoux, P.-Y. (1983) 'Le Djebel Akhdar (Cyrénaïque, Libye): évolution morphostructurale', *BAGF* 499, 37–41.

Bousquet, B. et al. (1984) 'Nature, répartition et histoire du risque sismique dans l'aire méditerranéenne', in *La mobilité des paysages Mediterranéens*, 278–301.

Bousquet, B., Pechoux, Y. and Dufaure, J. J. (1983) 'Temps historiques et évolution des paysages égéens', *Méditerranée* 2, 3–25.

Bousquet, B., Pechoux, Y. and Dufaure J. J. (1987) 'Ports antiques et lignes de rivage égéennes', in *Déplacements . . .* , 137–54.

Bousquet, B., Pechoux, Y., Dufaure, J. J. and Philip, H. (1981) 'Séismes et géomorphologie autour du bassin méditerranéen', *BAGF* 478, 145–53.

Bousquet, B. and Reddé, M. (1994) 'Les installations hydrauliques et les parcellaires dans la région de Tell Douch (Égypte) à l'époque romaine', in Menu, 73–88.

Boussac, M. F. and Rougemont, G. (1993) 'Observation sur le territoire des cités d'Amorgos', in *Les Cyclades: matériaux pour une étude de géographie historique*, Paris, 113–20.

Bowden, H. (1996) 'The Greek settlement at Naucratis: Herodotus and archaeology', in M. H. Hansen and K. A. Raaflaub (eds) *More Studies on the Ancient Greek Polis*, Stuttgart, 17–37.

Bowersock, G. W. (1974) '*The Social and Economic History of the Roman Empire* by Michael Ivanovitch Rostovtzeff', *Daedalus* 103, 15–23.

Bowersock, G. W. (1990) *Hellenism in Late Antiquity*, Ann Arbor.

Bowman, A. K. (1985) 'Land-holding in the Hermopolite nome in the fourth century A.D.', *JRS* 75, 136–55.

Bowman, A. K. (1986) *Egypt after the Pharaohs 332 B.C.–A.D. 642*, London.

Boxer, B. (1983) 'Environment and regional identity', in Pinkele and Pollis, 59–73.

Boyazoglou, J. and Flamant, J.-C. (1992) 'Mediterranean systems of animal production', in J. G. Galatly and D. L. Johnson (eds) *The World of Pastoralism: Herding Systems in Comparative Perspective*, New York, 353–93.

Boyd, S. A. and Mango, M. M. (eds) (1992) *Ecclesiastical Silver Plate in Sixth Century Byzantium*, Washington DC.

Bradford, E. (1964) *Ulysses Found*, London.

Bradley, R. N. (1912) *Malta and the Mediterranean Race*, London.

Braemer, F. (1998) 'Eléments naturels (vents, courants, avantages, inconvénients, risques) et itinéraires maritimes', in Rieth, 61–74.

Braithwaite, J. (1989) *Crime, Shame and Reintegration*, Cambridge.

Bramwell, A. (1989) *Ecology in the 20th Century: A History*, New Haven and London.

Brandes, S. (1987) 'Reflections on honor and shame in the Mediterranean', in Gilmore (ed.) 121–34.

Brandes, S. H. (1975) *Migration, Kinship and Community: Tradition and Transition in a Spanish Village*, London and New York.

Branigan, J. J. and Jarrett, H. R. (1969) *The Mediterranean Lands*, London.

Braudel, F. (1972a) *The Mediterranean and the Mediterranean World in the Age of Philip II* (*La Méditerrannée et le Monde Méditerranéen à l'époque de Philippe II*, 1st edn 1949, 2nd revised edn 1966), 2 vols (vol. 2 published 1973), London and New York.

Braudel, F. (1972b) 'Personal testimony', *Journal of Modern History* 44, 448–67.

Braudel, F. (1973) *Capitalism and Material Life, 1400–1800* (first published 1967, early version of Braudel 1981–4, vol. 1), London.

Braudel, F. (1977) *Afterthoughts on Material Civilisation and Capitalism*, Baltimore.

Braudel, F. (1980) *On History*, first published 1969, Chicago.

Braudel, F. (1981–4) *Civilization and Capitalism*, first published 1979, 3 vols, London.

Braudel, F. (1986) 'Fernand Braudel, l'antiquité et l'histoire ancienne' (interview with Andreau, J., Aymard, M., Etienne, R., 29 April 1985), *QS* 12, no. 24, 5–21.

Braudel, F. (1988–90) *The Identity of France* (vol. 1, *History and Environment*; vol. 2, *People and Production*; first published in 3 vols, 1986), London.

Braudel, F. (ed.) (1977) *La Méditerranée: l'espace et l'histoire*, Paris.

Braudel, F. (unpublished) *La Méditerranée: la longue marche d'une civilisation*.

Braudel, F. et al. (1986) *Une leçon d'histoire de Fernand Braudel: Châteauvallon, Journées Fernand Braudel, 18, 19 et 20 Octobre, 1985*, Paris.

Braudel, P. (1992) 'Les origines intellectuelles de Fernand Braudel: un témoignage', *Annales*, 237–44.

Braun, T. F. R. G. (1982) 'The Greeks in the Near East', in J. Boardman and N. G. L. Hammond (eds) *Cambridge Ancient History*, 2nd edn, vol. 3, part 3, Cambridge, 1–31.

Braun, T. F. R. G. (1995) 'Barley cakes and emmer bread', in Dobson, Harvey and Wilkins, 25–37.

Braunstein, P. (1983) 'Innovations in mining and metal-production in Europe in the late Middle Ages', *JEEH* 12.1, 573–91.

Bravo, B. (1980) 'Sulān: représailles et justice privée contre des étrangers dans les cités grecques. Étude de vocabulaire et des institutions', *ASNP* 10, 675–987.

Brenner, R. (1976) 'Agrarian class structure and economic development in pre-industrial Europe', *PP* 70, 30–75.

Brenner, R. (1982) 'The agrarian roots of European capitalism', *PP* 97, 16–113.

Brentano, R. (1974) (repr. 1991) *Rome before Avignon: A Social History of Thirteenth-Century Rome*, London.

Bresc, H. (1971) 'Pantelleria entre l'Islam et la chrétienté', *CT* 19, 105–27 (repr. in Bresc 1991).

Bresc, H. (1972) 'Les jardins de Palerme 1290–1460', *MEFRM* 84, 55–127 (repr. in Bresc 1991).

Bresc, H. (1986a) 'Pêche et coraillage aux derniers siècles du moyen âge: Sicile et Provence orientale', in *L'exploitation de la mer*, 107–16.

Bresc, H. (1986b) *Un monde méditerranéen: économie et société en Sicile, 1300–1450*, 2 vols, Rome.

Bresc, H. (1988) 'Désertions, regroupements, stratégies dans la Sicile des Vêpres', in Bazzana, 237–45.

Bresc, H. (1989) 'L'esclave dans le monde méditerranéen des XIVe et Xve siècles: problèmes politiques, religieux et moraux', in *XIII Congrès d'història de la Corona d'Aragó: Ponències*, Palma de Mallorca, 1.91–5.

Bresc, H. (1991) *Politique et société en Sicile XIIe–XVe siècles*, Variorum, Aldershot.

Bresson, A. (1993) 'Les cités grecques et leurs *emporia*', in Bresson and Rouillard, 163–226.

Bresson, A. and Rouillard, P. (eds) (1993) *L'Emporion*, Paris.

Brett, M. (1969) 'Ifrîqya as a market for Saharan trade from the tenth to the twelfth century A.D.', *Journal of African History* 10, 347–64.

Brettell, C. B. (1986) *Men who Migrate, Women who Wait: Population and History in a Portuguese Parish*, Princeton NJ.

Brewer, D. J. and Friedman, R. F. (1989) *Fish and Fishing in Ancient Egypt*, Warminster.

Brewer, J. and Bermingham, A. (1995) *The Consumption of Culture 1600–1800*, London.

Brewer, J. and Porter, R. (eds) (1993) *Consumption and the World of Goods*, London.

Brewer, J. and Staves, S. (1996) *Early Modern Conceptions of Property*, London.

Brewster, H. (1997) *River Gods of Greece: Myths and Mountain Waters in the Hellenic World*, London.

Briant, P. (1976) 'Brigandage, dissidence et conquête en Asie achéménide et hellénistique', *DHA* 2, 163–258.

Briant, P. (1982a) *État et pasteurs au Moyen-Orient ancien*, Cambridge.

Briant, P. (1982b) *Rois, tributs et paysans: études sur les formations tributaires du Moyen-Orient ancien*, Paris.

Brice, W. C. (ed.) (1978) *The Environmental History of the Near and Middle East*, London.

Bridbury, A. R. (1969) 'The Dark Ages', *EcHR* 22, 526–37.

Bridbury, A. R. (1982) *Medieval English Clothmaking: An Economic Survey*, London.

Brien-Poitevin, F. (1996) 'Consommations des coquillages marins en Provence à l'époque romaine', in F. Gateau et al., 137–42.

Brinkhuizen, D. C. and Clason, A. T. (eds) (1986) *Fish and Archaeology*, BAR 294, Oxford.

Britnell, R. H. (1991) 'The towns of England and northern Italy in the early fourteenth century', *EcHR* 44, 21–35.

Brogiolo, G. P. (ed.) (1996) *Città altomedievali nel mediterraneo occidentale*, Mantua.

Broodbank, C. (1993) 'Ulysses without sails: trade, distance, knowledge and power in the early Cyclades', *WA* 24, 315–31.

Broodbank, C. and Strasser, T. (1991) 'Migrant farmers and the Neolithic colonization of Crete', *Antiquity* 65, 233–45.

Brooke, C. N. L. (1989) *The Medieval Idea of Marriage*, Oxford.

Brooke, M. Z. (1970) *Le Play: Engineer and Social Scientist*, London.

Broshi, M. (1980) 'The population of the western Palestine in the Roman–Byzantine period', *BASOR* 236, 1–10.

Brothwell, D. and Dimbleby, G. (eds) (1981) *Environmental Aspects of Coast and Islands*, BAR 94, Oxford.

Broughton, T. R. S. (1938) 'Roman Asia Minor', in T. Frank et al., 4.419–918.

Brown, A. G. (1997) *Alluvial Geoarchaeology: Floodplain Archaeology and Environmental Change*, Cambridge.

Brown, A. G. and Ellis, C. (1995) 'People, climate and alluviation: theory, research design and new sedimentological and stratigraphical data from Etruria', *PBSR* 63, 45–73.

Brown, J. C. (1982) *In the Shadow of Florence: Provincial Society in Renaissance Pescia*, New York and Oxford.

Brown, J. P. (1969) *The Lebanon and Phoenicia*, Beirut.

Brown, L. (1981) *Innovation Diffusion: A New Perspective*, London.

Brown, P. (1981) *The Cult of the Saints: Its Rise and Function in Latin Christianity*, Chicago.

Brown, P. (1982a) 'Eastern and Western Christendom in late Antiquity: a parting of the ways', in P. Brown (1982c), 166–95.

Brown, P. (1982b) '*Mohammed and Charlemagne* by Henri Pirenne', in P. Brown (1982c), 63–79.

Brown P. (1982c) *Society and the Holy in Late Antiquity*, London.

Brown, P. (1995) *Authority and the Sacred: Aspects of the Christianization of the Roman World*, Cambridge.

Brown, P. (1996) *The Rise of Western Christendom*, Oxford and Cambridge MA.

Brown, T. S. (1984) *Gentlemen and Officers: Imperial Administration and Aristocratic Power in Byzantine Italy A.D. 554–800*, London.

Bruce-Mitford, T. (1980) *The Nymphaeum at Kafizin: The Inscribed Pottery*, Berlin and New York.

Bruck, G. vom (1996) 'Being worthy of protection: the dialectics of gender attributes in Yemen', *Social Anthropology* 4, 145–62.

Brückner, H. (1986) 'Man's impact on the evolution of the physical environment in the Mediterranean region in historical times', *GeoJournal* 13, 7–17.

Brückner, H. (1990) 'Changes in the Mediterranean ecosystem during antiquity: a geomorphological approach as seen in two examples' [Basilicata and Attica], in Bottema et al., 127–37.

Brugnone, A. (1980) 'Annotazioni sull'Apollo Archegete di Nasso', in *Philias Charin: Miscellanea di studi in onore di E. Manni*, Rome, 1.277–94.

Bruhns, H. (1985) 'De Werner Sombart à Max Weber et Moses I. Finley: la typologie de la ville antique et la question de la ville de consommation', in P. Leveau (ed.) *L'origine des richesses dépensées dans la ville antique: Actes du colloque organisé à Aix-en-Provence . . . 1984*, Aix-en-Provence, 255–73.

Brulé, P. (1978) *La piraterie crétoise héllénistique*, Paris.

Brulé, P. (1990) 'Enquête démographique sur la famille grecque antique', *REA* 92, 233–58.

Brun, P. (1993) 'La stèle des céréales de Cyrène et le commerce des grains en Égée au IVe siècle', *ZPE* 99, 185–96.

Brun, P. (1996) *Les archipels égéens dans l'antiquité grecque Ve–IIe siècle av. notre ère*, Paris.

Brun, P. (1997) 'Du fromage de Cythnos au marbre de Paros: la question des appellations contrôlées (?) dans l'antiquité grecque', *REA* 99, 401–9.

Brunaux, J. L. (ed.) (1991) *Les sanctuaires celtiques et leur rapport avec le monde méditerranéen*, Montagnac.

Bruneau, P. (1988) 'L'esclavage à Délos', in M.-M. Mactoux and E. Geny (eds) *Mélanges Pierre Lévêque*, Paris, 3.41–52.

Brunet, M. (1990a) 'Contribution à l'histoire rurale de Délos aux époques classique et héllénistique', *BCH* 114, 669–82.

Brunet, M. (1990b) 'Terrasses de cultures antiques: l'exemple de Délos, Cyclades', *Méditerranée* 3.4, 5–11.

Brunet, M. (1992) 'Campagnes de la Grèce antique: le danger du prisme Athénien: en marge des travaux de R. Osborne', *Topoi* 2 (1992), 33–51.

Brunhes, J. (1902) *L'irrigation: ses conditions géographiques, ses modes, et son organisation dans la Péninsule Ibérique et dans l'Afrique du Nord*, Paris.

Brunner, K. (1995) 'Continuity and discontinuity of Roman agricultural knowledge in the early Middle Ages', in D. Sweeney (ed.) *Agriculture in the Middle Ages: Technology, Practice, and Representation*, Philadelphia, 21–40.

Brunt, P. A. (1966) 'Athenian settlements abroad in the fifth century B.C.', in *Ancient Society and Institutions: Studies presented to Victor Ehrenberg*, Oxford, 71–92.

Brunt, P. A. (1975) 'Two great Roman landowners', *Latomus* 34, 619–35.

Brunt, P. A. (1987) *Italian Manpower 225 B.C.–A.D. 14*, 2nd edn, Oxford.

Bryan, R. and Yair, A. (1982) *Badlands Geomorphology*, Norwich.

Bryer, A. (1982) 'The question of Byzantine mines in the Pontos: Chalybian iron, Chaldian silver, Koloneian alum and the mummy of Cheriana', *AS* 32, 133–50.

Bryer, A. (1985) 'Byzantine porridge', in H. Mayr-Harting and R. I. Moore (eds) *Studies in Medieval History Presented to R. H. C. Davis*, London and Ronceverte, 1–6.

Bryer, A. (1986a) 'Rural Society in Matzouka', in Bryer and Lowry , 53–95.

Bryer, A. (1986b) 'The structure of the late Byzantine town: *dioikismos* and the *mesoi*', in Bryer and Lowry, 263–79.

Bryer, A. (1986c) 'Byzantine agricultural implements: the evidence of medieval illustrations of Hesiod's *Works and Days*', *ABSA* 81, 45–80.

Bryer, A. and Lowry, H. (eds) (1986) *Continuity and Change in Late Byzantine and Early Ottoman Society*, Birmingham and Washington DC.

Bryer, A. and Winfield, D. (1985) *The Byzantine Monuments and Topography of the Pontus*, Washington DC.

Buchholz, H.-G. (1975) *Methymna: Archäologische Beiträge zur Topographie und Geschichte von Nordlesbos*, Mainz.

Buck, W. J. (1893) *Wild Spain . . . Records of Sport with Rifle, Rod, and Gun, Natural History and Exploration*, London.

Buckland, P. C. (1991) 'Granaries, stores and insects: the archaeology of insect synanthropy', in Sigaut and Fournier (1991a), 69–81.

Budd, P. et al. (1995) 'Oxhide ingots, recycling and the Mediterranean metals trade', *JMA* 8.1, 1–32 (cf. 70–75).

Buisseret, D. (ed.) (1992) *Monarchs, Ministers and Maps: The Emergence of Cartography as a Tool of Government in early Modern Europe*, Chicago.

Bull, M. (1993) *Knightly Piety and the Lay Response to the First Crusade: The Limousin and Gascony c.970–c.1130*, Oxford.

Bulliet, R. W. (1975, new edn 1992) *The Camel and the Wheel*, Cambridge MA.

Burckhardt, J. (1959) *Judgements on History and Historians*, London.

Burford, A. (1960) 'Heavy transport in classical Greece', *EcHR* 13, 1–18.

Burford, A. (1993) *Land and Labor in the Greek World*, Baltimore.

Burguière, A. (1979) 'Histoire d'une histoire: la naissance des *Annales*', *Annales*, 1347–59.

Burke, P. (1987) *The Historical Anthropology of Early Modern Italy*, Cambridge.

Burke, P. (1990) *The French Historical Revolution: The 'Annales' School, 1929–89*, Oxford.

Burke, P. (ed.) (1991) *New Perspectives on Historical Writing*, Cambridge.

Burkert, W. (1983) *Homo Necans: The Anthropology of Ancient Greek Sacrificial Ritual and Myth*, Berkeley.

Burnouf, J., Bravard, J.-P. and Chouquer, G. (eds) (1996) *La dynamique des paysages protohistoriques, antiques, médiévaux et modernes*, Nice.

Burns, R. I. (1980) 'Piracy as an Islamic–Christian interface in the thirteenth century', *Viator* 11, 165–78.

Burr, V. (1952) *Nostrum Mare: Ursprung und Geschichte der Namen des Mittelmeeres und seiner Teilmeere im Altertum*, Stuttgart.

Burrin, P. J. and Scaife, R. G. (1988) 'Environmental thresholds, catastrophe theory, and landscape sensitivity: their relevance to the impact of man on valley alluviations', in Bintliff, Davidson and Grant, 211–32.

Busquet, R. and Pernoud, R. (1949) *Histoire du commerce de Marseille*, ed. G. Rambert, vol. 1, Paris.

Butlin, R. A. and Roberts N. (eds) (1995) *Ecological Relations in Historical Times: Human Impact and Adaptation*, Oxford.

Buttimer, A. (1971) *Society and Milieu in the French Geographic Tradition*, Chicago.

Buttimer, A. and Seamon, D. (eds) (1980) *The Human Experience of Space and Place*, London.

Butzer, K. W. (1976) *Early Hydraulic Civilization in Egypt: A Study in Cultural Ecology*, Chicago.

Butzer, K. W. (1982) *Archaeology as Human Ecology: Method and Theory for a Contextual Approach*, Cambridge.

Butzer, K. W. (1994) 'The Islamic traditions of agroecology: cross-cultural experience, ideas and innovation', *Ecumene: A Journal of Environment, Culture, Meaning* 1, 7–50.

Butzer, K. W. (1996) 'Ecology in the long term: settlement histories, agrosystemic strategies and ecological performance', *JFA* 23, 141–50.

Butzer, K. W., Butzer, E. K. and Mateu, J. F. (1982) 'Medieval Muslim communities of the Sierra de Espadán, Kingdom of Valencia', *Viator* 17, 339–413.

Butzer, K. W., Miralles, I. and Mateu, J. F. (1983) 'Urban geo-archaeology in mediaeval Alzira (prov. Valencia, Spain)', *JAS* 10, 333–49.

Butzer, K. W. et al. (eds) (1985) 'Irrigation agrosystems in eastern Spain: Roman or Islamic origins?', *AAAG* 75, 479–509.

Buxton, R. (1994) *Imaginary Greece*, Cambridge.

Buzaian, A. and Lloyd, J. A. (1996) 'Early urbanism in Cyrenaica: new evidence from Euesperides', *LS* 27, 129–152.

Byrne, E. H. (1930) *Genoese Shipping in the Twelfth and Thirteenth Centuries*, Cambridge MA.

Cabanes, P. (n.d.) 'La montagne, lieu de vie et de rencontre, en Épire et en Illyrie méridionale dans l'antiquité', in Fabre, 69–82.

Caferro, W. (1994) 'City and countryside in Siena in the second half of the fourteenth century', *JEH* 54, 85–103.

Cahen, C. (1953–4) 'Un texte peu connu relatif au commerce d'Amalfi au Xe siècle', *ASPN* 34, 3–8 (repr. Cahen 1974).

Cahen, C. (1963) 'L'alun avant Phocée: un chapitre d'histoire économique islamo-chrétienne au temps des Croisades', *RHES* 41.4, 433–47 (repr. Cahen 1974).

Cahen, C. (1965) 'Quelques problèmes concernant l'expansion économique musulmane au haut moyen âge', *SS* 12, 391–432, with discussion, 487–515.

Cahen, C. (1968) 'Quelques mots sur les Hilaliens et le nomadisme', *JESHO* 11, 130–3.

Cahen, C. (1973) 'Nomades et sédentaires dans le monde musulman du milieu du moyen âge', in D. S. Richards (ed.) *Islamic Civilisation 950–1150*, Oxford, 93–104.

Cahen, C. (1974) *Turcobyzantina et Oriens Christianus*, Variorum, London.

Cahen, C. (1978) 'Ports et chantiers navals dans le monde méditerranéen musulman jusqu'aux Croisades', *SS* 25, 299–313.

Cahen, C. (1980) 'Commercial relations between the Near East and western Europe from the VIIth to the XIth century', in K. I. Semaan (ed.) *Islam and the Medieval West: Aspects of Intercultural Relations*, Albany NY, 1–25.

Caillet, J.-P. (1996) 'Le trésor de l'antiquité à l'époque romane: bases de la recherche actuelle et éléments de problématique', in Caillet and Bazin, 5–18.

Caillet, J.-P. and Bazin P. (eds) (1996) *Les trésors des sanctuaires de l'antiquité à l'époque romane*, Paris.

Cairns, D. (1993) *Aidōs: The Psychology and Ethics of Honour and Shame in Ancient Greek Literature*, Oxford.

Calbi, A. (ed.) (1993) *Epigrafia del Villagio*, Faenza.

Callot, O. (1984) *Huileries antiques de Syrie du Nord*, Paris.

Callot, O. and Marcillet-Janbert, J. (1984) 'Hauts-Lieux de la Syrie du nord', in G. Roux (ed.) *Temples et sanctuaires*, Paris, 185–202.

Calvet, Y. and Geyer, B. (1992) *Barrages antiques de Syrie*, Lyon.

Cambitoglou, A. (ed.) (1988) *Zagora II: Excavation of a Geometric Town on the Island of Andros*, 2 vols, Athens.

Cameron, A. (1993) *The Mediterranean World in Late Antiquity AD 395–600*, London.

Cameron, A. and Herrin, J. (eds) (1984) *Constantinople in the Eighth Century: The 'Parastaseis Syntomoi Chronikai'*, Leiden.

Cameron, C. M. and Tomka, S. A. (eds) (1993) *Abandonment of Settlements and Regions: Ethnoarchaeological and Archaeological Approaches*, Cambridge.

Cameron Lyons, M. and Jackson, D. E. P. (1982) *Saladin: The Politics of the Holy War*, Cambridge.

Campbell, B. M. S., Galloway, J. A., Keene, D. and Murphy, M. (1993) *A Medieval Capital and its Grain Supply: Agrarian Production and Distribution in the London Region, c.1300*, London.

Campbell, J. K. (1964) *Honour, Family, and Patronage: A Study of Institutions and Moral Values in a Greek Mountain Community*, Oxford.

Campbell, J. K. (1965) 'Honour and the devil', in Peristiany (ed.), 141–70.

Campbell, J. K. (1983) 'Traditional values and continuities in Greek society', in R. Clogg (ed.) *Greece in the 1980s*, London, 184–207.

Campbell, J. K. (1992) 'Fieldwork among the Sarakatsani, 1954–55', in Pina-Cabral and Campbell, 148–66.

Campbell, T. (1987) 'Portolan charts from the late thirteenth century to 1500', in Harley and Woodward (1987–), 1.371–463.

Camporeale, G. (ed.) (1985) *L'Etruria mineraria*, Milan.

Camporesi, P. (1989) *Bread of Dreams: Food and Fantasy in Early Modern Europe*, Oxford.

Camps-Fabrer, H. (1953) *L'olivier et l'huile dans l'Afrique romaine*, Algiers.

Canard, M. (1964) 'Les relations politiques et sociales entre Byzance et les Arabes', *DOP* 18, 33–56.

Canivet, P. and Rey-Coquais, J.-P. (eds) (1992) *La Syrie de Byzance à l'Islam VIIe–VIIIe siècles*, Damascus.

Cantarella, E. (1991) 'Homicides of honor: the development of Italian adultery law over two millennia', in Kertzer and Saller, 229–44.

Capogrossi Colognesi, L. (1981a) 'Alcuni aspetti dell'organizzazione fondiaria romana nella tarda repubblica e nel principato', *Klio* 63.2, 347–57.

Capogrossi Colognesi, L. (1981b) 'Proprietà agraria e lavoro subordinato nei giuristi e nei agronomi latini tra repubblica e principato', in Giardina and Schiavone, 1.445–54.

Capogrossi Colognesi, L. (1986) 'Grandi proprietari contadini e coloni nell'Italia romana (I–III d.C.)', in Giardina, 1.325–65.

Capogrossi Colognesi, L. (1995) 'The limits of the ancient city and the evolution of the medieval city in the thought of Max Weber', in Cornell and Lomas, 27–37.

Capogrossi Colognesi, L. (ed.) (1982) *L'agricoltura romana*, Rome and Bari.

Carandini, A. (1981) 'Sviluppo e crisi delle manifatture rurali e urbane', in Giardina and Schiavone, 2.249–60.

Carandini, A. (1983) 'Columella's vineyard and the rationality of the Roman economy', *Opus* 2, 177–204.

Carandini, A. (1985) 'Orti e frutteti intorno a Roma', in *Misurare la terra: centuriazione e coloni nel mondo romano (Roma)*, Modena, 66–74.

Carandini, A. (1986) 'Il mondo della tarda antichità visto attraverso le merci', in Giardina, 3.3–19.

Carandini, A. (1989) 'L'economia italica fra tarda repubblica e medio Impero considerata dal punto di vista di una merce: il vino. Ricordando i tempi dello scavo ostiense, che sembrano così lontani', in *Amphores romaines et histoire économique*, 505–31.

Carbonell, C.-O. and Livet, G. (eds) (1983) *Au berceau des Annales*, Toulouse.

Carile, A. and Fedalto, G. (1978) *Le origini di Venezia*, Bologna.

Carlsen, J. (1994) '*CIL* X 8217 and the question of temple land in Roman Italy', in Carlsen et al., 9–16.

Carlsen, J., Ørsted, P. and Skydsgaard, J. E. (eds) (1994) *Land Use in the Roman Empire*, Rome.

Carlstein, T. (1982) *Time Resources, Society and Ecology: On the Capacity for Human Interaction in Space and Time*. Vol. 1: *Preindustrial Societies*, London.

Carlton, R. (1988) 'An ethnoarchaeological study of pottery production on the Dalmatian island of Iz', in J. C. Chapman (ed.) *Recent Developments in Yugoslav Archaeology*, Oxford, 101–23.

Carmichael, D. L., Hubert, J. and Schanche, A. (eds) (1994) *Sacred Sites, Sacred Places*, London.

Caro Baroja, J. (1963) 'The city and the country: reflections on some ancient commonplaces', in Pitt-Rivers, 27–40.

Caro Baroja, J. (1965) 'Honour and shame: a historical account of several conflicts', in Peristiany (ed.), 81–137.

Carozzi, C. (1983) 'La géographie de l'au-delà et sa signification pendant le haut moyenâge', *SS* 29, 423–85.

Carozzi, C. (1994) *Le voyage de l'âme dans l'au-delà d'après la littérature latine (Ve–XIIIe siècles)*, Rome.

Carrard, P. (1992) *Poetics of the New History: French Historical Discourse from Braudel to Chartier*, Baltimore and London.

Carrington, R. (1971) *The Mediterranean: Cradle of Western Culture*, New York.

Carter, F. W. (1977) 'Brač island, Dalmatia: a case for sequent occupance?', in F. W. Carter (ed.), 239–70.

Carter, F. W. (ed.) (1977) *An Historical Geography of the Balkans*, London, New York and San Francisco.

Carter, H. (1983) *An Introduction to Urban Historical Geography*, London.

Carter, J. C. (1994) 'Sanctuaries in the *chora* of Metaponto', in Alcock and Osborne, 161–98.

Cartledge, P. (1976) 'Seismicity and Spartan society', *LCM* 1, 25–8.

Cartledge, P. (1993) 'Classical Greek agriculture: recent work and alternative views', *JPS* 21, 127–36

Cartledge, P. (1995) 'Classical Greek agriculture II: two more alternative views', *JPS* 23, 131–9

Carver, M. O. H. (1993) *Arguments in Stone: Archaeological Research and the European Town in the First Millennium*, Oxford.

Cary, M. (1949) *The Geographic Background of Greek and Roman History*, Oxford.

Casanova, A. (1993) 'Types de pressoirs et types de production à partir de l'exemple de la Corse à la fin du XVIIIe siècle', in Amouretti and Brun, 359–78.

Casevitz, M. (1991) 'Le vocabulaire agricole dans le calendrier grec', in Cauvin, 109–12.

Casevitz, M. (1993) 'Emporion: emplois classiques et histoire du mot', in Bresson and Rouillard, 9–20.

Casey, James (1983) 'Household disputes and the law in early modern Andalusia', in J. Bossy (ed.) *Disputes and Settlements: Law and Human Relations in the West*, Cambridge, 189–217.

Casey, John (1990) *Pagan Virtue: An Essay in Ethics*, Oxford.

Casson, L. (1954) 'The grain trade of the Hellenistic world', *TAPA* 85, 168–87.

Casson, L. (1971) *Ships and Seamanship in the Ancient World*, Princeton NJ.

Casson, S. (1938) 'The modern pottery trade in the Aegean', *Antiquity* 12, 464–73.

Casson, S. (1952) 'The modern pottery trade in the Aegean: further notes', *Antiquity* 26, 187–90.

Castagnetti, A. (1990) 'La "Campanea" e i beni communi delle città', *SS* 37, 137–74.

Castan, Y. (1974) *Honnêteté et relations sociales en Languedoc, 1715–1780*, Paris.

Castella, D. (1990) *Le moulin hydraulique Gallo-romaine d'Avenches 'en Chaplix'*, Lausanne.

Castellani, V. (1993) [1995] 'Evidence for hydrogeological planning in ancient Cappadocia', *JAT/RTA* 3, 207–16.

Castro, A. (1971) *The Spaniards: An Introduction to their History*, Berkeley and Los Angeles.

Catani, E. (1985) 'La coltura della vite e la produzione del vino nella Cirenaica in età greca e romana: le fonti storiche e l'arte figurativea antica', in Barker, Lloyd and Reynolds, 145–64.

Cauvin, M.-C. (ed.) (1991) *Rites et rythmes agraires*, Lyon and Paris.

Cavaciocchi, D. (ed.) (1994) *Le migrazioni in Europa, secc. XIII–XVIII*, Florence.

Cavallo, S. and Cerutti, S. (1990) 'Female honor and social control of reproduction in Piedmont between 1600 and 1800', in Muir and Ruggiero, 73–109.

Cavanagh, W. G. (1991) 'Surveys, cities and synoicism', in Rich and Wallace-Hadrill, 97–118.

Cawkwell, G. (1992) 'Early colonisation', *CQ* 42, 289–303.

Cazzola, F. (1991) 'L'introduzione del mais in Italia e la sua utilizzazione alimentare (sec. XVI–XVII)', in Sigaut and Fournier (eds), 109–27.

Ceredi, G. (1567) *Tre discorsi sopra il modo d'alzar acque da' luoghi bassi*, Parma.

Chabal, L. (1997) *Forêts et sociétés en Languedoc (néolithique final, antiquité tardive): l'anthracologie, méthode et paléoécologie*, Paris.

Chabod, F. (1964) *Storia dell'Idea d'Europa*, Bari.

Chamorro, J. G. (1987) 'Recent archaeological discoveries relating to Tartessos', *AJA* 91, 197–232.

Chang, C. (1992) 'Archaeological landscapes: the ethnoarchaeology of pastoral land-use in the Grevena province of northern Greece', in Rossignol and Wandsnider, 65–89.

Chaniotis, A. (1988) 'Vinum Creticum excellens: zum Weinhandel Kretas', *Münsterische Beiträge zur antiken Handelsgeschichte* 7, 62–89.

Chaniotis, A. (1995) 'Problems of "pastoralism" and "transhumance" in classical and Hellenistic Crete', *Orbis Terrarum* 1, 38–89.

Chaouache, H. (1964) 'Les structures économiques de la Byzacène à travers l'antiquité et le moyen âge', *Cahiers de Tunisie* 12, 41–57.

Chapman, J. C., Shiel, R. and Batović, Š. (1996) *The Changing Face of Dalmatia: Archaeological and Ecological Studies in a Mediterranean Landscape*, London.

Chapman, R. (1990) *Emerging Complexity: The Later Prehistory of South-East Spain, Iberia and the West Mediterranean*, Cambridge.

Chapman, R. and Grant, A. (1997) 'Prehistoric subsistence and monuments in Mallorca', in Balmuth, 69–87.

Chapoutot-Remadi, M. (1980) 'Réflexions sur l'industrie textile dans le monde musulman au moyen âge: à propos d'un livre récent', *Annales*, 504–11.

Charanis, P. (1961) 'The transfer of populations as a policy in the Byzantine empire', *CSSH* 3, 140–54 (repr. Charanis 1972).

Charanis, P. (1966) 'Observations on the demography of the Byzantine Empire', in *Thirteenth International Congress of Byzantine studies, Main Papers* XIV, Oxford, 1–19 (repr. Charanis 1972).

Charanis, P. (1972) *Studies on the Demography of the Byzantine Empire*, Variorum, London.

Charles, M. P. (1984) 'Introductory remarks on the cereals', *Bulletin on Sumerian Agriculture* 1, 17–31.

Charlesworth, M. P. (1926) *Trade-Routes and Commerce of the Roman Empire*, London.

Chase, M. (1992) 'Can history be green? A prognosis', *RurH* 3.2, 243–51.

Chastagnol, A. (1981) 'L'inscription constantinienne d'Orcistus', *MEFRA* 93, 381–416.

Chaudhuri, K. N. (1985) *Trade and Civilisation in the Indian Ocean from the Rise of Islam to 1750*, Cambridge.

Chaudhuri, K. N. (1990) *Asia before Europe: Economy and Civilisation of the Indian Ocean from the Rise of Islam to 1750*, Cambridge.

Chaunu, P. and Chaunu, H. (1955–9) *Séville et l'Atlantique, 1504–1650*, 12 vols, Paris.

Chelbi F. et al. (1995) 'La baie d'Utique et son évolution depuis l'antiquité: une réévaluation géoarchéologique', *AA* 31, 7–51.

Chelhod, J. (1965) *Les structures du sacré chez les Arabes*, Paris.

Cherkauer, D. (1976) 'The stratigraphy and chronology of the River Treia alluvial deposits', in Potter, 106–20.

Chernoff, M. (1993) 'Natural resource use in an ancient Near East farming community', in D. Helms and D. E. Bowers (eds) *The History of Agriculture and the Environment*, Washington DC, 213–31.

Cherry, J. F. (1983) 'Frogs round the pond: perspectives on current archaeological survey projects in the Mediterranean region', in D. R. Keller and D. W. Rupp (eds) *Archaeological Survey in the Mediterranean Area*, BAR 155, Oxford, 375–416.

Cherry, J. F. (1988) 'Pastoralism and the role of animals in the pre- and protohistoric economies of the Aegean', in Whittaker (ed.), 6–34.

Cherry, J. F. (1990) 'The colonisation of the Mediterranean islands, a review of recent research', *JMA* 3, 105–21.

Cherry, J. F., Davis, J. L. and Mantzourani, E. (1991 [1992]) *Landscape Archaeology as Long-term History: Northern Keos in the Cycladic Islands from Earliest Settlements until Modern Times*, Los Angeles.

Chevallier, R. (1988) *Voyages et déplacements dans l'empire romain*, Paris.

Chevallier, R. (ed.) (1992) *Les eaux thermales et les cultes des eaux en Gaule et dans les provinces voisines*, Caesarodunum vol. 26, Tours.

Chipman, J. (ed.) (1988) *NATO's Southern Allies: Internal and External Challenges*, London.

Chirassi Colombo, I. (1975) 'Acculturation et cultes thérapeutiques', in F. Dunand and P. Lévêque (eds) *Les syncrétismes dans les religions de l'antiquité*, Leiden, 96–111.

Chittolini, G. (1990) 'Civic religion and the countryside in late medieval Italy', in T. Dean and C. Wickham (eds) *City and Countryside in Late Medieval and Renaissance Italy: Essays Presented to Philip Jones*, London, 69–80.

Chorley, R. J., Dunn, A. J. and Beckinsale, R. P. (1964) *The History of the Study of Landforms or the Development of Geomorphology*, London.

Christaller, W. (1966) *Central Places in Southern Germany* (first published, in German, 1933), Englewood Cliffs NJ.

Christensen, P. (1993) *The Decline of Iranshahr: Irrigation and Environment in the History of the Middle East, 500 B.C.–A.D. 1100*, Copenhagen.

Christian, W. A. (1981a) *Local Religion in Sixteenth Century Spain*, Princeton NJ.

Christian, W. A. (1981b) *Apparitions in Late Medieval and Renaissance Spain*, Princeton NJ.

Christian, W. A. (1989) *Person and God in a Spanish Valley*, 2nd revised edn (first published 1972), New York.

Christides, V. (1988) 'Naval history and naval technology in medieval times: the need for interdisciplinary studies', *Byzantion* 58, 309–32.

Christie, N. (1991) *Three South Etrurian Churches: Santa Cornelia, Santa Rufina and San Liberato*, London.

Christie, N. (1996) 'Barren fields: landscapes and settlements in late Roman and post-Roman Italy', in Salmon and Shipley, 254–83.

Christie, N. and Loseby, S. T. (eds) (1996) *Towns in Transition: Urban Evolution in Late Antiquity and the Early Middle Ages*, Aldershot.

Christien, J. (1989) 'Les liaisons entre Sparte et son territoire malgré l'encadrement montagneux', in Bergier, 18–44.

Chubb, J. (1982) *Patronage, Power, and Poverty in Southern Italy: A Tale of Two Cities*, Cambridge.

Cipolla, C. M. (1972) 'The diffusion of innovations in early modern Europe', *CSSH* 14, 46–52.

Cipolla, C. M. (1993) *Before the Industrial Revolution: European Society and Economy 1000–1700*, 3rd edn, London.

Citarella, A. O. (1968) 'Patterns in medieval trade: the commerce of Amalfi before the Crusades', *JEH* 28, 531–55.

Citarella, A. O. (1993) 'Merchants, markets and merchandise in southern Italy in the high Middle Ages', *SS* 40, 239–82.

Citter, C., Paroli, L., Pellecuer, C. and Péne, J.-M. (1996) 'Commerci nel Mediterraneo occidentale nell'alto medioevo', in Brogiolo, 121–42.

Clark, C. and Haswell, H. (1969) *The Economics of Subsistence Agriculture*, London.

Clark, D. (1982) *Urban Geography*, London.

Clark, E. C. (1974) 'The Ottoman industrial revolution', *IJMES* 5, 65–76.

Clark, P. and Lepetit, B. (eds) (1996) *Capital Cities and their Hinterlands in Early Modern Europe*, Aldershot.

Clark, S. (1985) 'The *Annales* Historians', in Q. Skinner (ed.) *The Return of Grand Theory in the Social Sciences*, Cambridge, 177–98.

Clarke, D. L. (1977) 'Introduction', in Clarke (ed.) *Spatial Archaeology*, London, 1–32.

Claude, D. (1985–7a) *Der Handel im westlichen Mittelmeer während des Frühmittelalters* = Düwel et al. (1985–7), vol. 2.

Claude, D. (1985–7b) 'Aspekte des Binnenhandels im Merowingerreich auf Grund der Schriftquellen', in Düwel et al., 3.7–99.

Clavel-Lévecque, M. (1978) 'Brigandage et piraterie, représentations idéologiques et pratiques impérialistes au dernier siècle de la République', *DHA* 4, 17–32.

Clementi, G. (1985) 'Discussione', *SS*. 31, 392–8.

Cline, E. H. (1994) *Sailing the Wine-Dark Sea: International Trade and the Late Bronze Age Aegean*, *BAR* 591, Oxford.

Clinkenbeard, B. (1982) 'Lesbian wine and storage amphoras: a progress report on identification', *Hesperia* 51, 254–6.

Clinkenbeard, B. (1986) 'Lesbian and Thasian wine amphoras: questions concerning collaboration', in Y. Garlan (ed.) *Recherches sur les amphores grecques*, Paris, 353–62.

Coates-Stephens, R. (1997) 'Dark Age Architecture in Rome', *PBSR* 65, 177–232.

Coccia, S. and Mattingly, D. J. (1992) 'Settlement history, environment and human exploitation of an intermontane basin in the Central Appennines: the Rieti survey 1988–1991, part I', *PBSR* 60, 213–89.

Coccia, S. and Mattingly, D. J. (1995) 'Settlement history, environment and human exploitation of an intermontane basin in the Central Appennines: the Rieti survey 1988–1991, part II', *PBSR* 63, 105–58.

Cohen, D. (1991a) *Law, Sexuality, and Society: The Enforcement of Morals in Classical Athens*, Cambridge.

Cohen, D. (1991b) 'The Augustan law on adultery: the social and cultural context', in Kertzer and Saller, 109–26.

Cohen, D. (1995) *Law, Violence and Community in Classical Athens*, Cambridge.

Cohen, E. (1992) 'Honor and gender in the streets of early modern Rome', *JIH* 22, 597–625.

Cohen, T. V. and Cohen, E. S. (1993) *Words and Deeds in Renaissance Rome: Trials before the Papal Magistrates*, Toronto, Buffalo, and London.

Cohn, B. S. (1988) *An Anthropologist among the Historians and Other Essays*, Delhi and Oxford.

Cohn, S. K., Jr. (1980) *The Laboring Classes in Renaissancxe Florence*, New York and London.

Colardelle, M. (ed.) (1996) *L'homme et la nature au moyen âge. Actes du Ve Congrès International d'Archéologie Médiévale (Grenoble)*, Paris.

Coldstream, J. N. (1994) 'Prospectors and pioneers: Pithekoussai, Kyme and central Italy', in F. De Angelis and G. Tsetskhladze (eds) (1994) *The Archaeology of Greek Colonisation: Studies presented to Sir John Boardman*, Oxford, 47–59.

Coldstream, J. N. (1995) 'The rich lady of the Areiopagus and her contemporaries', *Hesperia* 64, 391–403.

Cole, J. W. and Wolf, E. R. (1974) *The Hidden Frontier: Ecology and Ethnicity in an Alpine Valley*, New York and London.

Cole, S. G. (1989) 'The mysteries of Samothrace during the Roman period', *ANRW* 2.18.2, 1564–98.

Cole, S. G. (1994) 'Demeter in city and countryside', in Alcock and Osborne, 199–216.

Coleman, D. and Schofield, R. (eds) (1986) *The State of Population Theory: Forward from Malthus*, Oxford.

Coleman, S. and Elsner, J. (1995) *Pilgrimage Past and Present: Sacred Travel and Sacred Space in the World Religions*, London.

Colinvaux, P. A. (1980) *The Fates of Nations: A Biological Theory of History*, Harmondsworth.

Collomp, A. (1983) *La maison du père: famille et village en Haute-Provence aux XVIIe et XVIIIe siècles*, Paris.

Colonna, G. (ed.) (1988) *Etruria meridionale: conoscenza, conservazione, fruizione: Atti del convegno Viterbo . . . 1985*, Rome.

Columeau, P. (1996) 'Pratiques culturelles et spécialisation pastorale autour de l'Étang de Berre de l'âge du fer à la fin de l'antiquité', in F. Gateau et al., 128–36.

Comba, R. (1984) 'Emigrare nel medioevo: aspetti economico-sociali della mobilità geografica nei secoli XI–XVI', in R. Comba, G. Piccinni and G. Pinto (eds) *Strutture familiari, epidemie, migrazioni nell'Italia medievale*, Naples, 45–74.

Comet, G. (1992) *Le paysan et son outil: essai d'histoire technique des céréales: France, VIIIe–XVe siècle*, Rome.

Connelly, J. B. (1996) 'Yeronisos: sanctuary of Apollo', *Explorers Journal* 74.1, 14–18.

Connolly, C. (1981) *The Rock Pool*, first published 1936, Oxford.

Connor, W. R. (1988) 'Early Greek land warfare as symbolic expression', *PP* 119, 3–29.

Conophagos, C. (1980) *Le Laurium antique et la technique grecque de la production de l'argent*, Athens.

Conrad, L. I. (1992) 'The conquest of Arwâd: a source-critical study in the historiography of the early medieval Near East', in A. Cameron and L. I. Conrad (eds) *The Byzantine and Early Islamic Near East. I: Problems in the Literary Source Material*, Studies in Late Antiquity and Early Islam 1, Princeton NJ, 317–401.

Conrad, L. I. (ed.) (forthcoming) *Trade and Exchange in the Late Antique and Early Islamic Near East*, Princeton NJ.

Constable, O. R. (1994) *Trade and Traders in Muslim Spain: The Commercial Realignment of the Iberian Peninsula, 900–1500*, Cambridge.

Constantine, D. (1984) *Early Greek Travellers and the Hellenic Ideal*, Cambridge.

Cook, J. (1973) *The Troad*, Oxford.

Cook, M. A. (1972) *Population Pressure in Rural Anatolia*, London and New York.

Coon, C. S. (1958) *Caravan: The Story of the Middle East*, revised edn, New York.

Cooter, W. S. (1978) 'Ecological dimensions of medieval agrarian systems', *Agricultural History* 52, 458–77.

Corcoran, T. H. (1957) *The Roman Fishing Industry of the Late Republic and Early Empire*, dissertation, Northwestern University.

Cordano, F. (1993) *La geografia degli antichi*, Rome and Bari.

Cornell, T. J. and Lomas, K. (eds) (1995) *Urban Society in Roman Italy*, London.

Cornwall, A. and Lindisfarne, A. (eds) (1994) *Dislocating Masculinity: Comparative Ethnographies*, London and New York.

Corsaro, M. (1983) 'Le forme di dipendenza nella *chora* del re e in quella cittadina dell'Asia Minore ellenistica', in *Forme di contatto e processi di trasformazione nelle società antiche*, Pisa and Rome, 523–48.

Cosgrove, D. E. (1988) 'The geometry of landscape: practical and speculative arts in sixteenth century Venetian land-territories', in D. Cosgrove and S. Daniels (eds) *The Iconog-*

raphy of Landscape: Essays on the Symbolic Representation, Design and Use of Past Environments, Cambridge, 254–75.

Cosgrove, D. E. (1990) 'Platonism and practicality: hydrology, engineering and landscape in sixteenth century Venice', in Cosgrove and Petts, 35–53.

Cosgrove, D. E. and Petts, G. E. (1990) *Water, Engineering and Landscape: Water Control and Landscape Transformation in the Modern Period*, London.

Cosimato, D. and Natella, P. (1981) *Il territorio del Sarno: storia, società, arte*, Cava dei Tirreni.

Costa, J. (1898) *Colectivismo agrario en España*, Madrid.

Couchoud, P. L. and Svoronos, J. (1921) 'Le monument dit 'des Taureaux' à Délos et le culte du navire sacré', *BCH* 45, 270–94.

Courtot, R. (1989) *Campagnes et villes dans les huertas valenciennes*, Paris.

Cramer, P. (1993) *Baptism and Change in the Early Middle Ages, c.200–c.1150*, Cambridge.

Crane, E. (1983) *The Archaeology of Beekeeping*, London.

Crapanzano, V. (1973) *The Hamadsha: A Study in Moroccan Ethnopsychiatry*, Berkeley.

Crawford, D. J. = Thompson, D. J. (1971) *Kerkeosiris: An Egyptian Village in the Ptolemaic Period*, Cambridge.

Crawford, D. J. = Thompson, D. J. (1979) 'Food: tradition and change in Hellenistic Egypt', *WA* 11.2, 136–46.

Crawford, D. J. = Thompson, D. J. (1989) 'Agriculture', in *CAH*, 2nd edn, 7.1, 363–70.

Crawford, M. H. (1981) 'Italy and Rome', *JRS* 71, 153–60.

Creighton, O. H. and Segui, J. R. (1998) 'The ethnoarchaeology of abandonment and post-abandonment behaviour in pastoral sites: evidence from Famorca, Alacant, Spain', *JMA* 11, 31–52.

Cremasco, M. (1984) 'The military presence of the riparian countries', in Luciani, 206–38.

Cresswell, R. (1993) 'Of mills and waterwheels: the hidden parameters of technological choice', in Lemonnier (ed.), 181–23.

Cristofani, M. (1985) *Il commercio etrusco arcaico*, Rome.

Crombie, A. C. (ed.) (1963) *Scientific Change: Historical Studies in the Intellectual, Social and Technical Conditions for Scientific Discovery and Technical Invention from Antiquity to the Present*, London.

Crone, P. (1987) *Meccan Trade and the Rise of Islam*, Oxford.

Crone, P. (1989) *Pre-industrial Societies*, Oxford.

Crosby, A. (1986) *Ecological Imperialism*, Cambridge.

Crouch, D. (1993) *Water Management in Ancient Greek Cities*, New York.

Crumley, C. L. (1987) 'Historical ecology', in Crumley and Marquardt, 237–64.

Crumley, C. L. and Marquardt, W. H. (eds) (1987) *Regional Dynamics: Burgundian Landscapes in Historical Perspective*, London.

Cruzado, A. (1985) 'The chemistry of Mediterranean waters', in Margalef, 126–47.

Csapo, E. (1991) 'An international community of traders in late 8th–7th c. B.C. Kommos in southern Crete', *ZPE* 88, 211–16.

Cucchiari, S. (1981) 'The gender revolution and the transition from bisexual horde to patrilocal band: the origns of gender hierarchy', in Ortner and Whitehead (eds), 31–79.

Cuisenier, J. (ed.) (1979) *Europe as a Culture Area*, The Hague.

Curschmann, F. (1900) *Hungersnöte im Mittelalter: Ein Beitrag zur deutschen Wirtschaftsgeschichte des 8. bis 13. Jahrhunderts*, Leipzig.

Curtis, J. (ed.) (1988) *Bronzeworking Centres of Western Asia, c.1000 B.C.–539 B.C.*, London.

Curtis, R. I. (1991) *Garum and Salsamenta: Production and Commerce in Materia Medica*, Leiden.

Cutileiro, J. (1971) *A Portuguese Rural Society*, Oxford.

Cvijić, J. (1960) *Géographie des terrains calcaires*, Belgrade.

Dagron, G. (1977) 'Le christianisme dans la ville byzantine', *DOP* 31, 3–25 (repr. Dagron 1984).

Dagron, G. (1979) 'Entre village et cité: la bourgade rurale des IVe–VIIe siècles en Orient', *Koinónia* 3, 29–52 (repr. Dagron 1984).

Dagron, G. (1981) 'Quand la terre tremble ...', *Travaux et Mémoires* 8, 87–103 (repr. Dagron 1984).

Dagron, G. (1984) *La Romanité chrétienne en orient: héritages et mutations*, Variorum, London.

Dagron, G. (1990a) 'Das Firmament soll christlich werden: zu zwei Seefahrtkalendern des 10. Jahrhunderts', in G. Prinzing and D. Simon (eds) *Fest und Alltag in Byzanz*, Munich, 145–215.

Dagron, G. (1990b) 'L'homme sans honneur ou le saint scandaleux', *Annales*, 929–39.

Dagron, G. (1995) 'Poissons, pêcheurs et poissonniers de Constantinople', in Mango and Dagron, 57–73.

Dagron, G. (ed.) (1978) *Vie et miracles de Ste Thècle*, Brussels.

Daix, P. (1995) *Braudel*, Paris.

Dalby, A. (1992) 'Greeks abroad: social organization and food among the Ten Thousand', *JHS* 112, 16–30.

Dalché, P. G. (1995) *Carte marine et portulan au XIIe siècle: le Liber de existencia riveriarum et forma mari nostri Mediterranei*, Rome.

Dall'Aglio, P. L. (1997) 'Il "diluvium di Paolo Diacono" e le modificazioni ambientali tardoantiche: un problema di metodo', *Ocnus* 5, 97–104.

Dalton, G. (1960) 'A note of clarification on economic surplus', *AmAnth* 62, 483–90.

Dalton, G. (1963) 'Economic surplus, once again', *AmAnth* 65, 389–94.

Dalton, G. (1972) 'Peasantries in anthropology and history', *Current Anthropology* 13, 385–416.

Dalton, G. (1974) 'How exactly are peasants exploited?', *AmAnth* 76, 553–61.

Dar, S. (1995) 'Food and archaeology in Roman Palestine', in Dobson, Harvey and Wilkins, 326–35.

Darby, W. J., Ghalioungi, P. and Grivetti, L. (1977) *Food: The Gift of Osiris*, London.

Darmon, J.-P. (1964) 'Note sur le tarif de Zaraï', *CT* 12, 7–24.

Davidson, D. A. (1980) 'Erosion in Greece in the first and second millennia B.C.', in R. A. Cullingford, D. A. Davidson and J. Lewin (eds) *Timescales in Geomorphology*, Chichester, 143–58.

Davidson, D. A. and Shackley, M. L. (eds) (1976) *Geoarchaeology: Earth Science and the Past*, London.

Davies, J. L. (ed.) (1998) *Sandy Pylos: An Archaeological History from Nestor to Navarino*, Austin.

Davies, N. (1996) *Europe: A History*, Oxford and New York.

Davies, S. (1994) 'Tithe-collection in the Venetian Peloponnese 1696–1705', *ABSA* 89, 443–55.

Davis, D. B. (1966) *The Problem of Slavery in Western Culture*, Ithaca (2nd edn Oxford, 1988).

Davis, J. (1970a) 'Honour and politics in Pisticci', *Proceedings of the Royal Anthropological Institute for 1969*, 69–81.

Davis, J. (1970b) 'Morals and backwardness', *CSSH* 12, 340–53.

Davis, J. (1973) *Land and Family in Pisticci*, London.

Davis, J. (1977) *People of the Mediterranean: An Essay in Comparative Social Anthropology*, London, Henley and Boston.

Davis, J. (1980) 'Social anthropology and the consumption of history' (review essay), *Theory and Society* 9, 519–3.

Davis, J. (1987a) 'Family and state in the Mediterranean', in Gilmore (ed.), 22–34.

Davis, J. (1987b) *Libyan Politics: Tribe and Revolution*, London.

Davis, J. (1989) 'Col divorzio c'è differenza?', in Fiume, 47–59.

Davis, J. (1992a) 'Breve storia della civiltà contadina', *La Questione Agraria (Manlio Rossi-Doria e la Basilicata)* 36, C. Cecchi, M. de Benedictis, R. Mazzarone, A. Rossi-Doria and F. Vitelli (eds), 87–98.

Davis, J. (1992b) *Exchange*, Buckingham.

Davis, J. A. (1982) 'Innovation and technology in the Mediterranean countries, XIVth–XXth centuries', *JEEH* 2, 739–45.

Davis, J. L. (1991) 'Contributions to a Mediterranean rural archaeology: historical case studies from the Ottoman Cyclades', *JMA* 4, 131–216.

Davis, J. L. (1992) 'The islands of the Aegean', *AJA* 96, 699–756.

Davis, J. L. and Sutton, S. B. (1995) 'Response to A. J. Ammerman "The dynamics of modern land use and the Acconia survey"', *JMA* 8, 113–23.

Davis, N. Z. (1987) *Fiction in the Archives: Pardon Tales and their Tellers in Sixteenth-Century France*, Stanford CA.

Davis, R. (trans.) (1989) *The Book of Pontiffs (Liber Pontificalis)*, Liverpool.

Davis, R. (trans.) (1992) *The Lives of the Eighth-Century Popes (Liber Pontificalis)*, Liverpool.

Davis, R. C. (1997) 'Venetian shipbuilders and the fountain of wine', *PP* 156, 55–86.

Davite, C. and Moreno, D. (1996) 'Des "saltus" aux "alpes" dans les Appenins du Nord (Italie)'. Une hypothèse sur la place du haut moyen âge (560–680 ap. J.-C.) dans le diagramme pollinique du site de Prato Spilla', in Colardelle, 138–42.

Day, J. (1975) 'Malthus démenti: sous-peuplement chronique et calamités démographiques en Sardaigne au bas moyen-âge', *Annales*, 684–702.

Day, J. (1987) *The Medieval Market Economy*, Oxford.

de Bouard, M. (1938) 'Problèmes de subsistences dans un état médiéval: le marché et les prix des céréales au royaume angevin de Sicile (1266–1282)', *Annales*, 483–501.

de Cazenove, O. and Scheid, J. (eds) (1989) *Les bois sacrés: Actes du colloque international* (Naples 1989).

de Dainville, F. (1940) *La géographie des humanistes* (repr. Geneva, 1969), Paris.

De Garine, I. and Koppert, S. (1990) 'Social adaptation to season and uncertainty in food supply', in G. A. Harrison and J. C. Waterlow (eds) *Diet and Disease in Traditional and Developing Societies*, Cambridge, 240–89.

De Jesus, P. S. (1978) 'Metal resources in ancient Anatolia', *AS* 28, 97–102.

de Ligt, L. (1993) *Fairs and Markets in the Roman Empire*, Amsterdam.

De Magistris, E. (1995) 'Il mare di Elea', in *Tra Lazio e Campania: ricerche di storia e di topografia antica*, Naples, 7–78.

De Martino, F. (1990) 'Economia dell'oliveto nell'Italia romana', *PdelP* 254, 321–47.

De Neeve, P. W. (1984) *Peasants in Peril: Location and Economy in Italy in the Second Century B.C.*, Amsterdam.

De Neeve, P. W. (1990) 'A Roman landowner and his estates: Pliny the Younger', *Athenaeum* 60, 363–402.

de Planhol, X. (1966) 'Aspects of mountain life in Anatolia and Iran', in S. Eyre and G. Jones (eds) *Geography as Human Ecology: Methodology by Example*, London, 291–308.

de Planhol, X. (1968) *Les fondements géographiques de l'histoire de l'Islam*, Paris.

de Planhol, X. (1995) *L'eau de neige, le tiède et le frais*, Paris.

De Polignac, F. (1984) *La naissance de la cité grecque*, Paris (*Cults, Territory and the Origins of the Greek City-State*, Chicago, 1995).

De Polignac, F. (1994) 'Mediation, competition and sovereignty: the evolution of rural sanctuaries in Geometric Greece', in Alcock and Osborne, 3–18.

de Rachewiltz, S. and Riedmann, J. (eds) (1995) *Kommunikation und Mobilität im Mittelalter*, Thorbecke.

de Reparaz, A. (1990) 'La culture en terrasses, expression de la petite paysannerie méditerranéenne traditionelle', *Méditerranée* 3.4, 23–9.

de Slane, M. G. (ed. and trans.) (1965) al-Bakri (Abou-Obëid-el-Bekri) *Description de l'Afrique Septentrionale*, revised edn Paris.

De Ste Croix, G. E. M. (1956) 'Greek and Roman accounting', in A. C. Littleton and B. S. Yamey (eds) *Studies in the History of Accounting*, London, 14–74.

De Ste Croix, G. E. M. (1981) *The Class Struggle in the Ancient Greek World*, London.

de Vaumas, É. (1954) *Le Liban: montagne libanaise, Bekaa, Anti-Liban, Hermon, Haute Galilée libanaise. Étude de géographie physique*, Paris.

de Vries, J. (1984) *European Urbanization 1500–1800*, London.

de Vries, J. (1990) 'Problems in the measurement, description, and analysis of historical urbanization', in van der Woude, Hayami and de Vries, 43–60.

Deakin, R. (1855) *Flora of the Colosseum of Rome*, London.

Debord, P. (1982) *Aspects sociaux et économiques de la vie religieuse dans l'Anatolie gréco-romaine*, Leiden.

DeLaine, J. (1987) 'The "Cella Solealis" of the baths of Caracalla: a reappraisal', *PBSR* 42, 147–56.

Delaney, C. (1987) 'Seeds of honor, fields of shame', in Gilmore (ed.) 35–48.

Delaney, C. (1991) *The Seed and the Soil: Gender and Cosmology in Turkish Village Society*, Berkeley, Los Angeles and Oxford.

Delano Smith, C. (1979) *Western Mediterranean Europe: A Historical Geography of Italy, Spain and Southern France since the Neolithic*, London and New York.

Delano Smith, C. (1996) 'Where was the wilderness in Roman times?', in Salmon and Shipley, 154–79.

Delatte, A. (1947, 1958) *Les portolans grecs*, 2 vols, Liège and Brussels.

Delille, G. (1985) *Famille et propriété dans le royaume de Naples (XVe–XIXe siècle)*, Paris.

Dell, B., Hopkins, A. J. M. and Lamont, B. B. (1986) *Resilience in Mediterranean-Type Ecosystems*, Dordrecht, Boston and Lancaster.

Dell, H. (1967) 'The origin and development of Illyrian piracy', *Historia* 16, 344–58.

Delumeau, J. (1957–9) *Vie économique et sociale de Rome dans la seconde moitie du XVIe siecle*, 2 vols, Paris.

Deluz, C. (1987) 'Pèlerins et voyageurs face à la mer (XIIe–XVIe siècles)', in Dubois, Hocquet and Vauchez, 2.277–87.

Deman, A. (1975) 'Matériaux et réflexions pour servir à une étude du développement et du sous-développement dans les provinces de l'empire romain', *ANRW* 2.3, 3–97.

Demand, N. H. (1990) *Urban Relocation in Archaic and Classical Greece: Flight and Consolidation*, Bristol.

DeMolen, R. L. (ed.) (1974) *One Thousand Years: Western Europe in the Middle Ages*, Boston.

Déplacements des lignes de rivage en Méditerranée d'après les données de l'archéologie (1987), Paris.

Dermenghem, E. (1954) *Le culte des saints dans l'Islam maghrébin*, Paris.

Descoeudres, J.-P. (ed.) (1990) *Greek Colonists and Native Populations*, Oxford.

Despois, J. (1953) *Le Hodna, Algérie*, Paris.

Despy, G. and Verhulst, A. (eds) (1986) *La fortune historiographique des thèses d'Henri Pirenne*, Archives et Bibliothèques de Belgique, Brussels.

Deussen, P. W. (1994) 'The granaries of Morgantina and the *lex Hieronica*', in *Le ravitaillement en blé*, 231–5.

Devecian, K. (1928) *Pêche et pêcheries en Turquie*, Constantinople.

Devlin, J. (1987) *The Superstitious Mind: French Peasants and the Supernatural in the Nineteenth Century*, New Haven and London.

Di Castri, F., Goodall, D. W. and Specht, R. L. (eds) (1981) *Mediterranean-Type Shrublands*, Amsterdam and Oxford.

di Lusignano, S. (1573) *Chorograffia et breve historia universale dell'isola di Cipro*, Bologna.

di Segni, R. (1990) 'Spazi sacri e spazi maledetti nella Roma ebraica', in Boesch Gajano and Scaraffia, 113–20.

Diamond, J. (1997) *Guns, Germs and Steel*, London.

Dickie, J. (1992) 'Granada: a case-study of Arab urbanism in Muslim Spain', in S. K. Jayyusi (ed.) *Handbook of Oriental Studies XII: The Legacy of Muslim Spain*, Leiden, 88–111.

Dickinson, O. (1992) *The Aegean Bronze Age*, Cambridge.

Dickinson, R. E. (1969) *The Makers of Modern Geography*, London.

Dickinson, R. E. and Howarth, O. J. R. (1933) *The Making of Geography*, Oxford.

Dickson, D. B. (1989) 'Out of Utopia: Runnels' and van Andel's non-equilibrium growth model of the origins of agriculture', *JMA* 2.2, 297–302.

Dietler, M. (1995) 'The cup of Gyptis: rethinking the colonial encounter in early-Iron-Age western Europe and the relevance of world-systems models', *JEA* 3, 89–111.

Dilke, O. A. W. (1985) *Greek and Roman Maps*, London.

Dillard, H. (1984) *Daughters of the Reconquest: Women in Castilian Town Society, 1100–1300*, Cambridge.

Dillon, M. P. J. (1997a) 'The ecology of the Greek sanctuary', *ZPE* 118, 113–27.

Dillon, M. P. J. (1997b) *Pilgrims and Pilgrimage in Ancient Greece*, London and New York.

Dimen, M. and Friedl, E. (eds) (1976) *Regional Variation in Modern Greece and Cyprus: Towards a Perspective on the Ethnography of Greece, ANYAS* 268, New York.

Dinges, M. (1989) 'Die Ehre als Thema der Stadtgeschichte: eine Semantik im Übergang vom Ancien Régime zur Moderne', *Zeitschrift für Historische Forschung* 16, 409–40.

Dinzelbacher, P. (1990) 'Il ponte come luogo sacro nella realtà e nell'immaginario', in Boesch Gajano and Scaraffia, 51–60.

Dion, R. (1959) *L'histoire de la vigne et du vin en France des origines au XIXe siècle*, Paris.

Dixon, D. M. (1969) 'A note on cereals in ancient Egypt', in Ucko and Dimbleby, 131–42.

Djobadze, W. Z. (1986) *Archeological Investigations in the Region West of Antioch-on-the-Orontes*, Stuttgart.

Djurfeldt, G. (1993) 'Classes as clients of the state: landlords and labourers in Andalusia', *CSSH* 35, 159–82.

Dobby, E. G. H. (1936) 'The Ebro delta', *GJ* 87, 455–69.

Dobson, M., Harvey, D. and Wilkins, J. (eds) (1995) *Food in Antiquity*, Exeter.

Docavo Alberti, I. (1985a) 'La Albufera de Valencia y son entorno', in *Atti del convegno internazionale 'I Parchi costieri mediterranei 1973'*, 381–405.

Docavo Alberti, I. (1985b) 'El delta del Ebro', in *Atti del convegno internazionale 'I parchi costieri mediterranei 1973'*, 407–15.

Docter, R. F. and Niemeyer, H. G. (1994) 'Pithekoussai: the Carthaginian connection. On the archaeological evidence of Eubeo-Phoenician partnership in the 8th and 7th centuries B.C.', in *APOIKIA . . . scritti in onore di Giorgio Buchner*, 101–25.

Dodd, P. C. (1973) 'Family honor and the forces of change in Arab society', *IJMES* 4, 40–54.

Doehaerd, R. (1947) 'Ce qu'on vendait et comment on le vendait dans le Bassin parisien', *Annales*, 266–80.

Doehaerd, R. (1978) *The Early Middle Ages in the West: Economy and Society*, first published 1971, Amsterdam, New York and Oxford.

Domergue, C. (1990) *Les mines de la péninsule Ibérique dans l'antiquité romaine*, Rome.

Donham, D. L. (1981) 'Beyond the domestic mode of production', *Man* 16, 515–41.

Donkin, R. A. (1979) *Agricultural Terracing in the Aboriginal New World*, Tucson AZ.

Donner, F. M. (1989) 'The role of nomads in the Near East in late Antiquity (400–800 C.E.)', in F. M. Clover and R. S. Humphreys (eds) *Tradition and Innovation in Late Antiquity*, Madison WI, 73–85.

D'Onofrio, A. M. (1995) 'Santuari "rurali" e dinamiche insediative in Attica fra il protogeometrico e l'orientilizzante (1050–600 a.C.)', *AION*, new series 2, 57–88.

Donohue, V. A. (1992) 'The goddess of the Theban mountain', *Antiquity* 66, 871–85.

Dougherty, C. (1993) *The Poetics of Colonization*, New York.

Douglas, M. (1985) *Risk Acceptability according to the Social Sciences*, London.

Doukellis, P. N. and Mendoni, L. G. (eds) (1994) *Structures rurales et sociétés antiques: Actes du Colloque de Corfou . . . 1992*, Paris.

Doulgéri-Intzessiloglou, A. and Garlan, Y. (1990) 'Vin et amphores de Péparéthos et d'Ikos', *BCH* 114, 361–93.

Dover, K. J. (1974) *Greek Popular Morality in the Time of Plato and Aristotle*, Oxford.

Dover, K. J. (ed.) (1992) *Perceptions of the Ancient Greeks*, Oxford.

Dowdall, L. D. (1909) Aristotle, *De Mirabilibus Auscultationibus*, Oxford.

Downey, G. (1961) *A History of Antioch in Syria*, Princeton NJ.

Downey, G. (ed. and trans.) (1957) 'Nikolaos Mesarites: description of the Church of the Holy Apostles at Constantinople', *Transactions of the American Philosophical Society*, new series 47, 857–924.

Downie, R. A. (1970) *Frazer and the Golden Bough*, London.

Downing, T. E. and Gibson, M. (eds) (1974) *Irrigation's Impact on Society*, Tucson.

Downs, R. M. and Stea, D. (1977) *Maps in Minds: Reflections on Cognitive Mapping*, New York.

Downs, R. M. and Stea, D. (eds) (1973) *Image and Environment: Cognitive Mapping and Spatial Behaviour*, London.

Drake, S. (1976) 'An agricultural economist of the late Renaissance', in Hall and West, 53–73.

Dresch, P. (1989) *Tribes, Government, and History in Yemen*, Oxford.

Driessen, H. (1981) 'Anthropologists in Andalusia: the use of comparison and history', *Man* 16, 451–62.

du Boulay, J. (1974) *Portrait of a Greek Mountain Village*, Oxford.

du Boulay, J. (1976) 'Lies, mockery and family integrity', in J. G. Peristiany (ed.) *Mediterranean Family Structures*, Cambridge, 389–406.

du Boulay, J. and Williams, R. (1987) 'Amoral familism and the image of limited good', *Anthopological Quarterly* 60, 12–24.

Du latifundium au latifondo: un héritage de Rome, une création médiévale ou moderne? (1995), *Actes de la table ronde internationale du CNRS . . . Bordeaux . . . 1992*, Paris.

Dubisch, J. (1990) 'Pilgrimage and popular religion at a Greek holy shrine', in E. Badone (ed.) *Religious Orthodoxy and Popular Faith in European Society*, Princeton NJ, 113–39.

Dubisch, J. (1995) *In a Different Place: Pilgrimage, Gender, and Politics at a Greek Island Shrine*, Princeton NJ.

Dubois, H., Hocquet, J.-C. and Vauchez, A. (eds) (1987) *Horizons marins et itinéraires spirituels (Ve–XVIIIe siècles)*, 2 vols, Paris.

Duby, G. (1965) *Villages désertés et histoire économique*, Paris.

Duby, G. (1968) *Rural Economy and Country Life in the Medieval West*, London.

Duby, G. (1974) *The Early Growth of the European Economy: Warriors and Peasants from the Seventh to the Twelfth Century*, Ithaca.

Duby, G. (ed.) (1980–5) *Histoire de la France urbaine*, 5 vols, Paris.

Ducellier, A. (1980) 'Les séismes en Méditerranée orientale du XIème au XIIIème siècle: problèmes de méthode et résultats provisoires', in *Actes du XVe Congrès International d'Études Byzantines*, Athens, 4.103–13.

Ducellier, A. (1981) *La façade maritime de l'Albanie au moyen âge: Durazzo et Valona du XIe au XVe siècle*, Salonica.

Ducellier, A. (1991) 'Le bassin Adriatique, exutoire du commerce Balkanique à la fin du XVe siècle: la voie de mer', in Kravari, Lefort and Morrisson, 277–88.

Ducellier, A. and Balard, M. (eds) (1995) *Coloniser au moyen âge*, Paris.

Ducrey, P. (1983) 'Les Cyclades à l'époque hellénistique: la piraterie symptôme d'un malaise économique et social', in *Les Cyclades: matériaux pour une étude de géographie historique*, Paris, 143–8.

Dufaure, J.-J. (1976) 'La terrasse holocène d'Olympie et ses équivalents méditerranéens', *BAGF* 433, 85–94.

Dufaure, J.-J. and Vaudour, J. (1984) 'Aspects des grands karsts méditerranéens', in *La mobilité des paysages Mediterranéens*, 263–76.

Dufourcq, C.-E. (1975) *La vie quotidienne dans les ports méditerranéens au moyen âge: Provence, Languedoc, Catalogne*, Paris.

Dunand, F. (1979) 'L'artisanat du textile dans l'Égypte lagide', *Ktema* 4, 47–69.

Dunbabin, K. (1989) '*Baiarum grata voluptas*: pleasures and dangers of the baths', *PBSR* 44, 6–46.

Dunbabin, T. J. (1955) 'Sir John Myres 1869–1954', *PBA* 41, 348–65.

Duncan, N. (ed.) (1996) *BodySpace*, London.

Duncan-Jones, R. (1980) 'Demographic change and economic progress under the Roman Empire', in Gabba, 67–80.

Duncan-Jones, R. (1982) *The Economy of the Roman Empire: Quantitative Studies*, 2nd edn, Cambridge.

Duncan-Jones, R. (1990) *Structure and Scale in the Roman Economy*, Cambridge.

Dundes, A. (1988) *The Flood Myth*, Berkeley.

Dunn, A. (1992) 'The exploitation and control of woodland and scrubland in the Byzantine world', *BMGS* 16, 235–98.

Dunn, A. (1994) 'The transition from *polis* to *kastron* in the Balkans (III–VIIcc.): general and regional perspectives', *BMGS* 18, 60–80.

Dupré, N. (1987) 'Evolution de la ligne de rivage à l'embouchure de l'Èbre', in *Déplacements*, 25–34.

Dupront, A. (1973) 'Pélérinage et lieux sacrés', in *Mélanges . . . Braudel*, 2.189–206.

Durkheim, E. (1933) *The Division of Labor in Society*, first published 1893, New York and London.

Durliat, J. (1982) 'Taxes sur l'entrée des marchandises dans la cité de Carales/Cagliari à l'époque byzantine (582–602 ap. J.-C.)', *DOP* 36, 1–14.

Durliat, J. (1990) *De la ville antique à la ville byzantine: le problème des subsistances*, Rome.

Durliat, J. (1995) 'L'approvisionnement de Constantinople', in Mango and Dagron, 19–34.

Durrenberger, E. P. (ed.) (1984) *Chayanov, Peasants and Economic Anthropology*, New York.

Dussaud, R. (1927) *Topographie historique de la Syrie antique et médiévale*, Paris.

Düwel, K. and Claude, D. (eds) (1985–7) *Untersuchungen zu Handel und Verkehr der vor- und frühgeschichtlichen Zeit in Mittel- und Nordeuropa*. (1: *Methodische Grundlagen und Darstellungen zum Handel in vorgeschichtlicher Zeit und in der Antike*; 2: *Der Handel im westlichen Mittelmeer während des Frühmittlelalters* (monograph by D. Claude); 3: *Der Handel des frühen Mittelalters*; 4: *Der Handel der Karolinger- und Wikingerzeit*), *Abhandlungen der Akademie der Wissenschaften in Göttingen, philologisch-historische Klasse*, 3rd series, nos. 143, 144, 150, 156.

Dvornik, F. (1926) *La vie de Saint Grégoire le Décapolite et les Slaves Macédoniens au IXe siècle*, Paris.

Dyer, R. R. (1996) 'Timavus and the supine at Virgil, *Aen.* 1, 246', *CW* 89 (1996), 403–8.

Dyson, S. (1985) *The Creation of the Roman Frontier*, Princeton NJ.

Dyson, S. L. (1982) 'Archaeological survey in the Mediterranean basin: a review of recent research', *American Antiquity* 47, 87–96.

Dyson, S. L. (1992) *Community and Society in Roman Italy*, Baltimore and London.

Dyson-Hudson, R. and Dyson-Hudson, N. (1980) 'Nomadic pastoralism', *ARA* 9, 15–61.

Eade, J. and Sallnow, M. J. (eds) (1991) *Contesting the Sacred: The Anthropology of Christian Pilgrimage*, London.

East, W. D. G. (1940) *Mediterranean Problems*, London.

Eck, D. (1981) 'India's *tirthas*: crossings in sacred geography', *History of Religions* 20.4, 323–44.

Edelman, M. (1992) *The Logic of the Latifundio: The Large Estates of Northwestern Costa Rica since the Late Nineteenth Century*, Stanford CA.

Edlund, I. E. M. (1984) 'Sacred and secular: evidence of rural shrines and industry among Greeks and Etruscans', in Hackens et al., 277–90.

Edlund, I. E. M. (1985) 'Man, nature and the gods: a study of rural sanctuaries in Etruria and Magna Graecia from the seventh to the fourth century B.C.', in Malone and Stoddart, 21–32.

Edmondson, J. C. (1987) *Two Industries in Roman Lusitania: Mining and Garum Production*, Oxford.

Edmondson, J. C. (1989) 'Mining in the later Roman empire and beyond: continuity or disruption?', *JRS* 79, 84–102.

Edwards, J. (1982) *Christian Córdoba: The City and its Region in the Late Middle Ages*, Cambridge.

Edwards, J. (1987) '"Development" and "underdevelopment" in the western Mediterranean: the case of Córdoba and its region in the late fifteenth and early sixteenth centuries', *MHR* 2, 3–45.

Efstratiou, N. (1985) *Agios Petros: A Neolithic Site in the Northern Sporades. Aegean Relationships during the Neolithic of the Fifth Millennium B.C.*, Oxford.

Ehrenkreutz, A. (1972) 'Another orientalist's remarks concerning the Pirenne thesis', *JESHO* 15, 94–104.

Ehrenkreutz, A. (1981) 'Strategic implications of the slave trade between Genoa and Mamluk Egypt in the second half of the thirteenth century', in Udovitch, 335–45.

Eickelman, D. F. (1974) 'Is there an Islamic city? The making of a quarter in a Moroccan town', *IJMES* 5, 274–94.

Eickelman, D. F. (1976) *Moroccan Islam: Tradition and Society in a Pilgrimage Center*, Austin and London.

Eickelman, D. F. (1998) *The Middle East and Central Asia: An Anthropological Approach* (1st edn 1981), Englewood Cliffs NJ.

Eickelman, D. F. and Piscatori, J. (eds) (1990) *Muslim Travellers: Pilgrimage, Migration and the Religious Imagination*, London.

Eickhoff, E. (1966) *Seekrieg und Seepolitik zwischen Islam und Abendland: das Mittelmeer unter Byzantinischer und Arabischer Hegemonie (650–1040)*, Berlin.

Eisenstadt, S. N. (ed.) (1987) *Patterns of Modernity*, 2 vols, London.

Eisma, D. (1978) 'Stream deposition and erosion by the eastern shore of the Aegean', in Brice, 67–81.

Ellen, R. (1982) *Environment, Subsistence and System: The Ecology of Small-Scale Social Formations*, Cambridge.

Ellis, F. (1988) *Peasant Economics, Farm Household and Agrarian Development*, Cambridge.

Elsner, J. (1997) 'Hagiographic geography: travel and allegory in the *Life of Apollonius of Tyana*', *JHS* 117, 22–37.

Elster, J. (1983) *Explaining Technical Change*, Cambridge.

Elton, G. R. (1985) 'Europe and the Reformation', in D. Beales and G. Best (eds) *History, Society and the Churches: Essays in Honour of Owen Chadwick*, Cambridge, 89–104.

Elton, H. (1996) *Frontiers of the Roman Empire*, London.

Empereur, J.-Y. (1993) 'La production viticole dans l'Égypte ptolémaïque et romaine', in Amouretti and Brun, 39–47.

Empereur, J.-Y. and Garlan, Y. (eds) (1986) *Recherches sur les amphores grecques: actes du colloque international organisé par le Centre National de la Recherche Scientifique, l'Université de Rennes II et l' École Française d'Athènes . . . 1984*, Paris.

Empereur, J.-Y. and Picon, M. (1989) 'Les régions de production d'amphores impériales en Méditerranée orientale', in *Amphores romaines et histoire économique*, 223–48.

English, P. W. (1968) 'Qanats in the old world', *PAPS* 112, 170–81.

Ennen, E. (1987) *Die Europäische Stadt des Mittelalters*, 4th edn, Göttingen.

Épaulard, A., Monod, T., Lhote, H. and Mauny, R. (1956) Leo Africanus, *Description de l'Afrique*, Paris.

Epstein, A. L. (1984) *The Experience of Shame in Melanesia*, London.

Epstein, S. A. (1988) 'Labour in thirteenth-century Genoa', *MHR* 3, 114–40.

Epstein, S. A. (1996) *Genoa and the Genoese 958–1528*, Chapel Hill and London.

Epstein, S. R. (1991) 'Cities, regions and the late medieval crisis: Sicily and Tuscany compared', *PP* 130, 3–50.

Epstein, S. R. (1992) *An Island for Itself: Economic Development and Social Change in Late Medieval Sicily*, Cambridge.

Epstein, S. R. (1994) 'Regional fairs, institutional innovation and economic growth in late medieval Europe', *EcHR* 47, 3, 459–82.

Esler, P. F. (1994) *The First Christians in their Social Worlds*, London and New York.

Estrada, M., Vives, F. and Alcaraz, M. (1985) 'Life and the productivity of the open sea', in Margalef, 148–97.

Étienne, R. (1984) 'Astu et polis à Ténos', *Ktema* 9, 205–11.

Euzennat, M. (1992) 'L'hydraulique dans l'Afrique romaine', in Argoud et al., 75–94.

Evans, G. (1973) 'Recent coastal sedimentation: a review', in Blackman, 89–114.

Evans, G. E. (1960) *The Horse in the Furrow*, London.

Evans, J. D. (1977) 'Island archaeology in the Mediterranean', *WA* 9, 12–26.

Evans, J. K. (1980) 'Plebs rustica: the peasantry of classical Italy', *AJAH* 5, 19–47, 134–73.

Evans, J. K. (1981) 'Wheat production and its social consequences in the Roman world', *CQ* 31, 421–42.

Evans-Grubbs, J. (1989) 'Abduction marriage in aniquity: a law of Constantine (*CTh* IX. 24. 1) and its social context', *JRS* 79, 59–83.

Evans-Pritchard, E. E. (1949) *The Sanusi of Cyrenaica*, Oxford.

Evans-Pritchard, E. E. (1960) 'Introduction', in R. Hertz, *Death and the Right Hand*, ed. Evans-Pritchard, London, 9–24.

Evans-Pritchard, E. E. (1962) *Essays in Social Anthropology*, London.

Evans-Pritchard, E. E. (1981) *A History of Anthropological Thought*, London and Boston.

Eyre, C. J. (1994) 'The water regime for orchards and plantations in pharaonic Egypt', *Journal of Egyptian Archaeology* 80, 57–80.

Eyre, S. and Jones, E. (1966) *Geography as Human Ecology*, London.

Faber, G. L. (1883) *The Fisheries of the Adriatic and the Fish thereof*, London.

Fabian, J. (1983) *Time and the Other: How Anthropology Makes its Object*, New York.

Fabre, G. (1990–2) 'La catastrophe hydrologique éclair de Nîmes 3/10/1988', *BAGF* 67, 113–22.

Fabre, G. (ed.) (n. d.) *La montagne dans l'antiquité: Actes du colloque de la société des professeurs d'histoire ancienne de l'université . . . 1990*, Pau.

Fabre, P. (1981) *Les Grecs et la connaissance de l'occident*, Lille.

Fahmy, A. M. (1966) *Muslim Sea-Power in the Eastern Mediterranean from the Seventh to the Tenth Century A.D.*, 2nd edn, Cairo.

Fairbridge, R. W. (1972) 'Quaternary sedimentation in the Mediterranean region controlled by tectonics, paleoclimates and sea-level', in Stanley, 99–113.

Fairbridge, R. W. (1976) 'Shellfish-eating preceramic Indians in coastal Brazil', *Science* 191, 353–9.

Fanselow, F. (1990) 'The bazaar economy or how bizarre is the bazaar really?', *Man* 25, 250–65.

Fantechi, R. and Margaris, N. S. (eds) (1986) *Desertification in Europe*, Dordrecht.

Farès, B. (1932) *L'honneur chez les Arabes avant l'Islam: étude de sociologie*, Paris.

Farnoux, A. (1996) 'Les magasins à vivres (IIe et Ie millénaires): bilan de la journée d'étude', *Topoi* 6, 65–70.

Faroqhi, S. (1978) 'The early history of the Balkan fairs', *Südost-Forschungen* 37, 50–68.

Faroqhi, S. (1984) *Towns and Townsmen of Ottoman Anatolia: Trade, Crafts and Food Production in an Urban Setting, 1520–1650*, Cambridge.

Faroqhi, S. (1990–1) 'In search of Ottoman history', *JPS* 18, 211–41.

Farr, J. R. (1988) *Hands of Honor: Artisans and their World in Dijon, 1550–1650*, Ithaca and London.

Farrington, I. S. (1980) 'The archaeology of irrigation canals, with special reference to Peru', *WA* 11, 3, 287–305.

Favory, F. and J.-L. Fiches (eds) (1994) *Les campagnes de la France méditerranéenne dans l'antiquité et le haut moyen âge: études microrégionales*, Paris.

Febvre, L. (1925) *A Geographical Introduction to History*, first published 1922, London.

Febvre, L. (1935) 'Réflexions sur l'histoire des techniques', *Annales*, 29–32.

Febvre, L. (1940) 'Les surprises d'Hérodote, ou les acquisitions de l'agriculture méditerranéenne', *Annales*, 29–32.

Febvre, L. (1947) 'Vignes, vins, et vignerons', *Annales*, 281–7.

Febvre, L. (1973a) '*Frontière*: the word and the concept', in Febvre (1973b), 208–18.

Febvre, L. (1973b) *A New Kind of History: From the Writings of Lucien Febvre*, ed. P. Burke, London.

Fedeli, P. (1990) *La natura violata: ecologia e mondo Romano*, Palermo.

Fejfer, J. (ed.) (1995) *Ancient Akamas I*, Aarhus.

Fel, A. (1975) 'Paysages agraires et civilisation rurale de la vieille Corse', in *I paesaggi rurali europei*, 183–95.

Fenton, W. (1949) 'Collecting materials for a political history of the six nations', *PAPS* 93, 233–8.

Fentress, E., Judson, S., Blagg, T., De Vos, M. and Arthur, P. (1983) 'Excavations at Fosso della Crescenza, 1962', *PBSR* 51, 58–101.

Ferluga, J. (1987) 'Navigation et commerce dans l'Adriatique aux VIIe et VIIIe siècle', *BF* 12, 39–51.

Ferluga, J. (1993) 'Mercati e mercanti fra Mar Nero e Adriatico: il commercio nei Balcani dal VII all'XI secolo', *SS* 40, 443–89.

Fernandez, J. W. (1983) 'Consciousness and class in southern Spain', *American Ethnologist* 10, 165–73.

Fernández-Armesto, F. (1987) *Before Columbus: Exploration and Colonisation from the Mediterranean to the Atlantic, 1229–1492*, Basingstoke and London.

Fernández-Armesto, F. (1991) *Barcelona: A Thousand Years of the City's Past*, London.

Fernández-Miranda, M. (1997) 'Aspects of Talayotic culture', in Balmuth, 59–68.

Fernea, R. E. (1963–4) 'Conflict in irrigation', *CSSH* 6, 76–83.

Ferrante, L. (1989) 'Differenza sociale e differenza sessuale nelle questioni d'onore (Bologna sec. XVII)', in Fiume, 105–27.

Ferrante, L. (1990) 'Honor regained: women in the Casa del Soccorso di San Paolo in sixteenth-century Bologna', in Muir and Ruggiero, 46–72.

Février, P. A. (1974) 'Permanence et héritages de l'antiquité dans la topographie des villes de l'occident durant le haut moyen âge', *SS* 21, 41–138.

Figueira, T. J. (1981) *Aegina: Society and Politics*, Salem MA.

Fincardi, M. (1995) '"Ici pas de Madone": inondations et apparitions mariales dans les campagnes de la vallée du Pô', *Annales*, 829–54.

Fink, C. (1989) *Marc Bloch: A Life in History*, Cambridge.

Finlay, R. (1981) *Population and Metropolis: The Demography of London 1580–1650*, Cambridge.

Finley, M. I. (1958) review of A. E. R. Boak, *Manpower Shortage and the Fall of the Roman Empire in the West* (Ann Arbor and London 1955), *JRS* 48, 156–64.

Finley, M. I. (1965) 'Technological innovation and economic progress in the ancient world', *EcHR* 18, 29–45 (repr. Finley 1981b).

Finley, M. I. (1981a) 'The ancient city: from Fustel de Coulanges to Max Weber and beyond', in Finley (1981b), 1–23.

Finley, M. I. (1981b) *Economy and Society in Ancient Greece*, ed. B. D. Shaw and R. Saller, London.

Finley, M. I. (1985a) *The Ancient Economy*, 2nd edn, first published 1973, London.

Finley, M. I. (1985b) *Ancient History: Evidence and Models*, London.

Finley, M. I. (1987) 'Anthropology and the classics', in Finley, *The Use and Abuse of History*, first published 1975, Harmondsworth, 102–19.

Fischer, J. (1957) *Oriens-Occidens-Europa: Begriff und Gedanke 'Europa' in der späten Antike und im frühen Mittelalter* (Veröffentlichungen des Instituts für Europäische Geschichte, Mainz, 15), Wiesbaden.

Fischer, T. (1913) *Mittelmeerbilder*, Leipzig.

Fisher, G. (1957) *Barbary Legend: War, Trade and Piracy in North Africa, 1415–1830*, Oxford.

Fisher, N. and van Wees, H. (eds) (1998) *Archaic Greece: New Approaches and New Evidence*, London.

Fisher, N. R. (1992) *Hybris: A Study in the Values of Honour and Shame in Ancient Greece*, Warminster.

Fitton-Brown, A. D. (1985) 'The unreality of Ovid's Tomitan exile', *LCM* 10, 18–22.

Fiume, G. (ed.) (1989) *Onore e storia nelle società mediterranee*, Palermo.

Flemming, N. C. (1972) 'Eustatic and tectonic factors in the relative vertical displacement of the Aegean coast', in Stanley, 189–201.

Flemming, N. C. (1996) 'Sea level, neotectonics and changes in coastal settlements: threat and response', in Rice, 23–52.

Flemming, N. C., Czartoryska, M. M. G. and Hunter, P. M. (1973) 'Archaeological evidence for eustatic and tectonic components of relative sea-level change in the south Aegean', in Blackman, 1–66.

Flemming, N. C. and Masters, P. M. (eds) (1983) *Quaternary Coastlines and Marine Archaeology*, London.

Fletcher, Richard (1989) *The Quest for El Cid*, New York.

Fletcher, Roland (1995) *The Limits of Settlement Growth: A Theoretical Outline*, Cambridge.

Flint, V. I. J. (1991) *The Rise of Magic in Early Medieval Europe*, Oxford.

Foraboschi, D. (1994) 'Economie plurali ed interdependenze', in *L'Italie d'Auguste à Dioclétien: actes du colloque international 1992*, Rome, 215–18.

Forbes, H. (1976) 'The thrice-ploughed field', *Expedition* 18, 5–11.

Forbes, H. (1982) *Strategies and Soils: Technology, Production and Environment in the Peninsula of Methana, Greece*, Diss. Pennsylvania, published as *Strategies and Soils*, Ann Arbor, 1975.

Forbes, H. (1989) 'Of grandfathers and grand theories: the hierarchical ordering of responses to hazard in a Greek rural community', in Halstead and O'Shea (eds), 87–97.

Forbes, H. (1992) 'The ethnoarchaeological approach to ancient Greek agriculture', in B. Wells, 87–101.

Forbes, H. (1993) 'Ethnoarchaeology and the place of the olive in the economy of the South Argolid, Greece', in Amouretti and Brun, 213–26.

Forbes, H. (1996) 'The uses of the uncultivated landscape in modern Greece: a pointer to the value of the wilderness in antiquity?', in Salmon and Shipley, 68–97.

Forbes, H. (1998) 'European agriculture viewed bottom-side upwards: fodder- and forage-provision in a traditional Greek community', *Environmental Archaeology* 1, 19–34.

Forbes, H. and Foxhall, L. (1982) 'Sitometreia: the role of grain as a staple food in classical antiquity', *Chiron* 12, 41–89.

Forbes, H. and Foxhall, L. (1995) 'Ethnoarchaeology and storage in the ancient Mediterranean: beyond risk and survival?', in Dobson et al., 69–86.

Forbes, R. J. (1964) 'Washing, bleaching, fulling and felting', in *Studies in Ancient Technology* 4, Leiden, 82–98.

Forni, G. (1980a) 'Il *plaumaratum* (aratro a carrello) di Plinio nel quadro della storia dell'aratrocoltura in Italia', in Gabba, 99–120.

Forni, G. (1980b) 'Recent archaeological finds of tilling tools and fossil ard traces in Italy', *TT* 4, 1, 60–3.

Forni, G. (1989) 'Progrediti strumenti agricoli a fondamento della ricca economia lombarda in età romana imperiale', *RIL* 123, 59–75.

Forsyth, P. Y. (1996) 'The pre-eruption shapes of Bronze Age Thera: a new model', *AHB* 10, 1, 1–16.

Foss, C. (1994) 'The Lycian coast in the Byzantine age', *DOP* 48, 1–52.

Foss, C. (1995) 'The Near Eastern countryside in late antiquity: a review article', *JRA*, supplementary series 14, 213–34.

Foss, C. (1997) 'Syria in transition, A.D. 550–750', *DOP* 51, 189–269.

Fossey, J. M. (1979) 'The cities of the Kopaïs in the Roman period', *ANRW* 2.7.1, 549–91.

Fossier, R. (ed.) (1982–3) *Le moyen âge* (trans. as *The Cambridge Illustrated History of the Middle Ages*, Cambridge 1986–97), 3 vols, Paris.

Fotiadis, M. (1980) 'Transhumance: was it indeed practiced in the prehistoric Mediterranean?', *AJA* 84, 207.

Fotiadis, M. (1995) 'Modernity and the past-still-present: politics of time in the birth of regional archaeological projects in Greece', *AJA* 99, 59–78.

Foucault, M. (1972) *The Archaeology of Knowledge*, first published 1969, London.

Fowden, G. (1978) 'Bishops and temples in the eastern Roman empire, A.D. 320–453', *JThS* 29, 53–78.

Fowden, G. (1988) 'City and mountain in late Roman Attica', *JHS* 108, 48–59.

Fowden, G. (1990a) 'Religious developments in late Roman Lycia: topographical preliminaries', *Meletemata* 10, 343–70.

Fowden, G. (1990b) 'The Athenian Agora and the progress of Christianity', *JRA* 3, 494–501.

Fowden, G. (1993) *Empire to Commonwealth: Consequences of Monotheism in Late Antiquity*, Princeton NJ.

Fox, R. (1991) *The Inner Sea: The Mediterranean and its People*, London.

Fox, R. (1996) 'Introduction: methods and themes in the history of technology', in Fox (ed.), 1–15.

Fox, R. (ed.) (1996) *Technological Change: Methods and Themes in the History of Technology*, London.

Foxhall, L. (1990a) 'The dependent tenant: leasing and labour in Italy and Greece', *JRS* 80, 97–114.

Foxhall, L. (1990b) 'Olive cultivation within Greek and Roman agriculture: the ancient economy revisted', PhD thesis, University of Liverpool.

Foxhall, L. (1996) 'Feeling the earth move: cultivation techniques on steep slopes in classical antiquity', in Salmon and Shipley, 44–67.

Foxhall, L. (1998a) 'Cargoes of the heart's desire: the character of trade in the archaic Mediterranean world', in Fisher and van Wees, 295–310.

Foxhall, L. (1998b) 'Snapping up the unconsidered trifles: the use of agricultural residues in ancient Greek and Roman farming', *Environmental Archaeology* 1, 35–40.

Foxhall, L. (forthcoming) *Olive-Cultivation*.

Frake, C. (1985) 'Cognitive maps of time and tide', *Man* 20, 254–70.

Frances, E. (1966) 'L'empereur Nicéphore Ier et le commerce maritime byzantin', *Byzantinoslavica* 27, 41–7.

Francovich, R. and Noyé, G. (eds) (1994) *La storia dell'alto medioevo italiano (VI–X secolo) alla luce dell'archeologia*, Florence.

Frank, A. G. (1979) *Dependent Accumulation and Underdevelopment*, New York.

Frank, T. et al. (eds) (1933–40) *An Economic Survey of Ancient Rome*, 6 vols, Paterson NJ.

Frantz, A. (1965) 'From paganism to Christianity in the temples of Athens', *DOP* 19, 187–205.

Frantz-Murphy, G. (1986) *The Agrarian Administration of Egypt from the Arabs to the Ottomans*, Cairo.

Frayn, J. (1975) 'Wild and cultivated plants: a note on the peasant economy of Roman Italy', *JRS* 65, 32–9 (repr. in *Subsistence Farming in Roman Italy*, Fontwell and London 1979, ch. 4).

Frayn, J. (1984) *Sheep-Rearing and the Wool Trade in Italy during the Roman Period*, Liverpool.

Frayn, J. (1993) *Markets and Fairs in Roman Italy*, Oxford.

Frazer, J. (1898) *Pausanias's Description of Greece*, 6 vols, London.

Frazer, J. (1906) *Adonis, Attis, Osiris*, London, 2nd edn, 1907.

Frazer, J. (1911–35) *The Golden Bough*, 3rd edn, in 12 vols, London.

Frazer, J. (1936) *Aftermath: A Supplement to the Golden Bough*, London.

Frederiksen, M. W. (1975) 'Theory, evidence and the ancient economy', *JRS* 65, 164–71.

Frederiksen, M. W. (1980) 'Plinio il Vecchio e l'agricoltura in età imperiale romana: gli aspetti tecnici ed economici', in Gabba, 81–98.

Frederiksen, M. W. (1984) *Campania*, ed. N. Purcell, London.

Freedberg, D. (1989) *The Power of Images*, Princeton NJ.

Frei-Stolba, R. (1988) 'Viehzucht, Alpwirtschaft, Transhumanz: Bemerkungen zu Problemen der Wirtschaft in der Schweiz zur römischen Zeit', in Whittaker (ed.), 143–59.

Freitag, U. (1997) 'The critique of orientalism', in Hamilton, 620–38.

French, D. (1981) *Roads and Milestones of Asia Minor*, 1: *The Pilgrims' Road*, Oxford.

French, R. K. (1994) *Ancient Natural History: Histories of Nature*, London.

Frend, W. H. C. (1955) 'North Africa and Europe in the early Middle Ages', *TRHS* 5, 61–80.

Frenzel, B. (ed.) (1994) *Evaluation of Land-Surfaces Cleared from Forests in the Mediterranean Region during the Time of the Roman Empire*, Mainz.

Frézouls, E. (1987) *Sociétés urbaines, sociétés rurales dans l'Asie Mineure et la Syrie hellénistiques et romaines*, Strasbourg.

Friedl, E. (1962) *Vasilika: A Village in Modern Greece*, New York.

Friedman, S. W. (1997) *Marc Bloch, Sociology and Geography: Encountering Changing Disciplines*, Cambridge.

Frier, B. W. (1982) 'Roman life expectancy: Ulpian's evidence', *HSCP* 86, 213–51.

Frisch, P. (ed.) (1983) *Die Inschriften von Parion*, Inschriften griechischer Städte aus Kleinasien 25, Bonn.

Frost, H. (1995) 'Harbours and proto-harbours: early Levantine engineering', in Karageorghis and Michaelides, 1–22.

Frugoni, C. (1991) 'The city and the "new" saints', in J. Emlen, A. Molho and K. A. Raaflaub (eds) *City States in Classical Antiquity and Medieval Italy: Athens and Rome, Florence and Venice*, Stuttgart, 71–91.

Fukuyama, F. (1993) *The End of History and the Last Man*, London.

Fulford, M. (1984) 'Berenice and the economy of Cyrenaica', *LS* 15, 161–3.

Fulford, M. (1987) 'Economic interdependence among urban communities of the Roman Mediterranean', *WA* 19, 58–75.

Fumagalli, V. (1992) *L'uomo e l'ambiente nel medioevo*, Rome and Bari.

Fumagalli, V. (1994) *Landscapes of Fear: Perceptions of Nature and the City in the Middle Ages*, Oxford.

Gabba, E. (1981) 'True history and false history', *JRS* 71, 50–62.

Gabba, E. (1985) 'La transumanza nell'Italia romana, evidenza e problemi: qualche prospettiva per l'età altomedioevale', *SS* 31, 373–89.

Gabba, E. (1990) 'La transumanza nell'economia italico-romana', *Giornate internazionali di studio sulla transumanza*, 15–27.

Gabba, E. (ed.) (1980) *Tecnologia, economia e società nel mondo romano*, Como.

Gabba, E. and Pasquinucci, M. (1979) *Struture agrarie e allevamento transumante nell'Italia romana (III–I sec. a.C.)*, Pisa.

Gabbert, J. J. (1986) 'Piracy in the early Hellenistic period: a career open to talents', *GR* 3, 156–63.

Gabrieli, F. (1964) 'Greeks and Arabs in the central Mediterranean area', *DOP* 18, 57–65.

Gabrielsen, V. (1997) *The Naval Aristocracy of Hellenistic Rhodes*, Aarhus.

Gadban, C. (1987) 'Observations sur le statut des terres et l'organisation des villages dans la Béqa hellénistique et romaine', in E. Frézouls (ed.) *Sociétés urbaines, sociétés rurales dans l'Asie mineure et la Syrie hellénistiques et romaines*, Strasbourg, 217–38.

Gaffney, V. and Stančić, Z. (1991) *GIS Approaches to Regional Analysis*, Ljubljana.

Gaines, A.D. and Farmer, P. E. (1986) 'Visible saints: social cynosures and dysphoria in the Mediterranean tradition', *Culture, Medicine and Psychiatry* 10, 295–330.

Gale, N. H. (ed.) (1991) *Bronze Age Trade in the Central Mediterranean*, Göteborg.

Gale, N. H., Stos-Gale, Z. and Gilmore, G. R. (1985) 'Alloy types and copper sources of Anatolian copper alloy artefacts', *AS* 35, 143–74.

Galetti, P. (1988) 'Bosco e spazi incolti nel territorio piacentino durante l'alto medioevo', in Andreolli and Montanari, 263–86.

Galili, E., Schmueli, N. and Artzy, M. (1986) 'Bronze Age ship's cargo of copper and tin', *IJNA* 15, 25–37.

Gallant, T. W. (1985) *A Fisherman's Tale, Miscellanea Graeca* fasc. 7, Ghent.

Gallant, T. W. (1988) 'Greek bandits: lone wolves or a family affair?', *JMGS* 6, 269–90.

Gallant, T. W. (1989) 'Crisis and response: risk-buffering behavior in Hellenistic Greek communities', *JIH* 19.3, 393–419.

Gallant, T. W. (1991) *Risk and Survival in Ancient Greece*, Oxford.

Gallie, W. B. (1956) 'Essentially contested concepts', *Proceedings of the Aristotelian Society*, new series 56 (for 1955–6), 167–98.

Gallo, L. (1983) 'Alimentazione e classi sociali: una nota sull'orzo e frumento in Grecia', *Opus* 2, 449–72.

Gallo, L. (1989) [1991] 'Produzione cerealicola e demografia siciliana', *AION* 11, 31–53.

Gallo, L. (1992) 'La Sicilia occidentale e l'approviggionamento cerealicolo di Roma', *ASNP* 22, 365–98.

Galloway, J. A., Keene, D. and Murphy, M. (1996) 'Fuelling the city: production and distribution of firewood and fuel in London's region 1290–1400', *EcHR* 49, 447–72.

Galt, A. H. (1991a) 'Marital property in an Apulian town during the eighteenth and early nineteenth centuries', in Kertzer and Saller, 304–20.

Galt, A. H. (1991b) *Far from the Church Bells: Settlement and Society in an Apulian Town*, Cambridge.

Gamble, C. (1981) 'Social control and the economy', in Sheridan and Bailey, 215–29.

Gamble, J. C. and Yorke, R. A. (eds) (1978) *Progress in Underwater Science*, London.

Ganshof, F. L. (1938) 'Notes sur les ports de Provence du VIIIe au Xe siècle', *Revue historique* 183, 28–37.

Ganz, D. and Goffart, W. (1990) 'Charters earlier than 800 from French collections', *Speculum* 65, 906–32.

Garbrecht, G. (1980) 'The water supply system at Tuşpa (Urartu)', *WA* 11, 3, 306–12.

Garbrecht, G. (1984) 'Geschichtlichen Talsperren im östlichen Mittelmeerraum', *LIWBM* 82, 1–25.

Gardiner, G. (trans.) (1950) Turgenev, *On the Eve*, Harmondsworth.

Gargola, D. J. (1992) 'Grain distribution and the revenue of the Temple of Hera on Samos', *Phoenix* 46, 12–28.

Garlan, Y. (1978) 'Signification historique de la piraterie grecque', *DHA* 4, 1–16.

Garlan, Y. (1988) *Vin et amphores de Thasos*, Athens.

Garnsey, P. (1975–6) 'Peasants in ancient Roman society', *JPS* 3, 221–35 (repr. Garnsey 1998).

Garnsey, P. (1976) 'Economy and society of Mediolanum under the Principate', *PBSR* 44, 13–27 (repr. Garnsey 1998).

Garnsey, P. (1979) 'Where did Italian peasants live?', *PCPS* 29, 1–25.

Garnsey, P. (1980) 'Non-slave labour in the Roman world', in Garnsey (ed.), 34–47 (repr. Garnsey 1998).

Garnsey, P. (1988a) *Famine and Food Supply in the Graeco-Roman World: Responses to Risk and Crisis*, Cambridge.

Garnsey, P. (1988b) 'Mountain economies in southern Europe: thoughts on the early history, continuity and individuality of Mediteranean upland pastoralism', in Whittaker (ed.), 196–209 (repr. Garnsey 1998).

Garnsey, P. (1992) 'La fève: substance et symbole', in M. Aurell, O. Dumoulin and F. Thelamon (eds) *La sociabilité à table: commensalité et convivialité à travers les âges*, Rouen, 317–23 (trans. in Garnsey 1998).

Garnsey, P. (1998) *Cities, Peasants and Food in Classical Antiquity: Essays in Social and Economic History*, ed. W. Scheidel, Cambridge.

Garnsey, P. (ed.) (1980) *Non-Slave Labour in the Greco-Roman World*, Cambridge.

Garnsey, P., Hopkins, K. and Whittaker, C. R. (eds) (1983) *Trade in the Ancient Economy*, London.

Garnsey, P. and Morris, I. (1989) 'Risk and the polis: the evolution of institutionalized responses to food-supply problems in the ancient Greek state', in Halstead and O'Shea (eds), 98–105.

Garnsey, P. and Saller, R. (1987) *The Roman Empire: Economy, Society, Culture*, London.

Garnsey, P. and Whittaker, C. R. (1998) 'Trade, industry and the urban economy', in A. Cameron and P. Garnsey (eds) *The Cambridge Ancient History, Volume XIII: The Late Empire, A.D. 337–425*, Cambridge, 312–37.

Garnsey, P. and Whittaker, C. R. (eds) (1983) *Trade and Famine in Classical Antiquity*, Cambridge Philological Society supplementary vol. 8, Cambridge.

Garrioch, D. (1986) *Neighbourhood and Community in Paris, 1740–1790*, Cambridge.

Gateau, A. (ed. and trans.) (1947) *Conquête de l'Afrique du nord et de l'Espagne (Futúh' Ifríqiya wa'l-Andalus)*, 2nd edn, Algiers.

Gateau, F. (1996) *L'Étang de Berre*, Paris.

Gatto, G. (1979) 'Le voyage au paradis: la christianisation des traditions folkloriques au moyen âge', *Annales*, 929–942.

Gautheron, M. (ed.) (1991) *L'honneur: image de soi ou don de soi, un idéal équivoque*, Paris.

Gauthier, P. (1966) 'Les clérouques de Lesbos et la colonisation athénienne au Ve s.', *REG* 79, 64–88.

Gauthier, P. (1975) *Symbola: les étrangers et la justice dans les cités grecques*, Nancy.

Gauthier, P. (1979) 'EXAGŌGĒ SITOU: Samothrace, Hippomédon et les Lagides', *Historia* 28, 76–89.

Gauthier, P. (1982) 'Les villes athéniennes et un décret pour un commerçant (*IG* II² 903)', *REG* 95, 275–90.

Gauthier, P. (1987) 'Nouvelles récoltes et grain nouveau: à propos d'une inscription de Gazôros', *BCH* 111, 413–8.

Gauthier-Pilters, H. and Dagg, A. I. (1981) *The Camel: Its Evolution, Ecology, Behaviour and Relationship to Man*, Chicago.

Gavitt, P. (1990) *Charity and Children in Renaissance Florence: The Ospedale degli Innocenti, 1410–1536*, Ann Arbor.

Gayraud, M. (1981) *Narbonne antique des origines à la fin du IIIe siècle*, Narbonne.

Geary, P. (1978) *Furta Sacra: Thefts of Relics in the Central Middle Ages*, Princeton NJ.

Geary, P. (1986) 'Sacred commodities: the circulation of medieval relics', in Appadurai, 169–91.

Geertz, C. (1963) *Agricultural Involution: The Process of Ecological Change in Indonesia*, Berkeley.

Geertz, C. (1966) 'Religion as a cultural system', in M. Banton, *Anthropological Approaches to the Study of Religion*, London, 1–46 (repr. in Geertz, *The Interpretation of Cultures*, New York, 1973, 87–125).

Geertz, C. (1972) 'The wet and the dry: traditional irrigation in Bali and Morocco', *Human Ecology* 1, 23–39.

Geertz, C. (1984) 'Cultural and social change: the Indonesian case', *Man* 19, 511–33.

Geertz, C. (1990) 'History and anthropology', *New Literary History* 21, 321–35.

Gell, A. (1985) 'How to read a map: remarks on the practical logic of navigation', *Man* 20, 271–86.

Gell, A. (1995) 'The language of the forest: landscape and phonological iconism in Umeda', in Hirsch and O'Hanlon, 232–54.

Gell, W. (1807) *The Geography and Antiquities of Ithaca*, London.

Gellner, E. A. (1969) *Saints of the Atlas*, London.

Gellner, E. A. (1988) *Plough, Sword and Book: The Structure of Human History*, London.

Gemelli, G. (1995) *Fernand Braudel*, Paris.

Georgirenes, J. (1678) *A Description of the Present State of Samos, Nicaria, Patmos, and Mount Athos*, trans. [H. Denton], London.

Georgoudi, S. (1974) 'La transhumance dans la Grèce ancienne', *REG* 87, 155–85.

Gerschenkron, A. (1968) *Continuity in History and Other Essays*, Cambridge MA.

Gertwagen, R. (1988) 'The Venetian port of Candia, Crete (1299–1363): construction and maintenance', *MHR* 3, 141–58; also in Malkin and Hohlfelder, 141–58.

Gervers, V. (1983) 'Medieval garments in the Mediterranean world', in Harte and Ponting, 279–315.

Geyer, B. (ed.) (1990) *Techniques et pratiques hydro-agricoles traditionnelles en domaine irrigué: approche pluridisciplinaire des modes de culture avant la motorisation en Syrie. Actes du Colloque de Damas . . . 1987*, Bibliothèque archéologique et historique, 136, Paris.

Geyer, P. (ed.) (1898) *Itinera Hierosolymitana saeculi III–VIII*, Corpus Scriptorum Ecclesiaticorum Latinorum 39, Bonn.

Ghadban, C. (1987) 'Observations sur le statut des terres et l'organisation des villages dans le Beqa hellénistique et romaine', in Frézouls, 217–238.

Ghosh, P. (1997) 'The conception of Gibbon's *History*', in R. McKitterick and R. Quinault (eds) *Edward Gibbon and Empire*, Cambridge, 271–316.

Gianfrotta, P. A. (1981) 'Commerci e pirateria: prime testimonianze archeologiche sottomarine', *MEFRA* 93, 227–42.

Gianfrotta, P. A. and Pomey, P. (1980) *Archeologia subacquea: storia, techniche, scoperte e relitti*, Milan.

Giardina, A. (ed.) (1986) *Società romana e impero tardoantico*, 3 vols, Rome and Bari.

Giardina, A. and Schiavone, A. (eds) (1981) *Società romana e produzione schiavistica*, 3 vols, Rome and Bari.

Giardino, C. (1992) 'Nuragic Sardinia and the Mediterranean: metallurgy and maritime traffic', in Andrews and Tykot, 304–16.

Giardino, C. (1995) *Il Mediterraneo occidentale fra XIV ed VII secolo a.C.: cerchie minerarie e metallurgiche/The West Mediterranean between the 14th and 8th centures B.C.: Mining and Metallurgical Spheres*, BAR 612, Oxford.

Gibb, H. A. R. (1955) 'The fiscal rescript of 'Umar II', *Arabica* 2, 1–16.

Gibb, H. A. R. (1958) 'Arab–Byzantine relations under the Umayyad Caliphate', *DOP* 12, 219–33.

Gibbins, D. (1991) 'Archaeology in deep water: a preliminary view', *IJNA* 20, 163–8.

Gibbon, E. (1896) *The History of the Decline and Fall of the Roman Empire*, ed. J. B. Bury, vol. 1 of 7, London.

Giddens, A. (1981) *A Contemporary Critique of Historical Materialism*, vol. 1, London.

Giet, S. (ed.) (1968) Basil of Caesarea, *Homélies sur l'Hexaéméron*, 2nd edn, Paris.

Gil, M. (1974) 'The Râdhânite merchants and the Land of Râdhân', *JESHO* 17, 299–328.

Gil, M. (1986) 'Shlomo Dov Goitein, 1900–1985: a Mediterranean scholar', *MHR* 1, 9–12.

Gilbertson, D. D. (1986) 'Runoff (floodwater) farming and rural water-supply in arid lands', *Applied Geography* 6, 5–12.

Gill, D. W. J. (1988) 'Silver anchors and cargoes of oil: some observations on Phoenician trade in the western Mediterranean', *PBSR* 56, 1–12.

Gill, D. W. J. (1994) 'Positivism, pots and long-distance trade', in I. Morris, 99–107.

Gillis, C., Risberg, C. and Sjöberg, B. (eds) (1995) *Trade and Production in Premonetary Greece: Aspects of Trade*, Jonsered.

Gilman, A. and Thornes, J. B. (1985) *Land Use and Prehistory in South East Spain*, London.

Gilmore, D. D. (1982) 'Anthropology of the Mediterranean area', *ARA* 11, 175–205.

Gilmore, D. D. (1987a) 'Introduction: the shame of dishonour', in Gilmore (ed.), 2–21.

Gilmore, D. D. (1987b) 'Honor, honesty, shame: male status in contemporary Andalusia', in Gilmore (ed.), 90–103.

Gilmore, D. D. (1990) *Manhood in the Making: Cultural Concepts of Masculinity*, New Haven and London.

Gilmore, D. D. (ed.) (1987) *Honor and Shame and the Unity of the Mediterranean*, special publication of the American Anthropological Association no. 22, Washington DC.

Gilsenan, M. (1977) 'Against patron–client relations', in E. Gellner and J. Waterbury (eds) *Patrons and Clients in Mediterranean Societies*, London, 167–83.

Gilsenan, M. (1996) *Lords of the Lebanese Marches: Violence and Narrative in an Arab Society*, London and New York.

Gimpel, J. (1992) *The Medieval Machine: The Industrial Revolution of the Middle Ages*, 2nd edn, London.

Ginouvès, R., Guimier-Sorbets, A.-M., Jouanna, J. and Villard, L. (eds) (1994) *L'eau, la santé et la maladie dans le monde grec*, Paris.

Giovannini, A. (1985) 'Le sel et la fortune de Rome', *Athenaeum* 63, 373–87.

Giovannini, M. J. (1985) 'The dialectics of women's industrial work in a Sicilian town', *Anthropology* 9, 45–64.

Giovannini, M. J. (1987) 'Female chastity codes in the circum-Mediterranean: comparative perspectives', in Gilmore (ed.), 61–74.

Girard, F. et al. (1990) 'Les Norias hydrauliques du moyen-Oronte: patrimoine Syrien. Étude d'une technologie en voie de disparition', in Geyer, 367–82.

Girgis, M. D. (1987) *Mediterranean Africa*, Lanham MD, New York and London.

Gismondi, M. (1985) '"The gift of theory": a critique of the *histoire des mentalités*', *Social History* 10, 211–30.

Giuffrida Gentile, G. (1983) *La pirateria tirrenica: momenti e fortuna*, *Kokalos* supplement 6, Rome.

Glacken, C. J. (1967) *Traces on the Rhodian Shore: Nature and Culture in Western Thought from Ancient Times to the End of the Eighteenth Century*, Berkeley and Los Angeles.

Glick, T. F. (1970) *Irrigation and Society in Medieval Valencia*, Cambridge MA.

Glick, T. F. (1979) *Islamic and Christian Spain in the Early Middle Ages: Comparative Perspectives on Social and Cultural Formation*, Princeton NJ.

Glick, T. F. (1995) *From Muslim Fortress to Christian Castle*, Manchester.

Goar, J. (1647) *Euchologion sive rituale Graecorum*, Paris.

Goddard, V. (1987) 'Honour and shame: the control of women's sexuality and group identity in Naples', in P. Caplan (ed.) *The Cultural Construction of Sexuality*, London, 166–92.

Goddard, V. (1996) *Gender, Family and Work in Naples*, Oxford and Washington DC.

Goddard, V., Llobera, J. R. and Shore, C. (eds) (1994) *The Anthropology of Europe: Identity and Boundaries in Conflict*, Oxford and Providence RI.

Gödde, S. (1976) 'Données climatiques et risques d'incendie des forêts en Provence', *Méditerranée* 24, 1, 19–33.

Goffman, D. (1990) *Izmir and the Levantine World, 1550–1650*, Seattle and London.

Goitein, S. D. (1961) 'The main industries of the Mediterranean as reflected in the records of the Cairo Geniza', *JESHO* 4, 168–97.

Goitein, S. D. (1966a) *Studies in Islamic History and Institutions*, Leiden.

Goitein, S. D. (1966b) 'Medieval Tunisia: the hub of the Mediterranean', in Goitein (1966a), 308–28.

Goitein, S. D. (1967–88) *A Mediterranean Society: The Jewish Communities of the Arab World as Portrayed in the Documents of the Cairo Geniza*, 5 vols, Berkeley, Los Angeles and London.

Goitein, S. D. (1975) 'The life story of a scholar', in R. Attal (ed.) *A Bibliography of the Writings of Prof. Shelomo Dov Goitein*, Jerusalem.

Goitein, S. D. (trans.) (1973) *Letters of Medieval Jewish Traders*, Princeton NJ.

Golden, M. (1992) 'The uses of cross-cultural comparison in ancient social history', *Échos du Monde Classique/Classical Views* 36, 309–31.

Golden, M. and Toohey, P. (eds) (1997) *Inventing Ancient Culture: Historicism, Periodization, and the Ancient World*, London.

Goldschmidt, R. C. (1940) *Paulinus' Churches at Nola*, Amsterdam.

Goldsmith, J. L. (1984) 'The agrarian history of pre-industrial France: where do we go from here?', *JEEH* 13, 175–99.

Goldziher, I. (1971) *Muslim Studies*, ed. S. M. Stern, London.

Gomez Bellard, C. (1995) 'The first colonisation of Ibiza and Formentera', *WA* 26.3, 442–55.

Goodisson, W. (1822) *Historical and Topographical Essay upon the Islands of Corfu, etc.*, London.

Goodman, J. (1997) 'History and anthropology', in Bentley (ed.), 783–804.

Goodman, M. (1983) *State and Society in Roman Galilee, A.D. 132–212*, Totowa NJ.

Goody, J. (1971) *Technology, Tradition and the State in Africa*, Cambridge.

Goody, J. (1986) *Production and Reproduction: A Comparative Study of the Domestic Domain*, second edn, Cambridge.

Goody, J. (1996) *The East in the West*, Cambridge.

Goodyear, F. R. D. (1971) 'The *Dirae*', *PCPS* 17, 30–43.

Gose, P. (1993) 'Segmentary state formation and the ritual control of water under the Incas', *CSSH* 35, 480–514.

Gotteri, N. (1969) 'Gens, navires et marchandises à la douane de Palerme (1600–1605)', *MAH* 81, 783–860.

Gottmann, J. (1984) *Orbits: The Ancient Mediterranean Tradition of Urban Networks*, London.

Goudie, A. S. (1987) 'History and archaeology: the growth of a relationship', in Wagstaff, 11–25.

Gower Chapman, C. (1973) *Milocca: A Sicilian Village*, London.

Gowing, L. (1994) 'Language, power, and the law: women's slander litigation in early modern London', in J. Kermode and G. Walker (eds) *Women, Crime and the Courts in Early Modern England*, London, 26–47.

Gowing, L. (1996) *Domestic Dangers: Women, Words, and Sex in Early Modern London*, Oxford.

Goy, R. J. (1985) *Chioggia and the Villages of the Venetian Lagoon*, Cambridge.

Graham, A. J. (1978) 'The foundation of Thasos', *ABSA* 73, 61–98.

Graham-Campbell, J. (ed.) (1994) *The Archaeology of Pilgrimage*, London (also *WA* 26.1).

Grainger, D. (1990) *The Cities of Seleucid Syria*, Oxford.

Grant, E. (ed.) (1986) *Central Places, Archaeology and History*, Sheffield.

Grantham, G. W. (1997) 'Espaces privilégiés: productivité agraire et zones d'approvisionnement des villes dans l'Europe préindustrielles', *Annales*, 695–725.

Gras, M. (1993) 'Pour une Méditerranée des *emporia*', in Bresson and Rouillard, 103–12.

Graser, E. R. (1940) 'The Edict of Diocletian on maximum prices', in T. Frank et al., 5.305–421.

Grava, Y. (1980) 'Marchands, pêcheurs, et gens de mer sur les bords de l'Étang de Berre à la fin du moyen âge', in *Minorités en Méditerranée*, Aix.

Grayson, D. K. and Sheets, P. D. (eds) (1979) *Volcanic Activity and Human Ecology*, New York.

Greene, K. (1986) *The Archaeology of the Roman Economy*, London.

Greene, K. (1994) 'Technology and innovation in context: the Roman background to medieval and later developments', *JRA* 7, 22–33.

Greenhalgh, M. (1989) *The Survival of Roman Antiquities in the Middle Ages*, London.

Greenhill, B. (1976) *Archaeology of the Boat: A New Introductory Study*, London.

Gregorovius, F. (1911) *Roman Journals*, London.

Gregory, T. (1986) 'The survival of paganism in Christian Greece: a critical essay', *AJP* 107, 229–42.

Grenon, M. and Batisse, M. (eds) (1989) *Futures for the Mediterranean Basin: 'The Blue Plan'*, Oxford.

Gress, D. (1983) 'The pride and prejudice of Fernand Braudel', *The New Criterion*, April, 7–13.

Grieco, A. J. (1993) 'Olive tree cultivation and the alimentary use of olive oil in late medieval Italy (ca. 1300–1500)', in Amouretti and Brun, 297–306.

Grierson, P. (1992) 'The role of silver in the early Byzantine economy', in Boyd and Mango, 137–46.

Grigg, D. B. (1979) 'Esther Boserup's theory of agrarian change: a critical review', *Progress in Human Geography* 3, 64–84.

Grigg, D. B. (1980) 'Population pressure and agricultural change', in D. B. Grigg, *Population Growth and Agrarian Change: An Historical Perspective*, Cambridge, 134–76.

Grigg, D. B. (1982) *The Dynamics of Agricultural Change: The Historical Experience*, London.

Grigg, D. B. (1992) *The Transformation of Agriculture in the West*, Oxford.

Groenman-van Waateringe, W. (1996) 'Wasteland: buffer in the medieval economy', in Colardelle, 113–17.

Grosso, R. (1975) 'Histoire d'un paysage agraire: les prairies irriguées de la banlieue d'Avignon', in *I paesaggi rurali europei*, 263–72.

Grove, J. M., Moody, J. A. and Rackham, O. (eds) (1992) *Stability and Change in the Cretan Landscape*, Petromarula.

Groves, R. H. and Di Castri, F. (eds) (1991) *Biogeography of Mediterranean Invasions*, Cambridge.

Guest-Papamanoli, A. (1986) 'Une pêche au guet: le taliani. Origines et distribution géographique', in *L'exploitation de la mer*, 185–203.

Guichard, P. (1977) *Structures sociales 'orientales' et 'occidentales' dans l'Espagne musulmane*, Paris and The Hague.

Guidoboni, E. (1989) 'Sismicità e disastri sismici: il lungo periodo e i punti di vista', in Guidoboni (ed.), 12–24.

Guidoboni, E. (ed.) (1989) *I terremoti prima del Mille in Italia e nell'area mediterranea*, Bologna.

Guilaine, J. (1976) *Les premiers bergers et paysans de l'occident méditerranéen*, Paris.

Guilaine, J. (1994) *La mer partagée: la Méditerranée avant l'écriture, 7000–2000 av. J.-C.*, Baume-les-Dames.

Guillou, A. (1974) 'Production and profits in the Byzantine province of Italy (tenth to eleventh centuries): an expanding society', *DOP* 28, 89–109.

Gulick, J. (1973) 'Urban anthropology', in J. J. Honigmann (ed.) *Handbook of Social and Cultural Anthropology*, Chicago, 979–1029.

Gulick, J. (1983) *The Middle East: An Anthropological Perspective*, Lanham MD and London.

Gunder Frank, A. and Gills, B. K. (eds) (1993) *The World System: Five Hundred Years or Five Thousand?*, London.

Gunderson, G. (1976) 'Economic change and the demise of the Roman empire', *Explorations in Economic History* 13, 43–68.

Günsenin, N. (1993) 'Ganos: centre de production d'amphores à l'époque byzantine', *Anatolia Antiqua* 2, 193–201.

Gurevitch, A. (1988) *Medieval Popular Culture: Problems of Belief and Perception*, Cambridge.

Haas, P. M. (1990) *Saving the Mediterranean: The Politics of International Environmental Cooperation*, New York.

Habicht, C. (1985) *Pausanias' Guide to Ancient Greece*, Berkeley.

Hachmann, R. (1989) 'Kâmid el-Lôz 1963–1981: German excavations in Lebanon part I', *Berytus* 37, 5–187.

Hackens, T. (ed.) (1988) *Navies and Commerce of the Greeks, the Carthaginians and the Etruscans in the Tyrrhenian Sea, Convegno . . . Ravello 1987*, Strasbourg.

Hackens, T., Holloway, N. D. and Ross Holloway, R. (eds) (1984) *Crossroads of the Mediterranean: Papers delivered at the International Conference on the Archaeology of Early Italy . . . 1981*, Providence RI and Louvain-la-Neuve, Belgium.

Hackens, T. and Miró, M. (eds) (1990) *Le commerce maritime romain en Méditerranée occidentale. Convegno . . . Barcelona 1988*, Strasbourg.

Hadjisavvas, S. (1992) *Olive Oil Processing in Cyprus: From the Bronze Age to the Byzantine Period*, Nicosia.

Haggett, P., Cliff, A. D. and Frey, A. (1977) *Locational Analysis in Human Geography*, 2nd edn, London.

Haggis, D. C. (1996) 'The port of Tholos in eastern Crete and the role of a Roman *horreum* along the Egyptian corn-route', *OJA* 15, 183–209.

Hajjar, Y. (1985) *La triade de Héliopolis-Baalbek: iconographie, théologie, culte et sanctuaires*, Montreal.

Haldon, J. F. (1989) 'The feudalism debate once more: the case of Byzantium', *JPS* 17, 5–40.

Haldon, J. F. (1990) *Byzantium in the Seventh Century: The Transformation of a Culture*, Cambridge.

Haldon, J. F. (1994) 'Quelques remarques sur l'économie byzantine de 600 à 1100: esquisse comparative', in Francovich and Noyé, 71–84.

Hale, J. (1993) *The Civilization of Europe in the Renaissance*, London.

Halecki, O. (1950) *The Limits and Divisions of European History*, London and New York.

Hall, A. and Kenward, H. K. (eds) (1994) *Urban–Rural Connections: Perspectives from Environmental Archaeology*, Oxbow monograph 47, Oxford.

Hall, B. (1996) 'Lynn White's *Medieval Technology and Social Change* after thirty years', in Fox (ed.), 85–101.

Hall, B. S. and West, D. C. (eds) (1976) *On Pre-modern Technology and Science: A Volume of Studies in Honor of Lynn White, Jr.*, Malibu CA.

Halliday, W. R. (1910–11) 'Cenotaphs and sacred localities', *ABSA* 17, 181–92.

Hallof, K. (1994) 'Die Inschrift von Skaptopara: neue Dokumente und neue Lesungen', *Chiron* 24, 405–41.

Hallpike, C. R. (1972) *The Konso of Ethiopia: A Study of the Values of a Cushitic People*, Oxford.

Hallpike, C. R. (1986) *The Principles of Social Evolution*, Oxford.

Halstead, P. (1981a) 'From determinism to uncertainty: social storage and the rise of the Minoan palace', in Sheridan and Bailey, 187–213.

Halstead, P. (1981b) 'Counting sheep in Neolithic and Bronze Age Greece', in Hodder, Isaac and Hammond, 307–30.

Halstead, P. (1987) 'Traditional and ancient rural economy in Mediterranean Europe: plus ça change?', *JHS* 107, 77–87.

Halstead, P. (1989) 'The economy has a normal surplus: economic stability and social change among early farming communities of Thessaly', in Halstead and O'Shea (eds), 87–97.

Halstead, P. (1990a) 'Waste not, want not: traditional responses to crop failure in Greece', *RurH* 1, 147–64.

Halstead, P. (1990b) 'Quantifying Sumerian agriculture: some seeds of doubt and hope', *BSA* 5, 187–95.

Halstead, P. (1992a) 'Agriculture in the Bronze Age Aegean: towards a model of palatial economy', in B. Wells, 105–17.

Halstead, P. (1992b) 'The Mycenaean palatial economy: making the most of the gaps in the evidence', *PCPS* 38, 57–86.

Halstead, P. (1993) 'Banking on livestock: indirect storage in Greek agriculture', in *Domestic Animals of Mesopotamia I*, *BSA* 7, 63–75.

Halstead, P. (1995) 'Plough and power: the economic and social significance of cultivation with the ox-drawn ard in the Mediterranean', in *Domestic Animals of Mesopotamia II*, *BSA* 8, 11–22.

Halstead, P. and Jones, G. (1989) 'Agrarian ecology in the Greek island: time stress, scale and risk', *JHS* 109, 41–55.

Halstead, P. and O'Shea, J. (1982) 'A friend in need is a friend indeed: social storage and the origins of social ranking', in Renfrew and Shennan, 92–9.

Halstead, P. and O'Shea, J. (1989) 'Introduction: cultural responses to risk and uncertainty', in Halstead and O'Shea (eds), 1–7.

Halstead, P. and O'Shea, J. (eds) (1989) *Bad Year Economics: Cultural Responses to Risk and Uncertainty*, Cambridge.

Hamilton, J. (1856) *Wanderings in North Africa*, London.

Hammond, N. (1967) *Epirus*, Oxford.

Hanawalt, B. A. (ed.) (1986) *Women and Work in Pre-industrial Europe*, Bloomington.

Hanfmann, H. (1986) *Itinera Principum: Geschichte und Typologie der Kaiserreisen im Römischen Reich*, Stuttgart.

Hansen, M. H. (1985) *Demography and Democracy: The Number of Athenian Citizens in the Fourth Century B.C.*, Herning.

Hansen, M. H. and Raaflaub, K. (eds) (1995) *Studies in the Ancient Greek Polis*, Stuttgart.

Hanson, V. D. (1992) 'Practical aspects of grape-growing and the ideology of Greek viticulture', in B. Wells, 161–6.

Hanson, V. D. (1995) *The Other Greeks: The Family Farm and the Agrarian Roots of Western Civilization*, New York.

Hardesty, D. L. (1975) 'The niche concept: suggestions for its use in human ecology', *Human Ecology* 3, 71–85.

Hardy, D. (ed.) (1990) *Thera and the Aegean World III*, London.

Harlaftis, G. (1995) *A History of Greek-Owned Shipping: The Making of an International Tramp Fleet, 1830 to the Present Day*, London.

Harlan, J. G. (1951) 'Anatomy of gene centers', *American Naturalist* 85, 97–103.

Harlan, J. G. (1989) 'The tropical African cereals', in Harris and Hillman, 335–43.

Harley, J. B. and Woodward, D. (eds) (1987–) *The History of Cartography* (vol. 1: *Cartography in Prehistoric, Ancient and Medieval Europe and the Mediterranean*; vol. 2, book 1 (1992): *Cartography in the Traditional Islamic and South Asian Societies*), Chicago and London.

Harries, J. (1992) 'Death and the dead in the late Roman West', in S. Bassett (ed.) *Death in Towns: Urban Responses to the Dying and the Dead, 100–1600*, Leicester, 56–67.

Harris, D. R. (1996) *The Origins and Spread of Agriculture and Pastoralism*, London.

Harris, D. R. and Hillman, G. C. (1989) *Foraging and Farming: The Evolution of Plant Exploitation*, London.

Harris, W. V. (1980) 'Towards a study of the Roman slave trade', *MAAR* 36, 117–40.

Harrison, G. W. M. (1990) 'Gortyn in Byzantine Crete' (review), *JRA* 3, 503–5.

Harsgor, M. (1986) 'Braudel's sea revisited', *MHR* 1, 135–57.

Harte, N. B. and Ponting, K. G. (eds) (1983) *Cloth and Clothing in Medieval Europe*, London.

Hartmann, L. M. (1904) *Zur Wirtschaftsgeschichte Italiens im frühen Mittelalter: Analekten*, Gotha.

Harvey, A. (1989) *Economic Expansion in the Byzantine Empire A.D. 900–1200*, Cambridge.

Harvey, A. (1995) 'The middle Byzantine Empire: growth or stagnation?', *BMGS* 19, 243–61.

Hasluck, F. W. (1909–10) 'Terra Lemnia', *ABSA* 16, 220–31.

Hasluck, F. W. (1910–11) 'Depopulation in the Aegean islands and the Turkish conquest', *ABSA* 17, 151–81.

Hasluck, F. W. (1913–14) 'Ambiguous sanctuaries', *ABSA* 20, 94–122.

Hasluck, F. W. (1914–16) 'Stone cults', *ABSA* 21, 62–83.

Hasluck, F. W. (1926) *Letters on Religion and Folklore*, London.

Hasluck, F. W. (1929) *Christianity and Islam under the Sultans II*, Oxford.

Hastrup, K. (1985) *Culture and History in Medieval Iceland: An Anthropological Analysis of Structure and Change*, Oxford.

Hastrup, K. (ed.) (1992) *Other Histories*, London and New York.

Haudricourt, A.-G. (1987) *La technologie, science humaine: recherches d'histoire et d'ethnologie des techniques*, Paris.

Haudricourt, A.-G. and Delamarre, M. J.-B (1955) *L'homme et la charrue à travers le monde*, Paris.

Hauschild, T. (1992) 'Making history in southern Italy', in Hastrup, 29–44.

Haverkamp, A. (1987) '"Heilige Städte" im hohen Mittelalter', in F. Graus (ed.) *Mentalitäten im Mittelalter: methodische und inhaltliche Probleme*, Sigmaringen, 119–56.

Haverkamp, A. (1998) 'Cities as cultic centres in Germany and Italy during the Early and High Middle Ages', in Kedar and Werblowsky, 172–86.

Havighurst, A. F. (1958) *The Pirenne Thesis: Analysis, Criticism and Revision*, Boston.

Hawkes, J. G. (1983) *The Diversity of Crop Plants*, Cambridge MA.

Hawley, A. H. (1986) *Human Ecology: A Theoretical Essay*, Chicago.

Hay, D. (1968) *Europe: The Emergence of an Idea*, 2nd edn, Edinburgh.

Hayes, P. P. (1995) 'The geographical setting', in Fejfer, 63–72.

Haywood, J. (1991) *Dark Age Naval Power: A Re-assessment of Frankish and Anglo-Saxon Seafaring Activity*, London and New York.

Haywood, R. M. H. (1938) 'Roman Africa', in T. Frank et al., 5.1–119.

Healy, J. F. (1978) *Mining and Metallurgy in the Ancient World*, London.

Heaney, S. (1988) *The Government of the Tongue*, London.

Hedreen, G. (1991) 'The cult of Achilles in the Euxine', *Hesperia* 60, 313–30.

Heers, J. (1958) 'Types de navire et spécialisation des trafics en Méditerranée à la fin du moyen âge', in M. Mollat (ed.) *Le navire et l'économie maritime du moyen âge au XVIIIe siècle, principalement en Méditerranée: Actes du deuxième colloque international d'histoire maritime*, Paris, 107–17.

Heers, J. (1977) *Family Clans in the Middle Ages*, Amsterdam, New York and Oxford.

Heers, J. (1981) *Esclaves et domestiques au moyen âge dans le monde Méditerranéen*, Paris.

Heers, J. (1989) 'Paysages urbains et sociétés dans les différents types de villes portuaires en Méditerranée', in Poleggi, 11–24.

Hegyi, D. (1976) '*Temene hiera kai temene demosia*', *Oikoumene* 1, 77–88.

Heim, F. (1986) 'L'expérience mystique des pèlerins occidentaux en Terre Sainte aux alentours de 400', *Ktema* 11, 193–208.

Heine, P. (1982) *Weinstudien: Untersuchungen zu Anbau, Produktion und Konsum des Weins im arabisch-islamischen Mittelalter*, Wiesbaden.

Hellstrom, P. and Alroth, B. (eds) (1996) *Religion and Power in the Ancient Greek World: Proceedings of the Uppsala Symposium 1993*, Uppsala.

Helly, B. (1998) 'La sismicité est-elle un objet d'étude pour les archéologues?', in Olshausen and Sonnabend.

Helly, B. and Pollino, A. (eds) (1984) *Tremblements de terre: histoire et archéologie*, Valbonne.

Helms, M. W. (1988) *Ulysses' Sail*, Princeton NJ.

Heltzer, M. (1993) 'Olive oil and wine production in Phoenicia and the Mediterranean trade', in Amouretti and Brun, 49–54.

Hémardinquer, J. J. (1973) 'Les débuts du maïs en Méditerranéee (premier aperçu)', in *Mélanges . . . Braudel*, 1.227–33.

Hemphill, P. (1987) 'Report of fieldwork on Roman forestry in Italy', *AJA* 91, 304.

Henderson, J. (1994) *Piety and Charity in Late Medieval Florence*, Oxford.

Hendy, M. F. (1985) *Studies in the Byzantine Monetary Economy c.300–1450*, Cambridge.

Hendy, M. F. (1988) 'From public to private: the western barbarian coinages as a mirror of the disintegration of late Roman state structures', *Viator* 19, 29–78.

Hercher, R. (1871) *Epistolographi graeci*, Paris.

Herlihy, D. (1958a) *Pisa in the Early Renaissance: A Study of Urban Growth*, New Haven.

Herlihy, D. (1958b) 'The agrarian revolution in southern France and Italy, 801–1150', *Speculum* 33, 23–41.

Herlihy, D. (1967) *Medieval and Renaissance Pistoia: The Social History of an Italian Town, 1200–1430*, New Haven.

Herlihy, D. (1974) 'Ecological conditions and demographic change', in DeMolen, 3–46.

Herlihy, D. (1978) 'The distribution of wealth in a Renaissance community: Florence 1427', in Abrams and Wrigley, 131–57.

Herlihy, D. (1985) *Medieval Households*, Cambridge MA.

Herlihy, D. (1990) *Opera Muliebria: Women and Work in Medieval Europe*, New York.

Herlihy, D. and Klapisch-Zuber, C. (1985) *Tuscans and their Families: A Study of the Florentine Catasto of 1427* (abbreviated trans. of first edn of 1978), New Haven and London.

Herman, G. (1996) 'Ancient Athens and the values of Mediterranean society', *MHR* 11, 5–36.

Herrin, J. (1987) *The Formation of Christendom*, Oxford.

Herrmann, P. (1990) *Hilferufe aus römischen Provinzen: ein Aspekt der Krise des römischen Reiches im 3. Jhdt. n. Chr.*, Göttingen.

Hertz, R. (1913) 'Saint Besse, étude d'un culte alpestre', *Revue d'histoire des religions* 67, 115–80; trans. as 'St Besse: a study of an Alpine cult', in S. Wilson (1983), 55–100.

Herz, P. (1988) *Studien zur römischen Wirtschaftgesetzgebung: die Lebensmittelversorgung*, Stuttgart.

Herzfeld, M. (1980) 'Honour and shame: problems in the comparative analysis of moral systems', *Man* 15, 339–51.

Herzfeld, M. (1984) 'The horns of the Mediterraneanist dilemma', *American Ethnologist* 11, 439–54.

Herzfeld, M. (1985) *The Poetics of Manhood: Contest and Identity in a Cretan Mountain Village*, Princeton NJ.

Herzfeld, M. (1987a) ' "As in your own house": hospitality, ethnography, and the stereotype of Mediterranean society, in Gilmore (ed.), 75–89.

Herzfeld, M. (1987b) *Anthropology through the Looking-Glass: Critical Ethnography on the Margins of Europe*, Cambridge.

Herzfeld, M. (1991) *A Place in History: Social and Monumental Time in a Cretan Town*, Princeton NJ.

Hesnard, A. (1995) 'Les ports antiques de Marseille, Place Jules-Verne', *JRA* 8, 65–77.

Hess, A. C. (1978) *The Forgotten Frontier: A History of the Sixteenth-Century Ibero-African frontier*, Chicago.

Heurgon, J. (1952) 'La date des gobelets de Vicarello', *REA* 54, 39–50.

Heurgon, J. (1957) *Trois études sur le 'ver sacrum'*, Brussels.

Heurgon, J. (1982) 'A propos de l'inscription tyrrhénienne de Lemnos', *PdelP* 37, 189–92.

Hexter, J. H. (1979) 'Fernand Braudel and the Monde Braudellien . . .' (repr. from *Journal of Modern History* 44 (1972), 480–539) in *On Historians*, London, 61–145.

Higgins, M. D. and Higgins, R. (1996) *A Geological Companion to Greece and the Aegean*, London.

Higounet, C. (1966) 'Les forêts de l'Europe occidentale du Vème au XIème siècle', *SS* 13, 343–98.

Higounet-Nadal, A. (1978) *Périgueux aux XIVe et XVe siècles: étude de démographie historique*, Paris.

Hild, F. (1977) *Das byzantinische Strassensystem in Kappdokien*, Veröffentlichungen der Kommission für die Tabula Imperii Byzantini 2, Vienna.

Hill, D. R. (1980) *Islamic Technology: An Illustrated History*, Cambridge.

Hill, D. R. (1984) *A History of Engineering in Classical and Medieval Times*, London.

Hill, P. (1986) 'Why country people are not peasants', in Hill, *Development Economics on Trial: The Anthropological Case for a Prosecution*, Cambridge, 8–15.

Hill, S. and Bryer, A. (1995) 'Byzantine porridge: *Tracta*, *trachanas* and *tarhana*', in Dobson, Harvey and Wilkins, 44–54.

Hillgarth, J. N. (1975) *The Problem of a Catalan Mediterranean Empire, 1229–1327 (EHR* supplement 8), London.

Hillier, B. and Hanson, J. (1984) *The Social Logic of Space*, Cambridge.

Hills, R. L. (1994) *Power from Wind: A History of Windmill Technology*, Cambridge.

Hilton, R. H. and Sawyer, P. W. (1963) 'Technical determinism: the stirrup and the plough', *PP* 24, 90–100.

Himmelfarb, G. (1987) *The New History and the Old*, Harvard.

Himmelfarb, M. (1983) *Tours of Hell: An Apocalyptic Form in Jewish and Christian Literature*, Philadelphia.

Hindley, C. and Cohen, D. (1991) 'Debate: law, society and homosexuality in classical Athens', *PP* 133, 167–94.

Hingley, R. (ed. and trans.) (1965–80) *The Oxford Chekhov*, 9 vols, Oxford.

Hirsch, E. (1995) 'Landscape: between place and space', in Hirsch and O'Hanlon, 1–30.

Hirsch, E. and O'Hanlon, M. (eds) (1995) *The Anthropology of Landscape: Perspectives on Place and Space*, Oxford.

Hirschon, R. (1989) *Heirs of the Greek Catastrophe: The Social Life of Asia Minor Refugees in Piraeus* (repr. with new preface 1998), Oxford.

Hirth, K. G. (1978) 'Inter-regional trade and the formation of prehistoric gateway-communities' *American Antiquity* 43, 25–45.

Hitchner, R. B. (1988) 'The Kasserine archaeological survey, 1982–86', *Antiquités Africaines* 24, 7–41.

Hobsbawm, E. J. (1960) *Bandits*, Harmondsworth.

Hocquet, J.-Cl. (1978) *Le sel et la fortune de Venise*, Villeneuve-d'Ascq.

Hocquet, J.-Cl. (1985) *Le sel et le pouvoir: de l'an mil à la Révolution française*, Paris.

Hodder, I. (1988) 'Archaeology and theory', *Man* 23, 373–4.

Hodder, I. and Hassall, M. (1971) 'The non-random spacing of Romano-British walled towns', *Man* 6, 391–407.

Hodder, I., Isaac G. and Hammond, N. (eds) (1981) *Pattern of the Past: Studies in Honour of David Clarke*, Cambridge.

Hodge, A. T. (1992) *Roman Aqueducts and Water-Supply*, London.

Hodge, A. T. (ed.) (1991) *Future Currents in Aqueduct Studies*, Leeds.

Hodgen, M. T. (1936) *The Doctrine of Survivals: A Chapter in the History of Scientific Method in the Study of Man*, London.

Hodges, R. (1982a) *Dark Age Economics: The Origins of Towns and Trade A.D. 600–1000*, London.

Hodges, R. (1982b) 'The evolution of gateway settlements: their socio-economic implications', in Renfrew and Shennan, 117–23.

Hodges, R. (1988) *Primitive and Peasant Markets*, Oxford.

Hodges, R. (1990) 'Rewriting the rural history of early medieval Italy: twenty-five years of medieval archaeology reviewed', *RurH* 1/1, 17–36.

Hodges, R. (1994) 'In the shadow of Pirenne: San Vincenzo al Volturno and the revival of Mediterranean commerce', in Francovich and Noyé, 109–27.

Hodges, R. (1997) *Light in the Dark Ages: The Rise and Fall of San Vincenzo al Volturno*, London.

Hodges, R. and Bowden, W. (eds) (1998) *The Sixth Century: Production, Distribution and Demand*, Leiden, Boston and Cologne.

Hodges, R. and Hobley, B. (eds) (1988) *The Rebirth of Towns in the West AD 700–1050*, Council for British Archaeology Research Report 68, London.

Hodges, R. and Whitehouse, D. (1983) *Mohammed, Charlemagne and the Origins of Europe: Archaeology and the Pirenne Thesis*, London.

Hodkinson, S. (1988) 'Animal husbandry in the Greek polis', in Whittaker (ed.), 35–74.

Hodkinson, S. and Hodkinson, H. (1981) 'Mantinea and the Mantinike: settlement and society in a Greek polis', *ABSA* 76, 239–96.

Hoffman, G. and Schulz, H. D. (1988) 'Coastline shifts and holocene stratigraphy on the Mediterranean coast of Andalucia (southeastern Spain)', in Raban, 53–70.

Hoffman, G. L. (1997) *Imports and Immigrants: Near Eastern Contacts with Iron Age Crete*, Ann Arbor.

Hoffman, P. T. (1996) *Growth in a Traditional Society: The French Countryside, 1450–1815*, Princeton NJ.

Hogarth, D. G. (1906) 'Geographical conditions affecting population in the east Mediterranean lands', *Geographical Journal* 25, 465–77.

Hohenberg, P. M. and Lees, L. H. (1985) *The Making of Urban Europe 1000–1950*, London.

Holland, H. (1815) *Travels in the Ionian Isles, Albania, Thessaly, Macedonia &c during the Years 1812 and 1813*, London.

Holland, L. A. (1961) *Janus and the Bridge*, Rome.

Holland Rose, J. (1933) *The Mediterranean in the Ancient World*, Cambridge.

Hollingsworth, T. H. (1969) *Historical Demography*, London.

Holt, R. (1988) *The Mills of Medieval England*, Oxford.

Holt, R. (1996) 'Medieval technology and the historians: the evidence for the mill', in Fox (ed.), 103–21.

Holton, R. J. (1986) *Cities, Capitalism, and Civilization*, London.

Holum, K. G. (1990) 'Hadrian and St Helena: imperial travel and the origins of Christian Holy Land pilgrimage', in Ousterhout, 66–81.

Holy, L. (1989) *Kinship, Honour and Solidarity: Cousin Marriage in the Middle East*, Manchester and New York.

Hommes et richesses dans l'empire byzantin, vol. 1: *IVe–VIIe siècle* (1989) Paris.

Hopf, C. H. F. J. (ed.) (1873) *Chroniques gréco-romanes*, Berlin.

Hopkins, K. (1978a) 'Economic growth and towns in classical Antiquity', in Abrams and Wrigley, 35–77.

Hopkins, K. (1978b) *Conquerors and Slaves*, Cambridge.

Hopkins, K. (1980) 'Taxes and trade in the Roman empire (200 B.C.–A.D. 400)', *JRS* 70, 101–25.

Hopkins, K. (1983a) 'Models, ships and staples', in Garnsey and Whittaker, 84–109.

Hopkins, K. (1983b) 'Introduction', in Garnsey, Hopkins and Whittaker, ix–xxv.

Hopwood, K. (1989) 'Bandits, elites and rural order', in A. Wallace-Hadrill (ed.) *Patronage in Ancient Society*, London, 171–87.

Hopwood, K. (1991) 'Nomads or bandits? The pastoralist/sedentarist interface in Anatolia', *Byzforsch* 16, 179–94.

Horden, P. (1992) 'Disease, dragons and saints: the management of epidemics in the Dark Ages', in T. Ranger and P. Slack (eds) *Epidemics and Ideas: Essays on the Historical Perception of Pestilence*, Cambridge, 45–76.

Hornblower, S. (1982) *Mausolus*, Oxford.

Horowitz, R. (1983) *Honor and the American Dream: Culture and Identity in a Chicano Community*, New Brunswick NJ.

Hoselitz, B. F. (1954–5) 'Generative and parasitic cities', *Economic Development and Cultural Change* 3, 278–94.

Hourani, A. H. (1962) *Arabic Thought in the Liberal Age, 1797–1939*, Oxford.

Hourani, A. H. and Stern, S. M. (eds) (1969) *The Islamic City*, Oxford.

Hourani, G. F. (1963) *Arab Seafaring*, Beirut.

Hourmouziadis, G. H. (1982) *Magnesia, the Story of a Civilization*, Athens.

Houston, G. W. (1988) 'Ports in perspective: some comparative materials on Roman merchant ships and ports', *AJA* 92, 553–64.

Houston, J. M. (1964) *The Western Mediterranean World: An Introduction to Its Regional Landscapes*, London.

Howe, J. (1997) *Church Reform and Social Change in Eleventh-Century Italy: Dominic of Sora and his Patrons*, Philadelphia.

Howell, D. (1970) 'Health rituals at a Lebanese shrine', *Middle Eastern Studies* 6, 179–88.

Howgego, C. (1992) 'The supply and use of money in the Roman world 200 B.C. to A.D. 300', *JRS* 82, 1–31.

Hsü, K. (1983) *The Mediterranean was a Desert: A Voyage of the 'Glomar Challenger'*, Princeton NJ.

Hu, H. C. (1944) 'The Chinese concept of face', *AmAnth* 46, 45–64.

Hubert, E. (1990) *Espace urbain et habitat à Rome du Xe siècle à la fin du XIIIe siècle*, Rome.

Hübinger, P. E. (1968) *Bedeutung und Rolle des Islams beim Übergang von Altertum zum Mittelalter*, Darmstadt.

Huggett, R. (1980) *Systems Analysis in Geography*, Oxford.

Hughes, H. S. (1966) *The Obstructed Path: French Social Thought in the Years of Desperation, 1930–1960*, New York.

Hughes, J. D. (1975) *Ecology in Ancient Civilizations*, Albuquerque.

Hughes, J. D. (1983) 'How the ancients viewed deforestation', *JFA* 10, 436–45.

Hughes, J. D. (1994) *Pan's Travail: Environmental Problems of the Ancient Greeks and Romans*, Baltimore.

Hughes, J. D. and Thirgood, J. V. (1982) 'Deforestation in ancient Greece and Rome: a cause of collapse', *The Ecologist* 12, 196–208.

Humphreys, S. C. (1967) 'Archaeology and the economic and social history of classical Greece', *PdelP* 96, 374–400 (repr. Humphreys 1978).

Humphreys, S. C. (1969) 'History, economics and anthropology: the work of Karl Polanyi', *History and Theory* 8, 165–212 (repr. Humphreys 1978).

Humphreys, S. C. (1978) *Anthropology and the Greeks*, London.

Humphries, M. (1998) 'Trading gods in Northern Italy', in Parkins and Smith, 203–24.

Hunt, E. D. (1982) *Holy Land Pilgrimage in the Later Roman Empire, A.D. 312–460*, Oxford.

Hunt, R. C. and Hunt, E. (1974) 'Irrigation, conflict and politics: a Mexican case', in Downing and Gibson, 129–158.

Hunt, R. C. and Hunt, E. (1976) 'Canal irrigation and social organization', *Current Anthropology* 17.3, 389–411.

Huntington, E. (1910) 'The burial of Olympia: a study in climate and history', *Geographical Journal* 36, 657–86.

Huntington, E. (1915) *Civilization and Climate*, New Haven.

Huppert, G. (1997) 'The *Annales* experiment', in Bentley (ed.), 873–88.

Hutchinson, J. (1969) 'Erosion and land-use: the influence of agriculture on the Epirus region of Greece', *Agricultural History Review* 17, 85–90.

Hutson, S. (1971) 'Social ranking in a French Alpine community', in F. G. Bailey, 41–68.

I paesaggi rurali europei (1975): *Atti del convegno internazionale indetto a Perugia . . . 1973 dalla Conférence européenne permanente pour l'étude du paysage rural*, Perugia.

Iftikhar, A. and Ruttan, V. W. (eds) (1988) *Generation and Diffusion of Agricultural Innovations: The Role of Institutional Factors*, Aldershot and Brookfield VT.

Ilsley, J. S. (1996) *An Indexed Bibliography of Underwater Archaeology and Related Topics*, Oswestry.

Imamović, E. (1987) *Otoci Cres i Lošinj od ranog srednjeg vijeka do konca XVIII stoljeća*, Mali Lošinj.

Ingham, B. (1981) *Tropical Exports and Economic Development: New Perspectives on Producer Response in Three Low Income Countries*, London.

Ingold, T. (1981) 'The hunter and his spear: notes on the cultural mediation of social and ecological systems', in Sheridan and Bailey, 119–30.

Ingram, M. (1987) *Church Courts, Sex and Marriage in England, 1570–1640*, Cambridge.

Ioannides, G. C. (ed.) (1992) *Studies in Honour of Vassos Karageorghis*, Nicosia.

Irwin, R. (1984) *The Camel*, London.

Isager, S. (1990) 'Kings and gods in the Seleucid empire: a question of landed property in Asia Minor', in P. Bilde (eds) *Religion and Religious Practice in the Seleucid Kingdom*, Aarhus, 79–90.

Isager, S. (1992) 'Sacred animals in classical and Hellenistic Greece', in Linders and Alroth, 15–19.

Isager, S. and Skydsgaard, J. E. (1992) *Ancient Greek Agriculture: An Introduction*, London.

Islamoglu-Inan, H. (1988) 'Les paysans, le marché et l'état en Anatolie au XVIe siècle', *Annales*, 1025–43.

Isnard, H. (1947) 'Vigne et colonisation en Algérie', *Annales*, 288–300.

Isnard, H. (1973) *Pays et paysages méditerranéens*, Paris.

Israel, J. I. (1982) *The Dutch Republic and the Hispanic World, 1606–1661*, Oxford.

Issawi, C. (1980) *The Economic History of Turkey 1800–1914*, Chicago.

Issawi, C. (1981a) 'The Christian–Muslim frontier in the Mediterranean: a history of two peninsulas', in *The Arab World's Legacy: Essays by Charles Issawi*, Princeton NJ, 11–21.

Issawi, C. (1981b) 'The area and population of the Arab empire: an essay in speculation', in Udovitch, 375–396.

Issawi, C. (1991) 'Technology, energy and civilisation: some historical observations', *IJMES* 23, 281–9.

Jackson, A. H. (1995) 'An oracle for raiders', *ZPE* 108, 95–99.

Jackson, W. W. (1916) 'H. F. Tozer, 1829–1916' (obituary), *PBA* 7, 566–74.

Jacob, C. (1991) *Géographie et ethnographie en Grèce ancienne*, Paris.

Jacoby, D. (1989) 'L'évolution urbaine et la fonction méditerranéenne d'Acre à l'époque des Croisades', in Poleggi, 95–9 (repr. Jacoby 1997).

Jacoby, D. (1994a) 'The migration of merchants and craftsmen: a Mediterranean perspective (12th–15th century)', in Cavaciocchi, 533–60 (repr. Jacoby 1997).

Jacoby, D. (1994b) 'La production du sucre en Crète vénitienne: l'échec d'une entreprise économique', in C. Maltezou (ed.) *Rhodonia: Homage to M. I. Manoussakas*, Rethymno, 167–80 (repr. Jacoby 1997).

Jacoby, D. (1997) *Trade, Commodities and Shipping in the Medieval Mediterranean* Variorum.

Jaeger, C. S. (1985) *The Origins of Courtliness: Civilizing Trends and the Formation of Courtly Ideals, 939–1210*, Philadelphia.

Jal, A. (1988–) *Nouveau Glossaire Nautique*, ed. M. Mollat, Paris.

James, M. (1978) *English Politics and the Concept of Honour, 1485–1642* (*PP* supplement 3), Oxford.

James, P. et al. (1997) 'The physical environment of Methana: formation, explanation and change', in C. Mee and H. A. Forbes (eds) *A Rough and Rocky Place: The Landscape and Settlement History of the Methana Peninsula, Greece*, Liverpool, 5–32.

Jameson, M. H. (1988) 'Sacrifice and animal husbandry in classical Greece', in Whittaker (ed.), 87–119.

Jameson, M. H. (1989) 'Mountains and the Greek city states', in Bergier, 7–17.

Jameson, M. H., Runnels, C. N. and van Andel, T. H. (1994) *A Greek Countryside: The Southern Argolid from Prehistory to the Present Day*, Stanford CA.

Jamous, R. (1981) *Honneur et 'baraka': les structures sociales traditionelles dans le Rif*, Cambridge and Paris.

Jamous, R. (1992) 'From the death of men to the peace of God: violence and peace-making in the Rif', in Peristiany and Pitt-Rivers (eds), 167–91.

Janni, P. (1984) *La mappa e il periplo: cartografia antica e spazio odologico*, Rome.

Janssen, J. J. (1961) *Two Ancient Egyptian Ship's Logs: Leiden 350 verso and Turin 2008+2016*, Leiden.

Jashemski, W. (1979a) *The Gardens of Pompeii*, New Rochelle NY.

Jashemski, W. (1979b) 'Pompeii and Mount Vesuvius A.D. 79', in Grayson and Sheets, 587–622.

Jenkyns, R. (1980) *The Victorians and Ancient Greece*, Oxford.

Jennings, R. C. (1975) 'Women in early 17th century Ottoman judicial records: the Sharia court of Anatolian Kayseri', *JESHO* 18, 53–114.

Jézégou, M.-P. (1982) *L'épave II de l'Anse Saint-Gervais à Fos-sur-Mer*, dissertation, University of Provence, 2 vols, Aix-en-Provence.

Jézégou, M.-P. (1998) 'Le mobilier de l'épave Saint-Gervais 2 (VIIe s.) à Fos-sur-Mer (B.-du-Rh.)', in Bonifay, Carre and Rigoir, 343–51.

Johns, J. (1988) 'Sistemi socio-economici, ricognizione a scala regionale e campionamento ad uso probabilistico', in Noyé, 539–42.

Johnson, A. W. (1972) 'Individuality and experimentation in traditional agriculture', *Human Ecology* 1, 149–59.

Johnson, D. (1963) *Guizot: Aspects of French History, 1787–1874*, London.

Johnson, D. L. (1973) *Jabal al-Akhdar, Cyrenaica: An Historical Geography of Settlement and Livelihood*, University of Chicago Department of Geography Research Paper 148, Chicago.

Johnson, M. (1996) 'Water, animals and agricultural technology: a study of settlement patterns and economic change in neolithic southern Greece', *OJA* 15, 3, 267–305.

Johnston, R. J., and Smith, D. M (1994) *The Dictionary of Human Geography*, 3rd edn, Oxford.

Jones, A. H. M. (1960) 'The cloth industry under the Roman empire', *EcHR* 13, 183–92 (repr. in P. A. Brunt (ed.) *The Roman Economy*, Oxford, 1974).

Jones, A. H. M. (1964) *The Later Roman Empire, 284–602*, 2 vols, Oxford.

Jones, C. P. (1978) *The Roman World of Dio Chrysostom*, Cambridge MA.

Jones, E. L. (1981) *The European Miracle: Environments, Economies and Geo-Politics in the History of Europe and Asia*, Cambridge.

Jones, E. L. and Woolf, G. (1969) *Agrarian Change and Historical Development: The Historical Problems*, London.

Jones, G. (1987) 'Agricultural practice in Greek prehistory', *ABSA* 82, 115–23.

Jones, G. D. B. (1980) 'The Roman mines at Riotinto', *JRS* 70, 146–65.

Jones, Greta (1980) *Social Darwinism and English Thought: The Interaction Between Biological and Social Theory*, Brighton.

Jones, J. E. (1976) 'Hives and honey of Hymettus: bee-keeping in ancient Greece', *Archaeology* 29.2, 80–91.

Jones, P. (1997) *The Italian City-State from Commune to Signoria*, Oxford.

Jones, R. E. and Vagnetti, L. (1991) 'Traders and craftsmen in the central Mediterranean', in Gale, 125–45.

Jongman, W. (1988a) 'Adding it up', in Whittaker (ed.), 210–12.

Jongman, W. (1988b) *The Economy and Society of Pompeii*, Amsterdam.

Jordan, B. and Perlin, J. (1984) 'On the protection of sacred groves', in K. J. Rigby (ed.) *Studies Presented to Sterling Dow on his Eightieth Birthday*, Durham NC, 153–9.

Jordan, W. C. (1996) *The Great Famine: Northern Europe in the Early Fourteenth Century*, Princeton NJ.

Jost, M. (n.d.) 'La vie religieuse dans les montagnes d'Arcadie', in G. Fabre, 55–68.

Jourdin du Mollat, M. (1993) *Europe and the Sea*, Oxford.

Jowett, B. (trans.) (1871) *The Dialogues of Plato*, 4 vols, Oxford.

Judson, S. (1983) 'Alluviation and erosion', in E. Fentress et al.

Just, R. (1978) 'Some problems for Mediterranean anthropology', *Journal of the Anthropological Society of Oxford* 9, 81–97.

Jwaideh, W. (1959) *The Introductory Chapters of Yaqut's Mujam al-Buldan*, Leiden.

Kabbani, R. (1986) *Europe's Myths of Orient*, Bloomington IN.

Kahane, H. and Kahane R. (1970–6) 'Abendland und Byzanz: Sprache', in L. Wirth (ed.) *Reallexikon der Byzantinistik*, Amsterdam, vol. 1, 347–98.

Kahane, H. and Kahane, R. (1971) 'From landmark to toponym', in E. Coseriu and W.-D. Stempel (eds) *Sprache und Geschichte: Festschrift für Harri Meier zum 65. Geburtstag*, Munich, 253–8.

Kahane, H., Kahane R. and Bremner, L. (1967) *Glossario degli antichi portolani italiani*, Florence.

Kahane, H., Kahane, R. and Tietze, A. (1958) *The Lingua Franca in the Levant: Turkish Nautical Terms of Italian and Greek Origin*, Urbana IL.

Kaibel, G. (1885) 'Antike Windrosen', *Hermes* 20, 579–624.

Kaplan, M. (1986) 'L'économie paysanne dans l'Empire Byzantin du Ve au Xe siècle', *Klio* 68, 198–232.

Kaplan, M. (1992) *Les Hommes et la terre à Byzance du VIe au XIe siècle: propriété et exploitation du sol*, Byzantina Sorbonensia 10, Paris.

Kaplan, M. (1994) 'Réponse à A. P. Kazhdan', *Byzantinoslavica* 55, 88–95.

Kaplan, S. L. (1984) *Provisioning Paris: Merchants and Millers in the Grain and Flour Trade during the Eighteenth Century*, Ithaca NY.

Karageorghis, V. (1993) 'Le commerce chypriote avec l'occident au bronze récent', *CRAI* 557–88.

Karageorghis, V. and Michaelides, D. (1995) *Cyprus and the Sea*, Nicosia.

Karageorghis, V. and Michaelides, D. (1996) *The Development of the Cypriot Economy: From The Prehistoric Period to the Present Day*, Nicosia.

Kardulias, P. N. and Shutes, M. T. (1997) *Aegean Strategies: Studies of Culture and Environment on the European Fringe*, Lanham.

Kase, E. W. (ed.) (1991) *The Great Isthmus Corridor Route*, Dubuque.

Katchadourian, H. (1984) 'The historical background of psychiatry in Lebanon', *Bulletin of the History of Medicine* 54, 544–53.

Kaufman, G. (1989) *The Psychology of Shame: Theory and Treatment of Shame-Based Syndromes*, London.

Kaya, D. (1985) 'The sanctuary of the god Eurymedon at Tymbriada in Pisidia', *AS* 35, 39–56.

Kayser, B. (ed.) (1986) *Les sociétés rurales de la Méditerranée: un recueil de textes anthropologiques anglo-amercains*, Aix-en-Provence.

Kazhdan, A. P. (1993) 'State, feudal and private economy in Byzantium', *DOP* 47, 83–100.

Kazhdan, A. P. (1994) 'One more agrarian history of Byzantium', *Byzantinoslavica* 55, 66–88.

Kazhdan, A. P. and Constable, G. (1982) *People and Power in Byzantium*, Washington DC.

Kazhdan, A. P. and Wharton Epstein, A. (1985) *Change in Byzantine Culture in the Eleventh and Twelfth Centuries*, Berkeley.

Kearney, M. (1986) 'From the invisible hand to visible feet: anthropological studies of migration and development', *ARA* 15, 331–61.

Kearns, E. (1989 [1990]) *The Heroes of Attica*, London.

Keay, S. J. (1984) *Late Roman Amphorae in the Western Mediterranean: A Typology and Economic Study. The Catalan Evidence*, *BAR* 196, Oxford.

Kedar, B. Z. and Werblowsky, R. J. Z. (eds) (1998) *Sacred Space: Shrine, City, Land*, Basingstoke, London and Jerusalem.

Keddi, N. R. (1973) 'Is there a Middle East?', *IJMES* 4, 255–71.

Kehoe, D. P. (1988) *The Economics of Agriculture on Roman Imperial Estates in North Africa*, Göttingen.

Kehoe, D. P. (1989) 'Approaches to economic problems in the "Letters" of the Younger Pliny: the question of risk in agriculture', *ANRW* 33.1, 555–590.

Kehoe, D. P. (1990) 'Pastoralism and agriculture', *JRA* 3, 386–98.

Kehoe, D. P. (1992) *Management and Investment on Estates in Roman Egypt during the Early Empire*, Bonn.

Kehoe, D. P. (1993) review of Rathbone (1991), *JRA* 6, 476–84.

Kendrick, T. D. (1956) *The Lisbon Earthquake*, London.

Kennedy, H. (1985a) 'From *Polis* to *Madina*: urban change in late antiquity and early Islamic Syria', *PP* 106, 3–27.

Kennedy, H. (1985b) 'The last century of Byzantine Syria: a reinterpretation', *BF* 10, 141–83.

Kennet, D. (1994) 'Pottery as evidence for trade in medieval Cyrenaica', in J. Reynolds (ed.) *Cyrenaican Archaeology: An International Colloquium*, *LS* 25, London, 275–85.

Kenny, M. and Kertzer, D. I. (eds) (1983) *Urban Life in Mediterranean Europe: Anthropological Perspectives*, Urbana, Chicago and London.

Kent, J. H. (1948) 'The temple-estates of Delos, Rheneia and Mykonos', *Hesperia* 17, 243–338.

Kertzer, D. I. (1984) 'Anthropology and family history', *Journal of Family History* 9, 201–6.

Kertzer, D. I. (1993) *Sacrificed for Honor: Italian Infant Abandonment and the Politics of Reproductive Control*, Boston.

Kertzer, D. I. and Saller, R. P. (eds) (1991) *The Family in History from Antiquity to the Present*, New Haven and London.

Ketzer, D. I. and Brettell, C. (1987) 'Advances in Italian and Iberian family history', *Journal of Family History* 12, 87–120.

Khalaf, S. (1979) *Persistence and Change in Nineteenth Century Lebanon: A Sociological Essay*, Beirut.

Khazanov, A. M. (1984) *Nomads and the Outside World*, Cambridge.

Kiernan, V. G. (1988) *The Duel in European History: Honour and the Reign of Aristocracy*, Oxford.

Kilian, K. (1987) 'Zur Funktion der mykenischen Residenzen auf dem griechischen Festland', in R. Hägg and N. Marinatos (eds) *The Function of the Minoan Palaces: Proceedings of the Fourth International Symposium at the Swedish Institute in Athens . . . 1984*, Stockholm, 21–37.

Kimble, G. H. T. (1938) *Geography in the Middle Ages*, London.

King, G. and Cameron, A. (eds) (1994) *The Byzantine and Early Islamic Near East II: Land Use and Settlement Patterns*, Studies in Late Antiquity and Early Islam 4, Princeton NJ.

King, R. and Killingbeck, J. (1989) 'Carlo Levi, the mezzogiorno and emigration: fifty years of demographic change at Aliano', *Geography* 74, 128–43.

Kinser, S. (1981) '*Annaliste* paradigm? The geohistorical structuralism of Fernand Braudel', *AHR* 86, 63–105.

Kirchner, H. and Navarro, C. (1993) 'Objetivos, métodos y práctica de la arqueología hidráulica', *AM* 20, 121–50.

Kirigin, B. and Čače, S. (1998) 'Archaeological evidence for the cult of Diomedes in the Adriatic', in L. Braccesi (ed.) *Hesperia 9: studi sulla grecità di Occidente*, Rome, 63–110.

Kirsten, E. and Opelt, I. (1989) 'Eine Urkunde der Gründung von Arsinoe in Kilikia', *ZPE* 77, 55–66.

Klapisch-Zuber, C. (1986) 'Women servants in Florence during the fourteenth and fifteenth centuries', in B. A. Hanawalt (ed.) *Women and Work in Preindustrial Europe*, Bloomington IN.

Kloppenburg, J. R. (1988) *First the Seed: The Political Economy of Plant Biotechnology, 1492–2000*, Cambridge.

Knapp, A. B. (1986) *Copper Production and Divine Protection: Archaeology, Ideology and Social Complexity on Bronze Age Cyprus*, Göteborg.

Knapp, A. B. (1990) 'Ethnicity, entrepreneurship and exchange: Mediterranean inter-island relations in the Late Bronze Age', *ABSA* 85, 115–53.

Knapp, A. B. (ed.) (1992) *Archaeology, 'Annales', and Ethnohistory*, Cambridge.

Knapp, C. (1919–20) 'Irrigation among the Greeks and Romans', *Classical Weekly* 12, 73–4, 81–2; 13, 104.

Knauss, J. (1990a) 'Der Graben des Herakles in Becken von Pheneus und die Vertreibung der Stymphalischen Vögel', *MDAIA* 105, 1–52.

Knauss, J. (1990b) *Wasserbau und Geschichte: Minysche Epoche–Bayerische Zeit*, Munich.

Knauss, J. (1992) 'Die griechische Sintflut in Legende und Wirklichkeit', in Argoud et al., 127–47.

Knauss, J., Heinrich, B. and Kalcyk, H. (1984) *Die Wasserbauten des Minyer in der Kopais: die älteste Flussregulierung Europas*, Munich.

Kocturk, T. (1992) *A Matter of Honour: Experiences of Turkish Women Immigrants*, London.

Koder, J. (1988) 'Early modern times travellers as a source for the historical geography of Byzantium: the diary of Reinhold Lubenau', in H. Ahrweiler (ed.) *Géographie historique du monde méditerranéen*, Byzantina Sorbonensia 7, Paris, 141–8.

Koder, J. (1993) *Gemüse in Byzanz: Die Versorgung Konstantinopels mit Frischgemüse im Licht der Geoponika*, Vienna.

Koder, J. (1995) 'Fresh vegetables for the capital', in Mango and Dagron, 49–56.

Kolendo, J. (1994) 'Praedia suburbana e la loro redditività', in Carlsen, 59–72.

Kollmann, N. S. (1991) 'Women's honor in early modern Russia', in B. E. Clements, B. A. Engel and C. D. Worobec (eds) *Russia's Women: Accommodation, Resistance, Transformation*, Berkeley and Los Angeles, 60–73.

Kolodny, E. (1968) 'La Crète: mutations et évolutions d'une population insulaire grecque', *Revue Géographique de Lyon* 3, 227–90.

Kolodny, E. (1972) 'L'olivier dans la vie rurale des îles de Grèce', in *Les sociétés rurales méditerranéennes, actes du colloque de géographie agraire, Madrid 1971*, Aix-en-Provence, 157–62.

Kolodny, E. (1974) *La population des îles de Grèce: essai de géographie insulaire en Méditerranée orientale*, Aix-en-Provence.

Kopytoff, I. (1986) 'The cultural biography of things: commoditization as process', in Appadurai, 64–91.

Korfmann, M. (1988) 'East–west connections throughout the Mediterranean in the Early Neolithic period', *Berytus* 36, 9–26.

Korres, M. (1992) *Vom Penteli zum Parthenon*, Munich.

Koster, H. A. and Koster, J. B. (1976) 'Competition or symbiosis? Pastoral adaptive strategies in the southern Argolid', in M. Dimen and E. Friedl (eds) *Regional Variation in Modern*

Greece and Cyprus: Toward a Persepctive on the Ethnography of Greece, Annals of the New York Academy of Sciences 268, New York, 275–85.

Koumoulides, J. T. A. (1985) 'The monastery of Tatarna in Evritania (Greece), first preliminary report', *Greek Orthodox Theological Review* 30, 61–84.

Kraeling, C. H. (1938) *Gerasa, City of the Decapolis*, New Haven.

Kraft, J. C., Kayan, İ. and Aschenbrenner, S. E. (1985) 'Geological studies of coastal change applied to archaeological settings', in G. Rapp and J. A. Gifford (eds) *Archaeological Geology*, New Haven and London, 57–84.

Kraft, J. C., Kayan, İ. and Erol, O. (1982) 'Geology and paleogeographic reconstructions of the region of Troy', in Rapp and Gifford, 11–41.

Kramers, J. H. and Wiet, G. (trans.) (1964) Ibn Hauqal, *Configuration de la terre (Kitab Surat al-Ard)*, 2 vols, Beirut and Paris.

Krautheimer, R. (1980) *Rome: Profile of a City, 312–1308*, Princeton NJ.

Kravari, V., Lefort, J. and Morrisson, C. (eds) (1991) *Hommes et richesses dans l'empire byzantine tom. II, VIIIe–XVe siècle*, Paris.

Kressel, G. M. (1981) 'Sororicide/filiacide: homicide for family honour', *Current Anthropology* 22, 141–58.

Kressel, G. M. (1992) 'Shame and gender', *AQ* 65, 34–45.

Kressel, G. M. and Wikan, U. (1988) 'More on honour and shame' (debate on Wikan 1984), *Man* 23, 167–70.

Kretschmer, K. (1909) *Die italienischen Portolane des Mittelalters*, Berlin.

Kreutz, B. M. (1976) 'Ships, shipping, and the implications of change in the early medieval Mediterranean', *Viator* 7, 79–109.

Kreutz, B. M. (1988) 'The ecology of maritime success: the puzzling case of Amalfi', *MHR* 3, 103–13.

Kreutz, B. M. (1991) *Before the Normans: Southern Italy in the Ninth and Tenth Centuries*, Philadelphia.

Kreuzer, B. (1994) 'Überlegungen zum Handel mit bemalter Keramik im 6. Jahrhundert v. Chr. unter besonderer Berücksichtigung des Heraion von Samos', *Klio* 76, 103–19.

Kriss, R. and Kriss-Heinrich, H. (1955) *Peregrinatio Neohellenica*, Vienna.

Kriss, R. and Kriss-Heinrich, H. (1960–2) *Volksglaube im Bereich des Islam*, 2 vols, Wiesbaden.

Kroeber, A. L. (1939) *Cultural and Natural Areas of Native North America*, University of California Publications in American Archaeology and Ethnography 38, Berkeley.

Kroll, J. H. and Waggoner, N. M. (1984) 'Dating the earliest coins of Athens, Corinth and Aegina', *AJA* 88, 325–40.

Kuehn, T. (1991) *Law, Family, and Women: Toward a Legal Anthropology of Renaissance Italy*, Chicago and London.

Kuhnholtz-Lordat, G. (1939) *La terre incendiée. Essai d'agronomie comparée*, Nìmes.

Kuhrt, A. (1998) 'The old Assyrian merchants', in Parkins and Smith, 16–30.

Kuniholm, P. I. et al. (1996) 'Anatolian tree rings and the absolute chronology of the eastern Mediterranean 2220–718 B.C.', *Nature* 381, 27 June, 780–3.

Küthmann, H. (1966) 'Salz zum Würzen?', *JDAIAA*, 407–10.

Kyrris, C. P. (1984) 'The nature of the Arab–Byzantine relations in Cyprus from the middle of the seventh to the middle of the tenth century A.D.', *Graeco-Arabica* 3, 149–75.

L'exploitation de la mer de l'antiquité à nos jours: la mer, lieu de production. Actes du colloque . . . 1984, Antibes.

La mobilité des paysages mediterranéens: Hommage à Pierre Birot (1984), Toulouse.

Labarre, G. and Le Dinahet, M.-T. (1996) 'Les métiers du textile en Asie Mineure de l'époque hellénistique à l'époque impériale', in *Aspects de l'artisanat du textile dans le monde méditerranéen, Egypte, Grèce, monde romain*, Lyon, 49–117.

LaBianca, Ø. S. (1990) *Sedentarization and Nomadization: Food System Cycles at Hesban and Vicinity in Transjordan (Hesban 1)*, Berrien Springs MI.

Labrousse, E. (1973) 'En guise de toast à Fernand Braudel: aux vingt-cinq ans de *La Méditerrannée*', in *Mélanges . . . Braudel*, 1.7–17.

Labud, G. (1995) *Ricerche archeologico-ambientali dell'Istria settentrionale: la valle del fiume Risano*, Jonsered, Sweden.

Laet, S. J. de (1949) *Portorium: étude sur l'organisation douanière chez les Romains, surtout à l'époque du haut-empire*, repr. 1975, Ghent.

Laffineur, R. and Basch, L. (eds) (1991) *Thalassa: l'Égée préhistorique et la mer*, Liège.

Lagardère, V. (1993) *Campagnes et paysans d'al-Andalus (VIIIe s.–XVe s.)*, Paris.

Lagazzi, L. (1988) 'I segni sulla terra: sistemi di confinazione e di misurazione dei boschi nell'alto medioevo', in Andreolli and Montanari, 15–34.

Laiou, A. E. (1967) 'The provisioning of Constantinople during the winter of 1306–7', *Byzantion* 37, 91–113.

Laiou, A. E. (Laiou-Thomadakis) (1977) *Peasant Society in the Late Byzantine Empire*, Princeton NJ.

Laiou, A. E. (1980) 'Saints and society in the Byzantine empire', in Laiou (ed.), 84–114.

Laiou, A. E. (1981–2) 'The Byzantine economy in the Mediterranean trade system, thirteenth–fifteenth centuries', *DOP* 34–5, 177–222.

Laiou, A. E. (1990) 'Händler und Kaufleute auf dem Jahrmarkt', in G. Prinzing and D. Simon (eds) *Fest und Alltag in Byzanz*, Munich, 54–70.

Laiou, A. E. (1993) 'Sex, consent, and coercion in Byzantium', in Laiou (ed.) *Consent and Coercion to Sex and Marriage in Ancient and Medieval Societies*, Washington DC, 109–221.

Laiou, A. E. (ed.) (1980) *Charanis Studies: Essays in Honor of Peter Charanis*, New Brunswick NJ.

Lambeck, K. (1996) 'Sea-level change and shore-line evolution: Aegean Greece since the Upper Palaeolithic', *Antiquity* 269, 588–611.

Lamboley, J.-L. (1996) *Recherches sur les Messapiens, IVe–IIe siècle avant J.-C.*, Rome.

Lambrianides, K. et al. (1996) 'The Madra Çay Delta archaeological project, first preliminary report. Geomorphological survey and borehole sampling of the Altinova coastal plain on the Aegean coast of northwest Turkey', *AS* 46, 167–200.

Lambrinoudakis, V. (1986) 'Ancient farmhouses on Mount Aipos', in J. Boardman and C. E. Vaphopoulou-Richardson (eds) *Chios: A Conference at the Homereion in Chios 1984*, Oxford, 295–304.

Lambrou-Philippson, C. (1995) 'Smiths on board late Bronze Age ships', in *Tropis III: Third International Symposium on Ship Construction in Antiquity*, Athens, 243–7.

Lamonelli, A. (1990) 'I lavori alla peschiera del Marta', *Scritti in memoria di G. Marchetti Longhi*, Anagni, 233–49.

Lanciani, R. (1893) *Pagan and Christian Rome*, Boston and London.

Landels, J. G. (1978) *Engineering in the Ancient World*, London.

Landers, J. (1993) *Death and the Metropolis: Studies in the Demographic History of London 1670–1830*, Cambridge.

Lane, F. C. (1963) 'The economic meaning of the invention of the compass', *AHR* 68, reprinted in (1966) *Venice and History*, Baltimore, 331–44.

Lane, F. C. (1977) 'Double-entry bookkeeping and resident merchants', *JEEH* 6, 177–91 (repr. Lane 1987).

Lane, F. C. (1986) 'Technology and productivity in seaborne transportation', in A. Vannini Marx (ed.) *Trasporti e sviluppo economico, secoli XIII–XVIII: atti della 'quinta settimana di studio'... Prato 1973*, Florence, 233–44 (repr. Lane 1987).

Lane, F. C. (1987) *Studies in Venetian Social and Economic History*, eds. B. G. Kohl and R. C. Mueller, Variorum, London.

Lane Fox, R. J. (1986) *Pagans and Christians*, Harmondsworth.

Langdon, J. (1986) *Horses, Oxen and Technological Innovation: The Use of Draught Animals in English Farming from 1066 to 1500*, Cambridge.

Langdon, J. (1995) 'Double-shafted vehicles and other elements in the "revolution" of land transport in medieval Europe', in Raepsaet and Rommelaere, 113–26.

Langdon, M. K. (1976) *A Sanctuary of Zeus on Mt. Hymettus*, Princeton NJ.

Langton, J. and Hoppe, G. (1983) *Town and Country in the Development of Early Modern Western Europe* (Historical Geography Research Group research paper 11), Norwich.

Lansing, J. S. (1991) *Priests and Programmers: Technologies of Power in the Engineered Landscape of Bali*, Princeton NJ.

Lanz, C. F. W. (ed.) (1843) *Chronik des Edlen En Ramon Muntaner*, Stuttgart.

Laouina, A. et al. (1993) 'L'érosion anthropique en pays méditerranéen: le cas du Maroc septentrional', *BAGF* 70, 384–98.

Lapidus, I. M. (1969) 'The grain economy of Mamluk Egypt', *JESHO* 12, 1–15.

Lapidus, I. M. (1984) *Muslim Cities in the Later Middle Ages* (1st edn 1967), Cambridge.

Larner, J. (1990) 'Crossing the Romagnol Appennines in the Renaissance', in T. Dean and C. Wickham (eds) *City and Countryside in Late Medieval and Renaissance Italy: Essays Presented to Philip Jones*, London and Ronceverte, 147–70.

Laronde, A. (1987) *Cyrène et la Libye hellénistique – Libykai historiai – de l'époque républicaine au principat d'Auguste*, Paris.

Laronde, A. (1990) 'Greeks and Libyans in Cyrenaïca', in J.-P. Descoeudres (ed.) *Greek Colonists and Native Populations*, Oxford, 45–60.

Laronde, A. (1996a) 'Apollonia de Cyrénaïque: archéologie et histoire', *Journal des Savants*, 1–49.

Laronde, A. (1996b) 'L'exploitation de la chôra cyrénéenne à l'époque classique et hellénistique', *CRAI*, 503–527.

Larsen, J. A. O. (1968) *Greek Federal States, their Institutions and History*, Oxford.

Laslett, P. (1977) *Family Life and Illicit Love in Earlier Generations: Essays in Historical Sociology*, Cambridge.

Lassère, F. (1977) *Ubique populus: peuplement et mouvements de population dans l'Afrique romaine de la chute de Carthage à la fin de la dynastie des Sévères*, Paris.

Lattimore, O. (1940) *Inner Asian Frontiers of China*, 2nd edn 1988, Oxford.

Lauffer, S. (1971) *Diokletians Preisedikt*, Berlin.

Lauffer, S. (1985) 'Problèmes de Copaïs, solutions et énigmes', in *La Béotie antique*, Paris, 101–8.

Lauffer, S. (1986) *Kopais:Untersuchungen zur historischen Landeskunde Mittelgriechenlands*, Frankfurt.

Laurence, R. (1995) 'The organization of space in Pompeii', in Cornell and Lomas, 63–78.

Lavagne, H. (1988) *Operosa antra: recherches sur la grotte à Rome de Sylla à Hadrien*, Rome.

Laven, P. (1989) 'The Venetian rivers in the sixteenth century', in Bergier, 198–217.

Law, R. (1976) 'Horses, firearms and political power in pre-colonial West Africa', *PP* 72, 112–32.

Lawall, M. (1998) 'Ceramics and positivism revisited: Greek transport amphoras and history', in Parkins and Smith, 75–101.

Lawson, J. C. (1910) *Modern Greek Folklore and Ancient Greek Religion*, Cambridge.

Layton, R. (1973) 'Social systems theory and a village community in France', in Renfrew, 499–516.

Le Houerou, H. N. (1981) 'Impact of man and his animals on Mediterranean vegetation', in Di Castri et al., 479–521.

Le Houerou, H. N. (1987) 'Vegetation wildfires in the Mediterranean Basin: evolution and trends', *Ecologia Mediterranea* 13, 13–24.

Le Play, F. (1871) *L'organisation de la famille, selon le vrai modèle signalé par l'histoire de toutes les races et de tous les temps*, Paris.

Le ravitaillement en blé de Rome et des centres urbains des débuts de la république jusqu'au haut empire (1994), Centre J. Bérard, Rome.

Le Roy Ladurie, E. (1966) *Les paysans de Languedoc*, 2 vols, Paris.

Le Roy Ladurie, E. (1975) *Montaillou: village occitan de 1294 à 1324* (abridged English trans. 1978), Paris.

Le Roy Ladurie, E. (1978) *Le territoire de l'historien*, vol. 2, Paris.

Le Strange, G. (trans.) (1892) al-Muqaddasi (Mukaddasi), *Description of Syria*, Palestine Pilgrims' Text Society, London.

Leach, E. (1973), 'Concluding remarks', in Renfrew, 761–71.

Leake, W. M. (1830) *Travels in the Morea*, London.

Lebra, T. S. (1971) 'The social mechanism of guilt and shame: the Japanese case', *AQ* 44, 241–55.

Lee, D. (1973a) 'Science, philosophy and technology in the Greco-Roman world, I', *GR* 20, 65–78.

Lee, D. (1973b) 'Science, philosophy and technology in the Greco-Roman world, II', *GR* 20, 180–93.

Lee, R. B. and De Vore, I. (1968) *Man the Hunter*, New York.

Lee, R. D. (1986) 'Malthus and Boserup: a dynamic synthesis', in Coleman and Schofield, 96–130.

Lee Nolan, M. (1990) 'Shrine locations: ideals and realities in continental Europe', in Boesch Gajano and Scaraffia, 75–84.

Lefebvre, H. (1970) *La révolution urbaine*, Paris.

Lefebvre, H. (1991) *The Production of Space*, first published 1974, Oxford and Cambridge MA.

Lefebvre, H. and Régulier, C. (1996) 'Rhythmanalysis of Mediterranean cities' (first published 1986), in Lefebvre, *Writings on Cities*, Oxford and Malden MA, 228–40.

Lefebvre, T. [1929] 'La pêche en Turquie', *Annales de Géographie* 38, 470–9.

Lefebvre des Noettes, R. J. E. C. (1931) *L'attelage, le cheval de selle à travers les âges*, Paris.

Lefkowitz, M. and Rogers, G. M. (eds) (1996) *Black Athena Revisited*, Chapel Hill NC.

Lefort, J. (1982) *Villages de Macédoine: notices historiques et topographiques sur la Macédoine orientale au moyen âge*, Paris.

Lefort, J. (1991) 'L'organisation de l'espace rurale: Macédoine et Italie du Sud (Xe–XIIIe siècle)', in Kravari, Lefort, and Morrisson, 12–26.

Lefort, J. (1993) 'Rural economy and social relations in the countryside', *DOP* 47, 101–13.

Leftic, J., Milliman, J. D. and Sestini, G. (1992) *Climatic Change and the Mediterranean: Environmental and Societal Impacts of Climatic Change and Sea-Level Rise in the Mediterranean Region*, London.

LeGall, J. (1953) *Le Tibre, fleuve de Rome, dans l'antiquité*, Paris.

LeGall, J. (1994) 'Un mode de transport méconnu: les animaux de bât', in *Le ravitaillement en blé de Rome*, 69–72.

LeGoff, J. (1984) 'The learned and popular dimensions of journeys in the Otherworld in the Middle Ages', in S. Kaplan (ed.) *Understanding Popular Culture*, Berlin, 19–34.

Leighton, A. C. (1972) *Transport and Communication in Early Medieval Europe, A.D. 500–1100*, Newton Abbot.

Lemerle, P. (1979a) *Les plus anciens recueils des miracles de Saint Démétrius et la pénétration des Slaves dans les Balkans*, vol. 1: text, Paris.

Lemerle, P. (1979b) *The Agrarian History of Byzantium: From the Origins to the Twelfth Century. The Sources and Problems*, Galway.

Lemonnier, P. (1993) 'Introduction', in Lemonnier (ed.), 1–35.

Lemonnier, P. (ed.) (1993) *Technological Choices: Transformation in Material Cultures since the Neolithic*, London.

Lendon, J. F. (1997) *Empire of Honour: The Art of Government in the Roman World*, Oxford.

Lenormant, F. (1883) *A travers l'Apulie et la Lucanie: notes de voyage*, Paris.

Leonard, A. (1995) '"Canaanite jars" and the Late Bronze Age Aegeo-Levantine wine trade', in McGovern et al., 233–54.

Leonard, J. R. (1995) 'The anchorage at Kioni', in Fejfer, 133–70.

Leontidou, L. (1990) *The Mediterranean City in Transition: Social Change and Urban Development*, Cambridge.

Lepelley, C. (1989) 'Peuplement et richesses de l'Afrique romaine tardive', in *Hommes et richesses*.

Lepre, A. (1978) *Terra di Lavoro nell'età moderna*, Naples.

Les Phéniciens et le monde méditerranéen (1986), Luxemburg.

Leveau, P. (1983) 'La ville antique et l'organisation de l'espace rurale: villa, *ville, village*', *Annales*, 920–42.

Leveau, P. (1993a) 'Mentalité économique et grands travaux hydrauliques: le drainage du lac Fucin aux origines d'un modèle', *Annales*, 3–16.

Leveau, P. (1993b) 'Sociétés antiques et écologie des milieux montagnards et palustres. La construction des paysages méditerranéens', in Leveau and M. Provansal (eds.) *Archéologie et environnement*, Aix, 17–44.

Leveau, P. (1994) 'Dal paesaggio naturale al paesaggio coltivato. Dati archeologici relativi ai grandi lavori agricoli in età romana: il drenaggio dei paludi nella Bassa Provenza', in Carlsen et al., 73–8.

Leveau, P. (1995) 'Les moulins de Barbégal, les ponts-aqueducs du Vallon de l'Arc, et l'histoire naturelle de la Vallée des Baux', *CRAI*, 115–44.

Leveau, P. (1996) 'The Barbégal water mill in its environment: archaeology and the economic and social history of Antiquity', *JRA* 9, 137–53.

Leveau, P. (n.d.) 'L'occupation du sol dans les montagnes méditerranéennes pendant l'antiquité: apport de l'archéologie des paysages à la connaissance historique', in G. Fabre, 5–38.

Leveau, P. and Provansal, M. (1991) 'Construction deltaïque et histoire des systèmes agricoles, le cas d'un petit delta: l'Arc, Étang de Berre', *Revue archéologique de Narbonnaise* 23, 111–31.

Lévêque, P. (1993) 'La richesse foisonnante de l'*emporion*', in Bresson and Rouillard, 227–31.

Lever, A. (1986) 'Honour as a red herring', *Critique of Anthropology* 6, 83–106.

Levi, C. (1982) *Christ stopped at Eboli*, first published 1945, translation first published 1947, Harmondsworth.

Levi, D. (1981) 'Features and continuity of Cretan peak-cults', in A. Biran (ed.) *Temples and High Places in Biblical Times*, Jerusalem, 38–46.

Levi, G. (1991) 'On microhistory', in Burke, 93–113.

Lévi-Strauss, C. (1963) *Totemism*, first published 1962, Boston MA.

Lévi-Strauss, C. (1983) 'Histoire et ethnologie', *Annales*, 1217–31.

Levy, H. L. (1956) 'Property distribution by lot in present day Greece', *TAPA* 87, 42–6.

Lewicki, T. (1965) 'L'apport des sources arabes médiévales (IXe–Xe siècles) à la connaissance de l'Europe centrale et orientale', *SS* 12, 461–85.

Lewicki, T. (1978) 'Les voies maritimes de la Méditerranée dans le haut moyen âge d'après les sources arabes', *SS* 25, 439–69.

Lewin, J., Macklin, M. G. and Woodward, J. C. (eds) (1995) *Mediterranean Quaternary River Environments*, Rotterdam.

Lewis, A. R. (1951) *Naval Power and Trade in the Mediterranean, A.D. 500–1100*, Princeton NJ.

Lewis, A. R. (1978) 'Mediterranean maritime commerce, A.D. 300–1100: shipping and trade', *SS* 25, 481–501.

Lewis, B. (1988–9) 'The map of the Middle East: a guide for the perplexed', *The American Scholar* 58, 19–38.

Lewis, B. (1992) 'Legal and historical reflections on the position of Muslim populations under non-Muslim rule', *Journal Institute of Muslim Minority Affairs* [*sic*] 13, 1–16.

Lewis, B. and Holt, P. M. (eds) (1962) *Historians of the Middle East*, Oxford.

Lewis, B. and Said, E. W. (1982) 'Orientalism: an exchange', *New York Review of Books*, 12 August, 44–8 (revised in Lewis, *Islam and the West*, New York and Oxford 1993, 99–118).

Lewis G. (1972) 'The saint and the major-general', *AS* 22, 249–53.

Lewis, I. M. (ed.) (1968) *History and Social Anthropology*, ASA monograph no. 7, London.

Lewis, J. and Hudson, R. (eds) (1985) *Uneven Development in Southern Europe: Studies of Accumulation, Class, Migration and the State*, London.

Lewis, M. J. T. (1993) 'The Greeks and the early windmill', *History of Technology* 15, 141–89.

Lewis, N. N. (1987) *Nomads and Settlers in Syria and Jordan 1800–1900*, Cambridge MA.

Lewit, T. (1991) *Agricultural Production in the Roman Economy A.D. 200–400*, BAR 568, Oxford.

Lewthwaite, J. G. (1981) 'Plain tails from the hills: transhumance in Mediterranean archaeology', in Sheridan and Bailey, 57–66.

Lewthwaite, J. G. (1982) 'Acorns for the ancestors: the prehistoric exploitation of woodland in the west Mediterranean', in Bell and Limbrey, 217–30.

Lewthwaite, J. G. (1988) 'Trial by durée: a review of historico-geographical concepts relevant to the archaeology of settlement on Corsica and Sardinia', in Bintliff, Davidson and Grant, 61–86.

Leyser, K. (1992) 'Concepts of Europe in the Early and High Middle Ages', *PP* 137, 25–47.

Liebeschuetz, J. H. W. G. (1990) *Barbarians and Bishops: Army, Church and State in the Age of Arcadius and Chrysostom*, Oxford.

Lilie, R.-J. (1976) *Die byzantinische Reaktion auf die Ausbreitung der Araber*, Miscellanea Byzantina Monacensia 22, Munich.

Limbrey, S. (1990) 'Edaphic opportunism? A discussion of soil factors in relation to the beginnings of plant-husbandry in south-west Asia', *WA* 22.1, 45–52.

Linder, E. (1996) 'Human apprehension of the sea', in Rice, 15–22.

Linders, T. and Alroth, B. (eds) (1992) *The Economics of Cult in the Ancient Greek World: Proceedings of the Uppsala Symposium 1990, Boreas* 21, Uppsala.

Lindholm, C. (1982) *Generosity and Jealousy: The Swat Pukhtun of Northern Pakistan*, New York.

Lindholm, C. (1995) 'The new Middle Eastern ethnography' (review article), *Journal of the Royal Anthropological Institute (incorporating Man)*, 1, 805–20.

Lindholm, C. (1996) *The Islamic Middle East: An Historical Anthropology*, Oxford and Cambridge MA.

Lindisfarne, N. (1994) 'Variant masculinities, variant virginities: rethinking "honour and shame"', in Cornwall and Lindisfarne, 82–96.

Linehan, P. (1993) *History and the Historians of Medieval Spain*, Oxford.

Liphschitz, N. (1987) '*Ceratonia siliqua* in Israel: an ancient element or a newcomer?', *Israel Journal of Botany* 36, 191–7.

Lisón Arcal, J. C. (1986) *Cultura e identidad en la provincia de Huesca: una perspectiva desde la antropología social*, Zaragoza.

Lison-Tolosana, C. (1966) *Belmonte de los Caballeros: Anthropology and History in an Aragonese Community* (repr. Princeton NJ, 1983), Oxford.

Liu, X. (1996) *Silk and Religion: An Exploration of Material Life and the Thought of People, A.D. 600–1200*, Oxford 1996.

Livi-Bacci, M. (1991) *Population and Nutrition*, Cambridge.

Lixa Filgueiras, O. (ed.) (1988) *Local Boats, BAR* 438, Oxford.

Llobera, J. R. (1986) 'Fieldwork in southwestern Europe: anthropological panacea or epistemological straitjacket?', *Critique of Anthropology* 6, 25–33.

Lloyd, C. (1993) *Structures of History*, Oxford.

Lloyd, G. E. R. (1990) *Mentalities Demystified*, Cambridge.

Lloyd, J. (1991) 'Forms of rural settlement in the early Roman empire', in Barker and Lloyd, 233–40.

Lloyd, T. H. (1977) *The English Wool Trade in the Middle Ages*, Cambridge.

Lloyd-Jones, H. (1982) *Blood for the Ghosts: Classical Influences in the Nineteenth and Twentieth Centuries*, London.

Lloyd-Jones, H. (1990) 'Honour and shame in ancient Greek culture', in Lloyd-Jones, *Academic Papers: Greek Comedy, Hellenistic Literature, Greek Religion, Miscellanea*, Oxford, 253–80.

Lo Cascio, E. (1994) 'The size of the Roman population: Beloch and the meaning of the Augustan census figures', *JRS* 84, 23–40.

Lo Schiavo, F. (1986) 'Sardinian metallurgy, the archaeological background', in M. S. Balmuth (ed.) *Studies in Sardinian Archaeology 2: Sardinia in the Mediterranean*, Ann Arbor MI, 231–50.

Lobel, E. and Page, D. (eds) (1995) *Poetarum Lesbiorum Fragmenta*, Oxford.

Lock, P. (1990) 'D. G. Hogarth (1862–1927): "A specialist in the science of archaeology"', *ABSA* 85, 175–200.

Lock, P. (1995) *The Franks in the Aegean, 1204–1500*, London.

Lock, P. and Sanders, G. D. R. (1991) *The Archaeology of Medieval Greece*, Oxford.

Lockwood, W. G. (1975) *European Moslems: Economy and Ethnicity in Western Bosnia*, New York.

Lohmann, H. (1992) 'Agriculture and country life in classical Attica', in B. Wells, 29–66.

Lohmann, H. (1998) 'Die Santorin-Katastrophe – ein archäologischer Mythos?', in Olshausen and Sonnabend.

Lolos, Y. G. (1995) 'Late Cypro-Mycenaean seafaring: new evidence from sites in the Saronic and Argolic Gulfs', in Karageorghis and Michaelides, 65–88.

Lomas, K. (1995) 'Introduction', in Cornell and Lomas, 1–7.

Lombard, M. (1948) 'Mahomet et Charlemagne: le problème économique', *Annales*, 188–99.

Lombard, M. (1959) 'Le bois dans la Méditerranée musulmane, VIIème–XIème siècle', *Annales*, 234–54.

Lombard, M. (1974) *Les métaux dans l'ancien monde du Ve au XIe siècle*, Paris.

Lombard, M. (1975) *The Golden Age of Islam*, first published 1971, Amsterdam.

Lombard, M. (1978) *Les textiles dans le monde musulman, VIIIe–XIe siècle*, Paris.

Lombard, P. (1991) 'Du rhythme naturel au rhythme humain: vie et mort d'une technique traditionelle, le *qanāt*', in Cauvin, 69–86.

Lombardo, M. (1985) 'Il graffito', in M. Tagliente et al., 'Nuovi documenti su Pisticci in età arcaica', *PdelP* 223, 294–306.

Lombardo, M. (1995) 'Food and "frontier" in the Greek colonies of southern Italy', in Dobson, Harvey and Wilkins, 256–72.

Longobardi, C. (1936) *Land Reclamation in Italy*, London.

Lopez, R. S. (1933) *Genova marinara nel Duecento: Benedetto Zaccaria, ammiraglio e mercante*, Messina and Milan.

Lopez, R. S. (1945) 'Silk industry in the Byzantine empire', *Speculum* 20, 1–42 (repr. Lopez 1978).

Lopez, R. S. (1949) 'Du marché temporaire à la colonie permanente: l'évolution de la politique commerciale au moyen âge', *Annales*, 389–405 (repr. Lopez 1978).

Lopez, R. S. (1956) 'The evolution of land transport in the Middle Ages', *PP* 9, 17–29.

Lopez, R. S. (1959) 'The role of trade in the economic readjustment of Byzantium in the seventh century', *DOP* 13, 69–85 (repr. Lopez 1978).

Lopez, R. S. (1965) 'L'importanza del mondo Islamico nella vita economica Europea', *SS* 12, 433–60, with discussion 529–35.

Lopez, R. S. (1974) 'Foreigners in Byzantium', *Bulletin de l'Institut Historique Belge de Rome* 44, 341–52 (repr. Lopez 1978).

Lopez, R. S. (1976) *The Commercial Revolution of the Middle Ages, 950–1350*, Cambridge.

Lopez, R. S. (1978) *Byzantium and the World Around It: Economic and Institutional Relations*, Variorum, London.

Lopez, R. S. (1987) 'The trade of medieval Europe: the South', in Postan and Miller, 306–401, 902–4.

Lopez, R. S. and Raymond, I. W. (1955) *Medieval Trade in the Mediterranean World: Illustrative Documents translated with Introductions and Notes*, repr. New York 1990, London.

Loś, A. (1992) 'Les intérêts des affranchis dans l'agriculture italienne', *MEFRA* 104, 709–53.

Loseby, S. T. (1992) 'Marseille: a late antique success story?', *JRS* 82, 165–83.

Loseby, S. T. (1998) 'Marseille and the Pirenne Thesis I: Gregory of Tours, the Merovingian Kings and "un grand port"', in Hodges and Bowden, 203–29.

Loseby, S. T. (forthcoming a) 'Marseille and the Pirenne Thesis II: the death of Marseille', in Wickham and Hansen.

Loseby, S. T. (forthcoming b) 'The Mediterranean economy', in P. Fouracre (ed.) *The New Cambridge Medieval History* vol. 1: *500–700*, Cambridge.

Louis, P., Métral, F. and Métral, J. (eds) (1987) *L'homme et l'eau en Méditerranée et au Proche Orient IV: L'eau dans l'agriculture*, Lyon.

Loukopoulou, L. and Raptou, E. (1996) 'Mobilité et migration dans la Chypre antique', in Métral et al., 53–60.

Love, J. R. (1991) *Antiquity and Capitalism: Max Weber and the Sociological Foundations of Roman Civilization*, London.

Lucas, H. S. (1930) 'The great European famine of 1315, 1316, and 1317', *Speculum* 5, 343–77.

Luciani, G. (ed.) (1984) *The Mediterranean Region: Economic Interdependence and the Future of Society*, London, Canberra and New York.

Ludwig, E. (1929) *On Mediterranean Shores*, first published 1923, London.

Luft, U. (1994) 'L'irrigation au Moyen Empire', in Menu, 249–60.

Lutfi, H. (1985) *Al-Quds al-Mamlūkiyya: A History of Mamlūk Jerusalem based on the Haram Documents*, Berlin.

Luttrell, A. (1989) 'The Latins and life on the smaller Aegean islands, 1204–53', *MHR* 4, 146–57.

Luzzato, G. (1961) *Storia economica di Venezia dall'XI al XVI secolo*, Venice.

Lyon, B. (1974) *Henri Pirenne: A Biographical and Intellectual Study*, Ghent.

Lyon, B. (1980) 'Henri Pirenne and the origins of *Annales* history', *Annals of Scholarship* 1, 69–84.

MacArthur, R. H. and Wilson, E. O. (1967) *The Theory of Island Biogeography*, Princeton NJ.

MacCormack, S. (1990) '"Loca sancta": the organization of sacred topography in late Antiquity', in Ousterhout, 7–53.

Macfarlane, A. (1978) *The Origins of English Individualism: The Family, Property and Social Transition*, Oxford.

Macfarlane, A. (1984) 'The myth of the peasantry: family and economy in a northern parish', in R. M. Smith (ed.) *Land, Kinship and Life-Cycle*, 42–7.

Macfarlane, A. (1994) 'History and anthropology' (rev. of A. Gurevich, *Historical Anthropology of the Middle Ages*, Oxford 1992), *RurH* 5.1, 103–8.

MacKenzie, D. and Wajcman, J. (eds) (1985) *The Social Shaping of Technology: How the Refrigerator Got its Hum*, Milton Keynes and Philadelphia.

Mackie, N. K. (1983) 'Augustan colonies in Mauretania', *Historia* 32, 332–58.

MacLeod, A. E. (1991) *Accommodating Protest: Working Women, the New Veiling, and Change in Cairo*, New York.

MacMullen, R. (1970) 'Market-days in the Roman empire', *Phoenix* 24, 333–41.

MacMullen, R. (1980) 'Roman elite motivation: three questions', *PP* 88, 3–16.

Macve, R. H. (1985) 'Some glosses on "Greek and Roman accounting"', in *Crux: Essays in Greek History presented to G. E. M. de Ste Croix*, Liverpool, 233–64.

Magdalino, P. (1984) 'Byzantine snobbery', in M. Angold (ed.) *The Byzantine Aristocracy IX to XIII Centuries*, BAR 221, Oxford, 58–78.

Magdalino, P. (1989) 'Honour among Romaioi: the framework of social values in the world of Digenes Akrites and Kekaumenos', *BMGS* 13, 183–218.

Magdalino, P. (1995) 'The grain-supply of Constantinople, ninth–twelfth centuries', in Mango and Dagron, 35–48.

Maggi, R., Nisbet, R. and Barker, G. (eds) (1990) *Archeologia della pastorizia nell'Europa meridionale*, RSL 56, Bordighera.

Magnarella, P. J. (1992) 'Conceptualizing the circum-Mediterranean for purposes of social scientific research', *Journal of Mediterranean Studies* 2, 18–24.

Magoulias, H. J. (trans.) (1975) *Decline and Fall of Byzantium to the Ottoman Turks* [Ducas, *History*], Detroit MI.

Maier, F. G. and Karageorghis, V. (1984) *Paphos, History and Archaeology*, Nicosia.

Maitland, F. W. (1936) *Selected Essays*, ed. H. D. Hazeltine, G. T. Lapsley and P. H. Winfield, Cambridge.

Makris, J. (1992) 'Ethnography, history and collective representations: studying vendetta in Crete', in Pina-Cabral and Campbell (eds), 56–72.

Malamat, A. (1998) 'The Sacred Sea', in Kedar and Werblowsky, 45–54.

Malamut, E. (1988) *Les îles de l'empire byzantin (VIIIe–XIIe siècles)*, Byzantina Sorbonensia 8, 2 vols, Paris.

Malamut, E. (1993) *Sur la route des saints byzantins*, Paris.

Maldonado, A. (1985) 'Evolution of the Mediterranean basin and a detailed reconstruction of the Cenozoic paleoceanography', in Margalef, 17–59.

Malkin, I. (1987) *Religion and Colonization in Ancient Greece*, Leiden.

Malkin, I. (1994) *Myth and Territory in the Spartan Mediterranean*, Cambridge.

Malkin, I. (1996) 'Territorial Domination and the Greek Sanctuary', in Hellstrom and Alroth, 75–81.

Malkin, I. and Hohlfelder, R. L. (eds) (1988) *Mediterranean Cities: Historical Perspectives*, London.

Mallowan, M. E. L. (1939) 'Phoenician carrying-trade, Syria', *Antiquity* 13, 86–7.

Malone, C. and Stoddart, S. (eds) (1985) *Papers in Italian Archaeology, The Cambridge Conference Part IV: Classical and Medieval Archaeology*, BAR 246, Oxford.

Malone, C., Stoddart, S. and Allegrucci, F. (1994) *Territory, Time and State: The Archaeological Development of the Gubbio Basin*, Cambridge.

Malowist, M. (1972) *Croissance et régression en Europe XIVe–XVIIe siècles*, Cahiers des Annales 34, Paris.

Malpica, A. (ed.) (1995) *Paisajes del Azúcar*, Granada.

Maltezou, C. (1980) 'A contribution to the historical geography of the island of Kythira during the Venetian occupation', in Laiou (ed.), 151–75.

Manacorda, D. (1979) 'Le urne di Amalfi non sono amalfitane', *AC* 31, 318–37.

Manacorda, D. (1981) 'Produzione agricola, produzione ceramica e proprietari nell'*ager Cosanus* nel I a.C.', in Giardina and Schiavone, 2.3–54.

Mandelbaum, D. G. (1988) *Women's Seclusion and Men's Honor: Sex Roles in North India, Bangladesh, and Pakistan*, Tucson AZ.

Mane, P. (1983) *Calendriers et techniques agricoles: France–Italie, XIIe–XIIIe siècles*, Paris.

Mangin, W. (ed.) (1970) *Peasants in Cities: Readings in the Anthropology of Urbanization*, Boston.

Mango, C. (1963) 'Antique statuary and the Byzantine beholder', *DOP* 17, 53–75.

Mango, C. (1980) *Byzantium: The Empire of New Rome*, London.

Mango, C. (1984) 'Chypre, carrefour du monde Byzantin', *XVe congrès internationale d'études Byzantines: rapports et co-rapports*, 5.5, 3–13.

Mango, C. (1985) *Le développement urbain de Constantinople (IVe–VIIe siècles)*, Paris.

Mango, C. (1992) 'Diabolus Byzantinus', *DOP* 46, 215–23.

Mango, C. (ed. and trans.) (1990) *Nicephorus, Short History*, Washington DC.

Mango, C. and Dagron, G. (eds) (1995) *Constantinople and its Hinterland*, Aldershot.

Mango, M. M. (1992) 'The monetary value of silver revetments and objects belonging to churches, A.D. 300–700 in Boyd and Mango, 123–36.

Mann, H.-D. (1971) *Lucien Febvre: la pensée vivante d'un historien*, Paris.

Manning, S. (1988) 'The Bronze Age eruption of Thera: absolute dating, Aegean chronology and Mediterranean cultural interrelations', *JMA* 1, 17–82.

Mantelli, R. (1985) 'Industrialization in southern Italy before and after unification', *JEEH* 14, 577–83.

Manville, P. B. (1982) 'Geometric graves and the eighth century "population boom" in Attica', *AJA* 86, 275–6.

Marangou, A. (1994) 'Vin et amphores de Crète en Campanie', in Amouretti and Villard, 137–43.

Marangou-Lerat, A. (1995) *Le vin et les amphores de Crète de l'époque classique à l'époque impériale*, Athens.

Marasco, G. (1988) *Economia, commerci e politica nel Mediterraneo fra il 3 e il 2 s. a.C.*, Florence.

Maraval, P. (1984) 'Le temps du pèlerin (IVe–VIIe siècles)', in J.-M. Leroux (ed.) *Le temps chrétien de la fin de l'antiquité au moyen âge*, Paris, 479–88.

Maraval, P. (1985) *Lieux saints et pèlerinages d'Orient: histoire et géographie des origines à la conquête arabe*, Paris.

Marchese, R. T. (1986) *The Lower Maeander Flood-Plain: A Regional Settlement Study*, BAR 292, Oxford.

Marcus, M. (ed.) (1983) *Elites: Ethnographic Issues*, Santa Fe CA.

Marfoe, L. (1978) *Between Qadesh and Kumidi: A History of Frontier Settlement and Land Use in the Biqa, Lebanon*, dissertation, University of Chicago.

Marfoe, L. (1979) 'The integrative transformation: patterns of sociopolitical organisation in southern Syria', *BASOR* 234, 1–42.

Margadant, T. W. (1984) 'Tradition and modernity in rural France during the nineteenth century', *Journal of Modern History* 56, 667–97.

Margalef, R. (ed.) (1985) *The Western Mediterranean*, Oxford and New York.

Margaris, N. S. (1981) 'Adaptive strategies in plants dominating Mediterranean-type eco-systems', in Di Castri et al., 309–15.

Marin, B. (1996) 'Naples: capital of the Enlightenment', in Clark and Lepetit, 143–67.

Marino, J. A. (1988) *Pastoral Economics in the Kingdom of Naples*, Baltimore MD and London.

Marinone, N. (1992) *Il riso nell'antichità greca*, Bologna.

Markoe, G. (1985) *Phoenician Bronze and Silver Bowls from Cyprus and the Mediterranean*, Berkeley.

Markus, R. A. (1990) *The End of Ancient Christianity*, Cambridge.

Markus, R. A. (1994) 'How on earth could places become holy? Origins of the Christian idea of holy places', *Journal of Early Christian Studies* 2, 257–71.

Martin, L. H. (1990) 'Greek Goddesses and grain: the Sicilian connection', *Helios* 17, 251–61.

Marx, E. (1977) 'Communal and individual pilgrimage: the region of saints' tombs in South Sinai', in Werbner, 29–51.

Mason, S. (1995) 'Acornutopia? Determining the role of acorns in past human subsistence', in J. Wilkins, D. Harvey and M. Dobson (eds) *Food in Antiquity*, Exeter, 12–24.

Masschaele, J. (1993) 'Transport costs in medieval England', *EcHR* 46, 266–79.

Matthews, J. F. (1984) 'The tax law of Palmyra: evidence for economic history in a city of the Roman East', *JRS* 74, 157–80.

Mattingly, D. J. (1988) 'Megalithic madness and measurement: or how many olives could an olive press press?', *OJA* 7, 177–95.

Mattingly, D. J. (1994) 'Regional variation in Roman oleoculture: some problems of comparability', in Carlsen et al., 91–106.

Mattingly, D. J. (1996) 'First fruit? The olive in the Roman world', in Salmon and Shipley, 213–53.

Mattingly, D. J. (1997) 'Olive presses in Roman Africa: technical innovation or stagnation?', *L'Africa Romana* 11.3, 577–95.

Matvejević, P. (1991) *Mediterraneo: un nuovo breviario*, first published 1987, Rome.

Maucourant, J. (1996) 'Une analyse économique de la redistribution est-elle possible? Éléments de comparaison entre la "New Insitutional Economics" et l'approche substantive', *Topoi* 6, 131–58.

Maul, G. A. (1993) *Climatic Change in the Intra-Americas Sea: Implications of Future Climate on the Ecosystems and Socio-economic Structure in the Marine and Coastal Regions of the Caribbean Sea, Gulf of Mexico, Bahamas, and the Northeast Coast of South America*, London.

Maunier, R. (1927) 'Recherches sur les échanges rituels en Afrique du Nord', *L'Année sociologique*, new series 2 (for 1924–5), 11–97.

Mauss, M. (1969) *The Gift: Forms and Functions of Exchange in Archaic Societies*, first published 1925, London.

Mayerson, P. (1984) 'Wheat in the Roman world: an addendum', *CQ* 34, 243–5.

Mayerson, P. (1985) 'The wine and vineyards of Gaza in the Byzantine period', *BASOR* 257, 75–80.

Mazloum, S. (n.d.) *L'ancienne canalization d'eau d'Alep (le Qanāyé de Hailaān)*, Documents d'Études Orientales 5, Damascus.

Mazzaoui, M. F. (1981) *The Italian Cotton Industry in the Later Middle Ages 1100–1600*, Cambridge.

Mazzarino, S. (1961) 'In margine alle "Verrine": per un giudizio storico sull'orazione De Frumento', *Atti del I Congresso internazionale di studi ciceroniani, Roma 1959*, Rome, 2.99–118.

McCormick, M. (1995) 'Byzantium and the West, 700–900', in *New Cambridge Medieval History*, vol. 2, ed. R. McKitterick, Cambridge, 349–80.

McCormick, M. (1998) 'The imperial edge: Italo-Byzantine identity, movement and integration, A.D. 650–950', in Ahrweiler and Laiou, 17–52.

McDonnell, E. W. (1980) 'Monastic stability: some socio-economic considerations', in Laiou (ed.), 115–50.

McDonogh, G. W. (1986) *Good Families of Barcelona: A Social History of Power in the Industrial Era*, Princeton NJ.

McGovern, P. E., Fleming, S. J. and Katz, S. H. (eds) (1995) *The Origins and Ancient History of Wine*, Luxemburg.

McGowan, B. (1981) *Economic Life in Ottoman Europe: Taxation, Trade and the Struggle for Land, 1600–1800*, Cambridge and Paris.

McGrail, S. (1981) *Rafts, Boats and Ships from Prehistoric Times to the Mediaeval Era*, London.

McGrail, S. (1989) 'The shipment of traded goods and of ballast in Antiquity', *OJA* 8, 353–8.

McGrail, S. and Kentley, E. (eds) (1985) *Sewn Plank Boats*, BAR 279, Oxford.

McIntosh, R. P. (1985) *The Background of Ecology: Concept and Theory*, Cambridge.

McKechnie, P. (1989) *Outsiders in the Greek Cities in the Fourth Century B.C.*, London.

McKinney, J. C. (1966) *Constructive Typology and Social Theory*, New York.

McLoskey, D. N. (1976) 'English open fields as behaviour towards risk', in P. J. Uselding (ed.) *Research in Economic History*, supplement 1, 124–70.

McManners, J. (1982) *Popular Religion in Seventeenth and Eighteenth Century France*, London.

McNeil, I. (ed.) (1989) *An Encyclopaedia of the History of Technology*, London.

McNeill, J. R. (1992) *The Mountains of the Mediterranean World: An Environmental History*, Cambridge.

McNeill, W. H. (1980) *The Human Condition: An Ecological and Historical View*, Princeton NJ.

McNeill, W. H. (1986) 'Fernand Braudel', in McNeill, *Mythistory and Other Essays*, Chicago, 199–226.

McNeill, W. H. (1987) 'The eccentricity of wheels', *AHR* 92, 1111–26.

McPhee, P. (1992) *A Social History of France 1780–1880*, London and New York.

Medeiros, F. (1988) 'Espaces ruraux et dynamiques sociales en Europe du sud', *Annales*, 1081–1107.

Mee, C. and Forbes, H. A. (eds) (1997) *A Rough and Rocky Place: The Landscape and Settlement History of the Methana Peninsula, Greece*, Liverpool.

Meehan, D. (ed.) (1958) Adamnan, *De Locis Sanctis* (*On the Holy Places*), Scriptores Latini Hiberniae 3, Dublin.

Meek, C. (1978) *Lucca 1369–1400: Politics and Society in the Early Renaissance City-State*, Oxford.

Meeker, M. E. (1976) 'Meaning and society in the Near East: examples from the Black Sea Turks and the Levantine Arabs', *IJMES* 7, 243–70, 383–422.

Meeks, D. (1979) 'Les donations aux temples d'Égypte', in E. Lipinski (ed.) *State and Temple Economy in the Ancient Near East*, Louvain, 605–87.

Megas, G. A. (1958) *Greek Calendar Customs*, Athens.

Meiggs, R. (1982) *Trees and Timber in the Ancient Mediterranean World*, Oxford.

Meijer, F. and van Nijf, O. (1992) *Trade, Transport and Society in the Ancient World: A Sourcebook*, London and New York.

Meikle, S. (1995a) 'Modernism, economics and the ancient economy', *PCPS* 41, 174–91.

Meikle, S. (1995b) *Aristotle's Economic Thought*, Oxford.

Meillassoux, C. (1981) *Maidens, Meal and Money: Capitalism and the Domestic Community*, first published 1975, Cambridge.

Meillassoux, C. (1991) *The Anthropology of Slavery: The Womb of Iron and Gold*, first published 1986, London.

Meinardus, O. (1973) 'Testimonies to the economic vitality of Balat, the mediaeval Miletus [*sic*]', *Belleten* 37/147, 289–304.

Meinardus, O. (1980) 'St Michael's miracle of Khonai', *Ekklesia kai Theologia* 1, 459–69.

Mélanges en l'honneur de Fernand Braudel (1973) vol. 1: *Histoire économique du monde méditerranéen, 1450–1650;* vol. 2: *Méthodologie de l'histoire et des sciences humaines*, Toulouse.

Melas, E. M. (1985) *The Islands of Karpathos, Saros and Kasos in the Neolithic and Bronze Ages*, Göteborg.

Melas, I. (1955) *Istoria tis nisou Ikarias*, Athens.

Mele, A. (1979) *Il commercio greco arcaico: prexis ed emporie*, Naples.

Melena, J. L. (1983) 'Olive oil and other sorts of oil in the Cretan tablets', *Minos* 18, 89–123.

Melis, F. (1985) *I trasporti e le communicazioni nel medioevo*, ed. L. Frangioni, Florence.

Mendelson, S. and Crawford, P. (1998) *Women in Early Modern England*, Oxford.

Mendoni, L. G. (1989) 'More inscriptions from Ceos', *ABSA* 84, 289–96.

Mendras, H. (1979) *La fin des paysans*, Paris.

Menu, B. (1995) 'Fondations et concessions royales de terrres en Égypte ancienne', *DHA* 21, 11–55.

Menu, B. (ed.) (1994) *Les problèmes institutionnels de l'eau en Égypte ancienne et dans l'antiquité méditerranéenne*, Cairo.

Merkelbach, R. (1972) 'Aglauros (Die Religion der Epheben)', *ZPE* 9, 277–85.

Merlin, H. D. (1984) *On the Trail of the Ancient Opium Poppy*, London and Cranbury NJ.

Merrington, J. (1978) 'Town and country in the transition to capitalism' (repr. from *New Left Review* 93 (1975), 71–92) in R. Hilton (ed.) *The Transition from Feudalism to Capitalism*, London, 170–95.

Métral, F. (1991) 'Entre Palmyre et l'Euphrate: oasis et agriculture dans la région de Sukhné', in Cauvin, 87–108.

Métral, F. (1996) 'Du commerce itinérant à l'import-export: le commerce des produits pastoraux au proche-Orient: analyse d'un réseau', in Métral et al., 81–96.

Métral, F., Yon, M. and Ioannou, Y. (1996) *Chypre hier et aujourd'hui entre Orient et Occident*, Lyon and Paris.

Meuret, C. (1996) 'Le règlement de *Lamasba*: des tables de conversion appliquées à l'irrigation', *AA* 32, 87–112.

Mickwitz, G. (1937) 'Economic rationalism in Graeco-Roman agriculture', *EHR* 52, 577–89.

Milanese, M. (1987) *Scavi nell'oppidum preromano di Genova*, Rome.

Milanese, M. and Mannoni, T. (1986) 'Gli Etruschi a Genova e il commercio Mediterraneo', *Studi Etruschi* 52, 117–46.

Milieux calcaires et politique hydraulique (1991). *Actes du Congrès national des sociétés savantes: section de géographie physique et humaine*, Paris.

Millar, F. G. B. (1977) *The Emperor in the Roman World*, London.

Millar, F. G. B. (1990) 'The Roman *coloniae* of the Near East: a study of cultural relations', in H. Solin and M. Kajava (eds) *Roman Eastern Policy and Other Studies in Roman History*, Helsinki, 7–58.

Millar, F. G. B. (1993) *The Roman Near East, 31 B.C.–A.D. 337*, Cambridge MA.

Miller, J. A. (1984) *Imlil: A Moroccan Mountain Community in Change*, Boulder CO and London.

Millett, M. (1991) 'Roman towns and their territories: an archaeological perspective', in Rich and Wallace-Hadrill, 169–89.

Millett, P. (1984) 'Hesiod and his world', *PCPS* 30, 84–115.

Milojević, B. Z. (1939) *Les hautes montagnes de Yougoslavie*, Belgrade.

Miquel, A. (1967–88) *La géographie humaine du monde musulman jusqu'au milieu du XIe siècle*, 4 vols, Paris.

Miquel, A. (1980) 'Origine et carte des mers dans la géographie arabe aux approches de l'An Mil', *Annales*, 452–61.

Miquel, A. (trans.) (1963) al-Muqaddasi, *La meilleure répartition pour la connaissance des provinces* [*Ahsan at-taqasim fi ma'rifat al-aqalim*], Damascus.

Miranda, E. (1989) 'Osservazioni sul culto di Euploia', *Miscellanea greca e romana* 14, 123–44.

Miskimin, H. H., Herlihy, D. and Udovitch, A. L. (eds) (1977) *The Medieval City*, New Haven.

Mitchell, S. (1990) 'Festivals, games, and civic life in Roman Asia Minor' (review of Woerrle 1988), *JRS* 80, 183–93.

Mitchell, S. (1993) *Anatolia: Land, Men and Gods in Asia Minor*, 2 vols, Oxford.

Moeller, W. (1976) *The Wool Trade of Ancient Pompeii*, Leiden.

Mohammed, A. (1978) 'The nomadic and the sedentary: polar complimentaries – not polar opposites', in C. Nelson (ed.) *The Desert and the Sown: Nomads in the Wider Society*, Berkeley.

Moinier, B. (1986) 'Lecture moderne de Pline l'Ancien: communication sur la production et consommation de sel de mer dans le bassin méditerranéen', in *L'exploitation de la mer*, 73–106.

Mokyr, J. (1990) *The Lever of Riches: Technological Creativity and Economic Progress*, Oxford.

Mokyr, J. (1996) 'Evolution and technological change: a new metaphor for economic history?', in Fox (ed.), 63–83.

Molinari, A. (1994) 'Il popolamento rurale in Sicilia tra V e XIII secolo: alcuni spunti di reflessione', in Francovich and Noyé, 361–78.

Molinier, A. (1976) *Ardèche*, Paroisses et communes de France 7, Paris.

Mollat, M. (ed.) (1968) *Le rôle du sel dans l'histoire*, Paris.

Mollat du Jourdin, M. (1993) *Europe and the Sea*, Oxford and Cambridge MA.

Mollat du Jourdin, M. and de La Roncière, M. (1984) *Portulans: Sea Charts of the Early Explorers*, New York.

Möller, H., Petts, G. E. and Roux, A. L. (eds) (1989) *Historical Change of Large Alluvial Rivers: Western Europe*, Chichester.

Mols, R. (1954–6) *Introduction à la démographie des villes d'Europe du XIVe au XVIIIe siècle*, 3 vols, Louvain.

Momigliano, A. D. (1960) 'Sea-power in Greek thought' (repr. from *CR* 58 (1944), 1–7) in *Secondo contributo alla storia degli studi classici*, Rome, 57–67.

Momigliano, A. D. (1969a) *Studies in Historiography*, first published 1966, London.

Momigliano, A. D. (1969b) 'M. I. Rostovtzeff', in Momigliano (1969a), 91–104.

Momigliano, A. D. (1976) review of T. D. Barnes, *Tertullian: a Historical and Literary Study*, Oxford 1971, *JRS* 66, 273–6.

Momigliano, A. D. (1991) *The Classical Foundations of Modern Historiography*, Berkeley, Los Angeles and Oxford.

Montagu, J. (1799) *A Voyage Round the Mediterranean in the Years 1738 and 1739 to which are prefixed, Memoirs of the Noble Author's Life, by J. Cooke*, London.

Montanari, M. (1985a) 'Il cibo dei contadini: mutamenti economico-sociali e trasformazione del regime alimentare dei ceti rurali', in Andreolli et al., 195–216.

Montanari, M. (1985b) 'Tecniche e rapporti di produzione: le rese cerealicole dal IX al XIV secolo', in Andreolli et al., 43–68.

Moody, J. and Grove, A. T. (1990) 'Terraces and enclosure walls in the Cretan landscape', in Bottema et al., 183–91.

Moore, R. I. (1993) 'World history: world-economy or set of sets?' (review of Chaudhuri 1990 and Abu-Lughod 1989), *Journal of the Royal Asiatic Society*, 3rd series, 3, 99–105.

Moran, E. F. (ed.) (1984) *The Ecosystem Concept in Anthropology*, Boulder CO.

Moravcsik, G. and Jenkins, R. J. H. (eds and trans.) (1967) Constantine Porphyrogenitus, *De administrando imperio* (repr. 1985), Washington DC.

Morel, J.-P. (1978) 'La laine de Tarente', *Ktema* 3, 93–110.

Morel, J.-P. (1981) 'La produzione della ceramica campana: aspetti economici e sociali', in Giardina and Schiavone, 2.81–98.

Morel, J.-P. (1984) 'Greek colonisation in Italy and the West', in Hackens et al., 123–61.

Morel, J.-P. (1991) 'La romanisation du Samnium et de la Lucanie', in J. Mertens and R. Lambrechts (eds) *Comunità indigene e problemi della romanizzazione nell'Italia centro-meridionale (IVo–IIIo sec. av. C.)*, Brussels and Rome, 125–44.

Moreland, J. (1992) 'Restoring the dialectic: settlement patterns and documents in medieval central Italy', in Knapp, 112–29.

Moreland, J. (1993) 'Excavations at Casale San Donato, Castelnuovo di Farfa (RI), Lazio, 1992', *AM* 20, 185–228.

Moreland, J. (1994) 'Wilderness, wasteland, depopulation and the end of the Roman empire?', Accordia Research Papers 4 (for 1993), 89–110.

Morgan, C. (1994) 'The evolution of a sacral "landscape": Isthmia, Perachora and the early Corinthian state', in Alcock and Osborne, 105–142.

Morgan, C. (forthcoming) 'Ethne, ethnicity and early Greek states', in volume ed. M. Bats, Naples.

Morley, N. (1996) *Metropolis and Hinterland: The City of Rome and the Italian Economy, 200 B.C.–A.D. 200*, Cambridge.

Morley, N. (1997) 'Cities in context: urban systems in Roman Italy', in Parkins, 42–58.

Morris, D. (1977) *Manwatching: A Field Guide to Human Behaviour*, London.

Morris, I. (1986) 'Gift and commodity in archaic Greece', *Man* 21, 1–17.

Morris, I. (1987) *Burial and Ancient Society: The Rise of the Greek City-State*, Cambridge.

Morris, I. (1989) 'Circulation, deposition and the formation of the Greek Iron Age', *Man* 23, 502–19.

Morris, I. (1992) *Death-Ritual and Social Structure in Classical Antiquity*, Cambridge.

Morris, I. (1994) *Classical Greece: Ancient Histories and Modern Archaeologies*, Cambridge.

Morris, R. (1989) *Churches in the Landscape*, London.

Morrison, I. A. (1980) *Long Ships and Round Ships: Warfare and Trade in the Mediterranean 3000 B.C.–A.D. 500*, London.

Moryson, F. (1617) *An Itinerary*, London.

Moulin, A. (1991) *Peasantry and Society in France since 1789*, first published 1988, Cambridge and Paris.

Mueller, W. (1961) *Die heilige Stadt: Roma quadrata, himmlisches Jerusalem und die Mythe vom Weltnabel*, Stuttgart.

Muendel, J. (1985) 'The mountain men of the Casentino during the late Middle Ages', *ANYAS* 441, 29–70.

Muhawi, I. (1989) 'L'ideale onorifico nella società palestinese tradizionale', in Fiume, 263–76.

Muhly, J. D. (1996) 'The significance of metals in the late Bronze Age economy of Cyprus', in Karageorghis and Michaelides, 45–60.

Muhly, J. D., Maddin, R. and Stech, T. (1988) 'Cyprus, Crete and Sardinia: copper oxhide ingots and the metals trade', *Report of the Department of Antiquities, Cyprus*, 281–98.

Muhly, J. D., Maddin, R., Stech, T. and Özgen, E. (1985) 'Iron in Anatolia and the nature of the Hittite iron industry', *AS* 35, 67–84.

Muir, E. and Ruggiero, G. (eds) (1990) *Sex and Gender in Historical Perspective*, Baltimore and London.

Mumford, L. (1961) *The City in History: Its Origins, its Transformations, and its Prospects*, New York.

Murgatroyd, P. (1995) 'The sea of love', *CQ* 45, 9–25.

Murphy, M. (1998) 'Feeding medieval cities: some historical approaches', in M. Carlin and J. T. Rosenthal (eds) *Food and Eating in Medieval Europe*, London and Rio Grande, 117–31.

Murray, O. (1991) 'Arnaldo Momigliano in England', *History and Theory* 30, 49–64.

Murray, O. (1992) 'The ecology and agrarian history of ancient Greece', *Opus* 11 [1994], 11–23.

Murray, O. and Price, S. (eds) (1990) *The Greek City: From Homer to Alexander*, Oxford.

Murray, W. M. (1984) 'The ancient dam of the Mytikas valley', *AJA* 88, 195–203.

Murray, W. M. (1995) 'Ancient sailing winds in the eastern Mediterranean: the case for Cyprus', in Karageorghis and Michaelides, 33–44.

Muthesius, A. (1997) *Byzantine Silk Weaving: AD 400 to AD 1200*, Vienna.

Myres, J. L. (1906) 'On the list of "Thalassocracies" in Eusebius', *JHS* 26, 84–130.

Myres, J. L. (1943) *Mediterranean Culture*, Frazer Lecture, Cambridge.

Myres, J. L. (1953) *Geographic History in Greek Lands*, Oxford.

Nachmani, A. (1987) *Israel, Turkey and Greece: Uneasy Relations in the Eastern Mediterranean*, London.

Narciso, E. (ed.) (1991) *La cultura della transumanza*, Naples.

Naveh, Z. (1990) 'Ancient man's impact on the Mediterranean landscape in Israel – ecological and evolutionary perspectives', in Bottema, 45–50.

Naveh, Z. and Kutiel, P. (1990) 'Changes in the Mediterranean vegetation of Israel in response to human habitation and land-use', in Woodwell, 259–99.

Naveh, Z. and Vernet, J.-L. (1991) 'The palaeohistory of the Mediterranean biota', in Groves and Di Castri, 19–32.

Navigation et gens de mer en Méditerranée de la préhistoire à nos jours (1980), Paris.

Neboit, R. (1980) 'Morphogenèse et occupation humaine dans l'antiquité', *BAGF* 57, 21–27.

Neboit, R. (1984) 'Érosion des sols et colonisation grecque en Sicile et en Grande Grèce', *BAGF* 61, 5–13.

Neboit, R., Dufaure, J.-J., Julian, M., Guigo, M., Holloway, N. D. and Ross Holloway, R. (1984a) 'Facteurs naturels et humains dans la morphogenèse méditerranéenne', in *La mobilité des paysages Mediterranéens*, 317–30.

Neboit, R., Sontadé, G., Maurer, G., Dufaure, J.-J., Beaudet, G., Mussot, R., Guigo, M. Gabert, P. and Vaudon, J. (1984b) 'Les travaux et les jours de l'érosion méditerranéenne', in *La mobilité des paysages Mediterranéens*, 302–16.

Neboit-Guilhot, R. (1990) 'Les mouvements de terrain en Basilicate (Italie méridionale)', *BAGF* 67, 123–31.

Neboit-Guilhot, R. (1992–3) 'Accumulation et creusement dans les vallées depuis 10,000 ans autour de la méditerranée', *BAGF*, 189–206.

Needham, R. (1975) 'Polythetic classification: convergence and consequences', *Man* 10, 349–69.

Neev, D., Bakler, L. and Emery, K. O. (1987) *Mediterranean Coasts of Israel and Sinai: Holocene Geomorphism from Geology, Geophysics and Archaeology*, New York.

Neev, D. and Emery, K. O. (1967) *The Dead Sea*, Tel Aviv.

Nef, J. U. (1987) 'Mining and metallurgy in medieval civilisation', in Postan and Miller, 691–761.

Nelson, C. (ed.) (1974) *The Desert and the Sown: Nomads in the Wider Society*, Institute of International Studies, University of California, research series no. 21, Berkeley.

Nenci, G. (1982) 'L'allume di Focea', *PdelP* 37, 183–8.

Netting, R. McC. (1974a) 'The system nobody knows: village irrigation in the Swiss Alps', in Downing and Gibson, 67–78.

Netting, R. McC. (1974b) 'Agrarian ecology', *ARA* 3, 21–56.

Netting, R. McC. (1981) *Balancing on an Alp: Ecological Change and Continuity in a Swiss Mountain Community*, Cambridge.

Neuschel, K. B. (1989) *Word of Honor: Interpreting Noble Culture in Sixteenth-Century France*, Ithaca NY.

Nevo, Y. D. (1991) *Pagans and Herders: A Re-examination of the Negev Runoff Cultivation Systems in the Byzantine and Early Arab Periods*, Midreshet Ben-Gurion, Negev, Israel.

Newbigin, M. I. (1924) *The Mediterranean Lands: An Introductory Study in Human and Historical Geography*, London.

Newman, L. F. (ed.) (1990) *Hunger in History: Food Shortage, Poverty, and Deprivation*, Cambridge MA and Oxford.

Nicholas, D. (1997a) *The Growth of the Medieval City from Late Antiquity to the Early Fourteenth Century*, London and New York.

Nicholas, D. (1997b) *The Later Medieval City*, London and New York.

Nicolet, C. (1977–8) *Rome et la conquête du monde méditerranéen*, 2 vols, Paris.

Nicolet, C. (1988) *L'inventaire du monde*, Paris.

Niemeyer, H.-G. (1990) 'The Phoenicians in the Mediterranean: a non-Greek model for expansion and settlement in Antiquity', in Descoeudres, 469–89.

Niemeyer, H.-G. (ed.) (1982) *Phönizier im Westen*, Madrider Beiträge 8, Mainz am Rhein.

Nixon, I. G. (1985) 'The eruption of Thera and its effects', *JAS* 12, 9–24.

Nixon, L. and Price, S. (1990) 'The size and resources of Greek cities', in Murray and Price, 137–70.

Nolan, M. L. (1990) 'Shrine locations: ideals and realities in continental Europe', in Boesch Gajano and Scaraffia, 75–84.

Norberg, D. L. (ed.) (1982) Gregory the Great, *Registrum Epistularum*, Turnhout.

Nordenstam, T. (1968) *Sudanese Ethics*, Uppsala.

Nouschi, A. (1983) 'Les savoirs dans les pays méditerranéens: conservations, transmissions et acquisitions', in Aymard (ed.), 235–9.

Novák, V. (1989) *Fuzzy Sets and their Applications*, Bristol.

Noyé, G. (ed.) (1988) *Structures de l'habitat et occupation du sol dans les pays méditerranéens: les méthodes et l'apport de l'archéologie extensive*, Rome and Madrid.

Nutton, V. (1985) 'The drug trade in antiquity', *Journal of the Royal Society of Medicine* 78, 138–45.

Nye, R. A. (1993) *Masculinity and Male Codes of Honor in Modern France*, New York and Oxford.

Oaks, L. (1987) 'Epona in the Aeduan landscape: transfunctional deity under changing rule', in Crumley and Marquardt, 295–333.

Obrist, B. (1997) 'Wind diagrams and medieval cosmology', *Speculum* 72, 1–32.

Oded, B. (1979) *Mass Deportations and Deportees in the Neo-Assyrian Empire*, Wiesbaden.

Oehler, H. (1913) *Paradoxographi Florentini anonymi Opusculum de aquis mirabilibus*, Tübingen.

Oikonomides, N. (1968) *Actes de Dionysiou*, Archives de l'Athos 4, Paris.

Oikonomides, N. (1986) 'Silk trade and production in Byzantium from the sixth to the ninth century: the seals of Kommerkiarioi', *DOP* 40, 33–53.

Oikonomides, N. (1989) 'Commerce et production de la soie à Byzance', in *Hommes et richesses*, 187–92.

Okey, R. (1992) 'Central Europe/Eastern Europe: behind the definitions', *PP* 137, 102–33.

Oldroyd, D. R. (1996) *Thinking about the Earth: A History of Ideas in Geology*, London.

Oleson, J.-P. (1984) *Greek and Roman Water-Lifting Devices: The History of a Technology*, Buffalo.

Olmo, H. P. (1995) 'The origin and domestication of the Vinifera grape', in McGovern, Fleming and Katz, 31–43.

Olshausen, E. and Sonnabend, H. (eds) (1998) *Naturkatastrophen in der antiken Welt: Stuttgarter Kolloquium zur historischen Geographie des Altertums 6*, Geographica Historica 10, Stuttgart.

Olson, S. D. (1991) 'Firewood and charcoal in classical Athens', *Hesperia* 60, 411–20.

O'Neill, B. J. (1987) *Social Inequality in a Portuguese Hamlet: Land, Late Marriage, and Bastardy, 1870–1978*, Cambridge.

O'Neill, R. (ed.) (1988) *Prospects for Security in the Mediterranean*, Basingstoke.

Opelt, I. and Kirsten, E. (1989) 'Eine Urkunde der Gründung von Arsinoe in Kilikien', *ZPE* 77, 55–66.

Origo, I. (1979) *The Merchant of Prato: Francesco di Marco Datini, 1335–1410*, Harmondsworth.

Origone, S. (1992) *Bisanzio e Genova*, Genoa.

Orlove, B. S. (1980) 'Ecological anthropology', *ARA* 9, 235–73.

Ormerod, H. A. (1924) *Piracy in the Ancient World: An Essay in Mediterranean History*, Liverpool and London.

Orrieux, C. (1985) *Zénon de Caunos*, Paris.

Ortalli, G. (1993) 'Il mercante e lo stato: strutture della Venezia altomedievale', *SS* 40, 85–135.

Ortner, S. B. (1978) 'The virgin and the state', *Feminist Studies* 4, 19–37.

Ortner, S. B. (1981) 'Gender and sexuality in hierarchical societies: the case of Polynesia and some comparative implications', in Ortner and Whitehead (eds), 359–409.

Ortner, S. B. and Whitehead, H. (1981) 'Introduction: accounting for sexual meanings', in Ortner and Whitehead (eds), 1–27.

Ortner, S. B. and Whitehead, H. (eds) (1981) *Sexual Meanings: The Cultural Construction of Gender and Sexuality*, Cambridge.

Orvietani Busch, S. (1995) 'An interdisciplinary and comparative approach to northern Tuscan ports in the Early and High Middle Ages', in L. J. Simon (ed.) *Iberia and the Mediterranean World of the Middle Ages: Studies in Honor of Robert I. Burns*, Leiden, 161–84.

Osborne, R. G. (1985) 'Buildings and residence on the land in classical and Hellenistic Greece: the contribution of epigraphy', *ABSA* 80, 119–28.

Osborne, R. G. (1987) *Classical Landscape with Figures*, London.

Osborne, R. G. (1991a) 'Pride and prejudice, sense and subsistence: exchange and society in the Greek city', in Rich and Wallace-Hadrill (1991), 119–46.

Osborne, R. G. (1991b) 'The potential mobility of human populations', *OJA* 10, 231–52.

Osborne, R. G. (1992) '"Is it a farm?" The definition of agricultural sites and settlements in ancient Greece', in B. Wells, 21–27 (with discussion, 58–60).

Osborne, R. G. (1996a) '*Classical Landscape* revisited', *Topoi* 6, 49–64.

Osborne, R. G. (1996b) 'Pots, trade and the archaic Greek economy', *Antiquity* 70, 31–44.

Osborne, R. G. (1998) 'Early Greek colonization? The nature of Greek settlement in the west', in Fisher and van Wees, 251–70.

O'Shea, J. (1981) 'Coping with scarcity: exchange and social storage', in Sheridan and Bailey, 167–83.

Otranto, G. and Carletti, C. (1990) *Il santuario di S. Michele Archangelo sul Gargano dalle origini al X secolo*, Bari.

Ousterhout, R. (ed.) (1990) *The Blessings of Pilgrimage*, Urbana.

Owen Hughes, D. (1977) 'Kinsmen and neighbours in medieval Genoa', in Miskimin, Herlihy and Udovitch, 95–111.

Pagano, M. (1994) 'Commercio e consumo di grano a Ercolano', in *Le ravitaillement en blé de Rome*, 141–7.

Pairman Brown, J. (1969) *The Lebanon and Phoenicia*, vol. 1: *The Physical Setting and the Forest*, Beirut.

Pallot, J. and Shaw, D. J. B. (1990) *Landscape and Settlement in Romanov Russia, 1613–1917*, Oxford.

Palmer, R. (1994) *Wine in the Mycenaean Palace Economy*, Liège and Austin.

Palmer, R. (1995) 'Wine and viticulture in the Linear A and B texts of the Bronze Age Aegean', in McGovern, Fleming and Katz, 269–85.

Panella, C. (1981) 'La distribuzione e i mercati', in Giardina and Schiavone, 2.55–80.

Panella, C. (1986) 'Le merci: produzione, itinerari e destini', in Giardina, 3.431–59.

Panella, C. (1989a) 'Gli scambi nel Mediterraneo occidentale dal IV al VII secolo dal punto di vista di alcune "merci"', in *Hommes et richesses*, 135–41.

Panella, C. (1989b) 'Le anfore italiche del II secolo d. C.', in *Amphores romaines et histoire économique*, 139–178.

Panella, C. and Tchernia, A. (1994) 'Produits agricoles transportés en amphores: l'huile et surtout le vin', in *L'Italie d'Auguste à Dioclétien*, Rome, 145–65.

Papadopoulos, J. K. (1996) 'Euboians in Macedonia: a closer look', *OJA* 15, 151–81.

Papadopoulos, J. K. (1997) 'Phantom Euboians', *JMA* 10. 2, 191–219.

Parain, C. (1936) *La Méditerranée: les hommes et leurs travaux*, Paris.

Pardo, I. (1996) *Managing Existence in Naples: Morality, Action and Structure*, Cambridge.

Pardo, L. (1942) *La Albufera de Valencia: estudio limnografico, biologico, economico y antropologico*, Madrid.

Parise, N. F. (1978) '"Baratto silenzioso" fra punici e libi', in *Cirene e la Grecia*, Quaderni di Archeologia della Libia 8, Rome, 75–80.

Park, C. C. (1994) *Sacred Worlds: An Introduction to Geography and Religion*, London.

Parker, A. J. (1984) 'Shipwrecks and ancient trade in the Mediterranean', *Archaeological Review from Cambridge* 3, 99–113.

Parker, A. J. (1992a) *Ancient Shipwrecks of the Mediterranean and the Roman Provinces*, BAR 580, Oxford.

Parker, A. J. (1992b) 'Cargoes, containers and storage: the ancient Mediterranean', *IJNA* 21, 89–100.

Parker, A. J. (1996) 'Sea transport and trade in the ancient Mediterranean', in Rice, 97–110.

Parker, G. (1980) 'Homage to Braudel', *London Review of Books*, 4–17 September, 8–9.

Parker, R. C. T. (1996) *Athenian Religion: A History*, Oxford.

Parkin, T. G. (1992) *Demography and Roman Society*, Baltimore MD.

Parkins, H. M. (ed.) (1997) *Roman Urbanism: Beyond the Consumer City*, London.

Parkins, H. M. and Smith, C. J. (eds) (1998) *Trade, Traders and the Ancient City*, London.

Paskoff, R., Slim, H. and Trousset, P. (1991) 'Le littoral de la Tunisie dans l'antiquité', *CRAI*, 515–46.

Pasquali, G. (1988) 'Il bosco litoraneo nel medioevo, da Rimini al delta del Po', in Andreolli and Montanari, 263–86.

Pastner, C. McC. (1972) 'A social structural and historical analysis of honor, shame and purdah', AQ 45, 248–61.

Patai, R. (1952) 'The Middle East as a culture area', *Middle East Journal* 6, 1–21.

Paterson, J. (1998) 'Trade and traders in the Roman world: scale, structure, and organisation', in Parkins and Smith, 149–67.

Patterson, J. (1987) 'Crisis? What crisis? Rural change and urban development in early imperial Appennine Italy', *PBSR* 55, 115–46.

Patterson, O. (1982) *Slavery and Social Death: A Comparative Study*, Cambridge MA and London.

Patton, M. (1996) *Islands in Time: Island Sociogeography and Mediterranean Prehistory*, London.

Pavis d'Escurac, H. (1980) 'Irrigation et vie paysanne dans l'Afrique du nord antique', *Ktema* 5, 177–91.

Payne, S. G. (1986) 'The concept of "southern Europe" and political development', *MHR* 1, 100–116.

Peacock, D. P. S. (1982) *Pottery in the Roman World: An Ethnoarchaeological Approach*, London.

Pearson, H. (1957) 'The economy has no surplus', in Polanyi, Arensberg and Pearson, 320–41.

Peatfield, A. A. D. (1983) 'The topography of Minoan peak sanctuaries', *ABSA* 78, 273–80.

Peatfield, A. A. D. (1992) 'Rural ritual in Bronze Age Crete: the peak sanctuary at Atsipadhes', *CAJ* 2, 59–87.

Peet, R. (1985) 'The social origins of environmental determinism', *AAAG* 75.3, 309–33.

Pellegrini, G. B. (1978) 'La terminologia marinara di origine araba in italiano e nelle lingue europee', *SS* 25, 797–841.

Pelosi, A. (1991) 'Dinamiche territoriali del VII secolo a.C. nell'area Sirite-Metapontina', *Dd'A* 3.9, 49–74.

Pemble, J. (1987) *The Mediterranean Passion: Victorians and Edwardians in the South*, Oxford.

Penhallurick, R. D. (1986) *Tin in Antiquity: Its Mining and Trade throughout the Ancient World with particular reference to Cornwall*, London.

Peretti, A. (1979) *Il periplo di Scilace: studio sul primo portolano del Mediterraneo*, Pisa.

Perevolotsky, A. (1981) 'Orchard agriculture in the high mountain region of southern Sinai', *Human Ecology* 9, 331–57.

Pergola, P. and Vismara, C. (eds) (1989) *Castellu (Haute-Corse): un établissement rural de l'antiquité tardive: fouilles récentes (1981–1985)*, Documents d'archéologie française 18, Paris.

Perikos, J. (1993) *The Chios Gum Mastic*, Athens.

Peristiany, J. G. (1965) 'Introduction', in Peristiany (ed.), 9–18.

Peristiany, J. G. (ed.) (1965) *Honour and Shame: The Values of Mediterranean Society*, London.

Peristiany, J. G. and Pitt-Rivers, J. (1992) 'Introduction', in Peristiany and Pitt-Rivers (eds), 1–17.

Peristiany, J. G. and Pitt-Rivers, J. (eds) (1992) *Honor and Grace in Anthropology*, Cambridge.

Perkins, D. H. (1969) *Agricultural Development in China 1368–1968*, Chicago.

Perreault, J. Y. (1993) 'Les *emporia* grecs du levant: mythe ou réalité?', in Bresson and Rouillard, 59–83.

Perrot, J.-C. (1981) 'Le présent et la durée dans l'oeuvre de Fernand Braudel', *Annales*, 3–15.

Persson, G. (1988) *Pre-industrial Economic Growth: Social Organisation and Technological Progress in Europe*, Oxford.

Pertz, G. H. (1872) *Diplomata regum Francorum e stirpe Merowingica, Monumenta Germaniae Historica, Diplomatum Imperii* 1, Hanover.

Pesez, J.-M. (1991) 'Outils et techniques agricoles du monde médiéval', in J. Guilaine (ed.) *Pour une archéologie agraire*, Paris, 131–64.

Peters, F. E. (1988) 'The commerce of Mecca before Islam', in F. Kazemi and R. D. McChesney, *A Way Prepared: Essays on Islamic Culture in Honor of Richard Bayly Winder*, New York, 3–26.

Petersen, A. (1994) 'The archaeology of the Syrian and Iraqi Hajj', in Graham-Campbell, 97–56.

Petitmergin, P. (1967) 'Inscriptions de la région de Milev', *MAH* 79, 190–205.

Petrucci, A. (1963) 'Aspetti del culto e dei pellegrinagi di S. Michele arcangelo sul Monte Gargano', in *Pellegrinagi e culto dei santi*, Todi, 147–80.

Petrusewicz, M. (1996) *Latifundium: Moral Economy and Political Life in a European Periphery*, Ann Arbor MI.

Petts, G. E. (1990) 'Forested river corridors, a lost resource', in Cosgrove and Petts, 12–34.

Peyer, H. C. (1950) *Zur Getreidepolitik oberitalienscher Städte im 13. Jahrhundert*, Vienna.

Pfaffenberger, B. (1992) 'Social anthropology of technology', *ARA* 21, 491–516.

Philippson, A. (1904) *Das Mittelmeergebiet: seine geographische und kulturelle Eigenart* (2nd edn 1907), Leipzig.

Philippson, A. (1939) *Das Byzantinische Reich als Geographische Erscheinung*, Leiden.

Philippson, A. (1950–9) *Die griechischen Landschaften*, 4 vols, Frankfurt am Main.

Phillips, W. D. (1985) *Slavery from Roman Times to the Early Transatlantic Trade*, Manchester.

Picard, J.-C. (1981) 'Conscience urbaine et culte des saints: de Milan sous Liutprand à Vérone sous Pépin Ier d'Italie', in *Hagiographie, cultures et sociétés: IVe–XIIe siècles: actes du colloque organisé à Nanterre et à Paris . . . 1979*, Paris.

Picard, J.-C. (1986–9) *Topographie chrétienne des cités de la Gaule*, 6 vols, Paris.

Piccaluga, G. F. (1990) 'Il "monte santo" nella cultura rinascimentale: simbolo, immagine della memoria, realtà geografica', in Boesch Gajano and Scaraffia, 297–314.

Pichard, G. (1995) 'Les crues sur le bas Rhône de 1500 à nos jours: pour une histoire hydro-climatique', *Méditerranée* 82.3, 4, 105–16.

Picon, P. (1996) 'Towards a history of technological thought', in Fox (ed.), 37–49.

Piejko, F. (1991) 'Antiochus III and Ptolemy son of Thraseas: the inscription of Hefzibah reconsidered', *AntC* 60, 245–59.

Pietri, L. (1990) 'Loca sancta: la géographie de la sainteté dans l'hagiographie gauloise (IVe–VIe s.)', in Boesch Gajano and Scaraffia, 23–36.

Piggott, S. (1983) *The Earliest Wheeled Transport from the Atlantic Coast to the Caspian Sea*, London.

Piggott, S. (1985) Review of T. Champion et al., *Prehistoric Europe* (London 1984), *Antiquity* 59, 145–6.

Pignatti, S. (1983) 'Human impact on the vegetation of the Mediterranean', in W. Holzner, I. Ikusima and M. J. A. Werger (eds), *Man's Impact on Vegetation*, The Hague, 151–62.

Pina-Cabral, J. de (1986) *Sons of Adam, Daughters of Eve: The Peasant Worldview of the Alto Minho*, Oxford.

Pina-Cabral, J. de (1989) 'The Mediterranean as a category of regional comparison: a critical view', *Current Anthropology* 30, 399–406.

Pina-Cabral, J. de (1992a) 'The gods of the Gentiles are demons: the problem of pagan survivals in European culture', in Hastrup, 45–61.

Pina-Cabral, J. de (1992b) 'Against translation: the role of the researcher in the production of ethnographic knowledge', in Pina-Cabral and Campbell, 1–23.

Pina-Cabral, J. de and Campbell, J. K. (eds) (1992) *Europe Observed*, Basingstoke and London.

Pini, A. I. (1976) 'Pesci, pescivendoli e mercanti di pesce in Bologna medievale', *Il Canobio* 1, 329–49.

Pini, A. I. (1989) *Vite e vino nel medioevo*, Bologna.

Pini, A. I. (1990) 'Vite e olivo nell'alto medioevo', *SS* 37, 329–70.

Pinkele, C. F. and Pollis, A. (eds) (1983) *The Contemporary Mediterranean World*, New York.

Pinto, G. (ed.) (1978) *Il libro del Biadaiolo: carestie e annona a Firenze dalla metà del '200 al 1348*, Biblioteca storica toscana 18, Florence.

Pippidi, D. M. (ed.) (1976) *Assimilation et résistance à la culture gréco-romaine dans le monde ancien*, Paris.

Pirazzoli, P. A. (1976) 'Sea level variations in the northwest Mediterranean during Roman times', *Science* 194, 519–21.

Pirazzoli, P. A. (1988) 'Sea-level changes and crustal movements in the Hellenic Arc (Greece): the contribution of archaeological and historical data', in Raban, 157–84.

Pirenne, H. (1925) *Medieval Cities: Their Origins and the Revival of Trade*, Princeton NJ.

Pirenne, H. (1929) *Histoire de Belgique*, vol. 1 (of 7), *Des origines au commencement du XIVe siècle*, 5th edn, Brussels.

Pirenne, H. (1939) *Mohammed and Charlemagne*, first published 1937, London.

Pi-Sunyer, O. (1974) 'Elites and noncorporate groups in the European Mediterranean: a reconsideration of the Catalan case', *CSSH* 16, 117–31.

Pitkin, D. S. (1963) 'Mediterranean Europe', *AQ* 36, 120–9.

Pitkin, D. S. (1985) *The House that Giacomo Built: History of an Italian Family, 1898–1978*, Cambridge.

Pitte, J. R. (1986) *Terres de castanide: hommes et paysages du chataignier de l'antiquité à nos jours*, Paris.

Pitt-Rivers, J. A. (1971) *The People of the Sierra*, 1st edn 1954, Chicago and London.

Pitt-Rivers, J. A. (1977) *The Fate of Shechem: Essays in the Anthropology of the Mediterranean*, Cambridge.

Pitt-Rivers, J. A. (1991) 'La maladie de l'honneur', in Gautheron, 20–36.

Pitt-Rivers, J. A. (1997) 'Honour', *PBA* 94, 229–51.

Pitt-Rivers, J. A. (ed.) (1963) *Mediterranean Countrymen: Essays in the Sociology of the Mediterranean*, Paris and The Hague.

Pitts, L. F. (1985) *Inchtuthil: The Roman Legionary Fortress Excavations 1952–65*, Gloucester.

Pleket, H. W. (1993) 'Agriculture in the Roman Empire in comparative perspective', in *De Agricultura: In Memoriam Peter W. De Neeve*, Amsterdam, 317–42.

Plezia, M. (n. d.) *Aristotelis epistularum fragmenta*, Warsaw.

Polanyi, K. (1963) 'Ports of trade in early societies', *JEH* 23, 30–45 (repr. in Polanyi, *Primitive, Archaic and Modern Economies: Essays of Karl Polanyi*, ed. G. Dalton, New York 1968, 175–203).

Polanyi, K., Arensberg, C. and Pearson, H. W. (1957) *Trade and Market in the Early Empires: Economies in History and Theory*, Chicago.

Poleggi, E. (ed.) (1989) *Città portuali del Mediterraneo, storia e archeologia*, Genoa.

Polk, W. R. (1974) *The Golden Ode*, Chicago.

Pollard, S. (1997) *Marginal Europe: The Contribution of Marginal Lands since the Middle Ages*, Oxford.

Pomey, P. and Tchernia, A. (1977) 'Le tonnage maximum des navires de commerce romains', *Archaeonautica* 2, 233–51.

Poncet, J. (1967) 'Le mythe de la catastrophe hilalienne', *Annales*, 1099–1120.

Ponsich, M. and Tarradell, M. (1965) *Garum et industries de salaison dans la Méditerranée occidentale*, Paris.

Pooley, C. G. and Whyte, I. D. (1991) *Migrants, Emigrants and Immigrants: A Social History of Migration*, London.

Pope, K. O. and van Andel, T. H. (1984) 'Late quaternary alluviation and soil-formation in the southern Argolid: its history, causes and archaeological implications', *JAS* 11.4, 281–306.

Popham, M. R. and Lemos, I. S. (1995) 'A Euboean warrior-trader', *OJA* 14, 151–7.

Popp, H. (1986) 'L'agriculture irriguée dans la Vallée de Sous (Maroc): formes et conflits d'utilisation d'eau', *Méditerranée* 4, 33–47.

Porten, B. and Yardeni, A. (eds and trans.) (1993) *Textbook of Aramaic Documents from Ancient Egypt*, vol. 3: *Literature, Accounts, Lists*, Jerusalem.

Postan, M. M. and Miller, E. (eds) (1987) *Trade and Industry in the Middle Ages* (*The Cambridge Economic History of Europe*, vol. 2), 2nd edn, Cambridge.

Postgate, J. N. (1974) *Taxation and Conscription in the Assyrian Empire*, Rome.

Potter, T. W. (1978) 'Population hiatus and continuity: the case of the South Etruria Survey', in H. Blake, T. W. Potter and D. Whitehouse (eds) *Papers in Italian Archaeology I: The Lancaster Seminar*, *BAR* 41, Oxford, 99–116.

Potter, T. W. (1979) *The Changing Landscape of South Etruria*, London.

Potter, T. W. (1987) *Roman Italy*, London and Berkeley.

Potter, T. W. (1991) 'Towns and territories in southern Etruria', in Rich and Wallace-Hadrill, 191–209.

Potter, T. W. (ed.) (1976) *A Faliscan Town in South Etruria: Excavations at Narce 1966–71*, London.

Pouilloux, J. (1986) 'Notice sur la vie et les travaux de Louis Robert', *CRAI*, 356–66.

Pounds, N. J. G. (1969) 'The urbanization of the classical world', *AAAG* 59, 135–57.

Pounds, N. J. G. (1973) *An Historical Geography of Europe 450 B.C.–A.D. 1330*, Cambridge.

Pounds, N. J. G. (1974) *An Economic History of Medieval Europe*, London.

Poussou, J.-P. (1994) 'De l'intérêt de l'étude historique des mouvements migratoires européens du milieu du moyen âge à la fin du XIXe siècle', in Cavaciocchi, 21–43.

Powell, J. (1996) *Fishing in the Prehistoric Aegean*, Jonsered.

Prescott, H. F. M. (1950) *Friar Felix at Large: A Fifteenth Century Pilgrimage to the Holy Land*, New Haven.

Price, R. (1983) *The Modernization of Rural France: Communications Networks and Agricultural Market Structures in Nineteenth-Century France*, London.

Pridham, G. (ed.) (1984) *The New Mediterranean Democracies: Regime Transition in Spain, Greece and Portugal*, London.

Pringle, D. (1986) *The Red Tower (al-Burj al-Ahmar): Settlement in the Plain of Sharon at the time of the Crusaders and Mamluks, A.D. 1099–1516*, British School of Archaeology in Jerusalem monograph series 1, London.

Pritchett, W. Kendrick (1979) 'Military epiphanies', in *The Greek State at War*, Berkeley, 3.11–46.

Pritchett, W. Kendrick (1991) 'Spanositia and the problem of the grain route', in *The Greek State at War*, Berkeley, 5.465–72.

Prontera, F. (1981) 'A proposito del libro di Pédech sulla geografia dei Greci', *Dd'A* 3, 128–35.

Prosdocimi, A. (1976) 'Cippo Abellano', in *Popoli e Civilazioni dell'Italia Antica* 6, Rome, 825–912.

Pryor, J. H. (1987) *Commerce, Shipping and Naval Warfare in the Medieval Mediterranean*, Variorum, London.

Pryor, J. H. (1988) *Geography, Technology, and War: Studies in the Maritime History of the Mediterranean, 649–1571*, Cambridge.

Psychoyos, O. (1988) *Déplacements de la ligne de rivage et sites archéologiques dans les régions côtières de la Mer Égée au Néolithique et à l'Âge de Bronze*, Jonsered.

Pullen, D. J. (1992) 'Ox and plow in the early Bronze Age Aegean', *AJA* 96, 45–54.

Purcell, N. (1985) 'Wine and wealth in ancient Italy', *JRS* 75, 1–19.

Purcell, N. (1987a) 'Tomb and suburb', in H. von Hesberg and P. Zanker (eds) *Römische Gräberstrassen: Selbstdarstelung-Status-Standard*, Bayerische Akademie der Wissenschaften, philologisch-historische Klasse, Abhandlungen, new series 96, Munich, 25–41.

Purcell, N. (1987b) 'Town in country and country in town', in E. B. MacDougall (ed.) *Ancient Roman Villa Gardens*, Dumbarton Oaks colloquium on the history of landsape architecture 10, Washington DC, 185–203.

Purcell, N. (1990a) 'Mobility and the polis', in Murray and Price, 27–56.

Purcell, N. (1990b) 'The creation of provincial landscape: the Roman impact on Cisalpine Gaul', in T. F. C. Blagg and M. Millett (eds) *The Early Roman Empire in the West*, Oxford, 6–29.

Purcell, N. (1990c) 'The economy of an ancient town', *CR* 40, 111–15.

Purcell, N. (1992) 'The city of Rome', in R. Jenkyns (ed.) *The Legacy of Rome: A New Appraisal*, Oxford, 421–53.

Purcell, N. (1993) 'Continuity and change: the Mediterranean from antiquity to the present', *Der altsprachliche Unterricht* 2, *Das Mittelmeer*, 16–28.

Purcell, N. (1994) 'Women and wine in ancient Rome', in M. MacDonald (ed.) *Gender, Drink and Drugs*, Oxford and Providence RI, 191–208.

Purcell, N. (1995a) 'Field survey of an asteroid', *Antiquity* 69, 186–9, reviewing Cherry et al. (1991).

Purcell, N. (1995b) 'Eating fish: the paradoxes of seafood', in Dobson et al., 132–49.

Purcell, N. (1995c) 'The Roman *villa* and the landscape of production', in Cornell and Lomas, 151–79.

Purcell, N. (1996a) 'The ports of Rome: evolution of a *façade maritime*', in A. Claridge and A. Gallina Zevi (eds) *'Roman Ostia' Revisited: Archaeological and Historical Papers in Memory of Russell Meiggs*, London, 267–79.

Purcell, N. (1996b) 'Rome and the management of water: environment, culture and power', in Salmon and Shipley, 180–212.

Quaini, M. (1975) 'Per lo studio dei caratteri originali del paesaggio agrario della Liguria pre-industriale', in *I paesaggi rurali europei*, 451–69.

Quézel, P. (1981) 'Floristic composition and phytosociological structure of sclerophyllous matorral around the Mediterranean', in Di Castri et al., 106–21.

Quigley, C. (1973) 'Mexican national character and circum-Mediterranean personality structure', *AmAnth* 75, 319–22.

Quilici, L. (1979) *Roma primitiva e le origini della civiltà laziale*, Rome.

Quilici, L. (1988) 'Il Piano del Salvatore presso Briatico: prospezioni archeologiche', *AC* 40, 105–17.

Quilici, L. and Quilici Gigli, S. (1995a) *Agricoltura e commerci nell'Italia antica*, Rome.

Quilici, L. and Quilici Gigli, S. (1995b) *Interventi di bonifica agraria nell'Italia romana*, Rome.

Quilici Gigli, S. (1983) 'Sistemi di cunicoli nel territorio tra Velletri e Cisterna', *Quaderni del Centro di Studio per l'Archeologia Etrusco-italica*, 112–23.

Quilici Gigli, S. (1987) 'Su alcuni segni dell'antico paesaggio agrario presso Roma', *Archeologia Laziale* 8, 152–66.

Quilici Gigli, S. (1995) 'Bonifica agraria e difesa dei territori montani: alcuni interventi nella bassa Sabina', in Quilici and Quilici Gigli (1995b), 129–56.

Quilici Gigli, S. (1997) *Uomo, acqua e paesaggio: atti dell'incontro di studio sul tema: irreggimentazione delle acque e trasformazione del paesaggio*, Rome.

Quilici Gigli, S. (n.d.) 'Antiche opere di bonifica idraulica nella zona Pontina settentrionale', in *Satricum: un progetto di valorizzazione per la cultura e il territorio di Latina*, 50–5.

Raban, A. (1990) 'Man-instigated coastal changes along the Israeli shore of the Mediterranean in ancient times', in Bottema et al., 101–11.

Raban, A. (ed.) (1985) *Harbour Archaeology*, BAR 257, Oxford.

Raban, A. (ed.) (1988) *Archaeology of Coastal Changes*, BAR 404, Oxford.

Rabie, H. (1981) 'Some technical aspects of agriculture in medieval Egypt', in Udovitch, 59–60.

Raby, J. (1995) 'Terra Lemnia and the potteries of the Golden Horn: an antique revival under Ottoman auspices', *BF* 21 (1995) 305–42.

Racine, P. (1987) 'A propos de l'hinterland de Venise au XIIIe siècle', *BF* 12, 539–56.

Rackham, O. (1982) 'Land-use and the native vegetation of Greece', in Bell and Limbrey, 177–98.

Rackham, O. (1983) 'Observations on the historical ecology of Boeotia', *ABSA* 78, 291–351.

Rackham, O. (1990a) 'Ancient landscapes', in Murray and Price, 85–111.

Rackham, O. (1990b) 'Observations on the historical ecology of Santorini', in D. A. Hardy (ed.) *Thera and the Aegean World* III, vol. 2: *Earth Sciences*, London, 384–91.

Rackham, O. (1996) 'Ecology and pseudo-ecology: the example of ancient Greece', in Salmon and Shipley, 16–43.

Rackham, O. and Moody, J. (1992) 'Terraces', in B. Wells, 123–33.

Rackham, O. and Moody, J. (1997) *The Making of the Cretan Landscape*, Manchester.

Raepsaet, G. (1979) 'La faiblesse de l'attelage antique: la fin d'un mythe?', *AntC* 48, 171–6.

Raepsaet, G. (1982) 'Attelages antiques du nord de la Gaule: les systèmes de traction par équides', *Trierer Zeitschrift* 45, 215–73.

Raepsaet, G. (1994) 'Le renouveau de l'histoire des techniques: quelques jalons récents', *AntC* 63, 325–9.

Raepsaet, G. (1995) 'Les prémices de la mécanisation agricole entre Seine et Rhin de l'antiquité au 13e siècle', *Annales*, 911–42.

Raepsaet, G. and Rommelaere, C. (1995) *Brancards et transport attelé entre Seine et Rhin de l'antiquité au moyen âge*, Treignes.

Ramin J. and Veyne, P. (1981) 'Droit romain et société: les hommes libres qui passent pour esclaves et l'esclavage volontaire', *Historia* 30, 472–97.

Ramsay, W. M. (1890) *A Historical Geography of Asia Minor*, London.

Ramsay, W. M. (1892) 'Permanent attachment of religious veneration to localities', in *Transactions of the Oriental Congress in London*, London.

Ramsay, W. M. (1908) *Pauline and Other Studies in Early Christian history*, 2nd edn, London.

Ramsay, W. M. and Bell, G. L. (1909) *The Thousand and One Churches*, London.

Randles, W. G. L. (1980) *De la terre plate au globe terrestre: une mutation épistémologique rapide, 1480–1520*, Paris.

Randsborg, K. (1991) *The First Millennium A.D. in Europe and the Mediterranean: An Archaeological Essay*, Cambridge.

Randsborg, K. (1992) 'Barbarians, classical antiquity and the rise of western Europe: an archaeological essay', *PP* 137, 8–24.

Randsborg, K. (1994) 'A Greek episode: the early Hellenistic settlement of the western Crimea', *Acta Archaeologica*, 171–96.

Ranke, L. von (1824) *Geschichte der Romanischen und Germanischen Völker von 1494 bis 1514*, Leipzig.

Raphael, C. N. (1978) 'The erosional history of the Plain of Elis in the Peloponnese', in Brice, 51–66.

Rapp, G. and Gifford, J. A. (1982) *Troy: The Archaeological Geology*, Princeton NJ.

Rappaport, R. (1979) *Ecology, Meaning and Religion*, Berkeley.

Rappaport, R. (1984) *Pigs for the Ancestors: Ritual in the Ecology of a New Guinea People*, 2nd edn (first published 1968), New Haven.

Rathbone, D. (1983) 'The grain trade and grain shortage in the Hellenistic East', in Garnsey and Whittaker, 45–53.

Rathbone, D. (1991) *Economic Rationalism and Rural Society in Third-Century Egypt: The Heroninos Archive and the Appianus Estate*, Cambridge.

Rathbone, D. (1994) 'More (or less?) economic rationalism in Roman agriculture' (rev. of Kehoe 1992), *JRA* 7, 432–6.

Raynal, R. (1977) 'Milieux forestiers réels, potentiels et illusoires', in Raynal (ed.) *Les milieux et les hommes dans l'organisation de l'espace des régions méditerranéennes*, Strasbourg, 49–62.

Reboul, C. (1989) *Monsieur le Capital et Madame la Terre: fertilité agronomique et fertilité économique*, Paris.

Reddé, M. (1986) *Mare Nostrum*, Rome.

Redding, R. W. (1993) 'Subsistence security as a selective practice favoring increasing cultural complexity', in *Domestic Animals of Mesopotamia I, BSA* 7, 77–98.

Reddy, W. M. (1997) *The Invisible Code: Honor and Sentiment in Postrevolutionary France 1814–1848*, Berkeley and London.

Redfield, R. (1956) *Peasant Society and Culture*, Chicago.

Reece, D. (1969) 'Technological weakness of the ancient world', *GR* 16, 32–47.

Reed, M. (1996) 'London and its hinterland 1600–1800: the view from the provinces', in Clark and Lepetit, 51–83.

Reekmans, T. (1994) 'The behaviour of consumers in the Zenon papyri', *Ancient Society* 25, 119–40.

Reger, G. (1994a) *Regionalism and Change in the Economy of Independent Delos 314–167 B.C.*, Berkeley.

Reger, G. (1994b) 'The political history of the Kyklades', *Historia* 43, 32–69.

Reher, D. S. (1990) *Town and Country in Pre-industrial Spain: Cuenca, 1550–1870*, Cambridge.

Reinert, S. W. (1988) 'The Muslim presence in Constantinople, 9th–15th centuries: some preliminary observations', in Ahrweiler and Laiou, 125–50.

Rendeli, M. (1993) *Città aperte: ambiente e paesaggio rurale organizzato nell'Etruria meridionale costiera durante l'età orientalizzante e arcaica*, Rome.

Renfrew, A. C. (1972) *The Emergence of Civilization: The Cyclades and the Aegean in the Third Millennium B.C.*, London.

Renfrew, A. C. (1978) 'The anatomy of innovation', in D. Green, C. Haselgrove and M. Spriggs (eds) *Social Organization and Settlement, BAR* 47, Oxford, 89–117.

Renfrew, A. C. (1982a) *Towards an Archaeology of Mind*, Inaugural Lecture, Cambridge.

Renfrew, A. C. (1982b) 'Polity and power: interaction, intensification and exploitation', in Renfrew and Wagstaff, 264–90.

Renfrew, A. C. (1985) *The Archaeology of Cult: The Sanctuary at Phylakopi*, London.

Renfrew, A. C. (1987) *Archaeology and Language: The Puzzle of Indo-European Origins*, London.

Renfrew, A. C. (1996) 'Kings, tree rings and the Old World', *Nature* 381, 27 June, 733–4.

Renfrew, A. C. (ed.) (1973) *The Explanation of Culture Change: Models in Prehistory*, London.

Renfrew, A. C. and Shennan, S. (eds) (1982) *Ranking, Resource and Exchange*, Cambridge.

Renfrew, A. C. and Wagstaff, J. M. (eds) (1982) *An Island Polity: The Archaeology of Exploitation in Melos*, Cambridge.

Renouard, Y. (1936) 'Une expédition de céréales des Pouilles en Arménie', *MAH* 53, 287–329.

Revel, J. (1979) 'A capital city's privileges: food supplies in early-modern Rome', in R. Forster and O. Ranum (eds) *Food and Drink in History: Selections from the 'Annales'* 5, 37–49.

Revere, R. B. (1957) ' "No man's coast": ports of trade in the east Mediterranean', in Polanyi, Arensberg and Pearson, 38–63.

Rey-Coquais, J. P. (1987) 'Des montagnes au désert: Baetocécé, le *pagus Augustus* de Niha, la Ghouta à l'est de Damas', in Frézouls, 191–216.

Reyerson, K. L. (1979) 'Patterns of population attraction and mobility: the case of Montpellier, 1293–1348', *Viator* 10, 257–81.

Reyerson, K. L. (1995) *Society, Law, and Trade in Medieval Montpellier*, Variorum, Aldershot.

Reynolds, P. (1995) *Trade in the Western Mediterranean, A.D. 400–700: The Ceramic Evidence*, *BAR* 604, Oxford.

Rheubottom, D. (1985) 'The seed of evil within', in D. Parkin (ed.) *The Anthropology of Evil*, Oxford, 77–91.

Rice, E. E. (1988) 'Adoption in Rhodian society', in S. Dietz and I. Papachristodoulou (eds) *Archaeology in the Dodecanese*, Copenhagen, 138–44.

Rice, E. E. (ed.) (1996) *The Sea and History*, Stroud.

Rich, J. and Wallace-Hadrill, A. (eds) (1991) *City and Country in the Ancient World*, London and New York.

Richard, J. (1977) 'The eastern Mediterranean and its relations with its hinterland (11th–15th centuries)', in Richard, *Les relations entre l'Orient et l'Occident au moyen âge*, Variorum, London, I. 1–39.

Richard, J.-P. (1985) 'Agriculture in the Latin empire of Constantinople', in 'Agricultural conditions in the Crusader states', in Zacour and Hazard, 251–94, at 285–94.

Richards, P. (1985) *Indigenous Agricultural Revolution*, London.

Richardson, H. W. (1973) 'Theory of the distribution of city sizes: review and prospects', *Regional Studies* 7, 239–51.

Richardson, J. S. (1983) 'The *Tabula Contrebiensis*: Roman law in Spain in the early first century B.C.', *JRS* 73, 33–41.

Richter, U. (1991) 'Mensch und Umwalt in der Antike: neuere Literatur', *Environmental History Newsletter* 3, 85–7.

Rickman, G. E. (1971) *Roman Granaries and Store Buildings*, Cambridge.

Rickman, G. E. (1980) *The Corn Supply of Ancient Rome*, Oxford.

Rickman, G. E. (1985) 'Towards a study of Roman ports', in Raban, 105–14.

Rickman, G. E. (1988) 'The archaeology and history of Roman ports', *IJNA* 17, 257–67.

Rickman, G. E. (1991) 'Problems of transport and development of ports', in D. van Berchem and A. Giovannini (eds) *Nourrir la plèbe: Actes du colloque tenu à Genève les 28 et 29 IX 1989 en hommage à Denis van Berchem*, Basle, 103–18.

Rickman, G. E. (1996) 'Mare nostrum', in Rice, 1–14.

Rickman, G. E. and Raban, A. (1988) 'The archaeology and history of Roman ports', *International Journal of Nautical Archaeoalogy* 17, 257–67.

Rico, C. (1995) 'La diffusion par mer des matériaux de construction en terre cuite: un aspect mal connu du commerce antique en Méditerranée occidentale', *MEFRA* 107, 767–800.

Ricoeur, P. (1984–8) *Time and Narrative*, 3 vols, Chicago and London.

Ridgway, D. (1997) 'Nestor's cup and the Etruscans', *OJA* 16, 325–44.

Ridgway, D. and Serra Ridgway, F. R. (1992) 'Sardinia and history', in Andrews and Tykot, 355–63.

Riemann, O. (1879) *Recherches archéologiques sur les îles ioniennes*, Paris.

Riera, I. (ed.) (1994) *Utilitas necessaria: sistemi idraulici nell'Italia romana*, Milan.

Rieth, E. (ed.) (1998) *Méditerranée antique: pêche, navigation, commerce*, Paris.

Rigsby, K. J. (1996) *Asylia: Territorial Inviolability in the Hellenistic World*, Berkeley.

Riis, P. J. (1970) *Sukas I: The North-East Sanctuary and the first Settling of Greeks in Syria and Palestine*, Copenhagen.

Riley, J. A. (1981) 'Italy and the east Mediterranean in the Hellenistic and early Roman periods: the evidence of coarse pottery', in G. Barker and R. Hodges (eds) *Archaeology and Italian Society, BAR* 102, Oxford, 69–78.

Ringrose, D. R. (1983) *Madrid and the Spanish Economy, 1560–1850*, Berkeley, Los Angeles and London.

Risberg, C. (1992) 'Metal working in Greek sanctuaries', in Linders and Alroth, 33–40.

Riu, M. (1983) 'The woollen industry in Catalonia in the later Middle Ages', in Harte and Ponting, 205–29.

Rivera Nuñez, D. and Walker, M. J. (1989) 'A review of palaeobotanical findings of early *Vitis* in the Mediterranean and of the origins of cultivated grape-vines, with special reference to new pointers to prehistoric exploitation in the western Mediterranean', *Review of Palaeobotany and Palynology* 61, 205–37.

Rizakis, A. D. (1997) 'Roman colonies in the province of Achaia: territories, land and population', in S. E. Alcock (ed.) *The Early Roman Empire in the East*, Oxford, 15–36.

Robert, L. (1949) 'Les chèvres d'Héraklea', in Robert, *Hellenica* VII, Paris, 161–70.

Robert, L. (1955) 'Inscriptions des Dardanelles', in Robert, *Hellenica* X, Paris, 272–4.

Robert, L. (1980) *A travers l'Asie mineure: poètes et prosateurs, monnaies grecques, voyageurs et géographie*, Paris.

Robert, L. (1982) 'Documents de l'Asie Mineure XXI: au nord de Sardes, Lycophron et le marais d'Echidna, Strabon et le lac Koloe', *BCH* 106, 334–59.

Robert, L. (1983) 'Documents de l'Asie Mineure XXIII: Sardes et les roseaux du lac Koloe', *BCH* 107, 497–8.

Roberts, N. (1982) 'Forest re-advance and the Anatolian Neolithic', in Bell and Limbrey, 231–46.

Roberts, N. (1990) 'Human-induced landscape change in south and southwest Turkey during the later Holocene', in Bottema et al., 53–67.

Robertson Smith, W. (1889) *Lectures on the Religion of the Semites*, London, 2nd edn, 1894.

Rocchi, D. (1988) *Frontiera e confine nella Grecia antica*, Rome.

Rodero, A. (1995) *Las anforas preromanas en Andalusia*, Faenza.

Rodley, L. (1985) *Cave monasteries of Byzantine Cappadocia*, Cambridge.

Rogers, G. M. (1991) *The Sacred Identity of Ephesos: Foundation Myths of a Roman City*, London.

Rogers, S. C. (1991) *Shaping Modern Times in Rural France: The Transformation and Reproduction of an Aveyronnais Community*, Princeton NJ.

Roper, L. (1994) *Oedipus and the Devil: Witchcraft, Sexuality and Religion in Early Modern Europe*, London and New York.

Roques, D. (1987) *Synésios de Cyrène et la Cyrénaïque du Bas-Empire*, Paris.

Rose, V. (1863) *Aristoteles pseudepigraphus*, Leipzig.

Rosen, L. (1984) *Bargaining for Reality: The Construction of Social Relations in a Muslim Community*, Chicago and London.

Rosenberg, N. (1994) *Exploring The Black Box: Technology, Economics, and History*, Cambridge.

Rosenthal, F. (trans.) (1967) Ibn Khaldun, *The Muqaddimah: An Introduction to History*, 2nd edn, 3 vols, London.

Ross Holloway, R. (1990) '*Koine* and commerce in the Sicilian Bronze Age', *MHR* 5, 3–13.

Ross Holloway, R. (1991) *The Archaeology of Ancient Sicily*, London.

Ross Holloway, R. and Lukesch, S. (1991) 'Ustica 1990', *JDAIAA* 3, 359–65.

Rossignol, J. and Wandsnider, L. (eds) (1992) *Space, Time and Archaeological Landscapes*, New York.

Rostovtzeff, M. (1941) *The Social and Economic History of the Hellenistic World*, 3 vols, Oxford.

Rostovtzeff, M. (1957) *The Social and Economic History of the Roman Empire* (first published 1926), 2nd edn revised P. M. Fraser, 2 vols, Oxford.

Rotberg, R. I. and Rabb T. K. (eds) (1983) *Hunger and History: The Impact of Changing Food Production and Consumption Patterns on Society*, Cambridge.

Rougé, J. (1952) 'La navigation hivernale sous l'empire romain', *REA* 54, 316–25.

Rougé, J. (1966a) 'Le droit de naufrage et ses limitations en Méditerranée avant l'établissement de la domination de Rome', in *Mélanges d'archéologie et d'histoire offerts à A. Piganiol*, Paris, 3.1467–79.

Rougé, J. (1966b) *Recherches sur l'organisation du commerce maritime en Méditerranée sous l'empire romain*, Paris.

Rougé, J. (1981) *Ships and Fleets of the Ancient Mediterranean*, first published 1975, Middletown CT.

Rougé, J. (1984) 'Le confort des passagers à bord des navires antiques', *Archeonautica* 4, 223–42.

Rougemont, G. (1990) 'Géographie historique des Cyclades: l'homme et le milieu dans l'archipel', *Journal des Savants*, 199–220.

Rouillard, P. (1993) 'L'emporion chez Strabon', in Bresson and Rouillard, 23–34.

Roussel, P. (1931) 'Le miracle de Zeus Panamaros', *BCH* 55, 70–116.

Rousselle, A. (1990) *Croire et guérir: la foi en Gaule dans l'antiquité tardive*, Paris.

Rousselle, A. (ed.) (1995) *Frontières terrestres, frontières célestes dans l'antiquité*, Paris.

Rowland, R. J. (1990) 'The production of Sardinian grain in the Roman period', *MHR* 5, 14–20.

Rowlands, M. J. (1984) 'Conceptualizing the European Bronze and Early Iron Ages', in Bintliff, 147–56.

Rowlands, M. J. (1987) 'The concept of Europe in prehistory', *Man* 22, 558–9.

Roxborough, I. (1988) 'Modernization theory revisited' (review article), *CSSH* 30, 753–61.

Rubensohn, O. (1962) *Das Delion von Paros*, Wiesbaden.

Rubin, M. (1992) 'Religious culture in town and country: reflections on a great divide', in D. Abulafia, M. Franklin and M. Rubin (eds) *Church and City 1000–1500: Essays in Honour of Christopher Brooke*, Cambridge, 3–22.

Rubin, Z. (1986) 'The Mediterranean and the dilemma of the Roman empire in late Antiquity', *MHR* 1, 13–62.

Ruggiero, G. (1985) *The Boundaries of Eros: Sex Crime and Sexuality in Renaissance Venice*, New York and Oxford.

Runnels, C. N. (1989) 'Trade models in the study of agricultural origins and dispersals', *JMA* 2.1, 149–56.

Runnels, C. N. and van Andel, T. H. (1987) 'The evolution of settlement in the southern Argolid, Greece: an economic explanation', *Hesperia* 61, 303–34.

Runnels, C. N. and van Andel, T. H. (1988) 'Trade and the origins of agriculture in the eastern Mediterranean', *JMA* 1, 83–109.

Rupke, N. A. (1996) 'Eurocentric ideology of continental drift', *History of Science* 105, 251–72.

Ruschenbusch, E. (1988) 'Getreideerträge in Griechenland in der Zeit von 1921 bis 1938 n. Chr. als Maßstab für die Antike', *ZPE* 72, 141–53.

Ruskin, J. (1851–3) *The Stones of Venice*, 3 vols, London.

Russell, J. C. (1972) *Medieval Regions and their Cities*, Newton Abbot.

Russell, K. W. (1988) *After Eden: The Behavioural Ecology of Early Food Production in the Near East and North Africa*, BAR 391, Oxford.

Russell, R. J. (1942) 'Geomorphology of the Rhone delta', *AAAG* 32, 149–254.

Russell, R. J. (1954) 'Alluvial morphology of Anatolian rivers', *AAAG* 44, 363–91.

Russi, A. (1989) 'La grotta con iscrizioni sull'isolotto del Faro di Vieste (Foggia). Note preliminari', *Miscellanea Greca e Romana: studi pubblicati dall'Istituto Italiano per la storia antica* 14, 299–309.

Rutherford, I. (1995) 'Theoric crisis: the dangers of pilgrimage in Greek religion and society', *Studi e Materiali per la Storia delle Religioni* 61, 274–92.

Rutherfurd-Dyer, G. (1983) 'Homer's wine-dark sea', *GR* 30, 125–8.

Rutkowski, B. (1986) *Cult Places in the Aegean*, New Haven.

Rutman, D. B. (1986) 'History and anthropology: Clio's dalliances', *Historical Methods* 19, 120–3.

Ryder, M. L. (1993) 'Sheep and goat husbandry with particular reference to textile fibre and milk production', in *Domestic Animals of Mesopotamia I, BSA* 7, 9–32.

Safilios-Rothschild, C. (1969) '"Honour" crimes in contemporary Greece', *British Journal of Sociology* 20, 205–18.

Safrai, Z. (1994) *The Economy of Roman Palestine*, London and New York.

Şahin, Ç. (1987) 'Zwei Inschriften aus dem Südwestlichen Kleinasien', *EA* 10, 1–2.

Sahlins, M. (1974) *Stone Age Economics*, first published 1972, London.

Sahlins, M. (1983) 'Other times, other customs: the anthropology of history', *AmAnth* 85, 517–44.

Sahlins, P. (1989) *Boundaries: The Making of France and Spain in the Pyrenees*, Berkeley.

Said, E. W. (1978) *Orientalism*, London.

Said-Zammit, G. A. (1997) *Population, Landuse and Settlement on Punic Malta: A Contextual Analysis of the Burial Evidence*, BAR 682, Oxford.

Sakellariou, M. B. (1958) *La migration grecque en Ionie*, Athens.

Salibi, K. (1988) *A House of Many Mansions: The History of Lebanon Reconsidered*, Berkeley, Los Angeles and London.

Sallares, R. (1991) *The Ecology of the Ancient Greek World*, London.

Saller, R. P. (1994) *Patriarchy, Property and Death in the Roman Family*, Cambridge.

Salmeri, G. (1992) 'Miniere di zolfo in Sicilia ed in Grecia in età imperiale', in Salmeri, *Sicilia romana: storia e storiografia*, Catania, 29–43.

Salmeri, G. (1998) 'Per una lettura dei capitoli V–VII della *Storia economica dell'Impero Romano* di M. Rostovtzeff', *Athenaeum* 86, 57–84.

Salmi-Bianchi, J.-M. (1969), review of Berthier (1969), *Annales*, 1176–80.

Salmon J. and Shipley, G. (eds) (1996) *Human Landscapes in Classical Antiquity: Environment and Culture*, London.

Salmon, P. (1974) *Population et dépopulation dans l'empire romain*, Brussels.

Salomon, J.-N. and Maire, R. (eds) (1992) *Karst et évolutions climatiques*, Talence.

Salomon, R. (1936) *Opicinus de Canistris: Weltbild und Bekenntnisse eines Avignonesischen Klerikers des 14. Jahrhunderts*, London.

Salviat, F. (1986) 'Le vin de Thasos: amphores, vin et sources écrites', in Empereur and Garlan, 145–96.

Samuel, A. E., Hastings, W. K., Bowman, A. K. and Bagnall, R. S. (1971) *Death and Taxes: Ostraka in the Royal Ontario Museum I*, Toronto.

Sánchez-Albornoz, C. (1975) *Spain: A Historical Enigma*, first published 1956, 2 vols, Madrid.

Sandars, N. K. (1978) *The Sea Peoples: Warriors of the Ancient Mediterranean 1250–1150 B.C.*, London.

Sanders, G. D. R. (1984) 'Reassessing ancient populations', *ABSA* 79, 251–62.

Sanders, G. D. R. and Whitbread, I. K. (1990) 'Central places and major roads in the Peloponnese', *ABSA* 85, 333–61.

Sanders, I. F. (1976) 'Settlement in the Hellenistic and Roman periods on the Plain of the Mesara, Crete', *ABSA* 71, 131–8.

Sandy, D. B. (1989) *The Production and Use of Vegetable Oils in Ptolemaic Egypt*, Atlanta.

Sandys, G. (1615) *A Relation of a Journey begun An. Dom. 1610, containing a Description of the Turkish Empire, of Ægypt, of the Holy Land*, London.

Sant Cassia, P. (1991) 'Authors in search of a character: personhood, agency and identity in the Mediterranean', *Journal of Mediterranean Studies* 1, 1–17.

Sant Cassia, P. (1993) 'Banditry, myth, and terror in Cyprus and other Mediterranean societies', *CSSH* 35, 773–95.

Santamaria, U. and Bailey, A. (1984) 'A note on Braudel's structure as duration', *History and Theory* 23, 78–83.

Saprykin, S. J. (1994) *Ancient Farms and Land Plots on the Khora of Khersonesos Taurike (Research in the Herakleian Peninsula 1974–1990)*, Amsterdam.

Sarikakis, T. C. (1986) 'Commercial relations between Chios and other Greek cities in Antiquity', in J. Boardman and C. E. Vaphopoulou-Richardson (eds) *Chios: A Conference at the Homereion in Chios 1984*, Oxford, 121–31.

Sarpaki, A. (1992) 'The paleoethnobotanical approach: the Mediterranean triad, or is it a quartet?', in B. Wells, 61–76.

Sartre, M. (n. d.) 'Transhumance, économie et société de montagne en Syrie du sud', in G. Fabre, 39–54.

Sartre, M. and Tranoy, A. (1990) *La Méditerranée antique*, Paris.

Sathas, C. N. (ed.) (1882) *Monumenta Historiae Hellenicae*, vol. 3, Cancellariae Secretae pars II, Paris.

Saunders, P. (1986) *Social Theory and the Urban Question*, 2nd edn, London.

Sawyer, P. H. (1971) *The Age of the Vikings*, 2nd edn, London.

Sawyer, P. H. (1982) *Kings and Vikings: Scandinavia and Europe A.D. 700–1100*, London and New York.

Scaglione, A. (1991) *Knights at Court: Courtliness, Chivalry and Courtesy from Ottonian Germany to the Italian Renaissance*, Berkeley, Los Angeles and Oxford.

Scarborough, V. L. (1991) 'Water management adaptations in non-industrial complex societies: an archaeological perspective', *Archaeological Method and Theory* 3, 101–54.

Scargill, D. I. (1979) *The Form of Cities*, London.

Schallin, A.-L. (1993) *Islands under Influence: The Cyclades in the Late Bronze Age and the Nature of Mycenaean Presence*, Jonsered.

Schama, S. (1995) *Landscape and Memory*, London.

Schapera, I. A. (1962) 'Should anthropologists be historians?', *Journal of the Royal Anthropological Institute* 92, 143–56.

Scheid, J. (1989) '*Lucus, nemus*: qu'est-ce qu'un bois sacré?', in de Cazenove and Scheid, 13–20.

Scheidel, W. (1994) 'Grain cultivation in the economy of Roman Italy', in Carlsen et al., 159–66.

Scheidel, W. (1995) 'The most silent women of Greece and Rome: rural labour and women's life in the ancient world', 2 parts, *GR* 42, 202–17; 43, 1–10.

Scheidel, W. (1997) 'Quantifying the sources of slaves in the early Roman empire', *JRS* 87, 156–69.

Schioler, T. (1989) 'The watermills at the Crocodile River: a turbine mill dated to 345–380 A.D.', *Palestine Exploration Quarterly* 121, 133–43.

Schirmer, W. (1995) 'Archaeology in Turkey', *AJA* 99, 229–30.

Schmal, H. (ed.) (1981) *Patterns of European Urbanization since 1500*, London.

Schmidt, J. (1939) *Heilige Berge Griechenlands in alter und neuer Zeit*, Athens.

Schmiedt, G. (1972) *Il livello antico del Mar Tirreno: testimonianze dei resti archeologichi*, Florence.

Schmiedt, G. (1978) 'I porti italiani nell'alto medioevo', *SS* 25, 129–254.

Schneider, J. (1971) 'Of vigilance and virgins: honor, shame and access to resources in Mediterranean society', *Ethnology* 10, 1–24.

Schneider, J. (1978) 'Peacocks and penguins: the political economy of European cloth and colours', *American Ethnologist* 5, 413–47.

Schneider, J. (1987) 'The anthropology of cloth', *ARA* 16, 409–48.

Schneider, J. and Schneider, P. (1976) *Culture and Political Economy in Western Sicily*, New York.

Schneider, P., Schneider, J. and Hansen, E. (1972), 'Modernization and development: the role of regional elites and noncorporate groups in the European Mediterranean', *CSSH* 14, 328–50.

Schüle, W. (1968) 'Feldbewässerung in Alteuropa', *Madrider Mitteilungen* 8, 79–99.

Scotoni, L. (1992) 'L'Umbilicus Italiae secondo Varrone e il centro geografico dell'Italia odierna', *RL* 9.5.3, 193–212.

Scott, T. (ed.) (1998) *The Peasantries of Europe from the Fourteenth to the Eighteenth Centuries*, London and New York.

Scully, V. (1962) *The Earth, the Temple and the Gods*, revised edn 1979, New Haven.

Segal, J. B. (1970) *Edessa, the Blessed City*, Oxford.

Segura Graíño, C. (ed.) (1992) *Los regadíos hispanos en la Edad Media*, Madrid.

Segura Graíño, C. (ed.) (1994) *Caminos y caminantes por las tierras del Madrid medieval*, Madrid.

Seiber, J. (1977) *The Urban Saint in Early Byzantine Social History*, BAR 37, Oxford.

Seibert, J. (1979) *Die politischen Flüchtlinge und Verbannten in der griechischen Geschichte: von den Anfängen bis zur Unterwerfung durch die Römer*, Darmstadt.

Selli, R., Stanley, D. J. and Wezel, F.-C. (1985) *Geological Evolution of the Mediterranean Basin: Raimondo Selli Commemorative Volume*, New York.

Selma, S. (1991) 'El molí hidràulic de Farina I. L'organització de l'espai rural Andalusí: dos exemples d'estudi arqueològic espaial a La Serra d'Espadà (Castelló)', *MCV* Ant/MA 27.1, 43–64.

Selwyn, T. (1995) 'Landscapes of liberation and imprisonment: towards an anthropology of the Israeli landscape', in Hirsch and O'Hanlon, 114–34.

Semple, E. C. (1911) *Influences of Geographic Environment on the Basis of Ratzel's System of Anthropo-geography*, New York.

Semple, E. C. (1922) 'The influence of geographical conditions upon ancient Mediterranean stock-raising', *AAAG* 12, 3–38.

Semple, E. C. (1932) *The Geography of the Mediterranean Region: Its Relation to Ancient History*, London.

Sen, A. K. (1972) *On Economic Inequality*, enlarged edn 1997, Oxford.

Sen, A. K. (1981) *Poverty and Famines: An Essay on Entitlement and Deprivation*, Oxford.

Sen, A. K. (1993) 'The causation and prevention of famines: a reply', *JPS* 21, 29–40.

Sereni, E. (1955) *Comunità rurali nell'Italia antica*, Rome.

Serjeant, R. B. (1972) *Islamic Textiles: Materials for a History up to the Mongol Conquest*, Beirut.

Setton, K. M. (1944) 'Athens in the later twelfth century', *Speculum* 19, 179–207.

Sharlin, A. (1978) 'Natural decrease in early modern cities: a reconsideration', *PP* 79, 126–38.

Sharpe, J. A. (n. d.) [1980], *Defamation and Sexual Slander in Early Modern England: The Church Courts at York*, Borthwick Papers 58, York.

Shavit, Y. (1987) *The New Hebrew Nation: A Study in Israeli Heresy and Fantasy*, London.

Shavit, Y. (1988) 'The Mediterranean world and "Mediterraneanism": the origins, meaning, and application of a geo-cultural notion in Israel', *MHR* 3, 96–117.

Shaw, B. D. (1979) 'The camel in Roman North Africa and the Sahara: history, biology and human economy', *Bulletin de l'Institut Fondamental d'Afrique Noire*, series B, 41, 663–721 (repr. Shaw 1995a).

Shaw, B. D. (1981) 'Rural markets in North Africa and the political economy of the Roman Empire', *AA* 17, 37–83 (repr. Shaw 1995b).

Shaw, B. D. (1982) 'Lamasba: an ancient irrigation community', *AA* 18, 61–103 (repr. Shaw 1995a).

Shaw, B. D. (1982–3) '"Eaters of flesh, drinkers of milk": the ancient Mediterranean ideology of the pastoral nomad', *Ancient Society* 13–14, 5–31 (repr. Shaw 1995b).

Shaw, B. D. (1984a) 'Water and society in the ancient Maghrib: technology, property and development', *AA* 20, 121–73 (repr. Shaw 1995a).

Shaw, B. D. (1984b) 'Bandits in the Roman empire', *PP* 105, 3–52.

Shaw, B. D. (1984c) 'Anatomy of the vampire bat', *Economy and Society* 13, 208–48.

Shaw, B. D. (1986) 'Autonomy and tribute: mountain and plain in Mauretania Tingitana', in P.-R. Baduel (ed.) *Désert et montagne: hommage à Jean Dresch, Revue de l'Occident musulmane et de la Méditerranée* 41–2, 66–89 (repr. Shaw 1995b).

Shaw, B. D. (1987) 'The family in late Antiquity: the experience of Augustine', *PP* 115, 3–51.

Shaw, B. D. (1989) 'Our daily bread', *Social History of Medicine* 2.2, 205–13.

Shaw, B. D. (1990) 'Bandit highlands and lowland peace: the mountains of Isauria-Cilicia' (2 parts), *JESHO* 33, 199–233, 237–70.

Shaw, B. D. (1991) 'The noblest monuments and the smallest things: wells, walls and aqueducts in the making of Roman Africa', in A. T. Hodge (ed.) *Future Currents in Aqueduct Studies*, Leeds, 63–91 (repr. Shaw 1995a).

Shaw, B. D. (1995a) *Environment and Society in Roman North Africa*, Variorum, Aldershot.

Shaw, B. D. (1995b) *Rulers, Nomads and Christians in Roman North Africa*, Variorum, Aldershot.

Shaw, J. W. (1989) 'Phoenicians in southern Crete', *AJA* 93, 165–83.

Shefton, B. W. (1982) 'Greeks and Greek imports in the south of the Iberian peninsula: the archaeological evidence', in Niemeyer, 337–70.

Shepherd, R. (1993) *Ancient Mining*, London.

Sheridan, A. and Bailey G. (eds) (1981) *Economic Archaeology: Towards an Integration of Ecological and Social Approaches*, BAR 96, Oxford.

Sherratt, A. G. (1980) 'Water, soil and seasonality in early cereal cultivation', *WA* 11.3, 313–30 (repr. Sherratt 1997b).

Sherratt, A. G. (1981) 'Plough and pastoralism: aspects of the secondary products revolution', in Hodder, Isaac and Hammond, 261–305 (repr. Sherratt 1997b).

Sherratt, A. G. (1982) 'Mobile resources, settlement and exchange in early agricultural Europe', in Renfrew and Shennan, 13–26 (repr. Sherratt 1997b).

Sherratt, A. G. (1983) 'The secondary exploitation of animals in the Old World', *WA*, 15.1, 90–104 (repr. Sherratt 1997b).

Sherratt, A. G. (1992) 'What can archaeologists learn from Annalistes?', in Knapp, 135–42.

Sherratt, A. G. (1995a) 'Reviving the grand narrative: archaeology and long-term change', *JEA* 3, 1–32.

Sherratt, A. G. (1995b) 'Alcohol and its alternatives: symbol and substance in pre-industrial cultures', in J. Goodman, P. E. Lovejoy and A. G. Sherratt (eds) *Consuming Habits: Drugs in History and Anthropology*, London, 11–46.

Sherratt, A. G. (1995c) '*Fata morgana*: illusion and reality in "Greek–barbarian relations"', *CAJ* 5.1, 139–48, with 152.

Sherratt, A. G. (1997a) 'The evolution of the plough in temperate Europe', in Sherratt (1997b), 95 (Table 3.2).

Sherratt, A. G. (1997b) *Economy and Society in Prehistoric Europe: Changing Perspectives*, Edinburgh and Princeton NJ.

Sherratt, A. G. (1997c) 'Climatic cycles and behavioural revolutions: the emergence of modern humans and the beginning of farming', *Antiquity* 71, 271–87.

Sherratt, A. G. (1997d) 'Changing perspectives on European prehistory', in Sherratt (1997b), 1–34.

Sherratt, A. G. and Sherratt, E. S. (1991) 'From luxuries to commodities: the nature of Mediterranean Bronze Age trading systems', in Gale, 351–84.

Sherwin-White, A. N. (1973) *The Roman Citizenship*, 2nd edn, Oxford.

Shoshan, B. (1980) 'Grain riots and the moral economy: Cairo, 1350–1517', *JIH* 10, 459–78.

Siebert, G. (1996) *Nature et paysage dans la pensée et l'environnement des civilisations antiques: actes du colloque de Strasbourg . . . 1992*, Paris.

Siewert, P. (1977) 'The ephebic oath in fifth century Athens', *JHS* 107, 102–11.

Sigal, P.-A. (1969) 'Les miracles de Saint Gibrien à Reims', *Annales*, 1522–39.

Sigaut, F. (1975) *L'agriculture et le feu*, Paris.

Sigaut F. (1988) 'A method for identifying grain storage techniques and its application for European agricultural history', *TT* 6.1, 3–32.

Sigaut, F. (1991) 'Les techniques de récolte des grains: identification, localisation, problèmes d'interprétation', in Cauvin, 31–44.

Sigaut, F. (1995) 'Réflexions sur le thème du colloque dans le contexte générale de l'histoire du transport attelé', in Raepsaet and Rommelaere, 7–11.

Sigaut, F. and Fournier, D. (1991) 'La préparation alimentaire des céréales: fil directeur dans l'histoire technique et économique de l'Europe', in Sigaut and Fournier (eds), 9–16.

Sigaut, F. and Fournier, D. (eds) (1991) *La préparation alimentaire des céréales*, Rixensart, Belgium.

Silver, M. (1985) *Economic Structures of the Ancient Near East*, London and Sydney.

Silver, M. (1995) *Economic Structures of Antiquity*, Westport CT.

Silverman, S. F. (1966) 'An ethnographic approach to social stratification: prestige in a central Italian community', *AmAnth* 68, 899–921.

Silverman, S. F. (1975) *Three Bells of Civilisation: The Life of an Umbrian Hill-Town*, New York and London.

Silverman, S. F. (1986) 'Anthropology and history: understanding the boundaries', *Historical Methods* 19, 123–6.

Simek, R. (1996) *Heaven and Earth in the Middle Ages: The Physical World before Columbus*, Woodbridge.

Simkhovitch, V. G. (1921) *Towards the Understanding of Jesus and Two Additional Historical Studies: Rome's Fall Reconsidered, and Hay and History*, London.

Simon, J. L. (1981) *The Ultimate Resource* (revised edn, Princeton NJ, 1998), London.

Simon, R. (1989) *Meccan Trade and Islam: Problems of Origin and Structure*, Budapest.

Singleton, V. L. (1995) 'An enologist's commentary on ancient wines', in McGovern, Fleming and Katz, 67–77.

Sinn, U. (1990) 'Das Heraion von Perachora: eine sakrale Schutzzone in der korinthischen Peraia', *MDAIA* 105, 53–116.

Sinn, U. (1996) 'The influence of Greek sanctuaries on the consolidation of economic power', in Hellstrom and Alroth, 67–74.

Sion, J. (1935) 'Quelques problèmes de transport dans l'antiquité: le point de vue d'un géographe méditerranéen', *Annales*, 628–33.

Siraj, A. (1995) *L'image de la Tingitanie: l'historiographie arabe médiévale et l'antiquité nord-africaine*, Rome.

Sirks, B. (1991) *Food for Rome: The Legal Structure of the Transportation and Processing of Supplies for the Imperial Distributions in Rome and Constantinople*, Amsterdam.

Sjoberg, G. (1960) *The Preindustrial City: Past and Present* (2nd edn 1965), Glencoe IL.

Skydsgaard, J. E. (1988) 'Transhumance in ancient Greece', in Whittaker, 75–86.

Slaughter, C. (1984) 'Social evolution: some sociological aspects', in Bintliff (ed.), 41–68.

Slicher van Bath, B. H. (1963) *The Agrarian History of Western Europe, A.D. 500–1850*, London.

Slot, B. (1982) *Archipelagus Turbatus: les Cyclades entre colonisation Latine et occupation ottomane, ca. 1500–1718*, Leiden.

Slot, B. (1991) 'The Frankish archipelago', *BF* 16, 195–207.

Slotsky, A. L. (1997) *The Bourse of Babylon: Market Quotations in the Astronomical Diaries of Babylonia*, Bethesda MD.

Slouschz, N. (1948) *The Book of the Seas* (in Hebrew), Tel Aviv.

Sluyter, A. (1994) 'Intensive wetland agriculture in Mesoamerica: space, time and form', *AAAG* 84, 4, 557–84.

Smith, B. L. and Reynolds, H. B. (1987) *The City as a Sacred Centre: Essays on Six Asian Contexts*, Leiden.

Smith, C. A. (1976) 'Regional economic systems: linking geographical models and economic problems', in C. A. Smith (ed.) *Regional Analysis*, vol. 1: *Economic Systems*, New York, 3–63.

Smith, C. A. (1990) 'Types of city-size distributions: a comparative analysis', in van der Woude, Hayami and de Vries, 20–42.

Smith, C. J. (1998) 'Traders and artisans in archaic central Italy', in Parkins and Smith, 31–51.

Smith, N. A. F. (1971) *A History of Dams*, London.

Smith, N. A. F. (1976) *Man and Water*, London.

Smith, R. M. (1991) 'Demographic developments in rural England, 1300–48: a survey', in B. M. S. Campbell (ed.) *Before the Black Death: Studies in the 'Crisis' of the Early Fourteenth Century*, Manchester, 25–78.

Smith, T. (1987) *Mycenaean Trade and Interaction in the West Central Mediterranean, 1600 B.C.–1000 B.C.*, Oxford.

Smith, W. (1998) 'Fuel for thought: archaeobotanical evidence for the use of alternatives to wood fuel in late Antique North Africa', *JMA* 11.2, 191–205.

Smithson, M. (1987) *Fuzzy Set Analysis for Behavioral and Social Sciences*, New York and London.

Smyth, M. P. (1989) 'Domestic storage behavior in Mesoamerica: an ethnoarchaeological approach', *Archaeological Method and Theory* 1, 89–138.

Snodgrass, A. (1979) *Archaic Greece*, London.

Snodgrass, A. (1990) 'Survey archaeology and the rural landscape of the Greek city', in Murray and Price, 113–36.

Snodgrass, A. M. (1995) 'The Euboeans in Macedonia: a new precedent for westward expansion', *APOIKIA, scritti in onore di Giorgio Buchner*, 87–94.

Sodini, J.-P. (1989) 'Le commerce des marbres à l'époque protobyzantine', in *Hommes et richesses*, 163–86.

Sodini, J.-P. (1993) 'La contribution de l'archéologie à la connaissance du monde byzantine (IVe–VIIe siècles)', *DOP* 47, 139–84.

Sodini, J.-P. et al. (1980) 'Déhès (Syrie du nord), campagnes I–III (1976–8): recherches sur l'habitat rural', *Syria* 57, 1–304.

Sombart, W. (1916–27) *Der Moderne Kapitalismus*, 2nd edn, 3 vols, Munich and Leipzig.

Sordi, M. (1988) *Geografia e storiografia nel mondo classico*, Milan.

Sordi, M. (ed.) (1994) *Emigrazione e immigrazione nel mondo antico*, Milan.

Sordi, M. (ed.) (1995) *Coercizione e mobilità umana nel mondo antico*, Milan.

Sordinas, A. (1979) 'The Ropas plow from the island of Corfu, Greece', *TT* 3.3, 139–49.

Sorensen, M. L. S. and Thomas, R. (1989) *The Bronze Age–Iron Age Transition in Europe: Aspects of Continuity and Change in European Societies c.1200–500 B.C.*, BAR 483, Oxford.

Southern, R. W. (1953) *The Making of the Middle Ages*, London.

Southern, R. W. (1962) *Western Views of Islam in the Middle Ages*, Cambridge MA.

Soverini, L. (1990–2) 'Il "commercio nel tempio": osservazioni sul regolamento della *kapeleia* a Samo (*SEG* XXVIII, 545)', *Opus* 9–10, 59–122.

Soyez, B. (1977) *Byblos et la fête des Adonies*, Leiden.

Spate, O. H. K. (1978) 'The Pacific as an artefact', in N. Gunson (ed.) *The Changing Pacific: Essays in Honour of H. E. Maude*, Melbourne, 32–45.

Spate, O. H. K. (1979–89) *The Pacific since Magellan*, 3 vols, Canberra.

Spencer, N. (1995) *Time, Tradition and Society in Greek Archaeology: Bridging the 'Great Divide'*, London.

Spencer, N. (1996) 'To Pyrrhaiōn Oros to pityōdes': an archaeological and epigraphical approach to a topographical problem', *ZPE* 112, 252–62.

Spicciani, A. (1981) 'The "poveri vergognosi" in fifteenth-century Florence: the first thirty years' activity of the Buonomini di S. Martino', in T. Riis (ed.) *Aspects of Poverty in Early Modern Europe*, Florence, 119–82.

Spieser, J. M. (1984) *Thessalonique et ses monuments du IVe siècle au VIe siècle: contribution à l'étude d'une ville paléochrétienne*, Paris.

Spooner, B. (1973) *Population Growth: Anthropological Implications*, Cambridge, MA.

Spooner, B. (1974) 'Irrigation and society: the Iranian plateau', in Downing and Gibson, 43–57.

Spufford, M. (1984) *The Great Reclothing of Rural England: Petty Chapmen and their Wares in the Seventeenth Century*, London.

Spurr, M. S. (1986) *Arable Cultivation in Roman Italy, ca. 200 B.C.–ca. A.D. 200*, London.

Squatriti, P. (1995) 'Water, nature and culture in early medieval Lucca', *Early Medieval Europe* 4, 21–40.

Squatriti, P. (1997) '"Advent and conquests" of the water mill in Italy', in E. B. Smith and M. Wolfe (eds) *Technology and Resource Use in Medieval Europe: Cathedrals, Mills and Mines*, Aldershot, 125–38.

Squatriti, P. (1998) *Water and Society in Early Medieval Italy, AD 400–1000*, Cambridge.

Standing, G. (1980–1) 'Migration and modes of exploitation: social origins of immobility and mobility', *JPS* 8, 173–211.

Stanley, D. J. (ed.) (1972) *The Mediterranean Sea: A Natural Sedimentation Laboratory*, Stroudsburg PA.

Starr, C. (1982) *The Roman Empire 27 B.C.–A.D. 476: A Study in Survival*, New York.

Stech, T. (1988) 'Cyprus, Crete and Sardinia: the organisation of the metals trade and the role of Cyprus', *RDAC*, 281–98.

Steinmetzler, J. (1956) *Die Anthropogeographie Friedrich Ratzels und ihre ideengeschichtlichen Wurzeln*, Bonner geographische Abhandlungen 19, Bonn.

Stevenson, A. C. and Harrison, R. J. (1992) 'Ancient forests in Spain: a model for land-use and dry forest management in south west Spain from 4000 B.C. to A.D. 1900', *PPS* 58, 227–47.

Stewart, C. (1991) *Demons and the Devil: Moral Imagination in Modern Greek Culture*, Princeton NJ.

Stewart, F. H. (1994) *Honor*, Chicago and London.

Stillman, N. A. (1974) 'A case of labour problems in medieval Egypt', *IJMES* 5, 194–201.

Stiros, S. and Jones, R. E. (eds) (1996) *Archaeoseismology*, Athens.

Stoddart, S. et al. (1993) 'Cult in an island society: prehistoric Malta in the Tarxien period', *CAJ* 3, 3–19.

Stoianovich, T. (1976) *French Historical Method: The Annales Paradigm*, Ithaca.

Stol, M. (1994) 'Beer in Neo-Babylonian times', in L. Milano (ed.) *Drinking in Neo-Babylonian Times*, Padua, 155–83.

Stoneman, R. (1987) *Land of Lost Gods: The Search for Classical Greece*, London.

Stopford, J. (1992) 'After Dark Age economics', *RurH* 3.1, 119–21.

Stos-Gale, Z. A. and Gale, N. H. (1992) 'New light on the provenience of the copper oxhide ingots found on Sardinia', in Andrews and Tykot, 317–37.

Strubbe, J. H. M., Tybout, R. A. and Versnel, H. S. (1996) *Energeia: Studies on Ancient History and Epigraphy Presented to H. W. Pleket*, Amsterdam.

Structures féodales et féodalisme dans l'Occident méditerranéen (Xe–XIIIe siècles). Bilan et perspectives de recherches (1980), Rome.

Stuard, S. M. (1986) 'To town to serve: urban domestic slavery in medieval Ragusa', in B. A. Hanawalt (ed.) *Women and Work in Pre-industrial Europe*, Bloomington IN, 39–55.

Stuard, S. M. (1995) 'Ancillary evidence for the decline of mediaeval slavery', *PP* 149, 3–28.

Stucchi, S. (1989) 'Problems concerning the coming of the Greeks to Cyrenaica and their relations with their neighbours', *Mediterranean Archaeology* 2, 73–84.

Sumption, J. (1975) *Pilgrimage: An Image of Mediaeval Religion*, London.

Susini, G. (1963–4) 'Supplemento epigrafico di Caso, Scarpanto, Saro, Calchi, Alinnia e Tilo', *AnnA* 41–2, 203–92.

Suto, Y. (1993) 'Isolated farms in classical Attica', *Kodai* 4, 1–19.

Sutton, S. B. (1988) 'What is a village in a nation of migrants?', *JMGS* 6, 187–215.

Sutton, S. B. (1994) 'Settlement patterns, settlement perceptions: rethinking the Greek village', in N. Kardulias (ed.) *Beyond the Site: Regional Studies in the Aegean*, Lanham MD, 313–35.

Svoronos, N. (1956) 'Sur quelques formes de la vie rurale à Byzance: petite et grande exploitation', *Annales*, 325–35.

Swinburne, H. C. (1790) *Travels in the Two Sicilies*, 2nd edn, London.

Syme, R. (1995) *Anatolica: Studies in Strabo*, ed. A. R. Birley, Oxford.

Symonds, J. A. (1877) *Studies of the Greek Poets: First Series*, 2nd edn, London.

Tainter, J. A. (1988) *The Collapse of Complex Societies*, Cambridge.

Talbi, M. (1981) 'Law and society in Ifrīqiya (Tunisia) in the third Islamic century: agriculture and the role of slaves in the country's economy', in Udovitch, 209–49.

Talbot, C. H. (trans.) (1954) *The Anglo-Saxon Missionaries in Germany*, London and New York.

Tambiah, S. J. (1982) *Do Kamo: Person and Myth in a Melanesian Village*, Berkeley.

Tambiah, S. J. (1990) *Magic, Science, Religion and the Scope of Rationality*, Cambridge.

Tangri, D. (1989) 'On trade and assimilation in European agricultural origins', *JMA* 2.1, 139–48.

Tapper, N. (1991) *Bartered Brides: Politics, Gender and Marriage in an Afghan Tribal Society*, Cambridge.

Tarn, W. W. (1913) *Antigonos Gonatas*, Oxford.

Tarr, L. (1969) *The History of the Carriage*, Budapest.

Tate, G. (1989) 'Les campagnes de la Syrie du nord à l'époque proto-Byzantine', in *Hommes et richesses*, 63–77.

Tate, G. (1992a) *Les campagnes de la Syrie du nord du IIe au VIIe siècle*, Paris.

Tate, G. (1992b) 'Prospérité des villages de la Syrie du nord au VIe siècle', in Boyd and Mango, 93–8.

Taussig, M. (1982) 'Peasant economics and the development of agriculture in the Cauca valley, Colombia', in J. Harriss (ed.) *Rural Development: Theories of Peasant Economy and Agrarian Change*, London, 2nd edn, 178–205.

Taylor, E. G. R. (1930) *Tudor Geography, 1485–1583*, London.

Taylor, E. G. R. (1934) *Later Tudor and Early Stuart Geography, 1583–1650* (repr. New York 1968), London.

Taylor, E. G. R. (1956) *The Haven-Finding Art: A History of Navigation from Odysseus to Captain Cook*, London.

Taylor, G. (1985) *Pride, Shame and Guilt: Emotions of Self-Assessment*, Oxford.

Taylor, J. E. (1993) *Christians and the Holy Places: The Myth of Jewish-Christian Origins*, Oxford.

Tchalenko, G. (1953–8) *Villages antiques de la Syrie du nord: le massif du Bélus à l'époque romaine*, 3 vols, Paris.

Tchernia, A. (1983) 'Italian wine in Gaul at the end of the Republic', in Garnsey, Hopkins and Whittaker, 87–104.

Tchernia, A. (1986) *Le vin de l'Italie romaine*, Paris.

Tchernia, A. (1989) 'Encore sur les modèles économiques et les amphores', in *Amphores romaines et histoire économique*, 529–36.

Teall, J. L. (1959) 'The grain supply of the Byzantine empire 330–1025', *DOP* 13, 87–139.

Teall, J. L. (1971) 'The Byzantine agricultural tradition', *DOP* 25, 33–59.

Teixidor, J. (1984) *Un port romain du désert: Palmyre, Semitica* 34, Paris.

Tenenti, A. (1967) *Piracy and the Decline of Venice 1580–1615*, London.

Theroux, P. (1995) *The Pillars of Hercules: A Grand Tour of the Mediterranean*, London.

Thirgood, J. V. (1981) *Man and the Mediterranean Forest*, London.

Thiriet, F. (1953) 'Venise et l'occupation de Ténédos au XIVe siècle', *MAH* 65, 219–45.

Thiriet, F. (1981) 'Les routes maritimes dans l'Adriatique', in *I rapporti demografici e popolativi: congresso sulle relazioni tra le due sponde adriatiche* 2, Rome, 75–89.

Thirsk, J. (1997) *Alternative Agriculture: A History, from the Black Death to the Present Day*, Oxford.

Thomas, K. (1963) 'History and anthropology', *PP* 24, 3–24.

Thomas, K. (1971) *Religion and the Decline of Magic: Studies in Popular Beliefs in Sixteenth- and Seventeenth-Century England*, London.

Thomas, N. (1989) *Out of Time: History and Evolution in Anthropological Discourse*, Cambridge.

Thomas, R. and Wilson, A. (1994) 'Water supply for Roman farms in Latium and south Etruria', *PBSR* 62, 139–96.

Thompson, D. J. (= Crawford, D. J.) (1984) 'Agriculture', *CAH*, 2nd edn, 7.1, 363–70.

Thompson, E. P. (1976) 'The grid of inheritance: a comment', in J. Goody, J. Thirsk and E. P. Thompson (eds) *Family and Inheritance: Rural Society in Western Europe, 1200–1800*, repr. 1978, Cambridge, 328–60.

Thompson, L. A. (1982) 'On "development" in the early Roman empire', *Klio* 64, 383–401.

Thornes, J. B. (1987) 'The palaeo-ecology of erosion', in Wagstaff, 37–55.

Thornes, J. B. (1988) 'Erosional equilibria under grazing', in Bintliff, Davidson and Grant, 193–210.

Thornes, J. B. (ed.) (forthcoming) *Deforestation in the Mediterranean*, London.

Thulin, C. O. (ed.) (1913) *Corpus Agrimensorum Romanorum*, Leipzig.

Tillion, G. (1983) *The Republic of Cousins: Women's Oppression in Mediterranean Society*, first published 1966, London.

Tipps, D. C. (1973) 'Modernization theory and the comparative study of societies: a critical perspective', *CSSH* 15, 199–226.

Toch, M. (1989) 'Peasants of the mountains, peasants of the valleys and medieval state building: the case of the Alps', in Bergier, 65–70.

Tölle-Kastenbein, R. (1990) *Antike Wasserkultur*, Munich.

Tomber, R. (1993) 'Quantitative approaches to the investigation of long-distance exchange', *JRA* 6, 142–66.

Tonkin, E., McDonald, M. and Chapman, M. (eds) (1989) *History and Ethnicity*, London.

Topping, P. (1980) 'Albanian settlements in medieval Greece: some Venetian testimonies', in Laiou (ed.), 261–71.

Tora, Y. (1993) *Salt Production Techniques in Ancient China*, Leiden.

Torelli, M. (1969) 'Un templum augurale di età repubblicana a Bantia', *RL* 8.24, 1–21.

Torelli, M. (1980) 'Innovazioni nelle techniche edilizie romane tra il I sec. a.C. e il I sec. d.C.', in Gabba, 139–62.

Tortella, G. (1994) 'Patterns of economic retardation and recovery in south-western Europe in the nineteenth and twentieth centuries', *EcHR* 47, 1–21.

Tortorella, S. (1986) 'La ceramica fine di mensa africana dal IV al VII secolo d.C.', in Giardina, 3.211–25.

Toubert, P. (1973) *Les structures du Latium médiéval: le Latium méridional et la Sabine du IXe siècle à la fin du XIIe siècle*, Paris.

Toubert, P. (1987) 'Un mythe historiographique: la sériculture italienne du haut moyen âge, IXe–Xe siècle', in Dubois, Hocquet and Vauchez, 2.215–42.

Toubert, P. (1988) 'Introduction', in Bazzana, 7–9.

Touma, T. (1986) *Paysans et institutions féodales chez les Druses et les Maronites du Liban*, 2 vols, Beirut.

Toynbee, A. (1934–61) *A Study of History*, 12 vols, London.

Tozer, H. F. (1882) *Lectures on the Geography of Greece*, Oxford.

Tozer, H. F. (1890) *The Islands of the Aegean*, Oxford.

Trabaud, L. (1981) 'Man and fire: impacts on Mediterranean vegetation', in Di Castri et al., 523–37.

Trabaud, L. (1991) 'Is fire an agent favouring plant invasions?', in Groves and Di Castri, 179–90.

Trabaud, L. and Lepart, J. (1981) 'Diversity and stability in garrigue ecosystems after fire', *Vegetatio* 46, 105–16.

Tracy, S. V. (1986) 'Darkness from light: the beacon fire in the *Agamamnon*', *CQ* 36, 257–60.

Traina, G. (1983) *Le valli grandi Veronesi in età romana*, Pisa.

Traina, G. (1986) 'Paesaggio e decadenza: la palude nella trasformazione del mondo antico', in Giardina, 3.711–30.

Traina, G. (1988) *Paludi e bonifiche del mondo antico*, Rome.

Traina, G. (1989) 'Tracce di un'immagine: il terremoto fra prodigio e fenomeno', in Guidoboni, 104–13.

Traina, G. (1990) *Ambiente e paesaggi di Roma antica*, Rome.

Traina, G. (1994) 'Paesaggi tardoantichi: alcuni problemi', in Francovich and Noyé, 85–98.

Trautmann, T. R. (1992) 'The revolution in ethnological time', *Man* 27, 379–97.

Treadgold, W. (1988) *The Byzantine Revival 780–842*, Stanford CA.

Treister, M. Y. (1995) 'North Syrian metalworkers in archaic Greek settlements', *OJA* 14, 159–78.

Treister, M. Y. (1996) *The Role of Metals in Ancient Greek History*, Leiden.

Trevor-Roper, H. R. (1972) 'Fernand Braudel, the *Annales*, and the Mediterranean', *Journal of Modern History* 44, 468–79.

Trexler, R. (1974) 'Measures against water pollution in fifteenth century Florence', *Viator* 5, 455–67.

Trombley, F. R. (1985a) 'Paganism in the Greek world at the end of antiquity: the case of rural Anatolia and Greece', *HTR* 78, 327–52.

Trombley, F. R. (1985b) 'Monastic foundations in sixth century Anatolia and their role in the social and economic life of the countryside', *Greek Orthodox Theological Review* 30, 45–59.

Trombley, F. R. (1993–4) *Hellenic Religion and Christianization, c.370–529*, 2 vols, Leiden.

Trombley, F. R. (1994) 'Religious transition in sixth century Syria', *BF* 20, 153–95.

Trousset, P. (1986) 'Les oasis présahariennes dans l'antiquité: partage de l'eau et division du temps', *AA* 22, 163–93.

Trump, D. H. (1980) *The Prehistory of the Mediterranean*, Harmondsworth.

Tsetskhladze, G. (1995) 'Did the Greeks go to Colchis for metal?', *OJA* 14, 307–3.

Tsuji, S. (ed.) (1995) *The Survey of Early Byzantine Sites in Ölüdeniz Area (Lycia, Turkey): The First Preliminary Report*, Memoirs of the Faculty of Letters, Osaka University 35, Osaka.

Tuan, Yi-Fu (1968) *The Hydrological Cycle and the Wisdom of God*, Toronto.

Tuan, Yi-Fu (1974) *Topophilia: A Study of Environmental Perception, Attitudes, and Values*, Englewood Cliffs NJ.

Tucciarone, R. (1991) *I Saraceni nel Ducato di Gaeta e nell'Italia centromeridionale*, Gaeta.

Turner, F. M. (1981) *The Greek Heritage in Victorian Britain*, New Haven and London.

Turner, V. (1974) *Dramas, Fields, and Metaphors*, Ithaca.

Turner, V. and Turner, E. (1978) *Image and Pilgrimage in Christian Culture: Anthropological Perspectives*, New York.

Tvengsberg, P. M. (1995) 'Rye and swidden cultivation: tillage without tools', *TT* 7.4, 131–46.

Tzedakis, Y. (1989) 'Les routes minoennes: rapport préliminaire – défense de la circulation ou circulation de la défense', *BCH* 113, 43–75.

Ucko, P. J. and Dimbleby, G. W. (eds) (1969) *The Domestication and Exploitation of Plants and Animals*, London.

Ucko, P. J., Tringham, R. and Dimbleby, H. W. (eds) (1972) *Man, Settlement and Urbanism*, London.

Udovitch, A. L. (1978) 'Time, the sea and society: duration of commercial voyages on the southern shores of the Mediterranean during the high Middle Ages', *SS* 25, 503–46, with discussion, 547–63.

Udovitch, A. L. (1993) 'Muslims and Jews in the world of Frederic II: boundaries and communication', *Princeton Papers in Near Eastern Studies* 2, 83–104.

Udovitch, A. L. (ed.) (1981) *The Islamic Middle East, 700–1900: Studies in Economic and Social History*, Princeton NJ.

Ugolini, F. C. and Zakoski, R. J. (1979) 'Soils derived from tephra', in Grayson and Sheets, 83–124.

Unwin, P. T. H. (1991) *Wine and the Vine: An Historical Geography of Viticulture and the Wine Trade*, London.

Usai, A. (1969) *Il pane di ghiande e la geofagia in Sardegna*, Cagliari.

Vacalopoulos, A. E. (1980) 'The flight of the inhabitants of Greece to the Aegean islands, Crete and Mane, during the Turkish invasions (fourteenth and fifteenth centuries)', in Laiou (ed.), 272–83.

Valensi, L. (1985) *Tunisian Peasants in the Eighteenth and Nineteenth Centuries*, Cambridge and Paris.

van Andel, T. H. and Runnels, C. N. (1987) *Beyond the Acropolis: A Rural Greek Past*, Stanford.

van Andel, T. H. and Runnels, C. N. (1988) 'An essay on the "emergence of civilisation" in the Aegean world', *Antiquity* 62, 234–47.

van Andel, T. H., Runnels, C. N. and Pope, K. O. (1986) 'Five thousand years of land use and abuse in the southern Argolid, Greece', *Hesperia* 55, 103–28.

van Andel, T. H. and Zangger, E. (1990a) 'Landscape stability and destabilisation in the prehistory of Greece', in Bottema et al., 139–57.

van Andel, T. H. and E. Zangger (1990b) 'Land-use and soil erosion in prehistoric and historical Greece', *JFA* 17, 379–96.

van Binsbergen, W. M. J. (1985) 'The cult of saints in north-western Tunisia: an analysis of contemporary pilgrimage structures', in E. Gellner (ed.) *Islamic Dilemmas. Reformers, Nationalists and Industrialization: The Southern Shore of the Mediterranean* (Religion and Society 25), Berlin, 199–239.

van der Leeuw, S. (1994) 'Social and environmental change', *CAJ* 4, 130–9.

van der Woude, A., de Vries, J. and Hayami, A. (1990) 'Introduction: the hierarchies, provisioning, and demographic patterns of cities', in van der Woude, Hayami and de Vries (eds), 1–19.

van der Woude, A., Hayami, A. and de Vries, J. (eds) (1990) *Urbanization in History: A Process of Dynamic Interactions*, Oxford.

van Dieten, J. A. (1975) Niketas Choniates, *Historia* (trans. H. Magoulias, *O City of Byzantium*, Detroit 1984), New York and Berlin.

van Doorninck, F. H., Jr. (1991) 'The medieval shipwreck at Serçe Limani: an early 11th-century Fatimid–Byzantine commercial voyage', *Graeco-Arabica* 4, 45–52.

van Hoof, A. J. L. (1988) 'Ancient robbers: reflections behind the facts', *Ancient Society* 19, 105–24.

Van Nieuwenhuijze, C. A. O. (ed.) (1972) *Emigration and Agriculture in the Mediterranean Basin*, The Hague.

Van Zuidam, R.-A. (1975) 'Geomorphology and archaeology: evidence of interaction at historical sites in the Zaragoza region, Spain', *Zeitschrift für Geomorphologie* 19.3, 319–28.

Vandenabeele, F. (1991) 'Salt on Cyprus in Antiquity', in H. Thoen (ed.) *Liber Amicorum J. A. E. Nenquin: Studia Archaeologica*, Ghent, 85–6.

Vandermersch, C. (1994) *Vins et amphores de Grande Grèce et de Sicile IVe–IIIe s. av. J.-C.*, Naples.

Vandermersch, C. (1996) 'Vigne, vin et économie dans l'Italie du sud grecque à l'époque archaïque', *Ostraka* 5, 155–85.

Vanderpool, E. (1965) 'The Acharnian Aqueduct', in *Charisterion eis Anastasion K. Orlandon*, Athens, 1.166–75.

Varilioglu, G. (1988) 'Une inscription de Mercure aux Portes de Cilicie', *EA* 11, 59–64.

Varisco, D. M. (1983) '*Sayl* and *ghayl*: the ecology of water allocation in Yemen', *Human Ecology* 11, 365–85.

Vauchez, A. (1987) 'Le trafiquant céleste: Saint Homebon de Crémone (ob. 1197)', in Dubois, Hocquet and Vauchez, 1.115–22.

Veeser, H. (ed.) (1989) *The New Historicism*, London.

Velkov, V. and Domaradzka, L. (1994) 'Kotys I (383/2–359 av. J.-C.) et l'*emporion* Pistiros de Thrace', *BCH* 118, 1–15.

Vera, D. (1983) 'Strutture agrarie e strutture patrimoniali nella tarda antichità: l'aristocrazia romana fra agricoltura e commercio', *Opus* 2, 489–533.

Vera, D. (1986) 'Forme e funzione delle rendita fondiaria nella tarda antichità', in Giardina, 1.367–447.

Verdon, M. (1979) 'The stem family: towards a general theory', *JIH* 10, 81–105.

Verhulst, A. (1989) 'The origins of towns in the Low Countries and the Pirenne thesis', *PP* 122, 3–35.

Verhulst, A. (1990) 'The "agricultural revolution" of the Middle Ages reconsidered', in S. Bachrach and D. Nicholas (eds) *Law, Custom and the Social Fabric in Medieval Europe: Essays in Honour of Bryce Lyon*, Kalamazoo, 17–28.

Verlinden, C. (1977) *L'esclavage dans l'Europe médiévale*, vol. 2, Ghent.

Vernant, J.-P. (1983) *Myth and Thought among the Greeks*, first published 1965, London.

Vernet, J.-L. (1997) *L'homme et la forêt méditerranéenne de la préhistoire à nos jours*, Paris.

Viazzo, P. P. (1989) *Upland Communities: Environment, Population and Social Structure in the Alps since the Sixteenth Century*, Cambridge.

Vidal de la Blache, P. (1896) 'Les voies de commerce dans la géographie de Ptolémée', *CRAI* 24, 456–83.

Vidal de la Blache, P. (1911) 'Les genres de la vie dans la géographie humaine', *AG* 20, 193–212, 289–304.

Vidal de la Blache, P. (1926) *Principles of Human Geography*, New York.

Vidal de la Blache, P. (1928) *The Personality of France* (trans. from *Tableau de la géographie de la France*, Paris 1911), London.

Vidal-Naquet, P. A. (1992) 'Genèse d'un haut-lieu', in *Sainte-Victoire: hommes et paysages* (*Méditerranée* 1.2), 7–16.

Vieillard, R. (1942) *Recherches sur les origines de la Rome chrétienne*, Mâcon.

Vigneron, P. (1968) *Le cheval dans l'antiquité gréco-romaine*, Nancy.

Vilar, P. (1962) *La Catalogne dans l'Espagne moderne*, 3 vols, Paris.

Villedieu, F. (1984) *Turris Libisonis: fouille d'un site romain tardif à Porto Torres, sardaigne*, *BAR* 224, Oxford.

Violante, A. (1989) 'Suolo e paesaggio agrario nell'Italia romana: l'apporto delle sistemazioni idrauliche', in G. Botta (ed.) *Studi geografici sul paesaggio*, Milan, 109–26.

Virgilio, B. (1981) *Il 'tempio-stato' di Pessinunte fra Pergamo e Roma nel II–I sec. a. C.*, Pisa.

Vita-Finzi, C. (1966) 'The new Elysian fields', *AJA* 70, 175–8.

Vita-Finzi, C. (1969) *The Mediterranean Valleys*, Cambridge.

Vita-Finzi, C. (1972) 'Supply of fluvial sediment to the Mediterranean during the last 2,000 years', in Stanley, 43–6.

Vogt, E. Z. (1968) 'Some aspects of Zincantan settlement patterns and ceremonial organization', in K. C. Chang (ed.) *Settlement Archaeology*, Palo Alto CA, 154–73.

von Falkenhausen, V. (1989) 'Réseaux routiers et ports dans l'Italie méridionale Byzantine (VIe–XIe s.), in *He kathēmerinē Zōē sto Byzantinio*, Athens, 710–31.

von Thünen, J. H. (1966) *The Isolated State*, first published 1826–63, Oxford.

von Wartburg, M. L. (1995) 'Desing [*sic*] and technology of the medieval refineries of the sugar cane in Cyprus: a case of estudy [*sic*] in industrial archaeology', in Malpica, 81–116.

Vovelle, M. (1990) *Ideologies and Mentalities*, Cambridge.

Vroom, J. (1998) 'Early modern archaeology in central Greece: the contrast of artefact-rich and sherdless sites', *JMA* 11.2, 131–64.

Vryonis, S., Jr. (1956) 'Isidore Glebas and the Turkish *devshirme*', *Speculum* 31, 433–43.

Vryonis, S., Jr. (1962) 'The question of the Byzantine mines', *Speculum* 37, 1–17.

Vryonis, S., Jr. (1975) 'Nomadization and Islamization in Asia Minor', *DOP* 29, 47–71.

Vryonis, S., Jr. (1980) 'Travelers as a source for the societies of the Middle East, 900–1600', in Laiou (ed.), 284–311.

Vryonis, S., Jr. (1981) 'The *panegyris* of the Byzantine saint', in S. Hackel (ed.) *The Byzantine Saint*, London, 196–226.

Vryonis, S., Jr. (1988) 'The Byzantine legacy in folk life and tradition in the Balkans', in L. Clucas (ed.) *The Byzantine Legacy in Eastern Europe*, Boulder CO, 107–45.

Wade, R. (1971) 'Political behaviour and world view in a central Italian village', in F. G. Bailey, 252–80.

Wagstaff, J. M. (1975) 'A note on settlement numbers in ancient Greece', *JHS* 95, 163–8.

Wagstaff, J. M. (1981) 'Buried assumptions: some problems in the interpretation of the "Younger Fill" raised by recent data from Greece', *JAS* 8, 247–64.

Wagstaff, J. M. (1985) *The Evolution of Middle Eastern Landscapes: An Outline to A.D. 1840*, London.

Wagstaff, J. M. (1992) 'Agricultural terraces: the Vasilikos valley, Cyprus', in Bell and Boardman, 155–66.

Wagstaff, J. M. (ed.) (1987) *Landscape and Culture: Geographical and Archaeological Perspectives*, Oxford.

Wagstaff, J. M., Augustson, S. and Gamble, C. (1982) 'Alternative subsistence strategies', in Renfrew and Wagstaff, 172–80.

Wagstaff, J. M. and Cherry, J. F. (1982) 'Settlement and population change', in Renfrew and Wagstaff, 136–55.

Walcot, P. (1970) *Greek Peasants Ancient and Modern: A Comparison of Social and Moral Values*, Manchester.

Waldren, W. H. (1985) *The Deya Conference of Prehistory: Early Settlement in the Western Mediterranean Islands*, *BAR* 229, Oxford.

Waldron, T. (1983) *Lead and Lead Poisoning in Antiquity*, London.

Walker, D. S. (1962) *The Mediterranean Lands*, 2nd edn, London.

Walker, P. W. L. (1990) *Holy City, Holy Places: Christian Attitudes to Jerusalem and the Holy Land in the Fourth Century*, Oxford.

Wall, R. (1983) 'Introduction', in R. Wall, P. Laslett and J. Robin (eds) *Family Forms in Historic Europe*, Cambridge, 1–63.

Wallace-Hadrill, A. (1991) 'Elites and trade in the Roman town', in Rich and Wallace-Hadrill, 241–72 (revised in Wallace-Hadrill, *Houses and Society in Pompeii and Herculaneum*, Princeton NJ, 1994, ch. 6).

Wallerstein, I. (1974–89) *The Modern World-System*, New York.

Walter, J. and Schofield, R. (eds) (1989) *Famine, Disease and the Social Order in Early Modern Society*, Cambridge.

Wang, P. P. and Chang, S. K. (eds) (1980) *Fuzzy Sets*, New York.

Wanklyn, H. (1961) *Friedrich Ratzel: A Biographical Memoir and Bibliography*, Cambridge.

Ward-Perkins, B. (1984) *From Classical Antiquity to the Middle Ages: Urban Public Building in Northern and Central Italy, AD 300–850*, Oxford.

Ward-Perkins, B. (1986) review of Hodges and Whitehouse (1983), *EHR* 101, 466–7.

Ward-Perkins, B. (1988) 'The towns of northern Italy: rebirth or renewal?', in Hodges and Hobley, 16–27.

Ward-Perkins, B. (1995) 'Can the survival of an ancient town-plan be used as evidence of Dark-Age urban life?', in G. Cavalieri Manasse and E. Roffa (eds) *Splendida Civitas Nostra: studi archeologici in onore di Antonio Frova*, Rome, 223–9.

Ward-Perkins, B. (1996) 'Urban survival and urban transformation in the eastern Mediterranean', in Brogiolo, 153–53.

Ward-Perkins, B. (1997) 'Continuitists, catastrophists, and the towns of post-Roman Northern Italy', *PBSR* 65, 157–76.

Ward-Perkins, B. (forthcoming) 'Specialized production and exchange', in A. Cameron, B. Ward-Perkins and M. Whitby (eds) *CAH* 14, ch. 13.

Ward-Perkins, J. B. (1992) *Marble in Antiquity*, London.

Warren, P. (1995) 'Minoan Crete and pharaonic Egypt', in W. V. Davies and L. Schofield (eds) *Egypt, the Aegean and the Levant: Interconnections in the Second Millennium B.C.*, London, 1–18.

Warren, P. and Miles, G. C. (1972) 'An Arab building at Knossos', *ABSA* 67, 285–96.

Watrous, L. V. (1993) 'A survey of the Western Mesara plain in Crete: preliminary report of the 1984, 1986 and 1987 field seasons', *Hesperia* 62, 191–248.

Watson, A. M. (1981) 'Towards denser and more continuous settlement: new crops and farming techniques in the early Middle Ages', in J. A. Raftis (ed.) *Pathways to Medieval Peasants*, Toronto, 65–82.

Watson, A. M. (1983) *Agricultural Innovation in the Early Islamic World*, Cambridge.

Watson, A. M. (1994) 'The imperfect transmission of Arab agriculture into Christian Europe', in *Kommunikation zwischen Orient und Okzident: Alltag und Sachkultur*, Vienna, 199–212.

Watts, D. (1987) *The West Indies: Patterns of Development, Culture and Environmental Change since 1492*, Cambridge.

Webb, J. M. and Frankel, D. (1994) 'Making an impression: storage and surplus finance in late Bronze Age Cyprus', *JMA* 7, 1, 5–26.

Weber, E. (1977) *Peasants into Frenchmen: The Modernization of Rural France 1870–1914*, London.

Weber, M. (1949) *The Methodology of the Social Sciences*, Glencoe IL.

Weber, M. (1958) *The City* (first published 1921), New York and London.

Weber, M. (1968) *Economy and Society: An Outline of Interpretive Sociology* (trans. from 4th German edn 1956), 3 vols, New York.

Weeber, K.-W. (1990) *Smog über Attika*, Zurich and Munich.

Weiss, R. (1965) *The Renaissance Discovery of Classical Antiquity*, Oxford.

Welinder, S. (1983) *The Ecology of Long-Term Change*, Lund.

Wells, B. (ed.) (1992) *Agriculture in Ancient Greece*, Stockholm.

Wells, C. (1984) *The Roman Empire*, London.

Wells, P. S. (1980) *Culture Contact and Culture Change*, Cambridge.

Wengrow, D. (1996) 'Egyptian taskmasters and heavy burdens: highland exploitation and the collared-rim pithoi of the Bronze/Iron Age Levant', *OJA* 15.3, 307–26.

Werbner, R. P. (1989) *Ritual Passage, Sacred Journey: The Process and Organization of Religious Movement*, Washington DC.

Werbner, R. P. (ed.) (1977) *Regional Cults*, London.

Wertime, T. A. (1983) 'The furnace and the goat: the pyrotechnologic industries and Mediterranean deforestation in antiquity', *JFA* 10, 445–52.

Wertime, T. A. and Muhly, J. D. (1980) *The Coming of the Age of Iron*, New Haven.

Wes, M. A. (1990) *Michael Rostovtzeff, Historian in Exile: Russian Roots in an American Context*, Stuttgart.

Westra, L. and Robinson, T. (eds) (1997) *The Greeks and the Environment*, Lanham MD.

Weulersse, J. (1940a) *L'Oronte*, Tours.

Weulersse, J. (1940b) *Le pays des Alaouites*, Tours.

Whitbread, I. K. (1995) *Greek Transport Amphorae: A Petrological and Archaeological Study*, Athens.

Whitby, M. (1998) 'The grain trade of Athens in the fourth century B.C.', in Parkins and Smith, 102–28.

White, C. (1980) *Patrons and Partisans: A Study of Politics in Two Southern Italian 'Comuni'*, Cambridge.

White, K. D. (1970) *Roman Farming*, London.

White, K. D. (1984) *Greek and Roman Technology*, London.

White, L. T. (1962) *Medieval Technology and Social Change*, Oxford.

White, L. T. (1980) 'Technological development in the transition from Antiquity to the Middle Ages', in Gabba, 235–51.

Whitehead, D. (1977) *The Ideology of the Athenian Metic*, Cambridge.

Whitehouse, D. (1988) 'Rome and Naples: survival and revival in central and southern italy', in Hodges and Hobley, 28–31.

Whitney, E. (1993) 'Lynn White, ecotheology and history', *Environmental Ethics* 15.2, 151–69.

Whittaker, C. R. (1976) '*Agri deserti*', in M. I. Finley (ed.) *Studies in Ancient Property*, Cambridge, 137–65.

Whittaker, C. R. (1978) 'Land and labour in North Africa', *Klio* 60, 331–62.

Whittaker, C. R. (1983a) 'Trade and frontiers of the Roman empire', in Garnsey and Whittaker, 110–27.

Whittaker, C. R. (1983b) 'Late Roman trade and traders', in Garnsey, Hopkins and Whittaker, 163–80.

Whittaker, C. R. (1988) 'Trade and the aristocracy in the Roman empire', *Opus* 4, 49–75.

Whittaker, C. R. (1989) 'Amphorae and trade', in *Amphores romaines et histoire économique*, 537–9.

Whittaker, C. R. (1990), 'The consumer city revisited: the *vicus* and the city', *JRA* 3, 110–18.

Whittaker, C. R. (1994) *Frontiers of the Roman Empire: A Social and Economic Study*, Baltimore.

Whittaker, C. R. (1995) 'Do theories of the ancient city matter?', in Cornell and Lomas, 9–26.

Whittaker, C. R. (ed.) (1988) *Pastoral Economies in Classical Antiquity*, Cambridge Philological Society supplementary volume 14, Cambridge.

Whittle, A. (1985) *Neolithic Europe: A Survey*, Cambridge.

Whittow, M. (1990) 'Ruling the late Roman and early Byzantine city: a continuous history', *PP* 129, 3–29.

Whittow, M. (n.d.) 'Pastoralism and underdevelopment in the early medieval Near East', unpublished.

Wickham, C. (1979) 'Historical and topographical notes on early mediaeval south Etruria: part II', *PBSR* 47, 66–95.

Wickham, C. (1981) *Early Medieval Italy: Central Power and Local Society 400–1000*, London and Basingstoke.

Wickham, C. (1982), review of *Structures féodales et féodalisme dans l'Occident méditerranéen* (1980), *EHR* 95, 835–7.

Wickham, C. (1983–5) 'Pastoralism and underdevelopment in the Middle Ages', *SS* 31, 434–48.

Wickham, C. (1984) 'The other transition: from the ancient world to feudalism', *PP* 103, 3–36.

Wickham, C. (1988a) 'Marx, Sherlock Holmes, and late Roman commerce' (review-article), *JRS* 78, 183–93.

Wickham, C. (1988b) *The Mountains and the City: The Tuscan Appennines in the Early Middle Ages*, Oxford.

Wickham, C. (1988c) 'L'incastellamento ed i suoi destini, undici anni dopo il *Latium* di Toubert', in Noyé, 411–20.

Wickham, C. (1990) 'European forests in the early Middle Ages: landscape and land clearance', *SS* 37, 479–545.

Wickham, C. (1998) 'Overview: production, distribution and demand', in Hodges and Bowden, 279–92.

Wickham, C. (forthcoming) 'Trade and exchange, 550–750: the view from the West', in Conrad.

Wickham, C. and Hansen, I. (eds) (forthcoming) *The Long Eighth Century*, Leiden.

Wiesner, M. E. (1993) *Women and Gender in Early Modern Europe*, Cambridge.

Wikan, U. (1980) *Life Among the Poor in Cairo*, first published 1976, London.

Wikan, U. (1984) 'Shame and honour: a contestable pair', *Man* 19, 635–52.

Wikander, O. (1991) 'Water mills and aqueducts', in A. T. Hodge, 141–8.

Wilken, R. L. (1992) *The Land Called Holy: Palestine in Christian History and Thought*, New Haven.

Wilkes, J. J. (1969) *Dalmatia*, London.

Wilkes, J. J. (1983) 'Romans, Dacians and Sarmatians', in B. Hartley and J. Wacher (eds) *Rome and her Northern Provinces: Papers Presented to Sheppard Frere*, Gloucester, 255–89.

Wilkinson, R. G. (1973) *Poverty and Progress: An Ecological Model of Economic Development*, London.

Willemsen, H. and Brenne, S. (1991) 'Verzeichnis der Kerameikos-Ostraka', *MDAIA* 106, 147–56.

Williams, A. (ed.) (1984) *Southern Europe Transformed: Political and Economic Change in Greece, Italy, Portugal and Spain*, London.

Williams, B. (1993) *Shame and Necessity*, Berkeley, Los Angeles and London.

Williams, P. W. (ed.) (1993) *Karst Terrains: Environmental Changes and Human Impact*, Cremlingen-Destedt.

Williams-Thorpe, O. (1988) 'Provenancing and archaeology of Roman millstones from the Mediterranean area', *JAS* 15, 3, 253–306.

Wilson, A. J. N. (1966) *Emigration from Italy in the Republican Age of Rome*, Manchester.

Wilson, P. J. (1969) 'Reputation and respectability: a suggestion for Caribbean ethnology', *Man* 4, 70–84.

Wilson, S. (1988) *Feuding, Conflict and Banditry in Nineteenth-Century Corsica*, Cambridge.

Wilson, S. (ed.) (1983) *Saints and their Cults: Studies in Religious Sociology, Folklore and History*, Cambridge.

Winckelmann, J. J. (1755) *Gedanken über die Nachahmung der griechischen Werke in der Mahlerei und Bildhauer-Kunst*, Dresden.

Winfield, D. (1977) 'The northern routes across Anatolia', *AS* 27, 151–66.

Winnifrith, T. J. (1987) *The Vlachs: The History of a Balkan People*, London.

Wipszycka, E. (1965) *L'industrie textile dans l'Égypte romaine*, Wrocław, Warsaw and Krakow.

Wirth, L. (1938) 'Urbanism as a way of life', *American Journal of Sociology* 46, 743–55.

Wiseman, P. (1987) 'Julius Caesar and the Hereford World Map', *History Today* 37, November, 53–7.

Wittfogel, K. A. (1929) 'Geopolitik, geographischer Materialismus und Marxismus', *Unter den Banner des Marxismus* 3, 17–51; 4, 485–522; 6, 698–735.

Wittfogel, K. A. (1957) *Oriental Despotism: A Comparative Study of Total Power*, New Haven.

Wolf, E. R. (1966) *Peasants*, Englewood Cliffs NJ.

Wolf, J. G. and Crook, J. (1989) *Rechtsurkunden in Vulgärlatein aus den Jahren 37–39 n. Chr.*, Heidelberg.

Wolff, P. (1988) 'The French city of the Mediterranean Midi', *MHR* 3.2, 21–53.

Wood, I. (1994) *The Merovingian Kingdoms 450–751*, Harlow.

Woodhouse, J. (1991) 'Tales from another country: fictional treatments of the Russian peasantry 1847–61', *RurH* 2.2, 171–86.

Woodhouse, W. J. (1897) *Aetolia: Its Geography, Topography and Antiquities*, Oxford.

Woodwell, G. M. (1990) *The Earth in Transition*, New York.

Woolf, G. (1990) 'World-systems analysis and the Roman empire', *JRA* 3, 44–58.

Woolf, S. (1992) 'The construction of a European world-view in the Revolutionary–Napoleonic years', *PP* 137, 72–101.

Wörrle, M. (1981) 'Wasserrecht und -verwaltung in griechischer Zeit', in *Vorträge der Tagung Wasser im antiken Hellas, LIWBM* 71, 71–97.

Wörrle, M. (1988) *Stadt und Fest in kaiserzeitlichen Kleinasien: Studien zu einer agonistischen Stiftung aus Oenoanda*, Munich.

Wright, G. R. H. (1992) 'The Cypriot rural sanctuary: an illuminating document in comparative religion', in Ioannides, 269–83.

Wright, J. K. (1965) *The Geographical Lore of the Time of the Crusades: A Study in the History of Medieval Science and Tradition in Western Europe*, first published 1925, New York.

Wrigley, E. A. (1969) *Population and History*, London.

Wrigley, E. A. (1978a) 'A simple model of London's importance in changing English society and economy 1650–1750' (repr. from *PP* 36 (1967), 44–70), in Abrams and Wrigley (1978), 215–43.

Wrigley, E. A. (1978b) 'Parasite or stimulus: the town in a pre-industrial economy', in Abrams and Wrigley (1978), 295–309.

Wrigley, E. A. (1987) *People, Cities and Wealth: The Transformation of Traditional Society*, Oxford and New York.

Wrigley, E. A. (1990) 'Brake or accelerator? Urban growth and population growth before the Industrial Revolution', in van der Woude, Hayami and de Vries, 101–12.

Wrigley, E. A. (1991) 'City and country in the past: a sharp divide or a continuum?', *Historical Research* 64, 107–20.

Wylie, J. (1993) 'Crises of glut in the Faroe Islands and Dominica', *CSSH* 35, 353–89.

Yajima, H. (1986) *Arwad Island: A Case Study of Maritime Culture on the Syrian Coast, Studia Culturae Islamicae* 8, Tokyo.

Yamey, B. S. (1975) 'Notes on double-entry bookkeeping and economic progress', *JEEH* 4, 717–23.

Yanuchevitch, Z., Nikolayenko, G. and Kuzminova, N. (1985) 'La viticulture à Chersonèse de Taurique au IVe-IIe siècle avant notre ère d'après les recherches archéologiques et paléobotaniques', *Revue archéologique*, 115–22.

Yon, M. (1992) 'The goddess of the salt lake', in Ioannides, 301–6.

Zaccagnini, C. (1983) 'Patterns of mobility among ancient near Eastern craftsmen', *JNES* 42, 245–6.

Zaccagnini, C. (1993) 'In margine all'*emporion*: modelli di scambio nelle economie del Vicino Oriente antico', in Bresson and Rouillard, 127–43.

Zachariadou, E. A. (1977) 'Prix et marchés de céréales en Romanie (1343–1405)', *Nuova Rivista Storica* 61, 291–306.

Zachariadou, E. A. (1983) *Trade and Crusade: Venetian Crete and the Emirates of Menteshe and Aydın*, Venice.

Zachariadou, E. A. (1987) 'Notes sur la population de l'Asie Mineure Turque au XIVe siècle', *BF* 12, 223–31.

Zacour, N. P. and Hazard, H. W. (eds) (1985) *The Impact of the Crusades on the Near East* (*A History of the Crusades*, ed. K. Setton, vol. 5), Madison WI.

Zakri, S. (1990) 'Pratiques hydro-agricoles traditionelles d'après les manuscrits arabes d'agronomie à la période médiévale dans le monde musulman', in Geyer, 35–51.

Zamagni, V. (1993) *The Economic History of Italy 1860–1990: Recovery after Decline*, Oxford.

Zangger, E. (1991) 'Prehistoric coastal environments in Greece: the vanished landscapes of Dimini Bay and Lake Lerna', *JFA* 18.1, 1–16.

Zangger, E. (1992a) *The Flood from Heaven*, London and Basingstoke.

Zangger, E. (1992b) 'Prehistoric and historic soils in Greece: assessing the natural resources for agriculture', in B. Wells, 13–19.

Zangger, E. (1992c) 'Neolithic to present soil-erosion in Greece', in Bell and Boardman, 133–48.

Zangger, E. (1998) 'The port of Nestor', in J. L. Davies, 69–74.

Zaqzouq, A. R. (1990) 'Les Norias: anciens moyens d'irrigation les plus importants dans la région de Hama', in Geyer, 337–65.

Zawadzki, T. (1952–3) 'Quelques remarques sur l'étendue et l'accroissement des domaines des grands temples en Asie mineure', *Eos* 46, 83–96.

Zeumer, K. (1886) *Formulae Merowingici et Karolini Aevi*, Hanover.

Zevi, F. (1989) 'Introduzione', in *Amphores romaines et histoire économique*, 3–19.

Zevi, F. (1995) 'Demarato e i re "Corinzi" di Roma', in A. Storchi Marino (ed.) *L'incidenza dell'antico: studi in memore di Ettore Lepore*, Naples, 291–314.

Zevi, F. and Andreae, B. (1982) 'Gli scavi sottomarini di Baia', *PdelP* 37, 114–156.

Zifferaro, A. (1995) 'Economia, divinità e frontiere: sul ruolo di alcuni santuari di confine in Etruria meridionale', *Ostraka* 4.2, 333–50.

Zimmerer, K. S. (1994) 'Human geography and the "new ecology": the prospect and promise of integration', *AAAG* 84 (1), 108–25.

Zintzen, C. (1967) *Damascii Vitae Isidori Reliquiae*, Hildesheim.

Zohary, D. (1989) 'Domestication of the Southwest Asian Neolithic crop assemblage of cereals, pulses and flax: the evidence from the living plants', in Harris and Hillman, 358–73.

Zohary, D. (1995) 'The domestication of the grapevine *Vitis vinifera L.* in the Near East', in McGovern, Fleming and Katz, 23–43.

Zohary, D. and Hopf, M. (1988) *Domestication of Plants in the Old World: The Origin and Spread of Cultivated Plants in West Asia, Europe and the Nile Valley*, Oxford.

Zones cotières et plaines littorales dans le monde méditerranéen médiéval: défense, peuplement et mise en valeur (1996), Rome.

Zug Tucci, H. (1978) 'Un aspetto trascurato del commercio medievale del vino', in *Studi in memoria di Federigo Melis*, 4 vols, Naples, 3.311–48.

Zug Tucci, H. (1985) 'Il mondo medioevale dei pesci, tra realtà e immaginazione', *SS* 31, 291–372.

INDEX

?. of honor — never clear

509- elite & secluded
    lower visible

> what about male promiscuity?
_____

whether Med. view is valid (or not).
is it useful? what, if anything, do
we get out of it?

honor / shame 488

points out natural weakness of women 494

497 - status

488 - other cul-
      Shame + honor

⌐ 512
  ∴ by control of women

  519 GK. stuff

500 women @ work

historiography of anthropology?

       12/9
   10 am

a hopeless task?

1,2;4,11,12